THE COLLEGE SHAKESPEARE

15 Plays and the Sonnets

THE COLLEGE
Shakespeare
15 PLAYS AND THE SONNETS

BERTRAND EVANS

UNIVERSITY OF CALIFORNIA, BERKELEY

THE MACMILLAN COMPANY, NEW YORK
COLLIER-MACMILLAN PUBLISHERS, LONDON

The Macmillan Company
866 Third Avenue, New York, New York 10022

Collier-Macmillan Canada, Ltd., Toronto, Ontario

Library of Congress catalog card number: 72–78610

Printing: 1 2 3 4 5 6 7 8   Year: 3 4 5 6 7 8 9

A Note on This Edition

SELECTION OF PLAYS

This edition includes fifteen major plays and all the sonnets. Tragedies are most fully represented, with seven out of ten included; history plays are represented by three that are generally accounted outstanding; comedies have been chosen from the early, middle, and late periods and include each subspecies, with a fantasy, two romantic comedies, a "dark comedy," and a romance.

TEXT

Texts of the plays are complete and are as authoritative as modern scholarship can make them; readings have been checked against both Quarto and Folio versions. Though obviously a good many emendations offered during the past two hundred years have been incorporated, effort has always been made to retain the readings of earliest texts except where they appear truly corrupt. Spelling is modernized, and a serious effort has been made to bring the punctuation thoroughly into accord with contemporary American practice. With past participles of verbs, an apostrophe has been used where the ending is unaccented in verse lines; where no apostrophe is used, it is to be assumed that the ending is sounded: "We are *impressed* and *engag'd* to fight." In prose lines no such distinction has been made, and it is assumed that there readers will pronounce past participles according to modern practice.

FOOTNOTES

The decision about which words, lines, and passages need footnotes and which can be let pass without them is easily the most severe that an editor of Shakespeare must make. Since this edition is intended primarily for college undergraduates rather than, for example, research scholars, the guiding principle has been to annotate where annotation will be immediately useful or absolutely essential—to be helpful without being too helpful. Most teachers want their students to "figure out" meanings independently but also to have relevant information immediately available for passages that may prove unintelligible without it. The present editor has sought to avoid packing footnotes with superfluous information, however interesting it may be intrinsically, and to provide the exact tool where and when it is needed; to this end he has drawn on the experience of thirty years of conducting undergraduates through the plays. But how well or ill he has succeeded in walking the fine line between too little and too much, teachers and readers will soon discover for themselves.

INTRODUCTIONS AND AFTERWORDS

Besides a general introduction to Shakespeare and his age, this edition includes general introductions to Shakespeare's tragedies, histories, and comedies. But a special, and perhaps unique, feature of the edition is its inclusion of separate afterwords for the individual plays to replace the introductions of traditional editions. The pedagogical rationale of this reversal of usual practice is obvious: it makes for a more satisfying literary experience to read a work through first independently, and to make up one's own mind about it, than to absorb—perhaps unconsciously—a critic-reader's point of view in advance of one's firsthand experience. The afterwords are placed after each play and are intended to serve a twofold purpose: first, to supply readers with some general critical perspective on the play; and, second, to stimulate thought, discussion, debate, especially at points where the afterword's criticism of the play and the reader's immediate experience of the play come in conflict. All the plays of Shakespeare leave ample room for such conflict; that is one of the proofs of their greatness.

B. E.

Contents

SHAKESPEARE AND HIS AGE

LIFE

The facts of William Shakespeare's life that are known with certainty might conveniently be recorded on a single page; indeed, even among these "certainties" items inevitably occur that are the results of informed conjecture. The future poet-dramatist was baptized in the Church of the Holy Trinity at Stratford-on-Avon on April 26, 1564, and because baptism commonly took place within three days of birth, it is usual to assign April 23 as his birth date. Though there is not exact documentary proof, there is no reason to doubt that he was the son of John Shakespeare, a member of the Glovers' guild and dealer in country produce such as skins and wool, and his wife Mary Arden, daughter of a wealthy landowner in the neighborhood of Wilmcote. In 1568 John Shakespeare became High Bailiff (mayor) of Stratford and was evidently, for a period of ten years or more, a citizen of prominence; thereafter his fortunes appear to have declined. The John Shakespeares had eight children in all, among whom William was the third.

On November 28, 1582, when he was eighteen years of age, Shakespeare was married to Anne Hathway, or Hathaway, in the parish of Old Stratford. At her death in 1623 her age was recorded as sixty-seven years; thus we know that she was some eight years older than her husband. We know, too, that the couple had three children: Susanna, born 1583, and the twins Hamnet and Judith, born 1585. Hamnet died at the age of eleven, Judith at the age of seventy-seven, having had three sons who died before her and left no heirs. Susanna lived until 1649 and left one daughter, Elizabeth Hall, who died without issue in 1670. Thus the direct line of William Shakespeare's descent came to an end.

Unquestionably Shakespeare attended school in Stratford at the free grammar school, where he would have received the rudiments of a classical education, for the curriculum of the Elizabethan grammar school consisted almost entirely of Latin. Ben Jonson, much later, commented that Shakespeare had "small Latin and less Greek," and, indeed, he had conceivably no Greek at all; but in the grammar school he would have read *Aesop's Fables*, Cicero, Ovid, Terence, Plautus, and probably the tragedies of Seneca. If his learning was not that of a scholar, it was nevertheless near the equivalent of that of a modern college graduate who has majored in Latin. Best evidence for this conclusion is contained in the plays themselves, which often evince what looks to have been an easy and long acquaintance with Latin authors and their language. *Love's Labor's Lost* and *The Merry Wives of Windsor* are the most obvious cases in point.

For the date and reason of Shakespeare's leaving Stratford for London there are no facts; we can only guess. He may have departed with traveling players from the city, who had begun visiting Stratford in 1568, when he would have been four years of age. His father's declining fortunes, which presumably affected his own, may have driven him, in a quite ordinary way, to leave the country in pursuit of his fortune in the city. But in any event, at some time prior to 1592 he was active and successful in London, for in 1592 was published an angry testimonial to that effect: "there is an upstart crow, beautified with our feathers, that with his *Tygers heart wrapt in a players hide*, supposes he is as well able to bumbast out a blanke verse as the best of you; and being an absolute *Johannes Factotum*, is in his own conceit the only Shak-scene in a countrie." These were the remarks of one Robert Greene, prose writer and dramatist of no mean success at his height, who had, however, fallen upon evil days. That they refer to Shakespeare, not only the mention of "Shak-scene" suggests, but a line in Shakespeare's own *3Henry VI*—"O tiger's heart wrapt in a woman's hide"—makes strongly plausible. If Shakespeare had risen far enough to seem a threat to an established rival dramatist by 1592, it is reasonable to assume that he had been in London for several years and had possibly arrived there as early as 1585.

In 1593 and 1594 Shakespeare published, respectively, the narrative poems "Venus and Adonis" and "Lucrece," dedicating them to the Earl of Southampton. In the latter year also an anonymous poet commented on "Lucrece," which was evidently popular at once, mentioning Shakespeare's name: "Yet Tarquin plucked his glistering grape,/ And Shake-speare paints poor Lucrece' rape." In 1594–1595 Shakespeare's name appeared for the first time in connection with a theatrical company, the Lord Chamberlain's, a company of actors with which it is probable that he remained throughout his career, though the company itself underwent various changes of name according to the identity of the patron under whose sponsorship it was licensed. What is noteworthy about this first mention is that Shakespeare's name appears along with only two other names, those of William Kempe and Richard Burbage, the foremost actors of their time for comedy and tragedy. Both actors' lists and tradition supply evidence that, at least until the turn of the century, Shakespeare was actor as well as poet and playwright; he is known to have acted in two of Ben Jonson's plays, and tradition specifically connects his name with the roles of old Adam in *As You Like It* and the Ghost in *Hamlet*.

Various other factual items, fairly numerous but scattered, provide at least a skeletal outline of Shakespeare's growing success and prosperity. Presumably at the poet's urging, John Shakespeare in 1596 applied for and was granted a coat of arms. Though his own fortunes in Stratford had turned sour, the father was henceforth a "gentleman," and the dramatist's own social prestige was correspondingly enhanced. In the following year, Shakespeare bought and repaired New Place, the second largest house in Stratford, which was passed on by will at his death in 1616 and remained in the family until 1670, when his last descendant died. Shakespeare's name figures thereafter in various suits and transactions involving money matters. In 1599 he became part owner of the Globe Theater. In 1602 he purchased more than a hundred acres in Old Stratford, and additional land in the vicinity of New Place. Ten years later he purchased a "dwelling-house . . . with the appurtenances" in Blackfriars, London, and during the next two years he was involved with legal difficulties respecting title to this place.

By far the largest evidence of Shakespeare's material success, however, is expressed by his will, filed after his death on April 23, 1616, which makes bequests of very substantial character to his two daughters, his sister, and various other members of his family, and remembers numerous friends, fellow actors, and residents of Stratford with smaller but appropriate amounts. But certainly the most famous (and tantalizing) item in the will is that which comes nearly at its end: "Item, I give unto my wife my second best bed with the furniture."

Shakespeare was buried on April 25, 1616, in Holy Trinity Church, Stratford. He had presumably retired to Stratford a few years earlier, possibly as early as 1611. A few years later an elaborate monument was installed in the chancel of the church, supporting a bust within an arch. Over the grave itself was placed a stone bearing an epitaph that may or may not have been written by the dramatist:

Good friend for Jesus sake forbeare
To digg the dust enclosed heare!
Bleste be the man that spares thes stones,
And curst be he that moves my bones.

Curiosity, both scholarly and merely human, has, from time to time, impelled a movement to disregard the epitaph's injunction and to open the grave. So far, however, Shakespeare's bones have remained undisturbed.

LONDON AND THE THEATER

When Shakespeare arrived in London, in 1585 or soon after, it was already a metropolis of about 200,000 people, and it was bustling with life. Elizabeth had been on the throne for nearly thirty years, England was at peace, though fearful of invasion, the middle class was prosperous and rapidly gaining in power that it was not at all reluctant to assert. Trade was flourishing, for England had expanded her shipping until it included commerce with virtually every part of the world. London was the great center into which streamed young men from all walks of life, intent on making their way in the world economically, socially, and intellectually. Along with ambitions to participate in the robust life of the marketplace, they brought also an insatiable demand for pleasures of all sorts, and entertainment —from bearbaiting to tragic drama—grew and flourished with the times.

In 1588, perhaps just after Shakespeare had become adjusted to the life of the city, Sir Francis Drake and his light, gallant ships (aided by a fierce storm that scattered the enemy) totally defeated the dread Spanish Armada, and England was suddenly freed from the threat of invasion that had hitherto dampened spirits that were otherwise wholly exuberant. At once, at home and abroad, Englishmen were infected with the sense of their own greatness, proud of their past, confident of their present, hopeful of what seemed their boundless future. They had time and money for culture and entertainment, and this great age teemed with geniuses able and eager to give them all that they desired of both. In all the world's history there was never a more propitious time or place for a young poet of prodigious talent to appear on the scene.

Until 1576 the city had no theater as such. Plays were acted at court, in the Inns of Court—the law schools which had long been and would long remain the centers of intellectual activity—in great private homes along the Thames, and, indeed, wherever a company of actors could set up their modest equipment and attract a crowd. Plays and players were regarded as a mixed blessing: though they provided much-needed entertainment, they also attracted crowds that attracted pickpockets and other unsavory denizens of the city streets. Further, gatherings increased the likelihood of the spread of the plague, a danger never far from the minds of Englishmen in Shakespeare's time; twice during his career it broke out with terrible effects. It was no doubt the Lord Mayor's insistence on new regulations that prompted James Burbage, in 1576, to build a professional house for the acting of plays; this was the Theater. In the same year another theater was constructed, known as the Curtain. The two housed rival companies of players, and, to judge from what followed during the next dozen years, there is no doubt that competition was an invigorating condition.

For Shakespeare the immediate center of activity was the Theater, a towering circular structure with no roof but with several stages, or acting surfaces, that formalized the features found in the courtyards where many plays continued to be performed. The main stage was a great, square platform that extended far out, so that spectators stood or sat on three sides of the performers. At the rear of this platform was an inner stage with a curtain that could be used as the occasion required. Above the main stage, set back to the wall at the second-story level, was an upper stage. And above this, at the third-story level, was yet another acting area where, for example, a guard might stand as on a tower or where heralds might trumpet the arrival of a king. Doorways to right and left of the main stage, as well as usable windows to right and left of the upper stage, provided actors with ample facilities for speedy exits and entrances. There is no question that the Elizabethan stage was built for action, uninhibited and spectacular.

Shakespeare's three-level, multiple-playing-surface theater differed enormously from our conventional modern theater, which is walled in on three sides and uses a curtain across its proscenium arch to separate spectators and performers and to mark a formal distinction between acts. In the Elizabethan theater, scene followed scene in swift succession, with no interruption; as one group of actors swept out through the doorway at either side, their flying banners and coattails frequently still visible, a second group entered from the opposite side, or on another level, or on the inner stage at the rear, already speaking the opening lines of the next scene. Shakespeare's theater thus maintained the illusion of unbroken action, and thus, in two action-packed hours (the "two hours' traffic of our stage" mentioned in the Prologue of *Romeo and Juliet*) could present plays that on the modern stage, with its conventional division of scenes and acts and its changes of scenery, require three or four hours.

The number of playhouses increased with the growing public demand for theatrical entertainment. At the same time the Inns of Court—especially Gray's Inn (where Shakespeare's *Comedy of Errors* was acted in 1594) and the Middle Temple (where his *Twelfth Night* was acted in 1602)—alive with members who never ceased to be enthusiastic participants in dramatic events not only as spectators but as playwrights and performers as well, provided strong and salutary influence. More than once the public theaters fell into disrepute and were periodically enjoined by the Lord Mayor to cease their activities or were severely restrained by ordinances. The Puritans (whose power would ultimately prove sufficient to close English theaters for eighteen years, 1642–1660) were already expressing their antipathy to entertainment in general and dramatic entertainment in particular. Yet the public craving for plays was not to be denied. As early as 1576 the children of the Chapel Royal were acting in a converted hall in Blackfriars Monastery, and the name of Blackfriars continued for many years to be associated with child actors; but in 1608 Shakespeare's company took over the theater and used it for winter performances. In 1592 the Rose was built; the Rose was destined to be chief rival to Shakespeare's company for years thereafter. In 1599 Shakespeare's company (then known as the Chamberlain's Men) pulled down the old Theater and moved the timbers to the south bank of the Thames, where was constructed the playhouse called the Globe, with which Shakespeare's name is always most intimately associated, for on its stage were performed most of his greatest plays, beginning with *As You Like It* and *Julius Caesar* in 1599 and 1600. The Globe burned to the ground in 1613 during the performance of Shakespeare's last play, *Henry VIII*, when wadding shot from cannon on stage ignited its roof.

So central is the Globe in the life of Shakespeare and Elizabethan-Jacobean drama in general that it requires more than passing notice here. Thus, in part, a great French historian of the nineteenth century, H. A. Taine, has reconstructed the scene:

On a dirty site, on the banks of the Thames, rose the principal theatre, the Globe, a sort of hexagonal tower, surrounded by a muddy ditch, surmounted by a red flag. The common people could enter as well as the rich: there were sixpenny, twopenny, even penny seats; but they could not see it without money. If it rained, and it often rains in London, the people in the pit, butchers, mercers, bakers, sailors, apprentices, received the streaming rain upon their heads. . . . While waiting for the piece, they amuse themselves after their fashion, drink beer, crack nuts, eat fruits, howl, and now and then resort to their fists; they have been known to fall upon the actors and turn the theatre upside down. At other times they have gone in disgust to the tavern to give the poet a hiding, or toss him in a blanket. . . . Above them, on the stage, were the spectators able to pay a shilling, the elegant people, the gentlefolk. These were sheltered from the rain, and if they chose to pay an extra shilling could have a stool. . . . It often happened that stools were lacking; then they stretched themselves on the ground: they were not dainty at such times. They play cards, smoke, insult the pit, who give it them back without stinting, and throw apples at them into the bargain. As for the gentlefolk, they gesticulate, swear in Italian, French, English; crack aloud jokes in dainty, composite, high-colored words: in short, they have the energetic, original, gay manners of artists, the same humor, the same absence of constraint, and, to complete the resemblance, the same desire to make themselves singular, the same imaginative cravings, the same absurd and picturesque devices, beards cut to a point, into the shape of a fan, a spade, the letter T, gaudy and expensive dresses, copied from five or six neighboring nations, embroidered, laced with gold, motley, continually heightened in effect, or changed for others: there was, as it were, a carnival in their brains as on their backs.

Before such spectators, in an atmosphere more suggestive of a circus than of a formal tragedy or comedy, Shakespeare's plays were acted, and for such a theater they were written. They were presented with virtually no scenery and without visual indication of changes in location other than the rapid shifts from one playing surface to another. The same platform might stand, in swift succession, and without change of furnishings, for a room in a duke's palace, a seacoast, or a mansion in the suburbs. The lines spoken by the actors often identified the location of the scene ("This is Illyria, lady"), but all else was left to the active imagination of the audience: the spectator's mind's eye, briefed by the poet's lines, supplied the descriptive details of tomb, battlement, presence chamber, or wild heath.

FELLOWS AND CONTEMPORARIES

By 1600 there were some eleven theaters operating in and about London besides the private Blackfriars theater and a hall used by the boys of St. Paul's Cathedral. The seating (and standing) capacities of these are not known with certainty, but they apparently ranged from 100 or more seats in the smaller halls up to an estimated 2,000 at the Fortune, built on the Bankside in 1600. It has been estimated that an average of 1,250 spectators attended each of the theaters when the season was in full swing.

Obviously, to supply so large a market only an abundance of playwrights, as well as actors and actors' companies, could suffice, and the Elizabethan Age proved prolific in men of genius. Shakespeare's immediate predecessors included John Lyly (1553–1606), a lyric poet and writer of prose romances as well as plays, who wrote mainly for the children's companies and left a total of eight plays, of which the best remembered are *Endymion* and *Mother Bombie*; Thomas Kyd (1558–1594), a specialist in the "revenge" or "tragedy of blood" play, author of *The Spanish Tragedy* and a version of *Hamlet*; Robert Greene (1558–1592), also a writer of prose romances and pamphlets, who nevertheless won his most lasting fame by alluding to a certain unknown, who happened to be Shake-speare, as an "upstart crow"; George Peele (1558–1598), a good lyricist but poor drama-tist whose best-known play is *The Old Wives' Tale*; and the greatest of the lot by far, Christopher Marlowe (1564–1593). Marlowe might have proved a worthy rival of Shake-speare had he not died at the age of twenty-nine, leaving behind only four plays, which, however, gave a mighty thrust to Elizabethan drama, most notably in their develop-ment of dramatic blank verse (Marlowe's "mighty line") and their contribution to the basic idea of a *tragedy of character* that was to become Shakespeare's unchallenged forte between 1600 and 1608, the period of the tragedies. With *Tamburlaine, Dr. Faustus, The Jew of Malta,* and *Edward II,* Marlowe taught the young Shakespeare lessons in comedy, history, and tragedy.

The contribution of these dramatic pioneers to the history of Shakespeare's own artistic production is inestimable. It has been well said that, just when Shakespeare had finished his apprenticeship and was set to begin his career in earnest, all his great pio-neering predecessors had done their work, were dead, and had laid their gifts at his feet. Shakespeare was not of the first wave of Elizabethan dramatists; he was of the second wave. It was his fortune to reap the harvest that the pioneers had sown.

But of course he was not alone in the second wave; many other men of genius also stood on the shoulders of the pioneers. Of all these unquestionably the greatest was Ben Jonson (1573–1637), who but for Shakespeare would stand as the pre-eminent Eliza-bethan-Jacobean dramatist. Author of some fifty plays, with a classical learning that put Shakespeare's "small Latin and less Greek" to shame, Jonson wrote realistic, satiric, often harsh comedies, with "humor" characters that tend toward caricatures and the grotesque but are still, at the best, entertaining either on the stage or in the text. Prob-ably most notable of all his comedies were *Every Man in His Humor,* staged at the Curtain in 1598; *Volpone,* 1605; and *The Alchemist* (identified by Coleridge as containing one of three perfect plots in literature), 1610. Jonson's tragedies have been said to "smell of the lamp," and the fact is that they make dull reading for all but confirmed Jonsonians.

Other contemporaries and immediate successors of Shakespeare include George Chapman (1559–1634), a translator of Homer and writer of high-heroic tragedies, most characteristic of which is *Bussy D'Ambois*; Thomas Dekker (1570–1641), whose *Shoe-maker's Holiday* of 1599 is a richly comic play that brilliantly unites working-class, middle-class, and aristocratic elements within its complex plot; Thomas Middleton (1570–1627), whose name is connected with more than twenty plays, most notable of which, in com-edy, is *A Trick to Catch the Old One* and, in tragedy, the sensational *Changeling*; Thomas Heywood (1572–1650), whose name is connected with more than 200 plays, including virtually every variety known to the age, and best remembered for one fine play, *A Woman Kilde with Kindness,* sentimental, sensational, but moving with something like genuine tragic force; Francis Beaumont (1585–1616) and John Fletcher (1579–1625), col-laborators on an enormous number of plays, with Beaumont writing one of his own be-sides, and Fletcher fifteen. Most famous of their collaborations is *The Knight of the Burning Pestle,* a mock-heroic satire that is still sometimes acted today and is unfailingly enter-taining. Fletcher's own best work is in *The Faithfull Shepheardesse* (1610), a pastoral, and *The Wild-Goose Chase* (1621), a witty comedy that looks ahead to the Restoration and the lively comedies after 1660. Other Jacobean dramatists include Philip Massinger (1583–1640), another prolific dramatist whose best work is the satiric comedy *A New Way to Pay Old Debts*; John Webster (1580–1625), sometimes characterized as Shakespeare's most notable successor in tragedy, whose *Duchess of Malfi* (1613) specializes in the sensational but has some tragic force; John Ford (1586–1640), noted for one "heartbreak" tragedy, *The Broken Heart* (1629); and James Shirley (1596–1666), also a prolific dramatist for both

6

comedy and tragedy, whose best plays are *The Cardinal* (1641) and *The Lady of Pleasure* (1635). It was on the plays of Ford and Shirley that the Puritans, in 1642, rang down the curtain for nearly eighteen years. Curiously, the works of neither dramatist particularly deserved even a rigid Puritan's censure.

THE CANON AND CHRONOLOGY

Early in this prodigious half a century, the dramatic productivity of which is barely suggested by the foregoing review, stand the thirty-seven plays that are attributed to Shakespeare (with such qualifications as are noted below). The following table lists the generally accepted works, with approximate dates. Plays included in the present volume are printed in *italics* so that readers can place them in relation to the total canon. Though it is true that scholars do not know with certainty the exact year in which a single one of the plays was composed, intensive study, much of it done earlier in this century, has achieved consensus on some plays and fair agreement on most others. In the following table, the dates at the left represent, in the narrowest sense, "theatrical years," and, in the widest sense, two-year spans within which, in the opinion of modern scholars, a particular play was written. In parenthesis after each play is recorded the range of

YEAR	COMEDY	HISTORY	TRAGEDY
1590–1591	Comedy of Errors (1589–1594)	2 Henry VI (1590–1592)	
1591–1592		1, 3 Henry VI (1590–1595)	Titus Andronicus (1591–1594)
1592–1593	Two Gentlemen (1591–1594)		
1593–1594	Love's Labor's Lost (1588–1595)	Richard III (1592–1595)	
1594–1595	Taming of Shrew (1593–1596)	King John (1593–1596)	
1595–1596	*Midsummer Night's Dream* (1594–1596)	Richard II (1594–1596)	Romeo & Juliet (1591–1596)
1596–1597	Merchant of Venice (1594–1597)	*1 Henry IV* (1596–1598)	
1597–1598	*Much Ado* (1597–1599)	2 Henry IV (1596–1598)	
1598–1599		*Henry V* (1598–1599)	
1599–1600	As You Like It (1599–1600)		*Julius Caesar* (1599–1600)
1600–1601	Merry Wives (1597–1601)		
	Twelfth Night (1599–1601)		
1601–1602	All's Well (1593–1602)		Hamlet (1601–1603)
1602–1603	Troilus and Cressida (1601–1602)		
1603–1604	*Measure for Measure* (1603–1605)		Othello (1603–1604)
1604–1605			*King Lear* (1605–1606)
1605–1606			*Macbeth* (1605–1606)
1606–1607			Antony & Cleopatra (1606–1607)
1607–1608	Pericles (1607–1608)		Timon (1605–1608)
1608–1609			*Coriolanus* (1607–1609)
1609–1610	Cymbeline (1609–1610)		
1610–1611	*Winter's Tale* (1610–1611)		
1611–1612	Tempest (1610–1612)		
1612–1613		Henry VIII (1612–1613)	

estimates, sometimes broad indeed, made by various scholars from Malone (1778) to the present.

Of the plays listed, all but two, *Pericles* and *Henry VIII*, are now taken to be entirely Shakespeare's. In *Pericles* the first two acts and part of the third have been thought to be by someone other than Shakespeare, though they have in any event clearly been re-worked by Shakespeare. Numerous efforts have been made to show that Fletcher, especially, had a hand in *Henry VIII*, but the greater portion of the play as it stands is now taken to be Shakespeare's own. In addition to the plays listed, an even dozen more have been attached to Shakespeare's name, some with slight and some with greater claim. Of all those listed in the Shakespeare "apocrypha," probably *The Two Noble Kinsmen* deserves, and has received, most serious consideration.

The dating of the plays is a complex process that involves use of many sorts of evidence both internal and external. Internal evidence includes primarily topical allusions and style. In *Henry V*, for example, there is a clear reference to the Earl of Essex's departure for Ireland in the spring of 1599:

> As, by a lower but loving likelihood,
> Were now the general of our gracious Empress,
> As in good time he may, from Ireland coming,
> Bringing rebellion broached on his sword . . . .

The high hopes for Essex's success against the Irish rebels were blasted, and he returned in dismal failure in the fall of 1599, by which or after which time the Prologue's remarks would have been ill timed. The allusion accords with other sorts of evidence that point to 1599, and the reader will observe in the preceding chart that *Henry V* is one of a few plays on which there is consensus among scholars. But internal evidence also includes less exact, though enormously helpful, stylistic indications. Generally speaking, Shakespeare wrote more regular iambic pentameter, with a good deal of rhyme, in his early period; he inclined also toward figurative writing that might often be more decorative than dramatic. He involved his speakers in elaborate syntax and the spinning out of ideas until sometimes the crux of their argument is lost in the embroidery; almost any extended passage from *The Two Gentlemen of Verona* or *Love's Labor's Lost* exemplifies the tendency to prolixity and overrefinement. In the middle period, beginning with approximately 1597, he wrote a more balanced style, taking greater liberties with the regularity of blank verse, using hardly more words than were needed to convey his sense, and generally con-fining imagery to what was strictly dramatic in function. In the later period, beginning about 1605, his style began to grow almost too condensed, encapsulated, with images provided with a cutting edge that reached to the marrow of the subject at hand. In this final period little or nothing is wasted or even attenuated by the words; the blank verse is so flexible that at the best it truly approximates the ease of fine conversation. There are numerous feminine endings (weak rather than strong syllable at the end of the line). It has been remarked, with a great deal of general truth, that in the beginning Shakespeare used too many words, in the middle period about the right number, and at the last too few. Dating by stylistic characteristics is quite inadequate for purposes of determining the exact year of a play, but it is virtually infallible in distinguishing between the early, the middle, and the late. Scholars are confused only when, as in the case of *All's Well That Ends Well*, Shakespeare seems to have revised an early play, but not wholly, so that the final work appears to include stylistic characteristics from as early as 1593 and as late as 1603.

External evidence is of course much more useful in pinpointing dates. Greene's mention of the "Tyger's heart wrapped in a players hide" in 1592 tells us without fail that *3Henry VI*, with its "Tyger's heart wrapped in a woman's hide," *must* have been in existence by that date. Specific dates of performances, recorded in certain diaries and other documents of the time, similarly fix the time by which a particular play must have existed. Not less importantly, the Stationers' Register, wherein were recorded works prior to publication, provides accurate evidence up to a point. (It does not reveal how long before publication a play was composed.) Some sixteen of Shakespeare's plays were published in quarto, presumably not long after they were written and acted, and their date of publication normally fixes the date of composition within one or two years. It is therefore with the remainder of the thirty-seven, the plays that were not published until the First Folio of 1623, that the severest dating problems occur. Probably the most useful single document of external evidence is Francis Meres' *Palladis Tamia*, which listed, in 1598, twelve of Shakespeare's plays and the "sugred Sonnets"; thus we know that these plays, at least, were in existence by that date. (Vexingly, Meres included one play, *Love's Labor's Won*, which exists nowhere under that title; it is sometimes identified with the early version of *All's Well*, and compounds the already-troublesome problem of dating that play.)

First to wrestle with the problem of dating the plays was Edmond Malone, who in 1778 published his "Attempt to Ascertain the Order in Which the Plays of Shakespeare Were Written." Malone did astonishingly well, all things considered, and went badly astray on only a few plays, such as *Pericles* and *The Winter's Tale*, which he placed in 1592 and 1594, respectively; *Taming of the Shrew*, which he placed in 1606; and *Twelfth Night*, which he placed in 1614. [Malone's wildest conjectures are not included in the foregoing chronological tabulation, but his judgment is represented in the dates assigned to a majority of the plays. Our own century, and modern scholarship, owes most of all, however, to Sir E. K. Chambers, whose *William Shakespeare: A Study of Facts and Problems* (1930) is the basis for all serious modern scholarship on the chronology of the plays.]

SHAKESPEARE'S USE OF SOURCES

Like other dramatists of his time, and, indeed, like most supreme masters, Shakespeare wasted very little time on the invention of plots. For the most part, he drew on four major sources: English chronicles, especially Holinshed's, which supplied material for all ten of his history plays and contributed also to *Macbeth* and *Cymbeline*; older plays, including both classical (Plautus's *Menaechmi*, source of *Comedy of Errors*) and near contemporary, such as the *Famous Victories of Henry the Fifth*, which, besides Holinshed, furnished materials for *Henry IV* and *Henry V*, and the early *Hamlet*, which influenced Shakespeare's; Plutarch's *Lives*, from which were drawn the three Roman plays and the basic elements of *Timon of Athens*; and a wide range of prose tales and romances, Italian, French, and English, dating from ancient and medieval times to the near contemporary. Besides the sources on which he drew for plots, Shakespeare was indebted to others for many ideas, images, characters, incidental elements of many sorts; if he had "small Latin and less Greek," yet his borrowings from classical authors were on a huge scale. Nor is he only a "name-dropper," like some of his fellow dramatists; classical details provide, in passing, the matter and spirit alike of countless passages: if true value in such things could be accurately assessed, we might find that Ovid was fully as important to him as Holinshed.

Shakespeare attempted few plays without an established plot to base his own work on. The plays whose plots appear to be Shakespeare's include *Love's Labor's Lost*, *A Midsummer Night's Dream*, *The Merry Wives of Windsor*, and *The Tempest*. But even though the plots of these may have been original, all of them borrow heavily from a variety of sources for their details.

On the other hand, Shakespeare's practice of changing plots and plot materials around to suit his own purposes was not only highly creative and original but quite unfettered. One of his characteristic habits was that of supplementing the main borrowed plot with elements gathered from a variety of other sources, or of joining two plots drawn from different sources, as in *King Lear*. Always given to a principle of abundance, he seems never to have found enough for his uses in any single borrowed plot. With *The Comedy of Errors*, for example, probably his very first attempt at comedy, he began with the plot devised by a master craftsman in the art of plotting, Plautus; but instead of following his master slavishly, he devised a complex frame within which to set the farcical action of Plautus; moreover, he added a second set of twins to the story in order to multiply the possibilities of comic incident. The result is that his *Errors* took on an extra dimension and a kind of richness that makes even it—one of his lightest, slightest plays—thoroughly Elizabethan and complex beside the spare classical original. Other examples abound, in virtually all the comedies, where the dramatist functions as a skilled assembler of elements drawn from the past and the contemporary, from numerous authors and countries, from tales, histories, plays—and welds them by the power of his own imagination to form a new and greater whole that seems, finally, to be totally his own. Such a work is *Cymbeline*, blending ancient Britons and Romans with contemporary Italian and English materials, ancient history and legend with modern romance and Italian tale. Shakespeare added or subtracted characters and incidents at will throughout his dramatic career, and always, after the initial, apprentice years, toward the end of fashioning a work of art, whether comedy, history, or tragedy, that would be richer and more satisfying. He did not hesitate to split the historical Hotspur's age in half to make him an appropriate rival for young Prince Hal. He did not hesitate to invent a Roderigo to be in love with Desdemona in order to free his Iago (who in Cinthio's tale was himself enamored of Desdemona) from an ordinary source of malice so that he could become more nearly a symbol of pure evil. He certainly did not hesitate to telescope the events of the long, drawn-out affair of Romeo and Juliet as told in Brooke's poem to form a five-day tragedy of concentrated force, or to develop a Mercutio from his own imagination. The Hamlet story, as he found it, was a sensational tale of revenge and crafty madness; *Hamlet* remains a sensational tale of revenge and crafty madness, and a profound tragedy of inexhaustible human interest. Like the other great tragedies, it has the power to involve us deeply in the life and fate of its protagonist and those bound with him in a conflict of good and evil, life and death. It is no exaggeration to assert that not a single source tale or plot used in the making of one of the tragedies even approximates this power. Shakespeare immeasurably improved the source material that he handled (though many critics prefer Chaucer's *Troilus and Criseyde* to Shakespeare's play).

In the last analysis the student of Shakespeare has to conclude that the dramatist did the literate world a service by wasting little of his skill, energy, and imagination on the invention of story and plot but instead concentrating all his powers upon "bodying forth" his original in the most compelling terms that his genius allowed. Some of his contemporaries—for example, Webster, at his worst—were scarcely better than plagiarists. Shakespeare was never a plagiarist, even though he often lifted whole passages from Plutarch verbatim; for where Plutarch's version served, it was best to use it, and to conserve energy for the more frequent moments when Plutarch was inadequate. So also for Holinshed, who merely furnished the monumental mass of material from which the monuments themselves, which we know as *Richard II*, *Henry IV*, *Henry V*, all had to be carved.

THE TEXTS

No manuscript of Shakespeare's has survived; hence all modern editions must be based on the best evidence we have from the early quartos (sixteen of the plays were printed in quarto before Shakespeare's death in 1616) and the First Folio of 1623, which is the sole source for all the plays not previously printed in quarto. There is no such thing as a flawless text in either the Folio or any of the quartos, but editors, who began working seriously at textual problems with the beginning of the eighteenth century, have been able to put into the hands of modern readers texts of the plays that in many cases reproduce exactly what Shakespeare actually wrote and in all the others presumably come near enough that general readers (if not fastidious Shakespearean scholars in every instance) can be assured that they are reading a text that is right in all essentials.

Certain of the plays were printed in quarto as many as six times during Shakespeare's lifetime—*Richard III* and *1Henry IV*, to be specific. Others were printed once, twice, or more; *Hamlet* had four quartos, *Richard II* five, and so on. For the conscientious editor the collation of readings from numerous quartos and the Folio is no easy task, but editors have been at it for centuries. In many instances the Folio text is better than that of any quarto; in others, the Folio text is obviously corrupt, but then the day is saved by an eminently readable quarto. The Folio editors imply that they worked directly from Shakespeare's manuscripts, for they praised their idol by boasting that they had "scarce received from him a blot in his papers." But, as is obvious to any editor of Shakespeare, they must have worked not from manuscripts but from deficient quartos in some instances, unless the printers were exceedingly careless and themselves corrupted the clear texts from which they worked. With rare exceptions, few quartos are trustworthy. Shakespeare presumably did not supervise the publication of any of his plays, and in many instances evidently had no part at all in their publication. Some texts appear to have been stolen from the theater by actors or others and placed surreptitiously into the hands of publishers. Certain quartos even read as though they had been dictated to printers from the memory of some minor actor in the company.

There remain disputed passages, even whole disputed scenes, in a modern edition. Numerous lines in several plays still seem corrupt despite the labors of editors both in the process of collation and in providing conjectural emendations. Something is desperately wrong—a line or two half lines, or more, missing probably—in the third and highly important speech of *Measure for Measure*, to take a major example. We still do not know whether Shakespeare's Hamlet said "this too, too solid flesh" or "this too, too sullied flesh." Neither can we be sure that the great eighteenth-century editor Theobald was right in his emendation of "and 'a babbled o' green fields" for "on a table of green fields" when the Hostess reports Falstaff's death in *Henry V*. The emendation is obviously brilliant, but who can say? Perhaps it is more brilliant than what Shakespeare actually wrote. The object of serious Shakespeareans, as opposed to that of sundry "adapters" and "improvers," since the opening of the eighteenth century has been not to "improve" Shakespeare but to restore what he himself put down in manuscript. For the modern editor, as for the general reader, often the tempting way out with a peculiarly knotty passage that defies ready interpretation is to declare the passage corrupt and offer a substitute. But at the present time, such has been the diligence of centuries of scholars, it is doubtful that this "easy way out" is truly justifiable in more than a dozen passages in the entire canon.

Hence the modern reader will do well to take the twentieth-century text as all but perfectly authentic and to cudgel his wits, where need be, in the interpretation of any troublesome passages that may at first appear to be "corrupt." "And such readers," to quote the Folio editors, without whose early labors we should have scarcely any text at all, "we wish him."

LANGUAGE AND VERSE

When Shakespeare wrote, poets, dramatists, and prose writers were excited, in some cases to the point of delirium, with the possibilities of expression that were being discovered in the English language. They reveled in its sounds, played fancy and elaborate tricks with its flexible structures, found delight in contriving new and striking patterns for conjoining or disjoining sound and sense. If they needed a verb and had none, they made one out of a noun; if they needed a noun and had none, they made one out of a verb. They spelled rather wildly. They liked to balance word against word, phrase against phrase, sentence against sentence, like fanciful architects constructing intricate forms either delicate or ponderous. They delighted in the music that could arise from particular combinations of vowel with vowel, consonant with consonant, and consonant with vowel. On the whole, they preferred elaboration and ornament to simple, direct statement; style, like the age itself, was ornate rather than simple. They were experimenters and innovators, who strove for interesting and varied effects. One book of songs and poems that appeared about the time Shakespeare arrived in London was entitled *A Gorgeous Gallery of Gallant Inventions*; another was *A Paradise of Dainty Devices*. Spenser, taking his cue from Chaucer two centuries earlier, showed what melodious lays the language was capable of. Lyly, with his *Euphues*, showed to what extravagant uses a clever fashioner could put it. Writers of poetry and prose were excited alike in exploring the potential of English; some, indeed, seem to have been like children with a versatile new toy.

Shakespeare took up this toy of language and never tired of playing with it from his first history to his last romance; certainly the very first fact to remember in reading any one of the plays is that he shared his age's delight in language and exploited it for all that it could be made to yield, of fun, music, beauty, terror, grief, excitement, profundity. In Shakespeare's works everyone is conscious of language and plays with it, too—kings, princes, heroes, heroines, villains, old men and children, professional jesters and country clowns, happy men, and those at the point of death. The first words we hear Hamlet speak contain a bitter pun: "A little more than kin and less than kind." Mercutio, lying on the ground with his lifeblood pouring out, gasps out a last grim pun that is reminiscent of his wit duels with Romeo: "Ask for me tomorrow and you shall find me a grave man." The merchant of Venice, facing Shylock's knife and his claimed debt of a pound of flesh to be cut from Antonio's breast, wryly remarks that if the Jew will only cut deep enough, "I'll pay it instantly, with all my heart." The pun was only one of several of Shakespeare's ways of playing with language, but it was unmistakably his favorite. Neither he nor any of his characters could ever resist the opportunities afforded by such pairs of words as *heart–hart, soul–sole, deer–dear, all–awl, Rome–room, knight–night, sun–son*. Often, especially in the earlier plays, the characters engage in verbal play at times when we might not expect them to be in a mood for it; thus Romeo, tearing his hair in the Friar's cell after learning that he is banished, imagines how a mere fly will be free to touch Juliet's skin: "This may flies do, while I from this must fly." Gaunt, in *Richard II*, on his deathbed, speaks a long passage throughout which he puns on his name. But not only the characters in the early plays speak so; old Siward, a general in *Macbeth*, on learning that his son died bravely in battle, takes the news philosophically—and with the inevitable play: "Had I as many sons as I have hairs/I would not wish them to a fairer death."

Shakespeare's language, with its spelling updated, as in most modern editions, does not look formidably different from our own. Some of his words are obsolete, some are archaic, and still others have shifted their meanings either slightly or drastically. Differences generally are merely trivial and by no means serious impediments to understanding. Shakespeare usually writes *an* for *if* (but he uses *if* as well, and sometimes *an if*). He writes *swounded* for *swooned*, *afeard* for *afraid*, *thorough* for *through*, *moe* for *more*, *methinks* for *I think* or *it seems to me*. When he writes *naughty*, he means something stronger, like *wicked*; but when he writes *Marry*, he means something far lighter and more familiar than *By the Virgin Mary*, from which the expression derives. When he writes *fond*, usually he means *foolish*, but often with a hint of the modern meaning as well; so also with *gentle*, which carries the sense of the noble, as in *gentleman*, but also often suggests mildness, tenderness, as today. When he writes *presently*, he means *right now*, not, as in our time, *after a while*. In reading the plays, one needs to be watchful, so as not to take *cousin* too literally, for example, when an uncle speaks to his nephew; *cousin* served Shakespeare as a general word expressing kinship. But in fact there are few words in Shakespeare's vocabulary that offer serious barriers to the modern reader. If *tall* usually means *brave*, and if *brave* usually means *fine* or *splendid*, no irreparable loss is sustained even if the reader momentarily mistakes the meaning.

Similarly, Shakespeare's grammatical usage differs from ours only in such ways as rather add to the pleasure of reading than create barriers. He likes double negatives, for example: "I cannot go no further," laments poor Celia, lagging behind Rosalind and Touchstone on their hike into the Forest of Arden. He also likes double superlatives: "This was the most unkindest cut of all," says Antony, referring to where Brutus had struck Caesar (in the genitals, according to Plutarch). He also likes plural subjects with singular verbs: "Three parts of him is ours"; but, again, he also likes a singular subject with a plural verb: "The posture of your blows are yet unknown." He regularly differs from us in the number of the word *news*, saying, "These news are." Sometimes he uses a nominative pronoun where we would use accusative: "No one but she," where we would say, "No one but her." Like other Elizabethan writers, he has great difficulty with the possessive form of "it," sometimes saying, "It lifted up it head"; but more often he uses the masculine *his* for our neuter *its*. Shakespeare's grammatical parallelism is occasionally awry (by our usage) also; and (worst of all) certain of his characters are not above dangling a modifier: the Ghost in *Hamlet* dangles two ("sleeping in mine orchard,/A serpent stung me" and "Sleeping within my orchard,/My custom always in the afternoon,/Upon my secure hour thy uncle stole"—the effect, perhaps, of his traumatic experience when Claudius poured juice of hebenon in his ear). But for the most part Shakespeare's structures, like his grammatical usage and his vocabulary, are our own and place few obstacles in the way of understanding.

Shakespeare's verse is predominantly blank verse—iambic pentameter without rhyme. An iamb consists of an unaccented followed by an accented syllable, as in the word *again*. Five (penta) groups (feet) of two syllables make the pentameter line:

So sha/ken as/ we are,/ so wan/ with care
Find we/ a time/ for fright/ ed peace/ to pant.

Of course, Shakespeare did not write every line of every play in exact iambic pentameter. As he matured (and he matured quickly), he learned to vary his metrical patterns, matching the accents with the thought expressed, the manner of the speaker, and the urgency of the moment; thus Macbeth in a moment of great excitement:

Whence is that knocking?

And Horatio, in a comparably tense moment in *Hamlet*:

Stay! Speak, speak! I charge thee, speak!

In some of his later passages, Shakespeare's verse does not sound like verse at all, but like potent prose; but its basis is always blank verse, on which variations are played. Thus King Lear, half way between madness and recovery:

> Pray do not mock me.
> I am a very foolish, fond old man,
> Fourscore and upward, not an hour more nor less;
> And, to deal plainly,
> I fear I am not in my perfect mind.

Shakespeare's prose, like his blank verse, bears comparison with the best that was written in his age. Exactly adapted to the speaker of the moment, it is elegant, standard, slangy, or gross, as the occasion requires. Only four of the plays have no prose; eight are roughly one-third prose; four are roughly one-half prose; and five have more prose than verse. Usually identified as the greatest poet-dramatist, Shakespeare was in fact the supreme prose writer of his age as well. The later comedies, in particular, use much prose, and one, *The Merry Wives of Windsor*, includes only a few lines of verse. Much less prose occurs in the tragedies, though *Hamlet*, surprisingly, is about one-third prose. (It is worth noting that *Hamlet* contains much more comedy than any other of the tragedies, and the fact gives the most important clue to Shakespeare's general practice in the distribution of prose and verse.) But the best illustration of his habits in choosing between verse and prose is provided by the two parts of *Henry IV* and *Henry V*, where verse is regularly used for the serious historical scenes and prose for the comic ones. In the most general terms, Shakespeare used prose or verse accordingly as one or the other is more appropriate to the level of the speakers, to the occasion, and to the matter being presented. "Low" characters regularly speak in prose; heroes and heroines, kings and princes speak in blank verse except in special moments: note King Henry during the "little touch of Harry in the night" in *Henry V*, when he speaks some of the finest prose of the age. For, indeed, not only Shakespeare's blank verse, but his prose, too, is fit for a king.

SHAKESPEARE'S COMEDIES

Shakespeare wrote comedies from the beginning to the end of his career except for a gap of about four years (between *Measure for Measure* and *Pericles*) during which all his creative energies went into the writing of five or six tragedies. In all, if we count the last "dramatic romances" as comedies, and if we count *Troilus and Cressida*, which some scholars prefer to categorize as tragedy and others as "comical satire," there are seventeen—nearly half the total number of his plays.

To say that the comedies are varied in manner, matter, and mood is to understate the reality. To this date no one has been quite successful in composing a definition of Shakespearean comedy that is at the same time broad enough to include all seventeen and precise enough to be of much use. It is manifestly incorrect to assert that they share a happy mood or that they aim primarily to evoke laughter, though it is a fact that all, even *Troilus and Cressida*, have some happy moments and exhibit some laughable persons and incidents; but exactly the same can be said of the tragedies, a few of which—*Hamlet*, for example—are as abundant in "comic" matter as most of the comedies and much more abundant than some others. It is often said that the only thing the seventeen comedies share is a happy ending—i.e., problems solved, families reunited, lovers married; and perhaps that is as well as one can do towards a definition, even though it immediately excludes *Troilus and Cressida*, which ends with the hateful war still dragging on and with a disillusioned and bitter Troilus, a fallen and lost Cressida, and a dead Hector. (It would be convenient to class *Troilus and Cressida* as tragedy on the grounds of its pervasively black mood; but one mark of all the other tragedies by Shakespeare is that the protagonists are dead, whereas both Troilus and Cressida, though battered, remain alive. Hector is dead, but Hector's is not a title role.)

But if it is not possible to define Shakespearean comedy usefully, it is possible to sketch the history of the comedies and to characterize certain smaller and larger groups over the period of just over twenty years that produced them. Thus the first three comedies—*The Comedy of Errors*, *The Two Gentlemen of Verona*, and *Love's Labor's Lost*—a remarkably varied assortment, may be identified appropriately as an experimental group in each of which Shakespeare tried out a different emphasis. The *Errors* is almost exclusively a comedy of situation, in which character counts for little, and language (though the play is not devoid of verbal games) is exploited less for comic effect than would be usual in the later comedies. *The Two Gentlemen*, on the other hand, though it, too, exploits situation, relies less heavily on that resource, and relies to a greater degree on language, using subtle and intricate verbal play not only in the strictly "comic" parts but in the "romantic" ones as well, where love and love ideas are held up to the light, twisted and turned, and examined from what may sometimes seem an excessive number of angles. This play also develops a few characters that are comic in their own right and that do not depend entirely either on the situations in which they find themselves or on linguistic eccentricities for the comic effects that they engender. Of the three earliest comedies, thus, *The Two Gentlemen* comes nearest to achieving a balance in its exploitation of the three great comic resources—situation, character, language. But this play is most interesting as the forerunner of the great romantic comedies soon to come, displaying as it does a heroine who dons male disguise and goes forth into the world; two heroes, one of whom looks forward to the good but somewhat dumb romantic hero and the other to the less than perfect, slightly villainous hero of whom Bertram in *All's Well That Ends Well* is the best example; and a "world" in which the trials of lovers are the matters of central concern. Finally, *Love's Labor's Lost* is a comedy of extravagance, excess, and eccentricity, by and large a satire on fashionable excesses in manners, philosophy, and, above all, language. *Love's Labor's Lost* is a showpiece of the early 1590's, when Shakespeare and the age were both young. On the modern stage, decked out in full splendor, the play is a feast for eye, ear, and mind, displaying extravagant costumery, language fantastical, learned, elegant, as well as grossly abused, and ideas noble but always at the edge of the absurd: "Navarre shall be the wonder of the world:/ Our court shall be a little Academe,/ Still and contemplative in living art." For three years the king and his three friends vow "to live and study" and "not to see a woman in that term . . . one day in a week to touch no food . . . and but one meal on every day beside . . . to sleep but three hours in the night." The comic idea of the play is the imposition of such stringencies upon the boundless energies of virile young men in the vigor of the restless and buoyant Renaissance. It is scarcely necessary to record here that the idealistic scheme of the king and his friends soon tumbles in a heap.

After the round of experimental comedies, and before the period of the major romantic comedies fully blossomed, Shakespeare wrote two others that differ widely from each other and also stand virtually alone and apart from all others. The first of these, *A Midsummer Night's Dream*, is a fantasy that blends elements of farce and the true romantic comedy species that follows. It was very possibly Shakespeare's first unqualified masterpiece. (See the afterword to this play.) No less anomalous than the *Dream* in the canon of comedies is *The Taming of the Shrew*, over the centuries one of Shakespeare's most popular acting plays. This play is unique in uniting within a common frame two plots, one dominated by a mixture of farce and burlesque, the other by the usual elements of the major romantic comedies. The first of these plots, the shrew plot, is mainly rollicking horseplay involved with the taming of "Kate the curst" by a bridegroom even more ferocious than she. The second plot, concerned with the wooing and winning of the shrew's sister, Bianca, employs multiple disguises among its characters and exploits incidents of mistaken identity among other devices that relate it to the romantic comedies. Shakespeare gave the *Shrew* an additional dimension by setting the entire play within an ingenious frame so that both the Kate plot and the Bianca plot constitute a play within a play, the whole being staged for the entertainment of a drunken beggar who has been made to believe that he is a lord. All in all, the *Shrew* represents one of Shakespeare's most remarkable accomplishments in the art of uniting distinct plots—in this case plots composed of sharply contrasting elements—within one brilliantly fused work of art.

During the next four or five years, from about 1596 to 1600–1601, Shakespeare wrote the major romantic comedies: *The Merchant of Venice, Much Ado About Nothing, As You Like It,* and *Twelfth Night*; incredibly, within this space of time he wrote the great history plays, both parts of *Henry IV* and *Henry V*, as well. Suddenly, after the very brief period of apprenticeship with the first comedies and histories and the single "lyrical year" of 1595–1596, he had reached full maturity, a time when there was no longer anything that as poet and dramatic craftsman he could not do with apparent ease. The romantic comedies retain the music of 1595, but it was now richer, more complex, more full-throated; in addition, it was turned on full force only when dramatically "right"—as in the duet of Lorenzo and Jessica at Portia's Belmost villa (*Merchant of Venice*) or in the delicate interviews of Viola-Cesario first with Orsino and then with Olivia in love-infected Illyria (*Twelfth Night*)—for now the dramatist Shakespeare controlled his lyric impulses and not they him. During this same period Shakespeare became absolute master of the art of characterization. If the romantic comedies do not boast such many-faceted and full-length portrait studies as the histories—Henry IV, Hal-Henry, Falstaff, Hotspur, Worcester—it is only because romantic comedy has less need for them. Yet the characters of Shylock and Portia in *The Merchant of Venice*; of Rosalind, Jaques, and Touchstone in *As You Like It*; of Viola, Sir Toby, and Feste in *Twelfth Night*; and of Benedick, Beatrice, and Dogberry in *Much Ado* are as solidly represented as the insubstantial world of romance can comfortably support.

For the worlds of all the romantic comedies are patently make-believe and gossamer, into which mundane reality can hardly intrude without destruction. Of these plays, perhaps more than any others by Shakespeare, Coleridge's words are deadly accurate: they entice the reader into a "willing suspension of disbelief." The reader who resists the enticement, who looks about him for the familiar signs of workaday fact and no nonsense, will miss entirely their point and the experience of them as works of art. Dealing centrally in Shakespeare's persistent trilogy of youth, love, and beauty, they require to be taken on their own terms. Not one of them states the single theme of all quite so precisely as does Lysander in *A Midsummer Night's Dream* (which is not one of them, but a fantasy that borders on their domain): "The course of true love never did run smooth." The heroes and heroines of the romantic comedies—Portia and Bassanio (and Nerissa and Gratiano), Hero and Claudio (and Beatrice and Benedick), Rosalind and Orlando (and Phebe and Silvius), Viola and Orsino (and Olivia and Sebastian)—are not afflicted by a single one of the woes of courtship that are spelled out by Lysander and his Hermia:

> LYSANDER. . . . . either it was different in blood—
>   HERMIA. O cross! Too high to be enthrall'd to low.
> LYSANDER. Or else misgraffed in respect of years—
>   HERMIA. O spite! Too old to be engag'd to young.
> LYSANDER. Or else it stood upon the choice of friends—
>   HERMIA. O hell! To choose love by another's eyes.

But every pair (and it is noteworthy that every comedy presents at least two pairs) has obstacles suited to its own condition. And of course it is also noteworthy (and quite predictable) that the obstacles that impede the course of true love are at last dissolved, and the multiple marriages that conclude *As You Like It* epitomize the happy resolutions to all problems of all the romantic comedies. For these are worlds in which, at last, all things come right, and Shakespeare nowhere shows a higher art than that with which he charms us into accepting these enchanted worlds.

Toward the close of the period of the romantic comedies, Shakespeare wrote (according to legend, in two weeks' time) a comedy that belongs to no group, *The Merry Wives of Windsor*. The Falstaff of the first and second parts of *Henry IV* reputedly won not only general public acclaim, but favor in very high circles indeed, and Queen Elizabeth herself is supposed to have commanded Shakespeare to write a new play showing Falstaff (whom Shakespeare had already killed off early in *Henry V*) in love. Now the Falstaff of the history plays is not only a man of wit, but "the cause that wit is in other men." In commanding Shakespeare (if in fact she did command him) to show Falstaff in love, the queen inevitably required the dramatist to make a fool of him, for the qualities (and the quantity) of Falstaff are not those of which romantic heroes are made. The resulting play shows Falstaff not at his best, but subjects him to humiliation from which there is no adequate redemption, even though this play, too, like the romantic comedies, ends with everyone happy. Says Mrs. Page, one of the "merry wives," "let us everyone go home,/ And laugh this sport o'er by a country fire,/ Sir John and all." *The Merry Wives* was Shakespeare's sole attempt at a domestic comedy of contemporary English upper middle-class society; it is a comedy dominated by the spirit of farce, and the speedy action is moved by a succession of intrigues, in greater number than elsewhere in Shakespeare, roughly a dozen in all, that are carried on by multiple groups of characters, some for the mere sport of it, some for love, some for gain, some for revenge, and some (to borrow Rosalind's phrasing in *As You Like It*) "for the love of mockery." Technically, and as pure entertainment, the play is a masterpiece, and except that it offends us sentimentally by making a fool of Falstaff we might prefer to give it higher rank in the canon of comedies than criticism has accorded it. There is a measure of satisfaction in the fact that Verdi chose the Falstaff of this play, not that of the Henry plays, for his most entertaining opera.

Shakespeare's comic world darkened directly after 1600, when the period of the major tragedies began. *All's Well That Ends Well, Measure for Measure*, and *Troilus and Cressida*, the so-called dark comedies, truly lack the glorious shine that characterizes the world of the romantic comedies. Though the first centers, like the romantic comedies, on a brilliant heroine and the obstacles that impede the course of true love, its action and its mood replace the former sportive chase with the grimly determined hunting down of the quarry: Helena fixes steely eyes upon her unwilling prey, weds him against his will, uses subterfuge to get herself with child by him, breaks his proud nature that had first attracted her ("His arched brows, his hawking eye, his curls"). Finally, in the presence of the king, she reduces him to the condition of a whimpering, squirming, lying wretch—and a docile, penitent husband: "I'll love her dearly, ever, ever dearly." Most of the heroes of the comedies leave a good deal to be desired in the way of personal character, and Bertram leaves everything to be desired. The best that can be said in his behalf is that a sharp-eyed, single-minded heroine of Helena's prowess wants him and is willing to run him to the ground; in the end, our satisfaction lies in our certainty that the pair deserve each other. The world of *Troilus and Cressida* is far worse, however, than that of *All's Well*, and its inhabitants, with a few exceptions such as Hector and Ulysses, are an unsavory lot. Both Trojans and Greeks are engaged in a war that they loathe, and the effects of the war have contaminated them to their very souls. "All the argument," says Thersites, a disgusting specimen himself, whom Shakespeare uses as spokesman to fix the tone and attitudes of the play, "is a cuckold and a whore": so much for Menelaus, from whom Helen was stolen, and for Helen, over whose abduction the war must be fought, and for the war itself. All that about the Trojan War which for Homer epitomized an heroic zenith Shakespeare plucks down to a miry nadir. The erstwhile incomparable Achilles is here a petty, vain, irresponsible sensualist who dawdles in his tent with Patroclus, his "masculine whore," according to Thersites, and finally kills the noble Hector—whose character stands out in the play like a diamond on a dung heap—not in valiant combat front to front but by setting his gang of Myrmidons upon him while he is unarmed. As for the hero and the heroine, Troilus is a whimpering schoolboy who, when the object of his lust (which he mistakes for love) is traded away to the Greek camp, goes into a tantrum and screams bombast at the enemy; and Cressida, whose measure is taken in precise detail by Ulysses at his first sight of her:

> Fie, fie upon her!
> There's language in her eye, her cheek, her lip,
> Nay, her foot speaks; her wanton spirits look out
> At every joint and motive of her body.

This Cressida, unlike Chaucer's Criseyde two centuries earlier, who was guilty of no more than inability to deal with circumstances, is here reduced to the status of mere strumpet. Says Thersites, observing her in company with her next lover after Troilus: "How the devil Luxury, with his fat rump and potato-finger, tickles these together! Fry, lechery, fry!" It is perhaps the key image of the play. But to say so much of the unappetizing atmosphere of *Troilus and Cressida* is not to condemn it as a bad play. It has proved increasingly exciting to the twentieth century, especially during the period since World War II; and it has in it two of the greatest speeches in all Shakespeare, Ulysses', "Troy, yet upon his basis, had been down" (I, iii) and the same speaker's incredibly moving speech to Achilles, "Time hath, my lord, a wallet at his back" (III, iii).[1]

Finally, after the tragedies, during the last four active years of his career, Shakespeare turned to a new and different subgenre that is conventionally called dramatic romance and that fits within the broader category of "comedy" because the four plays in the group have happy endings, however perilous their participants' journeys to them. In 1875 a Shakespearean of great fame, Edward Dowden, published a book that divided Shakespeare's career into four periods: "In the Workshop," "In the World," "In the Depths," "On the Heights." According to Dowden, Shakespeare's career as dramatist reflected his personal life, and he passed through the period of depression that produced the great tragedies and the "dark comedies" to emerge "on the heights" with *Pericles, Cymbeline, The Winter's Tale,* and *The Tempest.* No one living can say knowledgeably whether or not Shakespeare's personal life even remotely paralleled the vicissitudes of the characters who participate in his dramatic plots. It is probably more realistic to recognize that Shakespeare was always the dramatist and that his art moved with the fashion of the changing time. In and after 1608 the time was ready for "something else," and, with other, younger dramatists then active, Shakespeare gave it to them. What is more to the point, it is not at all certain that the four "romances" depict "on the heights" in any sense, biographical or dramatic. Though these plays end happily, they do so only after the participants have suffered deprivation and misery that would make tragedy's solution, death, seem a welcome respite.

In *Pericles* (which Shakespeare may have revised from another dramatist's unsatisfactory first two acts onwards) the wife, apparently dead in childbirth, is cast overboard into a raging sea and lost to her husband, the daughter lost to her father and reportedly dead, the father himself driven from his kingdom by threat of death. In the view of Pericles, the father, the world is no place of comfort:

> Alas, the seas hath cast me on the rocks,
> Wash'd me from shore to shore, and left me breath
> Nothing to think on but ensuing death.

In the view of Marina, the daughter, it is no better:

> Aye me! Poor maid,
> Born in a tempest when my mother died,
> This world to me is like a lasting storm,
> Whirring me from my friends.

---

[1]For the world of the third of these "unpleasant plays," *Measure for Measure,* see the text and Afterword for that play.
[2]For *The Winter's Tale,* probably the most representative of the romances, see the text and the Afterword to the play.

In the view of the audience, until the very end, hope appears as futile as it appears to the participants; yet Shakespeare calls upon all the resources of romance to end the play with universal harmony: wife is restored to husband, and daughter restored to both. *Pericles* in the text shows its imperfections; on the stage it can be a haunting experience the eeriness of which a spectator does not soon forget.

Cymbeline, like *Pericles*, deals with the older and the younger generations, with separation and reconciliation, loss and restoration. Wholly Shakespeare's, it is a strange and wondrous tale, more surely managed than that of *Pericles*, and growing to even greater complexity than is developed elsewhere among the dramatist's works: the elaborate denouement requires explanation of some twenty secrets that have been compounded in course of the action. The heroine, Imogen, was a favorite of the romantic critics Hazlitt and Coleridge and must, by any reasonable judgment, take her place with the great ones of the romantic comedies.[2]

Except for *Henry VIII*, very likely his only in part, Shakespeare ended his career with *The Tempest*, again a technical triumph that is related as fantasy to the much earlier *Midsummer Night's Dream* and, because of its "strange and wonderful" elements of romance, to the three plays that immediately preceded it. Because the supermagician of godlike proportions, Prospero, speaks words that can readily (and agreeably) be associated with Shakespeare's career

> . . . I have bedimm'd
> The noontide sun, call'd forth the mutinous winds,
> And 'twixt the green sea and the azur'd vault
> Set roaring war; to the dread rattling thunder
> Have I given fire, and rifted Jove's stout oak
> With his own bolt; the strong-bas'd promontory
> Have I made shake, and by the spurs pluck'd up
> The pine and cedar; graves at my command
> Have wak'd their sleepers, op'd, and let 'em forth
> By my so potent art. . . . .

the play is often taken as being autobiographical in part, with Prospero's abdication of his magical powers

> . . . this rough magic
> I here abjure, and . . . I'll break my staff,
> Bury it certain fathoms in the earth,
> And deeper than did ever plummet sound
> I'll drown my book.

interpreted as Shakespeare's farewell to the stage. But of course it is impossible for us to know whether, when he wrote *The Tempest*, at the age of forty-seven, Shakespeare had any thought that it was to be his final play. Besides the autobiographical interpretation, various elaborate allegorical systems of meaning have been worked out from time to time in which, for example, the spirit Ariel figures as Fancy and the play as a whole signifies the triumph of Art (Prospero) over Nature (the brutish Caliban). Because of its principal characters and its strange action that occurs on a small, mysterious island all in the space of about four hours, and of course because it *was* Shakespeare's final play, in which (if ever) we might expect him to leave behind some profound philosophical comment, *The Tempest* does indeed present stronger temptation to allegory hunters and pursuers of symbolic meanings than does any of the other plays, for, except at special moments and for special purposes (see Menenius's fable of the belly in *Coriolanus*), Shakespeare seems to have made little use of allegory. Generally speaking, his art was explicit and its direction exactly opposite to that of allegorical art: his characters are exactly what they are represented to be and do not "stand for" something else, and the actions in which they engage are literal and not figurative. Nevertheless the as yet unfathomed depths of *The Tempest*, which has often been called Shakespeare's consummate work of art, continue to tempt new probers in every generation and perhaps this play is the exception to the general rule.

A Midsummer Night's Dream

DRAMATIS PERSONÆ

THESEUS *Duke of Athens*
EGEUS *father to Hermia*
LYSANDER }
DEMETRIUS } *in love with Hermia*
PHILOSTRATE *master of the revels to Theseus*
QUINCE *a carpenter*
SNUG *a joiner*
BOTTOM *a weaver*
FLUTE *a bellows-mender*
SNOUT *a tinker*
STARVELING *a tailor*
HIPPOLYTA *queen of the Amazons, betrothed to Theseus*

HERMIA *daughter to Egeus, in love with Lysander*
HELENA *in love with Demetrius*
OBERON *king of the fairies*
TITANIA *queen of the fairies*
PUCK *or Robin Goodfellow*
PEASEBLOSSOM }
COBWEB }
MOTH } *fairies*
MUSTARDSEED }
OTHER FAIRIES *attending their King and Queen.*
Attendants on Theseus and Hippolyta

SCENE *Athens, and wood near it.*

ACT I

SCENE i
Athens. The palace of THESEUS.

[*Enter* THESEUS, HIPPOLYTA, PHILOSTRATE, *and*
ATTENDANTS.]
THESEUS. Now, fair Hippolyta, our nuptial hour
  Draws on apace; four happy days bring in
  Another moon. But, O, methinks, how slow
  This old moon wanes! She lingers° my desires
5 Like to a step-dame or a dowager
  Long withering out a young man's revenue.°
HIPPOLYTA. Four days will quickly steep them-
    selves in night;
  Four nights will quickly dream away the time;
  And then the moon, like to a silver bow

New-bent in heaven, shall behold the night   10
  Of our solemnities.°
THESEUS.   Go, Philostrate,
  Stir up the Athenian youth to merriments;
  Awake the pert° and nimble spirit of mirth;
  Turn melancholy forth to funerals;
  The pale companion° is not for our pomp.   15
                [*Exit* PHILOSTRATE.]
  Hippolyta, I woo'd thee with my sword°
  And won thy love doing thee injuries;
  But I will wed thee in another key,
  With pomp, with triumph, and with reveling.
      [*Enter* EGEUS, HERMIA, LYSANDER, *and*
           DEMETRIUS.]

lingers delays
Like . . . revenue like a stepmother or widowed mother
  who lives so long as to use up her son's inheritance

solemnities festivities   *pert* lively
companion i.e., melancholy
Hippolyta . . . sword Theseus had defeated the Amazons
  and taken their queen captive

Tyrranus Pedlar Egeus (handwritten)

20 EGEUS. Happy be Theseus, our renowned duke!
THESEUS. Thanks, good Egeus. What's the news
        with thee?
EGEUS. Full of vexation come I, with complaint
    Against my child, my daughter Hermia.
    Stand forth, Demetrius. My noble lord,
25 This man hath my consent to marry her.
    Stand forth, Lysander. And, my gracious Duke,
    This man hath bewitch'd the bosom of my
        child.
    Thou, thou, Lysander, thou hast given her
        rhymes
    And interchang'd love-tokens with my child.
30 Thou hast by moonlight at her window sung,
    With feigning voices, verses of feigning love,
    And stol'n the impression of her fantasy°
    With bracelets of thy hair, rings, gawds,°
        conceits,°
    Knacks, trifles, nosegays, sweetmeats—mes-
        sengers
35 Of strong prevailment in unharden'd youth.
    With cunning hast thou filch'd my daughter's
        heart,
    Turn'd her obedience, which is due to me,
    To stubborn harshness. And, my gracious Duke,
    Be it so° she will not here before your Grace
40 Consent to marry with Demetrius,
    I beg the ancient privilege of Athens:
    As she is mine, I may dispose of her,
    Which shall be either to this gentleman
    Or to her death, according to our law
45 Immediately° provided in that case.
THESEUS. What say you, Hermia? Be advis'd, fair
        maid.
    To you your father should be as a god,
    One that compos'd your beauties, yea, and one
    To whom you are but as a form in wax
50 By him imprinted and within his power
    To leave the figure or disfigure it.
    Demetrius is a worthy gentleman.
HERMIA. So is Lysander.
THESEUS.   In himself he is;
    But in this kind,° wanting° your father's voice,
55 The other must be held the worthier.
HERMIA. I would my father look'd but with my
        eyes.
THESEUS. Rather your eyes must with his judg-
        ment look.
HERMIA. I do entreat your Grace to pardon me.
    I know not by what power I am made bold

    Nor how it may concern° my modesty   60
    In such a presence here to plead my thoughts,
    But I beseech your Grace that I may know
    The worst that may befall me in this case
    If I refuse to wed Demetrius.
THESEUS. Either to die the death or to abjure   65
    Forever the society of men.
    Therefore, fair Hermia, question your desires.
    Know of° your youth, examine well your blood,°
    Whether, if you yield not to your father's choice,
    You can endure the livery of a nun,   70
    For aye° to be in shady cloister mew'd,
    To live a barren sister all your life,
    Chanting faint hymns to the cold fruitless moon.
    Thrice-blessed they that master so their blood
    To undergo such maiden pilgrimage,   75
    But earthlier happy is the rose distill'd
    Than that which, withering on the virgin thorn,
    Grows, lives, and dies in single blessedness.
HERMIA. So will I grow, so live, so die, my lord,
    Ere I will yield my virgin patent° up   80
    Unto his lordship, whose unwished yoke
    My soul consents not to give sovereignty.
THESEUS. Take time to pause, and by the next
        new moon—
    The sealing-day° betwixt my love and me
    For everlasting bond of fellowship—   85
    Upon that day either prepare to die
    For disobedience to your father's will,
    Or else to wed Demetrius, as he would,
    Or on Diana's° altar to protest
    For aye austerity and single life.   90
DEMETRIUS. Relent, sweet Hermia, and, Lysander,
        yield
    Thy crazed title to my certain right.
LYSANDER. You have her father's love, Demetrius;   *Joke* (handwritten)
    Let me have Hermia's. Do you marry him.
EGEUS. Scornful Lysander! True, he hath my love,   95
    And what is mine my love shall render him.
    And she is mine, and all my right of her
    I do estate° unto Demetrius.
LYSANDER. I am, my lord, as well deriv'd as he,
    As well possess'd; my love is more than his;   100
    My fortunes every way as fairly rank'd,
    If not with vantage,° as Demetrius';
    And, which is more than all these boasts can be,
    I am belov'd of beauteous Hermia.
    Why should not I then prosecute my right?   105
    Demetrius, I'll avouch it to his head,°

stol'n . . . fantasy falsely made an impression on her
    fancy
gawds trinkets   conceits fancy compliments
Be it so if it be that
Immediately expressly   kind case   wanting lacking

concern compromise   Know of take cognizance of
blood passions   aye ever
virgin patent privilege of virginity
sealing-day marriage day   Diana goddess of chastity
estate bequeath   vantage advantage
avouch . . . head swear it to his face

Made love to Nedar's daughter, Helena,
And won her soul; and she, sweet lady, dotes,
Devoutly dotes, dotes in idolatry,
110 Upon this spotted and inconstant man.
THESEUS. I must confess that I have heard so much,
And with Demetrius thought to have spoke
thereof;
But, being over-full of self-affairs,
My mind did lose it. But, Demetrius, come,
115 And come, Egeus, you shall go with me;
I have some private schooling for you both.
For you, fair Hermia, look you arm yourself
To fit your fancies to your father's will,
Or else the law of Athens yields you up—
120 Which by no means we may extenuate—
To death, or to a vow of single life.
Come, my Hippolyta. What cheer, my love?
Demetrius and Egeus, go along.
I must employ you in some business
125 Against° our nuptial, and confer with you
Of something nearly that° concerns yourselves.
EGEUS. With duty and desire we follow you.
        [Exeunt all but LYSANDER and HERMIA.]
LYSANDER. How now, my love! Why is your cheek
so pale?
How chance the roses there do fade so fast?
HERMIA. Belike° for want of rain, which I could
130 well
Beteem° them from the tempest of my eyes.
LYSANDER. Aye me! For aught that I could ever
read,
Could ever hear by tale or history,
The course of true love never did run smooth;
135 But either it was different in blood—
HERMIA. O cross!° Too high to be enthrall'd° to
low.
LYSANDER. Or else misgraffed° in respect of years—
HERMIA. O spite! Too old to be engag'd to young.
LYSANDER. Or else it stood upon the choice of
friends—
140 HERMIA. O hell! To choose love by another's eyes.
LYSANDER. Or, if there were a sympathy in choice,°
War, death, or sickness did lay siege to it,
Making it momentany° as a sound,
Swift as a shadow, short as any dream,
145 Brief as the lightning in the collied° night,
That, in a spleen,° unfolds both heaven and
earth,
And ere a man hath power to say "Behold!"

The jaws of darkness do devour it up.
So quick bright things come to confusion.
HERMIA. If then true lovers have been ever cross'd,° 150
It stands as an edict in destiny.°
Then let us teach our trial patience°
Because it is a customary cross,
As due to love as thoughts and dreams and
sighs,
Wishes and tears—poor Fancy's° followers.   155
LYSANDER. A good persuasion. Therefore, hear me,
Hermia.
I have a widow aunt, a dowager
Of great revenue, and she hath no child.
From Athens is her house remote seven leagues,
And she respects° me as her only son.   160
There, gentle Hermia, may I marry thee,
And to that place the sharp Athenian law
Cannot pursue us. If thou lov'st me, then,
Steal forth thy father's house tomorrow night,
And in the wood a league without the town,   165
Where I did meet thee once with Helena
To do observance to a morn of May,°
There will I stay for thee.
HERMIA.   My good Lysander!
I swear to thee, by Cupid's strongest bow,
By his best arrow with the golden head,   170
By the simplicity of Venus' doves,°
By that which knitteth souls and prospers loves,
And by that fire which burn'd the Carthage
queen
When the false Troyan under sail was seen°—
By all the vows that ever men have broke,   175
In number more than ever women spoke,
In that same place thou hast appointed me,
Tomorrow truly will I meet with thee.
LYSANDER. Keep promise, love. Look, here comes
Helena.
              [Enter HELENA.]
HERMIA. God speed fair Helena! Whither away?   180
HELENA. Call you me fair? That fair again unsay.
Demetrius loves you fair. O happy fair!
Your eyes are lode-stars, and your tongue's
sweet air
More tuneable than lark to shepherd's ear

Against in preparation for   *nearly that* that closely
Belike likely   *Beteem* supply   *cross* perversity
enthrall'd enslaved   *misgraffed* mismatched
if . . . choice if the lovers were well matched
momentany momentary   *collied* coal-black
spleen fit of anger

ever cross'd always thwarted
edict in destiny decree of fate
teach . . . patience learn to bear our troubles with
  patience
Fancy's love's   *respects* regards
morn of May May Day, when lovers traditionally
  celebrated woodland rites
simplicity of Venus' doves the chariot of the goddess of
  love was drawn by doves
Carthage . . . seen Dido burned herself on a funeral pyre
  when the Trojan Aeneas sailed away, deserting her

185 When wheat is green, when hawthorn buds ap-
pear.
Sickness is catching. O, were favor° so,
Yours would I catch, fair Hermia, ere I go;
My ear should catch your voice, my eye your
eye,
My tongue should catch your tongue's sweet
melody.
190 Were the world mine, Demetrius being bated,°
The rest I'd give to be to you translated.°
O, teach me how you look, and with what art
You sway the motion° of Demetrius' heart!
HERMIA. I frown upon him, yet he loves me still.
195 HELENA. O that your frowns would teach my
smiles such skill!
HERMIA. I give him curses, yet he gives me love.
HELENA. O that my prayers could such affection
move!
HERMIA. The more I hate, the more he follows me.
HELENA. The more I love, the more he hateth me.
200 HERMIA. His folly, Helena, is no fault of mine.
HELENA. None but your beauty. Would that fault
were mine!
HERMIA. Take comfort. He no more shall see my
face;
Lysander and myself will fly this place.
Before the time I did Lysander see,
205 Seem'd Athens as a paradise to me.
O, then, what graces in my love do dwell,
That he hath turn'd a heaven unto a hell!
LYSANDER. Helen, to you our minds we will unfold.
Tomorrow night, when Phœbe° doth behold
210 Her silver visage in the wat'ry glass,
Decking with liquid pearl the bladed grass,
A time that lovers' flights doth still° conceal,
Through Athens' gates have we devis'd to steal.
HERMIA. And in the wood, where often you and I
215 Upon faint primrose beds were wont to lie,
Emptying our bosoms of their counsel° sweet,
There my Lysander and myself shall meet,
And thence from Athens turn away our eyes
To seek new friends and stranger companies.
220 Farewell, sweet playfellow. Pray thou for us,
And good luck grant thee thy Demetrius!
Keep word, Lysander. We must starve our sight
From lovers' food till morrow deep midnight.
LYSANDER. I will, my Hermia.   [Exit HERMIA.]
225 Helena, adieu.
As you on him, Demetrius dote on you! [Exit]

HELENA. How happy some o'er other some can be!
Through Athens I am thought as fair as she.
But what of that? Demetrius thinks not so;
He will not know what all but he do know.
230 And as he errs, doting on Hermia's eyes,
So I, admiring of his qualities,
Things base and vile, holding no quantity,°
Love can transpose to form and dignity.   *see Bottom & Hipp*
Love looks not with the eyes, but with the mind,
235 And therefore is wing'd Cupid painted blind.
Nor hath Love's mind of any judgment taste;°
Wings, and no eyes, figure unheedy° haste.
And therefore is Love said to be a child,
Because in choice he is so oft beguil'd.
240 As waggish boys in game themselves forswear,°
So the boy Love is perjur'd everywhere.
For ere Demetrius look'd on Hermia's eyne,
He hail'd down oaths that he was only mine;
And when this hail some heat from Hermia
felt,
245 So he dissolv'd, and show'rs of oaths did melt.°
I will go tell him of fair Hermia's flight;
Then to the wood will he tomorrow night
Pursue her; and for this intelligence°
If I have thanks, it is a dear° expense.
250 But herein mean I to enrich my pain,
To have his sight thither and back again.°
[Exit]

SCENE ii
The same. QUINCE'S house.

[Enter QUINCE, SNUG, BOTTOM, FLUTE, SNOUT,
and STARVELING.]
QUINCE. Is all our company here?
BOTTOM. You were best to call them generally,°
man by man, according to the scrip.°
QUINCE. Here is the scroll of every man's name
which is thought fit, through all Athens, to play   5
in our interlude° before the duke and the duchess on his wedding day at night.

---

favor i.e., both beauty and affection   bated caught
translated transformed
sway the motion rule the emotions
Phœbe Diana, the moon   still always
counsel secrets

holding no quantity having no shape
Nor . . . taste nor has Love even a trace of judgment
figure unheedy signify careless
As . . . forswear as playful boys make vows they do not
intend to keep
For . . . melt the general sense is that before Demetrius
saw Hermia he swore that he was only Helena's, but he
forgot his oath as soon as he saw Hermia
intelligence information   dear costly
But . . . again I mean to get some pleasure for my pain
by having Demetrius's company in the woods
generally Bottom means separately   scrip list
interlude play

BOTTOM. First, good Peter Quince, say what the play treats on. Then read the names of the actors, and so grow to a point.

QUINCE. Marry,° our play is, The most lamentable comedy, and most cruel death of Pyramus and Thisby.

BOTTOM. A very good piece of work, I assure you, and a merry. Now, good Peter Quince, call forth your actors by the scroll. Masters, spread yourselves.

QUINCE. Answer as I call you. Nick Bottom, the weaver.

BOTTOM. Ready. Name what part I am for, and proceed.

QUINCE. You, Nick Bottom, are set down for Pyramus.

BOTTOM. What is Pyramus? A lover, or a tyrant?°

QUINCE. A lover, that kills himself most gallant° for love.

BOTTOM. That will ask some tears in the true performing of it. If I do it, let the audience look to their eyes; I will move storms, I will condole° in some measure. To the rest.° Yet my chief humor° is for a tyrant. I could play Ercles rarely, or a part to tear a cat in, to make all split.°

The raging rocks
And shivering shocks
Shall break the locks
　Of prison-gates;
And Phibbus' car°
Shall shine from far,
And make and mar
　The foolish Fates.

This was lofty! Now name the rest of the players. This is Ercles' vein, a tyrant's vein; a lover is more condoling.

QUINCE. Francis Flute, the bellows-mender.

FLUTE. Here, Peter Quince.

QUINCE. Flute, you must take Thisby on you.

FLUTE. What is Thisby? A wand'ring knight?

QUINCE. It is the lady that Pyramus must love.

FLUTE. Nay, faith, let not me play a woman; I have a beard coming.

QUINCE. That's all one. You shall play it in a mask, and you may speak as small° as you will.

BOTTOM. An I may hide my face, let me play Thisby too. I'll speak in a monstrous little voice, "Thisne! Thisne!" "Ah Pyramus, my lover dear! Thy Thisby dear, and lady dear!"

QUINCE. No, no! You must play Pyramus; and, Flute, you Thisby.

BOTTOM. Well, proceed.

QUINCE. Robin Starveling, the tailor.

STARVELING. Here, Peter Quince.

QUINCE. Robin Starveling, you must play Thisby's mother. Tom Snout, the tinker.

SNOUT. Here, Peter Quince.

QUINCE. You, Pyramus' father; myself, Thisby's father; Snug, the joiner, you, the lion's part. And, I hope, here is a play fitted.

SNUG. Have you the lion's part written? Pray you, if it be, give it me, for I am slow of study.

QUINCE. You may do it extempore, for it is nothing but roaring.

BOTTOM. Let me play the lion too. I will roar, that I will do any man's heart good to hear me; I will roar, that I will make the duke say, "Let him roar again, let him roar again."

QUINCE. An you should do it too terribly, you would fright the duchess and the ladies, that they would shriek; and that were enough to hang us all.

ALL. That would hang us, every mother's son.

BOTTOM. I grant you, friends, if you should fright the ladies out of their wits, they would have no more discretion but to hang us. But I will aggravate° my voice so that I will roar you as gently as any sucking dove; I will roar you an 'twere° any nightingale.

QUINCE. You can play no part but Pyramus; for Pyramus is a sweet-faced man, a proper° man as one shall see in a summer's day, a most lovely, gentleman-like man. Therefore you must needs play Pyramus.

BOTTOM. Well, I will undertake it. What beard were I best to play it in?

QUINCE. Why, what you will.

BOTTOM. I will discharge it in either your straw-color beard, your orange-tawny beard, your purple-in-grain beard, or your French-crown-color beard, your perfect yellow.°

QUINCE. Some of your French crowns have no hair

Marry　by the Virgin Mary (a mild and frequent oath)
lover . . . tyrant　i.e., stock figures in contemporary plays
gallant　gallantly　　*condole*　grieve
To the rest　i.e., get on with the other parts
humor　inclination
Ercles . . . split　Hercules was portrayed as a ranting figure in medieval plays, given to horrendous and ear-splitting sounds
Phibbus' car　the chariot of the sun god, Phoebus

small　shrilly
aggravate　Bottom's blunder for *moderate*
an 'twere　as if it were　　*proper*　handsome
I . . . yellow　Bottom alludes to variously dyed beards commonly seen on the stage

at all,° and then you will play barefaced. But, masters, here are your parts. And I am to entreat you, request you, and desire you, to con° them by tomorrow night; and meet me in the palace wood, a mile without the town, by moonlight. There will we rehearse, for if we meet in the city, we shall be dogged with company, and our devices° known. In the meantime I will

105

Some . . . all (Quince puns on Bottom's *crown*, meaning gold coin; Quince's *crown* refers to heads bald from the "French disease," syphilis)
con memorize   *devices* stage effects

draw a bill of properties such as our play wants. I pray you, fail me not.

110

BOTTOM. We will meet, and there we may rehearse most obscenely° and courageously. Take pains; be perfect. Adieu.

QUINCE. At the duke's oak we meet.

BOTTOM. Enough. Hold or cut bow-strings.°

115

[*Exeunt*]

obscenely Bottom's blunder for *obscurely* (his sense of *courageously* is undetermined)
Hold . . . bow-strings i.e., be there or else!

ACT II

Puck identified

SCENE i

A wood near Athens.

[*Enter, from opposite sides, a* FAIRY, *and* PUCK.]

PUCK. How now, spirit! Whither wander you?

FAIRY. Over hill, over dale,
  Thorough° bush, thorough brier,
  Over park, over pale,°
5 Thorough flood, thorough fire,
  I do wander everywhere,
  Swifter than the moon's sphere;
  And I serve the fairy queen,
  To dew her orbs upon the green.°
10 The cowslips tall her pensioners° be.
  In their gold coats spots you see;
  Those be rubies, fairy favors;
  In those freckles live their savors.°
  I must go seek some dewdrops here
15 And hang a pearl in every cowslip's ear.
  Farewell, thou lob° of spirits; I'll be gone.
  Our queen and all her elves come here anon.°

PUCK. The King doth keep his revels here tonight.
  Take heed the Queen come not within his sight,
20 For Oberon is passing fell and wrath°
  Because that she as her attendant hath
  A lovely boy, stolen from an Indian king.
  She never had so sweet a changeling,°

Thorough through *pale* fence
To . . . green allusion to the belief that the dark green circles of grass seen in pastures are the effects of fairies' attention
pensioners attendants
savors perfumes *lob* lout *anon* at once
passing . . . wrath surpassingly cruel and wrathful
changeling a child secretly substituted for another by spirits

And jealous Oberon would have the child
Knight of his train, to trace the forests wild;   25
But she perforce° withholds the loved boy,
Crowns him with flowers, and makes him all
  her joy.
And now they never meet in grove or green,
By fountain clear, or spangled starlight sheen,
But they do square,° that° all their elves for fear   30
Creep into acorn cups and hide them there.

FAIRY. Either I mistake your shape and making°
  quite,
  Or else you are that shrewd and knavish sprite
  Call'd Robin Goodfellow. Are not you he
  That frights the maidens of the villagery,   35
  Skim milk, and sometimes labor in the quern°
  And bootless° make the breathless housewife
    churn,
  And sometime make the drink to bear no
    barm,°
  Mislead night-wanderers, laughing at their
    harm?
  Those that Hobgoblin call you, and sweet Puck,   40
  You do their work, and they shall have good
    luck.
  Are not you he?

PUCK.   Thou speak'st aright.
  I am that merry wanderer of the night.
  I jest to Oberon and make him smile
  When I a fat and bean-fed horse beguile,   45
  Neighing in likeness of a filly foal.
  And sometimes lurk I in a gossip's° bowl
  In very likeness of a roasted crab,°

perforce forcibly   *square* quarrel   *that* so that
making form   *quern* hand mill   *bootless* useless
barm froth   *gossip's* housewife's   *crab* crabapple

practical Joke

And when she drinks, against her lips I bob
50 And on her wither'd dewlap pour the ale.
The wisest aunt, telling the saddest tale,
Sometime for three-foot stool mistaketh me;
Then slip I from her bum,° down topples she,
And "tailor" cries,° and falls into a cough,
55 And then the whole quire° hold their hips and
      laugh,
And waxen° in their mirth, and neeze,° and
      swear
A merrier hour was never wasted there.
But, room, fairy! Here comes Oberon.
FAIRY. And here my mistress. Would that he were
      gone!
      [*Enter, from one side,* OBERON, *with his train;
            from the other,* TITANIA, *with hers.*]
60 OBERON. Ill met by moonlight, proud Titania.
TITANIA. What, jealous Oberon! Fairies, skip
      hence.
I have forsworn his bed and company.
OBERON. Tarry, rash wanton! Am not I thy lord?
TITANIA. Then I must be thy lady. But I know
65 When thou hast stolen away from fairyland,
And in the shape of Corin sat all day
Playing on pipes of corn° and versing love
To amorous Phillida.° Why art thou here,
Come from the farthest steppe of India,
70 But that, forsooth,° the bouncing Amazon,
Your buskin'd° mistress and your warrior love,
To Theseus must be wedded, and you come
To give their bed joy and prosperity?
OBERON. How canst thou thus for shame, Titania,
75 Glance at my credit with Hippolyta,
Knowing I know thy love to Theseus?
Didst thou not lead him through the glimmer-
      ing night
From Perigenia, whom he ravished?
And make him with fair Ægle break his faith,
80 With Ariadne and Antiopa?°
TITANIA. These are the forgeries° of jealousy.
And never since the middle summer's spring
Met we on hill, in dale, forest, or mead,
By paved fountain or by rushy brook,
85 Or in the beached margent° of the sea,
To dance our ringlets° to the whistling wind,

But with thy brawls thou hast disturb'd our
      sport.
Therefore the winds, piping to us in vain,
As in revenge, have suck'd up from the sea
Contagious fogs, which, falling in the land,   90
Have every pelting° river made so proud
That they have overborne their continents.°
The ox hath therefore stretch'd his yoke in vain,
The ploughman lost his sweat, and the green
      corn°
Hath rotted ere his° youth attain'd a beard.   95
The fold° stands empty in the drowned field,
And crows are fatted with the murrion° flock.
The nine men's morris is fill'd up with mud,
And the quaint mazes in the wanton green,°
For lack of tread, are undistinguishable.   100
The human mortals want° their winter cheer;
No night is now with hymn or carol blest.
Therefore the moon, the governess of floods,
Pale in her anger, washes all the air,
That° rheumatic diseases do abound.   105
And thorough this distemperature° we see
The seasons alter: hoary-headed frosts
Fall in the fresh lap of the crimson rose,
And on old Hiems'° thin and icy crown
An odorous chaplet° of sweet summer buds   110
Is, as in mockery, set. The spring, the summer,
The childing° autumn, angry winter, change
Their wonted° liveries, and the mazed° world,
By their increase, now knows not which is
      which.
And this same progeny of evils comes   115
From our debate, from our dissension.
We are their parents and original.°
OBERON. Do you amend it, then; it lies in you.
Why should Titania cross her Oberon?
I do but beg a little changeling boy   120
To be my henchman.°
TITANIA.   Set your heart at rest:
The fairyland buys not the child of me.
His mother was a votaress of my order,
And in the spiced Indian air by night
Full often hath she gossip'd by my side   125
And sat with me on Neptune's yellow sands,

bum bottom
"tailor" cries meaning uncertain, possible contrast with
      header
quire company   *waxen* grow   *neeze* sneeze
Corin . . . Phillida conventional names in pastoral poetry
pipes of corn oaten straws, musical instruments
forsooth in truth   *buskin'd* booted
Perigenia . . . Antiopa some of the women in Theseus's
      life
forgeries imaginings   *margent* margin
ringlets circling dances

pelting petty   *continents* banks
corn grain (not maize)   *his* its
fold sheep pen   *murrion* plague-stricken
nine . . . morris game played on a square with pebbles or
      stones
quaint . . . green intricate paths in the wild grass
want lack   *That* so that
thorough . . . distemperature through this disorder
Hiems winter   *odorous chaplet* fragrant garland
childing fruitful   *wonted* customary
mazed amazed   *original* origin
henchman i.e., page

Marking th' embarked traders° on the flood,
When we have laugh'd to see the sails conceive°
And grow big-bellied with the wanton wind,
130 Which she, with pretty and with swimming gait
Following—her womb then rich with my
        young squire—
Would imitate, and sail upon the land
To fetch me trifles, and return again
As from a voyage, rich with merchandise.
135 But she, being mortal, of that boy did die;
And for her sake do I rear up her boy,
And for her sake I will not part with him.
OBERON. How long within this wood intend you
        stay?
TITANIA. Perchance till after Theseus' wedding day.
140 If you will patiently dance in our round
And see our moonlight revels, go with us;
If not, shun me, and I will spare your haunts.
OBERON. Give me that boy, and I will go with thee.
TITANIA. Not for thy fairy kingdom. Fairies, away!
145 We shall chide° downright, if I longer stay.
                [Exit TITANIA with her train.]
OBERON. Well, go thy way. Thou shalt not from
        this grove
Till I torment thee for this injury.
My gentle Puck, come hither. Thou remem-
        berest
Since° once I sat upon a promontory
150 And heard a mermaid on a dolphin's back
Uttering such dulcet and harmonious breath
That the rude sea grew civil at her song,
And certain stars shot madly from their spheres
To hear the sea-maid's music.
PUCK.   I remember.
OBERON. That very time I saw, but thou couldst
155   not,
Flying between the cold moon and the earth,
Cupid all arm'd. A certain aim he took
At a fair vestal° throned by the west,
And loos'd his love-shaft smartly from his bow
160 As it should pierce a hundred thousand hearts.
But I might see young Cupid's fiery shaft
Quench'd in the chaste beams of the wat'ry
        moon,
And the imperial vot'ress passed on
In maiden meditation, fancy-free.
165 Yet mark'd I where the bolt of Cupid fell.
It fell upon a little western flower,

Before milk-white, now purple with love's
        wound,
And maidens call it love-in-idleness.° *party*
Fetch me that flower, the herb I show'd thee
        once.
The juice of it on sleeping eyelids laid   170
Will make or man or° woman madly dote
Upon the next live creature that it sees.
Fetch me this herb, and be thou here again
Ere the leviathan can swim a league.
PUCK. I'll put a girdle round° about the earth   175
In forty minutes.
OBERON.   Having once this juice,
I'll watch Titania when she is asleep
And drop the liquor of it in her eyes.
The next thing then she waking looks upon,
Be it on lion, bear, or wolf, or bull,   180
On meddling monkey, or on busy ape,
She shall pursue it with the soul of love.
And ere I take this charm from off her sight—
As I can take it with another herb—
I'll make her render up her page to me.   185
But who comes here? I am invisible,
And I will overhear their conference.
        [Enter DEMETRIUS, HELENA following him.]
DEMETRIUS. I love thee not, therefore pursue me
        not.
Where is Lysander and fair Hermia?
The one I'll slay, the other slayeth me.   190
Thou told'st me they were stolen unto this
        wood,
And here am I, and wood within this wood°
Because I cannot meet my Hermia.
Hence! Get thee gone, and follow me no more.
HELENA. You draw me, you hardhearted ada-
        mant,°   195
But yet you draw not iron, for my heart
Is true as steel.° Leave you° your power to draw,
And I shall have no power to follow you.
DEMETRIUS. Do I entice you? Do I speak you fair?°
Or, rather, do I not in plainest truth   200
Tell you I do not nor I cannot love you?
HELENA. And even for that do I love you the more.
I am your spaniel; and, Demetrius,
The more you beat me, I will fawn on you.
Use me but as your spaniel, spurn me, strike me, 205
Neglect me, lose me—only give me leave,
Unworthy as I am, to follow you.

embarked traders merchant ships
conceive become pregnant   *spare* avoid
chide quarrel
Since when   *vestal* virgin (evidently in compliment
    to Queen Elizabeth, as is the entire passage; the Queen
    was possibly present on the occasion of the first
    performance)

love-in-idleness the pansy *or ... or* either ... or
put ... round fly around
wood ... wood mad within this wood
adamant a stone both hard and magnetic
But ... steel but in this case you (the magnet) attract
    not ordinary iron but true steel (my heart)
Leave you give up   *fair* courteously

Speed

What worser place can I beg in your love—
And yet a place of high respect with me—
210   Than to be used as you use your dog?
DEMETRIUS. Tempt not too much the hatred of my spirit,
For I am sick when I do look on thee.
HELENA. And I am sick when I look not on you.
DEMETRIUS. You do impeach° your modesty too much,
215   To leave the city and commit yourself
Into the hands of one that loves you not,
To trust the opportunity of night
And the ill counsel of a desert place
With the rich worth of your virginity.
220 HELENA. Your virtue is my privilege.° For that
It is not night when I do see your face,
Therefore I think I am not in the night;
Nor doth this wood lack worlds of company,
For you in my respect° are all the world.
225   Then how can it be said I am alone,
When all the world is here to look on me?
DEMETRIUS. I'll run from thee and hide me in the brakes,
And leave thee to the mercy of wild beasts.
HELENA. The wildest hath not such a heart as you.
230   Run when you will, the story shall be chang'd:
Apollo flies and Daphne holds the chase,°
The dove pursues the griffin, the mild hind
Makes speed to catch the tiger—bootless speed,
When cowardice pursues and valor flies.
DEMETRIUS. I will not stay thy questions;° let me
235   go.
Or, if thou follow me, do not believe
But I shall do thee mischief in the wood.
HELENA. Aye, in the temple, in the town, the field,
You do me mischief. Fie, Demetrius!
240   Your wrongs do set a scandal on my sex.
We cannot fight for love, as men may do;
We should be woo'd, and were not made to woo.   [Exit DEMETRIUS.]
I'll follow thee, and make a heaven of hell,
To die upon the hand I love so well.   [Exit]
OBERON. Fare thee well, nymph. Ere he do leave
245   this grove,
Thou shalt fly him, and he shall seek thy love.
          Re-enter PUCK.
Hast thou the flower there? Welcome, wanderer.
PUCK. Aye, there it is.
OBERON.   I pray thee, give it me.

I know a bank where the wild thyme blows,°
Where oxlips and the nodding violet grows,   250
Quite over-canopied with luscious woodbine,
With sweet musk-roses, and with eglantine.
There sleeps Titania sometime of the night,
Lull'd in these flowers with dances and delight;
And there the snake throws her enamell'd skin,   255
Weed° wide enough to wrap a fairy in.
And with the juice of this I'll streak her eyes
And make her full of hateful fantasies.°
Take thou some of it, and seek through this grove.
A sweet Athenian lady is in love   260
With a disdainful youth. Anoint his eyes;
But do it when the next thing he espies
May be the lady. Thou shalt know the man
By the Athenian garments he hath on.
Effect it with some care, that he may prove   265
More fond on her than she upon her love.
And look thou meet me ere the first cock crow.
PUCK. Fear not, my lord, your servant shall do so.
          [Exeunt]

SCENE ii
Another part of the wood.

[Enter TITANIA, with her train.]
TITANIA. Come, now a roundel° and a fairy song,
Then, for the third part of a minute, hence—
Some to kill cankers° in the musk-rose buds,
Some war with rere-mice° for their leathern wings
To make my small elves coats, and some keep back   5
The clamorous owl that nightly hoots and wonders
At our quaint spirits. Sing me now asleep,
Then to your offices and let me rest.

          Song
FIRST FAIRY. You spotted snakes with double tongue,
Thorny hedgehogs, be not seen;   10
Newts and blind-worms,° do no wrong,
Come not near our fairy queen.

CHORUS. Philomel,° with melody
Sing in our sweet lullaby;

impeach discredit   *privilege* safeguard
For that because   *respect* regard
Apollo . . . chase Daphne, a nymph, pursued by the
   sun god Apollo, prayed for help and was turned into a
   laurel tree; here Helena reverses the situation

stay thy questions stay to hear your arguments
blows blooms   *Weed* garment
fantasies imaginings   *roundel* round dance
cankers cankerworms   *rere-mice* bats
Newts . . . blind-worms lizardlike reptiles
Philomel (according to Greek mythology, the daughter of
   the king of Athens, having been wronged by Tereus,
   king of Thrace, was turned into a nightingale)

15 Lulla, lulla, lullaby; lulla, lulla, lullaby.
  Never harm,
  Nor spell, nor charm,
  Come our lovely lady nigh.
  So, good night, with lullaby.
20 FIRST FAIRY. Weaving spiders, come not here;
  Hence, you long-legg'd spinners, hence!
  Beetles black, approach not near;
  Worm nor snail, do no offense.

CHORUS. Philomel, with melody, &c.
        [TITANIA *sleeps.*]

25 SECOND FAIRY. Hence, away! Now all is well.
  One aloof stand sentinel.
       [*Exeunt* FAIRIES.]
  [*Enter* OBERON *and squeezes the flower on*
    TITANIA'S *eyelids.*]
OBERON. What thou seest when thou dost wake,
  Do it for thy true-love take;
  Love and languish for his sake.
30 Be it ounce,° or cat, or bear,
  Pard,° or boar with bristled hair,
  In thy eye that° shall appear
  When thou wak'st, it is thy dear.
  Wake when some vile thing is near.   [*Exit*]
    [*Enter* LYSANDER *and* HERMIA.]
LYSANDER. Fair love, you faint with wand'ring in
35 the wood;
  And to speak troth,° I have forgot our way.
  We'll rest us, Hermia, if you think it good,
  And tarry for the comfort of the day.
HERMIA. Be it so, Lysander. Find you out a bed,
40 For I upon this bank will rest my head.
LYSANDER. One turf shall serve as pillow for us
  both—
  One heart, one bed, two bosoms, and one troth.°
HERMIA. Nay, good Lysander. For my sake, my
  dear,
  Lie further off yet; do not lie so near.
LYSANDER. O, take the sense, sweet, of my inno-
45 cence!
  Love takes the meaning in love's conference.°
  I mean that my heart unto yours is knit,
  So that but one heart we can make of it:
  Two bosoms interchained with an oath,
50 So then two bosoms and a single troth.
  Then by your side no bed-room me deny;
  For lying so, Hermia, I do not lie.°

ounce lynx *cat..*wildcat *Pard* leopard
that whatever *troth* truth *troth* betrothal
take . . . conference believe in the innocence of my
 intentions, for in lovers' conversation love guides the
 understanding
For . . . lie pun: I am not lying to you in order to lie
 beside you

HERMIA. Lysander riddles very prettily.
  Now much beshrew° my manners and my pride
  If Hermia meant to say Lysander lied.   55
  But, gentle friend, for love and courtesy
  Lie further off; in humane modesty,
  Such separation as may well be said
  Becomes a virtuous bachelor and a maid,
  So far be distant. And good night, sweet friend. 60
  Thy love ne'er alter till thy sweet life end!
LYSANDER. Amen, amen, to that fair prayer, say I;
  And then end life when I end loyalty!
  Here is my bed. Sleep give thee all his rest!
HERMIA. With half that wish the wisher's eyes be
  press'd!   [*They sleep.*] 65
    [*Enter* PUCK.]
PUCK. Through the forest have I gone,
  But Athenian found I none
  On whose eyes I might approve
  This flower's force in stirring love.
  Night and silence.—Who is here?   70
  Weeds of Athens he doth wear.
  This is he my master said
  Despised the Athenian maid,
  And here the maiden, sleeping sound,
  On the dank and dirty ground.   75
  Pretty soul! She durst not lie
  Near this lack-love, this kill-courtesy.
  Churl, upon thy eyes I throw
  All the power this charm doth owe.
  When thou wak'st, let love forbid   80
  Sleep his seat on thy eyelid.
  So awake when I am gone,
  For I must now to Oberon.   [*Exit*]
  [*Enter* DEMETRIUS *and* HELENA, *running.*]
HELENA. Stay, though thou kill me, sweet Deme-
  trius.
DEMETRIUS. I charge thee, hence, and do not haunt
  me thus.   85
HELENA. O, wilt thou darkling° leave me? Do not
  so.
DEMETRIUS. Stay, on thy peril. I alone will go.
         [*Exit*]
HELENA. O, I am out of breath in this fond° chase!
  The more my prayer, the lesser is my grace.
  Happy is Hermia, wheresoe'er she lies,   90
  For she hath blessed and attractive eyes.
  How came her eyes so bright? Not with salt
  tears;
  If so, my eyes are oftener wash'd than hers.
  No, no, I am as ugly as a bear,
  For beasts that meet me run away for fear.   95
  Therefore no marvel though Demetrius

beshrew mischief on
darkling in the dark *fond* foolish

couplets

Do, as a monster, fly my presence thus.
What wicked and dissembling glass of mine
Made me compare with Hermia's sphery° eyne?
100 But who is here? Lysander! On the ground!
Dead? Or asleep? I see no blood, no wound.
Lysander, if you live, good sir, awake.
LYSANDER [*Awaking*] And run through fire I will
   for thy sweet sake.
Transparent° Helena! Nature shows art,
That through thy bosom makes me see thy
105   heart.
Where is Demetrius? O, how fit a word
Is that vile name to perish on my sword!
HELENA. Do not say so, Lysander; say not so.
What though he love your Hermia? Lord, what
   though?
110 Yet Hermia still loves you; then be content.
LYSANDER. Content with Hermia! No; I do repent
The tedious minutes I with her have spent.
Not Hermia but Helena I love.
Who will not change° a raven for a dove?
115 The will of man is by his reason sway'd,
And reason says you are the worthier maid.
Things growing are not ripe until their season.
So I, being young, till now ripe not to reason;
And touching now the point° of human skill,°
120 Reason becomes the marshal to my will
And leads me to your eyes, where I o'erlook°
Love's stories written in love's richest book.
HELENA. Wherefore was I to this keen mockery
   born?
When at your hands did I deserve this scorn?
125 Is't not enough, is't not enough, young man,
That I did never, no, nor never can,

Deserve a sweet look from Demetrius' eye,
But you must flout my insufficiency?
Good troth, you do me wrong, good sooth, you
   do,
In such disdainful manner me to woo.
130 But fare you well. Perforce I must confess
I thought you lord of more true gentleness.°
O, that a lady, of one man refus'd,
Should of another therefore be abus'd!   [*Exit*]
LYSANDER. She sees not Hermia. Hermia, sleep
   thou there. 135
And never mayst thou come Lysander near!
For as a surfeit of the sweetest things
The deepest loathing to the stomach brings,
Or as the heresies that men do leave
Are hated most of° those they did deceive, 140
So thou, my surfeit and my heresy,
Of all be hated, but the most of me!
And, all my powers, address° your love and
   might
To honor Helen and to be her knight!   [*Exit*]
HERMIA [*Awaking*] Help me, Lysander, help me!
Do thy best 145
To pluck this crawling serpent from my breast!
Aye me, for pity! What a dream was here!
Lysander, look how I do quake with fear.
Methought a serpent eat my heart away,
And you sat smiling at his cruel prey.° 150
Lysander! What, remov'd? Lysander! Lord!
What, out of hearing? Gone? No sound, no
   word?
Alack, where are you? Speak, an if you hear;
Speak, of all loves!° I swoon almost with fear.
No? Then I well perceive you are not nigh. 155
Either death or you I'll find immediately.
        [*Exit*]

sphery eyne   starry eyes
Transparent   because her heart is visible
change   exchange   *point*   height   *skill*   reason
o'erlook   study   *gentleness*   courtesy

of   by   *address*   apply   *prey*   preying
of all loves   for love's sake

ACT III

SCENE i
The wood. TITANIA *lying asleep.*

[*Enter* QUINCE, SNUG, BOTTOM, FLUTE, SNOUT,
and STARVELING.]
BOTTOM. Are we all met?
QUINCE. Pat, pat, and here's a marvelous convenient place for our rehearsal. This green plot
shall be our stage, this hawthorn-brake our

tiring-house,° and we will do it in action as we 5
will do it before the duke.
BOTTOM. Peter Quince—
QUINCE. What sayest thou, bully° Bottom?
BOTTOM. There are things in this comedy of Pyra-
mus and Thisby that will never please. First, 10
Pyramus must draw a sword to kill himself,

tiring-house   dressing room   *bully*   "old boy"

which the ladies cannot abide. How answer you
that?

SNOUT. By'r lakin,° a parlous° fear.

15 STARVELING. I believe we must leave the killing
out, when all is done.

BOTTOM. Not a whit. I have a device to make all
well. Write me a prologue, and let the prologue seem to say we will do no harm with our
20 swords, and that Pyramus is not killed indeed;
and, for the more better assurance, tell them
that I Pyramus am not Pyramus, but Bottom the
weaver. This will put them out of fear.

QUINCE. Well, we will have such a prologue, and
25 it shall be written in eight and six.°

BOTTOM. No, make it two more. Let it be written
in eight and eight.

SNOUT. Will not the ladies be afeard of the lion?

STARVELING. I fear it, I promise you.

30 BOTTOM. Masters, you ought to consider with
yourselves. To bring in—God shield us!—a lion
among ladies, is a most dreadful thing; for
there is not a more fearful wildfowl than your
lion living, and we ought to look to 't.

35 SNOUT. Therefore another prologue must tell he
is not a lion.

BOTTOM. Nay, you must name his name, and half
his face must be seen through the lion's neck;
and he himself must speak through, saying
40 thus, or to the same defect°—"Ladies"—or
"Fair ladies—I would wish you"—or "I would
request you"—or "I would entreat you—not to
fear, not to tremble. My life for yours. If you
think I come hither as a lion, it were pity of my
45 life.° No, I am no such thing; I am a man as
other men are." And there indeed let him
name his name and tell them plainly he is
Snug the joiner.

QUINCE. Well, it shall be so. But there is two hard
50 things: that is, to bring the moonlight into a
chamber; for, you know, Pyramus and Thisby
meet by moonlight.

SNOUT. Doth the moon shine that night we play
our play?

55 BOTTOM. A calendar, a calendar! Look in the
almanac; find out moonshine, find out moonshine.

QUINCE. Yes, it doth shine that night.

BOTTOM. Why, then may you leave a casement of
60 the great chamber window, where we play,

open, and the moon may shine in at the casement.

QUINCE. Aye, or else one must come in with a
bush of thorns and a lantern, and say he comes
to disfigure,° or to present, the person of moon- 65
shine. Then, there is another thing: we must
have a wall in the great chamber, for Pyramus
and Thisby, says the story, did talk through the
chink of a wall.

SNOUT. You can never bring in a wall. What say 70
you, Bottom?

BOTTOM. Some man or other must present wall.
And let him have some plaster, or some loam,
or some rough-cast about him, to signify wall;
and let him hold his fingers thus, and through 75
that cranny shall Pyramus and Thisby whisper.

QUINCE. If that may be, then all is well. Come, sit
down, every mother's son, and rehearse your
parts. Pyramus, you begin. When you have
spoken your speech, enter into that brake; and 80
so every one according to his cue.

[*Enter* PUCK *behind.*]

PUCK. What hempen homespuns° have we swag-
gering here,
So near the cradle of the fairy queen?
What, a play toward! I'll be an auditor—
An actor too perhaps, if I see cause. 85

QUINCE. Speak, Pyramus. Thisby, stand forth.

BOTTOM. "Thisby, the flowers of odious savors
sweet—"

QUINCE. Odorous, odorous.

BOTTOM.

—odors savors sweet.
So hath thy breath, my dearest Thisby dear. 90
But hark, a voice! Stay thou but here awhile,
And by and by I will to thee appear.

[*Exit*]

PUCK. A stranger Pyramus then e'er play'd here.

[*Exit*]

FLUTE. Must I speak now?

QUINCE. Aye, marry, must you; for you must 95
understand he goes but to see a noise that he
heard, and is to come again.

FLUTE.

Most radiant Pyramus, most lily-white of hue,
Of color like the red rose on triumphant brier,
Most brisky juvenal,° and eke° most lovely Jew, 100
As true as truest horse, that yet would never tire,
I'll meet thee, Pyramus, at Ninny's tomb.

By'r lakin by our "little lady" (the Virgin Mary)
parlous Snout's blunder for "perilous"
eight and six ballad stanza, alternate lines of eight and
  six syllables
defect Bottom's blunder for *effect*
it . . . life "too bad for me"

disfigure blunder for *prefigure*
hempen homespuns coarse homespun garments; hence,
  country bumpkins
brisky juvenal brisk juvenile   *eke* also

QUINCE. "Ninus'° tomb," man. Why, you must
not speak that yet; that you answer to Pyramus.
105 You speak all your part at once, cues and all.
Pyramus, enter. Your cue is past; it is, "never
tire."
FLUTE. "O—As true as truest horse, that yet would
never tire."
[*Re-enter* PUCK, *and* BOTTOM *with an ass's head.*]
BOTTOM. "If I were fair, Thisby, I were only
thine."
110 QUINCE. O monstrous! O strange! We are haunted.
Pray, masters! Fly, masters! Help!
[*Exeunt* QUINCE, SNUG, FLUTE, SNOUT, *and*
STARVELING.]
PUCK. I'll follow you, I'll lead you about a round,
Through bog, through bush, through brake,
through brier.
Sometime a horse I'll be, sometime a hound,
115 A hog, a headless bear, sometime a fire,
And neigh, and bark, and grunt, and roar, and
burn,
Like horse, hound, hog, bear, fire, at every turn.
[*Exit*]
BOTTOM. Why do they run away? This is a knavery
of them to make me afeard.
[*Re-enter* SNOUT.]
120 SNOUT. O Bottom, thou art changed! What do I
see on thee?
BOTTOM. What do you see? You see an ass-head of
your own, do you?   [*Exit* SNOUT.]
[*Re-enter* QUINCE.]
QUINCE. Bless thee, Bottom! Bless thee! Thou art
125 translated.°   [*Exit*]
BOTTOM. I see their knavery. This is to make an
ass of me, to fright me, if they could. But I will
not stir from this place, do what they can. I will
walk up and down here, and I will sing, that
130 they shall hear I am not afraid.

[*Sings*]   The ousel° cock so black of hue,
With orange-tawny bill,
The throstle° with his note so true,
The wren with little quill—

TITANIA. [*Awaking*] What angel wakes me from
135 my flowery bed?
BOTTOM.

[*Sings*] The finch, the sparrow, and the lark,
The plain-song cuckoo gray,
Whose note full many a man doth mark,
And dares not answer nay—

140 for, indeed, who would set his wit to so foolish a
bird? Who would give a bird the lie, though he
cry "cuckoo" never so?
TITANIA. I pray thee, gentle mortal, sing again.
Mine ear is much enamor'd of thy note;
So is mine eye enthralled to thy shape;   145
And thy fair virtue's force perforce doth move
me°
On the first view to say, to swear, I love thee.
BOTTOM. Methinks, mistress, you should have
little reason for that. And yet, to say the truth,
reason and love keep little company together   150
nowadays; the more the pity, that some honest
neighbors will not make them friends. Nay, I
can gleek° upon occasion.
TITANIA. Thou art as wise as thou art beautiful.
BOTTOM. Not so, neither. But if I had wit enough 155
to get out of this wood, I have enough to serve
mine own turn.
TITANIA. Out of this wood do not desire to go.
Thou shalt remain here, whether thou wilt or
no.
I am a spirit of no common rate.°   160
The summer still° doth tend° upon my state;
And I do love thee. Therefore, go with me;
I'll give thee fairies to attend on thee,
And they shall fetch thee jewels from the deep,
And sing, while thou on pressed flowers dost
sleep.   165
And I will purge thy mortal grossness so
That thou shalt like an airy spirit go.
Peaseblossom! Cobweb! Moth! And Mustard-
seed!
[*Enter* PEASEBLOSSOM, COBWEB, MOTH, *and*
MUSTARDSEED.]
PEASEBLOSSOM. Ready.
COBWEB. And I.   170
MOTH. And I.
MUSTARDSEED. And I.
ALL. Where shall we go?
TITANIA. Be kind and courteous to this gentleman.
Hop in his walks, and gambol in his eyes;   175
Feed him with apricocks and dewberries,
With purple grapes, green figs, and mulberries.
The honey bags steal from the humblebees,
And for night tapers° crop their waxen thighs
And light them at the fiery glow-worm's eyes   180
To have my love to bed and to arise.
And pluck the wings from painted butterflies,
To fan the moonbeams from his sleeping eyes.
Nod to him, elves, and do him courtesies.
PEASEBLOSSOM. Hail, mortal!   185

Ninus legendary founder of Nineveh
translated blunder for *transformed*   *ousel* blackbird
throstle thrush

fair . . . me the power of your beauty compels me
gleek wisecrack   *rate* rank   *still* always
tend attend   *tapers* candles

COBWEB. Hail!

MOTH. Hail!

MUSTARDSEED. Hail!

BOTTOM. I cry your worship's mercy,° heartily. I
190   beseech your worship's name.

COBWEB. Cobweb.

BOTTOM. I shall desire you of more acquaintance,
good Master Cobweb. If I cut my finger, I shall
make bold with you.° Your name, honest
195   gentleman?

PEASEBLOSSOM. Peaseblossom.

BOTTOM. I pray you, commend me to Mistress
Squash,° your mother, and to Master Peascod,
your father. Good Master Peaseblossom, I shall
200   desire you of more acquaintance too. Your name,
I beseech you, sir?

MUSTARDSEED. Mustardseed.

BOTTOM. Good Master Mustardseed, I know your
patience well. That same cowardly, giantlike
205   ox-beef hath devoured many a gentleman of
your house. I promise you your kindred hath
made my eyes water ere now. I desire your
more acquaintance, good Master Mustardseed.

TITANIA. Come, wait upon him; lead him to my
bower.
210 The moon methinks looks with a watery eye,
And when she weeps, weeps every little flower,
Lamenting some enforced° chastity.
Tie up my love's tongue, bring him silently.

[*Exeunt*]

SCENE ii
Another part of the wood.

[*Enter* OBERON.]

OBERON. I wonder if Titania be awak'd;
Then, what it was that next came in her eye,
Which she must dote on in extremity.

[*Enter* PUCK.]

Here comes my messenger.
                How now, mad spirit!
5 What night-rule° now about this haunted grove?

PUCK. My mistress with a monster is in love.
Near to her close and consecrated bower,
While she was in her dull and sleeping hour,
A crew of patches,° rude mechanicals,°
10 That work for bread upon Athenian stalls,°
Were met together to rehearse a play

Intended for great Theseus' nuptial day.
The shallowest thick-skin of that barren sort,°
Who Pyramus presented in their sport,
Forsook his scene and enter'd in a brake.   15
When I did him at this advantage take,
An ass's nole° I fixed on his head.
Anon his Thisby must be answered,
And forth my mimic° comes. When they him
spy,
As wild geese that the creeping fowler eye,   20
Or russet-pated choughs,° many in sort,
Rising and cawing at the gun's report,
Sever themselves and madly sweep the sky,
So, at his sight, away his fellows fly;
And, at our stamp,° here o'er and o'er one falls; 25
He murder cries, and help from Athens calls.
Their sense thus weak, lost with their fears thus
strong,
Made senseless things begin to do them wrong;
For briers and thorns at their apparel snatch;
Some sleeves, some hats, from yielders all things
catch.   30
I led them on in this distracted fear,
And left sweet Pyramus translated there,
When in that moment, so it came to pass,
Titania wak'd, and straightway lov'd an ass.

OBERON. This falls out better than I could devise. 35
But hast thou yet latch'd° the Athenian's eyes
With the love juice, as I did bid thee do?

PUCK. I took him sleeping—that is finish'd too—
And the Athenian woman by his side,
That, when he wak'd, of force° she must be
ey'd.   40

[*Enter* HERMIA *and* DEMETRIUS.]

OBERON. Stand close. This is the same Athenian.

PUCK. This is the woman, but not this the man.

DEMETRIUS. O, why rebuke you him that loves you
so?
Lay breath so bitter on your bitter foe.°

HERMIA. Now I but chide. But I should use thee
worse,   45
For thou, I fear, hast given me cause to curse.
If thou hast slain Lysander in his sleep,
Being o'er shoes in blood, plunge in the deep,°
And kill me too.
The sun was not so true unto the day   50
As he to me. Would he have stolen away
From sleeping Hermia? I'll believe as soon

I . . . mercy I beg your pardon
If . . . you cobweb was used to stop bleeding
Squash peapod   *enforced* violated
night-rule mischief   *patches* clowns
mechanicals workmen   *stalls* shops

barren sort stupid crew   *nole* head   *mimic* actor
choughs jackdaws   *in sort* together
at our stamp at my stamping
latch'd anointed   *of force* necessarily
Lay . . . foe do not scold anyone so bitterly except your
worst enemy
Being . . . deep having gone so far, go the whole way

This whole earth may be bor'd and that the moon

May through the center creep, and so displease

55 Her brother's noontide with th' Antipodes.°

It cannot be but thou hast murder'd him;

So should a murderer look, so dead,° so grim.

DEMETRIUS. So should the murder'd look, and so should I,

Pierc'd through the heart with your stern cruelty.

60 Yet you, the murderer, look as bright, as clear,

As yonder Venus in her glimmering sphere.

HERMIA. What's this to my Lysander? Where is he?

Ah, good Demetrius, wilt thou give him me?

DEMETRIUS. I had rather give his carcass to my hounds.

HERMIA. Out, dog! Out, cur! Thou driv'st me past

65 the bounds

Of maiden's patience. Hast thou slain him, then?

Henceforth be never number'd among men!

O, once tell true, tell true, even for my sake!

Durst° thou have look'd upon him being awake,

And hast thou kill'd him sleeping? O brave

70 touch!°

Could not a worm, an adder, do so much?

An adder did it; for with doubler tongue

Than thine, thou serpent, never adder stung.

DEMETRIUS. You spend your passion on a mispris'd° mood.

75 I am not guilty of Lysander's blood,

Nor is he dead, for aught that I can tell.

HERMIA. I pray thee, tell me then that he is well.

DEMETRIUS. An if I could, what should I get therefore?

HERMIA. A privilege never to see me more.

80 And from thy hated presence part I so.

See me no more, whether he be dead or no.

                                    [Exit]

DEMETRIUS. There is no following her in this fierce vein;

Here therefore for a while I will remain.

So sorrow's heaviness doth heavier grow

85 For debt that bankrupt sleep doth sorrow owe;

Which now in some slight measure it will pay,

If for this tender° here I make some stay.

                        [Lies down and sleeps.]

OBERON. What hast thou done? Thou hast mistaken quite,

And laid the love juice on some true-love's sight.

Of thy misprision° must perforce ensue   90

Some true love turn'd, and not a false turn'd true.

PUCK. Then fate o'er-rules, that, one man holding troth,

A million fail, confounding oath on oath.°

OBERON. About the wood go swifter than the wind,

And Helena of Athens look thou find.   95

All fancy-sick° she is and pale of cheer,

With sighs of love that costs the fresh blood dear.

By some illusion° see thou bring her here.

I'll charm his eyes against she do appear.

PUCK. I go, I go; look how I go,   100

Swifter than arrow from the Tartar's bow.°

                                    [Exit]

OBERON. Flower of this purple dye,

Hit with Cupid's archery,

Sink in apple of his eye.

When his love he doth espy,   105

Let her shine as gloriously

As the Venus of the sky.

When thou wak'st, if she be by,

Beg of her for remedy.

                        [Re-enter PUCK.]

PUCK. Captain of our fairy band,   110

Helena is here at hand;

And the youth, mistook by me,

Pleading for a lover's fee.°

Shall we their fond pageant° see?

Lord, what fools these mortals be!   115

OBERON. Stand aside. The noise they make

Will cause Demetrius to awake.

PUCK. Then will two at once woo one;

That must needs be sport alone.

And those things do best please me   120

That befall prepost'rously.

                        [Enter LYSANDER and HELENA.]

LYSANDER. Why should you think that I should woo in scorn?

Scorn and derision never come in tears.

Look, when I vow, I weep; and vows so born,

In their nativity all truth appears.°   125

How can these things in me seem scorn to you,

Bearing the badge of faith to prove them true?

misprision mistake
Then . . . oath then fate overrules my action in that, for
  every man who is true, a million are false and break
  oath on oath
fancy-sick lovesick   illusion deception
Tartar's bow the fierce Tartars of Siberia were famed
  bowmen
lover's fee i.e., a kiss   fond pageant foolish exhibition
vows . . . appears vows made when one is in tears are
  bound to be true

I'll . . . Antipodes I'll as readily believe that the earth
  may be bored through and that the moon may pass
  through the center and vex the sun's noonday on the
  other side
dead deadly   Durst dare   touch deed
mispris'd mistaken   tender offer

HELENA. You do advance your cunning more and
    more.
    When truth kills truth, O devilish-holy fray!
130   These vows are Hermia's. Will you give her o'er?
    Weigh oath with oath, and you will nothing
    weigh.
    Your vows to her and me, put in two scales,
    Will even weigh—and both as light as tales.
LYSANDER. I had no judgment when to her I swore.
HELENA. Nor none, in my mind, now you give her
135   o'er.
LYSANDER. Demetrius loves her, and he loves not
    you.
DEMETRIUS. [*Awaking*] O Helen, goddess, nymph,
    perfect, divine!
    To what, my love, shall I compare thine eyne?
    Crystal is muddy. O, how ripe in show
140   Thy lips, those kissing cherries, tempting grow!
    That pure congealed white, high Taurus'° snow,
    Fann'd with the eastern wind, turns to a crow
    When thou hold'st up thy hand. O, let me kiss
    This princess of pure white, this seal° of bliss!
145 HELENA. O spite! O hell! I see you all are bent
    To set against me for your merriment.
    If you were civil and knew courtesy,
    You would not do me thus much injury.
    Can you not hate me, as I know you do,
150   But you must join in souls to mock me too?
    If you were men, as men you are in show,
    You would not use a gentle° lady so,
    To vow, and swear, and superpraise my parts,
    When I am sure you hate me with your hearts.
155   You both are rivals, and love Hermia;
    And now both rivals, to mock Helena.
    A trim° exploit, a manly enterprise,
    To conjure tears up in a poor maid's eyes
    With your derision! None of noble sort
160   Would so offend a virgin, and extort
    A poor soul's patience, all to make you sport.
LYSANDER. You are unkind, Demetrius. Be not so.
    For you love Hermia; this you know I know.
    And here, with all good will, with all my heart,
165   In Hermia's love I yield you up my part;
    And yours of Helena to me bequeath,
    Whom I do love, and will do till my death.
HELENA. Never did mockers waste more idle
    breath.
DEMETRIUS. Lysander, keep thy Hermia; I will
    none.
170   If e'er I lov'd her, all that love is gone.
    My heart to her but as guest-wise sojourn'd,°
    And now to Helen is it home return'd,

    There to remain.
LYSANDER.   Helen, it is not so.
DEMETRIUS. Disparage not the faith thou dost not
    know,
    Lest, to thy peril, thou aby° it dear.   175
    Look, where thy love comes. Yonder is thy dear.
               [*Re-enter* HERMIA.]
HERMIA. Dark night, that from the eye his° func-
    tion takes,
    The ear more quick of apprehension makes;
    Wherein it doth impair the seeing sense,
    It pays the hearing double recompense.   180
    Thou art not by mine eye, Lysander, found;
    Mine ear, I thank it, brought me to thy sound.
    But why unkindly didst thou leave me so?
LYSANDER. Why should he stay, whom love doth
    press to go?
HERMIA. What love could press Lysander from my
    side?   185
LYSANDER. Lysander's love, that would not let him
    bide,
    Fair Helena, who more engilds the night
    Than all yon fiery oes and eyes° of light.
    Why seek'st thou me? Could not this make thee
    know
    The hate I bare thee made me leave thee so?   190
HERMIA. You speak not as you think. It cannot be.
HELENA. Lo, she is one of this confederacy!
    Now I perceive they have conjoin'd all three
    To fashion this false sport in spite of° me.
    Injurious Hermia! Most ungrateful maid!   195
    Have you conspir'd, have you with these con-
    triv'd
    To bait° me with this foul derision?
    Is all the counsel that we two have shar'd,
    The sister's vows, the hours that we have spent,
    When we have chid the hasty-footed time   200
    For parting us—O, is all forgot?
    All school-days' friendship, childhood inno-
    cence?
    We, Hermia, like two artificial° gods,
    Have with our needles created both one flower,
    Both on one sampler, sitting on one cushion,   205
    Both warbling of one song, both in one key,
    As if our hands, our sides, voices, and minds,
    Had been incorporate. So we grew together
    Like to a double cherry, seeming parted,
    But yet an union in partition—   210
    Two lovely berries molded on one stem;
    So, with two seeming bodies, but one heart,
    Two of the first, like coats in heraldry,

Taurus mountain range in Asia Minor   *seal* pledge
gentle wellborn   *trim* fine   *sojourn'd* visited

aby pay for   *his* its   *oes . . . eyes* i.e., stars
in spite of to spite   *bait* taunt
artificial creative (artistically skilled)

Due but to one, and crowned with one crest.°
215 And will you rend our ancient love asunder
To join with men in scorning your poor friend?
It is not friendly, 'tis not maidenly.
Our sex, as well as I, may chide you for it,
Though I alone do feel the injury.
220 HERMIA. I am amazed at your passionate words.
I scorn you not. It seems that you scorn me.
HELENA. Have you not set Lysander, as in scorn,
To follow me and praise my eyes and face?
And made your other love, Demetrius,
225 Who even but now did spurn me with his foot,
To call me goddess, nymph, divine and rare,
Precious, celestial? Wherefore speaks he this
To her he hates? And wherefore doth Lysander
Deny your love, so rich within his soul,
230 And tender me, forsooth, affection,
But by your setting on, by your consent?
What though I be not so in grace° as you,
So hung upon with love, so fortunate,
But miserable most, to love unlov'd?
235 This you should pity rather than despise.
HERMIA. I understand not what you mean by this.
HELENA. Aye, do, persever, counterfeit sad looks,
Make mouths upon° me when I turn my back;
Wink each at other; hold the sweet jest up.
240 This sport, well carried, shall be chronicled.°
If you have any pity, grace, or manners,
You would not make me such an argument.°
But fare ye well: 'tis partly my own fault,
Which death or absence soon shall remedy.
245 LYSANDER. Stay, gentle Helena; hear my excuse.
My love, my life, my soul, fair Helena!
HELENA. O excellent!
HERMIA.   Sweet, do not scorn her so.
DEMETRIUS. If she cannot entreat, I can compel.
LYSANDER. Thou canst compel no more than she
entreat.
Thy threats have no more strength than her
250 weak prayers.
Helen, I love thee; by my life, I do.
I swear by that which I will lose for thee,
To prove him false that says I love thee not.
DEMETRIUS. I say I love thee more than he can do.
LYSANDER. If thou say so, withdraw, and prove it
255 too.
DEMETRIUS. Quick, come!
HERMIA.   Lysander, whereto tends all this?
LYSANDER. Away, you Ethiope!
DEMETRIUS.   No, no, sir—

Seem to break loose! Take on as you would
follow,
But yet come not. You are a tame man, go!
LYSANDER. Hang off, thou cat, thou burr! Vile
thing, let loose,   260
Or I will shake thee from me like a serpent!
HERMIA. Why have you grown so rude? What
change is this?
Sweet love—
LYSANDER.   Thy love! Out, tawny° Tartar, out!
Out, loathed med'cine! Hated potion, hence!
HERMIA. Do you jest?
HELENA.   Yes, sooth, and so do you.   265
LYSANDER. Demetrius, I will keep my word with
thee.
DEMETRIUS. I would I had your bond, for I perceive
A weak bond° holds you. I'll not trust your
word.
LYSANDER. What, should I hurt her, strike her, kill
her dead?
Although I hate her, I'll not harm her so.   270
HERMIA. What, can you do me greater harm than
hate?
Hate me! Wherefore? O me! What news, my
love!
Am not I Hermia? Are not you Lysander?
I am as fair now as I was erewhile.
Since night you lov'd me; yet since night you
left me.   275
Why, then you left me—O, the gods forbid!—
In earnest, shall I say?
LYSANDER.   Aye, by my life,
And never did desire to see thee more.
Therefore be out of hope, of question, of doubt;
Be certain, nothing truer; 'tis no jest   280
That I do hate thee, and love Helena.
HERMIA. O me! You juggler! You canker-blossom!
You thief of love! What, have you come by
night
And stolen my love's heart from him?
HELENA.   Fine, i'faith!
Have you no modesty, no maiden shame,   285
No touch of bashfulness? What, will you tear
Impatient answers from my gentle tongue?
Fie, fie! You counterfeit, you puppet, you!
HERMIA. Puppet? Why so? Aye, that way goes the
game!
Now I perceive that she hath made compare   290
Between our statures; she hath urg'd her height,
And with her personage, her tall personage,

Two . . . crest having two bodies but one heart
  (Helena's figure comes from heraldry, with two coats
  united under one crest)
grace favor   mouths upon faces at
chronicled recorded   argument subject for jest

tawny dark
bond . . . bond [the first bond is a written contract, which
  is stronger than oral agreement (word); second bond is
  Hermia, still holding Lysander]

Her height, forsooth,° she hath prevail'd with
   him.
And are you grown so high in his esteem
295 Because I am so dwarfish and so low?
How low am I, thou painted maypole? Speak.
How low am I? I am not yet so low
But that my nails can reach unto thine eyes.
HELENA. I pray you, though you mock me, gentle-
   men,
300 Let her not hurt me. I was never curst;°
I have no gift at all in shrewishness;
I am a right° maid for my cowardice.
Let her not strike me. You perhaps may think,
Because she is something lower than myself,
That I can match her.
305 HERMIA.   Lower! Hark, again.
HELENA. Good Hermia, do not be so bitter with
   me.
I evermore did love you, Hermia,
Did ever keep your counsels, never wrong'd
   you,
Save that, in love unto Demetrius,
310 I told him of your stealth unto this wood.
He follow'd you; for love I follow'd him;
But he hath chid me hence, and threaten'd me
To strike me, spurn me, nay, to kill me too.
And now, so you will let me quiet go,
315 To Athens will I bear my folly back
And follow you no further. Let me go.
You see how simple and how fond I am.
HERMIA. Why, get you gone. Who is't that hinders
   you?
HELENA. A foolish heart that I leave here behind.
HERMIA. What, with Lysander?
320 HELENA.   With Demetrius.
LYSANDER. Be not afraid; she shall not harm thee,
   Helena.
DEMETRIUS. No, sir, she shall not, though you take
   her part.
HELENA. O, when she's angry, she is keen and
   shrewd!°
She was a vixen when she went to school,
325 And though she be but little, she is fierce.
HERMIA. Little again! Nothing but low and little!
Why will you suffer her to flout° me thus?
Let me come to her.
LYSANDER.   Get you gone, you dwarf,
You minimus, of hind'ring knot-grass° made,
You bead, you acorn.
330 DEMETRIUS.   You are too officious

In her behalf that scorns your services.
Let her alone. Speak not of Helena;
Take not her part; for, if thou dost intend
Never so little show of love to her,
Thou shalt aby it.
LYSANDER.   Now she holds me not;   335
Now follow, if thou dar'st, to try whose right,
Of thine or mine, is most in Helena.
DEMETRIUS. Follow! Nay, I'll go with thee, cheek by
   jowl.   [Exeunt LYSANDER and DEMETRIUS.]
HERMIA. You, mistress, all this coil is 'long° of you.
Nay, go not back.
HELENA.   I will not trust you, I,   340
Nor longer stay in your curst company.
Your hands than mine are quicker for a fray;
My legs are longer, though, to run away.
                         [Exit]
HERMIA. I am amaz'd, and know not what to say.
                         [Exit]
OBERON. This is thy negligence. Still thou mis-
   tak'st,   345
Or else committ'st thy knaveries wilfully.
PUCK. Believe me, king of shadows, I mistook.
Did not you tell me I should know the man
By the Athenian garments he had on?
And so far blameless proves my enterprise,   350
That I have 'nointed an Athenian's eyes;
And so far am I glad it so did sort,
As this their jangling I esteem a sport.
OBERON. Thou see'st these lovers seek a place to
   fight.
Hie therefore, Robin, overcast the night;   355
The starry welkin° cover thou anon
With drooping fog as black as Acheron,°
And lead these testy rivals so astray
As one come not within another's way.
Like to Lysander sometime frame thy tongue,   360
Then stir Demetrius up with bitter wrong,
And sometime rail thou like Demetrius,
And from each other look thou lead them thus
Till o'er their brows death-counterfeiting sleep
With leaden legs and batty wings doth creep.   365
Then crush this herb into Lysander's eye,
Whose liquor hath this virtuous property°
To take from thence all error with his might,
And make his eyeballs roll with wonted° sight.
When they next awake, all this derision   370
Shall seem a dream and fruitless vision;
And back to Athens shall the lovers wend,
With league° whose date till death shall never
   end.

---

forsooth in truth   *curst* shrewish   *right* true
shrewd shrewish   *flout* mock
hind'ring knot-grass weed that stunts growth of other
   plants

coil is 'long quarrel is because   *welkin* sky
Acheron river in Hades   *virtuous property* potent force
wonted accustomed   *league* union

Whiles I in this affair do thee employ,
375　I'll to my queen and beg her Indian boy.
And then I will her charmed eye release
From monster's view, and all things shall be
　peace.
PUCK. My fairy lord, this must be done with haste,
For night's swift dragons° cut the clouds full
　fast,
380　And yonder shines Aurora's harbinger,°
At whose approach, ghosts, wand'ring here and
　there,
Troop home to churchyards. Damned spirits
　all,
That in crossways and floods have burial,
Already to their wormy beds are gone;
385　For fear lest day should look their shames upon,
They wilfully themselves exile from light,
And must for aye consort with black-brow'd
　night.
OBERON. But we are spirits of another sort.
I with the morning's love have oft made sport,
390　And, like a forester, the groves may tread
Even till the eastern gate, all fiery-red,
Opening on Neptune with fair blessed beams,
Turns into yellow gold his salt green streams.
But, notwithstanding, haste; make no delay.
395　We may effect this business yet ere day. [Exit]
PUCK. Up and down, up and down,
I will lead them up and down.
I am fear'd in field and town.
Goblin, lead them up and down.
400　Here comes one.
　　　　[Re-enter LYSANDER.]
LYSANDER. Where art thou, proud Demetrius?
　Speak thou now.
PUCK. Here, villain, drawn and ready. Where art
　thou?
LYSANDER. I will be with thee straight.
PUCK. 　　　　　　　Follow me, then,
　To plainer ground.
　　　[Exit LYSANDER, as following the voice.]
　　　　[Re-enter DEMETRIUS.]
DEMETRIUS. 　　　Lysander! Speak again.
405　Thou runaway, thou coward, art thou fled?
Speak! In some bush? Where dost thou hide thy
　head?
PUCK. Thou coward, art thou bragging to the
　stars,
Telling the bushes that thou look'st for wars,
And wilt not come? Come, recreant; come,
　thou child;

night's . . . dragons　the chariot of the night was drawn by
　dragons
Aurora's harbinger　forerunner of the dawn (the morning
　star)

I'll whip thee with a rod. He is defil'd   410
That draws a sword on thee.
DEMETRIUS. 　　　　　Yea, art thou there?
PUCK. Follow my voice. We'll try no manhood
　here. 　　　　　　　　　[Exeunt]
　　　　[Re-enter LYSANDER.]
LYSANDER. He goes before me and still dares me
　on.
When I come where he calls, then he is gone.
The villain is much lighter-heel'd than I.   415
I follow'd fast, but faster he did fly,
That° fallen am I in dark uneven way,
And here will rest me. [Lies down] Come, thou
　gentle day!
For if but once thou show me thy grey light,
I'll find Demetrius, and revenge this spite.   420
　　　　　　　　　　[Sleeps.]
　　　[Re-enter PUCK and DEMETRIUS.]
PUCK. Ho, ho, ho! Coward, why com'st thou not?
DEMETRIUS. Abide me, if thou dar'st; for well I
　wot°
Thou runn'st before me, shifting every place,
And dar'st not stand nor look me in the face.
Where art thou now?
PUCK. 　　　　　Come hither. I am here.   425
DEMETRIUS. Nay, then, thou mock'st me. Thou
　shalt buy this dear
If ever I thy face by daylight see.
Now, go thy way. Faintness constraineth° me
To measure out my length on this cold bed.
By day's approach look to be visited.   430
　　　　　　　[Lies down and sleeps.]
　　　　[Re-enter HELENA.]
HELENA. O weary night, O long and tedious night,
　Abate° thy hours! Shine comforts from the east,
That I may back to Athens by daylight come
　From these that my poor company detest;
And sleep, that sometimes shuts up sorrow's
　eye,   435
Steal me awhile from mine own company.
　　　　　　　[Lies down and sleeps.]
PUCK. Yet but three? Come one more;
Two of both kinds makes up four.
Here she comes, curst and sad.
Cupid is a knavish lad,   440
Thus to make poor females mad.
　　　　[Re-enter HERMIA.]
HERMIA. Never so weary, never so in woe,
　Bedabbled with the dew and torn with briers,
I can no further crawl, no further go;
　My legs can keep no pace with my desires.   445
Here will I rest me till the break of day.

That　so that　　wot　know　　constraineth　compels
Abate　shorten

Heavens shield Lysander, if they mean a fray!
                [*Lies down and sleeps.*]

PUCK. On the ground
   Sleep sound.
450   I'll apply
   To your eye,
   Gentle lover, remedy.
          [*Squeezing the juice on* LYSANDER'S *eye.*]
   When thou wak'st,
   Thou tak'st

   True delight   455
   In the sight
Of thy former lady's eye.
And the country proverb known,
That every man should take his own,
In your waking shall be shown: 460
   Jack shall have Jill;
   Naught shall go ill;
The man shall have his mare again, and all shall
   be well.   [*Exit*]

ACT IV

SCENE i

The same. LYSANDER, DEMETRIUS,
HELENA, *and* HERMIA, *lying asleep.*

[*Enter* TITANIA *and* BOTTOM; PEASEBLOSSOM,
COBWEB, MOTH, MUSTARDSEED, *and other*
FAIRIES *attending;* OBERON *behind unseen.*]

TITANIA. Come, sit thee down upon this flowery
   bed,
   While I thy amiable cheeks do coy°
And stick musk-roses in thy sleek smooth head
And kiss thy large ears, my gentle joy.

5 BOTTOM. Where's Peaseblossom?

PEASEBLOSSOM. Ready.

BOTTOM. Scratch my head, Peaseblossom. Where's
   Mounsieur Cobweb?

COBWEB. Ready.

10 BOTTOM. Mounsieur Cobweb, good mounsieur,
   get you your weapons in your hand and kill me
   a red-hipped humble-bee on the top of a thistle;
   and, good mounsieur, bring me the honey-bag.
   Do not fret yourself too much in the action,
15   mounsieur; and, good mounsieur, have a care
   the honey-bag break not; I would be loath to
   have you overflown with a honey-bag, signior.
   Where's Mounsieur Mustardseed?

MUSTARDSEED. Ready.

20 BOTTOM. Give me your neaf,° Mounsieur Mustardseed. Pray you leave your courtesy,° good
   mounsieur.

MUSTARDSEED. What's your will?

BOTTOM. Nothing, good mounsieur, but to help
25   Cavalery° Cobweb to scratch. I must to the

barber's, mounsieur, for methinks I am marvelous hairy about the face, and I am such a
tender ass, if my hair do but tickle me, I must
scratch.

TITANIA. What, wilt thou hear some music, my
   sweet love?   30

BOTTOM. I have a reasonable good ear in music.
   Let's have the tongs and the bones.°

TITANIA. Or say, sweet love, what thou desirest to
   eat.

BOTTOM. Truly, a peck of provender. I could
   munch your good dry oats. Methinks I have a   35
   great desire to a bottle° of hay. Good hay, sweet
   hay, hath no fellow.°

TITANIA. I have a venturous fairy that shall seek
   The squirrel's hoard and fetch thee new nuts.

BOTTOM. I had rather have a handful or two of   40
   dried peas. But, I pray you, let none of your
   people stir me. I have an exposition° of sleep
   come upon me.

TITANIA. Sleep thou, and I will wind thee in my
   arms.
   Fairies, be gone, and be all ways away.   45
                 [*Exeunt* FAIRIES.]
So doth the woodbine the sweet honeysuckle
Gently entwist; the female ivy so
Enrings the barky fingers of the elm.
O, how I love thee! How I dote on thee!
                 [*They sleep.*]

             [*Enter* PUCK.]

OBERON. [*Advancing*] Welcome, good Robin. See'st
   thou this sweet sight?   50
   Her dotage now I do begin to pity.

---

coy caress
neaf fist   *leave . . . courtesy* i.e., stop your bowing
Cavalery Cavalier

tongs . . . bones rustic musical instruments
bottle bundle   *fellow* equal
exposition blunder for *disposition*

For, meeting her of late behind the wood,
Seeking sweet favors for this hateful fool,
I did upbraid her and fall out with her,
55   For she his hairy temples then had rounded
With coronet of fresh and fragrant flowers,
And that same dew which sometime on the
   buds
Was wont to swell like round and orient pearls
Stood now within the pretty flowerets' eyes
60   Like tears that did their own disgrace bewail.
When I had at my pleasure taunted her,
And she in mild terms begg'd my patience,
I then did ask of her her changeling child,
Which straight she gave me, and her fairy sent
65   To bear him to my bower in fairyland.
And now I have the boy, I will undo
This hateful imperfection of her eyes.
And, gentle Puck, take this transformed scalp
From off the head of this Athenian swain,
70   That, he awaking when the other° do,
May all to Athens back again repair
And think no more of this night's accidents°
But as the fierce vexation of a dream.
But first I will release the fairy queen.
75   Be as thou wast wont to be;
      See as thou wast wont to see.
      Dian's bud o'er Cupid's flower
      Hath such force and blessed power.°
Now, my Titania, wake you, my sweet queen.
80   TITANIA. My Oberon! What visions have I seen!
Methought I was enamor'd of an ass.
OBERON. There lies your love.
TITANIA. How came these things to pass?
O, how mine eyes do loathe his visage now!
85   OBERON. Silence awhile. Robin, take off this head.
Titania, music call, and strike more dead
Than common sleep of all these five the sense.
TITANIA. Music, ho! Music, such as charmeth
   sleep!   [Music, still.]
PUCK. Now, when thou wak'st, with thine own
   fool's eyes peep.
OBERON. Sound, music! Come, my queen, take
90   hands with me
And rock the ground whereon these sleepers be.
Now thou and I are new in amity
And will tomorrow midnight solemnly
Dance in Duke Theseus' house triumphantly
95   And bless it to all fair prosperity.
There shall the pairs of faithful lovers be
Wedded, with Theseus, all in jollity.

PUCK. Fairy king, attend and mark.
I do hear the morning lark.
OBERON. Then, my queen, in silence sad,°   100
Trip we after night's shade.
We the globe can compass soon,
Swifter than the wand'ring moon.
TITANIA. Come, my lord, and in our flight
Tell me how it came this night   105
That I sleeping here was found
With these mortals on the ground.   [Exeunt]
                        [Horns winded within.]
      [Enter THESEUS, HIPPOLYTA, EGEUS, and train.]
THESEUS. Go, one of you, find out the forester,
For now our observation° is perform'd;
And since we have the vaward° of the day,   110
My love shall hear the music of my hounds.
Uncouple in the western valley; let them go.
Dispatch,° I say, and find the forester.
                        [Exit an ATTENDANT.]
We will, fair queen, up to the mountain's top
And mark the musical confusion   115
Of hounds and echo in conjunction.
HIPPOLYTA. I was with Hercules and Cadmus once
When in a wood of Crete they bay'd° the bear
With hounds of Sparta. Never did I hear
Such gallant chiding; for, besides the groves,   120
The skies, the fountains, every region near
Seem'd all one mutual cry. I never heard
So musical a discord, such sweet thunder.
THESEUS. My hounds are bred out of the Spartan
   kind,
So flew'd,° so sanded,° and their heads are hung 125
With ears that sweep away the morning dew;
Crook-knee'd, and dew-lapp'd like Thessalian
   bulls,
Slow in pursuit, but match'd in mouth like bells,
Each under each. A cry more tuneable
Was never holla'd to nor cheer'd with horn   130
In Crete, in Sparta, nor in Thessaly.
Judge when you hear. But, soft! What nymphs
   are these?
EGEUS. My lord, this is my daughter here asleep,
And this, Lysander; this Demetrius is;
This Helena, old Nedar's Helena.   135
I wonder of their being here together.
THESEUS. No doubt they rose up early to observe
The rite of May, and, hearing our intent,
Came here in grace of our solemnity.

sad   sober
observation   observance (they have observed the rite of
   May)
vaward   early part
Dispatch   make haste   bay'd   brought to bay
flew'd   with hanging cheeks, or dewlaps
sanded   of sandy color

other   others   accidents   happenings
Dian's . . . power   the power of Diana (goddess of
   chastity) transcends that of Cupid (the love god)

Strong noter

140 But speak, Egeus; is not this the day
  That Hermia should give answer of her choice?
EGEUS. It is, my lord.
THESEUS. Go, bid the huntsmen wake them with
    their horns.
    [*Horns and shout within.* LYSANDER, DEMETRIUS,
    HELENA, *and* HERMIA *wake and start up.*]
  Good morrow, friends. Saint Valentine is past.
145 Begin these wood-birds but to couple now?°
LYSANDER. Pardon, my lord.
THESEUS.   I pray you all, stand up.
  I know you two are rival enemies.
  How comes this gentle concord in the world,
  That hatred is so far from jealousy°
150 To sleep by hate and fear no enmity?
LYSANDER. My lord, I shall reply amazedly,
  Half sleep, half waking. But as yet, I swear,
  I cannot truly say how I came here;
  But, as I think—for truly would I speak,
155 And now I do bethink me, so it is—
  I came with Hermia hither. Our intent
  Was to be gone from Athens, where we might,
  Without the peril of the Athenian law—
EGEUS. Enough, enough, my lord; you have
    enough.
160 I beg the law, the law, upon his head.
  They would have stolen away; they would,
    Demetrius,
  Thereby to have defeated you and me,
  You of your wife and me of my consent,
  Of my consent that she should be your wife.
DEMETRIUS. My lord, fair Helen told me of their
165   stealth,
  Of this their purpose hither to this wood,
  And I in fury hither follow'd them,
  Fair Helena in fancy° following me.
  But, my good lord, I wot not by what power—
170 But by some power it is—my love to Hermia,
  Melted as the snow, seems to me now
  As the remembrance of an idle gaud°
  Which in my childhood I did dote upon,
  And all the faith, the virtue of my heart,
175 The object and the pleasure of mine eye,
  Is only Helena. To her, my lord,
  Was I betroth'd ere I saw Hermia.
  But like a sickness did I loathe this food;
  But, as in health, come to my natural taste,
180 Now I do wish it, love it, long for it,
  And will for evermore be true to it.
THESEUS. Fair lovers, you are fortunately met.

Of this discourse we more will hear anon.
Egeus, I will overbear your will,
For in the temple, by and by, with us   185
These couples shall eternally be knit.
And, for the morning now is something° worn,
Our purpos'd hunting shall be set aside.
Away with us to Athens! Three and three,
We'll hold a feast in great solemnity.   190
  Come, Hippolyta.
    [*Exeunt* THESEUS, HIPPOLYTA, EGEUS, *and train.*]
DEMETRIUS. These things seem small and undistin-
    guishable,
  Like far-off mountains turned into clouds.
HERMIA. Methinks I see these things with parted
    eye,
  When everything seems double.
HELENA.   So methinks.   195
  And I have found Demetrius like a jewel,
  Mine own, and not mine own.
DEMETRIUS.   It seems to me
  That yet we sleep, we dream. Do not you think
  The Duke was here, and bid us follow him?
HERMIA. Yea, and my father.
HELENA.   And Hippolyta.   200
LYSANDER. And he did bid us follow to the temple.
DEMETRIUS. Why, then, we are awake. Let's follow
    him,
  And by the way let us recount our dreams.
                                      [*Exeunt*]
BOTTOM. [*Awaking*] When my cue comes, call me,
  and I will answer. My next is, "Most fair Pyra-   205
  mus." Heigh-ho! Peter Quince! Flute, the bellows-mender! Snout, the tinker! Starveling!
  God's my life, stolen hence and left me asleep! I
  have had a most rare vision. I have had a dream,
  past the wit of man to say what dream it was.   210
  Man is but an ass, if he go about to expound this
  dream. Methought I was—there is no man can
  tell what. Methought I was—and methought I
  had—but man is but a patched° fool, if he will
  offer to say what methought I had. The eye of   215
  man hath not heard, the ear of man hath not
  seen, man's hand is not able to taste, his tongue
  to conceive, nor his heart to report, what my
  dream was. I will get Peter Quince to write a
  ballad of this dream. It shall be called Bottom's 220
  Dream, because it hath no bottom; and I will
  sing it in the latter end of a play, before the
  Duke. Peradventure, to make it the more
  gracious, I shall sing it at her death.°   [*Exit*]

Saint . . . now birds were supposed to choose their mates
  on this day
jealousy suspicion   *fancy* love   *gaud* trifle

something somewhat
patched many-colored (costume of the professional fool)
her death i.e., Thisbe's

lover, madness
& poet

SCENE ii
Athens. QUINCE's *house.*

[*Enter* QUINCE, FLUTE, SNOUT, *and* STARVELING.]
QUINCE. Have you sent to Bottom's house? Is he
come yet?
STARVELING. He cannot be heard of. Out of doubt
he is transported.°
FLUTE. If he come not, then the play is marred. It 5
goes not forward, doth it?
QUINCE. It is not possible. You have not a man in all
Athens able to discharge Pyramus but he.
FLUTE. No, he hath simply the best wit of any
handicraft man in Athens. 10
QUINCE. Yea, and the best person too, and he is a
very paramour for a sweet voice.
FLUTE. You must say "paragon." A paramour is,
God bless us, a thing of naught.°
[*Enter* SNUG.]
SNUG. Masters, the Duke is coming from the 15
temple, and there is two or three lords and
ladies more married. If our sport had gone
forward, we had all been made men.
FLUTE. O sweet bully Bottom! Thus hath he lost
sixpence° a day during his life; he could not 20

have scaped sixpence a day. An the Duke had
not given him sixpence a day for playing Pyramus, I'll be hanged; he would have deserved it:
sixpence a day in Pyramus, or nothing.
[*Enter* BOTTOM.]
BOTTOM. Where are these lads? Where are these 25
hearts?
QUINCE. Bottom! O most courageous day! O most
happy hour!
BOTTOM. Masters, I am to discourse wonders. But
ask me not what; for if I tell you, I am no true 30
Athenian. I will tell you everything, right as it
fell out.
QUINCE. Let us hear, sweet Bottom.
BOTTOM. Not a word of me. All that I will tell you
is that the Duke hath dined. Get your apparel 35
together, good strings to your beards, new ribbons to your pumps; meet presently at the
palace; every man look o'er his part; for the
short and the long is, our play is preferred.°
In any case, let Thisby have clean linen; and let 40
not him that plays the lion pare his nails, for
they shall hang out for the lion's claws. And,
most dear actors, eat no onions nor garlic, for
we are to utter sweet breath; and I do not
doubt but to hear them say it is a sweet comedy. 45
No more words. Away! Go, away!   [*Exeunt*]

transported carried off   *naught* wickedness
sixpence i.e., as a pension from the Duke

preferred recommended (among other pieces)

ACT V

SCENE i
Athens. The palace of THESEUS.

[*Enter* THESEUS, HIPPOLYTA, PHILOSTRATE,
LORDS, *and* ATTENDANTS.]
HIPPOLYTA. 'Tis strange, my Theseus, that these
lovers speak of.
THESEUS. More strange than true. I never may be-
lieve
These antique° fables, nor these fairy toys.°
Lovers and madmen have such seething brains,
Such shaping fantasies° that apprehend 5
More than cool reason ever comprehends.
The lunatic, the lover, and the poet
Are of imagination all compact.°

antique ancient   *fairy toys* trifles about fairies
shaping fantasies creative imaginations
compact composed

One sees more devils than vast hell can hold,
That is, the madman. The lover, all as frantic, 10
Sees Helen's beauty in a brow of Egypt.°
The poet's eye, in a fine frenzy rolling,
Doth glance from heaven to earth, from earth
to heaven,
And as imagination bodies forth
The forms of things unknown, the poet's pen 15
Turns them to shapes and gives to airy nothing
A local habitation and a name.
Such tricks hath strong imagination
That if it would but apprehend some joy
It comprehends some bringer of that joy;° 20
Or in the night, imagining some fear,

Sees . . . Egypt sees the beauty of Helen of Troy in a
gypsy's face
if . . . that joy if it would merely invent some joy, it
imagines also the cause of that joy

How easy is a bush suppos'd a bear!
HIPPOLYTA. But all the story of the night told over
And all their minds transfigur'd° so together
25 More witnesseth than fancy's images,°
And grows to something of great constancy—
But, howsoever, strange and admirable.°
THESEUS. Here come the lovers, full of joy and
    mirth.
[*Enter* LYSANDER, DEMETRIUS, HERMIA, *and* HELENA.]
Joy, gentle friends! Joy and fresh days of love
Accompany your hearts!
30 LYSANDER.   More than to us
Wait in your royal walks, your board, your bed!
THESEUS. Come now. What masques,° what dances
    shall we have,
To wear away this long age of three hours
Between our after-supper and bedtime?
35 Where is our usual manager of mirth?
What revels are in hand? Is there no play
To ease the anguish of a torturing hour?
Call Philostrate.
PHILOSTRATE.   Here, mighty Theseus.
THESEUS. Say, what abridgement° have you for
    this evening?
What masque? What music? How shall we be-
40   guile
The lazy time, if not with some delight?
PHILOSTRATE. There is a brief° how many sports
    are ripe.°
Make choice of which your highness will see
    first.   [*Giving a paper.*]
THESEUS.
[*Reads*]   The battle with the Centaurs, to be sung
45   By an Athenian eunuch to the harp.

We'll none of that. That have I told my love
In glory of my kinsman Hercules.

[*Reads*]   The riot of the tipsy Bacchanals,
        Tearing the Thracian singer in their rage.°

50 That is an old device,° and it was play'd
When I from Thebes came last a conqueror.

[*Reads*] The thrice three Muses mourning for the
    death
        Of Learning,° late deceas'd in beggary.

That is some satire, keen and critical,
Not sorting with° a nuptial ceremony.   55

[*Reads*]   A tedious brief scene of young Pyramus
        And his love Thisby; very tragical mirth.

Merry and tragical! Tedious and brief!
That is, hot ice and wondrous strange snow.
How shall we find the concord of this discord?   60
PHILOSTRATE. A play there is, my lord, some ten
    words long,
Which is as brief as I have known a play,
But by ten words, my lord, it is too long,
Which makes it tedious; for in all the play
There is not one word apt, one player fitted.   65
And tragical, my noble lord, it is,
For Pyramus therein doth kill himself.
Which when I saw rehears'd, I must confess
Made mine eyes water; but more merry tears
The passion of loud laughter never shed.   70
THESEUS. What are they that do play it?
PHILOSTRATE. Hard-handed men that work in
    Athens here,
Which never labor'd in their minds till now,
And now have toil'd their unbreath'd° memo-
    ries
With this same play, against° your nuptial.   75
THESEUS. And we will hear it.
PHILOSTRATE.   No, my noble lord;
It is not for you. I have heard it over,
And it is nothing, nothing in the world—
Unless you can find sport in their intents,
Extremely stretch'd and conn'd with cruel
    pain,°   80
To do you service.
THESEUS.   I will hear that play,
For never anything can be amiss
When simpleness and duty tender it.
Go, bring them in; and take your places, ladies.
                      [*Exit* PHILOSTRATE.]
HIPPOLYTA. I love not to see wretchedness o'er-
    charg'd°   85
And duty in his service perishing.°
THESEUS. Why, gentle sweet, you shall see no such
    thing.
HIPPOLYTA. He says they can do nothing in this
    kind.°

---

transfur'd so together affected so similarly
More . . . images counts for more than figures drawn by
  love
admirable wonderful   *masques* spectacular court
  entertainments (*MND* itself is masquelike)
abridgement pastime   *brief* list   *ripe* ready
riot . . . rage when Bacchantes tore Orpheus apart
  (Ovid xi, 1)
device show
thrice . . . Learning (a common poetic theme; see
  Spenser's "The Teares of the Muses")

sorting with befitting   *unbreath'd* unexercised
against in anticipation of
Extremely . . . pain i.e., the players have outdone
  themselves and learned their parts with great strain
wretchedness o'ercharged i.e., poor wretches struggling
  beyond their abilities
duty . . . perishing duty destroying itself by its own
  efforts
in this kind i.e., cannot put on a play

THESEUS. The kinder we, to give them thanks for
    nothing.
90   Our sport shall be to take what they mistake;
    And what poor duty cannot do, noble respect
    Takes it in might, not merit.°
    Where I have come, great clerks have purposed
    To greet me with premeditated welcomes,
95   Where I have seen them shiver and look pale,
    Make periods in the midst of sentences,
    Throttle their practic'd accent in their fears,
    And, in conclusion, dumbly have broke off,
    Not paying me a welcome. Trust me, sweet,
100   Out of this silence yet I picked a welcome,
    And in the modesty of fearful duty
    I read as much as from the rattling tongue
    Of saucy and audacious eloquence.
    Love, therefore, and tongue-tied simplicity
105   In least speak most, to my capacity.°
              [Re-enter PHILOSTRATE.]
PHILOSTRATE. So please your Grace, the Prologue
    is address'd.°
THESEUS. Let him approach.
                 [Flourish of trumpets.]
      [Enter QUINCE for the PROLOGUE.]

        Prologue *Quince*
    If we offend, it is with our good will.
    That you should think, we come not to offend,
110 But with good will. To show our simple skill,
    That is the true beginning of our end.
    Consider, then, we come but in despite.
    We do not come, as minding to content you,
    Our true intent is. All for your delight,
115   We are not here. That you should here repent you,
    The actors are at hand; and, by their show,
    You shall know all, that you are like to know.

THESEUS. This fellow doth not stand upon points.°
LYSANDER. He hath rid his prologue like a rough
120   colt; he knows not the stop. A good moral, my
    lord: it is not enough to speak, but to speak
    true.
HIPPOLYTA. Indeed he hath played on his pro-
    logue like a child on a recorder; a sound, but
125   not in government.°
THESEUS. His speech was like a tangled chain—
    nothing impaired, but all disordered. Who is
    next?
      [Enter PYRAMUS and THISBE, WALL, MOON-
           SHINE, and LION.]

---

noble . . . merit the noble mind values the intent, not the
    performance
to my capacity i.e., as I see it   *address'd* ready
stand . . . points observe punctuation marks
in government under control

Prologue
Gentles, perchance you wonder at this show;
    But wonder on, till truth make all things plain. 130
This man is Pyramus, if you would know;
    This beauteous lady Thisby is certain.
This man, with lime and rough-cast, doth present
    Wall, that vile Wall which did these lovers sunder;
And through Wall's chink, poor souls, they are con-
    tent 135
    To whisper. At the which let no man wonder.
This man, with lanthorn, dog, and bush of thorn,
    Presenteth Moonshine; for, if you will know,
By moonshine did these lovers think no scorn
    To meet at Ninus' tomb, there, there to woo. 140
This grisly beast, which Lion hight° by name,
The trusty Thisby, coming first by night,
Did scare away, or rather did affright;
And, as she fled, her mantle she did fall,
    Which Lion vile with bloody mouth did stain. 145
Anon comes Pyramus, sweet youth and tall,
    And finds his trusty Thisby's mantle slain.
Whereat, with blade, with bloody blameful blade,
    He bravely broach'd his boiling bloody breast;
And Thisby, tarrying in mulberry shade, 150
    His dagger drew, and died. For all the rest,
Let Lion, Moonshine, Wall, and lovers twain
    At large discourse, while here they do remain.

      [Exeunt PROLOGUE, PYRAMUS, THISBE, LION, and
                        MOONSHINE.]
THESEUS. I wonder if the lion be to speak.
DEMETRIUS. No wonder, my lord. One lion may, 155
    when many asses do.
WALL. In this same interlude° it doth befall
    That I, one Snout by name, present a wall;
    And such a wall, as I would have you think,
    That had in it a crannied hole or chink, 160
    Through which the lovers, Pyramus and Thisby,
    Did whisper often very secretly.
    This loam, this rough-cast, and this stone, doth
    show
    That I am that same wall; the truth is so.
    And this the cranny° is, right and sinister,° 165
    Through which the fearful lovers are to whisper.
THESEUS. Would you desire lime and hair to
    speak better?
DEMETRIUS. It is the wittiest partition that ever I
    heard discourse, my lord. 170
THESEUS. Pyramus draws near the wall. Silence!
               [Re-enter PYRAMUS.]
Bottom
PYRAMUS. O grim-look'd night! O night with hue so
    black!
    O night, which ever art when day is not!
    O night, O night! Alack, alack, alack,
    I fear my Thisby's promise is forgot! 175

---

hight is called   *interlude* play   *cranny* crack
sinister left

moon gets cross

And thou, O wall, O sweet, O lovely wall,
  That stand'st between her father's ground and
    mine!
Thou wall, O wall, O sweet and lovely wall,
  Show me thy chink, to blink through with mine
    eyne!   [WALL *holds up his fingers.*]
180 Thanks, courteous wall. Jove shield thee well for this!
  But what see I? No Thisby do I see.
O wicked wall, through whom I see no bliss!
  Curs'd be thy stones for thus deceiving me!
THESEUS. The wall, methinks, being sensible,° should curse again.
185
PYRAMUS. No, in truth, sir, he should not. "Deceiving me" is Thisby's cue. She is to enter now, and I am to spy her through the wall. You shall see, it will fall pat as I told you. Yonder she
190 comes.
                    [*Re-enter* THISBE.]
THISBE. O wall, full often hast thou heard my moans,
  For parting my fair Pyramus and me!
My cherry lips have often kiss'd thy stones,
  Thy stones with lime and hair knit up in thee.
195 PYRAMUS. I see a voice. Now will I to the chink,
  To spy an I can hear my Thisby's face.
  Thisby!
THISBE. My love thou art, my love I think.
PYRAMUS. Think what thou wilt, I am thy lover's
    grace,
200 And, like Limander,° am I trusty still.
THISBE. And I like Helen,° till the Fates me kill.
PYRAMUS. Not Shafalus to Procrus was so true.
THISBE. As Shafalus to Procrus, I to you.
PYRAMUS. O, kiss me through the hole of this vile wall!
205 THISBE. I kiss the wall's hole, not your lips at all.
PYRAMUS. Wilt thou at Ninny's tomb meet me
    straightway?
THISBE. 'Tide life 'tide death,° I come without delay.
                    [*Exeunt* PYRAMUS *and* THISBE.]
WALL. Thus have I, Wall, my part discharged so;
  And, being done, thus Wall away doth go.
                                      [*Exit*]
210 THESEUS. Now is the mural down between the
    two neighbors.
DEMETRIUS. No remedy, my lord, when walls are
    so wilful to hear without warning.
HIPPOLYTA. This is the silliest stuff that ever I
215 heard.
THESEUS. The best in this kind are but shadows,
    and the worst are no worse, if imagination
    amend them.

being sensible having feelings
lover's grace gracious lover
Limander blunder for *Leander*, who swam the
  Hellespont to visit his beloved Hero and was drowned
Helen (surely *Hero*, and not Helen of Troy, is meant)
Shafalus to Procrus blunders for *Cephalus* and *Procris*,
  another tragic couple
'Tide . . . death come (betide) life, come death

HIPPOLYTA. It must be your imagination then, and 220
  not theirs.
THESEUS. If we imagine no worse of them than
  they of themselves, they may pass for excellent
  men. Here come two noble beasts in, a man and
  a lion.   *sing*   225
                    [*Re-enter* LION *and* MOONSHINE.]
LION. You, ladies, you, whose gentle hearts do fear
  The smallest monstrous mouse that creeps on floor,
May now perchance both quake and tremble here,
  When lion rough in wildest rage doth roar.
Then know that I, one Snug the joiner, am   230
  A lion fell,° nor else no lion's dam;°
For, if I should as lion come in strife
  Into this place, 'twere pity on my life.
THESEUS. A very gentle beast, and of a good con-
  science.   235
DEMETRIUS. The very best at a beast, my lord, that
  e'er I saw.
LYSANDER. This lion is a very fox for his valor.
THESEUS. True; and a goose for his discretion.
DEMETRIUS. Not so, my lord; for his valor cannot 240
  carry his discretion, and the fox carries the
  goose.
THESEUS. His discretion, I am sure, cannot carry
  his valor; for the goose carries not the fox. It is
  well. Leave it to his discretion, and let us listen 245
  to the moon.
MOONSHINE. This lanthorn doth the horned moon
  present—
DEMETRIUS. He should have worn the horns on his
  head.   250
THESEUS. He is no crescent, and his horns are invisible within the circumference.
MOONSHINE. This lanthorn doth the horned moon
    present;
  Myself the man i' the moon do seem to be.
THESEUS. This is the greatest error of all the rest. 255
  The man should be put into the lantern. How
  is it else the man i' the moon?
DEMETRIUS. He dares not come there for° the candle; for, you see, it is already in snuff.°
HIPPOLYTA. I am aweary of this moon. Would he 260
  would change!
THESEUS. It appears, by his small light of discretion, that he is in the wane; but yet, in courtesy,
  in all reason, we must stay the time.°
LYSANDER. Proceed, Moon.   265
MOONSHINE. All that I have to say is to tell you
  that the lanthorn is the moon; I, the man i' the
  moon; this thorn-bush, my thorn-bush; and
  this dog, my dog.

fell fierce   *dam* mother   *for* because of
in snuff in need of snuffing (with pun, angry)
stay the time see the end

270 DEMETRIUS. Why, all these should be in the lantern; for all these are in the moon. But, silence! Here comes Thisbe.

        [Re-enter THISBE.]

THISBE. This is old Ninny's tomb. Where is my love?

LION. [*Roaring*] Oh—

                               [THISBE *runs off.*]

275 DEMETRIUS. Well roared, Lion.

THESEUS. Well run, Thisbe.

HIPPOLYTA. Well shone, Moon. Truly, the moon shines with a good grace.

        [*The* LION *shakes* THISBE's *mantle, and exit.*]

THESEUS. Well moused, Lion.

280 DEMETRIUS. And then came Pyramus.

LYSANDER. And so the lion vanished.

        [Re-enter PYRAMUS.]

PYRAMUS. Sweet Moon, I thank thee for thy sunny beams;
   I thank thee, Moon, for shining now so bright;
For, by thy gracious, golden, glittering gleams,
285   I trust to take of truest Thisby sight.
      But stay, O spite!
      But mark, poor knight,
   What dreadful dole° is here!
      Eyes, do you see?
290   How can it be?
   O dainty duck! O dear!
      Thy mantle good,
      What, stain'd with blood!
   Approach, ye Furies fell!
295   O Fates, come, come,
      Cut thread and thrum;°
   Quail, crush, conclude, and quell!°

THESEUS. This passion, and the death of a dear friend, would go near to make a man look sad.

300 HIPPOLYTA. Beshrew my heart, but I pity the man.

PYRAMUS. O wherefore, Nature, didst thou lions frame?
   Since lion vile hath here deflower'd my dear:
Which is—no, no—which was the fairest dame
   That liv'd, that lov'd, that lik'd, that look'd with cheer.
305   Come, tears, confound;
      Out, sword, and wound
   The pap of Pyramus;
      Aye, that left pap,
      Where heart doth hop.   [*Stabs himself.*]
310 Thus die I, thus, thus, thus.
      Now am I dead,
      Now am I fled;
   My soul is in the sky.
      Tongue, lose thy light;
315   Moon, take thy flight.   [*Exit* MOONSHINE.]
   Now die, die, die, die, die.   [*Dies.*]

DEMETRIUS. No die, but an ace, for him;° for he is but one.

LYSANDER. Less than an ace, man; for he is dead; he is nothing.   320

THESEUS. With the help of a surgeon he might yet recover, and prove an ass.

HIPPOLYTA. How chance Moonshine is gone before Thisbe comes back and finds her lover?

THESEUS. She will find him by starlight. Here she 325 comes, and her passion ends the play.

        [Re-enter THISBE.]

HIPPOLYTA. Methinks she should not use a long one for such a Pyramus. I hope she will be brief.

DEMETRIUS. A mote° will turn the balance, which Pyramus, which Thisbe, is the better—he for a 330 man, God warrant us, she for a woman, God bless us.

LYSANDER. She hath spied him already with those sweet eyes.

DEMETRIUS. And thus she means, videlicet:°—   335

THISBE. Asleep, my love?
   What, dead, my dove?
O Pyramus, arise!
   Speak, speak. Quite dumb?
   Dead, dead? A tomb   340
Must cover thy sweet eyes.
   These lily lips,
   This cherry nose,
These yellow cowslip cheeks,
   Are gone, are gone.   345
   Lovers, make moan.
His eyes were green as leeks.
   O Sisters Three,°
   Come, come to me,
With hands as pale as milk;   350
   Lay them in gore,
   Since you have shore
With shears his thread of silk.
   Tongue, not a word.
   Come, trusty sword;   355
Come, blade, my breast imbrue.°

                    [*Stabs herself.*]

   And, farewell, friends;
   Thus Thisby ends.
Adieu, adieu, adieu.   [*Dies.*]

THESEUS. Moonshine and Lion are left to bury the 360 dead.

DEMETRIUS. Aye, and Wall too.

BOTTOM. [*Starting up*] No, I assure you; the wall is down that parted their fathers. Will it please

---

dole grief
Cut . . . thrum sever the thread, destroy everything (Bottom is a weaver, and so, apparently, was Pyramus)
Quail . . . quell overcome . . . kill

No . . . him pun on *die* and *dice* ("Ace" is a die with a single spot)
mote speck
And . . . videlicet and thus she laments, as follows
Sisters Three the three Fates, who spun men's destinies
imbrue make bloody

365 you to see the epilogue, or to hear a Bergomask°
dance between two of our company?
THESEUS. No epilogue, I pray you, for your play
needs no excuse. Never excuse; for when the
players are all dead, there need none to be
370 blamed. Marry, if he that writ it had played
Pyramus and hanged himself in Thisbe's garter,
it would have been a fine tragedy. And so it is,
truly, and very notably discharged. But, come,
your Bergomask. Let your epilogue alone.
                              [A dance.]
375 The iron tongue of midnight hath told twelve.
Lovers, to bed: 'tis almost fairy time.
I fear we shall out-sleep the coming morn,
As much as we this night have overwatch'd.°
This palpable-gross play hath well beguil'd
380 The heavy gait of night. Sweet friends, to bed.
A fortnight hold we this solemnity,
In nightly revels and new jollity.   [Exeunt.]
                    [Enter PUCK.]
PUCK. Now the hungry lion roars,
      And the wolf behowls the moon,
385 Whilst the heavy ploughman snores,
      All with weary task fordone.°
Now the wasted brands do glow,
      Whilst the screech-owl, screeching loud,
Puts the wretch that lies in woe
390   In remembrance of a shroud.
Now it is the time of night,
      That the graves, all gaping wide,
Every one lets forth his sprite
      In the church-way paths to glide.
395 And we fairies that do run
      By the triple Hecate's° team°
From the presence of the sun,
      Following darkness like a dream,
Now are frolic.° Not a mouse
400 Shall disturb this hallow'd house.
I am sent with broom before
To sweep the dust behind the door.
      [Enter OBERON and TITANIA with their train.]
OBERON. Through the house give glimmering
      light,
      By the dead and drowsy fire.
405 Every elf and fairy sprite
      Hop as light as bird from brier;

And this ditty, after me,
Sing, and dance it trippingly.
TITANIA. First, rehearse your song by rote,
To each word a warbling note.   410
Hand in hand, with fairy grace,
Will we sing, and bless this place.
                    [Song and dance.]
OBERON. Now, until the break of day,
Through this house each fairy stray.
To the best bride-bed will we,   415
Which by us shall blessed be;
And the issue there create
Ever shall be fortunate.
So shall all the couples three
Ever true in loving be;   420
And the blots of Nature's hand
Shall not in their issue stand;
Never mole, hare lip, nor scar,
Nor mark prodigious,° such as are
Despised in nativity,   425
Shall upon their children be.
With this field-dew consecrate,°
Every fairy take his gait;
And each several° chamber bless,
Through this palace, with sweet peace,   430
And the owner of it blest,
Ever shall in safety rest.
Trip away; make no stay;
Meet me all by break of day.
          [Exeunt OBERON, TITANIA, and train.]
PUCK. If we shadows have offended,   435
Think but this, and all is mended,
That you have but slumber'd here
While these visions did appear.
And this weak and idle theme,
No more yielding but a dream,   440
Gentles, do not reprehend.
If you pardon, we will mend.
And, as I am an honest Puck,
If we have unearned luck
Now to scape the serpent's tongue,°   445
We will make amends ere long,
Else the Puck a liar call.
So, good night unto you all.
Give me your hands,° if we be friends,
And Robin shall restore amends.   [Exit] 450

Bergomask   rustic dance of Bergamo in Italy
overwatch'd   stayed up overlong   fordone   worn out
triple Hecate's   (Hecate ruled as Diana, on earth,
   Cynthia, on the moon, and Proserpina, in Hades)
team   i.e., dragons, which drew Night's chariot
frolic   frolicsome

prodigious   unnatural   consecrate   consecrated
several   separate
Serpent's tongue   i.e., hissing
Give . . . hands   i.e., applaud

AFTERWORD

Even for Shakespeare, who from the first to the last preferred to mix his genres, the more the merrier, unlike the Greeks, who chose to separate comedy from tragedy and tragedy from comedy with strict decorum, *A Midsummer Night's Dream* is a rare composite of farce (the lovers in the woods), fantasy (the fairies), romantic comedy (the multiple love themes), classical romance (Theseus and Hippolyta), burlesque (the "tragical mirth" of Bottom's play), and masque (the play as a whole, "A Midsummer Night's Dream," staged within the frame of a wedding celebration).

Evidence exists that Shakespeare was asked (or ordered) to supply an entertainment to accommodate a special occasion, the marriage of a noble young couple, possibly the Earl of Derby and Elizabeth Vere, daughter of the Earl of Oxford, at one of the great houses along the Thames, with, very possibly, Queen Elizabeth herself in attendance. But whatever the occasion may have been, it so stimulated Shakespeare's imagination that he created his first unqualified masterpiece. All the earlier plays include some fine individual scenes, striking lines of verse, and memorable theatrical characters, as well as some notable imperfections; but *A Midsummer Night's Dream* is a flawless whole, a finished work of art, the final effect of which is to create a kind of spell.

In deference to the nature of this play, perhaps we may ourselves very briefly fantasize: for such a grand occasion, what kind of play should an ambitious, fast-rising young dramatist (Shakespeare was then barely thirty) strive to provide? Obviously it must be dreamlike, masquelike; it must sparkle with gorgeous poetry; it must be studded with prestigious classical allusions to compliment the occasion. So much for the general; but what specifically? If we may judge by the finished product, the play itself, Shakespeare's meditations must have gone somewhat as follows:

A play for a noble wedding! And with the queen there! Why, then, it must first of all be a play *about* a great wedding; a play about love and lovers—lots of lovers, all young and lusty, and all at last joyously married. And to compliment the noble couple being married, it must include one surpassingly noble pair of lovers. There must be moments of laughter, of high hilarity, for the occasion is a festive one; but there must also be suspenseful moments, when the lovers fear that nothing will come out right, for certainly the course of true love never did run smooth. There must be moonlight, always moonlight, for the goddess of the moon is the goddess of love and lovers. Indeed, why not somehow work more than a single moon into the play, and then hope that, besides, the real moon will also be shining that night, above the Thames? ("Doth the moon shine that night we play our play?") What else? Why, fairies, too—and not just fairies, but royal ones, a fairy king and queen, to make a double compliment to royalty. What else for the grand finale? Why, include *a play within the play*, which will stand in relation to the noble marriage that takes place within our play as our play stands in relation to the noble marriage that *really* takes place on the Thames! Thus there will be two audiences (the wedding party and guests who watch the play within our play, and the wedding party and guests who watch our play and also watch our wedding party and guests as these watch the play within our play). But what should our play within the play be about? Why, certainly, it must concern yet another famous couple, another tale of love. And, above all, because the queen herself is to be present, let there be words meant for her ears especially—some flattering allusion to the "fair vestal throned in the west"—and because she, after witnessing the multiple weddings both within the play and without, will nevertheless herself continue to be the Virgin Queen, let some rich line obliquely commemorate that probability as well. ("And the imperial vot'ress passed on,/ In maiden meditation, fancy-free.")

For his setting that must compliment the occasion, Shakespeare chose Athens, for nothing less than noble Greece would do; yet it is a delightful fact that his Athens is very like the London of his day and the woods very like those he played in as a boy at Stratford, filled with just such flowers, vines, and shrubs. His two pairs of young Athenian lovers are also very like the young gallants and ladies of his own time and country. But for the especially magnificent noble couple who must have stature and glamor enough that their own impending marriage, which frames the whole play, would flatter the noble pair who were the "real" bride and bridegroom—that choice was a challenge indeed, and Shakespeare met it brilliantly, for he chose Theseus—brother of Hercules, slayer of the Cretan Minotaur, lover of Ariadne, conqueror of the fabled Amazons—and Hippolyta herself, the Amazons' glittering queen. These are names that might make Homer's own ears tremble, and what a compliment to that noble pair being married on the Thames! And what a double-edged and silken-smooth compliment-lesson for both the noble hosts and the guest of honor when Theseus, throughout the play the epitome of royal grace, not once but repeatedly speaks of the graciousness with which great princes should receive the bumbling efforts of humble subjects:

> For never anything can be amiss,
> When simpleness and duty tender it.

So he addresses Hippolyta, who has momentarily forgotten royalty's duty to be royal not only in manner but also in manners; and, again:

> The kinder we, to give them thanks for nothing.
> Our sport shall be to take what they mistake;
> And what poor duty cannot do, noble respect
> Takes it in might, not merit.

(Possibly Shakespeare's "lesson for princes" relayed through Theseus is not only graceful but also a trifle sly: it is to be hoped that the dramatist's own company were at least as well rewarded for their efforts as (presumably) are Quince's troupe, and Bottom especially, for enacting Pyramus—"He could not have 'scaped sixpence a day during his life.")

As for that assemblage of "hard-handed men . . . which never labor'd in their minds till now" who stage the "lamentable comedy" of Pyramus and Thisbe before Theseus's court even as the Lord Chamberlain's men staged their spectacle of "very midsummer madness" for noble lords and ladies on the Thames, their collective contribution to the evening's merriment is itself of legendary proportions. And if we could but know all the intimate facts we might discover yet another dimension to their comedy, including multiple "in" jokes. For undoubtedly Shakespeare satirized (but with great good humor) not only many contemporary theatrical conventions and extraordinary improvisations of staging ("one must come in with a bush of thorns and a lantern, and say he comes to disfigure, or to present, Moonshine"), but also individual actors of his company. Was there a Bottom among them, who habitually wanted to claim all the good parts ("Let me play the lion too")? A Snug who was "slow of study"? A Flute of course there was, to play women's parts. Was Shakespeare's Flute also, like Quince's, given to speaking all his part at once, "cues and all"? And what of Peter Quince himself, the ring master of this undirectable crew? Was there an identifiable Quince among them? (On the modern stage a strange added dimension results when the make-up artist gives Quince just a suggestion of the familiar beard and hair-line of a Shakespeare portrait.)

When the moon-mad young couples, the wrangling fairy king and queen with their separate retinues, and Bottom with his crew of "patches, rude mechanicals" simultaneously inhabit the enchanted woods at night on the outskirts of Athens, the comic possibilities open to an inventive dramatist's exploitation are without limit. Deception, counterdeception, self-deception keep all lines of action going forward, each with its own measure of excitement and suspense. The lovers, two of them put beside themselves by the juice of Oberon's "little western flower" (the pansy) squeezed on their eyelids, grow frenzied, pursue one another, dash headlong through the forest until they sink exhausted. The fairy queen, tiny but awesome in her feminine fury, succumbs to drops of the same flower, wakes and dotes on Bottom, the "shallowest thickskin of that barren sort"—Bottom, and not merely Bottom, as would be bad enough, but Bottom "translated" with an ass's head. During this great middle section of the play, such is the power of dramatic illusion that dream and reality intermingle, slip in and out of each other, and it is as difficult for the spectators as for the participants to tell where the one ends and the other begins. Nor is there any compelling reason to distinguish, for the whole intent of the play is that all should melt and resolve itself into the single experience that is "a midsummer night's dream," where in the end, as in romantic comedy, all is well: Theseus and Hippolyta are married; the erstwhile misaligned lovers are realigned and married; the fairy king and queen have reconciled their differences; the actors are applauded for their "very tragical mirth"; and all ends in the glow of the omnipresent moon. Here, in this enchanted world, all mortal problems (and immortal ones as well) have been handily resolved by the simple expedient of applying the appropriate juice to erring eyelids.

Even in the romantic comedies that follow, problems are not so easily resolved. In the "dark comedies" they are resolved only after severe trials and general unpleasantness. In the tragedies they are resolved only by death. Perhaps, indeed, the difficulties of the *Dream* will seem too easily overcome unless we remember its origin as a festive play wherein the special occasion itself is an integral part of the total work of art, as in some of the later Elizabethan and Jacobean masques when theatrical spectacle and audience become involved with one another. Possibly we cannot fully experience the play unless we somehow manage to visualize its initial production when the occasion literally was part of the total experience. In the modern audience we need to think of ourselves as looking over the shoulders of the wedding celebrants of 1595 while they watch the play; and for the final scene we should think of looking over their shoulders while they look over the shoulders of Theseus, Hippolyta, and their guests who watch Bottom's Pyramus performed. Thus, in the finished perspective, Bottom's "lamentable comedy" has *three* sets of auditors, each in a circle outside the other. So imagined, Shakespeare's little entertainment written "to order" becomes a richly complex work of art indeed.

But the artistic perfection of *A Midsummer Night's Dream* has not always been appreciated. The unaccountable Samuel Pepys, who regularly attended the theater for reasons other than the play itself, wrote in his diary in 1662: "To the King's Theatre, where we saw 'Midsummer Night's Dream,' which I had never seen before, nor shall ever again, for it is the most insipid, ridiculous play that ever I saw in my life." (Pepys' sour comment is reminiscent of Hippolyta's—which, however, is spoken lightly—on Bottom's play: "This is the silliest stuff that ever I heard.") The great Dr. Johnson, about a century later, found it necessary to "defend" the play on the grounds that "Fairies in his time were much in fashion"; Dr. Johnson would have done better to say nothing. With the nineteenth century the play as an artistic work came abruptly into its own; the famed romantics, Coleridge, Hazlitt, and Lamb, loved the play—that is, the text of the play, for

Hazlitt and Lamb especially could never bear to see Shakespeare acted. Said Hazlitt, after witnessing a disastrous production, "Fairies are not incredible, but fairies six feet high are so." Hazlitt argued that, "All that is finest in the play is lost in the representation."

But the fact is that, Hazlitt and Lamb to the contrary notwithstanding, the *Dream* is a superb acting play, as its history on the stage makes indisputable. For it has long remained among the most popular of all stage plays. The quarto of 1600 advertises the text as having been "Sundry times publickely acted" before that date, and the frequency with which the play was reprinted during the next twenty-five years evinces its continuing popularity until the closing of the theaters in 1642. When the theaters reopened with the Restoration of 1660, the text itself fell afoul of successive "adapters" (including, in the next century, the great actor David Garrick), who supplied the stage with false versions, some of which held the stage until the middle of the nineteenth century, when the "true text" was restored. The play has inspired ballet, symphony, and no fewer than eight operatic versions.

A NOTE ON THE COMPOSITION OF THE PLAY

A Midsummer Night's Dream is generally regarded as having been written about 1595 and first performed before a private audience in that year. The plot is original with Shakespeare, but for various elements in the story he drew on Chaucer's "Knight's Tale" and Plutarch's "Life of Theseus" in the *Lives*. The story of Pyramus and Thisbe was available in Ovid's *Metamorphoses*, and certain details in the affairs of the lovers correspond to elements in Jorge De Montemayor's prose romance of *Diana Enamorada*.

SHAKESPEARE'S TRAGEDIES

Ten of Shakespeare's plays are conventionally classed as tragedies; in addition, *Troilus and Cressida* is sometimes classed as a tragedy, and two of the history plays, *Richard II* and *Richard III*, have some claim to the title. Shakespeare did not write tragedies as consistently throughout his career as he wrote comedies, but the range (with some wide gaps in the first decade) extends from *Titus Andronicus* (about 1591) to *Coriolanus* (1608).

It is not at all certain that, with the first of these, Shakespeare was consciously aiming at a form so ancient, dignified, exalted, and rigidly defined as tragedy, which had come down from classical times paired with the epic as the highest form of literary art. Thus, in part, Aristotle had defined tragedy in the *Poetics*

> Tragedy . . . is an imitation of an action that is serious, complete, and of a certain magnitude; in language embellished with each kind of artistic ornament, the several kinds being found in separate parts of the play; in the form of action, not of narrative; through pity and fear effecting the proper purgation of these emotions.

With *Titus Andronicus* Shakespeare was presumably not at all aware of Aristotle's definition. What he was aware of was the current fashion for what is sometimes called the drama of blood, a form ultimately inspired by the Roman revenge tragedies of Seneca, and he appears to have set out with the intention of outdoing his competitors. Hence *Titus* is rather a concoction than a tragedy, a veritable chamber of horrors in which heads, hands, and tongues are lopped off; the whole action, including the last appalling bloodbath, exhibits a succession of killings and other atrocities. To assert that these incidents constitute "an action that is serious, complete, and of a certain magnitude" assembled for the purpose of "effecting the proper purgation" of pity and fear would clearly be to protest too much, for the play was manifestly designed to entertain an audience that liked violence. The atrocities that take place along the way to the sensational ending do not result from the workings of either fate, fortune, or human character as they do in formal tragedies from the Greeks onward, but, as has been aptly said, are "at the will of the dramatist." However, they were entirely appropriate to the popular theatrical mode in which the young Shakespeare was working, and the play was evidently an instant hit; it was repeatedly performed and three times reprinted in quarto before the Folio of 1623. Hazlitt quite properly called it "an accumulation of vulgar physical horrors," for so it is, and written in a language that is overblown, bombastic, turgid. However, when well staged, it can prove astonishingly exciting theatrical fare even today, and demonstrates that, from the very beginning, Shakespeare knew how to please an audience.

Next, in two English history plays, *Richard III* and *Richard II*, Shakespeare took a long step toward the kind of tragedy that would assume its characteristic form soon afterward in *Julius Caesar*. Both Richards are protagonists whose own characters and deeds are largely responsible for their undoing. There is thus strong argument for including both of these plays within the general classification of "Shakespearean tragedy." Yet both are unmistakably also, and primarily, works of another genre, the "chronicle play," and the concept of tragedy as representing the downfall of an individual hero is secondary in them to the idea of re-creating events of the historical periods that are depicted.

With *Romeo and Juliet*, beautiful and moving drama though it is—". . . never was a story of more woe/ Than this of Juliet and her Romeo"—Shakespeare actually took a step backward from the histories' advance toward the later form of "Shakespearean tragedy." For the initial Prologue, augmented by a succession of pointed comments on fate and fortune throughout the play, spells out Shakespeare's intention of a tragedy in which not individual human character but fate or fortune bears the main responsibility for the catastrophe. Arthur Brooke, in his poem of "Romeus and Juliet," an immediate source of the play, uses the word *fortune* more than seventy times, and the emphasis is echoed in the play, sometimes by Romeo ("O, I am fortune's fool"). Character is strongly developed in the play and is vitally instrumental, but it serves as a means through which fate works toward its end rather than as cause in itself of the catastrophe. The lovers are star-crossed, their doom fixed at birth; what impels them to disaster is fate's will, not theirs.

With *Julius Caesar*, just before the close of the century, Shakespeare first worked out the general pattern that, with many variations but with no basic changes, was to serve for all his following tragedies. Since this tragedy and all the others except *Antony and Cleopatra* and *Timon of Athens* are included, with critical afterwords, in this volume, the following introductory remarks are directed mainly to the subject of tragedy and Shakespearean tragedy in general. Because so very much depends, in this latter species of tragedy, on the character of the protagonist, it will be well to establish some sort of base from which to observe the succession of individual heroes; and since, for a very long time now, the starting point for considerations of tragedy has been Aristotle, we may appropriately begin with his crucial remarks on the nature of the tragic hero:

> It follows plainly . . . that the change of fortune presented must not be the spectacle of a virtuous man brought from prosperity to adversity: for this moves neither pity nor fear; it merely shocks us. Nor, again, that of a bad man passing from adversity to prosperity: for nothing can be more alien to the spirit of Tragedy; it possesses no single tragic quality; it neither satisfies the moral sense, nor calls forth pity or fear. Nor, again, should the downfall of the utter villain be exhibited. A plot of this kind would, doubtless, satisfy the moral sense, but it would inspire neither pity nor fear; for pity is aroused by unmerited misfortune, fear by the misfortune of a man like ourselves. Such an event, therefore, will be neither pitiful nor terrible. There remains, then, the character between these extremes—that of a man who is not eminently good and just, yet whose misfortune is brought about not by vice or depravity, but by some error or frailty. He must be one who is highly renowned and prosperous—a personage like Oedipus, Thyestes, or other illustrious men of such families.[1]

Now it is certain that Aristotle, who died in 322 B.C., never examined a Shakespearean tragedy, and it is nearly as certain that Shakespeare had no direct acquaintance with Aristotle. Nevertheless, expressed in broad terms as they are, Aristotle's observations apply about as well to Shakespeare's tragedies as to those of Aeschylus, Sophocles, and Euripides—though Shakespeare's tragedies and classical tragedies are notably different even in basic ways.

Like the Aristotelian tragic hero, all of Shakespeare's protagonists are men of high place. Brutus is a patrician, higher in his inherited nobility, if not in his political position,

---

[1]*Poetics*. Translated by S. H. Butcher.

than Caesar. Hamlet is of royal blood, a prince who might have been a king had not Claudius "popped in between the election and my hopes." Othello was of royal lineage in his native land ("I fetch my life and being/ From men of royal siege") and is Venice's general and governor of Cyprus. Lear is "every inch a king." Macbeth is a general, the king's kinsman, and makes himself a king. Antony is a general and a "triple pillar" of the world, and Cleopatra is a queen. Timon is a noble lord of Athens. Coriolanus is a patrician, and a general successively of Rome and Antium. Aristotle and Shakespeare were not alone in supposing that only a man of high place was a proper subject for tragedy. For better or worse, the idea ruled practicing dramatists virtually exclusively until the beginning of the eighteenth century; indeed, until our own century was well begun the idea was not firmly established that a traveling salesman like Willy Loman might be as fit for formal tragedy as a king. Nor is the old argument silenced yet; not a critic, but Rosencrantz of *Hamlet*—who was speaking about another matter—stated it best as he addresses the king:

> The cease of majesty
> Dies not alone, but, like a gulf, doth draw
> What's near it with it. It is a massy wheel,
> Fix'd on the summit of the highest mount,
> To whose huge spokes ten thousand lesser things
> Are mortis'd and adjoin'd; which, when it falls,
> Each small annexment, petty consequence,
> Attends the boist'rous ruin.

Stripping away Rosencrantz's metaphors, some of them wildly mixed, we find the kernel: the fall of a king makes a greater crash than the fall of a common man; hence it is better suited for what Aristotle called an action "of a certain magnitude."

Thus the idea of the public renown or "prosperity" of the tragic hero, a matter of first importance for both the Greeks and Shakespeare, is clear and even obvious. What is less simple is the idea of the hero's *character*.

The hero must not be wholly good, says Aristotle, or the spectacle of his destruction will be merely shocking; neither must he be wholly wicked, for then, though his destruction will gratify our feelings, it will move neither pity nor terror. So the proper tragic hero must stand somewhere between these extremes, his misfortune "brought about . . . by some error or frailty." The relevance of Aristotle's observations to the characters of Shakespeare's tragic heroes is a valid point to consider in the study of the tragedies included in this volume. Especially so is the question of these heroes' relative closeness to or remoteness from the Aristotelian ideal of the hero who stands in the middle between good and bad.

It may be said that, in this regard, Shakespeare's heroes divide about equally between earlier and later, the early ones falling to the "good" side of the scale, the later ones falling to the "bad" side. A modern scholar has argued that the early ones—i.e., Brutus, Hamlet, Othello, Lear—are "nothing if not noble"; they are doers of duty, ministers of justice, men of honor. It might be argued that Brutus, Hamlet, and Othello are all rather *too* good to suit the Aristotelian principle, but that Lear fits it perfectly, standing exactly astride the dividing line between the good and the bad. Whereas the early heroes have been pronounced noble, the later ones, all falling to the "bad" side of the line, have been said to be "deeply flawed," with their taints of evil running inward to their very cores. Thus Coriolanus is said to be afflicted with a deadly pride; Timon's ostensibly selfless nobility is said to be, in reality, a form of selfishness, hence his transformation to sheer bestiality once his flatterers have deserted him; Antony's "taints and honors/ Wag'd equal" in him, but his lust destroys all his good; and as for Macbeth, perhaps Aristotle would disqualify him as being too wicked for a proper subject of tragedy even as Brutus is too good. But it is among the proofs of Shakespeare's greatness that there is no single, simple answer to the question of the balance of good and evil in his tragic heroes, some of whom, like Hamlet and Antony in particular, approach the infinite complexity that characterizes human individuals in real, as opposed to theatrical, life. On the evidence of Shakespeare's texts themselves it is even possible to build some sort of case *against* the nobility of Hamlet's motives and *for* the nobility of Macbeth's impulses, if not for his actions. Though it has often been said that tragedy, at bottom, depicts the eternal struggle between good and evil, yet the assertion should not imply that the good and the bad in the characters of the heroes are therefore sharply differentiated, readily categorized. Brutus is "nothing if not noble"—yet he murdered, in Antony's words, "the noblest man/ That ever liv'd in the tide of times." Othello, too, is "nothing if not noble"—yet, in the interest of justice as he sees it, he murders his own wife, an utter innocent. Where, then, does "good" cease and "evil" begin? None of Shakespeare's tragic heroes makes or invites an undebatable answer.

Not at all easy, either, is the fixing of the degree to which one of Shakespeare's heroes is responsible for the catastrophe that overtakes him and, usually, those about him. Aristotle said that in a proper tragedy the misfortune "is brought about . . . by some error or frailty" in the hero's nature. For A. C. Bradley, whose *Shakespearean Tragedy* (1904) still remains the single most influential text on the subject, "The calamities of tragedy do not simply happen, nor are they sent; they proceed mainly from actions, and those the actions of men." He adds, significantly, "What we feel strongly, as a tragedy advances to its close, is that the calamities and catastrophe follow inevitably from the deeds of men, and that the main source of these deeds is character." If it is an exaggeration to say that, with Shakespeare, "character is destiny," yet "it is the exaggeration of a vital truth." A much-used (no doubt overused) "working definition" states that Shakespearean tragedy "represents the downfall of a great man through a flaw in his own make-up." This is a very great oversimplification of both Aristotle and Bradley, and no doubt a still greater oversimplification of the tragedies contained in this volume. Yet another much-used definition, and perhaps more accurate but only by being much more general, is that of another influential student of the drama, George Pierce Baker: "Tragedy is a sequence of incidents or episodes so presented as to emphasize with seriousness their causal relationship." Baker's definition unfortunately omits one of the constants of Shakespeare's tragedies, the fact that all of them end in catastrophe; lacking this specification, the definition is as applicable to the best-designed comedies as to the tragedies, for "causal relationships" are just as vitally a part of *A Midsummer Night's Dream* as of *Othello*.

In any event, most attempts to define Shakespearean tragedy underscore the idea that the catastrophe ending the play does not "just happen" but is shown to have been *brought about*—that is to say that, running through the incidents that comprise the action, is a chain of inevitability, or, at the worst, of *simulated* inevitability, so that, in the end, the audience is made to feel that, however terrible the denouement, it *had to be*. The sense of inevitability is, in any event, a common denominator of all Shakespeare's tragedies (probably excepting *Titus Andronicus*) and, for that matter, of Greek tragedy as well. Though accidents, or seeming accidents, do occur in Shakespeare's tragedies (Friar John's detention in a house suspected of plague in *Romeo and Juliet* and Hamlet's timely encounter with the pirates on his way to death in England are celebrated instances), yet "accident" is per se inimical to the essential idea of tragedy, wherein all dramatists who have known what they were about have been careful, even to the point of insistence, that what comes about does so inevitably.

Thus in a tragedy of character, as Shakespeare's tragedies are, beginning with *Julius Caesar*, the dramatist's necessity is to show that the hero acts as he does act *because he is as he is*—and in the given circumstances in which he acts, his decisions prove fatal. He has "free will," indeed, but only within the limits fixed by his own nature. His actions are as much at the command of his own character as the Greek hero's were at the command of the gods. Thus Brutus, being Brutus and not someone of different convictions, *chooses* to kill Caesar, *chooses* to spare Antony, *chooses* to let Antony speak at Caesar's funeral, and so on, until at last he has run out of space for any decision but death. Hence all his actions are, in Bradley's words, "characteristic actions," actions dictated by his own character. But certainly Brutus, though the model after whom the later heroes were fashioned, is also an exceptional case; in being "themselves the authors of their proper woe," the later heroes appear to follow Brutus only in varying degrees. Interestingly enough, it is probably Coriolanus, the last hero of the series, who conforms most closely to Brutus's pattern.

Always a questionable issue also is that of the relative responsibility of persons other than the hero for his ultimate demise. Without Cassius, Brutus might not have chosen to kill Caesar; without the Witches and his wife, Macbeth might not have chosen to kill Duncan; without the Ghost, Hamlet would presumably not have pursued Claudius to a catastrophe that wipes out all members of both the royal family and the family of Polonius; without Iago, Othello would presumably not have suffocated his wife and slain himself; without Cleopatra, Antony would presumably not have set aside his duty to Rome and run afoul of Octavius Caesar. Are these, then—most of whom directly precipitated the heroes' fatal decisions and actions—equally responsible for the several catastrophes? Or more responsible? Or partially responsible? Or do they, after all, figure only as elements of the situations within which the heroes themselves choose their "characteristic actions"? For indeed a man of a different nature from Brutus's could easily have resisted Cassius's urging, and a man of a different nature from Othello's could have resisted Iago's. A Hamlet, placed in the initial situation of Macbeth, would never have murdered Duncan, regardless of wife or witches; but a Macbeth in Hamlet's place, no doubt, would have killed Claudius within an hour after hearing the Ghost's word—though whether, in the long run, he would have come off any better than Hamlet does is an issue in itself.

The afterwords to the tragedies in this volume raise these among other questions and other sorts of questions; but it is in the texts themselves that readers must seek the only answers that can satisfy.

Romeo and Juliet

DRAMATIS PERSONÆ

ESCALUS   *Prince of Verona*
PARIS   *a young nobleman, kinsman to the Prince*
MONTAGUE ⎱ *heads of two houses at variance with each*
CAPULET ⎰ *other*
AN OLD MAN   *of the Capulet family*
ROMEO   *son to Montague*
MERCUTIO   *kinsman to the Prince, and friend to Romeo*
BENVOLIO   *nephew to Montague, and friend to Romeo*
TYBALT   *nephew to Lady Capulet*
FRIAR LAURENCE   *a Franciscan*
FRIAR JOHN   *of the same order*
BALTHASAR   *servant to Romeo*
SAMPSON ⎱ *servants to Capulet*
GREGORY ⎰

PETER   *servant to Juliet's nurse*
ABRAHAM   *servant to Montague*
AN APOTHECARY
THREE MUSICIANS
PAGE *to Paris; another* PAGE; *an* OFFICER
LADY MONTAGUE   *wife to Montague*
LADY CAPULET   *wife to Capulet*
JULIET   *daughter to Capulet*
NURSE   *to Juliet*

CITIZENS *of Verona;* KINSFOLK *of both houses;* MASKERS, GUARDS, WATCHMEN, *and* ATTENDANTS

CHORUS

SCENE   *Verona; Mantua*

PROLOGUE

[*Enter* CHORUS.]
CHORUS. Two households, both alike in dignity,
    In fair Verona, where we lay our scene,
From ancient grudge break to new mutiny,°
    Where civil blood makes civil hands unclean.
5 From forth the fatal loins of these two foes
    A pair of star-cross'd° lovers take their life,
Whose misadventur'd piteous overthrows
    Do with their death bury their parents' strife.
The fearful passage of their death-mark'd love
    And the continuance of their parents' rage,   10
Which but their children's end naught could
    remove,
    Is now the two hours' traffic of our stage;
The which if you with patient ears attend,
What here shall miss, our toil shall strive to
    mend.

mutiny violence   *star-cross'd* doomed by the stars

Puns, jokes,
double entendres

ACT I

SCENE i
Verona. A public place.

[*Enter* SAMPSON *and* GREGORY, *of the house of Capulet, with swords and bucklers.*]

SAMPSON. Gregory, on my word, we'll not carry coals.°

GREGORY. No, for then we should be colliers.

SAMPSON. I mean, an° we be in choler,° we'll draw.

5 GREGORY. Aye, while you live, draw your neck out o' the collar.°

SAMPSON. I strike quickly, being moved.

GREGORY. But thou art not quickly moved to strike.

10 SAMPSON. A dog of the house of Montague moves me.

GREGORY. To move is to stir, and to be valiant is to stand; therefore, if thou art moved, thou runn'st away.

15 SAMPSON. A dog of that house shall move me to stand. I will take the wall° of any man or maid of Montague's.

GREGORY. That shows thee a weak slave, for the weakest goes to the wall.°

20 SAMPSON. 'Tis true, and therefore women, being the weaker vessels, are ever thrust to the wall. Therefore I will push Montague's men from the wall and thrust his maids to the wall.

GREGORY. The quarrel is between our masters

25 and us their men

SAMPSON. 'Tis all one. I will show myself a tyrant. When I have fought with the men, I will be cruel with the maids. I will cut off their heads.

GREGORY. The heads of the maids?

30 SAMPSON. Aye, the heads of the maids, or their maidenheads; take it in what sense thou wilt.

GREGORY. They must take it in sense° that feel it.

SAMPSON. Me they shall feel while I am able to stand, and 'tis known I am a pretty piece of

35 flesh.

GREGORY. 'Tis well thou art not fish. If thou hadst, thou hadst been poor John.° Draw thy tool;

here comes two of the house of Montagues.

[*Enter* ABRAHAM *and* BALTHASAR.]

SAMPSON. My naked weapon is out. Quarrel; I will back thee.   40

GREGORY. How! Turn thy back and run?

SAMPSON. Fear me not.°

GREGORY. No, marry.° I fear thee!

SAMPSON. Let us take the law of° our sides; let them begin.   45

GREGORY. I will frown as I pass by, and let them take it as they list.°

SAMPSON. Nay, as they dare. I will bite my thumb° at them, which is a disgrace to them if they bear it.   *ACTION*   50

ABRAHAM. Do you bite your thumb at us, sir?

SAMPSON. I do bite my thumb, sir.

ABRAHAM. Do you bite your thumb at us, sir?

SAMPSON. [*Aside to* GREGORY] Is the law of our side if I say aye?   55

GREGORY. No.

SAMPSON. No, sir, I do not bite my thumb at you, sir. But I bite my thumb, sir.

GREGORY. Do you quarrel, sir?

ABRAHAM. Quarrel, sir! No, sir.   60

SAMPSON. But if you do, sir, I am for you. I serve as good a man as you.

ABRAHAM. No better.

SAMPSON. Well, sir.

[*Enter* BENVOLIO.]

GREGORY. [*Aside to* SAMPSON] Say "better." Here   65
comes one of my master's kinsmen.

SAMPSON. Yes, better, sir.

ABRAHAM. You lie.

SAMPSON. Draw, if you be men. Gregory, remember thy swashing blow.   [*They fight*]   70

BENVOLIO. Part, fools!

[*Beating down their weapons.*]
Put up your swords; you know not what you do.

[*Enter* TYBALT.]

TYBALT. What, art thou drawn among these heartless hinds?°

Turn thee, Benvolio, look upon thy death.

BENVOLIO. I do but keep the peace. Put up thy sword,   75

---

carry coals i.e., submit to insults   *an* *if*
choler anger   *collar* i.e., the hangman's noose
take the wall seize the inside walk (safer and cleaner from filth tossed out of windows)
weakest . . . wall i.e., is brushed aside (proverbial)
take . . . sense feel it physically
poor John salted fish (cheap food)

Fear me not don't fear that I'll run
marry by the Virgin Mary   *of* on   *list* like
bite my thumb a gross, insulting gesture
heartless hinds cowardly servants

Or manage it to part these men with me.

TYBALT. What, drawn, and talk of peace! I hate the word,
As I hate hell, all Montagues, and thee.
Have at thee, coward!   [*They fight.*]
[*Enter several of both houses, who join the fray;
then enter* CITIZENS *and* PEACE OFFICERS,
with clubs.]

FIRST OFFICER. Clubs, bills, and partisans!° Strike!
80   Beat them down!
Down with the Capulets! Down with the Montagues!
[*Enter old* CAPULET *in his gown, and* LADY CAPULET.]

CAPULET. What noise is this? Give me my long sword, ho!

LADY CAPULET. A crutch, a crutch! Why call you for a sword?

CAPULET. My sword, I say! Old Montague is come,
85   And flourishes his blade in spite of me.
[*Enter old* MONTAGUE *and* LADY MONTAGUE.]

MONTAGUE. Thou villain Capulet!—Hold me not, let me go.

LADY MONTAGUE. Thou shalt not stir one foot to seek a foe.
[*Enter* PRINCE ESCALUS, *with his train.*]

PRINCE. Rebellious subjects, enemies to peace,
Profaners of this neighbor-stained steel°—
Will they not hear? What, ho! You men, you
90   beasts,
That quench the fire of your pernicious rage
With purple fountains issuing from your veins!
On pain of torture, from those bloody hands
Throw your mistemper'd° weapons to the ground
95   And hear the sentence of your moved prince.
Three civil brawls, bred of an airy word,
By thee, old Capulet and Montague,
Have thrice disturb'd the quiet of our streets
And made Verona's ancient citizens
100   Cast by their grave beseeming ornaments°
To wield old partisans, in hands as old,
Canker'd with peace, to part your canker'd° hate.
If ever you disturb our streets again,
Your lives shall pay the forfeit of the peace.
105   For this time, all the rest depart away.
You, Capulet, shall go along with me,

And, Montague, come you this afternoon,
To know our farther pleasure in this case,
To old Freetown, our common judgment place.
Once more, on pain of death, all men depart.   110
[*Exeunt all but* MONTAGUE, LADY MONTAGUE, *and* BENVOLIO.]

MONTAGUE. Who set this ancient quarrel new abroach?°
Speak, nephew, were you by when it began?

BENVOLIO. Here were the servants of your adversary
And yours close fighting ere I did approach.
I drew to part them. In the instant came   115
The fiery Tybalt, with his sword prepar'd,
Which, as he breath'd defiance to my ears,
He swung about his head and cut the winds,
Who, nothing hurt withal,° hiss'd him in scorn.
While we were interchanging thrusts and blows,   120
Came more and more and fought on part and part,
Till the prince came, who parted either part.

LADY MONTAGUE. O, where is Romeo? Saw you him today?
Right glad I am he was not at this fray.

BENVOLIO. Madam, an hour before the worshipp'd sun   125
Peer'd forth the golden window of the east,
A troubled mind drave me to walk abroad,
Where, underneath the grove of sycamore
That westward rooteth from the city's side,
So early walking did I see your son.   130
Towards him I made, but he was ware° of me
And stole into the covert of the wood.
I, measuring his affections° by my own,
Which then most sought where most might not be found,°
Being one too many by my weary self,   135
Pursu'd my humor,° not pursuing his,
And gladly shunn'd who gladly fled from me.

MONTAGUE. Many a morning hath he there been seen,
With tears augmenting the fresh morning's dew,
Adding to clouds more clouds with his deep sighs.   140
But all so soon as the all-cheering sun
Should in the farthest east begin to draw
The shady curtains from Aurora's° bed,
Away from light steals home my heavy° son,

---

bills . . . partisans spears with cutting edges
Profaners . . . steel those who disgrace their swords by staining them with civil blood
mistemper'd tempered for a wrong purpose
grave beseeming ornaments garments suited to age and gravity
Canker'd . . . canker'd rusted . . . malignant

abroach afoot   *nothing hurt withal* not hurt thereby
ware aware
measuring his affections judging his feelings
Which . . . found (my feelings) sought solitude
humor inclination   *Aurora* the sun goddess
heavy melancholy

Romeo, the lover by the books

6 Keymoran

145 And private in his chamber pens himself,
Shuts up his windows, locks fair daylight out,
And makes himself an artificial night.
Black and portentous must this humor° prove
Unless good counsel may the cause remove.
BENVOLIO. My noble uncle, do you know the
150   cause?
MONTAGUE. I neither know it nor can learn of him.
BENVOLIO. Have you importun'd him by any
    means?
MONTAGUE. Both by myself and many other
    friends.
But he, his own affections' counselor,
155 Is to himself—I will not say how true—
But to himself so secret and so close,
So far from sounding° and discovery
As is the bud bit with an envious° worm
Ere he can spread his sweet leaves to the air
160 Or dedicate his beauty to the sun.
Could we but learn from whence his sorrows
    grow,
We would as willingly give cure as know.
                [Enter ROMEO.]
BENVOLIO. See where he comes. So please you step
    aside,
I'll know his grievance or be much deni'd.
MONTAGUE. I would thou wert so happy° by thy
165   stay
To hear true shrift.° Come, madam, let's away.
          [Exeunt MONTAGUE and LADY.]
BENVOLIO. Good morrow, cousin.
ROMEO.   Is the day so young?
BENVOLIO. But new struck nine.
ROMEO.   Aye me! Sad hours seem long.
Was that my father that went hence so fast?
BENVOLIO. It was. What sadness lengthens Romeo's
170   hours?
ROMEO. Not having that which, having, makes
    them short.
BENVOLIO. In love?
ROMEO. Out—
BENVOLIO. Of love?
175 ROMEO. Out of her favor where I am in love.
BENVOLIO. Alas, that love, so gentle in his view,°
Should be so tyrannous and rough in proof!°
ROMEO. Alas, that love, whose view is muffled
    still,°
Should without eyes see pathways to his will!°

Where shall we dine? O me! What fray was
    here?   180
Yet tell me not, for I have heard it all.
Here's much to do with hate, but more with
    love.
Why, then, O brawling love! O loving hate!
O anything, of nothing first create!°
O heavy lightness! Serious vanity!   185
Misshapen chaos of well-seeming forms!
Feather of lead, bright smoke, cold fire, sick
    health!
Still-waking° sleep, that is not what it is!
This love feel I, that feel no love in this.
Dost thou not laugh?
BENVOLIO.   No, coz,° I rather weep.   190
ROMEO. Good heart, at what?
BENVOLIO.   At thy good heart's oppression.
ROMEO. Why, such is love's transgression.
Griefs of mine own lie heavy in my breast,
Which thou wilt propagate, to have it prest
With more of thine.° This love that thou hast
    shown   195
Doth add more grief to too much of mine own.
Love is a smoke rais'd with the fume° of sighs;
Being purg'd,° a fire sparkling in lovers' eyes;
Being vex'd, a sea nourish'd with lovers' tears.
What is it else? A madness most discreet,   200
A choking gall, and a preserving sweet.
Farewell, my coz.
BENVOLIO.   Soft! I will go along.
An if° you leave me so, you do me wrong.
ROMEO. Tut, I have lost myself; I am not here.
This is not Romeo, he's some other where. 205
BENVOLIO. Tell me in sadness,° who is that you
    love?
ROMEO. What, shall I groan and tell thee?
BENVOLIO.   Groan! Why, no.
But sadly tell me who.
ROMEO. Bid a sick man in sadness make his will—
Ah, word ill urg'd to one that is so ill!   210
In sadness, cousin, I do love a woman.
BENVOLIO. I aim'd so near when I suppos'd you
    lov'd.
ROMEO. A right good markman! And she's fair I
    love.
BENVOLIO. A right fair mark, fair coz, is soonest hit.
ROMEO. Well, in that hit you miss. She'll not be hit 215
With Cupid's arrow; she hath Dian's wit,°

---

humor mood   sounding sounding-out
envious malicious   happy fortunate
To . . . shrift i.e., to get the truth
view appearance   in proof on being experienced
whose . . . still whose sight is always blindfolded; i.e.,
   love is blind
see . . . will should conquer us

create created   Still-waking ever-waking   coz cousin
Which . . . thine you will increase my griefs by adding
   yours
fume vapor   purg'd cleared   An if if
in sadness seriously
Dian's wit Diana, huntress goddess of chastity, had the
   wit to stay single

And in strong proof of chastity well arm'd,
From love's weak childish bow she lives un-
   harm'd.
She will not stay° the siege of loving terms,
220 Nor bide th' encounter of assailing eyes,
Nor ope her lap to saint-seducing gold.
O, she is rich in beauty, only poor
That, when she dies, with beauty dies her store.°
BENVOLIO. Then she hath sworn that she will still
   live chaste?
ROMEO. She hath, and in that sparing° makes huge
225   waste;
For beauty, starv'd with her severity,
Cuts beauty off from all posterity.
She is too fair, too wise, wisely too fair,
To merit bliss by making me despair.
230 She hath forsworn to love, and in that vow
Do I live dead that live to tell it now.
BENVOLIO. Be rul'd by me. Forget to think of her.
ROMEO. O teach me how I should forget to think.
BENVOLIO. By giving liberty unto thine eyes;
   Examine other beauties.
235 ROMEO.   'Tis the way
To call hers, exquisite, in question more.°
These happy masks that kiss fair ladies' brows,
Being black, put us in mind they hide the fair.
He that is strucken blind cannot forget
240 The precious treasure of his eyesight lost.
Show me a mistress that is passing° fair,
What doth her beauty serve but as a note
Where I may read who pass'd that passing fair?
Farewell. Thou canst not teach me to forget.
BENVOLIO. I'll pay that doctrine,° or else die in
245   debt.   [Exeunt]

SCENE ii
A street.

[Enter CAPULET, PARIS, and SERVANT.]
CAPULET. But Montague is bound as well as I,
In penalty alike, and 'tis not hard, I think,
For men so old as we to keep the peace.
PARIS. Of honorable reckoning° are you both,
5   And pity 'tis you liv'd at odds so long.
But now, my lord, what say you to my suit?

CAPULET. But saying o'er what I have said before.
My child is yet a stranger in the world;
She hath not seen the change of fourteen years.
Let two more summers wither in their pride   10
Ere we may think her ripe to be a bride.
PARIS. Younger than she are happy mothers made.
CAPULET. And too soon marr'd are those so early
   made.
The earth hath swallow'd all my hopes but she;
She is the hopeful lady of my earth.   15
But woo her, gentle Paris, get her heart;
My will to her consent is but a part.
An she agree, within her scope of choice
Lies my consent and fair according voice.
This night I hold an old accustom'd feast   20
Whereto I have invited many a guest
Such as I love; and you among the store,
One more, most welcome, makes my number
   more.
At my poor house look to behold this night
Earth-treading stars that make dark heaven
   light.   25
Such comfort as do lusty young men feel
When well-apparel'd April on the heel
Of limping Winter treads, even such delight
Among fresh female buds shall you this night
Inherit° at my house. Hear all, all see,   30
And like her most whose merit most shall be—
Which, on more view of many, mine, being one,
May stand in number,° though in reck'ning
   none.°
Come, go with me. Go, sirrah, trudge about
Through fair Verona; find those persons out   35
Whose names are written there, and to them
   say
My house and welcome on their pleasure stay.
                  [Exeunt CAPULET and PARIS.]
SERVANT. Find them out whose names are written
here! It is written that the shoemaker should
meddle with his yard and the tailor with his   40
last, the fisher with his pencil and the painter
with his nets. But I am sent to find those persons
whose names are here writ, and can never find
what names the writing person hath here writ.
I must to the learned. In good time.   45
                  [Enter BENVOLIO and ROMEO.]
BENVOLIO. Tut, man, one fire burns out another's
   burning;
One pain is lessen'd by another's anguish.
Turn giddy, and be holp° by backward turning.

---

stay wait for
O . . . store though rich in beauty, she is poor because,
  having no descendants, her store of beauty dies with
  her (see Sonnets 1–14)
sparing saving
in question more into greater estimate
passing surpassingly
I'll . . . doctrine I'll prove my point
reck'ning reputation

Inherit have
stand in number count among the crowd
in reck'ning none not noteworthy in herself
holp helped

One desperate grief cures with another's lan-
guish;
50 Take thou some new infection to thy eye,
And the rank poison of the old will die.
ROMEO. Your plantain leaf° is excellent for that.
BENVOLIO. For what, I pray thee?
ROMEO.   For your broken shin.°
BENVOLIO. Why, Romeo, art thou mad?
ROMEO. Not mad, but bound more than a mad-
55   man is,
Shut up in prison, kept without my food,
Whipt and tormented and—God-den, good
fellow.
SERVANT. God gi' god-den.° I pray, sir, can you
read?
ROMEO. Aye, mine own fortune in my misery.
60 SERVANT. Perhaps you have learned it without
book.° But, I pray, can you read anything you
see?
ROMEO. Aye, if I know the letters and the language.
SERVANT. Ye say honestly. Rest you merry!
65 ROMEO. Stay, fellow; I can read.

[Reads] Signior Martino and his wife and daughters; County Anselme and his beauteous sisters
the lady widow of Vitruvio; Signior Placentio
and his lovely nieces; Mercutio and his brother
70   Valentine; mine uncle Capulet, his wife and
daughters; my fair niece Rosaline; Livia; Signior
Valentio and his cousin Tybalt; Lucio and the
lively Helena.

A fair assembly. Whither should they come?
75 SERVANT. Up.
ROMEO. Whither?
SERVANT. To supper; to our house.
ROMEO. Whose house?
SERVANT. My master's.
ROMEO. Indeed, I should have ask'd you that
80   before.
SERVANT. Now I'll tell you without asking. My
master is the great rich Capulet, and if you be
not of the house of Montagues, I pray come and
crush a cup of wine. Rest you merry!   [Exit]
85 BENVOLIO. At this same ancient feast of Capulet's
Sups the fair Rosaline whom thou so lov'st,
With all th' admired beauties of Verona.
Go thither, and with unattainted° eye
Compare her face with some that I shall show,
90 And I will make thee think thy swan a crow.

ROMEO. When the devout religion of mine eye
Maintains such falsehood, then turn tears to
fires;
And these, who, often drown'd, could never die,
Transparent heretics, be burnt for liars!
One fairer than my love! Th' all-seeing sun   95
Ne'er saw her match since first the world begun.
BENVOLIO. Tut, you saw her fair, none else being
by,
Herself pois'd° with herself in either eye.
But in that crystal scales let there be weigh'd
Your lady's love against some other maid   100
That I will show you shining at this feast,
And she shall scant show well that now seems
best.
ROMEO. I'll go along, no such sight to be shown,
But to rejoice in splendor of mine own.
                                    [Exeunt]

SCENE iii
A room in CAPULET's house.

[Enter LADY CAPULET and NURSE.]
LADY CAPULET. Nurse, where's my daughter? Call
her forth to me.
NURSE. Now, by my maidenhead at twelve year
old,
I bade her come. What, lamb! What, lady-
bird!—
God forbid!—Where's this girl? What, Juliet!
                    [Enter JULIET.]
JULIET. How now! Who calls?
NURSE.   Your mother.
JULIET.   Madam, I am here.   5
What is your will?
LADY CAPULET. This is the matter. Nurse, give
leave awhile;
We must talk in secret.—Nurse, come back
again;
I have remember'd me, thou's° hear our coun-
sel.
Thou know'st my daughter's of a pretty° age.   10
NURSE. Faith, I can tell her age unto an hour.
LADY CAPULET. She's not fourteen.
NURSE.   I'll lay fourteen of my teeth—
And yet, to my teen° be it spoken, I have but
four—
She's not fourteen. How long is it now
To Lammastide?°
LADY CAPULET.   A fortnight and odd days.   15

---

plantain leaf medication used for superficial wounds
broken shin scraped skin, not broken bone
God gi' god-den God give you good evening
learned . . . book memorized it
unattainted unbiased

pois'd balanced   thou's thou shalt   pretty goodly
teen sorrow   Lammastide August 1

Early nurse

NURSE. Even or odd, of all days in the year,
    Come Lammas Eve at night shall she be fourteen.
    Susan and she—God rest all Christian souls!—
    Were of an age. Well, Susan is with God;
20 She was too good for me. But, as I said,
    On Lammas Eve at night shall she be fourteen.
    That shall she, marry; I remember it well.
    'Tis since the earthquake now eleven years,
    And she was wean'd—I never shall forget it—
25 Of all the days of the year, upon that day;
    For I had then laid wormwood to my dug,
    Sitting in the sun under the dovehouse wall.
    My lord and you were then at Mantua.—
    Nay, I do bear a brain.—But, as I said,
30 When it did taste the wormwood on the nipple
    Of my dug, and felt it bitter, pretty fool,
    To see it tetchy° and fall out with the dug!
    Shake, quoth the dovehouse. 'Twas no need, I trow,°
    To bid me trudge.
35 And since that time it is eleven years,
    For then she could stand high-lone—nay, by the rood,°
    She could have run and waddled all about;
    For even the day before, she broke° her brow.
    And then my husband—God be with his soul!
40 A' was a merry man—took up the child.
    "Yea," quoth he, "dost thou fall upon thy face?
    Thou wilt fall backward when thou hast more wit,
    Wilt thou not, Jule?" And, by my holidame,°
    The pretty wretch left crying, and said "Aye."
45 To see now how a jest shall come about!
    I warrant, an I should live a thousand years,
    I never should forget it. "Wilt thou not, Jule?" quoth he,
    And, pretty fool, it stinted,° and said "Aye."
LADY CAPULET. Enough of this. I pray thee, hold thy peace.
NURSE. Yes, madam. Yet I cannot choose but
50   laugh,
    To think it should leave crying and say "Aye."
    And yet, I warrant, it had upon it° brow
    A bump as big as a young cock'rel's stone°—
    A perilous knock, and it cried bitterly.
    "Yea," quoth my husband, "fall'st upon thy
55   face?
    Thou wilt fall backward when thou com'st to age,
    Wilt thou not, Jule?" It stinted and said "Aye."

JULIET. And stint thou too, I pray thee, nurse, say I.
NURSE. Peace, I have done. God mark° thee to his
        grace!
    Thou wast the prettiest babe that e'er I nurs'd   60
    An I might live to see thee married once,
    I have my wish.
LADY CAPULET. Marry, that "marry" is the very
        theme
    I come to talk of. Tell me, daughter Juliet,
    How stands your disposition to be married?   65
JULIET. It is an honor that I dream not of.
NURSE. An honor! Were not I thine only nurse,
    I would say thou hadst suck'd wisdom from thy
        teat.
LADY CAPULET. Well, think of marriage now.
        Younger than you
    Here in Verona, ladies of esteem,   70
    Are made already mothers. By my count,
    I was your mother much upon these years
    That you are now a maid. Thus then in brief:
    The valiant Paris seeks you for his love.
NURSE. A man, young lady! Lady, such a man   75
    As all the world—why, he's a man of wax.°
LADY CAPULET. Verona's summer hath not such a
        flower.
NURSE. Nay, he's a flower; in faith, a very flower.
LADY CAPULET. What say you? Can you love the
        gentleman?
    This night you shall behold him at our feast.   80
    Read o'er the volume of young Paris' face,
    And find delight writ there with beauty's pen.
    Examine every married lineament,°
    And see how one another lends content;
    And what obscur'd in this fair volume lies,   85
    Find written in the margent° of his eyes.
    This precious book of love, this unbound lover,
    To beautify him, only lacks a cover.
    The fish lives in the sea, and 'tis much pride
    For fair without the fair within to hide.°   90
    That book in many's eyes doth share the glory
    That in gold clasps locks in the golden story.
    So shall you share all that he doth possess,
    By having him making yourself no less.
NURSE. No less! Nay, bigger. Women grow by
        men.   95
LADY CAPULET. Speak briefly. Can you like of Paris'
        love?
JULIET. I'll look to like, if looking liking move.

tetchy irritable   trow guess   rood Cross
broke i.e., the skin   holidame Holy Dame
stinted stopped   it its
cock'rel's stone rooster's testicle

mark choose
man of wax i.e., handsome as a wax model
married lineament harmonious feature
margent marginal gloss
The fish . . . hide the (beautiful) fish is enclosed by the
    (beautiful) sea, and it is perfect that what is fair within
    be enclosed by what is also fair

Obedient
J.

But no more deep will I endart mine eye
Than your consent gives strength to make it
fly.
          [*Enter a* SERVINGMAN.]
100 SERVINGMAN. Madam, the guests are come, supper
    served up, you called, my young lady asked for,
    the nurse cursed in the pantry, and everything
    in extremity. I must hence to wait. I beseech you,
    follow straight.°
    LADY CAPULET. We follow thee. [*Exit* SERVINGMAN]
105   Juliet, the county° stays.
    NURSE. Go, girl, seek happy nights to happy days.
                            [*Exeunt*]

SCENE iv
A street.

[*Enter* ROMEO, MERCUTIO, BENVOLIO, *with five
or six other* MASKERS, *and* TORCHBEARERS.]
ROMEO. What, shall this speech be spoke for our
    excuse?
    Or shall we on without apology?
BENVOLIO. The date is out of such prolixity.°
    We'll have no Cupid hoodwink'd° with a scarf,
5   Bearing a Tartar's painted bow of lath,
    Scaring the ladies like a crowkeeper,°
    Nor no without-book prologue, faintly spoke
    After the prompter, for our entrance.
    But let them measure° us by what they will,
10   We'll measure them a measure,° and be gone.
ROMEO. Give me a torch. I am not for this ambling;°
    Being but heavy, I will bear the light.
MERCUTIO. Nay, gentle Romeo, we must have you
    dance.
ROMEO. Not I, believe me. You have dancing shoes
15   With nimble soles. I have a soul of lead
    So stakes me to the ground I cannot move.
MERCUTIO. You are a lover; borrow Cupid's wings,
    And soar with them above a common bound.
ROMEO. I am too sore enpiercèd with his shaft
20   To soar with his light feathers, and so bound
    I cannot bound a pitch above dull woe.
    Under love's heavy burthen do I sink.
MERCUTIO. And to sink in it, should you burthen
    love—

Too great oppression for a tender thing.
ROMEO. Is love a tender thing? It is too rough,   25
    Too rude, too boisterous, and it pricks like
    thorn.
MERCUTIO. If love be rough with you, be rough
    with love;
    Prick love for pricking, and you beat love down.
    Give me a case to put my visage in.
    A visor for a visor!° What care I   30
    What curious eye doth quote° deformities?
    Here are the beetle° brows shall blush for me.
BENVOLIO. Come, knock and enter, and no sooner
    in
    But every man betake him to his legs.
ROMEO. A torch for me. Let wantons° light of
    heart   35
    Tickle the senseless rushes° with their heels,
    For I am proverb'd with a grandsire phrase:°
    I'll be a candleholder,° and look on.
    The game was ne'er so fair, and I am done.°
MERCUTIO. Tut, dun's the mouse,° the constable's
    own word.°   40
    If thou art dun, we'll draw thee from the mire°
    Of this sir-reverence° love wherein thou stick'st
    Up to the ears. Come, we burn daylight,° ho.
ROMEO. Nay, that's not so.°
MERCUTIO.   I mean, sir, in delay
    We waste our lights in vain, like lamps by day.   45
    Take our good meaning, for our judgment sits
    Five times in that ere once in our five wits.°
ROMEO. And we mean well in going to this mask;
    But 'tis no wit to go.
MERCUTIO.   Why, may one ask?
ROMEO. I dreamt a dream tonight.
MERCUTIO.   And so did I.   50
ROMEO. Well, what was yours?
MERCUTIO.   That dreamers often lie.

---

straight straightaway   *county* count
The date . . . prolixity such an elaborate device is out of
    fashion (Benvolio refers to the practice of uninvited
    maskers announcing their arrival through a costumed
    messenger provided with a set speech)
hoodwink'd blindfolded   *crowkeeper* scarecrow
measure judge
measure . . . measure dance one dance with them
ambling dancing

visor . . . visor an ugly mask for an ugly face
quote note   *beetle* beetling
wantons sports   *rushes* floor-coverings
proverb'd . . . phrase provided with an ancient proverb
candleholder bystander
The game . . . done I'll quit the game at its height
    (proverbial)
dun's the mouse be quiet (a stock phrase)
constable's own word i.e., as the constable warns while
    lying in ambush
dun . . . mire if you are Dun (horse's name), we'll pull
    you from the mud (reference to a game played with a
    log representing the horse)
sir-reverence contemptuous epithet
burn daylight waste time
Nay . . . so i.e., it's nighttime (Romeo pretends to take
    the literal meaning)
Take . . . wits i.e., take our intended meaning as
    recognized by your commonsense, which is much more
    likely to be right than any witty interpretation

Q. Mab *Mercutio*

ROMEO. In bed asleep, while they do dream things
  true.
MERCUTIO. O, then I see Queen Mab° hath been
  with you.
  She is the fairies' midwife,° and she comes
55 In shape no bigger than an agate stone
  On the forefinger of an alderman,
  Drawn with a team of little atomies°
  Athwart men's noses as they lie asleep.
  Her wagon spokes made of long spinners'° legs;
60 The cover, of the wings of grasshoppers;
  Her traces, of the smallest spider's web;
  Her collars, of the moonshine's wat'ry beams;
  Her whip, of cricket's bone; the lash, of film;
  Her wagoner, a small grey-coated gnat,
65 Not half so big as a round little worm
  Prick'd from the lazy finger of a maid.°
  Her chariot is an empty hazelnut
  Made by the joiner squirrel or old grub,
  Time out o' mind the fairies' coachmakers.
70 And in this state she gallops night by night
  Through lovers' brains, and then they dream of
  love;
  O'er courtiers' knees, that dream on curtsies
  straight;
  O'er lawyers' fingers, who straight dream on
  fees;
  O'er ladies' lips, who straight on kisses dream,
75 Which oft the angry Mab with blisters plagues,
  Because their breaths with sweetmeats tainted
  are.
  Sometime she gallops o'er a courtier's nose,
  And then dreams he of smelling out a suit;°
  And sometime comes she with a tithe pig's tail
80 Tickling a parson's nose as a' lies asleep;
  Then dreams he of another benefice.
  Sometime she driveth o'er a soldier's neck,
  And then dreams he of cutting foreign throats,
  Of breaches, ambuscadoes, Spanish blades,
85 Of healths five fathom deep; and then anon
  Drums in his ear, at which he starts and wakes,
  And being thus frighted swears a prayer or two
  And sleeps again. This is that very Mab
  That plats° the manes of horses in the night
90 And bakes the elf-locks° in foul sluttish hairs,

Queen Mab the Fairy Queen (Celtic)
midwife i.e., who delivers men's dreams
atomies minute creatures *spinners* spiders
worm . . . maid worms were said to breed in the fingers
  of lazy maids
smelling . . . suit finding one with a petition to be
  presented to the king, thus gaining a fee
tithe pig every tenth pig went to the parson
healths . . . deep (drinking) toasts from mugs thirty feet
  deep
plats tangles *elf-locks* knots

Which once untangled much misfortune bodes°
  This is the hag, when maids lie on their backs,
  That presses them and learns them first to bear,
  Making them women of good carriage.
  This is she—
ROMEO.   Peace, peace, Mercutio, peace! 95
  Thou talk'st of nothing.
MERCUTIO.   True, I talk of dreams,
  Which are the children of an idle brain,
  Begot of nothing but vain° fantasy,
  Which is as thin of substance as the air
  And more inconstant than the wind, who woos 100
  Even now the frozen bosom of the north,
  And, being anger'd, puffs away from thence,
  Turning his face to the dew-dropping south.
BENVOLIO. This wind you talk of blows us from
  ourselves;
  Supper is done, and we shall come too late. 105
ROMEO. I fear, too early; for my mind misgives
  Some consequence, yet hanging in the stars,
  Shall bitterly begin his fearful date
  With this night's revels and expire the term
  Of a despised life clos'd in my breast 110
  By some vile forfeit of untimely death.
  But He that hath the steerage of my course
  Direct my sail! On, lusty gentlemen.
BENVOLIO. Strike, drum. [*Exeunt*]

SCENE v
A hall in CAPULET'S *house.*

[MUSICIANS *waiting. Enter* SERVINGMEN, *with
  napkins.*]
FIRST SERVINGMAN. Where's Potpan, that he helps
  not to take away? He shift a trencher!° He scrape
  a trencher!
SECOND SERVINGMAN. When good manners shall
  lie all in one or two men's hands, and they un- 5
  washed too, 'tis a foul thing.
FIRST SERVINGMAN. Away with the joint-stools, remove the court-cupboard, look to the plate.
  Good thou, save me a piece of marchpane;° and,
  as thou lovest me, let the porter let in Susan 10
  Grindstone and Nell. Antony, and Potpan!
SECOND SERVINGMAN. Aye, boy, ready.
FIRST SERVINGMAN. You are looked for and called
  for and sought for, in the great chamber.
THIRD SERVINGMAN. We cannot be here and there 15
  too. Cheerly, boys; be brisk a while, and the
  longer liver take all.° [*They retire behind.*]

bodes threatens *vain* empty
trencher platter *marchpane* sweetmeat
longer . . . all proverbial exhortation to be cheerful

Hot Capulet

[*Enter* CAPULET, *with* JULIET *and others of his
    house, meeting the* GUESTS *and* MASKERS.]

CAPULET. Welcome, gentlemen! Ladies that have
    their toes
Unplagu'd with corns will have a bout with you.
20 Ah ha, my mistresses! Which of you all
Will now deny to dance? She that makes dainty,
She, I'll swear, hath corns. Am I come near ye
    now?
Welcome, gentlemen! I have seen the day
That I have worn a visor, and could tell
25 A whispering tale in a fair lady's ear
Such as would please. 'Tis gone, 'tis gone, 'tis
    gone.
You are welcome, gentlemen! Come, musicians,
    play.
A hall, a hall! Give room! And foot it, girls.
                        [*Music plays, and they dance.*]
More light, you knaves, and turn the tables up,
30 And quench the fire, the room is grown too hot.
Ah, sirrah, this unlook'd-for sport comes well.
Nay, sit, nay, sit, good cousin Capulet,
For you and I are past our dancing days.
How long is 't now since last yourself and I
Were in a mask?
35 SECOND CAPULET.   By 'r lady, thirty years.
CAPULET. What, man! 'Tis not so much, 'tis not so
    much.
'Tis since the nuptial of Lucentio,
Come Pentecost as quickly as it will,
Some five and twenty years; and then we
    mask'd.
SECOND CAPULET. 'Tis more, 'tis more. His son is
40   elder, sir;
His son is thirty.
CAPULET.   Will you tell me that?
His son was but a ward° two years ago.
ROMEO. [*To a* SERVINGMAN] What lady's that,
    which doth enrich the hand
Of yonder knight?
45 SERVINGMAN. I know not, sir.
ROMEO. O, she doth teach the torches to burn
    bright!
It seems she hangs upon the cheek of night
Like a rich jewel in an Ethiop's ear,
Beauty too rich for use, for earth too dear!°
50 So shows a snowy dove trooping with crows
As yonder lady o'er her fellows shows.
The measure done, I'll watch her place of stand,
And, touching hers, make blessed my rude
    hand.
Did my heart love till now? Forswear it, sight!
55 For I ne'er saw true beauty till this night.

ward minor   *dear* precious

TYBALT. This, by his voice, should be a Montague.
Fetch me my rapier, boy. What, dares the slave
Come hither, cover'd with an antic face,°
To fleer° and scorn at our solemnity?°
Now, by the stock and honor of my kin,   60
To strike him dead I hold it not a sin.
CAPULET. Why, how now, kinsman! Wherefore
    storm you so?
TYBALT. Uncle, this is a Montague, our foe,
A villain that is hither come in spite
To scorn at our solemnity this night.   65
CAPULET. Young Romeo is it?
TYBALT.   'Tis he, that villain Romeo.
CAPULET. Content thee, gentle coz, let him alone.
He bears him like a portly° gentleman,
And, to say truth, Verona brags of him
To be a virtuous and well-govern'd youth.   70
I would not for the wealth of all this town
Here in my house do him disparagement.
Therefore be patient; take no note of him.
It is my will, the which if thou respect,
Show a fair presence and put off these frowns,   75
An ill-beseeming semblance for a feast.
TYBALT. It fits, when such a villain is a guest.
I'll not endure him.
CAPULET.   He shall be endur'd.
What, goodman boy! I say, he shall. Go to.
Am I the master here, or you? Go to.   80
You'll not endure him! God shall mend my
    soul!
You'll make a mutiny among my guests!
You will set cock-a-hoop!° You'll be the man!
TYBALT. Why, uncle, 'tis a shame.
CAPULET.   Go to, go to.
You are a saucy boy. Is't so, indeed?   85
This trick may chance to scathe you.° I know
    what:
You must contrary me! Marry, 'tis time.—
Well said, my hearts!—You are a princox.° Go.
Be quiet, or—More light, more light!—For
    shame!
I'll make you quiet.—What, cheerly, my hearts!   90
TYBALT. Patience perforce with wilful choler meet-
    ing
Makes my flesh tremble in their different greet-
    ing.°
I will withdraw; but this intrusion shall,

antic face grotesque mask
fleer mock   *solemnity* festivity
portly dignified   *set cock-a-hoop* start a rumpus
This trick . . . you your quarrelsome habit may get you
    into trouble   *princox* smart aleck
Patience . . . greeting enforced patience thwarting wilful
    anger makes my flesh tremble

Now seeming sweet, convert° to bitterest gall.

[*Exit*]

ROMEO. [*To* JULIET] If I profane with my unworthi-
95   est hand
    This holy shrine, the gentle fine° is this:
    My lips, two blushing pilgrims, ready stand
        To smooth that rough touch with a tender
        kiss.

JULIET. Good pilgrim,° you do wrong your hand
        too much,
100   Which mannerly devotion shows in this;
    For saints have hands that pilgrims' hands do
        touch,
        And palm to palm is holy palmers' kiss.

ROMEO. Have not saints lips, and holy palmers
        too?

JULIET. Aye, pilgrim, lips that they must use in
        prayer.

ROMEO. O, then, dear saint, let lips do what hands
105   do:
    They pray. Grant thou, lest faith turn to des-
        pair.

JULIET. Saints do not move, though grant for
        prayers' sake.

ROMEO. Then move not, while my prayer's effect I
    take.
    Thus from my lips by thine my sin is purg'd.

[*Kisses her.*]

JULIET. Then have my lips the sin that they have
110   took.

ROMEO. Sin from my lips? O trespass sweetly
        urg'd!
    Give me my sin again.   [*Kisses her.*]

JULIET.   You kiss by the book.°

NURSE. Madam, your mother craves a word with
        you.

ROMEO. What is her mother?

NURSE.   Marry, bachelor,

Her mother is the lady of the house,   115
And a good lady, and a wise and virtuous.
I nurs'd her daughter, that you talk'd withal.
I tell you, he that can lay hold of her
Shall have the chinks.°

ROMEO.   Is she a Capulet?
O dear account! My life is my foe's debt.   120

BENVOLIO. Away, be gone; the sport is at the best.

ROMEO. Aye, so I fear; the more is my unrest.

CAPULET. Nay, gentlemen, prepare not to be gone;
    We have a trifling foolish banquet towards.
    Is it e'en so? Why, then, I thank you all,   125
    I thank you, honest gentlemen. Good night.
    More torches here! Come on then, let's to bed.
    Ah, sirrah, by my fay,° it waxes late.
    I'll to my rest.

                [*Exeunt all but* JULIET *and* NURSE.]

JULIET. Come hither, nurse. What is yond gentle-
    man?   130

NURSE. The son and heir of old Tiberio.

JULIET. What's he that now is going out of door?

NURSE. Marry, that, I think, be young Petruchio.

JULIET. What's he that follows there, that would
    not dance?

NURSE. I know not.   135

JULIET. Go ask his name. If he be married,
    My grave is like to be my wedding bed.

NURSE. His name is Romeo, and a Montague,
    The only son of your great enemy.

JULIET. My only love sprung from my only hate! 140
    Too early seen unknown, and known too late!
    Prodigious° birth of love it is to me,
    That I must love a loathed enemy.

NURSE. What's this? What's this?

JULIET.   A rhyme I learn'd even now
    Of one I danc'd withal.   145

                [*One calls within "Juliet."*]

NURSE.   Anon, anon!°
    Come, let's away; the strangers all are gone.

                                        [*Exeunt*]

---

convert change   *holy shrine* i.e., her hand
gentle fine mild penalty
Good pilgrim Juliet picks up, and both continue, the
    religious imagery that Romeo began at the start of the
    sonnet "If I profane . . ."
kiss . . . book according to rules

Shall . . . chinks will come into money
fay faith   *Prodigious* monstrous
anon at once

ACT II

PROLOGUE

[Enter CHORUS.]
CHORUS. Now old desire° doth in his deathbed lie,
   And young affection gapes to be his heir;
   That fair for which love groan'd for and would
      die,
   With tender Juliet match'd, is now not fair.
5 Now Romeo is belov'd and loves again,
   Alike° bewitched by the charm of looks;
   But to his foe suppos'd he must complain,
   And she steal love's sweet bait from fearful
      hooks.
   Being held a foe, he may not have access
10   To breathe such vows as lovers use° to swear;
   And she, as much in love, her means much less
    To meet her new beloved anywhere.
   But passion lends them power, time means, to
     meet,
   Temp'ring extremities with extreme sweet.°

                              [Exit]

SCENE i
A lane by the wall of CAPULET's *orchard.*

[Enter ROMEO, *alone.]*
ROMEO. Can I go forward when my heart is here?
   Turn back, dull earth,° and find thy center° out.
   [He climbs the wall, and leaps down within it.]
   [Enter BENVOLIO *with* MERCUTIO.]*
BENVOLIO. Romeo! My cousin Romeo!
MERCUTIO.   He is wise,
   And, on my life, hath stol'n him home to bed.
BENVOLIO. He ran this way and leap'd this orchard
5   wall.
   Call, good Mercutio.
MERCUTIO.   Nay, I'll conjure° too.
   Romeo! Humors! Madman! Passion! Lover!
   Appear thou in the likeness of a sigh.
   Speak but one rhyme, and I am satisfied.

Cry but "aye me!" pronounce but "love" and
   "dove,"   10
   Speak to my gossip° Venus one fair word,
   One nickname for her purblind son and heir,
   Young Adam Cupid,° he that shot so trim
   When King Cophetua° lov'd the beggar maid!
   He heareth not, he stirreth not, he moveth not; 15
   The ape is dead,° and I must conjure him.
   I conjure thee by Rosaline's bright eyes,
   By her high forehead and her scarlet lip,
   By her fine foot, straight leg, and quiv'ring
     thigh,
   And the demesnes° that there adjacent lie,   20
   That in thy likeness thou appear to us!
BENVOLIO. An if he hear thee, thou wilt anger him.
MERCUTIO. This cannot anger him. 'Twould anger
   him
   To raise a spirit in his mistress' circle°
   Of some strange nature, letting it there stand   25
   Till she had laid it and conjur'd it down;
   That were some spite. My invocation
   Is fair and honest, and in his mistress' name
   I conjure only but to raise up him.
BENVOLIO. Come, he hath hid himself among
   these trees,   30
   To be consorted° with the humorous° night.
   Blind is his love, and best befits the dark.
MERCUTIO. If love be blind, love cannot hit the
   mark.
   Now will he sit under a medlar° tree
   And wish his mistress were that kind of fruit 35
   As maids call medlars when they laugh alone.
   O, Romeo, that she were, O, that she were
   An open et cetera,° thou a poperin° pear!

old desire i.e., Romeo's love for Rosaline
Alike mutually   *use* are accustomed
Temp'ring . . . sweet balancing extreme difficulties (of
  meeting) with extreme pleasure (in meeting)
dull earth my body   *thy center* Juliet
conjure Mercutio mockingly recites a "spell," as if
  Romeo were a spirit that can be summoned

gossip confidante
Adam Cupid i.e., good archer, after Adam Bell, hero of a
  famous ballad
King Cophetua ballad hero who made the beggar maid
  his queen
The ape is dead reference to a performing ape that
  played dead
demesnes areas
mistress' circle the conjurer's circle in which the
  summoned spirit appears and "plays dead" until
  properly "conjured"; with extended and gross pun
consorted associated   *humorous* moody
medlar a species of pear
open et cetera (used like *so-and-so*, to stand for an
  improper word or phrase)
poperin species of pear (but ribald imagery runs
  throughout the passage)

Romeo, good night. I'll to my truckle-bed;°
40 This field bed is too cold for me to sleep.
Come, shall we go?
BENVOLIO.   Go then, for 'tis in vain
To seek him here that means not to be found.

[*Exeunt*]

SCENE ii
CAPULET's *orchard*.

[*Enter* ROMEO.]

ROMEO. He jests at scars that never felt a wound.
[JULIET *appears above at a window*.]
But, soft! What light through yonder window
breaks?
It is the east, and Juliet is the sun!
Arise, fair sun, and kill the envious moon,
5   Who is already sick and pale with grief
That thou her maid art far more fair than she.
Be not her maid, since she is envious;
Her vestal livery is but sick and green,
And none but fools do wear it; cast it off.
10 It is my lady; O, it is my love!
O that she knew she were!
She speaks, yet she says nothing.° What of that?
Her eye discourses; I will answer it.
I am too bold, 'tis not to me she speaks:
15 Two of the fairest stars in all the heaven,
Having some business, do entreat her eyes
To twinkle in their spheres till they return.
What if her eyes were there, they in her head?
The brightness of her cheek would shame those
stars
20 As daylight doth a lamp; her eyes in heaven
Would through the airy region stream so bright
That birds would sing and think it were not
night.
See how she leans her cheek upon her hand!
O that I were a glove upon that hand,
That I might touch that cheek!
25 JULIET.   Aye me!
ROMEO. She speaks.
O speak again, bright angel! For thou art
As glorious to this night, being o'er my head,
As is a winged messenger of heaven
Unto the white-upturned wond'ring eyes
30 Of mortals that fall back to gaze on him
When he bestrides the lazy-pacing clouds
And sails upon the bosom of the air.

JULIET. O Romeo, Romeo! Wherefore art thou
Romeo?
Deny thy father and refuse thy name;
Or, if thou wilt not, be but sworn my love   35
And I'll no longer be a Capulet.
ROMEO. [*Aside*] Shall I hear more, or shall I speak
at this?
JULIET. 'Tis but thy name that is my enemy;
Thou art thyself, though not a Montague.
What's Montague? It is nor hand, nor foot,   40
Nor arm, nor face, nor any other part
Belonging to a man. O be some other name!
What's in a name? That which we call a rose
By any other name would smell as sweet;
So Romeo would, were he not Romeo call'd,   45
Retain that dear perfection which he owes°
Without that title. Romeo, doff thy name,
And for thy name, which is no part of thee,
Take all myself.
ROMEO.   I take thee at thy word.
Call me but love, and I'll be new baptiz'd;   50
Henceforth I never will be Romeo.
JULIET. What man art thou that thus bescreen'd in
night
So stumblest on my counsel?
ROMEO.   By a name
I know not how to tell thee who I am.
My name, dear saint, is hateful to myself,   55
Because it is an enemy to thee.
Had I it written, I would tear the word.
JULIET. My ears have yet not drunk a hundred
words
Of thy tongue's uttering, yet I know the sound.
Art thou not Romeo, and a Montague?   60
ROMEO. Neither, fair maid, if either thee dislike.°
JULIET. How cam'st thou hither, tell me, and
wherefore?
The orchard walls are high and hard to climb
And the place death, considering who thou art,
If any of my kinsmen find thee here.   65
ROMEO. With love's light wings did I o'er-perch
these walls,
For stony limits cannot hold love out;
And what love can do, that dares love attempt.
Therefore thy kinsmen are no let° to me.
JULIET. If they do see thee, they will murder thee. 70
ROMEO. Alack, there lies more peril in thine eye
Than twenty of their swords. Look thou but
sweet,
And I am proof against their enmity.
JULIET. I would not for the world they saw thee
here.

---

truckle-bed trundle-bed, or baby bed
yet . . . nothing i.e., her speech is inaudible

owes owns   *dislike* displease   *let* hindrance

The desire to discover

ROMEO. I have night's cloak to hide me from their
75   eyes,
       And but° thou love me, let them find me here.
       My life were better ended by their hate
       Than death prorogued,° wanting° of thy love.
JULIET. By whose direction found'st thou out this
       place?
ROMEO. By love, that first did prompt me to in-
80   quire;
       He lent me counsel, and I lent him eyes.
       I am no pilot; yet wert thou as far
       As that vast shore wash'd with the farthest sea,
       I would adventure for such merchandise.
JULIET. Thou know'st the mask of night is on my
85   face,
       Else would a maiden blush bepaint my cheek
       For that which thou hast heard me speak to-
       night.
       Fain would I dwell on form, fain, fain deny
       What I have spoke. But farewell compliment!°
90   Dost thou love me? I know thou wilt say "Aye,"
       And I will take thy word. Yet if thou swear'st,
       Thou mayst prove false: at lovers' perjuries,
       They say, Jove laughs. O gentle Romeo,
       If thou dost love, pronounce it faithfully;
95   Of if thou think'st I am too quickly won,
       I'll frown and be perverse and say thee nay,
       So thou wilt woo; but else, not for the world.
       In truth, fair Montague, I am too fond,
       And therefore thou mayst think my 'havior
       light.
100   But trust me, gentleman, I'll prove more true
       Than those that have more cunning to be
       strange.
       I should have been more strange, I must confess,
       But that thou overheard'st, ere I was ware,
       My true love's passion; therefore pardon me,
105   And not impute this yielding to light love,
       Which the dark night hath so discovered.
ROMEO. Lady, by yonder blessed moon I swear,
       That tips with silver all these fruit-tree tops—
JULIET. O swear not by the moon, th' inconstant
       moon,
110   That monthly changes in her circled orb,
       Lest that thy love prove likewise variable.
ROMEO. What shall I swear by?
JULIET.   Do not swear at all;
       Or, if thou wilt, swear by thy gracious self,
       Which is the god of my idolatry,
       And I'll believe thee.
115 ROMEO.   If my heart's dear love—
JULIET. Well, do not swear. Although I joy in thee,

       I have no joy of this contract° tonight.
       It is too rash, too unadvis'd, too sudden,
       Too like the lightning, which doth cease to be
       Ere one can say "It lightens." Sweet, good night! 120
       This bud of love, by summer's rip'ning breath,
       May prove a beauteous flow'r when next we
       meet.
       Good night, good night! As sweet repose and rest
       Come to thy heart as that within my breast!
ROMEO. O wilt thou leave me so unsatisfied?   125
JULIET. What satisfaction canst thou have tonight?
ROMEO. Th' exchange of thy love's faithful vow for
       mine.
JULIET. I gave thee mine before thou didst request
       it.
       And yet I would it were to give again.
ROMEO. Wouldst thou withdraw it? For what
       purpose, love?   130
JULIET. But to be frank, and give it thee again.
       And yet I wish but for the thing I have.
       My bounty is as boundless as the sea,
       My love as deep; the more I give to thee,
       The more I have, for both are infinite.   135
       I hear some noise within; dear love, adieu!
                           [NURSE calls within.]
       Anon, good nurse! Sweet Montague, be true.
       Stay but a little, I will come again.   [Exit]
ROMEO. O blessed, blessed night! I am afeard,
       Being in night, all this is but a dream,   140
       Too flattering-sweet to be substantial.
                  [Re-enter JULIET, above.]
JULIET. Three words, dear Romeo, and good night
       indeed.
       If that thy bent° of love be honorable,
       Thy purpose marriage, send me word tomorrow
       By one that I'll procure to come to thee,   145
       Where and what time thou wilt perform the
       rite,
       And all my fortunes at thy foot I'll lay
       And follow thee my lord throughout the
       world.
NURSE. [Within] Madam!
JULIET. I come anon.—But if thou mean'st not
       well,   150
       I do beseech thee—
NURSE. [Within] Madam!
JULIET.   By and by, I come—
       To cease thy suit, and leave me to my grief.
       Tomorrow will I send.
ROMEO.   So thrive my soul—
JULIET. A thousand times good night!   [Exit] 155
ROMEO. A thousand times the worse, to want thy
       light.

---

but unless   *prorogued* postponed   *wanting* lacking
compliment ceremony

contract betrothal   *bent* intention

Love goes toward love as schoolboys from their
    books,
But love from love, toward school with heavy
    looks.   *[Retiring slowly.]*
             [Re-enter JULIET, *above.]*
JULIET. Hist! Romeo, hist!—O, for a falconer's
    voice,
160   To lure this tassel-gentle° back again!
    Bondage is hoarse° and may not speak aloud,
    Else would I tear the cave where Echo lies
    And make her airy tongue more hoarse than
    mine
    With repetition of my Romeo's name.
165   Romeo!
ROMEO. It is my soul that calls upon my name.
    How silver-sweet sound lovers' tongues by night,
    Like softest music to attending ears!
JULIET. Romeo!
ROMEO.   My dear?
JULIET.   At what o'clock tomorrow
    Shall I send to thee?
170 ROMEO.   By the hour of nine.
JULIET. I will not fail. 'Tis twenty years till then.
    I have forgot why I did call thee back.
ROMEO. Let me stand here till thou remember it.
JULIET. I shall forget, to have thee still stand there,
175   Rememb'ring how I love thy company.
ROMEO. And I'll still stay, to have thee still forget,
    Forgetting any other home but this.
JULIET. 'Tis almost morning. I would have thee
    gone,
    And yet no farther than a wanton's° bird,
180   Who lets it hop a little from her hand
    Like a poor prisoner in his twisted gyves,°
    And with a silk thread plucks it back again,
    So loving-jealous of his liberty.
ROMEO. I would I were thy bird.
JULIET.   Sweet, so would I.
185   Yet I should kill thee with much cherishing.
    Good night, good night! Parting is such sweet
    sorrow
    That I shall say good night till it be morrow.
                             [Exit]
ROMEO. Sleep dwell upon thine eyes, peace in thy
    breast!
    Would I were sleep and peace, so sweet to rest!
190   Hence will I to my ghostly° father's cell,
    His help to crave and my dear hap° to tell.
                             [Exit]

SCENE iii
FRIAR LAURENCE'S *cell.*

[Enter FRIAR LAURENCE, *with a basket.]*
FRIAR LAURENCE. The gray-eyed morn smiles on
    the frowning night,
    Check'ring the eastern clouds with streaks of
    light,
    And flecked darkness like a drunkard reels
    From forth day's path and Titan's° fiery wheels.
    Now, ere the sun advance his burning eye,   5
    The day to cheer and night's dank dew to dry,
    I must upfill this osier cage° of ours
    With baleful weeds and precious-juiced flowers.
    The earth that's nature's mother is her tomb;
    What is her burying grave, that is her womb,   10
    And from her womb children of divers kind
    We sucking on her natural bosom find,
    Many for many virtues excellent,
    None but for some, and yet all different.
    O, mickle° is the powerful grace that lies   15
    In herbs, plants, stones, and their true qualities,
    For naught so vile that on the earth doth live,
    But to the earth some special good doth give;
    Nor aught so good, but, strain'd from that fair
    use,
    Revolts from true birth,° stumbling on abuse.   20
    Virtue itself turns vice, being misapplied,
    And vice sometime's by action dignified.
    Within the infant rind of this small flower
    Poison hath residence, and medicine° power;
    For this, being smelt, with that part cheers each
    part;   25
    Being tasted, slays all senses with the heart.
    Two such opposed kings encamp them still
    In man as well as herbs, grace and rude will;°
    And where the worser is predominant,
    Full soon the canker° death eats up that plant.   30
                  [Enter ROMEO.]*
ROMEO. Good morrow, father.
FRIAR LAURENCE.   Benedicite!°
    What early tongue so sweet saluteth me?
    Young son, it argues a distemper'd head
    So soon to bid good morrow to thy bed.
    Care keeps his watch in every old man's eye   35
    And where care lodges, sleep will never lie;
    But where unbruised youth with unstuff'd°
    brain

---

tassel-gentle male falcon
Bondage is hoarse i.e., parental control requires secrecy
wanton's spoiled child's   *gyves* fetters
ghostly spiritual   *dear hap* good fortune

Titan's the sun's   *osier cage* willow basket
mickle great   *true birth* its proper nature
medicine medicinal
grace . . . will heavenly virtue and bestial impulse
canker cankerworm
Benedicite bless you   *unstuff'd* free from care

Couplets

Doth couch his limbs, there golden sleep doth reign.
Therefore thy earliness doth me assure
40   Thou art up-rous'd by some distemperature;
Or if not so, then here I hit it right—
Our Romeo hath not been in bed tonight.
ROMEO. That last is true; the sweeter rest was mine.
FRIAR LAURENCE. God pardon sin! Wast thou with Rosaline?
45   ROMEO. With Rosaline, my ghostly father? No.
I have forgot that name and that name's woe.
FRIAR LAURENCE. That's my good son. But where hast thou been then?
ROMEO. I'll tell thee ere thou ask it me again.
I have been feasting with mine enemy,
50   Where on a sudden one hath wounded me
That's by me wounded. Both our remedies
Within thy help and holy physic° lies.
I bear no hatred, blessed man, for, lo,
My intercession° likewise steads° my foe.
FRIAR LAURENCE. Be plain, good son, and homely° in thy drift;
55   Riddling confession finds but riddling shrift.°
ROMEO. Then plainly know my heart's dear love is set
On the fair daughter of rich Capulet.
As mine on hers, so hers is set on mine,
And all combin'd, save what thou must com-
60   bine
By holy marriage. When and where and how
We met, we woo'd, and made exchange of vow,
I'll tell thee as we pass; but this I pray,
That thou consent to marry us today.
FRIAR LAURENCE. Holy Saint Francis, what a change
65   is here!
Is Rosaline, that thou didst love so dear,
So soon forsaken? Young men's love then lies
Not truly in their hearts, but in their eyes.
Jesu Maria, what a deal of brine
70   Hath wash'd thy sallow cheeks for Rosaline!
How much salt water thrown away in waste
To season love, that of it doth not taste!°
The sun not yet thy sighs from heaven clears;
Thy old groans ring yet in mine ancient ears.
75   Lo, here upon thy cheek the stain doth sit
Of an old tear that is not wash'd off yet.
If e'er thou wast thyself and these woes thine,
Thou and these woes were all for Rosaline.
And art thou chang'd? Pronounce this sentence
then:

Women may fall when there's no strength in
men.   80
ROMEO. Thou chid'st me oft for loving Rosaline.
FRIAR LAURENCE. For doting, not for loving, pupil mine.
ROMEO. And bad'st me bury love.
FRIAR LAURENCE.   Not in a grave
To lay one in, another out to have!
ROMEO. I pray thee, chide not. She whom I love now   85
Doth grace° for grace and love for love allow.
The other did not so.
FRIAR LAURENCE.   O, she knew well
Thy love did read by rote and could not spell.°
But come, young waverer, come, go with me.
In one respect° I'll thy assistant be,   90
For this alliance may so happy prove
To turn your households' rancor to pure love.
ROMEO. O, let us hence; I stand on° sudden haste.
FRIAR LAURENCE. Wisely and slow; they stumble
that run fast.   [Exeunt]

SCENE iv
A street.

[Enter BENVOLIO and MERCUTIO.]
MERCUTIO. Where the devil should this Romeo be?
Came he not home tonight?
BENVOLIO. Not to his father's; I spoke with his man.
MERCUTIO. Why, that same pale hard-hearted wench, that Rosaline,
Torments him so that he will sure run mad.   5
BENVOLIO. Tybalt, the kinsman to old Capulet,
Hath sent a letter to his father's house.
MERCUTIO. A challenge, on my life.
BENVOLIO. Romeo will answer it.
MERCUTIO. Any man that can write may answer a   10
letter.
BENVOLIO. Nay, he will answer the letter's master,
how he dares, being dared.
MERCUTIO. Alas, poor Romeo, he is already dead!
Stabbed with a white wench's black eye, shot   15
thorough the ear with a love-song, the very pin°
of his heart cleft with the blind bow-boy's butt-
shaft. And is he a man to encounter Tybalt?
BENVOLIO. Why, what is Tybalt?
MERCUTIO. More than prince of cats,° I can tell   20

---

physic medicine   *intercession* plea   *steads* aids
homely simple   *shrift* absolution
that . . . taste i.e., love is sweet, not salty

grace favor   *read . . . spell* i.e., merely going through
the conventional motions
In one respect for one purpose
stand on am in need of   *pin* center (bullseye)
prince of cats Tybalt (Tybert, Thibert) was the cat in the
tale of Reynard the Fox

you. O, he's the courageous captain of compliments.° He fights as you sing prick-song,° keeps time, distance, and proportion, rests me his minim rest,° one, two—and the third in your
25 bosom. The very butcher of a silk button,° a duelist, a duelist; a gentleman of the very first house,° of the first and second cause.° Ah, the immortal passado! The punto reverso! The hai!°

BENVOLIO. The what?

30 MERCUTIO. The pox of° such antic, lisping, affecting fantasticoes,° these new tuners of accents!° "By Jesu, a very good blade! A very tall° man! A very good whore!" Why, is not this a lamentable thing, grandsire,° that we should be thus
35 afflicted with these strange flies, these fashionmongers, these perdona-mi's,° who stand so much on the new form° that they cannot sit at ease on the old bench? O, their bones, their bones!°

[*Enter* ROMEO.]

40 BENVOLIO. Here comes Romeo, here comes Romeo.

MERCUTIO. Without his roe, like a dried herring. O flesh, flesh, how art thou fishified! Now is he for the numbers° that Petrarch° flowed in. Laura to
45 his lady was but a kitchen wench—marry, she had a better love to berhyme her; Dido,° a dowdy; Cleopatra, a gypsy; Helen° and Hero,° hildings and harlots; Thisbe,° a gray eye or so, but not to the purpose. Signior Romeo, bon
50 jour! There's a French salutation to your French slop.° You gave us the counterfeit fairly last night.

ROMEO. Good morrow to you both. What counterfeit did I give you?

MERCUTIO. The slip, sir, the slip.° Can you not 55 conceive?°

ROMEO. Pardon, good Mercutio, my business was great, and in such a case as mine a man may strain courtesy.

MERCUTIO. That's as much as to say such a case° as 60 yours constrains a man to bow in the hams.

ROMEO. Meaning, to curtsy.

MERCUTIO. Thou hast most kindly hit it.

ROMEO. A most courteous exposition.

MERCUTIO. Nay, I am the very pink of courtesy. 65

ROMEO. Pink for flower.

MERCUTIO. Right.

ROMEO. Why, then is my pump well flowered.°

MERCUTIO. Well said. Follow me this jest now, till thou hast worn out thy pump, that, when the 70 single sole of it is worn, the jest may remain, after the wearing, solely singular.

ROMEO. O single-soled jest, solely singular for the singleness!

MERCUTIO. Come between us, good Benvolio; my 75 wits faint.

ROMEO. Switch and spurs, switch and spurs,° or I'll cry a match.°

MERCUTIO. Nay, if thy wits run the wild-goose chase,° I have done; for thou hast more of the 80 wild goose in one of thy wits than, I am sure, I have in my whole five. Was I with you there for the goose?°

ROMEO. Thou wast never with me for anything when thou wast not there for the goose.° 85

MERCUTIO. I will bite thee by the ear for that jest.

ROMEO. Nay, good goose, bite not.

MERCUTIO. Thy wit is a very bitter sweeting;° it is a most sharp sauce.

ROMEO. And is it not well served in to a sweet 90 goose?

MERCUTIO. O, here's a wit of cheveril° that stretches from an inch narrow to an ell broad!

ROMEO. I stretch it out for that word "broad," which added to the goose, proves thee far and 95 wide a broad goose.

---

compliments formalities   *prick-song* written music
minim rest shortest pause in musical notation
butcher . . . button i.e., a precise marksman with rapier point
first house finest school (of fencing)
first . . . cause i.e., causes of challenging (dueling terms)
passado . . . hai dueling terms for thrusts and strokes
pox of plague on   *fantasticoes* coxcombs
new . . . accents users of fancy new jargon
tall brave   *grandsire* i.e., "fellow oldster"
perdona-mi's i.e., fops with affected manners
form fashion (with pun on *bench* or class as in school)
bones i.e., the old bench is too hard for them
numbers poetic meters
Petrarch Italian poet (1304–1374) famed for sonnets to Laura
Dido Queen of Carthage, loved and left by Aeneas
Helen over whom the Trojan war was fought
Hero for whom Leander swam the Hellespont
Thisbe beloved of Pyramus (see *A Midsummer Night's Dream*, V, i)
French slop baggy trousers

counterfeit . . . slip (a pun; *slip* means both "escape" and "counterfeit coin")
conceive understand
case (punning on Romeo's word, Mercutio implies a crippling affliction)
pump . . . flowered my shoe is well "pinked," or ornamented
Switch and spurs i.e., urge your wits to do their utmost
cry a match claim the victory
run . . . chase i.e., play follow-the-leader in this race of wits
Was . . . goose i.e., did I score by calling you "goose"
goose with pun, prostitute
bitter sweeting tart apple   *cheveril* kidskin

nurse

MERCUTIO. Why, is not this better now than groaning for love? Now art thou sociable, now art thou
Romeo, now art thou what thou art, by art as
100 well as by nature. For this driveling love is like a
great natural° that runs lolling up and down to
hide his bauble in a hole.

BENVOLIO. Stop there, stop there.

MERCUTIO. Thou desirest me to stop in my tale
105 against the hair.°

BENVOLIO. Thou wouldst else have made thy tale
large.°

MERCUTIO. O, thou art deceived; I would have
made it short, for I was come to the whole
110 depth of my tale, and meant indeed to occupy
the argument° no longer.

ROMEO. Here's goodly gear!°

[*Enter* NURSE *and* PETER.]

MERCUTIO. A sail, a sail!

BENVOLIO. Two, two—a shirt and a smock.°

115 NURSE. Peter!

PETER. Anon.

NURSE. My fan, Peter.

MERCUTIO. Good Peter, to hide her face, for her
fan's the fairer of the two.

120 NURSE. God ye good morrow, gentlemen.

MERCUTIO. God ye good den, fair gentlewoman.

NURSE. Is it good den?

MERCUTIO. 'Tis no less, I tell you, for the bawdy
hand of the dial is now upon the prick° of noon.

125 NURSE. Out upon you! What a man are you!

ROMEO. One, gentlewoman, that God hath made
for himself to mar.

NURSE. By my troth, it is well said. "For himself to
mar," quoth a'?° Gentlemen, can any of you
130 tell me where I may find the young Romeo?

ROMEO. I can tell you, but young Romeo will be
older when you have found him than he was
when you sought him. I am the youngest of that
name, for fault° of a worse.

135 NURSE. You say well.

MERCUTIO. Yea, is the worst well? Very well took,
i' faith; wisely, wisely.

NURSE. If you be he, sir, I desire some confidence
with you.

140 BENVOLIO. She will indite° him to some supper.

MERCUTIO. A bawd, a bawd, a bawd! So ho!

ROMEO. What hast thou found?

MERCUTIO. No hare, sir, unless a hare, sir, in a
lenten pie, that is something stale and hoar° ere
it be spent.°   [*Sings.*] 145

> An old hare hoar,
> And an old hare hoar,
> Is very good meat in lent:
> But a hare that is hoar,
> Is too much for a score,   150
> When it hoars ere it be spent.

Romeo, will you come to your father's? We'll to
dinner thither.

ROMEO. I will follow you.

MERCUTIO. Farewell, ancient lady; farewell, [*singing*] 155
"lady, lady, lady."

[*Exeunt* MERCUTIO *and* BENVOLIO.]

NURSE. Marry, farewell! I pray you, sir, what
saucy merchant was this that was so full of his
ropery?°

ROMEO. A gentleman, nurse, that loves to hear 160
himself talk and will speak more in a minute
than he will stand to in a month.

NURSE. An a' speak anything against me, I'll take
him down, an a' were lustier than he is, and
twenty such Jacks; and if I cannot, I'll find those 165
that shall. Scurvy knave! I am none of his flirt-
gills; I am none of his skains-mates.° [*Turning to*
PETER] And thou must stand by too, and suffer
every knave to use me at his pleasure!

PETER. I saw no man use you at his pleasure; if I 170
had, my weapon should quickly have been out, I
warrant you. I dare draw as soon as another
man if I see occasion in a good quarrel and the
law on my side.

NURSE. Now, afore God, I am so vexed that every 175
part about me quivers. Scurvy knave! Pray you,
sir, a word. And as I told you, my young lady
bade me inquire you out. What she bade me
say, I will keep to myself. But first let me tell ye,
if ye should lead her into a fool's paradise, as 180
they say, it were a very gross kind of behavior,
as they say, for the gentlewoman is young, and
therefore, if you should deal double with her,
truly it were an ill thing to be offered to any
gentlewoman, and very weak dealing.   185

ROMEO. Nurse, commend me to thy lady and mistress. I protest unto thee—

NURSE. Good heart, and, i' faith, I will tell her as
much. Lord, Lord, she will be a joyful woman.

---

natural idiot   *against . . . hair* contrary to my
   inclination (with gross pun)
large indecent (with gross pun)
occupy . . . argument continue the subject
goodly gear rich stuff; i.e., "more sport"
shirt . . . smock i.e., a male and a female
prick stroke   *quoth a'* said he   *fault* lack
indite invite (Benvolio mocks her misuse of
   confidence for *conference*)

hoar moldy   *spent* used
ropery (misused for *roguery*)
flirt-gills . . . skains-mates (terms for loose women)

190 ROMEO. What wilt thou tell her, nurse? Thou dost
       not mark me.
     NURSE. I will tell her, sir, that you do protest;
       which, as I take it, is a gentlemanlike offer.
     ROMEO. Bid her devise
195   Some means to come to shrift this afternoon,
       And there she shall at Friar Laurence' cell
       Be shriv'd and married. Here is for thy pains.
     NURSE. No, truly, sir; not a penny.
     ROMEO. Go to; I say you shall.
200 NURSE. This afternoon, sir? Well, she shall be there.
     ROMEO. And stay, good nurse, behind the abbey
       wall.
       Within this hour my man shall be with thee
       And bring thee cords made like a tackled stair,°
       Which to the high top-gallant° of my joy
205   Must be my convoy in the secret night.
       Farewell. Be trusty, and I'll quit° thy pains.
       Farewell. Commend me to thy mistress.
     NURSE. Now God in heaven bless thee! Hark you,
       sir.
     ROMEO. What say'st thou, my dear nurse?
210 NURSE. Is your man secret? Did you ne'er hear say,
       Two may keep counsel, putting one away?
     ROMEO. I warrant thee, my man's as true as steel.
     NURSE. Well, sir, my mistress is the sweetest lady—
       Lord, Lord! When 'twas a little prating thing—
215   O, there is a nobleman in town, one Paris, that
       would fain lay knife aboard.° But she, good soul,
       had as lieve see a toad, a very toad, as see him.
       I anger her sometimes, and tell her that Paris is
       the properer° man; but, I'll warrant you, when
220   I say so, she looks as pale as any clout° in the
       versal° world. Doth not rosemary and Romeo
       begin both with a letter?
     ROMEO. Aye, nurse. What of that? Both with an R.
     NURSE. Ah, mocker! That's the dog's name.° R is
225   for the—No. I know it begins with some other
       letter. And she hath the prettiest sententious° of
       it, of you and rosemary, that it would do you
       good to hear it.
     ROMEO. Commend me to thy lady.
     NURSE. Aye, a thousand times. [Exit ROMEO]
230   Peter!
     PETER. Anon.
     NURSE. Peter, take my fan and go before, and
       apace.   [Exeunt]

SCENE v
CAPULET's orchard.

[Enter JULIET.]

JULIET. The clock struck nine when I did send the
     nurse;
   In half an hour she promis'd to return.
   Perchance she cannot meet him. That's not so.
   O, she is lame! Love's heralds should be
     thoughts,
   Which ten times faster glide than the sun's
     beams,   5
   Driving back shadows over louring hills.
   Therefore do nimble-pinion'd doves draw love,°
   And therefore hath the wind-swift Cupid wings.
   Now is the sun upon the highmost hill
   Of this day's journey, and from nine till twelve   10
   Is three long hours; yet she is not come.
   Had she affections° and warm youthful blood,
   She would be as swift in motion as a ball.
   My words would bandy° her to my sweet love
   And his to me.   15
   But old folks, many feign as° they were dead—
   Unwieldy, slow, heavy, and pale as lead.
        [Enter NURSE, with PETER.]
   O God, she comes! O honey nurse, what news?
   Hast thou met with him? Send thy man away.
NURSE. Peter, stay at the gate.   [Exit PETER.]   20
JULIET. Now, good sweet nurse—O Lord, why
     look'st thou sad?
   Though news be sad, yet tell them merrily;
   If good, thou sham'st the music of sweet news
   By playing it to me with so sour a face.
NURSE. I am aweary; give me leave a while.   25
   Fie, how my bones ache! What a jaunce° have I
     had!
JULIET. I would thou hadst my bones and I thy
     news.
   Nay, come, I pray thee, speak. Good, good
     nurse, speak.
NURSE. Jesu, what haste? Can you not stay awhile?
   Do you not see that I am out of breath?   30
JULIET. How art thou out of breath when thou hast
     breath
   To say to me that thou art out of breath?
   Th' excuse that thou dost make in this delay
   Is longer than the tale thou dost excuse.
   Is thy news good, or bad? Answer to that.   35

tackled stair rope ladder   top-gallant i.e., summit
quit requite, reward
lay . . . aboard i.e., carve this bird for himself
properer handsomer   clout cloth   versal universal
dog's name "dog's letter" for its growling sound
sententious sentences

doves . . . love Venus's chariot was drawn by doves
affections passions
bandy bat to and fro like a shuttlecock
feign as act as if
jaunce jaunt

Say either, and I'll stay the circumstance.
Let me be satisfied. Is't good or bad?
NURSE. Well, you have made a simple choice. You
  know not how to choose a man. Romeo! No, not
40 he. Though his face be better than any man's,
  yet his leg excels all men's; and for a hand, and a
  foot, and a body, though they be not to be talked
  on, yet they are past compare. He is not the
  flower of courtesy, but, I'll warrant him, as
45 gentle as a lamb. Go thy ways, wench; serve
  God. What, have you dined at home?
JULIET. No, no. But all this did I know before.
  What says he of our marriage? What of that?
NURSE. Lord, how my head aches! What a head
  have I!
50 It beats as it would fall in twenty pieces.
  My back o' t' other side—ah, my back, my back!
  Beshrew° your heart for sending me about
  To catch my death with jauncing up and down!
JULIET. I' faith, I am sorry that thou art not well.
  Sweet, sweet, sweet nurse, tell me, what says my
55 love?
NURSE. Your love says, like an honest gentleman,
  and a courteous, and a kind, and a handsome,
  and, I warrant, a virtuous—Where is your
  mother?
60 JULIET. Where is my mother! Why, she is within.
  Where should she be? How oddly thou repliest!
  "Your love says, like an honest gentleman,
  Where is your mother?"
NURSE.   O God's lady dear!
  Are you so hot? Marry, come up, I trow.°
65 Is this the poultice for my aching bones?
  Henceforward do your messages yourself.
JULIET. Here's such a coil!° Come, what says
  Romeo?
NURSE. Have you got leave to go to shrift today?
JULIET. I have.
NURSE. Then hie you hence to Friar Laurence'
70 cell.
  There stays a husband to make you a wife.
  Now comes the wanton blood up in your cheeks!
  They'll be in scarlet straight at any news.
  Hie you to church; I must another way
75 To fetch a ladder by the which your love
  Must climb a bird's nest soon when it is dark.
  I am the drudge, and toil in your delight,
  But you shall bear the burden soon at night.
  Go. I'll to dinner. Hie you to the cell.
JULIET. Hie to high fortune! Honest nurse, fare-
80 well.   [Exeunt]

Beshrew mischief on   Marry . . . trow (by the Virgin)
you're due for a come-uppance, I trust   coil fuss

SCENE vi
FRIAR LAURENCE'S *cell.*

[*Enter* FRIAR LAURENCE *and* ROMEO.]
FRIAR LAURENCE. So smile the heavens upon this
    holy act
  That after-hours with sorrow chide us not!
ROMEO. Amen, amen! But come what sorrow can,
  It cannot countervail° th' exchange of joy
  That one short minute gives me in her sight.   5
  Do thou but close our hands with holy words,
  Then love-devouring death do what he dare—
  It is enough I may but call her mine.
FRIAR LAURENCE. These violent delights have
    violent ends,
  And in their triumph die like fire and powder,   10
  Which as they kiss consume. The sweetest honey
  Is loathsome in his° own deliciousness,
  And in the taste confounds° the appetite.
  Therefore, love moderately; long love doth so.
  Too swift arrives as tardy as too slow.   15
      [*Enter* JULIET.]
  Here comes the lady. O, so light a foot
  Will ne'er wear out the everlasting flint.
  A lover may bestride the gossamer°
  That idles in the wanton summer air,
  And yet not fall; so light is vanity.°   20
JULIET. Good even to my ghostly confessor.
FRIAR LAURENCE. Romeo shall thank thee, daugh-
    ter, for us both.
JULIET. As much to him, else is his thanks too
    much.
ROMEO. Ah, Juliet, if the measure of thy joy
  Be heap'd like mine, and that thy skill be more   25
  To blazon° it, then sweeten with thy breath
  This neighbor air, and let rich music's tongue
  Unfold th' imagin'd happiness that both
  Receive in either by this dear encounter.
JULIET. Conceit,° more rich in matter than in
    words,   30
  Brags of his substance, not of ornament:
  They are but beggars that can count their
    worth.
  But my true love is grown to such excess
  I cannot sum up sum of half my wealth.
FRIAR LAURENCE. Come, come with me, and we
    will make short work;   35
  For, by your leaves, you shall not stay alone
  Till holy church incorporate two in one.
                                        [*Exeunt*]

countervail outbalance   *his* its   *confounds* destroys
gossamer spider's webbing   *vanity* earthly joys
blazon describe   *Conceit* imagination

ACT III

SCENE i
A public place.

[*Enter* MERCUTIO, BENVOLIO, PAGE, *and*
SERVANTS.]

BENVOLIO. I pray thee, good Mercutio, let's retire.
 The day is hot, the Capulets abroad,
 And if we meet we shall not 'scape a brawl,
 For now these hot days is the mad blood
 stirring.

5 MERCUTIO. Thou art like one of those fellows that
 when he enters the confines of a tavern claps
 me his sword upon the table and says "God
 send me no need of thee!" and by the operation°
 of the second cup draws it on the drawer,° when
10 indeed there is no need.

BENVOLIO. Am I like such a fellow?

MERCUTIO. Come, come, thou art as hot a Jack in
 thy mood as any in Italy, and as soon moved to
 be moody, and as soon moody to be moved.

15 BENVOLIO. And what to?

MERCUTIO. Nay, an there were two such, we should
 have none shortly, for one would kill the other.
 Thou! Why, thou wilt quarrel with a man that
 hath a hair more or a hair less in his beard than
20 thou hast. Thou wilt quarrel with a man for
 cracking nuts, having no other reason but because
 thou hast hazel eyes; what eye but such an eye
 would spy out such a quarrel? Thy head is as full
 of quarrels as an egg is full of meat, and yet thy
25 head hath been beaten as addle as an egg for
 quarreling. Thou hast quarreled with a man for
 coughing in the street, because he hath wakened
 thy dog that hath lain asleep in the sun. Didst
 thou not fall out with a tailor for wearing his
30 new doublet° before Easter? With another, for
 tying his new shoes with old riband? And yet
 thou wilt tutor me from quarreling!

BENVOLIO. An I were so apt to quarrel as thou art,
 any man should buy the fee simple° of my life
35 for an hour and a quarter.°

MERCUTIO. The fee simple! O simple!

 [*Enter* TYBALT *and others.*]

BENVOLIO. By my head, here come the Capulets.

MERCUTIO. By my heel, I care not.

TYBALT. Follow me close, for I will speak to them.
 Gentlemen, good den. A word with one of you.   40

MERCUTIO. And but one word with one of us?
 Couple it with something; make it a word and a
 blow.

TYBALT. You shall find me apt enough to that, sir,
 an you will give me occasion.   45

MERCUTIO. Could you not take some occasion without giving?

TYBALT. Mercutio, thou consort'st° with Romeo—

MERCUTIO. Consort!° What, dost thou make us
 minstrels? An thou make minstrels of us, look   50
 to hear nothing but discords. Here's my fiddlestick;° here's that shall make you dance.
 'Zounds,° consort!

BENVOLIO. We talk here in the public haunt of
 men.
 Either withdraw unto some private place,   55
 Or reason coldly of your grievances,
 Or else depart. Here all eyes gaze on us.

MERCUTIO. Men's eyes were made to look, and let
 them gaze.
 I will not budge for no man's pleasure, I.

 [*Enter* ROMEO.]

TYBALT. Well, peace be with you, sir. Here comes
 my man.   60

MERCUTIO. But I'll be hang'd, sir, if he wear your
 livery.°
 Marry, go before to field; he'll be your follower.
 Your worship in that sense may call him man.

TYBALT. Romeo, the love I bear thee can afford
 No better term than this—thou art a villain.   65

ROMEO. Tybalt, the reason that I have to love thee
 Doth much excuse the appertaining° rage
 To such a greeting. Villain am I none.
 Therefore farewell; I see thou know'st me not.

TYBALT. Boy, this shall not excuse the injuries   70
 That thou hast done me; therefore turn and
 draw.

ROMEO. I do protest I never injur'd thee,
 But love thee better than thou canst devise
 Till thou shalt know the reason of my love.

---

operation drinking   drawer waiter
doublet jacket   fee simple clear title
for . . . quarter i.e., just about long enough to be killed

consort'st associate
Consort a troupe of musicians; Mercutio's deliberate
  misinterpretation
fiddlestick i.e., sword   'Zounds God's wounds
if . . . livery (Mercutio deliberately takes man to mean
  "servant")
appertaining appropriate

75 And so, good Capulet—which name I tender
   As dearly as mine own—be satisfied.
   MERCUTIO. O calm, dishonorable, vile submission!
   Alla stoccata° carries it away.   [*Draws.*]
   Tybalt, you rat-catcher, will you walk?
80 TYBALT. What wouldst thou have with me?
   MERCUTIO. Good king of cats, nothing but one of
   your nine lives, that I mean to make bold withal,
   and, as you shall use me hereafter, dry-beat the
   rest of the eight. Will you pluck your sword out
85 of his pilcher° by the ears? Make haste, lest mine
   be about your ears ere it be out.
   TYBALT. I am for you.   [*Drawing.*]
   ROMEO. Gentle Mercutio, put thy rapier up.
   MERCUTIO. Come, sir, your passado.°
                               [*They fight.*]
90 ROMEO. Draw, Benvolio. Beat down their weapons.
   Gentlemen, for shame, forbear this outrage!
   Tybalt, Mercutio, the prince expressly hath
   Forbid this bandying in Verona streets.
   Hold, Tybalt! Good Mercutio!
        [TYBALT *under* ROMEO's *arm stabs* MERCUTIO
                 and flies with his followers.]
   MERCUTIO.   I am hurt.
95 A plague o' both your houses! I am sped.°
   Is he gone, and hath nothing?
   BENVOLIO.   What, art thou hurt?
   MERCUTIO. Aye, aye, a scratch, a scratch; marry,
     'tis enough.
   Where is my page? Go, villain, fetch a surgeon.
                               [*Exit* PAGE.]
   ROMEO. Courage, man; the hurt cannot be much.
100 MERCUTIO. No, 'tis not so deep as a well nor so wide
   as a churchdoor; but 'tis enough, 'twill serve.
   Ask for me tomorrow, and you shall find me a
   grave man. I am peppered, I warrant, for this
   world. A plague o' both your houses! 'Zounds, a
105 dog, a rat, a mouse, a cat, to scratch a man to
   death! A braggart, a rogue, a villain, that fights
   by the book of arithmetic! Why the devil came
   you between us? I was hurt under your arm.
   ROMEO. I thought all for the best.
110 MERCUTIO. Help me into some house, Benvolio,
   Or I shall faint. A plague o' both your houses!
   They have made worms' meat of me. I have it,
   And soundly too. Your houses!
             [*Exeunt* MERCUTIO *and* BENVOLIO.]
   ROMEO. This gentleman, the prince's near ally,
115 My very friend, hath got this mortal hurt
   In my behalf; my reputation stain'd
   With Tybalt's slander—Tybalt, that an hour

Hath been my kinsmen! O sweet Juliet,
Thy beauty hath made me effeminate,
And in my temper soften'd valor's steel!
        [*Re-enter* BENVOLIO.]
BENVOLIO. O Romeo, Romeo, brave Mercutio's
   dead!
That gallant spirit hath aspir'd the clouds,
Which too untimely here did scorn the earth.
ROMEO. This day's black fate on moe° days doth
   depend;
This but begins the woe others must end.   125
        [*Re-enter* TYBALT.]
BENVOLIO. Here comes the furious Tybalt back
   again.
ROMEO. Alive, in triumph, and Mercutio slain!
Away to heaven, respective lenity,°
And fire-eyed fury be my conduct now!
Now, Tybalt, take the "villain" back again   130
That late thou gav'st me; for Mercutio's soul
Is but a little way above our heads,
Staying for thine to keep him company.
Either thou or I or both must go with him.
TYBALT. Thou wretched boy that didst consort
   him here   135
Shalt with him hence.
ROMEO.   This shall determine that.
        [*They fight;* TYBALT *falls.*]
BENVOLIO. Romeo, away, be gone!
The citizens are up, and Tybalt slain.
Stand not amaz'd. The prince will doom thee
   death
If thou art taken. Hence, be gone, away!   140
ROMEO. O, I am fortune's fool!°
BENVOLIO.   Why dost thou stay?
                               [*Exit* ROMEO.]
        [*Enter* CITIZENS.]
FIRST CITIZEN. Which way ran he that kill'd
   Mercutio?
Tybalt, that murderer, which way ran he?
BENVOLIO. There lies that Tybalt.
FIRST CITIZEN.   Up, sir, go with me.
I charge thee in the prince's name, obey.   145
   [*Enter* PRINCE, *attended;* MONTAGUE, CAPULET,
             their WIVES, *and others.*]
PRINCE. Where are the vile beginners of this fray?
BENVOLIO. O noble Prince, I can discover° all
The unlucky manage° of this fatal brawl.
There lies the man, slain by young Romeo,
That slew thy kinsman, brave Mercutio.   150
LADY CAPULET. Tybalt, my cousin! O my brother's
   child!

Alla stoccata literally, at the thrust; here, this fancy
   fencing master   *pilcher* scabbard
passado lunge   *sped* done for

moe more   *respective lenity* prudent mildness
fool plaything
discover disclose   *manage* circumstance

...ousin! Husband! O, the blood is

...nsman! Prince, as thou art true,

...urs, shed blood of Montague.

...sin!

...o, who began this bloody fray?

BENVOLIO. Tybalt, here slain, whom Romeo's
   hand did slay—
   Romeo that spoke him fair, bid him bethink
   How nice° the quarrel was, and urg'd withal°
160 Your high displeasure. All this uttered
   With gentle breath, calm look, knees humbly
     bow'd
   Could not take truce with° the unruly spleen°
   Of Tybalt deaf to peace, but that he tilts
   With piercing steel at bold Mercutio's breast,
165 Who, all as hot, turns deadly point to point,
   And, with a martial scorn, with one hand beats
   Cold death aside, and with the other sends
   It back to Tybalt, whose dexterity
   Retorts it. Romeo—he cries aloud
   "Hold, friends! Friends, part!" and swifter than
170   his tongue
   His agile arm beats down their fatal points
   And 'twixt them rushes; underneath whose arm
   An envious° thrust from Tybalt hit the life
   Of stout Mercutio, and then Tybalt fled,
175 But by and by comes back to Romeo,
   Who had but newly entertain'd revenge,
   And to 't they go like lightning; for ere I
   Could draw to part them was stout Tybalt
     slain,
   And as he fell did Romeo turn and fly.
180 This is the truth, or let Benvolio die.
   LADY CAPULET. He is a kinsman to the Montague.
   Affection makes him false. He speaks not true.
   Some twenty of them fought in this black strife,
   And all those twenty could but kill one life.
185 I beg for justice, which thou, Prince, must give.
   Romeo slew Tybalt, Romeo must not live.
   PRINCE. Romeo slew him, he slew Mercutio.
   Who now the price of his dear blood doth owe?
   MONTAGUE. Not Romeo, Prince; he was Mercutio's
     friend.
   His fault concludes but what the law should
190   end,
   The life of Tybalt.
   PRINCE.   And for that offense
   Immediately we do exile him hence.
   I have an interest in your hate's proceeding.
   My blood for your rude brawls doth lie a-
     bleeding;

But I'll amerce° you with so strong a fine   195
That you shall all repent the loss of mine.
I will be deaf to pleading and excuses;
Nor tears nor prayers shall purchase out
   abuses;°
Therefore use none. Let Romeo hence in haste,
Else when he's found that hour is his last.   200
Bear hence this body, and attend our will.
Mercy but murders, pardoning those that kill.
                       [*Exeunt*]

SCENE ii
CAPULET'S *orchard.*

[*Enter* JULIET.]

JULIET. Gallop apace, you fiery-footed steeds,
   Towards Phœbus' lodging.° Such a wagoner
   As Phaethon° would whip you to the west
   And bring in cloudy night immediately.
   Spread thy close curtain, love-performing night,   5
   That runaways' eyes° may wink° and Romeo
   Leap to these arms untalk'd of and unseen.
   Lovers can see to do their amorous rites
   By their own beauties; or, if love be blind,
   It best agrees with night. Come, civil night,   10
   Thou sober-suited matron all in black,
   And learn me how to lose a winning match
   Play'd for a pair of stainless maidenhoods.
   Hood my unmann'd° blood bating° in my
     cheeks
   With thy black mantle till strange° love grown
     bold   15
   Think true love acted simple modesty.
   Come, night; come, Romeo; come, thou day in
     night,
   For thou wilt lie upon the wings of night
   Whiter than new snow on a raven's back.
   Come, gentle night; come, loving, black-
     brow'd night;
   Give me my Romeo; and when he shall die,   20
   Take him and cut him out in little stars,
   And he will make the face of heaven so fine
   That all the world will be in love with night
   And pay no worship to the garish sun.
   O, I have bought the mansion of a love   25

nice trivial   *withal* besides   *take truce with* pacify
spleen temper   *envious* malicious

amerce penalize   *purchase out abuses* pay for misdeeds
fiery-footed . . . lodging horses that draw the sun's
   chariot toward the West
Phaethon the sun-god's son, with whom the horses ran
   away when he tried to drive them
runaways' eyes (uncertain reference; possibly refers to
   Phaethon's runaways)
wink be closed   *unmann'd* untamed
bating beating   *strange* unfamiliar

Rhetoric

But not possess'd it, and, though I am sold,
Not yet enjoy'd. So tedious is this day
As is the night before some festival
30   To an impatient child that hath new robes
And may not wear them. O, here comes my
    nurse,
And she brings news, and every tongue that
    speaks
But Romeo's name speaks heavenly eloquence.
        [*Enter* NURSE, *with cords.*]
Now, nurse, what news? What hast thou there?
    The cords
That Romeo bid thee fetch?
35   NURSE.   Aye, aye, the cords.
        [*Throws them down.*]
JULIET. Aye me! What news? Why dost thou
    wring thy hands?
NURSE. Ah, well-a-day! He's dead, he's dead, he's
    dead.
We are undone, lady, we are undone.
Alack the day! He's gone, he's kill'd, he's dead.
JULIET. Can heaven be so envious?
40   NURSE.   Romeo can,
Though heaven cannot. O Romeo, Romeo!
Who ever would have thought it? Romeo!
JULIET. What devil art thou that dost torment me
    thus?
This torture should be roar'd in dismal hell.
45   Hath Romeo slain himself? Say thou but "I,"°
And that bare vowel "I" shall poison more
Than the death-darting eye of cockatrice.°
I am not I, if there be such an I,
Or those eyes shut that make thee answer "I."
50   If he be slain, say "I," or if not, no.
Brief sounds determine of my weal or woe.
NURSE. I saw the wound, I saw it with mine eyes—
God save the mark!—here on his manly breast:
A piteous corse,° a bloody piteous corse;
55   Pale, pale as ashes, all bedaub'd in blood,
All in gore blood. I swounded° at the sight.
JULIET. O, break, my heart! Poor bankrupt, break
    at once!
To prison, eyes, ne'er look on liberty!
Vile earth, to earth° resign, end motion here,
60   And thou and Romeo press one heavy bier!
NURSE. O Tybalt, Tybalt, the best friend I had!
O courteous Tybalt! Honest gentleman!
That ever I should live to see thee dead!
JULIET. What storm is this that blows so contrary?
65   Is Romeo slaughter'd, and is Tybalt dead?
My dear-lov'd cousin, and my dearer lord?

"*I*"   (with play on *aye*)
cockatrice   the basilisk, that slew with a glance
corse corpse   *swounded* swooned
earth . . . earth   body . . . earth

Then, dreadful trumpet, sound the general
    doom!
For who is living, if those two are gone?
NURSE. Tybalt is gone, and Romeo banished;
Romeo that kill'd him, he is banished.
JULIET. O God! Did Romeo's hand shed Tybalt's
    blood?
NURSE. It did, it did; alas the day, it did!
JULIET. O serpent heart, hid with a flow'ring face!
Did ever dragon keep so fair a cave?
Beautiful tyrant! Fiend angelical!   75
Dove-feather'd raven! Wolvish-ravening lamb!
Despised substance of divinest show!
Just opposite to what thou justly seem'st,
A damned saint, an honorable villain!
O nature, what hadst thou to do in hell   80
When thou didst bower the spirit of a fiend
In mortal paradise of such sweet flesh?
Was ever book containing such vile matter
So fairly bound? O, that deceit should dwell
In such a gorgeous palace!
NURSE.   There's no trust,   85
No faith, no honesty in men; all perjur'd,
All forsworn, all naught, all dissemblers.
Ah, where's my man? Give me some aqua vitæ.°
These griefs, these woes, these sorrows make me
    old.
Shame come to Romeo!
JULIET.   Blister'd be thy tongue   90
For such a wish! He was not born to shame.
Upon his brow shame is asham'd to sit,
For 'tis a throne where honor may be crown'd
Sole monarch of the universal earth.
O, what a beast was I to chide at him!   95
NURSE. Will you speak well of him that kill'd your
    cousin?
JULIET. Shall I speak ill of him that is my husband?
Ah, poor my lord, what tongue shall smooth
    thy name,
When I, thy three-hours wife, have mangled it?
But wherefore, villain, didst thou kill my
    cousin?   100
That villain cousin would have kill'd my
    husband.
Back, foolish tears, back to your native spring;
Your tributary drops belong to woe,
Which you mistaking offer up to joy.
My husband lives that Tybalt would have slain;   105
And Tybalt's dead that would have slain my
    husband.
All this is comfort; wherefore weep I then?
Some word there was, worser than Tybalt's
    death,

aqua vitae spirits

That murder'd me. I would forget it fain;
110 But, O, it presses to my memory
Like damned guilty deed to sinners' minds:
"Tybalt is dead, and Romeo banished;"
That "banished," that one word "banished,"
Hath slain ten thousand Tybalts. Tybalt's
death
115 Was woe enough, if it had ended there;
Or, if sour woe delights in fellowship,
And needly° will be rank'd with other griefs,
Why follow'd not, when she said "Tybalt's
dead,"
Thy father, or thy mother, nay, or both,
Which modern° lamentation might have
120 mov'd?
But with a rearward following Tybalt's death,
"Romeo is banished"—to speak that word
Is father, mother, Tybalt, Romeo, Juliet,
All slain, all dead. "Romeo is banished."
125 There is no end, no limit, measure, bound,
In that word's death; no words can that woe
sound.
Where is my father and my mother, nurse?
NURSE. Weeping and wailing over Tybalt's corse.
Will you go to them? I will bring you thither.
JULIET. Wash they his wounds with tears: mine
130 shall be spent
When theirs are dry, for Romeo's banishment.
Take up those cords. Poor ropes, you are
beguil'd,
Both you and I; for Romeo is exil'd.
He made you for a highway to my bed,
135 But I, a maid, die maiden-widowed.
Come, cords; come, nurse. I'll to my wedding
bed,
And death, not Romeo, take my maidenhead!
NURSE. Hie to your chamber. I'll find Romeo
To comfort you. I wot° well where he is.
140 Hark ye, your Romeo will be here at night.
I'll to him; he is hid at Laurence' cell.
JULIET. O, find him! Give this ring to my true
knight,
And bid him come to take his last farewell.
[Exeunt]

SCENE iii
FRIAR LAURENCE'S *cell.*

[*Enter* FRIAR LAURENCE.]
FRIAR LAURENCE. Romeo, come forth; come forth,
thou fearful man.
Affliction is enamor'd of thy parts,

And thou art wedded to calamity.
[*Enter* ROMEO.]
ROMEO. Father, what news? What is the prince's
doom?
What sorrow craves acquaintance at my hand,   5
That I yet know not?
FRIAR LAURENCE.   Too familiar
Is my dear son with such sour company.
I bring thee tidings of the prince's doom.
ROMEO. What less than doomsday is the prince's
doom?
FRIAR LAURENCE. A gentler judgment vanish'd
from his lips,   10
Not body's death, but body's banishment.
ROMEO. Ha, banishment! Be merciful, say "death,"
For exile hath more terror in his look,
Much more than death. Do not say "banish-
ment."
FRIAR LAURENCE. Here from Verona art thou
banished.   15
Be patient, for the world is broad and wide.
ROMEO. There is no world without Verona walls
But purgatory, torture, hell itself.
Hence banished is banish'd from the world,
And world's exile is death: then "banished"   20
Is death misterm'd. Calling death "banished,"
Thou cut'st my head off with a golden axe
And smil'st upon the stroke that murders me.
FRIAR LAURENCE. O deadly sin! O rude unthank-
fulness!
Thy fault our law calls death; but the kind
prince,   25
Taking thy part, hath rush'd° aside the law
And turn'd that black word death to banish-
ment.
This is dear mercy, and thou seest it not.
ROMEO. 'Tis torture, and not mercy. Heaven is
here
Where Juliet lives, and every cat and dog   30
And little mouse, every unworthy thing,
Live here in heaven and may look on her,
But Romeo may not. More validity,°
More honorable state, more courtship° lives
In carrion flies than Romeo. They may seize   35
On the white wonder of dear Juliet's hand
And steal immortal blessing from her lips,
Who, even in pure and vestal° modesty,
Still blush, as thinking their own kisses sin.
But Romeo may not; he is banished.   40
This may flies do, but I from this must fly;
They are free men, but I am banished.
And say'st thou yet that exile is not death?

---

needly necessarily   *modern* moderate   *wot* know
rush'd brushed   *validity* worth
courtship privilege of courting   *vestal* virginal

Hadst thou no poison mix'd, no sharp-ground knife,
45 No sudden mean of death, though ne'er so mean,
But "banished" to kill me?—"Banished"?
O friar, the damned use that word in hell;
Howling attends it. How hast thou the heart,
Being a divine, a ghostly confessor,
50 A sin-absolver, and my friend profess'd,
To mangle me with that word "banished"?
FRIAR LAURENCE. Thou fond mad man, hear me but speak a word.
ROMEO. O, thou wilt speak again of banishment.
FRIAR LAURENCE. I'll give thee armor to keep off that word—
55 Adversity's sweet milk, philosophy,
To comfort thee, though thou art banished.
ROMEO. Yet "banished"? Hang up philosophy!
Unless philosophy can make a Juliet,
Displant° a town, reverse a prince's doom,
60 It helps not, it prevails not. Talk no more.
FRIAR LAURENCE. O, then I see that madmen have no ears.
ROMEO. How should they, when that wise men have no eyes?
FRIAR LAURENCE. Let me dispute with thee of thy estate.°
ROMEO. Thou canst not speak of that thou dost not feel.
65 Wert thou as young as I, Juliet thy love,
An hour but married, Tybalt murdered,
Doting like me, and like me banished,
Then mightst thou speak, then mightst thou tear thy hair
And fall upon the ground as I do now,
70 Taking the measure of an unmade grave.
                              [Knocking within.]
FRIAR LAURENCE. Arise; one knocks. Good Romeo, hide thyself.
ROMEO. Not I, unless the breath of heartsick groans
Mistlike enfold me from the search of eyes.
                              [Knocking.]
FRIAR LAURENCE. Hark, how they knock! Who's there? Romeo, arise;
75 Thou wilt be taken.—Stay awhile!—Stand up;
                              [Knocking.]
Run to my study.—By and by!—God's will,
What simpleness is this!—I come, I come!
                              [Knocking.]
Who knocks so hard? Whence come you? What's your will?
NURSE. [Within] Let me come in, and you shall know my errand.
I come from Lady Juliet.

Displant move   *estate* condition

FRIAR LAURENCE.   Welcome, then.   80
                              [Enter NURSE.]
NURSE. O holy friar, O, tell me, holy friar,
Where is my lady's lord, where's Romeo?
FRIAR LAURENCE. There on the ground, with his own tears made drunk.
NURSE. O, he is even in my mistress' case,
Just in her case!
FRIAR LAURENCE.   O woeful sympathy!   85
Piteous predicamẽnt!
NURSE.   Even so lies she,
Blubbering and weeping, weeping and blubbering.
Stand up, stand up; stand, an you be a man.
For Juliet's sake, for her sake, rise and stand;
Why should you fall into so deep an O?   90
ROMEO. Nurse!
NURSE. Ah sir! Ah sir! Well, death's the end of all.
ROMEO. Spak'st thou of Juliet? How is it with her?
Doth she not think me an old murderer,
Now I have stain'd the childhood of our joy   95
With blood remov'd but little from her own?
Where is she? And how doth she? And what says
My conceal'd lady to our cancel'd love?
NURSE. O, she says nothing, sir, but weeps and weeps,
And now falls on her bed, and then starts up,   100
And Tybalt calls, and then on Romeo cries,
And then down falls again.
ROMEO.   As if that name,
Shot from the deadly level of a gun,
Did murder her, as that name's cursed hand
Murder'd her kinsman. O, tell me, friar, tell me,   105
In what vile part of this anatomy
Doth my name lodge? Tell me, that I may sack
The hateful mansion.   [Drawing his sword.]
FRIAR LAURENCE.   Hold thy desperate hand.
Art thou a man? Thy form cries out thou art;
Thy tears are womanish. Thy wild acts denote   110
Th' unreasonable fury of a beast.
Unseemly woman in a seeming man!
Or ill-beseeming beast in seeming both!
Thou hast amaz'd me. By my holy order,
I thought thy disposition better temper'd.   115
Hast thou slain Tybalt? Wilt thou slay thyself?
And slay thy lady that in thy life lives,
By doing damned hate upon thyself?
Why rail'st thou on thy birth, the heaven, and earth?
Since birth and heaven and earth, all three do meet   120
In thee at once, which thou at once wouldst lose.
Fie, fie! Thou sham'st thy shape, thy love, thy wit,

Which, like a usurer, abound'st in all,
And usest none in that true use indeed
Which should bedeck thy shape, thy love, thy
125   wit.
Thy noble shape is but a form of wax,
Digressing from the valor of a man;
Thy dear love sworn, but hollow perjury,
Killing that love which thou hast vow'd to
   cherish;
130 Thy wit, that ornament to shape and love,
Misshapen in the conduct of them both,
Like powder in a skilless soldier's flask,
Is set afire by thine own ignorance,
And thou dismember'd with thine own de-
   fense.
135 What, rouse thee, man! Thy Juliet is alive,
For whose dear sake thou wast but lately dead;
There art thou happy. Tybalt would kill thee,
But thou slew'st Tybalt; there art thou happy
   too.
The law that threaten'd death becomes thy
   friend
140 And turns it to exile; there art thou happy.
A pack of blessings lights upon thy back;
Happiness courts thee in her best array;
But like a misbehav'd and sullen wench
Thou pout'st upon thy fortune and thy love.
145 Take heed, take heed, for such die miserable.
Go, get thee to thy love, as was decreed;
Ascend her chamber, hence, and comfort her.
But look thou stay not till the watch be set,
For then thou canst not pass to Mantua,
150 Where thou shalt live till we can find a time
To blaze° your marriage, reconcile your friends,
Beg pardon of the prince, and call thee back
With twenty hundred thousand times more
   joy
Than thou went'st forth in lamentation.
155 Go before, nurse. Commend me to thy lady,
And bid her hasten all the house to bed,
Which heavy sorrow makes them apt unto.
Romeo is coming.
NURSE. O Lord, I could have stay'd here all the
   night
160 To hear good counsel. O, what learning is!
My lord, I'll tell my lady you will come.
ROMEO. Do so, and bid my sweet prepare to chide.
NURSE. Here, sir, a ring she bid me give you, sir.
Hie you, make haste, for it grows very late.
                                  [Exit]
165 ROMEO. How well my comfort is reviv'd by this!
FRIAR LAURENCE. Go hence; good night; and here
   stands all your state:

blaze   make public

Either be gone before the watch be set,
Or by the break of day disguis'd from hence.
Sojourn in Mantua. I'll find out your man,
And he shall signify from time to time   170
Every good hap to you that chances here.
Give me thy hand. 'Tis late; farewell; good
   night.
ROMEO. But that a joy past joy calls out on me,
It were a grief, so brief° to part with thee.
Farewell.   [Exeunt]   175

SCENE iv
A room in CAPULET'*s house.*

[*Enter* CAPULET, LADY CAPULET, *and* PARIS.]
CAPULET. Things have fall'n out, sir, so unluckily
That we have had no time to move our daugh-
   ter.
Look you, she lov'd her kinsman Tybalt dearly,
And so did I. Well, we were born to die.
'Tis very late; she'll not come down tonight.   5
I promise you, but for your company,
I would have been abed an hour ago.
PARIS. These times of woe afford no time to woo.
Madam, good night. Commend me to your
   daughter.
LADY CAPULET. I will, and know her mind early
   tomorrow;   10
Tonight she's mew'd up to her heaviness.°
CAPULET. Sir Paris, I will make a desperate tender°
Of my child's love. I think she will be rul'd
In all respects by me; nay more, I doubt it not.
Wife, go you to her ere you go to bed.   15
Acquaint her here of my son Paris' love,
And bid her, mark you me, on Wednesday
   next—
But, soft! What day is this?
PARIS.   Monday, my lord.
CAPULET. Monday! Ha, ha! Well, Wednesday is too
   soon;
O' Thursday let it be. O' Thursday, tell her,   20
She shall be married to this noble earl.
Will you be ready? Do you like this haste?
We'll keep no great ado—a friend or two;
For, hark you, Tybalt being slain so late,
It may be thought we held him carelessly,   25
Being our kinsman, if we revel much.
Therefore we'll have some half a dozen friends,
And there an end. But what say you to Thurs-
   day?

brief abruptly
mew'd . . . heaviness closed in with her grief
tender offer

PARIS. My lord, I would that Thursday were to-
    morrow.
CAPULET. Well, get you gone. O' Thursday be it
30   then.
    Go you to Juliet ere you go to bed;
    Prepare her, wife, against this wedding day.
    Farewell, my lord. Light to my chamber, ho!
    Afore me,° it is so very very late,
35   That we may call it early by and by.
    Good night.   [Exeunt]

SCENE v
CAPULET's orchard.

[Enter ROMEO and JULIET, above, at the window.]
JULIET. Wilt thou be gone? It is not yet near day.
    It was the nightingale, and not the lark,
    That pierc'd the fearful hollow of thine ear;
    Nightly she sings on yond pomegranate tree.
5   Believe me, love, it was the nightingale.
ROMEO. It was the lark, the herald of the morn,
    No nightingale. Look, love, what envious streaks
    Do lace the severing clouds in yonder east.
    Night's candles are burnt out, and jocund day
10   Stands tiptoe on the misty mountain tops.
    I must be gone and live, or stay and die.
JULIET. Yond light is not daylight; I know it, I.
    It is some meteor that the sun exhales
    To be to thee this night a torchbearer
15   And light thee on thy way to Mantua.
    Therefore stay yet; thou need'st not to be gone.
ROMEO. Let me be ta'en, let me be put to death;
    I am content, so thou wilt have it so.
    I'll say yon grey is not the morning's eye,
20   'Tis but the pale reflex of Cynthia's brow;°
    Nor that is not the lark, whose notes do beat
    The vaulty heaven so high above our heads.
    I have more care to stay than will to go.
    Come, death, and welcome! Juliet wills it so.
25   How is't, my soul? Let's talk. It is not day.
JULIET. It is, it is. Hie hence, be gone, away!
    It is the lark that sings so out of tune,
    Straining harsh discords and unpleasing sharps.
    Some say the lark makes sweet division;°
30   This doth not so, for she divideth us.
    Some say the lark and loathed toad change°
    eyes;
    O, now I would they had chang'd voices too,
    Since arm from arm that voice doth us affray,°

Hunting thee hence with hunts-up° to the day.
    O, now be gone; more light and light it grows. 35
ROMEO. More light and light, more dark and dark
    our woes!
             [Enter NURSE, to the chamber.]
NURSE. Madam!
JULIET. Nurse?
NURSE. Your lady mother is coming to your
    chamber.
    The day is broke; be wary, look about.   [Exit] 40
JULIET. Then, window, let day in, and let life out.
ROMEO. Farewell, farewell! One kiss, and I'll
    descend.   [Descends]
JULIET. Art thou gone so? My lord, my love, my
    friend!
    I must hear from thee every day in the hour,
    For in a minute there are many days. 45
    O, by this count I shall be much in years
    Ere I again behold my Romeo!
ROMEO. Farewell!
    I will omit no opportunity
    That may convey my greetings, love, to thee. 50
JULIET. O, think'st thou we shall ever meet again?
ROMEO. I doubt it not, and all these woes shall
    serve
    For sweet discourses in our time to come.
JULIET. O God! I have an ill-divining soul.
    Methinks I see thee, now thou art below, 55
    As one dead in the bottom of a tomb.
    Either my eyesight fails or thou look'st pale.
ROMEO. And trust me, love, in my eye so do you.
    Dry sorrow drinks our blood. Adieu, adieu!
                         [Exit]
JULIET. O fortune, fortune, all men call thee fickle. 60
    If thou art fickle, what dost thou with him
    That is renown'd for faith? Be fickle, fortune;
    For then, I hope, thou wilt not keep him long,
    But send him back.
LADY CAPULET. [Within] Ho, daughter! Are you up? 65
JULIET. Who is 't that calls? It is my lady mother!
    Is she not down so late, or up so early?
    What unaccustom'd cause procures her hither?
              [Enter LADY CAPULET.]
LADY CAPULET. Why, how now, Juliet!
JULIET.   Madam, I am not well.
LADY CAPULET. Evermore weeping for your
    cousin's death? 70
    What, wilt thou wash him from his grave with
    tears?
    And if thou couldst, thou couldst not make him
    live;
    Therefore have done. Some grief shows much of
    love,

Afore me (milder oath than "before God")
reflex . . . brow reflection of the moon
division melody   *change* exchange   *affray* affright   *hunts-up* hunter's waking song

But much of grief shows still some want of wit.

75 JULIET. Yet let me weep for such a feeling loss.

LADY CAPULET. So shall you feel the loss, but not the friend
Which you weep for.

JULIET.   Feeling so the loss,
I cannot choose but ever weep the friend.

LADY CAPULET. Well, girl, thou weep'st not so much for his death

80   As that the villain lives which slaughter'd him.

JULIET. What villain, madam?

LADY CAPULET.   That same villain, Romeo.

JULIET. [Aside] Villain and he be many miles asunder.
God pardon him! I do, with all my heart;
And yet no man like he doth grieve my heart.

LADY CAPULET. That is because the traitor mur-

85   derer lives.

JULIET. Aye, madam, from the reach of these my hands.
Would none but I might venge my cousin's death!

LADY CAPULET. We will have vengeance for it, fear thou not;
Then weep no more. I'll send to one in Mantua,

90   Where that same banish'd runagate° doth live,
Shall give him such an unaccustom'd dram°
That he shall soon keep Tybalt company.
And then, I hope, thou wilt be satisfied.

JULIET. Indeed, I never shall be satisfied

95   With Romeo, till I behold him—dead—
Is my poor heart so for a kinsman vex'd.
Madam, if you could find out but a man
To bear a poison, I would temper it
That° Romeo should, upon receipt thereof,

100   Soon sleep in quiet. O, how my heart abhors
To hear him nam'd and cannot come to him,
To wreak the love I bore my cousin
Upon his body that hath slaughter'd him!

LADY CAPULET. Find thou the means, and I'll find such a man.

105   But now I'll tell thee joyful tidings, girl.

JULIET. And joy comes well in such a needy time.
What are they, I beseech your ladyship?

LADY CAPULET. Well, well, thou hast a careful father, child—
One who, to put thee from thy heaviness,

110   Hath sorted out a sudden day of joy
That thou expect'st not, nor I look'd not for.

JULIET. Madam, in happy time, what day is that?

LADY CAPULET. Marry, my child, early next Thursday morn,

The gallant, young, and noble gentleman,
The County Paris, at Saint Peter's Church,   115
Shall happily make thee there a joyful bride.

JULIET. Now, by Saint Peter's Church and Peter too,
He shall not make me there a joyful bride!—
I wonder at this haste, that I must wed
Ere he that should be husband comes to woo.   120
I pray you, tell my lord and father, madam,
I will not marry yet; and, when I do, I swear,
It shall be Romeo, whom you know I hate,
Rather than Paris. These are news indeed!

LADY CAPULET. Here comes your father; tell him so yourself,   125
And see how he will take it at your hands.

[Enter CAPULET and NURSE.]

CAPULET. When the sun sets, the air doth drizzle dew;
But for the sunset of my brother's son
It rains downright.
How now! A conduit,° girl? What, still in tears?   130
Evermore showering? In one little body
Thou counterfeit'st a bark, a sea, a wind
For still° thy eyes, which I may call the sea,
Do ebb and flow with tears; the bark thy body is,
Sailing in this salt flood; the winds, thy sighs,   135
Who, raging with thy tears and they with them,
Without a sudden calm will overset
Thy tempest-tossed body. How now, wife!
Have you deliver'd to her our decree?

LADY CAPULET. Aye, sir; but she will none, she gives you thanks.   140
I would the fool were married to her grave!

CAPULET. Soft! Take me with you, take me with you, wife.
How! Will she none? Doth she not give us thanks?
Is she not proud? Doth she not count her blest,
Unworthy as she is, that we have wrought   145
So worthy a gentleman to be her bridegroom?

JULIET. Not proud, you have, but thankful that you have.
Proud can I never be of what I hate,
But thankful even for hate that is meant love.

CAPULET. How, how! How, how! Chop-logic! What is this?   150
"Proud," and "I thank you," and "I thank you not,"
And yet "not proud." Mistress minion,° you,
Thank me no thankings, nor proud me no prouds,

---

runagate runaway
unaccustom'd dram i.e., of poison   That so that

conduit waterpipe   still always
Mistress minion "spoiled darling" (ironic)

But fettle your fine joints 'gainst° Thursday next
155 To go with Paris to Saint Peter's Church,
Or I will drag thee on a hurdle° thither.
Out, you green-sickness carrion! Out, you bag-
gage!
You tallow-face!
LADY CAPULET.   Fie, fie! What, are you mad?
JULIET. Good father, I beseech you on my knees,
160 Hear me with patience but to speak a word.
CAPULET. Hang thee, young baggage! Disobedient
wretch!
I tell thee what: get thee to church o' Thursday
Or never after look me in the face.
Speak not, reply not, do not answer me;
My fingers itch. Wife, we scarce thought us
165 blest
That God had lent us but this only child.
But now I see this one is one too much,
And that we have a curse in having her.
Out on her, hilding!°
NURSE.   God in heaven bless her!
170 You are to blame, my lord, to rate° her so.
CAPULET. And why, my lady wisdom? Hold your
tongue,
Good prudence; smatter° with your gossips, go.
NURSE. I speak no treason.
CAPULET.   O, God ye god-den.
NURSE. May not one speak?
CAPULET.   Peace, you mumbling fool!
175 Utter your gravity o'er a gossip's bowl,
For here we need it not.
LADY CAPULET.   You are too hot.
CAPULET. God's bread! It makes me mad.
Day, night, hour, tide, time, work, play,
Alone, in company, still my care hath been
To have her match'd. And having now pro-
180 vided
A gentleman of noble parentage,
Of fair demesnes, youthful, and nobly train'd,
Stuff'd, as they say, with honorable parts,
Proportion'd as one's thought would wish a
man—
185 And then to have a wretched puling fool,
A whining mammet,° in her fortune's tender,°
To answer "I'll not wed; I cannot love,
I am too young; I pray you, pardon me."
But, an you will not wed, I'll pardon you:
Graze where you will, you shall not house with
190 me.

fettle . . . 'gainst get yourself ready for
hurdle frame for dragging criminals to execution
hilding wretch   *rate* berate   *smatter* jabber
mammet doll   *in . . . tender* when she is offered good
fortune

Look to 't, think on 't, I do not use to jest.
Thursday is near; lay hand on heart, advise.
An you be mine, I'll give you to my friend;
An you be not, hang, beg, starve, die in the
streets,
For by my soul I'll ne'er acknowledge thee,   195
Nor what is mine shall never do thee good.
Trust to 't, bethink you; I'll not be forsworn.°
[Exit]
JULIET. Is there no pity sitting in the clouds
That sees into the bottom of my grief?
O, sweet my mother, cast me not away!   200
Delay this marriage for a month, a week;
Or, if you do not, make the bridal bed
In that dim monument where Tybalt lies.
LADY CAPULET. Talk not to me, for I'll not speak a
word.
Do as thou wilt, for I have done with thee.   205
[Exit]
JULIET. O God!—O nurse, how shall this be pre-
vented?
My husband is on earth, my faith in heaven;
How shall that faith return again to earth
Unless that husband send it me from heaven
By leaving earth? Comfort me, counsel me.   210
Alack, alack, that heaven should practice
stratagems
Upon so soft a subject as myself!
What say'st thou? Hast thou not a word of joy?
Some comfort, nurse.
NURSE.   Faith, here it is.
Romeo is banish'd, and all the world to nothing 215
That he dares ne'er come back to challenge you;
Or, if he do, it needs must be by stealth.
Then, since the case so stands as now it doth,
I think it best you married with the county.
O, he's a lovely gentleman!   220
Romeo's a dishclout to him. An eagle, madam,
Hath not so green, so quick, so fair an eye
As Paris hath. Beshrew my very heart,
I think you are happy in this second match,
For it excels your first; or if it did not,   225
Your first is dead, or 'twere as good he were
As living here and you no use of him.
JULIET. Speak'st thou from thy heart?
NURSE. And from my soul too; else beshrew them
both.
JULIET. Amen!   230
NURSE. What?
JULIET. Well, thou hast comforted me marvelous
much.
Go in, and tell my lady I am gone,
Having displeas'd my father, to Laurence' cell

be forsworn break my oath

89

235 To make confession and to be absolv'd.
NURSE. Marry, I will, and this is wisely done.
                                    [Exit]
JULIET. Ancient damnation! O most wicked fiend!
  Is it more sin to wish me thus forsworn,
  Or to dispraise my lord with that same tongue

Which she hath prais'd him with above com- 240
    pare
So many thousand times? Go, counselor;
Thou and my bosom henceforth shall be twain.
I'll to the friar, to know his remedy.
If all else fail, myself have power to die.   [Exit]

A C T   I V

SCENE i
FRIAR LAURENCE'S cell.

[Enter FRIAR LAURENCE and PARIS.]
FRIAR LAURENCE. On Thursday, sir? The time is
    very short.
PARIS. My father Capulet will have it so,
  And I am nothing slow to slack his haste.
FRIAR LAURENCE. You say you do not know the
    lady's mind.
5   Uneven is the course; I like it not.
PARIS. Immoderately she weeps for Tybalt's
    death,
  And therefore have I little talk'd of love,
  For Venus smiles not in a house of tears.
  Now, sir, her father counts it dangerous
10 That she doth give her sorrow so much sway,
  And in his wisdom hastes our marriage
  To stop the inundation of her tears,
  Which, too much minded by herself alone,
  May be put from her by society.
15 Now do you know the reason of this haste.
FRIAR LAURENCE. [Aside] I would I knew not why it
    should be slow'd.
  Look, sir, here comes the lady toward my cell.
                    [Enter JULIET.]
PARIS. Happily met, my lady and my wife!
JULIET. That may be, sir, when I may be a wife.
PARIS. That may be must be, love, on Thursday
20   next.
JULIET. What must be shall be.
FRIAR LAURENCE.   That's a certain text.
PARIS. Come you to make confession to this father?
JULIET. To answer that, I should confess to you.
PARIS. Do not deny to him that you love me.
25 JULIET. I will confess to you that I love him.
PARIS. So will ye, I am sure, that you love me.
JULIET. If I do so, it will be of more price
    Being spoke behind your back than to your face.
PARIS. Poor soul, thy face is much abus'd with
    tears.
30 JULIET. The tears have got small victory by that,

For it was bad enough before their spite.
PARIS. Thou wrong'st it more than tears with that
    report.
JULIET. That is no slander, sir, which is a truth,
  And what I spake, I spake it to my face.
PARIS. Thy face is mine, and thou hast slander'd it. 35
JULIET. It may be so, for it is not mine own.
  Are you at leisure, holy father, now,
  Or shall I come to you at evening mass?
FRIAR LAURENCE. My leisure serves me, pensive
    daughter, now.
  My lord, we must entreat the time alone.   40
PARIS. God shield° I should disturb devotion!
  Juliet, on Thursday early will I rouse ye.
  Till then, adieu, and keep this holy kiss.   [Exit]
JULIET. O, shut the door, and when thou hast done
    so,
  Come weep with me; past hope, past cure, past
    help!   45
FRIAR LAURENCE. Ah, Juliet, I already know thy
    grief;
  It strains me past the compass of my wits.
  I hear thou must, and nothing may prorogue it,
  On Thursday next be married to this county.
JULIET. Tell me not, friar, that thou hear'st of this, 50
  Unless thou tell me how I may prevent it.
  If in thy wisdom thou canst give no help,
  Do thou but call my resolution wise,
  And with this knife I'll help it presently.°
  God join'd my heart and Romeo's, thou our
    hands;   55
  And ere this hand, by thee to Romeo's seal'd,
  Shall be the label° to another deed,
  Or my true heart with treacherous revolt
  Turn to another, this shall slay them both.
  Therefore, out of thy long-experienc'd time,   60
  Give me some present counsel; or, behold,
  'Twixt my extremes° and me this bloody knife
  Shall play the umpire, arbitrating that

shield forbid   *presently* instantly   *label* seal
extremes difficulties

Which the commission° of thy years and art
65 Could to no issue of true honor bring.
Be not so long to speak; I long to die
If what thou speak'st speak not of remedy.
FRIAR LAURENCE. Hold, daughter. I do spy a kind of
hope,
Which craves as desperate an execution
70 As that is desperate which we would prevent.
If, rather than to marry County Paris,
Thou hast the strength of will to slay thyself,
Then is it likely thou wilt undertake
A thing like death to chide away this shame
That cop'st° with death himself to 'scape from
75 it;
And, if thou dar'st, I'll give thee remedy.
JULIET. O, bid me leap, rather than marry Paris,
From off the battlements of yonder tower,
Or walk in thievish ways; or bid me lurk
Where serpents are; chain me with roaring
80 bears;
Or shut me nightly in a charnel house,°
O'er-cover'd quite with dead men's rattling
bones,
With reeky° shanks and yellow chapless° skulls;
Or bid me go into a new-made grave
85 And hide me with a dead man in his shroud—
Things that to hear them told have made me
tremble—
And I will do it without fear or doubt,
To live an unstain'd wife to my sweet love.
FRIAR LAURENCE. Hold, then. Go home, be merry,
give consent
90 To marry Paris. Wednesday is tomorrow.
Tomorrow night look that thou lie alone;
Let not thy nurse lie with thee in thy chamber.
Take thou this vial, being then in bed,
And this distilled liquor drink thou off,
95 When presently through all thy veins shall run
A cold and drowsy humor°—for no pulse
Shall keep his° native progress, but surcease.°
No warmth, no breath shall testify thou liv'st.
The roses in thy lips and cheeks shall fade
100 To paly ashes, thy eyes' windows fall
Like death when he shuts up the day of life.
Each part, depriv'd of supple government,°
Shall, stiff and stark and cold, appear like death.
And in this borrow'd likeness of shrunk death
105 Thou shalt continue two and forty hours,
And then awake as from a pleasant sleep.
Now when the bridegroom in the morning
comes

To rouse thee from thy bed, there art thou dead.
Then, as the manner of our country is,
In thy best robes uncover'd on the bier   110
Thou shalt be borne to that same ancient vault
Where all the kindred of the Capulets lie.
In the meantime, against° thou shalt awake,
Shall Romeo by my letters know our drift,°
And hither shall he come. And he and I   115
Will watch thy waking, and that very night
Shall Romeo bear thee hence to Mantua.
And this shall free thee from this present shame
If no inconstant toy° nor womanish fear
Abate° thy valor in the acting it.   120
JULIET. Give me, give me! O, tell not me of fear!
FRIAR LAURENCE. Hold; get you gone, be strong and
prosperous
In this resolve. I'll send a friar with speed
To Mantua with my letters to thy lord.
JULIET. Love give me strength! And strength shall
help afford.°   125
Farewell, dear father!   [Exeunt]

SCENE ii
Hall in CAPULET's house.

[Enter CAPULET, LADY CAPULET, NURSE, and
two SERVINGMEN.]
CAPULET. So many guests invite as here are writ.
                          [Exit FIRST SERVANT.]
Sirrah, go hire me twenty cunning cooks.
SECOND SERVINGMAN. You shall have none ill, sir,
for I'll try if they can lick their fingers.
CAPULET. How canst thou try them so?   5
SECOND SERVINGMAN. Marry, sir, 'tis an ill cook that
cannot lick his own fingers; therefore he that
cannot lick his fingers goes not with me.
CAPULET. Go, be gone.   [Exit SECOND SERVANT.]
We shall be much unfurnish'd for this time.   10
What, is my daughter gone to Friar Laurence?
NURSE. Aye, forsooth.
CAPULET. Well, he may chance to do some good on
her.
A peevish self-will'd harlotry° it is.
                          [Enter JULIET.]
NURSE. See where she comes from shrift with
merry look.   15
CAPULET. How now, my headstrong! Where have
you been gadding?
JULIET. Where I have learn'd me to repent the sin
Of disobedient opposition

commission authority   cop'st vies
charnel house vault of bones   reeky reeking
chapless jawless   humor impulse   his its
surcease cease   government control

against before   drift purpose
toy whim   Abate lessen
help afford furnish help   harlotry hussy

To you and your behests, and am enjoin'd
20 By holy Laurence to fall prostrate here
To beg your pardon. Pardon, I beseech you!
Henceforward I am ever rul'd by you.
CAPULET. Send for the county; go tell him of this.
I'll have this knot knit up tomorrow morning.
25 JULIET. I met the youthful lord at Laurence' cell
And gave him what becomed° love I might,
Not stepping o'er the bounds of modesty.
CAPULET. Why, I am glad on 't; this is well. Stand
up.
This is as 't should be. Let me see the county.
30 Aye, marry, go, I say, and fetch him hither.
Now, afore God, this reverend holy friar,
All our whole city is much bound to him.
JULIET. Nurse, will you go with me into my closet
To help me sort such needful ornaments
35 As you think fit to furnish me tomorrow?
LADY CAPULET. No, not till Thursday; there is time
enough.
CAPULET. Go, nurse, go with her. We'll to church
tomorrow.
                    [Exeunt JULIET and NURSE.]
LADY CAPULET. We shall be short in our provision.
'Tis now near night.
CAPULET.   Tush, I will stir about,
And all things shall be well, I warrant thee,
40 wife.
Go thou to Juliet, help to deck up her.
I'll not to bed tonight; let me alone;
I'll play the housewife for this once. What, ho!
They are all forth. Well, I will walk myself
45 To County Paris to prepare him up
Against tomorrow. My heart is wondrous light
Since this same wayward girl is so reclaim'd.
                    [Exeunt]

SCENE iii
JULIET's chamber.

[Enter JULIET and NURSE.]
JULIET. Aye, those attires are best. But, gentle
nurse,
I pray thee, leave me to myself tonight;
For I have need of many orisons°
To move the heavens to smile upon my state,
Which well thou know'st is cross° and full of
5 sin.
                    [Enter LADY CAPULET.]
LADY CAPULET. What, are you busy, ho? Need you
my help?

becomed becoming   orisons prayers
cross ill-starred (see Prologue)

JULIET. No, madam; we have cull'd° such neces-
saries
As are behoveful° for our state° tomorrow.
So please you, let me now be left alone,
And let the nurse this night sit up with you,   10
For I am sure you have your hands full all
In this so sudden business.
LADY CAPULET.   Good night.
Get thee to bed and rest, for thou hast need.
                    [Exeunt LADY CAPULET and NURSE.]
JULIET. Farewell! God knows when we shall meet
again.
I have a faint cold fear thrills through my veins   15
That almost freezes up the heat of life.
I'll call them back again to comfort me.
Nurse!—What should she do here?
My dismal scene I needs must act alone.
Come, vial.   20
What if this mixture do not work at all?
Shall I be married then tomorrow morning?
No, no: this shall forbid it. Lie thou there.
                    [Laying down a dagger.]
What if it be a poison which the friar
Subtly hath minister'd to have me dead,   25
Lest in this marriage he should be dishonor'd
Because he married me before to Romeo?
I fear it is; and yet, methinks, it should not,
For he hath still been tried° a holy man.
How if, when I am laid into the tomb,   30
I wake before the time that Romeo
Come to redeem me? There's a fearful point.
Shall I not then be stifled in the vault,
To whose foul mouth no healthsome air
breathes in,
And there die strangled ere my Romeo comes?   35
Or, if I live, is it not very like
The horrible conceit° of death and night,
Together with the terror of the place,
As in a vault, an ancient receptacle
Where for this many hundred years the bones   40
Of all my buried ancestors are pack'd,
Where bloody Tybalt, yet but green in earth,
Lies fest'ring in his shroud; where, as they say,
At some hours in the night spirits resort—
Alack, alack, is it not like that I   45
So early waking, what with loathsome smells
And shrieks like mandrakes° torn out of the
earth,

cull'd picked out   behoveful necessary
state ceremony   tried proved
conceit imagining
mandrakes (the forked root of the mandrake, much
    mentioned in Shakespeare, has a human shape; its
    shriek at being torn from earth reputedly killed or
    drove men mad)

That living mortals hearing them run mad—
O, if I wake, shall I not be distraught,
50   Environed with all these hideous fears,
And madly play with my forefathers' joints
And pluck the mangled Tybalt from his shroud
And in this rage with some great kinsman's bone,
As with a club, dash out my desperate brains?
55   O, look! Methinks I see my cousin's ghost
Seeking out Romeo, that did spit his body
Upon a rapier's point. Stay, Tybalt, stay!
Romeo, I come! This do I drink to thee.
        [*She falls upon her bed, within the curtains.*]

SCENE iv
Hall in CAPULET's *house.*

[*Enter* LADY CAPULET *and* NURSE.]

LADY CAPULET. Hold, take these keys and fetch more spices, nurse.
NURSE. They call for dates and quinces in the pastry.
        [*Enter* CAPULET.]
CAPULET. Come, stir, stir, stir! The second cock hath crow'd,
The curfew bell hath rung; 'tis three o'clock.
5   Look to the bak'd meats, good Angelica.
Spare not for cost.
NURSE.   Go, you cot-quean,° go.
Get you to bed; faith, you'll be sick tomorrow
For this night's watching.°
CAPULET. No, not a whit. What! I have watch'd ere now
10   All night for lesser cause and ne'er been sick.
LADY CAPULET. Aye, you have been a mouse-hunt° in your time,
But I will watch you from such watching now.
        [*Exeunt* LADY CAPULET *and* NURSE.]
CAPULET. A jealous hood,° a jealous hood!
    [*Enter three or four* SERVINGMEN *with spits and logs and baskets.*]
                Now, fellow,
What is there?
FIRST SERVINGMAN. Things for the cook, sir, but I
15   know not what.
CAPULET. Make haste, make haste.
        [*Exit* FIRST SERVINGMAN.]
Sirrah, fetch drier logs.
Call Peter—he will show thee where they are.

---

cot-quean (like *squaw-man*)   *watching* staying awake
mouse-hunt girl-chaser
jealous hood (i.e., she wears the "cap of jealousy," is jealous)

SECOND SERVINGMAN. I have a head, sir, that will find out logs,
And never trouble Peter for the matter.   20
CAPULET. Mass,° and well said; a merry whoreson,° ha!
Thou shalt be loggerhead.° [*Exit* SECOND SERVINGMAN] Good faith, 'tis day.
The county will be here with music straight,
For so he said he would. [*Music within*] I hear him near.   25
Nurse! Wife! What, ho! What, nurse, I say!
        [*Re-enter* NURSE.]
Go waken Juliet. Go and trim her up.
I'll go and chat with Paris. Hie, make haste,
Make haste. The bridegroom he is come already.
Make haste, I say.   [*Exeunt*]   30

SCENE v
JULIET's *chamber.*

[*Enter* NURSE.]

NURSE. Mistress! What, mistress! Juliet! Fast,° I warrant her, she.
Why, lamb! Why, lady! Fie, you slug-abed!
Why, love, I say! Madam! Sweetheart! Why, bride!
What, not a word? You take your pennyworths now—
Sleep for a week; for the next night, I warrant,   5
The County Paris hath set up his rest°
That you shall rest but little. God forgive me,
Marry, and amen. How sound is she asleep!
I needs must wake her. Madam, madam, madam!
Aye, let the county take you in your bed;   10
He'll fright you up, i' faith. Will it not be?
        [*Undraws the curtains.*]
What, dress'd! And in your clothes! And down again!
I must needs wake you. Lady! Lady! Lady!—
Alas, alas! Help, help! My lady's dead!
O, well-a-day, that ever I was born!   15
Some aqua-vitæ, ho! My lord! My lady!
        [*Enter* LADY CAPULET.]
LADY CAPULET. What noise is here?
NURSE.   O lamentable day!
LADY CAPULET. What is the matter?
NURSE.   Look, look! O heavy day!
LADY CAPULET. O me, O me! My child, my only life,

Mass by the mass   *whoreson* rascal
loggerhead blockhead
Fast fast asleep   *hath . . . rest* has resolved

20   Revive, look up, or I will die with thee.
      Help, help! Call help.
                    [*Enter* CAPULET.]
      CAPULET. For shame, bring Juliet forth. Her lord is
          come.
      NURSE. She's dead, deceas'd, she's dead; alack the
          day!
      LADY CAPULET. Alack the day, she's dead, she's
          dead, she's dead!
      CAPULET. Ha! Let me see her. Out, alas! She's
25   cold;
      Her blood is settled and her joints are stiff;
      Life and these lips have long been separated.
      Death lies on her like an untimely frost
      Upon the sweetest flower of all the field.
      NURSE. O lamentable day!
30   LADY CAPULET.   O woeful time!
      CAPULET. Death, that hath ta'en her hence to make
          me wail,
      Ties up my tongue and will not let me speak.
              [*Enter* FRIAR LAURENCE, *and* PARIS, *with*
                          MUSICIANS.]
      FRIAR LAURENCE. Come, is the bride ready to go to
          church?
      CAPULET. Ready to go, but never to return.
35   O son, the night before thy wedding day
      Hath Death lain with thy wife. See, there she
          lies,
      Flower as she was, deflowered by him.
      Death is my son-in-law, Death is my heir;
      My daughter he hath wedded. I will die
40   And leave him all. Life, living, all is Death's.
      PARIS. Have I thought long to see this morning's
          face,
      And doth it give me such a sight as this?
      LADY CAPULET. Accurst, unhappy, wretched, hate-
          ful day!
      Most miserable hour that e'er time saw
45   In lasting labor of his pilgrimage!
      But one, poor one, one poor and loving child,
      But one thing to rejoice and solace in,
      And cruel death hath catch'd it from my sight!
      NURSE. O woe! O woeful, woeful, woeful day!
50   Most lamentable day, most woeful day,
      That ever, ever I did yet behold!
      O day! O day! O day! O hateful day!
      Never was seen so black a day as this.
      O woeful day, O woeful day!
55   PARIS. Beguil'd, divorced, wronged, spited, slain!
      Most detestable° death, by thee beguil'd,
      By cruel cruel thee quite overthrown!
      O love! O life! Not life, but love in death!

CAPULET. Despis'd, distressed, hated, martyr'd,
    kill'd!
Uncomfortable time, why cam'st thou now   60
To murder, murder our solemnity?°
O child! O child! My soul, and not my child!
Dead art thou! Alack, my child is dead,
And with my child my joys are buried!
FRIAR LAURENCE. Peace, ho, for shame! Confusion's°
    cure lives not   65
In these confusions. Heaven and yourself
Had part in this fair maid; now heaven hath all,
And all the better is it for the maid.
Your part in her you could not keep from death,
But heaven keeps his part in eternal life.   70
The most you sought was her promotion,
For 'twas your heaven she should be advanc'd.
And weep ye now, seeing she is advanc'd
Above the clouds, as high as heaven itself?
O, in this love, you love your child so ill   75
That you run mad, seeing that she is well.
She's not well married that lives married long,
But she's best married that dies married young.
Dry up your tears, and stick your rosemary°
On this fair corse, and, as the custom is,   80
In all her best array bear her to church.
For though fond nature bids us all lament,
Yet nature's tears are reason's merriment.°
CAPULET. All things that we ordained festival,
Turn from their office to black funeral.   85
Our instruments to melancholy bells,
Our wedding cheer to a sad burial feast,
Our solemn hymns to sullen dirges change,
Our bridal flowers serve for a buried corse,
And all things change them to the contrary.   90
FRIAR LAURENCE. Sir, go you in, and, madam, go
    with him,
And go, Sir Paris. Every one prepare
To follow this fair corse unto her grave.
The heavens do lour upon you for some ill;
Move them no more by crossing their high will. 95
        [*Exeunt* CAPULET, LADY CAPULET, PARIS, *and*
                                        FRIAR.]
FIRST MUSICIAN. Faith, we may put up our pipes
    and be gone.
NURSE. Honest good fellows, ah, put up, put up,
    For well you know this is a pitiful case.   [*Exit*]
FIRST MUSICIAN. Aye, by my troth, the case° may 100
    be amended.
                [*Enter* PETER.]

---

solemnity festivity   *Confusion's* destruction's
rosemary for remembrance
Yet . . . merriment what moves our natural impulses to
    tears is to our reason cause to rejoice
case . . . case (pun on *situation* and *instrument case*)

---

detestable (accent on first syllable)

PETER. Musicians, O, musicians, "Heart's ease,
    Heart's ease."
    O, an you will have me live, play "Heart's
105   ease."
FIRST MUSICIAN. Why "Heart's ease"?
PETER. O, musicians, because my heart itself plays
    "My heart is full of woe." O, play me some
    merry dump° to comfort me.
110 FIRST MUSICIAN. Not a dump we; 'tis no time to
    play now.
PETER. You will not then?
FIRST MUSICIAN. No.
PETER. I will then give it you soundly.
115 FIRST MUSICIAN. What will you give us?
PETER. No money, on my faith, but the gleek;° I
    will give you the minstrel.°
FIRST MUSICIAN. Then will I give you the serving-
    creature.
120 PETER. Then will I lay the serving-creature's
    dagger on your pate. I will carry no crotchets.°
    I'll re you, I'll fa you. Do you note me?
FIRST MUSICIAN. And you re us and fa us, you note
    us.
125 SECOND MUSICIAN. Pray you, put up your dagger,
    and put out your wit.
PETER. Then have at you with my wit! I will dry-

dump mournful dance tune
gleek gibe
give . . . minstrel insult you musicians by calling you
    minstrels
carry no crotchets stand for no whimsical notions (with
    pun on *quarter notes*)

beat you with an iron wit, and put up my iron
dagger. Answer me like men:

    When griping grief the heart doth wound   130
    And doleful dumps the mind oppress,
    Then music with her silver sound—

Why "silver sound"? Why "music with her
silver sound"?—What say you, Simon Cat-   135
ling?
FIRST MUSICIAN. Marry, sir, because silver hath a
    sweet sound.
PETER. Pretty! What say you, Hugh Rebeck?
SECOND MUSICIAN. I say "silver sound" because
    musicians sound for silver.   140
PETER. Pretty too! What say you, James Sound-
    post?
THIRD MUSICIAN. Faith, I know not what to say.
PETER. O, I cry you mercy;° you are the singer. I
    will say for you.° It is "music with her silver   145
    sound" because musicians have no gold for
    sounding:

    Then music with her silver sound
    With speedy help doth lend redress

[Exit]
FIRST MUSICIAN. What a pestilent knave is this   150
    same!
SECOND MUSICIAN. Hang him, Jack! Come, we'll in
    here, tarry for the mourners, and stay dinner.
[Exeunt]

cry you mercy beg your pardon
you are . . . for you (implying that singers cannot speak
    and must be spoken for)

ACT V

SCENE i
Mantua. A street.

[Enter ROMEO.]
ROMEO. If I may trust the flatt'ring truth of sleep,
    My dreams presage some joyful news at hand.
    My bosom's lord sits lightly in his throne,
    And all this day an unaccustom'd spirit
5   Lifts me above the ground with cheerful
        thoughts.
    I dreamt my lady came and found me dead—
    Strange dream, that gives a dead man leave to
        think!—
    And breath'd such life with kisses in my lips
    That I reviv'd and was an emperor.
10   Ah me! How sweet is love itself possess'd,

When but love's shadows are so rich in joy!
[Enter BALTHASAR, booted.]
News from Verona! How now, Balthasar!
Dost thou not bring me letters from the friar?
How doth my lady? Is my father well?
How fares my Juliet? That I ask again,   15
For nothing can be ill if she be well.
BALTHASAR. Then she is well, and nothing can be
    ill.
Her body sleeps in Capels' monument,
And her immortal part with angels lives.
I saw her laid low in her kindred's vault,
And presently took post° to tell it you.   20
O, pardon me for bringing these ill news,

presently . . . post instantly hired posthorses

Since you did leave it for my office, sir.

ROMEO. Is it e'en so? Then I defy you, stars!
   Thou know'st my lodging. Get me ink and
25   paper,
   And hire posthorses; I will hence tonight.

BALTHASAR. I do beseech you, sir, have patience.
   Your looks are pale and wild and do import°
   Some misadventure.

ROMEO.   Tush, thou art deceiv'd.
30   Leave me and do the thing I bid thee do.
   Hast thou no letters to me from the friar?

BALTHASAR. No, my good lord.

ROMEO.   No matter. Get thee gone
   And hire those horses; I'll be with thee straight.
                     [*Exit* BALTHASAR.]
   Well, Juliet, I will lie with thee tonight.
35   Let's see for means:—O mischief, thou art swift
   To enter in the thoughts of desperate men!
   I do remember an apothecary,
   And hereabouts a' dwells, which late I noted
   In tatter'd weeds,° with overwhelming brows,
40   Culling of simples.° Meager were his looks;
   Sharp misery had worn him to the bones.
   And in his needy shop a tortoise hung,
   An alligator stuff'd, and other skins
   Of ill-shap'd fishes; and about his shelves
45   A beggarly account of empty boxes,
   Green earthen pots, bladders, and musty seeds,
   Remnants of packthread and old cakes of roses
   Were thinly scatter'd to make up a show.
   Noting this penury, to myself I said,
50   And if a man did need a poison now,
   Whose sale is present death in Mantua,
   Here lives a caitiff° wretch would sell it him.
   O, this same thought did but forerun my need,
   And this same needy man must sell it me.
55   As I remember, this should be the house.
   Being holiday, the beggar's shop is shut.
   What, ho! Apothecary!
               [*Enter* APOTHECARY.]

APOTHECARY.   Who calls so loud?

ROMEO. Come hither, man. I see that thou art
     poor;
   Hold, there is forty ducats. Let me have
60   A dram of poison, such soon-speeding gear°
   As will disperse itself through all the veins,
   That° the life-weary taker may fall dead
   And that the trunk may be discharg'd of breath
   As violently as hasty powder fir'd
65   Doth hurry from the fatal cannon's womb.

APOTHECARY. Such mortal drugs I have, but
   Mantua's law

Is death to any he that utters° them.

ROMEO. Art thou so bare and full of wretchedness,
   And fear'st to die? Famine is in thy cheeks,
   Need and oppression starveth in thy eyes,   70
   Contempt and beggary hangs upon thy back.
   The world is not thy friend, nor the world's law.
   The world affords no law to make thee rich.
   Then be not poor, but break it and take this.

APOTHECARY. My poverty but not my will con-
   sents.   75

ROMEO. I pay thy poverty and not thy will.

APOTHECARY. Put this in any liquid thing you will
   And drink it off, and if you had the strength
   Of twenty men it would dispatch you straight.

ROMEO. There is thy gold, worse poison to men's
   souls,   80
   Doing more murder in this loathsome world,
   Than these poor compounds that thou mayst
     not sell.
   I sell thee poison, thou hast sold me none.
   Farewell. Buy food and get thyself in flesh.
   Come, cordial and not poison, go with me   85
   To Juliet's grave; for there must I use thee.
                             [*Exeunt*]

SCENE ii
FRIAR LAURENCE'S *cell*.

[*Enter* FRIAR JOHN.]

FRIAR JOHN. Holy Franciscan friar! Brother, ho!
              [*Enter* FRIAR LAURENCE.]

FRIAR LAURENCE. This same should be the voice of
   Friar John.
   Welcome from Mantua. What says Romeo?
   Or, if his mind be writ, give me his letter.

FRIAR JOHN. Going to find a barefoot brother out,   5
   One of our order, to associate° me,
   Here in this city visiting the sick,
   And finding him, the searchers of the town,
   Suspecting that we both were in a house
   Where the infectious pestilence° did reign,   10
   Seal'd up the doors and would not let us forth;
   So that my speed to Mantua there was stay'd.

FRIAR LAURENCE. Who bare my letter then to
   Romeo?

FRIAR JOHN. I could not send it—here it is again—
   Nor get a messenger to bring it thee,   15
   So fearful were they of infection.

FRIAR LAURENCE. Unhappy fortune! By my brotherhood,
   The letter was not nice,° but full of charge

---

import signify   *weeds* garments
Culling of simples sorting herbs   *caitiff* miserable
soon-speeding gear quick-acting stuff   *That* so that

utters dispenses   *associate* accompany
infectious pestilence the plague   *nice* trivial

Of dear import,° and the neglecting it
20 May do much danger. Friar John, go hence;
Get me an iron crow° and bring it straight
Unto my cell.
FRIAR JOHN. Brother, I'll go and bring it thee.
                                        [*Exit*]
FRIAR LAURENCE. Now must I to the monument
alone.
25 Within this three hours will fair Juliet wake.
She will beshrew° me much that Romeo
Hath had no notice of these accidents.°
But I will write again to Mantua
And keep her at my cell till Romeo come,
30 Poor living corse, clos'd in a dead man's tomb!
                                        [*Exit*]

SCENE iii
A churchyard; in it a monument belonging to the
CAPULETS.

[*Enter* PARIS *and his* PAGE, *bearing flowers and
a torch.*]
PARIS. Give me thy torch, boy. Hence, and stand
aloof;
Yet put it out, for I would not be seen.
Under yond yew trees lay thee all along,
Holding thine ear close to the hollow ground;
5 So shall no foot upon the churchyard tread,
Being loose, unfirm, with digging up of graves,
But thou shalt hear it. Whistle then to me
As signal that thou hear'st something approach.
Give me those flowers. Do as I bid thee, go.
10 PAGE. [*Aside*] I am almost afraid to stand alone
Here in the churchyard; yet I will adventure.
                                        [*Retires.*]
PARIS. Sweet flower, with flowers thy bridal bed I
strew—
O woe! Thy canopy is dust and stones—
Which with sweet water nightly I will dew,
Or, wanting° that, with tears distill'd by
15   moans.
The obsequies that I for thee will keep
Nightly shall be to strew thy grave and weep.
                                [*The* PAGE *whistles.*]
The boy gives warning something doth ap-
proach.
What cursed foot wanders this way tonight
20 To cross my obsequies and true love's rite?
What, with a torch! Muffle me, night, awhile.
                                        [*Retires.*]
[*Enter* ROMEO *and* BALTHASAR, *with a torch,
mattock, etc.*]

ROMEO. Give me that mattock and the wrenching
iron.
Hold, take this letter; early in the morning
See thou deliver it to my lord and father.
Give me the light. Upon thy life I charge thee,   25
Whate'er thou hear'st or seest, stand all aloof
And do not interrupt me in my course.
Why I descend into this bed of death
Is partly to behold my lady's face,
But chiefly to take thence from her dead finger 30
A precious ring, a ring that I must use
In dear employment. Therefore hence, be gone.
But if thou, jealous,° dost return to pry
In what I farther shall intend to do,
By heaven I will tear thee joint by joint   35
And strew this hungry churchyard with thy
limbs.
The time and my intents are savage wild,
More fierce and more inexorable far
Than empty tigers or the roaring sea.
BALTHASAR. I will be gone, sir, and not trouble you. 40
ROMEO. So shalt thou show me friendship. Take
thou that.
Live and be prosperous, and farewell, good
fellow.
BALTHASAR. [*Aside*] For all this same, I'll hide me
hereabout.
His looks I fear, and his intents I doubt.°
                                        [*Retires.*]
ROMEO. Thou detestable° maw, thou womb of
death,   45
Gorg'd with the dearest morsel of the earth,
Thus I enforce thy rotten jaws to open,
And in despite° I'll cram thee with more food.
                                [*Opens the tomb.*]
PARIS. This is that banish'd haughty Montague
That murder'd my love's cousin, with which
grief   50
It is supposed the fair creature died,
And here is come to do some villainous shame
To the dead bodies. I will apprehend him.
                                [*Comes forward.*]
Stop thy unhallow'd toil, vile Montague!
Can vengeance be pursu'd further than death?   55
Condemned villain, I do apprehend thee.
Obey, and go with me, for thou must die.
ROMEO. I must indeed, and therefore came I
hither.
Good gentle youth, tempt not a desperate man.
Fly hence and leave me. Think upon these gone;   60
Let them affright thee. I beseech thee, youth,
Put not another sin upon my head

---

dear import great importance   *crow* crowbar
beshrew scold   *accidents* events   *wanting* lacking

jealous suspicious   *doubt* mistrust
detestable (accent on first syllable)   *despite* scorn

By urging me to fury. O, be gone!
By heaven, I love thee better than myself,
65 For I come hither arm'd against myself.
Stay not, be gone. Live, and hereafter say
A madman's mercy bid thee run away.
PARIS. I do defy thy conjurations°
And apprehend thee for a felon here.
ROMEO. Wilt thou provoke me? Then have at
70   thee, boy!   [*They fight.*]
PAGE. O Lord, they fight! I will go call the watch.
                                       [*Exit*]
PARIS. O, I am slain! [*Falls*] If thou be merciful,
Open the tomb, lay me with Juliet.   [*Dies.*]
ROMEO. In faith, I will. Let me peruse this face.
75 Mercutio's kinsman, noble County Paris!
What said my man, when my betossed soul
Did not attend him as we rode? I think
He told me Paris should have married Juliet.
Said he not so? Or did I dream it so?
80 Or am I mad, hearing him talk of Juliet,
To think it was so? O, give me thy hand,
One writ with me in sour misfortune's book!
I'll bury thee in a triumphant grave.
A grave? O, no, a lantern,° slaughter'd youth;
85 For here lies Juliet, and her beauty makes
This vault a feasting presence° full of light.
Death, lie thou there, by a dead man interr'd.
                        [*Laying* PARIS *in the monument.*]
How oft when men are at the point of death
Have they been merry! Which their keepers call
90 A lightning° before death. O, how may I
Call this a lightning? O my love, my wife!
Death, that hath suck'd the honey of thy breath,
Hath had no power yet upon thy beauty.
Thou art not conquer'd; beauty's ensign yet
95 Is crimson in thy lips and in thy cheeks,
And Death's pale flag is not advanced there.
Tybalt, liest thou there in thy bloody sheet?
O, what more favor can I do to thee
Than with that hand that cut thy youth in
    twain
100 To sunder his that was thine enemy?
Forgive me, cousin! Ah, dear Juliet,
Why art thou yet so fair? Shall I believe
That unsubstantial Death is amorous,
And that the lean abhorred monster keeps
105 Thee here in dark to be his paramour?
For fear of that I still will stay with thee
And never from this palace of dim night
Depart again. Here, here will I remain

conjurations   commands
lantern   windowed turret
feasting presence   state chamber, where a sovereign greets
    visitors
lightning   lightening (of the spirit)

With worms that are thy chambermaids. O,
    here
Will I set up my everlasting rest   110
And shake the yoke of inauspicious stars
From this world-wearied flesh. Eyes, look your
    last!
Arms, take your last embrace! And, lips, O you
The doors of breath seal with a righteous kiss
A dateless bargain to engrossing° death!   115
Come, bitter conduct,° come, unsav'ry guide!
Thou desperate pilot, now at once run on
The dashing rocks thy sea-sick weary bark.°
Here's to my love! [*Drinks*] O true apothecary!
Thy drugs are quick. Thus with a kiss I die. 120
                                        [*Dies.*]
[*Enter, at the other end of the churchyard,* FRIAR
    LAURENCE, *with a lantern, crow, and spade.*]
FRIAR LAURENCE. Saint Francis be my speed! How
    oft tonight
Have my old feet stumbled at graves! Who's
    there?
BALTHASAR. Here's one, a friend, and one that
    knows you well.
FRIAR LAURENCE. Bliss be upon you! Tell me, good
    my friend,
What torch is yond that vainly lends his light 125
To grubs and eyeless skulls? As I discern,
It burneth in the Capels' monument.
BALTHASAR. It doth so, holy sir, and there's my
    master,
One that you love.
FRIAR LAURENCE.   Who is it?
BALTHASAR.   Romeo.
FRIAR LAURENCE. How long hath he been there?
BALTHASAR.   Full half an hour. 130
FRIAR LAURENCE. Go with me to the vault.
BALTHASAR.   I dare not, sir.
My master knows not but I am gone hence,
And fearfully did menace me with death
If I did stay to look on his intents.
FRIAR LAURENCE. Stay, then; I'll go alone. Fear
    comes upon me;
O, much I fear some ill unthrifty° thing.   135
BALTHASAR. As I did sleep under this yew tree
    here,
I dreamt my master and another fought
And that my master slew him.
FRIAR LAURENCE. Romeo!   [*Advances.*]
Alack, alack, what blood is this which stains   140
The stony entrance of this sepulchre?
What mean these masterless and gory swords

engrossing   all-absorbing
bitter conduct   (i.e., the poison)
pilot . . . bark   my soul . . . my body
unthrifty   unfortunate

To lie discolor'd by this place of peace?
　　　　　　　　　　　　　　　[Enters the tomb.]
Romeo! O, pale! Who else? What, Paris too?
145　And steep'd in blood? Ah, what an unkind hour
Is guilty of this lamentable chance!
The lady stirs. 　　　　　　　[JULIET wakes.]
JULIET. O comfortable° friar! Where is my lord?
I do remember well where I should be,
150　And there I am. Where is my Romeo?
　　　　　　　　　　　　　　　[Noise within.]
FRIAR LAURENCE. I hear some noise. Lady, come
　　from that nest
Of death, contagion, and unnatural sleep.
A greater power than we can contradict
Hath thwarted our intents. Come, come away.
155　Thy husband in thy bosom there lies dead,
And Paris too. Come, I'll dispose of thee
Among a sisterhood of holy nuns.
Stay not to question, for the watch is coming.
Come, go, good Juliet; I dare no longer stay.
160　JULIET. Go, get thee hence, for I will not away.
　　　　　　　　　　　　　[Exit FRIAR LAURENCE.]
What's here? A cup, clos'd in my true love's
　　hand?
Poison, I see, hath been his timeless end.
O churl! Drunk all, and left no friendly drop
To help me after? I will kiss thy lips;
165　Haply° some poison yet doth hang on them,
To make me die with a restorative. [Kisses him]
Thy lips are warm!
FIRST WATCHMAN. [Within] Lead, boy. Which way?
JULIET. Yea, noise? Then I'll be brief. O happy
　　dagger!
　　　　　　　　　　　　[Snatching ROMEO's dagger.]
This is thy sheath. [Stabs herself] There rust, and
170　let me die.
　　　　　　　　　　[Falls on ROMEO's body, and dies.]
　　　　　　　[Enter WATCH, with the PAGE of PARIS.]
PAGE. This is the place; there, where the torch
　　doth burn.
FIRST WATCHMAN. The ground is bloody; search
　　about the churchyard.
Go, some of you, whoe'er you find attach.°
Pitiful sight! Here lies the county slain,
175　And Juliet bleeding, warm, and newly dead,
Who here hath lain this two days buried.
Go, tell the prince; run to the Capulets;
Raise up the Montagues. Some others search.
We see the ground whereon these woes do lie,
180　But the true ground of all these piteous woes
We cannot without circumstance descry.
　　　　　[Re-enter some of the WATCH, with BALTHASAR.]

SECOND WATCHMAN. Here's Romeo's man; we
　　found him in the churchyard.
FIRST WATCHMAN. Hold him in safety till the prince
　　come hither.
　　　　　　　　　[Re-enter FRIAR LAURENCE, and
　　　　　　　　　　　　another WATCHMAN.]
THIRD WATCHMAN. Here is a friar that trembles,
　　sighs, and weeps.
We took this mattock and this spade from him　185
As he was coming from this churchyard's side.
FIRST WATCHMAN. A great suspicion; stay the friar
　　too.
　　　　　　　　[Enter the PRINCE and ATTENDANTS.]
PRINCE. What misadventure is so early up,
That calls our person from our morning rest?
　　　　[Enter CAPULET, LADY CAPULET, and others.]
CAPULET. What should it be that they so shriek
　　abroad? 　　　　　　　　　　　　　　190
LADY CAPULET. The people in the street cry Romeo,
Some Juliet, and some Paris, and all run
With open outcry toward our monument.
PRINCE. What fear is this which startles in our ears?
FIRST WATCHMAN. Sovereign, here lies the County
　　Paris slain, 　　　　　　　　　　　　195
And Romeo dead, and Juliet, dead before,
Warm and new kill'd.
PRINCE. Search, seek, and know how this foul mur-
　　der comes.
FIRST WATCHMAN. Here is a friar, and slaughter'd
　　Romeo's man,
With instruments upon them fit to open　　200
These dead men's tombs.
CAPULET. O heavens! O wife, look how our
　　daughter bleeds!
This dagger hath mista'en, for, lo, his house
Is empty on the back of Montague,
And it missheathed in my daughter's bosom!　205
LADY CAPULET. O me! This sight of death is as a
　　bell
That warns my old age to a sepulcher.
　　　　　　　　　[Enter MONTAGUE and others.]
PRINCE. Come, Montague, for thou art early up
To see thy son and heir more early down.
MONTAGUE. Alas, my liege, my wife is dead to-
　　night; 　　　　　　　　　　　　　　210
Grief of my son's exile hath stopp'd her breath.
What further woe conspires against mine age?
PRINCE. Look, and thou shalt see.
MONTAGUE. O thou untaught! What manners is in
　　this,
To press before thy father to a grave? 　　215
PRINCE. Seal up the mouth of outrage for awhile,
Till we can clear these ambiguities
And know their spring, their head, their true
　　descent;

comfortable comforting　　haply perhaps
attach arrest

And then will I be general of your woes
220   And lead you even to death. Meantime forbear,
And let mischance be slave to patience.
Bring forth the parties of suspicion.

FRIAR LAURENCE. I am the greatest, able to do least,
Yet most suspected, as the time and place
225   Doth make against me, of this direful murder;
And here I stand, both to impeach and purge
Myself condemned and myself excus'd.

PRINCE. Then say at once what thou dost know in
this.

FRIAR LAURENCE. I will be brief, for my short date
of breath
230   Is not so long as is a tedious tale.
Romeo, there dead, was husband to that Juliet,
And she, there dead, that Romeo's faithful wife.
I married them, and their stol'n marriage day
Was Tybalt's doomsday, whose untimely death
Banish'd the new-made bridegroom from this
235   city,
For whom, and not for Tybalt, Juliet pin'd.
You, to remove that siege of grief from her,
Betroth'd and would have married her perforce
To County Paris. Then comes she to me
240   And with wild looks bid me devise some mean
To rid her from this second marriage,
Or in my cell there would she kill herself.
Then gave I her, so tutor'd by my art,
A sleeping potion, which so took effect
245   As I intended, for it wrought on her
The form of death. Meantime I writ to Romeo
That he should hither come as° this dire night
To help to take her from her borrow'd grave,
Being the time the potion's force should cease.
250   But he which bore my letter, Friar John,
Was stay'd by accident, and yesternight
Return'd my letter back. Then all alone
At the prefixed hour of her waking
Came I to take her from her kindred's vault,
255   Meaning to keep her closely° at my cell
Till I conveniently could send to Romeo.
But when I came, some minute ere the time
Of her awaking, here untimely lay
The noble Paris and true Romeo dead.
260   She wakes, and I entreated her come forth
And bear this work of heaven with patience.
But then a noise did scare me from the tomb,
And she too desperate would not go with me,
But, as it seems, did violence on herself.
265   All this I know; and to the marriage
Her nurse is privy.° And if aught in this
Miscarried by my fault, let my old life

Be sacrific'd some hour before his time
Unto the rigor of severest law.

PRINCE. We still° have known thee for a holy man.   270
Where's Romeo's man? What can he say in this?

BALTHASAR. I brought my master news of Juliet's
death,
And then in post° he came from Mantua
To this same place, to this same monument.
This letter he early bid me give his father   275
And threaten'd me with death, going in the
vault,
If I departed not and left him there.

PRINCE. Give me the letter; I will look on it.
Where is the county's page that rais'd the
watch?
Sirrah, what made° your master in this place?   280

PAGE. He came with flowers to strew his lady's
grave,
And bid me stand aloof, and so I did.
Anon comes one with light to ope the tomb,
And by and by my master drew on him;
And then I ran away to call the watch.   285

PRINCE. This letter doth make good the friar's
words,
Their course of love, the tidings of her death.
And here he writes that he did buy a poison
Of a poor 'pothecary, and therewithal
Came to this vault to die and lie with Juliet.   290
Where be these enemies? Capulet! Montague!
See what a scourge is laid upon your hate,
That heaven finds means to kill your joys with
love!
And I, for winking at your discords too,
Have lost a brace of kinsmen. All are punish'd. 295

CAPULET. O brother Montague, give me thy hand.
This is my daughter's jointure,° for no more
Can I demand.

MONTAGUE.   But I can give thee more.
For I will raise her statue in pure gold,
That° whiles Verona by that name is known   300
There shall no figure at such rate be set
As that of true and faithful Juliet.

CAPULET. As rich shall Romeo's by his lady's lie;
Poor sacrifices of our enmity!

PRINCE. A glooming peace this morning with it
brings;   305
The sun for sorrow will not show his head.
Go hence to have more talk of these sad things;
Some shall be pardon'd and some punished.
For never was a story of more woe
Than this of Juliet and her Romeo.   [Exeunt]   310

---

still always   *in post* posthaste
made was he doing   *jointure* marriage portion
That so that

as on   *closely* secretly
privy partner in the secret

AFTERWORD

Hero and Leander, Pyramus and Thisbe, Antony and Cleopatra, Troilus and Cressida, Paris and Helen, Tristan and Isolde, Siegfried and Brünnhilde, Pelleas and Melisande, Paola and Francesca, Romeo and Juliet: these are among the world's most famous lovers of fact or fiction; and if a universal vote were taken there is little question whose fame would be found to transcend that of all others,

> For never was a story of more woe
> Than this of Juliet and her Romeo.

Their story was first fully told (though not originated) by Matteo Bandello, a sixteenth-century Italian writer of licentious romances. It was translated into French by Belleforest, in his *Histoires Tragiques* (1565, when Shakespeare was a year old) and into English by William Painter, in his *Palace of Pleasure* (1566). But it had earlier been introduced into England, with a limited degree of charm, by Arthur Brooke in a longish narrative poem, "The Tragicall Historye of Romeus and Juliet" (1562). This version was reprinted (in the edition that Shakespeare no doubt used) in 1587, a year before the Spanish Armada and perhaps two years before Shakespeare, just arriving from Stratford, began to write for the London stage. Popular as were the earlier versions in their times, it is doubtful that, except for Shakespeare's version, most modern readers would ever have heard of Romeo and Juliet.

More than one critic categorically has pronounced *Romeo and Juliet* Shakespeare's best-loved play. Not only does it read as well as it acts and act as well as it reads, but it has lent itself with great distinction to the operatic stage, to the ballet, and in recent times, to a steady succession of filmings. If it is not his greatest tragedy—and, indeed, it has some-times, on rather narrow grounds, been denied the title of "true tragedy" entirely—yet it has strong claim to be called the most beautiful and the most moving of them all. Much of its beauty and moving power resides in its poetry. Evidently, in what may have been the single year in which he wrote *A Midsummer Night's Dream*, *Richard II*, and *Romeo and Juliet*, Shakespeare felt like singing, for sing he did in all three—a comedy, a history, and a tragedy. One is set in ancient Athens, one in medieval England, and the last in Renaissance Italy. One is dreamlike and marvelous, its enchanted woodlands peopled by a royal band of fairies; one is bustling with angry political factions, rival kings, armed men, and a brutal struggle for power; and one is a tragic love story of two shining young innocents. In materials and settings it would be difficult to find three plays more unlike. The fact made little difference to Shakespeare in this "lyric year": he sang gloriously in all of them and thus made them, despite their differences, more alike than unlike.

Everywhere, in that year, the language that he wrote for his characters to speak vibrates with song. Here is Oberon in the *Dream*:

> I know a bank where the wild thyme blows,
> Where oxlips and the nodding violet grows,
> Quite over-canopied with luscious woodbine,
> With sweet musk-roses and with eglantine....

Here is King Richard:

> ... within the hollow crown
> That rounds the mortal temples of a king

> Keeps Death his court, and there the antic sits,
> Scoffing his state and grinning at his pomp,
> Allowing him a breath, a little scene
> To monarchize, be fear'd, and kill with looks,
> Infusing him with self and vain conceit,
> As if this flesh which walls about our life
> Were brass impregnable; and humor'd thus
> Comes at the last and with a little pin
> Bores through his castle wall, and—farewell king!

And from the same play is John of Gaunt, in a burst of patriotic music that flows throughout forty lines:

> This royal throne of kings, this sceptred isle,
> This earth of majesty, this seat of Mars,
> This other Eden, demi-Paradise,
> This fortress built by Nature for herself . . . .

In *Romeo and Juliet* it is this same potent thrust of poetry that, as by magic, lifts and holds the action somewhere betwixt earth and heaven. Here is Romeo's ecstatic outburst at first sight of Juliet:

> O she doth teach the torches to burn bright!
> It seems she hangs upon the cheek of night
> As a rich jewel in an Ethiop's ear,
> Beauty too rich for use, for earth too dear!

Such sounds as these—which, as one famous Shakespearean pointed out, had never before been heard on the English stage—are sustained throughout the great moments of the action. Here is Juliet as she impatiently awaits the coming of Romeo for their wedding night:

> Come, gentle night, come, loving, black-brow'd night,
> Give me my Romeo, and when he shall die
> Take him and cut him out in little stars,
> And he will make the face of heaven so fine
> That all the world will be in love with night
> And pay no worship to the garish sun.

And here is Romeo again, this time with his tones darkened by grief as he bends over his bride's body in the Capulet tomb:

> O my love, my wife!
> Death that hath suck'd the honey of thy breath
> Hath had no power yet upon thy beauty.
> Thou art not conquer'd; beauty's ensign yet
> Is crimson in thy lips and in thy cheeks,
> And Death's pale flag is not advanced there . . .

Nearly three centuries later the great composer Gounod would express the passions of these lovers in some of the world's most potent music; but, indeed, Shakespeare's *Romeo and Juliet* is virtually operatic as it stands, with the very words of the libretto furnishing their own music.

It would be false to suggest, of course, that all the poetry of the play is equally rich, genuine, and dramatically "right." The reader misses a great deal who fails to distinguish the artificial, affected poetic language of the early Romeo, playing at being in love with Rosaline, from that which he speaks in the great moments after he meets Juliet. Here he is at first, having come in just after the street brawl with which the play opens:

> O me! What fray was here?
> Yet tell me not, for I have heard it all.
> Here's much to do with hate, but more with love.
> Why, then, O brawling love! O loving hate!
> O anything, of nothing first create!
> O heavy lightness! Serious vanity!
> Misshapen chaos of well-seeming forms!
> Feather of lead, bright smoke, cold fire, sick health!
> Still-waking sleep, that is not what it is!
> This love feel I, that feel no love in this.

Such lines as these, stuffed with the fashionable conceits and paradoxes that characterized much poetry of the time, have no doubt influenced the decisions of star actors during past centuries who chose to play Mercutio rather than Romeo. Like other "fashionable" lovers, who indulged themselves rather in expressing than in truly feeling, Romeo has a go at defining or "anatomizing" love:

> Love is a smoke rais'd with the fume of sighs;
> Being purg'd, a fire sparkling in lovers' eyes;
> Being vex'd, a sea nourish'd with lovers' tears.
> What is it else? A madness most discreet.
> A choking gall, and a preserving sweet.

Romeo and Juliet would be an unbearable work indeed if Shakespeare had allowed his hero to speak such stuff throughout. But of course he uses the device of affected poetry for dramatic purpose; and when, at the first sight of Juliet, the great poetry of genuine passion appears, we recognize the sheer dramatic brilliance of the contrast. Even so, Romeo occasionally relapses into his old habits, formed when he was courting the disdainful Rosaline, and when he does so the effect is sheer delight for the reader who recognizes what has happened. Thus, under the balcony, Romeo tries some of the fashionable lover's extravagant "protestations" on Juliet, only to find that she will have none of them: "Do not swear at all." He starts off again, "If my heart's dear love," and she cuts him off abruptly: "Well, do not swear." Here, no doubt, Romeo's passion is as genuine as her own; but, in conversation with his true love, he slips back too easily into the false language that he had learned before, and speaks "by the book." Later, too, at a moment of terrible crisis, after the banishment, when he lies on the floor of the Friar's cell in desperation, some psychological quirk momentarily shifts him back to the old devices of verbal play, and he says, "This may flies do, when I from this must fly," and, again, to the Nurse, ". . . what says/ My conceal'd lady to our cancel'd love?" At a moment of great crisis, old habit has reasserted itself; the earlier "phony" language of love reappears.

But one of the great pleasures in the study of the play comes in observing Romeo's growth from boy to man in the space of less than a week, and, simultaneously with this growth, his growth as a poet. The affected style of the early anatomizer of love wears quickly away, and as his experiences of life, love, and grief assail him in swift succession, his poetic powers deepen, very much as do those of Richard II, after his return from the disastrous Irish expedition, and those of Macbeth once he has done the murder and begun to feel its consequences. Shakespeare's major poets all grow before our very eyes.

Romeo and Juliet, of course, are not the only poets of the play; in 1595–1596 Shakespeare tended to make everyone a poet. Mercutio, not only in the Queen Mab speech but also in the sheer inventiveness of his bawdy wit, is "of imagination all compact." Capulet, who in his moods swings to and fro like a pendulum, sometimes engages in showy plays of fancy, as when he chides Juliet for weeping overmuch, as he supposes, for Tybalt's death. No doubt the wildest flight of all is given to Lady Capulet, ultrafashionable young mother of the times, when, in an excess of maternal persuasiveness, she compares the princely Paris to a book that "only lacks a cover." Especially during the first two acts, the strained affectations of poetic convention and the extravagant conceits of overly inventive imaginations stand in sharp contrast to the poetry of genuine passion, whether of love or of grief, that, after the middle of Act III, begins to drown out all other sounds. In the end even old Montague, who has not been given a chance to say much of anything before, utters a compressed line or two that cut as deeply as any in the play; thus, when he confronts Romeo's body in the tomb:

> O thou untaught! What manners is in this,
> To press before thy father to a grave?

So it is unquestionably the poetry that beyond all else makes *Romeo and Juliet* so moving and so memorable. But of course poetry alone does not provide a dramatic experience in the theater; there must also be action and characters who live and claim our sympathies. The action of *Romeo and Juliet* is peculiarly swift and impresses with its swiftness from the opening scene, when we are simultaneously introduced to the situation of the feud, shown a new eruption of it, and swept up in the action that will lead ultimately to the dead bodies in the Capulet tomb, for this particular outbreak results in the Prince's edict that, when the next outbreak occurs, requires, at the very least, Romeo's banishment. The play opens on a Sunday morning. That evening, Romeo and Juliet first meet. Just after Monday noon they are married, and that same afternoon Romeo is banished. Early Tuesday morning they part in fear that they will never meet again. Very late Tuesday night or very early Wednesday morning, Juliet takes the potion. She is laid in the Capulet tomb on Wednesday and wakes there late Thursday night. Time, in the final scene, is telescoped, with several hours compressed into the half hour or less of playing time. The play ends on Friday, near dawn; but there will be no dawn, for "The sun, for sorrow, will not show his head." Throughout, Shakespeare marks the passage of time almost from hour to hour. We are told when it is morning, afternoon, evening. We are told when the dial's hand is "on the prick of noon." The Friar does not loosely foretell when Juliet will awaken, but states it precisely: "two and forty hours." It is not idly that the dramatist keeps us thus informed; our sense of the swiftness with which the fateful events follow one another is crucial to our sense of the tragedy itself. We must understand that, once afoot, the force that destroys the lives of the lovers moves with terrifying speed.

Finally, we must ask, what *is* this force? At the time he wrote this play Shakespeare had not yet worked out the general pattern that we mean when we say, in the wake of A. C. Bradley, "Shakespearean tragedy," wherein the primary force of ruin resides in the character of the protagonist and makes him, at last, responsible for his own fate. That pattern would emerge, fully drawn, in Shakespeare's next attempt, *Julius Caesar*. In *Romeo and Juliet*, as the Prologue directly advises us, it is Fate that brings about the deaths of the lovers in order to end their families' feud. What the action that follows represents, then, is Fate at work toward the accomplishment of this end. Fate does its work through a chain of what, casually observed, look only like accidents. In the main, Fate works through the actions of persons who would not knowingly harm the lovers but who, nevertheless, finally destroy them. Thus Mercutio, Romeo's friend though a Capulet, not knowing the true reason for Romeo's refusal to fight Tybalt, fights Tybalt himself and is killed under Romeo's arm. His death obliges Romeo to kill Tybalt; Romeo's banishment ensues and brings on the events that lead to the catastrophe. The always well-intentioned Benvolio, interceding between servants in the opening brawl in order to keep the peace, unintentionally thus invites the fiery Tybalt into the fray, which becomes general and leads to the Prince's fatal edict. Paris, who loves Juliet and could never wish to harm her, knowing nothing of her prior marriage, urges his own suit, which Capulet accepts in Juliet's name, and the result is that Juliet must swallow the Friar's potion in order to escape. Capulet himself, who, though at times furious with her, loves his daughter beyond life itself ("The earth hath swallowed all my hopes but she") knowing nothing of Juliet's marriage to Romeo, gives his consent to a hasty marriage in the hope that Juliet's grief— for Tybalt, as he erroneously supposes—may be alleviated. Moreover, his anger at her refusal to marry Paris turns later to such joy, when she seemingly agrees to do so, that he advances the wedding date by twenty-four hours. The result is that Juliet must drink the potion a day earlier, the Friar has that much less time in which to get the truth to Romeo in Mantua—and Balthasar, the servant who is always "as true as steel," gets to his master with false word of her death. But for the change of date, Friar Laurence would have had more than enough time, despite Friar John's brief detention under quarantine, to have sent the true word to Romeo.

Thus Fate weaves its deadly pattern, which is the plot of the tragedy, out of the actions of persons who would not knowingly have harmed the lovers but who, acting unknowingly, destroy them. The examples cited above are only the more obvious ones; others include virtually all the persons who have any part in the action, so that, by the end, all have contributed, unwittingly, the links that forge the doom promised in the Prologue. Obviously, Romeo and Juliet themselves, young, impulsive, and passionate as they are, contribute also to the end; Fate works through them even as it does through Capulet's unwitting acts. In the end, Romeo kills himself because he does not know that Juliet is alive, and the final link has been set in place. But *Romeo and Juliet* is a different kind of tragedy from *Julius Caesar* and the others that follow, wherein, though indeed there may be an external force at work, as in *Macbeth* most notably, it is the inner nature of the protagonist and not an external force that determines the course of events and brings on death. To deny to *Romeo and Juliet* the title of "true tragedy" on the grounds of its difference from the others seems preposterous; it is different, but it is tragedy indeed, and contains the power to move readers and spectators as few other tragedies do.

A NOTE ON THE COMPOSITION OF THE PLAY

Romeo and Juliet is usually assigned to the year 1595; it was "often plaid publiquely" before its first publication in the Quarto of 1597. Shakespeare drew on Arthur Brooke's poem "The Tragicall Historye of Romeus and Juliet" and on William Painter's prose version printed in the *Palace of Pleasure*, both of which versions came from a tale by Matteo Bandello, which came in turn from yet earlier versions.

SHAKESPEARE'S HISTORY PLAYS

The "chronicle play," a native dramatic genre which undertook to represent segments of English history on the stage, was already long established when Shakespeare arrived in London from Stratford. Very possibly, though uncertainly, his initial theatrical assignments consisted of retouching older works of this kind. By 1592 at the latest, he had written all three parts of *King Henry VI*; history plays would make the heaviest demands on his creative energies during the decade. After 1599 he set English history aside for almost thirteen years, but returned to it with his final play, *Henry VIII* (probably written with a collaborator). Thus his career began and ended with English history.

In quantitative as well as temporal terms, history looms large in the total canon: ten plays, a total of fifty acts, somewhat more than 30,500 lines, mainly blank verse—more than he gave to tragedy (30,000) but fewer than he gave to romantic comedy, "dark" comedy, and dramatic romance combined (45,800). If we add to the ten English history plays the tragedies *Macbeth* and *King Lear* and the romance of *Cymbeline*, all derived from native historical and legendary materials, and if, further, we add to these the great Roman tragedies *Julius Caesar*, *Antony and Cleopatra*, and *Coriolanus*, all closely reworked from classical biographies of famous historical personages, and certainly not less "historical" than the English histories, we find that, numerically and quantitatively, history provided the basic substance for nearly half the total of Shakespeare's plays.

His early, heavy emphasis on history is easily accounted for. English patriotic fervor reached a fine frenzy a year or two after Shakespeare reached London from Stratford. Not only the defeat of the Spanish Armada by Sir Francis Drake and other doughty seamen in 1588, but sundry other contemporary manifestations of burgeoning national greatness during the immediate period made Englishmen proud of their present, optimistic about the future, and eager to hear about their past. Industrious historians like Edward Hall, John Foxe, John Stow, and—most importantly for Shakespeare—Raphael Holinshed produced an astonishing quantity of historical writing which told the patriotic Englishman how glorious, if often gory, had been the island's past. Such historians were the researchers, the "leg men," the collectors of fact and legend who, themselves infatuated by the events they narrated, supplied the raw material that kindled and fed the imaginations of dramatists and poets.

For of course the poets, too, quickly took up the theme of England's greatness and the wonders of her past. Between 1585 and 1615, metrical chronicles—that is, narrative and descriptive poems—on native subjects flourished, and in these the poets celebrated the theme of England's glory past and present. Among the best (and longest) was Samuel Daniel's "Civil Wars Between the Two Houses of Lancaster and York," a poem that swelled to gigantic dimensions between 1595 and 1605. In large measure, Daniel was doing in narrative verse what Shakespeare, almost simultaneously, was doing in dramatic verse. William Warner's "Albion's England" grew to an incredible sixteen books between 1586 and 1612. The finest and most prolific of the rhyming chroniclers was Michael Drayton, also a sonneteer of the first order, who wrote the "Barons' Wars," "England's Historical

Epistles," and, among the most remarkable descriptive poems in the language, "Poly-olbion, A Choreographical Description of Great Britain." Such works were enormous not only in their proportions but in their popularity; volumes that modern readers would be reluctant to open at all were rushed through edition after edition during the very time that Shakespeare was writing the 30,000 lines of his eight history plays.

If Shakespeare lent his energies to the glorification of England, the benefits were nevertheless mutual. The fact that he worked so early, regularly, and long with history had tremendous impact on his habits as a dramatist and on the character of all his plays. History, and especially history as it was recorded in the English chronicles from which he chiefly worked, was packed with men and events. The dramatist's first necessity was to find how to handle masses of material—persons, incidents, enormous periods of time. With history Shakespeare found himself in the position of a sculptor confronted with a gigantic block from which he must carve a finished statue of relatively small dimensions. He was obliged to reduce it, to sift and select for what would be most significant, to shape it somehow to actable form that would suit the "two hours' traffic of our stage." If there is a single characteristic of Shakespeare's plays—histories, comedies, tragedies alike—that transcends the rest, it is *abundance*. Whether we consider characters, incidents, plots, images, comic figures and situations, or whatever, we always find them present in profusion in the plays. Images pile atop images, incidents atop incidents; Shakespeare never offers a single comic character, but crowds in half a dozen, each of a distinct variety; the mature plays at the center of his career are like three-ring circuses, with action bustling in each ring. Whatever else he may or may not be, Shakespeare is never thin, skimpy in any of the departments of his art. In the middle plays his appetite for dramatic elements of all sorts is voracious; he reaches out in every direction to pull in ever more and pack it into the teeming cauldron at the center. No doubt that, in part at least, this career-long habit of requiring abundance even unto superfluity took its origin in his first necessity as a dramatist, when he labored over mountains of raw historical matter that must somehow be reduced to reasonable compass and beaten into unified and significant dramatic form.

The point is not that his long preoccupation with historical materials made Shakespeare an historian, for it did not; it made him a dramatist, for here he learned his trade. If the habit of abundance underlies his workmanship, the habit of *conflict* pervades it. In the century of history that he dramatized for the main group of history plays, conflict is incessant—conflict between kings, dukes, earls, kingmakers and kingbreakers, those rising and those falling; the conflict of factionalism and of outright war. Treating the English Wars of the Roses, the Peasants' Revolt, the wars of England and France, he could not easily have avoided making conflict a primary condition of dramatic action even if he had wished to do so, or of growing to think of it, indeed, as the very *sine qua non* of dramatic situation and dramatic interest. It was in the histories that Shakespeare mastered the art of representing conflict, though of course conflict is not a staple of the history plays alone; it is at the heart of Shakespearean tragedy, conflict between hero and villain, hero and environment, hero and himself. *Hamlet*, in the hero's own apt description, is "a battle of mighty opposites," and the phrase fits the other tragedies equally well. But, indeed, even Shakespearean comedy is compact of conflict—between rival lovers, hero and heroine, masters and servants, husbands and wives, Jews and Christians, the old and the young. A light fantasy like *A Midsummer Night's Dream* is not only of imagination but of conflict "all compact." Dramatic conflict is not limited to physical confrontations; the very wit duels that occur in nearly all the plays and that virtually dominate some of them is among the more obvious forms that it assumes. Thus most of the sheer excitement, physical and emotional, that characterizes Shakespeare everywhere rises from some base of conflict, the habit of which was at least in part instilled by his experience with the conflicts of history.

Shakespeare would never have become the Shakespeare we know if he had not mastered, early and well, the art of *characterization*, and, once again, it was in writing the first histories that he practiced and acquired that skill in portraiture which, along with the gift of poetry, contributes the ultimate distinction to his plays. It is too emphatic to assert that he would never have mastered the art of characterization but for his early concentration on history; but history provided him with a field for practice such as no other source material could do, and, further, confronted the dramatist with urgent pressure to learn the art. For the chronicles that were his sources teemed with historical personages, most of whom were differentiated by the historians only by name and lineage. Though "real-life" persons, they had no ready-made reality; a dramatic character does not acquire reality merely by having an historical name; historical reality does not automatically confer dramatic reality. In the first three history plays, Shakespeare placed on the stage about one hundred speaking and named characters. He did not succeed in giving individualizing human traits to very many of them; but even in the first histories he achieved several notably sharp delineations, and by the time he wrote the second group of histories he was able to invest all the major characters and masses of minor ones with dramatic reality of astonishing clarity and depth. Among the later history plays are portraits as fully achieved as are those of Hamlet, Lear, Othello, and Macbeth. More pointedly here, perhaps Hamlet, Lear, Othello, and Macbeth would not exist in the dimensions in which we have them had not Shakespeare served his apprenticeship and moved on to the rank of master craftsman by concentrating on the kings, dukes, earls, and their uncles and their cousins and their aunts who made up the roster of English history as he received it in the chronicles and transmuted it to theatrical spectacle.

Finally, from the necessities imposed on him by the rambling and disjointed chronicles, Shakespeare learned and learned well the lesson of dramatic *focus*, without which we should have no tragedy of *Hamlet, Lear, Othello,* or *Macbeth*—indeed, no Shakespearean tragedy at all as we know it. Shakespeare's first histories have virtually no focus; they present successions of events, or episodes, often connected by one messenger after another, each entering in order to announce a new situation or a change in the old one. Even as late as the fourth history, *Richard III*, events threaten to dominate men and to subordinate drama to history. But even before the fourth play, certain individuals had begun to emerge as human beings rather than as mere speakers in a chronicle of incidents. Shakespeare would no doubt have learned to focus upon a center even without undergoing apprenticeship in the unfocused raw materials of history, but he would not have learned his lesson so rapidly; as it was, he mastered his art within five or six plays—well in advance of the period of the great tragedies, which are essentially stories of a single, central hero to whom events are subordinated.

In all, Shakespeare wrote ten history plays—but not in the order in which the kings who give them their titles ruled. He began with a trilogy, *Henry VI, Part 1, Henry VI, Part 2,* and *Henry VI, Part 3;* then he completed the cycle with *Richard III*, making the so-called "first tetralogy," or group of four plays covering a single span of history. Somewhere in the course of writing these plays, he evidently perceived the necessity of exploring the origins of the civil disturbances and outright wars that are depicted in these plays. Hence, having already written what amounted to the end of the story, which came with the violent overthrow and death of Richard III in the battle of Bosworth Field (1485), he dropped back nearly a century to the reign of an earlier Richard and wrote *Richard II, Henry IV, Part 1, Henry IV, Part 2,* and *Henry V*. The following table will clarify the relationship of the historical order to Shakespeare's order of composing the plays.

REGNAL YEARS	ORDER OF COMPOSITION
Richard II, 1377–1399	First Tetralogy
Henry IV, 1399–1413	1, 2, 3 Henry VI (1591–1592)
Henry V, 1413–1422	Richard III (1592–1593)
Henry VI, 1422–1461	Second Tetralogy
Richard III, 1483–1485	Richard II (1595)
	1, 2 Henry IV (1597–1598)
	Henry V (1598–1599)

Aside from the central group of eight plays that cover a single historical sequence, Shakespeare wrote two other histories not particularly relevant here: *King John* (ruled 1199–1216), uncertainly dated but probably 1596–1597; *Henry VIII* (ruled 1509–1547), dated 1612–1613.

The contrast in dramatic craftsmanship between the first and second tetralogies, which is to say between the first and second halves of the decade 1590–1600, during which time Shakespeare's growth as writer of comedy and tragedy kept the pace as well, is very striking. The three parts of *Henry VI*, though they show marked advance beyond the crude chronicle plays written by other playwrights during the three decades before 1590, contain stirring moments, spectacular battle scenes, much impressive pageantry, and an occasional sharp portrait. However, they lack focus and are chronicles of events rather than dramas of individual lives. Human character is subordinated to historical incident; they are all but devoid of the leavening effects of comedy; they contain lengthy, artificial "set" speeches. They have few artistically potent scenes; more often, their art is too obvious, too patently devised—as, for example, in *3Henry VI* (II, v) when, during the civil wars, Shakespeare has, from one side of the stage, "Enter a Father that has killed his son, bringing in the body," and, from the other side, "Enter a Son that has killed his father, dragging in the body," each of whom, in turn, laments the "heavy times begetting such events." Meanwhile, from above, King Henry looks on, and he too delivers a soliloquy of lamentation: "Here sits a King more woeful than you are." A surprisingly effective and moving scene when it is acted, its art is nevertheless too evidently "arranged" and calls attention to itself as Shakespeare's later, greater scenes do not.

But in the latter half of *3Henry VI*, Shakespeare begins to emphasize the character, not merely the role, of the hump-backed Duke of Gloucester, who dominates the final scenes and virtually singlehandedly converts history to living drama. As King Richard III in the final play of the first group (and historically the last of the complete cycle of eight plays) he achieves a dramatic stature that towers over any other that Shakespeare had yet attempted. Garrick, Kemble, Kean, the Booths, Irving—all relished Richard's powerful role no less than they did Hamlet's, and especially Kean, noted for romantic and fiery histrionics, exceeded all his other roles in the performance of the part. To this day the twisted, halting, evil Richard remains a favorite of actors and audiences. In our own century Sir Laurence Olivier's film of *Richard III* remains a classic that was not at all eclipsed by the same actor's *Henry V* and *Hamlet* on film, though of course the latter are greater plays. In America, shortly after the "talkies" succeeded silent films, John Barrymore executed a short feature presenting himself as the hump-backed duke standing atop a heap of skulls; as a virtuoso performance, which, indeed, is what the entire role of Richard is, the Barrymore rendition has never been, and perhaps never will be, surpassed. Even so, *Richard III* as a whole exhibits most of the faults of its immediate predecessors: it subordinates character to event, is melodramatic and spectacular rather than probing, represents a ranting style of speech, and, in short, shows Shakespeare still indecisive about which, in a play, should rule—historical or dramatic fidelity. Like the early Henry plays, it is overly crowded with incidents merely because they were there, in history. He shortly learned better—as the three histories included in this volume will make apparent. The first of these is *Richard II*.

Richard II

DRAMATIS PERSONÆ

KING RICHARD THE SECOND
JOHN OF GAUNT *Duke of Lancaster* } *uncles to the*
EDMUND OF LANGLEY *Duke of York* } *King*
HENRY *surnamed* BOLINGBROKE, *Duke of Hereford,*
  son to John of Gaunt; afterwards KING HENRY IV.
DUKE OF AUMERLE *son to the Duke of York*
THOMAS MOWBRAY *Duke of Norfolk*
DUKE OF SURREY
EARL OF SALISBURY
LORD BERKELEY
BUSHY }
BAGOT } *servants to King Richard*
GREEN }
EARL OF NORTHUMBERLAND
HENRY PERCY *surnamed Hotspur, his son*
LORD ROSS

LORD WILLOUGHBY
LORD FITZWATER
BISHOP *of Carlisle*
ABBOT *of Westminster*
LORD MARSHAL
SIR STEPHEN SCROOP
SIR PIERCE OF EXTON
CAPTAIN *of a band of Welshmen*
QUEEN *to King Richard*
DUCHESS OF YORK
DUCHESS OF GLOUCESTER
LADY *attending on the Queen*
LORDS, HERALDS, OFFICERS, SOLDIERS, *two* GAR-
  DENERS, KEEPER, MESSENGER, GROOM, *and other*
  ATTENDANTS.
SCENE *England and Wales*

ACT I

SCENE i
London. KING RICHARD'S *palace.*

[*Enter* KING RICHARD, JOHN OF GAUNT, *with other*
NOBLES *and* ATTENDANTS.]

KING RICHARD. Old John of Gaunt, time-honor'd
    Lancaster,
  Hast thou, according to thy oath and band,°
  Brought hither Henry Hereford thy bold son,
  Here to make good the boist'rous late appeal,°
5 Which then our leisure would not let us hear,
  Against the Duke of Norfolk, Thomas Mow-
    bray?
GAUNT. I have, my liege.
KING RICHARD. Tell me, moreover, hast thou
    sounded him

If he appeal the duke on ancient malice,°
Or worthily, as a good subject should,   10
On some known ground of treachery in him?
GAUNT. As near as I could sift him on that argu-
    ment,
  On some apparent danger seen in him
  Aim'd at your highness—no inveterate malice.
KING RICHARD. Then call them to our presence.
    Face to face   15
  And frowning brow to brow, ourselves will hear
  Th' accuser and th' accused freely speak;
  High-stomach'd° are they both, and full of ire,
  In rage deaf as the sea, hasty as fire.
        [*Enter* BOLINGBROKE *and* MOWBRAY.]
BOLINGBROKE. Many years of happy days befall   20

band bond   *appeal* accusation (of treason)

on . . . malice from ancient grudge
High-stomach'd high-spirited

III

My gracious sovereign, my most loving liege!
MOWBRAY. Each day still better other's happiness,
Until the heavens, envying earth's good hap,°
Add an immortal title to your crown!
KING RICHARD. We thank you both. Yet one but
25   flatters us,
As well appeareth by the cause you come,
Namely, t'appeal each other of high treason.
Cousin of Hereford, what dost thou object
Against the Duke of Norfolk, Thomas Mow-
bray?
BOLINGBROKE. First, heaven be the record of my
30   speech!
In the devotion of a subject's love,
Tend'ring the precious safety of my prince,
And free from other misbegotten hate,
Come I appellant° to this princely presence.
35 Now, Thomas Mowbray, do I turn to thee;
And mark my greeting well, for what I speak
My body shall make good upon this earth,
Or my divine soul answer it in heaven.
Thou art a traitor and a miscreant,°
40 Too good to be so, and too bad to live,
Since the more fair and crystal is the sky,
The uglier seem the clouds that in it fly.
Once more, the more to aggravate the note,°
With a foul traitor's name stuff I thy throat
45 And wish, so please my sovereign, ere I move,
What my tongue speaks my right drawn sword
may prove.
MOWBRAY. Let not my cold words here accuse°
my zeal:
'Tis not the trial of a woman's war,
The bitter clamor of two eager tongues,
50 Can arbitrate this cause betwixt us twain.
The blood is hot that must be cool'd for this.
Yet can I not of such tame patience boast
As to be hush'd and naught at all to say.
First, the fair reverence of your highness curbs
me
55 From giving reins and spurs to my free speech,
Which else would post° until it had return'd
These terms of treason doubled down his throat.
Setting aside his high blood's royalty,
And let him be no kinsman to my liege,
60 I do defy him, and I spit at him,
Call him a sland'rous coward and a villain,
Which to maintain I would allow him odds
And meet him, were I tied° to run afoot

Even to the frozen ridges of the Alps
Or any other ground inhabitable°   65
Where ever Englishman durst set his foot.
Meantime let this defend my loyalty:
By all my hopes, most falsely doth he lie.
BOLINGBROKE. Pale trembling coward, there I
throw my gage,°
Disclaiming here the kindred of the king,   70
And lay aside my high blood's royalty,
Which fear, not reverence, makes thee to
except.
If guilty dread have left thee so much strength
As to take up mine honor's pawn, then stoop.
By that and all the rites of knighthood else   75
Will I make good against thee, arm to arm,
What I have spoke or thou canst worse devise.
MOWBRAY. I take it up, and by that sword I swear,
Which gently laid my knighthood on my
shoulder,
I'll answer thee in any fair degree°   80
Or chivalrous design of knightly trial.
And when I mount, alive may I not light
If I be traitor or unjustly fight!
KING RICHARD. What doth our cousin lay to Mow-
bray's charge?
It must be great that can inherit us°   85
So much as of a thought of ill in him.
BOLINGBROKE. Look, what I speak, my life shall
prove it true—
That Mowbray hath receiv'd eight thousand
nobles°
In name of lendings for your highness' soldiers,
The which he hath detain'd for lewd employ-
ments   90
Like a false traitor and injurious villain.
Besides I say and will in battle prove,
Or here or° elsewhere to the furthest verge
That ever was survey'd by English eye,
That all the treasons for these eighteen years   95
Complotted and contrived in this land
Fetch from false Mowbray their first head and
spring.
Further I say, and further will maintain
Upon his bad life to make all this good,
That he did plot the Duke of Gloucester's death, 100
Suggest° his soon-believing adversaries,
And consequently,° like a traitor coward,
Sluic'd out his innocent soul through streams of
blood

---

hap luck   appellant as accuser
miscreant (villainous) unbeliever
aggravate the note add to the insult
accuse seem to qualify
post ride hard   tied bound (obliged)

inhabitable uninhabitable
gage glove, as token of defiance
fair degree i.e., according to chivalric rules
inherit us cause me to possess   nobles gold coins
Or . . . or either . . . or   Suggest incite
consequently subsequently

Which blood, like sacrificing Abel's,° cries
105   Even from the tongueless caverns of the earth
To me for justice and rough chastisement.
And by the glorious worth of my descent
This arm shall do it, or this life be spent.
KING RICHARD. How high a pitch his resolution soars!
110   Thomas of Norfolk, what say'st thou to this?
MOWBRAY. O, let my sovereign turn away his face
And bid his ears a little while be deaf
Till I have told this slander of his blood
How God and good men hate so foul a liar.
KING RICHARD. Mowbray, impartial are our eyes
115   and ears.
Were he my brother, nay, my kingdom's heir,
As he is but my father's brother's son,
Now by my sceptre's awe I make a vow,
Such neighbor nearness to our sacred blood
120   Should nothing privilege him, nor partialize
Th' unstooping firmness of my upright soul.
He is our subject, Mowbray; so art thou.
Free speech and fearless I to thee allow.
MOWBRAY. Then, Bolingbroke, as low as to thy heart,
Through the false passage of thy throat, thou
125   liest.
Three parts of that receipt I had for Calais
Disburs'd I duly to his highness' soldiers;
The other part reserv'd I by consent,
For that° my sovereign liege was in my debt
130   Upon remainder of a dear account°
Since last I went to France to fetch his queen.
Now swallow down that lie. For Gloucester's death,
I slew him not, but to my own disgrace
Neglected my sworn duty in that case.
135   For you, my noble Lord of Lancaster,
The honorable father to my foe,
Once did I lay an ambush for your life,
A trespass that doth vex my grieved soul.
But ere I last receiv'd the sacrament
140   I did confess it and exactly begg'd
Your grace's pardon, and I hope I had it.
This is my fault. As for the rest appeal'd,
It issues from the rancor of a villain,
A recreant and most degenerate traitor—
145   Which in myself I boldly will defend,
And interchangeably hurl down my gage
Upon this overweening traitor's foot,
To prove myself a loyal gentleman
Even in the best blood chamber'd in his bosom.
150   In haste whereof, most heartily I pray

Your highness to assign our trial day.
KING RICHARD. Wrath-kindled gentlemen, be rul'd by me:
Let's purge this choler° without letting blood.
This we prescribe, though no physician;
Deep malice makes too deep incision.   155
Forget, forgive, conclude, and be agreed.
Our doctors say this is no month to bleed.
Good uncle, let this end where it begun;
We'll calm the Duke of Norfolk, you your son.
GAUNT. To be a make-peace shall become my age.   160
Throw down, my son, the Duke of Norfolk's gage.
KING RICHARD. And, Norfolk, throw down his.
GAUNT. When, Harry, when?
Obedience bids I should not bid again.
KING RICHARD. Norfolk, throw down, we bid;
there is no boot.°
MOWBRAY. Myself I throw, dread sovereign, at thy foot.   165
My life thou shalt command, but not my shame.
The one my duty owes,° but my fair name,
Despite of death that lives upon my grave,
To dark dishonor's use thou shalt not have.
I am disgrac'd, impeach'd, and baffled° here,   170
Pierc'd to the soul with slander's venom'd spear,
The which no balm can cure but his heartblood
Which breath'd this poison.
KING RICHARD.   Rage must be withstood.
Give me his gage. Lions make leopards tame.
MOWBRAY. Yea, but not change his spots. Take but my shame,   175
And I resign my gage. My dear dear lord,
The purest treasure mortal times afford
Is spotless reputation. That away,
Men are but gilded loam or painted clay.
A jewel in a ten-times-barr'd-up chest   180
Is a bold spirit in a loyal breast.
Mine honor is my life; both grow in one;
Take honor from me, and my life is done.
Then, dear my liege, mine honor let me try;°
In that I live, and for that will I die.   185
KING RICHARD. Cousin, throw up your gage. Do you begin.
BOLINGBROKE. O, God defend my soul from such deep sin!
Shall I seem crestfall'n in my father's sight?
Or with pale beggar-fear impeach my height°
Before this out-dar'd dastard? Ere my tongue   190

---

sacrificing Abel's (see *Genesis*, iv, 10)
For that because   *dear account* large debt

choler anger
no boot i.e., no other choice   *owes* owns
baffled degraded   *try* prove   *height* high rank

Shall wound my honor with such feeble wrong,
Or sound so base a parle, my teeth shall tear
The slavish motive of recanting fear
And spit it bleeding in his high disgrace
Where shame doth harbor, even in Mowbray's
195 face.   [*Exit* GAUNT.]
KING RICHARD. We were not born to sue, but to
    command;
Which since we cannot do to make you friends,
Be ready, as your lives shall answer it,
At Coventry, upon Saint Lambert's day.°
200 There shall your swords and lances arbitrate
The swelling diff'rence of your settled hate.
Since we cannot atone° you, we shall see
Justice design the victor's chivalry.°
Lord marshal, command our officers at arms
205 Be ready to direct these home alarms.°
                                        [*Exeunt*]

SCENE ii
The DUKE OF LANCASTER's *palace.*

[*Enter* JOHN OF GAUNT *with the* DUCHESS OF
    GLOUCESTER.]
GAUNT. Alas, the part I had in Woodstock's° blood
Doth more solicit me than your exclaims
To stir against the butchers of his life!
But since correction lieth in those hands°
5   Which made the fault that we cannot correct,
Put we our quarrel to the will of heaven,
Who when they see the hours ripe on earth
Will rain hot vengeance on offenders' heads.
DUCHESS OF GLOUCESTER. Finds brotherhood in
    thee no sharper spur?
10 Hath love in thy old blood no living fire?
Edward's° seven sons, whereof thyself art one,
Were as seven vials of his sacred blood,
Or seven fair branches springing from one root.
Some of those seven are dried by nature's
    course,
15 Some of those branches by the Destinies° cut,
But Thomas,° my dear lord, my life, my
    Gloucester,

One vial full of Edward's sacred blood,
One flourishing branch of his most royal root,
Is crack'd and all the precious liquor spilt,
Is hack'd down and his summer leaves all faded, 20
By envy's hand and murder's bloody axe.
Ah, Gaunt, his blood was thine! That bed, that
    womb,
That metal, that self-mould° that fashion'd thee
Made him a man; and though thou liv'st and
    breath'st,
Yet art thou slain in him. Thou dost consent 25
In some large measure to thy father's death
In that thou seest thy wretched brother die,
Who was the model of thy father's life.
Call it not patience, Gaunt; it is despair.
In suff'ring thus thy brother to be slaughter'd, 30
Thou show'st the naked pathway to thy life,
Teaching stern murder how to butcher thee.
That which in mean men we entitle patience
Is pale cold cowardice in noble breasts.
What shall I say? To safeguard thine own life, 35
The best way is to venge my Gloucester's death.
GAUNT. God's is the quarrel, for God's substitute,°
His deputy anointed in His sight,
Hath caus'd his death; the which if wrongfully,
Let heaven revenge, for I may never lift 40
An angry arm against His minister.
DUCHESS OF GLOUCESTER. Where then, alas, may I
    complain myself?
GAUNT. To God, the widow's champion and
    defense.
DUCHESS OF GLOUCESTER. Why, then, I will. Fare-
    well, old Gaunt.
Thou goest to Coventry, there to behold 45
Our cousin Hereford and fell° Mowbray fight.
O, sit my husband's wrongs on Hereford's
    spear,
That it may enter butcher Mowbray's breast!
Or, if misfortune miss the first career,°
Be Mowbray's sins so heavy in his bosom 50
That they may break his foaming courser's back
And throw the rider headlong in the lists,
A caitiff recreant to° my cousin Hereford!
Farewell, old Gaunt. Thy sometimes° brother's
    wife
With her companion grief must end her life. 55
GAUNT. Sister, farewell; I must to Coventry.
As much good stay with thee as go with me!
DUCHESS OF GLOUCESTER. Yet one word more.
    Grief boundeth° where it falls,

Saint Lambert's day September 17   *atone* reconcile
Justice . . . chivalry i.e., trial by combat will disclose who
    is true
home alarms domestic troubles
Woodstock the Duke of Gloucester, Gaunt's brother
those hands King Richard's hands
Edward Edward III [father of Gaunt, Gloucester,
    Edward the Black Prince (Richard's father), William of
    Hatfield, Duke of Clarence, Duke of York, William of
    Windsor (died in infancy)]
Destinies the three Fates
Thomas i.e., of Woodstock, Duke of Gloucester

self-mould selfsame mould
God's substitute i.e., Richard   *fell* cruel
career charge   *caitiff recreant to* slave vanquished by
sometimes sometime; i.e., "late"
boundeth i.e., like a ball

Not with the empty hollowness,° but weight.°
60 I take my leave before I have begun,
For sorrow ends not when it seemeth done.
Commend me to thy brother, Edmund York.
Lo, this is all.—Nay, yet depart not so.
Though this be all, do not so quickly go;
65 I shall remember more. Bid him—ah, what?—
With all good speed at Plashy visit me.
Alack, and what shall good old York there see
But empty lodgings and unfurnish'd walls,
Unpeopled offices, untrodden stones?
And what hear there for welcome but my
70   groans?
Therefore commend me; let him not come
    there,
To see out sorrow that dwells everywhere.
Desolate, desolate, will I hence and die.
The last leave of thee takes my weeping eye.
                              [Exeunt]

SCENE iii
The lists at Coventry.

[*Enter the* LORD MARSHAL *and the* DUKE OF
AUMERLE.]
MARSHAL. My Lord Aumerle, is Harry Hereford
    arm'd?
AUMERLE. Yea, at all points, and longs to enter in.
MARSHAL. The Duke of Norfolk, sprightfully and
    bold,
Stays but the summons of th' appellant's
    trumpet.
AUMERLE. Why, then, the champions are prepar'd,
5   and stay
For nothing but his majesty's approach.
[*The trumpets sound, and the* KING *enters with his
nobles,* GAUNT, BUSHY, BAGOT, GREEN, *and others.
When they are set, enter* MOWBRAY *in arms,
defendant, with a* HERALD.]
KING RICHARD. Marshal, demand of yonder
    champion
The cause of his arrival here in arms.
Ask him his name, and orderly proceed
10 To swear him in the justice of his cause.
MARSHAL. In God's name and the king's, say who
    thou art
And why thou com'st thus knightly clad in
    arms,
Against what man thou com'st, and what thy
    quarrel.
Speak truly, on thy knighthood and thy oath,
15 As so defend thee heaven and thy valor!

MOWBRAY. My name is Thomas Mowbray, Duke
    of Norfolk,
Who hither come engaged by my oath—
Which God defend° a knight should violate!—
Both to defend my loyalty and truth
To God, my king, and my succeeding issue   20
Against the Duke of Hereford that appeals me;
And, by the grace of God and this mine arm,
To prove him, in defending of myself,
A traitor to my God, my king, and me.
And as I truly fight, defend me heaven!   25
    [*The trumpets sound. Enter* BOLINGBROKE,
      appellant, in armor, with a HERALD.]
KING RICHARD. Marshal, ask yonder knight in
    arms
Both who he is and why he cometh hither
Thus plated° in habiliments of war,
And formally, according to our law,
Depose him° in the justice of his cause.   30
MARSHAL. What is thy name? And wherefore
    com'st thou hither
Before King Richard in his royal lists?
Against whom comest thou? And what's thy
    quarrel?
Speak like a true knight, so defend thee heaven!
BOLINGBROKE. Harry of Hereford, Lancaster, and
    Derby   35
Am I, who ready here do stand in arms
To prove by God's grace and my body's valor
In lists, on Thomas Mowbray, Duke of Norfolk,
That he is a traitor, foul and dangerous
To God of heaven, King Richard, and to me;   40
And as I truly fight, defend me heaven!
MARSHAL. On pain of death, no person be so bold
Or daring-hardy° as to touch the lists
Except the marshal and such officers
Appointed to direct these fair designs.   45
BOLINGBROKE. Lord marshal, let me kiss my
    sovereign's hand
And bow my knee before his majesty,
For Mowbray and myself are like two men
That vow a long and weary pilgrimage;
Then let us take a ceremonious leave   50
And loving farewell of our several friends.
MARSHAL. Th' appellant in all duty greets your
    highness
And craves to kiss your hand and take his leave.
KING RICHARD. We will descend and fold him in
    our arms.
Cousin of Hereford, as thy cause is right,   55
So be thy fortune in this royal fight!

---

empty hollowness i.e., of a ball   *weight* heavily

defend forbid   *plated* armor-plated
Depose him i.e., take his deposition
daring-hardy overbold

Farewell, my blood, which if today thou shed,
Lament we may, but not revenge thee dead.
BOLINGBROKE. O, let no noble eye profane a tear°
60　For me if I be gor'd with Mowbray's spear.
As confident as is the falcon's flight
Against a bird do I with Mowbray fight.
My loving lord, I take my leave of you;
Of you, my noble cousin, Lord Aumerle;
65　Not sick, although I have to do with death,
But lusty, young, and cheerly drawing breath.
Lo, as at English feasts, so I regreet°
The daintiest last, to make the end most sweet.
O thou, the earthly author of my blood,
70　Whose youthful spirit, in me regenerate,
Doth with a twofold vigor lift me up
To reach at victory above my head,
Add proof° unto mine armor with thy prayers
And with thy blessings steel my lance's point
75　That it may enter Mowbray's waxen° coat
And furbish new the name of John a° Gaunt
Even in the lusty havior of his son.
GAUNT. God in thy good cause make thee pros-
　　perous!
Be swift like lightning in the execution,
80　And let thy blows, doubly redoubled,
Fall like amazing thunder on the casque
Of thy adverse pernicious enemy.
Rouse up thy youthful blood, be valiant, and
　　live.
BOLINGBROKE. Mine innocency and Saint George to
　　thrive!
85　MOWBRAY. However God or fortune cast my lot,
There lives or dies, true to King Richard's
　　throne,
A loyal, just, and upright gentleman.
Never did captive with a freer heart
Cast off his chains of bondage and embrace
90　His golden uncontroll'd enfranchisement
More than my dancing soul doth celebrate
This feast of battle with mine adversary.
Most mighty liege, and my companion peers,
Take from my mouth the wish of happy years.
95　As gentle and as jocund as to jest
Go I to fight. Truth hath a quiet breast.
KING RICHARD. Farewell, my lord. Securely I espy
Virtue with valor couched in thine eye.
Order the trial, marshal, and begin.
MARSHAL. Harry of Hereford, Lancaster, and
100　Derby,
Receive thy lance; and God defend the right!

BOLINGBROKE. Strong as a tower in hope, I cry
　　amen.
MARSHAL. Go bear this lance to Thomas, Duke of
　　Norfolk.
FIRST HERALD. Harry of Hereford, Lancaster, and
　　Derby
Stands here for God, his sovereign, and himself　105
On pain to be found false and recreant,
To prove the Duke of Norfolk, Thomas Mow-
　　bray,
A traitor to his God, his king, and him,
And dares him to set forward to the fight.
SECOND HERALD. Here standeth Thomas Mowbray,
　　Duke of Norfolk,　　　　　　　　　　　　110
On pain to be found false and recreant,
Both to defend and to approve
Henry of Hereford, Lancaster, and Derby
To God, his sovereign, and to him disloyal,
Courageously and with a free desire　　　　　115
Attending but the signal to begin.
MARSHAL. Sound, trumpets, and set forward,
　　combatants.　　　　　　　　[A charge sounded.]
Stay! The king hath thrown his warder down.
KING RICHARD. Let them lay by their helmets and
　　their spears
And both return back to their chairs again.　120
Withdraw with us, and let the trumpets sound
While we return these dukes what we decree.
　　　　　　　　　　　　　　　[A long flourish.]
Draw near
And list what with our council we have done.
For that our kingdom's earth should not be
　　soil'd　　　　　　　　　　　　　　　125
With that dear blood which it hath fostered,
And for our eyes do hate the dire aspect
Of civil wounds plough'd up with neighbors'
　　sword,
And for we think the eagle-winged pride
Of sky-aspiring and ambitious thoughts　　　130
With rival-hating envy set on you
To wake our peace, which in our country's
　　cradle
Draws the sweet infant breath of gentle sleep—
Which so rous'd up with boist'rous untun'd
　　drums,
With harsh-resounding trumpets' dreadful bray　135
And grating shock of wrathful iron arms
Might from our quiet confines fright fair peace
And make us wade even in our kindred's
　　blood—
Therefore we banish you our territories.
You, cousin Hereford, upon pain of life,　　　140
Till twice five summers have enrich'd our fields,
Shall not regreet our fair dominions,
But tread the stranger paths of banishment.

profane a tear　i.e., to lose would be to prove his treason;
　　hence a tear for his loss would be unholy
regreet　greet　　proof　armor
waxen　i.e., as though it were made of wax　　a　of

BOLINGBROKE. Your will be done. This must my
   comfort be:
145   That sun that warms you here shall shine on me,
   And those his golden beams to you here lent
   Shall point on me and gild my banishment.
KING RICHARD. Norfolk, for thee remains a heavier
   doom,
   Which I with some unwillingness pronounce.
150   The sly slow hours shall not determinate
   The dateless limit of thy dear° exile;
   The hopeless word of "never to return"
   Breathe I against thee, upon pain of life.
MOWBRAY. A heavy sentence, my most sovereign
   liege,
   And all unlook'd for from your highness'
155   mouth.
   A dearer merit, not so deep a maim
   As to be cast forth in the common air,
   Have I deserved at your highness' hands.
   The language I have learn'd these forty years,
160   My native English, now I must forgo,
   And now my tongue's use is to me no more
   Than an unstringed viol or a harp,
   Or like a cunning instrument cas'd up,
   Or, being open, put into his hands
165   That knows no touch to tune the harmony.
   Within my mouth you have enjail'd my tongue,
   Doubly portcullis'd° with my teeth and lips,
   And dull unfeeling barren ignorance
   Is made my jailer to attend on me.
170   I am too old to fawn upon a nurse,
   Too far in years to be a pupil now.
   What is thy sentence then but speechless death,
   Which robs my tongue from breathing native
   breath?
KING RICHARD. It boots° thee not to be com-
   passionate.
175   After our sentence plaining° comes too late.
MOWBRAY. Then thus I turn me from my country's
   light
   To dwell in solemn shades of endless night.
KING RICHARD. Return again and take an oath with
   thee.
   Lay on our royal sword your banish'd hands;
180   Swear by the duty that you owe to God—
   Our part therein we banish with yourselves—
   To keep the oath that we adminster.
   You never shall, so help you truth and God,
   Embrace each other's love in banishment,
185   Nor never look upon each other's face,
   Nor never write, regreet, nor reconcile

This louring° tempest of your home-bred hate,
   Nor never by advised purpose meet
   To plot, contrive, or complot any ill
   'Gainst us, our state, our subjects, or our land.   190
BOLINGBROKE. I swear.
MOWBRAY. And I, to keep all this.
BOLINGBROKE. Norfolk, so far as° to mine enemy:
   By this time, had the king permitted us,
   One of our souls had wander'd in the air,   195
   Banish'd this frail sepulcher of our flesh,
   As now our flesh is banish'd from this land.
   Confess thy treasons ere thou fly the realm;
   Since thou hast far to go, bear not along
   The clogging burthen of a guilty soul.   200
MOWBRAY. No, Bolingbroke. If ever I were traitor,
   My name be blotted from the book of life
   And I from heaven banish'd as from hence!
   But what thou art, God, thou, and I do know,
   And all too soon, I fear, the king shall rue.   205
   Farewell, my liege. Now no way can I stray;
   Save back to England, all the world's my way.
                             [*Exit*]
KING RICHARD. Uncle, even in the glasses of thine
   eyes
   I see thy grieved heart. Thy sad aspect
   Hath from the number of his banish'd years   210
   Pluck'd four away. [*To* BOLINGBROKE] Six frozen
   winters spent,
   Return with welcome home from banishment.
BOLINGBROKE. How long a time lies in one little
   word!
   Four lagging winters and four wanton springs
   End in a word. Such is the breath of kings.   215
GAUNT. I thank my liege, that in regard of me
   He shortens four years of my son's exile.
   But little vantage shall I reap thereby,
   For ere the six years that he hath to spend
   Can change their moons and bring their times
   about,   220
   My oil-dried lamp and time-bewasted light
   Shall be extinct with age and endless night:
   My inch of taper will be burnt and done,
   And blindfold death not let me see my son.
KING RICHARD. Why, uncle, thou hast many years
   to live.   225
GAUNT. But not a minute, king, that thou canst
   give.
   Shorten my days thou canst with sullen sorrow,
   And pluck nights from me, but not lend a
   morrow;
   Thou canst help time to furrow me with age,
   But stop no wrinkle in his pilgrimage.   230

---

dear costly (heavy)
portcullis'd locked in as with a grating
boots avails   *plaining* complaining

louring lowering (threatening)
so far as i.e., so far as I may speak

Thy word is current° with him for my death,
But dead, thy kingdom cannot buy my breath.
KING RICHARD. Thy son is banish'd upon good
   advice,
Whereto thy tongue a party-verdict gave.
235   Why at our justice seem'st thou then to lour?°
GAUNT. Things sweet to taste prove in digestion
   sour.
You urg'd me as a judge, but I had rather
You would have bid me argue like a father.
O, had it been a stranger, not my child,
To smooth his fault I should have been more
240   mild.
A partial slander° sought I to avoid,
And in the sentence my own life destroy'd.
Alas, I look'd when some of you should say
I was too strict to make mine own away;
245   But you gave leave to my unwilling tongue
Against my will to do myself this wrong.
KING RICHARD. Cousin, farewell, and, uncle, bid
   him so.
Six years we banish him, and he shall go.
      [Flourish. Exeunt KING RICHARD and TRAIN.]
AUMERLE. Cousin, farewell. What presence must
   not know,°
250   From where you do remain let paper show.
MARSHAL. My lord, no leave take I, for I will ride
As far as land will let me, by your side.
GAUNT. O, to what purpose dost thou hoard thy
   words,
That thou return'st no greeting to thy friends?
BOLINGBROKE. I have too few to take my leave of
255   you,
When the tongue's office should be prodigal
To breathe the abundant dolor of the heart.
GAUNT. Thy grief is but thy absence for a time.
BOLINGBROKE. Joy absent, grief is present for that
   time.
260   GAUNT. What is six winters? They are quickly gone.
BOLINGBROKE. To men in joy; but grief makes one
   hour ten.
GAUNT. Call it a travel that thou tak'st for pleasure.
BOLINGBROKE. My heart will sigh when I miscall it
   so,
Which finds it an enforced pilgrimage.
265   GAUNT. The sullen passage of thy weary steps
Esteem as foil° wherein thou art to set
The precious jewel of thy home return.
BOLINGBROKE. Nay, rather, every tedious stride I
   make

Will but remember me what a deal of world
I wander from the jewels that I love.   270
Must I not serve a long apprenticehood
To foreign passages, and in the end,
Having my freedom, boast of nothing else
But that I was a journeyman to grief?°
GAUNT. All places that the eye of heaven visits   275
Are to a wise man ports and happy havens.
Teach thy necessity to reason thus:
There is no virtue like necessity.
Think not the king did banish thee,
But thou the king. Woe doth the heavier sit   280
Where it perceives it is but faintly borne.
Go, say I sent thee forth to purchase honor,
And not the king exil'd thee; or suppose
Devouring pestilence hangs in our air
And thou art flying to a fresher clime.   285
Look, what thy soul holds dear, imagine it
To lie that way thou go'st, not whence thou
   com'st.
Suppose the singing birds musicians,
The grass whereon thou tread'st the presence°
   strew'd,°
The flowers fair ladies, and thy steps no more   290
Than a delightful measure or a dance;
For gnarling° sorrow hath less power to bite
The man that mocks at it and sets it light.
BOLINGBROKE. O, who can hold a fire in his hand
By thinking on the frosty Caucasus?   295
Or cloy the hungry edge of appetite
By bare imagination of a feast?
Or wallow naked in December snow
By thinking on fantastic summer's heat?
O, no! The apprehension of the good   300
Gives but the greater feeling to the worse.
Fell° sorrow's tooth doth never rankle more
Than when he bites, but lanceth not the sore.
GAUNT. Come, come, my son, I'll bring thee on
   thy way.
Had I thy youth and cause, I would not stay.   305
BOLINGBROKE. Then, England's ground, farewell;
   sweet soil, adieu,
My mother, and my nurse, that bears me yet!
Where'er I wander, boast of this I can,
Though banish'd, yet a trueborn Englishman.
                                          [Exeunt]

---

current valid (legal tender)   lour look black
partial slander i.e., charge of partiality
What . . . know i.e., what you cannot say before the king
foil bright metal used to set off a gem (see 1HIV, I,
   ii, 232)

journeyman to grief hired worker in the service of grief
   (with pun: journeyer to grief)
presence the royal Presence Chamber
strew'd i.e., with rushes
gnarling snarling (but suggesting also growling,
   gnawing)
Fell cruel

SCENE iv
The court.

[*Enter the* KING, *with* BAGOT *and* GREEN *at one door, and the* DUKE OF AUMERLE *at another.*]

KING RICHARD. We did observe. Cousin Aumerle,
  How far brought you high Hereford on his way?
AUMERLE. I brought high Hereford, if you call him
    so,
  But to the next highway, and there I left him.
KING RICHARD. And say what store of parting tears
5   were shed?
AUMERLE. Faith, none for me—except the north-
    east wind,
  Which then blew bitterly against our faces,
  Awak'd the sleeping rheum, and so by chance
  Did grace our hollow parting with a tear.
KING RICHARD. What said our cousin when you
10   parted with him?
AUMERLE. "Farewell."
  And, for my heart disdained that my tongue
  Should so profane the word, that taught me
    craft
  To counterfeit oppression of such grief
15 That words seem'd buried in my sorrow's grave.
  Marry,° would the word "farewell" have
    lengthen'd hours
  And added years to his short banishment,
  He should have had a volume of farewells;
  But since it would not, he had none of me.
KING RICHARD. He is our cousin, cousin; but 'tis
20   doubt,
  When time shall call him home from banish-
    ment,
  Whether our kinsman come to see his friends.
  Ourself and Bushy, Bagot here, and Green
  Observ'd his courtship to the common people—
25 How he did seem to dive into their hearts
  With humble and familiar courtesy,
  What reverence he did throw away on slaves,
  Wooing poor craftsmen with the craft of smiles
  And patient underbearing° of his fortune
30 As 'twere to banish their affects° with him.
  Off goes his bonnet to an oyster-wench;

A brace of draymen bid God speed him well
  And had the tribute of his supple knee
  With "Thanks, my countrymen, my loving
    friends,"
  As were our England in reversion° his,   35
  And he our subjects' next degree in hope.°
GREEN. Well, he is gone, and with him go these
    thoughts.
  Now for the rebels which stand out in Ireland,
  Expedient manage° must be made, my liege,
  Ere further leisure yield them further means   40
  For their advantage and your highness' loss.
KING RICHARD. We will ourself in person to this
    war,
  And for our coffers, with too great a court
  And liberal largess,° are grown somewhat
    light,
  We are enforc'd to farm° our royal realm,   45
  The revenue whereof shall furnish us
  For our affairs in hand. If that come short,
  Our substitutes at home shall have blank
    charters,
  Whereto, when they shall know what men are
    rich,
  They shall subscribe them for large sums of
    gold   50
  And send them after to supply our wants;
  For we will make for Ireland presently.°
                              [*Enter* BUSHY.]
  Bushy, what news?
BUSHY. Old John of Gaunt is grievous sick, my
    lord,
  Suddenly taken, and hath sent posthaste   55
  T' entreat your majesty to visit him.
KING RICHARD. Where lies he?
BUSHY. At Ely House.
KING RICHARD. Now put it, God, in the physician's
    mind
  To help him to his grave immediately!   60
  The lining of his coffers shall make coats°
  To deck our soldiers for these Irish wars.
  Come, gentlemen, let's all go visit him.
  Pray God we may make haste—and come too
    late!
ALL. Amen.   [*Exeunt*]   65

Marry by the Virgin   *underbearing* endurance
affects affections

in reversion by right of succession
next . . . hope i.e., heir presumptive
Expedient manage quick action
liberal largess lavish gift-giving   *farm* lease
presently immediately   *coats* i.e., of mail

ACT II

SCENE i
Ely House.

[*Enter* JOHN OF GAUNT *sick, with the* DUKE OF
YORK, *etc.*]

GAUNT. Will the king come, that I may breathe
  my last
  In wholesome counsel to his unstaid youth?
YORK. Vex not yourself, nor strive not with your
  breath,
  For all in vain comes counsel to his ear.
5 GAUNT. O, but they say the tongues of dying men
  Enforce attention like deep harmony.
  Where words are scarce, they are seldom spent
    in vain,
  For they breathe truth that breathe their words
    in pain.
  He that no more must say is listen'd more
  Than they whom youth and ease have taught
10   to glose;°
  More are men's ends mark'd than their lives
    before.
  The setting sun, and music at the close,
  As the last taste of sweets, is sweetest last,
  Writ in remembrance more than things long
    past.
  Though Richard my life's counsel would not
15   hear,
  My death's sad tale may yet undeaf his ear.
YORK. No, it is stopp'd with other, flatt'ring
  sounds—
  As praises, of whose taste the wise are fond;
  Lascivious meters, to whose venom sound
20 The open ear of youth doth always listen;
  Report of fashions in proud Italy,
  Whose manners still° our tardy apish nation
  Limps after in base imitation.
  Where doth the world thrust forth a vanity—
25 So it be new, there's no respect° how vile—
  That is not quickly buzz'd into his ears?
  Then all too late comes counsel to be heard
  Where will doth mutiny with wit's regard.°
  Direct not him whose way himself will choose.
  'Tis breath thou lack'st, and that breath wilt
30   thou lose.

glose speak flatteringly
still always   *there's no respect* it matters not
Where . . . regard where personal inclination mutinies
  against the way of wisdom

GAUNT. Methinks I am a prophet new inspir'd
  And thus expiring do foretell of him:
  His rash fierce blaze of riot cannot last,
  For violent fires soon burn out themselves;
  Small showers last long, but sudden storms are
35   short;
  He tires betimes° that spurs too fast betimes;°
  With eager feeding food doth choke the feeder;
  Light vanity, insatiate cormorant,°
  Consuming means, soon preys upon itself.
40 This royal throne of kings, this scepter'd isle,
  This earth of majesty, this seat of Mars,
  This other Eden, demi-paradise,
  This fortress built by Nature for herself
  Against infection and the hand of war,
45 This happy breed of men, this little world,
  This precious stone set in the silver sea
  Which serves it in the office of a wall
  Or as a moat defensive to a house
  Against the envy of less happier lands,
  This blessed plot, this earth, this realm, this
    England,
50 This nurse, this teeming womb of royal kings,
  Fear'd by their breed° and famous by their
    birth,
  Renowned for their deeds as far from home,
  For Christian service and true chivalry,
55 As is the sepulcher in stubborn Jewry
  Of the world's ransom, blessed Mary's Son:
  This land of such dear souls, this dear dear land,
  Dear for her reputation through the world,
  Is now leas'd out—I die pronouncing it—
60 Like to a tenement or pelting° farm.
  England, bound in with the triumphant sea,
  Whose rocky shore beats back the envious siege
  Of wat'ry Neptune, is now bound in with
    shame,
  With inky blots and rotten parchment bonds.°
65 That England that was wont to conquer others,
  Hath made a shameful conquest of itself.
  Ah, would the scandal vanish with my life,
  How happy then were my ensuing death!
  Enter KING RICHARD *and* QUEEN, AUMERLE,
  BUSHY, GREEN, BAGOT, ROSS, *and* WILLOUGHBY.]

betimes early   *cormorant* glutton
Fear'd . . . breed feared for their (warlike) ancestry
pelting paltry
inky . . . bonds i.e., the documents by which Richard
leased out the lands

YORK. The king is come. Deal mildly with his youth,
70 For young hot colts being rag'd do rage the more.
QUEEN. How fares our noble uncle Lancaster?
KING RICHARD. What comfort, man? How is't with aged Gaunt?
GAUNT. O, how that name befits my composition!
Old Gaunt indeed, and gaunt in being old.
75 Within me grief hath kept a tedious fast,
And who abstains from meat that is not gaunt?
For sleeping England long time have I watch'd;
Watching breeds leanness, leanness is all gaunt.
The pleasure that some fathers feed upon
80 Is my strict fast—I mean my children's looks—
And therein fasting hast thou made me gaunt.
Gaunt am I for the grave, gaunt as a grave,
Whose hollow womb inherits naught but bones.
KING RICHARD. Can sick men play so nicely with their names?
85 GAUNT. No, misery makes sport to mock itself.
Since thou dost seek to kill my name in me,
I mock my name, great king, to flatter thee.
KING RICHARD. Should dying men flatter with those that live?
GAUNT. No, no, men living flatter those that die.
KING RICHARD. Thou, now a-dying, say'st thou
90 flatt'rest me.
GAUNT. O, no! Thou diest, though I the sicker be.
KING RICHARD. I am in health, I breathe, and see thee ill.
GAUNT. Now, He that made me knows I see thee ill,
Ill in myself to see, and in thee seeing ill.
95 Thy deathbed is no lesser than thy land,
Wherein thou liest in reputation sick;
And thou, too careless patient as thou art,
Commit'st thy anointed body to the cure
Of those physicians that first wounded thee.
100 A thousand flatt'rers sit within thy crown,
Whose compass is no bigger than thy head;
And yet, incaged in so small a verge,°
The waste is no whit lesser than thy land.
O, had thy grandsire with a prophet's eye
105 Seen how his son's son should destroy his sons,
From forth thy reach he would have laid thy shame,
Deposing thee before thou wert possess'd,°
Which art possess'd now to depose thyself.
Why, cousin, wert thou regent of the world,
110 It were a shame to let this land by lease;
But, for thy world enjoying but this land,
Is it not more than shame to shame it so?
Landlord of England art thou now, not king.

Thy state of law° is bondslave to the law;
And thou—
KING RICHARD. A lunatic lean-witted fool,   115
Presuming on an ague's privilege,°
Dar'st with thy frozen admonition
Make pale our cheek, chasing the royal blood
With fury from his native residence?
Now by my seat's right royal majesty,   120
Wert thou not brother to great Edward's son,
This tongue that runs so roundly in thy head
Should run thy head from thy unrev'rent shoulders.
GAUNT. O, spare me not, my brother Edward's son,
For that I was his father Edward's son;   125
That blood already, like the pelican,°
Hast thou tapp'd out and drunkenly carous'd.
My brother Gloucester, plain well-meaning soul—
Whom fair befall in heaven 'mongst happy souls!—
May be a precedent and witness good   130
That thou respect'st not spilling Edward's blood.
Join with the present sickness that I have,
And thy unkindness be like crooked age
To crop at once a too-long-wither'd flower.
Live in thy shame, but die not shame with thee!   135
These words hereafter thy tormentors be!
Convey me to my bed, then to my grave.
Love they to live that love and honor have.
              [Exit, borne by his ATTENDANTS.]
KING RICHARD. And let them die that age and sullens have;
For both hast thou, and both become the grave.   140
YORK. I do beseech your majesty, impute his words
To wayward sickliness and age in him.
He loves you, on my life, and holds you dear
As Harry Duke of Hereford, were he here.
KING RICHARD. Right, you say true: as Hereford's love, so his;   145
As theirs, so mine, and all be as it is.
              [Enter NORTHUMBERLAND.]
NORTHUMBERLAND. My liege, old Gaunt commends him to your majesty.
KING RICHARD. What says he?
NORTHUMBERLAND.   Nay, nothing; all is said.
His tongue is now a stringless instrument;
Words, life, and all, old Lancaster hath spent.   150

Thy . . . law your status as king is now reduced to that of mortgagee
ague's privilege i.e., the license of sick people to be insulting
pelican (which supposedly fed its young with its own blood)

verge boundary   *possess'd* i.e., of the crown

YORK. Be York the next that must be bankrupt so!
　　Though death be poor, it ends a mortal woe.
KING RICHARD. The ripest fruit first falls, and so
　　doth he;
　　His time is spent, our pilgrimage must be.
155　So much for that. Now for our Irish wars.
　　We must supplant those rough rug-headed
　　　kerns°
　　Which live like venom° where no venom else
　　But only they have privilege to live.
　　And for these great affairs do ask some charge,
160　Towards our assistance we do seize to us
　　The plate, coin, revenues, and movables
　　Whereof our uncle Gaunt did stand possess'd.
YORK. How long shall I be patient? Ah, how long
　　Shall tender duty make me suffer wrong?
　　Not Gloucester's death nor Hereford's banish-
165　　ment,
　　Not Gaunt's rebukes nor England's private
　　　wrongs,
　　Nor the prevention of poor Bolingbroke
　　About his marriage,° nor my own disgrace
　　Have ever made me sour my patient cheek
170　Or bend one wrinkle on my sovereign's face.
　　I am the last of noble Edward's sons,
　　Of whom thy father, Prince of Wales, was first.
　　In war was never lion rag'd more fierce,
　　In peace was never gentle lamb more mild
175　Than was that young and princely gentleman.
　　His face thou hast, for even so look'd he,
　　Accomplish'd with the number of thy hours;
　　But when he frown'd, it was against the French
　　And not against his friends. His noble hand
180　Did win what he did spend, and spent not that
　　Which his triumphant father's hand had won.
　　His hands were guilty of no kindred blood,
　　But bloody with the enemies of his kin.
　　O Richard! York is too far gone with grief,
185　Or else he never would compare between.
KING RICHARD. Why, uncle, what's the matter?
YORK.　　　　　　　　　　　　　　O my liege,
　　Pardon me if you please; if not, I, pleas'd
　　Not to be pardon'd, am content withal.
　　Seek you to seize and gripe into your hands
190　The royalties and rights of banish'd Hereford?
　　Is not Gaunt dead, and doth not Hereford live?
　　Was not Gaunt just, and is not Harry true?
　　Did not the one deserve to have an heir?
　　Is not his heir a well-deserving son?

Take Hereford's rights away, and take from
　　time　　　　　　　　　　　　　　　　　195
　　His charters and his customary rights;
　　Let not tomorrow then ensue today;
　　Be not thyself; for how art thou a king
　　But by fair sequence and succession?
　　Now, afore God—God forbid I say true!—　200
　　If you do wrongfully seize Hereford's rights,
　　Call in the letters patents° that he hath
　　By his attorneys-general to sue
　　His livery,° and deny his offer'd homage,
　　You pluck a thousand dangers on your head,　205
　　You lose a thousand well-disposed hearts,
　　And prick my tender patience to those thoughts
　　Which honor and allegiance cannot think.
KING RICHARD. Think what you will. We seize into
　　our hands
　　His plate, his goods, his money, and his lands.　210
YORK. I'll not be by the while. My liege, farewell:
　　What will ensue hereof, there's none can tell;
　　But by bad courses may be understood
　　That their events can never fall out good.
　　　　　　　　　　　　　　　　　　[Exit]

KING RICHARD. Go, Bushy, to the Earl of Wiltshire
　　straight;　　　　　　　　　　　　　　215
　　Bid him repair to us to Ely House
　　To see° this business. Tomorrow next
　　We will for Ireland, and 'tis time, I trow.
　　And we create, in absence of ourself,
　　Our uncle York lord governor of England,　220
　　For he is just and always lov'd us well.
　　Come on, our queen. Tomorrow must we part;
　　Be merry, for our time of stay is short.
　　　　　[Flourish. Exeunt KING, QUEEN, AUMERLE,
　　　　　　　　　　　BUSHY, GREEN, and BAGOT.]
NORTHUMBERLAND. Well, lords, the Duke of
　　Lancaster is dead.
ROSS. And living too, for now his son is duke.　225
WILLOUGHBY. Barely in title, not in revenues.
NORTHUMBERLAND. Richly in both, if justice had her
　　right.
ROSS. My heart is great, but it must break with
　　silence
　　Ere't be disburden'd with a liberal° tongue.
NORTHUMBERLAND. Nay, speak thy mind, and let
　　him ne'er speak more　　　　　　　　230
　　That speaks thy words again to do thee harm!
WILLOUGHBY. Tends that thou wouldst speak to the
　　Duke of Hereford?
　　If it be so, out with it boldly, man;
　　Quick is mine ear to hear of good towards him.

---

rug-headed kerns　shag-haired foot-soldiers
venom　i.e., venomous snakes
prevention . . . marriage　(Richard prevented Bolingbroke's
　marriage in exile to the French king's cousin by citing
　"heinous offenses")

letters patents　legal authorization from the king
to sue . . . livery　i.e., to regain his father's lands
see　attend to　　*liberal*　free

235 Ross. No good at all that I can do for him,
 Unless you call it good to pity him,
 Bereft and gelded of his patrimony.
 Northumberland. Now, afore God, 'tis shame
   such wrongs are borne
 In him a royal prince and many moe°
240 Of noble blood in this declining land.
 The king is not himself, but basely led
 By flatterers, and what they will inform,
 Merely in hate, 'gainst any of us all,
 That will the king severely prosecute
245 'Gainst us, our lives, our children, and our heirs.
 Ross. The commons hath he pill'd° with grievous
   taxes,
   And quite lost their hearts. The nobles hath he
   fin'd
   For ancient quarrels, and quite lost their hearts.
 Willoughby. And daily new exactions are devis'd,
250 As blanks,° benevolences, and I wot not what.
 But what, o' God's name, doth become of this?
 Northumberland. Wars have not wasted it, for
   warr'd he hath not,
 But basely yielded upon compromise
 That which his noble ancestors achiev'd with
   blows.
255 More hath he spent in peace than they in wars.
 Ross. The Earl of Wiltshire hath the realm in
   farm.
 Willoughby. The king's grown bankrupt, like a
   broken man.
 Northumberland. Reproach and dissolution hang-
   eth over him.
 Ross. He hath not money for these Irish wars,
260 His burthenous taxations notwithstanding,
 But by the robbing of the banish'd duke.
 Northumberland. His noble kinsman. Most de-
   generate king!
 But, lords, we hear this fearful tempest sing,
 Yet seek no shelter to avoid the storm;
265 We see the wind sit sore upon our sails,
 And yet we strike not, but securely° perish.
 Ross. We see the very wreck that we must suffer,
 And unavoided is the danger now
 For suffering so the causes of our wreck.
 Northumberland. Not so. Even through the hol-
270   low eyes of death
 I spy life peering; but I dare not say
 How near the tidings of our comfort is.
 Willoughby. Nay, let us share thy thoughts, as
   thou dost ours.
 Ross. Be confident to speak, Northumberland.
275 We three are but thyself, and, speaking so,

Thy words are but as thoughts. Therefore be
   bold.
 Northumberland. Then thus: I have from le
   Port Blanc, a bay
 In Brittany, receiv'd intelligence
 That Harry Duke of Hereford, Rainold Lord
   Cobham,
 The son of Richard Earl of Arundel,   280
 That late broke from the Duke of Exeter,
 His brother, Archbishop late of Canterbury,
 Sir Thomas Erpingham, Sir John Ramston,
 Sir John Norbery, Sir Robert Waterton, and
   Francis Quoint,
 All these well furnish'd by the Duke of Bretagne 285
 With eight tall ships, three thousand men of
   war,
 Are making hither with all due expedience
 And shortly mean to touch our northern shore.
 Perhaps they had ere this, but that they stay
 The first departing of the king for Ireland.   290
 If then we shall shake off our slavish yoke,
 Imp out° our drooping country's broken wing,
 Redeem from broking pawn the blemish'd
   crown,
 Wipe off the dust that hides our sceptre's gilt,
 And make high majesty look like itself,   295
 Away with me in post to Ravenspurgh,
 But if you faint, as fearing to do so,
 Stay and be secret, and myself will go.
 Ross. To horse, to horse! Urge doubts to them that
   fear.
 Willoughby. Hold out my horse, and I will first be
   there.   [Exeunt] 300

SCENE ii
Windsor Castle.

[Enter Queen, Bushy, and Bagot.]
 Bushy. Madam, your majesty is too much sad.
 You promis'd, when you parted with the king,
 To lay aside life-harming heaviness
 And entertain a cheerful disposition.
 Queen. To please the king I did; to please myself 5
 I cannot do it. Yet I know no cause
 Why I should welcome such a guest as grief,
 Save bidding farewell to so sweet a guest
 As my sweet Richard. Yet again, methinks,
 Some unborn sorrow, ripe in fortune's womb,   10
 Is coming towards me, and my inward soul
 With nothing trembles. At some thing it grieves,
 More than with parting from my lord the king.

---

moe more   pill'd peeled (skinned)
blanks enforced loans   securely overconfidently

Imp out engraft new feathers (falconry image)

BUSHY. Each substance of a grief hath twenty
    shadows
15 Which shows like grief itself but is not so;
    For sorrow's eye, glazed with blinding tears,
    Divides one thing entire to many objects,
    Like perspectives,° which rightly gaz'd upon
    Show nothing but confusion, ey'd awry,
20 Distinguish form. So your sweet majesty,
    Looking awry upon your lord's departure,
    Find shapes of grief, more than himself, to wail;
    Which, look'd on as it is, is naught but shadows
    Of what it is not. Then, thrice-gracious queen,
    More than your lord's departure weep not.
25   More's not seen;
    Or if it be, 'tis with false sorrow's eye,
    Which for things true weeps things imaginary.
QUEEN. It may be so, but yet my inward soul
    Persuades me it is otherwise. Howe'er it be,
30 I cannot but be sad, so heavy sad
    As, though on thinking on no thought I think,
    Makes me with heavy nothing faint and shrink.
BUSHY. 'Tis nothing but conceit,° my gracious lady.
QUEEN. 'Tis nothing less.° Conceit is still° deriv'd
35 From some forefather grief;° mine is not so,
    For nothing hath begot my something grief;
    Or something hath the nothing that I grieve.
    'Tis in reversion that I do possess;°
    But what it is, that is not yet known; what
40 I cannot name; 'tis nameless woe, I wot.°
        [*Enter* GREEN.]
GREEN. God save your majesty! And well met,
    gentlemen.
    I hope the king is not yet shipp'd for Ireland.
QUEEN. Why hop'st thou so? 'Tis better hope he is,
    For his designs crave haste, his haste good hope.
    Then wherefore dost thou hope he is not
45   shipp'd?
GREEN. That he, our hope, might have retir'd° his
    power
    And driven into despair an enemy's hope,
    Who strongly hath set footing in this land.
    The banish'd Bolingbroke repeals° himself,
50 And with uplifted arms is safe arriv'd
    At Ravenspurgh.
QUEEN.   Now God in heaven forbid!

GREEN. Ah madam, 'tis too true. And that° is
    worse,
    The Lord Northumberland, his son young
    Henry Percy,
    The Lords of Ross, Beaumond, and Willoughby,
    With all their powerful friends, are fled to him. 55
BUSHY. Why have you not proclaim'd Northum-
    berland
    And all the rest revolted faction traitors?
GREEN. We have—whereupon the Earl of Wor-
    cester
    Hath broke his staff,° resign'd his stewardship,
    And all the household servants fled with him   60
    To Bolingbroke.
QUEEN. So, Green, thou art the midwife to my
    woe,
    And Bolingbroke my sorrow's dismal heir.
    Now hath my soul brought forth her prodigy,
    And I, a gasping new-deliver'd mother,   65
    Have woe to woe, sorrow to sorrow join'd.
BUSHY. Despair not, madam.
QUEEN. Who shall hinder me?
    I will despair, and be at enmity
    With coz'ning° hope. He is a flatterer,
    A parasite, a keeper-back of death,   70
    Who gently would dissolve the bands of life,
    Which false hope lingers° in extremity.
        [*Enter* YORK.]
GREEN. Here comes the Duke of York.
QUEEN. With signs of war about his aged neck;
    O, full of careful business° are his looks!   75
    Uncle, for God's sake, speak comfortable
    words.
YORK. Should I do so, I should belie my thoughts,
    Comfort's in heaven, and we are on the earth,
    Where nothing lives but crosses, cares, and grief.
    Your husband, he is gone to save far off,   80
    Whilst others come to make him lose at home.
    Here am I left to underprop his land,
    Who, weak with age, cannot support myself.
    Now comes the sick hour that his surfeit° made;
    Now shall he try his friends that flatter'd him.   85
        [*Enter a* SERVANT.]
SERVANT. My lord, your son was gone before I
    came.
YORK. He was? Why, so! Go all which way it will!
    The nobles they are fled, the commons they are
    cold,
    And will, I fear, revolt on Hereford's side.
    Sirrah, get thee to Plashy, to my sister Glouces-
    ter;   90

---

perspectives ingeniously devised pictures that change
   according to the angle from which they are viewed
conceit fancy
'Tis . . . less it is anything but mere fancy
still always
forefather grief former (real) grief
'Tis . . . possess I shall inherit this as-yet-unidentified
   grief in the future
wot know   *retir'd* called back
repeals recalls from banishment

that what   *staff* the sign of his office
coz'ning cheating   *lingers* forces to linger
careful business anxiety   *surfeit* waste, excess

Bid her send me presently° a thousand pound.
Hold, take my ring.
SERVANT. My lord, I had forgot to tell your lord-
 ship,
Today, as I came by, I called there;
95 But I shall grieve you to report the rest.
YORK. What is't, knave?
SERVANT. An hour before I came, the duchess died.
YORK. God for his mercy! What a tide of woes
Comes rushing on this woeful land at once!
100 I know not what to do. I would to God,
So my untruth had not provok'd him to it,
The king had cut off my head with my brother's.
What, are there no posts dispatch'd for Ireland?
How shall we do for money for these wars?
Come, sister—cousin, I would say—pray, pardon
105 me.
Go, fellow, get thee home, provide some carts
And bring away the armor that is there.
      [Exit SERVANT.]
Gentlemen, will you go muster men?
If I know how or which way t' order these
 affairs
110 Thus thrust disorderly into my hands,
Never believe me. Both are my kinsmen.
Th' one is my sovereign, whom both my oath
And duty bids defend; th' other again
Is my kinsman, whom the king hath wrong'd,
115 Whom conscience and my kindred bids to right.
Well, somewhat° we must do. Come, cousin, I'll
Dispose of you.
Gentlemen, go muster up your men
And meet me presently at Berkeley.
120 I should to Plashy too,
But time will not permit. All is uneven,
And everything is left at six and seven.
     [Exeunt YORK and QUEEN.]
BUSHY. The wind sits fair for news to go to Ireland,
But none returns. For us to levy power
125 Proportionable to the enemy
Is all unpossible.
GREEN. Besides, our nearness to the king in love
Is near the hate of those love not the king.
BAGOT. And that's the wav'ring commons, for
 their love
130 Lies in their purses, and whoso empties them
By so much fills their hearts with deadly hate.
BUSHY. Wherein the king stands generally con-
 demn'd.
BAGOT. If judgment lie in them, then so do we,
Because we ever have been near the king.
GREEN. Well, I will for refuge straight to Bristol
135 castle.

The Earl of Wiltshire is already there.
BUSHY. Thither will I with you, for little office
The hateful commons will perform for us,
Except like curs to tear us all to pieces.
Will you go along with us?   140
BAGOT. No, I will to Ireland to his majesty.
Farewell. If heart's presages be not vain,
We three here part that ne'er shall meet again.
BUSHY. That's as York thrives to beat back Boling-
 broke.
GREEN. Alas, poor duke! The task he undertakes 145
Is numb'ring sands and drinking oceans dry.
Where one on his side fights, thousands will fly.
Farewell at once, for once, for all, and ever.
BUSHY. Well, we may meet again.
BAGOT.   I fear me, never.
         [Exeunt]

SCENE iii
Wilds in Gloucestershire.

[*Enter* BOLINGBROKE *and* NORTHUMBERLAND,
with Forces.]

BOLINGBROKE. How far is it, my lord, to Berkeley
 now?
NORTHUMBERLAND. Believe me, noble lord,
I am a stranger here in Gloucestershire.
These high wild hills and rough uneven ways
Draws out our miles and makes them weari-
 some;   5
And yet your fair discourse hath been as sugar,
Making the hard way sweet and delectable.
But I bethink me what a weary way
From Ravenspurgh to Cotswold will be found
In Ross and Willoughby, wanting° your com-
 pany,   10
Which I protest hath very much beguil'd
The tediousness and process of my travel.
But theirs is sweeten'd with the hope to have
The present benefit which I possess,
And hope to joy is little less in joy   15
Than hope enjoy'd. By this the weary lords
Shall make their way seem short, as mine hath
 done
By sight of what I have, your noble company.
BOLINGBROKE. Of much less value is my company
Than your good words. But who comes here? 20
      [*Enter* HENRY PERCY.]
NORTHUMBERLAND. It is my son, young Harry Percy,
Sent from my brother Worcester, whenceso-
 ever.
Harry, how fares your uncle?

---

presently immediately *somewhat* something   *wanting* lacking

HENRY PERCY. I had thought, my lord, to have
    learn'd his health of you.
25 NORTHUMBERLAND. Why, is he not with the queen?
HENRY PERCY. No, my good lord. He hath forsook
    the court,
    Broken his staff of office, and dispers'd
    The household of the king.
NORTHUMBERLAND.   What was his reason?
    He was not so resolv'd when last we spake
    together.
HENRY PERCY. Because your lordship was pro-
30   claimed traitor.
    But he, my lord, is gone to Ravenspurgh
    To offer service to the Duke of Hereford,
    And sent me over by Berkeley to discover
    What power the Duke of York had levied there,
35   Then with directions to repair to Ravenspurgh.
NORTHUMBERLAND. Have you forgot the Duke of
    Hereford, boy?
HENRY PERCY. No, my good lord, for that is not
    forgot
    Which ne'er I did remember. To my know-
    ledge,
    I never in my life did look on him.
NORTHUMBERLAND. Then learn to know him now;
40   this is the duke.
HENRY PERCY. My gracious lord, I tender you my
    service,
    Such as it is, being tender, raw, and young,
    Which elder days shall ripen and confirm
    To more approved service and desert.
BOLINGBROKE. I thank thee, gentle Percy; and be
45   sure
    I count myself in nothing else so happy
    As in a soul rememb'ring my good friends;
    And, as my fortune ripens with thy love,
    It shall be still thy true love's recompense.
    My heart this covenant makes, my hand thus
50   seals it.
NORTHUMBERLAND. How far is it to Berkeley? And
    what stir
    Keeps good old York there with his men of war?
HENRY PERCY. There stands the castle by yon tuft of
    trees,
    Mann'd with three hundred men, as I have
    heard,
    And in it are the Lords of York, Berkeley, and
55   Seymour,
    None else of name and noble estimate.
        [Enter Ross and WILLOUGHBY.]
NORTHUMBERLAND. Here come the Lords of Ross
    and Willoughby,
    Bloody with spurring, fiery-red with haste.
BOLINGBROKE. Welcome, my lords. I wot your love
    pursues

    A banish'd traitor. All my treasury   60
    Is yet but unfelt thanks, which more enrich'd
    Shall be your love and labor's recompense.
ROSS. Your presence makes us rich, most noble
    lord.
WILLOUGHBY. And far surmounts our labor to
    attain it.
BOLINGBROKE. Evermore thanks, th' exchequer of
    the poor,   65
    Which till my infant fortune comes to years
    Stands for my bounty. But who comes here?
        [Enter BERKELEY.]
NORTHUMBERLAND. It is my Lord of Berkeley, as I
    guess.
BERKELEY. My Lord of Hereford, my message is to
    you.
BOLINGBROKE. My lord, my answer is—to Lan-
    caster;   70
    And I am come to seek that name in England;
    And I must find that title in your tongue
    Before I make reply to aught you say.
BERKELEY. Mistake me not, my lord; 'tis not my
    meaning
    To raze one title of your honor out.   75
    To you, my lord, I come, what lord you will,
    From the most gracious regent of this land,
    The Duke of York, to know what pricks you on
    To take advantage of the absent time
    And fright our native peace with self-borne
    arms.   80
        [Enter YORK attended.]
BOLINGBROKE. I shall not need transport my words
    by you;
    Here comes his grace in person. My noble uncle!
        [Kneels.]
YORK. Show me thy humble heart, and not thy
    knee,
    Whose duty is deceivable and false.
BOLINGBROKE. My gracious uncle!   85
YORK. Tut, tut!
    Grace me no grace, nor uncle me no uncle.
    I am no traitor's uncle, and that word "grace"
    In an ungracious mouth is but profane.
    Why have those banish'd and forbidden legs   90
    Dar'd once to touch a dust of England's ground?
    But then more why: Why have they dar'd to
    march
    So many miles upon her peaceful bosom,
    Frighting her pale-fac'd villages with war
    And ostentation of despised arms?   95
    Com'st thou because th' anointed king is hence?
    Why, foolish boy, the king is left behind,
    And in my loyal bosom lies his power.
    Were I but now the lord of such hot youth
    As when brave Gaunt, thy father, and myself   100

Rescu'd the Black Prince,° that young Mars of men,
From forth the ranks of many thousand French,
O, then how quickly should this arm of mine,
Now prisoner to the palsy, chastise thee
105　And minister correction to thy fault!
BOLINGBROKE. My gracious uncle, let me know my fault.
On what condition stands it and wherein?
YORK. Even in condition of the worst degree—
In gross rebellion and detested treason.
110　Thou art a banish'd man, and here art come
Before the expiration of thy time,
In braving° arms against thy sovereign.
BOLINGBROKE. As I was banish'd, I was banish'd Hereford;
But as I come, I come for Lancaster.
115　And, noble uncle, I beseech your grace
Look on my wrongs with an indifferent° eye.
You are my father, for methinks in you
I see old Gaunt alive. O, then, my father,
Will you permit that I shall stand condemn'd
120　A wand'ring vagabond, my rights and royalties
Pluck'd from my arms perforce and given away
To upstart unthrifts? Wherefore was I born?
If that my cousin king be King of England,
It must be granted I am Duke of Lancaster.
125　You have a son, Aumerle, my noble cousin;
Had you first died, and he been thus trod down,
He should have found his uncle Gaunt a father
To rouse his wrongs and chase them to the bay.
I am denied to sue my livery here,
130　And yet my letters-patents give me leave.
My father's goods are all distrain'd° and sold,
And these and all are all amiss employ'd.
What would you have me do? I am a subject,
And I challenge law. Attorneys are denied me,
135　And therefore personally I lay my claim
To my inheritance of free descent.
NORTHUMBERLAND. The noble duke hath been too much abus'd.
ROSS. It stands your grace upon to do him right.
WILLOUGHBY. Base men by his endowments° are made great.
140　YORK. My lords of England, let me tell you this:
I have had feeling of my cousin's wrongs
And labor'd all I could to do him right.
But in this kind to come, in braving° arms,
Be his own carver and cut out his way,

To find out right with wrong, it may not be,　145
And you that do abet him in this kind
Cherish rebellion and are rebels all.
NORTHUMBERLAND. The noble duke hath sworn his coming is
But for his own, and for the right of that
We all have strongly sworn to give him aid　150
And let him ne'er see joy that breaks that oath!
YORK. Well, well, I see the issue of these arms.
I cannot mend it, I must needs confess,
Because my power is weak and all ill left.
But if I could, by Him that gave me life,　155
I would attach° you all and make you stoop
Unto the sovereign mercy of the king.
But since I cannot, be it known to you
I do remain as neuter. So fare you well,
Unless you please to enter in the castle　160
And there repose you for this night.
An offer, uncle, that we will accept.
But we must win your grace to go with us
To Bristol castle, which they say is held
By Bushy, Bagot, and their complices,　165
The caterpillars° of the commonwealth,
Which I have sworn to weed and pluck away.
YORK. It may be I will go with you; but yet I'll pause,
For I am loath to break our country's laws.
Nor friends nor° foes, to me welcome you are.　170
Things past redress are now with me past care.
[Exeunt]

SCENE iv
A camp in Wales.

[Enter SALISBURY and a Welsh CAPTAIN.]
CAPTAIN. My Lord of Salisbury, we have stay'd ten days
And hardly kept our countrymen together,
And yet we hear no tidings from the king;
Therefore we will disperse ourselves. Farewell.
SALISBURY. Stay yet another day, thou trusty Welshman.　5
The king reposeth all his confidence in thee.
CAPTAIN. 'Tis thought the king is dead; we will not stay.
The bay trees in our country are all wither'd,
And meteors fright the fixed stars of heaven;
The pale-fac'd moon looks bloody on the earth,　10
And lean-look'd prophets whisper fearful change;
Rich men look sad, and ruffians dance and leap,

Black Prince　Edward III's first son, father of Richard
braving　challenging, rebellious　　indifferent　impartial
distrain'd　confiscated
stands . . . upon　is your grace's duty
by his endowments　from his (stolen) properties
braving　defiant

attach　arrest　　caterpillars　devouring parasites
Nor . . . nor　neither . . . nor

The one in fear to lose what they enjoy,
The other to enjoy by rage° and war.
15 These signs forerun the death or fall of kings.
Farewell. Our countrymen are gone and fled,
As well assur'd Richard their king is dead.

                                  [Exit]
SALISBURY. Ah, Richard, with the eyes of heavy
    mind

rage outrage

I see thy glory like a shooting star
Fall to the base earth from the firmament.   20
Thy sun sets weeping in the lowly west,
Witnessing storms to come, woe, and unrest.
Thy friends are fled to wait upon thy foes,
And crossly° to thy good all fortune goes.

                                  [Exit]

crossly contrary

ACT III

SCENE i
Bristol. Before the castle.

[Enter BOLINGBROKE, YORK, NORTHUMBERLAND,
  ROSS, PERCY, WILLOUGHBY, *with* BUSHY *and*
    GREEN, *prisoners.*]
BOLINGBROKE. Bring forth these men.
  Bushy and Green, I will not vex your souls—
  Since presently your souls must part° your
    bodies—
  With too much urging° your pernicious lives,
5 For 'twere no charity;° yet, to wash your blood
  From off my hands, here in the view of men
  I will unfold some causes of your deaths.
  You have misled a prince, a royal king,
  A happy gentleman in blood and lineaments,
10 By you unhappied and disfigur'd clean.°
  You have in manner° with your sinful hours
  Made a divorce betwixt his queen and him,
  Broke° the possession of a royal bed,
  And stain'd the beauty of a fair queen's cheeks
  With tears drawn from her eyes by your foul
15   wrongs.
  Myself, a prince by fortune of my birth,
  Near to the king in blood, and near in love
  Till you did make him misinterpret me,
  Have stoop'd my neck under your injuries
20 And sigh'd my English breath in foreign clouds,
  Eating the bitter bread of banishment,
  Whilst you have fed upon my signories,°
  Dispark'd° my parks and fell'd my forest woods,
  From my own windows torn my household
    coat,

part depart   *urging* making a point of
charity kindness   *lineaments* physical appearance
clean completely   *in manner* in effect
Broke compromised
signories domains   *Dispark'd* made public

Raz'd out my imprese,° leaving me no sign   25
Save men's opinions and my living blood
To show the world I am a gentleman.
This and much more, much more than twice all
  this,
Condemns you to the death. See them deliver'd
  over
To execution and the hand of death.   30
BUSHY. More welcome is the stroke of death to me
  Than Bolingbroke to England. Lords, farewell.
GREEN. My comfort is that heaven will take our
  souls
  And plague injustice with the pains of hell.
BOLINGBROKE. My Lord Northumberland, see
  them dispatch'd.   35
    [Exeunt NORTHUMBERLAND *and others, with the*
                               prisoners.]
  Uncle, you say the queen is at your house.
  For God's sake, fairly let her be entreated.°
  Tell her I send to her my kind commends;
  Take special care my greetings be deliver'd.
YORK. A gentleman of mine I have dispatch'd   40
  With letters of your love to her at large.
BOLINGBROKE. Thanks, gentle uncle. Come, lords,
  away,
  To fight with Glendower and his complices.°
  Awhile to work, and after holiday.   [Exeunt]

SCENE ii
The coast of Wales. A castle in view.

[Drums: *flourish and colors. Enter* KING RICHARD,
  the BISHOP OF CARLISLE, AUMERLE, *and Soldiers.*]
KING RICHARD. Barkloughly castle call they this at
  hand?

Raz'd . . . imprese eradicated my ducal emblem
entreated treated   *complices* accomplices

AUMERLE. Yea, my lord. How brooks your grace
    the air,
    After your late tossing on the breaking seas?
KING RICHARD. Needs must I like it well. I weep for
    joy
5   To stand upon my kingdom once again.
    Dear earth, I do salute thee with my hand,
    Though rebels wound thee with their horses'
      hoofs.
    As a long-parted mother with her child
    Plays fondly with her tears and smiles in meet-
      ing,
10   So, weeping, smiling, greet I thee, my earth,
    And do thee favors with my royal hands.
    Feed not thy sovereign's foe, my gentle earth,
    Nor with thy sweets comfort his rav'nous
      sense,
    But let thy spiders, that suck up thy venom,
15   And heavy-gaited toads lie in their way,
    Doing annoyance to the treacherous feet
    Which with usurping steps do trample thee.
    Yield stinging nettles to mine enemies,
    And when they from thy bosom pluck a flower,
20   Guard it, I pray thee, with a lurking adder,
    Whose double tongue may with a mortal touch
    Throw death upon thy sovereign's enemies.
    Mock not my senseless conjuration, lords.
    This earth shall have a feeling and these stones
25   Prove armed soldiers ere her native king
    Shall falter under foul rebellion's arms.
CARLISLE. Fear not, my lord. That Power that made
    you king
    Hath power to keep you king in spite of all.
    The means that heaven yields must be em-
      brac'd,
30   And not neglected; else, if heaven would
    And we will not, heaven's offer we refuse—
    The proffer'd means of succor and redress.
AUMERLE. He means, my lord, that we are too
    remiss,
    Whilst Bolingbroke, through our security,°
    Grows strong and great in substance and in
35   power.
KING RICHARD. Discomfortable° cousin! Know'st
    thou not
    That when the searching eye of heaven is hid
    Behind the globe and lights the lower world,°
    Then thieves and robbers range abroad unseen
40   In murders and in outrage, boldly here;
    But when from under this terrestrial ball
    He fires the proud tops of the eastern pines
    And darts his light through every guilty hole,

Then murders, treasons, and detested sins,
The cloak of night being pluck'd from off their
    backs,   45
Stand bare and naked, trembling at themselves?
So when this thief, this traitor Bolingbroke,
Who all this while hath revel'd in the night,
Whilst we were wand'ring with th' Antipodes,°
Shall see us rising in our throne, the east,   50
His treasons will sit blushing in his face,
Not able to endure the sight of day,
But self-affrighted tremble at his sin.
Not all the water in the rough rude sea
Can wash the balm off from an anointed king; 55
The breath of worldly men cannot depose
The deputy elected by the Lord.
For every man that Bolingbroke hath press'd°
To lift shrewd steel against our golden crown,
God for his Richard hath in heavenly pay   60
A glorious angel. Then, if angels fight,
Weak men must fall, for heaven still guards the
    right.
           [Enter SALISBURY.]
Welcome, my lord. How far off lies your power?
SALISBURY. Nor near nor farther off, my gracious
    lord,
    Than this weak arm. Discomfort guides my
    tongue   65
    And bids me speak of nothing but despair.
    One day too late, I fear me, noble lord,
    Hath clouded all thy happy days on earth.
    O, call back yesterday, bid time return,
    And thou shalt have twelve thousand fighting
    men!   70
    Today, today, unhappy day, too late,
    O'erthrows thy joys, friends, fortune, and thy
    state.
    For all the Welshmen, hearing thou wert dead,
    Are gone to Bolingbroke, dispers'd, and fled.
AUMERLE. Comfort, my liege. Why looks your
    grace so pale?   75
KING RICHARD. But now the blood of twenty
    thousand men
    Did triumph in my face, and they are fled;
    And, till so much blood thither come again,
    Have I not reason to look pale and dead?
    All souls that will be safe, fly from my side, 80
    For time hath set a blot upon my pride.
AUMERLE Comfort, my liege. Remember who you
    are.
KING RICHARD. I had forgot myself. Am I not king?
    Awake, thou coward majesty! Thou sleep'st.
    Is not the king's name twenty thousand names? 85

---

security overconfidence   *Discomfortable* discomforting
lower world i.e., the other side of the earth

Antipodes i.e., the other side of the earth
press'd drafted

Arm, arm, my name! A puny subject strikes
At thy great glory. Look not to the ground,
Ye favorites of a king. Are we not high?°
High be our thoughts. I know my uncle York
Hath power enough to serve our turn. But who
90   comes here?

[Enter SCROOP.*]*

SCROOP. More health and happiness betide my
liege
Than can my care-tun'd tongue deliver him!
KING RICHARD. Mine ear is open and my heart
prepar'd.
The worst is worldly loss thou canst unfold.
95   Say, is my kingdom lost? Why, 'twas my care,
And what loss is it to be rid of care?
Strives Bolingbroke to be as great as we?
Greater he shall not be; if he serve God,
We'll serve Him too and be his fellow so.
100   Revolt our subjects? That we cannot mend—
They break their faith to God as well as us.
Cry woe, destruction, ruin, and decay;
The worst is death, and death will have his day.
SCROOP. Glad am I that your highness is so arm'd
105   To bear the tidings of calamity.
Like an unseasonable stormy day
Which makes the silver rivers drown their
shores
As if the world were all dissolv'd to tears,
So high above his limits swells the rage
110   Of Bolingbroke, cov'ring your fearful land
With hard bright steel and hearts harder than
steel.
White-beards have arm'd their thin and hairless
scalps
Against thy majesty; boys with women's voices
Strive to speak big and clap their female joints
115   In stiff unwieldy arms against thy crown;
The very beadsmen° learn to bend their bows
Of double-fatal yew° against thy state;
Yea, distaff women° manage rusty bills°
Against thy seat. Both young and old rebel,
120   And all goes worse than I have power to tell.
KING RICHARD. Too well, too well thou tell'st a
tale so ill.
Where is the Earl of Wiltshire? Where is Bagot?
What is become of Bushy? Where is Green?
That they have let the dangerous enemy
125   Measure our confines with such peaceful steps?
If we prevail, their heads shall pay for it.

I warrant they have made peace with Boling-
broke.
SCROOP. Peace have they made with him indeed,
my lord.
KING RICHARD. O villains, vipers, damn'd without
redemption!
Dogs easily won to fawn on any man!   130
Snakes in my heart-blood warm'd that sting my
heart!
Three Judases, each one thrice worse than Judas!
Would they make peace? Terrible hell make
war
Upon their spotted° souls for this offense!
SCROOP. Sweet love, I see, changing his property,°   135
Turns to the sour'st and most deadly hate.
Again uncurse their souls; their peace is made
With heads, and not with hands. Those whom
you curse
Have felt the worst of death's destroying wound
And lie full low, grav'd in the hollow ground.   140
AUMERLE. Is Bushy, Green, and th' Earl of Wilt-
shire dead?
SCROOP. Aye, all of them at Bristol lost their heads.
AUMERLE. Where is the duke my father with his
power?
KING RICHARD. No matter where; of comfort no
man speak.
Let's talk of graves, of worms, and epitaphs,   145
Make dust our paper, and with rainy eyes
Write sorrow on the bosom of the earth.
Let's choose executors and talk of wills.
And yet not so, for what can we bequeath
Save our deposed bodies to the ground?   150
Our lands, our lives, and all are Bolingbroke's,
And nothing can we call our own but death
And that small model of the barren earth
Which serves as paste and cover to our bones.
For God's sake let us sit upon the ground   155
And tell sad stories of the death of kings:
How some have been depos'd, some slain in
war,
Some haunted by the ghosts they have depos'd,
Some poison'd by their wives, some sleeping
kill'd—
All murder'd. For within the hollow crown   160
That rounds the mortal temples of a king
Keeps Death his court, and there the antic° sits,
Scoffing his state and grinning at his pomp,
Allowing him a breath, a little scene
To monarchize, be fear'd, and kill with looks,   165
Infusing him with self and vain conceit
As if this flesh which walls about our life

high i.e., on Fortune's wheel
beadsmen pensioners paid to pray for their benefactor
double-fatal yew yew-wood, poisonous in itself, and used
for bow-wood
distaff women women who spin; i.e., old women
bills seven-foot spears with axes at the end

spotted stained (with treason)
property true nature   *antic* buffoon (Death)

Were brass impregnable. And humor'd thus,
Comes at the last and with a little pin
Bores through his castle wall—and farewell
170   king!
Cover your heads and mock not flesh and blood
With solemn reverence. Throw away respect,
Tradition, form, and ceremonious duty,
For you have but mistook me all this while.
175   I live with bread like you, feel want,
Taste grief, need friends. Subjected thus,
How can you say to me I am a king?
CARLISLE. My lord, wise men ne'er sit and wail
their woes,
But presently° prevent the ways to wail.
180   To fear the foe, since fear oppresseth strength,
Gives in your weakness strength unto your foe,
And so your follies fight against yourself.
Fear, and be slain; no worse can come to fight.
And fight and die is death destroying death,
185   Where fearing dying pays death servile breath.
AUMERLE. My father hath a power. Inquire of him,
And learn to make a body of a limb.
KING RICHARD. Thou chid'st me well. Proud
Bolingbroke, I come
To change° blows with thee for our day of doom.
190   This ague fit of fear is overblown;
An easy task it is to win our own.
Say, Scroop, where lies our uncle with his
power?
Speak sweetly, man, although thy looks be
sour.
SCROOP. Men judge by the complexion of the sky
195   The state and inclination of the day.
So may you by my dull and heavy eye,
My tongue hath but a heavier tale to say.
I play the torturer by small and small°
To lengthen out the worst that must be spoken.
200   Your uncle York is join'd with Bolingbroke
And all your northern castles yielded up
And all your southern gentlemen in arms
Upon° his party.
KING RICHARD.   Thou hast said enough.
Beshrew° thee, cousin, which didst lead me
205   forth°   [To AUMERLE]
Of that sweet way I was in to despair!
What say you now? What comfort have we
now?
By heaven, I'll hate him everlastingly
That bids me be of comfort anymore.
210   Go to Flint castle. There I'll pine away.
A king, woe's slave, shall kingly woe obey.

That power I have, discharge and let them go
To ear° the land that hath some hope to grow,
For I have none. Let no man speak again
To alter this, for counsel is but vain.   215
AUMERLE. My liege, one word.
KING RICHARD.   He does me double wrong
That wounds me with the flatt'ries of his tongue.
Discharge my followers. Let them hence away
From Richard's night to Bolingbroke's fair day.
[Exeunt]

SCENE iii
Wales. Before Flint castle.

[*Enter, with drum and colors,* BOLINGBROKE, YORK,
NORTHUMBERLAND, *Attendants, and forces.*]
BOLINGBROKE. So that by this intelligence we learn
The Welshmen are dispers'd and Salisbury
Is gone to meet the king, who lately landed
With some few private friends upon this coast.
NORTHUMBERLAND. The news is very fair and good,
my lord.   5
Richard not far from hence hath hid his head.
YORK. It would beseem the Lord Northumberland
To say "King Richard." Alack the heavy day
When such a sacred king should hide his head.
NORTHUMBERLAND. Your grace mistakes; only to
be brief   10
Left I his title out.
YORK.   The time hath been,
Would you have been so brief with him, he
would
Have been so brief with you, to shorten you,
For taking so the head,° your whole head's
length.
BOLINGBROKE. Mistake not, uncle, further than you
should.   15
YORK. Take not, good cousin, further than you
should,
Lest you mistake the heavens are o'er our heads.
BOLINGBROKE. I know it, uncle, and oppose not
myself
Against their will. But who comes here?
[*Enter* HENRY PERCY.]
Welcome, Harry. What, will not this castle
yield?   20
HENRY PERCY. The castle royally is mann'd, my
lord,
Against thy entrance.
BOLINGBROKE. Royally!
Why, it contains no king?
HENRY PERCY.   Yes, my good lord,

presently immediately   *change* exchange
by . . . small little by little
Upon i.e., siding with   *Beshrew* curse   *forth* out

ear plough   *taking . . . head* omitting his title

25   It doth contain a king. King Richard lies
       Within the limits of yon lime and stone,
       And with him are the Lord Aumerle, Lord
          Salisbury,
       Sir Stephen Scroop, besides a clergyman
       Of holy reverence—who, I cannot learn.
   NORTHUMBERLAND. O, belike it is the Bishop of
30   Carlisle.
   BOLINGBROKE. Noble lords,
       Go to the rude ribs° of that ancient castle.
       Through brazen trumpet send the breath of
          parley
       Into his ruin'd ears, and thus deliver:
35   Henry Bolingbroke
       On both his knees doth kiss King Richard's
          hand
       And sends allegiance and true faith of heart
       To his most royal person; hither come
       Even at his feet to lay my arms and power,
40   Provided that my banishment repeal'd
       And lands restor'd again be freely granted.°
       If not, I'll use th' advantage of my power
       And lay the summer's dust with showers of
          blood
       Rain'd from the wounds of slaughter'd English-
          men—
       The which how far off from the mind of Boling-
45   broke
       It is such crimson tempest should bedrench
       The fresh green lap of fair King Richard's land,
       My stooping duty° tenderly shall show.
       Go signify as much, while here we march
50   Upon the grassy carpet of this plain.
       Let's march without the noise of threat'ning
          drum,
       That from this castle's tatter'd battlements
       Our fair appointments° may be well perus'd.
       Methinks King Richard and myself should meet
55   With no less terror than the elements
       Of fire and water, when their thund'ring shock
       At meeting tears the cloudy cheeks of heaven.
       Be he the fire, I'll be the yielding water;
       The rage be his, whilst on the earth I rain
60   My waters—on the earth and not on him.
       March on, and mark King Richard how he
          looks.
       [Parle without, and answer within. Then a flourish.
       Enter on the walls, KING RICHARD, *the* BISHOP OF
         CARLISLE, AUMERLE, SCROOP, *and* SALISBURY.]

    See, see, King Richard doth himself appear,
       As doth the blushing discontented sun
       From out the fiery portal of the east
       When he perceives the envious clouds are bent   65
       To dim his glory and to stain the track
       Of his bright passage to the occident.
   YORK. Yet looks he like a king. Behold his eye,
       As bright as is the eagle's, lightens forth
       Controlling majesty. Alack, alack, for woe,   70
       That any harm should stain so fair a show!
   KING RICHARD. We are amaz'd, and thus long have
         we stood
       To watch the fearful bending of thy knee
                       [To NORTHUMBERLAND.]
       Because we thought ourself thy lawful king.
       And if we be, how dare thy joints forget   75
       To pay their awful° duty to our presence?
       If we be not, show us the hand of God
       That hath dismiss'd us from our stewardship;
       For well we know no hand of blood and bone
       Can gripe the sacred handle of our sceptre   80
       Unless he do profane, steal, or usurp.
       And though you think that all, as you have done,
       Have torn their souls by turning them from us,
       And we are barren and bereft of friends,
       Yet know my master, God omnipotent,   85
       Is must'ring in his clouds on our behalf
       Armies of pestilence; and they shall strike
       Your children yet unborn and unbegot
       That lift your vassal hands against my head
       And threat the glory of my precious crown.   90
       Tell Bolingbroke—for yond methinks he
         stands—
       That every stride he makes upon my land
       Is dangerous treason. He is come to open
       The purple testament° of bleeding war,
       But ere the crown he looks for live in peace,   95
       Ten thousand bloody crowns of mothers' sons
       Shall ill become the flower of England's face,
       Change the complexion of her maid-pale peace
       To scarlet indignation, and bedew
       Her pasture's grass with faithful English blood. 100
   NORTHUMBERLAND. The king of heaven forbid our
         lord the king
       Should so with civil and uncivil arms
       Be rush'd upon! Thy thrice-noble° cousin
       Harry Bolingbroke doth humbly kiss thy hand,
       And by the honorable tomb he swears,   105
       That stands upon your royal grandsire's bones,
       And by the royalties of both your bloods,

---

   ribs walls
   Provided . . . granted provided that my recall from
     banishment and the restoration of my lands be freely
     granted
   stooping duty i.e., bowing of the knees
   fair appointments impressive equipment

   awful awed
   purple testament bloody will (i.e., to enforce his claim by
     resort to arms)
   thrice-noble (a frequent epithet in Shakespeare, never
     conclusively explained)

Currents that spring from one most gracious head,
And by the buried hand of warlike Gaunt,
110 And by the worth and honor of himself,
Comprising all that may be sworn or said,
His coming hither hath no further scope
Than for his lineal royalties,° and to beg
Enfranchisement immediate on his knees;
115 Which on thy royal party° granted once,
His glittering arms he will commend to rust,
His barbed steeds to stables, and his heart
To faithful service of your majesty.
This swears he, as he is a prince, is just;
120 And, as I am a gentleman, I credit him.

KING RICHARD. Northumberland, say thus the king returns.
His noble cousin is right welcome hither,
And all the number of his fair demands
Shall be accomplish'd without contradiction.
125 With all the gracious utterance thou hast,
Speak to his gentle hearing kind commends.
We do debase ourselves, cousin, do we not,
                              [To AUMERLE.]
To look so poorly and to speak so fair?
Shall we call back Northumberland and send
130 Defiance to the traitor, and so die?

AUMERLE. No, good my lord, let's fight with gentle words
Till time lend friends and friends their helpful swords.

KING RICHARD. O God, O God!—That e'er this tongue of mine,
That laid the sentence of dread banishment
135 On yon proud man, should take it off again
With words of sooth!° O that I were as great
As is my grief, or lesser than my name!
Or that I could forget what I have been,
Or not remember what I must be now!
Swell'st thou, proud heart? I'll give thee scope
140 to beat,
Since foes have scope to beat both thee and me.

AUMERLE. Northumberland comes back from Bolingbroke.

KING RICHARD. What must the king do now? Must he submit?
The king shall do it. Must he be depos'd?
145 The king shall be contented. Must he lose
The name of king? O' God's name, let it go.
I'll give my jewels for a set of beads,
My gorgeous palace for a hermitage,
My gay apparel for an almsman's° gown,

My figur'd goblets for a dish of wood,   150
My sceptre for a palmer's° walking-staff,
My subjects for a pair of carved saints,
And my large kingdom for a little grave,
A little little grave, an obscure° grave,
Or I'll be buried in the king's highway,   155
Some way of common trade, where subjects' feet
May hourly trample on their sovereign's head;
For on my heart they tread now whilst I live,
And buried once, why not upon my head?
Aumerle, thou weep'st, my tender-hearted cousin! 160
We'll make foul weather with despised tears;
Our sighs and they shall lodge° the summer corn
And make a dearth in this revolting land.
Or shall we play the wantons° with our woes
And make some pretty match with shedding tears?   165
As thus, to drop them still° upon one place
Till they have fretted° us a pair of graves
Within the earth; and, therein laid—"There lies
Two kinsmen digg'd their graves with weeping eyes!"
Would not this ill do well? Well, well, I see   170
I talk but idly, and you laugh at me.
Most mighty prince, my Lord Northumberland,
What says King Bolingbroke? Will his majesty
Give Richard leave to live till Richard die?
You make a leg,° and Bolingbroke says aye.   175

NORTHUMBERLAND. My lord, in the base court° he doth attend
To speak with you, may it please you to come down.

KING RICHARD. Down, down I come, like glist'ring° Phaeton,°
Wanting° the manage° of unruly jades.
In the base court? Base court, where kings grow base 180
To come at traitors' calls and do them grace.
In the base court? Come down? Down, court!
Down, king!
For night-owls shriek where mounting larks should sing.   [Exeunt from above.]

BOLINGBROKE. What says his majesty?

---

lineal royalties hereditary rights
Enfranchisement recall from banishment
on . . . party by your royal authority   *sooth* flattery
almsman poor man dependent on alms

palmer pilgrim   *obscure* (accented on first syllable)
lodge flatten   *play the wantons* sport frivolously
still always   *fretted* dug constant wearing
make a leg i.e., bow   *base court* lower courtyard
glist'ring glittering
Phaeton sun god's son who drove his father's chariot too near the earth and scorched it (symbol of colossal failure)
Wanting lacking   *manage* control

NORTHUMBERLAND.   Sorrow and grief of heart
  Makes him speak fondly,° like a frantic man.
185 Yet he is come.
    [Enter KING RICHARD and his attendants below.]
BOLINGBROKE. Stand all apart,
  And show fair duty to his majesty.
                    [He kneels down.]
  My gracious lord—
KING RICHARD. Fair cousin, you debase your
190   princely knee
  To make the base earth proud with kissing it.
  Me rather had my heart might feel your love
  Than my unpleas'd eye see your courtesy.
  Up, cousin, up; your heart is up, I know—
195 Thus high at least, although your knee be low.
BOLINGBROKE. My gracious lord, I come but for
  mine own.
KING RICHARD. Your own is yours, and I am yours,
  and all.
BOLINGBROKE. So far be mine, my most redoubted°
  lord,
  As my true service shall deserve your love.
KING RICHARD. Well you deserve. They well
200   deserve to have
  That know the strong'st and surest way to get.
  Uncle, give me your hands. Nay, dry your eyes;
  Tears show their love, but want their remedies.°
  Cousin, I am too young to be your father,
205 Though you are old enough to be my heir.
  What you will have, I'll give, and willing too;
  For do we must what force will have us do.
  Set on towards London, cousin, is it so?
BOLINGBROKE. Yea, my good lord.
KING RICHARD.   Then I must not say no.
                    [Flourish. Exeunt]

SCENE iv
Langley. The DUKE OF YORK's garden.

[Enter the QUEEN and two LADIES.]
QUEEN. What sport shall we devise here in this
  garden
  To drive away the heavy thought of care?
LADY. Madam, we'll play at bowls.
QUEEN. 'Twill make me think the world is full of
  rubs
5 And that my fortune runs against the bias.°
LADY. Madam, we'll dance.
QUEEN. My legs can keep no measure in delight
  When my poor heart no measure keeps in grief.

Therefore no dancing, girl; some other sport.
LADY. Madam, we'll tell tales.   10
QUEEN. Of sorrow or of joy?
LADY.   Of either, madam.
QUEEN. Of neither, girl.
  For if of joy, being altogether wanting,
  It doth remember me the more of sorrow;
  Or if of grief, being altogether had,   15
  It adds more sorrow to my want of joy.
  For what I have I need not to repeat,
  And what I want it boots° not to complain.
LADY. Madam, I'll sing.
QUEEN.   'Tis well that thou hast cause;
  But thou shouldst please me better wouldst
  thou weep.   20
LADY. I could weep, madam, would it do you good.
QUEEN. And I could sing, would weeping do me
  good,
  And never borrow any tear of thee.
    [Enter a GARDENER, and two SERVANTS.]
  But stay, here come the gardeners.
  Let's step into the shadow of these trees.   25
  My wretchedness unto a row of pins
  They'll talk of state, for everyone doth so
  Against° a change. Woe is forerun with woe.
              [QUEEN and LADIES retire.]
GARDENER. Go bind thou up yon dangling apri-
  cocks,
  Which like unruly children make their sire   30
  Stoop with oppression of their prodigal weight.
  Give some supportance to the bending twigs.
  Go thou, and like an executioner
  Cut off the heads of too-fast-growing sprays
  That look too lofty in our commonwealth.   35
  All must be even° in our government.
  You thus employ'd, I will go root away
  The noisome weeds, which without profit suck
  The soil's fertility from wholesome flowers.
SERVANT. Why should we in the compass of a pale° 40
  Keep law and form and due proportion,
  Showing, as in a model, our firm estate,
  When our sea-walled garden, the whole land,
  Is full of weeds, her fairest flowers chok'd up,
  Her fruit-trees all unprun'd, her hedges ruin'd, 45
  Her knots disorder'd, and her wholesome herbs
  Swarming with caterpillars?
GARDENER.   Hold thy peace.
  He that hath suffer'd this disorder'd spring
  Hath now himself met with the fall of leaf.
  The weeds which his broad-spreading leaves did
  shelter,
  That seem'd in eating him to hold him up,   50

---

fondly foolishly   *redoubted* dread
want . . . remedies lack power to remedy
rubs . . . bias impediments . . . curvature (bowling terms)

boots avails   *against* in expectation of
even tidy   *compass . . . pale* limits of a park

Are pluck'd up root and all by Bolingbroke.
I mean the Earl of Wiltshire, Bushy, Green.
SERVANT. What, are they dead?
GARDENER.   They are, and Bolingbroke
55 Hath seiz'd the wasteful king. O, what pity is it
That he had not so trimm'd and dress'd his
    land
As we this garden! We at time of year
Do wound the bark, the skin of our fruit trees,
Lest, being over-proud° in sap and blood,
60 With too much riches it confound itself.
Had he done so to great and growing men,
They might have liv'd to bear and he to taste
Their fruits of duty. Superfluous branches
We lop away, that bearing boughs may live.
65 Had he done so, himself had borne the crown,
Which waste of idle hours hath quite thrown
    down.
SERVANT. What, think you then the king shall be
    depos'd?
GARDENER. Depress'd he is already, and depos'd
'Tis doubt° he will be. Letters came last night
70 To a dear friend of the good Duke of York's
That tell black tidings.
QUEEN. O, I am press'd° to death through want of
    speaking!
                              [Coming forward.]
Thou old Adam's° likeness, set to dress this
    garden,
How dares thy harsh rude tongue sound this
    unpleasing news?
75 What Eve, what serpent, hath suggested thee
To make a second fall of cursed man?
Why dost thou say King Richard is depos'd?
Dar'st thou, thou little better thing than earth,

Divine his downfall? Say where, when, and how
Cam'st thou by this ill tidings? Speak, thou
    wretch.   80
GARDENER. Pardon me, madam. Little joy have I
To breathe this news; yet what I say is true.
King Richard, he is in the mighty hold
Of Bolingbroke. Their fortunes both are
    weigh'd.
In your lord's scale is nothing but himself   85
And some few vanities that make him light;
But in the balance of great Bolingbroke,
Besides himself, are all the English peers,
And with that odds he weighs King Richard
    down.
Post you to London, and you will find it so;   90
I speak no more than everyone doth know.
QUEEN. Nimble mischance, that art so light of foot,
Doth not thy embassage° belong to me,
And am I last that knows it? O, thou think'st
To serve me last that I may longest keep   95
Thy sorrow in my breast. Come, ladies, go
To meet at London London's king in woe.
What, was I born to this that my sad look
Should grace the triumph of great Bolingbroke?
Gardener, for telling me these news of woe,   100
Pray God the plants thou graft'st may never
    grow.   [Exeunt QUEEN and LADIES.]
GARDENER. Poor queen! So that thy state might be
    no worse,
I would my skill were subject to thy curse.
Here did she fall a tear; here in this place
I'll set a bank of rue, sour herb of grace.°   105
Rue, even for ruth,° here shortly shall be seen
In the remembrance of a weeping queen.
                              [Exeunt]

over-proud swollen   doubt feared   embassage message   grace repentance
press'd oppressed   Adam i.e., the first gardener   ruth pity

A C T   I V

SCENE i
Westminster Hall.

[Enter, *as to the Parliament,* BOLINGBROKE,
AUMERLE, NORTHUMBERLAND, PERCY, FITZWATER,
SURREY, *the* BISHOP OF CARLISLE, *the* ABBOT OF
WESTMINSTER, *and another* LORD, HERALD,
OFFICERS, *and* BAGOT.]
BOLINGBROKE. Call forth Bagot.
Now, Bagot, freely speak thy mind—

What thou dost know of noble Gloucester's
    death,
Who wrought it with the king, and who per-
    form'd
The bloody office of his timeless end.   5
BAGOT. Then set before my face the Lord Aumerle.
BOLINGBROKE. Cousin, stand forth and look upon
    that man.
BAGOT. My Lord Aumerle, I know your daring
    tongue

Scorns to unsay what once it hath deliver'd.
In that dead time when Gloucester's death was
10   plotted,
I heard you say, "Is not my arm of length,
That reacheth from the restful English court
As far as Calais, to mine uncle's head?"
Amongst much other talk, that very time,
15 I heard you say that you had rather refuse
The offer of an hundred thousand crowns
Than Bolingbroke's return to England,
Adding withal how blest this land would be
In this your cousin's death.
    AUMERLE.   Princes and noble lords,
20   What answer shall I make to this base man?
Shall I so much dishonor my fair stars,
On equal terms to give him chastisement?
Either I must, or have mine honor soil'd
With the attainder° of his sland'rous lips.
25   There is my gage, the manual seal of death°
That marks thee out for hell. I say thou liest
And will maintain what thou hast said is false
In thy heartblood, though being all too base
To stain the temper of my knightly sword.
BOLINGBROKE. Bagot, forbear; thou shalt not take
30   it up.
AUMERLE. Excepting one, I would he were the best
In all this presence that hath mov'd me so.
FITZWATER. If that thy valor stand on sympathy,°
There is my gage, Aumerle, in gage to thine.
By that fair sun which shows me where thou
35   stand'st,
I heard thee say, and vauntingly thou spak'st it,
That thou wert cause of noble Gloucester's
death.
If thou deny'st it twenty times, thou liest,
And I will turn thy falsehood to thy heart,
40   Where it was forged, with my rapier's point.
AUMERLE. Thou dar'st not, coward, live to see that
day.
FITZWATER. Now, by my soul, I would it were this
hour.
AUMERLE. Fitzwater, thou art damn'd to hell for
this.
HENRY PERCY. Aumerle, thou liest; his honor is as
true
45 In this appeal° as thou art all unjust;
And that thou art so, there I throw my gage
To prove it on thee to th' extremest point
Of mortal breathing. Seize it if thou dar'st.
AUMERLE. An if° I do not, may my hands rot off
50   And never brandish more revengeful steel

Over the glitt'ring helmet of my foe!
ANOTHER LORD. I task the earth t' the like,° for-
sworn Aumerle,
And spur thee on with full as many lies
As may be holloa'd in thy treach'rous ear
From sun to sun. There is my honor's pawn;   55
Engage it to the trial if thou dar'st.
AUMERLE. Who sets° me else? By heaven, I'll
throw° at all.
I have a thousand spirits in one breast
To answer twenty thousand such as you.
SURREY. My Lord Fitzwater, I do remember well   60
The very time Aumerle and you did talk.
FITZWATER. 'Tis very true. You were in presence
then,
And you can witness with me this is true.
SURREY. As false, by heaven, as heaven itself is
true.
FITZWATER. Surrey, thou liest.
SURREY.   Dishonorable boy!   65
That lie shall lie so heavy on my sword
That it shall render vengeance and revenge
Till thou the lie-giver and that lie do lie
In earth as quiet as thy father's skull.
In proof whereof, there is my honor's pawn;   70
Engage it to the trial if thou dar'st.
FITZWATER. How fondly° dost thou spur a forward°
horse!
If I dare eat, or drink, or breathe, or live,
I dare meet Surrey in a wilderness
And spit upon him whilst I say he lies,   75
And lies, and lies. There is my bond of faith
To tie thee to my strong correction.°
As I intend to thrive in this new world,
Aumerle is guilty of my true appeal.
Besides, I heard the banish'd Norfolk say   80
That thou, Aumerle, didst send two of thy men
To execute the noble duke at Calais.
AUMERLE. Some honest Christian trust me with a
gage
That Norfolk lies. Here do I throw down this,
If he may be repeal'd,° to try his honor.   85
BOLINGBROKE. These differences shall all rest under
gage°
Till Norfolk be repeal'd. Repeal'd he shall be,
And, though mine enemy, restor'd again
To all his lands and signories.° When he's
return'd,

---

attainder slander
manual . . . death i.e., death warrant
sympathy equality   appeal accusation   An if if

I . . . like i.e., I throw down my gage also
sets challenges   *throw* cast (dicing metaphor)
fondly foolishly   *forward* spirited
tie . . . correction bind you to the chastisement I shall
    administer
repeal'd recalled from banishment
under gage i.e., as formal challenges   *signories* estates

90   Against Aumerle we will enforce his trial.
CARLISLE. That honorable day shall ne'er be seen.
Many a time hath banish'd Norfolk fought
For Jesu Christ in glorious Christian field,
Streaming the ensign° of the Christian cross
95   Against black pagans, Turks, and Saracens,
And toil'd with works of war, retir'd himself
To Italy, and there at Venice gave
His body to that pleasant country's earth
And his pure soul unto his captain Christ,
100   Under whose colors he had fought so long.
BOLINGBROKE. Why, bishop, is Norfolk dead?
CARLISLE. As surely as I live, my lord.
BOLINGBROKE. Sweet peace conduct his sweet soul
    to the bosom
Of good old Abraham!° Lords appellants,°
105   Your differences shall all rest under gage
Till we assign you to your days of trial.
            [Enter YORK, attended.]
YORK. Great Duke of Lancaster, I come to thee
From plume-pluck'd Richard, who with willing
    soul
Adopts thee heir and his high sceptre yields
110   To the possession of thy royal hand.
Ascend his throne, descending now from him,
And long live Henry, fourth of that name!
BOLINGBROKE. In God's name, I'll ascend the regal
    throne.
CARLISLE. Marry, God forbid!
115   Worst° in this royal presence may I speak,
Yet best beseeming me to speak the truth.
Would God that any in this noble presence
Were enough noble to be upright judge
Of noble Richard! Then true noblesse° would
120   Learn° him forbearance from so foul a wrong.
What subject can give sentence on his king?
And who sits here that is not Richard's subject?
Thieves are not judg'd but they are by to hear,
Although apparent° guilt be seen in them.
125   And shall the figure of God's majesty,
His captain, steward, deputy elect,
Anointed, crowned, planted many years,
Be judg'd by subject and inferior breath,
And he himself not present? O, forfend° it, God,
130   That in a Christian climate souls refin'd
Should show so heinous, black, obscene a deed!
I speak to subjects, and a subject speaks,
Stirr'd up by God, thus boldly for his king.
My Lord of Hereford here, whom you call king,
Is a foul traitor to proud Hereford's king,   135
And if you crown him, let me prophesy
The blood of English shall manure the ground
And future ages groan for this foul act;
Peace shall go sleep with Turks and infidels,
And in this seat of peace tumultuous wars   140
Shall kin with kin and kind with kind confound;
Disorder, horror, fear, and mutiny
Shall here inhabit, and this land be call'd
The field of Golgotha° and dead men's skulls.
O, if you raise this house against this house,   145
It will the woefulest division prove
That ever fell upon this cursed earth.
Prevent it, resist it, let it not be so,
Lest child, child's children, cry against you
    "Woe!"
NORTHUMBERLAND. Well have you argued, sir, and
    for your pains,   150
Of capital treason we arrest you here.
My Lord of Westminster, be it your charge
To keep him safely till his day of trial.
May it please you, lords, to grant the commons'
    suit?°
BOLINGBROKE. Fetch hither Richard, that in com-
    mon view   155
He may surrender; so we shall proceed
Without suspicion.
YORK.   I will be his conduct.   [Exit]
BOLINGBROKE. Lords, you that here are under our
    arrest,
Procure your sureties for your days of answer.°
Little are we beholding to your love,   160
And little look'd for at your helping hands.
    [Re-enter YORK, with RICHARD, and OFFICERS
            bearing the regalia.]
KING RICHARD. Alack, why am I sent for to a king
Before I have shook off the regal thoughts
Wherewith I reign'd? I hardly yet have learn'd
T' insinuate,° flatter, bow, and bend my limbs.   165
Give sorrow leave awhile to tutor me
To this submission. Yet I well remember
The favors° of these men. Were they not mine?
Did they not sometime° cry "All hail!" to me?
So Judas did to Christ: but He in twelve   170
Found truth in all but one; I, in twelve thousand,
    none.
God save the king! Will no man say amen?
Am I both priest and clerk? Well then, amen.

Streaming the ensign   flying the flag
bosom . . . Abraham   rest in Paradise (see Luke 16:22)
appellants   accusers   Worst   i.e., with least prestige
noblesse   nobility   Learn   teach
Although apparent   even though evident
forfend   forbid

Golgotha   site of the Crucifixion, the "place of a skull"
commons' suit   that charges against Richard be made
    public
sureties . . . answer   guarantors of your appearance for
    trial
insinuate   ingratiate   favors   faces
sometime   formerly

God save the king! although I be not he;
175 And yet, amen, if heaven do think him me.
To do what service am I sent for hither?
YORK. To do that office of thine own good will
Which tired majesty did make thee offer—
The resignation of thy state and crown
180 To Henry Bolingbroke.
KING RICHARD. Give me the crown. Here, cousin,
seize the crown.
Here, cousin,
On this side my hand and on that side yours.
Now is this golden crown like a deep well
185 That owes° two buckets, filling one another,
The emptier ever dancing in the air,
The other down, unseen, and full of water.
That bucket down and full of tears am I,
Drinking my griefs, whilst you mount up on
high.
BOLINGBROKE. I thought you had been willing to
190 resign.
KING RICHARD. My crown I am, but still my griefs
are mine.
You may my glories and my state depose,
But not my griefs; still am I king of those.
BOLINGBROKE. Part of your cares you give me with
your crown.
KING RICHARD. Your cares set up do not pluck my
195 cares down.
My care is loss of care, by old care done;
Your care is gain of care, by new care won.
The cares I give, I have, though given away;
They tend the crown, yet still with me they stay.
BOLINGBROKE. Are you contented to resign the
200 crown?
KING RICHARD. Aye, no; no, aye; for I must nothing
be
Therefore no no, for I resign to thee.
Now mark me how I will undo myself:
I give this heavy weight from off my head
205 And this unwieldy sceptre from my hand,
The pride of kingly sway from out my heart;
With mine own tears I wash away my balm,°
With mine own hands I give away my crown,
With mine own tongue deny my sacred state,
210 With mine own breath release all duty's rites;
All pomp and majesty I do forswear;
My manors, rents, revenues I forgo;
My acts, decrees, and statutes I deny.
God pardon all oaths that are broke to me!
215 God keep all vows unbroke that swear to thee!
Make me, that nothing have, with nothing
griev'd,

And thou with all pleas'd, that hast all achiev'd!
Long mayst thou live in Richard's seat to sit,
And soon lie Richard in an earthy pit!
God save King Harry, unking'd Richard says, 220
And send him many years of sunshine days!
What more remains?
NORTHUMBERLAND. No more but that you read
These accusations and these grievous crimes
Committed by your person and your followers
Against the state and profit of this land, 225
That, by confessing them, the souls of men
May deem that you are worthily depos'd.
KING RICHARD. Must I do so? And must I ravel out
My weav'd-up folly? Gentle Northumberland,
If thy offenses were upon record, 230
Would it not shame thee in so fair a troop
To read a lecture of them? If thou wouldst,
There shouldst thou find one heinous article
Containing the deposing of a king
And cracking the strong warrant of an oath,° 235
Mark'd with a blot, damn'd in the book of
heaven.
Nay, all of you that stand and look upon
Whilst that my wretchedness doth bait myself,
Though some of you with Pilate wash your
hands,
Showing an outward pity, yet you Pilates 240
Have here deliver'd me to my sour cross,
And water cannot wash away your sin.
NORTHUMBERLAND. My lord, dispatch; read o'er
these articles.
KING RICHARD. Mine eyes are full of tears. I cannot
see;
And yet salt water blinds them not so much 245
But they can see a sort of traitors here.
Nay, if I turn mine eyes upon myself,
I find myself a traitor with the rest,
For I have given here my soul's consent
T' undeck the pompous° body of a king, 250
Made glory base and sovereignty a slave,
Proud majesty a subject, state a peasant.
NORTHUMBERLAND. My lord—
KING RICHARD. No lord of thine, thou haught°
insulting man,
Nor no man's lord. I have no name, no title, 255
No, not that name was giv'n me at the font,
But 'tis usurp'd. Alack the heavy day,
That I have worn so many winters out
And know not now what name to call myself!
O that I were a mockery king of snow, 260
Standing before the sun of Bolingbroke,
To melt myself away in waterdrops!

---

owes° owns
balm° holy oil with which the king was anointed

cracking . . . oath (see III, iii, 101–120)
pompous° decked with pomp   haught° haughty

Good king, great king, and yet not greatly good,
An if my word be sterling yet in England,
265 Let it command a mirror hither straight,
That it may show me what a face I have,
Since it is bankrupt of his° majesty.
BOLINGBROKE. Go some of you and fetch a looking-
glass.   [*Exit an* ATTENDANT.]
NORTHUMBERLAND. Read o'er this paper while the
glass doth come.
KING RICHARD. Fiend, thou torment'st me ere I
270 come to hell!
BOLINGBROKE. Urge it no more, my Lord North-
umberland.
NORTHUMBERLAND. The commons will not then be
satisfied.
KING RICHARD. They shall be satisfied. I'll read
enough
When I do see the very book indeed
275 Where all my sins are writ, and that's myself.
[*Re-enter* ATTENDANT, *with a glass.*]
Give me the glass, and therein will I read.
No deeper wrinkles yet? Hath sorrow struck
So many blows upon this face of mine,
And made no deeper wounds? O flatt'ring glass,
280 Like to my followers in prosperity,
Thou dost beguile me! Was this face the face
That every day under his household roof
Did keep ten thousand men? Was this the face
That like the sun did make beholders wink?
285 Was this the face that fac'd° so many follies
And was at last outfac'd by Bolingbroke?
A brittle° glory shineth in this face.
As brittle as the glory is the face,
[*Dashes the glass against the ground.*]
For there it is, crack'd in a hundred shivers.°
290 Mark, silent king, the moral of this sport,
How soon my sorrow hath destroy'd my face.
BOLINGBROKE. The shadow of your sorrow hath
destroy'd
The shadow of your face.
KING RICHARD.   Say that again.
The shadow of my sorrow! Ha! Let's see.
295 'Tis very true, my grief lies all within,
And these external manners of laments
Are merely shadows to the unseen grief
That swells with silence in the tortur'd soul;

There lies the substance, and I thank thee, king,
For thy great bounty that not only giv'st   300
Me cause to wail but teachest me the way
How to lament the cause. I'll beg one boon
And then be gone and trouble you no more.
Shall I obtain it?
BOLINGBROKE. Name it, fair cousin.
KING RICHARD. "Fair cousin"? I am greater than a
king.   305
For when I was a king, my flatterers
Were then but subjects; being now a subject,
I have a king here to my flatterer.
Being so great, I have no need to beg.
BOLINGBROKE. Yet ask.   310
KING RICHARD. And shall I have?
BOLINGBROKE. You shall.
KING RICHARD. Then give me leave to go.
BOLINGBROKE. Whither?
KING RICHARD. Whither you will, so I were from
your sights.   315
BOLINGBROKE. Go some of you, convey him to the
Tower.
KING RICHARD. O, good! Convey? Conveyers° are
you all
That rise thus nimbly by a true king's fall.
[*Exeunt* KING RICHARD, *some* LORDS, *and a* GUARD.]
BOLINGBROKE. On Wednesday next we solemnly
set down
Our coronation. Lords, prepare yourselves.   320
[*Exeunt all except the* BISHOP OF CARLISLE, *the*
ABBOT OF WESTMINSTER, *and* AUMERLE.]
ABBOT. A woeful pageant have we here beheld.
CARLISLE. The woe's to come; the children yet
unborn
Shall feel this day as sharp to them as thorn.
AUMERLE. You holy clergymen, is there no plot
To rid the realm of this pernicious blot?   325
ABBOT. My lord,
Before I freely speak my mind herein,
You shall not only take the sacrament
To bury mine intents, but also to effect
Whatever I shall happen to devise.   330
I see your brows are full of discontent,
Your hearts of sorrow, and your eyes of tears.
Come home with me to supper, and I'll lay°
A plot shall show us all a merry day.   [*Exeunt*]

---

his its   *fac'd* countenanced   *brittle* fragile
shivers splinters

Convey . . . Conveyers (with sense of *steal . . . thieves*)
lay lay out

ACT V

SCENE i
London. A street leading to the Tower

[*Enter* QUEEN *and* LADIES.]

QUEEN. This way the king will come; this is the
    way
    To Julius Cæsar's ill-erected tower,°
    To whose flint bosom my condemned lord
    Is doom'd a prisoner by proud Bolingbroke.
5   Here let us rest, if this rebellious earth
    Have any resting for her true king's queen.

        [*Enter* RICHARD *and* GUARD.]

    But soft, but see—or rather do not see—
    My fair rose° wither. Yet look up, behold,
    That you in pity may dissolve to dew
10   And wash him fresh again with truelove tears.
    Ah, thou, the model where old Troy did stand,
    Thou map of honor, thou King Richard's tomb,
    And not King Richard, thou most beauteous
        inn;
    Why should hard-favor'd grief be lodg'd in thee
15 When triumph is become an alehouse guest?°

KING RICHARD. Join not with grief, fair woman, do
    not so,
    To make my end too sudden. Learn, good soul,
    To think our former state a happy dream,
    From which awak'd, the truth of what we are
20 Shows us but this: I am sworn brother, sweet,
    To grim Necessity, and he and I
    Will keep a league till death. Hie thee to France
    And cloister thee in some religious house.
    Our holy lives must win a new world's° crown,
    Which our profane hours here have stricken
25   down.

QUEEN. What, is my Richard both in shape and
    mind
    Transform'd and weaken'd? Hath Bolingbroke
    depos'd
    Thine intellect? Hath he been in thy heart?

Julius Caesar's . . . tower (the Tower of London, built,
  according to legend, by Caesar, was used as a prison,
  hence *ill*)
rose i.e., Richard
Ah . . . guest i.e., Richard is the ruin (Troy, symbol of
  ruin) of his former self, a mere outline (map) of honor
  and tomb of his own greatness, a beauteous lodging
  where resides ugly-faced grief while triumph resides in
  an alehouse (Bolingbroke)
new world's i.e., heavenly

    The lion dying thrusteth forth his paw
    And wounds the earth, if nothing else, with
        rage   30
    To be° o'erpower'd; and wilt thou, pupil-like,
    Take thy correction mildly, kiss the rod,
    And fawn on rage with base humility,
    Which art a lion and a king of beasts?

KING RICHARD. A king of beasts, indeed; if aught
    but beasts,   35
    I had been still a happy king of men.
    Good sometime queen, prepare thee hence for
    France.
    Think I am dead, and that even here thou
    tak'st,
    As from my deathbed, thy last living leave.
    In winter's tedious nights sit by the fire   40
    With good old folks and let them tell thee tales
    Of woeful ages long ago betid;°
    And ere thou bid goodnight, to quit their griefs,°
    Tell thou the lamentable tale of me
    And send the hearers weeping to their beds—   45
    For why, the senseless brands will sympathize°
    The heavy accent of thy moving tongue,
    And in compassion weep the fire out;
    And some will mourn in ashes, some coal-
    black,
    For the deposing of a rightful king.   50

        [*Enter* NORTHUMBERLAND *and others.*]

NORTHUMBERLAND. My lord, the mind of Boling-
    broke is chang'd;
    You must to Pomfret, not unto the Tower.
    And, madam, there is order ta'en for you;
    With all swift speed you must away to France.

KING RICHARD. Northumberland, thou ladder
    wherewithal   55
    The mounting Bolingbroke ascends my throne,
    The time shall not be many hours of age
    More than it is, ere foul sin gath'ring head
    Shall break into corruption. Thou shalt think,
    Though he divide the realm and give thee half, 60
    It is too little, helping him to all;
    And he shall think that thou, which know'st the
    way
    To plant unrightful kings, wilt know again,

To be at being   *betid* happened
quit . . . griefs recompense them for their woeful tales
For . . . sympathize for even the insensate firelogs will be
  moved by

Being ne'er so little urg'd, another way
To pluck him headlong from the usurp'd
65   throne.
The love of wicked men converts° to fear,
That fear to hate, and hate turns one or both
To worthy° danger and deserved death.
NORTHUMBERLAND. My guilt be on my head, and
there an end.
Take leave and part, for you must part forth-
70   with.
KING RICHARD. Doubly divorc'd! Bad men, you
violate
A twofold marriage: 'twixt my crown and me,
And then betwixt me and my married wife.
Let me unkiss the oath 'twixt thee and me;
75   And yet not so, for with a kiss 'twas made.
Part us, Northumberland; I towards the north,
Where shiv'ring cold and sickness pines° the
clime,
My wife to France, from whence, set forth in
pomp,
She came adorned hither like sweet May,
80   Sent back like Hallowmas° or short'st of day.
QUEEN. And must we be divided? Must we part?
KING RICHARD. Aye, hand from hand, my love, and
heart from heart.
QUEEN. Banish us both and send the king with me.
NORTHUMBERLAND. That were some love but little
policy.
85   QUEEN. Then whither he goes, thither let me go.
KING RICHARD. So two, together weeping, make
one woe.
Weep thou for me in France, I for thee here;
Better far off than near, be ne'er the near.°
Go, count thy way with sighs; I mine with
groans.
QUEEN. So longest way shall have the longest
90   moans.
KING RICHARD. Twice for one step I'll groan, the
way being short,
And piece the way out with a heavy heart.
Come, come, in wooing sorrow let's be brief,
Since, wedding it, there is such length in grief.
One kiss shall stop our mouths, and dumbly
95   part;°
Thus give I mine, and thus take I thy heart.
QUEEN. Give me mine own again; 'twere no good
part
To take on me to keep and kill thy heart.

So, now I have mine own again, be gone,
That I may strive to kill it with a groan.   100
KING RICHARD. We make woe wanton° with this
fond delay.
Once more, adieu; the rest let sorrow say.
                                    [Exeunt]

SCENE ii
The DUKE OF YORK's *palace.*

[*Enter* YORK *and his* DUCHESS.]
DUCHESS OF YORK. My lord, you told me you would
tell the rest,
When weeping made you break the story off
Of our two cousins coming into London.
YORK. Where did I leave?
DUCHESS OF YORK.   At that sad stop, my lord,
Where rude misgovern'd hands from windows'
tops   5
Threw dust and rubbish on King Richard's
head.
YORK. Then, as I said, the duke, great Bolingbroke,
Mounted upon a hot and fiery steed
Which his aspiring rider seem'd to know,
With slow but stately pace kept on his course   10
Whilst all tongues cried "God save thee, Boling-
broke!"
You would have thought the very windows
spake,
So many greedy looks of young and old
Through casements darted their desiring eyes
Upon his visage, and that all the walls   15
With painted imag'ry had said° at once
"Jesu preserve thee! Welcome, Bolingbroke!"
Whilst he, from one side to the other turning,
Bareheaded, lower than his proud steed's neck,
Bespake them thus: "I thank you, countrymen."   20
And thus still doing, thus he pass'd along.
DUCHESS OF YORK. Alack, poor Richard! Where
rode he the whilst?
YORK. As in a theater the eyes of men,
After a well-grac'd actor leaves the stage,
Are idly bent on him that enters next,   25
Thinking his prattle to be tedious,
Even so, or with much more contempt, men's
eyes
Did scowl on gentle Richard; no man cried
"God save him!"
No joyful tongue gave him his welcome home,

---

converts changes   *worthy* well-earned
pines afflicts   *Hallowmas* November 1
Better . . . near better to be far off than to be near but
never nearer (i.e., better to be distantly separated than
close but yet separated)
dumbly part separate in silence

make woe wanton make woe a strumpet (cheapen our
grief)
fond delay sentimental exhibition
painted . . . said i.e., "speaking pictures" painted on
cloths

30 But dust was thrown upon his sacred head,
    Which with such gentle sorrow he shook off,
    His face still combating with tears and smiles—
    The badges of his grief and patience—
    That had not God, for some strong purpose, steel'd
35 The hearts of men, they must perforce° have melted
    And barbarism itself have pitied him.
    But heaven hath a hand in these events,
    To whose high will we bound our calm contents.°
    To Bolingbroke are we sworn subjects now,
40 Whose state° and honor I for aye allow.
    DUCHESS OF YORK. Here comes my son Aumerle.
    YORK.   Aumerle that was,
    But that is lost for being Richard's friend;
    And, madam, you must call him Rutland° now.
    I am in parliament pledge for his truth
45 And lasting fealty to the new-made king.
                [Enter AUMERLE.]
    DUCHESS OF YORK. Welcome, my son. Who are the violets° now
    That strew the green lap of the new-come spring?
    AUMERLE. Madam, I know not, nor I greatly care not.
    God knows I had as lief be none as one.
    YORK. Well, bear you well in this new spring of time,
50 Lest you be cropp'd before you come to prime.
    What news from Oxford? Hold those justs and triumphs?°
    AUMERLE. For aught I know, my lord, they do.
    YORK. You will be there, I know.
55 AUMERLE. If God prevent not, I purpose so.
    YORK. What seal is that that hangs without thy bosom?
    Yea, look'st thou pale? Let me see the writing.
    AUMERLE. My lord, 'tis nothing.
    YORK. No matter, then, who see it.
    I will be satisfied; let me see the writing.
60 AUMERLE. I do beseech your grace to pardon me.
    It is a matter of small consequence
    Which for some reasons I would not have seen.
    YORK. Which for some reasons, sir, I mean to see.
    I fear, I fear—

    DUCHESS OF YORK.   What should you fear?
    'Tis nothing but some bond° that he is enter'd into
65 For gay apparel 'gainst° the triumph day.
    YORK. Bound to himself! What doth he with a bond
    That he is bound to? Wife, thou art a fool.
    Boy, let me see the writing.
    AUMERLE. I do beseech you, pardon me; I may not show it.
70 YORK. I will be satisfied; let me see it, I say.
            [He plucks it out of his bosom and reads it.]
    Treason! Foul treason! Villain! Traitor! Slave!
    DUCHESS OF YORK. What is the matter, my lord?
    YORK. Ho! Who is within there?
                [Enter a SERVANT.]
                              Saddle my horse.
    God for his mercy, what treachery is here!
75 DUCHESS OF YORK. Why, what is it, my lord?
    YORK. Give me my boots, I say. Saddle my horse.
                [Exit SERVANT.]
    Now, by mine honor, by my life, by my troth,
    I will appeach° the villain.
    DUCHESS OF YORK.   What is the matter?
    YORK. Peace, foolish woman.
80 DUCHESS OF YORK. I will not peace. What is the matter, Aumerle?
    AUMERLE. Good mother, be content; it is no more
    Than my poor life must answer.
    DUCHESS OF YORK.   Thy life answer!
    YORK. Bring me my boots. I will unto the king.
                [Re-enter SERVANT with boots.]
    DUCHESS OF YORK. Strike him, Aumerle. Poor boy, th' art amaz'd.
85 Hence, villain! Never more come in my sight.
    YORK. Give me my boots, I say.
    DUCHESS OF YORK. Why, York, what wilt thou do?
    Wilt thou not hide the trespass of thine own?
    Have we more sons? Or are we like to have?
90 Is not my teeming date drunk up with time?°
    And wilt thou pluck my fair son from mine age
    And rob me of a happy mother's name?
    Is he not like thee? Is he not thine own?
    YORK. Thou fond mad woman,
95 Wilt thou conceal this dark conspiracy?
    A dozen of them here have ta'en the sacrament
    And interchangeably° set down their hands
    To kill the king at Oxford.
    DUCHESS OF YORK.   He shall be none;
    We'll keep him here. Then what is that to him? 100

---

perforce of necessity
To . . . contents i.e., we are content, trusting in heaven's
    will ("in thy will is our peace")
state high place
Rutland (he has been deprived of his ducal title of
    Aumerle)
violets i.e., the new king's favorites
justs . . . triumphs tournaments . . . festivities

bond agreement to pay   'gainst in preparation for
appeach publicly charge
teeming . . . time time of childbearing past
interchangeably (i.e., each has a copy of the document
    signed by all)

YORK. Away, fond woman! Were he twenty times
　　my son,
　I would appeach him.
DUCHESS OF YORK.　　Hadst thou groan'd for him
　As I have done, thou wouldst be more pitiful.
　But now I know thy mind: thou dost suspect
105　That I have been disloyal to thy bed
　And that he is a bastard, not thy son.
　Sweet York, sweet husband, be not of that mind.
　He is as like thee as a man may be,
　Not like to me, or any of my kin,
　And yet I love him.
110　YORK.　　　　Make way, unruly woman! [Exit]
　DUCHESS OF YORK. After, Aumerle! Mount thee
　　upon his horse;
　Spur post,° and get before him to the king,
　And beg thy pardon ere he do accuse thee.
　I'll not be long behind; though I be old,
115　I doubt not but to ride as fast as York.
　And never will I rise up from the ground
　Till Bolingbroke have pardon'd thee. Away, be
　　gone!　　　　　　　　　　　　[Exeunt]

SCENE iii
Windsor Castle.

[Enter BOLINGBROKE, HENRY PERCY, and other
　　LORDS.]
BOLINGBROKE. Can no man tell me of my unthrifty°
　　son?
　'Tis full three months since I did see him last.
　If any plague hang over us, 'tis he.
　I would to God, my lords, he might be found.
5　Inquire at London, 'mongst the taverns there,
　For there, they say, he daily doth frequent,
　With unrestrained loose companions—
　Even such, they say, as stand in narrow lanes
　And beat our watch and rob our passengers,°
10　Which he, young wanton and effeminate boy,
　Takes on the point of honor to support
　So dissolute a crew.°
HENRY PERCY. My lord, some two days since I saw
　　the prince
　And told him of those triumphs° held at Oxford.
15　BOLINGBROKE. And what said the gallant?
HENRY PERCY. His answer was he would unto the
　　stews°

Spur post ride hard
unthrifty prodigal　　　*passengers* travelers
Which . . . crew (an ungrammatical sentence with two
　subjects) he (the Prince) considers it a matter of honor
　to support his low companions who commit unlawful
　acts
triumphs festivities　　　*stews* brothels

And from the common'st creature pluck a
　glove
And wear it as a favor, and with that
He would unhorse the lustiest challenger.
BOLINGBROKE. As dissolute as desperate; yet
　　through both　　　　　　　　　　　　　20
　I see some sparks of better hope, which elder
　　years
　May happily bring forth. But who comes here?
　　　　　　　　　　　　　[Enter AUMERLE.]
AUMERLE. Where is the king?
BOLINGBROKE. What means our cousin that he
　　stares and looks
　So wildly?　　　　　　　　　　　　　　25
AUMERLE. God save your grace! I do beseech your
　　majesty
　To have some conference with your grace alone.
BOLINGBROKE. Withdraw yourselves and leave us
　　here alone.
　　　　　　　　　　[Exeunt PERCY and LORDS.]
　What is the matter with our cousin now?
AUMERLE. Forever may my knees grow to the
　　earth,　　　　　　　　　　　　　　30
　My tongue cleave to my roof within my mouth,
　Unless a pardon ere I rise or speak.
BOLINGBROKE. Intended or committed was this
　　fault?
　If on the first, how heinous e'er it be,
　To win thy after-love I pardon thee.　　　35
AUMERLE. Then give me leave that I may turn the
　　key,
　That no man enter till my tale be done.
BOLINGBROKE. Have thy desire.
YORK. [Within] My liege, beware; look to thyself.
　Thou hast a traitor in thy presence there.　40
BOLINGBROKE. Villain, I'll make thee safe.
　　　　　　　　　　　　　　[Drawing.]
AUMERLE. Stay thy revengeful hand; thou hast no
　　cause to fear.
YORK. [Within] Open the door, secure,° foolhardy
　　king.
　Shall I for love speak treason to thy face?
　Open the door, or I will break it open.　　45
　　　　　　　　　　　　　[Enter YORK.]
BOLINGBROKE. What is the matter, uncle? Speak.
　Recover breath; tell us how near is danger,
　That we may arm us to encounter it.
YORK. Peruse this writing here, and thou shalt
　　know
　The treason that my haste forbids me show.　50
AUMERLE. Remember, as thou read'st, thy promise
　　pass'd.
　I do repent me; read not my name there;

---

secure overconfident

My heart is not confederate with my hand.

YORK. It was, villain, ere thy hand did set it down.
55 I tore it from the traitor's bosom, king;
Fear, and not love, begets his penitence.
Forget to pity him, lest thy pity prove
A serpent that will sting thee to the heart.

BOLINGBROKE. O heinous, strong, and bold con-
spiracy!
60 O loyal father of a treacherous son!
Thou sheer, immaculate, and silver fountain
From whence this stream through muddy
passages
Hath held his current and defil'd himself!°
Thy overflow of good converts to bad,
65 And thy abundant goodness shall excuse
This deadly blot in thy digressing° son.

YORK. So shall my virtue be his vice's bawd,
And he shall spend mine honor with his shame
As thriftless sons their scraping fathers' gold.
70 Mine honor lives when his dishonor dies,
Or my sham'd life in his dishonor lies.
Thou kill'st me in his life; giving him breath,
The traitor lives, the true man's put to death.

DUCHESS OF YORK. [Within] What ho, my liege!
For God's sake, let me in.

BOLINGBROKE. What shrill-voiced suppliant makes
75 this eager cry?

DUCHESS OF YORK. A woman, and thy aunt, great
king; 'tis I.
Speak with me, pity me, open the door.
A beggar begs that never begg'd before.

BOLINGBROKE. Our scene is alter'd from a serious
thing,
And now chang'd to "The Beggar and the
80 King."°
My dangerous cousin, let your mother in.
I know she's come to pray for your foul sin.

YORK. If thou do pardon, whosoever pray,
More sins for this forgiveness prosper may.
85 This fester'd joint cut off, the rest rest sound;
This let alone will all the rest confound.

[Enter DUCHESS OF YORK.]

DUCHESS OF YORK. O king, believe not this hard-
hearted man!
Love loving not itself, none other can.°

YORK. Thou frantic woman, what dost thou make
here?
90 Shall thy old dugs once more a traitor rear?

DUCHESS OF YORK. Sweet York, be patient. Hear
me, gentle liege.   [Kneels]

BOLINGBROKE. Rise up, good aunt.

DUCHESS OF YORK.   Not yet, I thee beseech.
Forever will I walk upon my knees
And never see day that the happy sees
Till thou give joy—until thou bid me joy   95
By pardoning Rutland, my transgressing boy.

AUMERLE. Unto my mother's prayers I bend my
knee.   [Kneels]

YORK. Against them both my true joints bended
be.   [Kneels]
Ill mayst thou thrive if thou grant any grace!

DUCHESS OF YORK. Pleads he in earnest? Look upon
his face.   100
His eyes do drop no tears, his prayers are in
jest;
His words come from his mouth, ours from our
breast.
He prays but faintly and would be denied;
We pray with heart and soul and all beside.
His weary joints would gladly rise, I know;   105
Our knees shall kneel till to the ground they
grow.
His prayers are full of false hypocrisy;
Ours of true zeal and deep integrity.
Our prayers do out-pray his; then let them have
That mercy which true prayer ought to have.   110

BOLINGBROKE. Good aunt, stand up.

DUCHESS OF YORK.   Nay, do not say "Stand up."
Say "Pardon" first, and afterwards "Stand up."
An if I were thy nurse, thy tongue to teach,
"Pardon" should be the first word of thy
speech.
I never long'd to hear a word till now;   115
Say "Pardon," king; let pity teach thee how.
The word is short, but not so short as sweet;
No word like "pardon" for kings' mouths so
meet.

YORK. Speak it in French, king; say "Pardonne
moi."°

DUCHESS OF YORK. Dost thou teach pardon pardon
to destroy?   120
Ah, my sour husband, my hard-hearted lord,
That set'st the word itself against the word!
Speak "Pardon" as 'tis current in our land;
The chopping° French we do not understand.
Thine eye begins to speak; set thy tongue there. 125
Or in thy piteous heart plant thou thine ear,
That hearing how our plaints and prayers do
pierce,
Pity may move thee "Pardon" to rehearse.°

---

his . . . himself its . . . itself
digressing i.e., deviating from the course
Our scene . . . King our action is changing from tragedy
  to comedy (with allusion to a ballad about King
  Cophetua and the beggar maid)
Love . . . can who cannot love his own (son) can love no
  one

Pardonne moi excuse me (i.e., reject the plea)
chopping changing (of meaning)   rehearse repeat

BOLINGBROKE. Good aunt, stand up.
DUCHESS OF YORK.   I do not sue to stand;
130   Pardon is all the suit I have in hand.
BOLINGBROKE. I pardon him, as God shall pardon
    me.
DUCHESS OF YORK. O happy vantage of a kneeling
    knee!
    Yet am I sick for fear. Speak it again;
    Twice saying "Pardon" doth not pardon twain,°
    But makes one pardon strong.
135 BOLINGBROKE.   With all my heart
    I pardon him.
DUCHESS OF YORK.   A god on earth thou art.
BOLINGBROKE. But for our trusty brother-in-law,°
    and the abbot,°
    With all the rest of that consorted crew,
    Destruction straight shall dog them at the heels.
140   Good uncle, help to order several powers
    To Oxford, or where'er these traitors are.
    They shall not live within this world, I swear,
    But I will have them, if I once know where.
    Uncle, farewell, and cousin too, adieu.
    Your mother well hath pray'd, and prove you
145   true.
DUCHESS OF YORK. Come, my old son. I pray God
    make thee new.   [Exeunt]

                    SCENE iv
                    The same.

            [Enter EXTON and SERVANT.]
EXTON. Didst thou not mark the king, what words
    he spake?—
    "Have I no friend will rid me of this living fear?"
    Was it not so?
SERVANT.   These were his very words.
EXTON. "Have I no friend?" quoth he. He spake it
    twice,
5   And urg'd it twice together,° did he not?
SERVANT. He did.
EXTON. And speaking it, he wishtly° look'd on me,
    As who should say, "I would thou wert the man
    That would divorce this terror from my
    heart"—
10   Meaning the king at Pomfret. Come, let's go.
    I am the king's friend, and will rid his foe.
                    [Exeunt]

twain doubly
brother-in-law Exeter (ringleader of the Oxford
    conspirators and husband of Bolingbroke's sister)
abbot of Westminster
urg'd . . . together insisted by repeating
wishtly wishfully, wistfully

                    SCENE v
                    Pomfret Castle.

            [Enter KING RICHARD.]
KING RICHARD. I have been studying how I may
    compare
    This prison where I live unto the world,
    And for because the world is populous,
    And here is not a creature but myself,
    I cannot do it; yet I'll hammer it out.   5
    My brain I'll prove the female to my soul,
    My soul the father, and these two beget
    A generation of still-breeding° thoughts,
    And these same thoughts people this little world
    In humors° like the people of this world,   10
    For no thought is contented. The better sort,
    As thoughts of things divine, are intermix'd
    With scruples and do set the word itself
    Against the word,
    As thus, "Come, little ones," and then again,   15
    "It is as hard to come as for a camel
    To thread the postern° of a small needle's eye."
    Thoughts tending to ambition, they do plot
    Unlikely wonders—how these vain weak nails
    May tear a passage through the flinty ribs   20
    Of this hard world, my ragged° prison walls,
    And, for they cannot, die in their own pride.
    Thoughts tending to content flatter themselves
    That they are not the first of fortune's slaves,
    Nor shall not be the last, like silly beggars   25
    Who sitting in the stocks refuge° their shame
    That many have and others must sit there;
    And in this thought they find a kind of ease,
    Bearing their own misfortunes on the back
    Of such as have before endur'd the like.   30
    Thus play I in one person many people,
    And none contented. Sometimes am I king;
    Then treasons make me wish myself a beggar,
    And so I am. Then crushing penury
    Persuades me I was better when a king;   35
    Then am I king'd again; and by and by
    Think that I am unking'd by Bolingbroke,
    And straight am nothing. But whate'er I be,
    Nor I nor° any man that but man is
    With nothing shall be pleas'd till he be eas'd   40
    With being nothing. Music do I hear?
                    [Music.]
    Ha, ha! Keep time! How sour sweet music is
    When time is broke and no proportion kept!

still-breeding always multiplying
humors varied dispositions   postern narrow doorway
ragged rough   refuge find refuge for
Nor . . . nor neither . . . nor

                    145

So is it in the music of men's lives.
45 And here have I the daintiness of ear
To check° time broke in a disorder'd string,
But for the concord of my state and time
Had not an ear to hear my true time broke.
I wasted time, and now doth time waste me,
For now hath time made me his numb'ring°
50   clock:
My thoughts are minutes, and with sighs they
       jar
Their watches° on unto mine eyes, the outward
       watch,
Whereto my finger, like a dial's point,
Is pointing still, in cleansing them from tears.
55 Now sir, the sound that tells what hour it is
Are clamorous groans, which strike upon my
       heart,
Which is the bell. So sighs and tears and groans
Show minutes, times, and hours. But my time
Runs posting on in Bolingbroke's proud joy
While I stand fooling here, his Jack o' the
60   clock.°
This music mads me; let it sound no more;
For though it have holp madmen to their wits,
In me it seems it will make wise men mad.
Yet blessing on his heart that gives it me!
65 For 'tis a sign of love, and love to Richard
Is a strange brooch° in this all-hating world.
       [Enter a GROOM OF THE STABLE.]
GROOM. Hail, royal prince!
KING RICHARD.   Thanks, noble peer;
The cheapest of us is ten groats too dear.°
What art thou? And how com'st thou hither,
70 Where no man never comes but that sad dog
That brings me food to make misfortune live?
GROOM. I was a poor groom of thy stable, king,
When thou wert king, who, traveling towards
       York,
With much ado at length have gotten leave
75 To look upon my sometimes royal master's face.
O, how it yearn'd° my heart when I beheld
In London streets, that coronation day,
When Bolingbroke rode on roan Barbary,
That horse that thou so often hast bestrid,
80 That horse that I so carefully have dress'd!
KING RICHARD. Rode he on Barbary? Tell me,
       gentle friend,
How went he under him?

check rebuke   numb'ring i.e., marking the minutes
jar . . . watches tick their intervals
Jack . . . clock mechanical figure which struck the hour
brooch ornament
royal . . . dear i.e., to call me "royal" (coin worth ten
   shillings) is to overrate me by ten groats (forty pence)
yearn'd grieved

GROOM. So proudly as if he disdain'd the ground.
KING RICHARD. So proud that Bolingbroke was on
       his back!
That jade hath eat bread from my royal hand;   85
This hand hath made him proud with clapping
       him.
Would he not stumble? Would he not fall
       down,
Since pride must have a fall, and break the
       neck
Of that proud man that did usurp his back?
Forgiveness, horse! Why do I rail on thee,   90
Since thou, created to be aw'd by man,
Wast born to bear? I was not made a horse,
And yet I bear a burthen like an ass,
Spurr'd, gall'd, and tir'd by jauncing° Boling-
       broke.
       [Enter KEEPER, with a dish.]
KEEPER. Fellow, give place; here is no longer stay.   95
KING RICHARD. If thou love me, 'tis time thou wert
       away.
GROOM. What my tongue dares not, that my heart
       shall say.   [Exit]
KEEPER. My lord, will't please you to fall to?
KING RICHARD. Taste of it first, as thou art wont to
       do.
KEEPER. My lord, I dare not. Sir Pierce of Exton,   100
who lately came from the king, commands the
contrary.
KING RICHARD. The devil take Henry of Lancaster
and thee!
                                        [Beats the KEEPER.]
KEEPER. Help, help, help!
       [Enter EXTON and SERVANTS, armed.]
KING RICHARD. How now! What means Death in
this rude assault?   105
Villain, thy own hand yields thy death's instru-
       ment.
[Snatching an axe from a SERVANT and killing him.]
Go thou and fill another room in hell.
       [He kills another. Then EXTON strikes him down.]
That hand shall burn in never-quenching fire
That staggers thus my person. Exton, thy fierce
       hand   110
Hath with the king's blood stain'd the king's
own land.
Mount, mount, my soul! Thy seat is up on high,
Whilst my gross flesh sinks downward, here to
die.   [Dies]
EXTON. As full of valor as of royal blood!
Both have I spill'd. O would the deed were
good!
For now the devil, that told me I did well,   115

jauncing prancing

Says that this deed is chronicled in hell.
This dead king to the living king I'll bear.
Take hence the rest, and give them burial here.

[*Exeunt*]

SCENE vi
Windsor Castle.

[*Flourish. Enter* BOLINGBROKE, YORK, *with other*
LORDS, *and* ATTENDANTS.]

BOLINGBROKE. Kind uncle York, the latest news we
hear
Is that the rebels have consum'd with fire
Our town of Cicester in Gloucestershire;
But whether they be ta'en or slain we hear not.

[*Enter* NORTHUMBERLAND.]

Welcome, my lord. What is the news?

NORTHUMBERLAND. First, to thy sacred state wish I
all happiness.

5   The next news is, I have to London sent
The heads of Oxford, Salisbury, Blunt, and
Kent.
The manner of their taking may appear
At large discoursed in this paper here.

BOLINGBROKE. We thank thee, gentle Percy, for thy
pains,
10   And to thy worth will add right worthy gains.

[*Enter* FITZWATER.]

FITZWATER. My lord, I have from Oxford sent to
London
The heads of Brocas and Sir Bennet Seely,
Two of the dangerous consorted traitors
That sought at Oxford thy dire overthrow.

BOLINGBROKE. Thy pains, Fitzwater, shall not be
15   forgot;
Right noble is thy merit, well I wot.

[*Enter* HENRY PERCY, *and the* BISHOP OF CARLISLE.]

HENRY PERCY. The grand conspirator, Abbot of
Westminster,

With clog° of conscience and sour melancholy   20
Hath yielded up his body to the grave;
But here is Carlisle living, to abide
Thy kingly doom and sentence of his pride.

BOLINGBROKE. Carlisle, this is your doom:
Choose out some secret place, some reverend
room,°   25
More than thou hast, and with it joy thy life;
So as thou liv'st in peace, die free from strife.
For though mine enemy thou hast ever been,
High sparks of honor in thee have I seen.

[*Enter* EXTON, *with persons bearing a coffin.*]

EXTON. Great king, within this coffin I present   30
Thy buried fear. Herein all breathless lies
The mightiest of thy greatest enemies,
Richard of Bordeaux, by me hither brought.

BOLINGBROKE. Exton, I thank thee not, for thou
hast wrought
A deed of slander, with thy fatal hand,   35
Upon my head and all this famous land.

EXTON. From your own mouth, my lord, did I this
deed.

BOLINGBROKE. They love not poison that do poison
need,
Nor do I thee. Though I did wish him dead,
I hate the murderer, love him murdered.   40
The guilt of conscience take thou for thy labor,
But neither my good word nor princely favor.
With Cain go wander thorough° shades of night,
And never show thy head by day nor light.
Lords, I protest my soul is full of woe   45
That blood should sprinkle me to make me
grow.
Come, mourn with me for that I do lament,
And put on sullen black incontinent.°
I'll make a voyage to the Holy Land
To wash this blood off from my guilty hand.   50
March sadly after. Grace my mournings here
In weeping after this untimely bier.   [*Exeunt*]

---

clog burden   *reverend room* holy refuge   *thorough* through   *incontinent* immediately

AFTERWORD

When he wrote *Richard II*, Shakespeare had behind him the experience of writing four history plays (possibly five, if the undatable *King John* intervened between *Richard III* and *Richard II*, as some believe) besides a similar number of comedies and one "drama of blood" (*Titus Andronicus*). *Richard II* forms the clearest link between the earlier "apprentice" histories and the plays of early maturity that immediately followed, for it exposes in approximately equal proportions the major defects of its predecessors and the marks of the mature craftsmanship to come.

Besides linking apprenticeship and maturity, *Richard II* has special connections with three groups of Shakespeare's plays: the "lyrical plays," the histories, and the tragedies (for it is identified by its Folio title as a tragedy). It is unique among Shakespeare's plays in being so multiply associated.

Richard II's nearest lyrical associates, of course, are the comedy *A Midsummer Night's Dream* and the tragedy *Romeo and Juliet*; all three were probably composed within a single theatrical year (1595–1596). To a degree, at least, the lyricism of these three plays transcends the relationship of each to its particular genre of comedy, tragedy, history, for they are all primarily lyrical dramas and secondarily comedy, tragedy, history. Each makes abundantly clear that in this "lyric year" Shakespeare was fascinated by the musical possibilities of language. At the worst, in this year, he was capable of making characters speak lyrically whose natures suggest anything but a tuneful disposition, and in situations where music is somewhat less than appropriate; but at the best he used the musical power of language not as ornament only but as a potent dramatic force. All three of the plays exhibit him at his best and at his worst in this regard, though clearly the lyric excesses of the comedy and the tragedy are less conspicuous than those of the history. The "shallowest thickskin," Bottom, of the *Dream*, can speak lyrically in prose—"I have had a most rare vision. I have had a dream past the wit of man to say what dream it was"—and the general tone of the fantasy easily accommodates him; but the Duchess of York breaks into rhyme in *Richard II* at an inopportune moment, and the effect is, to say the least, conspicuous.

Except for occasional individual lines like Richard's sudden "We were not born to sue, but to command," *Richard II* is not notably musical until the beginning of Act II, when dying Gaunt pours forth such a eulogy of England as had never been heard before on the English stage, and never since: "Methinks I am a prophet new-inspir'd." In that famous speech lyricism is unmistakably dramatic and functional, for it serves to stir the patriotic emotions of its hearers and thus to underscore the central theme of the play, and of all the history plays—the glory of England. But Shakespeare reserves his most potent dramatic application of lyricism until the second scene of Act III, when Richard, supposedly lost and dead in Ireland, returns to English soil: "I weep for joy/ To stand upon my kingdom once again." In this speech of about twenty-five lines, Shakespeare begins to turn the power of music to shrewd dramatic purpose—restoration of Richard to a place of sympathy in the hearts of the audience. Earlier, Richard's conduct (most particularly when he savagely rebukes and ridicules the dying Gaunt in Act II and, upon Gaunt's death, confiscates his estate) has alienated the audience and possibly even won its abhorrence. But once Bolingbroke (in general the counterpoint to the lyric strain throughout the play) has unlawfully recalled himself from banishment and begun his ruthless march to the throne, Shakespeare sets about to recover sympathy for Richard. He does so in various ways, but chiefly by bestowing upon the falling king a lyric voice that claims first the ear and then the heart, despite the weaknesses that, at the same time, it discloses in his character. From the second scene of Act III until his last words before his violent death, Richard speaks no passages of length that are not musically eloquent in the extreme and compulsive in their bid for our sympathy; indeed, sometimes substance that is in itself anything but lyrical is miraculously made so and seems virtually to demand that it be sung:

> Where is the Earl of Wiltshire? Where is Bagot?
> What is become of Bushy? Where is Green?

But the most noteworthy lyric flights are in the long passages, as in III, ii, "Let's talk of graves, of worms, and epitaphs"; in III, iii, "What must the king do now?"; in Act IV, scene i, "Now mark me how I will undo myself"; and in Act V, scene v, "I have been studying how I may compare/ This prison where I live unto the world." Like Romeo and like Macbeth, Richard becomes a greater poet as his experience of life deepens, and like them he deserves to rank with Shakespeare's greatest "poets."

Richard's is the chief lyric voice of the play; but Gaunt's single tremendous outburst of patriotic feeling, already noted, is richly musical. Besides Gaunt is the Bishop of Carlisle, to whose mouth, in IV, i, Shakespeare entrusts one of the most splendid utterances of the play, "Worst in this royal presence may I speak," wherein he asserts the divine right of kings and proclaims a warning of what will follow if Richard is deposed. Shakespeare's own audiences had already seen the tetralogy of *Henry VI–Richard III*, and of course they were familiar with the civil wars, hardly more than a hundred years in the past; hence they recognized the prophetic truth of Carlisle's dire warning:

> Disorder, horror, fear, and mutiny
> Shall here inhabit, and this land be called
> The field of Golgotha and dead men's skulls.

Thus in Richard, Gaunt, and Carlisle, to mention the most notable cases, Shakespeare makes shrewd dramatic use of lyric power, not only in reclaiming a degree of much-needed sympathy for his hero, but in reinforcing the major themes of the play.

His poetics, however, are not flawlessly employed throughout. Some of the verbal play, as in the parting scene of the king and queen (V, i), is tangled and excessive in its use of "conceits" that seem rather to bury than to express the sentiments that they are meant to convey; thus Richard,

> So two, together weeping, make one woe.
> Weep thou for me in France, I for thee here;
> Better far off than near, be ne'er the near.

Again,

> Come, come, in wooing sorrow let's be brief,
> Since, wedding it, there is such length in grief.
> One kiss shall stop our mouths, and dumbly part;
> Thus give I mine, and thus take I thy heart.

The Queen replies,

> Give me mine own again; 'twere no good part
> To take on me to keep and kill thy heart.
> So, now I have mine own again, be gone,
> That I may strive to kill it with a groan.

Clearly, Shakespeare invented this parting scene as a device for making Richard's plight more poignant, and on the stage, indeed, with the performers playing it as a heartbreaking moment, it is compelling; yet it is doubtful that, on the whole, the Queen does much for Richard as a means of claiming our sympathy. When she speaks, she injects a verbal artificiality into the poetics of the play that borders on cuteness; such is the effect of her conversations with Bushy and Bagot in Act II, scene ii, and with the Ladies and the Gardener in Act III, scene iv, where the dialogue looks back toward Shakespeare's early comedies rather than forward to the mature histories and tragedies. So too does the curious scene in which the Duchess of York bursts in upon Bolingbroke to beg amnesty for her son Aumerle (V, iii); so out of key is the poetic (and dramatic) quality of this scene that some scholars have suspected it as an interpolation by another hand than Shakespeare's, and it is easy to wish that it may have been just that. Finally, also curiously, some of the most awkward lines of the play are spoken by Henry Percy, the Hotspur of *1Henry IV*, and the finest "poet" of that play.

Characterization in *Richard II*, like the verse, looks both back toward earlier plays and forward toward mature ones. In the main it marks an advance beyond that of the *Henry VI* group, but is much inferior to that of *Henry IV*. *Romeo and Juliet*, a tragedy of the same year, exhibits a higher development of the art of character portrait: there the hero and the heroine, Mercutio, Capulet, and the Nurse are brilliant creations; even Benvolio and Tybalt are "free-standing," if limited, figures. With the exceptions of Richard and Bolingbroke (and the rampant-mother figure of the Duchess of York) none of the characters of *Richard II* comes alive. Most merely speak their lines to convey what is required at the moment, and others, like Gaunt, York, and Carlisle, though they seem impressive enough at particular moments, are so not as individual human beings with identities of their own, but as spokesmen for specific political points of view; they are primarily embodiments of particular ideas.

Even Richard and Bolingbroke are not fully realized characters, though at times each reveals traits that mark him as a man, and more than merely as a historical contrast to the other. These occasions are rare but striking: Richard, discovering in the mirror that he has "no deeper wrinkles yet," momentarily steps out of the picture frame in which he is identified as king by divine right and shows a glimpse of deeper humanity; Bolingbroke at the end, fretting about his wayward son, momentarily steps out of his role of ideological adversary and speaks like a father. Noteworthy is the degree of presumably deliberate ambiguity in the portraits of both men. Shakespeare's political balance is precariously situated throughout the play. *Richard II* is the keystone of all the eight histories that trace the problem of usurpation from its origin to its violent resolution in the overthrow of Richard III nearly a hundred years later. Richard II was a weak and vacillating king, wasteful, irresponsible, governed by favoritism and whim; but he *was* "king by divine right." Bolingbroke, who becomes King Henry IV, was grossly wronged by Richard and was, besides, far the shrewder and abler man—a kind of king by nature; but he usurped the throne of a king who ruled "by divine right." Richard abused the realm beyond bearing; but his overthrow and murder led to many years of bloody civil war—a fact of which Shakespeare was all the more aware for having just depicted those wars in the plays of *Henry VI* and *Richard III*.

In the final analysis it is impossible to determine where Shakespeare's personal sympathies lay or even where he wished the sympathies of his audience to lie. Early in the play we are repelled by Richard, who handles the Mowbray–Bolingbroke dispute ineptly and highhandedly. Later, at the time of his snarling words addressed to the dying Gaunt (who has just endeared himself to the audience by speaking the most stirring lines in the play, the tribute to England) he makes himself so odious that the likelihood of his ever again being restored to our favor seems slim indeed. Further, the frivolous conversation of Richard's queen with Bushy and Bagot reflects even more unfavorably upon the king's side; and much later the queen's savage reprimand of the Gardener, with her curse—"Pray God the plants thou graft'st may never grow"—serves to alienate our sympathies further. But, as has been remarked, when Richard returns from Ireland and finds himself helpless against a ruthless alliance of ambitious men who aim to crush him, Shakespeare turns the full force of poetry to the purpose of compelling sympathy for the underdog king, and this force he maintains with rising insistence until the end of the play, when Richard dies more heroically than he had lived, wielding an ax against the assassins who come at him from all sides.

The handling of Bolingbroke is similarly ambiguous. During the opening scene we are left in the dark as to who is right and who is wrong—Mowbray or Bolingbroke. Indeed at the end of the play, when Mowbray's heroic service in the Crusades and his death are saluted, the issue is left unresolved. When Richard seizes Bolingbroke's estate and titles after the death of Gaunt, it is Bolingbroke who is clearly the wronged man and Richard who is the villain. Even when Bolingbroke returns to England and begins his march toward London and the throne, we are in an emotional limbo. Both Northumberland and Bolingbroke swear that their sole aim is recovery of the rightful and hereditary dukedom of Lancaster, illegally stripped from Bolingbroke by Richard. Does Shakespeare mean that we should take their words at face value? Or are we to recognize one or the other's as cold-blooded lies? At once thereafter Bolingbroke's highhanded treatment of the king and the ruthlessness of his drive for the throne swing the sympathies wholly to Richard. Again, Bolingbroke's mercy extended to Aumerle, his kindness to the Duchess of York, his statesmanlike manner of speech invite our sympathies to him and away from Richard. However, the assassination of Richard by Exton, acting on a reported cue from Bolingbroke, once more reverses our allegiance. After Richard's death, Bolingbroke's solicitude for his son's welfare and his repudiation of Richard's murderer—coupled with his vow to "make a voyage to the Holy Land/ To wash this blood off from my guilty hand"—make a final plea for our favor. Whether they are successful must be decided by the individual reader or spectator, for Shakespeare leaves the deepest issues of the play unresolved at the end.

No other play of Shakespeare's pursues a course of such plotted ambiguities, wherein our sympathies are buffeted first this way and then that. Bolingbroke was both usurper and murderer, but he had been wronged by a worse king than he himself would become. Moreover, he was the father of a prince whom Shakespeare would soon represent on the stage as the ideal monarch. All elements considered, perhaps the dramatist pursued the only reasonable course in leaving the central issues unresolved at this point; he would take them up anew in the histories that followed.

Finally, with *Richard II* Shakespeare came nearer to writing a tragedy in the pattern of "Shakespearean tragedy," as the term is applied to the succession of tragedies from *Julius Caesar* to *Coriolanus*, than he had previously come. *Titus Andronicus*, designated as tragedy by the Folio, is a "drama of blood" without much real claim to the nobler title. *Richard III* shows drama enmeshed in historical events and presents the account of a man too wicked, in Aristotle's terms, to be a proper hero of tragedy; *Romeo and Juliet* is ruled by the stars rather than by human character—and character is the essence of "Shakespearean tragedy." Perhaps *Richard II*, like *Richard III*, is somewhat too consciously a chronicle of historical events to be an unquestionable tragedy, and perhaps, too, the fact that its interest is about equally divided between two protagonists, one falling, the other rising, blunts some of its tragic force. Yet there can be no reasonable doubt that it clearly anticipates the pattern of the tragic masterpieces soon to follow.

A NOTE ON THE COMPOSITION OF THE PLAY

Richard II was written in 1595 and first performed in that year. It was first printed in quarto in 1597. Shakespeare's main source, as for all the chronicle plays, was Raphael Holinshed's *Chronicles*.

Henry IV, Part 1

DRAMATIS PERSONÆ

KING HENRY   *the Fourth*
HENRY   *Prince of Wales* ⎫
JOHN   *of Lancaster* ⎭ *sons to the King*
EARL OF WESTMORLAND
SIR WALTER BLUNT
THOMAS PERCY   *Earl of Worcester*
HENRY PERCY   *Earl of Northumberland*
HENRY PERCY   *surnamed* HOTSPUR, *his son*
EDMUND MORTIMER   *Earl of March*
RICHARD SCROOP   *Archbishop of York*
ARCHIBALD   *Earl of Douglas*
OWEN GLENDOWER
SIR RICHARD VERNON
SIR JOHN FALSTAFF

SIR MICHAEL   *a friend to the Archbishop of York*
POINS
GADSHILL
PETO
BARDOLPH
LADY PERCY   *wife to Hotspur and sister to Mortimer*
LADY MORTIMER   *daughter to Glendower and wife to Mortimer*
MISTRESS QUICKLY   *hostess of a tavern in Eastcheap*
LORDS, OFFICERS, SHERIFF, VINTNER, CHAMBERLAIN, DRAWERS, *two* CARRIERS, TRAVELERS, *and* ATTENDANTS.

SCENE   *England and Wales*

ACT I

SCENE i
London. The palace.

[*Enter* KING HENRY, LORD JOHN OF LANCASTER, *the* EARL OF WESTMORELAND, SIR WALTER BLUNT, *and others.*]

KING. So shaken as we are, so wan with care,
Find we° a time for frighted peace to pant
And breathe short-winded accents of new broils
To be commenc'd in stronds° afar remote.
5   No more the thirsty entrance of this soil
Shall daub her lips with her own children's blood.
No more shall trenching° war channel her fields
Nor bruise her flow'rets with the armed hoofs
Of hostile paces. Those opposed eyes,
10   Which, like the meteors of a troubled heaven,

All of one nature, of one substance bred,
Did lately meet in the intestine° shock
And furious close° of civil butchery,
Shall now in mutual well-beseeming° ranks
March all one way and be no more oppos'd   15
Against acquaintance, kindred, and allies.
The edge of war, like an ill-sheathed knife,
No more shall cut his° master. Therefore, friends,
As far as to the sepulcher of Christ,
Whose soldier now, under whose blessed cross   20
We are impressed° and engag'd to fight,
Forthwith a power of English shall we levy
Whose arms were moulded in their mothers' womb
To chase these pagans in those holy fields

Find we let us find   *stronds* strands
trenching trench-carving

intestine internal   *close* encounter
mutual well-beseeming uniformly well disciplined
his its   *impressed* enlisted

153

25 Over whose acres walk'd those blessed feet
Which fourteen hundred years ago were nail'd
For our advantage on the bitter cross.
But this our purpose° now is twelve month old,
And bootless° 'tis to tell you we will go.
30 Therefore we meet not now.° Then let me hear
Of you, my gentle cousin° Westmoreland,
What yesternight our council did decree
In forwarding this dear expedience.°
WESTMORELAND. My liege, this haste was hot in
question,°
35 And many limits of the charge set down°
But yesternight, when all athwart° there came
A post from Wales loaden with heavy news,
Whose worst was that the noble Mortimer,
Leading the men of Herefordshire to fight
40 Against the irregular and wild Glendower,
Was by the rude hands of that Welshman taken,
A thousand of his people butchered,
Upon whose dead corpse° there was such misuse,
Such beastly shameless transformation
45 By those Welshwomen done, as may not be
Without much shame retold or spoken of.
KING. It seems then that the tidings of this broil
Brake off our business for the Holy Land.
WESTMORELAND. This match'd with other did, my
gracious lord.
50 For more uneven° and unwelcome news
Came from the north, and thus it did import.
On Holyrood° day the gallant Hotspur there,
Young Harry Percy, and brave Archibald,
That ever-valiant and approved° Scot,
55 At Holmedon met,
Where they did spend a sad and bloody hour,
As by discharge of their artillery
And shape of likelihood° the news was told;
For he that brought them, in the very heat
60 And pride of their contention° did take horse,
Uncertain of the issue any way.
KING. Here is a dear, a true industrious friend,
Sir Walter Blunt, new lighted from his horse,
Stain'd with the variation of each soil

Betwixt that Holmedon and this seat of ours,   65
And he hath brought us smooth and welcome
news.
The Earl of Douglas is discomfited.
Ten thousand bold Scots, two and twenty
knights
Balk'd° in their own blood did Sir Walter see
On Holmedon's plains. Of prisoners Hotspur
took   70
Mordake, Earl of Fife and eldest son
To beaten Douglas; and the Earl of Athol,
Of Murray, Angus, and Menteith.
And is not this an honorable spoil?
A gallant prize? Ha, cousin, is it not?   75
WESTMORELAND. In faith,
It is a conquest for a prince to boast of.
KING. Yea, there thou mak'st me sad and mak'st
me sin
In envy that my Lord Northumberland
Should be the father to so blest a son—   80
A son who is the theme of honor's tongue,
Amongst a grove the very straightest plant,
Who is sweet Fortune's minion° and her pride—
Whilst I, by looking on the praise of him,
See riot and dishonor stain the brow   85
Of my young Harry. O that it could be prov'd
That some night-tripping fairy had exchang'd
In cradle clothes our children where they lay,
And call'd mine Percy, his Plantagenet!°
Then would I have his Harry and he mine.   90
But let him from my thoughts. What think you,
coz,
Of this young Percy's pride? The prisoners
Which he in this adventure hath surpris'd
To his own use° he keeps, and sends me word
I shall have none but Mordake Earl of Fife.   95
WESTMORELAND. This is his uncle's teaching, this is
Worcester,
Malevolent to you in all aspects,
Which makes him prune himself and bristle up
The crest of youth against your dignity.
KING. But I have sent for him to answer this,   100
And for this cause awhile we must neglect
Our holy purpose to Jerusalem.
Cousin, on Wednesday next our council we
Will hold at Windsor; so inform the lords.
But come yourself with speed to us again,   105
For more is to be said and to be done
Than out of anger can be uttered.
WESTMORELAND. I will, my liege.   [Exeunt]

---

this our purpose   see *Richard II* (v, vi, 49–50)
bootless   needless
Therefore . . . now   it is not for that reason that we meet
now
gentle cousin   noble kinsman
dear expedience   much-desired mission
haste . . . question   urgent issue was being hotly debated
limits . . . down   logistical details determined
all athwart   thwarting everything   *corpse*   corpses
uneven   disturbing
Holyrood day   Holy Cross day, September 14
approved   tested, proven
shape of likelihood   indication of probability
pride . . . contention   height of the battle

Balk'd   lying in ridge rows
minion   darling
Plantagenet   family name of the royal family
use   profit

SCENE ii

London. An apartment of the PRINCE's.

[Enter the PRINCE OF WALES and FALSTAFF.]

FALSTAFF. Now, Hal, what time of day is it, lad?

PRINCE. Thou art so fat-witted with drinking of old
sack° and unbuttoning thee after supper and
sleeping upon benches after noon that thou hast
5 forgotten to demand that truly which thou
wouldst truly know. What a devil hast thou to
do with the time of the day? Unless hours were
cups of sack, and minutes capons, and clocks the
tongues of bawds, and dials the signs of leaping-
10 houses,° and the blessed sun himself a fair hot
wench in flame-colored taffeta, I see no reason
why thou shouldst be so superfluous to demand
the time of the day.

FALSTAFF. Indeed, you come near me now, Hal, for
15 we that take purses go by the moon and the
seven stars,° and not by Phœbus,° he, "that
wandering knight so fair."° And, I prithee,
sweet wag, when thou art king, as, God save
thy Grace—majesty I should say, for grace°
20 thou wilt have none—

PRINCE. What, none?

FALSTAFF. No, by my troth, not so much as will
serve to be prologue to an egg and butter.°

PRINCE. Well, how then? Come, roundly,° roundly.

25 FALSTAFF. Marry, then, sweet wag, when thou art
king, let not us that are squires of the night's
body be called thieves of the day's beauty.° Let
us be Diana's foresters,° gentlemen of the shade,
minions of the moon; and let men say we be
30 men of good government,° being governed, as
the sea is, by our noble and chaste mistress the
moon, under whose countenance° we steal.

PRINCE. Thou sayest well, and it holds well too,
for the fortune of us that are the moon's men
35 doth ebb and flow like the sea, being governed,
as the sea is, by the moon. As, for proof now: a

purse of gold most resolutely snatched on
Monday night and most dissolutely spent on
Tuesday morning; got with swearing "Lay by"
and spent with crying "Bring in"°—now in as   40
low an ebb as the foot of the ladder, and by and
by in as high a flow as the ridge of the gallows.°

FALSTAFF. By the Lord, thou sayest true, lad. And is
not my hostess of the tavern a most sweet
wench?   45

PRINCE. As the honey of Hybla,° my old lad of the
castle.° And is not a buff jerkin a most sweet
robe of durance?°

FALSTAFF. How now, how now, mad wag! What, in
thy quips and thy quiddities?° What a plague   50
have I to do with a buff jerkin?

PRINCE. Why, what a pox have I to do with my
hostess of the tavern?

FALSTAFF. Well, thou hast called her to a reckoning
many a time and oft.   55

PRINCE. Did I ever call for thee to pay thy part?

FALSTAFF. No, I'll give thee thy due—thou has paid
all there.

PRINCE. Yea, and elsewhere, so far as my coin
would stretch, and where it would not I have   60
used my credit.

FALSTAFF. Yea, and so used it that, were it not here
apparent that thou art heir apparent°—But, I
prithee, sweet wag, shall there be gallows
standing in England when thou art king, and   65
resolution thus fobbed° as it is with the rusty
curb of old father antic° the law? Do not thou,
when thou art king, hang a thief.

PRINCE. No. Thou shalt.

FALSTAFF. Shall I? O, rare! By the Lord, I'll be a   70
brave° judge.

PRINCE. Thou judgest false already. I mean thou
shalt have the hanging of the thieves and so become a rare hangman.

FALSTAFF. Well, Hal, well; and in some sort it   75
jumps with my humor° as well as waiting in the
court, I can tell you.

PRINCE. For obtaining of suits?

---

sack sweet white wine   leaping-houses brothels
seven stars the Pleiades   Phoebus the sun god
"that . . . fair" reference to a chivalric romance the hero
  of which was the Knight of the Sun
Grace . . . grace pun: Grace as title and grace as virtue
not . . . butter (third sense of grace as prayer before
  dining, the supposition being that "egg and butter"
  would merit the briefest of thanksgiving)
roundly fully
squires . . . beauty puns: night's body (the moon) but also
  knight's body, day's beauty but also day's booty
Diana's foresters i.e., let night robbers be called
  euphemistically "the moon's foresters"
good government well-behaved
countenance pun: face but also sanction

"Bring in" i.e., tavern refreshments
foot . . . gallows ominous warning that the robber will
  climb the ladder to be hanged
Hybla in Sicily
old . . . castle reference to Oldcastle, Falstaff's original
  name in the play
buff . . . durance pun: leather jacket worn by sheriff;
  durance, both durable and imprisonment
quips . . . quiddities verbal joustings
here apparent . . . heir apparent obvious pun that
  Falstaff abandons
fobbed thwarted   antic buffoon   brave fine
jumps . . . humor suits my disposition

FALSTAFF. Yea, for obtaining of suits,° whereof the
80   hangman hath no lean wardrobe. 'Sblood,° I am
      as melancholy as a gib° cat or a lugged° bear.
PRINCE. Or an old lion, or a lover's lute.
FALSTAFF. Yea, or the drone of a Lincolnshire
      bagpipe.
85 PRINCE. What sayest thou to a hare, or the melan-
      choly of Moorditch?°
FALSTAFF. Thou hast the most unsavory similes,
      and art indeed the most comparative, rascalliest,
      sweet young prince. But, Hal, I prithee, trouble
90   me no more with vanity.° I would to God thou
      and I knew where a commodity of good names
      were to be bought. An old lord of the council
      rated° me the other day in the street about you,
      sir, but I marked him not; and yet he talked
95   very wisely, but I regarded him not; and yet he
      talked wisely, and in the street too.
PRINCE. Thou didst well, for wisdom cries out in
      the streets and no man regards it.°
FALSTAFF. O, thou hast damnable iteration,° and
100   art indeed able to corrupt a saint. Thou hast
      done much harm upon me, Hal. God forgive
      thee for it! Before I knew thee, Hal, I knew
      nothing, and now am I, if a man should speak
      truly, little better than one of the wicked. I
105   must give over this life, and I will give it over.
      By the Lord, an I do not, I am a villain. I'll be
      damned for never a king's son in Christendom.
PRINCE. Where shall we take a purse tomorrow,
      Jack?
110 FALSTAFF. 'Zounds, where thou wilt, lad; I'll make
      one. An I do not, call me villain and baffle° me.
PRINCE. I see a good amendment of life in thee—
      from praying to purse-taking.
FALSTAFF. Why, Hal, 'tis my vocation, Hal; 'tis no
115   sin for a man to labor in his vocation.°
                    [Enter POINS.]
      Poins! Now shall we know if Gadshill° have set a

match.° O, if men were to be saved by merit,
what hole in hell were hot enough for him?
This is the most omnipotent villain that ever
cried "Stand" to a true° man.   120
PRINCE. Good morrow, Ned.
POINS. Good morrow, sweet Hal. What says
   Monsieur Remorse? What says Sir John Sack
   and Sugar? Jack, how agrees the devil and thee
   about thy soul that thou soldest him on Good   125
   Friday last for a cup of Madeira and a cold
   capon's leg?
PRINCE. Sir John stands to his word, the devil shall
   have his bargain; for he was never yet a breaker
   of proverbs. He will give the devil his due.   130
POINS. Then art thou damned for keeping thy
   word with the devil.
PRINCE. Else he had been damned for cozening°
   the devil.
POINS. But, my lads, my lads, tomorrow morning,   135
   by four o'clock early, at Gadshill! There are
   pilgrims going to Canterbury with rich offerings,
   and traders riding to London with fat purses. I
   have vizards° for you all; you have horses for
   yourselves. Gadshill lies tonight in Rochester. I   140
   have bespoke supper tomorrow night in Eastcheap. We may do it as secure as sleep. If you
   will go, I will stuff your purses full of crowns; if
   you will not, tarry at home and be hanged.
FALSTAFF. Hear ye, Yedward; if I tarry at home and 145
   go not, I'll hang you for going.
POINS. You will, chops?
FALSTAFF. Hal, wilt thou make one?
PRINCE. Who, I rob? I a thief? Not I, by my faith.
FALSTAFF. There's neither honesty, manhood, nor   150
   good fellowship in thee, nor thou camest not
   of the blood royal, if thou darest not stand° for
   ten shillings.
PRINCE. Well then, once in my days I'll be a mad-
   cap.   155
FALSTAFF. Why, that's well said.
PRINCE. Well, come what will, I'll tarry at home.
FALSTAFF. By the Lord, I'll be a traitor then, when
   thou art king.
PRINCE. I care not.   160
POINS. Sir John, I prithee, leave the prince and me
   alone. I will lay him down such reasons for this
   adventure that he shall go.
FALSTAFF. Well, God give thee the spirit of persuasion and him the ears of profiting, that what   165
   thou speakest may move and what he hears
   may be believed, that the true prince may, for

suits . . . suits   pun: lawsuits, but also clothing
   (hangmen claimed the victims' garments)
'Sblood   violent oath, by God's blood   gib   tom
lugged   shackled
Moorditch   local joke: an open and filthy sewer draining
   Moorfield Marshes in North London
vanity   idle things   rated   berated
for wisdom . . . it   paraphrased from Proverbs 1:20–24
damnable iteration   habit of twisting phrases when
   repeating or quoting
An   if
baffle   to degrade a knight by stripping him of armor,
   shield, etc.
'tis . . . vocation   (see I Corinthians 7:20)
Gadshill   (Shakespeare uses the name of a location
   notorious for robberies as the name of his most
   professional robber)

set a match   arranged time and place for a robbery
true   honest   cozening   cheating   vizards   masks
stand   i.e., take a stand as a highway robber

recreation sake, prove a false thief; for the poor abuses of the time want countenance.° Farewell.

170 You shall find me in Eastcheap.

PRINCE. Farewell, thou latter spring! Farewell, All-hallown summer!° [*Exit* FALSTAFF.]

POINS. Now, my good sweet honey lord, ride with us tomorrow. I have a jest to execute that I can-

175 not manage alone. Falstaff, Bardolph, Peto, and Gadshill shall rob those men that we have already waylaid; yourself and I will not be there; and when they have the booty, if you and I do not rob them, cut this head off from my

180 shoulders.

PRINCE. How shall we part with them in setting forth?

POINS. Why, we will set forth before or after them, and appoint them a place of meeting, wherein

185 it is at our pleasure to fail, and then will they adventure upon the exploit themselves—which they shall have no sooner achieved, but we'll set upon them.

PRINCE. Yea, but 'tis like that they will know us by

190 our horses, by our habits,° and by every other appointment, to be ourselves.

POINS. Tut! Our horses they shall not see; I'll tie them in the wood. Our vizards we will change after we leave them. And, sirrah, I have cases of

195 buckram for the nonce,° to immask our noted outward garments.

PRINCE. Yea, but I doubt° they will be too hard for us.

POINS. Well, for two of them, I know them to be as

200 truebred cowards as ever turned back; and for the third, if he fight longer than he sees reason, I'll forswear arms. The virtue of this jest will be the incomprehensible lies that this same fat rogue will tell us when we meet at supper—

205 how thirty, at least, he fought with, what wards,° what blows, what extremities he endured. And in the reproof of this lies the jest.

PRINCE. Well, I'll go with thee. Provide us all things necessary and meet me tomorrow night

210 in Eastcheap; there I'll sup. Farewell.

POINS. Farewell, my lord.

PRINCE. I know you all and will awhile uphold The unyok'd humor° of your idleness. Yet herein will I imitate the sun,

215 Who doth permit the base contagious clouds°

To smother up his beauty from the world, That, when he please again to be himself, Being wanted,° he may be more wonder'd at By breaking through the foul and ugly mists

220 Of vapors that did seem to strangle him. If all the year were playing holidays, To sport would be as tedious as to work; But when they seldom come, they wish'd for come, And nothing pleaseth but rare accidents. So, when this loose behavior I throw off 225 And pay the debt I never promised, By how much better than my word I am, By so much shall I falsify men's hopes; And like bright metal on a sullen ground,° My reformation, glitt'ring o'er my fault, 230 Shall show more goodly and attract more eyes Than that which hath no foil to set it off. I'll so offend to° make offense a skill, Redeeming time° when men think least I will.

[*Exit*]

SCENE iii
London. The palace.

[*Enter the* KING, NORTHUMBERLAND, WORCESTER, HOTSPUR, SIR WALTER BLUNT, *with others.*]

KING. My blood hath been too cold and temperate, Unapt to stir at these indignities, And you have found me;° for accordingly You tread upon my patience. But be sure I will from henceforth rather be myself, 5 Mighty and to be fear'd, than my condition,° Which hath been smooth as oil, soft as young down, And therefore lost that title of respect Which the proud soul ne'er pays but to the proud.

WORCESTER. Our house, my sovereign liege, little deserves 10 The scourge of greatness to be used on it— And that same greatness too which our own hands Have holp° to make so portly.

NORTHUMBERLAND. My lord—

---

poor . . . countenance i.e., Falstaff suggests that robbery, like other "good causes," should not lack patronage
All-hallown summer Indian Summer
habits garments *nonce* occasion *doubt* suspect
wards parries *unyok'd humor* unrestrained whimsy
contagious clouds clouds were thought to carry pestilence

wanted lacked *sullen ground* dull background
to as to
Redeeming time making up for wasted time
found me found me out
I will . . . condition I will act like myself (as a king) rather than as my natural (mild) disposition would lead me to act
holp helped

15 KING. Worcester, get thee gone, for I do see
        Danger and disobedience in thine eye.
        O, sir, your presence is too bold and peremptory,
        And majesty might never yet endure
        The moody frontier of a servant brow.
20   You have good leave to leave us. When we need
        Your use and counsel, we shall send for you.
                                    [Exit WORCESTER.]
                                    [To NORTHUMBERLAND.]
        You were about to speak.
    NORTHUMBERLAND.   Yea, my good lord.
        Those prisoners in your highness' name de-
            manded,
25   Which Harry Percy here at Holmedon took,
        Were, as he says, not with such strength denied
        As is deliver'd to your majesty.
        Either envy, therefore, or misprision°
        Is guilty of this fault and not my son.
    HOTSPUR. My liege, I did deny no prisoners.
30   But I remember, when the fight was done,
        When I was dry with rage and extreme toil,
        Breathless and faint, leaning upon my sword,
        Came there a certain lord, neat and trimly
            dress'd,
35   Fresh as a bridegroom, and his chin new reap'd
        Show'd like a stubble-land at harvest-home.
        He was perfumed like a milliner,
        And 'twixt his finger and his thumb he held
        A pouncet-box,° which ever and anon
        He gave his nose and took 't away again,
40   Who° therewith angry, when it next came there,
        Took it in snuff;° and still he smil'd and talk'd,
        And as the soldiers bore dead bodies by,
        He call'd them untaught knaves, unmannerly,
        To bring a slovenly unhandsome corse°
45   Betwixt the wind and his nobility.
        With many holiday and lady terms
        He question'd me; amongst the rest, demanded
        My prisoners in your majesty's behalf.
        I then, all smarting with my wounds being cold,
50   To be so pester'd with a popinjay,°
        Out of my grief and my impatience,
        Answer'd neglectfully I know not what—
        He should, or he should not; for he made me
            mad
        To see him shine so brisk and smell so sweet
55   And talk so like a waiting-gentlewoman
        Of guns and drums and wounds—God save the
            mark!—
        And telling me the sovereign'st thing on earth

        Was parmaceti for an inward bruise,°
        And that it was great pity, so it was,
        This villainous saltpeter° should be digg'd   60
        Out of the bowels of the harmless earth,
        Which many a good tall° fellow had destroy'd
        So cowardly, and but for these vile guns,
        He would himself have been a soldier.
        This bald unjointed chat of his, my lord,   65
        I answer'd indirectly, as I said;
        And I beseech you, let not his report
        Come current° for an accusation
        Betwixt my love and your high majesty.
    BLUNT. The circumstance consider'd, good my
        lord,   70
        Whate'er Lord Harry Percy then had said
        To such a person and in such a place,
        At such a time, with all the rest retold,
        May reasonably die and never rise
        To do him wrong, or any way impeach   75
        What then he said, so he unsay it now.
    KING. Why, yet he doth deny his prisoners,
        But with proviso and exception
        That we at our own charge shall ransom straight
        His brother-in-law, the foolish Mortimer,   80
        Who, on my soul, hath wilfully betray'd
        The lives of those that he did lead to fight
        Against that great magician, damn'd Glen-
            dower,
        Whose daughter, as we hear, the Earl of March°
        Hath lately married. Shall our coffers, then,   85
        Be emptied to redeem a traitor home?
        Shall we buy treason and indent° with fears,
        When they have lost and forfeited themselves?
        No, on the barren mountains let him starve;
        For I shall never hold that man my friend   90
        Whose tongue shall ask me for one penny cost
        To ransom home revolted Mortimer.
    HOTSPUR. Revolted Mortimer!
        He never did fall off, my sovereign liege,
        But by the chance of war. To prove that true   95
        Needs no more but one tongue for all those
            wounds,
        Those mouthed wounds, which valiantly he
            took
        When on the gentle Severn's sedgy bank,
        In single opposition, hand to hand,
        He did confound° the best part of an hour   100
        In changing hardiment° with great Glendower.

---

misprision misapprehension
pouncet-box perfume box   Who i.e., the nose
Took . . . snuff pun: reacted with anger, but also inhaled
    abruptly (tobacco snuff was not used until after 1600)
corse corpse   popinjay parrot

parmaceti . . . bruise salve for an inner hurt (a broken
    heart)
saltpeter gunpowder   tall brave
Come current pass at face value (like good money)
Earl of March Mortimer   indent bargain
confound consume, waste
changing hardiment exchanging valor

Three times they breath'd and three times did
they drink,
Upon agreement, of swift Severn's flood,
Who then, affrighted with their bloody looks,
105 Ran fearfully among the trembling reeds
And hid his crisp° head in the hollow bank
Bloodstained with these valiant combatants.
Never did base and rotten policy°
Color her working with such deadly wounds,
110 Nor never could the noble Mortimer
Receive so many, and all willingly.
Then let not him be slander'd with revolt.
KING. Thou dost belie him, Percy, thou dost belie
him.
He never did encounter with Glendower.
115 I tell thee
He durst as well have met the devil alone
As Owen Glendower for an enemy.
Art thou not asham'd? But, sirrah, henceforth
Let me not hear you speak of Mortimer.
Send me your prisoners with the speediest
120 means,
Or you shall hear in such a kind from me
As will displease you. My Lord Northumber-
land,
We license your departure with your son.
Send us your prisoners, or you will hear of it.
[*Exeunt* KING HENRY, BLUNT, *and train.*]
125 HOTSPUR. An if the devil come and roar for them,
I will not send them. I will after straight
And tell him so, for I will ease my heart
Albeit I make a hazard of my head.
NORTHUMBERLAND. What, drunk with choler?°
Stay and pause a while.
Here comes your uncle.
[*Re-enter* WORCESTER.]
130 HOTSPUR.   Speak of Mortimer!
'Zounds, I will speak of him, and let my soul
Want mercy if I do not join with him.
Yea, on his part I'll empty all these veins
And shed my dear blood drop by drop in the
dust,
135 But I will lift the downtrod Mortimer
As high in the air as this unthankful king,
As this ingrate and canker'd° Bolingbroke.°
NORTHUMBERLAND. Brother, the king hath made
your nephew mad.
WORCESTER. Who struck this heat up after I was
gone?
140 HOTSPUR. He will, forsooth,° have all my prisoners;

And when I urg'd the ransom once again
Of my wife's brother, then his cheek look'd pale,
And on my face he turn'd an eye of death,
Trembling even at the name of Mortimer.
WORCESTER. I cannot blame him. Was not he
proclaim'd,   145
By Richard that dead is, the next of blood?
NORTHUMBERLAND. He was. I heard the proclama-
tion;
And then it was when the unhappy king—
Whose wrongs in us God pardon!—did set
forth
Upon his Irish expedition,   150
From whence he intercepted did return
To be depos'd and shortly murdered.
WORCESTER. And for whose death we in the world's
wide mouth
Live scandaliz'd and foully spoken of.
HOTSPUR. But, soft, I pray you. Did King Richard
then   155
Proclaim my brother Edmund Mortimer
Heir to the crown?
NORTHUMBERLAND.   He did. Myself did hear it.
HOTSPUR. Nay, then I cannot blame his cousin king
That wish'd him on the barren mountains
starve.
But shall it be that you, that set the crown   160
Upon the head of this forgetful man
And for his sake wear the detested blot
Of murderous subornation,° shall it be
That you a world of curses undergo,
Being the agents or base second means,   165
The cords, the ladder, or the hangman rather?
O, pardon me that I descend so low
To show the line and the predicament°
Wherein you range under this subtle king.
Shall it for shame be spoken in these days,   170
Or fill up chronicles in time to come,
That men of your nobility and power
Did gage° them both in an unjust behalf,
As both of you—God pardon it!—have done,
To put down Richard, that sweet lovely rose,   175
And plant this thorn, this canker,° Bolingbroke?
And shall it in more shame be further spoken
That you are fool'd, discarded, and shook off
By him for whom these shames ye underwent?
No! Yet time serves wherein you may redeem   180
Your banish'd honors and restore yourselves
Into the good thoughts of the world again,

crisp ripply   *policy* political cunning
choler anger   *canker'd* malignant
Bolingbroke the king's former name, from Bolingbroke
    Castle, where he was born (here used insultingly)
forsooth in truth (sarcastic)

blot . . . subornation the stain of those suborned (incited)
    to commit murder
line . . . predicament level . . . category   *gage* engage
canker wild dog rose, but also the destructive
    cankerworm, the "worm i' the bud" —*Twelfth Night*, II,
    iv, 112)

Revenge the jeering and disdain'd contempt
Of this proud king who studies day and night
185 To answer all the debt he owes to you
Even with the bloody payment of your deaths.
Therefore, I say—
WORCESTER.   Peace, cousin, say no more.
And now I will unclasp a secret book,
And to your quick-conceiving discontents
190 I'll read you matter deep and dangerous,
As full of peril and adventurous spirit
As to o'erwalk a current roaring loud
On the unsteadfast footing of a spear.
HOTSPUR. If he fall in, good night! Or sink or°
swim.
195 Send danger from the east unto the west,
So honor cross it from the north to south,
And let them grapple. O, the blood more stirs
To rouse a lion than to start a hare!
NORTHUMBERLAND. Imagination of some great ex-
ploit
200 Drives him beyond the bounds of patience.
HOTSPUR. By heaven, methinks it were an easy
leap
To pluck bright honor from the pale-fac'd moon
Or dive into the bottom of the deep,
Where fathom line could never touch the
ground,
205 And pluck up drowned honor by the locks,
So he that doth redeem her thence might wear
Without corrival° all her dignities.
But out upon this half-fac'd fellowship!°
WORCESTER. He apprehends a world of figures here,
210 But not the form of what he should attend.
Good cousin, give me audience for a while.
HOTSPUR. I cry you mercy.
WORCESTER.   Those same noble Scots
That are your prisoners—
HOTSPUR.   I'll keep them all!
By God, he shall not have a Scot of them;
215 No, if a Scot would save his soul, he shall not.
I'll keep them, by this hand.
WORCESTER.   You start away
And lend no ear unto my purposes.
Those prisoners you shall keep.
HOTSPUR.   Nay, I will; that's flat.
220 He said he would not ransom Mortimer,
Forbade my tongue to speak of Mortimer;
But I will find him when he lies asleep,
And in his ear I'll holla "Mortimer!"
Nay,
225 I'll have a starling shall be taught to speak
Nothing but "Mortimer" and give it him

To keep his anger still in motion.
WORCESTER. Hear you, cousin, a word.
HOTSPUR. All studies here I solemnly defy
Save how to gall and pinch this Bolingbroke.
And that same sword-and-buckler° Prince of
Wales,   230
But that I think his father loves him not
And would be glad he met with some mis-
chance,
I would have him poison'd with a pot of ale.
WORCESTER. Farewell, kinsman. I'll talk to you
When you are better temper'd to attend.   235
NORTHUMBERLAND. Why, what a wasp-stung and
impatient fool
Art thou to break into this woman's mood,
Tying thine ear to no tongue but thine own!
HOTSPUR. Why, look you, I am whipp'd and
scourg'd with rods,
Nettled, and stung with pismires° when I hear   240
Of this vile politician, Bolingbroke.
In Richard's time—what do you call the place?—
A plague upon it, it is in Gloucestershire,
'Twas where the madcap duke his uncle kept,
His uncle York, where I first bow'd my knee   245
Unto this king of smiles, this Bolingbroke—
'Sblood!—
When you and he came back from Ravenspurgh.
NORTHUMBERLAND. At Berkeley castle.
HOTSPUR. You say true.   250
Why, what a candy deal of courtesy
This fawning greyhound then did proffer me!
Look, "when his infant fortune came to age,"
And "gentle Harry Percy," and "kind cousin."
O, the devil take such cozeners! God forgive me!   255
Good uncle, tell your tale, for I have done.
WORCESTER. Nay, if you have not, to it again;
We will stay your leisure.
HOTSPUR.   I have done, i' faith.
WORCESTER. Then once more to your Scottish
prisoners.
Deliver them up without their ransom straight   260
And make the Douglas' son your only mean°
For powers in Scotland, which, for divers reasons
Which I shall send you written, be assur'd,
Will easily be granted. You, my lord,
     [To NORTHUMBERLAND.]
Your son in Scotland being thus employ'd,   265
Shall secretly into the bosom creep
Of that same noble prelate well belov'd,
The archbishop.
HOTSPUR. Of York, is it not?
WORCESTER. True, who bears hard   270

Or ... or either ... or   corrival sharer
half-fac'd fellowship this contemptible sharing

sword-and-buckler low fellow (gentlemen wore rapiers)
pismires ants   mean means

His brother's death at Bristol, the Lord Scroop.
I speak not this in estimation
As what I think might be, but what I know
Is ruminated, plotted, and set down
275　And only stays but to behold the face
Of that occasion that shall bring it on.
HOTSPUR. I smell it. Upon my life, it will do well.
NORTHUMBERLAND. Before the game's afoot, thou
still let'st slip.°
HOTSPUR. Why, it cannot choose but be a noble
plot.
280　And then the power of Scotland and of York
To join with Mortimer, ha?
WORCESTER.　　　　　　　And so they shall.
HOTSPUR. In faith, it is exceedingly well aim'd.
WORCESTER. And 'tis no little reason bids us speed
To save our heads by raising of a head;°
285　For, bear ourselves as even as we can,

The king will always think him in our debt
And think we think ourselves unsatisfied
Till he hath found a time to pay us home.
And see already how he doth begin
To make us strangers to his looks of love.　　290
HOTSPUR. He does, he does. We'll be reveng'd on
him.
WORCESTER. Cousin, farewell. No further go in
this
Than I by letters shall direct your course.
When time is ripe, which will be suddenly,
I'll steal to Glendower and Lord Mortimer,　　295
Where you and Douglas and our powers at once,
As I will fashion it, shall happily meet
To bear our fortunes in our own strong arms,
Which now we hold at much uncertainty.
NORTHUMBERLAND. Farewell, good brother. We
shall thrive, I trust.　　　　　　　　　　300
HOTSPUR. Uncle, adieu. O, let the hours be short
Till fields and blows and groans applaud our
sport!　　　　　　　　　　　[Exeunt]

Before . . . slip　a figure drawn from falconry
head　army

A C T　I I

SCENE i
Rochester. An inn yard.

[*Enter a* CARRIER *with a lantern in his hand.*]
FIRST CARRIER. Heigh-ho! An it be not four by the
day, I'll be hanged. Charles' wain° is over the
new chimney, and yet our horse not packed.
What, ostler!
5　OSTLER. [*Within*] Anon, anon.
FIRST CARRIER. I prithee, Tom, beat Cut's saddle,
put a few flocks in the point.° Poor jade is wrung
in the withers out of all cess.°
[*Enter another* CARRIER.]
SECOND CARRIER. Peas and beans° are as dank here
10　as a dog, and that is the next way to give poor
jades the bots.° This house is turned upside
down since Robin Ostler died.
FIRST CARRIER. Poor fellow never joyed since the
price of oats rose. It was the death of him.
15　SECOND CARRIER. I think this be the most villainous
house in all London road for fleas. I am stung
like a tench.

FIRST CARRIER. Like a tench!° By the mass, there is
ne'er a king christen° could be better bit than I
have been since the first cock.　　　　　　20
SECOND CARRIER. Why, they will allow us ne'er a
jordan,° and then we leak° in your chimney, and
your chamber-lye° breeds fleas like a loach.°
FIRST CARRIER. What, ostler! Come away and be
hanged! Come away.　　　　　　　　　25
SECOND CARRIER. I have a gammon° of bacon and
two razes° of ginger to be delivered as far as
Charing Cross.
FIRST CARRIER. God's body! The turkeys in my
pannier° are quite starved. What, ostler! A　30
plague on thee! Hast thou never an eye in thy
head? Canst not hear? An 'twere not as good
deed as drink to break the pate on thee, I am a
very villain. Come, and be hanged! Hast no
faith in thee?　　　　　　　　　　　35
[*Enter* GADSHILL.]
GADSHILL. Good morrow, carriers. What's o'clock?
FIRST CARRIER. I think it be two o'clock.

tench　a fish sometimes infested by lice
king christen　Christian king　　*jordan*　chamber pot
leak　urinate　　*chamber-lye*　urine
loach　louse-infested fish　　*gammon*　leg
razes　roots　　*pannier*　basket

Charles' wain　Charlemagne's wagon, the Big Dipper
flocks . . . point　wads of wool at the front of the saddle
wrung . . . cess　excessively galled at the nape of the neck
Peas and beans　cheap horse food　　*bots*　worms

GADSHILL. I prithee lend me thy lantern, to see my
gelding in the stable.

40 FIRST CARRIER. Nay, by God, soft,° I know a trick
worth two of that, i' faith.

GADSHILL. I pray thee, lend me thine.

SECOND CARRIER. Aye, when? Canst tell? Lend me
thy lantern, quoth he? Marry, I'll see thee
45 hanged first.

GADSHILL. Sirrah carrier, what time do you mean
to come to London?

SECOND CARRIER. Time enough to go to bed with a
candle, I warrant thee. Come, neighbor Mugs,
50 we'll call up the gentlemen. They will along
with company, for they have great charge.°
                              [*Exeunt* CARRIERS.]

GADSHILL. What, ho! Chamberlain!

CHAMBERLAIN. [*Within*] At hand, quoth pickpurse.

GADSHILL. That's even as fair as° "at hand, quoth
55 the chamberlain,"° for thou variest no more
from picking of purses than giving direction doth
from laboring. Thou layest the plot how?°
                     [*Enter* CHAMBERLAIN.]

CHAMBERLAIN. Good morrow, Master Gadshill. It
holds current° that I told you yesternight.
60 There's a franklin° in the wild° of Kent hath
brought three hundred marks with him in
gold. I heard him tell it to one of his company
last night at supper, a kind of auditor, one that
hath abundance of charge too, God knows what.
65 They are up already and call for eggs and butter.
They will away presently.°

GADSHILL. Sirrah, if they meet not with Saint
Nicholas' clerks,° I'll give thee this neck.

CHAMBERLAIN. No, I'll none of it. I pray thee, keep
70 that for the hangman, for I know thou worship-
pest Saint Nicholas as truly as a man of falsehood
may.

GADSHILL. What talkest thou to me of the hangman? If I hang I'll make a fat pair of gallows, for
75 if I hang, old Sir John hangs with me, and thou
knowest he is no starveling. Tut! There are other
Trojans° that thou dreamest not of, the which
for sport sake are content to do the profession
some grace; that would, if matters should be
80 looked into, for their own credit sake, make all

whole.° I am joined with no foot landrakers, no
long-staff sixpenny strikers, none of these mad
mustachio purple-hued malt-worms,° but with
nobility and tranquillity, burgomasters and
great oneyers, such as can hold in, such as will 85
strike sooner than speak, and speak sooner than
drink, and drink sooner than pray. And yet,
'zounds, I lie, for they pray continually to their
saint, the commonwealth—or rather, not pray
to her, but prey on her, for they ride up and 90
down on her and make her their boots.°

CHAMBERLAIN. What, the commonwealth their
boots? Will she hold out water in foul way?

GADSHILL. She will, she will; justice hath liquored°
her. We steal as in a castle,° cocksure; we have 95
the receipt of fernseed,° we walk invisible.

CHAMBERLAIN. Nay, by my faith, I think you are
more beholding to the night than to fernseed for
your walking invisible.

GADSHILL. Give me thy hand. Thou shalt have a 100
share in our purchase,° as I am a true man.

CHAMBERLAIN. Nay, rather let me have it as you
are a false thief.

GADSHILL. Go to; *homo* is a common name to all
men.° Bid the ostler bring my gelding out of 105
the stable. Farewell, you muddy° knave.
                                    [*Exeunt*]

SCENE ii
The highway, near Gadshill.

[*Enter* PRINCE HENRY *and* POINS.]

POINS. Come, shelter, shelter. I have removed
Falstaff's horse, and he frets like a gummed
velvet.°

PRINCE. Stand close.
                [*Enter* FALSTAFF.]

FALSTAFF. Poins! Poins, and be hanged! Poins! 5

if . . . whole if the robbery were investigated, would
  patch things up for their own good
no . . . malt-worms no common footpads, no small-time
  robbers, no ale-guzzlers with soaked mustaches
boots pun: booty
liquored greased for waterproofing; with pun: bribed
in a castle in complete safety (with allusion to Falstaff's
  earlier name, Oldcastle)
receipt of fernseed recipe for invisibility (fernseed gathered
  on St. John s Eve supposedly made one invisible)
purchase loot
homo . . . men i.e., since *homo* fits all men, I am a true
  (genuine, real) man, hence a true (honest) man
muddy muddle-headed
frets . . . velvet (cheap velvet was gummed to give it the
  appearance of quality but showed its inferiority when
  patches rubbed off)

soft easy there!
great charge valuable commodities
even . . . as just the same as
chamberlain man in charge of letting rooms;
  notoriously leagued with highwaymen
Thou . . . how "What's the deal?"
holds current still stands   *franklin* landholder
wild forest   *presently* immediately
Saint Nicholas' clerks thieves, of whom the saint was
  patron
Trojans sports

PRINCE. Peace, ye fat-kidneyed rascal! What a
    brawling dost thou keep!
FALSTAFF. Where's Poins, Hal?
PRINCE. He is walked up to the top of the hill. I'll
10   seek him.
FALSTAFF. I am accursed to rob in that thief's com-
    pany. The rascal hath removed my horse and
    tied him I know not where. If I travel but four
    foot by the squire° further afoot, I shall break
15   my wind. Well, I doubt not but to die a fair
    death for all this, if I 'scape hanging for killing
    that rogue. I have forsworn his company hourly
    any time this two and twenty years, and yet I
    am bewitched with the rogue's company. If the
20   rascal have not given me medicines to make me
    love him, I'll be hanged. It could not be else; I
    have drunk medicines. Poins! Hal! A plague
    upon you both! Bardolph! Peto! I'll starve ere
    I'll rob a foot further. An 'twere not as good a
25   deed as drink, to turn true man and to leave
    these rogues, I am the veriest varlet that ever
    chewed with a tooth. Eight yards of uneven
    ground is threescore and ten miles afoot with
    me, and the stony-hearted villains know it well
30   enough. A plague upon it when thieves cannot
    be true one to another! [They whistle] Whew! A
    plague upon you all! Give me my horse, you
    rogues; give me my horse, and be hanged!
PRINCE. Peace, ye fat-guts! Lie down; lay thine ear
35   close to the ground and list if thou canst hear the
    tread of travelers.
FALSTAFF. Have you any levers to lift me up again,
    being down? 'Sblood, I'll not bear mine own
    flesh so far afoot again for all the coin in thy
40   father's exchequer. What a plague mean ye to
    colt° me thus?
PRINCE. Thou liest; thou art not colted, thou art
    uncolted.
FALSTAFF. I prithee, good Prince Hal, help me to my
45   horse, good king's son.
PRINCE. Out, ye rogue! Shall I be your ostler?
FALSTAFF. Go hang thyself in thine own heir-
    apparent garters!° If I be ta'en, I'll peach° for
    this. An I have not ballads made° on you all and
50   sung to filthy tunes, let a cup of sack be my
    poison. When a jest is so forward, and afoot too,
    I hate it.
[Enter GADSHILL, BARDOLPH, and PETO with him.]
GADSHILL. Stand.

FALSTAFF. So I do, against my will.
POINS. O, 'tis our setter.° I know his voice. Bar-   55
    dolph, what news?
BARDOLPH. Case ye,° case ye; on with your vizards.
    There's money of the king's coming down the
    hill; 'tis going to the king's exchequer.
FALSTAFF. You lie, ye rogue; 'tis going to the king's   60
    tavern.
GADSHILL. There's enough to make us all.
FALSTAFF. To be hanged.
PRINCE. Sirs, you four shall front them in the
    narrow lane; Ned Poins and I will walk lower. If   65
    they 'scape from your encounter, then they
    light on us.
PETO. How many be there of them?
GADSHILL. Some eight or ten.
FALSTAFF. 'Zounds, will they not rob us?   70
PRINCE. What, a coward, Sir John Paunch?
FALSTAFF. Indeed, I am not John of Gaunt, your
    grandfather, but yet no coward, Hal.
PRINCE. Well, we leave that to the proof.
POINS. Sirrah Jack, thy horse stands behind the   75
    hedge.
    When thou needest him, there thou shalt find
    him.
    Farewell, and stand fast.
FALSTAFF. Now cannot I strike him, if I should be   80
    hanged.
PRINCE. Ned, where are our disguises?
POINS. Here, hard by. Stand close.
                        [Exeunt PRINCE and POINS.]
FALSTAFF. Now, my masters, happy man be his
    dole,° say I. Every man to his business.   85
                        [Enter the TRAVELERS.]
FIRST TRAVELER. Come, neighbor. The boy shall
    lead our horses down the hill; we'll walk afoot
    awhile, and ease our legs.
THIEVES. Stand!
TRAVELERS. Jesus bless us!   90
FALSTAFF. Strike! Down with them! Cut the
    villains' throats! Ah, whoreson caterpillars!°
    Bacon-fed knaves! They hate us youth. Down
    with them! Fleece them.
TRAVELERS. O, we are undone, both we and ours   95
    forever!
FALSTAFF. Hang ye, gorbellied° knaves, are ye
    undone? No, ye fat chuffs;° I would your store
    were here! On, bacons, on! What, ye knaves!

---

squire carpenter's square   colt trick
heir-apparent garters (Hal, as crown prince, would of
    course be enrolled in the Order of the Garter, highest
    order of British knighthood)
peach turn informer   ballads made ballads on timely
    subjects were sung and sold on Elizabethan streets

setter Gadshill, who "set the match"
Case ye put on your masks
happy . . . dole happiness be his lot
caterpillars parasites   gorbellied fat-paunched
fat chuffs stuffed misers (Falstaff's epithets revolve
    around the idea of "over-fed capitalists" who deprive
    the poor)

100 Young men must live. You are grandjurors,° are ye? We'll jure ye, 'faith.

[*Here they rob them and bind them. Exeunt.*]
[*Re-enter* PRINCE HENRY *and* POINS *disguised.*]

PRINCE. The thieves have bound the true men. Now could thou and I rob the thieves and go merrily to London, it would be argument° for a
105 week, laughter for a month, and a good jest for ever.

POINS. Stand close. I hear them coming.

[*Enter the* THIEVES *again.*]

FALSTAFF. Come, my masters, let us share, and then to horse before day. An the Prince and Poins be
110 not two arrant cowards, there's no equity stirring.° There's no more valor in that Poins than in a wild duck.

PRINCE. Your money!

POINS. Villains!

[*As they are sharing, the* PRINCE *and* POINS *set upon them. They all run away, and* FALSTAFF, *after a blow or two, runs away too, leaving the booty behind them.*]

115 PRINCE. Got with much ease. Now merrily to horse. The thieves are all scatter'd and possess'd with fear
So strongly that they dare not meet each other;
Each takes his fellow for an officer.
Away, good Ned. Falstaff sweats to death
120 And lards the lean earth as he walks along.
Were't not for laughing, I should pity him.

POINS. How the rogue roar'd!   [*Exeunt*]

SCENE iii
Warkworth Castle.

[*Enter* HOTSPUR *alone, reading a letter.*]

HOTSPUR. "But, for mine own part, my lord, I could be well contented to be there, in respect of the love I bear your house." He could be contented. Why is he not, then? In respect of the
5 love he bears our house. He shows in this he loves his own barn better than he loves our house. Let me see some more. "The purpose you undertake is dangerous." Why, that's certain. 'Tis dangerous to take a cold, to sleep, to
10 drink. But I tell you, my lord fool, out of this nettle, danger, we pluck this flower, safety. "The purpose you undertake is dangerous, the friends you have named uncertain, the time

itself unsorted,° and your whole plot too light for the counterpoise of so great an opposition."
15 Say you so, say you so? I say unto you again, you are a shallow cowardly hind,° and you lie. What a lack-brain is this! By the Lord, our plot is a good plot as ever was laid, our friends true and constant. A good plot, good friends, and full of
20 expectation; an excellent plot, very good friends. What a frosty-spirited rogue is this! Why, my lord of York commends the plot and the general course of the action. 'Zounds, an I were now by this rascal, I could brain him with his lady's fan.
25 Is there not my father, my uncle, and myself? Lord Edmund Mortimer, my lord of York, and Owen Glendower? Is there not besides the Douglas? Have I not all their letters to meet me in arms by the ninth of the next month, and are
30 they not some of them set forward already? What a pagan rascal is this! An infidel! Ha! You shall see now, in very sincerity of fear and cold heart will he to the king and lay open all our proceedings. O, I could divide myself and go to
35 buffets° for moving such a dish of skim milk with so honorable an action! Hang him! Let him tell the king—we are prepared. I will set forward tonight.

[*Enter* LADY PERCY.]

How now, Kate! I must leave you within these two hours.   40

LADY PERCY. O, my good lord, why are you thus alone?
For what offense have I this fortnight been
A banish'd woman from my Harry's bed?
Tell me, sweet lord, what is't that takes from thee
Thy stomach, pleasure, and thy golden sleep?   45
Why dost thou bend thine eyes upon the earth
And start so often when thou sit'st alone?
Why hast thou lost the fresh blood in thy cheeks
And given my treasures and my rights of thee
To thick-eyed musing and curs'd melancholy?   50
In thy faint slumbers I by thee have watch'd°
And heard thee murmur tales of iron wars,
Speak terms of manage to thy bounding steed,
Cry "Courage! To the field!" And thou hast talk'd
Of sallies and retires, of trenches, tents,   55
Of palisadoes, frontiers, parapets,°

---

grandjurors affluent men such as would be chosen jurors
argument subject for discussion
no . . . stirring no sane judgment left in the world

unsorted unsuited   *hind* female deer, epitome of timidity; but also peasant, incapable of noble valor
divide . . . buffets separate myself into two who would box each other
watch'd lain awake
palisadoes . . . parapets barricades and similar devices for defense

Of basilisks, of cannon, culverin,°
Of prisoners' ransom and of soldiers slain,
And all the currents° of a heady fight.
60 Thy spirit within thee hath been so at war
And thus hath so bestirr'd thee in thy sleep
That beads of sweat have stood upon thy brow
Like bubbles in a late-disturbed stream,
And in thy face strange motions° have appear'd
65 Such as we see when men restrain their breath
On some great sudden hest.° O, what portents
    are these?
Some heavy business hath my lord in hand,
And I must know it, else he loves me not.
HOTSPUR. What, oh!
                    [Enter SERVANT.]
              Is Gilliams with the packet gone?
70 SERVANT. He is, my lord, an hour ago.
HOTSPUR. Hath Butler brought those horses from
    the sheriff?
SERVANT. One horse, my lord, he brought even
    now.
HOTSPUR. What horse? A roan, a crop-ear, is it not?
SERVANT. It is, my lord.
HOTSPUR.   That roan shall be my throne.
75 Well, I will back him straight. O esperance!°
Bid Butler lead him forth into the park.
                              [Exit SERVANT.]
LADY PERCY. But hear you, my lord.
HOTSPUR. What sayest thou, my lady?
LADY PERCY. What is it carries you away?
80 HOTSPUR. Why, my horse, my love, my horse.
LADY PERCY. Out, you mad-headed ape!
A weasel hath not such a deal of spleen°
As you are toss'd with. In faith,
I'll know your business, Harry, that I will.
85 I fear my brother Mortimer doth stir
About his title and hath sent for you
To line° his enterprise. But if you go—
HOTSPUR. So far afoot, I shall be weary, love.
LADY PERCY. Come, come, you paraquito, answer
    me
90 Directly unto this question that I ask.
In faith, I'll break thy little finger, Harry,
An if thou wilt not tell me all things true.
HOTSPUR. Away,
Away, you trifler! Love! I love thee not,
95 I care not for thee, Kate. This is no world
To play with mammets° and to tilt with lips.
We must have bloody noses and crack'd crowns,

And pass them current too.° God's me, my
    horse!
What say'st thou, Kate? What wouldst thou
    have with me?
LADY PERCY. Do you not love me? Do you not, in-
    deed?   100
Well, do not then, for since you love me not,
I will not love myself. Do you not love me?
Nay, tell me if you speak in jest or no.
HOTSPUR. Come, wilt thou see me ride?
And when I am o' horseback, I will swear   105
I love thee infinitely. But hark you, Kate.
I must not have you henceforth question me
Whither I go, nor reason whereabout.
Whither I must, I must; and, to conclude,
This evening must I leave you, gentle Kate.   110
I know you wise, but yet no farther wise
Than Harry Percy's wife. Constant you are,
But yet a woman. And for secrecy,
No lady closer—for I well believe
Thou wilt not utter what thou dost not know. 115
And so far will I trust thee, gentle Kate.
LADY PERCY. How! So far?
HOTSPUR. Not an inch further. But hark you, Kate.
Whither I go, thither shall you go too.
Today will I set forth, tomorrow you.   120
Will this content you, Kate?
LADY PERCY.   It must of force.
                              [Exeunt]

                    SCENE iv
        The Boar's-Head Tavern in Eastcheap.

              [Enter the PRINCE, and POINS.]
PRINCE. Ned, prithee come out of that fat room°
    and lend me thy hand to laugh a little.
POINS. Where hast been, Hal?
PRINCE. With three or four loggerheads amongst
    three or four-score hogsheads. I have sounded   5
    the very base-string of humility. Sirrah, I am
    sworn brother to a leash of drawers° and can
    call them all by their christen names, as Tom,
    Dick, and Francis. They take it already upon
    their salvation that though I be but Prince of   10
    Wales, yet I am the king of courtesy, and tell me
    flatly I am no proud Jack, like Falstaff, but a
    Corinthian,° a lad of mettle, a good boy, by the
    Lord, so they call me, and when I am king of

---

basilisks . . . culverin varieties of cannon
currents courses   motions emotions
hest command
O esperance hope (the Percys' motto)
spleen seat of irritability, excitability   line back up
mammets dolls

crack'd . . . too broken heads passed freely among us;
    with pun: cracked coins, not legal tender but
    nevertheless "passed current," made acceptable
fat room vat room
drawers wine-drawers, waiters
Corinthian gay blade, sport

15 England, I shall command all the good lads° in Eastcheap. They call drinking deep, dyeing scarlet, and when you breathe in your watering,° they cry "hem!" and bid you play° it off. To conclude, I am so good a proficient in one

20 quarter of an hour that I can drink with any tinker in his own language during my life. I tell thee, Ned, thou hast lost much honor, that thou wert not with me in this action. But, sweet Ned —to sweeten which name of Ned, I give thee

25 this pennyworth of sugar, clapped even now into my hand by an under-skinker,° one that never spake other English in his life than "Eight shillings and sixpence," and "You are welcome," with this shrill addition, "Anon, anon, sir!

30 Score a pint of bastard in the Half-Moon,"° or so. But, Ned, to drive away the time till Falstaff come, I prithee, do thou stand in some byroom while I question my puny drawer to what end he gave me the sugar, and do thou never leave

35 calling "Francis," that his tale to me may be nothing but "Anon."° Step aside, and I'll show thee a precedent.

POINS. Francis!

PRINCE. Thou art perfect.

40 POINS. Francis!

[Enter FRANCIS.]

FRANCIS. Anon, anon, sir. Look down into the Pomgarnet, Ralph.

PRINCE. Come hither, Francis.

FRANCIS. My lord?

45 PRINCE. How long hast thou to serve, Francis?

FRANCIS. Forsooth, five years, and as much as to—

POINS. [Within] Francis!

FRANCIS. Anon, anon, sir.

PRINCE. Five year! By'r lady, a long lease for the

50 clinking of pewter. But, Francis, darest thou be so valiant as to play the coward with thy indenture° and show it a fair pair of heels and run from it?

FRANCIS. O Lord, sir, I'll be sworn upon all the

55 books in England, I could find in my heart—

POINS. [Within] Francis!

FRANCIS. Anon, sir.

PRINCE. How old art thou, Francis?

FRANCIS. Let me see—about Michaelmas° next I

60 shall be—

POINS. [Within] Francis!

FRANCIS. Anon, sir. Pray stay a little, my lord.

PRINCE. Nay, but hark you, Francis. For the sugar thou gavest me, 'twas a pennyworth, was't not?

FRANCIS. O Lord I would it had been two! 65

PRINCE. I will give thee for it a thousand pound. Ask me when thou wilt, and thou shalt have it.

POINS. [Within] Francis!

FRANCIS. Anon, anon.

PRINCE. Anon, Francis? No, Francis; but tomorrow, 70 Francis; or, Francis, o' Thursday; or indeed, Francis, when thou wilt. But, Francis!

FRANCIS. My lord?

PRINCE. Wilt thou rob this leathern jerkin, crystal-button, not-pated, agate-ring, puke-stocking, 75 caddis-garter, smooth-tongue, Spanish-pouch°—

FRANCIS. O Lord, sir, who do you mean?

PRINCE. Why, then, your brown bastard is your only drink; for look you, Francis, your white canvas doublet will sully. In Barbary, sir, it can- 80 not come to so much.°

FRANCIS. What, sir?

POINS. [Within] Francis!

PRINCE. Away, you rogue! Dost thou not hear them call? 85

[Here they both call him; the DRAWER stands amazed, not knowing which way to go.]

[Enter VINTNER.]

VINTNER. What, standest thou still, and hearest such a calling? Look to the guests within. [Exit FRANCIS.] My lord, old Sir John, with half a dozen more, are at the door. Shall I let them in?

PRINCE. Let them alone awhile, and then open the 90 door. [Exit VINTNER.] Poins!

[Re-enter POINS.]

POINS. Anon, anon, sir.

PRINCE. Sirrah, Falstaff and the rest of the thieves are at the door. Shall we be merry?

POINS. As merry as crickets, my lad. But hark ye— 95 what cunning match have you made with this jest of the drawer? Come, what's the issue?

PRINCE. I am now of all humors that have showed themselves humors since the old days of goodman Adam to the pupil age of this present 100 twelve o'clock at midnight.°

[Re-enter FRANCIS.]

What's o'clock, Francis?

---

good lads i.e., thieves, rogues
breathe . . . watering stop for breath instead of draining the glass at one draught
play drink   *under-skinker* apprentice tapster
Score . . . Half-Moon charge up a pint of sweet wine to the (room named) Half-Moon
Anon at once   *indenture* contract of apprenticeship
Michaelmas September 29

leathern . . . Spanish-pouch description of Francis' own master, who wears a leather jacket, crystal buttons, cropped hair, dark wool stockings, yarn garters, and an imported moneybag
Why . . . much mainly nonsense shouted at Francis to confuse him
I am . . . midnight I am in the best humor that any man has been in from the first moment to the present

FRANCIS. Anon, anon, sir.   [*Exit*]

105 PRINCE. That ever this fellow should have fewer
words than a parrot, and yet the son of a woman!
His industry° is upstairs and downstairs, his
eloquence the parcel of a reckoning.° I am not
yet of Percy's mind, the Hotspur of the north—
110 he that kills me some six or seven dozen of Scots
at a breakfast, washes his hands, and says to his
wife "Fie upon this quiet life! I want work." "O
my sweet Harry," says she, "how many hast
thou killed today?" "Give my roan horse a
115 drench,"° says he, and answers "Some fourteen,"
an hour after; "a trifle, a trifle." I prithee, call in
Falstaff. I'll play Percy, and that damned brawn°
shall play Dame Mortimer his wife. "Rivo!"°
says the drunkard. Call in ribs, call in tallow.°

[*Enter* FALSTAFF, GADSHILL, BARDOLPH, *and*
PETO; FRANCIS *following with wine.*]

POINS. Welcome, Jack. Where hast thou been?

120 FALSTAFF. A plague of all cowards, I say, and a
vengeance too! Marry,° and amen! Give me a
cup of sack, boy. Ere I lead this life long, I'll sew
nether stocks° and mend them and foot them
too. A plague of all cowards! Give me a cup of
125 sack, rogue. Is there no virtue extant?

[*He drinks.*]

PRINCE. Didst thou never see Titan° kiss a dish of
butter—pitiful-hearted Titan—that melted at
the sweet tale of the sun? If thou didst, then
behold that compound.°

130 FALSTAFF. You rogue, here's lime in this sack too.
There is nothing but roguery to be found in
villainous man. Yet a coward is worse than a cup
of sack with lime in it. A villainous coward! Go
thy ways, old Jack; die when thou wilt. If man-
135 hood, good manhood, be not forgot upon the
face of the earth, then am I a shotten herring.°
There lives not three good men unhanged in
England, and one of them is fat and grows old.
God help the while!° A bad world, I say. I would
140 I were a weaver; I could sing psalms or anything.
A plague of all cowards, I say still.

PRINCE. How now, woolsack! What mutter you?

FALSTAFF. A king's son! If I do not beat thee out of
thy kingdom with a dagger of lath,° and drive
145 all thy subjects afore thee like a flock of wild

geese, I'll never wear hair on my face more. You
Prince of Wales!

PRINCE. Why, you whoreson round man, what's
the matter?

150 FALSTAFF. Are not you a coward? Answer me to
that. And Poins there?

POINS. 'Zounds, ye fat paunch, an ye call me
coward, by the Lord, I'll stab thee.

FALSTAFF. I call thee coward! I'll see thee damned
155 ere I call thee coward. But I would give a
thousand pound I could run as fast as thou canst.
You are straight enough in the shoulders, you
care not who sees your back. Call you that
backing of your friends? A plague upon such
160 backing! Give me them that will face me. Give
me a cup of sack. I am a rogue if I drunk today.

PRINCE. O villain! Thy lips are scarce wiped since
thou drunkest last.

FALSTAFF. All's one for that. [*He drinks*] A plague of
165 all cowards, still say I.

PRINCE. What's the matter?

FALSTAFF. What's the matter! There be four of us
here have ta'en a thousand pound this day
morning.

170 PRINCE. Where is it, Jack? Where is it?

FALSTAFF. Where is it! Taken from us it is. A hundred upon poor four of us.

PRINCE. What, a hundred, man?

FALSTAFF. I am a rogue if I were not at half-sword
175 with a dozen of them two hours together. I have
'scaped by miracle. I am eight times thrust
through the doublet, four through the hose, my
buckler cut through and through, my sword
hacked like a hand-saw—*ecce signum!*° I never
180 dealt better since I was a man. All would not do.
A plague of all cowards! Let them speak. If they
speak more or less than truth, they are villains
and the sons of darkness.

PRINCE. Speak, sirs. How was it?

185 GADSHILL. We four set upon some dozen—

FALSTAFF. Sixteen at least, my lord.

GADSHILL. And bound them.

PETO. No, no, they were not bound.

FALSTAFF. You rogue, they were bound, every man
190 of them.

GADSHILL. As we were sharing, some six or seven
fresh men set upon us—

FALSTAFF. And unbound the rest, and then come
in the other.

195 PRINCE. What, fought you with them all?

FALSTAFF. All! I know not what you call all, but if I
fought not with fifty of them, I am a bunch of
radish. If there were not two or three and fifty

---

industry occupation
parcel . . . reckoning itemizing of a bill
drench dose of medicine   *brawn* pig
"Rivo!" a drinking cry   *ribs . . . tallow* i.e., Falstaff
Marry by the Virgin   *nether stocks* stockings
Titan the sun   *compound* melted butter (Falstaff)
shotten herring empty, having discharged its eggs
the while these times
dagger of lath wooden dagger such as used by actors

ecce signum behold the evidence

200 upon poor old Jack, then am I no two-legged
creature.

PRINCE. Pray God you have not murdered some of
them.

FALSTAFF. Nay, that's past praying for. I have pep-
205 pered two of them, two I am sure I have paid,
two rogues in buckram suits. I tell thee what,
Hal, if I tell thee a lie, spit in my face, call me
horse. Thou knowest my old ward.° Here I lay,
and thus I bore my point. Four rogues in buckram let drive at me—

210 PRINCE. What, four? Thou saidst but two even
now.

FALSTAFF. Four, Hal; I told thee four.

POINS. Aye, aye, he said four.

FALSTAFF. These four came all a-front, and mainly°
215 thrust at me. I made me no more ado but took
all their seven points in my target, thus.

PRINCE. Seven? Why, there were but four even
now.

FALSTAFF. In buckram?

220 POINS. Aye, four, in buckram suits.

FALSTAFF. Seven by these hilts, or I am a villain
else.

PRINCE. Prithee, let him alone; we shall have more
anon.

225 FALSTAFF. Dost thou hear me, Hal?

PRINCE. Aye, and mark thee too, Jack.

FALSTAFF. Do so, for it is worth the listening to.
These nine in buckram that I told thee of—

PRINCE. So, two more already.

230 FALSTAFF. Their points being broken—

POINS. Down fell their hose.°

FALSTAFF. Began to give me ground. But I followed
me close, came in foot and hand, and with a
thought seven of the eleven I paid.

235 PRINCE. O monstrous! Eleven buckram men
grown out of two!

FALSTAFF. But, as the devil would have it, three misbegotten knaves in Kendal green came at my
back and let drive at me; for it was so dark, Hal,
240 that thou couldst not see thy hand.

PRINCE. These lies are like their father that begets
them, gross as a mountain, open, palpable. Why,
thou clay-brained guts, thou knotty-pated fool,
thou whoreson, obscene, greasy tallow-catch—

245 FALSTAFF. What, art thou mad? Art thou mad? Is
not the truth the truth?

PRINCE. Why, how couldst thou know these men in
Kendal green, when it was so dark thou couldst
not see thy hand? Come, tell us your reason.

What sayest thou to this?   250

POINS. Come, your reason, Jack, your reason.

FALSTAFF. What, upon compulsion? 'Zounds, an I
were at the strappado, or all the racks° in the
world, I would not tell you on compulsion. Give
you a reason on compulsion! If reasons° were as 255
plentiful as blackberries, I would give no man a
reason upon compulsion, I.

PRINCE. I'll be no longer guilty of this sin. This
sanguine coward, this bed-presser, this horse-
back-breaker, this huge hill of flesh—   260

FALSTAFF. 'Sblood, you starveling, you elfskin, you
dried neat's tongue, you bull's pizzle, you stock-
fish! O for breath to utter what is like thee! You
tailor's yard, you sheath, you bow case, you vile
standing tuck°—   265

PRINCE. Well, breathe a while, and then to it again.
And when thou hast tired thyself in base comparisons, hear me speak but this.

POINS. Mark, Jack.

PRINCE. We too saw you four set on four and   270
bound them, and were masters of their wealth.
Mark now, how a plain tale shall put you down.
Then did we two set on you four, and, with a
word, outfaced you from your prize, and have it,
yea, and can show it you here in the house. And, 275
Falstaff, you carried your guts away as nimbly,
with as quick dexterity, and roared for mercy,
and still run and roared, as ever I heard bullcalf.
What a slave art thou, to hack thy sword as thou
hast done, and then say it was in fight! What   280
trick, what device, what starting-hole° canst
thou now find out to hide thee from this open
and apparent shame?

POINS. Come, let's hear, Jack. What trick hast thou
now?   285

FALSTAFF. By the Lord, I knew ye as well as he that
made ye. Why, hear you, my masters. Was it for
me to kill the heir apparent? Should I turn upon
the true prince? Why, thou knowest I am as
valiant as Hercules. But beware instinct; the   290
lion will not touch the true prince. Instinct is a
great matter; I was now a coward on instinct. I
shall think the better of myself and thee during
my life—I for a valiant lion, and thou for a true
prince. But, by the Lord, lads, I am glad you have 295
the money. Hostess, clap to the doors. Watch
tonight, pray tomorrow. Gallants, lads, boys,
hearts of gold, all the titles of good fellowship
come to you! What, shall we be merry? Shall we
have a play extempore?   300

---

ward stance   mainly mightily
points . . . hose pun: sword points, but also stocking
    fasteners

strappado . . . racks devices of torture
reason . . . reasons pun: raisins   tuck rapier
starting-hole refuge, such as a mousehole

PRINCE. Content—and the argument° shall be thy running away.

FALSTAFF. Ah, no more of that, Hal, an thou lovest me!

[*Enter* HOSTESS.]

305 HOSTESS. O Jesu, my lord the prince!

PRINCE. How now, my lady the hostess! What sayest thou to me?

HOSTESS. Marry, my lord, there is a nobleman of the court at door would speak with you. He says 310 he comes from your father.

PRINCE. Give him as much as will make him a royal man, and send him back again to my mother.

FALSTAFF. What manner of man is he?

HOSTESS. An old man.

315 FALSTAFF. What doth gravity out of his bed at midnight? Shall I give him his answer?

PRINCE. Prithee, do, Jack.

FALSTAFF. Faith, and I'll send him packing.   [*Exit*]

PRINCE. Now, sirs, by'r lady, you fought fair. So did 320 you, Peto; so did you, Bardolph. You are lions too, you ran away upon instinct, you will not touch the true prince; no, fie!

BARDOLPH. Faith, I ran when I saw others run.

PRINCE. Faith, tell me now in earnest, how came 325 Falstaff's sword so hacked?

PETO. Why, he hacked it with his dagger, and said he would swear truth out of England but he would make you believe it was done in fight, and persuaded us to do the like.

330 BARDOLPH. Yea, and to tickle our noses with speargrass to make them bleed, and then to beslubber our garments with it and swear it was the blood of true men. I did that I did not this seven year before—I blushed to hear his monstrous devices.

335 PRINCE. O villain, thou stolest a cup of sack eighteen years ago, and wert taken with the manner,° and ever since thou hast blushed extempore. Thou hadst fire and sword on thy side, and yet thou rannest away. What instinct hadst thou for 340 it?

BARDOLPH. My lord, do you see these meteors? Do you behold these exhalations?°

PRINCE. I do.

BARDOLPH. What think you they portend?

345 PRINCE. Hot livers and cold purses.°

BARDOLPH. Choler,° my lord, if rightly taken.

PRINCE. No, if rightly taken, halter.°

[*Re-enter* FALSTAFF.]

Here comes lean Jack, here comes barebone. How now, my sweet creature of bombast!° How 350 long is't ago, Jack, since thou sawest thine own knee?

FALSTAFF. My own knee! When I was about thy years, Hal, I was not an eagle's talon in the waist; I could have crept into any alderman's thumb-ring. A plague of sighing and grief! It 355 blows a man up like a bladder. There's villainous news abroad. Here was Sir John Bracy from your father; you must to the court in the morning. That same mad fellow of the north, Percy, and he of Wales, that gave Amamon the bastinado° 360 and made Lucifer cuckold,° and swore the devil his true liegeman upon the cross of a Welsh hook°—what a plague call you him?

POINS. O, Glendower.

FALSTAFF. Owen, Owen, the same; and his son-in- 365 law Mortimer, and old Northumberland, and that sprightly Scot of Scots, Douglas, that runs o'horseback up a hill perpendicular—

PRINCE. He that rides at high speed and with his pistol kills a sparrow flying? 370

FALSTAFF. You have hit it.

PRINCE. So did he never the sparrow.

FALSTAFF. Well, that rascal hath good mettle in him; he will not run.

PRINCE. Why, what a rascal art thou then, to praise 375 him so for running!

FALSTAFF. O' horseback, ye cuckoo. But afoot he will not budge a foot.

PRINCE. Yes, Jack, upon instinct.

FALSTAFF. I grant ye, upon instinct. Well, he is there 380 too, and one Mordake, and a thousand bluecaps° more. Worcester is stolen away tonight. Thy father's beard is turned white with the news. You may buy land now as cheap as stinking mackerel. 385

PRINCE. Why, then, it is like, if there come a hot June and this civil buffeting hold, we shall buy maidenheads as they buy hobnails, by the hundreds.

---

argument plot

taken . . . manner verbal play: caught in the act, but also seized by the habit

meteors . . . exhalations Bardolph's face is a mass of streaks, bumps, and boils

Hot . . . purses i.e., livers heated by drink, purses emptied to pay the tapster

Choler fiery temperament

if . . . halter pun: *rightly understood,* but also *justly apprehended; halter* in opposition to *choler–collar,* but also hangman's noose

bombast stuffing

gave . . . bastinado gave Amamon (name of a fiend) a beating

made . . . cuckold i.e., gave the devil his horns (a frequent Elizabethan joke; a cuckold, the husband of a faithless wife, is always pictured as having horns)

Welsh hook weapon with both point and hook

bluecaps the blue-bonnetted Scots

390 FALSTAFF. By the mass, lad, thou sayest true; it is like we shall have good trading that way. But tell me, Hal, art not thou horrible afeard? Thou being heir apparent, could the world pick thee out three such enemies again as that fiend

395 Douglas, that spirit Percy, and that devil Glendower? Art thou not horribly afraid? Doth not thy blood thrill at it?

PRINCE. Not a whit, i' faith; I lack some of thy instinct.

400 FALSTAFF. Well, thou wilt be horribly chid tomorrow when thou comest to thy father. If thou love me, practice an answer.

PRINCE. Do thou stand for my father, and examine me upon the particulars of my life.

405 FALSTAFF. Shall I? Content. This chair shall be my state,° this dagger my scepter, and this cushion my crown.

PRINCE. Thy state is taken for a joined-stool, thy golden scepter for a leaden dagger, and thy
410 precious rich crown for a pitiful bald crown!

FALSTAFF. Well, an the fire of grace be not quite out of thee, now shalt thou be moved. Give me a cup of sack to make my eyes look red, that it may be thought I have wept; for I must speak in
415 passion, and I will do it in King Cambyses' vein.°

PRINCE. Well, here is my leg.

FALSTAFF. And here is my speech. Stand aside, nobility.

420 HOSTESS. O Jesu, this is excellent sport, i' faith!

FALSTAFF. Weep not, sweet queen, for trickling tears are vain.

HOSTESS. O, the father, how he holds his countenance!

425 FALSTAFF. For God's sake, lords, convey my tristful queen,
For tears do stop the floodgates of her eyes.

HOSTESS. O Jesu, he doth it as like one of these harlotry° players as ever I see!

430 FALSTAFF. Peace, good pintpot; peace, good ticklebrain. Harry, I do not only marvel where thou spendest thy time, but also how thou art accompanied. For though the camomile,° the more it is trodden on the faster it grows, yet youth, the
435 more it is wasted the sooner it wears. That thou art my son, I have partly thy mother's word, partly my own opinion, but chiefly a villainous

trick of thine eye and a foolish hanging of thy nether lip that doth warrant me. If then thou be son to me, here lies the point: why, being son to 440 me, art thou so pointed at? Shall the blessed sun of heaven prove a micher° and eat blackberries? A question not to be asked. Shall the son of England prove a thief and take purses? A question to be asked. There is a thing, Harry, 445 which thou hast often heard of, and it is known to many in our land by the name of pitch. This pitch, as ancient writers do report, doth defile; so doth the company thou keepest. For, Harry, now I do not speak to thee in drink but in tears, 450 not in pleasure but in passion, not in words only, but in woes also. And yet there is a virtuous man whom I have often noted in thy company, but I know not his name.

PRINCE. What manner of man, an it like your 455 majesty?

FALSTAFF. A goodly portly man, i' faith, and a corpulent, of a cheerful look, a pleasing eye, and a most noble carriage, and, as I think, his age some fifty, or, by'r lady, inclining to three score. 460 And now I remember me, his name is Falstaff. If that man should be lewdly given, he deceiveth me; for, Harry, I see virtue in his looks. If then the tree may be known by the fruit, as the fruit by the tree, then, peremptorily I speak it, there 465 is virtue in that Falstaff. Him keep with, the rest banish. And tell me now, thou naughty varlet, tell me, where hast thou been this month?

PRINCE. Dost thou speak like a king? Do thou stand for me, and I'll play my father. 470

FALSTAFF. Depose me? If thou dost it half so gravely, so majestically, both in word and matter, hang me up by the heels for a rabbit-sucker° or a poulter's hare.°

PRINCE. Well, here I am set. 475

FALSTAFF. And here I stand. Judge, my masters.

PRINCE. Now, Harry, whence come you?

FALSTAFF. My noble lord, from Eastcheap.

PRINCE. The complaints I hear of thee are grievous.

FALSTAFF. 'Sblood, my lord, they are false.—Nay, 480 I'll tickle ye for a young prince, i' faith.

PRINCE. Swearest thou, ungracious boy? Henceforth ne'er look on me. Thou art violently carried away from grace. There is a devil haunts thee in the likeness of an old fat man; a tun of 485 man° is thy companion. Why dost thou converse

---

state   chair of state
King Cambyses' vein   in the style of a ranting theatrical king, specifically from T. Preston's tragedy, Cambyses, King of Persia
harlotry   rascally   camomile   an aromatic herb (the lines mimic a passage in John Lyly's Euphues)

micher   truant (moocher?)
rabbit-sucker   unweaned rabbit
poulter's hare   rabbit hung up in a poulterer's shop
a tun of man   a wine barrel of a man

with that trunk of humors,° that bolting-hutch°
of beastliness, that swollen parcel of dropsies,
that huge bombard° of sack, that stuffed cloak-
490   bag of guts, that roasted Manningtree° ox with
the pudding in his belly, that reverend vice, that
gray iniquity, that father ruffian, that vanity in
years? Wherein is he good, but to taste sack and
drink it? Wherein neat and cleanly, but to carve
495   a capon and eat it? Wherein cunning, but in
craft? Wherein crafty, but in villainy? Wherein
villainous, but in all things? Wherein worthy,
but in nothing?

FALSTAFF. I would your grace would take me with
500   you. Whom means your grace?

PRINCE. That villainous abominable misleader of
youth, Falstaff, that old white-bearded Satan.

FALSTAFF. My lord, the man I know.

PRINCE. I know thou dost.

505   FALSTAFF. But to say I know more harm in him
than in myself, were to say more than I know.
That he is old, the more the pity, his white hairs
do witness it; but that he is, saving your
reverence, a whoremaster, that I utterly deny.
510   If sack and sugar be a fault, God help the wicked!
If to be old and merry be a sin, then many an old
host that I know is damned. If to be fat be to be
hated, then Pharaoh's lean kine° are to be loved.
No, my good lord. Banish Peto, banish Bardolph,
515   banish Poins; but for sweet Jack Falstaff, kind
Jack Falstaff, true Jack Falstaff, valiant Jack Falstaff, and therefore more valiant, being, as he is,
old Jack Falstaff, banish not him thy Harry's
company, banish not him thy Harry's company.
520   Banish plump Jack, and banish all the world.

PRINCE. I do, I will.   [A knocking heard.]
                [Exeunt HOSTESS, FRANCIS, and BARDOLPH.]
                [Re-enter BARDOLPH, running.]

BARDOLPH. O, my lord, my lord! The sheriff with
a most monstrous watch is at the door.

FALSTAFF. Out, ye rogue! Play out the play. I have
525   much to say in the behalf of that Falstaff.
                [Re-enter the HOSTESS.]

HOSTESS. O Jesu, my lord, my lord!—

PRINCE. Heigh, heigh! The devil rides upon a fiddlestick.° What's the matter?

HOSTESS. The sheriff and all the watch are at the
530   door. They are come to search the house. Shall I
let them in?

FALSTAFF. Dost thou hear, Hal? Never call a true

piece of gold a counterfeit. Thou art essentially
mad, without seeming so.

PRINCE. And thou a natural coward, without   535
instinct.

FALSTAFF. I deny your major.° If you will deny the
sheriff, so; if not, let him enter. If I become not a
cart° as well as another man, a plague on my
bringing up! I hope I shall as soon be strangled   540
with a halter as another.

PRINCE. Go, hide thee behind the arras;° the rest
walk up above. Now, my masters, for a true
face and good conscience.

FALSTAFF. Both which I have had, but their date is   545
out, and therefore I'll hide me.

PRINCE. Call in the sheriff.
                [Exeunt all except the PRINCE and PETO.]
                [Enter SHERIFF and the CARRIER.]
Now, master sheriff, what is your will with me?

SHERIFF. First, pardon me, my lord. A hue and cry
Hath follow'd certain men unto this house.   550

PRINCE. What men?

SHERIFF. One of them is well known, my gracious
lord,
A gross fat man.

CARRIER.   As fat as butter.

PRINCE. The man, I do assure you, is not here,
For I myself at this time have employ'd him.   555
And, sheriff, I will engage my word to thee
That I will, by tomorrow dinnertime,
Send him to answer thee, or any man,
For anything he shall be charg'd withal:
And so let me entreat you leave the house.   560

SHERIFF. I will, my lord. There are two gentlemen
Have in this robbery lost three hundred marks.

PRINCE. It may be so. If he have robb'd these men,
He shall be answerable; and so farewell.

SHERIFF. Good night, my noble lord.   565

PRINCE. I think it is good morrow, is it not?

SHERIFF. Indeed, my lord, I think it be two o'clock.
                [Exeunt SHERIFF and CARRIER.]

PRINCE. This oily rascal is known as well as Paul's.°
Go, call him forth.

PETO. Falstaff!—Fast asleep behind the arras, and   570
snorting like a horse.

PRINCE. Hark, how hard he fetches breath. Search
his pockets.
                [He searches his pockets, and finds certain papers.]
What hast thou found?

PETO. Nothing but papers, my lord.   575

PRINCE. Let's see what they be. Read them.

---

trunk of humors bag of unhealthy excesses
bolting-hutch flour bin for sifting   bombard winebag
Manningtree a town in Essex
Pharaoh's lean kine (see Genesis 41:18–21)
devil . . . fiddlestick i.e., something big is up

major major premise of your logic
become . . . cart look good on the cart hauling the
    condemned to the gallows   arras curtain
Paul's St. Paul's Cathedral

PETO. [*Reads*] *Item, A capon,* . . . . *2s. 2d.*°
        Item, Sauce, ...   *4d.*
        Item, Sack, two gallons, . . . *5s. 8d.*
580   *Item, Anchovies and sack after*
        supper, ... *2s. 6d.*
        Item, Bread, ...   *ob.*°

PRINCE. O monstrous! But one half-pennyworth of
bread to this intolerable deal of sack! What there
585   is else, keep close; we'll read it at more advan-

tage. There 'let him sleep till day. I'll to the
court in the morning. We must all to the wars,
and thy place shall be honorable. I'll procure
this fat rogue a charge of foot;° and I know his
death will be a march of twelve-score.° The 590
money shall be paid back again with advantage.
Be with me betimes in the morning; and so,
good morrow, Peto.
PETO. Good morrow, good my lord.   [*Exeunt*]

2s. 2d. two shillings and two pennies
ob. obolus (halfpenny)

foot infantry   *twelve-score* yards

A C T I I I

SCENE i
Bangor. The ARCHDEACON'S *house.*

[*Enter* HOTSPUR, WORCESTER, MORTIMER, *and*
GLENDOWER.]

MORTIMER. These promises are fair, the parties
   sure,
  And our induction° full of prosperous hope.
HOTSPUR. Lord Mortimer and cousin Glendower,°
  Will you sit down?
5 And uncle Worcester. A plague upon it!
  I have forgot the map.
GLENDOWER.   No, here it is.
  Sit, cousin Percy; sit, good cousin Hotspur,
  For by that name as oft as Lancaster°
  Doth speak of you, his cheek looks pale, and
   with
10 A rising sigh he wisheth you in heaven.
HOTSPUR. And you in hell, as oft as he hears Owen
  Glendower spoke of.
GLENDOWER. I cannot blame him. At my nativity°
  The front° of heaven was full of fiery shapes,
  Of burning cressets;° and at my birth
15 The frame and huge foundation of the earth
  Shak'd like a coward.
HOTSPUR. Why, so it would have done at the same
  season if your mother's cat had but kittened,
  though yourself had never been born.
GLENDOWER. I say the earth did shake when I was
20 born.

HOTSPUR. And I say the earth was not of my mind,
  If you suppose as fearing you it shook.
GLENDOWER. The heavens were all on fire, the
  earth did tremble.
HOTSPUR. O, then the earth shook to see the
  heavens on fire,
  And not in fear of your nativity.   25
  Diseased nature oftentimes breaks forth
  In strange eruptions; oft the teeming earth
  Is with a kind of colic pinch'd and vex'd
  By the imprisoning of unruly wind
  Within her womb; which, for enlargement°
   striving,   30
  Shakes the old beldam earth and topples down
  Steeples and mossgrown towers. At your birth
  Our grandam earth, having this distemperature,
  In passion shook.
GLENDOWER.   Cousin, of many men
  I do not bear these crossings. Give me leave 35
  To tell you once again that at my birth
  The front of heaven was full of fiery shapes,
  The goats ran from the mountains, and the
   herds
  Were strangely clamorous to the frighted fields.
  These signs have mark'd me extraordinary, 40
  And all the courses of my life do show
  I am not in the roll of common men.
  Where is he living, clipp'd in with the sea
  That chides the banks of England, Scotland,
   Wales,
  Which calls me pupil, or hath read° to me? 45
  And bring him out that is but woman's son
  Can trace me in the tedious ways of art,°
  And hold me pace in deep experiments.

---

induction beginning
cousin Glendower (an extreme case of typically loose
  Elizabethan usage of *cousin*: Hotspur's wife's brother is
  the husband of Glendower's daughter)
Lancaster surname of the royal family
nativity birth   *front* forehead (Latin *frons*)
cressets torchlights

enlargement release   *read* instructed
art i.e., magic art

HOTSPUR. I think there's no man speaks better
    Welsh.
50   I'll to dinner.
MORTIMER. Peace, cousin Percy; you will make him
    mad.
GLENDOWER. I can call spirits from the vasty deep.°
HOTSPUR. Why, so can I, or so can any man.
    But will they come when you do call for them?
GLENDOWER. Why, I can teach you, cousin, to
55   command
    The devil.
HOTSPUR. And I can teach thee, coz, to shame the
    devil
    By telling truth: tell truth, and shame the devil.
    If thou have power to raise him, bring him
    hither,
    And I'll be sworn I have power to shame him
60   hence.
    O, while you live, tell truth, and shame the
    devil!
MORTIMER. Come, come, no more of this un-
    profitable chat.
GLENDOWER. Three times hath Henry Bolingbroke
    made head°
    Against my power; thrice from the banks of
    Wye
65   And sandy-bottom'd Severn have I sent him
    Bootless° home and weather-beaten back.
HOTSPUR. Home without boots, and in foul
    weather too!
    How 'scapes he agues, in the devil's name?
GLENDOWER. Come, here's the map. Shall we
    divide our right
70   According to our threefold order ta'en?°
MORTIMER. Th' archdeacon hath divided it
    Into three limits very equally.
    England, from Trent and Severn hitherto,
    By south and east is to my part assign'd.
75   All westward, Wales beyond the Severn shore,
    And all the fertile land within that bound,
    To Owen Glendower. And, dear coz, to you
    The remnant northward, lying off from Trent.
    And our indentures tripartite° are drawn,
80   Which being sealed interchangeably,°
    A business that this night may execute,
    Tomorrow, cousin Percy, you and I
    And my good Lord of Worcester will set forth
    To meet your father and the Scottish power,
85   As is appointed us, at Shrewsbury.
    My father Glendower is not ready yet,

Nor shall we need his help these fourteen days.
Within that space you may have drawn together
Your tenants, friends, and neighboring gentle-
    men.
GLENDOWER. A shorter time shall send me to you,
    lords.   90
    And in my conduct shall your ladies come,
    From whom you now must steal and take no
    leave,
    For there will be a world of water shed
    Upon the parting of your wives and you.
HOTSPUR. Methinks my moiety,° north from
    Burton here,   95
    In quantity equals not one of yours.
    See how this river comes me cranking in
    And cuts me from the best of all my land
    A huge half-moon, a monstrous cantle° out.
    I'll have the current in this place damn'd up,   100
    And here the smug and silver Trent shall run
    In a new channel, fair and evenly.
    It shall not wind with such a deep indent,
    To rob me of so rich a bottom here.
GLENDOWER. Not wind? It shall, it must; you see it
    doth.   105
MORTIMER. Yea, but
    Mark how he bears his course, and runs me up
    With like advantage on the other side,
    Gelding th' opposed continent° as much
    As on the other side it takes from you.   110
WORCESTER. Yea, but a little charge° will trench
    him here
    And on this north side win this cape of land,
    And then he runs straight and even.
HOTSPUR. I'll have it so. A little charge will do it.
GLENDOWER. I'll not have it alter'd.
HOTSPUR.   Will not you? 115
GLENDOWER. No, nor you shall not.
HOTSPUR.   Who shall say me nay?
GLENDOWER. Why, that will I.
HOTSPUR. Let me not understand you, then; speak
    it in Welsh.
GLENDOWER. I can speak English, lord, as well as
    you;   120
    For I was train'd up in the English court,
    Where, being but young, I framed to the harp
    Many an English ditty lovely well
    And gave the tongue a helpful ornament°—
    A virtue° that was never seen in you.

---

deep secret   *made head* raised an army
Bootless without gain   *order ta'en* division made
indentures tripartite three-party contracts
sealed interchangeably signed by each party

moiety portion   *cantle* chunk   *continent* bank
charge expense
I . . . ornament I composed harp music for many English
    songs, giving words the benefit of musical
    accompaniment
virtue accomplishment

125 HOTSPUR. Marry,
  And I am glad of it with all my heart.
  I had rather be a kitten and cry mew
  Than one of these same meter ballad-mongers.°
  I had rather hear a brazen canstick° turn'd
130 Or a dry wheel grate on the axletree,
  And that would set my teeth nothing on edge,
  Nothing so much as mincing poetry.
  'Tis like the forc'd gait of a shuffling nag.
  GLENDOWER. Come, you shall have Trent turn'd.
  HOTSPUR. I do not care. I'll give thrice so much
135   land
  To any well-deserving friend.
  But in the way of bargain, mark ye me,
  I'll cavil on the ninth part of a hair.
  Are the indentures drawn? Shall we be gone?
  GLENDOWER. The moon shines fair; you may
140   away by night.
  I'll haste the writer, and withal
  Break with° your wives of your departure
    hence.
  I am afraid my daughter will run mad,
  So much she doteth on her Mortimer.   [Exit]
  MORTIMER. Fie, cousin Percy! How you cross my
145   father!
  HOTSPUR. I cannot choose. Sometimes he angers me
  With telling me of the moldwarp° and the ant,
  Of the dreamer Merlin and his prophecies,
  And of a dragon and a finless fish,
150 A clip-wing'd griffin and a moulten° raven,
  A couching lion and a ramping °cat,
  And such a deal of skimble-skamble stuff
  As puts me from my faith. I tell you what—
  He held me last night at least nine hours
155 In reckoning up the several devils' names
  That were his lackeys. I cried "hum" and "well,
    go to,"
  But mark'd him not a word. O, he is as tedious
  As a tired horse, a railing wife,
  Worse than a smoky house. I had rather live
160 With cheese and garlic in a windmill, far,
  Than feed on cates° and have him talk to me
  In any summerhouse in Christendom.
  MORTIMER. In faith, he is a worthy gentleman,
  Exceedingly well read, and profited
165 In strange concealments,° valiant as a lion,
  And wondrous affable, and as bountiful
  As mines of India. Shall I tell you, cousin?

  He holds your temper in a high respect
  And curbs himself even of his natural scope
  When you come 'cross his humor; faith, he does. 170
  I warrant you that man is not alive
  Might so have tempted him as you have done,
  Without the taste of danger and reproof.
  But do not use it oft, let me entreat you.
  WORCESTER. In faith, my lord, you are too wilful-
    blame,°   175
  And since your coming hither have done enough
  To put him quite beside his patience.
  You must needs learn, lord, to amend this fault.
  Though sometimes it show greatness, courage,
    blood—
  And that's the dearest grace it renders you—   180
  Yet oftentimes it doth present° harsh rage,
  Defect of manners, want of government,°
  Pride, haughtiness, opinion,° and disdain—
  The least of which haunting a nobleman
  Loseth men's hearts and leaves behind a stain 185
  Upon the beauty of all parts besides,
  Beguiling° them of commendation.
  HOTSPUR. Well, I am school'd. Good manners be
    your speed!°
  Here come our wives, and let us take our leave.
    [Re-enter GLENDOWER with the LADIES.]
  MORTIMER. This is the deadly spite that angers
    me—   190
  My wife can speak no English, I no Welsh.
  GLENDOWER. My daughter weeps; she will not
    part with you.
  She'll be a soldier too, she'll to the wars.
  MORTIMER. Good father, tell her that she and my
    aunt Percy°
  Shall follow in your conduct speedily.   195
    [GLENDOWER speaks to her in Welsh, and she
                    answers him in the same.]
  GLENDOWER. She is desperate here, a peevish
    self-will'd harlotry,° one that no persuasion
    can do good upon.
            [The LADY speaks in Welsh.]
  MORTIMER. I understand thy looks. That pretty
    Welsh°
  Which thou pour'st down from these swelling
    heavens   200

---

meter ballad-mongers   contemptuous term for a rhymester
canstick   candlestick
Break with   inform   moldwarp   mole
moulten   moulted
couching . . . ramping   couchant and rampant (heraldic
  terms)
cates   delicacies   concealments   mysteries

wilful-blame   headstrong to the point of deserving blame
present   represent
want of government   lack of self-control
opinion   self-opinion   Beguiling   cheating
Good . . . speed   literally, good manners make you
  prosper; but here, have it you own way
aunt Percy   historians on whom Shakespeare drew
  confused two generations of Mortimers; here
  Mortimer should have said "sister"
harlotry   wench   That . . . Welsh   i.e., her tears

I am too perfect in,° and, but for shame,
In such a parley should I answer thee.
                 [*The* LADY *speaks again in Welsh.*]
I understand thy kisses and thou mine,
And that's a feeling disputation.°
205 But I will never be a truant, love,
Till I have learn'd thy language, for thy tongue
Makes Welsh as sweet as ditties highly penn'd,
Sung by a fair queen in a summer's bower,
With ravishing division,° to her lute.
GLENDOWER. Nay, if you melt, then will she run
210   mad.
                 [*The* LADY *speaks again in Welsh.*]
MORTIMER. O, I am ignorance itself in this!
GLENDOWER. She bids you on the wanton rushes
    lay you down
    And rest your gentle head upon her lap,
    And she will sing the song that pleaseth you,
215   And on your eyelids crown the god of sleep,
    Charming your blood with pleasing heaviness,
    Making such difference 'twixt wake and sleep
    As is the difference betwixt day and night
    The hour before the heavenly-harness'd team°
220   Begins his golden progress in the east.
MORTIMER. With all my heart I'll sit and hear her
    sing.
    By that time will our book, I think, be drawn.
GLENDOWER. Do so.
    And those musicians that shall play to you
    Hang in the air a thousand leagues from hence,
225   And straight they shall be here. Sit, and attend.
HOTSPUR. Come, Kate, thou art perfect in lying
    down. Come, quick, quick, that I may lay my
    head in thy lap.
LADY PERCY. Go, ye giddy goose.
                     [*The music plays.*]
HOTSPUR. Now I perceive the devil understands
230   Welsh,
    And 'tis no marvel—he is so humorous.°
    By'r lady, he is a good musician.
LADY PERCY. Then should you be nothing but
    musical, for you are altogether governed by
235   humors.° Lie still, ye thief, and hear the lady
    sing in Welsh.
HOTSPUR. I had rather hear Lady, my brach,°
    howl in Irish.
LADY PERCY. Wouldst thou have thy head broken?

HOTSPUR. No.   240
LADY PERCY. Then be still.
HOTSPUR. Neither; 'tis a woman's fault.°
LADY PERCY. Now God help thee!
HOTSPUR. To the Welsh lady's bed.
LADY PERCY. What's that?
HOTSPUR. Peace! She sings.   245
          [*Here the* LADY *sings a Welsh song.*]
HOTSPUR. Come, Kate, I'll have your song too.
LADY PERCY. Not mine, in good sooth.
HOTSPUR. Not yours, in good sooth! Heart! You
    swear like a comfit-maker's° wife. "Not you, in
    good sooth," and "as true as I live," and "as   250
    God shall mend me," and "as sure as day,"
    And giv'st such sarcenet surety° for thy oaths
    As if thou never walk'st further than Finsbury.°
    Swear me, Kate, like a lady as thou art,
    A good mouth-filling oath, and leave "in sooth"   255
    And such protest of pepper-gingerbread°
    To velvet guards° and Sunday citizens.
    Come, sing.
LADY PERCY. I will not sing.
HOTSPUR. 'Tis the next way to turn tailor,° or be   260
    redbreast teacher.° An the indentures be drawn,
    I'll away within these two hours, and so come in
    when ye will.   [*Exit*]
GLENDOWER. Come, come, Lord Mortimer. You
    are as slow
    As hot Lord Percy is on fire to go.   265
    By this our book is drawn; we'll but seal,
    And then to horse immediately.
MORTIMER.   With all my heart.
                        [*Exeunt*]

SCENE ii
London. The palace.

[*Enter the* KING, PRINCE OF WALES, *and others.*]
KING. Lords, give us leave. The Prince of Wales
    and I
    Must have some private conference. But be
    near at hand,

---

too . . . in understand too well
feeling disputation moving discussion
division harmony
heavenly-harness'd team sun-god's team
humorous eccentric
altogether . . . humors entirely ruled by whims and
  impulses
brach bitch

'tis . . . fault Hotspur jestingly reverses the usual charge
  that women talk too much
comfit-maker candy-maker
sarcenet surety flimsy (silken) assurance
never . . . Finsbury i.e., have not "been around" much;
  Finsbury Fields, near London
protest . . . gingerbread i.e., oaths no "hotter" than
  gingerbread
velvet guards figuratively, ladies who wear fancy
  trimmings, as on Sunday
turn tailor i.e., the tailor sings at his work (Hotspur
  treats middle-class manners and vocations with
  contempt)
redbreast teacher i.e., teach robins to sing

For we shall presently have need of you.
                              [*Exeunt* LORDS.]
I know not whether God will have it so
5   For some displeasing service I have done,
That, in his secret doom, out of my blood
He'll breed revengement and a scourge for me;
But thou dost in thy passages of life
Make me believe that thou art only mark'd
10 For the hot vengeance and the rod of heaven
To punish my mistreadings. Tell me else,
Could such inordinate and low desires,
Such poor, such bare, such lewd, such mean
    attempts,°
Such barren pleasures, rude society
15 As thou art match'd withal and grafted to,
Accompany the greatness of thy blood
And hold their level with° thy princely heart?
PRINCE. So please your majesty, I would I could
Quit° all offenses with as clear excuse
20 As well as I am doubtless I can purge
Myself of many I am charg'd withal.
Yet such extenuation let me beg
As, in reproof° of many tales devis'd
Which oft the ear of greatness needs must hear,
25 By smiling pick-thanks° and base newsmongers,
I may for some things true wherein my youth
Hath faulty wander'd and irregular
Find pardon on my true submission.
KING. God pardon thee! Yet let me wonder, Harry,
30 At thy affections,° which do hold a wing
Quite from the flight of all thy ancestors.
Thy place in council thou hast rudely lost,°
Which by thy younger brother is supplied,
And art almost an alien to the hearts
35 Of all the court and princes of my blood.
The hope and expectation of thy time
Is ruin'd, and the soul of every man
Prophetically doth forethink thy fall.
Had I so lavish of my presence been,
40 So common-hackney'd° in the eyes of men,
So stale and cheap to vulgar company,
Opinion,° that did help me to the crown,
Had still kept loyal to possession°
And left me in reputeless banishment,
45 A fellow of no mark nor likelihood.

By being seldom seen, I could not stir
But like a comet I was wonder'd at,
That men would tell their children "This is he."
Others would say "Where, which is Boling-
    broke?"
And then I stole all courtesy from heaven,   50
And dress'd myself in such humility
That I did pluck allegiance from men's hearts,
Loud shouts and salutations from their mouths,
Even in the presence of the crowned king.
Thus did I keep my person fresh and new,   55
My presence, like a robe pontifical,
Ne'er seen but wonder'd at. And so my state,
Seldom but sumptuous, showed like a feast
And won by rareness such solemnity.°
The skipping king, he ambled up and down   60
With shallow jesters and rash bavin wits,°
Soon kindled and soon burnt; carded° his state,
Mingled his royalty with capering fools,
Had his great name profaned with their scorns,
And gave his countenance, against his name,   65
To laugh at gibing boys and stand the push
Of every beardless vain comparative,°
Grew a companion to the common streets,
Enfeoff'd° himself to popularity—
That,° being daily swallow'd by men's eyes,   70
They surfeited with honey and began
To loathe the taste of sweetness, whereof a little
More than a little is by much too much.
So when he had occasion to be seen,
He was but as the cuckoo is in June,°   75
Heard, not regarded; seen, but with such eyes
As, sick and blunted with community,°
Afford no extraordinary gaze
Such as is bent on sunlike majesty
When it shines seldom in admiring eyes,   80
But rather drows'd and hung their eyelids down,
Slept in his face and render'd such aspect
As cloudy° men use to their adversaries,
Being with his presence glutted, gorg'd, and full.
And in that very line, Harry, standest thou,   85
For thou hast lost thy princely privilege
With vile participation. Not an eye
But is aweary of thy common sight,
Save mine, which hath desir'd to see thee more,

---

90 Which now doth that I would not have it do,
Make blind itself with foolish tenderness.°
PRINCE. I shall hereafter, my thrice gracious lord,
Be more myself.
KING.   For all the world
As thou art to this hour was Richard then
95 When I from France set foot at Ravenspurgh,
And even as I was then is Percy now.
Now, by my scepter and my soul to boot,
He hath more worthy interest to the state
Than thou, the shadow of succession;°
100 For of no right, nor color like to right,
He doth fill fields with harness° in the realm,
Turns head against the lion's armed jaws,
And, being no more in debt to years than thou,
Leads ancient lords and reverend bishops on
105 To bloody battles and to bruising arms.
What never-dying honor hath he got
Against renowned Douglas!—whose high deeds,
Whose hot incursions and great name in arms
Holds from all soldiers chief majority°
110 And military title capital°
Through all the kingdoms that acknowledge
Christ.
Thrice hath this Hotspur, Mars in swathling
clothes,°
This infant warrior, in his enterprises
Discomfited great Douglas, ta'en him once,
115 Enlarged° him and made a friend of him
To fill the mouth of deep defiance up°
And shake the peace and safety of our throne.
And what say you to this? Percy, Northumber-
land,
The Archbishop's grace of York, Douglas,
Mortimer
120 Capitulate against us and are up.°
But wherefore do I tell these news to thee?
Why, Harry, do I tell thee of my foes,
Which art my near'st and dearest enemy?
Thou that art like enough, through vassal fear,°
125 Base inclination, and the start of spleen,
To fight against me under Percy's pay,
To dog his heels and curtsy at his frowns
To show how much thou art degenerate.

PRINCE. Do not think so; you shall not find it so.
And God forgive them that so much have
sway'd   130
Your majesty's good thoughts away from me!
I will redeem all this on Percy's head,
And in the closing of some glorious day
Be bold to tell you that I am your son,
When I will wear a garment all of blood   135
And stain my favors° in a bloody mask,
Which, wash'd away, shall scour my shame with
it.
And that shall be the day, whene'er it lights,
That this same child of honor and renown,
This gallant Hotspur, this all-praised knight,   140
And your unthought-of Harry chance to meet.
For every honor sitting on his helm,
Would they were multitudes, and on my head
My shames redoubled! For the time will come
That I shall make this northern youth exchange 145
His glorious deeds for my indignities.
Percy is but my factor,° good my lord,
T' engross° up glorious deeds on my behalf,
And I will call him to so strict account
That he shall render every glory up,   150
Yea, even the slightest worship of his time,°
Or I will tear the reckoning from his heart.
This in the name of God I promise here,
The which if He be pleas'd I shall perform,
I do beseech your majesty may salve   155
The long-grown wounds of my intemperance.
If not, the end of life cancels all bands,°
And I will die a hundred thousand deaths
Ere break the smallest parcel of this vow.
KING. A hundred thousand rebels die in this.   160
Thou shalt have charge and sovereign trust
herein.
                    [Enter BLUNT.]
How now, good Blunt? Thy looks are full of
speed.
BLUNT. So hath the business that I come to speak of.
Lord Mortimer of Scotland hath sent word
That Douglas and the English rebels met   165
Th' eleventh of this month at Shrewsbury.
A mighty and a fearful head they are,
If promises be kept on every hand,
As ever offer'd foul play in a state.
KING. The Earl of Westmoreland set forth today, 170
With him my son, Lord John of Lancaster;
For this advertisement° is five days old.
On Wednesday next, Harry, you shall set for-
ward;

---

foolish tenderness i.e., tears
shadow of succession having shown no merit, Hal is the
    mere shadow of a rightful successor
harness armor
chief majority greatest acclaim   *capital* highest
Mars . . . clothes the god of war in swaddling clothes
Enlarged freed
To fill . . . up to round out the rebel forces
Capitulate . . . up ally themselves and are in revolt
vassal fear (only noblemen were thought capable of the
    noble virtue of courage; hence Henry charges Hal
    with the fear that would be natural to a slave)

favors features   *factor* agent   *engross* store, gather
worship . . . time honor of his lifetime   *bands* bonds
advertisement news

On Thursday we ourselves will march. Our
    meeting
175 Is Bridgenorth. And, Harry, you shall march
Through Gloucestershire, by which account
Our business valued,° some twelve days hence
Our general forces at Bridgenorth shall meet.
Our hands are full of business. Let's away;
180 Advantage feeds him fat while men delay.

                                          [Exeunt]

SCENE iii
Boar's-Head Tavern in Eastcheap.

[Enter FALSTAFF and BARDOLPH.]

FALSTAFF. Bardolph, am I not fallen away vilely
since this last action? Do I not bate? Do I not
dwindle? Why, my skin hangs about me like an
old lady's loose gown; I am withered like an old
5 applejohn. Well, I'll repent, and that suddenly,
while I am in some liking; I shall be out of heart
shortly, and then I shall have no strength to
repent. An I have not forgotten what the inside
of a church is made of, I am a peppercorn, a
10 brewer's horse.° The inside of a church! Company, villainous company, hath been the spoil of
me.

BARDOLPH. Sir John, you are so fretful, you cannot
live long.

FALSTAFF. Why, there is it. Come, sing me a bawdy
15 song; make me merry. I was as virtuously given
as a gentleman need to be, virtuous enough;
swore little, diced not above seven times a week,
went to a bawdy-house not above once in a
quarter—of an hour; paid money that I bor-
20 rowed—three or four times; lived well, and
in good compass. And now I live out of all
order, out of all compass.

BARDOLPH. Why, you are so fat, Sir John, that you
must needs be out of all compass, out of all
25 reasonable compass,° Sir John.

FALSTAFF. Do thou amend thy face, and I'll amend
my life. Thou art our admiral,° thou bearest
the lantern in the poop,° but 'tis in the nose of
thee. Thou art the Knight of the Burning Lamp.

30 BARDOLPH. Why, Sir John, my face does you no
harm.

FALSTAFF. No, I'll be sworn; I make as good use of
it as many a man doth of a death's-head or a
memento mori.° I never see thy face but I think
upon hellfire, and Dives that lived in purple;° 35
for there he is in his robes, burning, burning. If
thou wert any way given to virtue, I would
swear by thy face; my oath should be, "By this
fire, that's God's angel." But thou art altogether
given over, and wert indeed, but for the light in 40
thy face, the son of utter darkness. When thou
rannest up Gadshill in the night to catch my
horse, if I did not think thou hadst been an ignis
fatuus,° or a ball of wildfire, there's no purchase
in money. O, thou art a perpetual triumph, an 45
everlasting bonfire light! Thou hast saved me a
thousand marks in links° and torches, walking
with thee in the night betwixt tavern and
tavern, but the sack that thou hast drunk me
would have bought me lights as good cheap at 50
the dearest chandler's° in Europe. I have maintained that salamander° of yours with fire anytime this two and thirty years. God reward me
for it!

BARDOLPH. 'Sblood, I would my face were in your 55
belly!

FALSTAFF. God-a-mercy! So should I be sure to be
heartburned.

                        [Enter HOSTESS.]

How now, Dame Partlet° the hen! Have you
inquired yet who picked my pocket? 60

HOSTESS. Why, Sir John, what do you think, Sir
John? Do you think I keep thieves in my house?
I have searched, I have inquired, so has my husband, man by man, boy by boy, servant by
servant. The tithe° of a hair was never lost in my 65
house before.

FALSTAFF. Ye lie, hostess. Bardolph was shaved,
and lost many a hair; and I'll be sworn my
pocket was picked. Go to, you are a woman, go.

HOSTESS. Who, I? No; I defy thee. God's light, I was 70
never called so in mine own house before.

FALSTAFF. Go to, I know you well enough.

HOSTESS. No, Sir John; you do not know me, Sir
John. I know you, Sir John. You owe me money,
Sir John, and now you pick a quarrel to beguile 75
me of it. I bought you a dozen of shirts to your
back.

Our . . . valued estimating how much time our
    business will require
peppercorn . . . horse signifying what is shriveled, worn
    out
compass . . . compass order . . . circumference
admiral flagship   poop stern

memento mori reminder of death
Dives . . . purple the rich man in Luke 16:19–31
ignis fatuus will o' the wisp
links small torchlights
dearest chandler's most costly candlemaker's
salamander a lizard that supposedly lived in and ate fire
Dame Partlet hen in Reynard the Fox stories (see
    Chaucer's "Nun's Priest's Tale")
tithe tenth part

FALSTAFF. Dowlas,° filthy dowlas. I have given them away to bakers' wives, and they have made bolters° of them.

HOSTESS. Now, as I am a true woman, holland° of eight shillings an ell. You owe money here besides, Sir John, for your diet and by-drinkings, and money lent you, four and twenty pound.

FALSTAFF. He had his part of it; let him pay.

HOSTESS. He? Alas, he is poor; he hath nothing.

FALSTAFF. How! Poor? Look upon his face; what call you rich? Let them coin his nose, let them coin his cheeks. I'll not pay a denier.° What, will you make a younker° of me? Shall I not take mine ease in mine inn but I shall have my pocket picked? I have lost a seal-ring of my grandfather's worth forty mark.

HOSTESS. O Jesu, I have heard the prince tell him, I know not how oft, that that ring was copper!

FALSTAFF. How! The prince is a Jack,° a sneak-cup.° 'Sblood, an he were here, I would cudgel him like a dog, if he would say so.

[*Enter the* PRINCE *and* PETO, *marching, and* FALSTAFF *meets them playing on his truncheon like a fife.*]

How now, lad! Is the wind in that door,° i' faith? Must we all march?

BARDOLPH. Yea, two and two, Newgate fashion.°

HOSTESS. My lord, I pray you, hear me.

PRINCE. What sayest thou, Mistress Quickly? How doth thy husband? I love him well; he is an honest man.

HOSTESS. Good my lord, hear me.

FALSTAFF. Prithee, let her alone, and list to me.

PRINCE. What sayest thou, Jack?

FALSTAFF. The other night I fell asleep here behind the arras and had my pocket picked. This house is turned bawdy-house; they pick pockets.

PRINCE. What didst thou lose, Jack?

FALSTAFF. Wilt thou believe me, Hal? Three or four bonds of forty pound apiece, and a seal-ring of my grandfather's.

PRINCE. A trifle, some eight-penny matter.

HOSTESS. So I told him, my lord, and I said I heard your grace say so. And, my lord, he speaks most vilely of you, like a foul-mouthed man as he is, and said he would cudgel you.

PRINCE. What! He did not?

HOSTESS. There's neither faith, truth, nor womanhood in me else.

FALSTAFF. There's no more faith in thee than in a stewed prune, nor no more truth in thee than in a drawn fox, and for womanhood, Maid Marian may be the deputy's wife of the ward to thee.° Go, you thing, go.

HOSTESS. Say, what thing? What thing?

FALSTAFF. What thing! Why, a thing to thank God on.°

HOSTESS. I am no thing to thank God on, I would thou shouldst know it. I am an honest man's wife, and, setting thy knighthood aside, thou art a knave to call me so.

FALSTAFF. Setting thy womanhood aside, thou art a beast to say otherwise.

HOSTESS. Say, what beast, thou knave, thou?

FALSTAFF. What beast! Why, an otter.

PRINCE. An otter, Sir John! Why an otter?

FALSTAFF. Why, she's neither fish nor flesh; a man knows not where to have her.

HOSTESS. Thou art an unjust man in saying so. Thou or any man knows where to have me, thou knave, thou!

PRINCE. Thou sayest true, hostess, and he slanders thee most grossly.

HOSTESS. So he doth you, my lord, and said this other day you ought° him a thousand pound.

PRINCE. Sirrah, do I owe you a thousand pound?

FALSTAFF. A thousand pound, Hal! A million. Thy love is worth a million; thou owest me thy love.

HOSTESS. Nay, my lord, he called you Jack, and said he would cudgel you.

FALSTAFF. Did I, Bardolph?

BARDOLPH. Indeed, Sir John, you said so.

FALSTAFF. Yea, if he said my ring was copper.

PRINCE. I say 'tis copper. Darest thou be as good as thy word now?

FALSTAFF. Why, Hal, thou knowest, as thou art but man, I dare. But as thou art prince, I fear thee as I fear the roaring of the lion's whelp.

PRINCE. And why not as the lion?

FALSTAFF. The king himself is to be feared as the lion. Dost thou think I'll fear thee as I fear thy father? Nay, an I do, I pray God my girdle break.

PRINCE. O, if it should, how would thy guts fall about thy knees! But, sirrah, there's no room for faith, truth, nor honesty in this bosom of thine; it is all filled up with guts and midriff.

Dowlas coarse linen   *bolters* flour sifters
holland fine linen
denier French coin worth little
younker young greenhorn, "sucker"   *Jack* knave
sneak-cup (possibly "sneak-up") a cadger of drinks (?);
  in any event, a low type
Is . . . door "is that the way the wind blows?"
Newgate fashion like Newgate prisoners, chained together

Maid Marian . . . thee Maid Marian may be a pattern of propriety in comparison to you (Robin Hood's sweetheart was represented in May Day dances as a slattern)
on for   *ought* owed

Charge an honest woman with picking thy pocket! Why, thou whoreson, impudent, embossed° rascal, if there were anything in thy
175 pocket but tavern reckonings, memorandums of bawdy-houses, and one poor pennyworth of sugar-candy to make thee long winded, if thy pocket were enriched with any other injuries° but these, I am a villain. And yet you will
180 stand to it, you will not pocket up wrong. Art thou not ashamed?

FALSTAFF. Dost thou hear, Hal? Thou knowest in the state of innocency Adam fell, and what should poor Jack Falstaff do in the days of
185 villainy? Thou seest I have more flesh than another man, and therefore more frailty.° You confess then, you picked my pocket?

PRINCE. It appears so by the story.

FALSTAFF. Hostess, I forgive thee. Go, make ready
190 breakfast. Love thy husband, look to thy servants, cherish thy guests. Thou shalt find me tractable to any honest reason; thou seest I am pacified still.° Nay, prithee, be gone. [Exit HOSTESS] Now, Hal, to the news at court. For
195 the robbery, lad, how is that answered?

PRINCE. O, my sweet beef, I must still be good angel to thee. The money is paid back again.

FALSTAFF. O, I do not like that paying back; 'tis a double labor.

---

embossed swollen
pocket . . . injuries to "pocket up injuries" is to endure affronts; but Hal also plays on the literal application, the contents of Falstaff's pocket
flesh . . . frailty another of Falstaff's perversions of gospel (see Matthew 26:41)
pacified still always allow myself to be pacified

PRINCE. I am good friends with my father, and may 200 do anything.

FALSTAFF. Rob me the exchequer the first thing thou dost, and do it with unwashed hands° too.

BARDOLPH. Do, my lord.

PRINCE. I have procured thee, Jack, a charge of 205 foot.

FALSTAFF. I would it had been of horse. Where shall I find one that can steal well? O for a fine thief, of the age of two and twenty or thereabouts! I am heinously unprovided. Well, 210 God be thanked for these rebels, they offend none but the virtuous. I laud them, I praise them.

PRINCE. Bardolph!

BARDOLPH. My lord? 215

PRINCE. Go bear this letter to Lord John of Lancaster, to my brother John; this to my Lord of Westmoreland. [Exit BARDOLPH] Go, Peto, to horse, to horse, for thou and I have thirty miles to ride yet ere dinner time. [Exit PETO] Jack, 220 meet me tomorrow in the Temple hall at two o'clock in the afternoon.
There shalt thou know thy charge, and there receive
Money and order for their furniture.° 225
The land is burning. Percy stands on high,
And either we or they must lower lie.   [Exit]

FALSTAFF. Rare words! Brave world! Hostess, my breakfast, come! O, I could wish this tavern were my drum!   [Exit] 230

---

do . . . hands do it at once
furniture equipment

A C T   I V

SCENE i
The rebel camp near Shrewsbury.

[*Enter* HOTSPUR, WORCESTER, *and* DOUGLAS.]

HOTSPUR. Well said, my noble Scot. If speaking truth
In this fine age were not thought flattery,
Such attribution° should the Douglas have
As not a soldier of this season's stamp°

Should go so general current° through the world. 5
By God, I cannot flatter, I do defy°
The tongues of soothers.° But a braver° place
In my heart's love hath no man than yourself.
Nay, task° me to my word; approve° me, lord.

DOUGLAS. Thou art the king of honor. 10
No man so potent breathes upon the ground
But I will beard° him.

---

attribution tribute
of . . . stamp like a coin minted in this year

general current i.e., legal tender everywhere
defy detest   *soothers* flatterers   *braver* finer
task challenge   *approve* test   *beard* take him on

HOTSPUR.   Do so, and 'tis well.
          [*Enter a* MESSENGER *with letters.*]
    What letters hast thou there?—I can but thank
        you.
MESSENGER. These letters come from your father.
HOTSPUR. Letters from him! Why comes he not
15   himself?
MESSENGER. He cannot come, my lord; he is
    grievous sick.
HOTSPUR. 'Zounds! How has he the leisure to be
        sick
    In such a justling time? Who leads his power?
    Under whose government come they along?
MESSENGER. His letters bears his mind, not I, my
20   lord.
WORCESTER. I prithee tell me, doth he keep his
        bed?
MESSENGER. He did, my lord, four days ere I set
        forth,
    And at the time of my departure thence
    He was much fear'd by his physicians.
WORCESTER. I would the state of time had first
25   been whole
    Ere he by sickness had been visited.
    His health was never better worth than now.
HOTSPUR. Sick now! Droop now! This sickness
        doth infect
    The very lifeblood of our enterprise;
30 'Tis catching hither, even to our camp.
    He writes me here that inward sickness—
    And that his friends by deputation could not
    So soon be drawn,° nor did he think it meet
    To lay so dangerous and dear° a trust
35 On any soul remov'd but on his own.
    Yet doth he give us bold advertisement°
    That with our small conjunction° we should on
    To see how fortune is dispos'd to us;
    For, as he writes, there is no quailing now,
40 Because the king is certainly possess'd
    Of all our purposes. What say you to it?
WORCESTER. Your father's sickness is a maim to us.
HOTSPUR. A perilous gash, a very limb lopp'd off.
    And yet, in faith, it is not; his present want
45 Seems more than we shall find it. Were it good
    To set the exact wealth of all our states
    All at one cast?° To set so rich a main
    On the nice° hazard of one doubtful hour?
    It were not good, for therein should we read
50 The very bottom and the soul of hope,

The very list, the very utmost bound°
    Of all our fortunes.
DOUGLAS.   Faith, and so we should,
    Where now remains a sweet reversion.°
    We may boldly spend upon the hope of what
    Is to come in.   55
    A comfort of retirement lives in this.
HOTSPUR. A rendezvous, a home to fly unto,
    If that the devil and mischance look big
    Upon the maidenhead of our affairs.°
WORCESTER. But yet I would your father had been
        here.   60
    The quality and hair° of our attempt
    Brooks no division. It will be thought
    By some, that know not why he is away,
    That wisdom, loyalty, and mere dislike
    Of our proceedings kept the earl from hence.   65
    And think how such an apprehension
    May turn the tide of fearful faction
    And breed a kind of question in our cause;
    For well you know we of the off'ring° side
    Must keep aloof from strict arbitrement   70
    And stop all sight-holes, every loop from whence
    The eye of reason may pry in upon us.
    This absence of your father's draws a curtain
    That shows the ignorant a kind of fear
    Before not dreamt of.
HOTSPUR.   You strain too far.   75
    I rather of his absence make this use:
    It lends a luster and more great opinion,
    A larger dare to our great enterprise
    Than if the earl were here. For men must think,
    If we without his help can make a head   80
    To push against a kingdom, with his help
    We shall o'erturn it topsy-turvy down.
    Yet all goes well, yet all our joints are whole.
DOUGLAS. As heart can think. There is not such a
        word
    Spoke of in Scotland as this term of fear.   85
          [*Enter* SIR RICHARD VERNON.]
HOTSPUR. My cousin Vernon! Welcome, by my
    soul.
VERNON. Pray God my news be worth a welcome,
        lord.
    The Earl of Westmoreland, seven thousand
        strong,
    Is marching hitherwards; with him Prince John.
HOTSPUR. No harm. What more?

by . . . drawn could not be assembled by others serving
    as his deputies
dear important   *advertisement* advice
conjunction united forces
To . . . cast to risk all our fortunes on one throw
nice delicate

list . . . bound edge . . . limit
reversion future expectation
If . . . affairs if evil misfortune threatens our first
    venture
quality . . . hair nature . . . nature (synonyms, a frequent
    Shakespearean mannerism)
off'ring challenging

90 VERNON.   And further, I have learn'd
The king himself in person is set forth,
Or hitherwards intended speedily,
With strong and mighty preparation.
HOTSPUR. He shall be welcome too. Where is his
    son,
95 The nimble-footed madcap Prince of Wales,
And his comrades, that daff'd° the world aside
And bid it pass?
VERNON.   All furnish'd, all in arms,
All plum'd like estridges° that with the wind
Bated° like eagles having lately bath'd,
100 Glitt'ring in golden coats like images,
As full of spirit as the month of May,
And gorgeous as the sun at midsummer,
Wanton as youthful goats, wild as young bulls.
I saw young Harry with his beaver on,
105 His cuisses° on his thighs, gallantly arm'd,
Rise from the ground like feather'd Mercury
And vaulted with such ease into his seat
As if an angel dropp'd down from the clouds
To turn and wind a fiery Pegasus°
110 And witch° the world with noble horsemanship.
HOTSPUR. No more, no more. Worse than the sun
    in March,
This praise doth nourish agues. Let them come;
They come like sacrifices in their trim,°
And to the fire-ey'd maid° of smoky war
115 All hot and bleeding will we offer them.
The mailed Mars° shall on his altar sit
Up to the ears in blood. I am on fire
To hear this rich reprisal° is so nigh
And yet not ours. Come, let me taste my horse,
120 Who is to bear me like a thunderbolt
Against the bosom of the Prince of Wales.
Harry to Harry shall, hot horse to horse,
Meet and ne'er part till one drop down a corse.
O that Glendower were come!
VERNON.   There is more news.
125 I learn'd in Worcester, as I rode along,
He cannot draw his power this fourteen days.
DOUGLAS. That's the worst tidings that I hear of
    yet.
WORCESTER. Aye, by my faith, that bears a frosty
    sound.
HOTSPUR. What may the king's whole battle°
    reach unto?
VERNON. To thirty thousand.

HOTSPUR.   Forty let it be!   130
My father and Glendower being both away,
The powers of us may serve so great a day.
Come, let us take a muster speedily.
Doomsday is near; die all, die merrily.
DOUGLAS. Talk not of dying. I am out of fear   135
Of death or death's hand for this one half year.
                    [Exeunt]

SCENE ii
A public road near Coventry.

[Enter FALSTAFF and BARDOLPH.]

FALSTAFF. Bardolph, get thee before to Coventry;
    fill me a bottle of sack. Our soldiers shall march
    through; we'll to Sutton Co'fil'° tonight.
BARDOLPH. Will you give me money, captain?
FALSTAFF. Lay out, lay out.   5
BARDOLPH. This bottle makes an angel.°
FALSTAFF. An if it do, take it for thy labor, and if it
    make twenty, take them all;° I'll answer° the
    coinage. Bid my lieutenant Peto meet me at
    town's end.   10
BARDOLPH. I will, captain. Farewell.   [Exit]
FALSTAFF. If I be not ashamed of my soldiers, I am
    a soused gurnet.° I have misused the king's
    press° damnably. I have got, in exchange of a
    hundred and fifty soldiers, three hundred and   15
    odd pounds. I press me none but good house-
    holders, yeomen's sons; inquire me out con-
    tracted bachelors, such as had been asked twice
    on the banns;° such a commodity of warm
    slaves as had as lieve hear the devil as a drum;   20
    such as fear the report of a caliver° worse than a
    struck fowl or a hurt wild duck. I pressed me
    none but such toasts-and-butter, with hearts in
    their bellies no bigger than pins' heads, and they
    have bought out their services; and now my   25
    whole charge consists of ancients,° corporals,
    lieutenants, gentlemen of companies,° slaves as
    ragged as Lazarus in the painted cloth,° where
    the glutton's dogs licked his sores, and such as
    indeed were never soldiers, but discarded   30

---

daff'd brushed (doffed)   estridges ostriches
Bated fluttered, beat   cuisses protective plates
turn . . . Pegasus manage the winged horse of mythology
witch bewitch   trim finery
fire-ey'd maid Bellona, goddess of war
mailed Mars armored god of war   reprisal prize
battle force

Co'fil' Coldfield, in Warwickshire
makes an angel makes ten shillings that you owe me
An if . . . all Falstaff pretends to think that Bardolph
    means that the bottle will be minted into shillings
answer pay for   soused gurnet small pickled fish
king's press royal order for drafting troops
banns public announcement of intentions to wed
caliver musket   ancients standard bearers
gentlemen of companies gentlemen volunteers
Lazarus . . . cloth Lazarus (Luke 16) as he is depicted in
    cheap tapestries

unjust° servingmen, younger sons to younger brothers,° revolted tapsters, and ostlers trade-fallen—the cankers° of a calm world and a long peace, ten times more dishonorable ragged
35 than an old-faced ancient.° And such have I, to fill up the rooms of them that have bought out their services, that you would think that I had a hundred and fifty tattered prodigals lately come from swinekeeping, from eating draff° and
40 husks. A mad fellow met me on the way and told me I had unloaded all the gibbets and pressed the dead bodies. No eye hath seen such scarecrows. I'll not march through Coventry with them, that's flat. Nay, and the villains
45 march wide betwixt the legs, as if they had gyves° on, for indeed I had the most of them out of prison. There's but a shirt and a half in all my company, and the half shirt is two napkins tacked together and thrown over the shoulders
50 like a herald's coat without sleeves; and the shirt, to say the truth, stolen from my host at Saint Alban's, or the red-nose innkeeper of Daventry. But that's all one; they'll find linen enough on every hedge.°

[Enter the PRINCE and WESTMORELAND.]

55 PRINCE. How now, blown° Jack! How now, quilt!°

FALSTAFF. What, Hal! How now, mad wag! What a devil dost thou in Warwickshire? My good Lord of Westmoreland, I cry you mercy;° I
60 thought your honor had already been at Shrewsbury.

WESTMORELAND. Faith, Sir John, 'tis more than time that I were there, and you too; but my powers are there already. The king, I can tell
65 you, looks for us all. We must away all night.

FALSTAFF. Tut, never fear me. I am as vigilant as a cat to steal cream.

PRINCE. I think, to steal cream indeed, for thy theft hath already made thee butter. But tell me,
70 Jack, whose fellows are these that come after?

FALSTAFF. Mine, Hal, mine.

PRINCE. I did never see such pitiful rascals.

FALSTAFF. Tut, tut, good enough to toss; food for powder, food for powder! They'll fill a pit as

well as better. Tush, man, mortal men, mortal 75 men.

WESTMORELAND. Aye, but, Sir John, methinks they are exceeding poor and bare, too beggarly.

FALSTAFF. Faith, for their poverty, I know not where they had that; and for their bareness, I 80 am sure they never learned that of me.

PRINCE. No, I'll be sworn, unless you call three fingers on the ribs bare. But, sirrah, make haste. Percy is already in the field.

FALSTAFF. What, is the king encamped? 85

WESTMORELAND. He is, Sir John. I fear we shall stay too long.

FALSTAFF. Well,
To the latter end of a fray and the beginning of a feast
Fits a dull fighter and a keen guest.

[Exeunt]

SCENE iii
The rebel camp near Shrewsbury.

[Enter HOTSPUR, WORCESTER, DOUGLAS, and VERNON.]

HOTSPUR. We'll fight with him tonight.

WORCESTER. It may not be.

DOUGLAS. You give him then advantage.

VERNON. Not a whit.

HOTSPUR. Why say you so? Looks he not for supply?

VERNON. So do we.

HOTSPUR. His is certain, ours is doubtful.

WORCESTER. Good cousin, be advis'd; stir not tonight. 5

VERNON. Do not, my lord.

DOUGLAS. You do not counsel well.
You speak it out of fear and cold heart.

VERNON. Do me no slander, Douglas. By my life,
And I dare well maintain it with my life,
If well-respected honor bid me on,
I hold as little counsel with weak fear 10
As you, my lord, or any Scot that this day lives.
Let it be seen tomorrow in the battle
Which of us fears.

DOUGLAS. Yea, or tonight.

VERNON. Content.

HOTSPUR. Tonight, say I. 15

VERNON. Come, come, it may not be. I wonder much,
Being men of such great leading as you are,
That you foresee not what impediments
Drag back our expedition. Certain horse
Of my cousin Vernon's are not yet come up. 20

---

unjust dishonest
younger . . . brothers i.e., those doubly hopeless of inheritance
cankers cankerworms, social parasites
old-faced ancient patched flag *draff* slop
gyves fetters
on . . . hedge i.e., where it was spread to dry
blown swollen
Jack . . . quilt a jack is a soldier's padded, quilted jacket
I . . . mercy i.e., for having failed to see him

Your uncle Worcester's horse came but today,
And now their pride and mettle is asleep,
Their courage with hard labor tame and dull,
That not a horse is half the half of himself.
25 HOTSPUR. So are the horses of the enemy
In general journey-bated° and brought low.
The better part of ours are full of rest.
WORCESTER. The number of the king exceedeth
ours.
For God's sake, cousin, stay till all come in.
The trumpet sounds a parley.]
[*Enter* SIR WALTER BLUNT.]
30 BLUNT. I come with gracious offers from the king
If you vouchsafe° me hearing and respect.
HOTSPUR. Welcome, Sir Walter Blunt, and would
to God
You were of our determination!
Some of us love you well, and even those some
35 Envy your great deservings and good name
Because you are not of our quality,°
But stand against us like an enemy.
BLUNT. And God defend but still I should stand so,
So long as out of limit and true rule
40 You stand against anointed majesty.
But to my charge. The king hath sent to know
The nature of your griefs, and whereupon
You conjure from the breast of civil peace
Such bold hostility, teaching his duteous land
45 Audacious cruelty. If that the king
Have any way your good deserts forgot,
Which he confesseth to be manifold,
He bids you name your griefs, and with all
speed
You shall have your desires with interest
50 And pardon absolute for yourself and these
Herein misled by your suggestion.
HOTSPUR. The king is kind—and well we know the
king
Knows at what time to promise, when to pay.
My father and my uncle and myself
55 Did give him that same royalty he wears,
And when he was not six and twenty strong,
Sick in the world's regard, wretched and low,
A poor unminded outlaw sneaking home,
My father gave him welcome to the shore.
60 And when he heard him swear and vow to God
He came but to be Duke of Lancaster,
To sue his livery° and beg his peace
With tears of innocency and terms of zeal,
My father, in kind heart and pity mov'd,
65 Swore him assistance and perform'd it too.

Now when the lords and barons of the realm
Perceiv'd Northumberland did lean to him,
The more and less came in with cap and knee,°
Met him in boroughs, cities, villages,
Attended him on bridges, stood in lanes,   70
Laid gifts before him, proffer'd him their oaths,
Gave him their heirs, as pages follow'd him
Even at the heels in golden multitudes.
He presently, as greatness° knows itself,
Steps me° a little higher than his vow   75
Made to my father, while his blood was poor,
Upon the naked shore at Ravenspurgh;
And now, forsooth, takes on him to reform
Some certain edicts and some strait decrees
That lie too heavy on the commonwealth,   80
Cries out upon abuses, seems to weep
Over his country's wrongs. And by this face,
This seeming brow of justice, did he win
The hearts of all that he did angle for;
Proceeded further—cut me off the heads   85
Of all the favorites that the absent king
In deputation left behind him here
When he was personal° in the Irish war.
BLUNT. Tut, I came not to hear this.
HOTSPUR.   Then to the point.
In short time after, he depos'd the king;   90
Soon after that, depriv'd him of his life,
And in the neck of that, task'd° the whole state;
To make that worse, suffer'd his kinsman
March,°
Who is, if every owner were well plac'd,
Indeed his king, to be engag'd in Wales,   95
There without ransom to lie forfeited;
Disgrac'd me in my happy victories,
Sought to entrap me by intelligence,°
Rated mine uncle from the council board,
In rage dismiss'd my father from the court,   100
Broke oath on oath, committed wrong on
wrong,
And in conclusion drove us to seek out
This head of safety and withal to pry
Into his title, the which we find
Too indirect° for long continuance.   105
BLUNT. Shall I return this answer to the king?
HOTSPUR. Not so, Sir Walter. We'll withdraw
awhile.
Go to the king, and let there be impawn'd
Some surety for a safe return again,

The more . . . knee the greater and lesser nobility came
  with caps off and knees bent
greatness power *Steps me* steps (the dative *me*, which
  occurs often in Shakespeare, has no value)
personal in person *task'd* taxed
March Mortimer *intelligence* spies
indirect not in the direct line of succession

journey-bated travel-worn   *vouchsafe* grant
quality persuasion
sue his livery regain his inheritance

110 And in the morning early shall mine uncle
Bring him our purposes. And so farewell.
BLUNT. I would you would accept of grace and
love.
HOTSPUR. And may be so we shall.
BLUNT.   Pray God you do.
                          [*Exeunt*]

SCENE iv
York. The ARCHBISHOP'S *Palace.*

[*Enter the* ARCHBISHOP OF YORK *and* SIR
MICHAEL.]
ARCHBISHOP. Hie,° good Sir Michael; bear this
sealed brief°
With winged haste to the lord marshal,
This to my cousin Scroop, and all the rest
To whom they are directed. If you knew
How much they do import, you would make
5   haste.
SIR MICHAEL. My good lord,
I guess their tenor.
ARCHBISHOP.   Like enough you do.
Tomorrow, good Sir Michael, is a day
Wherein the fortune of ten thousand men
10   Must bide the touch;° for, sir, at Shrewsbury,
As I am truly given to understand,
The king with mighty and quick-raised power
Meets with Lord Harry. And I fear, Sir Michael,
What with the sickness of Northumberland,
15   Whose power was in the first proportion,

Hie hasten   *brief* letter
bide . . . touch stand . . . test

And what with Owen Glendower's absence
    thence,
Who with them was a rated sinew too
And comes not in, o'er-rul'd by prophecies,
I fear the power of Percy is too weak
To wage an instant trial with the king.   20
SIR MICHAEL. Why, my good lord, you need not
    fear;
There is Douglas and Lord Mortimer.
ARCHBISHOP. No, Mortimer is not there.
SIR MICHAEL. But there is Mordake, Vernon, Lord
    Harry Percy,
And there is my Lord of Worcester, and a head 25
Of gallant warriors, noble gentlemen.
ARCHBISHOP. And so there is. But yet the king
    hath drawn
The special head of all the land together:
The Prince of Wales, Lord John of Lancaster,
The noble Westmoreland and warlike Blunt,   30
And many moe corrivals° and dear men
Of estimation and command in arms.
SIR MICHAEL. Doubt not, my lord, they shall be
    well oppos'd.
ARCHBISHOP. I hope no less, yet needful 'tis to fear;
And, to prevent the worst, Sir Michael, speed.   35
For if Lord Percy thrive not, ere the king
Dismiss his power he means to visit us,
For he hath heard of our confederacy,
And 'tis but wisdom to make strong against
    him.
Therefore make haste. I must go write again   40
To other friends; and so farewell, Sir Michael.
                              [*Exeunt*]

moe corrivals more associates

A C T   V

SCENE i
The KING'S *camp near Shrewsbury.*

[*Enter the* KING, PRINCE OF WALES, LORD JOHN
OF LANCASTER, SIR WALTER BLUNT, *and*
FALSTAFF.]
KING. How bloodily the sun begins to peer
Above yon busky° hill! The day looks pale
At his distemperature.°
PRINCE.   The southern wind
Doth play the trumpet to his purposes

busky bushy   *distemperature* unhealthy look

And by his hollow whistling in the leaves   5
Foretells a tempest and a blust'ring day.
KING. Then with the losers let it sympathize,
For nothing can seem foul to those that win.
                          [*The trumpet sounds.*]
              [*Enter* WORCESTER *and* VERNON.]
How now, my Lord of Worcester! 'Tis not well
That you and I should meet upon such terms   10
As now we meet. You have deceiv'd our trust
And made us doff our easy robes of peace
To crush our old limbs in ungentle steel.
This is not well, my lord, this is not well.
What say you to it? Will you again unknit   15

185

This churlish knot of all-abhorred war
And move in that obedient orb again
Where you did give a fair and natural light,
And be no more an exhal'd meteor,
20 A prodigy of fear, and a portent
Of broached° mischief to the unborn times?
WORCESTER. Hear me, my liege:
For mine own part, I could be well content
To entertain the lag-end of my life
25 With quiet hours, for I do protest
I have not sought the day of this dislike.
KING. You have not sought it! How comes it, then?
FALSTAFF. Rebellion lay in his way, and he found it.
PRINCE. Peace, chewet,° peace!
WORCESTER. It pleas'd your majesty to turn your
30   looks
Of favor from myself and all our house;
And yet I must remember° you, my lord,
We were the first and dearest of your friends.
For you my staff of office did I break
35 In Richard's time, and posted day and night
To meet you on the way and kiss your hand
When yet you were in place and in account
Nothing so strong and fortunate as I.
It was myself, my brother, and his son
40 That brought you home and boldly did outdare
The dangers of the time. You swore to us,
And you did swear that oath at Doncaster,
That you did nothing purpose 'gainst the state
Nor claim no further than your new-fall'n right,
45 The seat of Gaunt, dukedom of Lancaster.
To this we swore our aid. But in short space
It rain'd down fortune show'ring on your head,
And such a flood of greatness fell on you—
What with our help, what with the absent king,
50 What with the injuries of a wanton° time,
The seeming sufferances° that you had borne,
And the contrarious winds that held the king
So long in his unlucky Irish wars
That all in England did repute him dead—
55 And from this swarm of fair advantages
You took occasion to be quickly woo'd
To gripe° the general sway° into your hand,
Forgot your oath to us at Doncaster,
And being fed by us, you us'd us so
60 As that ungentle gull, the cuckoo's bird,°
Useth the sparrow—did oppress our nest,
Grew by our feeding to so great a bulk

That even our love durst not come near your
    sight
For fear of swallowing, but with nimble wing
We were enforc'd for safety sake to fly   65
Out of your sight and raise this present head.
Whereby we stand opposed by such means
As you yourself have forg'd against yourself
By unkind usage, dangerous countenance,°
And violation of all faith and troth   70
Sworn to us in your younger enterprise.
KING. These things indeed you have articulate,°
Proclaim'd at market-crosses, read in churches
To face° the garment of rebellion
With some fine color that may please the eye   75
Of fickle changelings and poor discontents
Which gape and rub the elbow at the news
Of hurlyburly innovation—
And never yet did insurrection want
Such water-colors to impaint his cause   80
Nor moody beggars starving for a time
Of pellmell havoc and confusion.
PRINCE. In both your armies there is many a soul
Shall pay full dearly for this encounter
If once they join in trial. Tell your nephew   85
The Prince of Wales doth join with all the world
In praise of Henry Percy. By my hopes,
This present enterprise set off his head,°
I do not think a braver gentleman,
More active-valiant or more valiant-young,   90
More daring or more bold, is now alive
To grace this latter age with noble deeds.
For my part, I may speak it to my shame,
I have a truant been to chivalry,
And so I hear he doth account me too.   95
Yet this before my father's majesty:
I am content that he shall take the odds
Of his great name and estimation,
And will, to save the blood on either side,
Try fortune with him in a single fight.   100
KING. And, Prince of Wales, so dare we venture
    thee,
Albeit° considerations infinite
Do make against it. No, good Worcester, no,
We love our people well; even those we love
That are misled upon your cousin's° part,   105
And, will they take the offer of our grace,
Both he and they and you, yea, every man
Shall be my friend again and I'll be his.
So tell your cousin, and bring me word
What he will do. But if he will not yield,   110

---

broached let loose
chewet chough, or jackdaw, hence chatterer; but also a
    mince pie
remember remind   *wanton* unruly, wild
sufferances sufferings   *gripe* seize   *sway* rule
that ungentle . . . bird that rude offspring of the cuckoo,
    hatched in nests built by other birds and fed by them

dangerous countenance threatening mien
articulate explained in detail   *face* decorate
This . . . head being excused from blame for the present
    rebellion
Albeit but that   *cousin's* i.e., nephew's

Rebuke and dread correction wait on us,°
And they shall do their office. So, be gone.
We will not now be troubled with reply.
We offer fair; take it advisedly.
                    [*Exeunt* WORCESTER *and* VERNON.]
115 PRINCE. It will not be accepted, on my life.
The Douglas and the Hotspur both together
Are confident against the world in arms.
KING. Hence, therefore, every leader to his charge;
For on their answer will we set on them.
120 And God befriend us as our cause is just!
                    [*Exeunt all but the* PRINCE OF WALES *and*
                                        FALSTAFF.]
FALSTAFF. Hal, if thou see me down in the battle,
and bestride me, so; 'tis a point of friendship.
PRINCE. Nothing but a colossus can do thee that
friendship.
Say thy prayers, and farewell.
FALSTAFF. I would 'twere bedtime, Hal, and all
125 well.
PRINCE. Why, thou owest God a death.   [*Exit*]
FALSTAFF. 'Tis not due yet; I would be loath to
pay him before his day. What need I be so forward with him that calls not on me? Well, 'tis
130 no matter; honor pricks me on. Yea, but how if
honor prick me off when I come on? How then?
Can honor set to a leg? No. Or an arm? No. Or
take away the grief of a wound? No. Honor hath
no skill in surgery, then? No. What is honor? A
135 word. What is in that word honor? What is that
honor? Air. A trim reckoning!° Who hath it?
He that died o' Wednesday. Doth he feel it?
No. Doth he hear it? No. 'Tis insensible, then?
Yea, to the dead. But will it not live with the
140 living? No. Why? Detraction° will not suffer it.
Therefore I'll none of it. Honor is a mere
scutcheon;° and so ends my catechism.
                                        [*Exit*]

SCENE ii
The rebel camp.

[*Enter* WORCESTER *and* VERNON.]
WORCESTER. O, no, my nephew must not know,
Sir Richard,
The liberal and kind offer of the king.
VERNON. 'Twere best he did.
WORCESTER.   Then are we all undone.
It is not possible, it cannot be
5 The king should keep his word in loving us.

He will suspect us still and find a time
To punish this offense in other faults.
Suspicion all our lives shall be stuck full of eyes,
For treason is but trusted like the fox,
Who, ne'er so tame, so cherish'd and lock'd up,   10
Will have a wild trick of his ancestors.
Look how we can, or sad or° merrily,
Interpretation will misquote our looks,
And we shall feed like oxen at a stall,
The better cherish'd, still the nearer death.   15
My nephew's trespass may be well forgot;
It hath th' excuse of youth and heat of blood
And an adopted name of privilege,°
A hare-brain'd Hotspur, govern'd by a spleen.°
All his offenses live upon my head   20
And on his father's; we did train him on,°
And, his corruption being ta'en from us,
We, as the spring of all, shall pay for all.
Therefore, good cousin, let not Harry know,
In any case, the offer of the king.   25
VERNON. Deliver what you will; I'll say 'tis so.
Here comes your cousin.
                    [*Enter* HOTSPUR *and* DOUGLAS.]
HOTSPUR.   My uncle is return'd;
Deliver up my Lord of Westmoreland.
Uncle, what news?
WORCESTER. The king will bid you battle pres-
ently.°   30
DOUGLAS. Defy him by the Lord of Westmoreland.
HOTSPUR. Lord Douglas, go you and tell him so.
DOUGLAS. Marry, and shall, and very willingly.
                                        [*Exit*]
WORCESTER. There is no seeming mercy in the
king.
HOTSPUR. Did you beg any? God forbid!   35
WORCESTER. I told him gently of our grievances,
Of his oath-breaking, which he mended° thus,
By now forswearing that he is forsworn.°
He calls us rebels, traitors, and will scourge
With haughty arms this hateful name in us.   40
                    [*Re-enter* DOUGLAS.]
DOUGLAS. Arm, gentlemen; to arms! For I have
thrown
A brave defiance in King Henry's teeth,
And Westmoreland, that was engag'd,° did bear
it,
Which cannot choose but bring him quickly on.

---

wait on us   are at our command
A trim reckoning   "a fine thing!"
Detraction   slander   *scutcheon*   shield borne at a funeral

or . . . or   whether . . . or
adopted . . . privilege   nickname that excuses his conduct
govern'd . . . spleen   ruled by impulse, whim
train . . . on   mislead him
presently   immediately   *mended*   patched over
forswearing . . . forsworn   falsely swearing that he broke a
   former vow
engag'd   held hostage (for Worcester's safe return)

WORCESTER. The Prince of Wales stepp'd forth
45   before the king,
      And, nephew, challenged you to single fight.
HOTSPUR. O would the quarrel lay upon our heads,
      And that no man might draw short breath
          today
      But I and Harry Monmouth! Tell me, tell me,
      How show'd his tasking?° Seem'd it in con-
50   tempt?
      VERNON. No, by my soul. I never in my life
      Did hear a challenge urg'd more modestly,
      Unless a brother should a brother dare
      To gentle exercise and proof of arms.
55   He gave you all the duties of a man,
      Trimm'd up your praises with a princely
          tongue,
      Spoke your deservings like a chronicle,
      Making you ever better than his praise
      By still dispraising praise valu'd° with you;
60   And, which became him like a prince indeed,
      He made a blushing cital° of himself
      And chid his truant youth with such a grace
      As if he master'd there a double spirit
      Of teaching and of learning instantly.°
65   There did he pause. But let me tell the world,
      If he outlive the envy of this day,
      England did never owe° so sweet a hope,
      So much misconstru'd in his wantonness.°
HOTSPUR. Cousin, I think thou art enamored
70   On his follies. Never did I hear
      Of any prince so wild a libertine.
      But be he as he will, yet once ere night
      I will embrace him with a soldier's arm
      That° he shall shrink under my courtesy.
      Arm, arm with speed, and, fellows, soldiers,
75   friends,
      Better consider what you have to do
      Than I, that have not well the gift of tongue,
      Can lift your blood up with persuasion.
              [Enter a MESSENGER.]
MESSENGER. My lord, here are letters for you.
80 HOTSPUR. I cannot read them now.
      O gentlemen, the time of life is short!
      To spend that shortness basely were too long
      If life did ride upon a dial's point
      Still ending at the arrival of an hour.°

      An if we live, we live to tread on kings;   85
      If die, brave death, when princes die with us!
      Now, for our consciences, the arms are fair°
      When the intent of bearing them is just.
              [Enter another MESSENGER.]
MESSENGER. My lord, prepare; the king comes on
      apace.
HOTSPUR. I thank him that he cuts me from my
      tale,   90
      For I profess not talking. Only this—
      Let each man do his best. And here draw I
      A sword whose temper I intend to stain
      With the best blood that I can meet withal
      In the adventure of this perilous day.   95
      Now, Esperance! Percy! And set on.
      Sound all the lofty instruments of war,
      And by that music let us all embrace;
      For, heaven to earth, some of us never shall
      A second time do such a courtesy.   100
              [The trumpets sound. They embrace, and exeunt.]

                        SCENE iii
                  Plain between the camps.

      [The KING enters with his power. Alarum to the
                        battle.
      Then enter DOUGLAS and SIR WALTER BLUNT.]
BLUNT. What is thy name, that in the battle thus
      Thou crossest me? What honor dost thou seek
      Upon my head?
DOUGLAS.   Know then, my name is Douglas,
      And I do haunt thee in the battle thus   5
      Because some tell me that thou art a king.
BLUNT. They tell thee true.
DOUGLAS. The Lord of Stafford dear today hath
      bought
      Thy likeness,° for instead of thee, King Harry,
      This sword hath ended him. So shall it thee,
      Unless thou yield thee as my prisoner.   10
BLUNT. I was not born a yielder, thou proud Scot,
      And thou shalt find a king that will revenge
      Lord Stafford's death.
              [They fight. DOUGLAS kills BLUNT.]
              [Enter HOTSPUR.]
HOTSPUR. O Douglas, hadst thou fought at Holme-
      don thus,
      I never had triumph'd upon a Scot.   15
DOUGLAS. All's done, all's won; here breathless lies
      the king.
HOTSPUR. Where?

---

tasking challenge   valu'd compared   cital recital
master'd . . . instantly could, at the moment,
    simultaneously teach and learn
owe possess
misconstru'd . . . wantonness misinterpreted in his wild
    youth
That so that
If . . . hour though life rode a clock's hand and ended
    with the hour

fair righteous
dear . . . likeness has paid dearly for appearing in your
    likeness

DOUGLAS. Here.

HOTSPUR. This, Douglas? No. I know this face full
well.

20   A gallant knight he was; his name was Blunt,
Semblably furnish'd° like the king himself.

DOUGLAS. A fool go with thy soul, whither it goes!
A borrow'd title hast thou bought too dear.
Why didst thou tell me that thou wert a king?

HOTSPUR. The king hath many marching in his
25   coats.

DOUGLAS. Now, by my sword, I will kill all his
coats;
I'll murder all his wardrobe piece by piece
Until I meet the king.

HOTSPUR.   Up, and away!
Our soldiers stand full fairly° for the day.
                                        [Exeunt]

[Alarum. Enter FALSTAFF, alone.]

30   FALSTAFF. Though I could 'scape shot-free° at
London, I fear the shot here; here's no scoring°
but upon the pate. Soft! Who are you? Sir
Walter Blunt. There's honor for you! Here's no
vanity!° I am as hot as molten lead, and as heavy
35   too. God keep lead out of me! I need no more
weight than mine own bowels. I have led my
ragamuffins where they are peppered. There's
not three of my hundred and fifty left alive,
and they are for the town's end, to beg during
40   life. But who comes here?

[Enter the PRINCE.]

PRINCE. What, stand'st thou idle here? Lend me
thy sword.
Many a nobleman lies stark and stiff
Under the hoofs of vaunting enemies,
Whose deaths are unreveng'd. Prithee, lend me
thy sword.

45   FALSTAFF. O Hal, I prithee, give me leave to breathe
a while. Turk Gregory° never did such deeds in
arms as I have done this day. I have paid Percy, I
have made him sure.

PRINCE. He is, indeed, and living to kill thee. I
50   prithee, lend me thy sword.

FALSTAFF. Nay, before God, Hal, if Percy be alive,
thou get'st not my sword; but take my pistol,
if thou wilt.

PRINCE. Give it me. What, is it in the case?

55   FALSTAFF. Aye, Hal; 'tis hot, 'tis hot. There's that
will sack a city.

Semblably furnish'd   dressed to resemble
fairly   hopefully   shot-free   without paying cash
scoring   charging on credit (with pun)
vanity   i.e., mere show
Turk Gregory   possible reference to Pope Gregory VII,
    famed for violence, signified here by Turk,
    synonymous with ferocity

[The PRINCE draws it out, and finds it to be a
                                        bottle of sack.]

PRINCE. What, is it a time to jest and dally now?
                        [He throws the bottle at him. Exit.]

FALSTAFF. Well, if Percy be alive, I'll pierce him. If
he do come in my way, so; if he do not, if I
come in his willingly, let him make a carbonado°   60
of me. I like not such grinning honor as Sir
Walter hath. Give me life, which if I can save, so;
if not, honor comes unlooked for, and there's an
end.   [Exit]

SCENE iv
Another part of the field.

[Alarum. Excursions. Enter the KING, the PRINCE,
LORD JOHN OF LANCASTER, and EARL OF
WESTMORELAND.]

KING. I prithee,
Harry, withdraw thyself; thou bleed'st too
much.
Lord John of Lancaster, go you with him.

LANCASTER. Not I, my lord, unless I did bleed too.

PRINCE. I beseech your majesty, make up,°   5
Lest your retirement do amaze your friends.

KING. I will do so.
My Lord of Westmoreland, lead him to his
tent.

WESTMORELAND. Come, my lord, I'll lead you to
your tent.

PRINCE. Lead me, my lord? I do not need your
help,   10
And God forbid a shallow scratch should drive
The Prince of Wales from such a field as this,
Where stain'd nobility lies trodden on
And rebels' arms triumph in massacres!

LANCASTER. We breathe too long. Come, cousin
Westmoreland,   15
Our duty this way lies; for God's sake, come.
            [Exeunt PRINCE JOHN and WESTMORELAND.]

PRINCE. By God, thou hast deceiv'd me, Lancaster;
I did not think thee lord of such a spirit.
Before, I lov'd thee as a brother, John,
But now I do respect thee as my soul.   20

KING. I saw him hold Lord Percy at the point
With lustier maintenance than I did look for
Of such an ungrown warrior.

PRINCE.   O this boy
Lends mettle to us all!   [Exit]

[Enter DOUGLAS.]

---

carbonado   barbecue   make up   go forward

DOUGLAS. Another king! They grow like Hydra's°
25   heads.
    I am the Douglas, fatal to all those
    That wear those colors on them. What art thou,
    That counterfeit'st the person of a king?
KING. The king himself, who, Douglas, grieves at
    heart
30   So many of his shadows thou hast met
    And not the very king. I have two boys
    Seek Percy and thyself about the field.
    But, seeing thou fall'st on me so luckily,
    I will assay thee. So, defend thyself.
35 DOUGLAS. I fear thou art another counterfeit,
    And yet, in faith, thou bear'st thee like a king.
    But mine I am sure thou art, who'er thou be,
    And thus I win thee.
       [*They fight; the* KING *being in danger, re-enter*
            PRINCE OF WALES.]
PRINCE. Hold up thy head, vile Scot, or thou art
    like
40   Never to hold it up again! The spirits
    Of valiant Shirley, Stafford, Blunt are in my
    arms.
    It is the Prince of Wales that threatens thee,
    Who never promiseth but he means to pay.
             [*They fight:* DOUGLAS *flies.*]
    Cheerly, my lord. How fares your grace?
45 Sir Nicholas Gawsey hath for succor sent,
    And so hath Clifton. I'll to Clifton straight.
KING. Stay and breathe awhile.
    Thou hast redeem'd thy lost opinion
    And show'd thou mak'st some tender of my life
50 In this fair rescue thou hast brought to me.
PRINCE. O God! They did me too much injury
    That ever said I hearken'd for your death.
    If it were so, I might have let alone
    Th' insulting hand of Douglas over you,
55   Which would have been as speedy in your end
    As all the poisonous potions in the world,
    And sav'd the treacherous labor of your son.
KING. Make up to Clifton. I'll to Sir Nicholas
    Gawsey.   [*Exit*]
           [*Enter* HOTSPUR.]
HOTSPUR. If I mistake not, thou art Harry Mon-
    mouth.
60 PRINCE. Thou speak'st as if I would deny my name.
HOTSPUR. My name is Harry Percy.
PRINCE.   Why, then I see
    A very valiant rebel of the name.
    I am the Prince of Wales; and think not, Percy,
    To share with me in glory any more.
65 Two stars keep not their motion in one sphere,

Nor can one England brook a double reign
Of Harry Percy and the Prince of Wales.
HOTSPUR. Nor shall it, Harry, for the hour is come
    To end the one of us, and would to God
    Thy name in arms were now as great as mine!   70
PRINCE. I'll make it greater ere I part from thee,
    And all the budding honors on thy crest
    I'll crop to make a garland for my head.
HOTSPUR. I can no longer brook thy vanities.
                  [*They fight.*]
          [*Enter* FALSTAFF.]
FALSTAFF. Well said, Hal! To it, Hal! Nay, you shall   75
    find no boy's play here, I can tell you.
       [*Re-enter* DOUGLAS; *he fights with* FALSTAFF,
         who falls down as if he were dead, and
         exit DOUGLAS. HOTSPUR *is wounded, and falls.*]
HOTSPUR. O, Harry, thou hast robb'd me of my
    youth!
    I better brook the loss of brittle life
    Than those proud titles thou hast won of me;
    They wound my thoughts worse than thy sword
       my flesh.   80
    But thought's the slave of life, and life time's
       fool,°
    And time, that takes survey of all the world,
    Must have a stop. O, I could prophesy,
    But that the earthy and cold hand of death
    Lies on my tongue. No, Percy, thou art dust,   85
    And food for—   [*Dies.*]
PRINCE. For worms, brave Percy. Fare thee well,
    great heart!
    Ill-weav'd ambition, how much art thou shrunk!
    When that this body did contain a spirit,
    A kingdom for it was too small a bound;°   90
    But now two paces of the vilest earth
    Is room enough. This earth that bears thee dead
    Bears not alive so stout a gentleman.
    If thou wert sensible of courtesy,
    I should not make so dear a show of zeal.   95
    But let my favors° hide thy mangled face,
    And even in thy behalf I'll thank myself
    For doing these fair rites of tenderness.
    Adieu, and take thy praise with thee to heaven!
    Thy ignominy sleep with thee in the grave,   100
    But not remember'd in thy epitaph!
          [*He spies* FALSTAFF *on the ground.*]
    What, old acquaintance! Could not all this flesh
    Keep in a little life? Poor Jack, farewell!
    I could have better spar'd a better man.
    O, I should have a heavy miss of thee   105
    If I were much in love with vanity!°

fool plaything   *bound* limit
favors i.e., scarf or other item of his own apparel
vanity frivolity

Hydra mythological monster that sprouted two new
   heads for each one struck off

Death hath not struck so fat a deer today,
Though many dearer, in this bloody fray.
Embowel'd will I see thee by and by;
110   Till then in blood by noble Percy lie.   [*Exit*]
FALSTAFF. [*Rising up*] Emboweled! If thou embowel
me today, I'll give you leave to powder me and
eat me too tomorrow. 'Sblood, 'twas time to
counterfeit, or that hot termagant Scot had paid
115   me scot and lot too. Counterfeit? I lie, I am no
counterfeit. To die is to be a counterfeit; for he is
but the counterfeit of a man who hath not the
life of a man. But to counterfeit dying, when a
man thereby liveth, is to be no counterfeit, but
120   the true and perfect image of life indeed. The
better part of valor is discretion; in the which
better part I have saved my life. 'Zounds,° I am
afraid of this gunpowder Percy, though he be
dead. How if he should counterfeit too, and rise?
125   By my faith, I am afraid he would prove the
better counterfeit. Therefore I'll make him sure;
yea, and I'll swear I killed him. Why may he not
rise as well as I? Nothing confutes me but eyes,
and nobody sees me. Therefore, sirrah [*stabbing
130   him*], with a new wound in your thigh, come you
along with me.   [*Takes up* HOTSPUR *on his back.*]
[*Re-enter the* PRINCE OF WALES *and* LORD JOHN
OF LANCASTER.]
PRINCE. Come, brother John; full bravely hast thou
flesh'd°
Thy maiden sword.
LANCASTER.   But, soft! Whom have we here?
Did you not tell me this fat man was dead?
135   PRINCE. I did; I saw him dead,
Breathless and bleeding on the ground. Art thou
alive?
Or is it fantasy that plays upon our eyesight?
I prithee, speak; we will not trust our eyes
Without our ears. Thou art not what thou
seem'st.
140   FALSTAFF. No, that's certain; I am not a double
man. But if I be not Jack Falstaff, then am I a
Jack.° There is Percy [*throwing the body down*]. If
your father will do me any honor, so; if not, let
him kill the next Percy himself. I look to be
145   either earl or duke, I can assure you.
PRINCE. Why, Percy I killed myself, and saw thee
dead.
FALSTAFF. Didst thou? Lord, Lord, how this world
is given to lying! I grant you I was down and out
150   of breath, and so was he. But we rose both at an
instant and fought a long hour by Shrewsbury
clock. If I may be believed, so: if not, let them

that should reward valor bear the sin upon their
own heads. I'll take it upon my death, I gave him
this wound in the thigh. If the man were alive   155
and would deny it, 'zounds, I would make him
eat a piece of my sword.
LANCASTER. This is the strangest tale that ever I
heard.
PRINCE. This is the strangest fellow, brother John.
Come, bring your luggage nobly on your back.   160
For my part, if a lie may do thee grace,
I'll gild it with the happiest terms I have.
[*A retreat is sounded.*]
The trumpet sounds retreat; the day is ours.
Come, brother, let us to the highest of the field
To see what friends are living, who are dead.   165
[*Exeunt* PRINCE OF WALES *and* LANCASTER.]
FALSTAFF. I'll follow, as they say, for reward. He
that rewards me, God reward him! If I do grow
great, I'll grow less, for I'll purge, and leave sack,
and live cleanly as a nobleman should do.
[*Exit*]

SCENE v
Another part of the field.

[*The trumpets sound. Enter the* KING, PRINCE OF
WALES, LORD JOHN OF LANCASTER, EARL OF
WESTMORELAND, *with* WORCESTER *and* VERNON
prisoners.]
KING. Thus ever did rebellion find rebuke.
Ill-spirited Worcester! Did not we send grace,
Pardon, and terms of love to all of you?
And wouldst thou turn our offers contrary?
Misuse the tenor of thy kinsman's trust?   5
Three knights upon our party slain today,
A noble earl, and many a creature else
Had been alive this hour
If like a Christian thou hadst truly borne
Betwixt our armies true intelligence.   10
WORCESTER. What I have done my safety urg'd me
to,
And I embrace this fortune patiently,
Since not to be avoided it falls on me.
KING. Bear Worcester to the death, and Vernon
too.
Other offenders we will pause upon.   15
[*Exeunt* WORCESTER *and* VERNON, *guarded.*]
How goes the field?
PRINCE. The noble Scot, Lord Douglas, when he
saw
The fortune of the day quite turn'd from him,
The noble Percy slain, and all his men
Upon the foot of fear,° fled with the rest.   20

Zounds by Christ's wounds   *flesh'd* initiated
Jack knave

Upon . . . fear running away in fear

191

And falling from a hill, he was so bruis'd
That the pursuers took him. At my tent
The Douglas is, and I beseech your grace
I may dispose of him.
KING.   With all my heart.
25   PRINCE. Then, brother John of Lancaster, to you
This honorable bounty° shall belong.
Go to the Douglas and deliver him
Up to his pleasure, ransomless and free.
His valor shown upon our crests today
30   Hath taught us how to cherish such high deeds
Even in the bosom of our adversaries.
LANCASTER. I thank your grace for this high
courtesy,
Which I shall give away° immediately.

KING. Then this remains, that we divide our power.
You, son John, and my cousin Westmoreland,   35
Towards York shall bend you with your dearest°
speed
To meet Northumberland and the prelate
Scroop,
Who, as we hear, are busily in arms.
Myself and you, son Harry, will towards Wales
To fight with Glendower and the Earl of March.   40
Rebellion in this land shall lose his sway,
Meeting the check of such another day.
And since this business so fair is done,
Let us not leave till all our own be won.
                                    [Exeunt]

bounty generosity
give away i.e., pass on to Douglas

dearest most urgent

AFTERWORD

1Henry IV is usefully identified as the first play of Shakespeare's full maturity, the time when there was no longer anything that he could not do superbly. In terms of historical chronology it is the second of the eight history plays that trace the course of men and events from the fall of Richard II in 1399 to the fall of Richard III in 1485; but in terms of Shakespeare's own development it is the fifth of the history cycle and approximately the fifteenth play of his career. His race, in short, was already between one third and one half run.

The greatest comedies and tragedies were all still to come; and among the plays that preceded these, *1Henry IV* best foretells what heights were to be attained in both genres. It is not a tragedy, but it is a serious drama of tremendous vitality, mass, and depth; it is not a comedy, but it includes much of Shakespeare's finest comedy—for it contains Falstaff, a dramatic creation over whom critics as diverse as Dr. Johnson, the apostle of classicism and common sense, and William Hazlitt, the romantics' own romantic, could grow ecstatic: "Falstaff, unimitated, unimitable Falstaff," wrote Johnson, "how shall I describe thee!"

The play all but bursts with its variety of dramatic distinctions. First among these is its blending of historical and fictional elements. We speak of "high plot" and "low plot," historical and comic plots, main and secondary plots, and indeed the episodes involved in these are clearly distinguished the one from the other. Yet Shakespeare's mastery shows most in the completeness with which a single whole is wrought that embraces all the elements, historical and fictional, even while their separate identities remain distinct. Further, not only are the elements woven into one massive, bustling whole, but the dramatist has also contrived to create parallels within the historical and fictional plots in such a way that each plot is enhanced by the existence of the other.

Individual participants serve as the most obvious links between the two large actions, the primary unifying device being Prince Hal himself, who moves easily from one to the other, necessarily carrying with him into one plot a considerable reminiscence of the other. When he is with Falstaff and others of the Boar's Head "underworld," he remains nevertheless the Crown Prince, an historical personage, and when he comes into the King's presence we are not allowed to forget the world from which he has just come: echoes of the Boar's Head follow him wherever he goes. Less conspicuous links, subtle in their effects as well as in their forms, occur everywhere: thus, near the end of the solidly historical opening scene, the King laments the fact that "riot and dishonor stain the brow/ Of my young Harry." The next scene opens with Hal in the midst of that "riot and dishonor"; Henry's mention of Hal has the effect of drawing the contrasting worlds together. Similarly, Hotspur, wholly committed to the historical scenes, alludes to the "sword-and-buckler Prince of Wales" and re-creates for the mind's eye Hal's whole recreational environment with his jesting threat to "have him poison'd with a pot of ale." Conversely, from their side, Falstaff and Hal toss satiric barbs at Hotspur, who "kills me some six or seven dozen of Scots at a breakfast"; at Glendower, who "swore the devil his true liegeman upon the cross of a Welsh hook"; and at Douglas, who "runs o' horseback up a hill perpendicular . . . and with his pistol kills a sparrow flying." Criss-crossing the double action, such allusions effectively bind the worlds together. The robbery at Gadshill is spoken of as an "action" and thus parallels and mildly burlesques the military action that soon engulfs all. The jesting thrusts and parries of the wit battles between Hal and Falstaff subtly parody the bitter disputes of the King and the rebel faction, which finally erupt into the deadly thrusts and parries of the battlefield, including those of Hal and

Hotspur. In a superbly artistic way, the third and climatic episode of the final scene of Act II, when Falstaff "rehearses" Hal for his forthcoming interview with his father, brings the court into the tavern. "This chair shall be my state," says Falstaff, playing the King, "this dagger my scepter, and this cushion my crown." And he goes on: "Give me a cup of sack, to make my eyes look red, that it may be thought I have wept." He commences his speech with a sweep of his hand at the Hostess and the assembled denizens of the Boar's Head: "Stand aside, nobility." Surely enough, thereafter, when the tavern goes to the court and Hal stands before his father, the King's first words echo Falstaff's: "Lords, give us leave." And at the end of his first long speech Henry's sight is blurred by tears: his eye "now doth that I would not have it do,/ Make blind itself with foolish tenderness." Who, hearing him, can forget Falstaff's demand for sack "to make my eyes look red"?

It is worth noting that Shakespeare's achievement here in blending history and comedy was a pioneering endeavor both for himself and for English drama. Earlier history plays sometimes sandwiched "interludes" of comic dialogue or action between historical scenes, but, typically, such comic "time outs" had no integral relationship with the main plot. Shakespeare's own history plays before *1Henry IV* were almost totally lacking in comic elements, except as the crude remarks of peasants in *Henry VI* or the grotesquely sardonic utterances of the king in *Richard III* produce comic effect. In *Richard II*, which just precedes *1Henry IV*, nothing is comic unless it be the frenzied conduct of the Duchess of York and the unexpected rhymed couplets that occur during her interview with Bolingbroke in Act V, scene v. In any event no history play before *1Henry IV* develops a comic plot interwoven with historical matter. Generally speaking, Shakespeare was no pioneer; he preferred to perfect what others pioneered. But in this instance he simultaneously pioneered and perfected.

Second only to this achievement in overall significance are the characterizations of *1Henry IV*. The extraordinary quality, range, and abundance of dramatic portraits make the play, in this respect, second to no other of Shakespeare's; it is truly a drama of character, even as the later tragedies are all tragedies of character. Here for the first time history has been fully subordinated to drama and drama not of events but of men. Shakespeare does not hesitate to halve the age of Hotspur so as to make the warrior the contemporary of Prince Hal, and to represent the fate of England as resting upon the personal confrontation of the two. Dramatic, not factual, considerations govern the decisions that the dramatist makes throughout the play: in the scale of dramatic values, not historical ones, the charming domestic scene of Hotspur and his wife—"In faith, I'll break thy little finger, Harry"—weighs as heavily as the confrontation of Henry and Worcester.

Five major characters—Henry, Hal, Hotspur, Worcester, and Falstaff—rank with the richest portraits in all Shakespeare. And of course the principals are not the only ones worth mentioning; we must add at least six minor figures as well: Northumberland, Mortimer, Glendower, Bardolph, Lady Percy, and Mistress Quickly, that hen-brained creature who, after fluttering through two more *Henry* plays, would eventually emerge in *The Merry Wives of Windsor* as the quickest wit of all. And there are yet more, infrequently seen and only one-dimensional, yet sharply etched: Blunt, Vernon, Douglas, and Gadshill. All told, the number is impressive and leaves no question that with this play Shakespeare entered fully into his great middle career that is marked by, as much as anything, the range and distinction of its human portraits.

To be fully seen some of the historical figures must be followed through two or three plays. Henry is one such. Prominent as the Bolingbroke of *Richard II*, where his character remains ambiguous until the second half, he exposes new depths, nooks, and crannies of personality in *1Henry IV*, then continues to reveal the qualities that make him at last profoundly human, with human frailties, in *2Henry IV*. A leading figure, thus, in three plays, he is assuredly one of Shakespeare's most remarkable full-length human studies. "Shrewd politician" by no means sums him up, although he is manifestly that; he is also a father who worries about his son, a king who worries about England, edgy, distrustful, a self-confessed hypocrite—"And then I stole all courtesy from heaven,/ And dress'd myself in such humility"—a sinner whose soul harbors a long and aching sense of guilt that is crusted over but always raw within for "the fault (he) made in compassing the crown," as Hal, who inherits the worry, says long after, in *Henry V*.

Hal, too, runs through three plays that tell the story of the boy who grows up to be a man, the prince who grows up to be not just a king but the hero-king par excellence. Perhaps he is never again so delightful or so ingratiating as in the carefree days early in *1Henry IV*. Yet even there he has appeared as neither delightful nor ingratiating to numerous eminent Shakespeareans who have found it impossible to forgive him for what seems the peculiarly cold, calculating, and hypocritical speech—just such a one as his father might have been capable of making—that ends the second scene of Act I: "I know you all and will awhile uphold/The unyok'd humor of your idleness." But that issue, and a fuller analysis of the Prince, will best be deferred until the evidence of *Henry V* has been added.

Hal is the hero of the three plays that end with *Henry V*, and when we look backward from this final one to the beginnings in *Richard II*, where he is merely mentioned, it may appear that he is not only the hero of the series but the very cause of its existence, for indeed all the preceding histories serve the purpose of preparing the Prince for his heroic role as king. Yet is is not Hal whom the star actors of three centuries have chosen to play; granted that when these grew older and fatter (Betterton, for example) they regularly turned to Falstaff: but while they were young and had the figure for it, they all chose the "hare-brain'd Hotspur, govern'd by a spleen." Now and again among Shakespeare's plays arises a character with whom the dramatist seems himself to have fallen in love. Mercutio of *Romeo and Juliet* is one such; Hamlet is another. But the great example is Hotspur. Hotspur is also a great example of Shakespeare's career-long habit of developing character beyond the mere needs of plot. In this case the dramatic structure required only a warlike opponent to be pitted against the Prince. The easy way would have been to invest Hotspur with only the rigidly martial qualities that distinguish Douglas, a strongly marked but single-dimensioned character who has nothing to say and nothing to show except what concerns the battlefield. Shakespeare quickly establishes the point that Hotspur is even a better warrior than Douglas; but, having done so, he proceeds to make Hal's rival the warmest human being in the play. Impulsive, wildly imaginative, absent-minded, incurably optimistic, wholly committed to "honor," alternately exasperating and lovable, a hater of poets—"meter ballad-mongers"—yet also the sole poet in the play, hot-headed Hotspur, often played in flaming red wig, is understandably the actors' darling, who, on the stage, steals the play not only from Hal and Henry but from Falstaff himself. Only the "wild and irregular" Glendower, in his single scene, sometimes takes the limelight from Hotspur. When Hal kills him, loud gasps often break from audiences, particularly young ones. In making Hotspur a kind of adorable monster, Shakespeare chose, as he often did, to walk the tightrope, for Hal must kill his rival and yet not only hold the audience's sympathy but take a mighty step forward, thereby, toward *Henry V* and his role of hero-king and ideal monarch. Shakespeare could have afflicted his rebel with obnoxious traits that the audience could hate, and there would have been no risk of alienating anyone from Hal. But by doing exactly the opposite, endearing Hotspur to us as few dramatic characters are endeared, risking a "boomerang" reaction, yet always

195

demanding our full allegiance to Hal, Shakespeare enormously enriched the dramatic as well as the human values of the play.

No brief commentary can do justice to Falstaff, a favorite of audiences, critics, and general readers since Shakespeare first brought him on stage in this play. A descendant of the *miles gloriosus*, or "braggart soldier," of Roman comedy, he owes something also to the "vice" figure of English morality plays; but what audiences find most delightful in him, his wit, is wholly Shakespeare's invention. Besides his obvious function of making us laugh, Falstaff serves Shakespeare's largest dramatic purposes in somewhat the same way that Hotspur does. "Percy is but my factor, good my lord," Hal tells his father, "T'engross up glorious deeds on my behalf," so that when Hal overcomes Hotspur he "inherits" all his glory, and thus Shakespeare advances his hero toward the ultimate destination of hero-king. Conversely, Falstaff, the gross "cloak-bag" of idleness and excesses, partly symbolizes Hal's misspent youth, gathering unto himself all manner of faults and vices, so that when Hal casts him off (as he does at the end of *2Henry IV*) the effect is that of purging himself of all his own past derelictions. But Shakespeare walked the tightrope here, too, and not a few critics, Hazlitt among them, have been unable to forgive Hal for his final rejection of the fat rogue. Indeed, some have been unable to forgive Shakespeare himself for his part in the dastardly deed: the late and very great Sir Arthur Quiller-Couch, for example, pointed out that Shakespeare applied for a coat of arms and "turned respectable" at the very time that he caused Hal to turn respectable and turn the unrespectable Falstaff away. At the beginning of *Henry V*, when Hal has become king, the Hostess reports bitterly that Falstaff is dying, for "The King has killed his heart," and shortly thereafter, very movingly, she reports the manner of his death. But Falstaff's popularity in Shakespeare's own age was evidently enormous, and he was not allowed to pass from memory by the simple expedient of the dramatist's killing him off so that he could not prove an embarrassment to the flawless Henry V. According to respectable evidence, Queen Elizabeth herself commanded Shakespeare to resurrect Falstaff in a new play showing him in love, and the result, reportedly finished within fourteen days, was *The Merry Wives of Windsor*; and of course Falstaff lives yet again in Verdi's opera of *Falstaff*, based on the plot of the *Merry Wives*.

Last of the major characters is Worcester, the crooked genius who foments the rebellion against the king, controls the uncontrollable Hotspur (after a fashion), and directs his energies to serve his (Worcester's) personal ends. Shakespeare's own shrewdness and dramatic economy in the portrait of Worcester are well exhibited in such a passage as the following, when the arch plotter is urging the necessity of rebellion:

> For, bear ourselves as even as we can,
> The king will always think him in our debt
> And think we think ourselves unsatisfied,
> Till he hath found a time to pay us home.

Psychology is Worcester's forte; he is past master in the art of prying into the minds of others—and in interpreting their motives after the pattern of his own duplicity. One more incident may suffice to exemplify his habit of crooked insinuation. On the eve of battle, word is brought that Northumberland is sick and cannot come to lead his forces. Hotspur, as we should expect, flies off the handle: "'Zounds. How has he the leisure to be sick/ In such a justling time." He goes on to demand who, then, will lead his father's army. But the crafty mind of Worcester takes another tack with a seemingly innocent question: "I prithee tell me, doth he keep his bed?" We do not learn for certain until the opening of *2Henry IV* that Northumberland is indeed only "crafty-sick," but the thought instantly crossed Worcester's busy, suspicious brain.

A potent complement to the individual characters in *1Henry IV* is Shakespeare's system, employed in other plays also but never so fully as here, of parallels and contrasts of one with another. "My reformation," says Hal in his controversial soliloquy, "Shall show more goodly and attract more eyes/ Than that which hath no foil to set it off." In this play nearly everyone has a "foil." Hal's political shrewdness parallels his father's, but with humor and humanity added, thanks at least in part to his education at the hands of Falstaff. But of course Hal's great foil is Hotspur, just as Henry's is Worcester, who seems to reflect and magnify in his singular dedication to self-interest the king's habit of "policy"; but whereas Worcester's concern is only for himself, Henry's is for his son and his country as well as for himself. Falstaff, with his famous disquisition upon honor and his lack of eagerness to take to the field, stands in signal contrast to Hotspur's eager pursuit of honor as a plume to be won and worn. Blunt, who without any fanfare dies for his king, shows up Hotspur's conception of honor as rather shallow; and Falstaff, eying the dead Blunt with his "grinning honor," represents an attitude that contrasts sharply with both Blunt's and Hotspur's. These are only a few of the more noteworthy instances; the play's tissue is composed of such parallels and contrasts.

If Shakespeare's arrival at full maturity is evinced in *1Henry IV* by his mastery of characterization, it is reflected also in his mastery of dramatic language, both prose and verse, which are almost equally represented in the play. The vernacular of the Carriers, barely awake and stumbling about in the darkness outside the inn at Rochester, stands as a worthy contrast to the eloquent verse of the court:

> FIRST CARRIER. I prithee, Tom, beat Cut's saddle, put a few flocks in the point. Poor jade is wrung in the withers out of all cess.
> SECOND CARRIER. Peas and beans are as dank here as a dog, and that is the next way to give poor jades the bots. This house is turned upside down since Robin Ostler died.
> FIRST CARRIER. Poor fellow never joyed since the price of oats rose. It was the death of him.

Without deprecating the stunning lyricism that is the glory of the plays just preceding this —*A Midsummer Night's Dream*, *Romeo and Juliet*, *Richard II*—we must nevertheless acknowledge that the melodious poetry of these is like the sound of a single virtuoso instrument, such as the violin; in contrast, the dramatic verse of *1Henry IV* reproduces the sounds of a whole orchestra. No one is lyrical, except Hotspur, who touches some rare heights but wildly scrambles his metaphors, as would be expected. It is a fact that in the earlier plays characters are sometimes inappropriately lyrical because, presumably, Shakespeare was himself carried away by "the concord of sweet sounds." In *1Henry IV* Hotspur is often carried away by his own sound, but never Shakespeare. What is remarkable here is the "rightness" of the language for the speaker, the matter, and the moment. Henry, Hal, Hotspur, Worcester, Falstaff speak each his own language. The play inaugurates the period of the great middle plays, from *Julius Caesar* to *Macbeth*, when the question whether the language is "right" for speaker and situation does not occur to the reader, let alone to an audience.

Finally, *1Henry IV* is distinguished, against strong odds, by the degree of its completeness as a work of art. Historically, it is one unit in a four-part sequence, and a yet smaller unit in an eight-part whole that traces the century-long consequences of the usurpation and murder of a king by divine right. It is thus, of necessity, a chapter in a large and complex book; yet by looking both before and after, it incorporates within itself the full range of its historical subject, constitutes something of a microcosm of the larger whole, and is artistically self-contained. It is noteworthy that the story of what occurred in the reign of Richard II that led to his downfall is recounted, unobtrusively, not once but three times in *1Henry IV*—by Henry, Worcester, and Hotspur. The King's and Worcester's versions are greatly at odds, for obvious reasons; Worcester's and Hotspur's differ hardly at all, for an equally apparent reason: all that Hotspur knows to say has been insinuated into his head by his uncle. In any event, what has preceded the opening of the play is thus made abundantly clear for an audience. As for what would follow—the resurgence of the rebels, the wars with France, the Wars of the Roses—the way is left open for that; but meanwhile the immediate rebellion has been stalled, Hotspur has been killed, and the Wayward Prince has proved himself in battle and won his father's esteem. The play is thus satisfyingly complete, with all the elements needed to make an artistic whole framed within its five acts; at the same time, its beginning and its ending constitute smooth transitions from the past and toward the future.

A NOTE ON THE COMPOSITION OF THE PLAY

Henry IV, Part 1 was written in 1597, according to good evidence, and was first published in 1598. The first record of performance is 1600, but it may well have been staged earlier. For the historical materials, Shakespeare drew upon Holinshed's *Chronicles of England, Scotland, and Ireland*, and for some of the comic incidents and characters he drew on a crude history-comedy called *The Famous Victories of Henry V*, which had been acted as early as 1588.

Henry V

DRAMATIS PERSONÆ

KING HENRY *the Fifth*
DUKE OF GLOUCESTER }
DUKE OF BEDFORD } *brothers to the King*
DUKE OF EXETER *uncle to the King*
DUKE OF YORK *cousin to the King*
EARLS OF SALISBURY, WESTMORELAND, *and*
  WARWICK
ARCHBISHOP OF CANTERBURY
BISHOP OF ELY
EARL OF CAMBRIDGE
LORD SCROOP
SIR THOMAS GREY
SIR THOMAS ERPINGHAM, GOWER, FLUELLEN,
  MACMORRIS, JAMY *officers in King Henry's army*
BATES, COURT, WILLIAMS *soldiers in the same*
PISTOL, NYM, BARDOLPH
BOY
A HERALD

CHARLES *the Sixth, King of France*
LEWIS *the Dauphin*
DUKES OF BURGUNDY, ORLEANS, *and* BOURBON
THE CONSTABLE *of France*
RAMBURES *and* GRANDPRÉ *French Lords*
GOVERNOR *of Harfleur*
MONTJOY *a French Herald*
AMBASSADORS *to the King of England*
ISABEL *Queen of France*
KATHARINE *daughter to Charles and Isabel*
ALICE *a lady attending on her*
HOSTESS *of a tavern in Eastcheap, formerly Mistress*
  Quickly, and now married to Pistol
LORDS, LADIES, OFFICERS, SOLDIERS, CITIZENS,
  MESSENGERS, *and* ATTENDANTS
CHORUS

SCENE *England; afterwards France*

PROLOGUE

[Enter CHORUS.]
CHORUS. O for a Muse of fire that would ascend
  The brightest heaven of invention,°
  A kingdom for a stage, princes to act,
  And monarchs to behold the swelling scene!
5 Then should the warlike Harry, like himself,
  Assume the port° of Mars, and at his heels,
  Leash'd in like hounds, should famine, sword,
    and fire
  Crouch for employment.° But pardon, gentles
    all,
The flat unraised spirits° that have dar'd
On this unworthy scaffold° to bring forth 10
So great an object. Can this cockpit° hold
The vasty fields of France? Or may we cram
Within this wooden O° the very casques°
That did affright the air at Agincourt?
O, pardon, since a crooked figure may 15
Attest° in little place a million,
And let us, ciphers to this great accompt,°

Muse . . . invention flaming inspiration that would scale
  the highest peak of poetic art
port bearing
Crouch for employment i.e., ready to leap forward at
  command

flat . . . spirits i.e., dull, uninspired actors
scaffold stage
cockpit cockfight arena; here, the theater
wooden O the circular, wooden theater, probably the
  Curtain
casques helmets   *Attest* represent
accompt account

199

On your imaginary forces° work.
Suppose within the girdle of these walls
20 Are now confin'd two mighty monarchies,
Whose high upreared and abutting fronts°
The perilous narrow ocean parts asunder.
Piece out our imperfections with your thoughts;
Into a thousand parts divide one man,
25 And make imaginary puissance.°
Think, when we talk of horses, that you see them

Printing their proud hoofs i' the receiving earth;
For 'tis your thoughts that now must deck our kings,
Carry them here and there, jumping o'er times,
Turning the accomplishment of many years   30
Into an hourglass. For the which supply,°
Admit me Chorus to this history,
Who prologue-like your humble patience pray,
Gently to hear, kindly to judge, our play.

[*Exit*]

imaginary forces imaginative faculties
high . . . fronts towering cliffs of Dover and Calais
  which confront each other across the Channel
puissance armed forces

For . . . supply for filling in the gaps in time

A C T   I

SCENE i
London. An ante-chamber in the KING'S *palace.*

[*Enter the* ARCHBISHOP OF CANTERBURY, *and the* BISHOP OF ELY.]

CANTERBURY. My lord, I'll tell you—that self° bill is urg'd
Which in the eleventh year of the last king's reign
Was like,° and had indeed against us pass'd,
But that the scambling° and unquiet time
5 Did push it out of farther question.
ELY. But how, my lord, shall we resist it now?
CANTERBURY. It must be thought on. If it pass against us,
We lose the better half of our possession.
For all the temporal lands° which men devout
10 By testament have given to the church
Would they strip from us, being valu'd thus:
As much as would maintain, to the king's honor,
Full fifteen earls and fifteen hundred knights,
Six thousand and two hundred good esquires,
15 And, to relief of lazars° and weak age,
Of indigent faint souls past corporal toil,
A hundred almshouses right well supplied;
And to the coffers of the king beside,

A thousand pounds by the year. Thus runs the bill.
ELY. This would drink deep.
CANTERBURY.   'Twould drink the cup and all.   20
ELY. But what prevention?
CANTERBURY. The king is full of grace and fair regard.
ELY. And a true lover of the holy church.
CANTERBURY. The courses of his youth promis'd it not.
The breath no sooner left his father's body   25
But that his wildness, mortified° in him,
Seem'd to die too. Yea, at that very moment,
Consideration° like an angel came
And whipp'd th' offending Adam° out of him,
Leaving his body as a paradise   30
T' envelop and contain celestial spirits.
Never was such a sudden scholar made;
Never came reformation in a flood
With such a heady currance,° scouring faults;
Nor never Hydra-headed° wilfulness   35
So soon did lose his seat, and all at once,
As in this king.
ELY.   We are bless'd in the change.
CANTERBURY. Hear him but reason in divinity,
And all-admiring with an inward wish

self same   *like* likely (to pass)
scambling tumultuous
temporal lands belonging to laymen and not used for
  ecclesiastical purposes
lazars beggars (literally, lepers)

mortified killed
Consideration disposition toward reflection
offending Adam i.e., native wickedness
heady currance strong current
Hydra-headed many-headed (the Hydra, slain by
  Hercules, had nine heads and grew two more for each
  one cut off)

40 You would desire the king were made a prelate.
   Hear him debate of commonwealth affairs,
   You would say it hath been all in all his study.
   List his discourse of war, and you shall hear
   A fearful battle render'd you in music.
45 Turn him to any cause of policy,°
   The Gordian knot° of it he will unloose,
   Familiar as his garter; that,° when he speaks,
   The air, a charter'd libertine,° is still,
   And the mute wonder° lurketh in men's ears
50 To steal his sweet and honey'd sentences;°
   So that the art and practic part of life
   Must be the mistress to this theoric°—
   Which is a wonder how his grace should glean
       it,
   Since his addiction was to courses vain,
55 His companies unletter'd, rude, and shallow,
   His hours fill'd up with riots, banquets, sports,
   And never noted in him any study,
   Any retirement, any sequestration
   From open haunts and popularity.°
60 ELY. The strawberry grows underneath the nettle,
   And wholesome berries thrive and ripen best
   Neighbor'd by fruit of baser quality.
   And so the prince obscur'd his contemplation
   Under the veil of wildness, which,° no doubt,
65 Grew like the summer grass, fastest by night,
   Unseen, yet crescive in his faculty.°
   CANTERBURY. It must be so, for miracles are ceas'd;
   And therefore we must needs admit the means°
   How things are perfected.
   ELY.   But, my good lord,
70 How now for mitigation of this bill
   Urg'd by the commons? Doth his majesty
   Incline to it, or no?
   CANTERBURY.   He seems indifferent,°
   Or rather swaying more upon our part
   Than cherishing th' exhibiters° against us.
75 For I have made an offer to his majesty,
   Upon our spiritual convocation°

cause of policy affair of state
Gordian knot cut through by Alexander the Great; a
   seemingly insoluble difficulty
that so that
air . . . libertine air is entirely free, like one licensed to
   do as he pleases
mute wonder silent wonderer, i.e., the air
sentences wise sayings
art . . . theoric practical experience must have taught
   him his philosophy
open . . . popularity public places and vulgar company
which i.e., his habit of contemplation
crescive . . . faculty growing by its natural power
admit . . . means accept the cause as natural
indifferent impartial   exhibiters promoters
Upon . . . convocation on the authority of our clerical
   assembly

   And in regard of causes now in hand,°
   Which I have open'd to his grace at large,
   As touching° France, to give a greater sum
   Than ever at one time the clergy yet   80
   Did to his predecessors part withal.
ELY. How did this offer seem receiv'd, my lord?
CANTERBURY. With good acceptance of his majesty,
   Save that there was not time enough to hear,
   As I perceiv'd his grace would fain have done, 85
   The severals and unhidden passages°
   Of his true titles to some certain dukedoms,
   And generally to the crown and seat of France,
   Deriv'd from Edward, his great-grandfather.
ELY. What was th' impediment that broke this off? 90
CANTERBURY. The French ambassador upon that
       instant
   Crav'd audience; and the hour, I think, is come
   To give him hearing. Is it four o'clock?
ELY. It is.
CANTERBURY. Then go we in to know his embassy—   95
   Which I could with a ready guess declare
   Before the Frenchman speak a word of it.
ELY. I'll wait upon you, and I long to hear it.
                                          [Exeunt]

                    SCENE ii
          The same. The Presence chamber.

   [Enter KING HENRY, GLOUCESTER, BEDFORD,
     EXETER, WARWICK, WESTMORELAND, and
                 ATTENDANTS.]
KING. Where is my gracious Lord of Canterbury?
EXETER. Not here in presence.
KING.   Send for him, good uncle.
WESTMORELAND. Shall we call in th' ambassador,
       my liege?
KING. Not yet, my cousin. We would be resolv'd,
   Before we hear him, of some things of weight   5
   That task° our thoughts concerning us and
       France.
   [Enter the ARCHBISHOP OF CANTERBURY and
              the BISHOP OF ELY.]
CANTERBURY. God and his angels guard your
       sacred throne
   And make you long become it!
KING.   Sure, we thank you.
   My learned lord, we pray you to proceed

causes . . . hand issues now pressing
touching concerning
severals . . . passages particulars and clear lines of
   succession
task tax

201

10 And justly and religiously unfold
Why the law Salique that they have in France
Or should or° should not bar us in our claim.
And God forbid, my dear and faithful lord,
That you should fashion, wrest, or bow your
reading,
15 Or nicely charge your understanding soul
With opening titles miscreate° whose right
Suits not in native colors with the truth;°
For God doth know how many now in health
Shall drop their blood in approbation°
20 Of what your reverence shall incite us to.
Therefore take heed how you impawn° our
person,
How you awake our sleeping sword of war.
We charge you in the name of God, take heed;
For never two such kingdoms did contend
Without much fall of blood, whose guiltless
25 drops
Are every one a woe, a sore complaint
'Gainst him whose wrongs give edge unto the
swords
That make such waste in brief mortality.
Under this conjuration speak, my lord,
30 For we will hear, note, and believe in heart
That what you speak is in your conscience
wash'd
As pure as sin with baptism.
CANTERBURY. Then hear me, gracious sovereign,
and you peers
That owe yourselves, your lives, and services
35 To this imperial throne. There is no bar
To make against your highness' claim to France
But this, which they produce from Pharamond,
"In terram Salicam mulieres ne succedant"—
"No woman shall succeed in Salique land."
40 Which Salique land the French unjustly gloze°
To be the realm of France, and Pharamond
The founder of this law and female bar.
Yet their own authors faithfully affirm
That the land Salique is in Germany,
45 Between the floods° of Sala and of Elbe,
Where Charles the Great, having subdu'd the
Saxons,
There left behind and settled certain French,
Who, holding in disdain the German women
For some dishonest manners of their life,

Establish'd then this law—to wit, no female   50
Should be inheritrix in Salique land;
Which Salique, as I said, 'twixt Elbe and Sala,
Is at this day in Germany call'd Meisen.
Then doth it well appear the Salique law
Was not devised for the realm of France,   55
Nor did the French possess the Salique land
Until four hundred one and twenty years
After defunction° of King Pharamond,
Idly suppos'd the founder of this law,
Who died within the year of our redemption   60
Four hundred twenty-six. And Charles the
Great
Subdu'd the Saxons and did seat the French
Beyond the river Sala in the year
Eight hundred five. Besides, their writers say,
King Pepin, which deposed Childeric,   65
Did, as heir general, being descended
Of Blithild, which was daughter to King Clo-
thair,
Make claim and title to the crown of France.
Hugh Capet also, who usurp'd the crown
Of Charles the duke of Lorraine, sole heir male   70
Of the true line and stock of Charles the Great,
To find° his title with some shows of truth—
Though, in pure truth, it was corrupt and
naught—
Convey'd° himself as heir to the Lady Lingare,
Daughter to Charlemain, who was the son   75
To Lewis the emperor, and Lewis the son
Of Charles the Great. Also King Lewis the
tenth,
Who was sole heir to the usurper Capet,
Could not keep quiet in his conscience,
Wearing the crown of France, till satisfied   80
That fair Queen Isabel, his grandmother,
Was lineal° of the Lady Ermengare,
Daughter to Charles the foresaid duke of
Lorraine,
By the which marriage the line of Charles the
Great
Was reunited to the crown of France.   85
So that, as clear as is the summer's sun,
King Pepin's title and Hugh Capet's claim,
King Lewis his satisfaction,° all appear
To hold in the right and title of the female.
So do the kings of France unto this day,   90
Howbeit they would hold up this Salique law
To bar your highness claiming from the female,
And rather choose to hide them in a net

Or . . . or either . . . or
nicely . . . miscreate burden your soul by being too
  ingenious in disclosing illegitimate titles
Suits . . . truth does not accord (without false coloration)
  with the truth
approbation proving (on the battlefield)
impawn commit, pledge
gloze interpret   *floods* waters

defunction decease   *find* provide
Convey'd falsely posed   *lineal* lineally descended
King . . . satisfaction King Lewis's claim (which satisfied
  his conscience)

Than amply to imbar their crooked titles°
95 Usurp'd from you and your progenitors.
KING. May I with right and conscience make this
  claim?
CANTERBURY. The sin upon my head, dread
  sovereign!
For in the book of Numbers is it writ,
When the man dies, let the inheritance
100 Descend unto the daughter. Gracious lord,
Stand for your own. Unwind your bloody flag.
Look back into your mighty ancestors.
Go, my dread lord, to your great-grandsire's
  tomb
From whom you claim; invoke his warlike spirit,
And your great-uncle's, Edward the Black
  Prince,
105 Who on the French ground play'd a tragedy,°
Making defeat on the full power of France,
Whiles his most mighty father on a hill
Stood smiling to behold his lion's whelp
110 Forage in blood of French nobility.
O noble English, that could entertain
With half their forces the full pride of France
And let another half stand laughing by,
All out of work and cold for action!
115 ELY. Awake remembrance of these valiant dead,
And with your puissant arm renew their feats.
You are their heir, you sit upon their throne,
The blood and courage that renowned them
Runs in your veins, and my thrice-puissant liege
120 Is in the very May morn of his youth,
Ripe for exploits and mighty enterprises.
EXETER. Your brother kings and monarchs of the
  earth
Do all expect that you should rouse yourself,
As did the former lions of your blood.
WESTMORELAND. They know your grace hath
125 cause and means and might;
So hath your highness.° Never king of England
Had nobles richer and more loyal subjects,
Whose hearts have left their bodies here in
  England
And lie pavilion'd° in the fields of France.
CANTERBURY. O, let their bodies follow, my dear
130 liege,

With blood and sword and fire to win your
  right.
In aid whereof we of the spiritualty
Will raise your highness such a mighty sum
As never did the clergy at one time
Bring in to any of your ancestors. 135
KING. We must not only arm t' invade the French,
But lay down our proportions° to defend
Against the Scot, who will make road° upon us
With all advantages.
CANTERBURY. They of those marches,° gracious
  sovereign, 140
Shall be a wall sufficient to defend
Our inland from the pilfering borderers.
KING. We do not mean the coursing snatchers°
  only,
But fear the main intendment of the Scot,
Who hath been still° a giddy° neighbor to us. 145
For you shall read that my great-grandfather
Never went with his forces into France
But that the Scot on his unfurnish'd° kingdom
Came pouring like the tide into a breach,
With ample and brim fulness of his force, 150
Galling the gleaned° land with hot assays,°
Girding with grievous siege castles and towns,
That° England, being empty of defense,
Hath shook and trembled at th' ill neighbor-
  hood.
CANTERBURY. She hath been then more fear'd than
  harm'd, my liege, 155
For hear her but exampled by herself.°
When all her chivalry hath been in France,
And she a mourning widow of her nobles,
She hath herself not only well defended,
But taken and impounded as a stray 160
The King of Scots,° whom she did send to France
To fill King Edward's fame with prisoner kings
And make her chronicle as rich with praise
As is the ooze and bottom of the sea
With sunken wreck and sumless treasuries. 165
WESTMORELAND. But there's a saying very old and
  true,
  "If that you will France win,
  Then with Scotland first begin."
For once the eagle England being in prey,

---

to hide . . . titles to hide within a tangle of fabrication rather than make their own false titles secure (i.e., the French kings hold their titles on the same grounds that they would deny Henry—female succession)
play'd a tragedy at the battle of Crecy (1346) when Edward III ("great-grandsire") wrought destruction on the French and his young son ("great-uncle") distinguished himself
So . . . highness i.e., as indeed you have
pavilion'd encamped

lay . . . proportions determine and set aside the forces needed
road inroad *marches* borders
coursing snatchers hit-and-run raiders *still* always
giddy untrustworthy *unfurnish'd* unprotected
gleaned i.e., stripped of defenders *assays* assaults
That so that
hear . . . herself hear a precedent from her own history
King of Scots David Bruce, taken prisoner while Edward III was at Crecy

170 To her unguarded nest the weasel Scot
    Comes sneaking and so sucks her princely eggs,
    Playing the mouse in absence of the cat,
    To tear and havoc more than she can eat.
    EXETER. It follows then the cat must stay at home.
175 Yet that is but a crush'd necessity,°
    Since we have locks to safeguard necessaries,
    And pretty traps to catch the petty thieves.
    While that the armed hand doth fight abroad,
    Th' advised head defends itself at home.
180 For government, though high and low and
        lower,
    Put into parts,° doth keep in one consent.°
    Congreeing° in a full and natural close,°
    Like music.
    CANTERBURY.   Therefore doth heaven divide
    The state of man in divers functions,
185 Setting endeavor in continual motion,
    To which is fixed, as an aim or butt,°
    Obedience. For so work the honeybees,
    Creatures that by a rule in nature teach
    The act of order to a peopled kingdom.
190 They have a king and officers of sorts,°
    Where some, like magistrates, correct at home,
    Others, like merchants, venture trade abroad,
    Others, like soldiers, armed in their stings,
    Make boot° upon the summer's velvet buds,
    Which pillage they with merry march bring
195   home
    To the tent royal of their emperor—
    Who, busied in his majesty, surveys
    The singing masons building roofs of gold,
    The civil° citizens kneading up the honey,
200 The poor mechanic porters crowding in
    Their heavy burdens at his narrow gate,
    The sad-eyed justice, with his surly hum,
    Deliv'ring o'er to executors° pale
    The lazy yawning drone. I this infer,
205 That many things, having full reference
    To one consent, may work contrariously.
    As many arrows, loosed several ways,
    Come to one mark, as many ways meet in one
        town,
    As many fresh streams meet in one salt sea,
210 As many lines close in the dial's center—
    So may a thousand actions, once afoot,
    End in one purpose and be all well borne
    Without defeat. Therefore to France, my liege.
    Divide your happy England into four,

    Whereof take you one quarter into France,   215
    And you withal shall make all Gallia shake.
    If we, with thrice such powers left at home,
    Cannot defend our own doors from the dog,
    Let us be worried and our nation lose
    The name of hardiness and policy.°   220
    KING. Call in the messengers sent from the
        Dauphin.   [Exeunt some ATTENDANTS.]
    Now are we well resolv'd; and by God's help
    And yours, the noble sinews of our power,
    France being ours, we'll bend it to our awe
    Or break it all to pieces. Or° there we'll sit,   225
    Ruling in large and ample empery°
    O'er France and all her almost kingly dukedoms,
    Or lay these bones in an unworthy urn,
    Tombless, with no remembrance over them.
    Either our history shall with full mouth   230
    Speak freely of our acts, or else our grave,
    Like Turkish mute,° shall have a tongueless
        mouth,
    Not worshipp'd with a waxen epitaph.°
            [Enter AMBASSADORS of France.]
    Now are we well prepar'd to know the pleasure
    Of our fair cousin Dauphin, for we hear   235
    Your greeting is from him, not from the king.
    FIRST AMBASSADOR. May't please your majesty to
        give us leave
    Freely to render what we have in charge?
    Or shall we sparingly show you far off
    The Dauphin's meaning and our embassy?   240
    KING. We are no tyrant, but a Christian king,
    Unto whose grace our passion is as subject
    As are our wretches fetter'd in our prisons.
    Therefore with frank and with uncurbed plain-
        ness
    Tell us the Dauphin's mind.
    FIRST AMBASSADOR.   Thus, then, in few.   245
    Your highness, lately sending into France,
    Did claim some certain dukedoms in the right
    Of your great predecessor, King Edward the
        third.
    In answer of which claim, the prince our master
    Says that you savor too much of your youth,   250
    And bids you be advis'd there's naught in France
    That can be with a nimble galliard° won;
    You cannot revel into dukedoms there.
    He therefore sends you, meeter° for your spirit,
    This tun° of treasure; and, in lieu° of this,   255

---

crush'd necessity strained conclusion
parts i.e., like parts in music   consent harmony
Congreeing harmonizing   close cadence
butt target   sorts different ranks   boot booty
civil orderly
executors executioners (accented like execute)

policy statesmanship   Or either   empery dominion
Turkish mute i.e., slave with tongue removed to ensure
  secrecy
Not . . . epitaph not honored even by an epitaph cut in
  (impermanent) wax
galliard lively dance   meeter fitter   tun cask
in lieu of in exchange for

Desires you let the dukedoms that you claim
Hear no more of you. This the Dauphin speaks.
KING. What treasure, uncle?
EXETER.   Tennis balls, my liege.
KING. We are glad the Dauphin is so pleasant with
     us;
260   His present and your pains we thank you for.
     When we have match'd our rackets to these
        balls,
     We will in France, by God's grace, play a set
     Shall strike his father's crown into the hazard.°
     Tell him he hath made a match with such a
        wrangler°
265   That all the courts° of France will be disturb'd
     With chases.° And we understand him well,
     How he comes o'er us° with our wilder days,
     Not measuring what use we made of them.
     We never valu'd this poor seat° of England,
270   And therefore, living hence, did give ourself
     To barbarous license, as 'tis ever common
     That men are merriest when they are from
        home.
     But tell the Dauphin I will keep my state,°
     Be like a king, and show my sail of greatness
275   When I do rouse me in my throne of France.
     For that I have laid by my majesty
     And plodded like a man for working days.
     But I will rise there with so full a glory
     That I will dazzle all the eyes of France,
280   Yea, strike the Dauphin blind to look on us.
     And tell the pleasant prince this mock of his
     Hath turn'd his balls to gun-stones, and his soul

Shall stand sore charged for the wasteful
     vengeance
That shall fly with them. For many a thousand
     widows
Shall this his mock mock out of their dear hus-
     bands,   285
Mock mothers from their sons, mock castles
     down,
And some are yet ungotten and unborn
That shall have cause to curse the Dauphin's
     scorn.
But this lies all within the will of God,
To whom I do appeal, and in whose name   290
Tell you the Dauphin I am coming on
To venge me as I may and to put forth
My rightful hand in a well-hallow'd cause.
So get you hence in peace, and tell the Dauphin
His jest will savor but of shallow wit   295
When thousands weep more than did laugh at
     it.
Convey them with safe conduct. Fare you well.
                              [Exeunt AMBASSADORS.]
EXETER. This was a merry message.
KING. We hope to make the sender blush at it.
     Therefore, my lords, omit no happy° hour   300
     That may give furtherance to our expedition.
     For we have now no thought in us but France,
     Save those to God, that run before our business.
     Therefore let our proportions° for these wars
     Be soon collected, and all things thought upon 305
     That may with reasonable swiftness add
     More feathers to our wings. For, God before,°
     We'll chide this Dauphin at his father's door.
     Therefore let every man now task his thought°
     That this fair action may on foot be brought.   310
                              [Exeunt. Flourish.]

hazard   area from which the ball is unreturnable; with
     pun: jeopardy
wrangler   opponent (with obvious pun)
courts   pun: tennis courts, courts of kings
chases   missed returns in tennis (with pun, pursuits)
comes o'er us   scores a point on us, taunts us
seat   throne   state   royal dignity

happy   favorable   proportions   forces
before   leading us
task . . . thought   i.e., put his mind to it

ACT · II

PROLOGUE

[Enter CHORUS.]
CHORUS. Now all the youth of England are on fire,
     And silken dalliance in the wardrobe lies.°
     Now thrive the armorers, and honor's thought
     Reigns solely in the breast of every man.

silken . . . lies   luxury is laid aside

They sell the pasture now to buy the horse,   5
Following the mirror° of all Christian kings
With winged heels, as English Mercuries.°
For now sits Expectation in the air,
And hides a sword from hilts unto the point

mirror   model
winged . . . Mercuries   Mercury, the gods' messenger,
     wore sandals with winged heels

10 With crowns imperial, crowns and coronets,
Promis'd to Harry and his followers.
The French, advis'd by good intelligence°
Of this most dreadful preparation,
Shake in their fear and with pale policy°
15 Seek to divert the English purposes.
O England! Model to° thy inward greatness,
Like little body with a mighty heart,
What mightst thou do, that honor would thee°
do,
Were all thy children kind and natural!
20 But see thy fault! France hath in thee found out
A nest of hollow bosoms which he fills
With treacherous crowns,° and three corrupted
men,
One, Richard Earl of Cambridge, and the
second,
Henry Lord Scroop of Masham, and the third,
25 Sir Thomas Grey, knight, of Northumberland,
Have, for the gilt° of France—O guilt indeed!—
Confirm'd conspiracy with fearful France.
And by their hands this grace of kings° must die,
If hell and treason hold their promises,
30 Ere he take ship for France, and in Southampton.
Linger° your patience on, and we'll digest
Th' abuse of distance, force a play.°
The sum is paid, the traitors are agreed,
The king is set from London, and the scene
35 Is now transported, gentles, to Southampton.
There is the playhouse now; there must you sit.
And thence to France shall we convey you safe
And bring you back, charming the narrow seas
To give you gentle pass; for, if we may,
40 We'll not offend one stomach° with our play.
But, till the king come forth, and not till then,
Unto Southampton do we shift our scene.

[*Exit*]

SCENE i
London. A street.

[*Enter* CORPORAL NYM *and* LIEUTENANT
BARDOLPH.]
BARDOLPH. Well met, Corporal Nym.
NYM. Good morrow, Lieutenant Bardolph.

intelligence espionage   *pale policy* frightened cunning
Model to miniature replica of
would thee would have thee
treacherous crowns i.e., money paid to buy treason
gilt gold
grace of kings one who adds grace even to kingship
Linger extend
digest . . . play shrink space and make a (well-ordered)
    play
offend . . .stomach i.e., by seasickness (with obvious pun)

BARDOLPH. What, are Ancient° Pistol and you
friends yet?
NYM. For my part, I care not. I say little, but when   5
time shall serve, there shall be smiles; but that
shall be as it may. I dare not fight, but I will
wink and hold out mine iron. It is a simple one,
but what though? It will toast cheese, and it will
endure cold as another man's sword will, and   10
there's an end.
BARDOLPH. I will bestow a breakfast to make you
friends, and we'll be all three sworn brothers to
France. Let it be so, good Corporal Nym.
NYM. Faith, I will live so long as I may, that's the   15
certain of it, and when I cannot live any longer,
I will do as I may. That is my rest, that is the
rendezvous of it.°
BARDOLPH. It is certain, corporal, that he is married
to Nell Quickly, and certainly she did you wrong,   20
for you were troth-plight° to her.
NYM. I cannot tell. Things must be as they may.
Men may sleep, and they may have their throats
about them at that time, and some say knives
have edges. It must be as it may. Though   25
patience be a tired mare, yet she will plod.
There must be conclusions. Well, I cannot tell.
[*Enter* PISTOL *and* HOSTESS.]
BARDOLPH. Here comes Ancient Pistol and his
wife. Good corporal, be patient here. How now,
mine host Pistol!   30
PISTOL. Base tike,° call'st thou me host?
Now, by this hand, I swear, I scorn the term.
Nor shall my Nell keep lodgers.
HOSTESS. No, by my troth, not long, for we cannot
lodge and board a dozen or fourteen gentle-   35
women that live honestly by the prick of their
needles, but it will be thought we keep a bawdy
house straight. [NYM *and* PISTOL *draw.*] O
welladay, Lady,° if he be not drawn now! We
shall see wilful adultery and murder committed.   40
BARDOLPH. Good lieutenant! Good corporal!
Offer nothing here.
NYM. Pish!
PISTOL. Pish for thee, Iceland dog! Thou prick-
ear'd cur of Iceland!°   45
HOSTESS. Good Corporal Nym, show thy valor, and
put up your sword.
NYM. Will you shog off? I would have you solus.°
PISTOL. "Solus," egregious dog? O viper vile!

Ancient ensign
That . . . it i.e., that's what I stand pat on; that's the
    whole of it
troth-plight betrothed   *tike* cur
Lady an oath, "by the Virgin Mary"
prick-ear'd . . . Iceland pointed-eared, ill-tempered dog
solus alone

50 The "solus" in thy most mervailous° face,
The "solus" in thy teeth, and in thy throat,
And in thy hateful lungs, yea, in thy maw,
  perdy,°
And, which is worse, within thy nasty mouth!
I do retort the "solus" in thy bowels,

55 For I can take,° and Pistol's cock is up,
And flashing fire will follow.
NYM. I am not Barbason;° you cannot conjure me.
I have an humor to knock you indifferently well.
If you grow foul with me, Pistol, I will scour you

60 with my rapier, as I may, in fair terms. If you
would walk off, I would prick your guts a little,
in good terms, as I may, and that's the humor of
it.
PISTOL. O braggart vile, and damned furious
  wight!

65 The grave doth gape, and doting death is near;
Therefore exhale.
BARDOLPH. Hear me, hear me what I say. He that
strikes the first stroke, I'll run him up to the
hilts, as I am a soldier.   [Draws.]
PISTOL. An oath of mickle° might, and fury shall

70 abate.
Give me thy fist, thy forefoot to me give.
Thy spirits are most tall.
NYM. I will cut thy throat, one time or other, in
fair terms.
That is the humor of it.

75 PISTOL. "Couple a gorge!"°
That is the word. I thee defy again.
O hound of Crete, think'st thou my spouse to
  get?
No; to the spital° go,
And from the powd'ring tub° of infamy

80 Fetch forth the lazar kite of Cressid's kind,°
Doll Tearsheet° she by name, and her espouse.
I have, and I will hold, the quondam Quickly°
For the only she; and—pauca,° there's enough.
Go to.

[Enter the BOY.]

BOY. Mine host Pistol, you must come to my   85
master,° and you, hostess. He is very sick, and
would to bed. Good Bardolph, put thy face
between his sheets, and do the office of a warm-
ing pan.° Faith, he's very ill.
BARDOLPH. Away, you rogue!   90
HOSTESS. By my troth, he'll yield the crow a pud-
ding° one of these days. The king has killed his
heart. Good husband, come home presently.°
        [Exeunt HOSTESS and BOY.]
BARDOLPH. Come, shall I make you two friends?
We must to France together. Why the devil   95
should we keep knives to cut one another's
throats?
PISTOL. Let floods o'erswell, and fiends for food
howl on!
NYM. You'll pay me the eight shillings I won of you
at betting?
PISTOL. Base is the slave that pays.   100
NYM. That now I will have. That's the humor of it.
PISTOL. As manhood shall compound.° Push home.
        [They draw.]
BARDOLPH. By this sword, he that makes the first
thrust, I'll kill him; by this sword, I will.
PISTOL. Sword is an oath, and oaths must have
their course.   105
BARDOLPH. Corporal Nym, an° thou wilt be
friends, be friends. An thou wilt not, why, then,
be enemies with me too. Prithee, put up.
NYM. I shall have my eight shillings I won of you at
betting?   110
PISTOL. A noble° shalt thou have, and present° pay,
And liquor likewise will I give to thee,
And friendship shall combine, and brotherhood.
I'll live by Nym, and Nym shall live by me.
Is not this just? For I shall sutler° be   115
Unto the camp, and profits will accrue.
Give me thy hand.
NYM. I shall have my noble?
PISTOL. In cash most justly paid.
NYM. Well, then, that's the humor of't.   120
        [Re-enter HOSTESS.]
HOSTESS. As ever you came of women, come in
quickly to Sir John. Ah, poor heart! He is so
shaked of a burning quotidian tertian° that it is

---

mervailous marvelous   *perdy* per Dieu
can take i.e., catch fire, be touched off
Barbason name of a friend, presumably coined by Nym
mickle great
"Couple a gorge" Pistol's French for *couper la gorge*, cut
  the throat
spital hospital
powd'ring tub hot tub for sweating out venereal disease
lazar . . . kind leprous beggar like Cressida (see
  Henryson's poem "Testament of Cresseid")
Doll Tearsheet female companion of Falstaff in
  2Henry IV
quondam Quickly the former Mistress Quickly is now
  Pistol's wife
pauca in few words

my master Falstaff
face . . . pan Bardolph's fiery face is described in Act
  III, scene vi
he'll . . . pudding the Boy will be hanged and left for
  crow feed
presently immediately
As . . . compound as valor shall decide   *an* if
noble a coin worth six shillings and eight pence
present immediate   *sutler* provisioner
quotidian tertian literally, a daily fever that recurs every
  third day (the Hostess, as usual, is confused in her terms

most lamentable to behold. Sweet men, come
125   to him.
NYM. The king hath run bad humors° on the
  knight, that's the even of it.
PISTOL. Nym, thou hast spoke the right;
  His heart is fracted and corroborate.°
130 NYM. The king is a good king. But it must be as it
  may; he passes some humors and careers.°
PISTOL. Let us condole the knight; for, lambkins,
  we will live.

SCENE ii
Southampton. A council chamber.

[*Enter* EXETER, BEDFORD, *and* WESTMORELAND.]
BEDFORD. 'Fore God, his grace is bold, to trust
  these traitors.
EXETER. They shall be apprehended by and by.°
WESTMORELAND. How smooth and even they do
  bear themselves!
  As if allegiance in their bosoms sat,
5   Crowned with faith and constant loyalty.
BEDFORD. The king hath note of all that they
  intend,
  By interception which they dream not of.
EXETER. Nay, but the man that was his bedfellow,
  Whom he hath dull'd and cloy'd with gracious
    favor—
10   That he should, for a foreign purse, so sell
  His sovereign's life to death and treachery!
  [*Trumpets sound. Enter* KING HENRY, SCROOP,
    CAMBRIDGE, GREY, *and* ATTENDANTS.]
KING. Now sits the wind fair, and we will aboard.
  My Lord of Cambridge, and my kind Lord of
    Masham,
  And you, my gentle knight, give me your
    thoughts.
15   Think you not that the powers we bear with us
  Will cut their passage through the force of
    France,
  Doing the execution and the act
  For which we have in head° assembled them?
SCROOP. No doubt, my liege, if each man do his
  best.
20 KING. I doubt not that, since we are well persuaded
  We carry not a heart with us from hence
  That grows not in a fair consent with ours,

Nor leave not one behind that doth not wish
  Success and conquest to attend on us.
CAMBRIDGE. Never was monarch better fear'd and
  lov'd   25
  Than is your majesty. There's not, I think, a
    subject
  That sits in heart-grief and uneasiness
  Under the sweet shade of your government.
GREY. True. Those that were your father's enemies
  Have steep'd their galls in honey, and do serve
    you   30
  With hearts create° of duty and of zeal.
KING. We therefore have great cause of thankful-
  ness,
  And shall forget the office° of our hand
  Sooner than quittance° of desert and merit
  According to the weight and worthiness.   35
SCROOP. So service shall with steeled sinews toil,
  And labor shall refresh itself with hope,
  To do your grace incessant services.
KING. We judge no less. Uncle of Exeter,
  Enlarge° the man committed yesterday   40
  That rail'd against our person. We consider
  It was excess of wine that set him on,
  And on his more advice° we pardon him.
SCROOP. That's mercy, but too much security.°
  Let him be punish'd, sovereign, lest example   45
  Breed, by his sufferance,° more of such a kind.
KING. O, let us yet be merciful.
CAMBRIDGE. So may your highness, and yet punish
  too.
GREY. Sir,
  You show great mercy if you give him life,   50
  After the taste° of much correction.
KING. Alas, your too much love and care of me
  Are heavy orisons° 'gainst this poor wretch!
  If little faults, proceeding on distemper,°
  Shall not be wink'd at, how shall we stretch our
    eye   55
  When capital crimes, chew'd, swallow'd, and
    digested,
  Appear before us? We'll yet enlarge that man,
  Though Cambridge, Scroop, and Grey, in their
    dear care
  And tender preservation of our person,
  Would have him punish'd. And now to our
    French causes.   60
  Who are the late commissioners?

---

run . . . humors i.e., afflicted him with ills
fracted . . . corroborate Pistol's nonsense: fractured and
  joined together
passes . . . careers indulges in some whims and wild
  gallops
apprehended . . . by arrested at once
in head i.e., as an army

create composed   *office* function
quittance requital, reward   *Enlarge* free
his . . . advice his better thoughts (his sobering up)
security overconfidence
by . . . sufferance by allowance made for him
taste experience   *heavy orisons* weighty prayers
distemper drunkenness

CAMBRIDGE. I one, my lord.
　　Your highness bade me ask for it° today.
SCROOP. So did you me, my liege.
65　GREY. And I, my royal sovereign.
KING. Then, Richard Earl of Cambridge, there is
　　yours;
　　There yours, Lord Scroop of Masham; and, sir
　　knight,
　　Grey of Northumberland, this same is yours.
　　Read them, and know I know your worthiness.
70　My Lord of Westmoreland, and uncle Exeter,
　　We will aboard tonight. Why, how now, gentle-
　　men!
　　What see you in those papers that you lose
　　So much complexion? Look ye, how they
　　change!
　　Their cheeks are papers. Why, what read you
　　there
75　That hath so cowarded and chas'd your blood
　　Out of appearance?
CAMBRIDGE. 　　　　　　I do confess my fault,
　　And do submit me to your highness' mercy.
GREY and SCROOP. To which we all appeal.
KING. The mercy that was quick° in us but late,
80　By your own counsel is suppress'd and kill'd.
　　You must not dare, for shame, to talk of mercy,
　　For your own reasons turn into your bosoms
　　As dogs upon their masters, worrying you.
　　See you, my princes and my noble peers,
　　These English monsters! My Lord of Cam-
　　bridge here,
85　You know how apt our love was to accord°
　　To furnish him with all appertinents°
　　Belonging to his honor; and this man
　　Hath, for a few light crowns, lightly conspir'd
90　And sworn unto the practices° of France
　　To kill us here in Hampton. To the which
　　This knight, no less for bounty bound to us
　　Than Cambridge is, hath likewise sworn. But, O,
　　What shall I say to thee, Lord Scroop? Thou
　　cruel,
95　Ingrateful, savage, and inhuman creature!
　　Thou that didst bear the key of all my counsels,
　　That knew'st the very bottom of my soul,
　　That almost mightst have coin'd me into gold,
　　Wouldst thou have practic'd on me for thy
　　use°—
100　May it be possible that foreign hire
　　Could out of thee extract one spark of evil
　　That might annoy my finger? 'Tis so strange

That, though the truth of it stands off as gross
As black and white, my eye will scarcely see it.
Treason and murder ever kept together,　　　105
As two yoke-devils sworn to either's purpose,
Working so grossly in a natural° cause
That admiration° did not hoop° at them.
But thou, 'gainst all proportion,° didst bring in
Wonder to wait on treason and on murder.　　110
And whatsoever cunning fiend it was
That wrought upon thee so preposterously
Hath got the voice° in hell for excellence.
All other devils that suggest by treasons
Do botch and bungle up damnation　　　　115
With patches, colors, and with forms being
　fetch'd
From glist'ring semblances of piety.°
But he that temper'd thee° bade thee stand up,
Gave thee no instance why thou shouldst do
　treason,
Unless to dub thee with the name of traitor.　120
If that same demon that hath gull'd° thee thus
Should with his lion gait° walk the whole
　world,
He might return to vasty Tartar° back,
And tell the legions "I can never win
A soul so easy as that Englishman's."　　　125
O, how hast thou with jealousy° infected
The sweetness of affiance!° Show° men dutiful?
Why, so didst thou. Seem they grave and
　learned?
Why, so didst thou. Come they of noble family?
Why, so didst thou. Seem they religious?　　130
Why, so didst thou. Or are they spare in diet,
Free from gross passion or of mirth or anger,
Constant in spirit, not swerving with the blood,°
Garnish'd and deck'd in modest complement,°
Not working with the eye without the ear,　　135
And but in purged judgment trusting neither?°
Such and so finely bolted° didst thou seem.

---

natural　i.e., natural for them　　*admiration*　wonder
hoop　whoop
'gainst . . . proportion　in contradiction of all natural form
　and order
voice　vote
botch . . piety　clumsily patch and cover over with
　external appearances, put together from shining,
　seemingly pious motives
temper'd thee　shaped you to his purpose　　*gull'd*　duped
lion gait　(see 1 Peter 5:8, "the devil, as a roaring lion,
　walketh about, seeking whom he may devour")
Tartar　hell　　*jealousy*　suspicion　　*affiance*　trust
show　seem
blood　passions　　*modest complement*　mild demeanor
Not . . . neither　not judging by the eye alone without
　hearing the case, and trusting neither eye nor ear but
　with free ("impartial") judgment
bolted　sifted, like flour; hence refined, purified

---

it　i.e., the official appointment
quick　living　　*accord*　agree
appertinents　things pertinent　　*practices*　intrigues
practic'd . . . use　plotted against me for your own ends

And thus thy fall hath left a kind of blot
To mark the full-fraught man and best indu'd°
140 With some suspicion. I will weep for thee,
For this revolt of thine, methinks, is like
Another fall of man.—Their faults are open.
Arrest them to the answer of the law;
And God acquit them of their practices!
145 EXETER. I arrest thee of high treason by the name of
Richard Earl of Cambridge.
I arrest thee of high treason by the name of
Henry Lord Scroop of Masham.
I arrest thee of high treason by the name of
150 Thomas Grey, knight, of Northumberland.
SCROOP. Our purposes God justly hath discover'd,°
And I repent my fault more than my death,
Which I beseech your highness to forgive,
Although my body pay the price of it.
CAMBRIDGE. For me, the gold of France did not
155 seduce,
Although I did admit it as a motive
The sooner to effect what I intended.
But God be thanked for prevention,
Which I in sufferance° heartily will rejoice,
160 Beseeching God and you to pardon me.
GREY. Never did faithful subject more rejoice
At the discovery of most dangerous treason
Than I do at this hour joy o'er myself,
Prevented from a damned enterprise.
165 My fault, but not my body, pardon, sovereign.
KING. God quit° you in his mercy! Hear your
sentence.
You have conspir'd against our royal person,
Join'd with an enemy proclaim'd, and from his
coffers
Receiv'd the golden earnest° of our death,
Wherein you would have sold your king to
170 slaughter,
His princes and his peers to servitude,
His subjects to oppression and contempt,
And his whole kingdom into desolation.
Touching our person seek we no revenge;
175 But we our kingdom's safety must so tender,
Whose ruin you have sought, that to her laws
We do deliver you. Get you therefore hence,
Poor miserable wretches, to your death,
The taste whereof God of his mercy give
180 You patience to endure, and true repentance
Of all your dear° offenses! Bear them hence.

[Exeunt CAMBRIDGE, SCROOP, and
GREY, guarded.]
Now, lords, for France, the enterprise whereof
Shall be to you, as us, like° glorious.
We doubt not of a fair and lucky war,
Since God so graciously hath brought to light   185
This dangerous treason lurking in our way
To hinder our beginnings. We doubt not now
But every rub° is smoothed on our way.
Then forth, dear countrymen. Let us deliver
Our puissance° into the hand of God,   190
Putting it straight in expedition.
Cheerly to sea; the signs° of war advance.
No king of England, if not king of France.

[Exeunt]

SCENE iii
London. Before a tavern.

[Enter PISTOL, HOSTESS, NYM, BARDOLPH, and
BOY.]
HOSTESS. Prithee, honeysweet husband, let me
bring thee to Staines.°
PISTOL. No; for my manly heart doth earn.°
Bardolph, be blithe. Nym, rouse thy vaunting
veins.
Boy, bristle thy courage up; for Falstaff he is
dead,   5
And we must earn° therefore.
BARDOLPH. Would I were with him, where-
some'er he is, either in heaven or in hell!
HOSTESS. Nay, sure, he's not in hell. He's in Arthur's
bosom,° if ever man went to Arthur's bosom.   10
A'° made a finer end and went away an it had
been any christom° child. A' parted even just
between twelve and one, even at the turning o'
the tide. For after I saw him fumble with the
sheets, and play with flowers, and smile upon   15
his fingers' ends, I knew there was but one way;
for his nose was as sharp as a pen, and a' babbled°
of green fields. "How now, Sir John!" quoth I.
"What, man! Be o' good cheer." So a' cried out
"God, God, God!" three or four times. Now I, 20
to comfort him, bid him a' should not think of

full-fraught . . . indu'd the fully laden and best endowed
(with estimable qualities) man
discover'd disclosed
sufferance i.e., in suffering death
quit acquit, absolve
golden earnest advance payment   dear grievous

like alike, equally
rub obstacle   puissance powers   signs standards
Staines (en route to Southampton)   earn grieve
Arthur's bosom the Hostess means Abraham's bosom,
i.e., heaven
A' he   christom just christened (innocent)
a' babbled . . . fields (the Folio reads "and a table of
greene fields"; present reading supplied by
Theobald, 1726)

God; I hoped there was no need to trouble himself with any such thoughts yet. So a' bade me
lay more clothes on his feet. I put my hand into
25 the bed and felt them, and they were as cold as
any stone; then I felt to his knees, and they were
as cold as any stone, and so upward and upward,
and all was as cold as any stone.
Nym. They say he cried out of sack.°
30 Hostess. Aye, that a' did.
Bardolph. And of women.
Hostess. Nay, that a' did not.
Boy. Yes, that a' did, and said they were devils
incarnate.°
35 Hostess. A' could never abide carnation; 'twas a
color he never liked.
Boy. A' said once, the devil would have him about
women.
Hostess. A' did in some sort, indeed, handle
40 women; but then he was rheumatic,° and talked
of the whore of Babylon.°
Boy. Do you not remember, a' saw a flea stick
upon Bardolph's nose, and a' said it was a black
soul burning in hellfire?
45 Bardolph. Well, the fuel is gone that maintained
that fire; that's all the riches I got in his service.
Nym. Shall we shog?° The king will be gone from
Southampton.
Pistol. Come, let's away. My love, give me thy
lips.
50 Look to my chattels and my movables.
Let senses rule; the word is "Pitch and Pay."°
Trust none;
For oaths are straws, men's faiths are wafer
cakes,°
And hold-fast is the only dog,° my duck.
55 Therefore, Caveto° be thy counselor.
Go, clear thy crystals.° Yokefellows in arms,
Let us to France, like horseleeches, my boys,
To suck, to suck, the very blood to suck!
Boy. And that's but unwholesome food, they
say.
60 Pistol. Touch her soft mouth, and march.
Bardolph. Farewell, hostess.   [Kissing her.]

Nym. I cannot kiss, that is the humor of it; but,
adieu.
Pistol. Let housewifery appear; keep close, I thee
command.
Hostess. Farewell; adieu.   [Exeunt] 65

SCENE iv
France. The KING'*s palace.*

[*Flourish. Enter the* FRENCH KING, *the* DAUPHIN,
the DUKES OF BERRI *and* BRETAGNE, *the*
CONSTABLE, *and others.*]

FRENCH KING. Thus comes the English with full
power upon us,
And more than carefully it us concerns
To answer royally in our defenses.
Therefore the Dukes of Berri and of Bretagne,
Of Brabant and of Orleans shall make forth,   5
And you, Prince Dauphin, with all swift dis-
patch,
To line° and new repair our towns of war
With men of courage and with means defendant.
From England his approaches makes as fierce
As waters to the sucking of a gulf.°   10
It fits us then to be as provident
As fear may teach us out of late examples°
Left by the fatal and neglected° English
Upon our fields.
DAUPHIN.   My most redoubted father,
It is most meet we arm us 'gainst the foe;   15
For peace itself should not so dull a kingdom,
Though war nor no known quarrel were in
question,
But that defenses, musters, preparations
Should be maintain'd, assembled, and collected
As were a war in expectation.   20
Therefore I say 'tis meet we all go forth
To view the sick and feeble parts of France.
And let us do it with no show of fear;
No, with no more than if we heard that England
Were busied with a Whitsun morris dance.°   25
For, my good liege, she is so idly king'd,
Her scepter so fantastically borne
By a vain, giddy, shallow, humorous° youth,
That fear attends her not.
CONSTABLE.   O peace, Prince Dauphin!
You are too much mistaken in this king.   30

---

cried . . . sack cried out against wine
incarnate in human shape
rheumatic (possibly the Hostess means *lunatic*)
whore of Babylon the "scarlet woman" of Revelations
    17:4–5
shog i.e., "shove off"
Let . . . Pay i.e., use common sense, and accept only
    cash
wafer cakes i.e., as easily broken as
hold-fast . . . dog see the proverb, "Brag is a good dog,
    but Hold-fast is a better"
Caveto beware, take care
clear . . . crystals wipe your eyes

line fortify   *gulf* Whirlpool
late examples i.e., the battles of Crécy and Poitiers (see
    lines 55–65 below)
neglected underestimated
Whitsun . . . dance i.e., with mere fun (folk dancing
    celebrated the arrival of summer)
humorous capricious

Question your grace the late ambassadors,
With what great state he heard their embassy,
How well supplied with noble counselors,
How modest in exception, and withal
35 How terrible in constant resolution,
And you shall find his vanities forespent°
Were but the outside of the Roman Brutus,°
Covering discretion with a coat of folly,
As gardeners do with ordure° hide those roots
40 That shall first spring and be most delicate.
DAUPHIN. Well, 'tis not so, my lord high constable;
But though we think it so, it is no matter.
In cases of defense 'tis best to weigh
The enemy more mighty than he seems.
45 So the proportions of defense are fill'd,°
Which of a weak and niggardly projection°
Doth, like a miser, spoil his coat with scanting
A little cloth.
FRENCH KING.   Think we King Harry strong;
And, princes, look you strongly arm to meet
50   him.
The kindred of him hath been flesh'd° upon us,
And he is bred out of that bloody strain
That haunted us in our familiar paths.
Witness our too much memorable shame
55 When Cressy° battle fatally was struck
And all our princes captiv'd by the hand
Of that black name, Edward, Black Prince of
    Wales,
Whiles that his mountain sire,° on mountain
    standing,
Up in the air, crown'd with the golden sun,
60 Saw his heroical seed, and smil'd to see him,
Mangle the work of nature and deface
The pattern that by God and by French fathers
Had twenty years° been made. This is a stem
Of that victorious stock, and let us fear
65 The native mightiness and fate of him.
    [Enter a MESSENGER.]
MESSENGER. Ambassadors from Harry King of
    England
Do crave admittance to your majesty.
FRENCH KING. We'll give them present audience.
    Go, and bring them.
    [Exeunt MESSENGER and certain LORDS.]

You see this chase is hotly follow'd, friends.
DAUPHIN. Turn head,° and stop pursuit; for
    coward dogs
Most spend their mouths when what they seem
    to threaten   70
Runs far before them. Good my sovereign,
Take up the English short, and let them know
Of what a monarchy you are the head.
Self-love, my liege, is not so vile a sin
As self-neglecting.
    [Re-enter LORDS, with EXETER and train.]
FRENCH KING.   From our brother England?   75
EXETER. From him; and thus he greets your
    majesty.
He wills you, in the name of God Almighty,
That you divest yourself, and lay apart
The borrow'd glories that by gift of heaven,
By law of nature and of nations, 'long   80
To him and to his heirs; namely, the crown
And all wide-stretched honors that pertain
By custom and the ordinance of times°
Unto the crown of France. That you may know
'Tis no sinister nor no awkward° claim,   85
Pick'd from the worm holes of long-vanish'd
    days,
Nor from the dust of old oblivion rak'd,
He sends you this most memorable line,°
In every branch truly demonstrative,°
Willing you overlook° this pedigree.   90
And when you find him evenly° deriv'd
From his most fam'd of famous ancestors,
Edward the Third, he bids you then resign
Your crown and kingdom, indirectly° held
From him the native and true challenger.   95
FRENCH KING. Or else what follows?
EXETER. Bloody constraint; for if you hide the
    crown
Even in your hearts, there will he rake for it.
Therefore in fierce tempest is he coming,
In thunder and in earthquake, like a Jove,   100
That, if requiring° fail, he will compel;
And bids you, in the bowels of the Lord,°
Deliver up the crown, and to take mercy
On the poor souls for whom this hungry war
Opens his vasty jaws; and on your head   105

forespent former
Brutus not Marcus, but Lucius Junius, whose pretended folly deceived the Tarquin, of whom he rid Rome
ordure manure
So . . . fill'd thus the defenses are made adequate
projection estimate
flesh'd initiated into bloody war   *Cressy* Crécy
mountain sire i.e., towering over other men
patterns . . . years i.e., young French soldiers of twenty years

Turn head make a stand
ordinance of times traditional usage
sinister . . . awkward irregular (left-handed) . . . indirect
line line of descent
demonstrative i.e., of the legitimacy of his claim
Willing . . . overlook urging you to examine
evenly directly
indirectly i.e., not in the direct line of descent
requiring demanding
in . . . Lord by the Lord's mercy

Turning the widows' tears, the orphans' cries,
The dead men's blood, the pining maidens groans
For husbands, fathers, and betrothed lovers
That shall be swallow'd in this controversy.
110 This is his claim, his threat'ning, and my message—
Unless the Dauphin be in presence here,
To whom expressly I bring greeting too.
FRENCH KING. For us, we will consider of this further.
Tomorrow shall you bear our full intent
Back to our brother England.
115 DAUPHIN.   For the Dauphin,
I stand here for him. What to him from England?
EXETER. Scorn and defiance, slight regard, contempt,
And anything that may not misbecome
The mighty sender, doth he prize you at.
120 Thus says my king. An if your father's highness
Do not, in grant of all demands at large,
Sweeten the bitter mock you sent his majesty,
He'll call you to so hot an answer of it
That caves and womby vaultages° of France
125 Shall chide your trespass, and return your mock
In second accent of his ordinance.°

womby vaultages   womblike caverns
second . . . ordinance   echo of his cannon

DAUPHIN. Say, if my father render fair return,
It is against my will; for I desire
Nothing but odds with England. To that end,
As matching to his youth and vanity,   130
I did present him with the Paris balls.
EXETER. He'll make your Paris Louvre° shake for it,
Were it the mistress court of mighty Europe.
And, be assur'd, you'll find a difference,
As we his subjects have in wonder found,   135
Between the promise of his greener days
And these he masters now. Now he weighs time
Even to the utmost gram. That you shall read
In your own losses, if he stay in France.
FRENCH KING. Tomorrow shall you know our mind at full.   140
EXETER. Dispatch us with all speed, lest that our king
Come here himself to question our delay;
For he is footed in this land already.
FRENCH KING. You shall be soon dispatch'd with fair conditions.
A night is but small breath and little pause   145
To answer matters of this consequence.
                              [Flourish. Exeunt.]

Paris Louvre   the royal palace (with pun lover for
mistress court in next line, with continuing play on
tennis court)

ACT III

PROLOGUE

[Enter CHORUS.]
CHORUS. Thus with imagin'd wing° our swift scene flies
In motion of no less celerity
Than that of thought. Suppose that you have seen
The well-appointed° king at Hampton pier
5 Embark his royalty, and his brave° fleet
With silken streamers the young Phœbus° fanning.
Play with your fancies, and in them behold
Upon the hempen tackle shipboys climbing;

imagin'd wing   imagination's wing
well-appointed   well equipped   brave   splendid
young Phoebus   the rising sun

Hear the shrill whistle which doth order give
To sounds confus'd; behold the threaden° sails, 10
Borne with th' invisible and creeping wind,
Draw the huge bottoms through the furrow'd sea,
Breasting the lofty surge. O, do but think
You stand upon the rivage° and behold
A city on th' inconstant billows dancing;   15
For so appears this fleet majestical,
Holding due course to Harfleur. Follow, follow.
Grapple your minds to sternage of this navy,
And leave your England as dead midnight still,°
Guarded with grandsires, babies, and old women,   20
Either past or not arriv'd to pith° and puissance;

threaden   linen   rivage   shore
as . . . still   i.e., as still as dead midnight   pith   strength

For who is he, whose chin is but enrich'd
With one appearing hair, that will not follow
These cull'd and choice-drawn cavaliers to
  France?
Work, work your thoughts, and therein see a
25 siege;
Behold the ordnance on their carriages,
With fatal mouths gaping on girded° Harfleur.
Suppose th' ambassador from the French
  comes back,
Tells Harry that the king doth offer him
30 Katharine his daughter, and with her, to dowry,
Some petty and unprofitable dukedoms.
The offer likes not, and the nimble gunner
With linstock° now the devilish cannon touches,
          [*Alarum, and chambers° go off.*]
And down goes all before them. Still be kind,
35 And eke out our performance with your mind.
          [*Exit*]

Dishonor not your mothers; now attest
That those whom you call'd fathers did beget
  you.
Be copy now to men of grosser blood,
And teach them how to war. And you, good
  yeomen,   25
Whose limbs were made in England, show us
  here
The mettle of your pasture.° Let us swear
That you are worth your breeding, which I
  doubt not,
For there is none of you so mean and base
That hath not noble luster in your eyes.   30
I see you stand like greyhounds in the slips,°
Straining upon the start. The game's afoot.
Follow your spirit, and upon this charge
Cry "God for Harry, England, and Saint
  George!"°

          [*Exeunt. Alarum, and chambers go off.*]

SCENE i
France. Before Harfleur.

[*Alarum. Enter* KING HENRY, EXETER, BEDFORD,
  GLOUCESTER, *and* SOLDIERS, *with scaling-ladders.*]
KING. Once more unto the breach, dear friends,
    once more,
  Or close the wall up with our English dead.
  In peace there's nothing so becomes a man
  As modest stillness and humility.
5 But when the blast of war blows in our ears,
  Then imitate the action of the tiger:
  Stiffen the sinews, summon up the blood,
  Disguise fair nature with hard-favor'd° rage;
  Then lend the eye a terrible aspect;
10 Let it pry through the portage° of the head
  Like the brass cannon; let the brow o'erwhelm
    it
  As fearfully as doth a galled rock
  O'erhang and jutty° his confounded° base,
  Swill'd with the wild and wasteful ocean.
15 Now set the teeth and stretch the nostril wide,
  Hold hard the breath, and bend up every spirit
  To his full height. On, on, you noblest English,
  Whose blood is fet° from fathers of war-proof!°
  Fathers that, like so many Alexanders,
20 Have in these parts from morn till even fought,
  And sheath'd their swords for lack of argument.

SCENE ii
The same.

[*Enter* NYM, BARDOLPH, PISTOL, *and* BOY.]
BARDOLPH. On, on, on, on, on! To the breach, to
  the breach!
NYM. Pray thee, corporal, stay. The knocks are too
  hot, and, for mine own part, I have not a case of
  lives. The humor of it is too hot, that is the very   5
  plainsong° of it.
PISTOL. The plainsong is most just, for humors do
  abound.

    Knocks go and come; God's vassals drop and die;
      And sword and shield
        In bloody field   10
    Doth win immortal fame.

BOY. Would I were in an alehouse in London! I
  would give all my fame for a pot of ale and
  safety.
PISTOL. And I: 15

    If wishes would prevail with me,
      My purpose should not fail with me,
        But thither would I hie.

BOY.

      As duly, but not as truly,°
        As bird doth sing on bough.   20

---

girded surrounded
linstock stick used in touching off the cannon
chambers small cannon
hard-favor'd stern-faced   *portage* porthole
jutty jut over   *confounded* overwhelmed
fet fetched   *war-proof* proved in war

mettle . . . pasture quality of your upbringing
slips leashes
Saint George patron saint of England (here pronounced
  jarge)
plainsong simple tune; here, plain truth
duly . . . truly surely . . . in tune

[*Enter* FLUELLEN.]

FLUELLEN. Up to the breach, you dogs! Avaunt, you
cullions!°   [*Driving them forward.*]

PISTOL. Be merciful, great duke, to men of mould.°
Abate thy rage, abate thy manly rage,
Abate thy rage, great duke!
Good bawcock,° bate thy rage; use lenity, sweet
25 chuck!

NYM. These be good humors! Your honor wins
bad humors.   [*Exeunt all but* BOY.]

BOY. As young as I am, I have observed these three
swashers.° I am boy to them all three, but all
30 they three, though they would serve me, could
not be man to me; for indeed three such antics°
do not amount to a man. For Bardolph, he is
white-livered and red-faced; by the means
whereof a' faces it out, but fights not. For Pistol,
35 he hath a killing tongue and a quiet sword; by
the means whereof a' breaks words, and keeps
whole weapons. For Nym, he hath heard that
men of few words are the best men, and therefore he scorns to say his prayers, lest a' should be
40 thought a coward; but his few bad words are
matched with as few good deeds, for a' never
broke any man's head but his own, and that was
against a post when he was drunk. They will
steal anything, and call it purchase. Bardolph
45 stole a lute case, bore it twelve leagues, and sold
it for three halfpence. Nym and Bardolph are
sworn brothers in filching, and in Calais they
stole a fire-shovel. I knew by that piece of service
the men would carry coals.° They would have
50 me as familiar with men's pockets as their gloves
or their handkerchers; which makes much
against my manhood, if I should take from
another's pocket to put into mine, for it is plain
pocketing up of wrongs.° I must leave them and
55 seek some better service. Their villainy goes
against my weak stomach, and therefore I must
cast it up.°   [*Exit*]
[*Re-enter* FLUELLEN, GOWER *following.*]

GOWER. Captain Fluellen, you must come presently to the mines;° the Duke of Gloucester
60 would speak with you.

FLUELLEN. To the mines! Tell you the duke it is not
so good to come to the mines, for look you, the
mines is not according to the disciplines of the
war.° The concavities of it is not sufficient, for
look you, th' athversary, you may discuss unto   65
the duke, look you, is dig himself four yard
under the countermines. By Cheshu, I think a'
will plow up all, if there is not better directions.

GOWER. The Duke of Gloucester, to whom the
order of the siege is given, is altogether directed   70
by an Irishman, a very valiant gentleman, i'
faith.

FLUELLEN. It is Captain Macmorris, is it not?

GOWER. I think it be.

FLUELLEN. By Cheshu, he is an ass, as in the world.   75
I will verify as much in his beard.° He has no
more directions in the true disciplines of the
wars, look you, of the Roman disciplines, than
is a puppy dog.
[*Enter* MACMORRIS *and* CAPTAIN JAMY.]

GOWER. Here a' comes, and the Scots captain,   80
Captain Jamy, with him.

FLUELLEN. Captain Jamy is a marvelous falorous
gentleman, that is certain, and of great expedi-
tion° and knowledge in th' aunchient wars,
upon my particular knowledge of his directions.   85
By Cheshu, he will maintain his argument as
well as any military man in the world, in the
disciplines of the pristine wars of the Romans.

JAMY. I say gud-day, Captain Fluellen.

FLUELLEN. God-den to your worship, good Captain   90
James.

GOWER. How now, Captain Macmorris! Have you
quit the mines? Have the pioners° given o'er?

MACMORRIS. By Chrish, la! Tish ill done. The
work ish give over, the trompet sound the   95
retreat. By my hand, I swear, and my father's
soul, the work ish ill done; it ish give over. I
would have blowed up the town, so Chrish
save me, la! in an hour. O'tish ill done, tish ill
done. By my hand, tish ill done!   100

FLUELLEN. Captain Macmorris, I beseech you now,
will you voutsafe me, look you, a few disputa-
tions with you, as partly touching or concerning
the disciplines of the war, the Roman wars, in
the way of argument, look you, and friendly   105
communications; partly to satisfy my opinion,
and partly for the satisfaction, look you, of my
mind, as touching the direction of the military
discipline; that is the point.

JAMY. It sall be vary gud, gud feith, gud captains   110

Avaunt . . . cullions be off, you rascals
men of mould i.e., mere mortals
bawcock fine cock (French *beau coq*)
swashers swaggerers   *antics* clowns
carry coals do dirty work, bear insults
pocketing . . . wrongs bearing insults (with double
  meaning)
cast it up give it over (with double meaning)
mines those dug beneath the enemy walls

disciplines . . . war military science based on classical
  examples
in . . . beard to his face
expedition facility in disputation
pioners diggers, miners

bath, and I sall quit you with gud leve,° as I may pick occasion; that sall I, marry.

MACMORRIS. It is no time to discourse, so Chrish save me. The day is hot, and the weather, and
115 the wars, and the king, and the dukes. It is no time to discourse. The town is beseeched, and the trumpet call us to the breach, and we talk, and, be Chrish, do nothing. 'Tis shame for us all, so God sa' me, 'tis shame to stand still; it is
120 shame, by my hand, and there is throats to be cut, and works to be done, and there ish nothing done, so Chrish sa' me, la!

JAMY. By the mess, ere theise eyes of mine take themselves to slomber, ay'll do gud service, or
125 ay'll lig i' the grund for it; ay, or got to death, and ay'll pay 't as valorously as I may, that sall I suerly do, that is the breff and the long. Marry, I wad full fain hear some question 'tween you tway.

130 FLUELLEN. Captain Macmorris, I think, look you, under your correction, there is not many of your nation—

MACMORRIS. Of my nation! What ish my nation? Ish a villain, and a bastard, and a knave, and a
135 rascal. What ish my nation? Who talks of my nation?

FLUELLEN. Look you, if you take the matter otherwise than is meant, Captain Macmorris, peradventure I shall think you do not use me
140 with that affability as in discretion you ought to use me, look you, being as good a man as yourself, both in the disciplines of war, and in the derivation of my birth, and in other particularities.

145 MACMORRIS. I do not know you so good a man as myself. So Chrish save me, I will cut off your head.

GOWER. Gentlemen both, you will mistake° each other.

150 JAMY. A! That's a foul fault.   [A parley sounded.]
GOWER. The town sounds a parley.
FLUELLEN. Captain Macmorris, when there is more better opportunity to be required, look you, I will be so bold as to tell you I know the discip-
155 lines of war; and there is an end.   [Exeunt]

SCENE iii
The same. Before the gates.

[The GOVERNOR and some CITIZENS on the walls; the English forces below. Enter KING HENRY and his train.]

KING. How yet resolves the governor of the town?
    This is the latest parle we will admit.
    Therefore to our best mercy give yourselves,
    Or like to men proud of destruction
    Defy us to our worst; for, as I am a soldier,   5
    A name that in my thoughts becomes me best,
    If I begin the battery once again,
    I will not leave the half-achiev'd Harfleur
    Till in her ashes she lie buried.
    The gates of mercy shall be all shut up,   10
    And the flesh'd° soldier, rough and hard of heart,
    In liberty of bloody hand shall range
    With conscience wide as hell, mowing like grass
    Your fresh-fair virgins and your flowering infants.
    What is it then to me if impious war,   15
    Array'd in flames like to the prince of fiends,
    Do, with his smirch'd complexion, all fell° feats
    Enlink'd to waste and desolation?
    What is 't to me, when you yourselves are cause,
    If your pure maidens fall into the hand   20
    Of hot and forcing violation?
    What rein can hold licentious wickedness
    When down the hill he holds his fierce career?
    We may as bootless° spend our vain command
    Upon th' enraged soldiers in their spoil   25
    As send precepts to the leviathan
    To come ashore. Therefore, you men of Harfleur,
    Take pity of your town and of your people
    Whiles yet my soldiers are in my command,
    Whiles yet the cool and temperate wind of grace   30
    O'erblows the filthy and contagious clouds
    Of heady murder, spoil, and villainy.
    If not, why, in a moment look to see
    The blind° and bloody soldier with foul hand
    Defile the locks of your shrill-shrieking daughters,   35
    Your fathers taken by the silver beards
    And their most reverend heads dash'd to the walls,
    Your naked infants spitted upon pikes,

---

quit . . . leve   answer with your good leave
will mistake   are determined to misunderstand

flesh'd   whose sword has tasted blood   fell   savage
bootless   uselessly   blind   i.e., to deeds of horror

Whiles the mad mothers with their howls confus'd
40   Do break the clouds as did the wives of Jewry
     At Herod's bloody-hunting slaughtermen.°
     What say you? Will you yield, and this avoid,
     Or, guilty in defense, be thus destroy'd?
     GOVERNOR. Our expectation hath this day an end.
45   The Dauphin, whom of succors we entreated,
     Returns us that his powers are yet not ready
     To raise so great a siege. Therefore, great king,
     We yield our town and lives to thy soft mercy.
     Enter our gates; dispose of us and ours;
50   For we no longer are defensible.
     KING. Open your gates. Come, uncle Exeter,
     Go you and enter Harfleur; there remain,
     And fortify it strongly 'gainst the French.
     Use mercy to them all. For us, dear uncle,
55   The winter coming on, and sickness growing
     Upon our soldiers, we will retire to Calais.
     Tonight in Harfleur will we be your guest;
     Tomorrow for the march are we addrest.
     [*Flourish. The* KING *and his train enter the town.*]

                    SCENE iv
               The FRENCH KING's *palace.*

          [*Enter* KATHARINE *and* ALICE.]

     KATHARINE.° Alice, tu as été en Angleterre, et tu
     parles bien le langage.
     ALICE. Un peu, madame.
     KATHARINE. Je te prie, m'enseignez; il faut que
5   j'apprenne à parler. Comment appelez-vous la
     main en Anglois?
     ALICE. La main? Elle est appelée de hand.
     KATHARINE. De hand. Et les doigts?
     ALICE. Les doigts? Ma foi, j'oublie les doigts; mais
10   je me souviendrai. Les doigts? Je pense qu'ils
     sont appelés de fingres; oui, de fingres.
     KATHARINE. La main, de hand; les doigts, de
     fingres. Je pense que je suis le bon écolier; j'ai
     gagné deux mots d'Anglois vîtement. Com-
15   ment appelez-vous les ongles?

Herod's . . . slaughtermen   (see Matthew 2:16–18)
Translation. KATHARINE. Alice, you have been in England,
    and you speak the language well.
ALICE. A little, madam.
KATHARINE. I pray you, teach me. I must learn to speak
    it. What do you call *la main* in English?
ALICE. *La main?* It is called de hand.
KATHARINE. De hand. And *les doights?*
ALICE. *Les doigts?* My faith, I forget *les doigts;* but I shall
    remember. *Les doigts?* I think they are called de fingres;
    yes, de fingres.
KATHARINE. *La main,* de hand; *les doigts,* de fingres. I think
    I am a good scholar; I have learned two English words
    quickly. What do you call *les ongles?*

     ALICE. Les ongles? Nous les appelons de nails.
     KATHARINE. De nails. Ecoutez; dites-moi si je
     parle bien: de hand, de fingres, et de nails.
     ALICE. C'est bien dit, madame; il est fort bon
     Anglois.   20
     KATHARINE. Dites-moi l'Anglois pour le bras.
     ALICE. De arm, madame.
     KATHARINE. Et le coude?
     ALICE. De elbow.
     KATHARINE. De elbow. Je m'en fais la répétition de   25
     tous les mots que vous m'avez appris dès à
     présent.
     ALICE. Il est trop difficile, madame, comme je
     pense.
     KATHARINE. Excusez-moi, Alice; écoutez: de hand,   30
     de fingres, de nails, de arma, de bilbow.
     ALICE. De elbow, madame.
     KATHARINE. O Seigneur Dieu, je m'en oublie! De
     elbow. Comment appelez-vous le col?
     ALICE. De neck, madame.   35
     KATHARINE. De nick. Et le menton?
     ALICE. De chin.
     KATHARINE. De sin. Le col, de nick; le menton, de
     sin.
     ALICE. Oui. Sauf votre honneur, en vérité, vous   40
     prononcez les mots aussi droit que les natifs
     d'Angleterre.
     KATHARINE. Je ne doute point d'apprendre, par le
     grace de Dieu, et en peu de temps.
     ALICE. N'avez vous pas déjà oublié ce que je vous   45
     ai enseigné?

ALICE. *Les ongles?* We call them de nails.
KATHARINE. De nails. Listen; tell me if I speak well: de
    hand, de fingres, and de nails.
ALICE. That is correct, my lady; it is very good English.
KATHARINE. Tell me the English for *le bras.*
ALICE. De arm, madam.
KATHARINE. And *le coude?*
ALICE. De elbow.
KATHARINE. De elbow. I shall repeat all the words you
    have taught me up to now.
ALICE. It is too hard, madam, I think.
KATHARINE. Pardon me, Alice; listen: de hand, de
    fingres, de nails, de arma, de bilbow.
ALICE. De elbow, my lady.
KATHARINE. Oh Lord, I forgot! De elbow. What do you
    call *le col?*
ALICE. De neck, madam.
KATHARINE. De nick. And *le menton?*
ALICE. De chin.
KATHARINE. De sin. *Le col,* de nick; *le menton,* de sin.
ALICE. Yes. Saving your grace, truly, you pronounce the
    words as well as the English do.
KATHARINE. I do not doubt that I shall learn, by the grace
    of God, and in a short while.
ALICE. Have you not already forgotten what I have
    taught you?

KATHARINE. Non, je reciterai à vous promptement:
de hand, de fingres, de mails—
ALICE. De nails, madame.
50 KATHARINE. De nails, de arm, de ilbow.
ALICE. Sauf votre honneur, de elbow.
KATHARINE. Ainsi dis-je; de elbow, de nick, et de
sin. Comment appelez-vous le pied et la robe?
ALICE. De foot, madame; et de coun.
55 KATHARINE. De foot et de coun! O Seigneur Dieu!
Ce sont mots de son mauvais, corruptible, gros,
et impudique, et non pour les dames d'honneur
d'user. Je ne voudrais prononcer ces mots
devant les seigneurs de France pour tout le
60 monde! Foh! le foot et le coun! Néanmoins,
je réciterai une autre fois ma lecon ensemble: de
hand, de fingres, de nails, de arm, de elbow, de
nick, de sin, de foot, de coun.
ALICE. Excellent, madame!
65 KATHARINE. C'est assez pour une fois. Allons-nous
à dîner.   [Exeunt]

SCENE v
The same.

[*Enter the* KING OF FRANCE, *the* DAUPHIN, *the*
DUKE OF BOURBON, *the* CONSTABLE OF
FRANCE, *and others.*]
FRENCH KING. 'Tis certain he hath pass'd the river
Somme.
CONSTABLE. And if he be not fought withal, my
lord,
Let us not live in France; let us quit all,
And give our vineyards to a barbarous people.
5 DAUPHIN. *O Dieu vivant!* Shall a few sprays° of us,
The emptying of our father's luxury,°
Our scions, put in° wild and savage stock,

KATHARINE. No, I shall recite for you at once: de hand, de
fingres, de mails.
ALICE. De nails, madam.
KATHARINE. De nails, de arm, de ilbow.
ALICE. Saving your grace, de elbow.
KATHARINE. That's what I said; de elbow, de nick, and de
sin. What do you call *le pied* and *la robe?*
ALICE. De foot, madam; and de coun.
KATHARINE. De foot and de coun! Oh, good Lord! These
are bad words, wicked, gross, and improper, and not
for ladies of honor to use. I would not pronounce these
words in front of French gentlemen for all the world!
Foh! le foot and le coun! Nevertheless, I shall recite all
my lesson once more: de hand, de fingres, de nails, de
arm, de elbow, de nick, de sin, de foot, de coun.
ALICE. Excellent, my lady.
KATHARINE. That's enough for one time. Let's go to
dinner.

sprays offshoots   *luxury* lust   *put in* grafted upon

Spirt° up so suddenly into the clouds,
And overlook° their grafters?
BOURBON. Normans, but bastard Normans, Nor-
man bastards!   10
Mort de ma vie! If they march along
Unfought withal, but I will sell my dukedom,
To buy a slobb'ry° and a dirty farm
In that nookshotten isle of Albion.°
CONSTABLE. *Dieu de batailles!* Where have they this
mettle?   15
Is not their climate foggy, raw, and dull,
On whom, as in despite, the sun looks pale,
Killing their fruit with frowns? Can sodden°
water,
A drench for sur-rein'd jades,° their barley
broth,°
Decoct° their cold blood to such valiant heat?   20
And shall our quick blood, spirited with wine,
Seem frosty? O, for honor of our land,
Let us not hang like roping° icicles
Upon our houses' thatch, whiles a more frosty
people
Sweat drops of gallant youth in our rich fields!— 25
Poor we may call them in their native lords.°
DAUPHIN. By faith and honor,
Our madams mock at us, and plainly say
Our mettle is bred out, and they will give
Their bodies to the lust of English youth,   30
To new-store France with bastard warriors.
BOURBON. They bid us to the English dancing
schools
And teach lavoltas high and swift corantos,°
Saying our grace is only in our heels
And that we are most lofty runaways.   35
FRENCH KING. Where is Montjoy the herald?
Speed him hence.
Let him greet England with our sharp defiance.
Up, princes! And, with spirit of honor edg'd
More sharper than your swords, hie to the field.
Charles Delabreth, high constable of France,   40
You Dukes of Orleans, Bourbon, and of Berri,
Alençon, Brabant, Bar, and Burgundy;
Jaques Chatillon, Rambures, Vaudemont,
Beaumont, Grandpré, Roussi, and Fauconberg,
Foix, Lestrale, Bouciqualt, and Charolois;   45

Spirt spurt, sprout   *overlook* overtop
slobb'ry muddy
nookshotten . . . Albion England, irregularly shaped, full
of angles and corners (see map of England)
sodden boiled
drench . . . jades medicinal dose for overridden horses
barley broth i.e., ale   *Decoct* warm up
roping dangling
Poor . . . lords we may better call our rich fields poor,
judging by those who are their lords
lavoltas . . . corantos fast-moving dances

High dukes, great princes, barons, lords, and
    knights,
For your great seats now quit you of great
    shames.°
Bar Harry England that sweeps through our
    land
With pennons painted in the blood of Harfleur.
50 Rush on his host,° as doth the melted snow
Upon the valleys, whose low vassal seat
The Alps doth spit and void his rheum° upon.
Go down upon him—you have power enough—
And in a captive chariot into Rouen
Bring him our prisoner.
55 CONSTABLE.   This becomes the great.
Sorry am I his numbers are so few,
His soldiers sick and famish'd in their march,
For I am sure, when he shall see our army,
He'll drop his heart into the sink of fear
60 And for achievement offer us his ransom.
FRENCH KING. Therefore, lord constable, haste on
    Montjoy,
And let him say to England that we send
To know what willing ransom he will give.
Prince Dauphin, you shall stay with us in Rouen.
65 DAUPHIN. Not so, I do beseech your majesty.
FRENCH KING. Be patient, for you shall remain with
    us.
Now forth, lord constable and princes all,
And quickly bring us word of England's fall.
                        [*Exeunt*]

SCENE vi
The English camp in Picardy.

[*Enter* GOWER *and* FLUELLEN, *meeting.*]
GOWER. How, now, Captain Fluellen! Come you
    from the bridge?
FLUELLEN. I assure you, there is very excellent
    services committed at the bridge.
5 GOWER. Is the Duke of Exeter safe?
FLUELLEN. The Duke of Exeter is as magnanimous
    as Agamemnon,° and a man that I love and
    honor with my soul, and my heart, and my duty,
    and my life, and my living, and my uttermost
10 power. He is not—God be praised and blessed!—
    any hurt in the world, but keeps the pridge most
    valiantly, with excellent discipline. There is an

For . . . shames in return for your high positions, now
    acquit yourselves of great (past) shames
host i.e., army
void . . . rheum expel its watery discharge (as from a
    cold in the head)
Agamemnon general of the Greek forces that besieged
    Troy

aunchient lieutenant there at the pridge. I think
in my very conscience he is as valiant a man as
Mark Antony, and he is a man of no estimation 15
in the world, but I did see him do as gallant
service.
GOWER. What do you call him?
FLUELLEN. He is called Aunchient Pistol.
GOWER. I know him not. 20
                [*Enter* PISTOL.]
FLUELLEN. Here is the man.
PISTOL. Captain, I thee beseech to do me favors.
    The Duke of Exeter doth love thee well.
FLUELLEN. Aye, I praise God, and I have merited
    some love at his hands. 25
PISTOL. Bardolph, a soldier firm and sound of
    heart,
    And of buxom° valor, hath, by cruel fate
    And giddy Fortune's furious fickle wheel,
    That goddess blind,
    That stands upon the rolling restless stone— 30
FLUELLEN. By your patience, Aunchient Pistol.
    Fortune is painted blind, with a muffler afore
    her eyes, to signify to you that Fortune is blind;
    and she is painted also with a wheel, to signify
    to you, which is the moral of it, that she is turn- 35
    ing, and inconstant, and mutability, and varia-
    tion; and her foot, look you, is fixed upon a
    spherical stone, which rolls, and rolls, and rolls.
    In good truth, the poet makes a most excellent
    description of it. Fortune is an excellent moral.° 40
PISTOL. Fortune is Bardolph's foe, and frowns on
    him,
    For he hath stolen a pax,° and hanged must a' be.
    A damned death!
    Let gallows gape for dog; let man go free
    And let not hemp his windpipe suffocate. 45
    But Exeter hath given the doom of death
    For pax of little price.
    Therefore, go speak—the duke will hear thy
    voice,
    And let not Bardolph's vital thread be cut
    With edge of penny cord and vile reproach. 50
    Speak, captain, for his life, and I will thee
    requite.
FLUELLEN. Aunchient Pistol, I do partly under-
    stand your meaning.
PISTOL. Why then, rejoice therefore.
FLUELLEN. Certainly, aunchient, it is not a thing to 55
    rejoice at; for if, look you, he were my brother, I
    would desire the duke to use his good pleasure,
    and put him to execution, for discipline ought to
    be used.

buxom robust   *moral* symbol
pax tablet stamped with a crucifix, used during Mass

PISTOL. Die and be damn'd! And figo for thy friend-
60   ship!

FLUELLEN. It is well.

PISTOL. The fig of Spain!°   [*Exit*]

FLUELLEN. Very good.

GOWER. Why, this is an arrant counterfeit rascal; I
65   remember him now—a bawd, a cutpurse.

FLUELLEN. I'll assure you, a' uttered as prave words
       at the pridge as you shall see in a summer's day.
       But it is very well; what he has spoke to me, that
       is well, I warrant you, when time is serve.°

70 GOWER. Why, 'tis a gull, a fool, a rogue, that now
       and then goes to the wars, to grace himself at his
       return into London under the form of a soldier.
       And such fellows are perfect in the great com-
       manders' names, and they will learn you by rote
75   where services were done—at such and such a
       sconce,° at such a breach, at such a convoy; who
       came off bravely, who was shot, who disgraced,
       what terms the enemy stood on; and this they
       con° perfectly in the phrase of war, which they
80   trick up with new-tuned oaths. And what a
       beard of the general's cut and a horrid suit of the
       camp will do among foaming bottles and ale-
       washed wits is wonderful to be thought on. But
       you must learn to know such slanders of the age,
85   or else you may be marvelously mistook.

FLUELLEN. I tell you what, Captain Gower. I do
       perceive he is not the man that he would gladly
       make show to the world he is. If I find a hole in
       his coat,° I will tell him my mind. [*Drum heard*]
90   Hark you, the king is coming, and I must speak
       with him from the pridge.

          [*Drum and Colors. Enter* KING HENRY,
              GLOUCESTER, *and* SOLDIERS.]

       God pless your majesty!

KING. How now, Fluellen! Camest thou from the
       bridge?

FLUELLEN. Aye, so please your majesty. The Duke
95   of Exeter has very gallantly maintained the
       pridge. The French is gone off, look you, and
       there is gallant and most prave passages.°
       Marry, th' athversary was have° possession of the
       pridge, but he is enforced to retire, and the Duke
100   of Exeter is master of the pridge. I can tell your
       majesty, the duke is a prave man.

KING. What men have you lost, Fluellen?

FLUELLEN. The perdition° of th' athversay hath
       been very great, reasonable great. Marry, for my

part, I think the duke hath lost never a man but   100
one that is like to be executed for robbing a
church, one Bardolph, if your majesty know the
man. His face is all bubukles, and whelks,° and
knobs, and flames o' fire, and his lips blows at
his nose, and it is like a coal of fire, sometimes   110
plue and sometimes red; but his nose is executed,
and his fire's out.

KING. We would have all such offenders so cut off,
and we give express charge that in our marches
through the country there be nothing compelled   115
from the villages, nothing taken but paid for,
none of the French upbraided or abused in disdainful language. For when lenity and cruelty
play for a kingdom, the gentler gamester is the
soonest winner.   120

          [*Tucket. Enter* MONTJOY.]

MONTJOY. You know me by my habit.°

KING. Well, then, I know thee. What shall I know
of thee?

MONTJOY. My master's mind.

KING. Unfold it.

MONTJOY. Thus says my king: Say thou to Harry of   125
England: Though we seemed dead, we did but
sleep; advantage° is a better soldier than rashness. Tell him we could have rebuked him at
Harfleur, but that we thought not good to
bruise an injury till it were full ripe. Now we   130
speak upon our cue, and our voice is imperial.
England shall repent his folly, see his weakness,
and admire° our sufferance. Bid him therefore
consider of his ransom, which must proportion
the losses we have borne, the subjects we have   135
lost, the disgrace we have digested; which in
weight to re-answer, his pettiness would bow
under. For our losses, his exchequer is too poor;
for the effusion of our blood, the muster of his
kingdom too faint a number; and for our dis-   140
grace, his own person, kneeling at our feet, but a
weak and worthless satisfaction. To this add
defiance, and tell him, for conclusion, he hath
betrayed his followers, whose condemnation is
pronounced.—So far my king and master; so   145
much my office.

KING. What is thy name? I know thy quality.

MONTJOY. Montjoy.

KING. Thou dost thy office fairly. Turn thee back,
And tell thy king I do not seek him now,   150
But could be willing to march on to Calais
Without impeachment.° For, to say the sooth,

---

fig . . . *Spain* an obscene gesture made by thrusting the
   thumb into the mouth or between the fingers
is serve shall serve *sconce* fortification
con memorize
hole . . . coat i.e., some fault in his record
passages deeds *was have* had *perdition* loss

bubukles . . . whelks inflamed bumps and boils
Tucket trumpet *habit* i.e., herald's coat
advantage favorable opportunity gained by waiting
admire wonder at
impeachment hindrance

Though 'tis no wisdom to confess so much
Unto an enemy of craft and vantage,
155 My people are with sickness much enfeebled,
My numbers lessen'd, and those few I have
Almost no better than so many French;
Who when they were in health, I tell thee,
  herald,
I thought upon one pair of English legs
Did march three Frenchmen. Yet, forgive me,
160   God,
That I do brag thus! This your air of France
Hath blown° that vice in me; I must repent.
Go therefore, tell thy master here I am:
My ransom is this frail and worthless trunk,
165 My army but a weak and sickly guard.
Yet, God before, tell him we will come on,
Though France himself and such another neigh-
  bor
Stand in our way. There's for thy labor, Mont-
  joy.
Go, bid thy master well advise himself.
170 If we may pass, we will; if we be hinder'd,
We shall your tawny° ground with your red
  blood
Discolor. And so, Montjoy, fare you well.
The sum of all our answer is but this:
We would not seek a battle, as we are;
175 Nor, as we are, we say we will not shun it.
So tell your master.
MONTJOY. I shall deliver so. Thanks to your high-
  ness.   [Exit]
GLOUCESTER. I hope they will not come upon us
  now.
KING. We are in God's hand, brother, not in theirs.
March to the bridge. It now draws toward
  night.
180 Beyond the river we'll encamp ourselves,
And on tomorrow bid them march away.
                                       [Exeunt]

SCENE vii
The French camp, near Agincourt.

[*Enter the* CONSTABLE *of France, the* LORD
RAMBURES, ORLEANS, DAUPHIN, *with others.*]
CONSTABLE. Tut! I have the best armor of the
  world. Would it were day!
ORLEANS. You have an excellent armor, but let my
  horse have his due.
5 CONSTABLE. It is the best horse of Europe.
ORLEANS. Will it never be morning?

DAUPHIN. My Lord of Orleans, and my lord high
  constable, you talk of horse and armor?
ORLEANS. You are as well provided of both as any
  prince in the world.   10
DAUPHIN. What a long night is this! I will not
  change my horse with any that treads but on
  four pasterns. Ça, ha! He bounds from the earth
  as if his entrails were hairs,° *le cheval volant*, the
  Pegasus, *chez les narines de feu!*° When I bestride 15
  him, I soar, I am a hawk. He trots the air, the
  earth sings when he touches it, the basest horn
  of his hoof is more musical than the pipe of
  Hermes.°
ORLEANS. He's of the color of the nutmeg.   20
DAUPHIN. And of the heat of the ginger. It is a beast
  for Perseus.° He is pure air and fire, and the dull
  elements of earth and water never appear in
  him, but only in patient stillness while his rider
  mounts him. He is indeed a horse, and all other 25
  jades you may call beasts.
CONSTABLE. Indeed, my lord, it is a most absolute
  and excellent horse.
DAUPHIN. It is the prince of palfreys. His neigh is
  like the bidding of a monarch, and his counte-   30
  nance enforces homage.
ORLEANS. No more, cousin.
DAUPHIN. Nay, the man hath no wit that cannot,
  from the rising of the lark to the lodging of the
  lamb, vary deserved praise on my palfrey. It is a 35
  theme as fluent as the sea: turn the sands into
  eloquent tongues, and my horse is argument°
  for them all. 'Tis a subject for a sovereign to
  reason° on, and for a sovereign's sovereign to
  ride on, and for the world, familiar to us and   40
  unknown, to lay apart their particular functions
  and wonder at him. I once writ a sonnet in his
  praise, and began thus: "Wonder of nature"—
ORLEANS. I have heard a sonnet begin so to one's
  mistress.   45
DAUPHIN. Then did they imitate that which I composed to my courser, for my horse is my mistress.
ORLEANS. Your mistress bears well.
DAUPHIN. Me well—which is the prescript° praise
  and perfection of a good and particular° mis-   50
  tress.
CONSTABLE. Nay, for methought yesterday your
  mistress shrewdly° shook your back.

---

blown fanned, like a blaze   *tawny* yellow

entrails . . . hairs i.e., like tennis balls, which were so
  stuffed
le . . . feu the flying horse, Pegasus, with nostrils of fire
Hermes (Mercury) the gods' messenger who piped
  Argus, the hundred-eyed monster, asleep
Perseus rider of Pegasus   *argument* subject
reason discourse   *prescript* prescribed
particular private   *shrewdly* shrewishly

DAUPHIN. So perhaps did yours.

55 CONSTABLE. Mine was not bridled.

DAUPHIN. O then belike she was old and gentle, and you rode, like a kern° of Ireland, your French hose off, and in your strait strossers.°

CONSTABLE. You have good judgment in horse-

60 manship.

DAUPHIN. Be warned by me, then. They that ride so, and ride not warily, fall into foul bogs. I had rather have my horse to° my mistress.

CONSTABLE. I had as lief have my mistress a jade.°

65 DAUPHIN. I tell thee, constable, my mistress wears his own hair.

CONSTABLE. I could make as true a boast as that, if I had a sow to my mistress.

DAUPHIN. "*Le chien est retourné à son propre vomisse-*

70 *ment, et la truie lavée au bourbier.*"° Thou makest use of anything.

CONSTABLE. Yet do I not use my horse for my mistress, or any such proverb so little kin to the purpose.

75 RAMBURES. My lord constable, the armor that I saw in your tent tonight, are those stars or suns upon it?

CONSTABLE. Stars, my lord.

DAUPHIN. Some of them will fall tomorrow, I hope.

80 CONSTABLE. And yet my sky shall not want.

DAUPHIN. That may be, for you bear a many superfluously, and 'twere more honor some were away.

CONSTABLE. Even as your horse bears your praises,

85 who would trot as well were some of your brags dismounted.

DAUPHIN. Would I were able to load him with his desert! Will it never be day? I will trot tomorrow a mile, and my way shall be paved with English

90 faces.

CONSTABLE. I will not say so, for fear I should be faced out of my way.° But I would it were morning, for I would fain be about the ears of the English.

95 RAMBURES. Who will go to hazard° with me for twenty prisoners?

CONSTABLE. You must first go yourself to hazard, ere you have them.

DAUPHIN. 'Tis midnight; I'll go arm myself.
                                                    [*Exit*]

ORLEANS. The Dauphin longs for morning.   100

RAMBURES. He longs to eat the English.

CONSTABLE. I think he will eat all he kills.

ORLEANS. By the white hand of my lady, he's a gallant prince.

CONSTABLE. Swear by her foot, that° she may tread 105
out the oath.

ORLEANS. He is simply the most active gentleman of France.

CONSTABLE. Doing is activity—and he will still° be doing.   110

ORLEANS. He never did harm, that I heard of.

CONSTABLE. Nor will do none tomorrow. He will keep that good name still.

ORLEANS. I know him to be valiant.

CONSTABLE. I was told that by one that knows him 115
better than you.

ORLEANS. What's he?

CONSTABLE. Marry, he told me so himself, and he said he cared not who knew it.

ORLEANS. He needs not; it is no hidden virtue in   120
him.

CONSTABLE. By my faith, sir, but it is; never any-body saw it but his lackey. 'Tis a hooded valor, and when it appears, it will bate.°

ORLEANS. Ill will never said well.   125

CONSTABLE. I will cap that proverb with "There is flattery in friendship."

ORLEANS. And I will take up that with "Give the devil his due."

CONSTABLE. Well placed. There stands your friend   130
for the devil. Have at the very eye of that proverb with "A pox of the devil."

ORLEANS. You are the better at proverbs, by how much "A fool's bolt is soon shot."

CONSTABLE. You have shot over.   135

ORLEANS. 'Tis not the first time you were overshot.
                              [*Enter a* MESSENGER.]

MESSENGER. My lord high constable, the English lie within fifteen hundred paces of your tents.

CONSTABLE. Who hath measured the ground?

MESSENGER. The Lord Grandpré.   140

CONSTABLE. A valiant and most expert gentleman. Would it were day! Alas, poor Harry of England! He longs not for the dawning as we do.

ORLEANS. What a wretched and peevish fellow is this King of England, to mope with his fat-   145
brained followers so far out of his knowledge!°

---

kern foot soldier

French hose . . . strait strossers loose, baggy breeches . . . tight-fitting underbreeches

to for

jade worn-out horse (with continuing play on *mistress*, here, *loose woman*)

"Le . . . bourbier" "the dog is turned to his own vomit again, and the sow that was washed to her wallowing in the mire" (see II Peter 2:222)

faced . . . way outfaced, put to flight

go to hazard make a wager

that so that   *still* always

'Tis . . . bate his valor is kept under cover (as a falcon is hooded) and when it appears it will fly away (as the falcon "bates," flaps its wings)

out . . . knowledge beyond his capacity

CONSTABLE. If the English had any apprehension, they would run away.

ORLEANS. That they lack, for if their heads had any
150   intellectual armor, they could never wear such heavy headpieces.

RAMBURES. That island of England breeds very valiant creatures; their mastiffs are of unmatchable courage.

155 ORLEANS. Foolish curs that run winking° into the mouth of a Russian bear and have their heads crushed like rotten apples! You may as well say that's a valiant flea that dare eat his breakfast on the lip of a lion.

160 CONSTABLE. Just, just; and the men do sympathize with the mastiffs in robustious and rough coming on, leaving their wits with their wives. And then give them great meals of beef, and iron and steel, they will eat like wolves, and fight like devils.   165

ORLEANS. Aye, but these English are shrewdly° out of beef.

CONSTABLE. Then shall we find tomorrow they have only stomachs to eat and none to fight. Now is it time to arm. Come, shall we about it? 170

ORLEANS. It is now two o'clock. But let me see, by ten
We shall have each a hundred Englishmen.

                            [*Exeunt*]

winking with their eyes shut

shrewdly bitterly

ACT IV

PROLOGUE

[*Enter* CHORUS.]

CHORUS. Now entertain conjecture° of a time
  When creeping murmur and the poring° dark
  Fills the wide vessel of the universe.
  From camp to camp through the foul womb of
    night
5 The hum of either army stilly sounds,
  That° the fix'd sentinels almost receive
  The secret whispers of each other's watch.
  Fire answers fire, and through their paly flames
  Each battle° sees the other's umber'd° face.
  Steed threatens steed, in high and boastful
10   neighs
  Piercing the night's dull ear; and from the tents
  The armorers, accomplishing° the knights,
  With busy hammers closing rivets up,
  Give dreadful note of preparation.
15 The country cocks do crow, the clocks do toll,
  And the third hour of drowsy morning name.
  Proud of their numbers and secure in soul,
  The confident and over-lusty° French
  Do the low-rated English play° at dice,
20 And chide the cripple tardy-gaited night
  Who, like a foul and ugly witch, doth limp
So tediously away. The poor condemned
  English,
Like sacrifices, by their watchful fires
Sit patiently and inly ruminate
The morning's danger, and their gesture sad 25
Investing lank-lean cheeks and war-worn coats
Presenteth them unto the gazing moon
So many horrid ghosts. O now, who° will
  behold
The royal captain of this ruin'd band
Walking from watch to watch, from tent to
  tent, 30
Let him cry "Praise and glory on his head!"
For forth he goes and visits all his host,
Bids them good morrow with a modest smile,
And calls them brothers, friends, and country-
  men.
Upon his royal face there is no note 35
How dread an army hath enrounded him;
Nor doth he dedicate° one jot of color
Unto the weary and all-watched° night,
But freshly looks and overbears attaint°
With cheerful semblance and sweet majesty, 40
That° every wretch, pining and pale before,
Beholding him, plucks comfort from his looks.
A largess universal like the sun
His liberal eye doth give to everyone,

entertain conjecture imagine
poring pore-filling, i.e., solid   *that* so that
battle army   *umber'd* shadowed
accomplishing outfitting   *over-lusty* too exuberant
play play for

who whoever   *dedicate* yield
all-watched sleepless   *overbears attaint* masters dismay
That so that

45   Thawing cold fear, that mean and gentle° all
     Behold, as may unworthiness define,°
     A little touch of Harry in the night.
     And so our scene must to the battle fly,
     Where—O for pity!—we shall much disgrace
50   With four or five most vile and ragged foils,°
     Right ill-dispos'd in brawl ridiculous,
     The name of Agincourt. Yet sit and see,
     Minding° true things by what their mockeries°
     be.   [*Exit*]

SCENE i
The English camp at Agincourt.

[*Enter* KING HENRY, BEDFORD, *and* GLOUCESTER.]
KING. Gloucester, 'tis true that we are in great
          danger;
     The greater therefore should our courage be.
     Good morrow, brother Bedford. God Almighty!
     There is some soul of goodness in things evil,
5   Would men observingly distill it out.
     For our bad neighbor makes us early stirrers,
     Which is both healthful and good husbandry.°
     Besides, they are our outward consciences
     And preachers to us all, admonishing
10   That we should dress us fairly for our end.
     Thus may we gather honey from the weed,
     And make a moral° of the devil himself.
          [*Enter* ERPINGHAM.]
     Good morrow, old Sir Thomas Erpingham.
     A good soft pillow for that good white head
15   Were better than a churlish turf of France.
ERPINGHAM. Not so, my liege. This lodging likes me
          better,
     Since I may say "Now lie I like a king."
KING. 'Tis good for men to love their present pains
     Upon example;° so the spirit is eas'd,
20   And when the mind is quicken'd, out of doubt
     The organs, though defunct and dead before,
     Break up their drowsy grave and newly move,
     With casted slough° and fresh legerity.°
     Lend me thy cloak, Sir Thomas. Brothers both,
25   Commend me to the princes in our camp;
     Do my good morrow to them, and anon°
     Desire them all to my pavilion.
GLOUCESTER. We shall, my liege.

ERPINGHAM. Shall I attend your grace?
KING.   No, my good knight.
     Go with my brothers to my lords of England.   30
     I and my bosom must debate awhile,
     And then I would no other company.
ERPINGHAM. The Lord in heaven bless thee, noble
          Harry!   [*Exeunt all but* KING.]
KING. God-a-mercy, old heart! Thou speak'st
          cheerfully.
          [*Enter* PISTOL.]
PISTOL. *Qui va là?*°   35
KING. A friend.
PISTOL. Discuss unto me. Art thou officer?
     Or art thou base, common, and popular?
KING. I am a gentleman of a company.°
PISTOL. Trail'st thou the puissant pike?°   40
KING. Even so. What are you?
PISTOL. As good a gentleman as the emperor.
KING. Then you are a better than the king.
PISTOL. The king's a bawcock,° and a heart of gold,
     A lad of life, an imp of fame,   45
     Of parents good, of fist most valiant.
     I kiss his dirty shoe, and from heartstring
     I love the lovely bully. What is thy name?
KING. Harry le Roy.°
PISTOL. Le Roy! A Cornish name. Art thou of
     Cornish crew?   50
KING. No, I am a Welshman.
PISTOL. Know'st thou Fluellen?
KING. Yes.
PISTOL. Tell him I'll knock his leek about his pate
     Upon Saint Davy's day.°   55
KING. Do not you wear your dagger in your cap
     that day, lest he knock that about yours.
PISTOL. Art thou his friend?
KING. And his kinsman too.
PISTOL. The figo for thee, then!   60
KING. I thank you. God be with you!
PISTOL. My name is Pistol call'd.   [*Exit*]
KING. It sorts° well with your fierceness.
          [*Enter* FLUELLEN *and* GOWER.]
GOWER. Captain Fluellen!
FLUELLEN. So! In the name of Jesu Christ, speak   65
     lower. It is the greatest admiration° in the
     universal world, when the true and aunchient
     prerogatifes and laws of the wars is not kept. If

---

mean . . . gentle lowly . . . noble
as . . . define as best our unworthy skill can represent it
foils rapiers   *Minding* imagining
mockeries imitations   *husbandry* management
make a moral find a moral in
Upon example by the example of others
slough skin   *legerity* agility   *anon* at once

Qui va là who goes there
gentleman . . . company volunteer gentleman, whose
     status was always ambiguous
Trail'st . . . pike do you carry the heavy lance; i.e., are
     you in the infantry
bawcock fine fellow   *le Roy* i.e., the king
leek . . . day on March 1 the Welchman wears a leek as
     his national emblem
sorts accords   *admiration* wonder

you would take the pains but to examine the
70 wars of Pompey the Great, you shall find, I
warrant you, that there is no tiddle taddle nor
pibble pabble in Pompey's camp; I warrant you,
you shall find the ceremonies of the wars, and
the cares of it, and the forms of it, and the
75 sobriety of it, and the modesty of it, to be
otherwise.
GOWER. Why, the enemy is loud; you hear him all
night.
FLUELLEN. If the enemy is an ass and a fool and a
80 prating coxcomb, is it meet, think you, that we
should also, look you, be an ass and a fool and a
prating coxcomb? In your own conscience,
now?
GOWER. I will speak lower.
85 FLUELLEN. I pray you and beseech you that you
will.   [*Exeunt* GOWER *and* FLUELLEN.]
KING. Though it appear a little out of fashion,
There is much care and valor in this Welshman.
[*Enter three soldiers,* JOHN BATES, ALEXANDER
COURT, *and* MICHAEL WILLIAMS.]
COURT. Brother John Bates, is not that the morning
90 which breaks yonder?
BATES. I think it be. But we have no great cause to
desire the approach of day.
WILLIAMS. We see yonder the beginning of the day,
but I think we shall never see the end of it. Who
95 goes there?
KING. A friend.
WILLIAMS. Under what captain serve you?
KING. Under Sir Thomas Erpingham.
WILLIAMS. A good old commander and a most
100 kind gentleman.
I pray you, what thinks he of our estate?°
KING. Even as men wrecked upon a sand, that look
to be washed off the next tide.
BATES. He hath not told his thought to the king?
105 KING. No, nor it is not meet he should. For, though
I speak it to you, I think the king is but a man,
as I am. The violet smells to him as it doth to
me; the element° shows to him as it doth to me;
all his senses have but human conditions. His
110 ceremonies° laid by, in his nakedness he appears
but a man; and though his affections are higher
mounted° than ours, yet, when they stoop,°
they stoop with the like wing. Therefore when
he sees reason of fears, as we do, his fears, out of
115 doubt, be of the same relish as ours are. Yet, in
reason, no man should possess him with any

appearance of fear, lest he, by showing it,
should dishearten his army.
BATES. He may show what outward courage he
will, but I believe, as cold a night as 'tis, he 120
could wish himself in Thames up to the neck;
and so I would he were, and I by him, at all
adventures, so we were quit here.
KING. By my troth, I will speak my conscience of
the king. I think he would not wish himself 125
anywhere but where he is.
BATES. Then I would he were here alone; so should
he be sure to be ransomed, and a many poor
men's lives saved.
KING. I dare say you love him not so ill, to wish him 130
here alone, howsoever you speak this to feel
other men's minds. Methinks I could not die
anywhere so contented as in the king's company,
his cause being just and his quarrel honorable.
WILLIAMS. That's more than we know. 135
BATES. Aye, or more than we should seek after,
for we know enough if we know we are the
king's subjects. If his cause be wrong, our
obedience to the king wipes the crime of it out
of us. 140
WILLIAMS. But if the cause be not good, the king
himself hath a heavy reckoning to make, when
all those legs and arms and heads, chopped off
in battle, shall join together at the latter day and
cry all "We died at such a place," some swearing, 145
some crying for a surgeon, some upon their
wives left poor behind them, some upon the
debts they owe, some upon their children
rawly left.° I am afeard there are few die well
that die in a battle, for how can they charitably 150
dispose of anything when blood is their argument? Now, if these men do not die well, it will
be a black matter for the king that led them to
it, whom to disobey were against all proportion
of subjection.° 155
KING. So, if a son that is by his father sent about
merchandise do sinfully miscarry° upon the sea,
the imputation of his wickedness, by your rule,
should be imposed upon his father that sent
him. Or if a servant, upon his master's com- 160
mand transporting a sum of money, be assailed
by robbers and die in many irreconciled iniquities,° you may call the business of the master the
author of the servant's damnation. But this is
not so. The king is not bound to answer the 165

---

estate position   *element* sky
ceremonies royal trappings
affections . . . mounted desires soar higher (falconry
  metaphor)
stoop swoop down

rawly left unprovided for
proportion of subjection appropriateness of behavior in a
  subject
sinfully miscarry perish in sin
irreconciled iniquities with his sins unconfessed and
  unabsolved

particular endings of his soldiers, the father of his son, nor the master of his servant; for they purpose not their death when they purpose their services. Besides, there is no king, be his
170 cause never so spotless, if it come to the arbitrement of° swords, can try it out with all unspotted soldiers. Some peradventure have on them the guilt of premeditated and contrived murder; some, of beguiling virgins with the broken seals
175 of perjury; some, making the wars their bulwark,° that have before gored the gentle bosom of peace with pillage and robbery. Now, if these men have defeated the law and outrun native punishment, though they can outstrip men,
180 they have no wings to fly from God. War is His beadle,° war is His vengeance; so that here men are punished for before-breach of the king's laws in now the king's quarrel. Where they feared the death, they have borne life away,
185 and where they would be safe, they perish; then if they die unprovided, no more is the king guilty of their damnation than he was before guilty of those impieties for the which they are now visited.° Every subject's duty is the king's,
190 but every subject's soul is his own. Therefore should every soldier in the wars do as every sick man in his bed, wash every mote out of his conscience. And dying so, death is to him advantage; or not dying, the time was blessedly
195 lost wherein such preparation was gained. And in him that escapes, it were not sin to think that, making God so free an offer, He let him outlive that day to see His greatness and to teach others how they should prepare.
200 WILLIAMS. 'Tis certain, every man that dies ill, the ill upon his own head, the king is not to answer it.

BATES. I do not desire he should answer for me, and yet I determine to fight lustily for him.
205 KING. I myself heard the king say he would not be ransomed.

WILLIAMS. Aye, he said so to make us fight cheerfully. But when our throats are cut, he may be ransomed and we ne'er the wiser.
210 KING. If I live to see it, I will never trust his word after.

WILLIAMS. You pay° him then! That's a perilous shot out of an elder-gun,° that a poor and a private displeasure can do against a monarch!
215 You may as well go about to turn the sun to

ice with fanning in his face with a peacock's feather. You'll never trust his word after! Come, 'tis a foolish saying.

KING. Your reproof is something too round.° I should be angry with you if the time were 220 convenient.

WILLIAMS. Let it be a quarrel between us if you live.

KING. I embrace it.

WILLIAMS. How shall I know thee again?

KING. Give me any gage° of thine, and I will wear 225 it in my bonnet. Then, if ever thou darest acknowledge it, I will make it my quarrel.

WILLIAMS. Here's my glove. Give me another of thine.

KING. There.   230

WILLIAMS. This will I also wear in my cap. If ever thou come to me and say, after tomorrow, "This is my glove," by his hand, I will take thee a box on the ear.

KING. If ever I live to see it, I will challenge it.   235

WILLIAMS. Thou darest as well be hanged.

KING. Well, I will do it, though I take thee in the king's company.

WILLIAMS. Keep thy word. Fare thee well.

BATES. Be friends, you English fools, be friends. 240 We have French quarrels enow,° if you could tell how to reckon.

KING. Indeed, the French may lay twenty French crowns° to one they will beat us, for they bear them on their shoulders. But it is no English 245 treason to cut French crowns,° and tomorrow the king himself will be a clipper.°

[Exeunt SOLDIERS.]

Upon the king! Let us our lives, our souls,
Our debts, our careful° wives,
Our children, and our sins lay on the king! 250
We must bear all. O hard condition,
Twin-born with greatness, subject to the breath
Of every fool whose sense° no more can feel
But his own wringing!° What infinite heart's-ease
Must kings neglect that private men enjoy!   255
And what have kings that privates have not too,
Save ceremony, save general ceremony?
And what art thou, thou idol ceremony?

something . . . round somewhat too direct
gage pledge
enow enough   *reckon* count
crowns French coins (with pun on *heads*)
English . . . crowns no treason for an Englishman to cut French heads (with pun: though treasonous for an Englishman to pare edges off English coins, not so for French coins)
clipper of French heads (with pun, of French coins)
careful full of care   *sense* sensibilities
wringing discomfort

arbitrement of settlement by
bulwark justification (for plundering)
beadle local law enforcement officer
visited punished
pay punish   *elder-gun* popgun

What kind of god art thou, that suffer'st more
260 Of mortal griefs than do thy worshipers?
   What are thy rents? What are thy comings-in?
   O ceremony, show me but thy worth!
   What is thy soul of adoration?°
   Art thou aught else but place, degree, and form,
265 Creating awe and fear in other men?—
   Wherein thou art less happy being fear'd
   Than they in fearing.
   What drink'st thou oft, instead of homage sweet,
   But poison'd flattery? O, be sick, great greatness,
270 And bid thy ceremony give thee cure!
   Think'st thou the fiery fever will go out
   With titles blown from adulation?°
   Will it give place to flexure and low bending?°
   Canst thou, when thou command'st the beg-
       gar's knee,
   Command the health of it? No, thou proud
275   dream
   That play'st so subtly with a king's repose.
   I am a king that find thee, and I know
   'Tis not the balm,° the scepter, and the ball,°
   The sword, the mace,° the crown imperial,
280 The intertissu'd robe of gold and pearl,
   The farced° title running 'fore the king,
   The throne he sits on, nor the tide of pomp
   That beats upon the high shore of this world—
   No, not all these, thrice-gorgeous ceremony,
285 Not all these, laid in bed majestical,
   Can sleep so soundly as the wretched slave,
   Who with a body fill'd and vacant mind
   Gets him to rest, cramm'd with distressful
       bread;
   Never sees horrid night, the child of hell,
290 But, like a lackey, from the rise to set
   Sweats in the eye of Phœbus° and all night
   Sleeps in Elysium;° next day after dawn,
   Doth rise and help Hyperion° to his horse,
   And follows so the ever-running year,
295 With profitable labor, to his grave.
   And, but for ceremony, such a wretch,
   Winding up days with toil and nights with
       sleep,
   Had the forehand° and vantage of a king.
   The slave, a member of the country's peace,

Enjoys it; but in gross brain little wots°   300
   What watch the king keeps to maintain the
       peace,
   Whose hours the peasant best advantages.
                    [Re-enter ERPINGHAM.]
ERPINGHAM. My lord, your nobles, jealous° of your
       absence,
   Seek through your camp to find you.
KING.   Good old knight,
   Collect them all together at my tent.   305
   I'll be before thee.
ERPINGHAM.   I shall do 't, my lord. [Exit]
KING. O God of battles! Steel my soldiers' hearts;
   Possess them not with fear; take from them
       now
   The sense of reck'ning,° if th' opposed numbers
   Pluck their hearts from them. Not today, O
       Lord,   310
   O, not today, think not upon the fault
   My father made in compassing the crown!°
   I Richard's body have interred new,
   And on it have bestow'd more contrite tears
   Than from it issu'd forced drops of blood.   315
   Five hundred poor I have in yearly pay,
   Who twice a day their wither'd hands hold up
   Toward heaven, to pardon blood; and I have
       built
   Two chantries, where the sad and solemn
       priests
   Sing still° for Richard's soul. More will I do,   320
   Though all that I can do is nothing worth,
   Since that my penitence comes after all,
   Imploring pardon.
                    [Re-enter GLOUCESTER.]
GLOUCESTER. My liege!
KING. My brother Gloucester's voice? Aye,   325
   I know thy errand; I will go with thee.
   The day, my friends, and all things stay for me.
                                        [Exeunt]

SCENE ii
The French camp.

[*Enter the* DAUPHIN, ORLEANS, RAMBURES, *and
                    others.*]
ORLEANS. The sun doth gild our armor; up, my
       lords!
DAUPHIN. *Montez à cheval!*° My horse! Varlet!°
   Laquais!° Ha!

---

soul of adoration   secret essence that evokes adoration
Think'st . . . adulation   do you think that empty titles
   bestowed by adulation will cure a fever
Will . . . bending   will (a king's) fever be cured by knee-
   bending (of flatterers)
balm   holy oil used in anointing kings
ball   symbol of sovereignty
mace   symbol of kingly power
farced   comically pompous   *Phœbus*   the sun
Elysium   Paradise   *Hyperion*   the sun
forehand   upperhand

wots   knows
jealous   apprehensive   reck'ning   counting
fault . . . crown   i.e., the usurpation of Richard's throne
   and his murder
still   always   *Montez à cheval*   mount up
Varlet   valet   *Laquais*   lackey

227

ORLEANS. O brave spirit!

DAUPHIN. *Via! Les eaux et la terre.*

5 ORLEANS. *Rien puis? L'air et le feu.*

DAUPHIN. *Ciel,*° cousin Orleans.

    [*Enter* CONSTABLE.]

  Now, my lord constable!

CONSTABLE. Hark, how our steeds for present
  service neigh!

DAUPHIN. Mount them, and make incision in their
  hides,

10 That their hot blood may spin in° English eyes
  And dout° them with superfluous courage,° ha!

RAMBURES. What, will you have them weep our
  horses' blood?

  How shall we then behold their natural tears?

    [*Enter* MESSENGER.]

MESSENGER. The English are embattled,° you
  French peers.

CONSTABLE. To horse, you gallant princes! Straight
15   to horse!

  Do but behold yon poor and starved band,

  And your fair show shall suck away their souls,

  Leaving them but the shales° and husks of
  men.

  There is not work enough for all our hands,

20 Scarce blood enough in all their sickly veins

  To give each naked curtle-axe° a stain,

  That our French gallants shall today draw out

  And sheathe for lack of sport. Let us but blow
  on them,

  The vapor of our valor will o'erturn them.

25 'Tis positive 'gainst all exceptions, lords,

  That our superfluous lackeys and our peasants,

  Who in unnecessary action swarm

  About our squares of battle, were enow

  To purge this field of such a hilding° foe,

30 Though we upon this mountain's basis by

  Took stand for idle speculation,°

  But that our honors must not. What's to say?

  A very little let us do,

  And all is done. Then let the trumpets sound

35 The tucket sonance° and the note to mount,

  For our approach shall so much dare° the field

  That England shall couch down in fear and yield.

    [*Enter* GRANDPRÉ.]

GRANDPRÉ. Why do you stay so long, my lords of
  France?

Yon island carrions, desperate of° their bones,

Ill-favoredly become° the morning field.   40

Their ragged curtains° poorly are let loose,

And our air shakes them passing° scornfully.

Big Mars seems bankrupt in their beggar'd host,

And faintly through a rusty beaver° peeps.

The horsemen sit like fixed candlesticks,   45

With torch staves in their hand, and their poor
  jades

Lob° down their heads, dropping the hides and
  hips,

The gum down-roping from their pale-dead
  eyes,

And in their pale dull mouths the gimmal'd° bit

Lies foul with chew'd grass, still and motionless;   50

And their executors, the knavish crows,

Fly o'er them, all impatient for their hour.

Description cannot suit itself in words

To demonstrate the life of such a battle°

In life so lifeless as it shows itself.   55

CONSTABLE. They have said their prayers, and they
  stay for death.

DAUPHIN. Shall we go send them dinners and fresh
  suits

  And give their fasting horses provender,

  And after fight with them?

CONSTABLE. I stay but for my guard. To the field!   60

  I will the banner from a trumpet take,

  And use it for my haste. Come, come, away!

  The sun is high, and we outwear the day.

    [*Exeunt*]

SCENE iii
The English camp.

[*Enter* GLOUCESTER, BEDFORD, EXETER,
ERPINGHAM, *with all his host;* SALISBURY
and WESTMORELAND.]

GLOUCESTER. Where is the king?

BEDFORD. The king himself is rode to view their
  battle.°

WESTMORELAND. Of fighting men they have full
  three score thousand.

EXETER. There's five to one. Besides, they all are
  fresh.

SALISBURY. God's arm strike with us! 'Tis a fearful
  odds.   5

  God be wi' you, princes all; I'll to my charge.

Via . . . Ciel Away! Water and earth . . . Nothing more?
  Air and fire . . . Heavens
spin in spurt into   *dout* put out
courage which supposedly resided in the blood
embattled drawn up in battle formation
shales shells   *curtle-axe* cutlass
hilding worthless   *speculation* observation
tucket sonance trumpet call   *dare* affright

desperate of fearful for
Ill-favoredly become look ugly upon   *curtains* banners
passing surpassingly   *beaver* visor   *Lob* hang
gimmal'd hinged   *battle* battle force
battle army

If we no more meet till we meet in heaven,
Then, joyfully, my noble Lord of Bedford,
My dear Lord Gloucester, and my good Lord
   Exeter,
10 And my kind kinsman, warriors all, adieu!
BEDFORD. Farewell, good Salisbury, and good luck
   go with thee!
EXETER. Farewell, kind lord; fight valiantly today.
And yet I do thee wrong to mind° thee of it,
For thou art fram'd° of the firm truth of valor.
                        [Exit SALISBURY.]
15 BEDFORD. He is as full of valor as of kindness,
   Princely in both.
             [Enter the KING.]
WESTMORELAND.   O that we now had here
But one ten thousand of those men in England
That do no work today!
KING.   What's he that wishes so?
My cousin Westmoreland? No, my fair cousin.
20 If we are mark'd to die, we are enow
To do our country loss, and if to live,
The fewer men, the greater share of honor.
God's will! I pray thee wish not one man more.
By Jove, I am not covetous for gold,
25 Nor care I who doth feed upon my cost;
It yearns° me not if men my garments wear;
Such outward things dwell not in my desires.
But if it be a sin to covet honor,
I am the most offending soul alive.
No, faith, my coz,° wish not a man from Eng-
30   land.
God's peace! I would not lose so great an honor
As one man more, methinks, would share from
   me
For the best hope I have. O, do not wish one
   more!
Rather proclaim it, Westmoreland, through my
   host,
35 That he which hath no stomach to this fight,
Let him depart; his passport shall be made
And crowns for convoy put into his purse.
We would not die in that man's company
That fears his fellowship to die° with us.
40 This day is call'd the feast of Crispian.°
He that outlives this day and comes safe home
Will stand a-tiptoe when this day is nam'd,
And rouse him at the name of Crispian.
He that shall live this day and see old age
45 Will yearly on the vigil feast his neighbors

And say, "Tomorrow is Saint Crispian."
Then will he strip his sleeve and show his scars,
And say, "These wounds I had on Crispin's
   day."
Old men forget; yet all shall be forgot,
But he'll remember with advantages°   50
What feats he did that day. Then shall our
   names,
Familiar in his mouth as household words,
Harry the king, Bedford and Exeter,
Warwick and Talbot, Salisbury and Gloucester,
Be in their flowing cups freshly remember'd.   55
This story shall the good man teach his son,
And Crispin Crispian shall ne'er go by
From this day to the ending of the world
But we in it shall be remembered,
We few, we happy few, we band of brothers.   60
For he today that sheds his blood with me
Shall be my brother; be he ne'er so vile,
This day shall gentle° his condition.
And gentlemen in England now abed
Shall think themselves accurs'd they were not
   here,   65
And hold their manhood cheap whiles any
   speaks
That fought with us upon Saint Crispin's day.
              [Re-enter SALISBURY.]
SALISBURY. My sovereign lord, bestow° yourself
   with speed.
The French are bravely in their battles° set,
And will with all expedience charge on us.   70
KING. All things are ready, if our minds be so.
WESTMORELAND. Perish the man whose mind is
   backward now!
KING. Thou dost not wish more help from Eng-
   land, coz?
WESTMORELAND. God's will! My liege, would you
   and I alone,
Without more help, could fight this royal
   battle!   75
KING. Why, now thou hast unwish'd five thousand
   men,
Which likes me better than to wish us one.
You know your places. God be with you all!
         [Tucket. Enter MONTJOY.]
MONTJOY. Once more I come to know of thee, King
   Harry,
If for thy ransom thou wilt now compound°   80
Before thy most assured overthrow.
For certainly thou art so near the gulf,°

---

mind remind   *fram'd* composed
yearns grieves   *coz* cousin   *to die* i.e., in death
This ... Crispian October 25 (twin brothers Crispinus
and Crispianus, martyred in 287A.D., are the patron
saints of shoemakers)

with advantages i.e., with exaggeration
gentle ennoble   *bestow* take your place
battles formations
compound discuss terms   *gulf* whirlpool

Thou needs must be englutted.° Besides, in mercy,
The constable desires thee thou wilt mind°
85 Thy followers of repentance, that their souls
May make a peaceful and a sweet retire
From off these fields, where, wretches, their poor bodies
Must lie and fester.
KING.   Who hath sent thee now?
MONTJOY. The Constable of France.
90 KING. I pray thee, bear my former answer back:
Bid them achieve° me and then sell my bones.
Good God! Why should they mock poor fellows thus?
The man that once did sell the lion's skin
While the beast liv'd was killed with hunting him.
95 A many of our bodies shall no doubt
Find native graves, upon the which, I trust,
Shall witness live in brass of this day's work.
And those that leave their valiant bones in France,
Dying like men, though buried in your dunghills,
They shall be fam'd; for there the sun shall
100 greet them
And draw their honors reeking up to heaven,
Leaving their earthly parts to choke your clime,
The smell whereof shall breed a plague in France.
Mark then abounding valor in our English,
105 That being dead, like to the bullet's grazing,
Break out into a second course of mischief,
Killing in relapse of mortality.°
Let me speak proudly: tell the constable
We are but warriors for the working-day;
110 Our gayness and our gilt are all besmirch'd
With rainy marching in the painful field.
There's not a piece of feather° in our host—
Good argument,° I hope, we will not fly—
And time hath worn us into slovenry.
115 But, by the mass, our hearts are in the trim,
And my poor soldiers tell me, yet ere night
They'll be in fresher robes, or they will pluck
The gay new coats o'er the French soldiers' heads
And turn them out of service.° If they do this—
120 As, if God please, they shall—my ransom then
Will soon be levied. Herald, save thou thy labor;

Come thou no more for ransom, gentle herald.
They shall have none, I swear, but these my joints,
Which if they have, as I will leave 'em them,
Shall yield them little, tell the constable.   125
MONTJOY. I shall, King Harry. And so fare thee well.
Thou never shalt hear herald any more.
                                        [Exit]
KING. I fear thou'lt once more come again for ransom.
                    [Enter YORK.]
YORK. My lord, most humbly on my knee I beg
The leading of the vaward.°   130
KING. Take it, brave York. Now, soldiers, march away.
And how thou pleaseth, God, dispose the day!
                                        [Exeunt]

SCENE iv
The field of battle.

[Alarum. Excursions. Enter PISTOL, FRENCH SOLDIER, and BOY.]
PISTOL. Yield, cur!
FRENCH SOLDIER. Je pense que vous êtes gentilhomme de bonne qualité.°
PISTOL. Qualitie calmie custure me!° Art thou a gentleman?
What is thy name? Discuss.   5
FRENCH SOLDIER. O Seigneur Dieu!
PISTOL. O Signieur Dew should be a gentleman.
Perpend° my words, O Signieur Dew, and mark.
O Signieur Dew, thou diest on point of fox,°
Except, O Signieur, thou do give to me   10
Egregious° ransom.
FRENCH SOLDIER. O, prenez miséricorde! Ayez pitié de moi!°
PISTOL. Moy shall not serve; I will have forty moys,
Or I will fetch thy rim° out at thy throat   15
In drops of crimson blood.
FRENCH SOLDIER. Est-il impossible d'échapper la force de ton bras?°

vaward vanguard
Je . . . qualité I think that you are a gentleman of high rank
Qualitie . . . me (Pistol's inexplicable "French")
Perpend ponder   fox sword
Egregious Pistol-ese for enormous
O . . . moi oh, have mercy; take pity on me
rim i.e., rim of the stomach
Est-il . . . bras is it impossible to escape the strength of your arms

englutted swallowed up   mind remind
achieve take
in . . . mortality in a deadly rebound
feather fancy plume   argument proof
turn . . . service dismiss them like servants

PISTOL. Brass, cur!

20   Thou damned and luxurious mountain goat,
      Offer'st me brass?

FRENCH SOLDIER. *O pardonnez moi!*

PISTOL. Say'st thou me so? Is that a ton of moys?
      Come hither, boy. Ask me this slave in French

25   What is his name.

BOY. *Écoutez. Comment êtes-vous appelé?°*

FRENCH SOLDIER. *Monsieur le Fer.*

BOY. He says his name is Master Fer.

PISTOL. Master Fer! I'll fer him, and firk, and
      ferret him.

30   Discuss the same in French unto him.

BOY. I do not know the French for fer, and ferret,
      and firk.

PISTOL. Bid him prepare, for I will cut his throat.

FRENCH SOLDIER. *Que dit-il, monsieur?°*

35   BOY. *Il me commande de vous dire que vous faites vous
      prêt, car ce soldat ici est disposé tout à cette heure de
      couper votre gorge.°*

PISTOL. Owy, cuppele gorge, permafoy,
      Peasant, unless thou give me crowns, brave
      crowns,

40   Or mangled shalt thou be by this my sword.

FRENCH SOLDIER. *O, je vous supplie, pour l'amour de
      Dieu, me pardonner! Je suis gentilhomme de bonne
      maison. Gardez ma vie, et je vous donnerai deux
      cents écus.*

45   PISTOL. What are his words?

BOY. He prays you to save his life. He is a gentle-
      man of a good house, and for his ransom he will
      give you two hundred crowns.

PISTOL. Tell him my fury shall abate, and I

50   The crowns will take.

FRENCH SOLDIER. *Petit monsieur, que dit-il?*

BOY. *Encore qu'il est contre son jurement de pardonner
      aucun prisonnier; néanmoins, pour les écus que vous
      l'avez promis, il est content de vous donner la liberté,
      le franchisement.°*

55   FRENCH SOLDIER. *Sur mes genoux je vous donne mille
      remercîmens, et je m'estime heureux que je suis tombé
      entre les mains d'un chevalier, je pense, le plus
      brave, vaillant, et très distingué seigneur d'Angle-
      terre.*

60   PISTOL. Expound unto me, boy.

BOY. He gives you, upon his knees, a thousand

thanks, and he esteems himself happy that he
hath fallen into the hands of one, as he thinks,
the most brave, valorous, and thrice-worthy   65
signieur of England.

PISTOL. As I suck blood, I will some mercy show.
      Follow me!

BOY. *Suivez-vous le grand capitaine.°* [*Exeunt* PISTOL,
      and FRENCH SOLDIER] I did never know so full a   70
      voice issue from so empty a heart. But the saying
      is true, "The empty vessel makes the greatest
      sound." Bardolph and Nym had ten times more
      valor than this roaring devil i' the old play, that
      every one may pare his nails with a wooden   75
      dagger;° and they are both hanged, and so
      would this be if he durst steal anything adven-
      turously. I must stay with the lackeys, with the
      luggage of our camp. The French might have a
      good prey of us, if he knew of it, for there is none   80
      to guard it but boys.   [*Exit*]

SCENE V
Another part of the field.

[*Enter* CONSTABLE, ORLEANS, BOURBON, DAUPHIN,
                and RAMBURES.]

CONSTABLE. *O diable!*

ORLEANS. *O Seigneur! Le jour est perdu, tout est
      perdu!°*

DAUPHIN. *Mort de ma vie!* All is confounded,° all!
      Reproach and everlasting shame   5
      Sits mocking in our plumes. *O méchante° fortune!*
      Do not run away.   [*A short alarum.*]

CONSTABLE.   Why, all our ranks are broke.

DAUPHIN. O perdurable° shame! Let's stab our-
      selves.
      Be these the wretches that we play'd at dice for?

ORLEANS. Is this the king we sent to for his ransom?   10

BOURBON. Shame and eternal shame, nothing but
      shame!
      Let us die in honor. Once more back again,
      And he that will not follow Bourbon now,
      Let him go hence, and with his cap in hand,
      Like a base pander,° hold the chamber door   15
      Whilst by a slave, no gentler than my dog,
      His fairest daughter is contaminated.

Écoutez . . . appelé listen . . . what is your name
Que . . . monsieur what does he say, sir
Il . . . gorge he orders me to tell you to get ready,
      because this soldier intends to cut your throat right
      now
Encore . . . franchisement it is still against his oath to
      pardon any prisoner; nevertheless, for the crowns that
      you have promised him he is happy to give you
      liberty, freedom

Suivez-vous . . . capitaine follow the great captain
roaring . . . dagger (the character of Pistol is descended
      from the roaring devil of early English miracle plays,
      who carried a wooden sword)
Le jour . . . perdu the day is lost, all is lost
confounded ruined
méchante wicked   *perdurable* everlasting
pander solicitor of customers for illicit purposes

CONSTABLE. Disorder, that hath spoil'd us, friend us
    now!
    Let us on heaps go offer up our lives.
20 ORLEANS. We are enow yet living in the field
    To smother up the English in our throngs,
    If any order might be thought upon.
    BOURBON. The devil take order now! I'll to the
        throng.
    Let life be short, else shame will be too long.
                                          [*Exeunt*]

SCENE vi
Another part of the field.

[*Alarum. Enter* KING HENRY *and forces,* EXETER,
            and others.]
KING. Well have we done, thrice valiant country-
    men.
    But all's not done; yet keep the French the field.
EXETER. The Duke of York commends him to your
    majesty.
KING. Lives he, good uncle? Thrice within this hour
5   I saw him down, thrice up again, and fighting.
    From helmet to the spur all blood he was.
EXETER. In which array, brave soldier, doth he lie,
    Larding° the plain; and by his bloody side,
    Yoke-fellow to his honor-owing° wounds,
10 The noble Earl of Suffolk also lies.
    Suffolk first died, and York, all haggled° over,
    Comes to him where in gore he lay insteep'd
    And takes him by the beard, kisses the gashes
    That bloodily did yawn upon his face,
15 And cries aloud, "Tarry, dear cousin Suffolk!
    My soul shall thine keep company to heaven,
    Tarry, sweet soul, for mine, then fly abreast,
    As in this glorious and well-foughten field
    We kept together in our chivalry!"
20 Upon these words I came and cheer'd him up.
    He smil'd me in the face, raught° me his hand,
    And with a feeble gripe says "Dear my lord,
    Commend my service to my sovereign."
    So did he turn, and over Suffolk's neck
25 He threw his wounded arm and kiss'd his lips,
    And so espous'd to death, with blood he seal'd
    A testament of noble-ending love.
    The pretty and sweet manner of it forc'd
    Those waters from me which I would have
        stopp'd,
30 But I had not so much of man in me,
    And all my mother came into mine eyes

Larding   enriching (with his blood)
honor-owing   honor-owning   *haggled*   hacked
raught   reached

And gave me up to tears.
KING. I blame you not;
    For, hearing this, I must perforce compound°
    With mistful eyes, or they will issue too.
                                          [*Alarum.*]
    But, hark! What new alarum is this same?   35
    The French have reinforc'd their scatter'd men.
    Then every soldier kill his prisoners;
    Give the word through.   [*Exeunt*]

SCENE vii
Another part of the field.

[*Enter* FLUELLEN *and* GOWER.]
FLUELLEN. Kill the poys and the luggage! 'Tis
    expressly against the law of arms. 'Tis as arrant a
    piece of knavery, mark you now, as can be
    offer't. In your conscience, now, is it not?
GOWER. 'Tis certain there's not a boy left alive, and   5
    the cowardly rascals that ran from the battle ha'
    done this slaughter. Besides, they have burned
    and carried away all that was in the king's tent,
    wherefore the king, most worthily, hath caused
    every soldier to cut his prisoner's throat. O, 'tis a   10
    gallant king!
FLUELLEN. Aye, he was porn at Monmouth, Cap-
    tain Gower. What call you the town's name
    where Alexander the Pig was born?
GOWER. Alexander the Great.   15
FLUELLEN. Why, I pray you, is not pig great? The
    pig, or the great, or the mighty, or the huge, or
    the magnanimous, are all one reckonings, save
    the phrase is a little variations.
GOWER. I think Alexander the Great was born in   20
    Macedon. His father was called Philip of Mace-
    don, as I take it.
FLUELLEN. I think it is in Macedon where Alexander
    is porn. I tell you, captain, if you look in the maps
    of the 'orld, I warrant you sall find, in the com-   25
    parisons between Macedon and Monmouth, that
    the situations, look you, is both alike. There is a
    river in Macedon, and there is also moreover a
    river at Monmouth. It is called Wye at Mon-
    mouth, but it is out of my prains what is the   30
    name of the other river; but 'tis all one, 'tis alike
    as my fingers is to my fingers, and there is
    salmons in both. If you mark Alexander's life
    well, Harry of Monmouth's life is come after it
    indifferent well,° for there is figures° in all   35
    things. Alexander, God knows, and you know,
    in his rages, and his furies, and his wraths, and

compound   come to terms
is . . . well   matches it pretty closely   *figures*   analogies

his cholers, and his moods, and his displeasures, and his indignations, and also being a little
40 intoxicates in his prains, did, in his ales and his angers, look you, kill his best friend, Cleitus.

GOWER. Our king is not like him in that. He never killed any of his friends.

FLUELLEN. It is not well done, mark you now, to
45 take the tales out of my mouth, ere it is made and finished. I speak but in the figures and comparisons of it. As Alexander killed his friend Cleitus, being in his ales and his cups, so also Harry Monmouth, being in his right wits and his
50 good judgments, turned away the fat knight with the great-belly doublet. He was full of jests, and gipes, and knaveries, and mocks. I have forgot his name.

GOWER. Sir John Falstaff.

55 FLUELLEN. That is he. I'll tell you there is good men porn at Monmouth.

GOWER. Here comes his majesty.

[*Alarum. Enter* KING HENRY *and forces;* WARWICK, GLOUCESTER, EXETER, *and others.*]

KING. I was not angry since I came to France
Until this instant. Take a trumpet, herald;
60 Ride thou unto the horsemen on yon hill.
If they will fight with us, bid them come down,
Or void the field. They do offend our sight.
If they'll do neither, we will come to them
And make them skirr° away, as swift as stones
65 Enforced from the old Assyrian slings.
Besides, we'll cut the throats of those we have,
And not a man of them that we shall take
Shall taste our mercy. Go and tell them so.

[*Enter* MONTJOY.]

EXETER. Here comes the herald of the French, my liege.

GLOUCESTER. His eyes are humbler than they us'd
70 to be.

KING. How now! What means this, herald?
Know'st thou not
That I have fin'd° these bones of mine for ransom?
Com'st thou again for ransom?

MONTJOY.   No, great king.
I come to thee for charitable license
75 That we may wander o'er this bloody field
To book° our dead and then to bury them;
To sort our nobles from our common men.
For many of our princes—woe the while!—
Lie drown'd and soak'd in mercenary blood;
80 So do our vulgar° drench their peasant limbs
In blood of princes, and their wounded steeds

Fret fetlock deep in gore, and with wild rage
Yerk° out their armed heels at their dead masters,
Killing them twice. O, give us leave, great king,
To view the field in safety and dispose   85
Of their dead bodies!

KING.   I tell thee truly, herald,
I know not if the day be ours or no,
For yet a many of your horsemen peer
And gallop o'er the field.

MONTJOY.   The day is yours.

KING. Praised be God, and not our strength, for it!   90
What is this castle call'd that stands hard by?

MONTJOY. They call it Agincourt.

KING. Then call we this the field of Agincourt,
Fought on the day of Crispin Crispianus.

FLUELLEN. Your grandfather of famous memory,   95
an 't please your majesty, and your great-uncle
Edward the Plack Prince of Wales, as I have read
in the chronicles, fought a most prave pattle here
in France.

KING. They did, Fluellen.   100

FLUELLEN. Your majesty says very true. If your
majesties is remembered of it, the Welshmen
did good service in a garden where leeks did
grow, wearing leeks in their Monmouth caps;
which, your majesty know, to this hour is an   105
honorable badge of the service, and I do believe
your majesty takes no scorn to wear the leek
upon Saint Tavy's° day.

KING. I wear it for a memorable honor,
For I am Welsh, you know, good countryman.   110

FLUELLEN. All the water in Wye cannot wash your
majesty's Welsh plood out of your pody, I can
tell you that. God pless it and preserve it, as long
as it pleases his grace, and his majesty too!

KING. Thanks, good my countryman.   115

FLUELLEN. By Jeshu, I am your majesty's countryman, I care not who know it; I will confess it to
all the 'orld. I need not to be ashamed of your
majesty, praised be God, so long as your majesty
is an honest man.   120

KING. God keep me so! Our heralds go with him.
Bring me just notice of the numbers dead
On both our parts. Call yonder fellow hither.

[*Exeunt* HERALDS *with* MONTJOY.]

EXETER. Soldier, you must come to the king.

KING. Soldier, why wearest thou that glove in thy   125
cap?

WILLIAMS. An 't please your majesty, 'tis the gage
of one that I should fight withal, if he be alive.

---

skirr scurry   *fin'd* wagered, staked
book register   *vulgar* commoners

Yerk kick
Saint Tavy's Saint David's, March 1, patron saint of Wales

KING. An Englishman?

130 WILLIAMS. An 't please your majesty, a rascal that swaggered with me last night, who, if alive and ever dare to challenge this glove, I have sworn to take him a box o' th' ear. Or if I can see my glove in his cap, which he swore, as he was a soldier, he
135 would wear if alive, I will strike it out soundly.

KING. What think you, Captain Fluellen? Is it fit this soldier keep his oath?

FLUELLEN. He is a craven and a villain else, an 't please your majesty, in my conscience.

140 KING. It may be his enemy is a gentleman of great sort, quite from the answer of his degree.°

FLUELLEN. Though he be as good a gentleman as the devil is, as Lucifer and Belzebub himself, it is necessary, look your grace, that he keep his vow
145 and his oath. If he be perjured, see you now, his reputation is as arrant a villain and a Jacksauce° as ever his black shoe trod upon God's ground and his earth, in my conscience, la!

KING. Then keep thy vow, sirrah, when thou
150 meetest the fellow.

WILLIAMS. So I will, my liege, as I live.

KING. Who servest thou under?

WILLIAMS. Under Captain Gower, my liege.

FLUELLEN. Gower is a good captain, and is good
155 knowledge and literatured in the wars.

KING. Call him hither to me, soldier.

WILLIAMS. I will, my liege.   [Exit]

KING. Here, Fluellen, wear thou this favor for me and stick it in thy cap. When Alençon and myself
160 were down together, I plucked this glove from his helm. If any man challenge this, he is a friend to Alençon, and an enemy to our person. If thou encounter any such, apprehend him, an thou dost me love.

165 FLUELLEN. Your grace doo's me as great honors as can be desired in the hearts of his subjects. I would fain see the man that has but two legs that shall find himself aggriefed at this glove, that is all. But I would fain see it once, an 't please God
170 of his grace that I might see.

KING. Knowest thou Gower?

FLUELLEN. He is my dear friend, an 't please you.

KING. Pray thee, go seek him, and bring him to my tent.

175 FLUELLEN. I will fetch him.   [Exit]

KING. My Lord of Warwick, and my brother Gloucester,
    Follow Fluellen closely at the heels.
    The glove which I have given him for a favor

May haply purchase him a box o' th' ear.
It is the soldier's. I by bargain should   180
Wear it myself. Follow, good cousin Warwick.
If that the soldier strike him, as I judge
By his blunt bearing he will keep his word,
Some sudden mischief may arise of it;
For I do know Fluellen valiant,   185
And, touch'd with choler, hot as gunpowder,
And quickly will return an injury.
Follow, and see there be no harm between them.
Go you with me, uncle of Exeter.   [Exeunt]

SCENE viii
Before KING HENRY's *pavilion.*

[*Enter* GOWER *and* WILLIAMS.]

WILLIAMS. I warrant it is to knight you, captain.
                [*Enter* FLUELLEN.]

FLUELLEN. God's will and his pleasure, captain, I beseech you now, come apace to the king. There is more good toward you peradventure than is in your knowledge to dream of.   5

WILLIAMS. Sir, know you this glove?

FLUELLEN. Know the glove! I know the glove is a glove.

WILLIAMS. I know this, and thus I challenge it.
                                          [*Strikes him.*]

FLUELLEN. 'Sblood!° An arrant traitor as any is in   10
the universal world, or in France, or in England!

GOWER. How now, sir! You villain!

WILLIAMS. Do you think I'll be forsworn?°

FLUELLEN. Stand away, Captain Gower. I will give treason his payment into plows, I warrant you.   15

WILLIAMS. I am no traitor.

FLUELLEN. That's a lie in thy throat. I charge you in his majesty's name, apprehend him. He's a friend of the Duke Alençon's.
        [*Enter* WARWICK *and* GLOUCESTER.]

WARWICK. How now, how now! What's the   20
matter?

FLUELLEN. My Lord of Warwick, here is—praised be God for it!—a most contagious treason come to light, look you, as you shall desire in a summer's day. Here is his majesty.   25
        [*Enter* KING HENRY *and* EXETER.]

KING. How now! What's the matter?

FLUELLEN. My liege, here is a villain and a traitor that, look your grace, has struck the glove which your majesty is take out of the helmet of Alençon.   30

WILLIAMS. My liege, this was my glove; here is the

---

quite . . . degree above his rank, hence not obliged to
    answer the challenge
Jacksauce saucy jack

S'blood by God's blood   *be forsworn* break my oath

fellow of it. And he that I gave it to in charge
promised to wear it in his cap. I promised to
strike him if he did. I met this man with my
35   glove in his cap, and I have been as good as my
word.

FLUELLEN. Your majesty hear now, saving your
majesty's manhood, what an arrant, rascally,
beggarly, lousy knave it is. I hope your majesty is
40   pear me testimony and witness, and will
avouchment, that this is the glove of Alençon,
that your majesty is give me; in your conscience,
now.

KING. Give me thy glove, soldier. Look, here is the
fellow of it.

45   'Twas I, indeed, thou promised'st to strike,
And thou hast given me most bitter terms.°

FLUELLEN. And please your majesty, let his neck
answer for it, if there is any martial law in the
world.

50   KING. How canst thou make me satisfaction?

WILLIAMS. All offenses, my lord, come from the
heart. Never came any from mine that might
offend your majesty.

KING. It was ourself thou didst abuse.

55   WILLIAMS. Your majesty came not like yourself.
You appeared to me but as a common man—
witness the night, your garments, your lowliness.
And what your highness suffered under that
shape, I beseech you to take it for your own
60   fault and not mine; for had you been as I took
you for, I made no offense. Therefore, I beseech
your highness, pardon me.

KING. Here, uncle Exeter, fill this glove with
crowns
And give it to this fellow. Keep it, fellow,
65   And wear it for an honor in thy cap
Till I do challenge it. Give him the crowns.
And, captain, you must needs be friends with
him.

FLUELLEN. By this day and this light, the fellow has
mettle enough in his belly. Hold, there is twelve
70   pence for you, and I pray you to serve God, and
keep you out of prawls, and prabbles, and
quarrels, and dissensions, and, I warrant you, it
is better for you.

WILLIAMS. I will none of your money.

75   FLUELLEN. It is with a good will, I can tell you. It
will serve you to mend your shoes. Come,
wherefore should you be so pashful? Your shoes
is not so good. 'Tis a good silling, I warrant you,
or I will change it.

[Enter an ENGLISH HERALD.]

80   KING. Now, herald, are the dead number'd?

HERALD. Here is the number of the slaughter'd
French.

KING. What prisoners of good sort are taken,
uncle?

EXETER. Charles Duke of Orleans, nephew to the
king,
John Duke of Bourbon, and Lord Bouciqualt.
Of other lords and barons, knights and squires,   85
Full fifteen hundred, besides commen men.

KING. This note doth tell me of ten thousand
French
That in the field lie slain. Of princes in this
number,
And nobles bearing banners,° there lie dead
One hundred twenty-six. Added to these,   90
Of knights, esquires, and gallant gentlemen,
Eight thousand and four hundred, of the which
Five hundred were but yesterday dubb'd
knights.
So that in these ten thousand they have lost
There are but sixteen hundred mercenaries;   95
The rest are princes, barons, lords, knights,
squires,
And gentlemen of blood and quality.
The names of those their nobles that lie dead:
Charles Delabreth, high constable of France;
Jaques of Chatillon, admiral of France;   100
The master of the crossbows, Lord Rambures;
Great Master of France, the brave Sir Guichard
Dolphin,
John Duke of Alençon, Anthony Duke of
Brabant,
The brother to the Duke of Burgundy,
And Edward Duke of Bar. Of lusty earls,   105
Grandpré and Roussi, Fauconberg and Foix,
Beaumont and Marle, Vaudemont and Lestrale.
Here was a royal fellowship of death!
Where is the number of our English dead?

[HERALD shows him another paper.]

Edward the Duke of York, the Earl of Suffolk,   110
Sir Richard Ketly, Davy Gam, esquire.
None else of name; and of all other men
But five and twenty. O God, thy arm was here!
And not to us, but to thy arm alone,
Ascribe we all! When, without stratagem,   115
But in plain shock and even play of battle,
Was ever known so great and little loss
On one part and on th' other? Take it, God,
For it is none but thine!

EXETER.   'Tis wonderful!

KING. Come, go we in procession to the village.   120
And be it death proclaimed through our host
To boast of this or take that praise from God

---

given . . . terms i.e., insulted me   *bearing banners* i.e., with coats of arms

Which is His only.

FLUELLEN. Is it not lawful, an 't please your ma-
125   jesty, to tell how many is killed?

KING. Yes, captain, but with this acknowledgment,
    That God fought for us.

FLUELLEN. Yes, my conscience, He did us great
    good.

KING. Do we all holy rites.   130
    Let there be sung "*Non nobis*" and "*Te Deum*,"
    The dead with charity enclos'd in clay.
    And then to Calais, and to England then,
    Where ne'er from France arriv'd more happy
    men.   [*Exeunt*]

A C T   V

PROLOGUE

[*Enter* CHORUS.]

CHORUS. Vouchsafe to those that have not read the
    story
    That I may prompt them; and of such as have,
    I humbly pray them to admit th' excuse
    Of time, of numbers, and due course of things
5   Which cannot in their huge and proper life
    Be here presented. Now we bear the king
    Toward Calais. Grant him there. There seen,
    Heave him away upon your winged thoughts
    Athwart the sea. Behold, the English beach
    Pales in the flood° with men, with wives, and
10   boys
    Whose shouts and claps out-voice the deep-
    mouth'd sea,
    Which like a mighty whiffler° 'fore the king
    Seems to prepare his way. So let him land,
    And solemnly see him set on to London.
15   So swift a pace hath thought that even now
    You may imagine him upon Blackheath,
    Where that his lords desire him to have borne
    His bruised helmet and his bended sword
    Before him through the city. He forbids it,
20   Being free from vainness and self-glorious pride,
    Giving full trophy, signal, and ostent°
    Quite from himself to God. But now behold,
    In the quick forge and working-house of
    thought,
    How London doth pour out her citizens!
25   The mayor and all his brethren in best sort,°
    Like to the senators of th' antique Rome
    With the plebeians swarming at their heels,
    Go forth and fetch their conquering Cæsar in—

As, by a lower but loving likelihood,°
Were now the general of our gracious empress   30
(As in good time he may) from Ireland coming,
Bringing rebellion broached° on his sword,°
How many would the peaceful city quit
To welcome him! Much more, and much more
    cause,
Did they this Harry. Now in London place him.   35
As yet the lamentation of the French
Invites the King of England's stay at home;
The Emperor's coming° in behalf of France
To order peace between them; and omit
All the occurrences, whatever chanc'd,   40
Till Harry's back-return again to France.
There must we bring him; and myself have
    play'd
The interim by rememb'ring° you 'tis past.
Then brook abridgment,° and your eyes
    advance
After your thoughts, straight back again to
    France.   [*Exit*]   45

SCENE i
France. The English camp.

[*Enter* FLUELLEN *an* GOWER.]

GOWER. Nay, that's right, but why wear you your
    leek today? Saint Davy's day is past.

FLUELLEN. There is occasions and causes why and
    wherefore in all things. I will tell you asse my

Pales . . . flood   walls in the sea
whiffler   officer who clears the way for the king
trophy . . . ostent   triumphal signs and shows
sort   attire

loving likelihood   much desired eventuality
broached   spitted
Were . . . sword   (contemporary allusion; the Earl of
    Essex led an expedition for Queen Elizabeth against the
    rebellious Irish in 1599, but failed)
Emperor's coming   (Sigismund, Holy Roman Emperor,
    came to England in 1416 to mediate between England
    and France)
rememb'ring   reminding
brook abridgment   tolerate the omission

5   friend, Captain Gower. The rascally, scauld°
beggarly, lousy, pragging knave, Pistol, which
you and yourself and all the world know to be
no petter than a fellow, look you now, of no
merits, he is come to me and prings me pread
10   and salt yesterday, look you, and bid me eat my
leek. It was in a place where I could not breed
no contention with him. But I will be so bold as
to wear it in my cap till I see him once again, and
then I will tell him a little piece of my desires.

                [ENTER PISTIL]

15   GOWER. Why, here he comes, swelling like a
turkey cock.

    FLUELLEN. 'Tis no matter for his swellings nor his
turkey cocks. God pless you, Aunchient Pistol!
You scurvy, lousy knave, God pless you.

    PISTOL. Ha! Art thou bedlam?° Dost thou thirst,
20   base Trojan,°
To have me fold up Parca's fatal web?°
Hence! I am qualmish at the smell of leek.

    FLUELLEN. I peseech you heartily, scurvy, lousy
knave, at my desires, and my requests, and my
25   petitions, to eat, look you, this leek. Because,
look you, you do not love it, nor your affections
and your appetites and your disgestions doo's
not agree with it, I would desire you to eat it.

    PISTOL. Not for Cadwallader° and all his goats.°

30   FLUELLEN. There is one goat for you. [Strikes him]
Will you be so good, scauld knave, as eat it?

    PISTOL. Base Trojan, thou shalt die.

    FLUELLEN. You say very true, scauld knave, when
God's will is. I will desire you to live in the
35   meantime, and eat your victuals. Come, there is
sauce for it. [Strikes him] You called me yesterday
mountain squire;° but I will make you today a
squire of low degree.° I pray you, fall to. If you
can mock a leek, you can eat a leek.

40   GOWER. Enough, captain. You have astonished
him.

    FLUELLEN. I say I will make him eat some part of
my leek, or I will peat his pate four days. Bite, I
pray you; it is good for your green wound and
45   your ploody coxcomb.

PISTOL. Must I bite?

FLUELLEN. Yes, certainly, and out of doubt and out
of question too, and ambiguities.

PISTOL. By this leek, I will most horribly revenge.
I eat and eat, I swear—   50

FLUELLEN. Eat, I pray you. Will you have some
more sauce to your leek? There is not enough
leek to swear by.

PISTOL. Quiet thy cudgel; thou dost see I eat.

FLUELLEN. Much good do you, scauld knave,   55
heartily. Nay, pray you, throw none away; the
skin is good for your broken coxcomb. When
you take occasions to see leeks hereafter, I pray
you, mock at 'em; that is all.

PISTOL. Good.   60

FLUELLEN. Aye, leeks is good. Hold you, there is a
groat° to heal your pate.

PISTOL. Me a groat!

FLUELLEN. Yes, verily and in truth, you shall take it,
or I have another leek in my pocket which you   65
shall eat.

PISTOL. I take thy groat in earnest° of revenge.

FLUELLEN. If I owe you anything, I will pay you in
cudgels. You shall be a woodmonger,° and buy
nothing of me but cudgels. God b' wi' you, and   70
keep you, and heal your pate.   [Exit]

PISTOL. All hell shall stir for this.

GOWER. Go, go; you are a counterfeit cowardly
knave. Will you mock at an ancient tradition,
begun upon an honorable respect and worn as a   75
memorable trophy of predeceased° valor, and
dare not avouch in your deeds any of your
words? I have seen you gleeking° and galling at
this gentleman twice or thrice. You thought,
because he could not speak English in the native   80
garb, he could not therefore handle an English
cudgel. You find it otherwise; and henceforth
let a Welsh correction teach you a good English
condition. Fare ye well.   [Exit]

PISTOL. Doth Fortune play the huswife° with me
now?   85
News have I that my Doll° is dead i' the spital°
Of malady of France,°
And there my rendezvous° is quite cut off.
Old I do wax, and from my weary limbs
Honor is cudgeled. Well, bawd° I'll turn,   90

---

scauld   scabby
bedlam   mad [from Bethlehem Hospital (Bedlam), the
    lunatic asylum]
Trojan   "sport"
fold . . . web   i.e., cut your life short (the Parcae were the
    Fates who sat weaving men's destinies)
Cadwallader   last king of Wales, defender against the
    Saxons
goats   associated with Wales (Pistol implies that
    Cadwallader ruled little else)
mountain squire   i.e., holder of worthless land
squire . . . degree   i.e., as opposed to "mountain"; but
    also the title of a contemporary romance

groat   fourpence
earnest   down payment   *woodmonger*   wood-dealer
predeceased   long-dead   *gleeking*   mocking
huswife   hussy
Doll   [possible misprint for *Nell* (the Mistress Quickly of
    1, 2Henry IV)]
spital   hospital   *malady of France*   venereal disease
rendezvous   i.e., place to return to
bawd   bawdy-house keeper

And something lean to cutpurse of quick hand.°
To England will I steal, and there I'll steal,
And patches will I get unto these cudgel'd
  scars
And swear I got them in the Gallia wars.

[*Exit*]

SCENE ii
France. A royal palace.

[*Enter, at one door,* KING HENRY, EXETER,
BEDFORD, GLOUCESTER, WARWICK,
WESTMORELAND, *and other* LORDS; *at another,*
the FRENCH KING, QUEEN ISABEL, *the*
PRINCESS KATHARINE, ALICE, *and other*
LADIES; *the* DUKE OF BURGUNDY, *and his train.*]

KING. Peace to this meeting, wherefore we are
  met!
Unto our brother France and to our sister
Health and fair time of day. Joy and good
  wishes
To our most fair and princely cousin Katharine.
5 And as a branch and member of this royalty,
By whom this great assembly is contriv'd,
We do salute you, Duke of Burgundy.
And, princes French, and peers, health to you
  all!
FRENCH KING. Right joyous are we to behold your
  face,
10 Most worthy brother England; fairly met.
So are you, princes English, every one.
QUEEN. So happy be the issue,° brother England,
Of this good day and of this gracious meeting,
As we are now glad to behold your eyes—
15 Your eyes, which hitherto have borne in them
Against the French, that met them in their
  bent,°
The fatal balls° of murdering basilisks.°
The venom of such looks, we fairly hope,
Have lost their quality, and that this day
20 Shall change all griefs and quarrels into love.
KING. To cry amen to that, thus we appear.
QUEEN. You English princes all, I do salute you.
BURGUNDY. My duty to you both, on equal love,
Great Kings of France and England! That I have
  labor'd
With all my wits, my pains, and strong en-
25   deavors

To bring your most imperial majesties
Unto this bar° and royal interview,
Your mightiness on both parts best can witness.
Since, then, my office hath so far prevail'd
30 That face to face and royal eye to eye
You have congreeted,° let it not disgrace me
If I demand, before this royal view,
What rub or what impediment there is
Why that the naked, poor, and mangled Peace,
35 Dear nurse of arts, plenties, and joyful births,
Should not in this best garden of the world,
Our fertile France, put up her lovely visage?
Alas, she hath from France too long been chas'd,
And all her husbandry doth lie on heaps,
40 Corrupting in it° own fertility.
Her vine, the merry cheerer of the heart,
Unpruned dies; her hedges even-pleach'd,°
Like prisoners wildly overgrown with hair,
Put forth disorder'd twigs; her fallow leas
45 The darnel, hemlock, and rank fumitory
Doth root upon, while that the coulter rusts
That should deracinate° such savagery.
The even mead, that erst° brought sweetly forth
The freckled cowslip, burnet, and green clover,
50 Wanting° the scythe, all uncorrected, rank,
Conceives by idleness, and nothing teems
But hateful docks, rough thistles, kecksies,°
  burrs,
Losing both beauty and utility.
And as our vineyards, fallows, meads, and
  hedges,
55 Defective in their natures, grow to wildness,
Even so our houses and ourselves and children
Have lost, or do not learn for want of time,
The sciences that should become our country,
But grow like savages—as soldiers will
60 That nothing do but meditate on blood—
To swearing and stern looks, diffus'd° attire,
And everything that seems unnatural.
Which to reduce into° our former favor°
You are assembled, and my speech entreats
65 That I may know the let° why gentle Peace
Should not expel these inconveniences
And bless us with her former qualities.
KING. If, Duke of Burgundy, you would° the peace
Whose want° gives growth to th' imperfections
70 Which you have cited, you must buy that peace
With full accord to all our just demands,

---

something . . . hand i.e., pick purses on the side
So . . . issue may the result be as happy
bent direct gaze; but also, line of fire
balls i.e., eyeballs, but also cannon balls
basilisks large cannon; but also mythical serpents that
  killed with a look

bar court   congreeted greeted one another   it its
even-pleach'd evenly interwoven   deracinate uproot
erst formerly   Wanting lacking
kecksies kex; dry stalks of hollow-stemmed plants
diffus'd disorderly   reduce into return to
favor appearance   let hindrance
would would have   want lack

Whose tenors and particular effects°
You have enschedul'd° briefly in your hands.
BURGUNDY. The king hath heard them, to the which as yet
There is no answer made.
75 KING.   Well, then, the peace
Which you before so urg'd lies in his answer.
FRENCH KING. I have but with a cursorary° eye
O'erglanc'd the articles. Pleaseth your Grace
To appoint some of your council presently
80 To sit with us once more, with better heed
To resurvey them, we will suddenly
Pass our accept and peremptory answer.°
KING. Brother, we shall. Go, uncle Exeter,
And brother Clarence, and you, brother Gloucester,
85 Warwick and Huntingdon, go with the king.
And take with you free power to ratify,
Augment, or alter, as your wisdoms best
Shall see advantageable for our dignity,
Anything in or out of our demands,
90 And we'll consign° thereto. Will you, fair sister,
Go with the princes, or stay here with us?
QUEEN. Our gracious brother, I will go with them.
Haply a woman's voice may do some good
When articles too nicely° urg'd be stood on.
95 KING. Yet leave our cousin Katharine here with us.
She is our capital demand, compris'd
Within the fore-rank of our articles.
QUEEN. She hath good leave.
[*Exeunt all except* HENRY, KATHARINE, *and* ALICE.]
KING.   Fair Katharine, and most fair,
Will you vouchsafe to teach a soldier terms
100 Such as will enter at a lady's ear
And plead his love suit to her gentle heart?
KATHARINE. Your majesty shall mock at me; I cannot speak your England.
KING. O fair Katharine, if you will love me soundly
105 with your French heart, I will be glad to hear you
confess it brokenly with your English tongue.
Do you like me, Kate?
KATHARINE. *Pardonnez-moi*, I cannot tell vat is "like me."
110 KING. An angel is like you, Kate, and you are like an angel.
KATHARINE. *Que dit-il? Que je suis semblable à les anges?*°
ALICE. *Oui, vraiment, sauf votre grace, ainsi dit-il.*°

KING. I said so, dear Katharine, and I must not 115 blush to affirm it.
KATHARINE. *O bon Dieu! Les langues des hommes sont pleines de tromperies.*
KING. What says she, fair one? That the tongues of men are full of deceits? 120
ALICE. *Oui*, dat de tongues of de mans is be full of deceits, dat is de princess.
KING. The princess is the better Englishwoman. I' faith, Kate, my wooing is fit for thy understanding. I am glad thou canst speak no better 125 English, for if thou couldst thou wouldst find me such a plain king that thou wouldst think I had sold my farm to buy my crown. I know no ways to mince it in love, but directly to say "I love you." Then if you urge me farther than to say 130 "Do you in faith?" I wear out my suit. Give me your answer, i' faith, do; and so clap hands and a bargain. How say you, lady?
KATHARINE. *Sauf votre honneur*, me understand vell.
KING. Marry, if you would put me to verses or to 135 dance for your sake, Kate, why, you undid me. For the one, I have neither words nor measure,° and for the other, I have no strength in measure,° yet a reasonable measure in strength. If I could win a lady at leapfrog, or by vaulting into my 140 saddle with my armor on my back—under the correction of bragging be it spoken—I should quickly leap into a wife. Or if I might buffet° for my love, or bound my horse° for her favors, I could lay on like a butcher and sit like a jacka- 145 napes,° never off. But, before God, Kate, I cannot look greenly° nor gasp out my eloquence, nor I have no cunning in protestation°—only downright oaths, which I never use till urged, nor never break for urging. If thou canst love a 150 fellow of this temper, Kate, whose face is not worth sunburning, that never looks in his glass for love of anything he sees there, let thine eye be thy cook. I speak to thee plain soldier. If thou canst love me for this, take me. If not, to say to 155 thee that I shall die, is true—but for thy love, by the Lord, no; yet I love thee too. And while thou livest, dear Kate, take a fellow of plain and uncoined° constancy, for he perforce must do thee right because he hath not the gift to woo in other 160 places. For these fellows of infinite tongue, that can rhyme themselves into ladies' favors, they do always reason themselves out again. What! A

---

tenors . . . effects general purport and details
enschedul'd itemized   *cursorary* cursory
Pass . . . answer render our decisive and final answer
consign seal   *nicely* fastidiously
Que . . . anges what does he say? that I am like the angels
Oui . . . dit-il yes, truly, save your grace, so he says

measure meter   *measure* dancing   *buffet* box
bound my horse i.e., make him prance
jackanapes monkey
greenly i.e., like a lovesick youth
protestation i.e., lovers' oaths
uncoined i.e., pure, unalloyed

speaker is but a prater; a rhyme is but a ballad.
165 A good leg will fall, a straight back will stoop, a
black beard will turn white, a curled pate will
grow bald, a fair face will wither, a full eye will
wax hollow. But a good heart, Kate, is the sun
and the moon; or, rather, the sun, and not the
170 moon, for it shines bright and never changes, but
keeps his course truly. If thou would have such a
one, take me; and take me, take a soldier; take
a soldier, take a king. And what sayest thou then
to my love? Speak, my fair, and fairly, I pray
175 thee.

KATHARINE. Is it possible dat I sould love de enemy
of France?

KING. No, it is not possible you should love the
enemy of France, Kate. But, in loving me you
180 should love the friend of France—for I love
France so well that I will not part with a village
of it; I will have it all mine. And, Kate, when
France is mine and I am yours, then yours is
France and you are mine.

185 KATHARINE. I cannot tell vat is dat.

KING. No, Kate? I will tell thee in French, which I
am sure will hang upon my tongue like a new-
married wife about her husband's neck, hardly
to be shook off. *Je quand sur le possession de*
190 *France, et quand vous avez le possession de moi*—let
me see, what then? Saint Denis° be my speed!—
donc votre est France et vous êtes mienne.° It is as
easy for me, Kate, to conquer the kingdom as to
speak so much more French. I shall never move
195 thee in French, unless it be to laugh at me.

KATHARINE. *Sauf votre honneur, le Francais que vous
parlez, il est meilleur que l'Anglais lequel je parle.°*

KING. No, faith, is 't not, Kate, but thy speaking of
my tongue, and I thine, most truly-falsely, must
200 needs be granted to be much at one.° But, Kate,
dost thou understand thus much English? Canst
thou love me?

KATHARINE. I cannot tell.

KING. Can any of your neighbors tell, Kate? I'll
205 ask them. Come, I know thou lovest me, and at
night, when you come into your closet, you'll
question this gentle-woman about me. And I
know, Kate, you will to her dispraise those parts
in me that you love with your heart; but, good
210 Kate, mock me mercifully, the rather, gentle
princess, because I love thee cruelly. If ever thou
beest mine, Kate—as I have a saving faith within

me tells me thou shalt—I get thee with scambling,° and thou must therefore needs prove a
good soldier-breeder. Shall not thou and I, 215
between Saint Denis and Saint George, compound a boy, half French, half English, that shall
go to Constantinople and take the Turk by the
beard?° Shall we not? What sayest thou, my fair
flower-de-luce?° 220

KATHARINE. I do not know dat.

KING. No, 'tis hereafter to know, but now to
promise. Do but now promise, Kate, you will
endeavor for your French part of such a boy, and
for my English moiety° take the word of a king 225
and a bachelor. How answer you, *la plus belle
Katharine du monde, mon très cher et devin déesse?°*

KATHARINE. Your majestee ave fausse French
enough to deceive de most sage demoiselle dat is
en France. 230

KING. Now, fie upon my false French! By mine
honor, in true English, I love thee, Kate. By
which honor I dare not swear thou lovest me;
yet my blood begins to flatter me that thou dost,
notwithstanding the poor and untempering° 235
effect of my visage. Now, beshrew° my father's
ambition! He was thinking of civil wars when he
got me; therefore was I created with a stubborn
outside, with an aspect of iron, that, when I come
to woo ladies, I fright them. But, in faith, Kate, 240
the elder I wax, the better I shall appear. My
comfort is that old age, that ill layer-up° of
beauty, can do no more spoil upon my face: thou
hast me, if thou hast me, at the worst; and thou
shalt wear me, if thou wear me, better and 245
better. And therefore tell me, most fair Katharine, will you have me? Put off your maiden
blushes; avouch the thoughts of your heart with
the looks of an empress; take me by the hand,
and say "Harry of England, I am thine." Which 250
word thou shalt no sooner bless mine ear withal,
but I will tell thee aloud "England is thine,
Ireland is thine, France is thine, and Henry
Plantagenet is thine," who, though I speak it
before his face, if he be not fellow with the best 255
king, ·thou shalt find the best king of good
fellows. Come, your answer in broken music,
for thy voice is music and thy English broken;
therefore, queen of all, Katharine, break thy

Saint Denis French patron saint
Je . . . mienne (Henry awkwardly translates his own
 words above)
Sauf . . . parle saving your honor, the French that you
 speak is better than the English that I speak
much at one about even

scambling fighting
go . . . beard i.e., win victory in the Crusade
flower-de-luce fleur-de-lis, the French royal emblem
moiety share
la plus . . . déesse the most beautiful Katharine in the
 world, my very dear and divine goddess
untempering incapable of softening
beshrew mischief on   *ill layer-up* poor preserver

260 mind to me in broken English. Wilt thou have
me?

KATHARINE. Dat is as it sall please *de roi mon père.*°

KING. Nay, it will please him well, Kate; it shall
please him, Kate.

265 KATHARINE. Den it sall also content me.

KING. Upon that I kiss your hand, and I call you my
queen.

KATHARINE. *Laissez, mon seigneur, laissez, laissez. Ma
foi, je ne veux point que vous abaissiez votre grandeur*
270 *en baisant la main d'une de votre seigneurie indigne
serviteur. Excusez-moi, je vous supplie, mon très-
puissant seigneur.*°

KING. Then I will kiss your lips, Kate.

KATHARINE. *Les dames et demoiselles pour être baisées*
275 *devant leur noces, il n'est pas la coutume de France.*°

KING. Madam my interpreter, what says she?

ALICE. Dat it is not be de fashion *pour les* ladies of
France—I cannot tell vat is *baiser* en Anglish.

KING. To kiss.

280 ALICE. Your majesty *entendre bettre que moi.*°

KING. It is not a fashion for the maids in France to
kiss before they are married, would she say?

ALICE. *Oui, vraiment.*°

KING. O Kate, nice customs curtsy to great kings.
285 Dear Kate, you and I cannot be confined within
the weak list° of a country's fashion. We are the
makers of manners, Kate, and the liberty that
follows our places stops the mouth of all find-
faults, as I will do yours for upholding the nice
290 fashion of your country in denying me a kiss.
Therefore, patiently and yielding. [*Kissing her*]
You have witchcraft in your lips, Kate. There is
more eloquence in a sugar touch of them than in
the tongues of the French council, and they
295 should sooner persuade Harry of England than a
general position of monarchs. Here comes your
father.

[*Re-enter the* FRENCH KING *and his* QUEEN,
BURGUNDY, *and other* LORDS.]

BURGUNDY. God save your majesty! My royal
cousin, teach you our princess English?

300 KING. I would have her learn, my fair cousin, how
perfectly I love her—and that is good English.

BURGUNDY. Is she not apt?

KING. Our tongue is rough, coz, and my condition°

is not smooth; so that, having neither the voice
nor the heart of flattery about me, I cannot so 305
conjure up the spirit of love in her that he will
appear in his true likeness.

BURGUNDY. Pardon the frankness of my mirth if I
answer you for that. If you would conjure in her,
you must make a circle; if conjure up love in her 310
in his true likeness, he must appear naked and
blind. Can you blame her then, being a maid yet
rosed over with the virgin crimson of modesty,
if she deny the appearance of a naked blind boy
in her naked seeing self? It were, my lord, a hard 315
condition° for a maid to consign° to.

KING. Yet they do wink and yield, as love is blind
and enforces.

BURGUNDY. They are then excused, my lord, when
they see not what they do. 320

KING. Then, good my lord, teach your cousin to
consent winking.

BURGUNDY. I will wink on her to consent, my lord,
if you will teach her to know my meaning, for
maids well summered and warm kept are like 325
flies at Bartholomewtide,° blind, though they
have their eyes; and then they will endure
handling, which before would not abide looking
on.

KING. This moral° ties me over to time and a hot 330
summer, and so I shall catch the fly, your cousin,
in the latter end, and she must be blind too.

BURGUNDY. As love is, my lord, before it loves.

KING. It is so; and you may, some of you, thank
love for my blindness, who cannot see many a 335
fair French city for one fair French maid that
stands in my way.

FRENCH KING. Yes, my lord, you see them perspectively,° the cities turned into a maid; for
they are all girdled with maiden walls that war 340
hath never entered.

KING. Shall Kate be my wife?

FRENCH KING. So please you.

KING. I am content, so° the maiden cities you talk
of may wait on her. So the maid that stood in the 345
way for my wish shall show me the way to my
will.

FRENCH KING. We have consented to all terms of
reason.

KING. Is 't so, my lords of England?

WESTMORELAND. The king hath granted every
article: 350
His daughter first, and then in sequel all,

---

de . . . père the king my father
Laissez . . . seigneur stop, my lord, stop, stop. My faith,
I do not wish you to lower your greatness by kissing
the hand of your unworthy servant. Excuse me, I beg
you, my most powerful lord.
Les . . . France it is not the custom in France for ladies
and young girls to kiss before their marriage
entendre . . . moi understands better than I
Oui, vraiment yes, truly   *list* limit
condition nature

consign agree   *Bartholomewtide* August 24
moral analogy
perspectively as through a glass that breaks and distorts
the image
so so long as   *addition* title

According to their firm proposed natures.

EXETER. Only he hath not yet subscribed this:
where your majesty demands that the King of
France, having any occasion to write for matter
of grant, shall name your highness in this form
and with this addition,° in French, *Notre très-cher*
fils Henri, Roi d'Angleterre, Héritier de France; and
thus in Latin, *Præclarissimus filius noster Henricus,*
Rex Angliæ, et Hæres Franciæ.°

FRENCH KING. Nor this I have not, brother, so
denied,
But your request shall make me let it pass.

KING. I pray you then, in love and dear alliance,
Let that one article rank with the rest,
And thereupon give me your daughter.

FRENCH KING. Take her, fair son, and from her
blood raise up
Issue to me, that the contending kingdoms
Of France and England, whose very shores look
pale
With envy of each other's happiness,
May cease their hatred, and this dear conjunc-
tion
Plant neighborhood° and Christian-like accord
In their sweet bosoms, that never war advance
His bleeding sword 'twixt England and fair
France.

ALL. Amen!

KING. Now, welcome, Kate; and bear me witness
all,
That here I kiss her as my sovereign queen.
[*Flourish.*]

QUEEN. God, the best maker of all marriages,
Combine your hearts in one, your realms in one!
As man and wife, being two, are one in love,
So be there 'twixt your kingdoms such a spousal
That never may ill office, or fell° jealousy,
Which troubles oft the bed of blessed marriage,

Thrust in between the paction° of these king-
doms
To make divorce of their incorporate league—
That English may as French, French Englishmen,
Receive each other. God speak this Amen!

ALL. Amen!

KING. Prepare we for our marriage; on which day
My Lord of Burgundy, we'll take your oath,
And all the peers', for surety° of our leagues.
Then shall I swear to Kate, and you to me,
And may our oaths well kept and prosp'rous be!
[*Sennet. Exeunt*]

EPILOGUE

[*Enter* CHORUS.]

CHORUS. Thus far, with rough and all-unable pen,
Our bending° author hath pursu'd the story,
In little room confining mighty men,
Mangling by starts° the full course of their
glory.
Small time, but in that small most greatly liv'd
This star of England. Fortune made his sword,
By which the world's best garden he achiev'd,
And of it left his son imperial lord.
Henry the Sixth, in infant bands crown'd King
Of France and England, did this king succeed;
Whose state so many had the managing
That they lost France and made his England
bleed.
Which oft our stage hath shown;° and, for their
sake,
In your fair minds let this acceptance take.°
[*Exit*]

---

paction union
surety ratification
bending i.e., under the weight
Mangling by starts i.e., presenting the story piecemeal
Which . . . shown (allusion to Shakespeare's own *1, 2, and*
3Henry VI, written nearly ten years earlier)
let . . . take let this play win your acceptance

Notre . . . Franciae our very dear son Henry, king of
England, heir of France, most renowned, etc.
neighborhood neighborliness *fell* fierce

AFTERWORD

As Shakespeare presents it, the story of the rascally and unpromising young Hal, Prince of Wales, who grew up to be the great statesman-soldier king, Henry V, is thoroughly in the tradition of one of literature's basic plots, the tale of the ugly duckling which grew up to be no duck at all but a beautiful white swan.

In reading this "Cronicle History of Henry the fift, With his battell fought at Agin Court in France. Togither with Auntient Pistoll . . . As it hath bene sundry times playd by the Right honorable the Lord Chamberlaine his servants," and in reflecting upon its immediate predecessors, *Richard II*, *Henry IV, Part 1*, and *Henry IV, Part 2*, an admirer of *Henry V*—both the play and the man—is tempted to conclude that Shakespeare conceived it as the end for which the other three plays were made. And indeed the first three do, in effect, exist in order to raise Hal-Henry up to the pinnacle on which the final play of the series sets and firmly holds him. All four are essentially the account of the wastrel youth who grows up to be a man, of the riotous prince who grows up to become England's hero-king.

Hal's story begins near the end of *Richard II*, when the ambitious and ruthless Bolingbroke, having deposed Richard and made himself Henry IV, asks his court whether any can tell him of his "unthrifty son," who reportedly frequents taverns with "unrestrained loose companions" and consorts even with men who commit robberies in narrow lanes. It is next picked up at the opening of *1Henry IV*, when the king again laments that "riot and dishonor" stain the reputation of his "young Harry" and expresses the wish that the heroic young Hotspur, son of Northumberland, might be proven to be his own son instead of Hal. Thereafter we are shown Hal himself among his "loose companions," including Falstaff, the fat knight who seems entirely given to drinking, waking at night, sleeping by day, robbing, and indulging his fantastic gift of wit in spectacular verbal duels with the Prince. We even see Hal take part in one robbery, but we are quickly assured that it was all in fun and that the money has been paid back. In fact, we are rather emphatically made to understand that though Hal has a reputation for wildness he is not *really* bad at all. Hal himself states in a famous and highly controversial soliloquy (*1HIV*, I, ii) that he is merely pretending to be idle so that when the time comes to throw off "this loose behavior" he will "show more goodly and attract more eyes" than if he had shown promise from the first. When serious rebellion threatens, Hal leaves the tavern, convinces his father that he is worthy of command, and goes to war. Shrewdly, Shakespeare places a description of the "new" Hal in the mouth of an enemy observer, for praise counts most when it comes from the other side:

> I saw young Harry with his beaver on,
> His cuisses on his thighs, gallantly arm'd,
> Rise from the ground like feather'd Mercury,
> And vaulted with such ease into his seat
> As if an angel dropp'd down from the clouds
> To turn and wind a fiery Pegasus
> And witch the world with noble horsemanship.

Hal distinguishes himself mightily in battle, first saving the life of his father and next defeating and killing the illustrious warrior Hotspur in hand-to-hand combat. At the end of this play, having defeated the rebels, Hal displays noble generosity by first asking his father's permission to free the heroic enemy Douglas, whose courage shown in the day's battle "taught us how to cherish such high deeds/ Even in the bosom of our adversaries," and then, more nobly still, turns over to his younger brother the actual honor of freeing the captive.

Shakespeare's campaign aimed at elevating Hal to the epic-hero status that would eventually be his in *Henry V* continues throughout *2Henry IV*. There new battles rage, and Hal continues to distinguish himself in valor and generosity. In this play, too, his conduct in taverns is restrained; though he plays tricks on Falstaff and continues to engage in wit duels with him, it is plain that his mind is growing increasingly aware of the great responsibility that will shortly be his. The wild abandon that characterized the comic scenes of *1Henry IV* is absent from Part 2. It is at the end of this play that Hal gives the final proofs of his mettle. When the old king dies (still, on his deathbed, not wholly confident of his son's worth), the Lord Chief Justice, with whom Hal as a wild youth had had serious difficulties (much more serious in history than in the play), expects to be summarily dismissed by the new king, if not imprisoned or executed. Instead, Hal commends his integrity, keeps him in office, and gives him this assurance:

> There is my hand.
> You shall be as a father to my youth,
> My voice shall sound as you do prompt mine ear,
> And I will stoop and humble my intents
> To your well-practic'd, wise directions.

But the final proof that Hal has grown up to kingly stature is given at the very end of the play, when without reservation or hint of regret he coldly rebukes, rejects, and banishes the friend of his misspent youth, Falstaff. Having just been crowned, Hal, with the Lord Chief Justice and the royal train, encounters Falstaff—who has waited in exuberant spirits, making confident wagers and expecting resumption, on a grand scale, of their old comradeship, together with new and royal favors. Falstaff greets Hal as of old: "God save thee, my sweet boy!" and adds, "My king! My Jove! I speak to thee, my heart!" Hal, with the crown newly set upon his head, stares icily upon his old comrade and speaks words that stand among the most chilling to be found in all Shakespeare:

> I know thee not, old man. Fall to thy prayers.
> How ill white hairs become a fool and jester!
> I have long dreamt of such a kind of man,
> So surfeit-swell'd, so old, and so profane;
> But, being awak'd, I do despise my dream.

He orders Falstaff "Not to come near our person by ten mile." And Falstaff, according to the Hostess's bitter charge in *Henry V*, goes home to die: "The King has killed his heart."

Over the centuries to the present, many critics, readers, and theatergoers have refused to forgive either Henry or Shakespeare for their treatment of Falstaff. The late great British Shakespearean Sir Arthur Quiller-Couch took furious occasion to remark that Shakespeare's composition of the rejection scene coincided with his own application for a coat of arms—the sign of his "turning respectable" and casting off whatever private Falstaffs he had in his own young days.

But of course Shakespeare's dramatic intention was diametrically opposed to this bitter view of latter-day and democratically oriented commentators: Shakespeare meant to serve unmistakable notice upon his immediate audiences that his hero was now ready to be a king. As a private man, certainly, Hal would never give up Falstaff. What Shakespeare appears to say is this: "Thus one must *be* to be a king." What our own age has found difficult to comprehend, the age of Elizabeth no doubt understood by common heritage.

So much, in part, is what lies behind the opening of *Henry V*. It was Shakespeare's purpose to raise his hero so high, in accomplishments and promise, that for the first and sole time in his dramatic career he would be moved to apologize for the inadequacies of himself as dramatic poet and the facilities of his crude theater, which, he makes the Chorus declare, could not possibly do justice to the greatness of his hero and his famous victories in France. What is needed is a kingdom for a stage, instead of the miserable "O" that the new Globe afforded, princes as actors, monarchs for audience. Only so might the hero-king be represented in the epic proportions that are his due. Though Shakespeare used a chorus elsewhere (*Romeo and Juliet*, *2Henry IV*, *Pericles*, *The Winter's Tale*), he never used one either before or after *Henry V* for such a purpose as here: to protest his own and his theater's inabilities to rise to the occasion.

The fact is that, except for Hal-Henry, Shakespeare was never much committed to high heroics. Talbot of *Henry VI, Part 1*, ten years earlier, appears to have been created "straight," without reservation. But the heroic Hotspur of *1Henry IV* Shakespeare would have us love for his whims, not his heroics. Achilles, the greatest of Greek warriors, he makes into a self-centered, murderous cad in *Troilus and Cressida*; Ajax is a plain blockhead; only the great Hector, in that play, earns respect, and he is so modest and noble that high heroics appears alien to his character. Orlando of *As You Like It*, the most— indeed, the only—heroic hero of the romantic comedies, is treated with tongue in cheek; he is the hero "As You Like Him," a lovable, robust booby, like our own L'il Abner. It is worthy of note that Henry as superhero appears mainly in the lines of the Chorus; there are a few exceptions, such as the stunning "Once more into the breach, dear friends" that opens Act III, scene i, and the yet-more-stunning "Crispin Crispian" speech, before Agincourt, in Act IV, scene iii. But otherwise the best of the hero king appears in his nonheroic moments, in the haunting IV, i, where he passes as "Harry le Roy," and gives us "A little touch of Harry in the night"; at the end of the same scene, when, with "Upon the King!" he gives us a profound look into "how it is" to be a king—and Shakespeare writes for the occasion one of the half dozen most tremendous utterances in all the plays; and, finally, in the wooing of Katharine (V, ii), whom he immediately calls Kate, as if she were a tavern wench back at the Boar's Head in London. It is in such moments, and not in the moments of battlefield heroics, that Shakespeare does best by his exalted hero; for in these moments we see less of the hero-king and more of the old Hal who polished his own wit against the hard edge of Falstaff's.

But of course he is no longer the carefree Hal. He has a few relaxed moments, but we are constantly reminded that he is tempered steel inside, of "the ice-brook's temper," like Othello's sword. When the French Dauphin sends him tennis balls as a taunting reminder of his playful youth, the King's reply glitters with wit, with double and triple puns pressing hard upon one another:

> We are glad the Dauphin is so pleasant with us;
> His present and your pains we thank you for.
> When we have match'd our rackets to these balls,
> We will in France, by God's grace, play a set
> Shall strike his father's crown into the hazard.
> Tell him he hath made a match with such a wrangler
> That all the courts of France will be disturb'd
> With chases.

But the speech, like Henry himself, contains a steely core; the words are arid, acrid, acid, uttered with tight lips:

> For many a thousand widows
> Shall this his mock mock out of their dear husbands,
> Mock mothers from their sons, mock castles down,
> And some are yet ungotten and unborn
> That shall have cause to curse the Dauphin's scorn.

The hardness of which Henry is capable within expresses itself in the summary manner with which he fits the noose of their own making about the throats of Cambridge, Scroop, and Grey; in the executions of Nym and Bardolph (Bardolph, the innocent one in *1Henry IV*, shy of intellect and devoid of wit, the constant butt of good-humored Falstaffian jests) for stealing in France; in his fury on learning that the French have slain the boys who belong to the English camp: "I was not angry since I came to France/ Until this instant"; and in his fearsome depiction of war:

> Now set the teeth and stretch the nostril wide,
> Hold hard the breath and bend up every spirit
> To his full height . . .

After all of Shakespeare's care, not all critics have especially liked either Henry or the play. Dr. Johnson deplored the familiarity with which the King woos Kate and found the fifth act empty and narrow. Hazlitt liked neither the historical Henry nor Shakespeare's portrait, except as we "like to gaze at a panther or a young lion in their cages in the Tower, and catch a pleasing horror from their glistening eyes, their velvet paws, and dreadless roar." Hazlitt lamented the dramatist's early removal of Falstaff and found the comic parts of *Henry V* greatly inferior to those of *Henry IV*, for without Falstaff the others, Pistol, Nym, and Bardolph, "are satellites without a sun." Twentieth-century critics have been, on the whole, lukewarm. In addition, actors have not been greatly drawn to Henry. The famous Garrick chose the part of the Chorus and left the heroic king to a fellow actor. In our own time only the film directed by and starring Sir Laurence Olivier has proved memorable.

In the face of fact, historical and contemporary, it is undeniable that audiences and readers fail to warm to King Henry as they warm to Mercutio, Romeo, Hamlet, Hotspur, Falstaff. Henry himself recognizes that there is much about him that forbids warmth, and in one of the richly human speeches of the play (V, ii) he acknowledges as much to Kate; but he concludes the speech most winningly: "If thou would have such a one, take me; and take me, take a soldier; take a soldier, take a king." But to grant that we do not take Henry to our hearts—as we did not take Hal, but preferred Hotspur and Falstaff—is to say nothing of the quality of the full dramatic portrait. Taken in its entirety, from the beginning of *1Henry IV*, through *2Henry IV*, to the end of *Henry V*, this study of boy, man, prince, king not only is among the greatest of Shakespeare's portraits, but is conceivably the very greatest, if we could judge such things quite objectively. We are put off a little by Henry, as we are put off greatly by Octavius Caesar in *Julius Caesar* and *Antony and Cleopatra*—and for something near the same reason: but we are quite amiss if we judge the portrayal by the portrait, the characterization by the character.

So also for the play as a whole. We are possibly put off by its exuberant nationalism— which, however, especially endeared it to Elizabethans and made it enormously popular with its first audiences: an elegy for the actor who played Shakespeare's great hero parts,

Richard Burbage, identifies him not with Hamlet, Othello, Macbeth, or Lear, but with Henry. Possibly Hazlitt was correct in complaining that the comic figures of *Henry V*, lacking Falstaff, were satellites with no sun; but it can be said in rebuttal that Falstaff's substitute, the "Auntient Pistoll," played to the hilt in the modern theater by an actor who understands the spirit of his outlandishness, can prove more hilarious than any other comic character in Shakespeare, Falstaff included. The scene of the "little touch of Harry in the night" long continues to haunt the memory as do only the finest of Shakespearean scenes. The English lesson given the Princess by her attendant unmistakably stands high among the most potent comic scenes in any dramatic literature. The stirring scenes, before Harfleur and elsewhere, *do* stir even the alien heart, much as Sir Philip Sidney confessed that the "Ballad of Chevy Chase" stirred his—"more than . . . a trumpet." Finally, the dramatic verse of *Henry V*, for its specific purposes, is unmatched. It is the antithesis to, say, *Romeo and Juliet*, wherein the beauty of the sound accentuates theme and mood; here is nothing decorative, but only a hard, muscular, taut line of verse, as tough as Henry's inner core during moments of heavy stress. Immediately after *Henry V*, *Hamlet* would restore rich music to Shakespeare's repertoire; but the predominant sounds of *Henry V* are hard, "right" for the matter they discuss:

> . . . why, in a moment look to see
> The blind and bloody soldier with foul hand
> Defile the locks of your shrill-shrieking daughters;
> Your fathers taken by the silver beards,
> And their most reverend heads dash'd to the walls. . . .

Here consonants knock hard against the actor's teeth, and vowels merely shift for themselves. If he wrote more magnificent verse many times elsewhere, Shakespeare never wrote more rigidly disciplined verse than he did for this play.

A NOTE ON THE COMPOSITION OF THE PLAY

Henry V is dated, more confidently than evidence allows for most of Shakespeare's plays, in 1599. It was "sundry times played" before 1600 and was published first in that year. Shakespeare drew his materials chiefly from Holinshed's *Chronicles* and from the anonymous play *The Famous Victories of Henry the Fifth*.

Much Ado About Nothing

DRAMATIS PERSONÆ

DON PEDRO *prince of Arragon*
DON JOHN *his bastard brother*
CLAUDIO *a young lord of Florence*
BENEDICK *a young lord of Padua*
LEONATO *governor of Messina*
ANTONIO *his brother*
BALTHASAR *attendant on Don Pedro*
CONRADE }
BORACHIO } *followers of Don John*
FRIAR FRANCIS
DOGBERRY *a constable*

VERGES *a headborough*
A SEXTON
A BOY

HERO *daughter to Leonato*
BEATRICE *niece to Leonato*
MARGARET }
URSULA } *gentlewomen attending on Hero*

MESSENGERS, WATCH, ATTENDANTS, &c.

SCENE: *Messina*

ACT I

SCENE i
Before LEONATO's *house.*

[*Enter* LEONATO, HERO, *and* BEATRICE, *with a* MESSENGER.]

LEONATO. I learn in this letter that Don Pedro of Arragon comes this night to Messina.

MESSENGER. He is very near by this. He was not three leagues off when I left him.

5 LEONATO. How many gentlemen have you lost in this action?

MESSENGER. But few of any sort, and none of name.

LEONATO. A victory is twice itself when the achiever brings home full numbers. I find here that Don

10 Pedro hath bestowed much honor on a young Florentine called Claudio.

MESSENGER. Much deserved on his part, and equally remembered° by Don Pedro. He hath borne himself beyond the promise of his age,

15 doing, in the figure of a lamb, the feats of a lion.

He hath indeed better bettered expectation than you must expect of me to tell you how.

LEONATO. He hath an uncle here in Messina will be very much glad of it.

MESSENGER. I have already delivered him letters, 20 and there appears much joy in him—even so much that joy could not show itself modest enough without a badge of bitterness.°

LEONATO. Did he break out into tears?

MESSENGER. In great measure. 25

LEONATO. A kind overflow of kindness. There are no faces truer than those that are so washed. How much better is it to weep at joy than to´joy at weeping!

BEATRICE. I pray you, is Signior Mountanto° 30 returned from the wars or no?

MESSENGER. I know none of that name, lady. There was none such in the army of any sort.

---

remembered rewarded

joy . . . bitterness i.e., unrestrained joy would have appeared immodest, so the uncle wept as well
Mountanto montanto, a fencing thrust

LEONATO. What is he that you ask for, niece?

35 HERO. My cousin means Signior Benedick of Padua.

MESSENGER. O, he's returned, and as pleasant as ever he was.

BEATRICE. He set up his bills° here in Messina and
40 challenged Cupid at the flight;° and my uncle's fool, reading the challenge, subscribed for° Cupid and challenged him at the bird-bolt.° I pray you, how many hath he killed and eaten in these wars? But how many hath he killed? For,
45 indeed, I promised to eat all of his killing.

LEONATO. Faith, niece, you tax Signior Benedick too much; but he'll be meet with° you, I doubt it not.

MESSENGER. He hath done good service, lady, in
50 these wars.

BEATRICE. You had musty victual, and he hath holp° to eat it. He is a very valiant trencher-man;° he hath an excellent stomach.

MESSENGER. And a good soldier too, lady.

55 BEATRICE. And a good soldier to a lady; but what is he to a lord?

MESSENGER. A lord to a lord, a man to a man; stuffed with all honorable virtues.

BEATRICE. It is so, indeed; he is no less than a
60 stuffed man. But for the stuffing—well, we are all mortal.

LEONATO. You must not, sir, mistake my niece. There is a kind of merry war betwixt Signior Benedick and her. They never meet but there's
65 a skirmish of wit between them.

BEATRICE. Alas! He gets nothing by that. In our last conflict four of his five wits went halting° off, and now is the whole man governed with one; so that if he have wit enough to keep himself
70 warm, let him bear it for a difference between himself and his horse; for it is all the wealth that he hath left to be known a reasonable creature. Who is his companion now? He hath every month a new sworn brother.

75 MESSENGER. Is't possible?

BEATRICE. Very easily possible. He wears his faith but as the fashion of his hat—it ever° changes with the next block.

MESSENGER. I see, lady, the gentleman is not in
80 your books.

BEATRICE. No; an he were, I would burn my study. But, I pray you, who is his companion? Is there no young squarer° now that will make a voyage with him to the devil?

MESSENGER. He is most in the company of the right 85 noble Claudio.

BEATRICE. O Lord, he will hang upon him like a disease. He is sooner caught than the pestilence, and the taker runs presently° mad. God help the noble Claudio! If he have caught the Bene- 90 dick, it will cost him a thousand pound ere a' be cured.

MESSENGER. I will hold friends with you, lady.

BEATRICE. Do, good friend.

LEONATO. You will never run mad, niece. 95

BEATRICE. No, not till a hot January.

MESSENGER. Don Pedro is approached.

[Enter DON PEDRO, DON JOHN, CLAUDIO,
BENEDICK, and BALTHASAR.]

DON PEDRO. Good Signior Leonato, you are come to meet your trouble. The fashion of the world is to avoid cost, and you encounter it. 100

LEONATO. Never came trouble to my house in the likeness of your Grace, for trouble being gone, comfort should remain; but when you depart from me, sorrow abides, and happiness takes his leave. 105

DON PEDRO. You embrace your charge too willing-ly. I think this is your daughter.

LEONATO. Her mother hath many times told me so.

BENEDICK. Were you in doubt, sir, that you asked 110 her?

LEONATO. Signior Benedick, no; for then were you a child.

DON PEDRO. You have it full,° Benedick. We may guess by this what you are, being a man. Truly, 115 the lady fathers herself.° Be happy, lady, for you are like an honorable father.

BENEDICK. If Signior Leonato be her father, she would not have his head on her shoulders for all Messina, as like him as she is. 120

BEATRICE. I wonder that you will still be talking, Signior Benedick. Nobody marks you.

BENEDICK. What, my dear Lady Disdain! Are you yet living?

BEATRICE. Is it possible disdain should die while she 125 hath such meet° food to feed it as Signior Bene-dick? Courtesy itself must convert to disdain if you come in her presence.

BENEDICK. Then is courtesy a turncoat. But it is

---

bills advertisements   *at the flight* i.e., archery
subscribed for represented
bird-bolt blunt arrow for bird shooting
be . . . with match   *holp* helped
valiant trencher-man great man with a dinner plate
halting limping   *ever* always

squarer quarreler   *presently* immediately
have it full i.e., are answered with as good a thrust as you
gave
fathers herself i.e., proves her legitimacy by her
appearance
meet appropriate

130 certain I am loved of all ladies, only you excepted. And I would I could find in my heart
that I had not a hard heart; for, truly, I love
none.

BEATRICE. A dear happiness to women; they would
135 else have been troubled with a pernicious suitor.
I thank God and my cold blood, I am of your
humor° for that. I had rather hear my dog bark
at a crow than a man swear he loves me.

BENEDICK. God keep your ladyship still in that
140 mind! So some gentleman or other shall 'scape
a predestinate° scratched face.

BEATRICE. Scratching could not make it worse, an°
'twere such a face as yours were.

BENEDICT. Well, you are a rare parrot-teacher.

145 BEATRICE. A bird of my tongue is better than a
beast of yours.

BENEDICK. I would my horse had the speed of your
tongue, and so good a continuer.° But keep your
way, i' God's name; I have done.

150 BEATRICE. You always end with a jade's trick.° I
know you of old.

DON PEDRO. That is the sum of all, Leonato.
Signior Claudio and Signior Benedick, my dear
friend Leonato hath invited you all. I tell him we
155 shall stay here at the least a month, and he
heartily prays some occasion may detain us
longer. I dare swear he is no hypocrite, but prays
from his heart.

LEONATO. If you swear, my lord, you shall not be
160 forsworn.° [To DON JOHN] Let me bid you welcome, my lord. Being reconciled to the prince
your brother, I owe you all duty.

DON JOHN. I thank you. I am not of many words,
but I thank you.

165 LEONATO. Please it your Grace lead on?

DON PEDRO. Your hand, Leonato; we will go
together.

[Exeunt all except BENEDICK and CLAUDIO.]

CLAUDIO. Benedick, didst thou note the daughter of
Signior Leonato?

170 BENEDICK. I noted her not; but I looked on her.

CLAUDIO. Is she not a modest young lady?

BENEDICK. Do you question me, as an honest man
should do, for my simple judgment? Or would
you have me speak after my custom, as being a
175 professed tyrant to their sex?

CLAUDIO. No, I pray thee speak in sober judgment.

BENEDICK. Why, i'faith, methinks she's too low for
a high praise, too brown for a fair praise, and too

little for a great praise. Only this commendation
I can afford her, that were she other than she is, 180
she were unhandsome; and being no other but
as she is, I do not like her.

CLAUDIO. Thou thinkest I am in sport. I pray thee
tell me truly how thou likest her.

BENEDICK. Would you buy her, that you inquire 185
after her?

CLAUDIO. Can the world buy such a jewel?

BENEDICK. Yea, and a case to put it into. But speak
you this with a sad° brow? Or do you play the
flouting Jack,° to tell us Cupid is a good hare- 190
finder and Vulcan a rare carpenter?° Come, in
what key shall a man take you, to go in the
song?°

CLAUDIO. In mine eye she is the sweetest lady that
ever I looked on. 195

BENEDICK. I can see yet without spectacles, and I
see no such matter. There's her cousin, an she
were not possessed with a fury, exceeds her as
much in beauty as the first of May doth the last
of December. But I hope you have no intent to 200
turn husband, have you?

CLAUDIO. I would scarce trust myself, though I had
sworn the contrary, if Hero would be my wife.

BENEDICK. Is't come to this? In faith, hath not the
world one man but he will wear his cap with 205
suspicion?° Shall I never see a bachelor of threescore again? Go to, i'faith; an thou wilt needs
thrust thy neck into a yoke, wear the print of it,
and sigh away Sundays.° Look, Don Pedro is
returned to seek you. 210

[Re-enter DON PEDRO.]

DON PEDRO. What secret hath held you here, that
you followed not to Leonato's?

BENEDICK. I would your Grace would constrain°
me to tell.

DON PEDRO. I charge thee on thy allegiance. 215

BENEDICK. You hear, Count Claudio. I can be secret
as a dumb man; I would have you think so; but,
on my allegiance, mark you this, on my allegiance. He is in love. With who? Now that is
your Grace's part. Mark how short his answer is. 220
With Hero, Leonato's short daughter.

CLAUDIO. If this were so, so were it uttered.

BENEDICK. Like the old tale, my lord: "It is not so,

---

humor disposition   predestinate predestined   an if
so . . . continuer   had as much endurance
jade's trick   of dropping out of the race like a worn-out
horse
be forsworn   break your oath

sad serious   flouting Jack mocker
Cupid . . . carpenter   i.e., mere absurdity, since Cupid is
blind and Vulcan a blacksmith
to . . . song   i.e., to suit your own whim
hath not . . . suspicion   does no man remain who will not
marry and fear the cuckold's horns (as husband of an
unfaithful wife)
sigh . . . Sundays   i.e., spend weekends of boredom
constrain force

225 nor 'twas not so, but, indeed, God forbid it
should be so."

CLAUDIO. If my passion change not shortly, God
forbid it should be otherwise.

DON PEDRO. Amen, if you love her, for the lady is
very well worthy.

230 CLAUDIO. You speak this to fetch me in,° my lord.

DON PEDRO. By my troth, I speak my thought.

CLAUDIO. And, in faith, my lord, I spoke mine.

BENEDICK. And, by my two faiths and troths, my
lord, I spoke mine.

235 CLAUDIO. That I love her, I feel.

DON PEDRO. That she is worthy, I know.

BENEDICK. That I neither feel how she should be
loved nor know how she should be worthy is
the opinion that fire cannot melt out of me. I
240 will die in it at the stake.

DON PEDRO. Thou wast ever an obstinate heretic in
the despite° of beauty.

CLAUDIO. And never could maintain his part in the
force of his will.

245 BENEDICK. That a woman conceived me, I thank
her; that she brought me up, I likewise give her
most humble thanks. But that I will have a
recheat winded° in my forehead, or hang my
bugle in an invisible baldrick,° all women shall
250 pardon me. Because I will not do them the
wrong to mistrust any, I will do myself the right
to trust none; and the fine° is, for the which I
may go the finer,° I will live a bachelor.

DON PEDRO. I shall see thee, ere I die, look pale
255 with love.

BENEDICK. With anger, with sickness, or with
hunger, my lord—not with love. Prove that
ever I lose more blood with love than I will get
again with drinking, pick out mine eyes with a
260 ballad-maker's pen and hang me up at the
door of a brothel-house for the sign of blind
Cupid.

DON PEDRO. Well, if ever thou dost fall from this
faith, thou wilt prove a notable argument.°

265 BENEDICK. If I do, hang me in a bottle like a cat°
and shoot at me; and he that hits me, let him
be clapped on the shoulder and called Adam.°

DON PEDRO. Well, as time shall try:°
"In time the savage bull doth bear the yoke."°

270 BENEDICK. The savage bull may; but if ever the
sensible Benedick bear it, pluck off the bull's
horns and set them in my forehead. And let me
be vilely painted, and in such great letters as
they write "Here is good horse to hire," let
275 them signify under my sign "Here you may see
Benedick the married man."

CLAUDIO. If this should ever happen, thou wouldst
be horn-mad.°

DON PEDRO. Nay, if Cupid have not spent all his
280 quiver in Venice,° thou wilt quake for this
shortly.

BENEDICK. I look for an earthquake too, then.

DON PEDRO. Well, you will temporize with the
hours.° In the meantime, good Signior Benedick,
285 repair to Leonato's. Commend me to him, and
tell him I will not fail him at supper; for indeed
he hath made great preparation.

BENEDICK. I have almost matter° enough in me for
such an embassage, and so I commit you—

290 CLAUDIO. To the tuition° of God. From my house,
if I had it—

DON PEDRO. The sixth of July. Your loving friend,
Benedick.

BENEDICK. Nay, mock not, mock not. The body of
295 your discourse is sometime guarded° with fragments, and the guards are but slightly basted on
neither. Ere you flout old ends° any further,
examine your conscience. And so I leave you.

[Exit]

CLAUDIO. My liege, your highness now may do me
good.

DON PEDRO. My love is thine to teach. Teach it
but how,   300
And thou shalt see how apt it is to learn
Any hard lesson that may do thee good.

CLAUDIO. Hath Leonato any son, my lord?

DON PEDRO. No child but Hero; she's his only heir.
Dost thou affect° her, Claudio?

CLAUDIO.   O, my lord,   305
When you went onward on this ended action,
I look'd upon her with a soldier's eye
That lik'd but had a rougher task in hand
Than to drive liking to the name of love.

---

fetch me in entrap me, get me to confess   *despite* disdain
recheat winded recall sounded to gather in the hounds
baldrick belt for the hunter's horn, continuing allusions
  to the cuckold's horns
fine sum
go the finer live more splendidly, having no wife to
  support
argument example
bottle . . . cat a cat hung in a basket was target in
  archery tournaments
Adam Adam Bell (archer celebrated in the ballad
  "Adam Bell")

try prove
"In . . . yoke" (quoted from Kyd's *The Spanish Tragedy*)
horn-mad mad with the cuckold's jealousy
Venice sin center of Europe
temporize . . . hours succumb to love eventually
matter sense   *tuition* protection
guarded ornamented
flout old ends mock (my) scraps of wit
affect have affection for

310 But now I am return'd and that war-thoughts
Have left their places vacant, in their rooms
Come thronging soft and delicate desires,
All prompting me how fair young Hero is,
Saying I lik'd her ere I went to wars.

315 DON PEDRO. Thou wilt be like a lover presently,
And tire the hearer with a book of words.
If thou dost love fair Hero, cherish it,
And I will break with° her and with her father,
And thou shalt have her. Was't not to this end

320 That thou began'st to twist so fine a story?
CLAUDIO. How sweetly you do minister to love,
That know love's grief by his complexion!°
But lest my liking might too sudden seem,
I would have salv'd it with a longer treatise.
DON PEDRO. What need the bridge much broader

325 than the flood?
The fairest grant is the necessity.°
Look, what will serve is fit. 'Tis once° thou lov'st,
And I will fit thee with the remedy.
I know we shall have reveling tonight.

330 I will assume thy part in some disguise
And tell fair Hero I am Claudio;
And in her bosom I'll unclasp my heart
And take her hearing prisoner with the force
And strong encounter of my amorous tale.

335 Then after to her father will I break,
And the conclusion is, she shall be thine.
In practice let us put it presently. [Exeunt]

SCENE ii
A room in LEONATO's house.

[Enter LEONATO and ANTONIO, meeting.]
LEONATO. How now, brother! Where is my
cousin,° your son? Hath he provided this music?
ANTONIO. He is very busy about it. But, brother, I
can tell you strange news that you yet dreamt
5 not of.
LEONATO. Are they good?
ANTONIO. As the event stamps them.° But they
have a good cover; they show well outward.
The prince and Count Claudio, walking in a
10 thick-pleached° alley in mine orchard, were thus
much overheard by a man of mine: the prince

discovered° to Claudio that he loved my niece
your daughter and meant to acknowledge it
this night in a dance; and if he found her accor-
dant, he meant to take the present time by the 15
top° and instantly break with you of it.
LEONATO. Hath the fellow any wit that told you
this?
ANTONIO. A good sharp fellow. I will send for him,
and question him yourself. 20
LEONATO. No, no. We will hold it as a dream till it
appear itself. But I will acquaint my daughter
withal, that she may be the better prepared for
an answer if peradventure this be true. Go you
and tell her of it. [Enter ATTENDANTS] Cousins, 25
you know what you have to do. O, I cry you
mercy, friend; go you with me, and I will use
your skill. Good cousin, have a care this busy
time. [Exeunt]

SCENE iii
The same.

[Enter DON JOHN and CONRADE.]
CONRADE. What the goodyear,° my lord! Why
are you thus out of measure sad?
DON JOHN. There is no measure in the occasion that
breeds;° therefore the sadness is without limit.
CONRADE. You should hear reason. 5
DON JOHN. And when I have heard it, what blessing brings it?
CONRADE. If not a present° remedy, at least a
patient sufferance.
DON JOHN. I wonder that thou, being (as thou 10
sayest thou art) born under Saturn,° goest about
to apply a moral medicine° to a mortifying
mischief.° I cannot hide what I am. I must be
sad when I have cause, and smile at no man's
jests; eat when I have stomach, and wait for no 15
man's leisure; sleep when I am drowsy, and
tend on° no man's business; laugh when I am
merry, and claw no man in his humor.°
CONRADE. Yea, but you must not make the full
show of this till you may do it without control- 20
ment. You have of late stood out against your

---

break with open the subject
his complexion its external appearance
The . . . necessity the most welcome gift is what meets
the need
once only once   cousin general term; here, nephew
As . . . them it depends on the outcome
cover exterior
thick-pleached i.e., with branches closely interwoven

discovered revealed   top forelock
goodyear an unexplained expletive, perhaps equivalent
to "what the devil!"
There is . . . breeds there is no limit to the cause of my
discontent
present immediate
born . . . Saturn i.e., born when the planet Saturn was
predominant, hence of morose disposition
moral medicine i.e., philosophy
mortifying mischief deadly affliction   tend on attend to
claw . . . humor cater to no man's disposition

brother, and he hath ta'en you newly into his grace, where it is impossible you should take true root but by the fair weather that you make

25 yourself. It is needful that you frame the season° for your own harvest.

Don John. I had rather be a canker° in a hedge than a rose in his grace, and it better fits my blood to be disdained of all than to fashion a

30 carriage° to rob love from any. In this, though I cannot be said to be a flattering honest man, it must not be denied but I am a plain-dealing villain. I am trusted with a muzzle and enfranchised with a clog;° therefore I have decreed

35 not to sing in my cage. If I had my mouth, I would bite; if I had my liberty, I would do my liking. In the meantime let me be that I am, and seek not to alter me.

Conrade. Can you make no use of your discontent?

40 Don John. I make all use of it, for I use it only. Who comes here?

[Enter Borachio.]

What news, Borachio?

Borachio. I came yonder from a great supper. The prince your brother is royally entertained

45 by Leonato, and I can give you intelligence of an intended marriage.

Don John. Will it serve for any model to build mischief on? What is he for a fool that betroths himself to unquietness?

Borachio. Marry, it is your brother's right hand.   50

Don John. Who? The most exquisite Claudio?

Borachio. Even he.

Don John. A proper squire!° And who, and who? Which way looks he?

Borachio. Marry, on Hero, the daughter and heir   55 of Leonato.

Don John. A very forward March-chick!° How came you to this?

Borachio. Being entertained° for a perfumer, as I was smoking° a musty room, comes me the   60 prince and Claudio, hand in hand, in sad° conference. I whipt me behind the arras and there heard it agreed upon that the prince should woo Hero for himself, and having obtained her, give her to Count Claudio.   65

Don John. Come, come, let us thither. This may prove food to my displeasure. That young start-up hath all the glory of my overthrow. If I can cross him any way, I bless myself every way. You are both sure, and will assist me?   70

Conrade. To the death, my lord.

Don John. Let us to the great supper. Their cheer is the greater that I am subdued. Would the cook were of my mind! Shall we go prove what's to be done?   75

Borachio. We'll wait upon your lordship.

[Exeunt]

---

frame the season   devise the occasion
canker   the despised dog rose
fashion a carriage   i.e., make myself agreeable
enfranchised . . . clog   set free within my shackles

proper squire   fine fellow
March-chick   chicken that is hatched before the normal season, hence, eager young thing
entertained employed   *smoking* perfuming
sad serious

ACT II

SCENE i
A hall in Leonato's house.

[*Enter* Leonato, Antonio, Hero, Beatrice, *and others.*]

Leonato. Was not Count John here at supper?

Antonio. I saw him not.

Beatrice. How tartly that gentleman looks! I never can see him but I am heart-burned an

5 hour after.

Hero. He is of a very melancholy disposition.

Beatrice. He were an excellent man that were made just in the midway between him and Benedick. The one is too like an image and says

nothing, and the other too like my lady's   10 eldest son, evermore tattling.

Leonato. Then half Signior Benedick's tongue in Count John's mouth, and half Count John's melancholy in Signior Benedick's face—

Beatrice. With a good leg and a good foot, uncle,   15 and money enough in his purse, such a man would win any woman in the world, if a' could get her goodwill.

Leonato. By my troth, niece, thou wilt never get thee a husband if thou be so shrewd° of thy   20 tongue.

---

shrewd   biting

ANTONIO. In faith, she's too curst.°

BEATRICE. Too curst is more than curst. I shall
lessen God's sending that way, for it is said,
25 "God sends a curst cow short horns," but to a
cow too curst he sends none.

LEONATO. So, by being too curst, God will send
you no horns.

BEATRICE. Just,° if he send me no husband, for the
30 which blessing I am at him upon my knees
every morning and evening. Lord, I could not
endure a husband with a beard on his face. I had
rather lie in the woolen.

LEONATO. You may light on a husband that hath
35 no beard.

BEATRICE. What should I do with him? Dress him
in my apparel and make him my waiting-
gentlewoman? He that hath a beard is more
than a youth, and he that hath no beard is less
40 than a man; and he that is more than a youth is
not for me, and he that is less than a man, I am
not for him. Therefore I will even take sixpence
in earnest° of the bear-ward,° and lead his apes
into hell.°

45 LEONATO. Well, then, go you into hell?

BEATRICE. No, but to the gate, and there will the
devil meet me, like an old cuckold, with horns
on his head, and say "Get you to heaven,
Beatrice, get you to heaven; here's no place for
50 you maids." So deliver I up my apes, and away
to Saint Peter for the heavens; he shows me
where the bachelors sit, and there live we as
merry as the day is long.

ANTONIO. [To HERO] Well, niece, I trust you will be
55 ruled by your father.

BEATRICE. Yes, faith. It is my cousin's duty to
make curtsy and say, "Father, as it please you."
But yet for all that, cousin, let him be a handsome fellow, or else make another curtsy and
60 say, "Father, as it please me."

LEONATO. Well, niece, I hope to see you one day
fitted with a husband.

BEATRICE. Not till God make men of some other
metal than earth. Would it not grieve a woman
65 to be overmastered with a piece of valiant dust?
To make an account of her life to a clod of wayward marl?° No, uncle, I'll none. Adam's sons
are my brethren, and, truly, I hold it a sin to
match in my kindred.

70 LEONATO. Daughter, remember what I told you.
If the prince do solicit you in that kind,° you
know your answer.

BEATRICE. The fault will be in the music, cousin, if
you be not wooed in good time. If the prince be
too important,° tell him there is measure in   75
everything, and so dance out the answer. For,
hear me, Hero: wooing, wedding, and repenting
is as a Scotch jig, a measure,° and a cinque pace.°
The first suit is hot and hasty, like a Scotch jig,
and full as fantastical; the wedding, mannerly-   80
modest as a measure, full of state and ancientry;°
and then comes repentance, and, with his bad
legs, falls into the cinque pace faster and faster
till he sink into his grave.

LEONATO. Cousin, you apprehend passing°   85
shrewdly.

BEATRICE. I have a good eye, uncle; I can see a
church by daylight.

LEONATO. The revelers are entering, brother.
Make good room.   [All put on their masks.]   90

[Enter DON PEDRO, CLAUDIO, BENEDICK,
BALTHASAR, DON JOHN, BORACHIO, MARGARET,
URSULA, and others, masked.]

DON PEDRO. Lady, will you walk° about with your
friend?

HERO. So you walk softly, and look sweetly, and
say nothing, I am yours for the walk—and
especially when I walk away.   95

DON PEDRO. With me in your company?

HERO. I may say so, when I please.

DON PEDRO. And when please you to say so?

HERO. When I like your favor,° for God defend the
lute should be like the case!°   100

DON PEDRO. My visor is Philemon's° roof; within
the house is Jove.

HERO. Why, then, your visor should be thatched.

DON PEDRO. Speak low, if you speak love.
                    [Drawing her aside.]   105

BALTHASAR. Well, I would you did like me.

MARGARET. So would not I, for your own sake, for I
have many ill qualities.

BALTHASAR. Which is one?

MARGARET. I say my prayers aloud.

BALTHASAR. I love you the better. The hearers may   110
cry "Amen."

MARGARET. God match me with a good dancer!

BALTHASAR. Amen.

MARGARET. And God keep him out of my sight
when the dance is done! Answer, clerk.°   115

---

curst shrewish   *Just* exactly   *in earnest* on account
bear-ward bear (and monkey) keeper
lead . . . hell proverbial penalty exacted of spinsters
marl clay   *solicit . . . kind* i.e., propose

important importunate   *measure* a stately dance
cinque pace a fast five-step dance
ancientry traditional formality   *passing* surpassingly
walk about dance a measure   *favor* face
lute . . . case i.e., that your face should be as ugly as your
mask
Philemon who with his wife Baucis gave shelter to Jupiter
clerk assistant to the parson

BALTHASAR. No more words. The clerk is answered.

URSULA. I know you well enough. You are Signior Antonio.

ANTONIO. At a word, I am not.

120 URSULA. I know you by the waggling of your head.

ANTONIO. To tell you true, I counterfeit him.

URSULA. You could never do him so ill-well unless you were the very man. Here's his dry hand up

125 and down. You are he, you are he.

ANTONIO. At a word, I am not.

URSULA. Come, come, do you think I do not know you by your excellent wit? Can virtue hide itself? Go to, mum, you are he. Graces will

130 appear, and there's an end.

BEATRICE. Will you not tell me who told you so?

BENEDICK. No, you shall pardon me.

BEATRICE. Nor will you not tell me who you are?

BENEDICK. Not now.

135 BEATRICE. That I was disdainful, and that I had my good wit out of the "Hundred Merry Tales"°— well, this was Signior Benedick that said so.

BENEDICK. What's he?

BEATRICE. I am sure you know him well enough.

140 BENEDICK. Not I, believe me.

BEATRICE. Did he never make you laugh?

BENEDICK. I pray you, what is he?

BEATRICE. Why, he is the prince's jester—a very dull fool, only his gift is in devising impossible

145 slanders. None but libertines delight in him, and the commendation is not in his wit, but in his villainy; for he both pleases men and angers them, and then they laugh at him and beat him. I am sure he is in the fleet.° I would he had

150 boarded me.

BENEDICK. When I know the gentleman, I'll tell him what you say.

BEATRICE. Do, do. He'll but break a comparison or two on me, which, peradventure not marked or

155 not laughed at, strikes him into melancholy; and then there's a partridge wing saved, for the fool will eat no supper that night. [Music] We must follow the leaders.

BENEDICK. In every good thing.

160 BEATRICE. Nay, if they lead to any ill, I will leave them at the next turning. [Dance. Then exeunt all except DON JOHN, and BORACHIO, and CLAUDIO.]

DON JOHN. Sure my brother is amorous on Hero, and hath withdrawn her father to break with him about it. The ladies follow her, and but one

165 visor remains.

BORACHIO. And that is Claudio. I know him by his bearing.

DON JOHN. Are not you Signior Benedick?

CLAUDIO. You know me well; I am he.

DON JOHN. Signior, you are very near my brother 170 in his love. He is enamored on Hero. I pray you, dissuade him from her. She is no equal for his birth. You may do the part of an honest man in it.

CLAUDIO. How know you he loves her?   175

DON JOHN. I heard him swear his affection.

BORACHIO. So did I too, and he swore he would marry her tonight.

DON JOHN. Come, let us to the banquet.
              [Exeunt DON JOHN and BORACHIO.]

CLAUDIO. Thus answer I in name of Benedick,   180
But hear these ill news with the ears of Claudio.
'Tis certain so—the prince woos for himself.
Friendship is constant in all other things
Save in the office and affairs of love;
Therefore all hearts in love use their own
    tongues.   185
Let every eye negotiate for itself,
And trust no agent, for beauty is a witch
Against whose charms faith melteth into blood.°
This is an accident° of hourly proof,
Which I mistrusted° not. Farewell, therefore,
    Hero!   190
              [Re-enter BENEDICK.]

BENEDICK. Count Claudio?

CLAUDIO. Yea, the same.

BENEDICK. Come, will you go with me?

CLAUDIO. Whither?

BENEDICK. Even to the next willow, about your   195
own business, County. What fashion will you wear the garland° of? About your neck, like an usurer's chain? Or under your arm, like a lieutenant's scarf? You must wear it one way, for the prince hath got your Hero.   200

CLAUDIO. I wish him joy of her.

BENEDICK. Why, that's spoken like an honest drovier;° so they sell bullocks. But did you think the prince would have served you thus?

CLAUDIO. I pray you, leave me.   205

BENEDICK. Ho! Now you strike like the blind man; 'twas the boy that stole your meat, and you'll beat the post.

CLAUDIO. If it will not be, I'll leave you.   [Exit]

BENEDICK. Alas, poor hurt fowl! Now will he creep 210

---

blood passion
accident . . . proof a fact proved true every hour
mistrusted suspected
garland i.e., garland of willow, sign of love forsaken
drovier drover, cattle-driver

into sedges. But that my Lady Beatrice should know me, and not know me! The prince's fool! Ha? It may be I go under that title because I am merry. Yea, but so I am apt to do myself wrong; I am not so reputed. It is the base, though bitter, disposition of Beatrice that puts the world into her person,° and so gives me out.° Well, I'll be revenged as I may.

[*Re-enter* Don Pedro.]

Don Pedro. Now, signior, where's the count? Did you see him?

Benedick. Troth, my lord, I have played the part of Lady Fame. I found him here as melancholy as a lodge in a warren.° I told him, and I think I told him true, that your grace had got the goodwill of this young lady, and I offered him my company to a willow-tree, either to make him a garland, as being forsaken, or to bind him up a rod, as being worthy to be whipped.

Don Pedro. To be whipped! What's his fault?

Benedick. The flat transgression of a schoolboy, who, being overjoyed with finding a bird's nest, shows it his companion, and he steals it.

Don Pedro. Wilt thou make a trust a transgression? The transgression is in the stealer.

Benedick. Yet it had not been amiss the rod had been made, and the garland too; for the garland he might have worn himself, and the rod he might have bestowed on you, who, as I take it, have stolen his bird's nest.

Don Pedro. I will but teach them to sing, and restore them to the owner.

Benedick. If their singing answer your saying,° by my faith, you say honestly.

Don Pedro. The Lady Beatrice hath a quarrel to you. The gentleman that danced with her told her she is much wronged by you.

Benedick. O, she misused me past the endurance of a block! An oak but with one green leaf on it would have answered her; my very visor began to assume life and scold with her. She told me, not thinking I had been myself, that I was the prince's jester, that I was duller than a great thaw,° huddling jest upon jest, with such impossible conveyance° upon me that I stood like a man at a mark,° with a whole army shooting at me. She speaks poniards, and every word stabs.

If her breath were as terrible as her terminations,° there were no living near her; she would infect to the north star. I would not marry her though she were endowed with all that Adam had left him before he transgressed. She would have made Hercules have turned spit,° yea, and have cleft his club to make the fire too. Come, talk not of her. You shall find her the infernal Ate° in good apparel.° I would to God some scholar would conjure° her, for certainly while she is here a man may live as quiet in hell as in a sanctuary, and people sin upon purpose because they would go thither. So, indeed, all disquiet, horror, and perturbation follows her.

Don Pedro. Look, here she comes.

[*Re-enter* Claudio, Beatrice, Hero, *and* Leonato.]

Benedick. Will your grace command me any service to the world's end? I will go on the slightest errand now to the Antipodes that you can devise to send me on. I will fetch you a toothpicker now from the furthest inch of Asia, bring you the length of Prester John's° foot, fetch you a hair off the great Cham's° beard, do you any embassage to the Pigmies—rather than hold three words' conference with this harpy. You have no employment for me?

Don Pedro. None but to desire your good company.

Benedick. O God, sir, here's a dish I love not. I cannot endure my Lady Tongue.   [*Exit*]

Don Pedro. Come, lady, come; you have lost the heart of Signior Benedick.

Beatrice. Indeed, my lord, he lent it me awhile, and I gave him use° for it, a double heart for his single one. Marry, once before he won it of me with false dice; therefore your Grace may well say I have lost it.

Don Pedro. You have put him down, lady, you have put him down.

Beatrice. So I would not he should do me, my lord, lest I should prove the mother of fools. I have brought Count Claudio, whom you sent me to seek.

Don Pedro. Why, how now, Count! Wherefore are you sad?

Claudio. Not sad, my lord.

Don Pedro. How then? Sick?

Claudio. Neither, my lord.

---

puts . . . person assumes that all the world thinks as she does
gives me out (mis)represents me
lodge . . . warren gamekeeper's lonely hut
If . . . saying if what you say proves true
great thaw when social activities were halted
impossible conveyance unbelievable barrage
mark target

terminations verbalizations
turned spit the roasting spit, a lowly task
Ate goddess of discord
in . . . apparel i.e., Beatrice, unlike Ate, dresses fashionably
scholar . . . conjure summoning or banishing evil spirits required a scholar's Latin
Prester John fabled Christian king of the Far East
Cham Mongol Khan   *use* interest

BEATRICE. The count is neither sad, nor sick, nor
305   merry, nor well, but civil count, civil as an
orange,° and something of that jealous complexion.°

DON PEDRO. I' faith, lady, I think your blazon° to
be true, though I'll be sworn, if he be so, his
310   conceit° is false. Here, Claudio, I have wooed in
thy name, and fair Hero is won. I have broke
with her father, and his good will obtained.
Name the day of marriage, and God give thee
joy!

315   LEONATO. Count, take of me my daughter, and
with her my fortunes. His Grace hath made the
match, and all grace say Amen to it.

BEATRICE. Speak, Count, 'tis your cue.

CLAUDIO. Silence is the perfectest herald of joy. I
320   were but little happy if I could say how much.
Lady, as you are mine, I am yours. I give away
myself for you, and dote upon the exchange.

BEATRICE. Speak, cousin; or, if you cannot, stop his
mouth with a kiss, and let not him speak neither.

325   DON PEDRO. In faith, lady, you have a merry
heart.

BEATRICE. Yea, my lord; I thank it, poor fool, it
keeps on the windy side of care. My cousin tells
him in his ear that he is in her heart.

330   CLAUDIO. And so she doth, cousin.

BEATRICE. Good Lord, for alliance!° Thus goes
everyone to the world° but I, and I am sunburnt.° I may sit in a corner and cry heigh-ho
for a husband!

335   DON PEDRO. Lady Beatrice, I will get you one.

BEATRICE. I would rather have one of your father's
getting.° Hath your Grace ne'er a brother like
you? Your father got excellent husbands, if a
maid could come by them.

340   DON PEDRO. Will you have me, lady?

BEATRICE. No, my lord, unless I might have another
for working days. Your Grace is too costly to
wear every day. But I beseech your Grace, pardon me. I was born to speak all mirth and no
345   matter.

DON PEDRO. Your silence most offends me, and to
be merry best becomes you, for, out of question,
you were born in a merry hour.

BEATRICE. No, sure, my lord, my mother cried;
350   but then there was a star danced, and under
that was I born. Cousins, God give you joy!

LEONATO. Niece, will you look to those things I
told you of?

BEATRICE. I cry you mercy, uncle. By your Grace's
pardon.   [Exit]   355

DON PEDRO. By my troth, a pleasant-spirited lady.

LEONATO. There's little of the melancholy element
in her, my lord. She is never sad but when she
sleeps, and not ever sad then; for I have heard
my daughter say she hath often dreamed of   360
unhappiness and waked herself with laughing.

DON PEDRO. She cannot endure to hear tell of a
husband.

LEONATO. O, by no means. She mocks all her
wooers out of suit.   365

DON PEDRO. She were an excellent wife for
Benedick.

LEONATO. O Lord, my lord, if they were but a
week married, they would talk themselves mad.

DON PEDRO. County Claudio, when mean you to   370
go to church?

CLAUDIO. Tomorrow, my lord. Time goes on
crutches till love have all his rites.

LEONATO. Not till Monday, my dear son, which is
hence a just seven-night, and a time too brief,   375
too, to have all things answer my mind.

DON PEDRO. Come, you shake the head at so long a
breathing.° But I warrant thee, Claudio, the time
shall not go dully by us. I will, in the interim,
undertake one of Hercules' labors, which is to   380
bring Signior Benedick and the Lady Beatrice
into a mountain of affection the one with the
other. I would fain have it a match, and I doubt
not but to fashion it if you three will but minister
such assistance as I shall give you direction.   385

LEONATO. My lord, I am for you though it cost me
ten nights' watchings.°

CLAUDIO. And I, my lord.

DON PEDRO. And you too, gentle Hero?

HERO. I will do any modest office, my lord, to help   390
my cousin to a good husband.

DON PEDRO. And Benedick is not the unhopefullest
husband that I know. Thus far can I praise him:
he is of a noble strain, of approved valor and
confirmed honesty. I will teach you how to   395
humor your cousin, that she shall fall in love
with Benedick; and I, with your two helps, will
so practice on° Benedick that, in despite of his
quick wit and his queasy stomach, he shall fall in
love with Beatrice. If we can do this, Cupid is no   400
longer an archer. His glory shall be ours, for we
are the only love-gods. Go in with me, and I
will tell you my drift.   [Exeunt]

---

civil . . . orange with pun on Seville, producer of
    sweet-sour oranges
that . . . complexion i.e., yellow, the color of jealousy
blazon description   *conceit* imagination
for alliance i.e., this marrying is a great thing
world i.e., worldly life   *sunburnt* i.e., not fair
getting begetting

breathing delay *watchings* wakings
practice on hoodwink

SCENE ii
The same.

[*Enter* Don John *and* Borachio.]

DON JOHN. It is so. The Count Claudio shall marry the daughter of Leonato.

BORACHIO. Yea, my lord, but I can cross it.

DON JOHN. Any bar, any cross, any impediment will be medicinable to me. I am sick in displeasure to him, and whatsoever comes athwart his affection ranges evenly° with mine. How canst thou cross this marriage?

BORACHIO. Not honestly, my lord, but so covertly that no dishonesty shall appear in me.

DON JOHN. Show me briefly how.

BORACHIO. I think I told your lordship, a year since, how much I am in the favor of Margaret, the waiting gentlewoman to Hero.

DON JOHN. I remember.

BORACHIO. I can, at any unseasonable instant of the night, appoint her to look out at her lady's chamber window.

DON JOHN. What life is in that, to be the death of this marriage?

BORACHIO. The poison of that lies in you to temper. Go you to the prince your brother. Spare not to tell him that he hath wronged his honor in marrying the renowned Claudio—whose estimation do you mightily hold up—to a contaminated stale,° such a one as Hero.

DON JOHN. What proof shall I make of that?

BORACHIO. Proof enough to misuse the prince, to vex Claudio, to undo Hero, and kill Leonato. Look you for any other issue?°

DON JOHN. Only to despite them I will endeavor anything.

BORACHIO. Go, then; find me a meet hour to draw Don Pedro and the Count Claudio alone. Tell them that you know that Hero loves me; intend a kind of zeal both to the prince and Claudio, as —in love of your brother's honor, who hath made this match, and his friend's reputation, who is thus like to be cozened° with the semblance of a maid—that you have discovered thus. They will scarcely believe this without trial. Offer them instances—which shall bear no less likelihood than to see me at her chamberwindow, hear me call Margaret, Hero, hear Margaret term me Claudio, and bring them to see this the very night before the intended wedding —for in the meantime I will so fashion the matter that Hero shall be absent—and there shall appear such seeming truth of Hero's disloyalty that jealousy° shall be called assurance° and all the preparation overthrown.

DON JOHN. Grow this to what adverse issue it can, I will put it in practice. Be cunning in the working this, and thy fee is a thousand ducats.

BORACHIO. Be you constant in the accusation, and my cunning shall not shame me.

DON JOHN. I will presently° go learn their day of marriage. [*Exeunt*]

SCENE iii
LEONATO'S *orchard.*

[*Enter* Benedick.]

BENEDICK. Boy!

[*Enter* Boy.]

BOY. Signior?

BENEDICK. In my chamber window lies a book. Bring it hither to me in the orchard.

BOY. I am here already, sir.

BENEDICK. I know that, but I would have thee hence and here again. [*Exit* Boy] I do much wonder that one man, seeing how much another man is a fool when he dedicates his behaviors to love, will, after he hath laughed at such shallow follies in others, become the argument° of his own scorn by falling in love. And such a man is Claudio. I have known when there was no music with him but the drum and the fife; and now had he rather hear the tabor and the pipe.° I have known when he would have walked ten mile afoot to see a good armor; and now will he lie ten nights awake carving the fashion of a new doublet.° He was wont to speak plain and to the purpose, like an honest man and a soldier, and now is he turned orthography;° his words are a very fantastical banquet—just so many strange dishes. May I be so converted, and see with these eyes? I cannot tell; I think not. I will not be sworn but love may transform me to an oyster; but I'll take my oath on it, till he have made an oyster of me, he shall never make me such a fool. One woman is fair, yet I am well; another is wise, yet I am well; another virtuous, yet I am well. But till all graces be in one woman, one woman shall not come in my grace. Rich she shall be, that's certain; wise, or I'll none; virtuous, or I'll never

ranges evenly parallels   *stale* harlot
issue outcome   *cozened* cheated
jealousy suspicion   *assurance* certainty
presently immediately   *argument* subject
tabor . . . pipe i.e., for dancing, socializing
doublet jacket   *orthography* i.e., linguistically pedantic

cheapen° her; fair, or I'll never look on her;
35 mild, or come not near me; noble, or not I for an
angel;° of good discourse, an excellent musician,
and her hair shall be of what color it please God.
Ha! The prince and Monsieur Love! I will hide
me in the arbor.   [*Withdraws.*]
    [*Enter* Don Pedro, Claudio, *and* Leonato.]
40 Don Pedro. Come, shall we hear this music?
Claudio. Yea, my good lord. How still the evening
is,
As hush'd on purpose to grace harmony!°
Don Pedro. See you where Benedick hath hid
himself?
Claudio. O, very well, my lord. The music ended,
45 We'll fit the kid-fox with a pennyworth.°
    [*Enter* Balthasar *with Music.*]
Don Pedro. Come, Balthasar, we'll hear that song
again.
Balthasar. O, good my lord, tax not so bad a
voice
To slander music any more than once.
Don Pedro. It is the witness still of excellency
50 To put a strange face on his° own perfections.
I pray thee, sing, and let me woo no more.
Balthasar. Because you talk of wooing, I will
sing.
Since many a wooer doth commence his suit
To her he thinks not worthy, yet he woos,
Yet will he swear he loves.
55 Don Pedro.   Nay, pray thee, come;
Or, if thou wilt hold longer argument,
Do it in notes.
Balthasar.   Note this before my notes;
There's not a note of mine that's worth the
noting.
Don Pedro. Why, these are very crotchets° that
he speaks;
60 Note, notes, forsooth, and nothing.°   [*Air.*]
Benedick. Now, divine air! Now is his soul
ravished! Is it not strange that sheeps' guts°
should hale souls out of men's bodies? Well, a
horn° for my money, when all's done.

cheapen bargain for
noble . . . angel i.e., of noble birth or unworthy me even
    if angelic (with pun on two coins, the noble and the
    angel)
to . . . harmony to do homage to the music
We'll . . . pennyworth i.e., give the sly fellow an earful
    (with allusion to fable told by Spenser of the
    overconfident kid who was seized by the fox)
his its
crotchets quarter notes; but also whimsical verbal play
nothing with pun on *noting*
sheeps' guts for stringed instruments
horn as being more manly (with usual allusion to the
    cuckold's horns)

The Song
Balthasar.

Sigh no more, ladies, sigh no more,   65
   Men were deceivers ever,
One foot in sea and one on shore,
   To one thing constant never.
Then sigh not so, but let them go,
   And be you blithe and bonny,   70
Converting all your sounds of woe
   Into Hey nonny, nonny.

Sing no more ditties, sing no moe°
   Of dumps° so dull and heavy;
The fraud of men was ever so,   75
   Since summer first was leavy.
Then sigh not so, &c.

Don Pedro. By my troth, a good song.
Balthasar. And an ill singer, my lord.
Don Pedro. Ha, no, no, faith; thou singest well   80
enough for a shift.°
Benedick. An he had been a dog that should have
howled thus, they would have hanged him. And
I pray God his bad voice bode no mischief. I had
as lief have heard the night-raven, come what   85
plague could have come after it.
Don Pedro. Yea, marry, dost thou hear, Balthasar?
I pray thee, get us some excellent music, for
tomorrow night we would have it at the Lady
Hero's chamber-window.   90
Balthasar. The best I can, my lord.
Don Pedro. Do so. Farewell. [*Exit* Balthasar]
Come hither, Leonato. What was it you told me
of today—that your niece Beatrice was in love
with Signior Benedick?   95
Claudio. O, aye, stalk on, stalk on; the fowl sits. I
did never think that lady would have loved any
man.
Leonato. No, nor I neither; but most wonderful
that she should so dote on Signior Benedick,   100
whom she hath in all outward behaviors seemed
ever to abhor.
Benedick. Is't possible? Sits the wind in that
corner?
Leonato. By my troth, my lord, I cannot tell what   105
to think of it but that she loves him with an
enraged affection. It is past the infinite of
thought.
Don Pedro. May be she doth but counterfeit.
Claudio. Faith, like enough.   110
Leonato. O God, counterfeit! There was never
counterfeit of passion came so near the life of
passion as she discovers it.

moe more   *dumps* melancholy songs
shift makeshift

Don Pedro. Why, what effects of passion shows
115 she?

Claudio. Bait the hook well; this fish will bite.

Leonato. What effects, my lord? She will sit you—
you heard my daughter tell you how.

Claudio. She did, indeed.

120 Don Pedro. How, how, I pray you? You amaze me.
I would have thought her spirit had been
invincible against all assaults of affection.

Leonato. I would have sworn it had, my lord—
especially against Benedick.

125 Benedick. I should think this a gull° but that the
white-bearded fellow speaks it. Knavery cannot,
sure, hide himself in such reverence.

Claudio. He hath ta'en the infection. Hold it up.

Don Pedro. Hath she made her affection known to
130 Benedick?

Leonato. No, and swears she never will. That's her
torment.

Claudio. 'Tis true, indeed; so your daughter says.
"Shall I," says she, "that have so oft encountered
135 him with scorn, write to him that I love him?"

Leonato. This says she now when she is beginning
to write to him; for she'll be up twenty times a
night, and there will she sit in her smock till she
hath writ a sheet of paper. My daughter tells us
140 all.

Claudio. Now you talk of a sheet of paper, I
remember a pretty jest your daughter told us of.

Leonato. O, when she had writ it, and was reading
it over, she found Benedick and Beatrice between
145 the sheet?

Claudio. That.

Leonato. O, she tore the letter into a thousand
halfpence,° railed at herself that she should be
so immodest to write to one that she knew
150 would flout her. "I measure him," says she, "by
my own spirit; for I should flout him if he writ
to me—yea, though I love him, I should."

Claudio. Then down upon her knees she falls,
weeps, sobs, beats her heart, tears her hair, prays,
155 curses—"O sweet Benedick! God give me
patience!"

Leonato. She doth indeed; my daughter says so.
And the ecstasy° hath so much overborne her
that my daughter is sometime afeard she will do
160 a desperate outrage to herself. It is very true.

Don Pedro. It were good that Benedick knew of it
by some other, if she will not discover° it.

Claudio. To what end? He would make but a
sport of it, and torment the poor lady worse.

Don Pedro. An he should, it were an alms° to hang 165
him. She's an excellent sweet lady, and, out of all
suspicion, she is virtuous.

Claudio. And she is exceeding wise.

Don Pedro. In everything but in loving Benedick.

Leonato. O, my lord, wisdom and blood° com- 170
bating in so tender a body, we have ten proofs to
one that blood hath the victory. I am sorry for
her, as I have just cause, being her uncle and her
guardian.

Don Pedro. I would she had bestowed this dotage 175
on me. I would have daffed all other respects°
and made her half myself. I pray you, tell Benedick of it and hear what a' will say.

Leonato. Were it good, think you?

Claudio. Hero thinks surely she will die, for she 180
says she will die if he love her not; and she will
die ere she make her love known; and she will
die if he woo her, rather than she will bate° one
breath of her accustomed crossness.

Don Pedro. She doth well. If she should make 185
tender° of her love, 'tis very possible he'll scorn
it; for the man, as you know all, hath a contemptible spirit.

Claudio. He is a very proper° man.

Don Pedro. He hath indeed a good outward hap- 190
piness.

Claudio. Before God! And in my mind, very wise.

Don Pedro. He doth indeed show some sparks
that are like wit.

Claudio. And I take him to be valiant. 195

Don Pedro. As Hector, I assure you. And in the
managing of quarrels you may say he is wise, for
either he avoids them with great discretion or
undertakes them with a most Christianlike fear.

Leonato. If he do fear God, a' must necessarily 200
keep peace. If he break the peace, he ought to
enter into a quarrel with fear and trembling.

Don Pedro. And so will he do, for the man doth
fear God, howsoever it seems not in him by some
large jests he will make. Well, I am sorry for 205
your niece. Shall we go seek Benedick, and tell
him of her love?

Claudio. Never tell him, my lord. Let her wear it
out with good counsel.

Leonato. Nay, that's impossible. She may wear 210
her heart out first.

Don Pedro. Well, we will hear further of it by
your daughter. Let it cool the while. I love Benedick well, and I could wish he would modestly

---

gull hoax
halfpence i.e., tiny pieces   *ecstasy* madness
discover reveal

alms charitable deed
blood passion   *respects* considerations
bate abate   *tender* offer
proper handsome

215 examine himself to see how much he is unworthy so good a lady.
LEONATO. My lord, will you walk? Dinner is ready.
CLAUDIO. If he do not dote on her upon this, I will
never trust my expectation.
220 DON PEDRO. Let there be the same net spread for
her; and that must your daughter and her
gentlewomen carry. The sport will be when
they hold one an opinion of another's dotage,
and no such matter. That's the scene that I
225 would see, which will be merely a dumb-show.
Let us send her to call him in to dinner.
          [*Exeunt* DON PEDRO, CLAUDIO, *and* LEONATO]
BENEDICK. [*Coming forward*] This can be no trick:
the conference was sadly° borne. They have the
truth of this from Hero. They seem to pity the
230 lady. It seems her affections have their full bent.
Love me! Why, it must be requited. I hear how
I am censured. They say I will bear myself
proudly if I perceive the love come from her.
They say too that she will rather die than give
235 any sign of affection. I did never think to marry.
I must not seem proud. Happy are they that hear
their detractions and can put them to mending.
They say the lady is fair—'tis a truth, I can bear
them witness; and virtuous—'tis so, I cannot
240 reprove° it; and wise, but for loving me—by my
troth, it is no addition to her wit, nor no great
argument of her folly, for I will be horribly in
love with her. I may chance have some odd

sadly seriously
reprove disprove

quirks and remnants of wit broken on me
because I have railed so long against marriage.
245 But doth not the appetite alter? A man loves the
meat in his youth that he cannot endure in his
age. Shall quips and sentences and these paper
bullets° of the brain awe a man from the career
of his humor?° No, the world must be peopled.
250 When I said I would die a bachelor, I did not
think I should live till I were married. Here
comes Beatrice. By this day, she's a fair lady! I
do spy some marks of love in her.
          [*Enter* BEATRICE.]
BEATRICE. Against my will I am sent to bid you
255 come in to dinner.
BENEDICK. Fair Beatrice, I thank you your pains.
BEATRICE. I took no more pains for those thanks
than you take pains to thank me. If it had been
painful, I would not have come.
260 BENEDICK. You take pleasure, then, in the message?
BEATRICE. Yea, just so much as you may take upon
a knife's point and choke a daw withal. You have
no stomach, signior. Fare you well.   [*Exit*]
BENEDICK. Ha! "Against my will I am sent to bid
265 you come in to dinner." There's a double meaning in that. "I took no more pains for those
thanks than you took pains to thank me."
That's as much as to say, "Any pains that I take
for you is as easy as thanks." If I do not take pity
270 of her, I am a villain; if I do not love her, I am a
Jew. I will go get her picture.   [*Exit*]

paper bullets i.e., harmless
career . . . humor indulging his own inclinations

ACT III

SCENE i
LEONATO's *orchard*.

[*Enter* HERO, MARGARET, *and* URSULA.]
HERO. Good Margaret, run thee to the parlor.
There shalt thou find my cousin Beatrice
Proposing° with the prince and Claudio.
Whisper her ear and tell her I and Ursula
5 Walk in the orchard and our whole discourse
Is all of her. Say that thou overheard'st us,
And bid her steal into the pleached bower,
Where honeysuckles, ripen'd by the sun,
Forbid the sun to enter, like favorites

Proposing conversing

Made proud by princes, that advance their pride   10
Against that power that bred it. There will she
     hide her
To 'listen our propose. This is thy office.
Bear thee well in it, and leave us alone.
MARGARET. I'll make her come, I warrant you,
     presently.°   [*Exit*]
HERO. Now, Ursula, when Beatrice doth come,   15
As we do trace this alley up and down,
Our talk must only be of Benedick.
When I do name him, let it be thy part
To praise him more than ever man did merit.
My talk to thee must be how Benedick   20

presently immediately

Is sick in love with Beatrice. Of this matter
Is little Cupid's crafty arrow made,
That only wounds by hearsay.
                    [Enter BEATRICE, behind.]
                                        Now begin—
For look where Beatrice, like a lapwing, runs
25 Close by the ground to hear our conference.
     URSULA. The pleasant'st angling is to see the fish
        Cut with her golden oars the silver stream
        And greedily devour the treacherous bait.
        So angle we for Beatrice, who even now
30   Is couched in the woodbine coverture.
        Fear you not my part of the dialogue.
     HERO. Then go we near her, that her ear lose
        nothing
        Of the false sweet bait that we lay for it.
                              [Approaching the bower.]
        No, truly, Ursula, she is too disdainful;
35   I know her spirits are as coy and wild
        As haggards° of the rock.
     URSULA.   But are you sure
        That Benedick loves Beatrice so entirely?
     HERO. So says the prince and my new-trothed
        lord.
     URSULA. And did they bid you tell her of it,
        madam?
40   HERO. They did entreat me to acquaint her of it;
        But I persuaded them, if they lov'd Benedick,
        To wish him wrestle with affection
        And never to let Beatrice know of it.
     URSULA. Why did you so? Doth not the gentleman
45   Deserve as full as fortunate a bed
        As ever Beatrice shall couch upon?
     HERO. O god of love! I know he doth deserve
        As much as may be yielded to a man.
        But Nature never fram'd a woman's heart
50   Of prouder stuff than that of Beatrice.
        Disdain and scorn ride sparkling in her eyes,
        Misprising° what they look on, and her wit
        Values itself so highly that to her
        All matter else seems weak. She cannot love,
55   Nor take no shape nor project of affection,°
        She is so self-endear'd.
     URSULA.   Sure, I think so,
        And therefore certainly it were not good
        She knew his love, lest she make sport at it.
     HERO. Why, you speak truth. I never yet saw man,
        How wise, how noble, young, how rarely
60   featur'd,
        But she would spell him backward.° If fair-
        fac'd,

She would swear the gentleman should be her
    sister;
If black, why, Nature, drawing of an antic,°
Made a foul blot; if tall, a lance ill-headed;
If low, an agate very vilely cut;   65
If speaking, why, a vane blown with all winds;
If silent, why, a block moved with none.
So turns she every man the wrong side out,
And never gives to truth and virtue that
Which simpleness and merit purchaseth.   70
URSULA. Sure, sure, such carping is not com-
    mendable.
HERO. No, not to be so odd and from° all fashions
    As Beatrice is cannot be commendable.
    But who dare tell her so? If I should speak,
    She would mock me into air. O, she would
        laugh me   75
    Out of myself, press me to death with wit!
    Therefore let Benedick, like cover'd fire,
    Consume away in sighs, waste inwardly.
    It were a better death than die with mocks,
    Which is as bad as die with tickling.   80
URSULA. Yet tell her of it. Hear what she will say.
HERO. No; rather I will go to Benedick
    And counsel him to fight against his passion.
    And, truly, I'll devise some honest slanders
    To stain my cousin with. One doth not know   85
    How much an ill word may empoison liking.
URSULA. O, do not do your cousin such a wrong!
    She cannot be so much without true judg-
        ment—
    Having so swift and excellent a wit
    As she is priz'd to have—as to refuse   90
    So rare a gentleman as Signior Benedick.
HERO. He is the only man of Italy,
    Always excepted my dear Claudio.
URSULA. I pray you, be not angry with me, madam,
    Speaking my fancy. Signior Benedick,   95
    For shape, for bearing, argument, and valor,
    Goes foremost in report through Italy.
HERO. Indeed, he hath an excellent good name.
URSULA. His excellence did earn it, ere he had it.
    When are you married, madam?   100
HERO. Why, every day, tomorrow. Come, go in.
    I'll show thee some attires and have thy
        counsel
    Which is the best to furnish me tomorrow.
URSULA. She's lim'd,° I warrant you. We have
        caught her, madam.
HERO. If it prove so, then loving goes by haps.   105
    Some Cupid kills with arrows, some with traps.
                        [Exeunt HERO and URSULA.]

---

haggards wild hawks   Misprising despising
Nor . . . affection nor even entertain any notion of love
spell him backward i.e., turn him topsy-turvy

antic comic figure   from contrary to
lim'd caught, like a bird with sticky birdlime

BEATRICE. [*Coming forward*] What fire is in mine
    ears? Can this be true?
  Stand I condemn'd for pride and scorn so
    much?
  Contempt, farewell! And maiden pride, adieu!
110 No glory lives behind the back of such.
  And, Benedick, love on; I will requite thee,
  Taming my wild heart to thy loving hand.
  If thou dost love, my kindness shall incite thee
  To bind our loves up in a holy band;
115 For others say thou dost deserve, and I
  Believe it better than reportingly.°   [*Exit*]

SCENE ii
A room in LEONATO'S *house.*

[*Enter* DON PEDRO, CLAUDIO, BENEDICK, *and*
LEONATO.]

DON PEDRO. I do but stay till your marriage be
  consummate, and then go I toward Arragon.
CLAUDIO. I'll bring you thither, my lord, if you'll
  vouchsafe me.
5 DON PEDRO. Nay, that would be as great a soil in
  the new gloss of your marriage as to show a
  child his new coat and forbid him to wear it. I
  will only be bold with Benedick for his company, for from the crown of his head to the sole
10 of his foot he is all mirth. He hath twice or
  thrice cut Cupid's bowstring, and the little hangman dare not shoot at him; he hath a heart as
  sound as a bell, and his tongue is the clapper, for
  what his heart thinks his tongue speaks.
15 BENEDICK. Gallants, I am not as I have been.
LEONATO. So say I. Methinks you are sadder.
CLAUDIO. I hope he be in love.
DON PEDRO. Hang him, truant! There's no true
  drop of blood in him to be truly touched with
20 love; if he be sad, he wants° money.
BENEDICK. I have the toothache.
DON PEDRO. Draw it.
BENEDICK. Hang it!
CLAUDIO. You must hang it first and draw it after-
25 wards.
DON PEDRO. What! Sigh for the toothache?
LEONATO. Where is but a humor or a worm.°
BENEDICK. Well, everyone can master a grief but
  he that has it.
30 CLAUDIO. Yet say I he is in love.

DON PEDRO. There is no appearance of fancy° in
  him unless it be a fancy that he hath to strange
  disguises—as to be a Dutchman today, a Frenchman tomorrow; or in the shape of two countries
  at once, as a German from the waist downward,   35
  all slops,° and a Spaniard from the hip upward,
  no doublet. Unless he have a fancy to this
  foolery, as it appears he hath, he is no fool for
  fancy, as you would have it appear he is.
CLAUDIO. If he be not in love with some woman,   40
  there is no believing old signs. A' brushes his hat
  o' mornings. What should that bode?
DON PEDRO. Hath any man seen him at the
  barber's?
CLAUDIO. No, but the barber's man hath been seen   45
  with him, and the old ornament° of his cheek
  hath already stuffed tennis balls.°
LEONATO. Indeed, he looks younger than he did by
  the loss of a beard.
DON PEDRO. Nay, a' rubs himself with civet.° Can   50
  you smell him out by that?
CLAUDIO. That's as much as to say the sweet
  youth's in love.
DON PEDRO. The greatest note of it is his melan-
  choly.   55
CLAUDIO. And when was he wont to wash his face?
DON PEDRO. Yea, or to paint himself? For the
  which I hear what they say of him.
CLAUDIO. Nay, but his jesting spirit, which is now
  crept into a lute string and now governed by   60
  stops.
DON PEDRO. Indeed, that tells a heavy tale for him.
  Conclude, conclude he is in love.
CLAUDIO. Nay, but I know who loves him.
DON PEDRO. That would I know too. I warrant, one   65
  that knows him not.
CLAUDIO. Yes, and his ill conditions, and, in despite
  of all, dies for him.
DON PEDRO. She shall be buried with her face up-
  wards.   70
BENEDICK. Yet is this no charm for the toothache.
  Old signior, walk aside with me. I have studied
  eight or nine wise words to speak to you which
  these hobby-horses° must not hear.
        [*Exeunt* BENEDICK *and* LEONATO.]
DON PEDRO. For my life, to break with him about   75
  Beatrice.
CLAUDIO. 'Tis even so. Hero and Margaret have by
  this played their parts with Beatrice, and then

---

reportingly from mere report   *wants* lacks
humor . . . worm "humors," or secretions downward
  from the head, and actual worms in the teeth,
  supposedly caused toothache

fancy love   *slops* baggy pants
ornament i.e., beard
tennis balls which were stuffed with hair
civet perfume from the civet cat
hobby-horses jokers

the two bears will not bite one another when
80 they meet.

[*Enter* DON JOHN.]

DON JOHN. My lord and brother, God save you!

DON PEDRO. Good den,° brother.

DON JOHN. If your leisure served, I would speak
with you.

85 DON PEDRO. In private?

DON JOHN. If it please you. Yet Count Claudio may
hear, for what I would speak of concerns him.

DON PEDRO. What's the matter?

DON JOHN. [*To* CLAUDIO] Means your lordship to be
90 married tomorrow?

DON PEDRO. You know he does.

DON JOHN. I know not that when he knows what I
know.

CLAUDIO. If there be any impediment, I pray you
95 discover it.

DON JOHN. You may think I love you not. Let that
appear hereafter, and aim better at me by that I
now will manifest. For my brother, I think he
holds you well, and in dearness of heart hath
100 help to effect your ensuing marriage—surely
suit ill spent and labor ill bestowed.

DON PEDRO. Why, what's the matter?

DON JOHN. I came hither to tell you; and, circumstances shortened, for she has been too long a
105 talking of, the lady is disloyal.

CLAUDIO. Who, Hero?

DON JOHN. Even she. Leonato's Hero, your Hero,
everyman's Hero.

CLAUDIO. Disloyal?

110 DON JOHN. The word is too good to paint out her
wickedness; I could say she were worse. Think
you of a worse title, and I will fit her to it.
Wonder not till further warrant. Go but with me
tonight. You shall see her chamber window
115 entered, even the night before her wedding day.
If you love her then, tomorrow wed her. But it
would better fit your honor to change your
mind.

CLAUDIO. May this be so?

120 DON PEDRO. I will not think it.

DON JOHN. If you dare not trust that you see, confess not that you know. If you will follow me, I
will show you enough, and when you have seen
more and heard more, proceed accordingly.

125 CLAUDIO. If I see anything tonight why I should not
marry her tomorrow, in the congregation where
I should wed, there will I shame her.

DON PEDRO. And as I wooed for thee to obtain her,
I will join with thee to disgrace her.

130 DON JOHN. I will disparage her no farther till you

are my witnesses. Bear it coldly° but till midnight, and let the issue show itself.

DON PEDRO. O day untowardly turned!

CLAUDIO. O mischief strangely thwarting!

DON JOHN. O plague right well prevented! So will 135
you say when you have seen the sequel.

[*Exeunt*]

SCENE iii
A street.

[*Enter* DOGBERRY *and* VERGES *with the* WATCH.]

DOGBERRY. Are you good men and true?

VERGES. Yea, or else it were pity but they should
suffer salvation,° body and soul.

DOGBERRY. Nay, there were a punishment too good
for them, if they should have any allegiance° in 5
them, being chosen for the prince's watch.

VERGES. Well, give them their charge, neighbor
Dogberry.

DOGBERRY. First, who think you the most desart-
less° man to be constable? 10

FIRST WATCH. Hugh Otecake, sir, or George Seacole, for they can write and read.

DOGBERRY. Come hither, neighbor Seacole. God
hath blessed you with a good name. To be a well-
favored° man is the gift of fortune; but to write 15
and read comes by nature.

SECOND WATCH. Both which, master constable—

DOGBERRY. You have. I knew it would be your
answer. Well, for your favor, sir, why, give God
thanks, and make no boast of it; and for your 20
writing and reading, let that appear when there
is no need of such vanity. You are thought here
to be the most senseless° and fit man for the
constable of the watch; therefore bear you the
lantern. This is your charge. You shall com- 25
prehend° all vagrom° men; you are to bid any
man stand, in the prince's name.

SECOND WATCH. How if a' will not stand?

DOGBERRY. Why, then, take no note of him, but
let him go; and presently call the rest of the 30
watch together, and thank God you are rid of a
knave.

VERGES. If he will not stand when he is bidden, he
is none of the prince's subjects.

Good den good evening

coldly coolly *salvation* blunder for *damnation*
allegiance blunder for *treachery*
desartless blunder for *deserving*
well-favored handsome
senseless blunder for *intelligent*
comprehend blunder for *apprehend*
vagrom blunder for *vagrant*

35 DOGBERRY. True, and they are to meddle with none
but the prince's subjects. You shall also make no
noise in the streets; for for the watch to babble
and to talk is most tolerable° and not to be
endured.

40 WATCH. We will rather sleep than talk. We know
what belongs to a watch.

DOGBERRY. Why, you speak like an ancient and
most quiet watchman, for I cannot see how
sleeping should offend. Only have a care that
45 your bills be not stolen. Well, you are to call at
all the alehouses and bid those that are drunk
get them to bed.

WATCH. How if they will not?

DOGBERRY. Why, then, let them alone till they are
50 sober. If they make you not then the better
answer, you may say they are not the men you
took them for.

WATCH. Well, sir.

DOGBERRY. If you meet a thief, you may suspect
55 him, by virtue of your office, to be no true° man;
and, for such kind of men, the less you meddle
or make with them, why, the more is for your
honesty.

WATCH. If we know him to be a thief, shall we not
60 lay hands on him?

DOGBERRY. Truly, by your office, you may; but I
think they that touch pitch will be defiled. The
most peaceable way for you, if you do take a
thief, is to let him show himself what he is, and
65 steal out of° your company.

VERGES. You have been always called a merciful
man, partner.

DOGBERRY. Truly, I would not hang a dog by my
mill, much more a man who hath any honesty
70 in him.

VERGES. If you hear a child cry in the night, you
must call to the nurse and bid her still it.

WATCH. How if the nurse be asleep and will not
hear us?

75 DOGBERRY. Why, then, depart in peace, and let the
child wake her with crying. For the ewe that will
not hear her lamb when it baas will never
answer a calf when he bleats.

VERGES. 'Tis very true.

80 DOGBERRY. This is the end of the charge.—You,
constable, are to present° the prince's own
person. If you meet the prince in the night, you
may stay him.

VERGES. Nay, by'r lady, that I think a' cannot.

DOGBERRY. Five shillings to one on't, with any man 85
that knows the statues,° he may stay him.
Marry, not without the prince be willing; for,
indeed, the watch ought to offend no man, and
it is an offense to stay a man against his will.

VERGES. By'r lady, I think it be so. 90

DOGBERRY. Ha, ah, ha! Well, masters, good night.
An there be any matter of weight chances, call
up me. Keep your fellows' counsels and your
own, and good night. Come, neighbor.

WATCH. Well, masters, we hear our charge. Let us 95
go sit here upon the church bench till two, and
then all to bed.

DOGBERRY. One word more, honest neighbors. I
pray you, watch about Signior Leonato's door;
for the wedding being there tomorrow, there is a 100
great coil° tonight. Adieu. Be vigitant,° I beseech
you.   [Exeunt DOGBERRY and VERGES.]
                    [Enter BORACHIO and CONRADE.]

BORACHIO. What, Conrade!

WATCH. [Aside] Peace! Stir not.

BORACHIO. Conrade, I say! 105

CONRADE. Here, man; I am at thy elbow.

BORACHIO. Mass, and my elbow itched; I thought
there would a scab° follow.

CONRADE. I will owe thee an answer for that. And
now forward with thy tale. 110

BORACHIO. Stand thee close, then, under this pent-
house, for it drizzles rain; and I will, like a true
drunkard, utter all to thee.

WATCH. [Aside] Some treason, masters. Yet stand
close. 115

BORACHIO. Therefore know I have earned of Don
John a thousand ducats.

CONRADE. Is it possible that any villainy should be
so dear?

BORACHIO. Thou shouldst rather ask if it were 120
possible any villainy should be so rich; for when
rich villains have need of poor ones, poor ones
may make what price they will.

CONRADE. I wonder at it.

BORACHIO. That shows thou art unconfirmed.° 125
Thou knowest that the fashion of a doublet, or a
hat, or a cloak, is nothing to a man.

CONRADE. Yes, it is apparel.

BORACHIO. I mean, the fashion.

CONRADE. Yes, the fashion is the fashion. 130

BORACHIO. Tush! I may as well say the fool's the
fool. But seest thou not what a deformed thief
this fashion is?

---

tolerable blunder for *intolerable*
bills watchmen's poles with axe and spearpoint
true honest
steal out of sneak away (with obvious, but unconscious, pun)
present represent

statues blunder for *statutes*   *coil* fuss
vigitant blunder for *vigilant*   *scab* with pun, low fellow
unconfirmed inexperienced

WATCH. [*Aside*] I know that Deformed. A' has been
a vile thief this seven year; a' goes up and down
like a gentleman. I remember his name.

BORACHIO. Didst thou not hear somebody?

CONRADE. No; 'twas the vane on the house.

BORACHIO. Seest thou not, I say, what a deformed
thief this fashion is? How giddily a' turns about
all the hot bloods between fourteen and five-
and-thirty? Sometimes fashioning them like
Pharaoh's soldiers in the reechy° painting, sometime like god Bel's° priests in the old church-
window, sometime like the shaven Hercules in
the smirched° worm-eaten tapestry, where his
codpiece° seems as massy as his club?

CONRADE. All this I see, and I see that the fashion
wears out more apparel than the man. But art
thou thyself giddy with the fashion too, that thou
hast shifted out of thy tale into telling me of the
fashion?

BORACHIO. Not so, neither. But know that I have
tonight wooed Margaret, the Lady Hero's
gentlewoman, by the name of Hero. She leans
me out at her mistress' chamber window, bids
me a thousand times good night—I tell this tale
vilely. I should first tell thee how the prince,
Claudio, and my master, planted and placed and
possessed by my master Don John, saw afar off
in the orchard this amiable encounter.

CONRADE. And thought they Margaret was Hero?

BORACHIO. Two of them did, the prince and
Claudio. But the devil my master knew she was
Margaret; and partly by his oaths, which first
possessed them, partly by the dark night, which
did deceive them, but chiefly by my villainy,
which did confirm any slander that Don John
had made, away went Claudio enraged—swore
he would meet her as he was appointed, next
morning at the temple, and there, before the
whole congregation, shame her with what he
saw o'er night, and send her home again without
a husband.

FIRST WATCH. We charge you, in the prince's name,
stand!

SECOND WATCH. Call up the right master constable.
We have here recovered° the most dangerous
piece of lechery° that ever was known in the
commonwealth.

FIRST WATCH. And one Deformed is one of them. I
know him; a' wears a lock.°

CONRADE. Masters, masters—

SECOND WATCH. You'll be made bring Deformed
forth, I warrant you.

CONRADE. Masters—

FIRST WATCH. Never speak. We charge you let us
obey you to go with us.

BORACHIO. We are like to prove a goodly commodity, being taken up of these men's bills.°

CONRADE. A commodity in question,° I warrant
you. Come, we'll obey you.   [*Exeunt*]

SCENE iv
HERO's *apartment*.

[*Enter* HERO, MARGARET, *and* URSULA.]

HERO. Good Ursula, wake my cousin Beatrice and
desire her to rise.

URSULA. I will, lady.

HERO. And bid her come hither.

URSULA. Well.   [*Exit*]

MARGARET. Troth, I think your other rebato° were
better.

HERO. No, pray thee, good Meg, I'll wear this.

MARGARET. By my troth's not so good, and I
warrant your cousin will say so.

HERO. My cousin's a fool, and thou art another. I'll
wear none but this.

MARGARET. I like the new tire° within excellently,
if the hair were a thought browner; and your
gown's a most rare fashion, i' faith. I saw the
Duchess of Milan's gown that they praise so.

HERO. O, that exceeds, they say.

MARGARET. By my troth's but a nightgown in
respect of yours—cloth o' gold, and cuts,° and
laced with silver, set with pearls, down sleeves,
side sleeves, and skirts, round underborne with
a bluish tinsel. But for a fine, quaint, graceful, and
excellent fashion, yours is worth ten on't.

HERO. God give me joy to wear it! For my heart is
exceeding heavy.

MARGARET. 'Twill be heavier soon by the weight of
a man.

HERO. Fie upon thee! Art not ashamed?

MARGARET. Of what, lady? Of speaking honorably?
Is not marriage honorable in a beggar? Is not
your lord honorable without marriage? I think
you would have me say "saving your reverence,

---

reechy begrimed
Bel Baal (from the Apocrypha)   *smirched* besmirched
codpiece exaggerated front part of men's breeches
recovered blunder for *discovered*
lechery blunder for *treachery*
lock lovelock (a curl of hair worn below the ear)

commodity . . . taken up . . . bills with puns on business
transactions
in question to be questioned; but also, of questionable
quality
rebato high, stiff ruff   *tire* headdress
cuts see-through slashes to show rich undercloth

a husband." An bad thinking do not wrest true speaking, I'll offend nobody. Is there any harm

35 in "the heavier for a husband"? None, I think, an it be the right husband and the right wife; otherwise 'tis light,° and not heavy. Ask my Lady Beatrice else; here she comes.

[*Enter* BEATRICE.]

HERO. Good morrow, coz.

40 BEATRICE. Good morrow, sweet Hero.

HERO. Why, how now? Do you speak in the sick tune?

BEATRICE. I am out of all other tune, methinks.

MARGARET. Clap's into "Light o' love." That goes

45 without a burden.° Do you sing it, and I'll dance it.

BEATRICE. Ye light o' love, with your heels! Then, if your husband have stables enough, you'll see he shall lack no barns.°

50 MARGARET. O illegitimate construction! I scorn that with my heels.

BEATRICE. 'Tis almost five o'clock, cousin. 'Tis time you were ready. By my troth, I am exceeding ill. Heigh-ho!

55 MARGARET. For a hawk, a horse, or a husband?

BEATRICE. For the letter that begins them all, H.°

MARGARET. Well, an you be not turned Turk, there's no more sailing by the star.°

BEATRICE. What means the fool, trow?

60 MARGARET. Nothing I; but God send everyone their heart's desire!

HERO. These gloves the count sent me; they are an excellent perfume.

BEATRICE. I am stuffed,° cousin; I cannot smell.

65 MARGARET. A maid, and stuffed! There's goodly catching of cold.

BEATRICE. O, God help me! God help me! How long have you professed apprehension?°

MARGARET. Ever since you left it. Doth not my wit

70 become me rarely?

BEATRICE. It is not seen enough. You should wear it in your cap. By my troth, I am sick.

MARGARET. Get you some of this distilled Carduus Benedictus,° and lay it to your heart. It is the

75 only thing for a qualm.°

HERO. There thou prickest her with a thistle.

BEATRICE. Benedictus! Why Benedictus? You have some moral in this Benedictus.

MARGARET. Moral! No, by my troth, I have no moral meaning. I meant, plain holy-thistle. You 80 may think perchance that I think you are in love. Nay, by'r lady, I am not such a fool to think what I list;° nor I list not to think what I can; nor, indeed, I cannot think, if I would think my heart out of thinking, that you are in love, or that you 85 will be in love, or that you can be in love. Yet Benedick was such another, and now is he become a man. He swore he would never marry; and yet now, in despite of his heart, he eats his meat without grudging. And how you may be 90 converted, I know not, but methinks you look with your eyes as other women do.

BEATRICE. What pace is this that thy tongue keeps?

MARGARET. Not a false gallop.

[*Re-enter* URSULA.]

URSULA. Madam, withdraw. The prince, the count, 95 Signior Benedick, Don John, and all the gallants of the town are come to fetch you to church.

HERO. Help to dress me, good coz, good Meg, good Ursula.   [*Exeunt*]

SCENE v
Another room in LEONATO'*s house.*

[*Enter* LEONATO, *with* DOGBERRY *and* VERGES.]

LEONATO. What would you with me, honest neighbor?

DOGBERRY. Marry, sir, I would have some confidence with you that decerns° you nearly.

LEONATO. Brief, I pray you, for you see it is a busy 5 time with me.

DOGBERRY. Marry, this it is, sir.

VERGES. Yes, in truth it is, sir.

LEONATO. What is it, my good friends?

DOGBERRY. Goodman Verges, sir, speaks a little off 10 the matter. An old man, sir, and his wits are not so blunt° as, God help, I would desire they were; but, in faith, honest as the skin between his brows.

VERGES. Yes, I thank God I am as honest as any man 15 living that is an old man and no honester than I.

DOGBERRY. Comparisons are odorous.° Palabras,° neighbor Verges.

LEONATO. Neighbors, you are tedious.

DOGBERRY. It pleases your worship to say so, but 20 we are the poor duke's° officers. But truly, for

---

light loose   *burden* refrain
barns with pun on *bairns*, children
H i.e., *ache* (pronounced the same)
star North Star (i.e., nothing can be counted on)
stuffed i.e., have a cold   *apprehension* sharp wit
Carduus Benedictus holy thistle, a cure-all; with pun on
    Benedick
qualm queasiness

list like   *confidence* blunder for *conference*
decerns blunder for *concerns*
blunt blunder for *sharp*   *odorous* blunder for *odious*
Palabras Spanish *pocas palabras*, few words
poor duke's i.e., duke's poor

mine own part, if I were as tedious° as a king, I could find in my heart to bestow it all of your worship.

25 LEONATO. All thy tediousness on me, ah?

DOGBERRY. Yea, an 'twere a thousand pound more than 'tis, for I hear as good exclamation° on your worship as of any man in the city; and though I be but a poor man, I am glad to hear it.

30 VERGES. And so am I.

LEONATO. I would fain know what you have to say.

VERGES. Marry, sir, our watch tonight, excepting your worship's presence,° ha' ta'en a couple of as arrant knaves as any in Messina.

35 DOGBERRY. A good old man, sir; he will be talking. As they say, "When the age is in, the wit is out." God help us! It is a world to see. Well said, i' faith, neighbor Verges. Well, God's a good man; an two men ride of a horse, one must ride behind. An

40 honest soul, i' faith, sir, by my troth he is, as ever broke bread. But God is to be worshipped; all men are not alike. Alas, good neighbor!

LEONATO. Indeed, neighbor, he comes too short of you.

45 DOGBERRY. Gifts that God gives.

LEONATO. I must leave you.

DOGBERRY. One word, sir. Our watch, sir, have indeed comprehended two aspicious° persons, and we would have them this morning examined before your worship. 50

LEONATO. Take their examination yourself and bring it me. I am now in great haste, as it may appear unto you.

DOGBERRY. It shall be suffigance.°

LEONATO. Drink some wine ere you go. Fare you 55 well.

[Enter a MESSENGER.]

MESSENGER. My lord, they stay for you to give your daughter to her husband.

LEONATO. I'll wait upon them. I am ready.

[Exeunt LEONATO and MESSENGER.]

DOGBERRY. Go, good partner, go, get you to Francis 60 Seacole. Bid him bring his pen and inkhorn to the jail. We are now to examination these men.

VERGES. And we must do it wisely.

DOGBERRY. We will spare for no wit, I warrant you. Here's that shall drive some of them to a non-come.° Only get the learned writer to set down 65 our excommunication,° and meet me at the jail.

[Exeunt]

---

tedious (Dogberry supposes the word complimentary)
exclamation blunder for *acclamation*
excepting . . . presence blunder for *begging your worship's pardon*

aspicious blunder for *suspicious*
suffigance blunder for *sufficient*
noncome i.e., *non plus*, confusion
excommunication blunder for *examination*

ACT IV

SCENE i
A church.

[*Enter* DON PEDRO, DON JOHN, LEONATO, FRIAR FRANCIS, CLAUDIO, BENEDICK, HERO, BEATRICE, *and* ATTENDANTS.]

LEONATO. Come, Friar Francis, be brief; only to the plain form of marriage, and you shall recount their particular duties afterwards.

FRIAR FRANCIS. You come hither, my lord, to marry
5 this lady.

CLAUDIO. No.

LEONATO. To be married to her, Friar. You come to marry her.

FRIAR FRANCIS. Lady, you come hither to be
10 married to this count.

HERO. I do.

FRIAR FRANCIS. If either of you know any inward

impediment why you should not be conjoined, I charge you, on your souls, to utter it.

CLAUDIO. Know you any, Hero?   15

HERO. None, my lord.

FRIAR FRANCIS. Know you any, Count?

LEONATO. I dare make his answer, none.

CLAUDIO. O, what men dare do! What men may do! What men daily do, not knowing what they 20 do!

BENEDICK. How now! Interjections? Why, then, some be of laughing, as, ah, ha, he!

CLAUDIO. Stand thee by, Friar. Father, by your leave,   25
Will you with free and unconstrained soul
Give me this maid, your daughter?

LEONATO. As freely, son, as God did give her me.

CLAUDIO. And what have I to give you back, whose worth

30 May counterpoise this rich and precious gift?

Don Pedro. Nothing, unless you render her again.

Claudio. Sweet Prince, you learn° me noble
  thankfulness.

  There, Leonato, take her back again.

  Give not this rotten orange to your friend.

35 She's but the sign and semblance of her honor.

  Behold how like a maid she blushes here!

  O, what authority and show of truth

  Can cunning sin cover itself withal!

  Comes not that blood as modest evidence

40 To witness simple virtue? Would you not swear,

  All you that see her, that she were a maid,

  By these exterior shows? But she is none.

  She knows the heat of a luxurious° bed;

  Her blush is guiltiness, not modesty.

Leonato. What do you mean, my lord?

45 Claudio.   Not to be married,

  Not to knit my soul to an approved° wanton.

Leonato. Dear my lord, if you, in your own proof,

  Have vanquish'd the resistance of her youth

  And made defeat of her virginity—

Claudio. I know what you would say. If I have

50 known her,

  You will say she did embrace me as a husband,

  And so extenuate the 'forehand sin.

  No, Leonato,

  I never tempted her with word too large,

55 But as a brother to his sister, show'd

  Bashful sincerity and comely love.

Hero. And seem'd I ever otherwise to you?

Claudio. Out on thee! Seeming! I will write
  against it.

  You seem to me as Dian in her orb,°

60 As chaste as is the bud ere it be blown.°

  But you are more intemperate in your blood

  Than Venus, or those pamper'd animals

  That rage in savage sensuality.

Hero. Is my lord well, that he doth speak so wide?°

Leonato. Sweet Prince, why speak not you?

65 Don Pedro.   What should I speak?

  I stand dishonor'd that have gone about

  To link my dear friend to a common stale.

Leonato. Are these things spoken, or do I but
  dream?

Don John. Sir, they are spoken, and these things
  are true.

Benedick. This looks not like a nuptial.

70 Hero.   True! O God!

Claudio. Leonato, stand I here?

Is this the prince? Is this the prince's brother?

Is this face Hero's? Are our eyes our own?

Leonato. All this is so. But what of this, my
  lord?

Claudio. Let me but move one question to your
  daughter,   75

  And, by that fatherly and kindly power

  That you have in her, bid her answer truly.

Leonato. I charge thee do so, as thou art my child.

Hero. O, God defend me! How am I beset!

  What kind of catechising call you this? 80

Claudio. To make you answer truly to your name.

Hero. Is it not Hero? Who can blot that name

  With any just reproach?

Claudio.   Marry, that can Hero;

  Hero itself can blot out Hero's virtue.

  What man was he talk'd with you yesternight 85

  Out at your window betwixt twelve and one?

  Now, if you are a maid, answer to this.

Hero. I talk'd with no man at that hour, my lord.

Don Pedro. Why, then are you no maiden.
  Leonato,

  I am sorry you must hear. Upon mine honor, 90

  Myself, my brother, and this grieved count

  Did see her, hear her, at that hour last night

  Talk with a ruffian at her chamber window,

  Who hath indeed, most like a liberal° villain,

  Confess'd the vile encounters they have had 95

  A thousand times in secret.

Don John. Fie, fie! They are not to be nam'd, my
  lord,

  Not to be spoke of.

  There is not chastity enough in language,

  Without offense to utter them. Thus, pretty
  lady,   100

  I am sorry for thy much misgovernment.°

Claudio. O Hero, what a Hero hadst thou been

  If half thy outward graces had been plac'd

  About thy thoughts and counsels of thy heart!

  But fare thee well, most foul, most fair! Farewell, 105

  Thou pure impiety and impious purity!

  For thee I'll lock up all the gates of love,

  And on my eyelids shall conjecture hang

  To turn all beauty into thoughts of harm,

  And never shall it more be gracious. 110

Leonato. Hath no man's dagger here a point for
  me?   [Hero swoons.]

Beatrice. Why, how now, cousin! Wherefore sink
  you down?

Don John. Come, let us go. These things, come
  thus to light,

  Smother her spirits up.

   [Exeunt Don Pedro, Don John, and Claudio.]

---

learn teach luxurious lustful approved proved
Dian . . . orb Diana was goddess of chastity and moon
  goddess
blown in full bloom so wide so wide of the mark

liberal gross misgovernment misconduct

BENEDICK. How doth the lady?

115 BEATRICE.   Dead, I think. Help, uncle!
    Hero! Why, Hero! Uncle! Signior Benedick!
      Friar!

LEONATO. O Fate! Take not away thy heavy hand.
    Death is the fairest cover for her shame
    That may be wish'd for.

BEATRICE.   How now, cousin Hero!

120 FRIAR FRANCIS. Have comfort, lady.

LEONATO. Dost thou look up?

FRIAR FRANCIS.   Yea, wherefore should she not?

LEONATO. Wherefore! Why, doth not every earthly
    thing
    Cry shame upon her? Could she here deny
    The story that is printed in her blood?
125   Do not live, Hero; do not ope thine eyes.
    For did I think thou wouldst not quickly die,
    Thought I thy spirits were stronger than thy
      shames,
    Myself would, on the rearward of reproaches,
    Strike at thy life. Griev'd I, I had but one?
130   Chid I for that at frugal nature's frame?
    O, one too much by thee! Why had I one?
    Why ever wast thou lovely in my eyes?
    Why had I not with charitable hand
    Took up a beggar's issue at my gates,
135   Who, smirched thus and mir'd with infamy,
    I might have said "No part of it is mine;
    This shame derives itself from unknown loins."
    But mine, and mine I lov'd, and mine I prais'd,
    And mine that I was proud on, mine so much
140   That I myself was to myself not mine,
    Valuing of her—why, she, O, she is fallen
    Into a pit of ink, that° the wide sea
    Hath drops too few to wash her clean again
    And salt too little which may season give
    To her foul-tainted flesh!

145 BENEDICK.   Sir, sir, be patient.
    For my part, I am so attir'd in wonder
    I know not what to say.

BEATRICE. O, on my soul, my cousin is belied!

BENEDICK. Lady, were you her bedfellow last night?

150 BEATRICE. No, truly, not, although, until last night,
    I have this twelvemonth been her bedfellow.

LEONATO. Confirm'd, confirm'd! O, that is stronger
    made
    Which was before barr'd up with ribs of iron!
    Would the two princes lie, and Claudio lie,
155   Who lov'd her so, that, speaking of her foulness,
    Wash'd it with tears? Hence from her! Let her
      die.

FRIAR FRANCIS. Hear me a little,
    For I have only been silent so long

that so that

And given way unto this course of fortune
By noting of the lady. I have mark'd   160
A thousand blushing apparitions
To start into her face, a thousand innocent
  shames
In angel whiteness beat away those blushes;
And in her eye there hath appear'd a fire
To burn the errors that these princes hold   165
Against her maiden truth. Call me a fool;
Trust not my reading nor my observations,
Which with experimental seal° doth warrant
The tenor of my book; trust not my age,
My reverence, calling, nor divinity,   170
If this sweet lady lie not guiltless here
Under some biting error.

LEONATO.   Friar, it cannot be.
Thou seest that all the grace that she hath left
Is that she will not add to her damnation
A sin of perjury; she not denies it.   175
Why seek'st thou, then, to cover with excuse
That which appears in proper nakedness?

FRIAR FRANCIS. Lady, what man is he you are
  accus'd of?

HERO. They know that do accuse me; I know none.
If I know more of any man alive   180
Than that which maiden modesty doth warrant,
Let all my sins lack mercy! O my father,
Prove you that any man with me convers'd
At hours unmeet, or that I yesternight
Maintain'd the change of words with any
  creature,   185
Refuse me, hate me, torture me to death!

FRIAR FRANCIS. There is some strange misprision° in
  the princes.

BENEDICK. Two of them have the very bent of
  honor;
And if their wisdoms be misled in this,
The practice of it lives in John the bastard,   190
Whose spirits toil in frame of villainies.

LEONATO. I know not. If they speak but truth of
  her,
These hands shall tear her. If they wrong her
  honor,
The proudest of them shall well hear of it.
Time hath not yet so dried this blood of mine,   195
Nor age so eat up my invention,
Nor fortune made such havoc of my means,
Nor my bad life reft° me so much of friends,
But they shall find, awak'd in such a kind,
Both strength of limb and policy of mind,   200
Ability in means and choice of friends,
To quit me of them throughly.°

experimental seal seal of experience
misprision mistaking   *reft* bereft
quit . . . throughly pay them back thoroughly

FRIAR FRANCIS.   Pause awhile,
And let my counsel sway you in this case.
Your daughter here the princes left for dead.
205   Let her awhile be secretly kept in,
And publish it that she is dead indeed.
Maintain a mourning ostentation,
And on your family's old monument
Hang mournful epitaphs, and do all rites
210   That appertain unto a burial.
  LEONATO. What shall become of this? What will
    this do?
  FRIAR FRANCIS. Marry, this, well carried, shall on
    her behalf
Change slander to remorse; that is some good.
But not for that dream I on this strange course,
215   But on this travail look for greater birth.
She dying, as it must be so maintain'd,
Upon the instant that she was accus'd,
Shall be lamented, pitied, and excus'd
Of every hearer. For it so falls out
220   That what we have we prize not to the worth
Whiles we enjoy it; but being lack'd and lost,
Why, then we rack° the value, then we find
The virtue that possession would not show us
Whiles it was ours. So will it fare with Claudio.
225   When he shall hear she died upon his words,
The idea of her life shall sweetly creep
Into his study of imagination,°
And every lovely organ of her life°
Shall come apparell'd in more precious habit,
230   More moving-delicate and full of life
Into the eye and prospect of his soul,
Than when she liv'd indeed; then shall he
    mourn,
If ever love had interest in his liver,°
And wish he had not so accused her—
235   No, though he thought his accusation true.
Let this be so, and doubt not but success
Will fashion the event° in better shape
Than I can lay it down in likelihood.
But if all aim but this be levell'd false,
240   The supposition of the lady's death
Will quench the wonder of her infamy.°
And if it sort not well, you may conceal her,
As best befits her wounded reputation,
In some reclusive and religious life,
245   Out of all eyes, tongues, minds, and injuries.

rack   stretch, as on the rack
study of imagination   contemplative thought
organ . . . life   aspect of her being
liver   the supposed seat of affection
event   outcome
But if . . . infamy   but if all else fails, at least the
supposition of Hero's death will cause her shame to be
forgotten

BENEDICK. Signior Leonato, let the friar advise you.
And though you know my inwardness° and love
Is very much unto the prince and Claudio,
Yet, by mine honor, I will deal in this
As secretly and justly as your soul   250
Should with your body.
  LEONATO.   Being that I flow in grief,
The smallest twine may lead me.
  FRIAR FRANCIS. 'Tis well consented. Presently
    away;
For to strange sores strangely they strain the
    cure.
Come, lady, die to live. This wedding day   255
Perhaps is but prolong'd.° Have patience and
    endure.
          [*Exeunt all but* BENEDICK *and* BEATRICE.]
  BENEDICK. Lady Beatrice, have you wept all this
    while?
  BEATRICE. Yea, and I will weep a while longer.
  BENEDICK. I will not desire that.   260
  BEATRICE. You have no reason; I do it freely.
  BENEDICK. Surely I do believe your fair cousin is
    wronged.
  BEATRICE. Ah, how much might the man deserve of
    me that would right her!   265
  BENEDICK. Is there any way to show such friendship?
  BEATRICE. A very even way, but no such friend.
  BENEDICK. May a man do it?
  BEATRICE. It is a man's office, but not yours.
  BENEDICK. I do love nothing in the world so well as   270
    you. Is not that strange?
  BEATRICE. As strange as the thing I know not. It
    were as possible for me to say I loved nothing so
    well as you. But believe me not; and yet I lie
    not; I confess nothing, nor I deny nothing. I am   275
    sorry for my cousin.
  BENEDICK. By my sword, Beatrice, thou lovest me.
  BEATRICE. Do not swear, and eat it.°
  BENEDICK. I will swear by it° that you love me, and
    I will make him eat it that says I love not you.   280
  BEATRICE. Will you not eat your word?
  BENEDICK. With no sauce that can be devised to it. I
    protest I love thee.
  BEATRICE. Why, then, God forgive me!
  BENEDICK. What offense, sweet Beatrice?   285
  BEATRICE. You have stayed me in a happy hour. I
    was about to protest I loved you.
  BENEDICK. And do it with all thy heart.
  BEATRICE. I love you with so much of my heart that
    none is left to protest.   290
  BENEDICK. Come, bid me do anything for thee.
  BEATRICE. Kill Claudio.

inwardness   deepest loyalty   *prolong'd*   postponed
eat it   i.e., your oath   *by it*   i.e., my sword

BENEDICK. Ha! Not for the wide world.

BEATRICE. You kill me to deny it. Farewell.

295 BENEDICK. Tarry, sweet Beatrice.

BEATRICE. I am gone, though I am here. There is no love in you. Nay, I pray you, let me go.

BENEDICK. Beatrice—

BEATRICE. In faith, I will go.

300 BENEDICK. We'll be friends first.

BEATRICE. You dare easier be friends with me than fight with mine enemy.

BENEDICK. Is Claudio thine enemy?

BEATRICE. Is he not approved° in the height° a
305 villain that hath slandered, scorned, dishonored my kinswoman? O that I were a man! What, bear her in hand until they come to take hands, and then, with public accusation, uncovered slander, unmitigated rancor—O God, that I were
310 a man! I would eat his heart in the marketplace.

BENEDICK. Hear me, Beatrice—

BEATRICE. Talk with a man out at a window! A proper saying!

BENEDICK. Nay, but, Beatrice—

315 BEATRICE. Sweet Hero! She is wronged, she is slandered, she is undone.

BENEDICK. Beat—

BEATRICE. Princes and counties! Surely, a princely testimony, a goodly count, Count Comfect°; a
320 sweet gallant, surely! O that I were a man for his sake! Or that I had any friend would be a man for my sake! But manhood is melted into courtesies, valor into compliment, and men are only turned into tongue, and trim° ones too. He
325 is now as valiant as Hercules that only tells a lie and swears it. I cannot be a man with wishing, therefore I will die a woman with grieving.

BENEDICK. Tarry, good Beatrice. By this hand, I love thee.

330 BEATRICE. Use it for my love some other way than swearing by it.

BENEDICK. Think you in your soul the Count Claudio hath wronged Hero?

BEATRICE. Yea, as sure as I have a thought or a soul.

335 BENEDICK. Enough, I am engaged. I will challenge him. I will kiss your hand, and so I leave you. By this hand, Claudio shall render me a dear account. As you hear of me, so think of me. Go, comfort your cousin. I must say she is dead. And
340 so, farewell.   [Exeunt]

SCENE ii
A prison.

[Enter DOGBERRY, VERGES, and SEXTON, in gowns; and the WATCH, with CONRADE and BORACHIO.]

DOGBERRY. Is our whole dissembly° appeared?

VERGES. O, a stool and a cushion for the sexton.

SEXTON. Which be the malefactors?

DOGBERRY. Marry, that am I and my partner.

VERGES. Nay, that's certain; we have the exhibi-   5
tion° to examine.

SEXTON. But which are the offenders that are to be examined? Let them come before master constable.

DOGBERRY. Yea, marry, let them come before me.   10
What is your name, friend?

BORACHIO. Borachio.

DOGBERRY. Pray, write down Borachio. Yours, sirrah?

CONRADE. I am a gentleman, sir, and my name is   15
Conrade.

DOGBERRY. Write down master gentleman Con-rade. Masters, do you serve God?

CONRADE and BORACHIO. Yea, sir, we hope.

DOGBERRY. Write down that they hope they serve   20
God. And write God first, for God defend° but God should go before such villains! Masters, it is proved already that you are little better than false knaves, and it will go near to be thought so shortly. How answer you for yourselves?   25

CONRADE. Marry, sir, we say we are none.

DOGBERRY. A marvelous witty fellow, I assure you. But I will go about with° him. Come you hither, sirrah; a word in your ear. Sir, I say to you it is thought you are false knaves.   30

BORACHIO. Sir, I say to you we are none.

DOGBERRY. Well, stand aside. 'Fore God, they are both in a tale.° Have you writ down that they are none?

SEXTON. Master constable, you go not the way to   35
examine. You must call forth the watch that are their accusers.

DOGBERRY. Yea, marry, that's the eftest° way. Let the watch come forth. Masters, I charge you in the prince's name, accuse these men.   40

FIRST WATCH. This man said, sir, that Don John, the prince's brother, was a villain.

DOGBERRY. Write down, Prince John a villain. Why,

---

approved proved
height highest degree
Count Comfect Count Candy   trim fine, dandified

dissembly blunder for assembly
exhibition blunder for commission
defend forbid   go about with deal with
in a tale i.e., in agreement
eftest (Dogberry's coinage)

this is flat perjury, to call a prince's brother
45 villain.
BORACHIO. Master constable—
DOGBERRY. Pray thee, fellow, peace. I do not like
    thy look, I promise thee.
SEXTON. What heard you him say else?
50 SECOND WATCH. Marry, that he had received a
    thousand ducats of Don John for accusing the
    Lady Hero wrongfully.
DOGBERRY. Flat burglary as ever was committed.
VERGES. Yea, by mass, that it is.
55 SEXTON. What else, fellow?
FIRST WATCH. And that Count Claudio did mean,
    upon his words, to disgrace Hero before the
    whole assembly, and not marry her.
DOGBERRY. O villain! Thou wilt be condemned into
60 everlasting redemption° for this.
SEXTON. What else?
WATCH. This is all.
SEXTON. And this is more, masters, than you can
    deny. Prince John is this morning secretly stolen
65 away. Hero was in this manner accused, in this
    very manner refused, and upon the grief of this
    suddenly died. Master constable, let these men
    be bound and brought to Leonato's. I will go
    before and show him their examination.   [Exit]

redemption blunder for damnation

DOGBERRY. Come, let them be opinioned.°   70
VERGES. Let them be in the hands—
CONRADE. Off, coxcomb!
DOGBERRY. God's my life, where's the sexton? Let
    him write down the prince's officer, coxcomb.
    Come, bind them. Thou naughty varlet!°   75
CONRADE. Away! You are an ass. You are an ass.
DOGBERRY. Dost thou not suspect° my place? Dost
    thou not suspect my years? O that he were here
    to write me down an ass! But, masters, remem-
    ber that I am an ass; though it be not written   80
    down, yet forget not that I am an ass. No, thou
    villain, thou art full of piety,° as shall be proved
    upon thee by good witness. I am a wise fellow;
    and, which is more, an officer; and, which is
    more, a householder; and, which is more, as   85
    pretty a piece of flesh as any is in Messina; and
    one that knows the law, go to; and a rich fellow
    enough, go to; and a fellow that hath had
    losses; and one that hath two gowns, and every-
    thing handsome about him. Bring him away. O   90
    that I had been writ down an ass!   [Exeunt]

opinioned blunder for pinioned
naughty varlet   wicked knave
suspect blunder for respect   piety blunder for impiety

ACT V

SCENE i
Before LEONATO's house.

[Enter LEONATO and ANTONIO.]
ANTONIO. If you go on thus, you will kill yourself,
    And 'tis not wisdom thus to second° grief
    Against yourself.
LEONATO.   I pray thee, cease thy counsel,
    Which falls into mine ears as profitless
5   As water in a sieve. Give not me counsel,
    Nor let no comforter delight mine ear
    But such a one whose wrongs do suit with mine.
    Bring me a father that so lov'd his child,
    Whose joy of her is overwhelm'd like mine,
10 And bid him speak of patience.
    Measure his woe the length and breadth of mine,
    And let it answer every strain for strain,
    As thus for thus, and such a grief for such,

second support

In every lineament, branch, shape, and form.
If such a one will smile and stroke his beard,   15
Bid sorrow wag,° cry "hem!" when he should
    groan,
Patch grief with proverbs, make misfortune
    drunk
With candle-wasters, bring him yet to me,
And I of him will gather patience.
But there is no such man. For, brother, men   20
Can counsel and speak comfort to that grief
Which they themselves not feel; but, tasting it,
Their counsel turns to passion, which before
Would give preceptial medicine to rage,
Fetter strong madness in a silken thread,   25
Charm ache with air and agony with words.
No, no; 'tis all men's office to speak patience
To those that wring° under the load of sorrow,

wag "go to"
"hem" a drinker's exclamation (see 1Henry IV, II, iv)
wring suffer pain

But no man's virtue nor sufficiency
30 To be so moral° when he shall endure
The like himself. Therefore give me no counsel.
My griefs cry louder than advertisement.°
ANTONIO. Therein do men from children nothing
differ.
LEONATO. I pray thee, peace. I will be flesh and
blood;
35 For there was never yet philosopher
That could endure the toothache patiently,
However they have writ° the style of gods
And made a push at chance and sufferance.°
ANTONIO. Yet bend not all the harm upon your-
self;
40 Make those that do offend you suffer too.
LEONATO. There thou speak'st reason. Nay, I will
do so.
My soul doth tell me Hero is belied,
And that shall Claudio know, so shall the prince,
And all of them that thus dishonor her.
ANTONIO. Here comes the prince and Claudio
45 hastily.
[Enter DON PEDRO and CLAUDIO.]
DON PEDRO. Good den, good den.
CLAUDIO. Good day to both of you.
LEONATO. Hear you, my lords—
DON PEDRO.   We have some haste, Leonato.
LEONATO. Some haste, my lord! Well, fare you
well, my lord.
50 Are you so hasty now? Well, all is one.
DON PEDRO. Nay, do not quarrel with us, good old
man.
ANTONIO. If he could right himself with quarreling,
Some of us would lie low.
CLAUDIO.   Who wrongs him?
LEONATO. Marry, thou dost wrong me, thou dis-
sembler, thou,
55 Nay, never lay thy hand upon thy sword;
I fear thee not.
CLAUDIO.   Marry, beshrew° my hand
If it should give your age such cause of fear.
In faith, my hand meant nothing to my sword.
LEONATO. Tush, tush, man; never fleer° and jest at
me.
60 I speak not like a dotard nor a fool,
As, under privilege of age, to brag
What I have done being young, or what would
do
Were I not old. Know, Claudio, to thy head,

Thou hast so wrong'd mine innocent child and
me
That I am forc'd to lay my reverence by,   65
And with grey hairs and bruise of many days
Do challenge thee to trial of a man.
I say thou hast belied mine innocent child.
Thy slander hath gone through and through her
heart,
And she lies buried with her ancestors—   70
O, in a tomb where never scandal slept
Save this of hers, fram'd by thy villainy!
CLAUDIO. My villainy?
LEONATO.   Thine, Claudio; thine, I say.
DON PEDRO. You say not right, old man.
LEONATO.   My lord, my lord,
I'll prove it on his body, if he dare,   75
Despite his nice fence° and his active practice,
His May of youth and bloom of lustihood.
CLAUDIO. Away! I will not have to do with you.
LEONATO. Canst thou so daff° me? Thou hast kill'd
my child.
If thou kill'st me, boy, thou shalt kill a man.   80
ANTONIO. He shall kill two of us, and men indeed.
But that's no matter; let him kill one first.
Win me and wear me; let him answer me.
Come, follow me, boy; come, sir boy, come,
follow me.
Sir boy, I'll whip you from your foining° fence;   85
Nay, as I am a gentleman, I will.
LEONATO. Brother—
ANTONIO. Content yourself. God knows I lov'd my
niece,
And she is dead, slander'd to death by villains
That dare as well answer a man indeed   90
As I dare take a serpent by the tongue.
Boys, apes, braggarts, Jacks,° milksops!
LEONATO.   Brother, Antony—
ANTONIO. Hold you content. What, man! I know
them, yea,
And what they weigh,° even to the utmost
scruple°—
Scambling,° out-facing,° fashion-monging° boys   95
That lie, and cog,° and flout, deprave,° and
slander,
Go anticly,° and show outward hideousness,
And speak off half a dozen dang'rous words
How they might hurt their enemies if they durst;
And this is all.   100

---

moral philosophical
advertisement advice   writ written in
made . . . sufferance brushed off mischance and
  suffering
beshrew curse   fleer sneer

nice fence fancy style of fencing   daff put aside
foining thrusting   Jacks knaves
weigh are worth; amount to   scruple tiniest unit
Scambling brawling   out-facing bullying
fashion-monging fashion-mongering, modish
cog cheat   deprave degrade
anticly like antics, buffoons

LEONATO. But, brother Antony—

ANTONIO.   Come, 'tis no matter.
  Do not you meddle; let me deal in this.

DON PEDRO. Gentlemen both, we will not wake°
  your patience.
  My heart is sorry for your daughter's death.
105 But, on my honor, she was charg'd with nothing
  But what was true, and very full of proof.

LEONATO. My lord, my lord—

DON PEDRO. I will not hear you.

LEONATO. No? Come, brother, away! I will be
  heard.

ANTONIO. And shall, or some of us will smart for
110 it.   [Exeunt LEONATO and ANTONIO.]

DON PEDRO. See, see, here comes the man we went
  to seek.

                [Enter BENEDICK.]

CLAUDIO. Now, signior, what news?

BENEDICK. Good day, my lord.

DON PEDRO. Welcome, signior. You are almost
115 come to part almost a fray.

CLAUDIO. We had like to have had our two noses
  snapped off with two old men without teeth.

DON PEDRO. Leonato and his brother. What
  thinkest thou? Had we fought, I doubt° we
120 should have been too young for them.

BENEDICK. In a false quarrel there is no true valor. I
  came to seek you both.

CLAUDIO. We have been up and down to seek thee,
  for we are high-proof melancholy and would
125 fain have it beaten away. Wilt thou use thy
  wit?

BENEDICK. It is in my scabbard. Shall I draw it?

DON PEDRO. Dost thou wear thy wit by thy side?

CLAUDIO. Never any did so, though very many have
130 been beside their wit. I will bid thee draw as we
  do the minstrels°; draw, to pleasure us.

DON PEDRO. As I am an honest man, he looks pale.
  Art thou sick, or angry?

CLAUDIO. What, courage, man! What though care
135 killed a cat, thou hast mettle enough in thee to
  kill care.

BENEDICK. Sir, I shall meet your wit in the career,°
  an you charge it against me. I pray you choose
  another subject.

140 CLAUDIO. Nay, then, give him another staff. This
  last was broke cross.°

DON PEDRO. By this light, he changes more and
  more. I think he be angry indeed.

CLAUDIO. If he be, he knows how to turn his girdle.°

BENEDICK. Shall I speak a word in your ear?   145

CLAUDIO. God bless me from a challenge!

BENEDICK. [Aside to CLAUDIO] You are a villain; I
  jest not. I will make it good how you dare, with
  what you dare, and when you dare. Do me right,
  or I will protest° your cowardice. You have killed 150
  a sweet lady, and her death shall fall heavy on
  you. Let me hear from you.

CLAUDIO. Well, I will meet you, so I may have good
  cheer.

DON PEDRO. What, a feast, a feast?   155

CLAUDIO. I'faith, I thank him; he hath bid me to a
  calf's-head and a capon, the which if I do not
  carve most curiously, say my knife's naught.°
  Shall I not find a woodcock° too?

BENEDICK. Sir, your wit ambles well; it goes easily. 160

DON PEDRO. I'll tell thee how Beatrice praised thy
  wit the other day. I said, thou hadst a fine wit.
  "True," said she, "a fine little one." "No," said
  I, "a great wit." "Right," says she, "a great gross
  one." "Nay," said I, "a good wit." "Just," said 165
  she, "it hurts nobody." "Nay," said I, "the
  gentleman is wise." "Certain," said she, "a wise
  gentleman." "Nay," said I, "he hath the
  tongues."° "That I believe," said she, "for he
  swore a thing to me on Monday night which he 170
  forswore on Tuesday morning; there's a double
  tongue; there's two tongues." Thus did she, an
  hour together, transshape° thy particular virtues.
  Yet at last she concluded with a sigh, thou wast
  the properest° man in Italy.   175

CLAUDIO. For the which she wept heartily and said
  she cared not.

DON PEDRO. Yea, that she did; but yet, for all that,
  an if she did not hate him deadly, she would love
  him dearly. The old man's daughter told us all. 180

CLAUDIO. All, all; and, moreover, God saw him
  when he was hid in the garden.

DON PEDRO. But when shall we set the savage
  bull's horns on the sensible Benedick's head?

CLAUDIO. Yea, and text underneath, "Here dwells 185
  Benedick the married man"?

BENEDICK. Fare you well, boy. You know my mind.
  I will leave you now to your gossip-like humor.
  You break jests as braggarts do their blades,
  which, God be thanked, hurt not. My lord, for 190
  your many courtesies I thank you. I must dis-
  continue your company. Your brother the

---

wake rouse; hence, make impatient   doubt suspect
draw . . . minstrels i.e., draw the minstrel's bow over
  the strings
career tilting-match charge
broke cross broken across, like the tilter's spear;
  i.e., Benedick's wit fell flat

turn his girdle (meaning uncertain; possibly, shift his
  girdle around so as to reach his weapon)
protest proclaim publicly   naught no good
woodcock foolish bird; here, Benedick
tongues i.e., foreign languages   transshape pervert
properest handsomest

bastard is fled from Messina. You have among
you killed a sweet and innocent lady. For my
195 Lord Lackbeard there, he and I shall meet. And
till then peace be with him. [*Exit*]

DON PEDRO. He is in earnest.

CLAUDIO. In most profound earnest, and, I'll
warrant you, for the love of Beatrice.

200 DON PEDRO. And hath challenged thee.

CLAUDIO. Most sincerely.

DON PEDRO. What a pretty thing man is when he
goes in his doublet and hose and leaves off his
wit!

205 CLAUDIO. He is then a giant to an ape. But then is an
ape a doctor° to such a man.

DON PEDRO. But, soft you, let me be. Pluck up, my
heart, and be sad.° Did he not say my brother
was fled?

[*Enter* DOGBERRY, VERGES, *and the* WATCH, *with*
CONRADE *and* BORACHIO.]

210 DOGBERRY. Come, you, sir. If justice cannot tame
you, she shall ne'er weigh more reasons° in her
balance.° Nay, an you be a cursing hypocrite
once, you must be looked to.

DON PEDRO. How now? Two of my brother's men
215 bound! Borachio one!

CLAUDIO. Hearken after their offense, my lord.

DON PEDRO. Officers, what offense have these men
done?

DOGBERRY. Marry, sir, they have committed false
220 report; moreover, they have spoken untruths;
secondarily, they are slanders; sixth and lastly,
they have belied a lady; thirdly, they have
verified unjust things; and, to conclude, they are
lying knaves.

225 DON PEDRO. First, I ask thee what they have done;
thirdly, I ask thee what's their offense; sixth and
lastly, why they are committed°; and, to conclude, what you lay to their charge.

CLAUDIO. Rightly reasoned, and in his own divi-
230 sion°; and, by my troth, there's one meaning
well suited.°

DON PEDRO. Who have you offended, masters,
that you are thus bound to your answer? This
learned constable is too cunning to be under-
235 stood. What's your offense?

BORACHIO. Sweet prince, let me go no farther to
mine answer. Do you hear me, and let this
count kill me. I have deceived even your very
eyes. What your wisdoms could not discover,

these shallow fools have brought to light, who, 240
in the night, overheard me confessing to this
man how Don John your brother incensed me to
slander the Lady Hero; how you were brought
into the orchard and saw me court Margaret in
Hero's garments; how you disgraced her when 245
you should marry° her. My villainy they have
upon record, which I had rather seal with my
death than repeat over to my shame. The lady is
dead upon mine and my master's false accusation, and, briefly, I desire nothing but the 250
reward of a villain.

DON PEDRO. Runs not this speech like iron through
your blood?

CLAUDIO. I have drunk poison whiles he utter'd it.

DON PEDRO. But did my brother set thee on to
this?

BORACHIO. Yea, and paid me richly for the practice
of it. 255

DON PEDRO. He is compos'd and fram'd of treachery,
And fled he is upon this villainy.

CLAUDIO. Sweet Hero! Now thy image doth
appear
In the rare semblance that I lov'd it first.

DOGBERRY. Come, bring away the plaintiffs.° By 260
this time our sexton hath reformed° Signior
Leonato of the matter. And, masters, do not
forget to specify, when time and place shall
serve, that I am an ass.

VERGES. Here, here comes master Signior Leonato, 265
and the sexton too.

[*Re-enter* LEONATO *and* ANTONIO, *with the* SEXTON.]

LEONATO. Which is the villain? Let me see his
eyes,
That when I note another man like him
I may avoid him. Which of these is he?

BORACHIO. If you would know your wronger, look
on me. 270

LEONATO. Art thou the slave that with thy breath
hast kill'd
Mine innocent child?

BORACHIO.   Yea, even I alone.

LEONATO. No, not so, villain; thou beliest thyself.
Here stand a pair of honorable men;
A third is fled that had a hand in it. 275
I thank you, princes, for my daughter's death.
Record it with your high and worthy deeds.
'Twas bravely done, if you bethink you of it.

CLAUDIO. I know not how to pray your patience;
Yet I must speak. Choose your revenge yourself; 280

---

doctor i.e., learned man   sad serious
reasons legal causes   balance scales
committed under arrest
in . . . division each in its proper category
one . . . suited one question variously phrased

should marry should have married
plaintiffs blunder for defendants
reformed blunder for informed

Impose me to what penance your invention
Can lay upon my sin. Yet sinn'd I not
But in mistaking.

DON PEDRO.   By my soul, nor I.
And yet, to satisfy this good old man,
285   I would bend under any heavy weight
That he'll enjoin me to.

LEONATO. I cannot bid you bid my daughter live;
That were impossible. But I pray you both,
Possess the people in Messina here
290   How innocent she died; and if your love
Can labor aught in sad invention,
Hang her an epitaph upon her tomb
And sing it to her bones. Sing it tonight.
Tomorrow morning come you to my house;
295   And since you could not be my son-in-law,
Be yet my nephew. My brother hath a daughter,
Almost the copy of my child that's dead,
And she alone is heir to both of us.
Give her the right you should have given her
     cousin,
And so dies my revenge.

300 CLAUDIO.   O noble sir,
Your overkindness doth wring tears from me!
I do embrace your offer, and dispose
For henceforth of poor Claudio.

LEONATO. Tomorrow, then, I will expect your
     coming;
305   Tonight I take my leave. This naughty° man
Shall face to face be brought to Margaret,
Who I believe was pack'd° in all this wrong,
Hir'd to it by your brother.

BORACHIO.   No, by my soul, she was not,
Nor knew not what she did when she spoke to
     me,
310   But always hath been just and virtuous
In anything that I do know by her.

DOGBERRY. Moreover, sir, which indeed is not
under white and black, this plaintiff here, the
offender, did call me ass. I beseech you, let it be
315   remembered in his punishment. And also the
watch heard them talk of one Deformed. They
say he wears a key in his ear and a lock hanging
by it, and borrows money in God's name, the
which he hath used so long and never paid that
320   now men grow hard-hearted and will lend
nothing for God's sake. Pray you, examine him
upon that point.

LEONATO. I thank thee for thy care and honest
pains.

325 DOGBERRY. Your worship speaks like a most thankful and reverend youth, and I praise God for you.

LEONATO. There's for thy pains.

DOGBERRY. God save the foundation!

LEONATO. Go, I discharge thee of thy prisoner, and
I thank thee.   330

DOGBERRY. I leave an arrant knave with your worship, which I beseech your worship to correct
yourself for the example of others. God keep
your worship! I wish your worship well; God
restore you to health! I humbly give you leave   335
to depart; and if a merry meeting may be
wished, God prohibit° it! Come, neighbor.
                    [Exeunt DOGBERRY and VERGES.]

LEONATO. Until tomorrow morning, lords, farewell.

ANTONIO. Farewell, my lords. We look for you
tomorrow.

DON PEDRO. We will not fail.

CLAUDIO.   Tonight I'll mourn with Hero.   340

LEONATO. [To the WATCH] Bring you these fellows
on. We'll talk with Margaret
How her acquaintance grew with this lewd
fellow.   [Exeunt, severally.]

SCENE ii
LEONATO's garden.

[Enter BENEDICK and MARGARET, meeting.]

BENEDICK. Pray thee, sweet Mistress Margaret,
deserve well at my hands by helping me to the
speech of Beatrice.

MARGARET. Will you, then, write me a sonnet in
praise of my beauty?   5

BENEDICK. In so high a style,° Margaret, that no
man living shall come over it; for, in most
comely truth, thou deservest it.

MARGARET. To have no man come over me! Why,
shall I always keep below stairs?   10

BENEDICK. Thy wit is as quick as the greyhound's
mouth; it catches.

MARGARET. And yours as blunt as the fencer's foils,
which hit but hurt not.

BENEDICK. A most manly wit, Margaret; it will not   15
hurt a woman. And so, I pray thee, call Beatrice.
I give thee the bucklers.°

MARGARET. Give us the swords; we have bucklers
of our own.

BENEDICK. If you use them, Margaret, you must   20
put in the pikes° with a vice,° and they are
dangerous weapons for maids.

prohibit blunder for _grant_
style of writing (with pun on _stile_)
I give . . . bucklers i.e., I give you the victory (the
  buckler was a shield)
pikes spikes   _vice_ screw

---

naughty wicked
pack'd one of the pack of conspirators

MARGARET. Well, I will call Beatrice to you, who I think hath legs.

25 BENEDICK. And therefore will come.

[*Exit* MARGARET.]

[*Sings*]　　　The god of love,
　　　　　　　That sits above,
　　　　　And knows me, and knows me,
　　　　　　How pitiful I deserve—

30 I mean in singing. But in loving, Leander the good swimmer,° Troilus° the first employer of panders, and a whole bookful of these quondam° carpetmongers,° whose names yet run smoothly in the even road of a blank verse, why, they 35 were never so truly turned over and over as my poor self in love. Marry, I cannot show it in rhyme; I have tried. I can find out no rhyme to "lady" but "baby," an innocent rhyme; for "scorn," "horn," a hard rhyme; for "school," 40 "fool," a babbling rhyme—very ominous endings. No, I was not born under a rhyming planet, nor I cannot woo in festival terms.

[*Enter* BEATRICE.]

Sweet Beatrice, wouldst thou come when I called thee?

45 BEATRICE. Yea, signior, and depart when you bid me.

BENEDICK. O, stay but till then!

BEATRICE. "Then" is spoken; fare you well now. And yet, ere I go, let me go with that I came 50 —which is, with knowing what hath passed between you and Claudio.

BENEDICK. Only foul words; and thereupon I will kiss thee.

BEATRICE. Foul words is but foul wind, and foul 55 wind is but foul breath, and foul breath is noisome; therefore I will depart unkissed.

BENEDICK. Thou hast frighted the word out of his right sense, so forcible is thy wit. But I must tell thee plainly, Claudio undergoes my challenge, 60 and either I must shortly hear from him, or I will subscribe° him a coward. And, I pray thee now, tell me for which of my bad parts didst thou first fall in love with me?

BEATRICE. For them all together, which main-65 tained so politic° a state of evil that they will

not admit any good part° to intermingle with them. But for which of my good parts did you first suffer love for me?

BENEDICK. Suffer love—a good epithet! I do suffer love indeed, for I love thee against my will.　70

BEATRICE. In spite of your heart, I think; alas, poor heart! If you spite it for my sake, I will spite it for yours; for I will never love that which my friend hates.

BENEDICK. Thou and I are too wise to woo peace-　75 ably.

BEATRICE. It appears not in this confession. There's not one wise man among twenty that will praise himself.

BENEDICK. An old, an old instance, Beatrice, that　80 lived in the time of good neighbors. If a man do not erect in this age his own tomb ere he dies, he shall live no longer in monument than the bell rings and the widow weeps.

BEATRICE. And how long is that, think you?　85

BENEDICK. Question: why, an hour in clamor and a quarter in rheum.° Therefore is it most expedient for the wise, if Don Worm, his conscience, find no impediment to the contrary, to be the trumpet of his own virtues, as I am to myself. So much for　90 praising myself, who, I myself will bear witness, is praiseworthy. And now tell me, how doth your cousin?

BEATRICE. Very ill.

BENEDICK. And how do you?　95

BEATRICE. Very ill too.

BENEDICK. Serve God, love me, and mend. There will I leave you too, for here comes one in haste.

[*Enter* URSULA.]

URSULA. Madam, you must come to your uncle. Yonder's old coil° at home. It is proved my Lady　100 Hero hath been falsely accused, the prince and Claudio mightily abused; and Don John is the author of all, who is fled and gone. Will you come presently?

BEATRICE. Will you go hear this news, signior?　105

BENEDICK. I will live in thy heart, die in thy lap, and be buried in thy eyes; and moreover I will go with thee to thy uncle's.　　　　　[*Exeunt*]

Leander . . . swimmer (who nightly swam the Hellespont to visit his beloved, also named Hero, and was finally drowned)
Troilus (see Chaucer's *Troilus and Criseyde* and Shakespeare's *Troilus and Cressida*)
quondam former
carpetmongers i.e., who shone more in loving than in fighting
subscribe publish　　*politic* tightly organized

part quality　　*rheum* tears　　*old coil* much ado

SCENE iii
A church.

[*Enter* DON PEDRO, CLAUDIO, *and three or four with tapers.*]

CLAUDIO. Is this the monument of Leonato?

A LORD. It is, my lord.

CLAUDIO. [*Reading out of a scroll*].

> Done to death by slanderous tongues
> 	Was the Hero that here lies.
> Death, in guerdon° of her wrongs,
> 	Gives her fame which never dies.
> So the life that died with shame
> Lives in death with glorious fame.

Hang thou there upon the tomb,

Praising her when I am dumb.

Now, music, sound, and sing your solemn hymn.

Song

> Pardon, goddess of the night,°
> Those that slew thy virgin knight;
> For the which, with songs of woe,
> Round about her tomb they go.
> 	Midnight, assist our moan;
> 	Help us to sigh and groan,
> 		Heavily, heavily.
> 	Graves, yawn, and yield your dead
> 	Till death be uttered,°
> 		Heavily, heavily.

CLAUDIO. Now, unto thy bones good night!
	Yearly will I do this rite.

DON PEDRO. Good morrow, masters. Put your torches out.
	The wolves have prey'd, and look, the gentle day,
	Before the wheels of Phœbus,° round about
	Dapples the drowsy east with spots of grey.
	Thanks to you all, and leave us. Fare you well.

CLAUDIO. Good morrow, masters. Each his several° way.

DON PEDRO. Come, let us hence and put on other weeds,°
	And then to Leonato's we will go.

CLAUDIO. And Hymen° now with luckier issue speed's°
	Than this for whom we render'd up this woe.
							[*Exeunt*]

guerdon reward
goddess . . . night goddess of chastity, the moon goddess Diana
uttered fully lamented
wheels of Phœbus the sun god's chariot
several separate	*weeds* garments
Hymen god of marriage	*speed's* prosper us

SCENE iv
A room in LEONATO'S *house.*

[*Enter* LEONATO, ANTONIO, BENEDICK, BEATRICE, MARGARET, URSULA, FRIAR FRANCIS, *and* HERO.]

FRIAR FRANCIS. Did I not tell you she was innocent?

LEONATO. So are the prince and Claudio, who accus'd her
	Upon the error that you heard debated.
	But Margaret was in some fault for this,
	Although against her will, as it appears
	In the true course of all the question.

ANTONIO. Well, I am glad that all things sort° so well.

BENEDICK. And so am I, being else by faith enforc'd
	To call young Claudio to a reckoning for it.

LEONATO. Well, daughter, and you gentlewomen all,
	Withdraw into a chamber by yourselves,
	And when I send for you, come hither mask'd.
							[*Exeunt* LADIES.]
	The prince and Claudio promis'd by this hour
	To visit me. You know your office, brother.
	You must be father to your brother's daughter
	And give her to young Claudio.

ANTONIO. Which I will do with confirm'd countenance.°

BENEDICK. Friar, I must entreat your pains, I think.

FRIAR FRANCIS. To do what, signior?

BENEDICK. To bind me, or undo me; one of them.
	Signior Leonato, truth it is, good signior,
	Your niece regards me with an eye of favor.

LEONATO. That eye my daughter lent her. 'Tis most true.

BENEDICK. And I do with an eye of love requite her.

LEONATO. The sight whereof I think you had from me,
	From Claudio, and the prince. But what's your will?

BENEDICK. Your answer, sir, is enigmatical.
	But, for my will, my will is, your goodwill
	May stand with ours, this day to be conjoin'd
	In the state of honorable marriage.
	In which, good friar, I shall desire your help.

LEONATO. My heart is with your liking.

FRIAR FRANCIS.						And my help.
	Here comes the prince and Claudio.
		[*Enter* DON PEDRO *and* CLAUDIO, *and two or three others.*]

DON PEDRO. Good morrow to this fair assembly.

sort turn out
confirm'd countenance straight face

LEONATO. Good morrow, prince; good morrow,
35   Claudio.
    We here attend° you. Are you yet° determin'd
    Today to marry with my brother's daughter?
CLAUDIO. I'll hold my mind, were she an Ethiope.
LEONATO. Call her forth, Brother; here's the friar
    ready.   [Exit ANTONIO.]
DON PEDRO. Good morrow, Benedick. Why, what's
40   the matter
    That you have such a February face,
    So full of frost, of storm, and cloudiness?
CLAUDIO. I think he thinks upon the savage bull.
    Tush, fear not, man; we'll tip° thy horns with
      gold,
45 And all Europa° shall rejoice at thee
    As once Europa° did at lusty Jove
    When he would play the noble beast in love.
BENEDICK. Bull Jove, sir, had an amiable low,
    And some such strange bull leap'd your father's
      cow
50 And got a calf in that same noble feat
    Much like to you, for you have just his bleat.
CLAUDIO. For this I owe you. Here comes other
      reck'nings.°
    [Re-enter ANTONIO, with the LADIES masked.]
    Which is the lady I must seize upon?
ANTONIO. This same is she, and I do give you her.
CLAUDIO. Why, then she's mine. Sweet, let me see
55   your face.
LEONATO. No, that you shall not till you take her
      hand
    Before this friar and swear to marry her.
CLAUDIO. Give me your hand. Before this holy
      friar,
    I am your husband, if you like of me.
60 HERO. And when I liv'd, I was your other wife;
                                    [Unmasking.]
    And when you lov'd, you were my other hus-
      band.
CLAUDIO. Another Hero!
HERO.   Nothing certainer.
    One Hero died defil'd; but I do live,
    And surely as I live, I am a maid.
65 DON PEDRO. The former Hero! Hero that is dead!
LEONATO. She died, my lord, but whiles her
      slander liv'd.
FRIAR FRANCIS. All this amazement can I qualify°
    When after that the holy rites are ended

attend await
yet still   tip . . . gold i.e., gild your cuckold's horns
Europa Europe
Europa maiden wooed and won by Jove in the form of a
    bull
reck'nings accounts to be settled
qualify dissipate

I'll tell you largely° of fair Hero's death.
    Meantime let wonder seem familiar,°   70
    And to the chapel let us presently.
BENEDICK. Soft and fair,° friar. Which is Beatrice?
BEATRICE. [Unmasking] I answer to that name. What
    is your will?
BENEDICK. Do not you love me?
BEATRICE.   Why, no, no more than reason.
BENEDICK. Why, then your uncle, and the prince,
    and Claudio   75
    Have been deceiv'd; they swore you did.
BEATRICE. Do not you love me?
BENEDICK.   Troth, no, no more than reason.
BEATRICE. Why, then my cousin, Margaret, and
    Ursula
    Are much deceiv'd, for they did swear you did.
BENEDICK. They swore that you were almost sick
    for me.   80
BEATRICE. They swore that you were well-nigh
    dead for me.
BENEDICK. 'Tis no such matter. Then you do not
    love me?
BEATRICE. No, truly, but in friendly recompense.
LEONATO. Come, cousin, I am sure you love the
    gentleman.
CLAUDIO. And I'll be sworn upon't that he loves
    her;   85
    For here's a paper, written in his hand,
    A halting° sonnet of his own pure brain,
    Fashion'd to Beatrice.
HERO.   And here's another,
    Writ in my cousin's hand, stolen from her
      pocket,
    Containing her affection unto Benedick.   90
BENEDICK. A miracle! Here's our own hands against
    our hearts. Come, I will have thee; but, by this
    light, I take thee for pity.
BEATRICE. I would not deny you; but, by this good
    day, I yield upon great persuasion, and partly to 95
    save your life, for I was told you were in a
    consumption.
BENEDICK. Peace! I will stop your mouth.
                                    [Kissing her.]
DON PEDRO. How dost thou, Benedick the married
    man?   100
BENEDICK. I'll tell thee what, Prince. A college of
    wit-crackers cannot flout me out of my humor.
    Dost thou think I care for a satire or an epigram?
    No. If a man will be beaten with brains, a' shall
    wear nothing handsome about him.° In brief, 105

largely fully   familiar ordinary
Soft and fair i.e., hold up a minute
halting limping   If . . . him i.e., if a man lets mere
    wit put him down, he deserves nothing fine about him

since I do purpose to marry, I will think nothing
to any purpose that the world can say against it;
and therefore never flout at me for what I have
said against it, for man is a giddy thing, and this
110   is my conclusion. For thy part, Claudio, I did
think to have beaten thee. But in that thou art
like to be my kinsman, live unbruised, and love
my cousin.

CLAUDIO. I had well hoped thou wouldst have
115   denied Beatrice, that I might have cudgeled thee
out of thy single life, to make thee a double-
dealer,° which, out of question, thou wilt be if
my cousin do not look exceeding narrowly to
thee.

120   BENEDICK. Come, come, we are friends. Let's have
a dance ere we are married, that we may lighten
our own hearts and our wives' heels.

LEONATO. We'll have dancing afterward.

BENEDICK. First, of my word; therefore play,
music. Prince, thou art sad. Get thee a wife,   125
get thee a wife. There is no staff more reverend
than one tipped with horn.

              [*Enter a* MESSENGER.]

MESSENGER. My lord, your brother John is ta'en in
flight
And brought with arm'd men back to Messina.

BENEDICK. Think not on him till tomorrow. I'll   130
devise thee brave° punishments for him. Strike
up, pipers.   [*Dance*]
                               [*Exeunt*]

---

double-dealer i.e., as a married man, no longer single—
and no doubt unfaithful to his wife   *brave* fine

AFTERWORD

The critical ranking of *Much Ado About Nothing* among Shakespeare's major romantic comedies remains controversial. For this play, perhaps better than any other, attests to the fact that even Shakespeare—at the top of his form and his powers, midway through his dramatic career, with some of the most masterly romantic comedies and nearly all of the mature histories behind him, and with the period of the greatest tragedies lying immediately ahead—was yet capable of composing a work that exhibits approximately as many faults as perfections, as many weak points as strong ones, as many visible and audible creaks, stresses, and strains in the superstructure as moments of smooth-flowing action and happy conjunctions of language, character, and incident. Much more subtly, it attests to the fact that none of these formal blemishes is to be taken altogether seriously. The very title, *Much Ado About Nothing*, implies an awesome warning to critics, especially pedantic ones. So let us beware.

Scholars of the last half century have tended to find the causes for the more obvious inconsistencies and other seeming defects in the probability that Shakespeare, about 1598, reworked a comedy that he had written, or at least begun, a few years earlier. Only about one fourth of the play as it stands is written in verse, the manner of which more resembles that of *The Two Gentlemen of Verona* (1592–1594) than that of *The Merchant of Venice* (1596–1597) and *Henry IV* (1597–1598). Very likely the early version was written mainly in verse and the added or expanded portions of 1598 written mainly in prose. Probably the expanded or added portions are represented principally by the subplot of Beatrice and Benedick and to a lesser extent by the sayings and doings of Dogberry and his cohorts—though these latter comic personages must already have figured largely in the earlier version that centered on the separation and reunion of Hero and Claudio.

The contrasting poetic–dramatic styles of the earlier and later periods of composition are unlikely to be noticed in the theater, but the close reader of the text is occasionally and, to a degree, disagreeably surprised by them. Mildly disturbing even to the theatrical audience—which, unlike the reader, is given no time to reflect—is the failure of minor details in the opening scenes to mesh exactly with subsequent developments. Thus, to begin with an exceedingly trivial but typical instance, in the seventh speech of the first scene, we hear that Claudio's "uncle here in Messina will be very much glad" of Claudio's good reputation earned in the wars. The conversation runs on for a few more lines, and—if we know the usual pattern of Shakespeare's initial exposition—we expect that this uncle will emerge sooner or later in the developing plot; for it is a fact that elsewhere, when Shakespeare mentions someone in the conspicuous position of the opening lines, that person will shortly come before us with relevant business. But we never again hear of Claudio's uncle.

Similarly trivial, and also similarly curious, are the opening lines of scene ii:

> LEONATO. How now, brother! Where is my cousin, your son? Hath he provided this music?
> ANTONIO. He is very busy about it. But, brother . . .

Once again, one who is identified in the first line of a Shakespearean scene is virtually guaranteed appearance, if not actual prominence thereafter. But if we ever meet this alleged son of Antonio's face to face, or ever again hear of him, it is by some other name.

Somewhat more mystifying, but still rather odd than significant, is the case of Beatrice's parentage. As Hero's cousin, we should involuntarily assume that she is Antonio's daughter. Why should she not be? But indeed she is not, though Antonio is the only brother of

Leonato who ever appears. Is she the daughter of a third brother, absent or dead? Or of a sister, absent or dead? Because Beatrice's role is of enormous importance, and because Antonio plays a conspicuous—though quite unnecessary—role, why should Shakespeare not make her Antonio's daughter? Or, for that matter, if she is not to be Antonio's daughter, why did Shakespeare introduce an Antonio, without whose assistance the plot could have survived quite handily, at all?

Late in the play, when the "substitute-Hero" requires a father to give her away in marriage, Leonato asks Antonio not, indeed, to pose as this imaginary Hero's father, but says, "You must be father to your brother's daughter." Are we then to suppose that this imagined father of an imagined Hero is yet a *fourth* brother? Alas, poor Antonio: he is denied the privilege of being the father of the priceless Beatrice, denied even the right to pose as the imaginary Hero's father, and allowed only to be father to a son who is once mentioned and never seen; perhaps it is no wonder that, in his mask, he is easily recognized by Ursula "by the waggling of your head."

Such odd marks of Shakespeare's apparent carelessness, presumably in the course of an overhasty and fairly drastic reworking of his source materials and his own earlier version, exemplify in miniature the faults that at once lie deeper in the fabric of the play and loom larger on its surface. These have to do with both structure and character, and, consequently, with plausibility. The least of them is the unexplained failure of Margaret to come forward with the truth when Hero's very life is at stake, because as Borachio later assures us, Margaret's own reputation is unstained by her participation in the villain's plot. (The unwary director of the play sometimes lets Margaret be present on the stage during the excruciating scene of the denunciation—as of course we should expect her to be; the advised director is careful to keep her out of sight, thus keeping Shakespeare's obvious fault from appearing as gross as it truly is.)

Perhaps more disconcerting to a student of the text, though hardly noticeable to the audience in the theater, is the fact of the "false start" made by the opening scenes. We are immediately introduced to a situation that looks to ripen into the main argument of the play, but it abruptly dissolves before our eyes. At the end of scene i, Don Pedro offers to woo Hero for Claudio—"Then after to her father will I break,/ And the conclusion is, she shall be thine." But in swift succession Don Pedro's intent is misrepresented to and misunderstood by Leonato, by the bastard brother Don John (and villains in Shakespeare, by and large, are *not* deceived by appearances), and, alas, by Claudio himself, who had initially embraced Don Pedro's offer. The misunderstandings persist into Act II, hard feelings arise, and there is growing indication that the main plot of *Much Ado* will turn upon a familiar Shakespearean theme, division between fast friends. But then, midway in Act II, with a single line, Don Pedro dissipates the storm clouds: "Here, Claudio, I have wooed in thy name, and fair Hero is won." Thus the plot line laid down by the first act and a half comes abruptly to an end, and Shakespeare begins, in Act II, scene ii, to lay the groundwork for what will become the central plot, Don John's defamation of Hero and Claudio's rejection of the heroine at the altar. Nowhere else in Shakespeare is there a parallel to what seems truly a false start in *Much Ado*, for very early in his career the dramatist became a master economist in the art of providing initial exposition, identifying not merely in the first act, but in the first scene, and sometimes in the opening lines of this scene, the gist of what subsequent acts would develop. It is therefore the more curious that the first one and a half acts of *Much Ado* point in a direction that is not taken.

At least one critic has argued vigorously that the opening scenes of the play are meant to illustrate "the way of the world of Much Ado"—showing by means of the early, groundless errors in connection with Don Pedro's wooing that the Messinians, residents and visitors alike, have a remarkable susceptibility to deception, and thus preparing the way for the grand deception and error by which Hero is nearly destroyed. And indeed Shakespeare's purpose may have been just that: to establish a climate for Messina which would make the main error more plausible. (To this end also, of course, the ease with which Beatrice and Benedick are individually and thoroughly deceived into thinking that each is loved by the other contributes; for if such bright ones succumb so readily to error, who can doubt the susceptibility of a Claudio?) On the other hand, we cannot be certain of the facts; Shakespeare may actually have begun to write one play, changed his mind, made some insufficient patches, and gone ahead with another.

More perplexing (if not acutely distressing) to most critics, and to audiences in the theater as well, are the personalities of the two principal characters of the primary plot, Hero and Claudio.

Elsewhere among the romantic comedies we find heroines who are in one or many ways extraordinary: the resourceful and persistent Julia of *The Two Gentlemen of Verona*; the robust, witty, and capable Rosalind of *As You Like It*; the ultrafeminine (but indomitable and victorious) Viola of *Twelfth Night*; the supremely self-possessed Portia of *The Merchant of Venice*. But in *Much Ado* we find only Hero—colorless, self-effacing, all but speechless—whose attractions for such a gallant as Claudio is reputed to be are unrevealed and not readily imaginable. Incredibly, Hero does not speak a single line between Claudio's first entrance upon the stage and his confession to Benedick that he has fallen in love. True, Claudio speaks of her as "a modest young lady," and with that assessment there can certainly be no quarrel. But it has often been said that poor Hero is the victim of the peculiar plot requirements of *Much Ado*: she must be as she is, or the main incident will not work. This is an unfortunate thing to have to say about a heroine or a plot, and one that need not be said about any of the other romantic comedies.

But even the silent and ironically named heroine Hero is not the play's greatest problem; that problem is the hero Claudio. Of him not the most tempting but the most charitable thing that may be said is that he, too, is a victim of plot requirements.

It is a fact (and, on the whole, a delightful one) that the heroes of the romantic comedies are rarely great prizes, except to the heroines who mysteriously aspire to catch them: Proteus of *The Two Gentlemen of Verona*, a changeable double-dealer, betrayer of his best (perhaps only) friend, deserter of his beloved, and would-be rapist of his new love; Bassanio of *The Merchant of Venice*, charming, but a wastrel, a fortune hunter, a gambler with his best friend's life (not his own), pursuer of Portia of the golden hair (and all that gold); Orsino, dilettantish duke of Illyria in *Twelfth Night*, who languishes luxuriously in lovesickness, feeding his condition with sweet music until he surfeits; and Orlando of *As You Like It*, easily the pick of the lot, the hero "as you like him" (with Shakespeare's tongue in cheek), muscular enough to break a professional wrestler's bones, loyal, noble, unspeakably heroic—and, beside the brilliant heroine, thoroughly "dumb," a Renaissance L'il Abner beyond price, at least for Rosalind. But certainly we are unlikely to wish any of these heroes changed by so much as a hair.

Claudio, however, is something else: callow at the outset and caddish as he continues, quick to believe that Don Pedro "woos for himself," quick to believe that his beloved is false (Hero, one of the least likely of all Shakespeare's heroines to be so), too quick and too eager in his decision to shame her at the altar, appallingly gross and abusive in carrying out the decision, insensitive and ugly in his jesting after the denunciation, instantly self-justifying on learning of Hero's "death" and innocence ("Yet err'd I not but in mistaking"), and, finally, unspeakably mercenary and shallow in his quick assent to marry "another Hero" —likewise an heiress—even "were she an Ethiope." Despite the valiant efforts of actors to make him palatable, modern audiences have been known to hiss Claudio at some of his less attractive moments, which occur each time he appears.

Some critics have sought to defend Claudio on the grounds of his immaturity and inexperience, others on the grounds that Elizabethan audiences saw with different eyes from ours and would have found nothing unduly reprehensible in anything that he says or does. But elsewhere we rarely need to justify Shakespeare's values and attitudes on such grounds; most often, his values seem contemporaneous with our own best ones. It is much more agreeable, in any event, to suppose that Shakespeare never liked Claudio any more than we do and that Benedick, without tongue in cheek, speaks for the author when at last he succinctly sums Claudio's personality:

> Bull Jove, sir, had an amiable low,
> And some such strange bull leap'd your father's cow
> And got a calf in that same noble feat
> Much like to you, for you have just his bleat.

It is pleasant also to imagine that Shakespeare would approve when modern audiences spontaneously applaud, as they often do, at the instant that Beatrice, in the midst of lovemaking with Benedick, screams "Kill Claudio!"

The final problem, which Shakespeare created also, presumably, in revising an earlier version of the play, concerns the Beatrice–Benedick combination, whose plot, in terms of the whole play, is unmistakably subordinate to the central plot of Hero–Claudio yet whose personalities and actions dim the central luminaries (to borrow a conceit from *Romeo and Juliet*) "as daylight doth the lamp." Perhaps it is not too far-fetched to conjecture that Shakespeare reworked his original plot and invented the bright new couple because he himself could not bear Hero and Claudio; but their magnitude does create an awkward dramatic situation, doing violence to strict dramatic protocol. For it is of course the famed "B and B" and not Hero and Claudio that modern audiences go to see, even as they went to see them three centuries and more ago. Wrote one Leonard Digges in 1640:

> . . . let but Beatrice
> And Benedicke be seene, loe in a trice
> The cockpit, Galleries, Boxes, all are full.

They are still full for these two, among the brightest lights in the Shakespearean galaxy. Theirs are the parts that the star actors have always chosen. Upon this pair of reluctant lovers the dramatist conferred such an abundance of wit that the performers must speak with machine-gun rapidity to get it all said, while the audience sits bolt upright on the edge of the chair, like tennis spectators, to catch sight of what passes between them. "Out o' question," hazards Don Pedro to Beatrice, "You were born in a merry hour." "No, sure, my lord," she replies,

> . . . my mother cried. But then there was a star danced,
> and under that star was I born.

Such is the spirit of both, and of the portions of the play that their presence dominates. Except for George Bernard Shaw—who denied that either has any true wit ("they contain at best nothing out of the common in thought or wit, and at worst a good deal of vulgar naughtiness")—and asserted that they are popular with audiences only because their platitudes are transformed by "the magic . . . of the Shakespearean music"—there have been no critical dissenters to the charms of this bright couple.

Perhaps, therefore, it is only the critic overly conscious of formal dramatic propriety who carps that they do, nevertheless, by their too potent magnetism, wrench the drama off its proper center, leaving audiences at the last to suppose that the play is essentially about them rather than about Hero and Claudio. Possibly in redrafting his early version Shakespeare did err in allowing "B and B"—creatures of his own imagination and not, like Claudio and Hero, inherited from earlier versions of the Italian tale—to usurp the center. But it would be a perverse theatergoer who would wish this pair dimmed in order to allow Claudio and Hero to appear to better advantage. For it is Beatrice and Benedick, after all, who, along with Dogberry (also Shakespeare's own addition to the story), not only save the play from its sundry formal faults but preserve it as a perennial joy on the stage.

For Dogberry, also Shakespeare's best specialist in the misuse of words, not even Shaw has an unkind word; on the contrary, Shaw calls him "a capital study of parochial character," and deplores performances in which the part is reduced. Dogberry's sublime unconsciousness of himself, and his administrative incompetence, contribute much to the play—not only in hilarity, but in exasperation and suspense, when he holds in his inept fingers the key to poor Hero's exoneration, and holds it an intolerably long while, so that we are obliged to hate and love him simultaneously. Perhaps it is not altogether sacrilegious to suggest also that his brand of unknowing humor provides an audience with much-needed respite from the prolonged wit duels with which Beatrice and Benedick titillate the intellect to the point of exhaustion.

With a pun in its very title ("nothing"–"noting"), *Much Ado About Nothing* transcends its near-brush with tragedy at the center and its host of technical flaws to emerge a happy comedy that affirms what *Twelfth Night* (whose subtitle, appropriately, is *What You Will*) would shortly reaffirm, that life is good and lighthearted life is best, that no one should take things too much to heart, least of all the incidents that comprise a comic play—or even the minor oversights of the playwright who has provided the entertainment.

A NOTE ON THE COMPOSITION OF THE PLAY

Much Ado About Nothing, in its present form, was written about 1598, "Sundrie times publikely acted" before 1600, and first published in the Quarto of 1600. Elements of the main plot appear in numerous early versions, but Shakespeare is believed to have drawn chiefly on Matteo Bandello's novella of "Timbreo and Fenecia" (1554). Dogberry, Verges, and the Benedick–Beatrice plot are Shakespeare's own inventions.

Twelfth Night

DRAMATIS PERSONÆ

ORSINO *Duke of Illyria*
SEBASTIAN *brother to Viola*
ANTONIO *a sea captain, friend to Sebastian*
A SEA CAPTAIN *friend to Viola*
VALENTINE ⎫
CURIO ⎭ *gentlemen attending on the Duke*
SIR TOBY BELCH *uncle to Olivia*
SIR ANDREW AGUECHEEK
MALVOLIO *steward to Olivia*

FABIAN ⎫
FESTE *a clown* ⎭ *servants to Olivia*
OLIVIA
VIOLA
MARIA *Olivia's woman*
LORDS, PRIESTS, SAILORS, OFFICERS, MUSICIANS, *and
other* ATTENDANTS

SCENE *A city in Illyria, and the seacoast near it.*

ACT I

SCENE i
An apartment in the DUKE'*s palace.*

[*Enter* DUKE, CURIO, *and other* LORDS; MUSICIANS
attending.]
DUKE. If music be the food of love, play on.
  Give me excess of it, that, surfeiting,
  The appetite may sicken, and so die.
  That strain again! It had a dying fall.
5 O, it came o'er my ear like the sweet sound
  That breathes upon a bank of violets,
  Stealing and giving odor! Enough, no more.
  'Tis not so sweet now as it was before.
  O spirit of love, how quick° and fresh art thou!
10 That,° notwithstanding° thy capacity
  Receiveth as the sea, naught enters there
  Of what validity° and pitch° soe'er
  But falls into abatement° and low price
  Even in a minute! So full of shapes° is fancy°
15 That it alone is high fantastical.°

quick lively   *That* so that
notwithstanding although   *validity* value
pitch height   *abatement* devaluation
shapes imaginings   *fancy* love
high fantastical purely imaginative

CURIO. Will you go hunt, my lord?
DUKE.   What, Curio?
CURIO. The hart.
DUKE. Why, so I do, the noblest that I have.
  O, when mine eyes did see Olivia first,
  Methought she purg'd the air of pestilence!   20
  That instant was I turn'd into a hart,
  And my desires, like fell° and cruel hounds,
  E'er since pursue me.°
        [*Enter* VALENTINE.]
                          How now! What news
    from her?
VALENTINE. So please my lord, I might not be
    admitted,
  But from her handmaid do return this answer: 25
  The element° itself, till seven years' heat,
  Shall not behold her face at ample view;
  But, like a cloistress, she will veiled walk
  And water once a day her chamber round

fell fierce
hart . . . me Actaeon, in Greek mythology, saw Diana
  bathing, was turned into a hart, and was pursued and
  killed by his own hounds (with obvious pun on
  hart–heart)
element sky

287

30 With eye-offending brine. All this to season°
A brother's dead love, which she would keep
    fresh
And lasting in her sad remembrance.
DUKE. O, she that hath a heart of that fine frame
To pay this debt of love but to a brother,
35 How will she love when the rich golden shaft°
Hath kill'd the flock of all affections else
That live in her—when liver, brain, and heart,
These sovereign thrones, are all supplied, and
    fill'd
Her sweet perfections with one self king!°
40 Away before me to sweet beds of flowers.
Love thoughts lie rich when canopied with
    bowers.   [Exeunt]

SCENE ii
The seacoast.

[Enter VIOLA, a CAPTAIN, and SAILORS.]
VIOLA. What country, friends, is this?
CAPTAIN. This is Illyria, lady.
VIOLA. And what should I do in Illyria?
My brother he is in Elysium.°
Perchance he is not drown'd. What think you,
5   sailors?
CAPTAIN. It is perchance that you yourself were
    sav'd.
VIOLA. O my poor brother! And so perchance may
he be.
CAPTAIN. True, madam, and, to comfort you with
    chance,
Assure yourself, after our ship did split,
When you and those poor number sav'd with
10   you
Hung on our driving boat, I saw your brother,
Most provident in peril, bind himself,
Courage and hopes both teaching him the
    practice,
To a strong mast that liv'd upon the sea,
15 Where, like Arion° on the dolphin's back,
I saw him hold acquaintance with the waves
So long as I could see.
VIOLA. For saying so, there's gold.
Mine own escape unfoldeth to my hope,
20 Whereto thy speech serves for authority,

The like of him.° Know'st thou this country?
CAPTAIN. Aye, madam, well, for I was bred and
    born
Not three hours' travel from this very place.
VIOLA. Who governs here?
CAPTAIN. A noble Duke, in nature as in name.   25
VIOLA. What is his name?
CAPTAIN. Orsino.
VIOLA. Orsino! I have heard my father name him.
He was a bachelor then.
CAPTAIN. And so is now, or was so very late,   30
For but a month ago I went from hence,
And then 'twas fresh in murmur—as, you know,
What great ones do the less will prattle of—
That he did seek the love of fair Olivia.
VIOLA. What's she?   35
CAPTAIN. A virtuous maid, the daughter of a
    count
That died some twelvemonth since, then leaving
    her
In the protection of his son, her brother,
Who shortly also died; for whose dear love,
They say, she hath abjur'd the company   40
And sight of men.
VIOLA.   O that I serv'd that lady
And might not be deliver'd° to the world
Till I had made mine own occasion mellow°
What my estate is!°
CAPTAIN.   That were hard to compass,
Because she will admit no kind of suit—   45
No, not the Duke's.
VIOLA. There is a fair behavior in thee, captain,
And though that nature with a beauteous wall
Doth oft close in pollution, yet of thee
I will believe thou hast a mind that suits   50
With this thy fair and outward character.
I prithee, and I'll pay thee bounteously,
Conceal me what I am and be my aid
For such disguise as haply° shall become
The form of my intent. I'll serve this Duke.   55
Thou shalt present me as an eunuch° to him.
It may be worth thy pains, for I can sing
And speak to him in many sorts of music
That will allow me very worth his service.
What else may hap, to time I will commit;   60
Only shape thou thy silence to my wit.
CAPTAIN. Be you his eunuch, and your mute I'll be.
When my tongue blabs, then let mine eyes not
    see.
VIOLA. I thank thee. Lead me on.   [Exeunt]

---

season preserve   *shaft* i.e., Cupid's arrow
when . . . king when the sovereign thrones of love,
intellect, and emotion are all occupied by one sole
king (her husband)
Elysium Paradise
Arion Greek singer who, about to be killed by pirates,
leaped overboard and was carried ashore by a dolphin
charmed by his song

The . . . him i.e., that he also escaped drowning
deliver'd made known
Till . . . mellow till the time was ripe
What . . . is i.e., that I am a gentlewoman
haply perhaps   *eunuch* boy singer

SCENE iii
OLIVIA's *house.*

[*Enter* SIR TOBY BELCH *and* MARIA.]

SIR TOBY. What a plague means my niece, to take the death of her brother thus? I am sure care's an enemy to life.

5 MARIA. By my troth,° Sir Toby, you must come in earlier o' nights. Your cousin,° my lady, takes great exceptions to your ill hours.

SIR TOBY. Why, let her except, before excepted.°

MARIA. Aye, but you must confine yourself within the modest limits of order.

10 SIR TOBY. Confine! I'll confine myself no finer than I am. These clothes are good enough to drink in, and so be these boots too. An° they be not, let them hang themselves in their own straps.

MARIA. That quaffing and drinking will undo you.
15 I heard my lady talk of it yesterday, and of a foolish knight that you brought in one night here to be her wooer.

SIR TOBY. Who, Sir Andrew Aguecheek?

MARIA. Aye, he.

20 SIR TOBY. He's as tall° a man as any's in Illyria.

MARIA. What's that to the purpose?

SIR TOBY. Why, he has three thousand ducats a year.

MARIA. Aye, but he'll have but a year in all these
25 ducats. He's a very fool and a prodigal.

SIR TOBY. Fie, that you'll say so! He plays o' the *viol-de-gamboys,*° and speaks three or four languages word for word without book,° and hath all the good gifts of nature.

30 MARIA. He hath indeed, almost natural;° for besides that he's a fool, he's a great quarreler, and but that he hath the gift of a coward to allay the gust° he hath in quarreling, 'tis thought among the prudent he would quickly have the
35 gift of a grave.

SIR TOBY. By this hand, they are scoundrels and substractors° that say so of him. Who are they?

MARIA. They that add, moreover, he's drunk nightly in your company.

SIR TOBY. With drinking healths to my niece. I'll 40 drink to her as long as there is a passage in my throat and drink in Illyria. He's a coward and a coystrill° that will not drink to my niece till his brains turn o' the toe like a parish top.° What, wench! Castiliano vulgo;° for here comes Sir 45 Andrew Agueface.

[*Enter* SIR ANDREW AGUECHEEK.]

SIR ANDREW. Sir Toby Belch! How now, Sir Toby Belch!

SIR TOBY. Sweet Sir Andrew!

SIR ANDREW. Bless you, fair shrew. 50

MARIA. And you too, sir.

SIR TOBY. Accost,° Sir Andrew, accost.

SIR ANDREW. What's that?

SIR TOBY. My niece's chambermaid.

SIR ANDREW. Good Mistress Accost, I desire better 55 acquaintance.

MARIA. My name is Mary, sir.

SIR ANDREW. Good Mistress Mary Accost—

SIR TOBY. You mistake, knight. "Accost" is front her, board her, woo her, assail her. 60

SIR ANDREW. By my troth, I would not undertake her in this company. Is that the meaning of "accost"?

MARIA. Fare you well, gentlemen.

SIR TOBY. An thou let part so, Sir Andrew, would 65 thou mightst never draw sword again.

SIR ANDREW. An you part so, mistress, I would I might never draw sword again. Fair lady, do you think you have fools in hand?

MARIA. Sir, I have not you by the hand. 70

SIR ANDREW. Marry,° but you shall have, and here's my hand.

MARIA. Now, sir, "thought is free."° I pray you, bring your hand to the buttery bar° and let it drink. 75

SIR ANDREW. Wherefore, sweetheart? What's your metaphor?

MARIA. It's dry,° sir.

SIR ANDREW. Why, I think so. I am not such an ass but I can keep my hand dry.° But what's your 80 jest?

MARIA. A dry jest, sir.

By my troth truly
cousin general term of kinship; here, niece
except . . . excepted play on the legal term *exceptis excipiendis,* "with the exception before named"; hence, let her except me before she takes exception
An if
tall brave
viol-de-gamboys Italian *viola da gamba,* the "leg-cello"
without book from memory
natural with pun on *fool*   *gust* taste
substractors detractors

coystrill knave
parish top large public top used by the whole parish
Castiliano vulgo i.e., "keep a straight face" (Castilians being notably sober)
Accost i.e., greet her
Marry by the Virgin Mary (a familiar mild oath)
"thought is free" i.e., I shall think what I will
buttery bar storeroom for liquor (but Maria intends an invitation to flirt)
It's dry a moist palm signifies a lustful nature
keep . . . dry an innocently gross remark bordering on scatology

SIR ANDREW. Are you full of them?

MARIA. Aye, sir, I have them at my fingers' ends.
85   Marry, now I let go your hand, I am barren.°

[*Exit*]

SIR TOBY. O knight, thou lackest a cup of canary.°
When did I see thee so put down?

SIR ANDREW. Never in your life, I think, unless you
see canary put me down. Methinks sometimes
90   I have no more wit than a Christian or an
ordinary man has. But I am a great eater of beef,
and I believe that does harm to my wit.

SIR TOBY. No question.

SIR ANDREW. An I thought that, I'd forswear it. I'll
95   ride home tomorrow, Sir Toby.

SIR TOBY. *Pourquoi*, my dear knight?

SIR ANDREW. What is "pourquoi"?° Do or not do?
I would I had bestowed that time in the tongues°
that I have in fencing, dancing, and bear-baiting.
100 O, had I but followed the arts!

SIR TOBY. Then hadst thou had an excellent head
of hair.

SIR ANDREW. Why, would that have mended my
hair?

105 SIR TOBY. Past question, for thou seest it will not
curl by nature.

SIR ANDREW. But it becomes me well enough, does
't not?

SIR TOBY. Excellent. It hangs like flax on a distaff,°
110 and I hope to see a housewife take thee between
her legs and spin it off.

SIR ANDREW. Faith, I'll home tomorrow, Sir Toby.
Your niece will not be seen, or if she be, it's four
to one she'll none of me. The count himself here
115 hard by woos her.

SIR TOBY. She'll none o' the count. She'll not
match above her degree, neither in estate, years,
nor wit; I have heard her swear 't. Tut, there's
life in 't,° man.

120 SIR ANDREW. I'll stay a month longer. I am a fellow
o' the strangest mind i' the world; I delight in
masques and revels sometimes altogether.

SIR TOBY. Art thou good at these kickshawses,°
knight?

125 SIR ANDREW. As any man in Illyria, whatsoever he
be, under the degree of my betters; and yet I
will not compare with an old man.°

SIR TOBY. What is thy excellence in a galliard,°
knight?

SIR ANDREW. Faith, I can cut a caper.   130

SIR TOBY. And I can cut the mutton° to 't.

SIR ANDREW. And I think I have the back-trick°
simply as strong as any man in Illyria.

SIR TOBY. Wherefore are these things hid? Wherefore have these gifts a curtain before 'em? Are   135
they like to take dust, like Mistress Mall's°
picture? Why dost thou not go to church in a
galliard and come home in a coranto?° My very
walk should be a jig; I would not so much as
make water but in a sink-a-pace.° What dost   140
thou mean? Is it a world to hide virtues in? I did
think, by the excellent constitution of thy leg, it
was formed under the star of a galliard.

SIR ANDREW. Aye, 'tis strong, and it does in-
different° well in a flame-colored stock.° Shall   145
we set about some revels?

SIR TOBY. What shall we do else? Were we not born
under Taurus?°

SIR ANDREW. Taurus! That's sides and heart.

SIR TOBY. No, sir; it is legs and thighs. Let me see 150
thee caper. Ha! Higher! Ha, ha! Excellent!

[*Exeunt*]

SCENE iv
The DUKE's *palace*.

[*Enter* VALENTINE, *and* VIOLA *in man's attire*.]

VALENTINE. If the Duke continue these favors
towards you, Cesario, you are like to be much
advanced. He hath known you but three days,
and already you are no stranger.

VIOLA. You either fear his humor or my negli-   5
gence,° that you call in question the continuance
of his love. Is he inconstant, sir, in his favors?

VALENTINE. No, believe me.

VIOLA. I thank you. Here comes the count.

[*Enter* DUKE, CURIO, *and* ATTENDANTS.]

DUKE. Who saw Cesario, ho?   10

VIOLA. On your attendance, my lord. Here.

---

barren i.e., of dry jokes
thou . . canary you need a drink of wine
Pourquoi why (French)
tongues languages (but immediately subject to Sir
Toby's pun on *tongs* for curling hair)
like . . . distaff straight strings of flax on a stick held
between the knees in spinning
life in 't still hope
kickshawes *quelque chose* (French), trifles
old man i.e., expert

galliard fast dance
caper . . . mutton (Sir Toby puns on *caper* as signifying
caper sauce, used with mutton)
back-trick backstep
Mistress Mall (topical allusion of unidentified meaning,
but *Mall* suggests *moll*)
coranto another fast dance
sink-a-pace cinque pace (French), a five-step dance
indifferent moderately   *stock* stocking
Taurus the zodiacal Bull, governing man's neck and
throat; hence both knights are mistaken
his . . . negligence his changeable disposition or my
neglect of duty

DUKE. Stand you awhile aloof. Cesario,
  Thou know'st no less but all; I have unclasp'd
  To thee the book even of my secret soul.
15 Therefore, good youth, address thy gait unto her.
  Be not denied access; stand at her doors,
  And tell them, there thy fixed foot shall grow
  Till thou have audience.
VIOLA.   Sure, my noble lord,
  If she be so abandon'd to her sorrow
20 As it is spoke, she never will admit me.
DUKE. Be clamorous and leap all civil bounds°
  Rather than make unprofited return.
VIOLA. Say I do speak with her, my lord, what
  then?
DUKE. O, then unfold the passion of my love,
25 Surprise her with discourse of my dear faith.
  It shall become thee well to act my woes;
  She will attend it better in thy youth
  Than in a nuncio's° of more grave aspect.
VIOLA. I think not so, my lord.
  DUKE.   Dear lad, believe it.
30 For they shall yet belie thy happy years
  That say thou art a man. Diana's lip
  Is not more smooth and rubious,° thy small
    pipe°
  Is as the maiden's organ, shrill and sound,
  And all is semblative° a woman's part.
35 I know thy constellation is right apt°
  For this affair. Some four or five attend him—
  All, if you will, for I myself am best
  When least in company. Prosper well in this,
  And thou shalt live as freely as thy lord
  To call his fortunes thine.
40 VIOLA.   I'll do my best
  To woo your lady. [Aside] Yet, a barful strife!°
  Whoe'er I woo, myself would be his wife.
                              [Exeunt]

SCENE v
OLIVIA's house.

[Enter MARIA and CLOWN.]
MARIA. Nay, either tell me where thou hast been,
  or I will not open my lips so wide as a bristle may
  enter in way of thy excuse. My lady will hang
  thee for thy absence.
5 CLOWN. Let her hang me. He that is well hanged in
  this world needs to fear no colors.°

MARIA. Make that good.
CLOWN. He shall see none to fear.
MARIA. A good lenten answer.° I can tell thee
  where that saying was born, of "I fear no colors." 10
CLOWN. Where, good Mistress Mary?
MARIA. In the wars; and that may you be bold to
  say in your foolery.
CLOWN. Well, God give them wisdom that have it,
  and those that are fools, let them use their 15
  talents.
MARIA. Yet you will be hanged for being so long
  absent; or, to be turned away, is not that as good
  as a hanging to you?
CLOWN. Many a good hanging prevents a bad 20
  marriage; and, for turning away, let summer
  bear it out.°
MARIA. You are resolute, then?
CLOWN. Not so, neither, but I am resolved on two
  points. 25
MARIA. That if one break, the other will hold;° or,
  if both break, your gaskins° fall.
CLOWN. Apt, in good faith, very apt. Well, go thy
  way. If Sir Toby would leave drinking, thou wert
  as witty a piece of Eve's flesh as any in Illyria. 30
MARIA. Peace, you rogue, no more o' that. Here
  comes my lady. Make your excuse wisely, you
  were best.   [Exit]
CLOWN. Wit, an 't be thy will, put me into good
  fooling! Those wits that think they have thee do 35
  very oft prove fools; and I, that am sure I lack
  thee, may pass for a wise man. For what says
  Quinapalus?° "Better a witty fool than a foolish
  wit."
    [Enter LADY OLIVIA with MALVOLIO.]
  God bless thee, lady!   40
OLIVIA. Take the fool away.
CLOWN. Do you not hear, fellows? Take away the
  lady.
OLIVIA. Go to, you're a dry fool; I'll no more of you.
  Besides, you grow dishonest. 45
CLOWN. Two faults, madonna, that drink and good
  counsel will amend. For give the dry fool drink,
  then is the fool not dry. Bid the dishonest man
  mend himself; if he mend, he is no longer dis-
  honest; if he cannot, let the botcher° mend him. 50
  Anything that's mended is but patched; virtue

---

civil bounds polite limits   nuncio's messenger's
rubious ruby-colored   pipe throat (voice)
is semblative resembles
thy . . . apt your stars are right
barful strife thorny inner conflict
fear no colors i.e., fear nothing

lenten answer lean answer, since Lent is a time of
fasting
let . . . out i.e., summer is as good time as any
if . . . hold pun on points, as referring to suspenders or
laces
gaskins breeches
Quinapalus a made-up authority (the Clown is given to
mock-learning)
botcher inexpert clothes-mender

that transgresses is but patched with sin; and sin that amends is but patched with virtue. If that this simple syllogism will serve, so; if it will not, what remedy? As there is no true cuckold° but calamity, so beauty's a flower. The lady bade take away the fool; therefore, I say again, take her away.

OLIVIA. Sir, I bade them take away you.

CLOWN. Misprision° in the highest degree! Lady, *cucullus non facit monachum;*° that's as much to say as I wear not motley in my brain.° Good madonna, give me leave to prove you a fool.

OLIVIA. Can you do it?

CLOWN. Dexteriously,° good madonna.

OLIVIA. Make your proof.

CLOWN. I must catechize you for it, madonna. Good my mouse of virtue, answer me.

OLIVIA. Well, sir, for want of other idleness, I'll bide your proof.

CLOWN. Good madonna, why mournest thou?

OLIVIA. Good fool, for my brother's death.

CLOWN. I think his soul is in hell, madonna.

OLIVIA. I know his soul is in heaven, fool.

CLOWN. The more fool, madonna, to mourn for your brother's soul being in heaven. Take away the fool, gentlemen.

OLIVIA. What think you of this fool, Malvolio? Doth he not mend?°

MALVOLIO. Yes, and shall do till the pangs of death shake him. Infirmity, that decays the wise, doth ever make the better fool.

CLOWN. God send you, sir, a speedy infirmity, for the better increasing your folly! Sir Toby will be sworn that I am no fox, but he will not pass his word for two pence that you are no fool.

OLIVIA. How say you to that, Malvolio?

MALVOLIO. I marvel your ladyship takes delight in such a barren rascal. I saw him put down the other day with an ordinary fool that has no more brain than a stone. Look you now, he's out of his guard° already. Unless you laugh and minister occasion° to him, he is gagged. I protest, I take these wise men that crow so at these set kind of fools no better than the fools' zanies.°

OLIVIA. O, you are sick of self-love, Malvolio, and taste with a distempered appetite. To be generous, guiltless, and of free disposition is to take those things for bird bolts that you deem cannon bullets.° There is no slander in an allowed° fool, though he do nothing but rail; nor no railing in a known discreet man, though he do nothing but reprove.

CLOWN. Now Mercury endue thee with leasing,° for thou speakest well of fools!

[*Re-enter* MARIA.]

MARIA. Madam, there is at the gate a young gentleman much desires to speak with you.

OLIVIA. From the Count Orsino, is it?

MARIA. I know not, madam. 'Tis a fair young man, and well attended.

OLIVIA. Who of my people hold him in delay?

MARIA. Sir Toby, madam, your kinsman.

OLIVIA. Fetch him off, I pray you; he speaks nothing but madman.° Fie on him! [*Exit* MARIA] Go you, Malvolio. If it be a suit from the count, I am sick, or not at home—what you will, to dismiss it. [*Exit* MALVOLIO] Now you see, sir, how your fooling grows old, and people dislike it.

CLOWN. Thou hast spoke for us, madonna, as if thy eldest son should be a fool—whose skull Jove cram with brains! For—here he comes— one of thy kin has a most weak *pia mater.*°

[*Enter* SIR TOBY.]

OLIVIA. By mine honor, half drunk. What is he at the gate, cousin?

SIR TOBY. A gentleman.

OLIVIA. A gentleman! What gentleman?

SIR TOBY. 'Tis a gentleman here—a plague o' these pickle-herring! How now, sot!

CLOWN. Good Sir Toby!

OLIVIA. Cousin, cousin, how have you come so early by this lethargy?°

SIR TOBY. Lechery! I defy lechery. There's one at the gate.

OLIVIA. Aye, marry, what is he?

SIR TOBY. Let him be the devil, an he will, I care not. Give me faith, say I. Well, it's all one.

[*Exit*]

OLIVIA. What's a drunken man like, fool?

CLOWN. Like a drowned man, a fool, and a mad man. One draught above heat makes him a fool, the second mads him, and a third drowns him.

OLIVIA. Go thou and seek the crowner° and let him sit o' my coz, for he's in the third degree of drink—he's drowned. Go look after him.

---

cuckold deceived husband   *Misprision* error
cucullus . . . monachum the cowl does not make the monk
motley . . . brain i.e., I am no fool even though I wear a fool's costume (motley)
Dexteriously dexterously   *mend* improve
out . . . guard lacks a witty reply
minister occasion feed him opportunity to show his wit
zanies assistants, stooges

take . . . bullets recognize as trivialities the things you regard as important
allowed licensed, privileged
Mercury . . . leasing may the god of thieves endow you with lying
madman lunacy   *pia mater* brain
lethargy drunken state   *crowner* coroner

CLOWN. He is but mad yet, madonna, and the fool
145   shall look to the madman.   [Exit]
                    [Re-enter MALVOLIO.]
MALVOLIO. Madam, yond young fellow swears he
       will speak with you. I told him you were sick; he
       takes on him to understand so much, and there-
       fore comes to speak with you. I told him you
150   were asleep; he seems to have a foreknowledge
       of that too, and therefore comes to speak with
       you. What is to be said to him, lady? He's
       fortified against any denial.
OLIVIA. Tell him he shall not speak with me.
155   MALVOLIO. Has been told so, and he says he'll
       stand at your door like a sheriff's post and be the
       supporter to a bench, but he'll speak with you.
OLIVIA. What kind o' man is he?
MALVOLIO. Why, of mankind.
160   OLIVIA. What manner of man?
MALVOLIO. Of very ill manner; he'll speak with
       you, will you or no.
OLIVIA. Of what personage and years is he?
MALVOLIO. Not yet old enough for a man nor
165   young enough for a boy, as a squash is before 'tis
       a peascod° or a codling when 'tis almost an
       apple: 'tis with him in standing water, between
       boy and man. He is very well-favored° and he
       speaks very shrewishly.° One would think his
170   mother's milk were scarce out of him.
OLIVIA. Let him approach. Call in my gentle-
       woman.
MALVOLIO. Gentlewoman, my lady calls.   [Exit]
                    [Re-enter MARIA.]
OLIVIA. Give me my veil. Come, throw it o'er my
175   face. We'll once more hear Orsino's embassy.
                [Enter VIOLA, and ATTENDANTS.]
VIOLA. The honorable lady of the house, which is
       she?
OLIVIA. Speak to me; I shall answer for her. Your
       will?
180   VIOLA. Most radiant, exquisite, and unmatchable
       beauty—I pray you, tell me if this be the lady of
       the house, for I never saw her. I would be loath
       to cast away my speech, for besides that it is
       excellently well penned, I have taken great
185   pains to con it. Good beauties, let me sustain no
       scorn; I am very comptible,° even to the least
       sinister usage.
OLIVIA. Whence come you, sir?
VIOLA. I can say little more than I have studied, and
190   that question's out of my part. Good gentle one,
       give me modest assurance if you be the lady of
       the house, that I may proceed in my speech.

OLIVIA. Are you a comedian?°
VIOLA. No, my profound heart; and yet, by the
       very fangs of malice, I swear I am not that I play.   195
       Are you the lady of the house?
OLIVIA. If I do not usurp myself, I am.
VIOLA. Most certain, if you are she, you do usurp
       yourself, for what is yours to bestow is not yours
       to reserve. But this is from° my commission. I   200
       will on with my speech in your praise and then
       show you the heart of my message.
OLIVIA. Come to what is important in 't. I forgive
       you the praise.
VIOLA. Alas, I took great pains to study it, and 'tis   205
       poetical.
OLIVIA. It is the more like to be feigned. I pray you,
       keep it in. I heard you were saucy at my gates,
       and allowed your approach rather to wonder at
       you than to hear you. If you be not mad, be gone;   210
       if you have reason, be brief. 'Tis not that time of
       moon with me to make one in so skipping a
       dialogue.°
MARIA. Will you hoist sail, sir? Here lies your way.
VIOLA. No, good swabber; I am to hull here a little   215
       longer. Some mollification for your giant, sweet
       lady. Tell me your mind, I am a messenger.
OLIVIA. Sure, you have some hideous matter to
       deliver, when the courtesy of it is so fearful.
       Speak your office.   220
VIOLA. It alone concerns your ear. I bring no over-
       ture of war, no taxation° of homage. I hold the
       olive in my hand; my words are as full of peace
       as matter.
OLIVIA. Yet you began rudely. What are you. What   225
       would you?
VIOLA. The rudeness that hath appeared in me
       have I learned from my entertainment.° What I
       am and what I would are as secret as maiden-
       head; to your ears, divinity, to any other's,   230
       profanation.
OLIVIA. Give us the place alone. We will hear this
       divinity. [Exeunt MARIA and ATTENDANTS] Now,
       sir, what is your text?
VIOLA. Most sweet lady—   235
OLIVIA. A comfortable doctrine, and much may be
       said of it. Where lies your text?
VIOLA. In Orsino's bosom.
OLIVIA. In his bosom! In what chapter of his
       bosom?   240
VIOLA. To answer by the method, in the first of his
       heart.
OLIVIA. O, I have read it; it is heresy. Have you no
       more to say?

peascod ripe peapod   well-favored handsome
shrewishly sharply   comptible sensitive

comedian actor   from aside from
make . . . dialogue take part in frivolous talk
taxation demand   entertainment i.e., at the door

293

245 VIOLA. Good madam, let me see your face.

OLIVIA. Have you any commission from your lord
to negotiate with my face? You are now out of
your text. But we will draw the curtain and show
you the picture. Look you, sir, such a one I was
250 this present. Is't not well done?   [*Unveiling.*]

VIOLA. Excellently done, if God did all.

OLIVIA. 'Tis in grain,° sir; 'twill endure wind and
weather.

VIOLA. 'Tis beauty truly blent, whose red and
255 white
Nature's own sweet and cunning hand laid on.
Lady, you are the cruel'st she alive
If you will lead these graces to the grave
And leave the world no copy.°

260 OLIVIA. O, sir, I will not be so hardhearted; I will
give out divers schedules° of my beauty. It shall
be inventoried, and every particle and utensil
labeled° to my will: as, item, two lips, indifferent
red; item, two gray eyes, with lids to them;
265 item, one neck, one chin, and so forth. Were you
sent hither to praise me?

VIOLA. I see what you are, you are too proud;
But, if you were the devil, you are fair.
My lord and master loves you. O, such love
Could be but recompens'd° though you were
270 crown'd
The nonpareil° of beauty!

OLIVIA.   How does he love me?

VIOLA. With adorations, fertile° tears,
With groans that thunder love, with sighs of fire.

OLIVIA. Your lord does know my mind; I cannot
love him.
275 Yet I suppose him virtuous, know him noble,
Of great estate, of fresh and stainless youth,
In voices well divulg'd,° free,° learn'd, and
valiant;
And in dimension and the shape of nature°
A gracious person. But yet I cannot love him;
280 He might have took his answer long ago.

VIOLA. If I did love you in my master's flame,
With such a suff'ring, such a deadly life,
In your denial I would find no sense.
I would not understand it.

OLIVIA.   Why, what would you?

285 VIOLA. Make me a willow° cabin at your gate
And call upon my soul within the house;

Write loyal cantons° of contemned° love
And sing them loud even in the dead of night;
Halloo your name to the reverberate hills
And make the babbling gossip° of the air   290
Cry out "Olivia!" O, you should not rest
Between the elements of air and earth,
But you should pity me!

OLIVIA.   You might do much.
What is your parentage?

VIOLA. Above my fortunes, yet my state is well.   295
I am a gentleman.

OLIVIA.   Get you to your lord.
I cannot love him. Let him send no more—
Unless, perchance, you come to me again,
To tell me how he takes it. Fare you well.
I thank you for your pains; spend this for me.   300

VIOLA. I am no fee'd post,° lady; keep your purse.
My master, not myself, lacks recompense.
Love make his heart of flint that you shall love,
And let your fervor, like my master's, be
Plac'd in contempt! Farewell, fair cruelty. [*Exit*] 305

OLIVIA. "What is your parentage?"
"Above my fortunes, yet my state is well.
I am a gentleman." I'll be sworn thou art;
Thy tongue, thy face, thy limbs, actions, and
spirit,
Do give thee five-fold blazon.° Not too fast; soft,
soft!   310
Unless the master were the man. How now!
Even so quickly may one catch the plague?
Methinks I feel this youth's perfections
With an invisible and subtle stealth
To creep in at mine eyes. Well, let it be.   315
What ho, Malvolio!

                    [*Re-enter* MALVOLIO.]

MALVOLIO.   Here, madam, at your service.

OLIVIA. Run after that same peevish messenger,
The county's° man. He left this ring behind him,
Would I or not. Tell him I'll none of it.
Desire him not to flatter with° his lord,   320
Nor hold him up with hopes; I am not for him.
If that the youth will come this way tomorrow,
I'll give him reasons for't. Hie thee, Malvolio.

MALVOLIO. Madam, I will.   [*Exit*]

OLIVIA. I do I know not what, and fear to find   325
Mine eye too great a flatterer for my mind.°
Fate, show thy force; ourselves we do not owe.°
What is decreed must be, and be this so. [*Exit*]

---

in grain i.e., natural
leave . . . copy fail to marry and have children (see the
  Sonnets, especially 1–14)
divers schedules various lists   *labeled* appended
but recompens'd barely repaid   *nonpareil* peerless one
fertile profuse   *voices . . . divulg'd* well spoken of
free generous   *dimension . . . nature* physical features
willow symbol of the dejected lover

cantons songs   *contemned* despised
babbling gossip echo
fee'd post paid (tipped) messenger
blazon advertisement   *county* count
flatter with encourage
Mine . . . mind my eye has so flatteringly presented
  Cesario as to overcome my judgment   *owe* own

ACT II

SCENE i
The seacoast.

[*Enter* ANTONIO *and* SEBASTIAN.]

ANTONIO. Will you stay no longer? Nor will you
not that I go with you?

SEBASTIAN. By your patience, no. My stars shine
darkly over me; the malignancy of my fate
5 might perhaps distemper yours. Therefore I shall
crave of you your leave that I may bear my evils
alone. It were a bad recompense for your love to
lay any of them on you.

ANTONIO. Let me yet know of you whither you are
10 bound.

SEBASTIAN. No, sooth, sir. My determinate voyage
is mere extravagancy.° But I perceive in you so
excellent a touch of modesty that you will not
extort from me what I am willing to keep in;
15 therefore it charges me in manners° the rather
to express myself. You must know of me then,
Antonio, my name is Sebastian, which I called
Roderigo. My father was that Sebastian of
Messaline whom I know you have heard of. He
20 left behind him myself and a sister, both born
in an hour. If the heavens had been pleased,
would we had so ended! But you, sir, altered
that, for some hour before you took me from the
breach° of the sea was my sister drowned.

25 ANTONIO. Alas the day!

SEBASTIAN. A lady, sir, though it was said she much
resembled me, was yet of many accounted
beautiful. But, though I could not with such
estimable wonder° overfar believe that, yet thus
30 far I will boldly publish her—she bore a mind
that envy could not but call fair. She is drowned
already, sir, with salt water, though I seem to
drown her remembrance again with more.

ANTONIO. Pardon me, sir, your bad entertain-
35 ment.°

SEBASTIAN. O good Antonio, forgive me your
trouble.

My . . . extravagancy I have determined merely to
   wander
it . . . manners courtesy obliges me
breach breakers
estimable wonder appreciative admiration
your bad entertainment the poor hospitality I have shown
   you

ANTONIO. If you will not murder me for my love,°
let me be your servant.

SEBASTIAN. If you will not undo what you have   40
done, that is, kill him whom you have recovered,
desire it not. Fare ye well at once. My bosom is
full of kindness,° and I am yet so near the
manners of my mother° that upon the least
occasion more mine eyes will tell tales of me. I   45
am bound to the Count Orsino's court. Fare-
well.   [*Exit*]

ANTONIO. The gentleness of all the gods go with
thee!
I have many enemies in Orsino's court,
Else would I very shortly see thee there.   50
But, come what may, I do adore thee so
That danger shall seem sport, and I will go.
                                                       [*Exit*]

SCENE ii
A street.

[*Enter* VIOLA, MALVOLIO *following.*]

MALVOLIO. Were not you even now with the
Countess Olivia?

VIOLA. Even now, sir. On a moderate pace I have
since arrived but hither.

MALVOLIO. She returns this ring to you, sir. You   5
might have saved me my pains, to have taken it
away yourself. She adds, moreover, that you
should put your lord into a desperate assurance
she will none of him; and one thing more, that
you be never so hardy to come again in his   10
affairs unless it be to report your lord's taking of
this. Receive it so.

VIOLA. She took the ring of me. I'll none of it.

MALVOLIO. Come, sir, you peevishly threw it to
her, and her will is it should be so returned. If it   15
be worth stooping for, there it lies in your eye; if
not, be it his that finds it.   [*Exit*]

VIOLA. I left no ring with her. What means this
lady?
Fortune forbid my outside have not charm'd
her!
She made good view of me; indeed, so much   20

If . . . love unless you wish to kill me by denying
kindness human feeling
manners . . . mother i.e., womanish feelings

295

That methought her eyes had lost her tongue,
For she did speak in starts distractedly.
She loves me, sure; the cunning of her passion
Invites me in this churlish messenger.
25 None of my lord's ring! Why, he sent her none.
I am the man. If it be so, as 'tis,
Poor lady, she were better love a dream.
Disguise, I see thou art a wickedness
Wherein the pregnant enemy° does much.
30 How easy is it for the proper-false°
In women's waxen hearts to set their forms!°
Alas, our frailty is the cause, not we!
For such as we are made of, such we be.
How will this fadge?° My master loves her
     dearly,
35 And I, poor monster, fond as much on him,
And she, mistaken, seems to dote on me.
What will become of this? As I am man,
My state is desperate for my master's love;
As I am woman—now alas the day!—
40 What thriftless sighs shall poor Olivia breathe!
O Time! Thou must untangle this, not I;
It is too hard a knot for me t'untie!   [*Exit*]

SCENE iii
OLIVIA's *house*.

[*Enter* SIR TOBY *and* SIR ANDREW.]

SIR TOBY. Approach, Sir Andrew. Not to be abed
after midnight is to be up betimes;° and
"*diluculo surgere*,"° thou know'st.
SIR ANDREW. Nay, by my troth, I know not. But I
5 know to be up late is to be up late.
SIR TOBY. A false conclusion. I hate it as an unfilled
can.° To be up after midnight and to go to bed
then, is early; so that to go to bed after midnight
is to go to bed betimes. Does not our life consist
10 of the four elements?°
SIR ANDREW. Faith, so they say, but I think it rather
consists of eating and drinking.
SIR TOBY. Thou'rt a scholar. Let us therefore eat
and drink. Marian, I say! A stoup of wine!
        [*Enter* CLOWN.]
15 SIR ANDREW. Here comes the fool, i' faith.
CLOWN. How now, my hearts! Did you never see
the picture of "we three"?°

SIR TOBY. Welcome, ass. Now let's have a catch.°
SIR ANDREW. By my troth, the fool has an excellent
breast. I had rather than forty shillings I had   20
such a leg, and so sweet a breath to sing, as the
fool has. In sooth, thou wast in very gracious
fooling last night, when thou spokest of Pigrogromitus, of the Vapians passing the equinoctial
of Queubus.° 'Twas very good, i' faith. I sent   25
thee sixpence for thy leman.° Hadst it?
CLOWN. I did impeticos thy gratillity, for Malvolio's
nose is no whipstock. My lady has a white hand,
and the Myrmidons are no bottle-ale houses.°
SIR ANDREW. Excellent! Why, this is the best   30
fooling, when all is done. Now, a song.
SIR TOBY. Come on, there is sixpence for you. Let's
have a song.
SIR ANDREW. There's a testril° of me too. If one
knight give a—   35
CLOWN. Would you have a love song, or a song of
good life?
SIR TOBY. A love song, a love song.
SIR ANDREW. Aye, aye. I care not for good life.
CLOWN.

[*Sings*] O mistress mine, where are you roaming?   40
          O, stay and hear; your true love's coming,
               That can sing both high and low.
          Trip no further, pretty sweeting;
          Journeys end in lovers' meeting,
               Every wise man's son doth know.   45

SIR ANDREW. Excellent good, i' faith.
SIR TOBY. Good, good.
CLOWN.

[*Sings*] What is love? 'Tis not hereafter;
          Present mirth hath present laughter;
               What's to come is still unsure.   50
          In delay there lies no plenty;
          Then come kiss me, sweet and twenty,
               Youth's a stuff will not endure.

SIR ANDREW. A mellifluous voice, as I am a true
knight.   55
SIR TOBY. A contagious breath.
SIR ANDREW. Very sweet and contagious, i' faith.
SIR TOBY. To hear by the nose, it is dulcet in contagion.° But shall we make the welkin° dance
indeed? Shall we rouse the night owl in a catch   60

---

pregnant enemy wily Satan
proper-false handsome but deceitful man
forms impressions   *fadge* work out   *betimes* early
"*diluculo surgere*" first part of proverb, "To rise early
  is healthful"
unfilled can i.e., of liquor
four elements air, water, fire, earth
"*we three*" picture of two asses, the spectator making
  the third

catch round   *Pigrogromitus . . . Queubus* mock-learning
leman sweetheart
impeticos . . . houses nonsensical double talk
testril sixpence
contagious breath catchy tune
To hear . . . contagion (punning reference to the Fool's
  bad breath as well as his sweet air)
welkin sky

that will draw three souls out of one weaver?° Shall we do that?

SIR ANDREW. An you love me, let's do't. I am dog at a catch.

65 CLOWN. By'r lady, sir, and some dogs will catch well.

SIR ANDREW. Most certain. Let our catch be, "Thou knave."

CLOWN. "Hold thy peace, thou knave," knight? I
70 shall be constrained in't to call thee knave, knight.

SIR ANDREW. 'Tis not the first time I have constrained one to call me knave. Begin, fool. It begins "Hold thy peace."

75 CLOWN. I shall never begin if I hold my peace.

SIR ANDREW. Good, i'faith. Come, begin.
[Catch sung.]

[Enter MARIA.]

MARIA. What a caterwauling do you keep here! If my lady have not called up her steward Malvolio and bid him turn you out of doors, never
80 trust me.

SIR TOBY. My lady's a Cataian, we are politicians, Malvolio's a Peg-a-Ramsey, and "Three merry men be we." Am not I consanguineous? Am I not of her blood? Tillyvally.° Lady! [Sings] "There
85 dwelt a man in Babylon, lady, lady!"

CLOWN. Beshrew me,° the knight's in admirable fooling.

SIR ANDREW. Aye, he does well enough if he be disposed, and so do I too. He does it with a better
90 grace, but I do it more natural.

SIR TOBY. [Sings] "O, the twelfth day of December"—

MARIA. For the love o'God, peace!

[Enter MALVOLIO.]

MALVOLIO. My masters, are you mad? Or what are
95 you? Have you no wit, manners, nor honesty, but to gabble like tinkers at this time of night? Do ye make an alehouse of my lady's house, that ye squeak out your coziers'° catches without any mitigation or remorse of voice? Is there no
100 respect of place, persons, nor time in you?

SIR TOBY. We did keep time, sir, in our catches. Sneck up!°

MALVOLIO. Sir Toby, I must be round° with you. My lady bade me tell you that, though she

harbors you as her kinsman, she's nothing allied 105 to your disorders. If you can separate yourself and your misdemeanors, you are welcome to the house; if not, an it would please you to take leave of her, she is very willing to bid you farewell. 110

SIR TOBY. "Farewell, dear heart, since I must needs be gone."

MARIA. Nay, good Sir Toby.

CLOWN. "His eyes do show his days are almost done." 115

MALVOLIO. Is't even so?

SIR TOBY. "But I will never die."

CLOWN. Sir Toby, there you lie.

MALVOLIO. This is much credit to you.

SIR TOBY. "Shall I bid him go?" 120

CLOWN. "What an if you do?"

SIR TOBY. "Shall I bid him go, and spare not?"

CLOWN. "O no, no, no, no, you dare not."

SIR TOBY. Out o' tune, sir; ye lie. Art any more than a steward? Dost thou think, because thou 125 art virtuous, there shall be no more cakes and ale?

CLOWN. Yes, by Saint Anne,° and ginger° shall be hot i' the mouth too.

SIR TOBY. Thou 'rt i' the right. Go, sir, rub your 130 chain with crumbs.° A stoup of wine, Maria!

MALVOLIO. Mistress Mary, if you prized my lady's favor at anything more than contempt, you would not give means for this uncivil rule.° She shall know of it, by this hand. [Exit] 135

MARIA. Go shake your ears.

SIR ANDREW. 'Twere as good a deed as to drink when a man's a-hungry, to challenge him the field and then to break promise with him and make a fool of him. 140

SIR TOBY. Do't, knight. I'll write thee a challenge, or I'll deliver thy indignation to him by word of mouth.

MARIA. Sweet Sir Toby, be patient for tonight. Since the youth of the count's was today with my 145 lady, she is much out of quiet. For Monsieur Malvolio, let me alone with him. If I do not gull° him into a nayword° and make him a common recreation,° do not think I have wit enough to lie straight in my bed. I know I can do it. 150

---

three . . . weaver weavers were likely to be Puritans and psalm singers
My lady's . . . Tillyvally (the passage is mainly drunken nonsense; but a Cataian is a native of Cathay, and Peg-a-Ramsey the name of a low ballad character)
Beshrew me mischief on me (familiar mild oath)
coziers' cobblers'   *sneck up* go hang
round direct

Saint Anne mother of the Virgin Mary (here a mild oath)
ginger used to spice ale
rub . . . crumbs (contemptuous reference to Malvolio's office as steward; crumbs were used for polishing silver)
uncivil rule disorderly conduct   *gull* fool
nayword common epithet
common recreation universal joke

Sir Toby. Possess° us, possess us; tell us something
of him.

Maria Marry, sir, sometimes he is a kind of
Puritan.

155 Sir Andrew. O, if I thought that, I'd beat him like
a dog!

Sir Toby. What, for being a Puritan? Thy exquisite
reason, dear knight?

Sir Andrew. I have no exquisite reason for't, but I
160 have reason good enough.

Maria. The devil a Puritan that he is, or anything
constantly, but a time-pleaser;° an affectioned°
ass, that cons state without book° and utters it
by great swarths;° the best persuaded of him-
165 self,° so crammed, as he thinks, with excellencies,
that it is his grounds of faith that all that look on
him love him. And on that vice in him will my
revenge find notable cause to work.

Sir Toby. What wilt thou do?

170 Maria. I will drop in his way some obscure epistles
of love, wherein, by the color of his beard, the
shape of his leg, the manner of his gait, the
expressure° of his eye, forehead, and complexion,
he shall find himself most feelingly personated.°
175 I can write very like my lady your niece; on
a forgotten matter we can hardly make distinction of our hands.

Sir Toby. Excellent! I smell a device.°

Sir Andrew. I have't in my nose too.

180 Sir Toby. He shall think, by the letters that thou
wilt drop, that they come from my niece and
that she's in love with him.

Maria. My purpose is, indeed, a horse of that color.

Sir Andrew. And your horse now would make him
185 an ass.

Maria. Ass, I doubt not.

Sir Andrew. O, 'twill be admirable!

Maria. Sport royal, I warrant you. I know my
physic will work with him. I will plant you two,
190 and let the fool make a third, where he shall find
the letter. Observe his construction° of it. For
this night, to bed, and dream on the event. Farewell.   [Exit]

Sir Toby. Good night, Penthesilea.°

195 Sir Andrew. Before me, she's a good wench.

Sir Toby. She's a beagle, true-bred, and one that
adores me. What o' that?

Sir Andrew. I was adored once too.

Sir Toby. Let's to bed, knight. Thou hadst need
send for more money.   200

Sir Andrew. If I cannot recover° your niece, I am
a foul way out.°

Sir Toby. Send for money, knight. If thou hast her
not i' the end, call me cut.°

Sir Andrew. If I do not, never trust me, take it   205
how you will.

Sir Toby. Come, come, I'll go burn some sack;° 'tis
too late to go to bed now. Come, knight; come,
knight.   [Exeunt]

SCENE iv
The Duke's palace.

[*Enter* Duke, Viola, Curio, *and others.*]

Duke. Give me some music. Now, good morrow,
friends.
Now, good Cesario, but that piece of song,
That old and antique° song we heard last night.
Methought it did relieve my passion much
More than light airs and recollected terms°   5
Of these most brisk and giddy-paced times.
Come, but one verse.

Curio. He is not here, so please your lordship, that
should sing it.

Duke. Who was it?   10

Curio. Feste, the jester, my lord, a fool that the
lady Olivia's father took much delight in. He is
about the house.

Duke. Seek him out, and play the tune the while.
                          [*Exit* Curio. *Music plays.*]
Come hither, boy. If ever thou shalt love,   15
In the sweet pangs of it remember me;
For such as I am all true lovers are,
Unstaid and skittish in all motions° else,
Save in the constant image of the creature
That is belov'd. How dost thou like this tune?   20

Viola. It gives a very echo to the seat
Where Love is thron'd.

Duke.   Thou dost speak masterly.°
My life upon't, young though thou art, thine
eye

Possess us let us know
time-pleaser fence straddler; sycophant
affectioned affected
cons . . . book apes stately behavior   *swarths* lumps
best . . . himself most conceited
expressure expression
personated represented   *device* plot
construction interpretation
Penthesilea Queen of Amazons (that Maria is tiny, see
also I, v, 216)

recover i.e., win   *foul way out* much out of pocket
cut horse with docked tail
burn . . . sack warm some sherry
antique quaint   *recollected terms* studied phrases
motions emotions   *masterly* knowingly

Hath stay'd upon some favor° that it loves.
Hath it not, boy?

25 VIOLA.   A little, by your favor.°
DUKE. What kind of woman is't?
VIOLA.   Of your complexion.
DUKE. She is not worth thee, then. What years,
    i'faith?
VIOLA. About your years, my lord.
DUKE. Too old, by heaven. Let still the woman
    take
30 An elder than herself; so wears she to him,
So sways she level° in her husband's heart.
For, boy, however we do praise ourselves,
Our fancies° are more giddy and unfirm,
More longing, wavering, sooner lost and worn
Than women's are.
35 VIOLA.   I think it well, my lord.
DUKE. Then let thy love be younger than thyself,
Or thy affection cannot hold the bent;°
For women are as roses, whose fair flower
Being once display'd, doth fall that very hour.
40 VIOLA. And so they are. Alas, that they are so—
To die, even when they to perfection grow!
        [Re-enter CURIO and CLOWN.]
DUKE. O, fellow, come, the song we had last night.
Mark it, Cesario, it is old and plain.
The spinsters and the knitters in the sun
And the free° maids that weave their thread
45   with bones°
Do use to chant it. It is silly sooth,°
And dallies with the innocence of love
Like the old age.°
CLOWN. Are you ready, sir?
50 DUKE. Aye, prithee, sing.   [Music.]
CLOWN.

                    Song

    Come away, come away, death,
        And in sad cypress° let me be laid.
    Fly away, fly away, breath,
        I am slain by a fair cruel maid.
55 My shroud of white, stuck all with yew,
        O, prepare it!
    My part of death, no one so true
        Did share it.

Not a flower, not a flower sweet,
    On my black coffin let there be strown.   60
Not a friend, not a friend greet
    My poor corpse, where my bones shall
        be thrown.
A thousand thousand sighs to save,
    Lay me, O, where
Sad true lover never find my grave   65
    To weep there!

DUKE. There's for thy pains.
CLOWN. No pains, sir; I take pleasure in singing,
    sir.
DUKE. I'll pay thy pleasure then.   70
CLOWN. Truly, sir, and pleasure will be paid,° one
    time or another.
DUKE. Give me now leave to leave thee.
CLOWN. Now, the melancholy god protect thee,
    and the tailor make thy doublet° of changeable 75
    taffeta,° for thy mind is a very opal.° I would
    have men of such constancy put to sea, that their
    business might be everything and their intent
    everywhere; for that's it that always makes a
    good voyage of nothing. Farewell.   [Exit]   80
DUKE. Let all the rest give place.
        [CURIO and ATTENDANTS retire.]
                    Once more, Cesario,
Get thee to yond same sovereign cruelty.
Tell her my love, more noble than the world,
Prizes not quantity of dirty lands.
The parts° that fortune hath bestow'd upon her,   85
Tell her I hold as giddily° as fortune.
But 'tis that miracle and queen of gems
That nature pranks° her in attracts my soul.
VIOLA. But if she cannot love you, sir?
DUKE. I cannot be so answer'd.
VIOLA.   Sooth, but you must.   90
Say that some lady, as perhaps there is,
Hath for your love as great a pang of heart
As you have for Olivia. You cannot love her;
You tell her so. Must she not then be answer'd?
DUKE. There is no woman's sides   95
Can bide the beating of so strong a passion
As love doth give my heart; no woman's heart
So big to hold so much. They lack retention.°
Alas, their love may be call'd appetite—
No motion of the liver,° but the palate—   100
That suffer surfeit, cloyment, and revolt.°

---

favor face
by your favor by your leave (with obvious, but not to
    Orsino, play)
sways she level she rules (holds sway)
Our fancies men's loves
hold the bent retain its intensity   *free* innocent
bones bobbins made of bones
silly sooth simple truth
Like . . . age as in the good old days
cypress cypress coffin (cypress is traditional symbol of
    mourning)

paid paid for   *doublet* jacket
changeable taffeta that changes under different lights
opal of changing color with the light
parts possessions   *giddily* lightly   *pranks* decks
retention powers of retaining
motion . . . liver no genuine effect of love, whereof the
    liver was considered the seat
surfeit . . . revolt excess, satiety, revulsion

But mine is all as hungry as the sea,
And can digest as much. Make no compare
Between that love a woman can bear me
And that I owe Olivia.

105 VIOLA.   Aye, but I know—
DUKE. What dost thou know?
VIOLA. Too well what love women to men may
    owe.
    In faith, they are as true of heart as we.
    My father had a daughter lov'd a man,
110 As it might be, perhaps, were I a woman,
    I should your lordship.
DUKE.   And what's her history?
VIOLA. A blank, my lord. She never told her love,
    But let concealment, like a worm i' the bud,°
    Feed on her damask cheek. She pin'd in thought,
115 And with a green and yellow melancholy
    She sat like patience on a monument,
    Smiling at grief. Was not this love indeed?
    We men may say more, swear more, but
        indeed
    Our shows are more than will,° for still° we
        prove
120 Much in our vows but little in our love.
DUKE. But died thy sister of her love, my boy?
VIOLA. I am all the daughters of my father's
        house,
    And all the brothers too. And yet I know not.
    Sir, shall I to this lady?
DUKE.   Aye, that's the theme.
125 To her in haste. Give her this jewel. Say
    My love can give no place, bide no denay.°
                                    [Exeunt]

SCENE v
OLIVIA's garden.

[Enter SIR TOBY, SIR ANDREW, and FABIAN.]
SIR TOBY. Come thy ways, Signior Fabian.
FABIAN. Nay, I'll come. If I lose a scruple° of this
    sport, let me be boiled to death with melan-
    choly.
5 SIR TOBY. Wouldst thou not be glad to have the
    niggardly rascally sheepbiter° come by some
    notable shame?
FABIAN. I would exult, man. You know, he brought
    me out o' favor with my lady about a bear-
10   baiting here.

SIR TOBY. To anger him we'll have the bear again,
    and we will fool him black and blue. Shall we
    not, Sir Andrew?
SIR ANDREW. An we do not, it is pity of our lives.°
SIR TOBY. Here comes the little villain.   15
                [Enter MARIA.]
    How now, my metal of India!°
MARIA. Get ye all three into the box-tree.° Mal-
    volio's coming down this walk. He has been
    yonder i' the sun practicing behavior to his own
    shadow this half hour. Observe him, for the
    love of mockery, for I know this letter will make
    a contemplative idiot of him. Close,° in the name
    of jesting! Lie thou there [throws down a letter],
    for here comes the trout that must be caught
    with tickling.°   [Exit]   25
                [Enter MALVOLIO.]
MALVOLIO. 'Tis but fortune; all is fortune. Maria
    once told me she did affect me.° And I have
    heard herself come thus near, that, should she
    fancy, it should be one of my complexion.
    Besides, she uses me with a more exalted   30
    respect than any one else that follows her. What
    should I think on't?
SIR TOBY. Here's an overweening rogue!
FABIAN. O, peace! Contemplation makes a rare
    turkey cock of him. How he jets° under his   35
    advanced plumes!
SIR ANDREW. 'Slight,° I could so beat the rogue!
SIR TOBY. Peace, I say.
MALVOLIO. To be Count Malvolio!
SIR TOBY. Ah, rogue!   40
SIR ANDREW. Pistol him, pistol him.
SIR TOBY. Peace, peace!
MALVOLIO. There is example for't; the lady of the
    Strachy married the yeoman of the wardrobe.°
SIR ANDREW. Fie on him, Jezebel!°   45
FABIAN. O, peace! Now he's deeply in; look how
    imagination blows° him.
MALVOLIO. Having been three months married to
    her sitting in my state°—
SIR TOBY. O, for a stone-bow° to hit him in the eye!   50
MALVOLIO. Calling my officers about me, in my

---

worm . . . bud cankerworm, which dooms the bloom
    from the beginning
more than will more than we live up to
still always
bide no denay endure no denial   scruple iota
sheepbiter a dog that nips sheep; hence a sneaky fellow

it . . . lives "it's too bad for us"
metal of India "golden one"
box-tree ornamental shrub   Close keep in hiding
trout . . . tickling i.e., an easily caught fish
she . . . me Olivia favored me   jets struts
'Slight by God's light
lady . . . wardrobe (a lost topical allusion; but the
    implication is obvious)
Jezebel infamous hussy of Israel, King Ahab's haughty
    queen (Kings 1: 16, 19; Kings 2: 9)
blows inflates him   state chair of state
stone-bow crossbow for hurling stones

branched° velvet gown; having come from a day-
bed, where I have left Olivia sleeping—
SIR TOBY. Fire and brimstone!
55 FABIAN. O, peace, peace!
MALVOLIO. And then to have the humor of state,°
and after a demure travel of regard,° telling
them I know my place as I would they should do
theirs, to ask for my kinsman Toby—
60 SIR TOBY. Bolts and shackles!
FABIAN. O, peace, peace, peace! Now, now.
MALVOLIO. Seven of my people, with an obedient
start, make out for him. I frown the while, and
perchance wind up my watch, or play with my
65 —some rich jewel. Toby approaches, curtsies
there to me—
SIR TOBY. Shall this fellow live?
FABIAN. Though our silence be drawn from us with
cars,° yet peace.
70 MALVOLIO. I extend my hand to him thus, quench-
ing my familiar smile with an austere regard of
control°—
SIR TOBY. And does not Toby take you a blow o'
the lips then?
75 MALVOLIO. Saying, "Cousin Toby, my fortunes
having cast me on your niece give me this prerogative of speech"—
SIR TOBY. What, what?
MALVOLIO. "You must amend your drunkenness."
80 SIR TOBY. Out, scab!
FABIAN. Nay, patience, or we break the sinews of
our plot.
MALVOLIO. "Besides, you waste the treasure of
your time with a foolish knight"—
85 SIR ANDREW. That's me, I warrant you.
MALVOLIO. "One Sir Andrew"—
SIR ANDREW. I knew 'twas I, for many do call me
fool.
MALVOLIO. What employment have we here?
[Taking up the letter.]
90 FABIAN. Now is the woodcock near the gin.°
SIR TOBY. O, peace! And the spirit of humors
initimate reading aloud to him!°
MALVOLIO. By my life, this is my lady's hand.
These be her very C's, her U's, and her T's, and
95 thus makes she her great P's. It is, in contempt
of° question, her hand.

SIR ANDREW. Her C's, her U's, and her T's—why
that?
MALVOLIO. [Reads] To the unknown beloved, this,
and my good wishes:—   100
Her very phrases! By your leave, wax. Soft! And
the impressure° her Lucrece,° with which she
uses to seal. 'Tis my lady. To whom should this
be?
FABIAN. This wins him, liver and all.   105
MALVOLIO.

[Reads]   Jove knows I love.
                  But who?
               Lips, do not move;
               No man must know.

"No man must know." What follows? The   110
numbers° altered!
"No man must know." If this should be thee,
Malvolió?
SIR TOBY. Marry, hang thee, brock!°
MALVOLIO.

[Reads] I may command where I adore,   115
       But silence, like a Lucrece knife,°
   With bloodless stroke my heart doth gore.
       M, O, A, I, doth sway my life.

FABIAN. A fustian° riddle!
SIR TOBY. Excellent wench, say I.   120
MALVOLIO. "M, O, A, I, doth sway° my life." Nay,
but first, let me see, let me see, let me see.
FABIAN. What dish o' poison has she dressed him!
SIR TOBY. And with what wing the staniel checks°
at it!   125
MALVOLIO. "I may command where I adore."
Why, she may command me: I serve her; she is
my lady. Why, this is evident to any formal°
capacity; there is no obstruction in this. And the
end—what should that alphabetical position   130
portend? If I could make that resemble something in me—Softly! M, O, A, I—
SIR TOBY. O, aye, make up that. He is now at a
cold scent.
FABIAN. Sowter will cry upon't for all this, though   135
it be as rank as a fox.°

branched embroidered
humor of state stately demeanor
travel of regard tour of inspection
with cars i.e., by force
regard of control look of authority
woodcock . . . gin a peculiarly stupid bird easily caught
  in a trap (gin)
spirit . . . him may the spirit that attends on whims put
  it into his mind to read aloud
in . . . of beyond

impressure seal
Lucrece Roman model of chastity whose head is on
  Olivia's seal (see Shakespeare's poem "The Rape of
  Lucrece")
numbers meter   brock badger
Lucrece knife ravished, Lucrece slew herself
fustian overdone, pompous   sway rule
staniel checks the kestrel, an inferior hunting falcon,
  turns away (checks) from the intended prey to dart at
  other game
formal normal
Sowter . . . fox Sowter (nickname for a stupid dog) will
  follow this cold scent though the falsity of it be as
  obvious as the fox's smell

MALVOLIO. M—Malvolio. M—why, that begins my name.

FABIAN. Did not I say he would work it out? The
140　cur is excellent at faults.

MALVOLIO. M—but then there is no consonancy in the sequel; that suffers under probation.° A should follow, but O does.

FABIAN. And O shall end, I hope.

145　SIR TOBY. Aye, or I'll cudgel him, and make him cry O!

MALVOLIO. And then I comes behind.

FABIAN. Aye, an you had any eye behind you, you might see more detraction at your heels than
150　fortunes before you.

MALVOLIO. M, O, A, I. This simulation° is not as the former; and yet, to crush° this a little, it would bow to me, for every one of these letters are in my name. Soft! Here follows prose.

155　[Reads] If this fall into thy hand, revolve.° In my stars I am above thee, but be not afraid of greatness. Some are born great, some achieve greatness, and some have greatness thrust upon 'em. Thy Fates open their hands; let thy blood and
160　spirit embrace them; and, to inure thyself to what thou art like to be, cast thy humble slough° and appear fresh. Be opposite with a kinsman, surly with servants; let thy tongue tang° arguments of state; put thyself into the
165　trick of singularity.° She thus advises thee that sighs for thee. Remember who commended thy yellow stockings, and wished to see thee ever cross-gartered:° I say, remember. Go to, thou art made, if thou desirest to be so; if not, let me
170　see thee a steward still, the fellow of servants, and not worthy to touch Fortune's fingers. Farewell. She that would alter services° with thee,
THE FORTUNATE UNHAPPY.

Daylight and champain° discovers° not more:
175　this is open. I will be proud, I will read politic authors, I will baffle° Sir Toby, I will wash off gross acquaintance, I will be point-devise the very man.° I do not now fool myself, to let imagination jade° me, for every reason excites
180　to this—that my lady loves me. She did commend my yellow stockings of late, she did

praise my leg being cross-gartered, and in this she manifests herself to my love, and with a kind of injunction drives me to these habits° of her liking. I thank my stars I am happy. I will be　185 strange,° stout,° in yellow stockings, and crossgartered, even with the swiftness of putting on. Jove and my stars be praised! Here is yet a postscript.

[Reads] Thou canst not choose but know who I　190 am. If thou entertainest my love, let it appear in thy smiling. Thy smiles become thee well; therefore in my presence still smile, dear my sweet, I prithee.

Jove, I thank thee. I will smile; I will do every-　195 thing that thou wilt have me.　[Exit]

FABIAN. I will not give my part of this sport for a pension of thousands to be paid from the Sophy.°

SIR TOBY. I could marry this wench for this　200 device°—

SIR ANDREW. So could I too.

SIR TOBY. And ask no other dowry with her but such another jest.

SIR ANDREW. Nor I neither.　205

FABIAN. Here comes my noble gull-catcher.
[Re-enter MARIA.]

SIR TOBY. Wilt thou set thy foot o' my neck?

SIR ANDREW. Or o' mine either?

SIR TOBY. Shall I play my freedom at trey-trip,° and become thy bondslave?　210

SIR ANDREW. I' faith, or I either?

SIR TOBY. Why, thou hast put him in such a dream that when the image of it leaves him he must run mad.

MARIA. Nay, but say true; does it work upon him?　215

SIR TOBY. Like aqua-vitæ° with a midwife.

MARIA. If you will then see the fruits of the sport, mark his first approach before my lady. He will come to her in yellow stockings, and 'tis a color she abhors, and cross-gartered, a fashion she　220 detests; and he will smile upon her, which will now be so unsuitable to her disposition, being addicted to a melancholy as she is, that it cannot but turn him into a notable contempt. If you will see it, follow me.　225

SIR TOBY. To the gates of Tartar,° thou most excellent devil of wit!

SIR ANDREW. I'll make one too.　[Exeunt]

---

suffers . . . probation fails under testing
simulation riddle　*crush* force　*revolve* ponder
slough snake skin　*tang* resound with
trick of singularity individualistic behavior
cross-gartered an affectation of crossing the garters both
　below and above the knee
alter services i.e., reverse the master–servant relationship
champain wide-open country　*discovers* reveals
baffle cut down (reduce in the degree of knighthood)
point-devise . . . man in every detail the proper gentleman
jade deceive

habits costumes　*strange* distant　*stout* haughty
Sophy Shah of Persia, renowned for wealth
device plot　*trey-trip* dice game in which three wins
aqua-vitae distilled spirits
Tartar Tartarus, the section of Hell reserved for the
　wickedest

ACT III

SCENE i
OLIVIA's *garden.*

[*Enter* VIOLA, *and* CLOWN *with a tabor.*]
VIOLA. Save thee, friend, and thy music. Dost thou
   live by thy tabor?°
CLOWN. No, sir, I live by the church.
VIOLA. Art thou a churchman?
5 CLOWN. No such matter, sir. I do live by the
   church; for I do live at my house, and my
   house doth stand by the church.
VIOLA. So thou mayst say the king lies by a beggar,
   if a beggar dwell near him; or, the church stands
10 by thy tabor, if thy tabor stand by the church.
CLOWN. You have said, sir. To see this age! A
   sentence is but a cheveril° glove to a good wit:
   how quickly the wrong side may be turned
   outward!
15 VIOLA. Nay, that's certain; they that dally° nicely
   with words may quickly make them wanton.°
CLOWN. I would, therefore, my sister had had no
   name, sir.
VIOLA. Why, man?
20 CLOWN. Why, sir, her name's a word, and to dally
   with that word might make my sister wanton.
   But indeed words are very rascals since bonds
   disgraced them.°
VIOLA. Thy reason, man?
25 CLOWN. Troth, sir, I can yield you none without
   words, and words are grown so false, I am loath
   to prove reason with them.
VIOLA. I warrant thou art a merry fellow and
   carest for nothing.
30 CLOWN. Not so, sir, I do care for something; but
   in my conscience, sir, I do not care for you. If
   that be to care for nothing, sir, I would it would
   make you invisible.
VIOLA. Art not thou the Lady Olivia's fool?
35 CLOWN. No, indeed, sir; the Lady Olivia has no
   folly. She will keep no fool, sir, till she be
   married, and fools are as like husbands as pil-
   chards° are to herrings: the husband's the bigger.

I am indeed not her fool, but her corrupter of
   words.   40
VIOLA. I saw thee late at the Count Orsino's.
CLOWN. Foolery, sir, does walk about the orb like
   the sun; it shines everywhere. I would be sorry,
   sir, but the fool should be as oft with your
   master as with my mistress. I think I saw your 45
   wisdom there.
VIOLA. Nay, an thou pass upon° me, I'll no more
   with thee. Hold, there's expenses for thee.
CLOWN. Now Jove, in his next commodity° of hair,
   send thee a beard!   50
VIOLA. By my troth, I'll tell thee, I am almost sick
   for one—[*Aside*] though I would not have it
   grow on my chin. Is thy lady within?
CLOWN. Would not a pair of these have bred, sir?°
VIOLA. Yes, being kept together and put to use.   55
CLOWN. I would play Lord Pandarus of Phrygia,
   sir, to bring a Cressida to this Troilus.°
VIOLA. I understand you, sir; 'tis well begged.
CLOWN. The matter, I hope, is not great, sir, beg-
   ging but a beggar. Cressida was a beggar.° My   60
   lady is within, sir. I will construe° to them
   whence you come. Who you are and what you
   would are out of my welkin;° I might say
   "element," but the word is overworn.   [*Exit*]
VIOLA. This fellow's wise enough to play the fool, 65
   And to do that well craves a kind of wit.
   He must observe their mood on whom he jests,
   The quality of persons, and the time,
   And, like the haggard,° check° at every feather
   That comes before his eye. This is a practice   70
   As full of labor as a wise man's art.
   For folly that he wisely shows is fit,
   But wise men, folly-fall'n, quite taint their wit.
      [*Enter* SIR TOBY, *and* SIR ANDREW.]
SIR TOBY. Save you, gentleman.
VIOLA. And you, sir.   75
SIR ANDREW. *Dieu vous garde, monsieur.*

---

pass upon jest at   *commodity* shipment
Would . . . sir i.e., give me a mate to this single coin
Lord Pandarus . . . Troilus Pandarus, Cressida's uncle,
   brought her lover Troilus to her (see Chaucer's *Troilus
   and Criseyde* and Shakespeare's *Troilus and Cressida*)
Cressida . . . beggar (in a fifteenth-century poem by
   Henryson, Cressida became a leper and begged at the
   roadside)
construe explain   *welkin* sky   *haggard* hawk
check dart

---

tabor small drum, used by jesters
cheveril kidskin, highly flexible
dally nicely play subtly   *wanton* inconstant
since . . . them i.e., since words are no longer good unless
   guaranteed by bonds
pilchards small herrings

VIOLA. *Et vous aussi; votre serviteur.*°

SIR ANDREW. I hope, sir, you are; and I am yours.

SIR TOBY. Will you encounter° the house? My
80   niece is desirous you should enter, if your trade
      be to her.

VIOLA. I am bound to° your niece, sir; I mean, she
      is the list° of my voyage.

SIR TOBY. Taste your legs, sir; put them to motion.

85   VIOLA. My legs do better understand me, sir, than
      I understand what you mean by bidding me
      taste my legs.

SIR TOBY. I mean, to go, sir, to enter.

VIOLA. I will answer you with gait and entrance.
90   But we are prevented.°

               [*Enter* OLIVIA *and* MARIA.]
      Most excellent accomplished lady, the heavens
      rain odors on you!

SIR ANDREW. That youth's a rare courtier: "Rain
      odors." Well.

95   VIOLA. My matter hath no voice, lady, but to your
      own most pregnant° and vouchsafed° ear.

SIR ANDREW. "Odors," "pregnant," and "vouch-
      safed." I'll get 'em all three all ready.

OLIVIA. Let the garden door be shut, and leave me
100   to my hearing.

               [*Exeunt* SIR TOBY, SIR ANDREW, *and* MARIA.]
      Give me your hand, sir.

VIOLA. My duty, madam, and most humble
      service.

OLIVIA. What is your name?

105   VIOLA. Cesario is your servant's name, fair princess.

OLIVIA. My servant, sir! 'Twas never merry world
      Since lowly feigning° was call'd compliment.
      You're servant to the Count Orsino, youth.

VIOLA. And he is yours, and his must needs be
      yours.
110   Your servant's servant is your servant, madam.

OLIVIA. For° him, I think not on him. For his
      thoughts,
      Would they were blanks, rather than fill'd with
      me!

VIOLA. Madam, I come to whet your gentle
      thoughts
      On his behalf.

OLIVIA.   O, by your leave, I pray you,
115   I bade you never speak again of him.
      But, would you undertake another suit,

I had rather hear you to solicit that
Than music from the spheres.°

VIOLA.   Dear lady—

OLIVIA. Give me leave, beseech you. I did send,
      After the last enchantment you did here,   120
      A ring in chase of you. So did I abuse
      Myself, my servant, and, I fear me, you.
      Under your hard construction° must I sit,
      To force that on you, in a shameful cunning,
      Which you knew none of yours. What might you 125
      think?
      Have you not set mine honor at the stake
      And baited it with all th' unmuzzled thoughts
      That tyrannous heart can think? To one of your
      receiving°
      Enough is shown. A cypress, not a bosom,
      Hides my heart. So, let me hear you speak.   130

VIOLA. I pity you.

OLIVIA.   That's a degree to love.

VIOLA. No, not a grize;° for 'tis a vulgar proof°
      That very oft we pity enemies.

OLIVIA. Why, then, methinks 'tis time to smile
      again.
      O world, how apt the poor are to be proud!   135
      If one should be a prey, how much the better
      To fall before the lion than the wolf!

                              [*Clock strikes.*]
      The clock upbraids me with the waste of time.
      Be not afraid, good youth, I will not have you;
      And yet, when wit and youth is come to harvest,   140
      Your wife is like to reap a proper° man.
      There lies your way, due west.

VIOLA.   Then westward-ho!
      Grace and good disposition attend your lady-
      ship!
      You'll nothing, madam, to my lord by me?

OLIVIA. Stay.   145
      I prithee tell me what thou think'st of me.

VIOLA. That you do think you are not what you
      are.

OLIVIA. If I think so, I think the same of you.

VIOLA. Then think you right. I am not what I am.

OLIVIA. I would you were as I would have you be!   150

VIOLA. Would it be better, madam, than I am?
      I wish it might, for now I am your fool.

OLIVIA. O, what a deal of scorn looks beautiful
      In the contempt and anger of his lip!
      A murd'rous guilt shows not itself more soon   155

Dieu . . . serviteur God protect you, sir. And you also,
    your servant
encounter go into (Sir Toby mocks the extravagant
    fashion of address)
bound to headed for (Viola affects nautical style)
list destination   *prevented* anticipated
pregnant receptive   *vouchsafed* willing
lowly feigning false humility   *For* as for

music . . . spheres (the universe, thought to consist of
    revolving concentric spheres containing the planets and
    stars, was believed to create music inaudible to man by
    its whirling motion)
hard construction harsh opinion
receiving understanding   *grize* step
vulgar proof common fact   *proper* handsome

Than love that would seem hid. Love's night is
noon.
Cesario, by the roses of the spring,
By maidhood, honor, truth, and everything,
I love thee so, that, maugre° all thy pride,
160 Nor wit nor° reason can my passion hide.
Do not extort thy reasons from this clause,
For that I woo, thou therefore hast no cause;
But rather reason thus with reason fetter:
Love sought is good, but given unsought is
better.
165 VIOLA. By innocence I swear, and by my youth,
I have one heart, one bosom, and one truth,
And that no woman has, nor never none
Shall mistress be of it save I alone.
And so adieu, good madam. Never more
170 Will I my master's tears to you deplore.
OLIVIA. Yet come again, for thou perhaps mayst
move
That heart which now abhors to like his love.

[Exeunt]

SCENE ii
OLIVIA's house.

[Enter SIR TOBY, SIR ANDREW, and FABIAN.]
SIR ANDREW. No, faith, I'll not stay a jot longer.
SIR TOBY. Thy reason, dear venom, give thy reason.
FABIAN. You must needs yield your reason, Sir
Andrew.
5 SIR ANDREW. Marry, I saw your niece do more
favors to the count's servingman than ever she
bestowed upon me. I saw't i' th' orchard.
SIR TOBY. Did she see thee the while, old boy? Tell
me that.
10 SIR ANDREW. As plain as I see you now.
FABIAN. This was a great argument of love in her
toward you.
SIR ANDREW. 'Slight, will you make an ass o' me?
FABIAN. I will prove it legitimate, sir, upon the
15 oaths of judgment and reason.
SIR TOBY. And they have been grand-jurymen
since before Noah was a sailor.
FABIAN. She did show favor to the youth in your
sight only to exasperate you, to awake your dor-
20 mouse valor, to put fire in your heart and brimstone in your liver. You should then have
accosted her, and with some excellent jests,
fire-new from the mint, you should have banged
the youth into dumbness. This was looked for at

your hand, and this was balked.° The double 25
gilt of this opportunity you let time wash off,°
and you are now sailed into the north of my
lady's opinion, where you will hang like an
icicle on a Dutchman's beard unless you do
redeem it by some laudable attempt either of 30
valor or policy.
SIR ANDREW. An't be any way, it must be with
valor, for policy I hate. I had as lief be a Brown-
ist° as a politician.
SIR TOBY. Why, then, build me° thy fortunes upon 35
the basis of valor. Challenge me the count's
youth to fight with him; hurt him in eleven
places. My niece shall take note of it, and assure
thyself, there is no love-broker in the world can
more prevail in man's commendation with 40
woman than report of valor.
FABIAN. There is no way but this, Sir Andrew.
SIR ANDREW. Will either of you bear me a challenge to him?
SIR TOBY. Go, write it in a martial hand. Be curst° 45
and brief. It is no matter how witty, so it be
eloquent and full of invention.° Taunt him with
the license of ink.° If thou thou'st° him so thrice,
it shall not be amiss. And as many lies as will lie
in thy sheet of paper, although the sheet were 50
big enough for the bed of Ware° in England,
set 'em down. Go, about it. Let there be gall
enough in thy ink; though thou write with a
goose-pen,° no matter. About it.
SIR ANDREW. Where shall I find you? 55
SIR TOBY. We'll call thee at the cubiculo.° Go.

[Exit SIR ANDREW.]

FABIAN. This is a dear manikin° to you, Sir Toby.
SIR TOBY. I have been dear to him,° lad, some two
thousand strong, or so.
FABIAN. We shall have a rare letter from him. But 60
you'll not deliver't?
SIR TOBY. Never trust me, then; and by all means
stir on the youth to an answer. I think oxen and
wainropes° cannot hale them together. For
Andrew, if he were opened and you find so 65

---

balked missed
double . . . wash off the best gold plate was given a
double dipping
Brownist Puritan extremist sect
build me build (the ethical dative *me* has no force)
curst bad-tempered   *invention* witty expression
Taunt . . . ink i.e., take advantage of the liberty of
taunting that writing (as opposed to direct
confrontation) allows
thou'st i.e., treat him as an inferior
bed of Ware which was nearly eleven feet square
goose-pen goosequill   *cubiculo* bedchamber
dear manikin dear little fellow, puppet
dear to him costly to him   *wainropes* wagon ropes

---

maugre in spite of   *Nor . . . nor* neither . . . nor

much blood in his liver° as will clog the foot of a
flea, I'll eat the rest of the anatomy.

FABIAN. And his opposite, the youth, bears in his
visage no great presage of cruelty.

[Enter MARIA.]

70 SIR TOBY. Look where the youngest wren of mine
comes.

MARIA. If you desire the spleen,° and will laugh
yourself into stitches, follow me. Yond gull
75 Malvolio is turned heathen, a very renegado,°
for there is no Christian that means to be saved
by believing rightly can ever believe such impossible passages of grossness.° He's in yellow
stockings.

SIR TOBY. And cross-gartered?

80 MARIA. Most villainously, like a pedant that keeps
a school i' the church. I have dogged him like his
murderer. He does obey every point of the letter
that I dropped to betray him. He does smile his
face into more lines than is in the new map with
85 the augmentation of the Indies;° you have not
seen such a thing as 'tis. I can hardly forbear
hurling things at him. I know my lady will
strike him. If she do, he'll smile and take 't for a
great favor.

90 SIR TOBY. Come, bring us, bring us where he is.

[Exeunt]

SCENE iii
A street.

[Enter SEBASTIAN and ANTONIO.]

SEBASTIAN. I would not by my will have troubled
you,
But since you make your pleasure of your pains,
I will no further chide you.

ANTONIO. I could not stay behind you. My desire,
5 More sharp than filed steel, did spur me forth;
And not all love to see you, though so much
As might have drawn one to a longer voyage,
But jealousy° what might befall your travel,
Being skilless in these parts—which to a stranger,
10 Unguided and unfriended, often prove
Rough and unhospitable. My willing love,
The rather by these arguments of fear,

Set forth in your pursuit.

SEBASTIAN.   My kind Antonio,
I can no other answer make but thanks,
And thanks, and ever thanks. Too oft good turns   15
Are shuffled off with such uncurrent° pay.
But were my worth as is my conscience firm,
You should find better dealing. What's to do?
Shall we go see the relics° of this town?

ANTONIO. Tomorrow, sir. Best first go see your
lodging.   20

SEBASTIAN. I am not weary, and 'tis long to night.
I pray you, let us satisfy our eyes
With the memorials and the things of fame
That do renown this city.

ANTONIO.   Would you'd pardon me.
I do not without danger walk these streets.   25
Once in a sea fight 'gainst the count his° galleys
I did some service of such note indeed
That were I ta'en here it would scarce be
answer'd.

SEBASTIAN. Belike you slew great number of his
people.

ANTONIO. Th' offense is not of such a bloody
nature,   30
Albeit the quality° of the time and quarrel
Might well have given us bloody argument.
It might have since been answer'd in repaying
What we took from them, which, for traffic's°
sake,
Most of our city did. Only myself stood out,   35
For which, if I be lapsed° in this place,
I shall pay dear.

SEBASTIAN.   Do not then walk too open.

ANTONIO. It doth not fit° me. Hold, sir, here's my
purse.
In the south suburbs at the Elephant
Is best to lodge. I will bespeak our diet   40
Whiles you beguile the time and feed your
knowledge
With viewing of the town. There shall you have
me.

SEBASTIAN. Why I your purse?

ANTONIO. Haply your eye shall light upon some
toy°
You have desire to purchase—and your store,   45
I think, is not for idle markets,° sir.

SEBASTIAN. I'll be your purse-bearer and leave you
For an hour.

ANTONIO.   To th' Elephant.

SEBASTIAN.   I do remember. [Exeunt]

blood . . . liver indicative of courage
spleen acute affliction from excessive laughter
renegado i.e., renegade Christian
impossible . . . grossness i.e., as were contained in the
   forged letter
new map . . . Indies map published in 1599 in Hakluyt's
   Voyages, using meridian lines and showing more of the
   East Indies than earlier maps
jealousy concern for

uncurrent not "passing current," hence, worthless
relics i.e., of antiquity
count his count's   quality nature   traffic's trade's
lapsed surprised   fit befit   toy trifle
idle markets casual purchases

SCENE iv
OLIVIA's *garden.*

[*Enter* OLIVIA *and* MARIA.]

OLIVIA. I have sent after him. He says he'll come.
How shall I feast him? What bestow of° him?
For youth is bought more oft than begg'd or
borrow'd.
I speak too loud.

5 Where is Malvolio? He is sad and civil,°
And suits well for a servant with my fortunes.
Where is Malvolio?

MARIA. He's coming, madam, but in very
strange manner. He is, sure, possessed,°
10 madam.

OLIVIA. Why, what's the matter? Does he rave?

MARIA. No, madam, he does nothing but smile.
Your ladyship were best to have some guard
about you if he come, for sure the man is
15 tainted in 's wits.

OLIVIA. Go call him hither. [*Exit* MARIA] I am as
mad as he,
If sad and merry madness equal be.

[*Re-enter* MARIA, *with* MALVOLIO.]

How now, Malvolio!

MALVOLIO. Sweet lady, ho, ho.

20 OLIVIA. Smilest thou?
I sent for thee upon a sad occasion.

MALVOLIO. Sad, lady? I could be sad. This does
make some obstruction in the blood, this cross-
gartering, but what of that? If it please the eye
25 of one, it is with me as the very true sonnet is,
"Please one, and please all."°

OLIVIA. Why, how dost thou, man? What is the
matter with thee?

MALVOLIO. Not black in my mind, though yellow
30 in my legs. It did come to his hands, and commands shall be executed. I think we do know the
sweet Roman hand.°

OLIVIA. Wilt thou go to bed, Malvolio?

MALVOLIO. To bed! Aye, sweetheart, and I'll come
35 to thee.

OLIVIA. God comfort thee! Why dost thou smile so
and kiss thy hand so oft?

MARIA. How do you, Malvolio?

MALVOLIO. At your request? Yes, nightingales
40 answer daws.°

---

of on   *sad . . . civil* sober . . . reserved
possessed mad
"Please . . . all" (quoted from a familiar ballad)
Roman hand Italian style recently adopted in aristocratic
society; archetype of modern script
nightingales . . . daws i.e., since noble birds condescend to
speak to inferior ones, I should reply to you

MARIA. Why appear you with this ridiculous
boldness before my lady?

MALVOLIO. "Be not afraid of greatness." 'Twas
well writ.

OLIVIA. What meanest thou by that, Malvolio?   45

MALVOLIO. "Some are born great"—

OLIVIA. Ha!

MALVOLIO. "Some achieve greatness"—

OLIVIA. What sayest thou?

MALVOLIO. "And some have greatness thrust   50
upon them."

OLIVIA. Heaven restore thee!

MALVOLIO. "Remember who commended thy
yellow stockings"—

OLIVIA. Thy yellow stockings!   55

MALVOLIO. "And wished to see thee cross-gartered."

OLIVIA. Cross-gartered!

MALVOLIO. "Go to, thou art made, if thou desirest
to be so"—   60

OLIVIA. Am I made?

MALVOLIO. "If not, let me see thee a servant still."

OLIVIA. Why, this is very midsummer madness.

[*Enter* SERVANT.]

SERVANT. Madam, the young gentleman of the
Count Orsino's is returned. I could hardly en-   65
treat him back. He attends your ladyship's
pleasure.

OLIVIA. I'll come to him. [*Exit* SERVANT] Good
Maria, let this fellow be looked to. Where's my
cousin Toby? Let some of my people have a   70
special care of him. I would not have him mis-
carry° for the half of my dowry.

[*Exeunt* OLIVIA *and* MARIA.]

MALVOLIO. O, ho! Do you come near me now? No
worse man than Sir Toby to look to me! This
concurs directly with the letter: she sends him   75
on purpose, that I may appear stubborn to him,
for she incites me to that in the letter. "Cast thy
humble slough," says she. "Be opposite with a
kinsman, surly with servants; let thy tongue
tang with arguments of state; put thyself into   80
the trick of singularity"—and consequently sets
down the manner how, as, a sad face, a reverend
carriage,° a slow tongue, in the habit° of some
sir of note, and so forth. I have limed° her, but it
is Jove's doing, and Jove make me thankful! And   85
when she went away now, "Let this fellow be
looked to." Fellow! Not Malvolio, nor after my
degree, but fellow. Why, everything adheres together, that no dram of a scruple, no scruple of a

---

miscarry come to harm (nautical image)
carriage bearing   *habit* dress
limed birdlimed; caught

90   scruple, no obstacle, no incredulous° or unsafe°
      circumstance—What can be said? Nothing that
      can be can come between me and the full
      prospect of my hopes. Well, Jove, not I, is the
      doer of this, and he is to be thanked.
          [*Re-enter* MARIA, *with* SIR TOBY *and* FABIAN.]
95   SIR TOBY. Which way is he, in the name of sanctity?
      If all the devils of hell be drawn in little° and
      Legion° himself possessed him, yet I'll speak to
      him.
      FABIAN. Here he is, here he is. How is 't with you,
100   sir? How is 't with you, man?
      MALVOLIO. Go off; I discard you. Let me enjoy my
      private.° Go off.
      MARIA. Lo, how hollow the fiend speaks within
      him! Did not I tell you? Sir Toby, my lady prays
105   you to have a care of him.
      MALVOLIO. Ah, ha! Does she so?
      SIR TOBY. Go to, go to; peace, peace. We must deal
      gently with him. Let me alone. How do you,
      Malvolio? How is 't with you? What, man! Defy
110   the devil. Consider, he's an enemy to mankind.
      MALVOLIO. Do you know what you say?
      MARIA. La you, an you speak ill of the devil, how he
      takes it at heart! Pray God he be not bewitched!
      FABIAN. Carry his water to the wise woman.°
115   MARIA. Marry, and it shall be done tomorrow
      morning, if I live. My lady would not lose him
      for more than I'll say.
      MALVOLIO. How now, mistress!
      MARIA. O Lord!
120   SIR TOBY. Prithee, hold thy peace; this is not the
      way. Do you not see you move him? Let me
      alone with him.
      FABIAN. No way but gentleness. Gently, gently, the
      fiend is rough, and will not be roughly used.
125   SIR TOBY. Why, how now, my bawcock!° How dost
      thou, chuck?°
      MALVOLIO. Sir!
      SIR TOBY. Aye, Biddy, come with me. What, man!
      'Tis not for gravity to play at cherry-pit° with
130   Satan; hang him, foul collier!°
      MARIA. Get him to say his prayers, good Sir Toby,
      get him to pray.

MALVOLIO. My prayers, minx!
MARIA. No, I warrant you, he will not hear of
      godliness.   135
MALVOLIO. Go hang yourselves all! You are idle
      shallow things. I am not of your element. You
      shall know more hereafter.   [*Exit*]
SIR TOBY. Is 't possible?
FABIAN. If this were played upon a stage now, I   140
      could condemn it as an improbable fiction.
SIR TOBY. His very genius° hath taken the infection
      of the device, man.
MARIA. Nay, pursue him now, lest the device take
      air and taint.°   145
FABIAN. Why, we shall make him mad indeed.
MARIA. The house will be the quieter.
SIR TOBY. Come, we'll have him in a dark room
      and bound.° My niece is already in the belief
      that he's mad. We may carry it thus, for our   150
      pleasure and his penance, till our very pastime,
      tired out of breath, prompt us to have mercy on
      him—at which time we will bring the device to
      the bar° and crown thee for a finder of madmen.
      But see, but see.   155
          [*Enter* SIR ANDREW.]
FABIAN. More matter for a May morning.
SIR ANDREW. Here's the challenge, read it. I war-
      rant there's vinegar and pepper in 't.
FABIAN. Is 't so saucy?
SIR ANDREW. Aye, is 't, I warrant him. Do but read.   160
SIR TOBY. Give me.

      [*Reads*] Youth, whatsoever thou art, thou art
      but a scurvy fellow.

FABIAN. Good, and valiant.
SIR TOBY.

      [*Reads*] Wonder not, nor admire° not in thy   165
      mind, why I do call thee so, for I will show thee
      no reason for 't.

FABIAN. A good note; that keeps you from the
      blow of the law.
SIR TOBY.

      [*Reads*] Thou comest to the lady Olivia, and in   170
      my sight she uses thee kindly. But thou liest in
      thy throat; that is not the matter I challenge
      thee for.

FABIAN. Very brief, and to exceeding good sense—
      less.   175

---

incredulous incredible   *unsafe* doubtful
drawn in little miniaturized (and packed into Malvolio's
    mind)
Legion the pack of devils cast out by Christ; see
    Mark 5:1–19
private privacy
Carry . . . woman i.e., for diagnosis (the "wise woman"
    no doubt also exorcised fiends)
bawcock French *beau coq*, "fine fellow"   *chuck* chick
cherry-pit child's game of throwing cherry stones into a
    hole
collier i.e., Satan, the "coal-dealer"

genius soul
device . . . taint lest our trick be spoiled
dark . . . bound a standard Elizabethan treatment for
    lunatics
bar court   *admire* be surprised

Sir Toby.

>　[*Reads*] I will waylay thee going home; where if
>　it be thy chance to kill me—

Fabian. Good.

Sir Toby.

>　[*Reads*] Thou killest me like a rogue and a
180　villain.

Fabian. Still you keep o' the windy° side of the law.
　Good.

Sir Toby.

>　[*Reads*] Fare thee well, and God have mercy
>　upon one of our souls! He may have mercy
185　upon mine, but my hope is better, and so look
>　to thyself. Thy friend, as thou usest him, and
>　thy sworn enemy,　　Andrew Aguecheek.

　If this letter move him not, his legs cannot. I'll
　give't him.

190　Maria. You may have very fit occasion for 't. He is
　now in some commerce with my lady, and will
　by and by depart.

Sir Toby. Go, Sir Andrew, scout me for him at the
　corner of the orchard like a bum-baily.° So soon
195　as ever thou seest him, draw, and, as thou
　drawest, swear horrible. For it comes to pass oft
　that a terrible oath, with a swaggering accent
　sharply twanged off, gives manhood more
　approbation° than ever proof itself would have
200　earned him. Away!

Sir Andrew. Nay, let me alone for swearing.°
　　　　　　　　　　　　　　　　　[*Exit*]

Sir Toby. Now will not I deliver his letter, for the
　behavior of the young gentleman gives him out
　to be of good capacity and breeding; his employ-
205　ment between his lord and my niece confirms no
　less. Therefore this letter, being so excellently
　ignorant, will breed no terror in the youth; he
　will find it comes from a clodpole. But, sir, I
　will deliver his challenge by word of mouth, set
210　upon Aguecheek a notable report of valor, and
　drive the gentleman, as I know his youth° will
　aptly receive it, into a most hideous opinion of
　his rage, skill, fury, and impetuosity. This will so
　fright them both that they will kill one another
215　by the look, like cockatrices.°
　　　　　[*Re-enter* Olivia, *with* Viola.]

Fabian. Here he comes with your niece. Give them
　way till he take leave, and presently° after him.

Sir Toby. I will meditate the while upon some
　horrid message for a challenge.
　　　　[*Exeunt* Sir Toby, Fabian, *and* Maria.]

Olivia. I have said too much unto a heart of stone,　220
　And laid mine honor too unchary° out.
　There's something in me that reproves my fault,
　But such a headstrong potent fault it is
　That it but mocks reproof.

Viola. With the same 'havior that your passion
　bears　　　　　　　　　　　　　　　225
　Goes on my master's grief.

Olivia. Here, wear this jewel for me, 'tis my
　picture.
　Refuse it not; it hath no tongue to vex you.
　And I beseech you come again tomorrow.
　What shall you ask of me that I'll deny,　　230
　That honor sav'd may upon asking give?

Viola. Nothing but this—your true love for my
　master.

Olivia. How with mine honor may I give him that
　Which I have given to you?

Viola.　　　　　　　　I will acquit you.

Olivia. Well, come again tomorrow. Fare thee
　well.　　　　　　　　　　　　　　235
　A fiend like thee might bear my soul to hell
　　　　　　　　　　　　　　　　　[*Exit*]
　　　　　[*Re-enter* Sir Toby *and* Fabian.]

Sir Toby. Gentleman, God save thee.

Viola. And you, sir.

Sir Toby. That defense thou hast, betake thee to 't.
　Of what nature the wrongs are thou hast done　240
　him, I know not, but thy intercepter, full of
　despite, bloody as the hunter, attends thee at the
　orchard end. Dismount thy tuck,° be yare° in thy
　preparation, for thy assailant is quick, skillful,
　and deadly.　　　　　　　　　　245

Viola. You mistake, sir; I am sure no man hath
　any quarrel to me. My remembrance is very
　free and clear from any image of offense done to
　any man.

Sir Toby. You'll find it otherwise, I assure you.　250
　Therefore, if you hold your life at any price,
　betake you to your guard; for your opposite
　hath in him what youth, strength, skill, and
　wrath can furnish man withal.

Viola. I pray you, sir, what is he?　　　　255

Sir Toby. He is knight, dubbed with unhatched
　rapier and on carpet consideration,° but he is a
　devil in private brawl. Souls and bodies hath he
　divorced three, and his incensement at this

---

windy　windward, sheltered　　　*bum-baily*　bailiff
approbation　reputation
let . . . swearing　leave that to me
youth　youthfulness
cockatrice　the basilisk, which killed with a glance
presently　immediately

unchary　carelessly　　*tuck*　rapier　　*yare*　quick
unhatched . . . consideration　unhacked rapier and by
　court favor (that is, Sir Andrew was knighted not for
　martial but for material reasons)

260 moment is so implacable that satisfaction can be
none but by pangs of death and sepulcher.
Hob, nob,° is his word, give 't or take 't.

VIOLA. I will return again into the house and desire
some conduct of the lady. I am no fighter. I have
265 heard of some kind of men that put quarrels
purposely on others, to taste their valor. Belike
this is a man of that quirk.

SIR TOBY. Sir, no. His indignation derives itself out
of a very competent° injury; therefore, get you
270 on and give him his desire. Back you shall not to
the house, unless you undertake that with me
which with as much safety you might answer
him; therefore, on, or strip your sword stark
naked. For meddle you must, that's certain, or
275 forswear to wear iron about you.

VIOLA. This is as uncivil as strange. I beseech you,
do me this courteous office, as to know of the
knight what my offense to him is. It is something of my negligence, nothing of my purpose.

280 SIR TOBY. I will do so. Signior Fabian, stay you by
this gentleman till my return.   [Exit]

VIOLA. Pray you, sir, do you know of this matter?

FABIAN. I know the knight is incensed against you,
even to a mortal arbitrement,° but nothing of
285 the circumstance more.

VIOLA. I beseech you, what manner of man is he?

FABIAN. Nothing of that wonderful promise, to
read him by his form, as you are like to find him
in the proof of his valor. He is, indeed, sir, the
290 most skillful, bloody, and fatal opposite that you
could possibly have found in any part of Illyria.
Will you walk towards him? I will make your
peace with him if I can.

VIOLA. I shall be much bound to you for 't. I am
295 one that had rather go with sir priest than sir
knight. I care not who knows so much of my
mettle.   [Exeunt]

            [Re-enter SIR TOBY, with SIR ANDREW.]

SIR TOBY. Why, man, he's a very devil. I have not
seen such a firago.° I had a pass with him, rapier,
300 scabbard, and all, and he gives me the stuck in°
with such a mortal motion that it is inevitable;
and on the answer,° he pays you as surely as your
feet hit the ground they step on. They say he has
been fencer to the Sophy.

305 SIR ANDREW. Pox on 't, I'll not meddle with him.

SIR TOBY. Aye, but he will not now be pacified.
Fabian can scarce hold him yonder.

Hob, nob   mere mumbo jumbo
competent   substantial
mortal arbitrement   deadly decision
firago   virago, mannish woman (but Sir Toby does not
   recognize the double joke)
stuck in   thrust   on the answer   at your return thrust

SIR ANDREW. Plague on 't, an I thought he had been
valiant and so cunning in fence, I'd have seen him
damned ere I'd have challenged him. Let him 310
let the matter slip, and I'll give him my horse,
gray Capilet.

SIR TOBY. I'll make the motion. Stand here, make a
good show on 't. This shall end without the
perdition of souls. [Aside] Marry, I'll ride your 315
horse as well as I ride you.

            [Re-enter FABIAN and VIOLA.]

[To FABIAN] I have his horse to take° up the
quarrel. I have persuaded him the youth's a
devil.

FABIAN. He is as horribly conceited° of him, and 320
pants and looks pale, as if a bear were at his
heels.

SIR TOBY. [To VIOLA] There's no remedy, sir. He
will fight with you for's oath sake. Marry, he
hath better bethought him of his quarrel, and he 325
finds that now scarce to be worth talking of.
Therefore draw, for the supportance° of his vow.
He protests he will not hurt you.

VIOLA. [Aside] Pray God defend me! A little thing
would make me tell them how much I lack of a 330
man.

FABIAN. Give ground, if you see him furious.

SIR TOBY. Come, Sir Andrew, there's no remedy.
The gentleman will, for his honor's sake, have
one bout with you; he cannot by the duello° 335
avoid it. But he has promised me, as he is a
gentleman and a soldier, he will not hurt you.
Come on; to 't.

SIR ANDREW. Pray God, he keep his oath!

VIOLA. I do assure you, 'tis against my will.   340
                           [They draw.]

            [Enter ANTONIO.]

ANTONIO. Put up your sword. If this young gentle-
man
Have done offense, I take the fault on me;
If you offend him, I for him defy you.

SIR TOBY. You, sir! Why, what are you?

ANTONIO. One, sir, that for his love dares yet do
more   345
Than you have heard him brag to you he will.

SIR TOBY. Nay, if you be an undertaker,° I am for
you.   [They draw.]

            [Enter OFFICERS.]

FABIAN. O good Sir Toby, hold! Here come the
officers.   350

SIR TOBY. I'll be with you anon.

take up   settle
horribly conceited   has as horrible an image
supportance   upholding   duello   dueling code
undertaker   meddler

VIOLA. Pray, sir, put your sword up, if you please.

SIR ANDREW. Marry, will I, sir. And, for that I
promised you, I'll be as good as my word. He
355 will bear you easily and reins well.

FIRST OFFICER. This is the man. Do thy office.

SECOND OFFICER. Antonio, I arrest thee at the suit of
Count Orsino.

ANTONIO. You do mistake me, sir.

FIRST OFFICER. No, sir, no jot. I know your favor°
360 well,
Though now you have no sea-cap on your head.
Take him away. He knows I know him well.

ANTONIO. I must obey. [*To* VIOLA] This comes with
seeking you.
But there's no remedy; I shall answer it.
365 What will you do, now my necessity
Makes me to ask you for my purse? It grieves me
Much more for what I cannot do for you
Than what befalls myself. You stand amaz'd;
But be of comfort.

370 SECOND OFFICER. Come, sir, away.

ANTONIO. I must entreat of you some of that
money.

VIOLA. What money, sir?
For the fair kindness you have show'd me here,
And, part,° being prompted by your present
trouble,
375 Out of my lean and low ability°
I'll lend you something. My having is not much;
I'll make division of my present° with you.
Hold, there's half my coffer.°

ANTONIO.   Will you deny me now?
Is't possible that my deserts to you
380 Can lack persuasion? Do not tempt my misery,
Lest that it make me so unsound a man
As to upbraid you with those kindnesses
That I have done for you.

VIOLA.   I know of none,
Nor know I you by voice or any feature.
385 I hate ingratitude more in a man
Than lying vainness, babbling drunkenness,
Or any taint of vice whose strong corruption
Inhabits our frail blood.

ANTONIO.   O heavens themselves!

SECOND OFFICER. Come, sir, I pray you, go.

ANTONIO. Let me speak a little. This youth that
390 you see here

I snatch'd one half out of the jaws of death,
Reliev'd him with such sanctity of love,
And to his image, which methought did promise
Most venerable worth, did I devotion.

FIRST OFFICER. What's that to us? The time goes by.
Away!   395

ANTONIO. But O how vile an idol proves this god!
Thou hast, Sebastian, done good feature shame.
In nature there's no blemish but the mind.
None can be call'd deform'd but the unkind.
Virtue is beauty, but the beauteous evil   400
Are empty trunks, o'erflourish'd by the devil.°

FIRST OFFICER. The man grows mad. Away with
him! Come, come, sir.

ANTONIO. Lead me on.   [*Exit with* OFFICERS.]

VIOLA. Methinks his words do from such passion
fly
That he believes himself. So do not I.   405
Prove true, imagination, O prove true,
That I, dear brother, be now ta'en for you!

SIR TOBY. Come hither, knight; come hither,
Fabian. We'll whisper o'er a couplet or two of
most sage saws.°   410

VIOLA. He nam'd Sebastian. I my brother know
Yet living in my glass;° even such and so
In favor was my brother, and he went
Still in this fashion, color, ornament,
For him I imitate. O, if it prove,   415
Tempests are kind and salt waves fresh in love!
[*Exit*]

SIR TOBY. A very dishonest paltry boy, and more a
coward than a hare. His dishonesty appears in
leaving his friend here in necessity and denying
him; and for his cowardship, ask Fabian.   420

FABIAN. A coward, a most devout coward, religious
in it.

SIR ANDREW. 'Slid,° I'll after him again and beat
him.

SIR TOBY. Do. Cuff him soundly, but never draw   425
thy sword.

SIR ANDREW. An I do not—   [*Exit*]

FABIAN. Come, let's see the event.°

SIR TOBY. I dare lay any money 'twill be nothing
yet.   [*Exeunt*] 430

---

favor face   part in part   ability means
present present means   coffer store

beauteous . . . devil those evil ones who are beautiful are
empty bodies flowered over by the devil
sage saws wise sayings   glass mirror, image
'Slid God's eyelid   event outcome

ACT IV

SCENE i
Before OLIVIA's *house.*

[*Enter* SEBASTIAN *and* CLOWN.]

CLOWN. Will you make me believe that I am not
    sent for you?

SEBASTIAN. Go to, go to, thou art a foolish fellow.
    Let me be clear of thee.

5   CLOWN. Well held out, i' faith! No, I do not know
    you; nor I am not sent to you by my lady, to bid
    you come speak with her; nor your name is not
    Master Cesario; nor this is not my nose neither.
    Nothing that is so is so.

10 SEBASTIAN. I prithee, vent thy folly somewhere
    else.
    Thou know'st not me.

CLOWN. Vent my folly! He has heard that word of
    some great man and now applies it to a fool.
15   Vent my folly! I am afraid this great lubber, the
    world, will prove a cockney.° I prithee now,
    ungird° thy strangeness and tell me what I shall
    vent to my lady. Shall I vent to her that thou art
    coming?

20 SEBASTIAN. I prithee, foolish Greek,° depart from
    me.
    There's money for thee. If you tarry longer,
    I shall give worse payment.

CLOWN. By my troth, thou hast an open hand.
25   These wise men that give fools money get them-
    selves a good report—after fourteen years'
    purchase.°

[*Enter* SIR ANDREW, SIR TOBY, *and* FABIAN.]

SIR ANDREW. Now, sir, have I met you again?
    There's for you.

30 SEBASTIAN. Why, there's for thee, and there, and
    there. Are all the people mad?

SIR TOBY. Hold, sir, or I'll throw your dagger o'er
    the house.

CLOWN. This will I tell my lady straight. I would
35   not be in some of your coats for twopence.
                             [*Exit*]

SIR TOBY. Come on, sir. Hold.

SIR ANDREW. Nay, let him alone. I'll go another

way to work with him; I'll have an action of
battery against him, if there be any law in
Illyria. Though I struck him first, yet it's no   40
matter for that.

SEBASTIAN. Let go thy hand.

SIR TOBY. Come, sir, I will not let you go. Come,
    my young soldier, put up your iron. You are well
    fleshed;° come on.   45

SEBASTIAN. I will be free from thee. What wouldst
    thou now?
    If thou dar'st tempt me further, draw thy sword.

SIR TOBY. What, what? Nay, then I must have an
    ounce or two of this malapert° blood from you.   50

[*Enter* OLIVIA.]

OLIVIA. Hold, Toby! On thy life, I charge thee,
    hold!

SIR TOBY. Madam!

OLIVIA. Will it be ever thus? Ungracious wretch,
    Fit for the mountains and the barbarous caves,
    Where manners ne'er were preach'd! Out of my
       sight!   55
    Be not offended, dear Cesario.
    Rudesby,° be gone!

[*Exeunt* SIR TOBY, SIR ANDREW, *and* FABIAN.]
                  I prithee, gentle friend,
    Let thy fair wisdom, not thy passion, sway°
    In this uncivil and unjust extent°
    Against thy peace. Go with me to my house   60
    And hear thou there how many fruitless pranks
    This ruffian hath botch'd up, that thou thereby
    Mayst smile at this. Thou shalt not choose but
       go.
    Do not deny. Beshrew° his soul for me!
    He started° one poor heart° of mine in thee.   65

SEBASTIAN. What relish is in this? How runs the
    stream?
    Or I am mad, or° else this is a dream.
    Let fancy still my sense in Lethe° steep;
    If it be thus to dream, still let me sleep!

OLIVIA. Nay, come, I prithee. Would thou'dst be
    rul'd by me!   70

SEBASTIAN. Madam, I will.

OLIVIA.   O, say so, and so be! [*Exeunt*]

---

cockney foppish, affected person   ungird put off
foolish Greek merry jester (Greeks were associated with
  revelry)
after . . . purchase i.e., after they have paid for fourteen
  years

well fleshed warmed up   malapert impertinent
Rudesby ruffian   sway rule   extent assault
Beshrew curse   started startled
heart with pun on hart   Or . . . or either . . . or
Lethe river of oblivion

SCENE ii
OLIVIA's *house.*

[*Enter* MARIA *and* CLOWN.]

MARIA. Nay, I prithee, put on this gown and this
beard. Make him believe thou art Sir Topas the
curate. Do it quickly. I'll call Sir Toby the whilst.
[*Exit*]

5 CLOWN. Well, I'll put it on, and I will dissemble°
myself in 't, and I would I were the first that ever
dissembled in such a gown. I am not tall enough
to become the function° well, nor lean enough
to be thought a good student, but to be said an
honest man and a good housekeeper goes as
10 fairly as to say a careful man and a great scholar.
The competitors° enter.

[*Enter* SIR TOBY *and* MARIA.]

SIR TOBY. Jove bless thee, master Parson.

CLOWN. *Bonos dies,*° Sir Toby. For, as the old hermit
of Prague,° that never saw pen and ink, very
15 wittily said to a niece of King Gorboduc,° "That
that is is." So I, being master Parson, am master
Parson; for what is "that" but "that," and "is"
but "is"?

SIR TOBY. To him, Sir Topas.

20 CLOWN. What, ho, I say! Peace in this prison!

SIR TOBY. The knave counterfeits well; a good
knave.

MALVOLIO. [*Within*] Who calls there?

CLOWN. Sir Topas the curate, who comes to visit
25 Malvolio the lunatic.

MALVOLIO. Sir Topas, Sir Topas, good Sir Topas, go
to my lady.

CLOWN. Out, hyperbolical° fiend! How vexest
thou this man! Talkest thou nothing but of
30 ladies?

SIR TOBY. Well said, master Parson.

MALVOLIO. Sir Topas, never was man thus wronged. Good Sir Topas, do not think I am mad. They
have laid me here in hideous darkness.

35 CLOWN. Fie, thou dishonest Satan! I call thee by the
most modest terms, for I am one of those gentle
ones that will use the devil himself with courtesy. Sayest thou that house is dark?

MALVOLIO. As hell, Sir Topas.

---

dissemble disguise
become the function i.e., imitate a cleric
competitors accomplices
Bonos dies good day
hermit of Prague more learned nonsense
King Gorboduc legendary king of Britain, but a mere
  name here
hyperbolical extravagant (but the Fool is only using
  impressive words)

CLOWN. Why, it hath bay windows transparent as   40
barricadoes, and the clerestories toward the
south north are as lustrous as ebony. And yet
complainest thou of obstruction?

MALVOLIO. I am not mad, Sir Topas. I say to you,
this house is dark.   45

CLOWN. Madman, thou errest. I say, there is no
darkness but ignorance, in which thou art more
puzzled than the Egyptians in their fog.°

MALVOLIO. I say this house is as dark as ignorance,
though ignorance were as dark as hell, and I say   50
there was never man thus abused. I am no more
mad than you are. Make the trial of it in any
constant question.°

CLOWN. What is the opinion of Pythagoras° concerning wild fowl?   55

MALVOLIO. That the soul of our grandam might
haply inhabit a bird.

CLOWN. What thinkest thou of his opinion?

MALVOLIO. I think nobly of the soul, and no way
approve his opinion.   60

CLOWN. Fare thee well. Remain thou still in darkness. Thou shalt hold the opinion of Pythagoras
ere I will allow of thy wits, and fear to kill a
woodcock, lest thou dispossess the soul of thy
grandam. Fare thee well.   65

MALVOLIO. Sir Topas, Sir Topas!

SIR TOBY. My most exquisite Sir Topas!

CLOWN. Nay, I am for all waters.°

MARIA. Thou mightst have done this without thy
beard and gown. He sees thee not.   70

SIR TOBY. To him in thine own voice, and bring me
word how thou findest him. I would we were
well rid of this knavery. If he may be conveniently delivered, I would he were; for I am
now so far in offense with my niece that I cannot   75
pursue with any safety this sport to the upshot.
Come by and by to my chamber.

[*Exeunt* SIR TOBY *and* MARIA.]

CLOWN.

[*Singing*]   Hey, Robin, jolly Robin
                  Tell me how thy lady does

MALVOLIO. Fool—   80

CLOWN. "My lady is unkind, perdy."°

MALVOLIO. Fool—

CLOWN. "Alas, why is she so?"

MALVOLIO. Fool, I say—

Egyptians . . . fog Moses brought a three-day fog upon
  Egypt (see Exodus 10:22)
constant question coherent argument
Pythagoras Greek philosopher who originated the
  doctrine of the transmigration of souls
Nay . . . waters i.e., I'm good at everything
perdy by God

85 CLOWN. "She loves another"—Who calls, ha?

MALVOLIO. Good fool, as ever thou wilt deserve
well at my hand, help me to a candle, and pen,
ink, and paper. As I am a gentleman, I will live
to be thankful to thee for 't.

90 CLOWN. Master Malvolio!

MALVOLIO. Aye, good fool.

CLOWN. Alas, sir, how fell you besides your five
wits?

MALVOLIO. Fool, there was never man so notori-
95 ously abused. I am as well in my wits, fool, as
thou art.

CLOWN. But as well? Then you are mad indeed, if
you be no better in your wits than a fool.

MALVOLIO. They have here propertied° me, keep
100 me in darkness, send ministers to me, asses,
and do all they can to face me out of my wits.

CLOWN. Advise you what you say; the minister is
here. Malvolio, Malvolio, thy wits the heavens
restore! Endeavor thyself to sleep, and leave thy
105 vain bibble babble.

MALVOLIO. Sir Topas—

CLOWN. Maintain no words with him, good fellow.
Who, I sir? Not I, sir. God be wi' you, good Sir
Topas. Marry, amen. I will, sir, I will.

110 MALVOLIO. Fool, fool, fool, I say—

CLOWN. Alas, sir, be patient. What say you, sir? I
am shent° for speaking to you.

MALVOLIO. Good fool, help me to some light and
some paper. I tell thee, I am as well in my wits
115 as any man in Illyria.

CLOWN. Well-a-day that you were, sir!

MALVOLIO. By this hand, I am. Good fool, some
ink, paper, and light, and convey what I will set
down to my lady. It shall advantage thee more
120 than ever the bearing of letter did.

CLOWN. I will help you to 't. But tell me true, are
you not mad indeed? Or do you but counterfeit?

MALVOLIO. Believe me, I am not; I tell thee true.

CLOWN. Nay, I'll ne'er believe a madman till I see
125 his brains. I will fetch you light and paper and
ink.

MALVOLIO. Fool, I'll requite it in the highest
degree. I prithee, be gone.

CLOWN.

[Singing]   I am gone, sir,
130   And anon, sir,
         I'll be with you again,
              In a trice,
              Like to the old vice,°
         Your need to sustain,

Who, with dagger of lath,°   135
In his rage and his wrath,
     Cries, ah, ha! to the devil.
Like a mad lad,
Pare thy nails, dad;
     Adieu, goodman devil.   [Exit] 140

SCENE iii
Before OLIVIA's garden.

[Enter SEBASTIAN.]

SEBASTIAN. This is the air, that is the glorious sun,
This pearl she gave me, I do feel 't and see 't—
And though 'tis wonder that enwraps me thus,
Yet 'tis not madness. Where's Antonio, then?
I could not find him at the Elephant.   5
Yet there he was,° and there I found this credit,°
That he did range the town to seek me out.
His counsel now might do me golden service.
For though my soul disputes well with my sense
That this may be some error, but no madness,   10
Yet doth this accident and flood of fortune
So far exceed all instance, all discourse,
That I am ready to distrust mine eyes
And wrangle with my reason that persuades me
To any other trust but that I am mad,   15
Or else the lady's mad. Yet, if 'twere so,
She could not sway° her house, command her
     followers,
Take and give back affairs and their dispatch
With such a smooth, discreet, and stable bearing
As I perceive she does. There's something in 't 20
That is deceivable. But here the lady comes.

[Enter OLIVIA and PRIEST.]

OLIVIA. Blame not this haste of mine. If you mean
     well,
Now go with me and with this holy man
Into the chantry° by. There, before him,
And underneath that consecrated roof,   25
Plight me the full assurance of your faith,
That my most jealous° and too doubtful soul
May live at peace. He shall conceal it
Whiles° you are willing it shall come to note,
What° time we will our celebration° keep   30

---

propertied confined   shent rebuked
old vice a stock character in early drama

---

dagger of lath wooden sword used by the "old vice" to
     beat the devil and endeavor to pare his nails
was had been   credit report
sway govern   chantry chapel
jealous apprehensive   Whiles until
What at which
celebration i.e., the formal marriage ceremony, as
     opposed to the betrothal ceremony that is to be
     carried out immediately

According to° my birth. What do you say?
SEBASTIAN. I'll follow this good man, and go with
  you,
And, having sworn truth, ever will be true.

According to   as befits (my high birth)

OLIVIA. Then lead the way, good father; and
  heavens so shine
That they may fairly° note this act of mine!   35
                                        [*Exeunt*]

fairly   favorably

ACT V

SCENE i
Before OLIVIA's *house*.

[*Enter* CLOWN *and* FABIAN.]
FABIAN. Now, as thou lovest me, let me see his
  letter.
CLOWN. Good Master Fabian, grant me another
  request.
5 FABIAN. Anything.
CLOWN. Do not desire to see this letter.
FABIAN. This is to give a dog, and in recompense
  desire my dog again.
      [*Enter* DUKE, VIOLA, CURIO, *and* LORDS.]
DUKE. Belong you to the Lady Olivia, friends?
10 CLOWN. Aye, sir, we are some of her trappings.
DUKE. I know thee well. How dost thou, my good
  fellow?
CLOWN. Truly, sir, the better for my foes and the
  worse for my friends.
15 DUKE. Just the contrary—the better for thy friends.
CLOWN. No, sir, the worse.
DUKE. How can that be?
CLOWN. Marry, sir, they praise me and make an
  ass of me. Now my foes tell me plainly I am an
20 ass, so that by my foes, sir, I profit in the knowledge of myself, and by my friends I am abused.°
  So that, conclusions to be as kisses, if your four
  negatives make your two affirmatives, why then,
  the worse for my friends and the better for my
25 foes.°
DUKE. Why, this is excellent.
CLOWN. By my troth, sir, no, though it please you
  to be one of my friends.
DUKE. Thou shalt not be the worse for me. There's
30 gold.
CLOWN. But that it would be double-dealing,° sir,
  I would you could make it another.

abused   deceived
conclusions . . . foes   mere mock logic (but many sober
  Shakespeare scholars have struggled to make sense of
  the nonsense)
double-dealing   deceiving, with pun: double-giving

DUKE. O, you give me ill counsel.
CLOWN. Put your grace in your pocket, sir, for this
  once, and let your flesh and blood obey it.°   35
DUKE. Well, I will be so much a sinner, to° be a
  doubledealer. There's another.
CLOWN. Primo, secundo, tertio is a good play, and
  the old saying is, the third pays for all. The
  triplex, sir, is a good tripping measure; or the   40
  bells of Saint Bennet,° sir, may put you in mind:
  one, two, three.
DUKE. You can fool no more money out of me at
  this throw.° If you will let your lady know I am
  here to speak with her, and bring her along with   45
  you, it may awake my bounty further.
CLOWN. Marry, sir, lullaby to your bounty till I
  come again. I go, sir, but I would not have you to
  think that my desire of having is the sin of
  covetousness. But, as you say, sir, let your   50
  bounty take a nap; I will awake it anon.
                                        [*Exit*]
VIOLA. Here comes the man, sir, that did rescue
  me.
      [*Enter* ANTONIO *and* OFFICERS.]
DUKE. That face of his I do remember well;
  Yet when I saw it last it was besmear'd
  As black as Vulcan° in the smoke of war.   55
  A baubling° vessel was he captain of,
  For shallow draught and bulk unprizable,°
  With which such scathful° grapple did he make
  With the most noble bottom° of our fleet
  That very envy and the tongue of loss   60
  Cried fame and honor on him. What's the
  matter?

Put . . . it   be unrespectable enough, for once, to take ill
  counsel, and give me another coin   *to*   as to
Saint Bennet   St. Benedict's church in London
throw   of the dice—i.e., the Clown's attempt to extract a
  third coin
Vulcan   Roman god of fire; the blacksmith god
baubling   piddling; toy
unprizable   not worth taking   *scathful*   scathing
bottom   ship

First Officer. Orsino, this is that Antonio
  That took the Phoenix and her fraught° from
    Candy,
  And this is he that did the Tiger board
65 When your young nephew Titus lost his leg.
  Here in the streets, desperate° of shame and
    state,
  In private brabble° did we apprehend him.
Viola. He did me kindness, sir, drew on my side,
  But in conclusion put strange speech upon me.
70 I know not what 'twas but distraction.°
Duke. Notable pirate! Thou salt-water thief!
  What foolish boldness brought thee to their
    mercies
  Whom thou in terms so bloody and so dear°
  Hast made thine enemies?
Antonio.   Orsino, noble sir,
75 Be pleas'd that I shake off these names you give
    me.
  Antonio never yet was thief or pirate,
  Though I confess, on base and ground enough,
  Orsino's enemy. A witchcraft drew me hither.
  That most ingrateful boy there by your side
80 From the rude sea's enrag'd and foamy mouth
  Did I redeem. A wreck past hope he was.
  His life I gave him and did thereto add
  My love, without retention or restraint,
  All his in dedication. For his sake
85 Did I expose myself, pure° for his love,
  Into the danger of this adverse° town;
  Drew to defend him when he was beset,
  Where being apprehended, his false cunning,
  Not meaning to partake with me in danger,
90 Taught him to face me out of his acquaintance,°
  And grew a twenty years removed° thing
  While one would wink; denied me mine own
    purse,
  Which I had recommended to his use
  Not half an hour before.
Viola.   How can this be?
95 Duke. When came he to this town?
Antonio. Today, my lord, and for three months
    before,
  No interim, not a minute's vacancy,
  Both day and night did we keep company.
      [Enter Olivia and Attendants.]
Duke. Here comes the countess. Now heaven
    walks on earth!
100 But for thee, fellow. Fellow, thy words are
    madness.

Three months this youth hath tended upon me.
  But more of that anon. Take him aside.
Olivia. What would my lord but that he may not
    have,
  Wherein Olivia may seem serviceable?
  Cesario, you do not keep promise with me.   105
Viola. Madam!
Duke. Gracious Olivia—
Olivia. What do you say, Cesario? Good my lord—
Viola. My lord would speak; my duty hushes me.
Olivia. If it be aught to the old tune, my lord,   110
  It is as fat and fulsome to mine ear
  As howling after music.
Duke.   Still so cruel?
Olivia. Still so constant, lord.
Duke. What, to perverseness? You uncivil lady,
  To whose ingrate and unauspicious altars   115
  My soul the faithful'st off'rings hath breath'd
    out
  That e'er devotion tender'd! What shall I do?
Olivia. Even what it please my lord, that shall be-
    come him.
Duke. Why should I not, had I the heart to do it,
  Like to th' Egyptian thief° at point of death,   120
  Kill what I love?—a savage jealousy
  That sometimes savors nobly.° But hear me this.
  Since you to non-regardance cast my faith,
  And that I partly know the instrument
  That screws me from my true place in your 125
    favor,
  Live you the marble-breasted tyrant still.
  But this your minion,° whom I know you love,
  And whom, by heaven I swear, I tender dearly,
  Him will I tear out of that cruel eye
  Where he sits crowned in his master's spite.   130
  Come, boy, with me. My thoughts are ripe in
    mischief.
  I'll sacrifice the lamb that I do love
  To spite a raven's heart within a dove.
Viola. And I, most jocund, apt, and willingly,
  To do° you rest, a thousand deaths would die. 135
Olivia. Where goes Cesario?
Viola.   After him I love
  More than I love these eyes, more than my life,
  More, by all mores, than e'er I shall love wife.
  If I do feign, you witnesses above
  Punish my life for tainting of my love!   140
Olivia. Aye me, detested! How am I beguil'd!
Viola. Who does beguile you? Who does do you
    wrong?

fraught freight   desperate reckless
brabble brawl   distraction madness   dear costly
pure purely   adverse hostile
face . . . acquaintance pretend not to know me
removed estranged

Egyptian thief in Heliodorus' romance a robber who
  sought to kill his sweetheart to prevent her capture by
  enemies
savors nobly smacks of nobility   minion darling
do give

OLIVIA. Hast thou forgot thyself? Is it so long?
  Call forth the holy father.
DUKE.   Come, away!
145 OLIVIA. Whither, my lord? Cesario, husband, stay.
DUKE. Husband!
OLIVIA.   Aye, husband. Can he that deny?
DUKE. Her husband, sirrah!
VIOLA.   No, my lord, not I.
OLIVIA. Alas, it is the baseness of thy fear
  That makes thee strangle thy propriety.°
150 Fear not, Cesario; take thy fortunes up.
  Be that thou know'st thou art, and then thou
    art
  As great as that thou fear'st.
                 [Enter PRIEST.]
                              O, welcome, father!
  Father, I charge thee by thy reverence
  Here to unfold, though lately we intended
155 To keep in darkness what occasion now
  Reveals before 'tis ripe, what thou dost know
  Hath newly pass'd between this youth and me.
PRIEST. A contract of eternal bond of love,
  Confirm'd by mutual joinder of your hands,
160 Attested by the holy close of lips,
  Strengthen'd by interchangement of your rings,
  And all the ceremony of this compact
  Seal'd in my function,° by my testimony.
  Since when, my watch hath told me, toward my
    grave
165 I have travel'd but two hours.
DUKE. O thou dissembling cub! What wilt thou be
  When time hath sow'd a grizzle on thy case?°
  Or will not else thy craft so quickly grow
  That thine own trip° shall be thine overthrow?
170 Farewell, and take her, but direct thy feet
  Where thou and I henceforth may never meet.
VIOLA. My lord, I do protest—
OLIVIA.   O, do not swear!
  Hold little° faith, though thou hast too much
    fear.
                 [Enter SIR ANDREW.]
SIR ANDREW. For the love of God, a surgeon! Send
175 one presently° to Sir Toby.
OLIVIA. What's the matter?
SIR ANDREW. He has broke my head across and has
  given Sir Toby a bloody coxcomb too. For the
  love of God, your help! I had rather than forty
180 pound I were at home.
OLIVIA. Who has done this, Sir Andrew?
SIR ANDREW. The count's gentleman, one Cesario.

We took him for a coward, but he's the very
  devil incardinate.°
DUKE. My gentleman, Cesario?   185
SIR ANDREW. 'Od's lifelings,° here he is! You
  broke my head for nothing, and that that I did, I
  was set on to do 't by Sir Toby.
VIOLA. Why do you speak to me? I never hurt you.
  You drew your sword upon me without cause,   190
  But I bespake you fair and hurt you not.
SIR ANDREW. If a bloody coxcomb be a hurt, you
  have hurt me. I think you set nothing by a
  bloody coxcomb.
                 [Enter SIR TOBY and CLOWN.]
  Here comes Sir Toby halting;° you shall hear 195
  more. But if he had not been in drink, he would
  have tickled you othergates° than he did.
DUKE. How now, gentleman! How is 't with you?
SIR TOBY. That's all one. Has hurt me, and there's
  th' end on 't. Sot, didst see Dick surgeon, sot? 200
CLOWN. O, he's drunk, Sir Toby, an hour agone.
  His eyes were set at eight i' th' morning.
SIR TOBY. Then he's a rogue, and a passy measures
  pavin.° I hate a drunken rogue.
OLIVIA. Away with him! Who hath made this   205
  havoc with them?
SIR ANDREW. I'll help you, Sir Toby, because we'll
  be dressed together.
SIR TOBY. Will you help? An ass-head and a cox-
  comb and a knave, a thin-faced knave, a gull! 210
OLIVIA. Get him to bed, and let his hurt be look'd
  to.
            [Exeunt CLOWN, FABIAN, SIR TOBY, and
                              SIR ANDREW.]
                 [Enter SEBASTIAN.]
SEBASTIAN. I am sorry, madam, I have hurt your
    kinsman,
  But had it been the brother of my blood,
  I must have done no less with wit and safety.   215
  You throw a strange regard upon me, and by
    that
  I do perceive it hath offended you.
  Pardon me, sweet one, even for the vows
  We made each other but so late ago.
DUKE. One face, one voice, one habit, and two   220
    persons,
  A natural perspective,° that is and is not!
SEBASTIAN. Antonio, O my dear Antonio!
  How have the hours rack'd and tortur'd me
  Since I have lost thee!

strange thy propriety   deny your identity
function   authority
sow'd . . . case   raised gray hairs on your skin
trip   trickery   little   a little   presently   immediately

incardinate   blunder for incarnate
'Od's lifelings   God's little lives
halting   limping   othergates   otherwise
passy . . . pavin   eight-bar double-slow dance
natural perspective   optical illusion produced by nature

225 ANTONIO. Sebastian are you?

SEBASTIAN.   Fear'st° thou that, Antonio?

ANTONIO. How have you made division of yourself?
    An apple cleft in two is not more twin
    Than these two creatures. Which is Sebastian?

OLIVIA. Most wonderful!

230 SEBASTIAN. Do I stand there? I never had a brother,
    Nor can there be that deity in my nature
    Of here and everywhere. I had a sister,
    Whom the blind waves and surges have de-
        vour'd.
    Of charity,° what kin are you to me?

235 What countryman? What name? What parent-
        age?

VIOLA. Of Messaline. Sebastian was my father;
    Such a Sebastian was my brother too.
    So went he suited to his watery tomb.
    If spirits can assume both form and suit,

240 You come to fright us.

SEBASTIAN.   A spirit I am indeed,
    But am in that dimension° grossly clad
    Which from the womb I did participate.°
    Were you a woman, as the rest goes even,
    I should my tears let fall upon your cheek,

245 And say "Thrice welcome, drowned Viola!"

VIOLA. My father had a mole upon his brow.

SEBASTIAN. And so had mine.

VIOLA. And died that day when Viola from her
        birth
    Had number'd thirteen years.

250 SEBASTIAN. O, that record is lively in my soul!
    He finished indeed his mortal act
    That day that made my sister thirteen years.

VIOLA. If nothing lets° to make us happy both
    But this my masculine usurp'd attire,

255 Do not embrace me till each circumstance
    Of place, time, fortune do cohere and jump°
    That I am Viola. Which to confirm,
    I'll bring you to a captain in this town,
    Where lie my maiden weeds, by whose gentle
        help

260 I was preserv'd to serve this noble count.
    All the occurrence of my fortune since
    Hath been between this lady and this lord.

SEBASTIAN. [To OLIVIA] So comes it, lady, you have
        been mistook.
    But nature to her bias drew in that.°

265 You would have been contracted to a maid,
    Nor are you therein, by my life, deceiv'd.
    You are betroth'd both to a maid and man.

DUKE. Be not amaz'd; right noble is his blood.
    If this be so, as yet the glass seems true,
    I shall have share in this most happy wreck.   270
    [To VIOLA] Boy, thou hast said to me a thousand
        times
    Thou never shouldst love woman like to me.

VIOLA. And all those sayings will I over-swear,
    And all those swearings keep as true in soul
    As doth that orbed continent° the fire   275
    That severs day from night.

DUKE.   Give me thy hand,
    And let me see thee in thy woman's weeds.

VIOLA. The captain that did bring me first on shore
    Hath my maid's garments. He upon some action
    Is now in durance,° at Malvolio's suit,   280
    A gentleman, and follower of my lady's.

OLIVIA. He shall enlarge° him; fetch Malvolio
        hither.
    And yet, alas, now I remember me,
    They say, poor gentleman, he's much distract.
        [Re-enter CLOWN with a letter, and FABIAN.]
    A most extracting° frenzy of mine own   285
    From my remembrance clearly banish'd his.
    How does he, sirrah?

CLOWN. Truly, madam, he holds Belzebub at the
    stave's end° as well as a man in his case may do.
    Has here writ a letter to you; I should have given 290
    't you today morning, but as a madman's
    epistles are no gospels, so it skills° not much
    when they are delivered.

OLIVIA. Open 't and read it.

CLOWN. Look then to be well edified when the fool   295
    delivers the madman. [Reads] By the Lord,
    madam—

OLIVIA. How now! Art thou mad?

CLOWN. No, madam, I do but read madness. An
    your ladyship will have it as it ought to be, you
    must allow Vox.°   300

OLIVIA. Prithee, read i' thy right wits.

CLOWN. So I do, madonna, but to read his right
    wits is to read thus. Therefore perpend,° my
    princess, and give ear.

OLIVIA. Read it you, sirrah.   [To FABIAN.]   305

FABIAN.

    [Reads] By the Lord, madam, you wrong me,
    and the world shall know it. Though you have
    put me into darkness and given your drunken
    cousin rule over me, yet have I the benefit of my

Fear'st doubt'st   Of charity in kindness
dimension form   participate inherit
lets hinders   jump agree
But . . . that nature followed her proper course in that

orbed continent the sun
in durance imprisoned   enlarge free
extracting distracting   holds . . . end holds the devil off
skills matters
Vox voice (the Clown had begun to read in Malvolio's
    loud voice)
perpend consider

310 senses as well as your ladyship. I have your own
letter that induced me to the semblance I put
on, with the which I doubt not but to do myself
much right, or you much shame. Think of me
as you please. I leave my duty a little unthought
315 of, and speak out of° my injury.
THE MADLY-USED MALVOLIO.

OLIVIA. Did he write this?
CLOWN. Aye, madam.
DUKE. This savors not much of distraction.
OLIVIA. See him deliver'd, Fabian. Bring him
hither.   [Exit FABIAN.]
320 My lord, so please you, these things further
thought on,
To think me as well a sister° as a wife,
One day shall crown th' alliance on 't, so please
you,
Here at my house and at my proper° cost.
DUKE. Madam, I am most apt t'embrace your offer.
325 [To VIOLA] Your master quits° you. And for
your service done him,
So much against the mettle of your sex,
So far beneath your soft and tender breeding,
And since you call'd me master for so long,
Here is my hand. You shall from this time be
330 Your master's mistress.
OLIVIA.   A sister! You are she.
[Re-enter FABIAN, with MALVOLIO.]
DUKE. Is this the madman?
OLIVIA.   Aye, my lord, this same.
How now, Malvolio!
MALVOLIO.   Madam, you have done me wrong,
Notorious wrong.
OLIVIA.   Have I, Malvolio? No.
MALVOLIO. Lady, you have. Pray you, peruse that
letter.
335 You must not now deny it is your hand.
Write from it, if you can, in hand or phase,
Or say 'tis not your seal, not your invention.°
You can say none of this. Well, grant it then,
And tell me, in the modesty of honor,°
340 Why you have given me such clear lights° of
favor,
Bade me come smiling and cross-garter'd to you,
To put on yellow stockings, and to frown
Upon Sir Toby and the lighter° people.
And, acting this in an obedient hope,
345 Why have you suffer'd me to be imprison'd,
Kept in a dark house, visited by the priest,

And made the most notorious geck and gull°
That e'er invention play'd on? Tell me why.
OLIVIA. Alas, Malvolio, this is not my writing,
Though, I confess, much like the character.   350
But out of question 'tis Maria's hand.
And now I do bethink me, it was she
First told me thou wast mad; then cam'st in
smiling,
And in such forms which here were presuppos'd°
Upon thee in the letter. Prithee, be content.   355
This practice° hath most shrewdly° pass'd upon
thee;
But when we know the grounds and authors of
it,
Thou shalt be both the plaintiff and the judge
Of thine own cause.
FABIAN.   Good madam, hear me speak,
And let no quarrel nor no brawl to come   360
Taint the condition of this present hour,
Which I have wonder'd° at. In hope it shall not,
Most freely I confess, myself and Toby
Set this device against Malvolio here,
Upon° some stubborn and uncourteous parts   365
We had conceiv'd against him. Maria writ
The letter at Sir Toby's great importance,°
In recompense whereof he hath married her.
How with a sportful malice it was follow'd
May rather pluck on laughter than revenge,   370
If that the injuries be justly weigh'd
That have on both sides pass'd.
OLIVIA. Alas, poor fool, how have they baffled°
thee!
CLOWN. Why, "some are born great, some achieve
greatness, and some have greatness thrown   375
upon them." I was one, sir, in this interlude, one
Sir Topas, sir. But that's all one. "By the Lord,
fool, I am not mad." But do you remember?
"Madam, why laugh you at such a barren rascal?
An you smile not, he's gagged." And thus the   380
whirligig of time brings in his revenges.
MALVOLIO. I'll be reveng'd on the whole pack of
you.   [Exit]
OLIVIA. He hath been most notoriously abus'd.
DUKE. Pursue him, and entreat him to a peace;   385
He hath not told us of the captain yet.
When that is known, and golden time convents,°
A solemn combination shall be made
Of our dear souls. Meantime, sweet sister,

I . . . of I momentarily forget my place
sister sister-in-law   *proper* own
quits releases   *from* differently from
invention composition   *in . . . honor* in plain decency
lights indications   *lighter* lesser

geck and gull fool and dupe
in . . . presuppos'd in the style of dress and manner that
was proposed beforehand
practice plot   *shrewdly* maliciously
wonder'd marveled   *Upon* because of
importance importunity
baffled abused   *convents* accords

390 We will not part from hence. Cesario, come—
For so you shall be, while you are a man.
But when in other habits you are seen,
Orsino's mistress and his fancy's° queen.
                              [*Exeunt all, except* CLOWN.]
CLOWN.

[*Sings*] When that I was and a little tiny boy,
395   With hey, ho, the wind and the rain,
A foolish thing was but a toy,
          For the rain, it raineth every day.

But when I came to man's estate,
          With hey, ho, the wind and the rain,
400 'Gainst knaves and thieves men shut their gate,
          For the rain, it raineth every day.

But when I came, alas! to wive,
          With hey, ho, the wind and the rain,
By swaggering could I never thrive,
          For the rain, it raineth every day.   405

But when I came unto my beds,
          With hey, ho, the wind and the rain,
With tosspots° still had drunken heads,
          For the rain, it raineth every day.

A great while ago the world begun,   410
          With hey, ho, the wind and the rain,
But that's all one, our play is done,
          And we'll strive to please you every day.
                              [*Exit*]

fancy's love's   *tosspots* drunkards

AFTERWORD

Not every critic has been overly fond of *Twelfth Night*. The romantics of the early nineteenth century generally adored it but were disposed to find Shakespeare too severe in his treatment of Malvolio, an impression that no doubt derived in part from the practice of contemporary actors in making him a grand and tragic figure. Thus Charles Lamb, writing in the first quarter of the century:

> Bensley . . . threw over the part an air of Spanish loftiness. He looked, spake, and moved like an old Castilian. He was starch, spruce, opinionated, but his superstructure of pride seemed bottomed upon a sense of worth. There was something in it beyond the coxcomb. It was big and swelling, but you could not be sure that it was hollow. You might wish to see it taken down, but you felt that it was upon an elevation. He was magnificent from the outset . . . you would have thought that the hero of La Mancha in person stood before you . . . I confess that I never saw the catastrophe of this character, while Bensley played it, without a kind of tragic interest.

Earlier, Dr. Johnson found Malvolio "truly comic; he is betrayed to ridicule merely by his pride." But Dr. Johnson also found the great "perplexity" of the main action, "though well enough contrived to divert in the stage," wanting in credibility; he added, with typical Johnsonian finality, the play "fails to produce the proper instruction required in the drama, as it exhibits no just picture of life."

Earlier still, Samuel Pepys, who saw the play repeatedly during the 1660's, liked it less well each time he went to the theater. In 1661 he found it all merely "a burthern to me." In 1663 it appeared "but a silly play." In 1669 it was "one of the weakest plays that ever I saw on the stage." Evidently for Pepys *Twelfth Night* came at last to rival *A Midsummer Night's Dream*, which, in 1662, he had pronounced to be "the most insipid, ridiculous play that ever I saw in my life."

A principal complaint of Pepys was that *Twelfth Night* does not "relate at all to the name or day." He meant, of course, Twelfth Night, the eve of Twelfth Day, January 6, the festivities of which brought the Christmas season to an end. Superficially, he was quite correct, of course; there is no mention of or specific relevance to this traditional "last fling" of Christmas celebration, though a biting reference to cakes and ale is addressed to Malvolio: "Dost thou think, because thou art virtuous, there shall be no more cakes and ale?" (It is this basic philosophical difference between Sir Toby and Maria, on the one hand, and Malvolio, on the other, that precipitates the forged letter and the rest of the prank that is the high point of the fun in *Twelfth Night*, for Malvolio is "a kind of puritan," who will neither indulge himself nor suffer others to indulge themselves.)

But in a profounder sense *Twelfth Night* does indeed relate to "the name or day," for as Twelfth Night is the "last fling" of Christmas, so was *Twelfth Night* the last fling of Shakespearean "romantic comedy": after it, abruptly, the dramatic world turned darker, bringing in the "bitter comedies" of *All's Well That Ends Well*, *Measure for Measure*, *Troilus and Cressida* and the tragedies of *Hamlet*, *Othello*, *King Lear*, *Macbeth*. And for the age, too, 1600, the year of *Twelfth Night*, was a "last fling" of sorts, when the glorious exuberance of Elizabeth's reign had begun to give way to the new and grimmer temper of the seventeenth century.

In the judgment of many critics, readers, and playgoers, *Twelfth Night* represents the pinnacle of Shakespearean comedy. It was written at the peak of Shakespeare's dramatic career, when he was perfect and easy master of poetic and dramatic techniques and while the spirit of the Renaissance still flowed robustly both in him and in the age. It is perhaps the gayest, the most hilarious of the romantic comedies:

> VIOLA. What country, friends, is this?
> CAPTAIN. This is Illyria, lady.

And Illyria indeed it is, a country hardly to be located geographically, but readily identifiable as a condition of mind and spirit, the name itself suggesting Elysia, illusion, delirium. What has made it the most popular of all the romantic comedies, the most frequently acted during more than three centuries, is no doubt its rollicking pace, its abundance of incident, its extraordinary measure of memorable comic figures: Sir Toby Belch, a kind of Illyrian Falstaff, and a lover of drink, as his name suggests, though he prefers to blame his condition on herring; Sir Andrew Aguecheek, the brainless knight; Maria, the diminutive dynamo of Olivia's household, perhaps second only to Beatrice of *Much Ado About Nothing* as the brightest female wit in all Shakespeare; Feste, the Clown, who shares with Touchstone of *As You Like It* and King Lear's bitter fool the highest place among professional jesters; and finally the sedate and humorless Malvolio, whose antics as the butt of Maria's merciless plot constitute the high point of the comic action. From the eighteenth century to our own day, in this play it is the role of Malvolio that the greatest actors, comic and tragic alike, have preferred to play.

Dr. Johnson, temperamentally incapable of entering into the spirit of Illyria, nevertheless acknowledged that the incidents are "well enough contrived to divert in the stage." He might well have added that these incidents are even more abundant than in any other of Shakespeare's comedies, that they are uncommonly lively, intricately interrelated, artistically balanced and controlled so that they underscore and enhance the effects of one another. In no other comedy are there plots so numerous and so diverse going forward either simultaneously or in swift succession. In her disguise, Viola deceives everyone in Illyria, and out of this enveloping and enduring situation come incessant confusion and comic incident. Meanwhile Sir Toby continues to gull Sir Andrew for the purpose of consuming the contents of his well-supplied purse, Sir Andrew being all the while sufficiently ingenuous to suppose that his amorous suit to Olivia stands a chance of success. Maria devises a wicked plot that is designed to put Malvolio in his place once and for all. The lovesick Orsino vainly persists in wooing the reluctant Olivia—who, equally vainly, strives to maintain an attitude of mourning in the midst of a household filled with zany servants and relatives. Viola, in boy's guise, falls in love with the Duke. Olivia falls in love with Viola. Sir Andrew's jealousy of Viola is kindled by Sir Toby, who brings the affair to the verge of a duel of singular ferocity. Throughout the play, while one plot is just being hatched, a second is nearing the point of overt action, a third is in the midst of its exploitation, and a fourth has just been brought to its conclusion. There are no dull moments in *Twelfth Night*.

But it is a fact that frivolity and wild abandon comprise only half the elements of a last fling. Characteristically such an occasion is marked also by a hint of underlying melancholy, a sadness for what has passed or is passing, an anxiety for the morrow; a note of suppressed desperation hangs over every final fling and is perhaps the true cause of the very wildness of the frivolity. *Twelfth Night* is Shakespeare's best case in point. It is replete with poignant stabs to the heart and with melancholy. These effects do not nullify the general hilarity; they enrich it and greatly deepen the total experience of the play.

It is noteworthy, on reflection, that none of the inhabitants of Illyria whose antics and predicaments make us laugh is himself happy. Orsino languishes in hopeless love of Olivia. Olivia has vowed to weep for seven years for her dead brother. Viola believes her own twin brother drowned, falls hopelessly in love with Orsino, is steadily distressed throughout the action, and feels incapable of coping with her man's role. Sir Andrew is frustrated in his pursuit of Olivia; perhaps Sir Toby's drinking problem is the result of personal, multiple frustrations; Maria's sharp practice of revenge against Malvolio and the fact that she ultimately elopes with Sir Toby imply frustrations of her own. The Clown, Feste, is anxious and in trouble when we first meet him, and all his songs are tinged with bittersweet reflection: "Then come kiss me, sweet and twenty,/ Youth's a stuff will not endure." The note of desperation hovers over the whole of the famous drunken cater-wauling scene (II, iii) that Malvolio interrupts. As for Malvolio himself, whose grotesque exhibition of his suppressed desires and ambitions provides the comic zenith of the play, he is surely one of the least content of mortals; his role is favored by tragic actors more famous in the roles of Hamlet, Othello, and Lear; and he has brought forth cries from the more sentimental critics of "By Heaven, the man is wronged!"

The note of poignancy that persists even in moments of hilarity is further accentuated by the special quality of femininity that Shakespeare bestows on the two leading women of the play and by the special quality of the poetry that he writes for them to speak. Olivia is one of Shakespeare's *gentlest* ladies, in both the modern and Elizabethan senses of the word. If the three situations in which she is shown—first striving to keep up an attitude of mourning in a household that makes mere sobriety impossible; then falling suddenly, unexpectedly ("Even so quickly may one catch the plague?") in love with a handsome youth whom we know to be no man at all; then mistaking Sebastian for Cesario and marrying him before he can catch his breath—if these situations are in themselves comic, bordering on the ludicrous, yet the lady herself is thoroughly noble and good, and the very fineness of her nature all but forbids a smile at her expense. Somewhat the same must be said of Viola, perhaps the most feminine and gentle of Shakespeare's adventurous heroines who go masquerading in the identities of young gentlemen, the least able of them all to carry off the role with relish and a swagger. When she finds herself in difficulties, she cries, "O Time! Thou must untangle this, not I!/ It is too hard a knot for me t'untie," and more than once she is at the point of abandoning her masquerade. She is a bright heroine, but she is not, like Rosalind of *As You Like It* and Portia of *The Merchant of Venice*—to say nothing of the awesome Helena of *All's Well That Ends Well*—capable of dealing handily with whatever awkward situation may arise.

In the midst of a laughable situation, Shakespeare writes poetry for the ladies that compels contrary emotions to come into play and wrestle with laughter for supremacy. "My father had a daughter lov'd a man," says Viola-Cesario to Orsino, "As it might be, perhaps, were I a woman,/ I should your lordship." "And what's her history," inquires the unsuspecting Duke. The tenderness with which Shakespeare everywhere surrounds his exquisitely feminine heroine is lavished upon the poetry of Viola's gently ironic reply:

> A blank, my lord. She never told her love,
> But let concealment, like a worm i' the bud,
> Feed on her damask cheek. She pin'd in thought,
> And with a green and yellow melancholy
> She sat like patience on a monument,
> Smiling at grief.

It is insufficient to assert that Shakespeare rarely wrote better poetry; but it is appropriate to insist that he never wrote "righter" poetry to satisfy all the complex demands of a particular occasion. But exactly the same must be said of lines that he gives to Olivia at the heart of a situation that is comic, potentially even grossly so. It is when Olivia confesses her love for "Cesario," whom we know to be a woman no less feminine than herself. "A cypress, not a bosom,/ Hides my heart," says Olivia, and she goes on:

> Cesario, by the roses of the spring,
> By maidhood, honor, truth, and everything,
> I love thee so that, maugre all thy pride,
> Nor wit nor reason can my passion hide.

With such language Shakespeare disarms laughter even in the midst of an hilarious situation; hilarity is tempered with sentiment, and the emotional demands placed upon the audience are multiple and complex, like the emotions that are implied in the idea of a "last fling." *Twelfth Night* is the richer for its blend of the comic and the poignant, and no comedy of Shakespeare's better achieves the rare artistic balance of these two.

But lest we grow too contemplative in analyzing this artistic blend, there is a final perfection in the note on which the play ends, a note that sets the ultimate perspective and that is no doubt responsible for the fact that audiences go away happier and more thoroughly satisfied from a brilliant *Twelfth Night* than from any other play that immediately comes to mind. "The rain, it raineth every day," sings the joyous-melancholy Clown, in reminding us not to take it all too seriously:

> A great while ago the world begun,
> With hey, ho, the wind and the rain,
> But that's all one, our play is done,
> And we'll strive to please you every day.

A NOTE ON THE COMPOSITION OF THE PLAY

The most probable date for the composition of *Twelfth Night* is 1600, and the play was probably first performed on Twelfth Night (January 6) in 1601. It was first published in the Folio of 1623. Shakespeare's immediate source for the main plot was Barnabe Riche's tale of "Apolonius and Silla," an English rendering of a much-told story probably deriving ultimately from an Italian play of the early sixteenth century; but, within the general frame, characterizations and dramatic detail were original with Shakespeare.

Julius Caesar

DRAMATIS PERSONÆ

JULIUS CÆSAR
OCTAVIUS CÆSAR
MARCUS ANTONIUS ⎬ *triumvirs after the death of*
M. AEMIL. LEPIDUS ⎭ *Julius Cæsar*
CICERO
PUBLIUS ⎬ *senators*
POPILIUS LENA ⎭
MARCUS BRUTUS
CASSIUS
CASCA
TREBONIUS ⎬ *conspirators against Julius*
LIGARIUS ⎭ *Cæsar*
DECIUS BRUTUS
METELLUS CIMBER
CINNA
FLAVIUS *and* MARULLUS   *tribunes*
ARTEMIDORUS   *of Cnidos, a teacher of Rhetoric*
A SOOTHSAYER
ANOTHER POET

LUCILIUS
TITINIUS
MESSALA ⎬ *friends to Brutus and Cassius*
YOUNG CATO
VOLUMNIUS
VARRO
CLITUS
CLAUDIUS ⎬ *servants to Brutus*
STRATO
LUCIUS
DARDANIUS
PINDARUS   *servant to Cassius*
CALPURNIA   *wife to Cæsar*
PORTIA   *wife to Brutus*
SENATORS, CITIZENS, GUARDS, ATTENDANTS, etc.

SCENE: *Rome; the neighborhood of Sardis; the neighborhood of Philippi*

ACT I

SCENE i
Rome. A street.

[*Enter* FLAVIUS, MARULLUS, *and certain* COMMONERS.]
FLAVIUS. Hence! Home, you idle creatures, get you
home.
Is this a holiday? What, know you not,
Being mechanical,° you ought not walk
Upon a laboring day without the sign°
5 Of your profession? Speak, what trade art thou?
CARPENTER. Why, sir, a carpenter.
MARULLUS. Where is thy leather apron and thy
rule?

What dost thou with thy best apparel on?
You, sir, what trade are you?
COBBLER. Truly, sir, in respect of° a fine workman, 10
I am but, as you would say, a cobbler.°
MARULLUS. But what trade art thou? Answer me
directly.
COBBLER. A trade, sir, that I hope I may use with a
safe conscience; which is indeed, sir, a mender of
bad soles. 15
MARULLUS. What trade, thou knave? Thou naughty
knave,° what trade?

in . . . of in comparison with
cobbler bungler (with pun)
naughty knave wicked rascal

mechanical workers   *sign* i.e., tools and garb

COBBLER. Nay, I beseech you, sir, be not out with
    me. Yet if you be out,° sir, I can mend you.
MARULLUS. What mean'st thou by that? Mend me,
20   thou saucy fellow!
COBBLER. Why, sir, cobble you.
FLAVIUS. Thou art a cobbler, art thou?
COBBLER. Truly, sir, all that I live by is with the
    awl. I meddle with no tradesman's matters, nor
25   women's matters, but with awl. I am indeed, sir,
    a surgeon to old shoes; when they are in great
    danger, I recover them. As proper° men as ever
    trod upon neat's leather° have gone upon my
    handiwork.
30 FLAVIUS. But wherefore art not in thy shop today?
    Why dost thou lead these men about the streets?
COBBLER. Truly, sir, to wear out their shoes, to get
    myself into more work. But indeed, sir, we make
    holiday to see Cæsar and to rejoice in his
35   triumph.
MARULLUS. Wherefore rejoice? What conquest
    brings he home?
    What tributaries° follow him to Rome
    To grace in captive bonds his chariot wheels?
    You blocks, you stones, you worse than senseless
    things!
40   O you hard hearts, you cruel men of Rome,
    Knew you not Pompey?° Many a time and oft
    Have you climb'd up to walls and battlements,
    To towers and windows, yea, to chimney tops,
    Your infants in your arms, and there have sat
45   The livelong day with patient expectation
    To see great Pompey pass the streets of Rome.
    And when you saw his chariot but appear,
    Have you not made an universal shout,
    That° Tiber trembled underneath her banks
50   To hear the replication° of your sounds
    Made in her concave shores?
    And do you now put on your best attire?
    And do you now cull out° a holiday?
    And do you now strew flowers in his way
55   That comes in triumph over Pompey's blood?°
    Be gone!
    Run to your houses, fall upon your knees,
    Pray to the gods to intermit° the plague
    That needs must light on this ingratitude.
FLAVIUS. Go, go, good countrymen, and for this
60   fault

    Assemble all the poor men of your sort.
    Draw them to Tiber banks and weep your tears
    Into the channel till the lowest stream
    Do kiss the most exalted shores of all.
                     [Exeunt all the COMMONERS.]
    See whe'er their basest metal° be not mov'd;   65
    They vanish tongue-tied in their guiltiness.
    Go you down that way towards the Capitol;
    This way will I. Disrobe the images
    If you do find them deck'd with ceremonies.°
MARULLUS. May we do so?   70
    You know it is the feast of Lupercal.°
FLAVIUS. It is no matter; let no images
    Be hung with Cæsar's trophies. I'll about
    And drive away the vulgar from the streets.
    So do you too, where you perceive them thick.   75
    These growing feathers pluck'd from Cæsar's
    wing
    Will make him fly an ordinary pitch,
    Who else would soar above the view of men
    And keep us all in servile fearfulness.   *[Exeunt]*

SCENE ii
A public place.

[*Flourish. Enter* CÆSAR; ANTONY, *for the course;*°
    CALPURNIA, PORTIA, DECIUS, CICERO, BRUTUS,
    CASSIUS, *and* CASCA; *a great crowd following,
        among them a* SOOTHSAYER.]
CÆSAR. Calpurnia!
CASCA.   Peace, ho! Cæsar speaks.
                            [Music ceases.]
CÆSAR.   Calpurnia!
CALPURNIA. Here, my lord.
CÆSAR. Stand you directly in Antonius' way
    When he doth run his course. Antonius!
ANTONY. Cæsar, my lord?   5
CÆSAR. Forget not in your speed, Antonius,
    To touch Calpurnia; for our elders say
    The barren, touched in this holy chase,
    Shake off their sterile curse.°
ANTONY.   I shall remember.
    When Cæsar says "do this," it is perform'd.   10
CÆSAR. Set on, and leave no ceremony out.
                            [Flourish.]
SOOTHSAYER. Cæsar!
CÆSAR. Ha! Who calls?
CASCA. Bid every noise be still. Peace yet again!

---

out . . . out angry . . . worn out   *proper* worthy
neat's leather cowhide   *tributaries* captives
Pompey Gnaeus Pompeius Magnus (defeated by Caesar
    in 48 B.C., thereafter murdered in Egypt)
That so that   *replication* echo
cull out i.e., proclaim
Pompey's blood Caesar had just defeated Pompey's sons
intermit withhold

their . . . metal (even) their gross emotions
ceremonies decorative trappings
Lupercal fertility festival in honor of Lupercus (Pan)
Antony . . . course i.e., dressed to run the race
sterile curse curse of sterility

15 CÆSAR. Who is it in the press that calls on me?
   I hear a tongue, shriller than all the music,
   Cry "Cæsar." Speak; Cæsar is turn'd to hear.
SOOTHSAYER. Beware the ides of March.
CÆSAR.   What man is that?
BRUTUS. A soothsayer° bids you beware the ides of
   March.°
20 CÆSAR. Set him before me. Let me see his face.
CASSIUS. Fellow, come from the throng; look upon
   Cæsar.
CÆSAR. What say'st thou to me now? Speak once
   again.
SOOTHSAYER. Beware the ides of March.
CÆSAR. He is a dreamer. Let us leave him. Pass.
   [Sennet. Exeunt all but BRUTUS and CASSIUS.]
25 CASSIUS. Will you go see the order of the course?
BRUTUS. Not I.
CASSIUS. I pray you, do.
BRUTUS. I am not gamesome.° I do lack some part
   Of that quick spirit° that is in Antony.
30 Let me not hinder, Cassius, your desires.
   I'll leave you.
CASSIUS. Brutus, I do observe you now of late.
   I have not from your eyes that gentleness
   And show of love as I was wont to have.
35 You bear too stubborn and too strange a hand
   Over your friend that loves you.
BRUTUS.   Cassius,
   Be not deceiv'd. If I have veil'd my look,
   I turn the trouble of my countenance
   Merely upon myself. Vexed I am
40 Of late with passions of some difference,°
   Conceptions only proper to° myself,
   Which give some soil° perhaps to my behaviors.
   But let not therefore my good friends be
   griev'd—
   Among which number, Cassius, be you one—
45 Nor construe any further my neglect
   Than that poor Brutus, with himself at war,
   Forgets the shows of love to other men.
CASSIUS. Then, Brutus, I have much mistook your
   passion;°
   By means whereof this breast of mine hath buried
50 Thoughts of great value, worthy cogitations.
   Tell me, good Brutus, can you see your face?
BRUTUS. No, Cassius, for the eye sees not itself
   But by reflection, by some other things.
CASSIUS. 'Tis just°—
55 And it is very much lamented, Brutus,

That you have no such mirrors as will turn
Your hidden worthiness into your eye,
That you might see your shadow. I have heard
Where many of the best respect° in Rome,
Except immortal Cæsar, speaking of Brutus   60
And groaning underneath this age's yoke,
Have wish'd that noble Brutus had his eyes.
BRUTUS. Into what dangers would you lead me,
   Cassius,
   That you would have me seek into myself
   For that which is not in me?   65
CASSIUS. Therefore, good Brutus, be prepar'd to
   hear;
   And since you know you cannot see yourself
   So well as by reflection, I your glass
   Will modestly discover° to yourself
   That of yourself which you yet know not of.   70
   And be not jealous on° me, gentle Brutus.
   Were I a common laugher, or did use
   To stale° with ordinary oaths my love
   To every new protester;° if you know
   That I do fawn on men and hug them hard,   75
   And after scandal° them; or if you know
   That I profess myself° in banqueting
   To all the rout—then hold me dangerous.
                          [Flourish and shout.]
BRUTUS. What means this shouting? I do fear the
   people
   Choose Cæsar for their king.
CASSIUS.   Aye, do you fear it?   80
   Then must I think you would not have it so.
BRUTUS. I would not, Cassius, yet I love him well.
   But wherefore do you hold me here so long?
   What is it that you would impart to me?
   If it be aught toward the general good,   85
   Set honor in one eye and death i' th' other,
   And I will look on both indifferently.°
   For let the gods so speed° me as I love
   The name of honor more than I fear death.
CASSIUS. I know that virtue to be in you, Brutus,   90
   As well as I do know your outward favor.°
   Well, honor is the subject of my story.
   I cannot tell what you and other men
   Think of this life, but, for my single self,
   I had as lief not be as live to be   95
   In awe of such a thing as I myself.
   I was born free as Cæsar; so were you.
   We both have fed as well, and we can both
   Endure the winter's cold as well as he.

---

soothsayer truth-teller, i.e., prophet
ides of March March 15   gamesome sportive
quick lively
passions . . . difference contradictory feelings
only proper to of concern only to   soil fault
passion feelings   just true

respect place   discover disclose
jealous on suspicious of   stale cheapen
protester i.e., of friendship   scandal slander
profess myself flaunt my friendliness
indifferently impartially   speed favor
favor appearance

100 For once upon a raw and gusty day,
    The troubled Tiber chafing with° her shores,
    Cæsar said to me, "Dar'st thou, Cassius, now
    Leap in with me into this angry flood
    And swim to yonder point?" Upon the word,
105 Accoutred as I was, I plunged in
    And bade him follow; so indeed he did.
    The torrent roar'd, and we did buffet it
    With lusty sinews, throwing it aside
    And stemming it with hearts of controversy.
110 But ere we could arrive the point propos'd,
    Cæsar cried, "Help me, Cassius, or I sink!"
    I, as Æneas° our great ancestor
    Did from the flames of Troy upon his shoulder
    The old Anchises bear, so from the waves of
    Tiber
115 Did I the tired Cæsar. And this man
    Is now become a god, and Cassius is
    A wretched creature and must bend his body
    If Cæsar carelessly but nod on him.
    He had a fever when he was in Spain,
120 And when the fit was on him, I did mark
    How he did shake. 'Tis true, this god did shake;
    His coward lips did from their color fly,
    And that same eye whose bend° doth awe the
    world
    Did lose his° luster. I did hear him groan.
    Aye, and that tongue of his that bade the
125 Romans
    Mark him and write his speeches in their books,
    Alas, it cried, "Give me some drink, Titinius,"
    As a sick girl. Ye gods! It doth amaze me
    A man of such a feeble temper should
130 So get the start of the majestic world
    And bear the palm° alone.   [Shout. Flourish.]
    BRUTUS. Another general shout!
    I do believe that these applauses are
    For some new honors that are heap'd on Cæsar.
    CASSIUS. Why, man, he doth bestride the narrow
135 world
    Like a Colossus,° and we petty men
    Walk under his huge legs and peep about
    To find ourselves dishonorable graves.
    Men at some time are masters of their fates;
140 The fault, dear Brutus, is not in our stars
    But in ourselves that we are underlings.

    Brutus and Cæsar: what should be in that
    Cæsar?
    Why should that name be sounded more than
    yours?
    Write them together, yours is as fair a name;
    Sound them, it doth become the mouth as well;   145
    Weigh them, it is as heavy; conjure with 'em,
    Brutus will start a spirit° as soon as Cæsar.
    Now, in the names of all the gods at once,
    Upon what meat doth this our Cæsar feed
    That he is grown so great? Age, thou art
    sham'd!   150
    Rome, thou hast lost the breed of noble bloods!
    When went there by an age, since the great
    flood,°
    But it was fam'd with more than with one man?
    When could they say till now that talk'd of
    Rome
    That her wide walls encompass'd but one man?   155
    Now is it Rome indeed, and room enough,
    When there is in it but one only man.
    O, you and I have heard our fathers say
    There was a Brutus° once that would have
    brook'd
    Th' eternal devil to keep his state in Rome   160
    As easily as a king.
    BRUTUS. That you do love me, I am nothing
    jealous;°
    What you would work me to, I have some aim.
    How I have thought of this and of these times,
    I shall recount hereafter; for this present,   165
    I would not, so with love I might entreat you,
    Be any further mov'd. What you have said
    I will consider; what you have to say
    I will with patience hear, and find a time
    Both meet to hear and answer such high things.   170
    Till then, my noble friend, chew upon this:
    Brutus had rather be a villager°
    Than to repute himself a son of Rome
    Under these hard conditions as this time
    Is like to lay upon us.   175
    CASSIUS. I am glad that my weak words
    Have struck but thus much show of fire from
    Brutus.
    BRUTUS. The games are done, and Cæsar is re-
    turning.
    CASSIUS. As they pass by, pluck Casca by the
    sleeve,

---

chafing with   raging at
Aeneas   who escaped the fall of Troy to become the
  legendary founder of the Roman people (see Virgil's
  Aeneid)
bend   glance   his   its
bear the palm   carry away the victor's prize
Colossus   giant statue which bestrode entrance to the
  harbor of Rhodes (the Seventh Wonder of the world)

start a spirit   call forth an apparition
great flood   not Noah's, but Deucalion's, its classical
  counterpart
Brutus   Lucius Junius Brutus, who drove the tyrannous
  Tarquins from Rome
jealous   doubtful   villager   i.e., peasant

180 And he will, after his sour fashion, tell you
What hath proceeded worthy note today.
      [*Re-enter* Cæsar *and his train.*]
BRUTUS. I will do so. But, look you, Cassius,
The angry spot doth glow on Cæsar's brow,
And all the rest look like a chidden train.
185 Calpurnia's cheek is pale, and Cicero
Looks with such ferret and such fiery eyes
As we have seen him in the Capitol,
Being cross'd in conference by some senators.
CASSIUS. Casca will tell us what the matter is.
190 CÆSAR. Antonius!
ANTONY. Cæsar?
CÆSAR. Let me have men about me that are fat—
Sleek-headed men, and such as sleep o' nights.
Yond Cassius has a lean and hungry look.
195 He thinks too much; such men are dangerous.
ANTONY. Fear him not, Cæsar; he's not dangerous.
He is a noble Roman, and well given.°
CÆSAR. Would he were fatter! But I fear him not.
Yet if my name were liable to fear,
200 I do not know the man I should avoid
So soon as that spare Cassius. He reads much;
He is a great observer, and he looks
Quite through the deeds of men. He loves no
      plays,
As thou dost, Antony; he hears no music,
205 Seldom he smiles, and smiles in such a sort
As if he mock'd himself and scorn'd his spirit
That could be mov'd to smile at anything.
Such men as he be never at heart's ease
Whiles they behold a greater than themselves,
210 And therefore are they very dangerous.
I rather tell thee what is to be fear'd
Than what I fear; for always I am Cæsar.
Come on my right hand, for this ear is deaf,
And tell me truly what thou think'st of him.
      [*Sennet. Exeunt* Cæsar *and all his train but*
      Casca.]
CASCA. You pull'd me by the cloak. Would you
215   speak with me?
BRUTUS. Aye, Casca. Tell us what hath chanc'd
      today,
That Cæsar looks so sad.
CASCA. Why, you were with him, were you not?
BRUTUS. I should not then ask Casca what had
      chanc'd.
220 CASCA. Why, there was a crown offered him, and
being offered him, he put it by with the back of
his hand, thus, and then the people fell a-
shouting.
BRUTUS. What was the second noise for?
225 CASCA. Why, for that too.

well given well disposed

CASSIUS. They shouted thrice. What was the last
      cry for?
CASCA. Why, for that too.
BRUTUS. Was the crown offered him thrice?
CASCA. Aye, marry, was 't, and he put it by
thrice, every time gentler than other; and at 230
every putting by mine honest neighbors
shouted.
CASSIUS. Who offered him the crown?
CASCA. Why, Antony.
BRUTUS. Tell us the manner of it, gentle Casca. 235
CASCA. I can as well be hanged as tell the manner
of it. It was mere foolery; I did not mark it. I saw
Mark Antony offer him a crown. Yet 'twas not a
crown neither, 'twas one of these coronets; and,
as I told you, he put it by once. But for all that, 240
to my thinking, he would fain have had it. Then
he offered it to him again; then he put it by
again. But to my thinking he was very loath to
lay his fingers off it. And then he offered it the
third time; he put it the third time by; and still 245
as he refused it the rabblement hooted and clapped their chopped° hands and threw up their
sweaty nightcaps and uttered such a deal of
stinking breath because Cæsar refused the
crown that it had almost choked Cæsar; for he 250
swounded° and fell down at it. And for mine
own part, I durst° not laugh for fear of opening
my lips and receiving the bad air.
CASSIUS. But, soft, I pray you. What, did Cæsar
      swound?
CASCA. He fell down in the marketplace and foam- 255
ed at the mouth and was speechless.
BRUTUS. 'Tis very like. He hath the falling-sickness.°
CASSIUS. No, Cæsar hath it not; but you, and I,
And honest Casca, we have the falling-sickness.
CASCA. I know not what you mean by that, but I 260
am sure Cæsar fell down. If the tag-rag people
did not clap him and hiss him according as he
pleased and displeased them, as they use to do
the players in the theater, I am no true man.
BRUTUS. What said he when he came unto himself? 265
CASCA. Marry, before he fell down, when he perceived the common herd was glad he refused
the crown, he plucked me ope his doublet° and
offered them his throat to cut. An° I had been a
man of any occupation, if I would not have 270
taken him at a word, I would I might go to hell
among the rogues. And so he fell. When he
came to himself again, he said, if he had done or
said anything amiss, he desired their worships to

chopped chapped, horny   *swounded* swooned
durst dared   *falling-sickness* epilepsy
doublet jacket   *An* if

275 think it was his infirmity. Three or four wenches
where I stood cried, "Alas, good soul!" and
forgave him with all their hearts. But there's no
heed to be taken of them; if Cæsar had stabbed
their mothers, they would have done no less.

280 BRUTUS. And after that he came, thus sad, away?
CASCA. Aye.
CASSIUS. Did Cicero say anything?
CASCA. Aye, he spoke Greek.
CASSIUS. To what effect?

285 CASCA. Nay, an I tell you that, I'll ne'er look you i'
the face again. But those that understood him
smiled at one another and shook their heads; but
for mine own part, it was Greek to me. I could
tell you more news, too. Marullus and Flavius,

290 for pulling scarfs off Cæsar's images, are put to
silence. Fare you well. There was more foolery
yet, if I could remember it.
CASSIUS. Will you sup with me tonight, Casca?
CASCA. No, I am promised forth.

295 CASSIUS. Will you dine with me tomorrow?
CASCA. Aye, if I be alive, and your mind hold, and
your dinner worth the eating.
CASSIUS. Good. I will expect you.
CASCA. Do so. Farewell, both.   [Exit]

300 BRUTUS. What a blunt fellow is this grown to be!
He was quick mettle° when he went to school.
CASSIUS. So is he now in execution
Of any bold or noble enterprise,
However he puts on this tardy form.°

305 This rudeness is a sauce to his good wit,
Which gives men stomach to digest his words
With better appetite.
BRUTUS. And so it is. For this time I will leave you.
Tomorrow, if you please to speak with me,

310 I will come home to you, or, if you will,
Come home to me and I will wait for you.
CASSIUS. I will do so. Till then, think of the world.
                              [Exit BRUTUS.]
Well, Brutus, thou art noble; yet I see
Thy honorable metal may be wrought

315 From that it is dispos'd.° Therefore it is meet
That noble minds keep ever with their likes;
For who so firm that cannot be seduc'd?
Cæsar doth bear me hard, but he loves Brutus.
If I were Brutus now and he were Cassius,

320 He should not humor° me. I will this night,
In several hands,° in at his windows throw,
As if they came from several citizens,
Writings, all tending to the great opinion

That Rome holds of his name, wherein obscurely
Cæsar's ambition shall be glanced at.   325
And after this let Cæsar seat him sure,
For we will shake him, or worse days endure.
                              [Exit]

SCENE iii
A street.

[*Thunder and lightning. Enter, from opposite sides,*
CASCA, *with his sword drawn, and* CICERO.]
CICERO. Good even, Casca. Brought you Cæsar
home?
Why are you breathless? And why stare you so?
CASCA. Are not you mov'd, when all the sway° of
earth
Shakes like a thing unfirm? O Cicero,
I have seen tempests when the scolding winds   5
Have riv'd the knotty oaks, and I have seen
Th' ambitious ocean swell and rage and foam
To be exalted with the threat'ning clouds;
But never till tonight, never till now,
Did I go through a tempest dropping fire.   10
Either there is a civil strife in heaven,
Or else the world, too saucy with the gods,
Incenses them to send destruction.
CICERO. Why, saw you anything more wonderful?°
CASCA. A common slave—you know him well by
sight—   15
Held up his left hand, which did flame and burn
Like twenty torches join'd, and yet his hand,
Not sensible of° fire, remain'd unscorch'd.
Besides—I ha' not since put up my sword—
Against° the Capitol I met a lion,   20
Who glaz'd° upon me and went surly by
Without annoying me; and there were drawn
Upon a heap° a hundred ghastly women
Transformed with their fear, who swore they
saw
Men all in fire walk up and down the streets.   25
And yesterday the bird of night° did sit
Even at noonday upon the marketplace,
Hooting and shrieking. When these prodigies°
Do so conjointly° meet, let not men say
"These are their reasons: they are natural."   30
For I believe they are portentous° things
Unto the climate that they point upon.°

---

quick mettle a lively one   tardy form dull manner
From . . . dispos'd from its natural inclination
humor influence
several hands different handwritings

sway fixed order   wonderful amazing
sensible of sensitive to   Against opposite to
glaz'd glared   drawn . . . heap crowded together
bird of night the owl   prodigies unnatural phenomena
conjointly meet coincide   portentous ominous
climate . . . upon country that they reveal themselves in

CICERO. Indeed, it is a strange-disposed time.
But men may construe things after their fashion,
Clean from the purpose of the things them-
selves.
35 Comes Cæsar to the Capitol tomorrow?
CASCA. He doth, for he did bid Antonius
Send word to you he would be there tomorrow.
CICERO. Good night then, Casca. This disturbed
sky
Is not to walk in.
40 CASCA.   Farewell, Cicero.
                                        [*Exit* CICERO.]
                    [*Enter* CASSIUS.]
CASSIUS. Who's there?
CASCA.   A Roman.
CASSIUS.   Casca, by your voice.
CASCA. Your ear is good. Cassius, what night is this!
CASSIUS. A very pleasing night to honest men.
CASCA. Who ever knew the heavens menace so?
CASSIUS. Those that have known the earth so full of
45   faults.
For my part, I have walk'd about the streets,
Submitting me unto the perilous night,
And thus unbraced,° Casca, as you see,
Have bar'd my bosom to the thunder-stone;
And when the cross blue lightning seem'd to
50   open
The breast of heaven, I did present myself
Even in the aim and very flash of it.
CASCA. But wherefore did you so much tempt the
heavens?
It is the part of men to fear and tremble
55 When the most mighty gods by tokens send
Such dreadful heralds to astonish us.
CASSIUS. You are dull, Casca, and those sparks of
life
That should be in a Roman you do want,°
Or else you use not. You look pale and gaze
60 And put on fear and cast yourself in wonder
To see the strange impatience of the heavens.
But if you would consider the true cause
Why all these fires, why all these gliding ghosts,
Why birds and beasts from quality and kind,°
65 Why old men, fools, and children calculate,°
Why all these things change from their ordi-
nance°
Their natures and preformed faculties°
To monstrous quality, why, you shall find
That heaven hath infus'd them with these
spirits

To make them instruments of fear and warning   70
Unto some monstrous state.
Now could I, Casca, name to thee a man
Most like this dreadful night
That thunders, lightens, opens graves, and roars
As doth the lion in the Capitol,   75
A man no mightier than thyself or me
In personal action, yet prodigious grown
And fearful, as these strange eruptions are.
CASCA. 'Tis Cæsar that you mean, is it not, Cassius?
CASSIUS. Let it be who it is: for Romans now   80
Have thews and limbs like to their ancestors;
But woe the while! Our fathers' minds are dead,
And we are govern'd with our mothers' spirits;
Our yoke and suff'rance show us womanish.
CASCA. Indeed they say the Senators tomorrow   85
Mean to establish Cæsar as a king,
And he shall wear his crown by sea and land
In every place save here in Italy.
CASSIUS. I know where I will wear this dagger then.
Cassius from bondage will deliver Cassius.   90
Therein, ye gods, you make the weak most
strong;
Therein, ye gods, you tyrants do defeat.
Nor stony tower, nor walls of beaten brass,
Nor airless dungeon, nor strong links of iron
Can be retentive to° the strength of spirit;   95
But life, being weary of these worldly bars,
Never lacks power to dismiss itself.
If I know this, know all the world besides,
That part of tyranny that I do bear
I can shake off at pleasure.   [*Thunder still.*] 100
CASCA.   So can I.
So every bondman in his own hand bears
The power to cancel his captivity.
CASSIUS. And why should Cæsar be a tyrant then?
Poor man! I know he would not be a wolf
But that he sees the Romans are but sheep.   105
He were no lion were not Romans hinds.°
Those that with haste will make a mighty fire
Begin it with weak straws. What trash is Rome,
What rubbish, and what offal, when it serves
For the base matter to illuminate   110
So vile a thing as Cæsar! But, O grief,
Where hast thou led me? I perhaps speak this
Before a willing bondman; then I know
My answer must be made. But I am arm'd,
And dangers are to me indifferent.   115
CASCA. You speak to Casca, and to such a man
That is no fleering° tell-tale. Hold, my hand.
Be factious° for redress of all these griefs,

---

unbraced unbuttoned   *want* lack
from . . . kind contrary to their natures
calculate interpret, prophesy   *ordinance* usual ways
preformed faculties inherited characters

be retentive to confine
hinds female deer, i.e., cowardly   *fleering* mocking
Be factious take sides

And I will set this foot of mine as far
As who goes farthest.
120 CASSIUS.   There's a bargain made.
Now know you, Casca, I have mov'd already
Some certain of the noblest-minded Romans
To undergo with me an enterprise
Of honorable-dangerous consequence;
125 And I do know, by this they stay for me
In Pompey's porch.° For now, this fearful night,
There is no stir or walking in the streets,
And the complexion of the element°
In favor's° like the work we have in hand,
130 Most bloody, fiery, and most terrible.
            [Enter CINNA.]
CASCA. Stand close awhile, for here comes one in
    haste.
CASSIUS. 'Tis Cinna; I do know him by his gait.
    He is a friend. Cinna, where haste you so?
CINNA. To find out you. Who's that? Metellus
    Cimber?
135 CASSIUS. No, it is Casca, one incorporate°
    To our attempts. Am I not stay'd for, Cinna?
CINNA. I am glad on 't. What a fearful night is this!
    There's two or three of us have seen strange
    sights.
CASSIUS. Am I not stay'd for? Tell me.
CINNA.   Yes, you are.
140 O Cassius, if you could

Pompey's porch   portico of huge theater built by Pompey
    and location of Pompey's statue
element sky   favor appearance
incorporate joined

But win the noble Brutus to our party—
CASSIUS. Be you content. Good Cinna, take this
    paper,
And look you lay it in the prætor's chair°
Where Brutus may but find it, and throw this
In at his window; set this up with wax   145
Upon old Brutus'° statue. All this done,
Repair to Pompey's porch, where you shall find
    us.
Is Decius Brutus and Trebonius there?
CINNA. All but Metellus Cimber; and he's gone
    To seek you at your house. Well, I will hie,   150
    And so bestow these papers as you bade me.
CASSIUS. That done, repair to Pompey's theater.
                              [Exit CINNA.]
Come, Casca, you and I will yet ere day
See Brutus at his house. Three parts of him
Is ours already, and the man entire   155
Upon the next encounter yields him ours.
CASCA. O, he sits high in all the people's hearts,
    And that which would appear offense in us
    His countenance,° like richest alchemy,
    Will change to virtue and to worthiness.   160
CASSIUS. Him and his worth and our great need of
    him
    You have right well conceited.° Let us go,
    For it is after midnight, and ere day
    We will awake him and be sure of him.
                                   [Exeunt]

praetor   next office under that of consul
old Brutus   i.e., Lucius Junius Brutus
countenance approval   conceited expressed

ACT II

SCENE i
Rome. BRUTUS'S *orchard.*

[Enter BRUTUS.]
BRUTUS. What, Lucius, ho!
    I cannot, by the progress of the stars,
    Give guess how near to day. Lucius, I say!
    I would it were my fault to sleep so soundly.
    When, Lucius, when? Awake, I say! What,
5   Lucius!
            [Enter LUCIUS.]
LUCIUS. Call'd you, my lord?
BRUTUS. Get me a taper in my study, Lucius.
    When it is lighted, come and call me here.
LUCIUS. I will, my lord.   [Exit]

BRUTUS. It must be by his death, and for my part   10
    I know no personal cause to spurn at him,
    But for the general. He would be crown'd.
    How that might change his nature, there's the
        question.
    It is the bright day that brings forth the adder,
    And that craves wary walking. Crown him—
        that—   15
    And then, I grant, we put a sting in him
    That at his will he may do danger° with.
    Th' abuse of greatness is when it disjoins
    Remorse° from power. And to speak truth of
        Cæsar,

danger harm   Remorse mercy

20 I have not known when his affections sway'd°
     More than his reason. But 'tis a common proof
     That lowliness is young ambition's ladder,
     Whereto the climber-upward turns his face;
     But when he once attains the upmost round,
25 He then unto the ladder turns his back,
     Looks in the clouds, scorning the base degrees
     By which he did ascend. So Cæsar may.
     Then, lest he may, prevent. And since the
          quarrel
     Will bear no color for the thing he is,
30 Fashion it thus:° that what he is, augmented,
     Would run to these and these extremities;
     And therefore think him as a serpent's egg
     Which hatch'd would as his kind grow mis-
          chievous,
     And kill him in the shell.
                    [Re-enter LUCIUS.]
35 LUCIUS. The taper burneth in your closet, sir.
     Searching the window for a flint, I found
     This paper thus seal'd up, and I am sure
     It did not lie there when I went to bed.
                         [Gives him the letter.]
     BRUTUS. Get you to bed again; it is not day.
40 Is not tomorrow, boy, the ides of March?
     LUCIUS. I know not, sir.
     BRUTUS. Look in the calendar and bring me word.
     LUCIUS. I will, sir.   [Exit]
     BRUTUS. The exhalations° whizzing in the air
45 Give so much light that I may read by them.
                    [Opens the letter and reads.]

     Brutus, thou sleep'st. Awake and see thyself.
     Shall Rome, &c. Speak, strike, redress.
     Brutus, thou sleep'st. Awake!

     Such instigations have been often dropp'd
50 Where I have took them up.
     "Shall Rome, &c." Thus must I piece it out:
     Shall Rome stand under one man's awe? What,
          Rome?
     My ancestors did from the streets of Rome
     The Tarquin drive when he was call'd a king.
55 "Speak, strike, redress." Am I entreated
     To speak and strike? O Rome, I make thee
          promise.
     If the redress will follow, thou receiv'st
     Thy full petition at the hand of Brutus!
                    [Re-enter LUCIUS.]
     LUCIUS. Sir, March is wasted fifteen days.
                         [Knocking within.]

BRUTUS. 'Tis good. Go to the gate; somebody
     knocks.   [Exit LUCIUS.]   60
     Since Cassius first did whet me against Cæsar,
     I have not slept.
     Between the acting of a dreadful thing
     And the first motion,° all the interim is
     Like a phantasma° or a hideous dream.   65
     The genius° and the mortal instruments°
     Are then in council, and the state of man,
     Like to a little kingdom, suffers then
     The nature of an insurrection.
               [Re-enter LUCIUS.]
LUCIUS. Sir, 'tis your brother Cassius at the door   70
     Who doth desire to see you.
BRUTUS.   Is he alone?
LUCIUS. No, sir, there are moe° with him.
BRUTUS.   Do you know them?
LUCIUS. No, sir. Their hats are pluck'd about their
          ears
     And half their faces buried in their cloaks,
     That° by no means I may discover them   75
     By any mark of favor.°
BRUTUS.   Let 'em enter.
                         [Exit LUCIUS.]
     They are the faction.° O conspiracy,
     Sham'st thou to show thy dangerous brow by
          night,
     When evils are most free? O then by day
     Where wilt thou find a cavern dark enough   80
     To mask thy monstrous visage? Seek none,
          conspiracy.
     Hide it in smiles and affability.
     For if thou path,° thy native semblance° on,
     Not Erebus° itself were dim enough
     To hide thee from prevention.°   85
     [Enter the conspirators, CASSIUS, CASCA, DECIUS,
          CINNA, METELLUS CIMBER, and TREBONIUS.]
CASSIUS. I think we are too bold upon your rest.
     Good morrow, Brutus. Do we trouble you?
BRUTUS. I have been up this hour, awake all night.
     Know I these men that come along with you?   90
CASSIUS. Yes, every man of them, and no man here
     Bùt honors you. And every one doth wish
     You had but that opinion of yourself
     Which every noble Roman bears of you.

---

motion idea   *phantasma* nightmare
genius one's private, guiding spirit
mortal instruments physical, mental, and emotional
     powers
moe more   *That* so that
mark of favor distinguishing feature
faction i.e., the conspirators   *path* walk
native semblance natural appearance
Erebus dismal antechamber to Hell
prevention being detected

affections sway'd feelings ruled
And since . . . thus since the case against Cæsar as he
     now is is insufficient, put it thus
exhalations meteors

This is Trebonius.
BRUTUS.   He is welcome hither.
CASSIUS. This, Decius Brutus.
95 BRUTUS.   He is welcome too.
CASSIUS. This, Casca; this, Cinna; and this, Metellus
    Cimber.
BRUTUS. They are all welcome.
    What watchful cares do interpose themselves
    Betwixt your eyes and night?
100 CASSIUS. Shall I entreat a word?   [*They whisper.*]
DECIUS. Here lies the east. Doth not the day break
    here?
CASCA. No.
CINNA. O, pardon, sir, it doth, and yon gray lines
    That fret the clouds are messengers of day.
CASCA. You shall confess that you are both de-
105   ceiv'd.
    Here, as I point my sword, the sun arises,
    Which is a great way growing on° the south,
    Weighing° the youthful season of the year.
    Some two months hence up higher toward the
    north
110 He first presents his fire, and the high° east
    Stands as the Capitol, directly here.
BRUTUS. Give me your hands all over, one by one.
CASSIUS. And let us swear our resolution.
BRUTUS. No, not an oath. If not the face of men,
115   The suff'rance° of our souls, the time's abuse—
    If these be motives weak, break off betimes,°
    And every man hence to his idle bed;
    So let high-sighted tyranny range on
    Till each man drop by lottery. But if these,
120 As I am sure they do, bear fire enough
    To kindle cowards and to steel with valor
    The melting spirits of women, then, country-
    men,
    What need we any spur but our own cause
    To prick us to redress? What other bond
125 Than secret Romans that have spoke the word
    And will not palter?° And what other oath
    Than honesty to honesty engag'd°
    That this shall be or we will fall for it?
    Swear priests and cowards and men cautelous,°
130 Old feeble carrions, and such suff'ring souls
    That welcome wrongs; unto bad causes swear
    Such creatures as men doubt.° But do not stain
    The even virtue of our enterprise
    Nor th' insuppressive° mettle of our spirits
135 To think that or° our cause or our performance

growing on tending toward   *Weighing* if you consider
high due   *suff'rance* i.e., what we have endured
betimes at once   *palter* equivocate
engag'd pledged   *cautelous* deceitful
doubt distrust   *insupressive* insupressible
or either

Did need an oath, when every drop of blood
That every Roman bears, and nobly bears,
Is guilty of a several bastardy
If he do break the smallest particle
Of any promise that hath pass'd from him.   140
CASSIUS. But what of Cicero? Shall we sound him?
    I think he will stand very strong with us.
CASCA. Let us not leave him out.
CINNA.   No, by no means.
METELLUS. O, let us have him, for his silver hairs
    Will purchase us a good opinion   145
    And buy men's voices to commend our deeds.
    It shall be said his judgment rul'd our hands;
    Our youths and wildness shall no whit appear,
    But all be buried in his gravity.
BRUTUS. O, name him not. Let us not break with°
    him,   150
    For he will never follow anything
    That other men begin.
CASSIUS.   Then leave him out.
CASCA. Indeed he is not fit.
DECIUS. Shall no man else be touch'd but only
    Cæsar?
CASSIUS. Decius, well urg'd. I think it is not meet 155
    Mark Antony, so well belov'd of Cæsar,
    Should outlive Cæsar. We shall find of him
    A shrewd contriver, and you know his means,
    If he improve° them, may well stretch so far
    As to annoy us all. Which to prevent,   160
    Let Antony and Cæsar fall together.
BRUTUS. Our course will seem too bloody, Caius
    Cassius,
    To cut the head off and then hack the limbs,
    Like wrath in death and envy° afterwards;
    For Antony is but a limb of Cæsar.   165
    Let us be sacrificers, but not butchers, Caius.
    We all stand up against the spirit of Cæsar,
    And in the spirit of men there is no blood.
    O that we then could come by Cæsar's spirit,
    And not dismember Cæsar! But, alas,   170
    Cæsar must bleed for it! And, gentle friends,
    Let's kill him boldly, but not wrathfully.
    Let's carve him as a dish fit for the gods,
    Not hew him as a carcass fit for hounds.
    And let our hearts, as subtle masters do,   175
    Stir up their servants to an act of rage
    And after° seem to chide 'em. This shall make
    Our purpose necessary and not envious;°
    Which so appearing to the common eyes,
    We shall be call'd purgers, not murderers.   180
    And for Mark Antony, think not of him,

break with confide in   *improve* exercise
envy malice   *after* afterwards
envious malicious

For he can do no more than Cæsar's arm
When Cæsar's head is off.
CASSIUS.   Yet I fear him,
For in th' ingrafted love he bears to Cæsar—
185 BRUTUS. Alas, good Cassius, do not think of him.
If he love Cæsar, all that he can do
Is to himself—take thought and die for Cæsar.
And that were much he should,° for he is given
To sports, to wildness, and much company.
190 TREBONIUS. There is no fear in him. Let him not die,
For he will live and laugh at this hereafter.
                         [*Clock strikes.*]
BRUTUS. Peace! Count the clock.
CASSIUS.   The clock hath stricken three.
TREBONIUS. 'Tis time to part.
CASSIUS.   But it is doubtful yet
Whether Cæsar will come forth today or no,
195 For he is superstitious grown of late,
Quite from the main opinion he held once
Of fantasy, of dreams, and ceremonies.°
It may be these apparent prodigies,
The unaccustom'd terror of this night,
200 And the persuasion of his augurers°
May hold him from the Capitol today.
DECIUS. Never fear that. If he be so resolv'd,
I can o'ersway him; for he loves to hear
That unicorns may be betray'd° with trees
205 And bears with glasses,° elephants with holes,
Lions with toils,° and men with flatterers.
But when I tell him he hates flatterers,
He says he does—being then most flattered.
Let me work,
210 For I can give his humor° the true bent,°
And I will bring him to the Capitol.
CASSIUS. Nay, we will all of us be there to fetch him.
BRUTUS. By the eighth hour. Is that the uttermost?
CINNA. Be that the uttermost, and fail not then.
215 METELLUS. Caius Ligarius doth bear Cæsar hard,
Who rated° him for speaking well of Pompey.
I wonder none of you have thought of him.
BRUTUS. Now, good Metellus, go along with him.
He loves me well, and I have given him reasons;
220 Send him but hither, and I'll fashion him.
CASSIUS. The morning comes upon 's. We'll leave
you, Brutus.
And, friends, disperse yourselves; but all re-
member
What you have said and show yourselves true
Romans.
BRUTUS. Good gentlemen, look fresh and merrily,

Let not our looks put on our purposes,   225
But bear it as our Roman actors do,
With untir'd spirits and formal constancy.°
And so, good morrow to you every one.
                         [*Exeunt all but* BRUTUS.]
Boy! Lucius! Fast asleep! It is no matter;
Enjoy the honey-heavy dew of slumber.   230
Thou hast no figures nor no fantasies°
Which busy care draws in the brains of men;
Therefore thou sleep'st so sound.
                         [*Enter* PORTIA.]
PORTIA.   Brutus, my lord!
BRUTUS. Portia, what mean you? Wherefore rise
you now?
It is not for your health thus to commit°   235
Your weak condition to the raw cold morning.
PORTIA. Nor for yours neither. You've ungently,
Brutus,
Stole from my bed, and yesternight at supper
You suddenly arose and walk'd about,
Musing and sighing, with your arms across,   240
And when I ask'd you what the matter was,
You star'd upon me with ungentle looks.
I urg'd you further; then you scratch'd your
head
And too impatiently stamp'd with your foot.
Yet I insisted, yet you answer'd not,   245
But with an angry wafture of your hand
Gave sign for me to leave you. So I did,
Fearing to strengthen that impatience
Which seem'd too much enkindled, and withal°
Hoping it was but an effect of humor,°   250
Which sometime hath his° hour with every man.
It will not let you eat, nor talk, nor sleep,
And, could it work so much upon your shape
As it hath much prevail'd on your condition,
I should not know you, Brutus. Dear my lord,   255
Make me acquainted with your cause of grief.
BRUTUS. I am not well in health, and that is all.
PORTIA. Brutus is wise, and were he not in health
He would embrace the means to come by it.
BRUTUS. Why, so I do. Good Portia, go to bed.   260
PORTIA. Is Brutus sick, and is it physical°
To walk unbraced and suck up the humors°
Of the dank morning? What, is Brutus sick,
And will he steal out of his wholesome bed
To dare the vile contagion of the night   265
And tempt the rheumy and unpurged° air

---

untir'd . . . constancy unaffected (unattired) manner and
    normal appearance
figures . . . fantasies mental pictures drawn by wild
    imaginings
commit expose   *withal* in addition   *humor* mood
his its   *physical* healthful   *humors* moistures
rheumy . . . unpurged damp and unhealthful

were . . . should is (too) much to expect
ceremonies omens   *augurers* interpreters of omens
betray'd tricked   *glasses* mirrors   *toils* traps
humor disposition   *bent* direction   *rated* berated

To add unto his sickness? No, my Brutus;
You have some sick offense within your mind,
Which by the right and virtue of my place
270 I ought to know of. And upon my knees
I charm you, by my once commended beauty,
By all your vows of love and that great vow
Which did incorporate and make us one,
That you unfold to me, yourself, your half,
275 Why you are heavy,° and what men tonight
Have had resort to you; for here have been
Some six or seven who did hide their faces
Even from darkness.
BRUTUS.   Kneel not, gentle Portia.
PORTIA. I should not need, if you were gentle
      Brutus.
280 Within the bond of marriage, tell me, Brutus,
Is it excepted I should know no secrets
That appertain to you? Am I yourself
But, as it were, in sort or limitation,°
To keep with you at meals, comfort your bed,
And talk to you sometimes? Dwell I but in the
285   suburbs
Of your good pleasure? If it be no more,
Portia is Brutus' harlot, not his wife.
BRUTUS. You are my true and honorable wife,
As dear to me as are the ruddy drops
290 That visit my sad heart.
PORTIA. If this were true, then should I know this
      secret.
I grant I am a woman, but withal
A woman that Lord Brutus took to wife;
I grant I am a woman, but withal°
295 A woman well reputed, Cato's° daughter.
Think you I am no stronger than my sex,
Being so father'd and so husbanded?
Tell me your counsels; I will not disclose 'em.
I have made strong proof of my constancy,°
300 Giving myself a voluntary wound°
Here in the thigh. Can I bear that with patience
And not my husband's secrets?
BRUTUS.   O ye gods,
Render me worthy of this noble wife!
                              [Knocking within.]
Hark, hark! One knocks. Portia, go in awhile,
305 And by and by thy bosom shall partake
The secrets of my heart.
All my engagements I will construe to thee,

heavy depressed
in . . . limitation only in a limited way
withal nevertheless
Cato Cato the Younger, Roman philosopher and patriot
constancy fortitude
voluntary wound (Plutarch's *Life of Brutus* reports that
   Portia "gave herself a great gash withal in her thigh"
   with a razor)

All the charactery° of my sad brows.
Leave me with haste. [*Exit* PORTIA] Lucius, who's
      that knocks?
            [*Re-enter* LUCIUS *with* LIGARIUS.]
LUCIUS. Here is a sick man that would speak with
      you.   310
BRUTUS. Caius Ligarius, that Metellus spake of.
Boy, stand aside. Caius Ligarius, how?
LIGARIUS. Vouchsafe° good morrow from a feeble
      tongue.
BRUTUS. O, what a time have you chose out, brave
      Caius,
To wear a kerchief! Would you were not sick! 315
LIGARIUS. I am not sick, if Brutus have in hand
Any exploit worthy the name of honor.
BRUTUS. Such an exploit have I in hand, Ligarius,
Had you a healthful ear to hear of it.
LIGARIUS. By all the gods that Romans bow before, 320
I here discard my sickness! Soul of Rome!
Brave son, deriv'd from honorable loins!
Thou, like an exorcist,° hast conjur'd up
My mortified° spirit. Now bid me run,
And I will strive with things impossible,   325
Yea, get the better of them. What's to do?
BRUTUS. A piece of work that will make sick men
      whole.°
LIGARIUS. But are not some whole that we must
      make sick?
BRUTUS. That must we also. What it is, my Caius,
I shall unfold to thee as we are going   330
To whom it must be done.
LIGARIUS.   Set on your foot,
And with a heart new-fir'd I follow you
To do I know not what. But it sufficeth
That Brutus leads me on.
BRUTUS.   Follow me then.
                                          [*Exeunt*]

SCENE ii
CÆSAR's *house.*

[*Thunder and lightning. Enter* CÆSAR *in his
            night gown.*]
CÆSAR. Nor heaven nor earth have been at peace
      tonight;
Thrice hath Calpurnia in her sleep cried out,
"Help, ho! They murder Cæsar!" Who's
      within?
                              [*Enter a* SERVANT.]
SERVANT. My lord?

charactery i.e., what is delineated by the facial features
Vouchsafe please to accept   exorcist conjurer
mortified dead-seeming   whole in health

5 CÆSAR. Go bid the priests do present° sacrifice,
   And bring me their opinions of success.
   SERVANT. I will, my lord.   [*Exit*]
                    [*Enter* CALPURNIA.]
   CALPURNIA. What mean you, Cæsar? Think you to
        walk forth?
   You shall not stir out of your house today.
   CÆSAR. Cæsar shall forth. The things that threat-
10   en'd me
   Ne'er look'd but on my back. When they shall
        see
   The face of Cæsar, they are vanished.
   CALPURNIA. Cæsar, I never stood on ceremonies,°
   Yet now they fright me. There is one within,
15 Besides the things that we have heard and seen,
   Recounts most horrid sights seen by the watch.
   A lioness hath whelped in the streets,
   And graves have yawn'd and yielded up their
        dead;
   Fierce fiery warriors fight upon the clouds
20 In ranks and squadrons and right form° of war,
   Which drizzled blood upon the Capitol.
   The noise of battle hurtled in the air,
   Horses did neigh, and dying men did groan,
   And ghosts did shriek and squeal about the
        streets.
25 O Cæsar! These things are beyond all use,°
   And I do fear them.
   CÆSAR.   What can be avoided
   Whose end is purpos'd by the mighty gods?
   Yet Cæsar shall go forth, for these predictions
   Are to° the world in general as to Cæsar.
   CALPURNIA. When beggars die, there are no
30   comets seen;
   The heavens themselves blaze forth the death of
        princes.
   CÆSAR. Cowards die many times before their
        deaths;
   The valiant never taste of death but once.
   Of all the wonders that I yet have heard,
   It seems to me most strange that men should
35   fear,
   Seeing that death, a necessary end,
   Will come when it will come.
                    [*Re-enter* SERVANTS.]
                         What say the augurers?
   SERVANT. They would not have you to stir forth
        today.
   Plucking the entrails of an offering forth,
40 They could not find a heart within the beast.

   CÆSAR. The gods do this in shame of cowardice.
   Cæsar should be a beast without a heart
   If he should stay at home today for fear.
   No, Cæsar shall not. Danger knows full well
   That Cæsar is more dangerous than he.   45
   We are two lions litter'd in one day,
   And I the elder and more terrible.
   And Cæsar shall go forth.
   CALPURNIA.   Alas, my lord,
   Your wisdom is consum'd in confidence.°
   Do not go forth today. Call it my fear   50
   That keeps you in the house and not your own.
   We'll send Mark Antony to the Senate House,
   And he shall say you are not well today.
   Let me, upon my knee, prevail in this.
   CÆSAR. Mark Antony shall say I am not well,   55
   And, for thy humor,° I will stay at home.
                    [*Enter* DECIUS.]
   Here's Decius Brutus; he shall tell them so.
   DECIUS. Cæsar, all hail! Good morrow, worthy
        Cæsar.
   I come to fetch you to the Senate House.
   CÆSAR. And you are come in very happy time   60
   To bear my greeting to the Senators
   And tell them that I will not come today.
   Cannot is false, and that I dare not, falser.
   I will not come today. Tell them so, Decius.
   CALPURNIA. Say he is sick.
   CÆSAR.   Shall Cæsar send a lie? 65
   Have I in conquest stretch'd mine arm so far
   To be afeard to tell graybeards the truth?
   Decius, go tell them Cæsar will not come.
   DECIUS. Most mighty Cæsar, let me know some
        cause,
   Lest I be laugh'd at when I tell them so.   70
   CÆSAR. The cause is in my will: I will not come.
   That is enough to satisfy the Senate.
   But, for your private satisfaction,
   Because I love you, I will let you know.
   Calpurnia here, my wife, stays me at home.   75
   She dreamt tonight she saw my statuë,
   Which like a fountain with an hundred spouts
   Did run pure blood, and many lusty Romans
   Came smiling and did bathe their hands in it.
   And these does she apply for warnings and
        portents   80
   And evils imminent, and on her knee
   Hath begg'd that I will stay at home today.
   DECIUS. This dream is all amiss interpreted;
   It was a vision fair and fortunate.
   Your statue spouting blood in many pipes,   85

---

present   immediate
stood on ceremonies   believed in omens
right form   regular formations
beyond all use   outside ordinary experience
are to   apply to

confidence   false security (see *Macbeth*, III, v, "Security is
   mortals' chiefest enemy")
humor   whim

In which so many smiling Romans bath'd,
Signifies that from you great Rome shall suck
Reviving blood, and that great men shall press°
For tinctures, stains, relics, and cognizance.°
90   This by Calpurnia's dream is signified.
CÆSAR. And this way have you well expounded it.
DECIUS. I have, when you have heard what I can
        say.
      And know it now: the Senate have concluded
      To give this day a crown to mighty Cæsar.
95   If you shall send them word you will not come,
      Their minds may change. Besides, it were a
        mock
      Apt to be render'd, for some one to say
      "Break up the Senate till another time,
      When Cæsar's wife shall meet with better
        dreams."
100 If Cæsar hide himself, shall they not whisper
      "Lo, Cæsar is afraid"?
      Pardon me, Cæsar, for my dear dear love
      To your proceeding bids me tell you this,
      And reason to my love is liable.°
CÆSAR. How foolish do your fears seem now,
105   Calpurnia!
      I am ashamed I did yield to them.
      Give me my robe, for I will go.
        [Enter PUBLIUS, BRUTUS, LIGARIUS, METELLUS,
            CASCA, TREBONIUS, and CINNA.]
      And look where Publius is come to fetch me.
PUBLIUS. Good morrow, Cæsar.
CÆSAR.   Welcome, Publius.
110 What, Brutus, are you stirr'd so early too?
      Good morrow, Casca. Caius Ligarius,
      Cæsar was ne'er so much your enemy
      As that same ague which hath made you lean.
      What is 't o'clock?
BRUTUS.   Cæsar, 'tis strucken eight.
115 CÆSAR. I thank you for your pains and courtesy.
        [Enter ANTONY.]
      See! Antony, that revels long o' nights,
      Is notwithstanding up. Good morrow, Antony.
ANTONY. So to most noble Cæsar.
CÆSAR.   Bid them prepare within.
      I am to blame to be thus waited for.
120 Now, Cinna; now, Metellus; what, Trebonius!
      I have an hour's talk in store for you;
      Remember that you call on me today.
      Be near me, that I may remember you.
TREBONIUS. Cæsar, I will. [Aside] And so near will I
        be
      That your best friends shall wish I had been
125   further.

press vie   cognizance identifiable emblems
liable subservient

CÆSAR. Good friends, go in and taste some wine
        with me,
      And we like friends will straightway go together.
BRUTUS. [Aside] That every like is not the same,°
        O Cæsar,
      The heart of Brutus earns° to think upon!
                                              [Exeunt]

SCENE iii
A street near the Capitol.

[Enter ARTEMIDORUS, reading a paper.]
ARTEMIDORUS.

      Cæsar, beware of Brutus; take heed of Cassius;
      come not near Casca; have an eye to Cinna;
      trust not Trebonius; mark well Metellus
      Cimber; Decius Brutus loves thee not; thou
      hast wronged Caius Ligarius. There is but one   5
      mind in all these men, and it is bent against
      Cæsar. If thou beest not immortal, look about
      you: security gives way to conspiracy.° The
      mighty gods defend thee!
                              Thy lover, ARTEMIDORUS. 10

      Here will I stand till Cæsar pass along,
      And as a suitor will I give him this.
      My heart laments that virtue cannot live
      Out of the teeth of emulation.°
      If thou read this, O Cæsar, thou mayst live;   15
      If not, the Fates with traitors do contrive.
                                              [Exit]

SCENE iv
Another part of the same street, before the house
of BRUTUS.

[Enter PORTIA and LUCIUS.]
PORTIA. I prithee, boy, run to the Senate House.
      Stay not to answer me, but get thee gone.
      Why dost thou stay?
LUCIUS.   To know my errand, madam.
PORTIA. I would have had thee there and here
        again
      Ere I can tell thee what thou shouldst do there. 5
      O constancy, be strong upon my side!
      Set a huge mountain 'tween my heart and
        tongue!

That . . . same that the appearance is not always the
   reality
earns grieves
security . . . conspiracy overconfidence opens the way for
   the conspirators
Out . . . emulation out of the reach of envy

I have a man's mind, but a woman's might.
How hard it is for women to keep counsel!
Art thou here yet?

10 LUCIUS.   Madam, what should I do?
Run to the Capitol and nothing else?
And so return to you and nothing else?

PORTIA. Yes, bring me word, boy, if thy lord look
    well,
For he went sickly forth. And take good note

15 What Cæsar doth, what suitors press to him.
Hark, boy! What noise is that?

LUCIUS. I hear none, madam.

PORTIA.   Prithee, listen well.
I heard a bustling rumor like a fray,°
And the wind brings it from the Capitol.

20 LUCIUS. Sooth,° madam, I hear nothing.
            [Enter the SOOTHSAYER.]

PORTIA. Come hither, fellow. Which way hast
    thou been?

SOOTHSAYER. At mine own house, good lady.

PORTIA. What is't clock?

SOOTHSAYER.   About the ninth hour, lady.

PORTIA. Is Cæsar yet gone to the Capitol?

SOOTHSAYER. Madam, not yet. I go to take my

25   stand

To see him pass on to the Capitol.

PORTIA. Thou hast some suit to Cæsar, hast thou
    not?

SOOTHSAYER. That I have, lady. If it will please
    Cæsar
To be so good to Cæsar as to hear me,
I shall beseech him to befriend himself.   30

PORTIA. Why, know'st thou any harm's intended
    towards him?

SOOTHSAYER. None that I know will be, much that
    I fear may chance.
Good morrow to you. Here the street is narrow;
The throng that follows Cæsar at the heels,
Of Senators, of prætors, common suitors,   35
Will crowd a feeble man almost to death.
I'll get me to a place more void° and there
Speak to great Cæsar as he comes along.   [Exit]

PORTIA. I must go in. Aye me, how weak a thing
The heart of woman is! O Brutus,   40
The heavens speed thee in thine enterprise!
Sure, the boy heard me. Brutus hath a suit
That Cæsar will not grant. O, I grow faint.
Run, Lucius, and commend me to my lord.
Say I am merry. Come to me again   45
And bring me word what he doth say to thee.
                        [Exeunt severally.]

bustling . . . fray confused noise as from a battle
Sooth in truth

void empty

ACT III

SCENE i
Rome. Before the Capitol; the Senate sitting above.

[*A crowd of people; among them* ARTEMIDORUS
and the SOOTHSAYER. *Flourish. Enter* CÆSAR,
BRUTUS, CASSIUS, CASCA, DECIUS, METELLUS,
TREBONIUS, CINNA, ANTONY, LEPIDUS, POPILIUS,
PUBLIUS, *and others.*]

CÆSAR. The ides of March are come.

SOOTHSAYER. Aye, Cæsar, but not gone.

ARTEMIDORUS. Hail, Cæsar! Read this schedule.°

DECIUS. Trebonius doth desire you to o'er-read,
At your best leisure, this his humble suit.

ARTEMIDORUS. O Cæsar, read mine first; for mine's

5   a suit
That touches° Cæsar nearer. Read it, great
Cæsar.

schedule document   touches concerns

CÆSAR. What touches us ourself shall be last
    serv'd.

ARTEMIDORUS. Delay not, Cæsar; read it instantly.

CÆSAR. What, is the fellow mad?

PUBLIUS.   Sirrah, give place.   10

CASSIUS. What, urge you your petitions in the
    street?
Come to the Capitol.
    [CÆSAR *goes up to the Senate House, the rest
        following.*]

POPILIUS. I wish your enterprise today may thrive.

CASSIUS. What enterprise, Popilius?

POPILIUS.   Fare you well.
                    [*Advances to* CÆSAR.]

BRUTUS. What said Popilius Lena?   15

CASSIUS. He wish'd today our enterprise might
    thrive.
I fear our purpose is discovered.

BRUTUS. Look, how he makes to Cæsar. Mark him.

CASSIUS.   Casca,
  Be sudden, for we fear prevention.
20 Brutus, what shall be done? If this be known,
  Cassius or Cæsar never shall turn back,
  For I will slay myself.
BRUTUS.   Cassius, be constant.°
  Popilius Lena speaks not of our purposes;
  For, look, he smiles, and Cæsar doth not change.
CASSIUS. Trebonius knows his time; for, look you,
25   Brutus,
  He draws Mark Antony out of the way.
                    [Exeunt ANTONY and TREBONIUS.]
DECIUS. Where is Metellus Cimber? Let him go,
  And presently prefer° his suit to Cæsar.
BRUTUS. He is address'd.° Press near and second
  him.
CINNA. Casca, you are the first that rears your
30   hand.
CÆSAR. Are we all ready? What is now amiss
  That Cæsar and his Senate must redress?
METELLUS. Most high, most mighty, and most
    puissant Cæsar,
  Metellus Cimber throws before thy seat
  An humble heart—   [Kneeling.]
35 CÆSAR.   I must prevent thee, Cimber.
  These couchings° and these lowly courtesies
  Might fire the blood of ordinary men
  And turn preordinance and first decree°
  Into the law of children. Be not fond,°
40 To think that Cæsar bears such rebel blood
  That will be thaw'd from the true quality
  With that which melteth fools, I mean sweet
    words,
  Low-crooked court'sies, and base spaniel-
    fawning.
  Thy brother by decree is banished.
45 If thou dost bend and pray and fawn for him,
  I spurn thee like a cur out of my way.
  Know Cæsar doth not wrong, nor without
    cause
  Will he be satisfied.
METELLUS. Is there no voice more worthy than my
    own,
50 To sound more sweetly in great Cæsar's ear
  For the repealing° of my banish'd brother?
BRUTUS. I kiss thy hand, but not in flattery, Cæsar,
  Desiring thee that Publius Cimber may
  Have an immediate freedom of repeal.°

CÆSAR. What, Brutus!
CASSIUS.   Pardon, Cæsar; Cæsar, pardon. 55
  As low as to thy foot doth Cassius fall
  To beg enfranchisement for Publius Cimber.
CÆSAR. I could be well mov'd if I were as you;
  If I could pray to move, prayers would move me.
  But I am constant as the northern star, 60
  Of whose true-fix'd and resting quality
  There is no fellow° in the firmament.
  The skies are painted with unnumber'd sparks;
  They are all fire and every one doth shine.
  But there's but one in all doth hold his place. 65
  So in the world; 'tis furnish'd well with men,
  And men are flesh and blood, and apprehen-
    sive.°
  Yet in the number I do know but one
  That unassailable holds on his rank,
  Unshak'd of motion. And that I am he, 70
  Let me a little show it, even in this—
  That I was constant Cimber should be banish'd,
  And constant do remain to keep him so.
CINNA. O Cæsar—
CÆSAR.   Hence! Wilt thou lift up Olympus?
DECIUS. Great Cæsar—
CÆSAR.   Doth not Brutus bootless° kneel? 75
CASCA. Speak, hands, for me!
          [CASCA first, then the other Conspirators and
                    MARCUS BRUTUS stab CÆSAR.]
CÆSAR. Et tu, Brute? Then fall, Cæsar!   [Dies.]
CINNA. Liberty! Freedom! Tyranny is dead!
  Run hence, proclaim, cry it about the streets.
CASSIUS. Some to the common pulpits,° and cry
    out 80
  "Liberty, freedom, and enfranchisement!"
BRUTUS. People, and Senators, be not affrighted.
  Fly not; stand still. Ambition's debt is paid.
CASCA. Go to the pulpit, Brutus.
DECIUS.   And Cassius too.
BRUTUS. Where's Publius? 85
CINNA. Here, quite confounded° with this mutiny.
METELLUS. Stand fast together, lest some friend of
    Cæsar's
  Should chance—
BRUTUS. Talk not of standing. Publius, good cheer.
  There is no harm intended to your person, 90
  Nor to no Roman else. So tell them, Publius.
CASSIUS. And leave us, Publius, lest that the people
  Rushing on us should do your age some mis-
    chief.

constant steadfast
presently prefer immediately offer   address'd ready
couchings prostrations
preordinance . . . decree the primary laws that underlie
  society
fond foolish   repealing recalling
freedom of repeal unconditional recall

fellow equal
apprehensive capable of apprehending
bootless uselessly
common pulpits public platforms for speakers
confounded shattered

BRUTUS. Do so. And let no man abide° this deed
  But we the doers.
    [*Re-enter* TREBONIUS.]
95 CASSIUS.   Where is Antony?
TREBONIUS. Fled to his house amaz'd.
  Men, wives, and children stare, cry out, and run
  As it were doomsday.
BRUTUS.   Fates, we will know your pleasures.
  That we shall die, we know; 'tis but the time,
100 And drawing days out, that men stand upon.°
CASSIUS. Why, he that cuts off twenty years of life
  Cuts off so many years of fearing death.
BRUTUS. Grant that, and then is death a benefit.
  So are we Cæsar's friends, that have abridg'd
  His time of fearing death. Stoop, Romans,
105   stoop,
  And let us bathe our hands in Cæsar's blood
  Up to the elbows, and besmear our swords.
  Then walk we forth, even to the marketplace,
  And waving our red weapons o'er our heads,
110 Let's all cry "Peace, freedom, and liberty!"
CASSIUS. Stoop then, and wash. How many ages
    hence
  Shall this our lofty scene be acted over
  In states unborn and accents yet unknown!
BRUTUS. How many times shall Cæsar bleed in
    sport,
115 That now on Pompey's basis° lies along
  No worthier than the dust!
CASSIUS.   So oft as that shall be,
  So often shall the knot of us be call'd
  The men that gave their country liberty.
DECIUS. What, shall we forth?
CASSIUS.   Aye, every man away.
120 Brutus shall lead, and we will grace his heels
  With the most boldest and best hearts of Rome.
    [*Enter a* SERVANT.]
BRUTUS. Soft! Who comes here? A friend of
  Antony's.
SERVANT. Thus, Brutus, did my master bid me
  kneel,
  Thus did Mark Antony bid me fall down,
125 And, being prostrate, thus he bade me say:
  Brutus is noble, wise, valiant, and honest;
  Cæsar was mighty, bold, royal, and loving;
  Say I love Brutus and I honor him;
  Say I fear'd Cæsar, honor'd him, and lov'd him.
130 If Brutus will vouchsafe° that Antony
  May safely come to him and be resolv'd

How Cæsar hath deserv'd to lie in death,
Mark Antony shall not love Cæsar dead
So well as Brutus living, but will follow
The fortunes and affairs of noble Brutus   135
Thorough° the hazards of this untrod state°
With all true faith. So says my master Antony.
BRUTUS. Thy master is a wise and valiant Roman;
  I never thought him worse.
  Tell him, so please him come unto this place,   140
  He shall be satisfied and, by my honor,
  Depart untouch'd.
SERVANT.   I'll fetch him presently.°
    [*Exit*]
BRUTUS. I know that we shall have him well to
  friend.
CASSIUS. I wish we may. But yet have I a mind
  That fears him much, and my misgiving still   145
  Falls shrewdly to the purpose.°
    [*Re-enter* ANTONY.]
BRUTUS. But here comes Antony. Welcome, Mark
  Antony.
ANTONY. O mighty Cæsar! Dost thou lie so low?
  Are all thy conquests, glories, triumphs, spoils
  Shrunk to this little measure? Fare thee well.   150
  I know not, gentlemen, what you intend,
  Who else must be let blood, who else is rank.°
  If I myself, there is no hour so fit
  As Cæsar's death's hour, nor no instrument
  Of half that worth as those your swords, made
    rich   155
  With the most noble blood of all this world.
  I do beseech ye, if you bear me hard,
  Now, whilst your purpled hands do reek and
    smoke,
  Fulfil your pleasure. Live a thousand years,
  I shall not find myself so apt° to die.   160
  No place will please me so, no mean° of death,
  As here by Cæsar, and by you cut off,
  The choice and master spirits of this age.
BRUTUS. O Antony, beg not your death of us.
  Though now we must appear bloody and cruel,   165
  As by our hands and this our present act
  You see we do; yet see you but our hands
  And this the bleeding business they have done.
  Our hearts you see not; they are pitiful;
  And pity to the general wrong of Rome—   170
  As fire drives out fire, so pity pity—
  Hath done this deed on Cæsar. For your part,
  To you our swords have leaden points, Mark
    Antony.

---

abide bear responsibility for
drawing . . . upon stretching out their lives, that men are
  concerned for
Pompey's basis i.e., the base of Pompey's statue
vouchsafe guarantee

Thorough through
untrod state uncharted future   *presently* immediately
still . . . purpose always proves accurate
rank overgrown, in need of "pruning"   *apt* ready
mean means

Our arms in strength of malice° and our hearts
175 Of brothers' temper do receive you in
With all kind love, good thoughts, and rever-
ence.
CASSIUS. Your voice shall be as strong as any man's
In the disposing of new dignities.
BRUTUS. Only be patient till we have appeas'd
180 The multitude, beside themselves with fear,
And then we will deliver you the cause
Why I, that did love Cæsar when I struck him,
Have thus proceeded.
ANTONY.   I doubt not of your wisdom.
Let each man render me his bloody hand;
185 First, Marcus Brutus, will I shake with you;
Next, Caius Cassius, do I take your hand;
Now, Decius Brutus, yours; now yours, Metel-
lus;
Yours, Cinna; and, my valiant Casca, yours;
Though last, not least in love, yours, good
Trebonius.
190 Gentlemen all—alas, what shall I say?
My credit now stands on such slippery ground
That one of two bad ways you must conceit°
me—
Either a coward or a flatterer.
That I did love thee, Cæsar, O, 'tis true.
195 If then thy spirit look upon us now,
Shall it not grieve thee dearer° than thy death
To see thy Antony making his peace,
Shaking the bloody fingers of thy foes,
Most noble! in the presence of thy corse?°
200 Had I as many eyes as thou hast wounds,
Weeping as fast as they stream forth thy blood,
It would become me better than to close°
In terms of friendship with thine enemies.
Pardon me, Julius! Here wast thou bay'd, brave
hart;
205 Here didst thou fall, and here thy hunters stand,
Sign'd in thy spoil and crimson'd in thy lethe.°
O world, thou wast the forest to this hart,
And this, indeed, O world, the heart of thee.
How like a deer strucken by many princes
210 Dost thou here lie!
CASSIUS. Mark Antony—
ANTONY.   Pardon me, Caius Cassius.
The enemies of Cæsar shall say this.
Then, in a friend, it is cold modesty.°

CASSIUS. I blame you not for praising Cæsar so,
But what compact mean you to have with us? 215
Will you be prick'd° in number of our friends,
Or shall we on and not depend on you?
ANTONY. Therefore I took your hands, but was
indeed
Sway'd from the point by looking down on
Cæsar.
Friends am I with you all and love you all, 220
Upon this hope that you shall give me reasons
Why and wherein Cæsar was dangerous.
BRUTUS. Or else were this a savage spectacle.
Our reasons are so full of good regard°
That were you, Antony, the son of Cæsar, 225
You should be satisfied.
ANTONY.   That's all I seek,
And am moreover suitor that I may
Produce his body to the marketplace,
And in the pulpit, as becomes a friend,
Speak in the order° of his funeral. 230
BRUTUS. You shall, Mark Antony.
CASSIUS.   Brutus, a word with you.
[Aside to BRUTUS] You know not what you do.
Do not consent
That Antony speak in his funeral.
Know you how much the people may be mov'd
By that which he will utter?
BRUTUS.   By your pardon— 235
I will myself into the pulpit first
And show the reason of our Cæsar's death.
What Antony shall speak, I will protest
He speaks by leave and by permission,
And that we are contented Cæsar shall 240
Have all true rites and lawful ceremonies.
It shall advantage more than do us wrong.
CASSIUS. I know not what may fall; I like it not.
BRUTUS. Mark Antony, here, take you Cæsar's
body.
You shall not in your funeral speech blame us, 245
But speak all good you can devise of Cæsar
And say you do 't by our permission.
Else shall you not have any hand at all
About his funeral. And you shall speak
In the same pulpit whereto I am going, 250
After my speech is ended.
ANTONY.   Be it so;
I do desire no more.
BRUTUS. Prepare the body, then, and follow us.
                    [Exeunt all but ANTONY.]
ANTONY. O, pardon me, thou bleeding piece of
earth,
That I am meek and gentle with these butchers! 255

---

in . . . malice (even) at their highest point of malice
conceit conceive   *dearer* more deeply
corse corpse
close join
Sign'd . . . lethe marked by your slaughter and
    reddened by your bloodstream (Lethe was the river of
    oblivion in Hades)
modesty moderation; i.e., "the least that I can do"

prick'd counted   *good regard* worthy purpose
order ritual

Thou art the ruins of the noblest man
That ever lived in the tide of times.
Woe to the hand that shed this costly blood!
Over thy wounds now do I prophesy—
260   Which like dumb mouths do ope their ruby lips
To beg the voice and utterance of my tongue—
A curse shall light upon the limbs of men;
Domestic fury and fierce civil strife
Shall cumber° all the parts of Italy;
265   Blood and destruction shall be so in use
And dreadful objects so familiar
That mothers shall but smile when they behold
Their infants quarter'd with the hands of war,
All pity chok'd with custom of fell deeds;°
270   And Cæsar's spirit ranging for revenge
With Ate° by his side come hot from hell
Shall in these confines° with a monarch's voice
Cry "Havoc!"° and let slip the dogs of war,
That this foul deed shall smell above the earth
275   With carrion men, groaning for burial.

[Enter a Servant.]

You serve Octavius Cæsar, do you not?
Servant. I do, Mark Antony.
Antony. Cæsar did write for him to come to Rome.
Servant. He did receive his letters and is coming,
280   And bid me say to you by word of mouth—
O Cæsar!   [Seeing the body.]
Antony. Thy heart is big; get thee apart and weep.
Passion,° I see, is catching, for mine eyes,
Seeing those beads of sorrow stand in thine,
285   Began to water. Is thy master coming?
Servant. He lies tonight within seven leagues of
Rome.
Antony. Post back with speed and tell him what
hath chanc'd.
Here is a mourning Rome, a dangerous Rome,
No Rome of safety for Octavius yet.
290   Hie hence and tell him so. Yet stay awhile;
Thou shalt not back till I have borne this corse
Into the marketplace. There shall I try,
In my oration, how the people take
The cruel issue of these bloody men;
295   According to the which thou shalt discourse
To young Octavius of the state of things.
Lend me your hand.

[Exeunt with Cæsar's body.]

cumber burden
custom . . . deeds cruel acts will have become so ordinary
Ate goddess of discord   *confines* regions
"Havoc" battlecry calling for pillage and general
   devastation
Passion emotion

SCENE ii
The Forum.

[Enter Brutus and Cassius, *and a throng of*
Citizens.]

Citizens. We will be satisfied! Let us be satisfied!
Brutus. Then follow me and give me audience,
   friends.
Cassius, go you into the other street
And part° the numbers.
Those that will hear me speak, let 'em stay
   here;   5
Those that will follow Cassius, go with him,
And public reasons shall be rendered
Of Cæsar's death.
First Citizen.   I will hear Brutus speak.
Second Citizen. I will hear Cassius and compare
   their reasons
When severally° we hear them rendered.   10

[Exit Cassius, *with some of the* Citizens.
Brutus *goes into the pulpit.*]

Third Citizen. The noble Brutus is ascended.
   Silence!
Brutus. Be patient till the last.
Romans, countrymen, and lovers! Hear me for
my cause, and be silent that you may hear.
Believe me for mine honor and have respect to   15
mine honor that you may believe. Censure me
in your wisdom and awake your senses that you
may the better judge. If there be any in this
assembly, any dear friend of Cæsar's, to him I
say that Brutus' love to Cæsar was no less than   20
his. If then that friend demand why Brutus rose
against Cæsar, this is my answer: not that I
loved Cæsar less, but that I loved Rome more.
Had you rather Cæsar were living and die all
slaves than that Cæsar were dead, to live all   25
freemen? As Cæsar loved me, I weep for him;
as he was fortunate, I rejoice at it; as he was
valiant, I honor him. But as he was ambitious, I
slew him. There is tears for his love, joy for his
fortune, honor for his valor, and death for his   30
ambition. Who is here so base that would be a
bondman? If any, speak, for him have I offended.
Who is here so rude° that would not be a
Roman? If any, speak, for him have I offended.
Who is here so vile that will not love his country?   35
If any, speak, for him have I offended. I pause for
a reply.
All. None, Brutus, none.
Brutus. Then none have I offended. I have done no
more to Cæsar than you shall do to Brutus. The   40

part divide   *severally* separately   *rude* barbarous question of his death is enrolled° in the Capitol, his glory not extenuated, wherein he was worthy, nor his offenses enforced,° for which he suffered death.

[*Enter* ANTONY *and others, with* CÆSAR'S *body.*]

45 Here comes his body, mourned by Mark Antony, who, though he had no hand in his death, shall receive the benefit of his dying, a place in the commonwealth—as which of you shall not? With this I depart—that, as I slew my best lover

50 for the good of Rome, I have the same dagger for myself when it shall please my country to need my death.

ALL. Live, Brutus! Live, live!

FIRST CITIZEN. Bring him with triumph home unto his house.

SECOND CITIZEN. Give him a statue with his ances-

55 tors.

THIRD CITIZEN. Let him be Cæsar.

FOURTH CITIZEN.   Cæsar's better parts Shall be crown'd in Brutus.

FIRST CITIZEN. We'll bring him to his house with shouts and clamors.

BRUTUS. My countrymen—

SECOND CITIZEN.   Peace! Silence! Brutus speaks.

60 FIRST CITIZEN. Peace, ho!

BRUTUS. Good countrymen, let me depart alone, And, for my sake, stay here with Antony. Do grace to Cæsar's corpse, and grace his speech Tending to Cæsar's glories, which Mark Antony

65 By our permission is allow'd to make. I do entreat you, not a man depart, Save I alone, till Antony have spoke.   [*Exit*]

FIRST CITIZEN. Stay, ho! and let us hear Mark Antony.

THIRD CITIZEN. Let him go up into the public chair;

70 We'll hear him. Noble Antony, go up.

ANTONY. For Brutus' sake, I am beholding to you.
                              [*Goes into the pulpit.*]

FOURTH CITIZEN. What does he say of Brutus?

THIRD CITIZEN.   He says for Brutus' sake He finds himself beholding° to us all.

FOURTH CITIZEN. 'Twere best he speak no harm of Brutus here.

FIRST CITIZEN. This Cæsar was a tyrant.

75 THIRD CITIZEN.   Nay, that's certain. We are blest that Rome is rid of him.

SECOND CITIZEN. Peace! Let us hear what Antony can say.

ANTONY. You gentle Romans—

ALL.   Peace, ho! Let us hear him.

ANTONY. Friends, Romans, countrymen, lend me your ears.

I come to bury Cæsar, not to praise him.   80
The evil that men do lives after them;
The good is oft interred with their bones.
So let it be with Cæsar. The noble Brutus
Hath told you Cæsar was ambitious.
If it were so, it was a grievous fault,   85
And grievously hath Cæsar answer'd it.
Here, under leave of Brutus and the rest—
For Brutus is an honorable man;
So are they all, all honorable men—
Come I to speak in Cæsar's funeral.   90
He was my friend, faithful and just to me.
But Brutus says he was ambitious—
And Brutus is an honorable man.
He hath brought many captives home to Rome,
Whose ransoms did the general coffers° fill.   95
Did this in Cæsar seem ambitious?
When that the poor have cried, Cæsar hath wept.
Ambition should be made of sterner stuff.
Yet Brutus says he was ambitious—
And Brutus is an honorable man.   100
You all did see that on the Lupercal
I thrice presented him a kingly crown,
Which he did thrice refuse. Was this ambition?
Yet Brutus says he was ambitious—
And, sure, he is an honorable man.   105
I speak not to disprove what Brutus spoke,
But here I am to speak what I do know.
You all did love him once, not without cause.
What cause withholds you then to mourn for him?
O judgment! Thou art fled to brutish beasts,   110
And men have lost their reason. Bear with me;
My heart is in the coffin there with Cæsar,
And I must pause till it come back to me.

FIRST CITIZEN. Methinks there is much reason in his sayings.

SECOND CITIZEN. If thou consider rightly of the matter,   115
Cæsar has had great wrong.

THIRD CITIZEN.   Has he, masters? I fear there will a worse come in his place.

FOURTH CITIZEN. Mark'd ye his words? He would not take the crown;
Therefore 'tis certain he was not ambitious.

FIRST CITIZEN. If it be found so, some will dear abide° it.   120

SECOND CITIZEN. Poor soul! His eyes are red as fire with weeping.

THIRD CITIZEN. There's not a nobler man in Rome than Antony.

---

question . . . enrolled   reasons for his death are recorded
enforced   distorted   *beholding*   obliged

general coffers   public treasury   *dear abide*   pay dearly for

FOURTH CITIZEN. Now mark him; he begins again
    to speak.
ANTONY. But yesterday the word of Cæsar might
125   Have stood against the world. Now lies he there,
    And none so poor to do him reverence.
    O masters, if I were dispos'd to stir
    Your hearts and minds to mutiny and rage,
    I should do Brutus wrong and Cassius wrong—
130   Who, you all know, are honorable men.
    I will not do them wrong; I rather choose
    To wrong the dead, to wrong myself and you,
    Than I will wrong such honorable men.
    But here's a parchment with the seal of Cæsar;
135   I found it in his closet; 'tis his will.
    Let but the commons hear this testament—
    Which, pardon me, I do not mean to read—
    And they would go and kiss dead Cæsar's
      wounds
    And dip their napkins° in his sacred blood,
140   Yea, beg a hair of him for memory,
    And, dying, mention it within their wills,
    Bequeathing it as a rich legacy
    Unto their issue.
FOURTH CITIZEN. We'll hear the will. Read it, Mark
    Antony.
145 ALL. The will, the will! We will hear Cæsar's will.
ANTONY. Have patience, gentle friends, I must not
    read it;
    It is not meet you know how Cæsar lov'd you.
    You are not wood, you are not stones, but men,
    And, being men, hearing the will of Cæsar,
150   It will inflame you, it will make you mad.
    'Tis good you know not that you are his heirs,
    For if you should, O what would come of it!
FOURTH CITIZEN. Read the will; we'll hear it,
    Antony,
    You shall read us the will, Cæsar's will.
155 ANTONY. Will you be patient? Will you stay awhile?
    I have o'ershot myself to tell you of it.
    I fear I wrong the honorable men
    Whose daggers have stabb'd Cæsar; I do fear it.
FOURTH CITIZEN. They were traitors! Honorable
    men!
160 ALL. The will! The testament!
SECOND CITIZEN. They were villains, murderers!
    The will! Read the will!
ANTONY. You will compel me then to read the will?
    Then make a ring about the corpse of Cæsar
165   And let me show you him that made the will.
    Shall I descend? And will you give me leave?
ALL. Come down.
SECOND CITIZEN. Descend.
             [*He comes down from the pulpit.*]

THIRD CITIZEN. You shall have leave.
FOURTH CITIZEN. A ring; stand round.   170
FIRST CITIZEN. Stand from the hearse, stand from
    the body.
SECOND CITIZEN. Room for Antony, most noble
    Antony.
ANTONY. Nay, press not so upon me; stand far
    off.
ALL. Stand back. Room! Bear back.
ANTONY. If you have tears, prepare to shed them
    now.   175
    You all do know this mantle. I remember
    The first time ever Cæsar put it on;
    'Twas on a summer's evening, in his tent,
    That day he overcame the Nervii.°
    Look, in this place ran Cassius' dagger through. 180
    See what a rent the envious Casca made.
    Through this the well-beloved Brutus stabb'd,
    And as he pluck'd his cursed steel away,
    Mark how the blood of Cæsar follow'd it,
    As rushing out of doors to be resolv'd   185
    If Brutus so unkindly knock'd or no.
    For Brutus, as you know, was Cæsar's angel:
    Judge, O you gods, how dearly Cæsar lov'd him!
    This was the most unkindest cut of all,
    For when the noble Cæsar saw him stab,   190
    Ingratitude, more strong than traitors' arms,
    Quite vanquish'd him. Then burst his mighty
      heart,
    And in his mantle muffling up his face,
    Even at the base of Pompey's statuë,
    Which all the while ran blood, great Cæsar fell. 195
    O what a fall was there, my countrymen!
    Then I, and you, and all of us fell down,
    Whilst bloody treason flourish'd over us.
    O now you weep, and I perceive you feel
    The dint of pity. These are gracious drops. 200
    Kind souls! What? Weep you when you but
      behold
    Our Cæsar's vesture wounded? Look you here—
    Here is himself, marr'd as you see with traitors.
FIRST CITIZEN. O piteous spectacle!
SECOND CITIZEN. O noble Cæsar!   205
THIRD CITIZEN. O woeful day!
FOURTH CITIZEN. O traitors, villains!
FIRST CITIZEN. O most bloody sight!
SECOND CITIZEN. We will be revenged.
ALL. Revenge! About! Seek! Burn! Fire! Kill! 210
    Slay!
    Let not a traitor live!
ANTONY.   Stay, countrymen.
FIRST CITIZEN. Peace there! Hear the noble Antony.

---

napkins handkerchiefs

Nervii Belgic tribe defeated in 57 B.C. thanks to Caesar's
personal skill and bravery

SECOND CITIZEN. We'll hear him, we'll follow him,
215   we'll die with him.
ANTONY. Good friends, sweet friends, let me not
         stir you up
      To such a sudden flood of mutiny.
      They that have done this deed are honorable;
      What private griefs they have, alas, I know not,
220   That made them do it. They are wise and
         honorable
      And will, no doubt, with reasons answer you.
      I come not, friends, to steal away your hearts.
      I am no orator, as Brutus is,
      But as you know me all, a plain blunt man
225   That love my friend. And that they know full
         well
      That gave me public leave to speak of him;
      For I have neither wit nor words nor worth,
      Action nor utterance nor the power of speech
      To stir men's blood. I only speak right on;
230   I tell you that which you yourselves do know,
      Show you sweet Cæsar's wounds, poor poor
         dumb mouths,
      And bid them speak for me. But were I Brutus,
      And Brutus Antony, there were an Antony
      Would ruffle up your spirits and put a tongue
235   In every wound of Cæsar that should move
      The stones of Rome to rise and mutiny!
ALL. We'll mutiny.
FIRST CITIZEN. We'll burn the house of Brutus.
THIRD CITIZEN. Away, then! Come, seek the
      conspirators.
ANTONY. Yet hear me, countrymen; yet hear me
240   speak.
ALL. Peace, ho! Hear Antony. Most noble Antony!
ANTONY. Why, friends, you go to do you know not
      what.
      Wherein hath Cæsar thus deserv'd your loves?
      Alas, you know not; I must tell you then.
245   You have forgot the will I told you of.
ALL. Most true, the will! Let's stay and hear the
      will.
ANTONY. Here is the will, and under Cæsar's seal.
      To every Roman citizen he gives,
      To every several° man, seventy-five drachmas.
SECOND CITIZEN. Most noble Cæsar! We'll revenge
250   his death.
THIRD CITIZEN. O royal Cæsar!
ANTONY. Hear me with patience.
ALL. Peace, ho!
ANTONY. Moreover, he hath left you all his walks,
255   His private arbors and new-planted orchards
      On this side Tiber; he hath left them you
      And to your heirs forever, common pleasures,

To walk abroad and recreate yourselves.
Here was a Cæsar! When comes such another?
FIRST CITIZEN. Never, never. Come, away, away!   260
      We'll burn his body in the holy place,
      And with the brands fire the traitors' houses.
      Take up the body.
SECOND CITIZEN. Go fetch fire.
THIRD CITIZEN. Pluck down benches.   265
FOURTH CITIZEN. Pluck down forms, windows, any-
      thing.   [Exeunt CITIZENS with the body.]
ANTONY. Now let it work. Mischief, thou art afoot;
      Take thou what course thou wilt.
            [Enter a SERVANT.]
                        How now, fellow!
SERVANT. Sir, Octavius is already come to Rome.   270
ANTONY. Where is he?
SERVANT. He and Lepidus are at Cæsar's house.
ANTONY. And thither will I straight to visit him.
      He comes upon a wish. Fortune is merry,
      And in this mood will give us anything.   275
SERVANT. I heard him say Brutus and Cassius
      Are rid like madmen through the gates of Rome.
ANTONY. Belike they had some notice of the people,
      How I had mov'd them. Bring me to Octavius.
                        [Exeunt]

                     SCENE iii
                      A street.

            [Enter CINNA the poet.]
CINNA. I dreamt tonight that I did feast with Cæsar,
      And things unluckily charge my fantasy.°
      I have no will to wander forth of doors,
      Yet something leads me forth.
            [Enter CITIZENS.]
FIRST CITIZEN. What is your name?   5
SECOND CITIZEN. Whither are you going?
THIRD CITIZEN. Where do you dwell?
FOURTH CITIZEN. Are you a married man or a
      bachelor?
SECOND CITIZEN. Answer every man directly.   10
FIRST CITIZEN. Aye, and briefly.
FOURTH CITIZEN. Aye, and wisely.
THIRD CITIZEN. Aye, and truly, you were best.
CINNA. What is my name? Whither am I going?
      Where do I dwell? Am I a married man or a   15
      bachelor? Then, to answer every man directly
      and briefly, wisely and truly, wisely I say, I am a
      bachelor.
SECOND CITIZEN. That's as much as to say they are
      fools that marry. You'll bear me a bang° for that,   20
      I fear. Proceed; directly.

_____

several individual

charge my fantasy burden my imagination
bear . . . bang get a blow

CINNA. Directly, I am going to Cæsar's funeral.
FIRST CITIZEN. As a friend or an enemy?
CINNA. As a friend.
25 SECOND CITIZEN. That matter is answered directly.
FOURTH CITIZEN. For your dwelling, briefly.
CINNA. Briefly, I dwell by the Capitol.
THIRD CITIZEN. Your name, sir, truly.
CINNA. Truly, my name is Cinna.
30 FIRST CITIZEN. Tear him to pieces; he's a con-
    spirator.
CINNA. I am Cinna the poet! I am Cinna the poet!
FOURTH CITIZEN. Tear him for his bad verses! Tear
    him for his bad verses!

CINNA. I am not Cinna the conspirator.   35
FOURTH CITIZEN. It is no matter. His name's Cinna;
    pluck but his name out of his heart, and turn
    him going.°
THIRD CITIZEN. Tear him, tear him! Come, brands,
    ho! Fire-brands! To Brutus', to Cassius'! Burn   40
    all! Some to Decius' house, and some to Casca's;
    some to Ligarius'! Away, go!   [Exeunt]

turn him going kill him

A C T   I V

SCENE i
A house in Rome.

[ANTONY, OCTAVIUS, *and* LEPIDUS, *seated at a table.*]
ANTONY. These many then shall die; their names
    are prick'd.°
OCTAVIUS. Your brother too must die. Consent you,
    Lepidus?
LEPIDUS. I do consent—
OCTAVIUS.   Prick him down, Antony.
LEPIDUS. Upon condition Publius shall not live,
5   Who is your sister's son, Mark Antony.
ANTONY. He shall not live. Look, with a spot I
    damn him.
    But, Lepidus, go you to Cæsar's house;
    Fetch the will hither, and we shall determine
    How to cut off some charge in legacies.°
10 LEPIDUS. What, shall I find you here?
OCTAVIUS. Or here or° at the Capitol.
                                [*Exit* LEPIDUS.]
ANTONY. This is a slight unmeritable man,
    Meet to be sent on errands. Is it fit,
    The three-fold world divided, he should stand
    One of the three to share it?
15 OCTAVIUS.   So you thought him,
    And took his voice who should be prick'd to die
    In our black sentence and proscription.°
ANTONY. Octavius, I have seen more days than you,
    And though we lay these honors on this man

To ease ourselves of divers° sland'rous loads,   20
He shall but bear them as the ass bears gold,
To groan and sweat under the business,
Either led or driven, as we point the way;
And having brought our treasure where we will,
Then take we down his load and turn him off,   25
Like to the empty ass, to shake his ears
And graze in commons.°
OCTAVIUS.   You may do your will;
But he's a tried and valiant soldier.
ANTONY. So is my horse, Octavius, and for that
    I do appoint him store of provender.°   30
    It is a creature that I teach to fight,
    To wind,° to stop, to run directly on,
    His corporal° motion govern'd by my spirit.
    And, in some taste,° is Lepidus but so;
    He must be taught, and train'd, and bid go
        forth,   35
    A barren-spirited fellow, one that feeds
    On objects, arts, and imitations,°
    Which, out of use and stal'd by other men,
    Begin his fashion.° Do not talk of him
    But as a property. And now, Octavius,   40
    Listen great things. Brutus and Cassius
    Are levying powers. We must straight make
        head.°

divers various   *commons* public pastures
appoint . . . provender allow him a supply of food
wind turn   *corporal* bodily
in . . . taste i.e., to some degree
objects . . . imitations curiosities, artificial and imitative
    works
Which . . . fashion which he does not take up until they
    have become outmoded
make head ready an army

prick'd marked
cut off . . . legacies i.e., reduce some of Caesar's bequests
Or . . . or either . . . or
black . . . proscription death sentences and proclamation
    of public enemies

Therefore let our alliance be combin'd,
Our best friends made, our means stretch'd,
45 And let us presently go sit in council,
How covert° matters may be best disclos'd
And open perils surest answered.°
OCTAVIUS. Let us do so, for we are at the stake°
And bay'd about with many enemies,
50 And some that smile have in their hearts, I fear,
Millions of mischiefs. [Exeunt]

SCENE ii
Camp near Sardis. Before BRUTUS's tent.

[Drum. Enter BRUTUS, LUCILIUS, LUCIUS, and
SOLDIERS; TITANIUS and PINDARUS meet them.]
BRUTUS. Stand, ho!
LUCILIUS. Give the word, ho! and stand.
BRUTUS. What now, Luculius! Is Cassius near?
LUCILIUS. He is at hand, and Pindarus is come
5 To do you salutation° from his master.
BRUTUS. He greets me well. Your master, Pindarus,
In his own change,° or by ill officers,
Hath given me some worthy cause to wish
Things done undone. But if he be at hand,
I shall be satisfied.
10 PINDARUS. I do not doubt
But that my noble master will appear
Such as he is, full of regard and honor.
BRUTUS. He is not doubted. A word, Lucilius,
How he receiv'd you. Let me be resolv'd.°
15 LUCILIUS. With courtesy and with respect enough,
But not with such familiar instances°
Nor with such free and friendly conference
As he hath us'd of old.
BRUTUS. Thou hast describ'd
A hot friend cooling. Ever note, Lucilius,
20 When love begins to sicken and decay,
It useth an enforced ceremony.°
There are no tricks in plain and simple faith;
But hollow men, like horses hot at hand,°
Make gallant show and promise of their mettle.
25 But when they should endure the bloody spur,
They fall their crests and like deceitful jades
Sink in the trial. Comes his army on?
LUCILIUS. They mean this night in Sardis to be
quarter'd;

covert hidden   surest answered best dealt with
at the stake i.e., like a chained bear beset by dogs
do you salutation greet you
In . . . change i.e., of his feelings toward me
resolv'd informed
familiar instances marks of familiarity
enforced ceremony strained formality
hot at hand chafing when restrained

The greater part, the horse° in general,
Are come with Cassius. [Low march within.]
BRUTUS. Hark! He is arriv'd. 30
March gently on to meet him.
[Enter CASSIUS and his powers.]
CASSIUS. Stand, ho!
BRUTUS. Stand, ho! Speak the word along.
FIRST SOLDIER. Stand!
SECOND SOLDIER. Stand! 35
THIRD SOLDIER. Stand!
CASSIUS. Most noble brother, you have done me
wrong.
BRUTUS. Judge me, you gods! Wrong I mine
enemies?
And, if not so, how should I wrong a brother?
CASSIUS. Brutus, this sober form of yours hides
wrongs; 40
And when you do them—
BRUTUS. Cassius, be content;
Speak your griefs° softly. I do know you well.
Before the eyes of both our armies here,
Which should perceive nothing but love from us,
Let us not wrangle. Bid them move away; 45
Then in my tent, Cassius, enlarge your griefs,
And I will give you audience.
CASSIUS. Pindarus,
Bid our commanders lead their charges off
A little from this ground.
BRUTUS. Lucilius, do you the like, and let no man 50
Come to our tent till we have done our con-
ference.
Let Lucius and Titinius guard our door.
[Exeunt]

SCENE iii
BRUTUS's tent.

[Enter BRUTUS and CASSIUS.]
CASSIUS. That you have wrong'd me doth appear in
this:
You have condemn'd and noted° Lucius Pella
For taking bribes here of the Sardians,
Wherein my letters, praying on his side
Because I knew the man, were slighted off. 5
BRUTUS. You wrong'd yourself to write in such a
case.
CASSIUS. In such a time as this it is not meet
That every nice° offense should bear his com-
ment.°

horse cavalry
griefs grievances   noted publicly accused
nice petty   bear his comment be noticed

BRUTUS. Let me tell you, Cassius, you yourself
10   Are much condemn'd to have an itching palm,°
        To sell and mart° your offices for gold
        To undeservers.
CASSIUS.   I an itching palm!
        You know that you are Brutus that speaks this,
        Or by the gods this speech were else your last.
BRUTUS. The name of Cassius honors this corrup-
15   tion,
        And chastisement doth therefore hide his° head.
CASSIUS. Chastisement!
BRUTUS. Remember March, the ides of March
          remember.
        Did not great Julius bleed for justice' sake?
20   What villain touch'd his body that did stab
        And not for justice? What, shall one of us
        That struck the foremost man of all this world
        But for supporting robbers,° shall we now
        Contaminate our fingers with base bribes
25   And sell the mighty space of our large honors°
        For so much trash as may be grasped thus?
        I had rather be a dog and bay the moon
        Than such a Roman.
CASSIUS.   Brutus, bait not me;
        I'll not endure it. You forget yourself,
30   To hedge me in.° I am a soldier, I,
        Older in practice, abler than yourself
        To make conditions.
BRUTUS.   Go to. You are not, Cassius.
CASSIUS. I am.
BRUTUS. I say you are not.
35 CASSIUS. Urge° me no more; I shall forget myself.
        Have mind upon your health; tempt me no
          farther.
BRUTUS. Away, slight man!
CASSIUS. Is't possible?
BRUTUS.   Hear me, for I will speak.
        Must I give way and room to your rash choler?°
40   Shall I be frighted when a madman stares?
CASSIUS. O ye gods, ye gods! Must I endure all this?
BRUTUS. All this! Aye, more. Fret till your proud
          heart break.
        Go show your slaves how choleric you are,
        And make your bondmen tremble. Must I
          budge?
45   Must I observe you? Must I stand and crouch
        Under your testy humor? By the gods,
        You shall digest the venom of your spleen°

Though it do split you; for from this day forth
        I'll use you for my mirth, yea, for my laughter,
        When you are waspish.
CASSIUS.   Is it come to this?   50
BRUTUS. You say you are a better soldier.
        Let it appear so; make your vaunting true,
        And it shall please me well. For mine own part,
        I shall be glad to learn of noble men.
CASSIUS. You wrong me every way; you wrong me,
          Brutus.   55
        I said an elder soldier, not a better.
        Did I say, better?
BRUTUS.   If you did, I care not.
CASSIUS. When Cæsar liv'd, he durst not thus have
          mov'd me.
BRUTUS. Peace, peace! You durst not so have
          tempted him.
CASSIUS. I durst not!   60
BRUTUS. No.
CASSIUS. What, durst not tempt him!
BRUTUS.   For your life you durst not.
CASSIUS. Do not presume too much upon my love;
        I may do that I shall be sorry for.
BRUTUS. You have done that you should be sorry
          for.   65
        There is no terror, Cassius, in your threats;
        For I am arm'd so strong in honesty
        That they pass by me as the idle wind
        Which I respect° not. I did send to you
        For certain sums of gold, which you denied me; 70
        For I can raise no money by vile means.
        By heaven, I had rather coin my heart
        And drop my blood for drachmas° than to
          wring
        From the hard hands of peasants their vile
          trash
        By any indirection.° I did send   75
        To you for gold to pay my legions,
        Which you denied me. Was that done like
          Cassius?
        Should I have answer'd Caius Cassius so?
        When Marcus Brutus grows so covetous,
        To lock such rascal counters° from his friends, 80
        Be ready, gods, with all your thunderbolts.
        Dash him to pieces!
CASSIUS.   I denied you not.
BRUTUS. You did.
CASSIUS.   I did not. He was but a fool
        That brought my answer back. Brutus hath
          riv'd° my heart.
        A friend should bear his friend's infirmities,   85

---

itching palm i.e., for bribes   *mart* market   *his* its
But . . . robbers i.e., protecting his dishonest favorites
sell . . . honors i.e., prostitute our best possession, our
    honor
hedge me in limit my authority   *Urge* harass
rash choler hot temper
spleen the supposed source of hot temper

respect regard   *drachmas* Greek coins
indirection dishonest means
rascal counters base coins   *riv'd* cleft

But Brutus makes mine greater than they are.
BRUTUS. I do not till you practice them on me.
CASSIUS. You love me not.
BRUTUS.   I do not like your faults.
CASSIUS. A friendly eye could never see such faults.
BRUTUS. A flatterer's would not, though they do
90   appear
    As huge as high Olympus.
CASSIUS. Come, Antony, and young Octavius,
    come,
    Revenge yourselves alone on Cassius;
    For Cassius is aweary of the world,
95   Hated by one he loves, brav'd° by his brother,
    Check'd° like a bondman, all his faults observ'd,
    Set in a notebook, learn'd and conn'd by rote°
    To cast into my teeth. O, I could weep
    My spirit from mine eyes! There is my dagger,
100   And here my naked breast; within, a heart
    Dearer than Plutus'° mine, richer than gold.
    If that thou be'st a Roman, take it forth.
    I, that denied thee gold, will give my heart.
    Strike as thou didst at Cæsar; for I know
    When thou didst hate him worst thou lov'dst
105   him better
    Than ever thou lov'dst Cassius.
BRUTUS.   Sheathe your dagger.
    Be angry when you will, it shall have scope;°
    Do what you will, dishonor shall be humor.°
    O Cassius, you are yoked with a lamb,
110   That carries anger as the flint bears fire,
    Who, much enforced,° shows a hasty spark
    And straight is cold again.
CASSIUS.   Hath Cassius liv'd
    To be but mirth and laughter to his Brutus
    When grief and blood ill-temper'd vexeth him?
115 BRUTUS. When I spoke that, I was ill-temper'd too.
CASSIUS. Do you confess so much? Give me your
    hand.
BRUTUS. And my heart too.
CASSIUS.   O Brutus!
BRUTUS.   What's the matter?
CASSIUS. Have not you love enough to bear with me
    When that rash humor° which my mother gave
    me
    Makes me forgetful?
120 BRUTUS.   Yes, Cassius, and from henceforth,
    When you are over-earnest with your Brutus,
    He'll think your mother chides, and leave you so.

POET. [Within] Let me go in to see the generals.
    There is some grudge between 'em; 'tis not
    meet
    They be alone.
LUCILIUS. [Within] You shall not come to them.   125
POET. [Within] Nothing but death shall stay me.
    [Enter POET, followed by LUCILIUS, TITINIUS, and
                LUCIUS.]
CASSIUS. How now! What's the matter?
POET. For shame, you generals! What do you
    mean?
    Love and be friends, as two such men should be;
    For I have seen more years, I'm sure, than ye.   130
CASSIUS. Ha, ha! How vilely doth this cynic° rhyme!
BRUTUS. Get you hence, sirrah; saucy fellow, hence!
CASSIUS. Bear with him, Brutus; 'tis his fashion.
BRUTUS. I'll know his humor when he knows his
    time.
    What should the wars do with these jigging
    fools?   135
    Companion, hence!
CASSIUS.   Away, away, be gone!
                     [Exit POET.]
BRUTUS. Lucilius and Titinius, bid the commanders
    Prepare to lodge their companies tonight.
CASSIUS. And come yourselves and bring Messala
    with you
    Immediately to us.
           [Exeunt LUCILIUS and TITINIUS.]
BRUTUS.   Lucius, a bowl of wine!   140
                     [Exit LUCIUS.]
CASSIUS. I did not think you could have been so
    angry.
BRUTUS. O Cassius, I am sick of many griefs.
CASSIUS. Of your philosophy you make no use,
    If you give place to accidental evils.°
BRUTUS. No man bears sorrow better. Portia is
    dead.   145
CASSIUS. Ha! Portia!
BRUTUS. She is dead.
CASSIUS. How 'scap'd I killing when I cross'd you
    so?
    O insupportable and touching loss!
    Upon what sickness?
BRUTUS.   Impatient of my absence,   150
    And grief that young Octavius with Mark
    Antony
    Have made themselves so strong—for with her
    death
    That tidings came—with this she fell distract,
    And, her attendants absent, swallow'd fire.

---

brav'd badgered   Check'd chastised
conn'd by rote memorized
Plutus Pluto, god of wealth   scope free range
dishonor . . . humor dishonest acts will be regarded as
   your whim
who much enforced which, being struck hard
rash humor quick temper

cynic i.e., rude fellow (the Cynic philosophers—e.g.,
   Diogenes—affected rude manners)
Of . . . evils i.e., Brutus, as a devotee of Stoicism, should
   bear everything evenly

Cassius. And died so?

Brutus.   Even so.

155 Cassius.   O ye immortal gods!

[*Re-enter* Lucius, *with wine and taper.*]

Brutus. Speak no more of her. Give me a bowl of
wine.

In this I bury all unkindness, Cassius.

[*Drinks.*]

Cassius. My heart is thirsty for that noble pledge.

Fill, Lucius, till the wine o'erswell the cup;

160 I cannot drink too much of Brutus' love.

[*Drinks.*]

Brutus. Come in, Titinius!   [*Exit* Lucius.]

[*Re-enter* Titinius, *with* Messala.]

Welcome, good Messala.

Now sit we close about this taper here

And call in question our necessities.

Cassius. Portia, art thou gone?

Brutus.   No more, I pray you.

165 Messala, I have here received letters

That young Octavius and Mark Antony

Come down upon us with a mighty power,

Bending their expedition toward Philippi.

Messala. Myself have letters of the selfsame
tenor.°

170 Brutus. With what addition?

Messala. That by proscription and bills of out-
lawry

Octavius, Antony, and Lepidus

Have put to death an hundred Senators.

Brutus. Therein our letters do not well agree;

175 Mine speak of seventy Senators that died

By their proscriptions, Cicero being one.

Cassius. Cicero one!

Messala.   Cicero is dead,

And by that order of proscription.

Had you your letters from your wife, my lord?

180 Brutus. No, Messala.

Messala. Nor nothing in your letters writ of her?

Brutus. Nothing, Messala.

Messala.   That, methinks, is strange.

Brutus. Why ask you? Hear you aught of her in
yours?

Messala. No, my lord.

185 Brutus. Now, as you are a Roman, tell me true.

Messala. Then like a Roman bear the truth I tell.

For certain she is dead, and by strange manner.

Brutus. Why, farewell, Portia. We must die,
Messala.

With meditating that she must die once°

190 I have the patience to endure it now.

Messala. Even so great men great losses should
endure.

tenor purport   *once* sometime

Cassius. I have as much of this in art° as you,

But yet my nature could not bear it so.

Brutus. Well, to our work alive. What do you
think

Of marching to Philippi presently?°   195

Cassius. I do not think it good.

Brutus.   Your reason?

Cassius.   This it is:

'Tis better that the enemy seek us.

So shall he waste his means, weary his soldiers,

Doing himself offense, whilst we lying still

Are full of rest, defense, and nimbleness.   200

Brutus. Good reasons must of force° give place to
better.

The people 'twixt Philippi and this ground

Do stand but in a forc'd affection,

For they have grudg'd us contribution.

The enemy, marching along by them,   205

By them shall make a fuller number up,

Come on refresh'd, new-added, and encourag'd;

From which advantage shall we cut him off

If at Philippi we do face him there,

These people at our back.

Cassius.   Hear me, good brother.   210

Brutus. Under your pardon. You must note beside

That we have tried the utmost of our friends;

Our legions are brim-full, our cause is ripe.

The enemy increaseth every day;

We, at the height, are ready to decline.   215

There is a tide in the affairs of men

Which taken at the flood leads on to fortune;

Omitted,° all the voyage of their life

Is bound in shallows and in miseries.

On such a full sea are we now afloat,   220

And we must take the current when it serves

Or lose our ventures.

Cassius.   Then, with your will,° go on;

We'll along ourselves and meet them at Philippi.

Brutus. The deep of night is crept upon our talk,

And nature must obey necessity,   225

Which we will niggard° with a little rest.

There is no more to say?

Cassius.   No more. Good night.

Early tomorrow will we rise and hence.

Brutus. Lucius! [*Re-enter* Lucius] My gown.

[*Exit* Lucius.]

Farewell, good Messala.

Good night, Titinius. Noble, noble Cassius,   230

Good night, and good repose.

Cassius.   O my dear brother!

This was an ill beginning of the night.

art theory
presently immediately   *of force* of necessity
Omitted neglected   *with . . . will* as you wish
niggard be miserly to; i.e., sleep only briefly

Never come such division 'tween our souls!
Let it not, Brutus.
BRUTUS.   Everything is well.
CASSIUS. Good night, my lord.
235 BRUTUS.   Good night, good brother.
TITINIUS *and* MESSALA. Good night, Lord Brutus.
BRUTUS.   Farewell, everyone.
                          [*Exeunt all but* BRUTUS.]
          [*Re-enter* LUCIUS, *with the gown.*]
     Give me the gown. Where is thy instrument?
LUCIUS. Here in the tent.
BRUTUS.   What, thou speak'st drowsily?
     Poor knave, I blame thee not; thou art o'er-
     watch'd.°
240 Call Claudius and some other of my men;
     I'll have them sleep on cushions in my tent.
LUCIUS. Varro and Claudius!
          [*Enter* VARRO *and* CLAUDIUS.]
VARRO. Calls my lord?
BRUTUS. I pray you, sirs, lie in my tent and sleep;
245 It may be I shall raise you by and by
     On business to my brother Cassius.
VARRO. So please you, we will stand and watch
     your pleasure.
BRUTUS. I will not have it so; lie down, good sirs,
     It may be I shall otherwise bethink me.
250 Look, Lucius, here's the book I sought for so;
     I put it in the pocket of my gown.
               [VARRO *and* CLAUDIUS *lie down.*]
LUCIUS. I was sure your lordship did not give it me.
BRUTUS. Bear with me, good boy, I am much
     forgetful.
     Canst thou hold up thy heavy eyes awhile,
255 And touch thy instrument a strain or two?
LUCIUS. Aye, my lord, an't please you.
BRUTUS.   It does, my boy.
     I trouble thee too much, but thou art willing.
LUCIUS. It is my duty, sir.
BRUTUS. I should not urge thy duty past thy might;
260 I know young bloods look for a time of rest.
LUCIUS. I have slept, my lord, already.
BRUTUS. It was well done, and thou shalt sleep
     again; ·
     I will not hold thee long. If I do live,
     I will be good to thee.   [*Music, and a song.*]
265 This is a sleepy tune. O murd'rous slumber,
     Lay'st thou thy leaden mace upon my boy
     That plays thee music? Gentle knave, good
     night;
     I will not do thee so much wrong to wake thee.
     If thou dost nod, thou break'st thy instrument.
270 I'll take it from thee; and, good boy, good night.

Let me see, let me see; is not the leaf turn'd
down
Where I left reading? Here it is, I think.
                              [*Sits down.*]
          [*Enter the* GHOST OF CÆSAR.]
How ill this taper burns! Ha! Who comes here?
I think it is the weakness of mine eyes
That shapes this monstrous apparition.   275
It comes upon me. Art thou anything?
Art thou some god, some angel, or some devil,
That mak'st my blood cold and my hair to
     stare?°
Speak to me what thou art.
GHOST. Thy evil spirit, Brutus.
BRUTUS.   Why comest thou?   280
GHOST. To tell thee thou shalt see me at Philippi.
BRUTUS. Well; then I shall see thee again?
GHOST. Aye, at Philippi.
BRUTUS. Why, I will see thee at Philippi then.
                              [*Exit* GHOST.]
Now I have taken heart, thou vanishest.   285
Ill spirit, I would hold more talk with thee.
Boy, Lucius! Varro! Claudius! Sirs, awake!
Claudius!
LUCIUS. The strings, my lord, are false.
BRUTUS. He thinks he still is at his instrument.   290
     Lucius, awake!
LUCIUS. My lord?
BRUTUS. Didst thou dream, Lucius, that thou so
     criedst out?
LUCIUS. My lord, I do not know that I did cry.
BRUTUS. Yes, that thou didst. Didst thou see any-
     thing?   295
LUCIUS. Nothing, my lord.
BRUTUS. Sleep again, Lucius. Sirrah Claudius!
     [*To* VARRO] Fellow thou, awake!
VARRO. My lord?
CLAUDIUS. My lord?   300
BRUTUS. Why did you so cry out, sirs, in your
     sleep?
VARRO *and* CLAUDIUS. Did we, my lord?
BRUTUS.   Aye. Saw you anything?
VARRO. No, my lord, I saw nothing.
CLAUDIUS.   Nor I, my lord.
BRUTUS. Go and commend me to my brother
     Cassius;
     Bid him set on his powers betimes before,°   305
     And we will follow.
VARRO *and* CLAUDIUS. It shall be done, my lord.
                              [*Exeunt*]

---

o'erwatch'd   gone too long without sleep

stare   start up
betimes before   i.e., at once, before mine

ACT V

SCENE i
The plains of Philippi.

[*Enter* OCTAVIUS, ANTONY, *and their* ARMY.]
OCTAVIUS. Now, Antony, our hopes are answered.
  You said the enemy would not come down,
  But keep the hills and upper regions.
  It proves not so; their battles° are at hand.
5 They mean to warn° us at Philippi here,
  Answering before we do demand of them.
ANTONY. Tut, I am in their bosoms,° and I know
  Wherefore they do it. They could be content
  To visit other places, and come down
10 With fearful bravery, thinking by this face
  To fasten in our thoughts that they have courage.
  But 'tis not so.
        [*Enter a* MESSENGER.]
MESSENGER.   Prepare you, generals.
  The enemy comes on in gallant show.
  Their bloody sign of battle is hung out,
15 And something to be done immediately.
ANTONY. Octavius, lead your battle softly on
  Upon the left hand of the even field.
OCTAVIUS. Upon the right hand I; keep thou the
  left.
ANTONY. Why do you cross me in this exigent?°
20 OCTAVIUS. I do not cross you; but I will do so.
                  [*March.*]
  [*Drum. Enter* BRUTUS, CASSIUS, *and their* ARMY;
    LUCILIUS, TITINIUS, MESSALA, *and others.*]
BRUTUS. They stand and would have parley.
CASSIUS. Stand fast, Titinius. We must out and
  talk.
OCTAVIUS. Mark Antony, shall we give sign of
  battle?
ANTONY. No, Cæsar, we will answer on their
  charge.
  Make forth; the generals would have some
25 words.
OCTAVIUS. Stir not until the signal.
BRUTUS. Words before blows. Is it so, countrymen?
OCTAVIUS. Not that we love words better, as you
  do.
BRUTUS. Good words are better than bad strokes,
  Octavius.

ANTONY. In your bad strokes, Brutus, you give
  good words.   30
  Witness the hole you made in Cæsar's heart,
  Crying "Long live! Hail, Cæsar!"
CASSIUS.   Antony,
  The posture° of your blows are yet unknown;
  But for your words, they rob the Hybla° bees
  And leave them honeyless.
ANTONY.   Not stingless too.   35
BRUTUS. O, yes, and soundless too,
  For you have stol'n their buzzing, Antony,
  And very wisely threat before you sting.
ANTONY. Villains, you did not so when your vile
  daggers
  Hack'd one another in the sides of Cæsar.   40
  You show'd your teeth like apes and fawn'd like
  hounds
  And bow'd like bondmen, kissing Cæsar's feet,
  Whilst damned Casca, like a cur, behind
  Struck Cæsar on the neck. O you flatterers!
CASSIUS. Flatterers! Now, Brutus, thank yourself.   45
  This tongue had not offended so today
  If Cassius might have rul'd.
OCTAVIUS. Come, come, the cause. If arguing make
  us sweat,
  The proof of it will turn to redder drops.
  Look;   50
  I draw a sword against conspirators;
  When think you that the sword goes up again?
  Never, till Cæsar's three and thirty wounds
  Be well aveng'd, or till another Cæsar
  Have added slaughter to the sword of traitors.   55
BRUTUS. Cæsar, thou canst not die by traitors'
  hands
  Unless thou bring'st them with thee.
OCTAVIUS.   So I hope;
  I was not born to die on Brutus' sword.
BRUTUS. O, if thou wert the noblest of thy strain,
  Young man, thou couldst not die more honor-
  able.   60
CASSIUS. A peevish schoolboy, worthless of such
  honor,
  Join'd with a masker and a reveler!
ANTONY. Old Cassius still!
OCTAVIUS.   Come, Antony; away!
  Defiance, traitors, hurl we in your teeth.

---

battles battalions   *warn* challenge
in . . . bosoms aware of what is in their hearts
exigent emergency

posture force
Hybla Sicilian town famed for honey

65 If you dare fight today, come to the field.
If not, when you have stomachs.

[*Exeunt* OCTAVIUS, ANTONY, *and their* ARMY.]

CASSIUS. Why, now, blow wind, swell billow, and
swim bark!
The storm is up, and all is on the hazard.°
BRUTUS. Ho, Lucilius! Hark, a word with you.
LUCILIUS.   [*Standing forth*] My lord?

[BRUTUS *and* LUCILIUS *converse apart*.]

CASSIUS. Messala!
MESSALA. [*Standing forth*] What says my general?
70 CASSIUS.   Messala,
This is my birthday; as° this very day
Was Cassius born. Give me thy hand, Messala.
Be thou my witness that, against my will,
As Pompey was,° am I compell'd to set
75 Upon one battle all our liberties.
You know that I held Epicurus strong,
And his opinion.° Now I change my mind,
And partly credit things that do presage.
Coming from Sardis, on our former ensign°
80 Two mighty eagles fell, and there they perch'd,
Gorging and feeding from our soldiers' hands,
Who to Philippi here consorted° us.
This morning are they fled away and gone,
And in their steads do ravens, crows, and kites
85 Fly o'er our heads and downward look on us
As we were sickly prey. Their shadows seem
A canopy most fatal, under which
Our army lies, ready to give up the ghost.
MESSALA. Believe not so.
CASSIUS.   I but believe it partly,
90 For I am fresh of spirit and resolv'd
To meet all perils very constantly.°
BRUTUS. Even so, Lucilius.
CASSIUS.   Now, most noble Brutus,
The gods today stand friendly, that we may,
Lovers in peace, lead on our days to age!
95 But since th' affairs of men rest still° incertain,
Let's reason with the worst that may befall.
If we do lose this battle, then is this
The very last time we shall speak·together.
What are you then determined to do?
100 BRUTUS. Even by the rule of that philosophy°
By which I did blame Cato for the death
Which he did give himself—I know not how,
But I do find it cowardly and vile,

For fear of what might fall,° so to prevent
The time of life—arming myself with patience 105
To stay° the providence of some high powers
That govern us below.
CASSIUS.   Then if we lose this battle,
You are contented to be led in triumph
Thorough the streets of Rome?
BRUTUS. No, Cassius, no. Think not, thou noble
Roman,   110
That ever Brutus will go bound to Rome;
He bears too great a mind. But this same day
Must end that work the ides of March begun;
And whether we shall meet again I know not.
Therefore our everlasting farewell take.   115
Forever and forever farewell, Cassius!
If we do meet again, why, we shall smile;
If not, why then this parting was well made.
CASSIUS. Forever and forever farewell, Brutus!
If we do meet again, we'll smile indeed;   120
If not, 'tis true this parting was well made.
BRUTUS. Why then, lead on. O that a man might
know
The end of this day's business ere it come!
But it sufficeth that the day will end,
And then the end is known. Come, ho! Away! 125

[*Exeunt*]

SCENE ii
The field of battle.

[*Alarum. Enter* BRUTUS *and* MESSALA.]

BRUTUS. Ride, ride, Messala, ride, and give these
bills°
Unto the legions on the other side.

[*Loud alarum.*]

Let them set on at once; for I perceive
But cold demeanor° in Octavius' wing,
And sudden push gives them the overthrow.   5
Ride, ride, Messala; let them all come down.

[*Exeunt*]

SCENE iii
Another part of the field.

[*Alarums. Enter* CASSIUS *and* TITINIUS.]

CASSIUS. O, look, Titinius, look, the villains fly!
Myself have to mine own turn'd enemy.
This ensign° here of mine was turning back;
I slew the coward, and did take it from him.

---

hazard at stake   *as* on
As Pompey was at Pharsalia in 48 B.C. Caesar forced
  Pompey to fight at a disadvantage
held . . . opinion believed in the Epicurean teachings on
  the absurdity of superstitition
former ensign foremost banner   consorted accompanied
constantly resolutely   *still* always
that philosophy Stoicism, which found suicide base

fall happen   *stay the providence* await the fate
bills orders   *cold demeanor* lack of spirit
ensign standard bearer

5 TITINIUS. O Cassius, Brutus gave the word too early,
  Who, having some advantage on Octavius,
  Took it too eagerly. His soldiers fell to spoil,
  Whilst we by Antony are all enclos'd.
                    [Enter PINDARUS.]
  PINDARUS. Fly further off, my lord, fly further off.
10 Mark Antony is in your tents, my lord.
  Fly, therefore, noble Cassius, fly far off.
  CASSIUS. This hill is far enough. Look, look, Titinius;
  Are those my tents where I perceive the fire?
  TITINIUS. They are, my lord.
  CASSIUS.   Titinius, if thou lovest me,
15 Mount thou my horse and hide thy spurs in him
  Till he have brought thee up to yonder troops
  And here again, that I may rest assur'd
  Whether yond troops are friend or enemy.
  TITINIUS. I will be here again, even with a thought.
                              [Exit]
20 CASSIUS. Go, Pindarus, get higher on that hill.
  My sight was ever thick;° regard Titinius,
  And tell me what thou not'st about the field.
                    [PINDARUS ascends the hill.]
  This day I breathed first: time is come round,
  And where I did begin, there shall I end;
25 My life is run his compass. Sirrah, what news?
  PINDARUS. [Above] O my lord!
  CASSIUS. What news?
  PINDARUS. [Above] Titinius is enclosed round about
  With horsemen that make to him on the spur;
30 Yet he spurs on. Now they are almost on him.
  Now, Titinius! Now some light. O, he lights too.
  He's ta'en. [Shout] And, hark! They shout for joy.
  CASSIUS. Come down; behold no more.
  O, coward that I am to live so long
35 To see my best friend ta'en before my face!
                    [PINDARUS descends.]
  Come hither, sirrah.
  In Parthia did I take thee prisoner,
  And then I swore thee, saving of thy life,
  That whatsoever I did bid thee do,
  Thou shouldst attempt it. Come now, keep thine
40   oath.
  Now be a freeman, and with this good sword
  That ran through Cæsar's bowels, search° this
    bosom.
  Stand not to answer. Here, take thou the hilts,
  And when my face is cover'd, as 'tis now,
  Guide thou the sword. [PINDARUS stabs him]
45   Cæsar, thou art reveng'd
  Ev'n with the sword that killed thee.   [Dies.]
  PINDARUS. So, I am free, yet would not so have
    been,
  Durst I have done my will. O Cassius!

Far from this country Pindarus shall run,
Where never Roman shall take note of him.   50
                              [Exit]
          [Re-enter TITINIUS with MESSALA.]
MESSALA. It is but change,° Titinius; for Octavius
  Is overthrown by noble Brutus' power
  As Cassius' legions are by Antony.
TITINIUS. These tidings will well comfort Cassius.
MESSALA. Where did you leave him?
TITINIUS.   All disconsolate,   55
  With Pindarus his bondman, on this hill.
MESSALA. Is not that he that lies upon the ground?
TITINIUS. He lies not like the living. O my heart!
MESSALA. Is not that he?
TITINIUS.   No, this was he, Messala,
  But Cassius is no more. O setting sun,   60
  As in thy red rays thou dost sink to night,
  So in his red blood Cassius' day is set,
  The sun of Rome is set! Our day is gone;
  Clouds, dews, and dangers come; our deeds are
    done!
  Mistrust of my success hath done this deed.   65
MESSALA. Mistrust of good success hath done this
    deed.
  O hateful error, melancholy's child,
  Why dost thou show to the apt thoughts of men
  The things that are not? O error, soon conceiv'd,
  Thou never com'st unto a happy birth,   70
  But kill'st the mother that engender'd thee!
TITINIUS. What, Pindarus! Where art thou,
    Pindarus?
MESSALA. Seek him, Titinius, whilst I go to meet
  The noble Brutus, thrusting this report
  Into his ears. I may say "thrusting" it,   75
  For piercing steel and darts envenomed
  Shall be as welcome to the ears of Brutus
  As tidings of this sight.
TITINIUS.   Hie you, Messala,
  And I will seek for Pindarus the while.
                              [Exit MESSALA.]
  Why didst thou send me forth, brave Cassius?   80
  Did I not meet thy friends? And did not they
  Put on my brows this wreath of victory
  And bid me give it thee? Didst thou not hear
    their shouts?
  Alas, thou has misconstru'd everything!
  But hold thee, take this garland on thy brow;   85
  Thy Brutus bid me give it thee, and I
  Will do his bidding. Brutus, come apace,
  And see how I regarded Caius Cassius.
  By your leave, gods: this is a Roman's part.
  Come, Cassius' sword, and find Titinius' heart.   90
                              [Kills himself.]

---

thick blurred   *search* probe   *change* exchange

[*Alarum. Re-enter* MESSALA, *with* BRUTUS, *young*
CATO, *and others.*]
BRUTUS. Where, where, Messala, doth his body lie?
MESSALA. Lo, yonder, and Titinius mourning it.
BRUTUS. Titinius' face is upward.
CATO.   He is slain.
BRUTUS. O Julius Cæsar, thou art mighty yet!
95   Thy spirit walks abroad, and turns our swords
      In our own proper° entrails.   [*Low alarums.*]
CATO.   Brave Titinius!
      Look, whether he have not crown'd dead
      Cassius!
BRUTUS. Are yet two Romans living such as these?
      The last of all the Romans, fare thee well!
100   It is impossible that ever Rome
      Should breed thy fellow. Friends, I owe moe
      tears
      To this dead man than you shall see me pay.
      I shall find time, Cassius, I shall find time.
      Come therefore, and to Thasos send his body.
105   His funerals shall not be in our camp,
      Lest it discomfort us. Lucilius, come,
      And come, young Cato. Let us to the field.
      Labeo and Flavius, set our battles on.
      'Tis three o'clock; and, Romans, yet ere night
110   We shall try fortune in a second fight.
                                         [*Exeunt*]

SCENE iv
Another part of the field.

[*Alarum. Enter, fighting,* SOLDIERS *of both armies;*
then BRUTUS, *young* CATO, LUCILIUS, *and others.*]
BRUTUS. Yet, countrymen, O, yet hold up your
      heads!   [*Exit*]
CATO. What bastard doth not? Who will go with
      me?
      I will proclaim my name about the field.
      I am the son of Marcus Cato, ho!
5   A foe to tyrants, and my country's friend;
      I am the son of Marcus Cato, ho!
LUCILIUS. And I am Brutus, Marcus Brutus, I;
      Brutus, my country's friend; know me for
      Brutus!
                  [*Cato is slain.*]
      O young and noble Cato, art thou down?
10   Why, now thou diest as bravely as Titinius,
      And mayst be honor'd, being Cato's son.
FIRST SOLDIER. Yield, or thou diest.
LUCILIUS.   Only I yield to die.°

[*Offering money*] There is so much that thou wilt
      kill me straight;
      Kill Brutus, and be honor'd in his death.
FIRST SOLDIER. We must not. A noble prisoner!   15
SECOND SOLDIER. Room, ho! Tell Antony, Brutus is
      ta'en.
FIRST SOLDIER. I'll tell the news. Here comes the
      general.
                  [*Enter* ANTONY.]
      Brutus is ta'en, Brutus is ta'en, my lord.
ANTONY. Where is he?
LUCILIUS. Safe, Antony. Brutus is safe enough;   20
      I dare assure thee that no enemy
      Shall ever take alive the noble Brutus.
      The gods defend him from so great a shame!
      When you do find him, or alive or° dead,
      He will be found like Brutus, like himself.   25
ANTONY. This is not Brutus, friend, but, I assure
      you,
      A prize no less in worth. Keep this man safe,
      Give him all kindness. I had rather have
      Such men my friends than enemies. Go on,
      And see whether Brutus be alive or dead   30
      And bring us word unto Octavius' tent
      How everything is chanc'd.°   [*Exeunt*]

SCENE v
Another part of the field.

[*Enter* BRUTUS, DARDANIUS, CLITUS, STRATO, *and*
VOLUMNIUS.]
BRUTUS. Come, poor remains of friends, rest on this
      rock.
CLITUS. Statilius show'd the torchlight, but, my
      lord,
      He came not back. He is or ta'en or° slain.
BRUTUS. Sit thee down, Clitus. Slaying is the word;
      It is a deed in fashion. Hark thee, Clitus.   5
                              [*Whispering.*]
CLITUS. What, I, my lord? No, not for all the world.
BRUTUS. Peace then, no words.
CLITUS.   I'll rather kill myself.
BRUTUS. Hark thee, Dardanius.   [*Whispering.*]
DARDANIUS.   Shall I do such a deed?
CLITUS. O Dardanius!
DARDANIUS. O Clitus!   10
CLITUS. What ill request did Brutus make to thee?
DARDANIUS. To kill him, Clitus. Look, he meditates.
CLITUS. Now is that noble vessel full of grief
      That it runs over even at his eyes.

---

own proper very own
Only . . . die I yield only that I may die

or . . . or whether . . . or   *is chanc'd* has come out
or . . . or either . . . or

BRUTUS. Come hither, good Volumnius; list a
15   word.
VOLUMNIUS. What says my lord?
BRUTUS.   Why, this, Volumnius:
    The ghost of Cæsar hath appear'd to me
    Two several° times by night, at Sardis once,
    And this last night here in Philippi fields.
    I know my hour is come.
20 VOLUMNIUS.   Not so, my lord.
BRUTUS. Nay, I am sure it is, Volumnius.
    Thou seest the world, Volumnius, how it goes;
    Our enemies have beat us to the pit.
                         [Low alarums.]
    It is more worthy to leap in ourselves
25   Than tarry till they push us. Good Volumnius,
    Thou know'st that we two went to school
      together.
    Even for that our love of old, I prithee,
    Hold thou my sword hilts, whilst I run on it.
VOLUMNIUS. That's not an office for a friend, my
    lord.   [Alarum still.]
30 CLITUS. Fly, fly, my lord; there is no tarrying here.
BRUTUS. Farewell to you, and you, and you,
    Volumnius.
    Strato, thou hast been all this while asleep.
    Farewell to thee too, Strato. Countrymen,
    My heart doth joy that yet in all my life
35   I found no man but he was true to me.
    I shall have glory by this losing day,
    More than Octavius and Mark Antony
    By this vile conquest shall attain unto.
    So fare you well at once, for Brutus' tongue
40   Hath almost ended his life's history.
    Night hangs upon mine eyes; my bones would
      rest,
    That have but labor'd to attain this hour.
            [Alarum. Cry within, "Fly, fly, fly!"]
CLITUS. Fly, my lord, fly.
BRUTUS.   Hence! I will follow.
    [Exeunt CLITUS, DARDANIUS, and VOLUMNIUS.]
    I prithee, Strato, stay thou by thy lord.
45   Thou art a fellow of a good respect.°
    Thy life hath had some smatch° of honor in it.

    Hold then my sword and turn away thy face
    While I do run upon it. Wilt thou, Strato?
STRATO. Give me your hand first. Fare you well,
    my lord.
BRUTUS. Farewell, good Strato. [Runs on his sword]
    Cæsar, now be still.   50
    I kill'd not thee with half so good a will. [Dies.]
[Alarum. Retreat. Enter OCTAVIUS, ANTONY, MESSALA,
                  LUCILIUS, and the ARMY.]
OCTAVIUS. What man is that?
MESSALA. My master's man. Strato, where is thy
    master?
STRATO. Free from the bondage you are in, Messala.
    The conquerors can but make a fire of him;   55
    For Brutus only overcame himself,
    And no man else hath honor by his death.
LUCILIUS. So Brutus should be found. I thank thee,
    Brutus,
    That thou hast prov'd Lucilius' saying true.
OCTAVIUS. All that serv'd Brutus, I will entertain°
    them.   60
    Fellow, wilt thou bestow thy time with me?
STRATO. Aye, if Messala will prefer° me to you.
OCTAVIUS. Do so, good Messala.
MESSALA. How died my master, Strato?
STRATO. I held the sword, and he did run on it.   65
MESSALA. Octavius, then take him to follow thee
    That did the latest service to my master.
ANTONY. This was the noblest Roman of them all,
    All the conspirators, save only he,
    Did that they did in envy of great Cæsar;   70
    He only, in a general honest thought
    And common good to all, made one of them.
    His life was gentle,° and the elements°
    So mix'd in him that Nature might stand up
    And say to all the world, "This was a man!"   75
OCTAVIUS. According to his virtue let us use him
    With all respect and rites of burial.
    Within my tent his bones tonight shall lie,
    Most like a soldier, order'd° honorably.
    So call the field to rest, and let's away   80
    To part° the glories of this happy day.
                               [Exeunt]

entertain employ   prefer recommend
gentle noble
elements i.e., that compose all matter
order'd arrayed and conducted with due ceremony
part share

several separate   respect reputation
smatch touch

AFTERWORD

"*Julius Caesar* is a landmark not merely in the history of Shakespearean tragedy," says a modern scholar, "but in the history of English tragedy. Before Brutus there had been no tragic hero on the English stage whose character had combined noble grandeur with fatal imperfection."[1]

The play was not Shakespeare's first attempt at tragedy. Nearly ten years before, he had written a "drama of blood," or "tragedy of blood," *Titus Andronicus*, filled with rape, mayhem, and murder, and calculated to catch on with the public taste, as it did. Next came two history plays, *Richard III* and *Richard II*, which came very close to our general idea of what constitutes "Shakespearean tragedy," but which are no doubt more accurately classified in the traditional way as chronicle history plays. Then, about five years before *Julius Caesar*, came *Romeo and Juliet*, unmistakably a tragedy of great beauty and moving power, but controlled by the stars (as the Prologue states) rather than by human character.

Hence *Julius Caesar* stands as the first play in which the dramatist, now arrived at full maturity in his craft, worked out the general pattern of "Shakespearean tragedy" as we commonly think of it. It is quite true that Shakespeare never afterward adhered exactly to his own model, for every later tragedy shows major differences, structural and other, from every other; but the basic principle of *Julius Caesar* also underlies the great works that followed in swift succession—*Hamlet, Othello, King Lear, Macbeth, Antony and Cleopatra,* and *Coriolanus*. (*Timon of Athens*, Shakespeare's only abortive tragedy, of which it has been said that he never succeeded in dragging its subject into the light, hardly deserves to be grouped with the others, even though it, too, clearly represents an attempt at a tragedy of character.)

Stripped to its essentials, the idea of this species of tragedy is that the hero himself— and not external forces, however influential they may be—is primarily responsible for his own downfall and death; his own character determines the way in which he responds to the elements of his situation, and the way that he chooses proves fatal. Shakespearean tragedy is thus, first of all, a tragedy not of fate or fortune, but of human character and human will. In a tragedy of fate, a supernatural and external force (which may, of course, work *through* the character of the protagonist and the characters of other participants) directs the actions of men and presses the tragic hero inexorably toward disaster. In a tragedy of fortune, the Lady Fortune herself, to use the medieval image, gives her great wheel a whimsical spin so that he who had stood at the top finds himself suddenly precipitated to the bottom. Says Chaucer's Monk in the *Canterbury Tales* (paraphrased), "Tragedy is to say a certain story of one who stood in great prosperity and falls into misery and ends wretchedly." Again in general terms, tragedy of fate is Greek; tragedy of fortune is medieval; and tragedy of character is Renaissance. (Christopher Marlowe, who with his *Tamburlaine* and *Doctor Faustus* before 1590 took a great step toward "Shakespearean tragedy," makes his Tamburlaine boast that he holds "the Fates" fast gripped in his own hands, and with his own hand "turns Fortune's wheel about"—a notable and most significant repudiation of external control and assertion of the primacy of the human will. Here, if not always elsewhere, Marlowe, like Shakespeare and like "Shakespearean tragedy," was thoroughly an expression of the Renaissance.)

That Shakespeare consciously intended *Julius Caesar* to be a tragedy of a new and distinct species is suggested by the deliberateness with which he delineates the crucial

[1]Willard Farnham, *Shakespeare's Tragic Frontier* (Berkeley: University of California Press, 1950).

358

features of its structure. Presumably because he was working out a new pattern, he marked the steps heavily; indeed, it has sometimes been remarked that he worked with too heavy a hand in labeling the "tragic flaw" of his protagonist and in demonstrating its causal relationship to the acts that lead to disaster for Brutus. First of all, in this pioneering draft, he establishes an enveloping situation, the environment or "world" within which the action is to occur, stressing, at the same time, its significance. The opening scene represents the historical fickleness of the Roman commoners, the perennial instability of their loyalties—a basic condition the relevance of which for Brutus and his allies is shortly afterward to be demonstrated. The general situation is next made specific, when the triumphant Caesar returns and is greeted with ominously divided reactions. Next—and now most carefully of all—Shakespeare brings his hero, Brutus, upon the stage and boldly identifies exactly that in his character which will eventually be his undoing. Not only does the dramatist make various other persons express themselves repeatedly throughout the play on the subject of Brutus's honor, but he makes the hero himself exhibit a preoccupation, amounting at times to a virtual obsession, with honor. In one way or another, sometimes head on, sometimes obliquely, Brutus evinces his addiction in nearly every speech he makes:

> If it be aught toward the general good,
> Set honor in one eye and death i' th' other,
> And I will look on both indifferently.
> For let the gods so speed me as I love
> The name of honor more than I fear death.

One advantage of the later tragic heroes is that none of them ever again so blatantly advertises his special, and fatal, blindness (though in the abortive *Timon* other persons are made to dwell excessively upon Timon's selfless generosity).

Having thus unmistakably labeled what will prove to be the "tragic flaw" of his hero, Shakespeare moves on to his temptation by Cassius, who shrewdly plays upon that in Brutus which is most likely to stir him to action, his dedication to the "general good" of Rome. Half convinced already, Brutus is easily caught by the tempter's bait. Shakespeare next exhibits him in a crucial moment of self-debate that ends in commitment:

> O Rome, I make thee promise:
> If the redress will follow, thou receivest
> Thy full petition at the hand of Brutus.

Then follows the fatal act itself—the assassination of "the foremost man of all this world," the deed being foreshadowed by a full complement of supernatural manifestations that proclaim its magnitude.

Shakespeare leaves no doubt that the decision to murder Caesar was motivated by Brutus's high-mindedness; the other conspirators are moved by impure considerations, but not the hero. His is a decision that is dictated by that in his nature which directs him along a particular course as inevitably as the stars guide the incidents of *Romeo and Juliet* to a predestined end. But the decision to kill Caesar is only the first of several disastrous decisions that Shakespeare shows to be dictated by Brutus's character. Indeed, even before the assassination, the hero errs fatally when he rejects the urging of Cassius and others that Antony be slain with Caesar. He does so with the same singularly high-minded brand of reasoning that everywhere characterizes his mind. Somewhat less significantly, he also rejects his fellows' suggestion that Cicero be invited to join their numbers. Says Metellus Cimber,

> . . . his silver hairs
> Will purchase us a good opinion
> And buy men's voices to commend our deeds.

But Brutus overrules them all. How great an error was the omission of Cicero, of course we cannot know; his silver hairs and silver tongue might or might not have counteracted Antony's powerful appeal to public opinion. In any event, the decision is illustrative of Brutus's character.

If any one error may be singled out as most disastrous of all, however, it is surely the decision to allow Antony to speak at Caesar's funeral. At the time Brutus makes this decision, Shakespeare has not fully characterized Antony; but he has shown enough for us to recognize how grave is Brutus's fault—and of course our sense of the impending danger is heightened by the shrewd Cassius's anguished exclamation: "You know not what you do!" But so unqualified is Brutus's confidence in the rightness of his cause that he supposes the public will need only to be told the simple truth in order to be won wholly to the conspirators' side. Of course neither Antony nor the commoner of Rome is ruled by the same uncompromising nobility that governs Brutus, and both betray his blind trust.

The remaining formal steps in the progress of this first "Shakespearean tragedy" follow rather routinely. Shakespeare marks the climax of the action, or turning point in the fortunes of the hero, with a single line spoken by the First Citizen at the end of the first section of Antony's oration: "Methinks there is much reason in his sayings." With this the tide turns, and what comes after is the "falling action" of the tragedy, wherein the affairs of Brutus and Cassius are shown undergoing rapid deterioration whereas those of Antony and Octavius, relentlessly pursuing, steadily improve. The deaths of Brutus and Cassius constitute the formal catastrophe, which puts an end to the enterprise and all of Brutus's high hopes for his country. Finally occurs the "lift" that regularly characterizes the ending of a Shakespearean tragedy. Brutus, before he dies, lauds the heroic qualities of Cassius and Titinius, and at the very last Antony and Octavius eulogize the fallen Brutus. We are thus left with a final, strong, and perhaps exhilarating sense of Brutus's nobility. It is noteworthy that Shakespeare passes no moral judgment on Brutus's act itself; his sole insistence is that the man himself believed it to be honorable.

Such, in broad terms, are the features of the pattern worked out in *Julius Caesar* for a species of tragedy in which the key element is the causal relationship of the hero's character to his ruin. In the later tragedies these features are never again so conspicuously exhibited. In *Hamlet*, *King Lear*, and *Antony and Cleopatra*, most notably, the pattern is deeply buried amidst the great complexities of both characters and incidents. Dominated by a single trait of character, Brutus is the least complex of the tragic heroes, and his virtually single-faceted nature served Shakespeare admirably in the making of a tragedy wherein the fall of the hero may be appropriately attributed to his "tragic flaw." For no other of his tragedies does this concept so adequately explain what it is, essentially, that happens in tragedy.

The working out of a basic tragic pattern does not, of course, constitute Shakespeare's whole achievement in this play. *Julius Caesar* offers a small but vivid and memorable assemblage of character portraits, most of which are in fact dramatically superior to the portrait of Brutus, where Shakespeare may have labored somewhat too concentratedly upon the single trait that determines his hero's tragic path. Cassius is in all ways a more interesting figure because he is not so narrowly conceived or so flatly drawn. Shrewd and envious he is, but shrewdness and enviousness do not, like Brutus's imperturbable righteousness, describe him wholly. Much that we may not have imagined to exist in the depths of Cassius's mind and heart is revealed in the great quarrel scene of Act IV, and we have even more to learn of the man in the final scenes. Of Brutus, in contrast, we have virtually nothing more to learn after his opening lines in the first scene of the play.

Caesar is another case of considerably greater character variety than is evinced in the portrait of Brutus. Never greatly admired by critics of the play, and described by an eminent Shakespearean (H. N. Hudson) at the beginning of this century as merely "a grand, strutting piece of puff-paste," this Caesar is in fact a worthy product of Shakespeare's mature skill. The dramatist treats him unreverentially, to be sure, making him pompous, overbearing, immoderately conscious of his own greatness, and generally unbearable. The appraisal of himself and his unshakable position in the universe that Shakespeare puts into his mouth just before he is stabbed comes over with such palpable irony encasing it that it is all but laughable. Yet if one examines the total portrait as it is gradually drawn from Caesar's first appearance until his final "*Et tu, Brute,*" he is sure to catch an occasional glimpse of "the foremost man of all this world." More interesting, too, than the portrait of Brutus is the portrait, briefly exposed as it is, of his wife, Portia. Regularly acted in the theater as a marblelike figure, standing as a stereotype of the Noble Roman Lady, Shakespeare's Portia is really a veritable packet of neuroses who once gave herself a wound—"a great gash in the thigh," said Plutarch—in order to prove her manly capability. She talks incessantly and unbearably in her recital of multiple grievances when she has her husband's long-suffering ear within sound of her voice; she rattles on incoherently to the boy Lucius as she dispatches him to the Capitol; and finally —offstage, in what would surely have been an intolerable scene of mixed self-justification and complaining had not Shakespeare graciously spared us the ordeal—she swallows fire and dies. Details for the portrait of Portia came from Plutarch and suggest that both writers read her character well. Brutus's alleged stoicism is perhaps not so well shown by the way he bears his wife's death as by his bearing with her alive.

Last of the brilliant portraits is that of Antony, who grows before our eyes more suddenly and vividly than does any other major figure in Shakespeare. His portrait is a masterpiece of economy. Though we see and hear of him early, we do not know quite what to make of him—or even whether we need make anything of him at all—until just after Brutus and his bloody fellows depart (III, i), leaving him alone with Caesar's body. And then, with a rush, all that Shakespeare had held back comes roaring forth: "O, pardon me, thou bleeding piece of earth,/ That I am meek and gentle with these butchers!"—and so on for twenty potent lines ending with "Cry 'Havoc!' and let slip the dogs of war." We are witnesses while he learns, by noting the effect upon himself of Caesar's servant's tears at first sight of Caesar's body, the trick of exhibiting "contagious" tears in public—and shortly thereafter he is saying to the funeral crowd, as he breaks down in tears,

> Bear with me;
> My heart is in the coffin there with Caesar,
> And I must pause till it come back to me.

Soon the whole mob is weeping, and Brutus is doomed.

Regrettably, Octavius Caesar is too briefly shown for us to form more than a preliminary notion of what he is and what he was to become. Shakespeare reserved for *Antony and Cleopatra* his subtle and deep studies of both Octavius and Antony. A few other persons in the play, though not examined in detail, are nevertheless made memorable by their brief moments on the stage. Caesar's wife, Calpurnia, appears in the opening scene but does not speak, and in the lone scene in which she does speak (II,ii) she is shown at a moment when her mind is consumed with fear for Caesar's safety; hence no rounded characterization is appropriate. But she is striking in her concern for her husband, and, dream-ridden though she is, one must prefer her to Portia. Casca's short appearances are the more effective because they furnish some blessed moments of comic relief—sorely needed in this otherwise totally austere play. It is noteworthy that in his very next tragedy, *Hamlet*, Shakespeare corrected the deficiency with a fuller complement of comic elements than is offered by any of the remaining tragedies.

It is at least partly because of its trio of attractive acting parts, in which famous actors can team up and sometimes alternate, that *Julius Caesar* has held a regular place on the stage for three centuries and more. In our own time, for example, James Mason, John Gielgud, and Marlon Brando joined their talents in a distinguished film version in the roles, respectively, of Brutus, Cassius, and Antony. If it is quite true that audiences do not warm to this rather cold tragedy as they do to *Hamlet* or *King Lear* (one critic has remarked that the play "rather thrills us mechanically than moves us deeply"), it is a fact that its main figures can be enormously effective on the stage and that its towering scenes—the assassination, the funeral oration of Antony, and the quarrel of Brutus and Cassius—are etched deeply on the minds of spectators who see them well done.

Finally, the dramatic verse of *Julius Caesar* has no doubt contributed much to the perennial success of the play with both spectators and readers. It is a relatively open and understandable language that Shakespeare writes for his Romans, never lyrical, like that of *Romeo and Juliet*, never sublime like that of *Lear* at its peaks, never spellbinding, like witchcraft itself, as in *Macbeth*. It is instead workmanlike rhetoric, marvelously appropriate to the speaker, the situation, and the immediate argument. At its best, as in Antony's speeches that follow the assassination, it rises to rare heights of eloquence. The Romans, like the Greeks, were famed for their rhetoric and oratory, and in all his classical plays Shakespeare made his characters speak as he presumably thought Greeks and Romans should speak, except for Casca perhaps; but Casca is straight off a London street.

A NOTE ON THE COMPOSITION OF THE PLAY

Julius Caesar was written and first performed at the new Globe Theater in 1599. It was first published in the Folio of 1623. Shakespeare's source was Plutarch's *Lives*, specifically the separate accounts of Caesar, Antony, and Brutus.

Hamlet

DRAMATIS PERSONÆ

CLAUDIUS   *king of Denmark*
HAMLET   *son to the late, and nephew to the present king*
POLONIUS   *lord chamberlain*
HORATIO   *friend to Hamlet*
LAERTES   *son to Polonius*
VOLTIMAND
CORNELIUS
ROSENCRANTZ
GUILDENSTERN   } *courtiers*
OSRIC
A GENTLEMAN
A PRIEST
MARCELLUS
BERNARDO   } *officers*

FRANCISCO   *a soldier*
REYNALDO   *servant to Polonius*
PLAYERS
TWO CLOWNS   *gravediggers*
FORTINBRAS   *prince of Norway*
A CAPTAIN
ENGLISH AMBASSADORS
GERTRUDE   *queen of Denmark, and mother to Hamlet*
OPHELIA   *daughter to Polonius*
LORDS, LADIES, OFFICERS, SOLDIERS, SAILORS, MES-
   SENGERS, *and other* ATTENDANTS
GHOST   *of Hamlet's Father*

SCENE: *Denmark*

ACT I

SCENE i
Elsinore. A platform before the castle.

[FRANCISCO *at his post. Enter to him* BERNARDO.]
BERNARDO. Who's there?
FRANCISCO. Nay, answer me. Stand, and unfold°
   yourself.
BERNARDO. Long live the king!
FRANCISCO. Bernardo?
5 BERNARDO. He.
FRANCISCO. You come most carefully upon your
   hour.
BERNARDO. 'Tis now struck twelve; get thee to bed,
   Francisco.
FRANCISCO. For this relief much thanks. 'Tis bitter
   cold,

unfold identify

And I am sick at heart.
BERNARDO. Have you had quiet guard?
FRANCISCO.   Not a mouse stirring.   10
BERNARDO. Well, good night.
   If you do meet Horatio and Marcellus,
   The rivals° of my watch, bid them make haste.
FRANCISCO. I think I hear them. Stand, ho! Who is
   there?
      [*Enter* HORATIO *and* MARCELLUS.]
HORATIO. Friends to this ground.
MARCELLUS.   And liegemen to the Dane.°   15
FRANCISCO. Give you good night.
MARCELLUS.   O, farewell, honest soldier.
   Who hath reliev'd you?
FRANCISCO.   Bernardo hath my place.
   Give you good night.   [*Exit*]

rivals partners
liegemen . . . Dane loyal subjects to the Danish king

MARCELLUS.   Holla! Bernardo!
BERNARDO.   Say,
What, is Horatio there?
HORATIO.   A piece of him.
BERNARDO. Welcome, Horatio; welcome, good
20   Marcellus.
MARCELLUS. What, has this thing appear'd again
tonight?
BERNARDO. I have seen nothing.
MARCELLUS. Horatio says 'tis but our fantasy,°
And will not let belief take hold of him
25   Touching° this dreaded sight twice seen of us.
Therefore I have entreated him along
With us to watch the minutes of this night,
That if again this apparition come,
He may approve our eyes° and speak to it.
HORATIO. Tush, tush, 'twill not appear.
30   BERNARDO.   Sit down a while,
And let us once again assail your ears,
That are so fortified against our story,
What we have two nights seen.
HORATIO.   Well, sit we down,
And let us hear Bernardo speak of this.
35   BERNARDO. Last night of all,
When yond same star that's westward from the
pole°
Had made his course t'illume that part of
heaven
Where now it burns, Marcellus and myself,
The bell then beating one—
              [Enter GHOST.]
MARCELLUS. Peace, break thee off. Look where it
40   comes again!
BERNARDO. In the same figure, like the king that's
dead.
MARCELLUS. Thou art a scholar;° speak to it,
Horatio.
BERNARDO. Looks it not like the king? Mark it,
Horatio.
HORATIO. Most like. It harrows me with fear and
wonder.
BERNARDO. It would be spoke to.
45   MARCELLUS.   Question it, Horatio.
HORATIO. What art thou that usurp'st this time of
night,
Together with that fair and warlike form
In which the majesty of buried Denmark°

Did sometimes march? By heaven I charge thee,
speak!
MARCELLUS. It is offended.
BERNARDO.   See, it stalks away!   50
HORATIO. Stay! Speak, speak! I charge thee, speak!
              [Exit GHOST.]
MARCELLUS. 'Tis gone, and will not answer.
BARNARDO. How now, Horatio! You tremble and
look pale.
Is not this something more than fantasy?
What think you on 't?   55
HORATIO. Before my God, I might not this believe
Without the sensible and true avouch°
Of mine own eyes.
MARCELLUS.   Is it not like the king?
HORATIO. As thou art to thyself.
Such was the very armor he had on   60
When he th' ambitious Norway combated.
So frown'd he once when in an angry parle.°
He smote the sledded Polacks° on the ice.
'Tis strange.
MARCELLUS. Thus twice before, and jump° at this
dead hour,
With martial stalk hath he gone by our watch. 65
HORATIO. In what particular thought to work I
know not.
But, in the gross and scope° of my opinion,
This bodes some strange eruption to our state.
MARCELLUS. Good now, sit down and tell me, he
that knows,   70
Why this same strict and most observant watch
So nightly toils the subject° of the land,
And why such daily cast of brazen cannon
And foreign mart° for implements of war,
Why such impress° of shipwrights, whose sore
task   75
Does not divide the Sunday from the week.
What might be toward,° that this sweaty haste
Doth make the night joint-laborer with the day.
Who is 't that can inform me?
HORATIO.   That can I—
At least the whisper goes so. Our last king,   80
Whose image even but now appear'd to us,
Was, as you know, by Fortinbras of Norway,
Thereto prick'd on by a most emulate pride,°
Dar'd to the combat, in which our valiant Ham-
let—
For so this side of our known world esteem'd
him—   85

---

fantasy imagination   *Touching* concerning
approve our eyes confirm the reality of what we have
  seen
pole Polestar
scholar i.e., who would presumably know how to address
  a spirit—or so Marcellus supposes
buried Denmark i.e., the buried king

sensible . . . avouch sensory testimony   *parle* parley
Polacks Poles   *jump* just
gross and scope i.e., in general, on the whole
subject subjects   *foreign mart* commerce
impress drafting   *toward* in the offing
emulate pride "touchy" rivalry

Did slay this Fortinbras; who by a seal'd compact,
Well ratified by law and heraldry,
Did forfeit, with his life, all those his lands
Which he stood seiz'd of, to the conqueror;
90 Against the which a moiety competent°
Was gaged° by our king, which had return'd
To the inheritance of Fortinbras
Had he been vanquisher, as, by the same covenant
And carriage° of the article design'd,
95 His fell to Hamlet. Now, sir, young Fortinbras,
Of unimproved° metal hot and full,
Hath in the skirts of Norway here and there
Shark'd up° a list of lawless resolutes,°
For food and diet,° to some enterprise
100 That hath a stomach° in 't. Which is no other—
As it doth well appear unto our state—
But to recover of us, by strong hand
And terms compulsatory, those foresaid lands
So by his father lost. And this, I take it,
105 Is the main motive of our preparations,
The source of this our watch, and the chief head°
Of this posthaste and romage° in the land.
    BERNARDO. I think it be no other but e'en so.
Well may it sort that this portentous figure
Comes armed through our watch, so like the
110 king
That was and is the question of these wars.
    HORATIO. A mote° it is to trouble the mind's eye.
In the most high and palmy state of Rome,
A little ere the mightiest Julius fell,
The graves stood tenantless, and the sheeted
115 dead
Did squeak and gibber in the Roman streets;
As° stars with trains of fire and dews of blood,
Disasters in the sun, and the moist star,°
Upon whose influence Neptune's empire stands,
120 Was sick almost to doomsday with eclipse.
And even the like precurse° of fierce events,
As harbingers preceding still° the fates
And prologue to the omen° coming on,
Have heaven and earth together demonstrated
125 Unto our climatures° and countrymen.

[*Re-enter* GHOST.]
But soft, behold! Lo, where it comes again!
I'll cross° it, though it blast me. Stay, illusion!
If thou hast any sound, or use of voice,
Speak to me.
If there be any good thing to be done,   130
That may to thee do ease and grace to me,
Speak to me.
If thou art privy to thy country's fate,
Which, happily, foreknowing may avoid,
O, speak!   135
Or if thou hast uphoarded in thy life
Extorted treasure in the womb of earth,
For which, they say, you spirits oft walk in death,
Speak of it. Stay, and speak! [*The cock crows*]
Stop it, Marcellus.
MARCELLUS. Shall I strike at it with my partisan?°   140
HORATIO. Do if it will not stand.
BERNARDO.   'Tis here!
HORATIO.   'Tis here!
MARCELLUS. 'Tis gone!   [*Exit* GHOST.]
We do it wrong, being so majestical,
To offer it the show of violence,
For it is as the air, invulnerable,   145
And our vain blows malicious mockery.
BERNARDO. It was about to speak when the cock
crew.
HORATIO. And then it started like a guilty thing
Upon a fearful summons. I have heard,
The cock, that is the trumpet to the morn,   150
Doth with his lofty and shrill-sounding throat
Awake the god of day, and at his warning,
Whether in sea or fire, in earth or air,
Th' extravagant and erring° spirit hies
To his confine. And of the truth herein   155
This present object made probation.°
MARCELLUS. It faded on the crowing of the cock.
Some say that ever 'gainst° that season comes
Wherein our Savior's birth is celebrated,
The bird of dawning singeth all night long;   160
And then, they say, no spirit dare stir abroad,
The nights are wholesome, then no planets
strike,°
No fairy takes° nor witch hath power to charm,
So hallow'd and so gracious is the time.
HORATIO. So have I heard and do in part believe it.   165
But look, the morn, in russet mantle clad,
Walks o'er the dew of yon high eastward hill.

moiety competent equal portion   *gaged* engaged
carriage terms   *unimproved* untested
Shark'd up thrown together indiscriminately
resolutes desperadoes
food and diet i.e., "bed and board"
stomach i.e., some challenge   *head* cause
posthaste and romage hustle and bustle
mote dust speck
As possibly *as well as* (more likely, an immediately
  preceding line has been lost)
moist star the moon   *precurse* forewarning
still constantly   *omen* disaster   *climatures* regions

cross confront   *partisan* pike   *erring* wandering
probation proof   *'gainst* in anticipation of
planets strike planets supposedly had power to influence
  life for good or ill
takes bewitches

Break we our watch up, and by my advice
Let us impart what we have seen tonight
170 Unto young Hamlet. For, upon my life,
This spirit, dumb to us, will speak to him.
Do you consent we shall acquaint him with it,
As needful in our loves, fitting° our duty?
MARCELLUS. Let's do 't, I pray. And I this morning know
175 Where we shall find him most conveniently.

[*Exeunt*]

SCENE ii

A room of state in the castle.

[*Flourish. Enter the* KING, QUEEN, HAMLET, POLONIUS,
LAERTES, VOLTIMAND, CORNELIUS, LORDS, *and*
ATTENDANTS.]

KING. Though yet of Hamlet our dear brother's death
The memory be green, and that it us befitted
To bear our hearts in grief and our whole kingdom
To be contracted in one brow of woe,
Yet so far hath discretion fought with nature
That we with wisest sorrow think on him
Together with remembrance of ourselves.
Therefore our sometime sister,° now our queen,
Th' imperial jointress° to this warlike state,
10 Have we, as 'twere with a defeated joy—
With an auspicious and a dropping eye,
With mirth in funeral and with dirge in marriage,
In equal scale weighing delight and dole°—
Taken to wife. Nor have we herein barr'd
15 Your better wisdoms, which have freely gone
With this affair along. For all, our thanks.
Now follows that° you know: young Fortinbras,
Holding a weak supposal° of our worth,
Or thinking by our late dear brother's death
20 Our state to be disjoint and out of frame,
Colleagued with° this dream of his advantage,
He hath not fail'd to pester us with message
Importing° the surrender of those lands
Lost by his father, with all bonds of law,
25 To our most valiant brother. So much for him.
Now for ourself, and for this time of meeting,
Thus much the business is: we have here writ
To Norway, uncle of young Fortinbras—

Who, impotent and bed-rid, scarcely hears
Of this his nephew's purpose—to suppress   30
His further gait° herein, in that the levies,
The lists, and full proportions are all made
Out of his subject. And we here dispatch
You, good Cornelius, and you, Voltimand,
For bearers of this greeting to old Norway,   35
Giving to you no further personal power
To business with the king more than the scope
Of these delated° articles allow.
Farewell, and let your haste commend your duty.
CORNELIUS *and* VOLTIMAND. In that and all things will we show our duty.   40
KING. We doubt it nothing. Heartily farewell.
[*Exeunt* VOLTIMAND *and* CORNELIUS.]
And now, Laertes, what's the news with you?
You told us of some suit. What is 't, Laertes?
You cannot speak of reason to the Dane
And lose your voice. What wouldst thou beg, Laertes,   45
That shall not be my offer, not thy asking?
The head is not more native° to the heart,
The hand more instrumental to the mouth,
Than is the throne of Denmark to thy father.
What wouldst thou have, Laertes?
LAERTES.   My dread lord,   50
Your leave and favor to return to France,
From whence though willingly I came to Denmark
To show my duty in your coronation,
Yet now, I must confess, that duty done,
My thoughts and wishes bend again toward France   55
And bow them to your gracious leave and pardon.
KING. Have you your father's leave? What says Polonius?
POLONIUS. He hath, my lord, wrung from me my slow leave
By laborsome petition, and at last
Upon his will I seal'd my hard° consent.   60
I do beseech you, give him leave to go.
KING. Take thy fair hour, Laertes. Time be thine,
And thy best graces° spend it at thy will!
But now, my cousin° Hamlet, and my son—
HAMLET. [*Aside*] A little more than kin, and less than kind.°
KING. How is it that the clouds still hang on you?   65

---

fitting befitting
sometime sister former sister-in-law   jointress partner
dole grief   that that which   supposal estimate
Colleagued with joined with   Importing bearing on

gait activity   delated detailed
native naturally bound   hard reluctant
graces qualities   cousin a general term; here, nephew
A little . . . kind i.e., more than the usual kinship and
     less than natural (a much-debated line)

HAMLET. Not so, my lord; I am too much i' the
 sun.°
QUEEN. Good Hamlet, cast thy nighted color off
 And let thine eye look like a friend on Denmark.
70 Do not for ever with thy vailed° lids
 Seek for thy noble father in the dust.
 Thou know'st 'tis common;° all that lives must
  die,
 Passing through nature to eternity.
HAMLET. Aye, madam, it is common.
QUEEN.   If it be,
75 Why seems it so particular with thee?
HAMLET. Seems, madam! Nay, it is; I know not
  "seems."
 'Tis not alone my inky cloak, good mother,
 Nor customary suits of solemn black,
 Nor windy suspiration of forc'd breath,°
80 No, nor the fruitful° river in the eye,
 Nor the dejected havior° of the visage,
 Together with all forms, moods, shapes of grief,
 That can denote me truly. These indeed seem,
 For they are actions that a man might play.
85 But I have that within which passeth° show;
 These but the trappings and the suits of woe.
KING. 'Tis sweet and commendable in your nature,
  Hamlet,
 To give these mourning duties to your father.
 But you must know, your father lost a father,
90 That father lost, lost his, and the survivor bound
 In filial obligation for some term
 To do obsequious sorrow. But to persever
 In obstinate condolement is a course
 Of impious stubbornness. 'Tis unmanly grief;
95 It shows a will most incorrect to heaven,
 A heart unfortified, a mind impatient,
 An understanding simple and unschool'd.
 For what we know must be and is as common
 As any the most vulgar thing to sense,
100 Why should we in our peevish opposition
 Take it to heart? Fie! 'Tis a fault to heaven,
 A fault against the dead, a fault to nature,
 To reason most absurd, whose common theme
 Is death of fathers, and who still hath cried,
105 From the first corse° till he that died today,
 "This must be so." We pray you, throw to
  earth
 This unprevailing woe, and think of us
 As of a father: for let the world take note,
 You are the most immediate to our throne,

And with no less nobility of love   110
Than that which dearest father bears his son
Do I impart° toward you. For your intent
In going back to school in Wittenberg,
It is most retrograde to our desire.
And we beseech you, bend you° to remain 115
Here in the cheer and comfort of our eye,
Our chiefest courtier, cousin, and our son.
QUEEN. Let not thy mother lose her prayers, Ham-
 let.
I pray thee, stay with us; go not to Wittenberg.
HAMLET. I shall in all my best obey you, madam. 120
KING. Why, 'tis a loving and a fair reply.
Be as ourself in Denmark. Madam, come;
This gentle and unforc'd accord of Hamlet
Sits smiling to my heart; in grace whereof,
No jocund health that Denmark drinks today, 125
But the great cannon to the clouds shall tell,
And the king's rouse° the heaven shall bruit°
 again,
Re-speaking earthly thunder. Come away.
    [Flourish. Exeunt all but HAMLET.]
HAMLET. O that this too too solid flesh would melt,
Thaw, and resolve itself into a dew!   130
Or that the Everlasting had not fix'd
His canon° 'gainst self-slaughter! O God! God!
How weary, stale, flat, and unprofitable
Seem to me all the uses° of this world!
Fie on 't! Ah fie! 'Tis an unweeded garden, 135
That grows to seed; things rank and gross in
 nature
Possess it merely.° That it should come to this!
But two months dead! Nay, not so much, not
 two.
So excellent a king, that was, to this,
Hyperion to a satyr.° So loving to my mother 140
That he might not beteem° the winds of heaven
Visit her face too roughly. Heaven and earth!
Must I remember? Why, she would hang on
 him
As if increase of appetite had grown
By what it fed on. And yet, within a month— 145
Let me not think on 't!—Frailty, thy name is
 woman!—
A little month, or ere those shoes were old
With which she follow'd my poor father's body
Like Niobe,° all tears, why she, even she—

---

too . . . sun i.e., in the royal favor (with pun)
vailed cast-down
common i.e., in common, shared by all
windy . . . breath heavy sighing
fruitful much-flowing *havior* behavior
passeth surpasses *corse* corpse

impart express *bend you* incline yourself
rouse draught *bruit* echo *canon* law *uses* affairs
merely wholly *Hyperion . . . satyr* the sun god compared
 to a beast, half man, half goat
beteem permit
Niobe mythological mother whose children were slain
 by gods and who was changed by Zeus into a rock that
 should drop tears forever

150 O God! A beast that wants discourse° of reason
Would have mourn'd longer—married with my
    uncle,
My father's brother, but no more like my father
Than I to Hercules. Within a month,
Ere yet the salt of most unrighteous tears
155 Had left the flushing in her galled eyes,
She married. O, most wicked speed, to post°
With such dexterity to incestuous sheets!
It is not nor it cannot come to good.
But break, my heart, for I must hold my tongue!
[*Enter* HORATIO, MARCELLUS, *and* BERNARDO.]
HORATIO. Hail to your lordship!
160 HAMLET.   I am glad to see you well.
    Horatio—or I do forget myself.
HORATIO. The same, my lord, and your poor ser-
    vant ever.
HAMLET. Sir, my good friend; I'll change° that
    name with you.
And what make you from Wittenberg, Horatio?
165 Marcellus?
MARCELLUS. My good lord!
HAMLET. I am very glad to see you. [*To* BERNARDO]
    Good even, sir.
But what, in faith, make you from Wittenberg?
HORATIO. A truant disposition, good my lord.
170 HAMLET. I would not hear your enemy say so,
Nor shall you do my ear that violence,
To make it truster of your own report
Against yourself. I know you are no truant.
But what is your affair in Elsinore?
175 We'll teach you to drink deep ere you depart.
HORATIO. My lord, I came to see your father's
    funeral.
HAMLET. I pray thee, do not mock me, fellow
    student;
I think it was to see my mother's wedding.
HORATIO. Indeed, my lord, it follow'd hard upon.
HAMLET. Thrift, thrift, Horatio! The funeral bak'd
180   meats
Did coldly furnish forth the marriage tables.
Would I had met my dearest° foe in heaven
Or ever° I had seen that day, Horatio!
My father!—methinks I see my father.
HORATIO. O where, my lord?
185 HAMLET.   In my mind's eye, Horatio.
HORATIO. I saw him once; he was a goodly king.
HAMLET. He was a man, take him for all in all.
I shall not look upon his like again.
HORATIO. My lord, I think I saw him yesternight.
190 HAMLET. Saw? Who?

HORATIO. My lord, the king your father.
HAMLET.   The king my father!
HORATIO. Season your admiration° for a while
With an attent ear, till I may deliver,
Upon the witness of these gentlemen,
This marvel to you.
HAMLET   For God's love, let me hear. 195
HORATIO. Two nights together had these gentle-
    men,
Marcellus and Bernardo, on their watch,
In the dead vast and middle of the night,
Been thus encounter'd. A figure like your
    father,
Armed at point exactly, cap-a-pe,°   200
Appears before them, and with solemn march
Goes slow and stately by them. Thrice he
    walk'd
By their oppress'd and fear-surprised eyes,
Within his truncheon's length, whilst they,
    distill'd
Almost to jelly with the act° of fear,   205
Stand dumb, and speak not to him. This to me
In dreadful secrecy impart they did,
And I with them the third night kept the
    watch;
Where, as they had deliver'd, both in time,
Form of the thing, each word made true and
    good,   210
The apparition comes. I knew your father;
These hands are not more like.
HAMLET.   But where was this?
MARCELLUS. My lord, upon the platform where we
    watch'd.
HAMLET. Did you not speak to it?
HORATIO.   My lord, I did,
But answer made it none; yet once methought 215
It lifted up it° head and did address
Itself to motion, like as it would speak.
But even then the morning cock crew loud,
And at the sound it shrunk in haste away
And vanish'd from our sight.
HAMLET.   'Tis very strange. 220
HORATIO. As I do live, my honor'd lord, 'tis true,
And we did think it writ down in our duty
To let you know of it.
HAMLET. Indeed, indeed, sirs. But this troubles me.
Hold you the watch tonight?
MARCELLUS *and* BERNARDO.   We do, my lord. 225
HAMLET. Arm'd, say you?
MARCELLUS *and* BERNARDO. Arm'd, my lord.
HAMLET.   From top to toe?

---

wants discourse lacks power
post hasten   *change* exchange
dearest extremest   *Or ever* before

season . . admiration control your wonder
at . . . cap-a-pe completely, head to foot   *act* effect
it its

MARCELLUS *and* BERNARDO. My lord, from head to
    foot.
HAMLET. Then saw you not his face?
HORATIO. O, yes, my lord; he wore his beaver up.
230 HAMLET. What, look'd he frowningly?
HORATIO. A countenance more in sorrow than in
    anger.
HAMLET. Pale, or red?
HORATIO. Nay, very pale.
HAMLET.   And fix'd his eyes upon you?
HORATIO. Most constantly.
HAMLET.   I would I had been there.
235 HORATIO. It would have much amaz'd you.
HAMLET. Very like, very like. Stay'd it long?
HORATIO. While one with moderate haste might
    tell° a hundred.
MARCELLUS *and* BERNARDO. Longer, longer.
HORATIO. Not when I saw 't.
HAMLET.   His beard was grizzled?° No?
240 HORATIO. It was as I have seen it in his life,
    A sable silver'd.°
HAMLET.   I will watch tonight;
    Perchance 'twill walk again.
HORATIO.   I warrant it will.
HAMLET. If it assume my noble father's person,
    I'll speak to it though hell itself should gape
245 And bid me hold my peace. I pray you all,
    If you have hitherto conceal'd this sight,
    Let it be tenable° in your silence still,
    And whatsoever else shall hap tonight,
    Give it an understanding, but no tongue.
250 I will requite° your loves. So fare you well.
    Upon the platform, 'twixt eleven and twelve,
    I'll visit you.
ALL.   Our duty to your honor.
HAMLET. Your loves, as mine to you. Farewell.
                    [Exeunt all but HAMLET.]
    My father's spirit in arms! All is not well;
    I doubt° some foul play. Would the night were
255 come!
    Till then sit still, my soul. Foul deeds will rise,
    Though all the earth o'erwhelm them, to men's
    eyes.   *[Exit]*

SCENE iii
A room in POLONIUS'S *house.*

[*Enter* LAERTES *and* OPHELIA.]
LAERTES. My necessaries are embark'd. Farewell.
    And, sister, as the winds give benefit
    And convoy is assistant,° do not sleep,
    But let me hear from you.
OPHELIA.   Do you doubt that?
LAERTES. For° Hamlet, and the trifling of his favor,   5
    Hold it a fashion, and a toy in blood,
    A violet in the youth of primy° nature,
    Forward, not permanent, sweet, not lasting,
    The perfume and suppliance° of a minute—
    No more.
OPHELIA.   No more but so?
LAERTES.   Think it no more.   10
    For nature crescent° does not grow alone
    In thews and bulk; but, as this temple waxes,°
    The inward service of the mind and soul
    Grows wide withal.° Perhaps he loves you now,
    And now no soil nor cautel° doth besmirch   15
    The virtue of his will. But you must fear,
    His greatness weigh'd, his will is not his own;
    For he himself is subject to his birth.
    He may not, as unvalu'd persons do,
    Carve° for himself, for on his choice depends   20
    The safety and health of this whole state,
    And therefore must his choice be circumscrib'd
    Unto the voice and yielding of that body
    Whereof he is the head. Then if he says he loves
      you,
    It fits your wisdom so far to believe it   25
    As he in his particular act and place
    May give his saying deed, which is no further
    Than the main voice of Denmark goes withal.
    Then weigh what loss your honor may sustain
    If with too credent ear you list° his songs,   30
    Or lose your heart, or your chaste treasure open
    To his unmaster'd importunity.
    Fear it, Ophelia, fear it, my dear sister,
    And keep you in the rear of your affection,
    Out of the shot and danger of desire.   35
    The chariest maid is prodigal enough,
    If she unmask her beauty to the moon.
    Virtue itself 'scapes not calumnious strokes.

---

as . . . assistant as winds are favorable and means of
    conveyance are available
For as for   *primy* springlike
perfume and suppliance the sweet diversion
nature crescent expanding nature
temple waxes body grows   *withal* also
cautel deceit   *carve* choose   *list* heed

---

tell count   *grizzled* gray
sable silver'd black mixed with white
tenable held   *requite* reward   *doubt* suspect

The canker galls the infants of the spring°
40 Too oft before their buttons° be disclos'd,
And in the morn and liquid dew of youth
Contagious blastments° are most imminent.
Be wary then. Best safety lies in fear.
Youth to itself rebels, though none else near.
45 OPHELIA. I shall th' effect of this good lesson keep
As watchman to my heart. But, good my
brother,
Do not, as some ungracious pastors do,
Show me the steep and thorny way to heaven,
Whilst, like a puff'd and reckless libertine,
50 Himself the primrose path of dalliance treads
And recks not his own rede.°
LAERTES.   O, fear me not!
I stay too long. But here my father comes.
           [*Enter* POLONIUS.]
A double blessing is a double grace;
Occasion smiles upon a second leave.
POLONIUS. Yet here, Laertes! Aboard, aboard, for
55   shame!
The wind sits in the shoulder of your sail,
And you are stay'd for. There; my blessing with
thee!
And these few precepts in thy memory
Look thou character.° Give thy thoughts no
tongue,
60 Nor any unproportion'd° thought his act.
Be thou familiar, but by no means vulgar.
Those friends thou hast, and their adoption
tried,°
Grapple them to thy soul with hoops of steel,
But do not dull thy palm with entertainment
Of each new-hatch'd unfledg'd comrade. Be-
65   ware
Of entrance to a quarrel, but being in,
Bear 't that th' opposed may beware of thee.
Give every man thy ear, but few thy voice.
Take each man's censure,° but reserve thy
judgment.
70 Costly thy habit as thy purse can buy,
But not express'd in fancy—rich, not gaudy;
For the apparel oft proclaims the man,
And they in France of the best rank and station
Are most select and generous° in that.
75 Neither a borrower nor a lender be,
For loan oft loses both itself and friend,
And borrowing dulls the edge of husbandry.

This above all: to thine own self be true,
And it must follow, as the night the day,
Thou canst not then be false to any man.   80
Farewell. My blessing season° this in thee!
LAERTES. Most humbly do I take my leave, my
lord.
POLONIUS. The time invites you; go, your servants
tend.°
LAERTES. Farewell, Ophelia, and remember well
What I have said to you.
OPHELIA.   'Tis in my memory lock'd, 85
And you yourself shall keep the key of it.
LAERTES. Farewell.   [*Exit*]
POLONIUS. What is 't, Ophelia, he hath said to you?
OPHELIA. So please you, something touching the
Lord Hamlet.
POLONIUS. Marry, well bethought.°   90
'Tis told me he hath very oft of late
Given private time to you, and yourself
Have of your audience been most free and
bounteous.
If it be so—as so 'tis put on° me,
And that in way of caution—I must tell you,   95
You do not understand yourself so clearly
As it behooves my daughter and your honor.
What is between you? Give me up the truth.
OPHELIA. He hath, my lord, of late made many
tenders°
Of his affection to me.   100
POLONIUS. Affection! Pooh! You speak like a
green girl,
Unsifted° in such perilous circumstance.
Do you believe his tenders, as you call them?
OPHELIA. I do not know, my lord, what I should
think.
POLONIUS. Marry, I'll teach you. Think yourself a
baby,   105
That you have ta'en these tenders for true pay,
Which are not sterling. Tender yourself more
dearly,°
Or—not to crack the wind of the poor phrase,
Running it thus—you'll tender me a fool.°
OPHELIA. My lord, he hath importun'd me with
love   110
In honorable fashion.
POLONIUS. Aye, fashion you may call it. Go to, go to.
OPHELIA. And hath given countenance° to his
speech, my lord,
With almost all the holy vows of heaven.

The canker . . . spring the cankerworm blights the early
    tender plants
buttons buds   *blastments* blights
recks . . . rede heeds . . . advice
character engrave   *unproportion'd* distorted
tried tested   *censure* opinion
generous discriminating

season preserve   *tend* attend
Marry . . . bethought by the Virgin, well remembered
put on put to   *tenders* offers   *unsifted* untested
Tender . . . dearly value . . . highly
tender . . . fool i.e., prove yourself a fool
countenance authority

POLONIUS. Aye, springes to catch woodcocks.° I do
115　know,
　　When the blood burns, how prodigal the soul
　　Lends the tongue vows. These blazes, daughter,
　　Giving more light than heat, extinct in both,
　　Even in their promise as it is a-making,
120　You must not take for fire. From this time
　　Be something scanter of your maiden presence.
　　Set your entreatments at a higher rate
　　Than a command to parley. For Lord Hamlet,
　　Believe so much in him that he is young
125　And with a larger tether may he walk
　　Than may be given you. In few,° Ophelia,
　　Do not believe his vows, for they are brokers,°
　　Not of that dye which their investments° show,
　　But mere implorators of unholy suits,
130　Breathing like sanctified and pious bawds
　　The better to beguile. This is for all:
　　I would not, in plain terms, from this time
　　forth,
　　Have you so slander any moment° leisure
　　As to give words or talk with the Lord Hamlet.
135　Look to 't, I charge you. Come your ways.°
　　OPHELIA. I shall obey, my lord.　　　　　　[Exeunt]

SCENE iv
The platform.

[Enter HAMLET, HORATIO, and MARCELLUS.]
HAMLET. The air bites shrewdly;° it is very cold.
HORATIO. It is a nipping and an eager° air.
HAMLET. What hour now?
HORATIO.　　　　　　　I think it lacks of twelve.
MARCELLUS. No, it is struck.
HORATIO. Indeed? I heard it not. It then draws near
5　the season
　　Wherein the spirit held his wont to walk.
　　　　[A flourish of trumpets, and ordnance shot off
　　　　　　　　　　　　　　　　　　within.]
　　What doth this mean, my lord?
HAMLET. The king doth wake tonight and takes his
　　rouse,°
　　Keeps wassail,° and the swagg'ring upspring°
　　reels.

springes . . . woodcocks snares to catch birds that
　(supposedly) had no brains
In few in brief　　brokers go-betweens
investments garments (outward appearances)
slander . . . moment abuse . . . momentary
Come your ways come along
shrewdly bitterly　　eager sharp
wakes . . . rouse stays awake and drinks
wassail revelry　　upspring a wild dance

And as he drains his draughts of Rhenish° down,　10
　　The kettledrum and trumpet thus bray out
　　The triumph of his pledge.°
HORATIO.　　　　　　　　Is it a custom?
HAMLET. Aye, marry, is 't.
　　But to my mind, though I am native here
　　And to the manner born, it is a custom　　　15
　　More honor'd in the breach than the observance.
　　This heavy-headed revel east and west
　　Makes us traduc'd° and tax'd of other nations.
　　They clip° us drunkards, and with swinish
　　phrase
　　Soil our addition;° and indeed it takes　　　20
　　From our achievements, though perform'd at
　　height,
　　The pith and marrow of our attribute.°
　　So oft it chances in particular men,
　　That for some vicious mole° of nature in them,
　　As in their birth—wherein they are not guilty,　25
　　Since nature cannot choose his° origin—
　　By the o'ergrowth of some complexion,°
　　Oft breaking down the pales and forts° of
　　reason,
　　Or by some habit that too much o'erleavens°
　　The form of plausive° manners, that these
　　men—　　　　　　　　　　　　　　　　30
　　Carrying, I say, the stamp of one defect,
　　Being nature's livery, or fortune's star°—
　　Their virtues else°—be they as pure as grace,
　　As infinite as man may undergo—
　　Shall in the general censure° take corruption　35
　　From that particular fault. The dram of evil
　　Doth all the noble substance often dout°
　　To his own scandal.°
　　　　　　　　　　[Enter GHOST.]
HORATIO.　　　　　　Look, my lord, it comes!
HAMLET. Angels and ministers of grace defend us!
　　Be thou a spirit of health or goblin damn'd,°　40
　　Bring with thee airs from heaven or blasts from
　　hell,
　　Be thy intents wicked or charitable,

Rhenish Rhine wine
triumph . . . pledge the achievement of draining his cup
　at one draught
traduc'd slandered　　clip call
with . . . addition besmirch our reputation by calling us
　swine
attribute reputation　　mole defect　　his its
complexion propensity　　pales and forts walls
o'erleavens lightens　　plausive acceptable
Being . . . star whether this fault is inborn or the result
　of chance
Their . . . else their other virtues
general censure public opinion　　dout cancel out
scandal shame
spirit . . . damn'd good spirit or fiend

Thou com'st in such a questionable shape
That I will speak to thee. I'll call thee Hamlet,
45 King, father, royal Dane. O, answer me!
Let me not burst in ignorance, but tell
Why thy canoniz'd bones, hearsed in death,
Have burst their cerements; why the sepulchre,
Wherein we saw thee quietly inurn'd,
50 Hath op'd his ponderous and marble jaws
To cast thee up again. What may this mean,
That thou, dead corse, again in complete steel,
Revisit'st thus the glimpses of the moon,
Making night hideous, and we fools of nature°
55 So horridly to shake our disposition
With thoughts beyond the reaches of our souls?
Say, why is this? Wherefore? What should we
do?

                    [GHOST *beckons* HAMLET.]
HORATIO. It beckons you to go away with it,
As if it some impartment° did desire
To you alone.
60 MARCELLUS.   Look, with what courteous action
It waves you to a more removed ground.
But do not go with it.
HORATIO.   No, by no means.
HAMLET. It will not speak; then will I follow it.
HORATIO. Do not, my lord.
HAMLET.   Why, what should be the fear?
65 I do not set my life at a pin's fee;
And for my soul, what can it do to that,
Being a thing immortal as itself?
It waves me forth again. I'll follow it.
HORATIO. What if it tempt you toward the flood,
my lord,
70 Or to the dreadful summit of the cliff
That beetles° o'er his base into the sea,
And there assume some other horrible form,
Which might deprive your sovereignty° of
reason
And draw you into madness? Think of it:
75 The very place puts toys of desperation,°
Without more motive, into every brain
That looks so many fathoms to the sea
And hears it roar beneath.
HAMLET.   It waves me still.
Go on; I'll follow thee.
MARCELLUS. You shall not go, my lord.
80 HAMLET.   Hold off your hands.
HORATIO. Be rul'd; you shall not go.
HAMLET.   My fate cries out,
And makes each petty artery in this body

As hardy as the Nemean lion's° nerve.
Still am I call'd. Unhand me, gentlemen.
By heaven, I'll make a ghost of him that lets° me.   85
I say, away! Go on; I'll follow thee.
                    [*Exeunt* GHOST *and* HAMLET.]
HORATIO. He waxes desperate with imagination.
MARCELLUS. Let's follow; 'tis not fit thus to obey
him.
HORATIO. Have after. To what issue will this come?
MARCELLUS. Something is rotten in the state of
Denmark.   90
HORATIO. Heaven will direct it.
MARCELLUS.   Nay, let's follow him.
                                              [*Exeunt*]

SCENE v
Another part of the platform.

[*Enter* GHOST *and* HAMLET.]
HAMLET. Whither wilt thou lead me? Speak; I'll go
no further.
GHOST. Mark me.
HAMLET.   I will.
GHOST.   My hour is almost come,
When I to sulphurous and tormenting flames
Must render up myself.
HAMLET.   Alas, poor ghost!
GHOST. Pity me not, but lend thy serious hearing   5
To what I shall unfold.
HAMLET.   Speak; I am bound to hear.
GHOST. So art thou to revenge, when thou shalt
hear.
HAMLET. What?
GHOST. I am thy father's spirit,
Doom'd for a certain term to walk the night,   10
And for the day confin'd to fast in fires,
Till the foul crimes done in my days of nature
Are burnt and purg'd away. But that I am forbid
To tell the secrets of my prison house,
I could a tale unfold whose lightest word   15
Would harrow up thy soul, freeze thy young
blood,
Make thy two eyes, like stars, start from their
spheres,
Thy knotted and combined locks to part
And each particular hair to stand on end,
Like quills upon the fretful porpentine.°   20
But this eternal blazon° must not be
To ears of flesh and blood. List, list, O, list!
If thou didst ever thy dear father love—

---

fools of nature i.e., limited by nature in what we can
  understand
impartment communication
beetles overhangs   *sovereignty* sovereign power
toys of desperation desperate ideas

Nemean lion slain by Hercules as one of his twelve labors
lets hinders   *porpentine* porcupine
eternal blazon revelation of truths of the afterlife

HAMLET. O God!

GHOST. Revenge his foul and most unnatural
25   murder.

HAMLET. Murder!

GHOST. Murder most foul, as in the best it is,
    But this most foul, strange, and unnatural.

HAMLET. Haste me to know't, that I with wings as
    swift
30   As meditation or the thoughts of love
    May sweep to my revenge.

GHOST.   I find thee apt,
    And duller shouldst thou be than the fat weed
    That roots itself in ease on Lethe° wharf,
    Wouldst thou not stir in this. Now, Hamlet,
    hear:
35   'Tis given out that, sleeping in my orchard,
    A serpent stung me; so the whole ear of Den-
    mark
    Is by a forged process of my death
    Rankly abus'd.° But know, thou noble youth,
    The serpent that did sting thy father's life
    Now wears his crown.

40 HAMLET   O my prophetic soul!
    My uncle!

GHOST. Aye, that incestuous, that adulterate beast,
    With witchcraft of his wit, with traitorous gifts—
    O wicked wit and gifts, that have the power
45   So to seduce!—won to his shameful lust
    The will of my most seeming-virtuous queen.
    O Hamlet, what a falling-off was there!
    From me, whose love was of that dignity
    That it went hand in hand even with the vow
50   I made to her in marriage; and to decline
    Upon a wretch, whose natural gifts were poor
    To those of mine!
    But virtue, as it never will be mov'd
    Though lewdness court it in a shape of heaven,
55   So lust, though to a radiant angel link'd,
    Will sate itself in a celestial bed
    And prey on garbage.
    But, soft! Methinks I scent the morning air;
    Brief let me be. Sleeping within my orchard,
60   My custom always of the afternoon,
    Upon my secure hour thy uncle stole,
    With juice of cursed hebenon° in a vial,
    And in the porches of my ears did pour
    The leperous distillment, whose effect
65   Holds such an enmity with blood of man
    That swift as quicksilver it courses through
    The natural gates and alleys of the body,

And with a sudden vigor it doth posset°
And curd, like eager droppings into milk,
The thin and wholesome blood. So did it mine;   70
And a most instant tetter bark'd about,°
Most lazar-like,° with vile and loathsome crust,
All my smooth body.
Thus was I, sleeping, by a brother's hand,
Of life, of crown, of queen at once dispatch'd: 75
Cut off even in the blossoms of my sin,
Unhousel'd, disappointed, unanel'd;°
No reck'ning made, but sent to my account
With all my imperfections on my head.

HAMLET. O, horrible! O, horrible! Most horrible!   80

GHOST. If thou hast nature in thee, bear it not;
Let not the royal bed of Denmark be
A couch for luxury° and damned incest.
But, howsoever thou pursu'st this act,
Taint not thy mind, nor let thy soul contrive   85
Against thy mother aught. Leave her to heaven,
And to those thorns that in her bosom lodge
To prick and sting her. Fare thee well at once!
The glowworm shows the matin° to be near,
And 'gins to pale his uneffectual fire.   90
Adieu, adieu, adieu! Remember me.   [Exit]

HAMLET. O all you host of heaven! O earth! What
    else?
    And shall I couple hell? O, fie! Hold, hold, my
    heart,
    And you, my sinews, grow not instant old,
    But bear me stiffly up. Remember thee!   95
    Aye, thou poor ghost, while memory holds a seat
    In this distracted globe.° Remember thee!
    Yea, from the table of my memory
    I'll wipe away all trivial fond° records,
    All saws of books, all forms, all pressures° past   100
    That youth and observation copied there;
    And thy commandment all alone shall live
    Within the book and volume of my brain,
    Unmix'd with baser matter. Yes, by heaven!
    O most pernicious woman!   105
    O villain, villain, smiling, damned villain!
    My tables°—meet it is I set it down
    That one may smile, and smile, and be a villain;
    At least I'm sure it may be so in Denmark.
                    [Writing.]
    So, uncle, there you are. Now to my word.   110

---

posset curdle
tetter bark'd about eruption formed a bark about
lazar-like leperlike
Unhousel'd . . . unanel'd without the Sacrament,
  unprepared, without extreme unction
luxury lust   *matin* morning
distracted globe confused head   *fond* foolish
saws . . . forms . . . pressures sayings, examples,
  impressions   *tables* tablet

Lethe river of oblivion in Hades
Rankly abus'd grossly deceived
hebenon a deadly plant (ebony, the yew, and henbane
  have been suggested)

It is "Adieu, adieu! Remember me."
I have sworn 't.
HORATIO *and* MARCELLUS. [*Within*] My lord, my
    lord!

        [*Enter* HORATIO *and* MARCELLUS.]

MARCELLUS. Lord Hamlet!
HORATIO.   Heaven secure him!
HAMLET. So be it!
115 MARCELLUS. Illo, ho, ho,° my lord!
HAMLET. Hillo, ho, ho, boy! Come, bird, come.
MARCELLUS. How is 't, my noble lord?
HORATIO.   What news, my lord?
HAMLET. O, wonderful!
HORATIO. Good my lord, tell it.
HAMLET.   No; you will reveal it.
HORATIO. Not I, my lord, by heaven.
120 MARCELLUS.   Nor I, my lord.
HAMLET. How say you, then? Would heart of man
    once think it?
    But you'll be secret?
HORATIO *and* MARCELLUS. Aye, by heaven, my lord.
HAMLET. There's ne'er a villain dwelling in all
    Denmark
    But he's an arrant knave.°
HORATIO. There needs no ghost, my lord, come
125   from the grave
    To tell us this.
HAMLET.   Why, right; you are i' the right.
    And so, without more circumstance at all,
    I hold it fit that we shake hands and part:
    You as your business and desire shall point you—
130   For every man hath business and desire,
    Such as it is; and for my own poor part,
    Look you, I'll go pray.
HORATIO. These are but wild and whirling words,
    my lord.
HAMLET. I'm sorry they offend you, heartily;
    Yes, faith, heartily.
135 HORATIO.   There's no offense, my lord.
HAMLET. Yes, by Saint Patrick, but there is, Horatio,
    And much offense too. Touching this vision
    here,
    It is an honest° ghost, that let me tell you.
    For your desire to know what is between us,
    O'ermaster 't as you may. And now, good
140   friends,
    As you are friends, scholars, and soldiers,
    Give me one poor request.
HORATIO. What is 't, my lord? We will.
HAMLET. Never make known what you have seen
    tonight.
HORATIO *and* MARCELLUS. My lord, we will not.

HAMLET.   Nay, but swear 't.
HORATIO.   In faith, 145
    My lord, not I.
MARCELLUS.   Nor I, my lord, in faith.
HAMLET. Upon my sword.
MARCELLUS.   We have sworn, my lord, already.
HAMLET. Indeed, upon my sword, indeed.
GHOST. [*Beneath*] Swear.
HAMLET. Ah, ha, boy! Say'st thou so? Art thou
    there, truepenny?°   150
    Come on, you hear this fellow in the cellarage.°
    Consent to swear.
HORATIO.   Propose the oath, my lord.
HAMLET. Never to speak of this that you have seen,
    Swear by my sword.
GHOST. [*Beneath*] Swear.   155
HAMLET. *Hic et ubique?*° Then we'll shift our
    ground.
    Come hither, gentlemen,
    And lay your hands again upon my sword.
    Never to speak of this that you have heard,
    Swear by my sword.   160
GHOST. [*Beneath*] Swear.
HAMLET. Well said, old mole! Canst work i' th'
    earth so fast?
    A worthy pioner!° Once more remove, good
    friends.
HORATIO. O day and night, but this is wondrous
    strange!
HAMLET. And therefore as a stranger give it wel-
    come.   165
    There are more things in heaven and earth,
      Horatio,
    Than are dreamt of in your philosophy.°
    But come.
    Here, as before, never, so help you mercy,
    How strange or odd soe'er I bear myself,   170
    As I perchance hereafter shall think meet
    To put an antic disposition° on,
    That you, at such times seeing me, never shall,
    With arms encumber'd° thus, or this headshake,
    Or by pronouncing of some doubtful phrase,   175
    As "Well, well, we know," or "We could, an if
    we would,"
    Or "If we list to speak," or "There be, an if they
    might,"
    Or such ambiguous giving out, to note
    That you know aught of me: this not to do,
    So grace and mercy at your most need help you,   180
    Swear.

Illo, ho, ho falconer's call
arrant knave villain   *honest* true

truepenny familiar expression, like *old fellow*
cellarage literally, the space beneath the stage
hic et ubique here and everywhere   *pioner* digger
your philosophy i.e., in philosophy (*your* is unemphatic)
antic disposition lunatic behavior   *encumber'd* crossed

GHOST. [*Beneath*] Swear.

HAMLET. Rest, rest, perturbed spirit! [*They swear*]
 So, gentlemen,
 With all my love I do commend me to you.
185 And what so poor a man as Hamlet is
 May do t' express his love and friending to you,
 God willing, shall not lack. Let us go in together.

And still° your fingers on your lips, I pray.
The time is out of joint. O cursed spite
That ever I was born to set it right!   190
Nay, come, let's go together.   [*Exeunt*]

still always

ACT II

SCENE i
A room in POLONIUS' *house.*

[*Enter* POLONIUS *and* REYNALDO.]

POLONIUS. Give him this money and these notes,
 Reynaldo.

REYNALDO. I will, my lord.

POLONIUS. You shall do marvel's° wisely, good
 Reynaldo,
 Before you visit him, to make inquire
 Of his behavior.

5 REYNALDO.   My lord, I did intend it.

POLONIUS. Marry, well said, very well said. Look
 you, sir,
 Inquire me first what Danskers° are in Paris,
 And how, and who, what means, and where
  they keep,°
 What company, at what expense, and finding
10 By this encompassment° and drift of question
 That they do know my son, come you more
  nearer
 Than your particular demands will touch it.°
 Take you, as 'twere, some distant knowledge of
  him,
 As thus, "I know his father and his friends,
15 And in part him." Do you mark this, Reynaldo?

REYNALDO. Aye, very well, my lord.

POLONIUS. "And in part him; but," you may say,
 "not well.
 But if 't be he I mean, he's very wild,
 Addicted so and so"—and there put on him
 What forgeries° you please; marry, none so
20 rank°
 As may dishonor him—take heed of that—
 But, sir, such wanton, wild, and usual slips

As are companions noted and most known
To youth and liberty.

REYNALDO.   As gaming, my lord.

POLONIUS. Aye, or drinking, fencing, swearing,
 quarreling,   25
 Drabbing.° You may go so far.

REYNALDO. My lord, that would dishonor him.

POLONIUS. Faith, no, as you may season it in the
 charge.
 You must not put another scandal on him,
 That he is open to incontinency;°   30
 That's not my meaning. But breathe his faults
  so quaintly°
 That they may seem the taints of liberty,
 The flash and outbreak of a fiery mind,
 A savageness in unreclaimed° blood,
 Of general assault.°

REYNALDO.   But, my good lord— 35

POLONIUS. Wherefore should you do this?

REYNALDO.   Aye, my lord,
 I would know that.

POLONIUS.   Marry, sir, here's my drift,
 And I believe it is a fetch of warrant.°
 You laying these slight sullies on my son,
 As 'twere a thing a little soil'd i' the working,° 40
 Mark you,
 Your party in converse, him you would sound,
 Having ever seen° in the prenominate° crimes
 The youth you breathe of guilty, be assur'd
 He closes with you in this consequence:° 45
 "Good sir," or so, or "friend," or "gentleman,"

marvel's marvelously
Danskers Danes *keep* live
encompassment roundabout approach
come . . . it thus (by indirect means) you are more
 likely to get the truth than by direct questions
forgeries false allegations *rank* gross

Drabbing frequenting brothels
incontinency dissoluteness *quaintly* cleverly
unreclaimed untamed
of . . . assault i.e., such as afflicts all young gallants
fetch of warrant guaranteed stratagem
a little . . . working i.e., minor smudges, nothing
 damaging
Having . . . seen if he has ever seen
prenominate aforesaid
closes . . . consequence will pick up your lead as follows

According to the phrase or the addition°
Of man and country.

REYNALDO.   Very good, my lord.

POLONIUS. And then, sir, does he this—he does—
50   what was I about to say? By the mass, I was about
to say something. Where did I leave?

REYNALDO. At "closes in the consequence," at
"friend or so," and "gentleman."

POLONIUS. At "closes in the consequence," aye,
marry.

He closes with you thus: "I know the gentle-
55   man;

I saw him yesterday, or t'other day,
Or then, or then, with such, or such, and, as you
say,

There was a'° gaming, there o'ertook in 's
rouse,°

There falling out at tennis." Or perchance,
60   "I saw him enter such a house of sale,"

Videlicet,° a brothel, or so forth.
See you now—

Your bait of falsehood takes this carp of truth.
And thus do we of wisdom and of reach,
65   With windlasses and with assays of bias,°

By indirections find directions out.
So, by my former lecture and advice,
Shall you my son. You have me, have you not?

REYNALDO. My lord, I have.

POLONIUS.   God be wi' ye; fare ye well.

70   REYNALDO. Good my lord!

POLONIUS. Observe his inclination in° yourself.

REYNALDO. I shall, my lord.

POLONIUS. And let him ply° his music.

REYNALDO.   Well, my lord.

POLONIUS. Farewell!   [Exit REYNALDO.]

                    [Enter OPHELIA.]

                How now, Ophelia! What's the matter?

OPHELIA. O, my lord, my lord, I have been so
75   affrighted!

POLONIUS. With what, i' the name of God?

OPHELIA. My lord, as I was sewing in my closet,
Lord Hamlet, with his doublet° all unbrac'd,°
No hat upon his head, his stockings foul'd,
80   Ungarter'd and down-gyved° to his ankle,

Pale as his shirt, his knees knocking each other,
And with a look so piteous in purport
As if he had been loosed out of hell
To speak of horrors, he comes before me.

POLONIUS. Mad for thy love?

OPHELIA.   My lord, I do not know,   85
But truly I do fear it.

POLONIUS.   What said he?

OPHELIA. He took me by the wrist and held me
hard;

Then goes he to the length of all his arm,
And with his other hand thus o'er his brow,
He falls to such perusal of my face   90
As he would draw it. Long stay'd he so.
At last, a little shaking of mine arm,
And thrice his head thus waving up and down,
He rais'd a sigh so piteous and profound
As it did seem to shatter all his bulk   95
And end his being. That done, he lets me go,
And with his head over his shoulder turn'd,
He seem'd to find his way without his eyes;
For out o' doors he went without their help,
And to the last bended their light on me.   100

POLONIUS. Come, go with me. I will go seek the
king.

This is the very ecstasy° of love,
Whose violent property fordoes° itself
And leads the will to desperate undertakings
As oft as any passion under heaven   105
That does afflict our natures. I am sorry.
What, have you given him any hard words of
late?

OPHELIA. No, my good lord, but, as you did
command,

I did repel his letters and deni'd
His access to me.

POLONIUS.   That hath made him mad.   110
I am sorry that with better heed and judgment
I had not quoted° him. I fear'd he did but trifle
And meant to wrack° thee; but beshrew my
jealousy!°

By heaven, it is as proper° to our age
To cast beyond ourselves in our opinions   115
As it is common for the younger sort
To lack discretion. Come, go we to the king.
This must be known, which, being kept close,
might move

More grief to hide than hate to utter love.°
Come.   [Exeunt]   120

---

addition   title
'a   he   rouse   carousal   Videlicet   namely
windlasses . . . bias   roundabout methods and indirect
    approaches   in   for
ply   keep at   doublet   jacket   unbrac'd   unfastened
down-gyved   fallen about his ankles like fetters (gyves) on
    a prisoner

ecstasy   madness   property fordoes   nature destroys
quoted   observed   wrack   ruin
beshrew my jealousy   curse my suspicion
proper   natural
This . . . love   this (love) must be made known lest, being
    kept secret, it cause more grief than it will cause
    displeasure by being divulged

SCENE ii
A room in the castle.

[*Flourish. Enter* KING, QUEEN, ROSENCRANTZ,
GUILDENSTERN, *and* ATTENDANTS.]

KING. Welcome, dear Rosencrantz and Guilden-
stern!
Moreover° that we much did long to see you,
The need we have to use you did provoke
Our hasty sending. Something have you heard
5 Of Hamlet's transformation; so I call it,
Sith° nor th' exterior nor the inward man
Resembles that it was. What it should be,
More than his father's death, that thus hath
put him
So much from th' understanding of himself,
10 I cannot dream of. I entreat you both
That, being of so young days brought up with
him
And sith so neighbor'd to his youth and havior,
That you vouchsafe your rest° here in our court
Some little time, so by your companies
15 To draw him on to pleasures and to gather
So much as from occasion you may glean,
Whether aught to us unknown afflicts him thus
That open'd lies within our remedy.
QUEEN. Good gentlemen, he hath much talk'd of
you,
20 And sure I am two men there are not living
To whom he more adheres. If it will please you
To show us so much gentry° and good will
As to expend your time with us a while
For the supply and profit of our hope,°
25 Your visitation shall receive such thanks
As fits a king's remembrance.
ROSENCRANTZ.   Both your majesties
Might, by the sovereign power you have of us,
Put your dread pleasures more into command
Than to entreaty.
GUILDENSTERN.   But we both obey,
30 And here give up ourselves, in the full bent°
To lay our service freely at your feet,
To be commanded.
KING. Thanks, Rosencrantz and gentle Guilden-
stern.
QUEEN. Thanks, Guildenstern and gentle Rosen-
crantz.
35 And I beseech you instantly to visit
My too much changed son. Go, some of you,

And bring these gentlemen where Hamlet is.
GUILDENSTERN. Heavens make our presence and
our practices
Pleasant and helpful to him!
QUEEN.   Aye, amen!
[*Exeunt* ROSENCRANTZ, GUILDENSTERN, *and some*
ATTENDANTS.]
[*Enter* POLONIUS.]
POLONIUS. Th' ambassadors from Norway, my
good lord,   40
Are joyfully return'd.
KING. Thou still hast been the father of good news.
POLONIUS. Have I, my lord? Assure you, my good
liege,
I hold my duty as I hold my soul,
Both to my God and to my gracious king.   45
And I do think, or else this brain of mine
Hunts not the trail of policy so sure°
As it hath us'd to do, that I have found
The very cause of Hamlet's lunacy.
KING. O, speak of that; that do I long to hear.   50
POLONIUS. Give first admittance to th' ambassa-
dors;
My news shall be the fruit to that great feast.
KING. Thyself do grace to them, and bring them in.
[*Exit* POLONIUS.]
He tells me, my dear Gertrude, he hath found
The head and source of all your son's distemper.   55
QUEEN. I doubt° it is no other but the main—
His father's death and our o'erhasty marriage.
KING. Well, we shall sift him.
[*Re-enter* POLONIUS, *with* VOLTIMAND *and*
CORNELIUS.]
                    Welcome, my good friends!
Say, Voltimand, what from our brother Norway?
VOLTIMAND. Most fair return of greetings and
desires.   60
Upon our first,° he sent out to suppress
His nephew's levies, which to him appear'd
To be a preparation 'gainst the Polack,
But better look'd into, he truly found
It was against your highness; whereat griev'd,   65
That so his sickness, age, and impotence
Was falsely borne in hand,° sends out arrests
On Fortinbras, which he, in brief, obeys,
Receives rebuke from Norway, and in fine°
Makes vow before his uncle never more   70
To give th' assay of arms against your majesty.
Whereon old Norway, overcome with joy,
Gives him three thousand crowns in annual fee,

Moreover besides the fact   *Sith* since
vouchsafe . . . rest please to remain
gentry courtesy   *For . . . hope* to help us bring about
  what we hope for   *bent* limit

Hunts . . . sure does not follow with as much certainty
doubt suspect
our first i.e., our initial presentation
borne in hand imposed on   *in fine* in conclusion

And his commission to employ those soldiers,
75 So levied as before, against the Polack,
With an entreaty, herein further shown,
                    [*Giving a paper.*]
That it might please you to give quiet pass
Through your dominions for this enterprise,
On such regards° of safety and allowance
As therein are set down.
80 KING.   It likes us well,
And at our more consider'd time we'll read,
Answer, and think upon this business.
Meantime we thank you for your well-took
    labor.
Go to your rest; at night we'll feast together.
Most welcome home!
                [*Exeunt* VOLTIMAND *and* CORNELIUS.]
85 POLONIUS.   This business is well ended.
My liege, and madam, to expostulate
What majesty should be, what duty is,
Why day is day, night night, and time is time,
Were nothing but to waste night, day, and time.
90 Therefore, since brevity is the soul of wit
And tediousness the limbs and outward
    flourishes,
I will be brief. Your noble son is mad.
Mad call I it, for, to define true madness,
What is 't but to be nothing else but mad?
But let that go.
95 QUEEN.   More matter, with less art.
POLONIUS. Madam, I swear I use no art at all.
That he is mad, 'tis true; 'tis true 'tis pity,
And pity 'tis 'tis true—a foolish figure,
But farewell it, for I will use no art.
100 Mad let us grant him then. And now remains
That we find out the cause of this effect,
Or rather say, the cause of this defect,
For this effect defective comes by cause.
Thus it remains, and the remainder thus.
105 Perpend.°
I have a daughter—have while she is mine—
Who in her duty and obedience, mark,
Hath given me this. Now gather and surmise.

        [*Reads*] To the celestial, and my soul's idol, the
110   most beautified Ophelia—

That's an ill phrase, a vile phrase—"beautified"
is a vile phrase. But you shall hear. Thus:

        [*Reads*] In her excellent white bosom, these, &c.

QUEEN. Came this from Hamlet to her?
POLONIUS. Good madam, stay awhile; I will be
115   faithful.   [*Reads*]

Doubt thou the stars are fire,
    Doubt that the sun doth move,
Doubt truth to be a liar,
    But never doubt I love.

    O dear Ophelia, I am ill at these numbers.° I 120
have not art to reckon my groans, but that I love
thee best, O most best, believe it. Adieu.
    Thine evermore, most dear lady, whilst this
machine is to him, HAMLET.

This in obedience hath my daughter shown me, 125
And more above,° hath his solicitings,
As they fell out by time, by means and place,
All given to mine ear.
KING.   But how hath she
Receiv'd his love?
POLONIUS.   What do you think of me?
KING. As of a man faithful and honorable. 130
POLONIUS. I would fain prove so. But what might
    you think,
When I had seen this hot love on the wing—
As I perceiv'd it, I must tell you that,
Before my daughter told me—what might you,
Or my dear majesty your queen here, think, 135
If I had play'd the desk or table-book,°
Or given my heart a winking, mute and dumb,
Or look'd upon this love with idle sight?
What might you think? No, I went round° to
    work,
And my young mistress thus I did bespeak: 140
"Lord Hamlet is a prince, out of thy star;
This must not be." And then I prescripts° gave
    her
That she should lock herself from his resort,
Admit no messengers, receive no tokens.
Which done, she took the fruits of my advice, 145
And he repulsed, a short tale to make,
Fell into a sadness, then into a fast,
Thence to a watch, thence into a weakness,
Thence to a lightness, and by this declension
Into the madness wherein now he raves 150
And all we mourn for.
KING.   Do you think 'tis this?
QUEEN. It may be, very like.
POLONIUS. Hath there been such a time, I'd fain
    know that,
That I have positively said "'tis so,"
When it prov'd otherwise?
KING.   Not that I know. 155
POLONIUS. [*Pointing to his head and shoulder*] Take
    this from this, if this be otherwise.

---

regards terms   Perpend consider

numbers verses   more above besides
play'd . . . table-book i.e., "played dumb" like any
    inanimate object
round directly   prescripts prescriptions

If circumstances lead me, I will find
Where truth is hid, though it were hid indeed
Within the center.
KING.   How may we try it further?
POLONIUS. You know, sometimes he walks four
160   hours together
Here in the lobby.
QUEEN.   So he does, indeed.
POLONIUS. At such a time I'll loose my daughter to
him.
Be you and I behind an arras° then;
Mark the encounter. If he love her not,
165   And be not from his reason fall'n thereon,
Let me be no assistant for a state,
But keep a farm and carters.
KING.   We will try it.
QUEEN. But look where sadly the poor wretch
comes reading.
POLONIUS. Away, I do beseech you, both away.
170   I'll board° him presently.
                [Exeunt KING, QUEEN, and ATTENDANTS.]
                [Enter HAMLET, reading.]
O, give me leave. How does my good Lord
Hamlet?
HAMLET. Well, God-a-mercy.
POLONIUS. Do you know me, my lord?
HAMLET. Excellent well; you are a fishmonger.
175   POLONIUS. Not I, my lord.
HAMLET. Then I would you were so honest a man.
POLONIUS. Honest, my lord!
HAMLET. Aye, sir. To be honest, as this world goes,
is to be one man picked out of ten thousand.
180   POLONIUS. That's very true, my lord.
HAMLET. For if the sun breed maggots in a dead
dog, being a god kissing carrion—Have you a
daughter?
POLONIUS. I have, my lord.
185   HAMLET. Let her not walk i' the sun. Conception is
a blessing, but as your daughter may conceive—
friend, look to 't.
POLONIUS. [Aside] How say you by that? Still harp-
ing on my daughter. Yet he knew me not at
190   first; he said I was a fishmonger. He is far gone;
and truly in my youth I suffered much extremity
for love—very near this. I'll speak to him again.
—What do you read, my lord?
HAMLET. Words, words, words.
195   POLONIUS. What is the matter, my lord?
HAMLET. Between who?°
POLONIUS. I mean the matter that you read, my
lord.

HAMLET. Slanders, sir, for the satirical rogue says
here that old men have gray beards, that their   200
faces are wrinkled, their eyes purging thick
amber and plum-tree gum, and that they have a
plentiful lack of wit, together with most weak
hams. All which, sir, though I most powerfully
and potently believe, yet I hold it not honesty to   205
have it thus set down; for yourself, sir, shall grow
old as I am, if like a crab you could go backward.
POLONIUS. [Aside] Though this be madness, yet
there is method in 't.—Will you walk out of the
air, my lord?   210
HAMLET. Into my grave?
POLONIUS. Indeed, that's out of the air. [Aside] How
pregnant sometimes his replies are! A happiness
that often madness hits on, which reason and
sanity could not so prosperously be delivered of.   215
I will leave him, and suddenly contrive the
means of meeting between him and my daughter.—My honorable lord, I will most humbly
take my leave of you.
HAMLET. You cannot, sir, take from me anything   220
that I will more willingly part withal—except
my life, except my life, except my life.
POLONIUS. Fare you well, my lord.
HAMLET. These tedious old fools!
                [Enter ROSENCRANTZ and GUILDENSTERN.]
POLONIUS. You go to seek the Lord Hamlet; there
he is.   225
ROSENCRANTZ. [To POLONIUS] God save you, sir!
                [Exit POLONIUS.]
GUILDENSTERN. My honored lord!
ROSENCRANTZ. My most dear lord!
HAMLET. My excellent good friends! How dost
thou, Guildenstern? Ah, Rosencrantz! Good   230
lads, how do you both?
ROSENCRANTZ. As the indifferent children of the
earth.
GUILDENSTERN. Happy in that we are not over-
happy;
On Fortune's cap we are not the very button.
HAMLET. Nor the soles of her shoe?   235
ROSENCRANTZ. Neither, my lord.
HAMLET. Then you live about her waist, or in the
middle of her favors?
GUILDENSTERN. Faith, her privates we.
HAMLET. In the secret parts of Fortune? O, most   240
true; she is a strumpet. What's the news?
ROSENCRANTZ. None, my lord, but that the world's
grown honest.
HAMLET. Then is doomsday near. But your news is
not true. Let me question more in particular.   245
What have you, my good friends, deserved at the
hands of Fortune, that she sends you to prison
hither?

---

arras tapestry   *board* address
Between who i.e., the quarrel is between whom (Hamlet
pretends to mistake Polonius's meaning)

GUILDENSTERN. Prison, my lord!

250 HAMLET. Denmark's a prison.

ROSENCRANTZ. Then is the world one.

HAMLET. A goodly one, in which there are many confines, wards, and dungeons, Denmark being one o' the worst.

255 ROSENCRANTZ. We think not so, my lord.

HAMLET. Why, then 'tis none to you; for there is nothing either good or bad, but thinking makes it so. To me it is a prison.

ROSENCRANTZ. Why, then your ambition makes it
260 one; 'tis too narrow for your mind.

HAMLET. O God, I could be bounded in a nutshell and count myself a king of infinite space, were it not that I have bad dreams.

GUILDENSTERN. Which dreams indeed are ambi-
265 tion; for the very substance of the ambitious is merely the shadow of a dream.

HAMLET. A dream itself is but a shadow.

ROSENCRANTZ. Truly, and I hold ambition of so airy and light a quality that it is but a shadow's
270 shadow.

HAMLET. Then are our beggars bodies, and our monarchs and outstretched heroes the beggars' shadows.° Shall we to the court? For, by my fay,° I cannot reason.

275 ROSENCRANTZ and GUILDENSTERN. We'll wait upon you.

HAMLET. No such matter. I will not sort° you with the rest of my servants; for, to speak to you like an honest man, I am most dreadfully attended.
280 But, in the beaten way of friendship, what make you at Elsinore?

ROSENCRANTZ. To visit you, my lord; no other occasion.

HAMLET. Beggar that I am, I am even poor in
285 thanks, but I thank you. And sure, dear friends, my thanks are too dear a halfpenny.° Were you not sent for? Is it your own inclining? Is it a free visitation? Come, deal justly with me. Come, come; nay, speak.

290 GUILDENSTERN. What should we say, my lord?

HAMLET. Why, anything, but to the purpose. You were sent for, and there is a kind of confession in your looks which your modesties have not craft enough to color. I know the good king and
295 queen have sent for you.

ROSENCRANTZ. To what end, my lord?

HAMLET. That you must teach me. But let me conjure you, by the rights of our fellowship, by

the consonancy of our youth, by the obligation of our ever-preserved love, and by what more 300 dear a better proposer could charge you withal, be even and direct with me, whether you were sent for, or no.

ROSENCRANTZ. [Aside to GUILDENSTERN] What say you? 305

HAMLET. [Aside] Nay then, I have an eye of you.— If you love me, hold not off.

GUILDENSTERN. My lord, we were sent for.

HAMLET. I will tell you why; so shall my anticipa- tion prevent your discovery, and your secrecy 310 to the king and queen moult no feather. I have of late—but wherefore I know not—lost all my mirth, forgone all custom of exercises; and indeed it goes so heavily with my disposition that this goodly frame, the earth, seems to me a 315 sterile promontory; this most excellent canopy, the air, look you, this brave° o'erhanging firmament, this majestical roof fretted° with golden fire, why, it appears no other thing to me than a foul and pestilent congregation of vapors. 320 What a piece of work is a man! How noble in reason! How infinite in faculty! In form and moving how express and admirable! In action how like an angel! In apprehension how like a god! The beauty of the world! The paragon of 325 animals! And yet, to me, what is this quin- tessence of dust? Man delights not me—no, nor woman neither, though by your smiling you seem to say so.

ROSENCRANTZ. My lord, there was no such stuff in 330 my thoughts.

HAMLET. Why did you laugh then, when I said "man delights not me"?

ROSENCRANTZ. To think, my lord, if you delight not in man, what lenten° entertainment the 335 players shall receive from you. We coted° them on the way, and hither are they coming to offer you service.

HAMLET. He that plays the king shall be welcome; his majesty shall have tribute of me. The 340 adventurous knight shall use his foil and target,° the lover shall not sigh gratis, the humorous man° shall end his part in peace, the clown shall make those laugh whose lungs are tickle o' the

---

Then . . . shadows since monarchs and heroes are given
  to ambition, they are only shadows, while beggars, not
  ambitious, are all substance   fay faith
sort class
too . . . halfpenny not even worth a halfpenny

brave splendid, showy   fretted ornamented
lenten i.e., meager
coted overtook   foil and target sword and shield
humorous man i.e., the actor of parts representing excess
  of one or another "humor" [thus Hotspur in Henry IV,
  dominated by his spleen, and Jaques in As You Like It,
  dominated by the black bile that makes for
  melancholy; Hamlet himself is (or pretends to be) the
  "humorous man" of Hamlet]

345 sere,° and the lady shall say her mind freely,
or the blank verse shall halt° for 't. What
players are they?

ROSENCRANTZ. Even those you were wont to take
such delight in, the tragedians of the city.

350 HAMLET. How chances it they travel? Their residence, both in reputation and profit, was better
both ways.

ROSENCRANTZ. I think their inhibition° comes by
the means of the late innovation.°

355 HAMLET. Do they hold the same estimation they
did when I was in the city? Are they so followed?

ROSENCRANTZ. No, indeed, are they not.

HAMLET. How comes it? Do they grow rusty?

ROSENCRANTZ. Nay, their endeavor keeps in the
360 wonted pace, but there is, sir, an eyrie of children, little eyases,° that cry out on the top of
question° and are most tyrannically° clapped for
't. These are now the fashion, and so be-rattle
the common stages—so they call them—that
365 many wearing rapiers are afraid of goose quills,°
and dare scarce come thither.

HAMLET. What, are they children? Who maintains
'em? How are they escoted?° Will they pursue
the quality° no longer than they can sing?° Will
370 they not say afterwards, if they should grow
themselves to common players°—as it is most
like, if their means are no better—their writers
do them wrong to make them exclaim against
their own succession?

375 ROSENCRANTZ. Faith, there has been much to do
on both sides, and the nation holds it no sin to
tarre° them to controversy. There was for a
while no money bid for argument° unless the
poet and the player went to cuffs in the ques-
380 tion.°

HAMLET. Is 't possible?

GUILDENSTERN. O, there has been much throwing
about of brains.

HAMLET. Do the boys carry it away?

ROSENCRANTZ. Aye, that they do, my lord— 385
Hercules and his load too.°

HAMLET. It is not very strange, for my uncle is king
of Denmark, and those that would make mows°
at him while my father lived give twenty, forty,
fifty, a hundred ducats apiece for his picture in 390
little.° 'Sblood,° there is something in this more
than natural, if philosophy could find it out.

                    [*Flourish of trumpets within.*]

GUILDENSTERN. There are the players.

HAMLET. Gentlemen, you are welcome to Elsinore.
Your hands, come then. The appurtenance° of 395
welcome is fashion and ceremony. Let me
comply with you in this garb,° lest my extent to
the players, which, I tell you, must show fairly
outwards,° should more appear like entertain-
ment° than yours. You are welcome. But my 400
uncle-father and aunt-mother are deceived.

GUILDENSTERN. In what, my dear lord?

HAMLET. I am but mad north-northwest. When the
wind is southerly, I know a hawk from a hand-
saw.° 405

                    [*Re-enter* POLONIUS.]

POLONIUS. Well be with you, gentlemen!

HAMLET. Hark you, Guildenstern, and you too—at
each ear a hearer. That great baby you see there
is not yet out of his swaddling clouts.

ROSENCRANTZ. Happily° he's the second time come 410
to them, for they say an old man is twice a child.

HAMLET. I will prophesy he comes to tell me of the
players; mark it.—You say right, sir; o' Monday
morning. 'Twas so, indeed.

POLONIUS. My lord, I have news to tell you. 415

HAMLET. My lord, I have news to tell you. When
Roscius° was an actor in Rome—

POLONIUS. The actors are come hither, my lord.

HAMLET. Buzz, buzz!°

POLONIUS. Upon my honor— 420

HAMLET. Then came each actor on his ass—

POLONIUS. The best actors in the world, either for

---

tickle . . . sere i.e., ready to laugh at the least
    provocation (a hair-triggered gun is "tickle o' the
    sere")
halt limp   *inhibition* hindrance
late innovation reference to the new fashion,
    contemporary with *Hamlet*, of having companies of
    children perform on London stages, threatening
    popularity of the regular acting companies
eyases nestling hawks
cry . . . question i.e., speak their parts in shrill voices
tyrannically excessively
many . . . quills gentlemen fear the satiric pens of
    playwrights
escoted supported   *quality* profession
no . . . sing i.e., until their voices change
common players i.e., adult actors on the public stage
tarre urge, kindle   *bid for argument* paid for a plot
poet . . . question playwright and actor contributed
    remarks to the controversy

Hercules . . . too Hercules briefly relieved Atlas of his
    burden (the world) (with possible reference also to the
    sign of the Globe Playhouse)
mows faces
in little in miniature   *'Sblood* by God's blood
appurtenance i.e., what properly accompanies
garb manner   *show . . . outwards* be fairly lavish
entertainment welcome
I know . . . handsaw i.e., "I'm not as mad as I seem"
    (with possible play on *hernshaw*, for *heron*)
Happily perhaps (haply)
Roscius Roman comic actor
Buzz, buzz i.e., "I told you so"

tragedy, comedy, history, pastoral, pastoral-
comical, historical-pastoral, tragical-historical,
425 tragical-comical-historical-pastoral, scene indi-
vidable, or poem unlimited. Seneca° cannot be
too heavy, nor Plautus° too light. For the law of
writ and the liberty,° these are the only men.
HAMLET. O Jephthah, judge of Israel,° what a
430 treasure hadst thou!
POLONIUS. What a treasure had he, my lord?
HAMLET. Why,

> One fair daughter and no more,
> The which he loved passing° well.

435 POLONIUS. [Aside] Still on my daughter.
HAMLET. Am I not i' the right, old Jephthah?
POLONIUS. If you call me Jephthah, my lord, I have
a daughter that I love passing well.
HAMLET. Nay, that follows not.
440 POLONIUS. What follows, then, my lord?
HAMLET. Why,

> As by lot, God wot,°

and then you know,

> It came to pass, as most like it was—

445 the first row of the pious chanson° will show you
more. For look where my abridgment° comes.
[Enter four or five PLAYERS.]
You are welcome, masters, welcome all. I am
glad to see thee well. Welcome, good friends.
O, my old friend! Why, thy face is valanced°
450 since I saw thee last; comest thou to beard me in
Denmark? What, my young lady and mistress!
By 'r lady, your ladyship is nearer to heaven
than when I saw you last, by the altitude of a
chopine.° Pray God your voice, like a piece of
455 uncurrent gold, be not cracked within the ring.°
Masters, you are all welcome. We'll e'en to 't
like French falconers, fly at anything we see.
We'll have a speech straight. Come, give us a
taste of your quality. Come, a passionate
460 speech.
FIRST PLAYER. What speech, my good lord?
HAMLET. I heard thee speak me a speech once, but
it was never acted; or, if it was, not above once.

For the play, I remember, pleased not the
million; 'twas caviar to the general.° But it was 465
—as I received it, and others whose judgments
in such matters cried in the top of mine°—an
excellent play, well digested° in the scenes, set
down with as much modesty as cunning. I
remember, one said there were no sallets° in the 470
lines to make the matter savory, nor no matter
in the phrase that might indict the author of
affectation, but called it an honest method, as
wholesome as sweet, and by very much more
handsome than fine.° One speech in it I chiefly 475
loved. 'Twas Aeneas' tale to Dido,° and there-
about of it especially, where he speaks of
Priam's° slaughter. If it live in your memory,
begin at this line. Let me see, let me see—

> The rugged Pyrrhus,° like the Hyrcanian beast°— 480

It is not so. It begins with Pyrrhus—

> The rugged Pyrrhus, he whose sable° arms,
> Black as his purpose, did the night resemble
> When he lay couched in the ominous horse,°
> Hath now this dread and black complexion
>   smear'd   485
> With heraldry° more dismal: head to foot
> Now is he total gules, horridly trick'd°
> With blood of fathers, mothers, daughters, sons,
> Bak'd and impasted° with the parching streets,
> That lend a tyrannous and a damned light   490
> To their lord's murder. Roasted in wrath and
>   fire,
> And thus o'er-sized with coagulate gore,
> With eyes like carbuncles, the hellish Pyrrhus
> Old grandsire Priam seeks.

So, proceed you.   495
POLONIUS. 'Fore God, my lord, well spoken, with
good accent and good discretion.
FIRST PLAYER.

> Anon he finds him
> Striking too short at Greeks. His antique sword,
> Rebellious to his arm, lies where it falls,   500

caviar . . general i.e., above the popular taste
cried . . . mine exceeded my judgment
digested composed
sallets salads; here, sharp witticisms   *fine* overfine
Aeneas' . . . Dido Aeneas described the fall of Troy to the
    Queen of Carthage (see *Aeneid*, Book II)
Priam king of Troy, father of Hector
Pyrrhus Achilles' son, who slew Priam to avenge his
    father's death
Hyrcanian beast Asian tiger (see *Macbeth*, III, iv)
sable black
ominous horse the wooden horse with which the Greeks
    gained entrance to Troy
heraldry heraldic painting; here, blood
gules . . . trick'd red . . . adorned   *impasted* crusted

Seneca Roman tragic playwright
Plautus Roman comic playwright
For . . . liberty i.e., for plays according to classical rules
    or plays more freely devised
ephthah . . . Israel whose vow compelled him to
    condemn his own daughter (see Judges xi)
passing surpassingly   *wot* knows
row . . . chanson verse . . . song
abridgment i.e., who cut my speech short
valanced bearded
chopine thick-soled shoe
uncurrent . . . ring coins were not passable if a crack
    extended inward to the ring enclosing the design

SOLILOQUY

Act II / Sc. ii   HAMLET

Repugnant to command. Unequal match'd,
Pyrrhus at Priam drives; in rage strikes wide;
But with the whiff and wind of his fell° sword
Th' unnerved father falls. Then senseless
    Ilium,°
505 Seeming to feel this blow, with flaming top
Stoops to his base, and with a hideous crash
Takes prisoner Pyrrhus' ear; for, lo! his sword,
Which was declining on the milky head
Of reverend Priam, seem'd i' the air to stick.
510 So, as a painted tyrant, Pyrrhus stood,
And like a neutral to his will and matter,
Did nothing.
But as we often see, against° some storm,
A silence in the heavens, the rack° stand still,
515 The bold winds speechless and the orb below
As hush as death, anon the dreadful thunder
Doth rend the region—so after Pyrrhus' pause
Aroused vengeance sets him new awork,
And never did the Cyclops'° hammers fall
520 On Mars's armor, forg'd for proof eterne,°
With less remorse than Pyrrhus' bleeding sword
Now falls on Priam.
Out, out, thou strumpet Fortune! All you gods,
In general synod° take away her power,
525 Break all the spokes and fellies° from her wheel,
And bowl the round nave° down the hill of
    heaven
As low as to the fiends!

POLONIUS. This is too long.
HAMLET. It shall to the barber's, with your beard.
530 Prithee, say on. He's for a jig or a tale of bawdry,
    or he sleeps. Say on. Come to Hecuba.° _women_
FIRST PLAYER.

    But who, O, who had seen the mobled° queen—

HAMLET. "The mobled queen"?
POLONIUS. That's good; "mobled queen" is good.
FIRST PLAYER.

    Run barefoot up and down, threat'ning the
535   flames
    With bisson rheum,° a clout° upon that head
    Where late the diadem stood, and for a robe,
    About her lank and all o'er-teemed° loins,
    A blanket, in the alarm of fear caught up.
    Who this had seen, with tongue in venom
540   steep'd

fell cruel   Ilium Troy   against before
rack cloud mass
Cyclops giant armor-makers for the gods
proof eterne eternal invulnerability   synod council
fellies wood segments joined to form circumference of a
    wheel
nave hub   Hecuba Priam's queen
mobled muffled   bisson rheum blinding tears
clout cloth-rag
o'er-teemed worn out from childbearing

'Gainst Fortune's state would treason have
    pronounc'd.
But if the gods themselves did see her then,
When she saw Pyrrhus make malicious sport
In mincing with his sword her husband's limbs,
The instant burst of clamor that she made,   545
Unless things mortal move them not at all,
Would have made milch° the burning eyes of
    heaven
And passion in the gods.

POLONIUS. Look whether he has not turned his
    color and has tears in 's eyes. Prithee, no more. 550
HAMLET. 'Tis well. I'll have thee speak out the rest
    of this soon. Good my lord, will you see the
    players well bestowed? Do you hear, let them
    be well used, for they are the abstract and brief
    chronicles of the time. After your death you   555
    were better have a bad epitaph than their ill
    report while you live.
POLONIUS. My lord, I will use them according to
    their desert.
HAMLET. God's bodykins,° man, much better. Use   560
    every man after his desert, and who shall 'scape
    whipping? Use them after your own honor and
    dignity. The less they deserve, the more merit is
    in your bounty. Take them in.
POLONIUS. Come, sirs.   565
HAMLET. Follow him, friends. We'll hear a play
    tomorrow.
    [Exit POLONIUS with all the PLAYERS but the FIRST.]
    Dost thou hear me, old friend? Can you play the
    Murder of Gonzago?
FIRST PLAYER. Aye, my lord.   570
HAMLET. We'll ha 't tomorrow night. You could,
    for a need, study a speech of some dozen or six-
    teen lines which I would set down and insert in
    't, could you not?
FIRST PLAYER. Aye, my lord.   575
HAMLET. Very well. Follow that lord, and look you
    mock him not. [Exit FIRST PLAYER] My good
    friends, I'll leave you till night. You are welcome
    to Elsinore.
ROSENCRANTZ. Good my lord!   580
HAMLET. Aye, so, God be wi' ye! [Exeunt ROSEN-
    CRANTZ and GUILDENSTERN] Now I am alone.
    O, what a rogue and peasant slave am I!
    Is it not monstrous that this player here,
    But in a fiction, in a dream of passion,
    Could force his soul so to his own conceit°   585
    That from her working all his visage wann'd,
    Tears in his eyes, distraction in 's aspect,
    A broken voice, and his whole function° suiting

soliloquy

Hamlet's view of self changing.

milch i.e., milky with tears   bodykins little body
conceit fancy   function manner of being

383

With forms° to his conceit? And all for nothing!
590 For Hecuba!
What's Hecuba to him or he to Hecuba,
That he should weep for her? What would he do
Had he the motive and the cue for passion
That I have? He would drown the stage with tears
595 And cleave the general ear with horrid speech,
Make mad the guilty and appall the free,°
Confound the ignorant, and amaze indeed
The very faculties of eyes and ears.
Yet I,
600 A dull and muddy-mettled° rascal, peak°
Like John-a-dreams, unpregnant of° my cause,
And can say nothing—no, not for a king,
Upon whose property and most dear life
A damn'd defeat was made. Am I a coward?
605 Who calls me villain? Breaks my pate across?
Plucks off my beard and blows it in my face?
Tweaks me by the nose? Gives me the lie i' the throat
As deep as to the lungs? Who does me this?
Ha!
610 'Swounds,° I should take it, for it cannot be
But I am pigeon-liver'd and lack gall
To make oppression bitter, or ere this
I should have fatted all the region kites
With this slave's offal. Bloody, bawdy villain!

Remorseless, treacherous, lecherous, kindless° villain!
O, vengeance!   615
Why, what an ass am I! This is most brave,
That I, the son of a dear father murder'd,
Prompted to my revenge by heaven and hell,
Must, like a whore, unpack my heart with words   620
And fall a-cursing like a very drab,
A scullion! Fie upon it! Foh!
About, my brain! Hum—I have heard
That guilty creatures, sitting at a play,
Have by the very cunning of the scene   625
Been struck so to the soul that presently°
They have proclaim'd their malefactions;
For murder, though it have no tongue, will speak
With most miraculous organ. I'll have these players
Play something like the murder of my father   630
Before mine uncle. I'll observe his looks;
I'll tent° him to the quick. If he but blench,°
I know my course. The spirit that I have seen
May be the devil, and the devil hath power
T' assume a pleasing shape. Yea, and perhaps   635
Out of my weakness and my melancholy,
As he is very potent with such spirits,
Abuses me to damn me. I'll have grounds
More relative° than this. The play's the thing
Wherein I'll catch the conscience of the king.   640
                                                    [Exit]

forms appearances   *free* innocent
muddy-mettled cloddish   *peak* mope
unpregnant of i.e., indifferent to
'Swounds by Christ's wounds

kindless unnatural   *presently* immediately
tent probe   *blench* wince   *relative* conclusive

ACT III

SCENE i
A room in the castle.

[*Enter* KING, QUEEN, POLONIUS, OPHELIA, ROSEN-
CRANTZ, *and* GUILDENSTERN.]
KING. And can you by no drift of circumstance
Get from him why he puts on° this confusion,
Grating so harshly all his days of quiet
With turbulent and dangerous lunacy?
ROSENCRANTZ. He does confess he feels himself dis-
5   tracted,
But from what cause he will by no means speak.

GUILDENSTERN. Nor do we find him forward to be
      sounded,°
But, with a crafty madness, keeps aloof
When we would bring him on to some confes-
      sion
Of his true state.
QUEEN.   Did he receive you well?   10
ROSENCRANTZ. Most like a gentleman.
GUILDENSTERN. But with much forcing of his dis-
      position.
ROSENCRANTZ. Niggard of question, but of our
      demands

puts on exhibits

forward . . . sounded cooperative in being questioned

Claudius's Guilt

Sol.
2 or 2B

Most free in his reply.

QUEEN.   Did you assay him

15   To any pastime?

ROSENCRANTZ. Madam, it so fell out that certain
    players

    We o'er-raught° on the way. Of these we told
    him,

    And there did seem in him a kind of joy

    To hear of it. They are about the court,

20   And, as I think, they have already order

    This night to play before him.

POLONIUS.   'Tis most true.

    And he beseech'd me to entreat your majesties

    To hear and see the matter.

KING. With all my heart; and it doth much content
    me

25   To hear him so inclin'd.

    Good gentlemen, give him a further edge,°

    And drive his purpose on to these delights.

ROSENCRANTZ. We shall, my lord.

            [*Exeunt* ROSENCRANTZ *and* GUILDENSTERN.]

KING.   Sweet Gertrude, leave us too;

    For we have closely° sent for Hamlet hither,

30   That he, as 'twere by accident, may here

    Affront° Ophelia.

    Her father and myself, lawful espials,

    Will so bestow ourselves that, seeing unseen,

    We may of their encounter frankly judge,

35   And gather by him, as he is behav'd,

    If 't be th' affliction of his love or no

    That thus he suffers for.

QUEEN.   I shall obey you.

    And for your part, Ophelia, I do wish

    That your good beauties be the happy cause

    Of Hamlet's wildness. So shall I hope your

40   virtues

    Will bring him to his wonted way again,

    To both your honors.

OPHELIA.   Madam, I wish it may.

                          [*Exit* QUEEN.]

POLONIUS. Ophelia, walk you here. Gracious, so
    please you,

    We will bestow ourselves. [*To* OPHELIA] Read on
    this book,

45   That show of such an exercise may color°

    Your loneliness. We are oft to blame in this—

    'Tis too much prov'd—that with devotion's
    visage

    And pious action we do sugar o'er

    The devil himself.

KING.   [*Aside*] O, 'tis too true!

How smart a lash that speech doth give my
    conscience!   50

The harlot's cheek, beautied with plast'ring art,

Is not more ugly to the thing that helps it

Than is my deed to my most painted word.

O heavy burden!

POLONIUS. I hear him coming. Let's withdraw, my
    lord.   [*Exeunt* KING *and* POLONIUS.]   55

            [*Enter* HAMLET.]

HAMLET. To be, or not to be: that is the question.

    Whether 'tis nobler in the mind to suffer°

    The slings and arrows of outrageous fortune,

    Or to take arms against a sea of troubles

    And by opposing end them. To die, to sleep—   60

    No more. And by a sleep to say we end

    The heartache and the thousand natural shocks

    That flesh is heir to: 'tis a consummation

    Devoutly to be wish'd. To die, to sleep.

    To sleep? Perchance to dream. Aye, there's the
    rub;   65

    For in that sleep of death what dreams may
    come

    When we have shuffled off this mortal coil°

    Must give us pause. There's the respect°

    That makes calamity of so long life;

    For who would bear the whips and scorns of
    time,   70

    Th' oppressor's wrong, the proud man's con-
    tumely,°

    The pangs of despis'd love, the law's delay,

    The insolence of office, and the spurns

    That patient merit of the unworthy takes,

    When he himself might his quietus° make   75

    With a bare bodkin?° Who would fardels° bear,

    To grunt and sweat under a weary life,

    But that the dread of something after death,

    The undiscover'd country from whose bourn°

    No traveler returns, puzzles the will   80

    And makes us rather bear those ills we have

    Than fly to others that we know not of?

    Thus conscience does make cowards of us all,

    And thus the native hue of resolution

    Is sicklied o'er with the pale cast of thought, 85

    And enterprises of great pith and moment

    With this regard their currents turn awry

    And lose the name of action. Soft you now!

    The fair Ophelia! Nymph, in thy orisons°

    Be all my sins remember'd.

OPHELIA.   Good my lord,   90

    How does your honor for this many a day?

---

suffer endure
shuffled . . . coil rid ourselves of the business of living
respect consideration   *contumely* contempt
quietus release   *bodkin* dagger   *fardels* burdens
bourn boundary   *orisons* prayers

o'er-raught overtook   *edge* incitement
closely privately
Affront confront   *color* evince

HAMLET. I humbly thank you, well, well, well.

OPHELIA. My lord, I have remembrances of yours
  That I have longed long to redeliver;
  I pray you, now receive them.

95 HAMLET.   No, not I.
  I never gave you aught.

OPHELIA. My honor'd lord, you know right well
    you did,
  And with them words of so sweet breath com-
    pos'd
  As made the things more rich. Their perfume
    lost,

100 Take these again; for to the noble mind
  Rich gifts wax poor when givers prove unkind.
  There, my lord.

HAMLET. Ha, ha! Are you honest?°

OPHELIA. My lord?

105 HAMLET. Are you fair?

OPHELIA. What means your lordship?

HAMLET. That if you be honest and fair, your
  honesty should admit no discourse to your
  beauty.

110 OPHELIA. Could beauty, my lord, have better commerce than with honesty?

HAMLET. Aye, truly, for the power of beauty will
  sooner transform honesty from what it is to a
  bawd than the force of honesty can translate
115 beauty into his° likeness. This was sometime a
  paradox, but now the time gives it proof. I did
  love you once.

OPHELIA. Indeed, my lord, you made me believe
  so.

120 HAMLET. You should not have believed me, for
  virtue cannot so inoculate our old stock but we
  shall relish° of it. I loved you not.

OPHELIA. I was the more deceived.

HAMLET. Get thee to a nunnery. Why wouldst thou
125 be a breeder of sinners? I am myself indifferent
  honest,° but yet I could accuse me of such things
  that it were better my mother had not borne
  me. I am very proud, revengeful, ambitious,
  with more offenses at my beck than I have
130 thoughts to put them in, imagination to give
  them shape, or time to act them in. What should
  such fellows as I do crawling between heaven and
  earth? We are arrant knaves all; believe none of
  us. Go thy ways to a nunnery. Where's your
135 father?

OPHELIA. At home, my lord.

HAMLET. Let the doors be shut upon him, that he
  may play the fool nowhere but in 's own house.
  Farewell.

OPHELIA. O, help him, you sweet heavens!   140

HAMLET. If thou dost marry, I'll give thee this
  plague for thy dowry: be thou as chaste as ice, as
  pure as snow, thou shalt not escape calumny.
  Get thee to a nunnery, go. Farewell. Or, if thou
  wilt needs marry, marry a fool, for wise men   145
  know well enough what monsters° you make of
  them. To a nunnery, go, and quickly too. Farewell.

OPHELIA. O heavenly powers, restore him!

HAMLET. I have heard of your paintings too, well 150
  enough. God hath given you one face, and you
  make yourselves another. You jig, you amble,
  and you lisp, and nickname God's creatures, and
  make your wantonness your ignorance.° Go to,
  I'll no more on 't; it hath made me mad. I say,   155
  we will have no more marriages. Those that are
  married already, all but one, shall live; the rest
  shall keep as they are. To a nunnery, go.

                                        [Exit]

OPHELIA. O, what a noble mind is here o'erthrown!
  The courtier's, soldier's, scholar's eye, tongue,
    sword,   160
  Th' expectancy and rose of the fair state,
  The glass of fashion and the mould of form,
  Th' observ'd of all observers—quite, quite down!
  And I, of ladies most deject and wretched,
  That suck'd the honey of his music vows,   165
  Now see that noble and most sovereign reason
  Like sweet bells jangled, out of tune and harsh;
  That unmatch'd form and feature of blown°
    youth
  Blasted with ecstasy.° O, woe is me
  T' have seen what I have seen, see what I see!   170
      [Re-enter KING and POLONIUS.]

KING. Love! His affections° do not that way tend,
  Nor what he spake, though it lack'd form a little,
  Was not like madness. There's something in his
    soul
  O'er which his melancholy sits on brood,
  And I do doubt° the hatch and the disclose°   175
  Will be some danger. Which for to prevent,
  I have in quick determination
  Thus set it down:—He shall with speed to
    England
  For the demand of our neglected tribute.
  Haply the seas and countries different   180
  With variable objects° shall expel

---

monsters i.e., cuckolds
nickname . . . ignorance employ gross names for things and
  excuse your indecency by pleading ignorance
blown full-blooming
Blasted . . . ecstasy shattered by madness
affections inclinations   doubt fear
disclose result   variable objects changing scenes

---

honest chaste   his its   relish retain a trace
indifferent honest averagely honorable

This something-settled° matter in his heart,
Whereon his brains still beating puts him thus
From fashion of himself. What think you on 't?
185 POLONIUS. It shall do well. But yet do I believe
The origin and commencement of his grief
Sprung from neglected love. How now, Ophelia!
You need not tell us what Lord Hamlet said.
We heard it all. My lord, do as you please.
190 But if you hold it fit, after the play
Let his queen mother all alone entreat him
To show his grief. Let her be round° with him;
And I'll be plac'd, so please you, in the ear
Of all their conference. If she find him not,
195 To England send him, or confine him where
Your wisdom best shall think.
KING.   It shall be so.
Madness in great ones must not unwatch'd go.
                                        [Exeunt]

SCENE ii
A hall in the castle.

[*Enter* HAMLET *and* PLAYERS.]
HAMLET. Speak the speech, I pray you, as I pronounced it to you, trippingly on the tongue. But
if you mouth it, as many of your players do, I had
as lief the towncrier spoke my lines. Nor do not
5 saw the air too much with your hand, thus, but
use all gently. For in the very torrent, tempest,
and, as I may say, whirlwind of your passion, you
must acquire and beget a temperance that may
give it smoothness. O, it offends me to the soul to
10 hear a robustious periwig-pated fellow tear a
passion to tatters, to very rags, to split the ears of
the groundlings,° who, for the most part, are
capable of nothing but inexplicable dumb-shows
and noise. I would have such a fellow whipped
15 for o'erdoing Termagant;° it out-herods Herod.°
Pray you, avoid it.
FIRST PLAYER. I warrant your honor.
HAMLET. Be not too tame neither, but let your own
discretion be your tutor. Suit the action to the
20 word, the word to the action, with this special
observance, that you o'erstep not the modesty
of nature; for anything so overdone is from° the

purpose of playing, whose end, both at the first
and now, was and is to hold, as 'twere, the
mirror up to nature—to show virtue her own   25
feature, scorn her own image, and the very age
and body of the time his form and pressure.°
Now this overdone or come tardy off, though it
make the unskillful laugh, cannot but make the
judicious grieve, the censure° of the which one   30
must in your allowance o'erweigh a whole
theater of others. O, there be players that I have
seen play, and heard others praise, and that
highly, not to speak it profanely, that neither
having the accent of Christians nor the gait of   35
Christian, pagan, nor man, have so strutted and
bellowed that I have thought some of nature's
journeymen° had made men, and not made
them well, they imitated humanity so abomi-
nably.   40
FIRST PLAYER. I hope we have reformed that in-
differently° with us, sir.
HAMLET. O, reform it altogether. And let those that
play your clowns speak no more than is set down
for them. For there be of° them that will them-   45
selves laugh to set on some quantity of barren
spectators to laugh too, though in the meantime
some necessary question of the play be then to be
considered. That's villainous, and shows a most
pitiful ambition in the fool that uses it. Go, make 50
you ready.   [*Exeunt* PLAYERS.]
[*Enter* POLONIUS, ROSENCRANTZ, *and* GUILDENSTERN.]
How now, my lord! Will the king hear this piece
of work?
POLONIUS. And the queen too, and that presently.
HAMLET. Bid the players make haste.   55
                                        [*Exit* POLONIUS.]
Will you two help to hasten them?
ROSENCRANTZ *and* GUILDENSTERN. We will, my lord.
          [*Exeunt* ROSENCRANTZ *and* GUILDSTERN.]
HAMLET. What ho! Horatio!
                              [*Enter* HORATIO.]
HORATIO. Here, sweet lord, at your service.
HAMLET. Horatio, thou art e'en as just a man   60
As e'er my conversation cop'd withal.°
HORATIO. O, my dear lord—
HAMLET.   Nay, do not think I flatter;
For what advancement may I hope from thee,
That no revenue hast but thy good spirits
To feed and clothe thee? Why should the poor
be flatter'd?   65
No, let the candied tongue lick absurd pomp,

---

something-settled somewhat fixed
round direct
groundlings lowest-paying spectators, who stood in the pit
   of the theater
Termagant Saracen god (portrayed as raging tyrant in
   early plays)
out-herods Herod i.e., to rant outrageously (as Herod
   was portrayed in early Biblical plays)
from aside from

age . . . pressure i.e., the true likeness of the times
censure judgment
journeymen learners, not yet master artisans
indifferently fairly well   *of* some of
As e'er . . . withal as I have ever known

And crook the pregnant hinges of the knee
Where thrift may follow fawning.° Dost thou
   hear?
Since my dear soul was mistress of her choice
70 And could of men distinguish, her election
Hath seal'd thee for herself. For thou hast been
As one, in suffering all, that suffers nothing,
A man that fortune's buffets and rewards
Hast ta'en with equal thanks. And blest are
   those
75 Whose blood° and judgment are so well com-
   mingled
That they are not a pipe for fortune's finger
To sound what stop she please. Give me that
   man
That is not passion's slave, and I will wear him
In my heart's core, aye, in my heart of heart,
80 As I do thee. Something too much of this.
There is a play tonight before the king.
One scene of it comes near the circumstance
Which I have told thee of my father's death.
I prithee, when thou seest that act afoot,
85 Even with the very comment of thy soul°
Observe my uncle. If his occulted° guilt
Do not itself unkennel in one speech,
It is a damned ghost that we have seen,
And my imaginations are as foul
90 As Vulcan's stithy.° Give him heedful note,
For I mine eyes will rivet to his face,
And after we will both our judgments join
In censure of his seeming.°
HORATIO.   Well, my lord.
If he steal aught the whilst this play is playing,
95 And 'scape detecting, I will pay the theft.
HAMLET. They are coming to the play; I must be
   idle.°
Get you a place.
   [*Danish march. A flourish. Enter* KING, QUEEN,
POLONIUS, OPHELIA, ROSENCRANTZ, GUILDENSTERN,
   and other LORDS *attendant, with the* GUARD
              carrying torches.]
KING. How fares our cousin Hamlet?
HAMLET. Excellent, i' faith; of the chameleon's
100 dish°—I eat the air, promise-crammed. You can-
   not feed capons so.

KING. I have nothing with° this answer, Hamlet;
   these words are not mine.
HAMLET. No, nor mine now. [*To* POLONIUS] My
   lord, you played once i' th' university, you say?   105
POLONIUS. That did I, my lord, and was accounted a
   good actor.
HAMLET. What did you enact?
POLONIUS. I did enact Julius Cæsar. I was killed i'
   the Capitol. Brutus killed me.   110
HAMLET. It was a brute part of him to kill so capital
   a calf there. Be the players ready?
ROSENCRANTZ. Aye, my lord. They stay upon your
   patience.
QUEEN. Come hither, my dear Hamlet, sit by me.   115
HAMLET. No, good mother, here's metal more
   attractive.
POLONIUS. [*To the* KING] O, ho! Do you mark that?
HAMLET. Lady, shall I lie in your lap?
         [*Lying down at* OPHELIA's *feet.*]
OPHELIA. No, my lord.   120
HAMLET. I mean, my head upon your lap?
OPHELIA. Aye, my lord.   CUNT-
HAMLET. Do you think I meant country matters?°
OPHELIA. I think nothing, my lord.
HAMLET. That's a fair thought to lie between   125
   maids' legs.
OPHELIA. What is, my lord?   N-THING
HAMLET. Nothing.
OPHELIA. You are merry, my lord.
HAMLET. Who, I?   130
OPHELIA. Aye, my lord.
HAMLET. O God, your only jig-maker. What should
   a man do but be merry? For look you how
   cheerfully my mother looks, and my father died
   within 's two hours.   135
OPHELIA. Nay, 'tis twice two months, my lord.
HAMLET. So long? Nay then, let the devil wear
   black, for I'll have a suit of sables.° O heavens!
   Die two months ago, and not forgotten yet?
   Then there's hope a great man's memory may   140
   outlive his life half a year. But, by 'r lady, he
   must build churches then; or else shall he suffer
   not thinking on, with the hobbyhorse, whose
   epitaph is, "For, O, for, O, the hobbyhorse is
   forgot."°   145
      Hautboys° play. The dumb-show enters.
   [*Enter a* KING *and a* QUEEN *very lovingly, the*

crook . . . fawning be quick to bow where profit will
   follow flattery
blood passion
comment . . . soul i.e., with your deepest concentration
occulted hidden
Vulcan's stithy the smithy of Vulcan, the blacksmith god
censure . . . seeming judgment of his behavior
idle i.e., act mad
chameleon's dish the chameleon was popularly thought
   to eat only air

have . . . with make no sense of
country matters rustic doings (with gross pun)
suit of sables i.e., sable fur, which would be unsuitable
   for mourning (with play on *sable* which also means
   "black")
"For . . . forgot" allusion to the hobbyhorse used in
   morris dances (see *Love's Labor's Lost*, III, i)
Hautboys oboes

QUEEN *embracing him and he her. She kneels, and makes show of protestation unto him. He takes her up, and declines his head upon her neck, lays him down upon a bank of flowers. She, seeing him asleep, leaves him. Anon comes in a fellow, takes off his crown, kisses it, and pours poison in the* KING's *ears, and exit. The* QUEEN *returns, finds the* KING *dead, and makes passionate action. The Poisoner, with some two or three Mutes, comes in again, seeming to lament with her. The dead body is carried away. The Poisoner woos the* QUEEN *with gifts. She seems loath and unwilling awhile, but in the end accepts his love.]*   [*Exeunt*]

OPHELIA. What means this, my lord?

HAMLET. Marry, this is miching mallecho.° It means mischief.

OPHELIA. Belike this show imports the argument°
150   of the play.

[*Enter* PROLOGUE.]

HAMLET. We shall know by this fellow. The players cannot keep counsel—they'll tell all.

OPHELIA. Will he tell us what this show meant?

HAMLET. Aye, or any show that you'll show him.
155   Be not you ashamed to show, he'll not shame to tell you what it means.

OPHELIA. You are naught,° you are naught. I'll mark the play.

Prologue

For us, and for our tragedy,
160   Here stooping to your clemency,
We beg your hearing patiently.

HAMLET. Is this a prologue, or the posy° of a ring?

OPHELIA. 'Tis brief, my lord.

HAMLET. As woman's love.

[*Enter two* PLAYERS, KING *and* QUEEN.]

PLAYER King. Full thirty times hath Phœbus' cart°
165   gone round
Neptune's salt wash° and Tellus' orbed ground,°
And thirty dozen moons with borrow'd sheen
About the world have times twelve thirties been
Since love our hearts and Hymen° did our hands
170   Unite commutual° in most sacred bands.

PLAYER QUEEN. So many journeys may the sun and moon
Make us again count o'er ere love be done!
But, woe is me, you are so sick of late,
So far from cheer and from your former state,

That I distrust you. Yet, though I distrust,°   175
Discomfort you, my lord, it nothing must.
For women's fear and love holds quantity
In neither aught, or in extremity.°
Now what my love is, proof hath made you know,
And as my love is siz'd, my fear is so.   180
Where love is great, the littlest doubts are fear;
Where little fears grow great, great love grows there.

PLAYER KING. Faith, I must leave thee, love, and shortly too;
My operant° powers their functions leave° to do.
And thou shalt live in this fair world behind,   185
Honor'd, belov'd; and haply one as kind
For husband shalt thou—

PLAYER QUEEN.   O, confound the rest!
Such love must needs be treason in my breast.
In second husband let me be accurst!
None wed the second but who kill'd the first.   190

HAMLET. [*Aside*] Wormwood,° wormwood.

PLAYER QUEEN. The instances that second marriage move
Are base respects of thrift,° but none of love.
A second time I kill my husband dead,
When second husband kisses me in bed.   195

PLAYER KING. I do believe you think what now you speak,
But what we do determine oft we break.
Purpose is but the slave to memory,
Of violent birth but poor validity,°
Which now, like fruit unripe, sticks on the tree,   200
But fall unshaken when they mellow be.
Most necessary 'tis that we forget
To pay ourselves what to ourselves is debt.
What to ourselves in passion we propose,
The passion ending, doth the purpose lose.   205
The violence of either grief or joy
Their own enactures° with themselves destroy.
Where joy most revels, grief doth most lament;
Grief joys, joy grieves, on slender accident.
This world is not for aye,° nor 'tis not strange   210
That even our loves should with our fortunes change.
For 'tis a question left us yet to prove,
Whether love lead fortune or else fortune love.
The great man down, you mark his favorite flies;
The poor advanc'd makes friends of enemies.   215
And hitherto doth love on fortune tend;
For who not needs shall never lack a friend,
And who in want a hollow friend doth try
Directly seasons him his enemy.
But, orderly to end where I begun,   220

---

miching mallecho presumably *skulduggery* (of unknown origin; possibly, Spanish *malhecho*, misdeed)
argument plot   *naught* naughty, wicked
posy poetic inscription on a ring, hence brief
Phoebus' cart the sun god's chariot
Neptune's . . . wash the sea god's ocean
Tellus' . . . ground the earth goddess' earth
Hymen god of marriage   *commutual* mutually

distrust fear for
In . . . extremity in none of either or excess of both
operant vital   *leave* cease
Wormwood a bitter herb
respects of thrift motives of profit   *validity* force
enactures doings   *aye* ever

Our wills and fates do so contrary run,
That our devices still are overthrown,
Our thoughts are ours, their ends none of our own;
So think thou wilt no second husband wed,
225 But die thy thoughts when thy first lord is dead.
PLAYER QUEEN. Nor earth to me give food nor heaven
　　light!
Sport and repose lock from me day and night!
To desperation turn my trust and hope!
An anchor's° cheer in prison be my scope!
230 Each opposite, that blanks° the face of joy,
Meet what I would have well and it destroy!
Both here and hence pursue me lasting strife,
If, once a widow, ever I be wife!

HAMLET. If she should break it now!

PLAYER KING. 'Tis deeply sworn. Sweet, leave me here
235 　　a while.
My spirits grow dull, and fain I would beguile
The tedious day with sleep.　　　　　　[Sleeps.]
PLAYER QUEEN.　　　　　　　Sleep rock thy brain,
And never come mischance between us twain!
　　　　　　　　　　　　　　　　　　[Exit]

HAMLET. Madam, how like you this play?
QUEEN. The lady doth protest too much,° me-
240 　　thinks.
HAMLET. O, but she'll keep her word.
KING. Have you heard the argument? Is there no
　　offense in 't?
HAMLET. No, no, they do but jest, poison in jest; no
245 　　offense i' the world.
KING. What do you call the play?
HAMLET. The Mouse-trap. Marry, how? Tropi-
　　cally.° This play is the image of a murder done
　　in Vienna. Gonzago is the duke's name; his wife
250 　　Baptista. You shall see anon. 'Tis a knavish piece
　　of work, but what o' that? Your majesty, and we
　　that have free° souls, it touches us not. Let the
　　galled jade° wince, our withers are unwrung.°
　　　　　　　　　　　　[Enter LUCIANUS.]
　　This is one Lucianus, nephew to the king.
255 OPHELIA. You are as good as a chorus, my lord.
HAMLET. I could interpret between you and your
　　love, if I could see the puppets dallying.°
OPHELIA. You are keen,° my lord, you are keen.
HAMLET. It would cost you a groaning to take off
260 　　my edge.
OPHELIA. Still better, and worse.

anchor's anchorite's (recluse's)　　*blanks* blanches
protest too much i.e., makes too encompassing vows
Tropically figuratively　　*free* i.e., free of guilt
galled jade the horse that has a sore (galled) spot
unwrung ungalled
I could . . . dallying I could act as commentator at a
　　puppet show featuring you and your lover if I could see
　　the figures in action
keen witty, sharp

HAMLET. So you must take your husbands. Begin,
　　murderer; pox, leave thy damnable faces, and
　　begin. Come: the croaking raven doth bellow
　　for revenge.　　　　　　　　　　　　　　265
LUCIANUS. Thoughts black, hands apt, drugs fit, and
　　time agreeing;
Confederate season,° else no creature seeing;
Thou mixture rank, of midnight weeds collected,
With Hecate's ban° thrice blasted, thrice infected,
Thy natural magic and dire property,°　　　　270
　　On wholesome life usurp immediately.
　　　　　　[Pours the poison into the sleeper's ear.]

HAMLET. He poisons him i' th' garden for's estate.
　　His name's Gonzago. The story is extant, and
　　written in very choice Italian. You shall see anon
　　how the murderer gets the love of Gonzago's　275
　　wife.
OPHELIA. The king rises.
HAMLET. What, frighted with false fire!
QUEEN. How fares my lord?
POLONIUS. Give o'er the play.　　　　　　　　280
KING. Give me some light. Away!
POLONIUS. Lights, lights, lights!
　　　　　　[Exeunt all but HAMLET and HORATIO.]
HAMLET.

Why, let the stricken deer go weep,
　　The hart ungalled play;
For some must watch, while some must sleep:　285
　　Thus runs the world away.

Would not this, sir, and a forest of feathers°—if
the rest of my fortunes turn Turk° with me—
with two Provincial roses on my razed shoes,°
get me a fellowship in a cry° of players, sir?　290
HORATIO. Half a share.
HAMLET. A whole one, I.

For thou dost know, O Damon° dear,
　　This realm dismantled was
Of Jove himself; and now reigns here　　　　295
　　A very, very—pajock.°

HORATIO. You might have rhymed.
HAMLET. O good Horatio, I'll take the ghost's word
　　for a thousand pound. Didst perceive?
HORATIO. Very well, my lord.　　　　　　　　300

Confederate season the time serving as accomplice
Hecate's ban the curse of Hecate, goddess of witchcraft (see
　　Macbeth)
property quality
forest of feathers plumes, actors' costumery
turn Turk turn false
Provincial . . . shoes rosettes worn on shoes that are
　　decoratively slashed
cry pack (company)
Damon of Damon and Pythias, archetypal friends
pajock peacock

H. & Guildenstern

HAMLET. Upon the talk of the poisoning?

HORATIO. I did very well note him.

HAMLET. Ah, ha! Come, some music! come, the recorders!

305   For if the king like not the comedy,
        Why then, belike, he likes it not, perdy.°

Come, some music!

[*Re-enter* ROSENCRANTZ *and* GUILDENSTERN.]

GUILDENSTERN. Good my lord, vouchsafe° me a word with you.

310 HAMLET. Sir, a whole history.

GUILDENSTERN. The king, sir—

HAMLET. Aye, sir, what of him?

GUILDENSTERN. Is in his retirement marvelous distempered.

315 HAMLET. With drink, sir?

GUILDENSTERN. No, my lord, rather with choler.°

HAMLET. Your wisdom should show itself more richer to signify this to the doctor; for, for me to put him to his purgation° would perhaps plunge
320 him into far more choler.

GUILDENSTERN. Good my lord, put your discourse into some frame, and start not so wildly from my affair.

HAMLET. I am tame, sir. Pronounce.

325 GUILDERNSTERN. The queen your mother, in most great affliction of spirit, hath sent me to you.

HAMLET. You are welcome.

GUILDENSTERN. Nay, good my lord, this courtesy is not of the right breed. If it shall please you to
330 make me a wholesome answer, I will do your mother's commandment. If not, your pardon and my return shall be the end of my business.

HAMLET. Sir, I cannot.

GUILDENSTERN. What, my lord?

335 HAMLET. Make you a wholesome answer; my wit's diseased. But, sir, such answer as I can make, you shall command; or rather, as you say, my mother. Therefore no more, but to the matter. My mother, you say—

340 ROSENCRANTZ. Then thus she says: your behavior hath struck her into amazement and admiration.°

HAMLET. O wonderful son, that can so 'stonish a mother! But is there no sequel at the heels of
345 this mother's admiration? Impart.

ROSENCRANTZ. She desires to speak with you in her closet ere you go to bed.

HAMLET. We shall obey, were she ten times our mother.
Have you any further trade with us?

ROSENCRANTZ. My lord, you once did love me.   350

HAMLET. So I do still, by these pickers and stealers.°

ROSENCRANTZ. Good my lord, what is your cause of distemper? You do surely bar the door upon your own liberty if you deny your griefs to your friend.   355

HAMLET. Sir, I lack advancement.

ROSENCRANTZ. How can that be, when you have the voice of the king himself for your succession in Denmark?

HAMLET. Aye, sir, but "while the grass grows"°—   360
the proverb is something musty.

[*Re-enter* PLAYERS *with recorders.*]
O, the recorders! Let me see one. To withdraw with you—why do you go about to recover the wind° of me, as if you would drive me into a toil?°   365

GUILDENSTERN. O, my lord, if my duty be too bold, my love is too unmannerly.

HAMLET. I do not well understand that. Will you play upon this pipe?   *See line 76*

GUILDENSTERN. My lord, I cannot.   370

HAMLET. I pray you.

GUILDENSTERN. Believe me, I cannot.

HAMLET. I do beseech you.

GUILDENSTERN. I know no touch of it, my lord.

HAMLET. It is as easy as lying. Govern these ventages with your fingers and thumb, give it breath with your mouth, and it will discourse most eloquent music. Look you, these are the stops.   375

GUILDENSTERN. But these cannot I command to any utterance of harmony. I have not the skill.   380

HAMLET. Why, look you now, how unworthy a thing you make of me! You would play upon me. You would seem to know my stops. You would pluck out the heart of my mystery. You   385
would sound me from my lowest note to the top of my compass. And there is much music, excellent voice, in this little organ; yet cannot you make it speak. 'Sblood, do you think I am easier to be played on than a pipe? Call me what   390
instrument you will, though you can fret° me, yet you cannot play upon me.

[*Re-enter* POLONIUS.]
God bless you, sir!

---

perdy corruption of French *par Dieu*
vouchsafe grant   *choler* anger
purgation purging, cure (Hamlet pretends to take *choler* as *indisposition*, or perhaps *colic*)
admiration wonder

pickers and stealers i.e., hands
"while . . . grows" "—the horse starves"
recover the wind as in hunting, to get downwind of the prey   *toil* trap
fret i.e., annoy (with pun on fingering the frets of the instrument)

POLONIUS. My lord, the queen would speak with
395   you, and presently.
HAMLET. Do you see yonder cloud that's almost in
       shape of a camel?
POLONIUS. By the mass, and 'tis like a camel, indeed.
HAMLET. Methinks it is like a weasel.
400 POLONIUS. It is backed like a weasel.
HAMLET. Or like a whale?
POLONIUS. Very like a whale.
HAMLET. Then I will come to my mother by and
       by. [*Aside*] They fool me to the top of my bent.°
405   —I will come by and by.
POLONIUS. I will say so.   [*Exit* POLONIUS.]
HAMLET. "By and by" is easily said. Leave me,
       friends.   [*Exeunt all but* HAMLET.]
       'Tis now the very witching time of night,
       When churchyards yawn, and hell itself breathes
       out
       Contagion to this world. Now could I drink hot
410   blood,
       And do such bitter business as the day
       Would quake to look on. Soft! Now to my
       mother.
       O heart, lose not thy nature; let not ever
       The soul of Nero° enter this firm bosom.
415   Let me be cruel, not unnatural.
       I will speak daggers to her, but use none.
       My tongue and soul in this be hypocrites;
       How in my words soever she be shent,°
       To give them seals° never, my soul, consent!
                                              [*Exit*]

              SCENE iii
          A room in the castle.

       [*Enter* KING, ROSENCRANTZ, *and* GUILDENSTERN.]
KING. I like him not,° nor stands it safe with us°
       To let his madness range. Therefore prepare you.
       I your commission will forthwith dispatch,
       And he to England shall along with you.
5   The terms of our estate° may not endure
       Hazard so near us as doth hourly grow
       Out of his lunacies.
GUILDENSTERN.   We will ourselves provide.
       Most holy and religious fear it is
       To keep those many many bodies safe
10   That live and feed upon your majesty.

They . . . bent they indulge my lunacy to the utmost
Nero who slew his mother   *shent* rebuked
give . . . seals confirm with actions
like him not distrust him   *us* me
our estate my sovereignty

ROSENCRANTZ. The single and peculiar life° is
       bound
       With all the strength and armor of the mind
       To keep itself from noyance;° but much more
       That spirit upon whose weal° depends and rests
       The lives of many. The cease° of majesty   15
       Dies not alone, but like a gulf doth draw
       What's near it with it. It is a massy wheel,
       Fix'd on the summit of the highest mount,
       To whose huge spokes ten thousand lesser things
       Are mortis'd and adjoin'd; which, when it falls,   20
       Each small annexment, petty consequence,
       Attends the boist'rous ruin. Never alone
       Did the king sigh, but with a general groan.
KING. Arm you, I pray you, to this speedy voyage,
       For we will fetters put upon this fear,   25
       Which now goes too free-footed.
ROSENCRANTZ *and* GUILDENSTERN. We will haste us.
       [*Exeunt* ROSENCRANTZ *and* GUILDENSTERN.]
                          [*Enter* POLONIUS.]
POLONIUS. My lord, he's going to his mother's
       closet.
       Behind the arras I'll convey myself
       To hear the process.° I'll warrant she'll tax him
       home;°
       And, as you said, and wisely was it said,   30
       'Tis meet that some more audience than a
       mother,
       Since nature makes them partial, should o'er-
       hear
       The speech of vantage.° Fare you well, my liege.
       I'll call upon you ere you go to bed
       And tell you what I know.
KING.   Thanks, dear my lord.   35
                              [*Exit* POLONIUS.]
       O, my offense is rank,° it smells to heaven;
       It hath the primal eldest curse° upon 't,
       A brother's murder. Pray can I not,
       Though inclination be as sharp as will.
       My stronger guilt defeats my strong intent,   40
       And like a man to double business bound,
       I stand in pause where I shall first begin,
       And both neglect. What if this cursed hand
       Were thicker than itself with brother's blood?
       Is there not rain enough in the sweet heavens   45
       To wash it white as snow? Whereto serves mercy
       But to confront the visage of offense?
       And what's in prayer but this twofold force,

primal . . . curse allusion to Cain's murder of Abel
single . . . life i.e., of the private citizen
noyance hurt   *weal* welfare   *cease* decease
process interview
tax him home "rake him over the coals"
of vantage i.e., from a concealed vantage point
rank rotten

50 To be forestalled ere we come to fall,
Or pardon'd being down? Then I'll look up;
My fault is past. But O, what form of prayer
Can serve my turn? "Forgive me my foul
   murder?"
That cannot be, since I am still possess'd
55 Of those effects for which I did the murder—
My crown, mine own ambition, and my queen.
May one be pardon'd and retain th' offense?
In the corrupted currents of this world,
Offense's gilded hand may shove by justice,
And oft 'tis seen the wicked prize itself
60 Buys out the law. But 'tis not so above;
There is no shuffling, there the action lies
In his true nature, and we ourselves compell'd
Even to the teeth and forehead of our faults
To give in evidence. What then? What rests?
65 Try what repentance can. What can it not?
Yet what can it when one can not repent?
O wretched state! O bosom black as death!
O limed° soul, that struggling to be free
Art more engag'd! Help, angels! Make assay!
Bow, stubborn knees, and, heart with strings of
70   steel,
Be soft as sinews of the new-born babe!
All may be well.   [He kneels.]
         [Enter HAMLET.]
HAMLET. Now might I do it pat, now he is praying,
And now I'll do 't. And so he goes to heaven,
75 And so am I reveng'd. That would be scann'd.°
A villain kills my father, and for that,
I, his sole son, do this same villain send
To heaven.
O, this is hire and salary, not revenge.
80 He took my father grossly, full of bread,
With all his crimes broad blown, as flush as
   May;
And how his audit° stands who knows save
   heaven?
But in our circumstance and course of thought,°
'Tis heavy with him. And am I then reveng'd,
85 To take him in the purging of his soul,
When he is fit and season'd for his passage?
No.
Up, sword, and know thou a more horrid hent.°
When he is drunk asleep, or in his rage,
90 Or in the incestuous pleasure of his bed;
At gaming, swearing, or about some act
That has no relish of salvation in 't—

limed   caught as with birdlime
would be scann'd   requires scrutinizing
audit   account in the judgment book
in . . . thought   according to what, in this life, we can
   surmise
hent   occasion

Then trip him, that his heels may kick at heaven
And that his soul may be as damn'd and black
As hell, whereto it goes. My mother stays.   95
This physic but prolongs thy sickly days.
                                        [Exit]
KING. [Rising] My words fly up, my thoughts re-
   main below.
Words without thoughts never to heaven go.
                                        [Exit]

                    SCENE iv
                The QUEEN's closet.

         [Enter QUEEN and POLONIUS.]
POLONIUS. He will come straight. Look you lay
   home to him.
Tell him his pranks have been too broad to bear
   with
And that your grace hath screen'd and stood
   between
Much heat and him. I'll sconce° me even here.
Pray you, be round with him.
HAMLET.   [Within] Mother, mother, mother!   5
QUEEN. I'll warrant you; fear me not. Withdraw, I
   hear him coming.
         [POLONIUS hides behind the arras.]
         [Enter HAMLET.]
HAMLET. Now, mother, what's the matter?
QUEEN. Hamlet, thou hast thy father much
   offended.
HAMLET. Mother, you have my father much
   offended.   10
QUEEN. Come, come, you answer with an idle°
   tongue.
HAMLET. Go, go, you question with a wicked
   tongue.
QUEEN. Why, how now, Hamlet!
HAMLET.   What's the matter now?
QUEEN. Have you forgot me?
HAMLET.   No, by the rood,° not so.
You are the queen, your husband's brother wife;   15
And—would it were not so!—you are my
   mother.
QUEEN. Nay, then, I'll set those to you that can
   speak.
HAMLET. Come, come, and sit you down; you shall
   not budge.
You go not till I set you up a glass
Where you may see the inmost part of you.   20
QUEEN. What wilt thou do? Thou wilt not murder
   me?
Help, help, ho!

sconce   ensconce   idle   foolish   rood   cross

[handwritten note at top: Symbolism end of slashing through the curtain. He acts, thinking her her the "truth," but he is deceived.]

POLONIUS. [Behind] What, ho! Help, help, help!

HAMLET. [Drawing] How now! A rat? Dead, for a
ducat, dead! [Makes a pass through the arras.]

POLONIUS. [Behind] O, I am slain! [Falls and dies.]

QUEEN. O me, what hast thou done?

25 HAMLET. Nay, I know not. Is it the king?

QUEEN. O, what a rash and bloody deed is this!

HAMLET. A bloody deed! Almost as bad, good
mother,
As kill a king and marry with his brother.

QUEEN. As kill a king!

HAMLET. Aye, lady, 'twas my word.
[Lifts up the arras and discovers POLONIUS.]

30 Thou wretched, rash, intruding fool, farewell!
I took thee for thy better. Take thy fortune;
Thou find'st to be too busy is some danger.
Leave wringing of your hands. Peace! Sit you
down
And let me wring your heart, for so I shall

35 If it be made of penetrable stuff,
If damned custom have not brass'd it so
That it be proof and bulwark against sense.°

QUEEN. What have I done that thou dar'st wag thy
tongue
In noise so rude against me?

HAMLET. Such an act

40 That blurs the grace and blush of modesty,
Calls virtue hypocrite, takes off the rose
From the fair forehead of an innocent love
And sets a blister there, makes marriage vows
As false as dicers' oaths. O, such a deed

45 As from the body of contraction° plucks
The very soul, and sweet religion makes
A rhapsody° of words. Heaven's face doth
glow°—
Yea, this solidity and compound mass,
With tristful visage, as against the doom,°
Is thought-sick at the act.

50 QUEEN. Aye me, what act,
That roars so loud and thunders in the index?°

HAMLET. Look here upon this picture and on this,
The counterfeit presentment of two brothers.
See what a grace was seated on this brow—

55 Hyperion's° curls, the front° of Jove himself,
An eye like Mars, to threaten and command;
A station° like the herald Mercury
New-lighted on a heaven-kissing hill;
A combination and a form indeed,

60 Where every god did seem to set his seal

sense feeling
body of contraction marriage contract
rhapsody jumble *glow* blush
against the doom in anticipation of doomsday
index preface *Hyperion* Apollo, the sun god
front forehead *station* bearing

To give the world assurance of a man.
This was your husband. Look you now what
follows.
Here is your husband, like a mildew'd ear,°
Blasting his wholesome brother. Have you eyes?

65 Could you on this fair mountain leave to feed,
And batten° on this moor? Ha! Have you eyes?
You cannot call it love, for at your age
The heyday in the blood is tame, it's humble,
And waits upon the judgment. And what
judgment

70 Would step from this to this? Sense sure you
have,
Else could you not have motion. But sure that
sense
Is apoplex'd, for madness would not err,
Nor sense to ecstasy was ne'er so thrall'd
But it reserv'd some quantity of choice

75 To serve in such a difference.° What devil was 't
That thus hath cozen'd you at hoodman-blind?°
Eyes without feeling, feeling without sight,
Ears without hands or eyes, smelling sans all,
Or but a sickly part of one true sense

80 Could not so mope.
O shame! Where is thy blush? Rebellious hell,
If thou canst mutine in a matron's bones,
To flaming youth let virtue be as wax
And melt in her own fire. Proclaim no shame

85 When the compulsive ardor gives the charge,
Since frost itself as actively doth burn,
And reason panders will.°

QUEEN. O Hamlet, speak no more.
Thou turn'st mine eyes into my very soul,
And there I see such black and grained° spots
As will not leave° their tinct.

90 HAMLET. Nay, but to live
In the rank sweat of an enseamed° bed,
Stew'd in corruption, honeying and making love
Over the nasty sty—

QUEEN. O, speak to me no more.
These words like daggers enter in my ears.
No more, sweet Hamlet!

95 HAMLET. A murderer and a villain,

mildew'd ear diseased head of grain
batten gorge yourself
sense . . . difference sense was never so enslaved to
madness but that it reserved enough ability to choose
where difference is so obvious
cozen'd . . . hoodman-blind cheated you at blindman's
buff
Proclaim . . . will do not call it shame when the
compelling passion (of youth) does the urging, since
age itself burns as passionately, and reason caters to the
baser instincts of the will
grained ingrained *leave* lose
enseamed grease-soaked

A slave that is not twentieth part the tithe°
Of your precedent lord, a vice of kings,
A cutpurse of the empire and the rule,
That from a shelf the precious diadem stole
And put it in his pocket!

100 QUEEN.   No more!
HAMLET. A king of shreds and patches—
                [*Enter* GHOST.]
  Save me, and hover o'er me with your wings,
  You heavenly guards! What would your gracious
      figure?
QUEEN. Alas, he's mad!
105 HAMLET. Do you not come your tardy son to chide,
  That, laps'd in time and passion,° lets go by
  Th' important acting of your dread command?
  O, say!
GHOST. Do not forget. This visitation
110 Is but to whet thy almost blunted purpose.
  But look, amazement on thy mother sits.
  O, step between her and her fighting soul.
  Conceit° in weakest bodies strongest works.
  Speak to her, Hamlet.
HAMLET.   How is it with you, lady?
115 QUEEN. Alas, how is 't with you,
  That you do bend your eye on vacancy
  And with th' incorporal° air do hold discourse?
  Forth at your eyes your spirits wildly peep,
  And, as the sleeping soldiers in th' alarm,
120 Your bedded hairs, like life in excrements,°
  Start up and stand on end. O gentle son,
  Upon the heat and flame of thy distemper
  Sprinkle cool patience. Whereon do you look?
HAMLET. On him, on him! Look you how pale he
      glares!
  His form and cause conjoin'd,° preaching to
125   stones,
  Would make them capable. Do not look upon
      me,
  Lest with this piteous action you convert°
  My stern effects.° Then what I have to do
  Will want true color°—tears perchance for
      blood.
QUEEN. To whom do you speak this?
130 HAMLET.   Do you see nothing there?
QUEEN. Nothing at all, yet all that is I see.
HAMLET. Nor did you nothing hear?
QUEEN.   No, nothing but ourselves.

HAMLET. Why, look you there! Look how it steals
      away!
  My father, in his habit as he liv'd!°
  Look where he goes even now out at the portal! 135
                [*Exit* GHOST.]
QUEEN. This is the very coinage of your brain.
  This bodiless creation ecstasy
  Is very cunning in.
HAMLET.   Ecstasy!
  My pulse as yours doth temperately keep time
  And makes as healthful music. It is not madness 140
  That I have utter'd. Bring me to the test,
  And I the matter will reword, which madness
  Would gambol° from. Mother, for love of grace,
  Lay not that flattering unction to your soul,
  That not your trespass but my madness speaks.° 145
  It° will but skin and film the ulcerous place,
  Whiles rank corruption, mining° all within,
  Infects unseen. Confess yourself to heaven;
  Repent what's past, avoid what is to come,
  And do not spread the compost on the weeds, 150
  To make them ranker. Forgive me this my
      virtue,
  For in the fatness of these pursy° times
  Virtue itself of vice must pardon beg,
  Yea, curb° and woo for leave to do him good.
QUEEN. O Hamlet, thou hast cleft my heart in
      twain.   155
HAMLET. O, throw away the worser part of it,
  And live the purer with the other half.
  Good night. But go not to my uncle's bed;
  Assume a virtue if you have it not.
  That monster, custom, who all sense doth eat 160
  Of habits evil, is angel yet in this,
  That to the use of actions fair and good
  He likewise gives a frock or livery
  That aptly is put on.° Refrain tonight,
  And that shall lend a kind of easiness 165
  To the next abstinence; the next more easy;
  For use° almost can change the stamp of nature
  And either tame the devil or throw him out
  With wondrous potency. Once more, good night.
  And when you are desirous to be blest, 170

---

twentieth . . . tithe i.e., one twentieth of one tenth part
laps'd . . . passion having let time pass and passion cool
Conceit imagination   *incorporal* bodiless
like . . . excrements like live outgrowths (hairs)
conjoin'd joined together   *convert* subdue
effects purposes
want . . . color lack even the appearance of what it
      should be

in . . . liv'd dressed in his usual attire
gambol shy away
for . . . speaks as you hope for salvation, do not deceive
      your soul by supposing my madness caused me to see
      what was nonexistent when in fact it was your sin that
      prevented you from seeing what was there
It i.e., the unction (salve)   *mining* undermining
fatness . . . pursy grossness . . . corrupt   *curb* bow
custom . . . on habitual practice, which destroys our
      sense of the evil of bad habits, is beneficent in that it
      also makes good habits easy to acquire
use habitual practice

sardonic humor   *puns*

I'll blessing beg of you. For this same lord,
               [*Pointing to* POLONIUS.]
I do repent. But heaven hath pleas'd it so

Core of Hamlet's problem

To punish me with this and this with me,
That I must be their scourge and minister.
175 I will bestow° him and will answer well
The death I gave him. So again good night.
I must be cruel only to be kind.
Thus bad begins, and worse remains behind.
One word more, good lady.
  QUEEN.   What shall I do?
180 HAMLET. Not this, by no means, that I bid you do:
Let the bloat king tempt you again to bed,
Pinch wanton° on your cheek, call you his
    mouse,
And let him, for a pair of reechy° kisses,
Or paddling in your neck with his damn'd
    fingers,
185 Make you to ravel all this matter out,
That I essentially am not in madness,
But mad in craft. 'Twere good you let him
    know;
For who that's but a queen, fair, sober, wise,
Would from a paddock, from a bat, a gib,°
190 Such dear concernings° hide? Who would do so?
No, in despite of sense and secrecy,
Unpeg the basket on the house's top,
Let the birds fly, and like the famous ape,
To try conclusions, in the basket creep

And break your own neck down.°   195
QUEEN. Be thou assur'd, if words be made of breath
And breath of life, I have no life to breathe
What thou hast said to me.
HAMLET. I must to England. You know that?
QUEEN. Alack, I had forgot. 'Tis so concluded on.   200
HAMLET. There's letters seal'd, and my two school-
    fellows,
Whom I will trust as I will adders fang'd,
They bear the mandate;° they must sweep my
    way,
And marshal me to knavery. Let it work;
For 'tis the sport to have the enginer   205
Hoist with his own petar.° And 't shall go hard,
But I will delve one yard below their mines
And blow them at the moon. O, 'tis most sweet
When in one line two crafts° directly meet.
This man shall set me packing.°   210
I'll lug the guts into the neighbor room.
Mother, good night. Indeed this counselor
Is now most still, most secret, and most grave,
Who was in life a foolish prating knave.
Come, sir, to draw toward an end with you.   215
Good night, mother.
[*Exeunt severally;* HAMLET *dragging in* POLONIUS.]

Unpeg . . . down presumably an allusion to some lost
  story of an ape that thus foolishly destroyed itself by
  imitating the birds
mandate order   *to have . . . petar* to have the maker
  of a destructive device blown up by it himself
crafts plots
set me packing i.e., packing him from the room; but also,
  packing myself out of Denmark

bestow stow   *wanton* lustfully   *reechy* lewd
paddock . . . gib toad . . . tomcat
dear concernings matters of vital concern

A C T   I V

SCENE i
A room in the castle.

[*Enter* KING, QUEEN, ROSENCRANTZ, *and*
      GUILDENSTERN.]
KING. There's matter in these sighs; those pro-
    found heaves
You must translate. 'Tis fit we understand them.
Where is your son?
QUEEN. Bestow this place on us a little while.
      [*Exeunt* ROSENCRANTZ *and* GUILDENSTERN.]
5   Ah, mine own lord, what have I seen tonight!
KING. What, Gertrude? How does Hamlet?
QUEEN. Mad as the sea and wind when both con-
    tend

Which is the mightier. In his lawless fit,
Behind the arras hearing something stir,
Whips out his rapier, cries "A rat, a rat!"   10
And in this brainish apprehension° kills
The unseen good old man.
KING.   O heavy deed!
It had been so with us had we been there.
His liberty is full of threats to all,
To you yourself, to us, to everyone.   15
Alas, how shall this bloody deed be answer'd?
It will be laid to us, whose providence
Should have kept short, restrain'd, and out of
    haunt°

brainish apprehension delusion   *haunt* company

20 This mad young man. But so much was our love,
We would not understand what was most fit,
But like the owner of a foul disease,
To keep it from divulging,° let it feed
Even on the pith of life. Where is he gone?
QUEEN. To draw apart the body he hath kill'd,
25 O'er whom his very madness, like some ore
Among a mineral of metals base,
Shows itself pure. He weeps for what is done.
KING. O Gertrude, come away!
The sun no sooner shall the mountains touch,
30 But we will ship him hence, and this vile deed
We must, with all our majesty and skill,
Both countenance° and excuse. Ho, Guilden-
stern!
    [Re-enter ROSENCRANTZ and GUILDENSTERN.]
Friends both, go join you with some further aid.
Hamlet in madness hath Polonius slain,
And from his mother's closet hath he dragg'd
35 him.
Go seek him out; speak fair, and bring the body
Into the chapel. I pray you, haste in this.
        [Exeunt ROSENCRANTZ and GUILDENSTERN.]
Come, Gertrude, we'll call up our wisest friends
And let them know both what we mean to do
40 And what's untimely done; so, haply, slander,
Whose whisper o'er the world's diameter
As level as the cannon to his blank°
'Transports his poison'd shot, may miss our name
And hit the woundless air. O, come away!
45 My soul is full of discord and dismay.   [Exeunt]

SCENE ii
Another room in the castle.

[Enter HAMLET.]
HAMLET. Safely stowed.
ROSENCRANTZ and GUILDENSTERN. [Within] Hamlet!
    Lord Hamlet!
HAMLET. But soft, what noise? Who calls on Ham-
    let?
5   O, here they come.
    [Enter ROSENCRANTZ and GUILDENSTERN.]
ROSENCRANTZ. What have you done, my lord, with
    the dead body?
HAMLET. Compounded it with dust, whereto 'tis
    kin.
ROSENCRANTZ. Tell us where 'tis, that we may take
    it thence
And bear it to the chapel.
10 HAMLET. Do not believe it.

divulging being divulged
countenance bear responsibility for   blank target

ROSENCRANTZ. Believe what?
HAMLET. That I can keep your counsel and not
    mine own. Besides, to be demanded of a sponge!
    What replication° should be made by the son of
    a king?   15
ROSENCRANTZ. Take you me for a sponge, my lord?
HAMLET. Aye, sir, that soaks up the king's coun-
    tenance,° his rewards, his authorities. But such
    officers do the king best service in the end. He
    keeps them, like an ape, in the corner of his jaw   20
    —first mouthed, to be last swallowed. When he
    needs what you have gleaned, it is but squeezing
    you, and, sponge, you shall be dry again.
ROSENCRANTZ. I understand you not, my lord.
HAMLET. I am glad of it. A knavish speech sleeps in 25
    a foolish ear.
ROSENCRANTZ. My lord, you must tell us where the
    body is, and go with us to the king.
HAMLET. The body is with the king, but the king is
    not with the body. The king is a thing—   30
GUILDENSTERN. A thing, my lord?
HAMLET. Of nothing. Bring me to him. Hide fox,
    and all after.   [Exeunt]

SCENE iii
Another room in the castle.

[Enter KING, attended.]
KING. I have sent to seek him, and to find the body.
How dangerous is it that this man goes loose!
Yet must not we put the strong law on him.
He's lov'd of the distracted multitude,
Who like not in their judgment, but their eyes;   5
And where 'tis so, th' offender's scourge is
    weigh'd,
But never the offense. To bear all smooth and
    even,
This sudden sending him away must seem
Deliberate pause.° Diseases desperate grown
By desperate appliance are reliev'd,   10
Or not at all.
            [Enter ROSENCRANTZ.]
            How now! What hath befall'n?
ROSENCRANTZ. Where the dead body is bestow'd,
    my lord,
We cannot get from him.
KING.   But where is he?
ROSENCRANTZ. Without, my lord, guarded, to
    know your pleasure.
KING. Bring him before us.   15
ROSENCRANTZ. Ho, Guildenstern! Bring in my lord.

replication reply   countenance favor
Deliberate pause duly deliberated

[*Enter* HAMLET *and* GUILDENSTERN.]

KING. Now, Hamlet, where's Polonius?

HAMLET. At supper.

KING. At supper! Where?

20 HAMLET. Not where he eats, but where he is eaten. A certain convocation of politic° worms are e'en at him. Your worm is your only emperor for diet. We fat all creatures else to fat us, and we fat ourselves for maggots. Your fat king and your

25 lean beggar is but variable service,° two dishes, but to one table. That's the end.

KING. Alas, alas!

HAMLET. A man may fish with the worm that hath eat of a king and eat of the fish that hath fed of

30 that worm.

KING. What dost thou mean by this?

HAMLET. Nothing but to show you how a king may go a progress through the guts of a beggar.

KING. Where is Polonius?

35 HAMLET. In heaven; send thither to see. If your messenger find him not there, seek him i' th' other place yourself. But indeed, if you find him not within this month, you shall nose him as you go up the stairs into the lobby.

40 KING. Go seek him there.   [*To some* ATTENDANTS.]

HAMLET. He will stay till you come.

[*Exeunt* ATTENDANTS.]

KING. Hamlet, this deed, for thine especial safety, Which we do tender° as we dearly grieve For that which thou hast done, must send thee hence

45 With fiery quickness. Therefore prepare thyself; The bark is ready and the wind at help, The associates tend,° and everything is bent For England.

HAMLET.   For England?

KING.   Aye, Hamlet.

HAMLET.   Good.

KING. So is it, if thou knew'st our purposes.

HAMLET. I see a cherub that sees them. But, come;

50 for England! Farewell, dear mother.

KING. Thy loving father, Hamlet.

HAMLET. My mother. Father and mother is man and wife; man and wife is one flesh, and so—my

55 mother. Come, for England!   [*Exit*]

KING. Follow him at foot;° tempt him with speed aboard. Delay it not; I'll have him hence tonight. Away! For everything is seal'd and done

That else leans on th' affair. Pray you, make haste.   60

[*Exeunt* ROSENCRANTZ *and* GUILDENSTERN.]

And, England, if my love thou hold'st at aught— As my great power thereof may give thee sense, Since yet thy cicatrice° looks raw and red After the Danish sword, and thy free awe°   65 Pays homage to us—thou mayst not coldly set Our sovereign process,° which imports at full, By letters congruing to that effect, The present° death of Hamlet. Do it, England; For like the hectic° in my blood he rages,   70 And thou must cure me. Till I know 't is done, Howe'er my haps,° my joys were ne'er begun.

[*Exit*]

SCENE iv
A plain in Denmark.

[*Enter* FORTINBRAS, *a* CAPTAIN *and* SOLDIERS, *marching.*]

FORTINBRAS. Go, captain, from me greet the Danish king. Tell him that by his license Fortinbras Craves the conveyance of a promis'd march Over his kingdom. You know the rendezvous. If that his majesty would aught with us,   5 We shall express our duty in his eye;° And let him know so.

CAPTAIN.   I will do 't, my lord.

FORTINBRAS. Go softly on.

[*Exeunt* FORTINBRAS *and* SOLDIERS.]

[*Enter* HAMLET, ROSENCRANTZ, GUILDENSTERN, *and others.*]

HAMLET. Good sir, whose powers are these?

CAPTAIN. They are of Norway, sir.   10

HAMLET. How purposed, sir, I pray you?

CAPTAIN. Against some part of Poland.

HAMLET. Who commands them, sir?

CAPTAIN. The nephew to old Norway, Fortinbras.

HAMLET. Goes it against the main of Poland, sir,   15 Or for some frontier?

CAPTAIN. Truly to speak, and with no addition,° We go to gain a little patch of ground That hath in it no profit but the name. To pay five ducats, five, I would not farm it;   20 Nor will it yield to Norway or the Pole A ranker° rate should it be sold in fee.°

---

politic   politically minded
variable service   alternate courses
tender   care for   tend   attend   at foot   at his heels

cicatrice   scar
free awe   i.e., not induced by overt threat
coldly . . . process   disregard my royal command
present   immediate   hectic   fever
haps   (personal) fortune   eye   presence
addition   exaggeration   ranker   higher   in fee   outright

[handwritten top margin: Soliloquy] *[handwritten: Contrast Fortinbras & Hamlet]*

HAMLET. Why, then the Polack never will defend
   it.
CAPTAIN. Yes, it is already garrison'd.
HAMLET. Two thousand souls and twenty thousand
   ducats   25
   Will not debate the question of this straw.°
   This is the imposthume° of much wealth and
      peace,
   That inward breaks and shows no cause without
   Why the man dies. I humbly thank you, sir.
CAPTAIN. God be wi' you, sir.   [*Exit*]
ROSENCRANTZ.   Will 't please you go,
   my lord?   30
HAMLET. I'll be with you straight. Go a little before.
                   [*Exeunt all but* HAMLET.]
[handwritten: topic] How all occasions do inform against° me
   And spur my dull revenge! What is a man,
   If his chief good and market of his time
   Be but to sleep and feed? A beast, no more.   35
   Sure, he that made us with such large discourse,°
   Looking before and after, gave us not
   That capability and godlike reason
   To fust° in us unus'd. Now whether it be
   Bestial oblivion or some craven scruple   40
   Of thinking too precisely on th' event—
   A thought which, quarter'd, hath but one part
      wisdom
   And ever three parts coward—I do not know
   Why yet I live to say "this thing's to do,"
   Sith I have cause, and will, and strength, and
      means   45
   To do 't. Examples gross as earth exhort me.
   Witness this army, of such mass and charge,°
[handwritten: Hamlet has misread Fortinbras] Led by a delicate and tender prince,
   Whose spirit with divine ambition puff'd
   Makes mouths at the invisible event,°   50
   Exposing what is mortal and unsure
   To all that fortune, death, and danger dare,
   Even for an eggshell.° Rightly to be great
   Is not to stir without great argument,
[handwritten: Hamlet's idea of greatness] But greatly to find quarrel in a straw   55
   When honor's at the stake. How stand I then,
   That have a father kill'd, a mother stain'd,
   Excitements of my reason and my blood,
   And let all sleep, while to my shame I see
   The imminent death of twenty thousand men,   60
   That for a fantasy and trick° of fame
   Go to their graves like beds, fight for a plot
   Whereon the numbers cannot try the cause,

---

debate . . . straw settle . . . trifle
imposthume abscess
inform against accuse, shame   discourse intelligence
fust decay   charge expense   event outcome
eggshell i.e., a trifle, nothing   trick toy

Which is not tomb enough and continent°
To hide the slain? O, from his time forth,   65
My thoughts be bloody or be nothing worth!
[handwritten: not moved to action yet.]   [*Exit*]

SCENE v
Elsinore. A room in the castle.

[*Enter* QUEEN, HORATIO, *and a* GENTLEMAN.]
QUEEN. I will not speak with her.
GENTLEMAN. She is importunate, indeed distract.
   Her mood will needs be pitied.
QUEEN.   What would she have?
GENTLEMAN. She speaks much of her father, says
   she hears
   There's tricks i' the world,° and hems and beats
      her heart,   5
   Spurns enviously at straws, speaks things in
      doubt°
   That carry but half sense. Her speech is nothing,
   Yet the unshap'd° use of it doth move
   The hearers to collection.° They aim° at it,
   And botch° the words up fit to their own
      thoughts,   10
   Which, as her winks and nods and gestures
      yield them,°
   Indeed would make one think there might be
      thought,
   Though nothing sure, yet much unhappily.
HORATIO. 'Twere good she were spoken with, for
   she may strew
   Dangerous conjectures in ill-breeding minds.   15
QUEEN. Let her come in.   [*Exit* GENTLEMAN.]
   [*Aside*] To my sick soul, as sin's true nature is,
   Each toy° seems prologue to some great amiss.°
   So full of artless jealousy° is guilt,
   It spills itself in fearing to be spilt.   20
      [*Re-enter* GENTLEMAN, *with* OPHELIA.]
OPHELIA. Where is the beauteous majesty of
   Denmark?
QUEEN. How now, Ophelia!
OPHELIA.

   [*Sings*] How should I your true love know
             From another one?
        By his cockle° hat and staff   25
        And his sandal shoon.°

---

continent container
tricks . . . world deceitful actions abroad
doubt suspicion   unshap'd random
collection interpretation   aim guess   botch patch
Which . . . them her words as expressed by her winks,
  nods, and gestures
toy trifle   amiss disaster
artless jealousy inept suspicion   cockle cockleshell
shoon shoes

QUEEN. Alas, sweet lady, what imports this song?
OPHELIA. Say you? Nay, pray you, mark.

30   [*Sings*] He is dead and gone, lady,
        He is dead and gone;
      At his head a grass-green turf,
        At his heels a stone.

Oh, oh!
QUEEN. Nay, but, Ophelia—
OPHELIA.   Pray you, mark.
35   [*Sings*] White his shroud as the mountain snow—
          [*Enter* KING.]
QUEEN. Alas, look here, my lord.
OPHELIA.

    [*Sings*]   Larded° with sweet flowers,
      Which bewept to the grave did go
       With true-love showers.

40 KING. How do you, pretty lady?
OPHELIA. Well, God 'ild° you! They say the owl
was a baker's daughter.° Lord, we know what
we are, but know not what we may be. God be
at your table!
45 KING. Conceit upon her father.
OPHELIA. Pray you, let's have no words of this;
but when they ask you what it means, say you
this:

    [*Sings*] Tomorrow is Saint Valentine's day,
50   All in the morning betime,
     And I a maid at your window,
       To be your Valentine.

     Then up he rose, and donn'd his clothes,
      And dupp'd° the chamber door;
55   Let in the maid, that out a maid
       Never departed more.

KING. Pretty Ophelia!
OPHELIA. Indeed, la, without an oath, I'll make an
end on 't:

60   [*Sings*] By Gis° and by Saint Charity,
      Alack, and fie for shame!
     Young men will do 't, if they come to 't;
      By Cock,° they are to blame.
     Quoth she, before you tumbled me,
65   You promis'd me to wed.

He answers:

     So would I ha' done, by yonder sun,
      An° thou hadst not come to my bed.

Larded decorated   'ild reward
owl . . . daughter allusion to the legend of the baker's
   daughter turned to an owl for begrudging Christ a
   piece of bread
dupp'd opened   Gis Jesus   Cock God   An if

KING. How long hath she been thus?
OPHELIA. I hope all will be well. We must be   70
patient. But I cannot choose but weep to think
they should lay him i' the cold ground. My
brother shall know of it. And so I thank you for
your good counsel. Come, my coach! Good
night, ladies; good night, sweet ladies; good   75
night, good night.   [*Exit*]
KING. Follow her close; give her good watch, I
pray you.   [*Exit* HORATIO.]
O, this is the poison of deep grief; it springs
All from her father's death. O Gertrude,
  Gertrude,
When sorrows come, they come not single
  spies,   80
But in battalions! First, her father slain.
Next, your son gone, and he most violent
  author
Of his own just remove. The people muddied,
Thick and unwholesome in their thoughts and
  whispers
For good Polonius' death, and we have done but
  greenly°   85
In hugger-mugger° to inter him. Poor Ophelia
Divided from herself and her fair judgment,
Without the which we are pictures, or mere
  beasts.
Last, and as much containing as all these,
Her brother is in secret come from France,   90
Feeds on his wonder, keeps himself in clouds,
And wants not buzzers° to infect his ear
With pestilent speeches of his father's death,
Wherein necessity, of matter° beggar'd,
Will nothing stick° our person to arraign   95
In ear and ear.° O my dear Gertrude, this,
Like to a murd'ring-piece, in many places
Gives me superfluous death.°   [*A noise within.*]
QUEEN.   Alack, what noise is this?
KING. Where are my Switzers?° Let them guard
  the door.
      [*Enter another* GENTLEMAN.]
What is the matter?
GENTLEMAN.   Save yourself, my lord.   100
The ocean, overpeering of his list,°
Eats not the flats with more impetuous haste
Than young Laertes, in a riotous head,°

---

greenly ineptly   hugger-mugger secrecy
buzzers gossips   matter substance, facts
nothing stick not hesitate
In ear . . . ear from ear to ear
Like . . . death like a gun loaded with shrapnel which
  gives many wounds any of which are fatal
Switzers Swiss bodyguards
overpeering . . . list overflowing the shore
head armed force

O'erbears your officers. The rabble call him
    lord;
105 And, as the world were now but to begin,
Antiquity forgot, custom not known,
The ratifiers and props° of every word,
They cry "Choose we; Laertes shall be king!"
Caps, hands, and tongues applaud it to the
    clouds,
110 "Laertes shall be king, Laertes king!"
QUEEN. How cheerfully on the false trail they cry!
O, this is counter,° you false Danish dogs!

                              [Noise within.]

KING. The doors are broke.
    [Enter LAERTES, armed; DANES following.]
LAERTES. Where is this king? Sirs, stand you all
    without.
DANES. No, let's come in.
115 LAERTES.   I pray you, give me leave.
DANES. We will, we will.
                  [They retire without the door.]
LAERTES. I thank you. Keep the door. O thou vile
    king,
Give me my father!
QUEEN.   Calmly, good Laertes.
LAERTES. That drop of blood that's calm proclaims
    me bastard,
120 Cries cuckold to my father, brands the harlot
Even here, between the chaste unsmirched
    brows
Of my true mother.
KING.   What is the cause, Laertes,
That thy rebellion looks so giantlike?
Let him go, Gertrude; do not fear our person.
125 There's such divinity doth hedge a king
That treason can but peep to what it would,°
Acts little of his will. Tell me, Laertes,
Why thou art thus incens'd. Let him go, Gert-
    rude.
Speak, man.
LAERTES. Where is my father?
KING.   Dead.
130 QUEEN.   But not by him.
KING. Let him demand his fill.
LAERTES. How came he dead? I'll not be juggled
    with.
To hell, allegiance! Vows, to the blackest devil!
Conscience and grace, to the profoundest pit!
135 I dare damnation. To this point I stand,
That both the worlds I give to negligence,°
Let come what comes; only I'll be reveng'd

Most throughly° for my father.
KING.   Who shall stay you?
LAERTES. My will, not all the world.
And for my means, I'll husband them so well   140
They shall go far with little.
KING.   Good Laertes,
If you desire to know the certainty
Of your dear father's death, is 't writ in your
    revenge
That, swoopstake,° you will draw both friend
    and foe,
Winner and loser?   145
LAERTES. None but his enemies.
KING.   Will you know them then?
LAERTES. To his good friends thus wide I'll ope my
    arms,
And, like the kind life-rend'ring pelican,°
Repast them with my blood.
KING.   Why, now you speak
Like a good child and a true gentleman.   150
That I am guiltless of your father's death
And am most sensibly in grief for it,
It shall as level to your judgment pierce
As day does to your eye.
DANES.   *[Within]* Let her come in.
LAERTES. How now! What noise is that?   155
             [Re-enter OPHELIA.]
O heat, dry up my brains! Tears seven times salt,
Burn out the sense and virtue of mine eye!
By heaven, thy madness shall be paid with
    weight,
Till our scale turn the beam. O rose of May!
Dear maid, kind sister, sweet Ophelia!   160
O heavens! Is 't possible a young maid's wits
Should be as mortal as an old man's life?
Nature is fine in love, and where 'tis fine
It sends some precious instance of itself
After the thing it loves.°   165
OPHELIA.

    [Sings] They bore him barefac'd on the bier;
        Hey non nonny, nonny, hey nonny,
        And in his grave rain'd many a tear—

Fare you well, my dove!
LAERTES. Hadst thou thy wits, and didst persuade
    revenge,   170
It could not move thus.

---

ratifiers and props i.e., antiquity and custom
counter the wrong scent
peep . . . would peep at but not reach its goal
give to negligence disregard

throughly thoroughly
swoopstake "wholesale"
life-rend'ring pelican which was supposed to feed its
    young with its own blood
Nature . . . loves nature is delicate in love and sends
    some precious part of itself (Ophelia's wits) after the
    thing it loves

OPHELIA.

> [*Sings*] You must sing down a-down,
> An you call him a-down-a.

O, how the wheel becomes it! It is the false
175 steward, that stole his master's daughter.
LAERTES. This nothing's more than matter.
OPHELIA. There's rosemary, that's for remembrance. Pray you, love, remember. And there is
pansies, that's for thoughts.
180 LAERTES. A document° in madness; thoughts and
remembrance fitted.
OPHELIA. There's fennel for you, and columbines.
There's rue for you, and here's some for me. We
may call it herb of grace o' Sundays. O, you
185 must wear your rue with a difference. There's a
daisy. I would give you some violets, but they
withered all when my father died. They say a'
made a good end—

> [*Sings*] For bonny sweet Robin is all my joy.

LAERTES. Thought and affliction, passion, hell
190 itself,
She turns to favor° and to prettiness.
OPHELIA.

> [*Sings*] And will a' not come again?
> And will a' not come again?
> No, no, he is dead,
195 Go to thy deathbed,
> He never will come again.
>
> His beard was as white as snow,
> All flaxen was his poll.°
> He is gone, he is gone,
200 And we cast away° moan.
> God ha' mercy on his soul!

And of° all Christian souls, I pray God. God be
wi' you.   [*Exit*]
LAERTES. Do you see this, O God?
KING. Laertes, I must commune with your grief,
205 Or you deny me right. Go but apart,
Make choice of whom your wisest friends you
will,
And they shall hear and judge 'twixt you and
me.
If by direct or by collateral° hand
They find us touch'd,° we will our kingdom
give,
210 Our crown, our life, and all that we call ours,
To you in satisfaction. But if not,

Be you content to lend your patience to us,
And we shall jointly labor with your soul
To give it due content.
LAERTES.   Let this be so.
His means of death, his obscure funeral,   215
No trophy, sword, nor hatchment° o'er his
bones,
No noble rite nor formal ostentation,°
Cry to be heard, as 'twere from heaven to earth,
That I must call 't in question.
KING.   So you shall.
And where th' offense is let the great axe fall.   220
I pray you, go with me.   [*Exeunt*]

SCENE vi
Another room in the castle.

[*Enter* HORATIO *and a* SERVANT.]
HORATIO. What are they that would speak with
me?
SERVANT. Seafaring men, sir. They say they have
letters for you.
HORATIO. Let them come in.   [*Exit* SERVANT.]
I do not know from what part of the world
I should be greeted, if not from Lord Hamlet.   5
[*Enter* SAILORS.]
FIRST SAILOR. God bless you, sir.
HORATIO. Let him bless thee too.
FIRST SAILOR. He shall, sir, an 't please him. There's
a letter for you, sir. It comes from the ambassa-   10
dor that was bound for England—if your name
be Horatio, as I am let to know it is.
HORATIO.

> [*Reads*] Horatio, when thou shalt have over-
> looked this, give these fellows some means to
> the king. They have letters for him. Ere we
> were two day old at sea, a pirate of very warlike   15
> appointment gave us chase. Finding ourselves
> too slow of sail, we put on a compelled valor,
> and in the grapple I boarded them. On the
> instant° they got clear of our ship, so I alone
> became their prisoner. They have dealt with   20
> me like thieves of mercy. But they knew what
> they did; I am to do a good turn for them. Let
> the king have the letters I have sent, and re-
> pair thou to me with as much speed as thou
> wouldst fly death. I have words to speak in   25
> thine ear will make thee dumb; yet are they
> much too light for the bore of the matter.°

---

document lesson
turns to favor makes charming
flaxen . . . poll white . . . hair   *cast away* waste
of on   *collateral* contributory
us touch'd me implicated

hatchment ornamental device
ostentation ceremony
On the instant at that instant
too light . . . matter i.e., the words are inadequate to
express their subject matter, like small shot fired
through a gun of large bore

Examine Shakespeare use of the mob an instrumental

These good fellows will bring thee where I am.
Rosencrantz and Guildenstern hold their
30   course for England. Of them I have much to tell
thee. Farewell.

                    He that thou knowest thine, HAMLET.

    Come, I will make you way for these your
        letters,
    And do 't the speedier that you may direct me
35   To him from whom you brought them.

                                          [*Exeunt*]

SCENE vii
Another room in the castle.

            [*Enter* KING *and* LAERTES.]
KING. Now must your conscience my acquittance
        seal,°
    And you must put me in your heart for friend,
    Sith you have heard, and with a knowing ear,
    That he which hath your noble father slain
    Pursu'd my life.
5   LAERTES.   It well appears. But tell me
    Why you proceeded not against these feats,
    So crimeful and so capital in nature,
    As by your safety, wisdom, all things else,
    You mainly° were stirr'd up.
    KING.   O, for two special reasons,
    Which may to you perhaps seem much un-
10   sinew'd,°
    But yet to me they're strong. The queen his
        mother
    Lives almost by his looks; and for myself—
    My virtue or my plague, be it either which—
    She's so conjunctive° to my life and soul,
15   That, as the star moves not but in his sphere,
    I could not but by her. The other motive
    Why to a public count° I might not go
    Is the great love the general gender° bear him,
    Who, dipping all his faults in their affection,
    Would, like the spring that turneth wood to
20   stone,°
    Convert his gyves° to graces; so that my arrows,
    Too slightly timber'd for so loud a wind,
    Would have reverted to my bow again
    And not where I had aim'd them.
25   LAERTES. And so have I a noble father lost,
    A sister driven into desperate terms,

Whose worth, if praises may go back again,
Stood challenger on mount of all the age
For her perfections.° But my revenge will come.
KING. Break not your sleeps for that. You must not
    think   30
That we are made of stuff so flat and dull
That we can let our beard be shook with danger
And think it pastime. You shortly shall hear
    more.
I lov'd your father, and we love ourself;
And that, I hope, will teach you to imagine—   35
            [*Enter a* MESSENGER, *with letters.*]
How now! What news?
MESSENGER.   Letters, my lord, from Hamlet.
This to your majesty, this to the queen.
KING. From Hamlet! Who brought them?
MESSENGER. Sailors, my lord, they say; I saw them
    not.
They were given me by Claudio; he receiv'd
    them   40
Of him that brought them.
KING.   Laertes, you shall hear them.
    Leave us.   [*Exit* MESSENGER.]

    [*Reads*] High and mighty, you shall know I am
    set naked on your kingdom. Tomorrow shall I
    beg leave to see your kingly eyes, when I shall,   45
    first asking your pardon thereunto, recount
    the occasion of my sudden and more strange
    return.   HAMLET.

What should this mean? Are all the rest come
    back?
Or is it some abuse, and no such thing?   50
LAERTES. Know you the hand?
KING. 'Tis Hamlet's character.° "Naked"!
    And in a postscript here, he says "alone."
    Can you advise me?
LAERTES. I'm lost in it, my lord. But let him come.   55
    It warms the very sickness in my heart
    That I shall live and tell him to his teeth,
    "Thus didest thou."
KING.   If it be so, Laertes—
    As how should it be so? How otherwise?—
    Will you be rul'd by me?
LAERTES.   Aye, my lord,   60
    So you will not o'errule me to a peace.
KING. To thine own peace. If he be now return'd,
    As checking at° his voyage, and that he means
    No more to undertake it, I will work him
    To an exploit now ripe in my device   65

---

acquittance seal acquit me   *mainly* on strong grounds
unsinew'd weak
conjunctive joined   *count* indictment
general gender common people
turneth . . . stone i.e., by coating it with lime
gyves fetters

Stood . . . perfections challenged the perfections of her
    finest contemporaries
character handwriting
checking at turning back from (hawking image)

Under the which he shall not choose but fall.
And for his death no wind of blame shall breathe,
But even his mother shall uncharge the practice°
And call it accident.

LAERTES.   My lord, I will be rul'd,
70 The rather if you could devise it so
That I might be the organ.°

KING.   It falls right.
You have been talk'd of since your travel much,
And that in Hamlet's hearing, for a quality
Wherein, they say, you shine. Your sum of parts
75 Did not together pluck such envy from him
As did that one, and that in my regard
Of the unworthiest siege.°

LAERTES.   What part is that, my lord?

KING. A very riband in the cap of youth,
Yet needful too; for youth no less becomes
80 The light and careless livery that it wears
Than settled age his sables and his weeds,°
Importing health and graveness. Two months since,
Here was a gentleman of Normandy.
I've seen myself, and serv'd against, the French,
And they can well° on horseback. But this
85   gallant
Had witchcraft in 't; he grew unto his seat,
And to such wondrous doing brought his horse
As had he been incorps'd and demi-natur'd°
With the brave beast. So far he topp'd my thought°
90 That I, in forgery of shapes and tricks,°
Come short of what he did.

LAERTES.   A Norman was 't?

KING. A Norman.

LAERTES. Upon my life, Lamond.

KING.   The very same.

LAERTES. I know him well. He is the brooch° indeed
95 And gem of all the nation.

KING. He made confession of° you,
And gave you such a masterly report
For art and exercise in your defense,
And for your rapier most especial,
100 That he cried out, 'twould be a sight indeed

If one could match you. The scrimers° of their nation,
He swore, had neither motion, guard, nor eye
If you oppos'd them. Sir, this report of his
Did Hamlet so envenom with his envy
That he could nothing do but wish and beg   105
Your sudden coming o'er to play with him.
Now, out of this—

LAERTES.   What out of this, my lord?

KING. Laertes, was your father dear to you?
Or are you like the painting of a sorrow,
A face without a heart?

LAERTES.   Why ask you this?   110

KING. Not that I think you did not love your father,
But that I know love is begun by time,
And that I see, in passages of proof,°
Time qualifies° the spark and fire of it.
There lives within the very flame of love   115
A kind of wick or snuff that will abate it,
And nothing is at a like goodness still,
For goodness, growing to a plurisy,°
Dies in his own too much. That we would do
We should do when we would; for this "would" changes
And hath abatements and delays as many   120
As there are tongues, are hands, are accidents,
And then this "should" is like a spendthrift° sigh
That hurts by easing.° But, to the quick o' th' ulcer.°
Hamlet comes back: what would you undertake,   125
To show yourself your father's son in deed
More than in words?

LAERTES.   To cut his throat i' the church.

KING. No place indeed should murder sanctuarize;
Revenge should have no bounds. But, good Laertes,
Will you do this: keep close within your chamber.   130
Hamlet return'd shall know you are come home.
We'll put on those shall praise your excellence
And set a double varnish on the fame
The Frenchman gave you; bring you in fine° together
And wager on your heads. He, being remiss,   135
Most generous and free from all contriving,°
Will not peruse the foils, so that with ease,

---

uncharge . . . practice   not suspect that there was a plot
organ   instrument (of death)   siege   place
sables . . . weeds   i.e., suitably sober garments
can well   are skilled
incorps'd and demi-natur'd   all of one body, like the centaur
topp'd my thought   exceeded my ideas of excellence
in . . . tricks   using whatever inventiveness of expression
brooch   shining ornament
made confession of   acknowledged knowing

scrimers   fencers   passages of proof   proven instances
qualifies   abates   plurisy   excess
spendthrift   wasteful
That . . . easing   sighing was supposed to rob the heart of blood
to . . . ulcer   to get to the point   in fine   in short
remiss . . . contriving   careless, noble-minded, and innocent of plotting

Or with a little shuffling, you may choose
A sword unbated,° and in a pass of practice°
Requite him for your father.

140 LAERTES.   I will do 't,
And for that purpose I'll anoint my sword.
I bought an unction° of a mountebank,°
So mortal that but dip a knife in it,
Where it draws blood no cataplasm° so rare,
145 Collected from all simples° that have virtue
Under the moon, can save the thing from death
That is but scratch'd withal. I'll touch my point
With this contagion, that,° if I gall him slightly,
It may be death.

KING.   Let's further think of this,
Weigh what convenience both of time and
150   means
May fit us to our shape.° If this should fail,
And that our drift° look through our bad per-
    formance,
'Twere better not assay'd. Therefore this project
Should have a back or second that might hold
155 If this did blast in proof.° Soft! Let me see.—
We'll make a solemn wager on your cunnings.
I ha 't:
When in your motion you are hot and dry—
As make your bouts more violent to that end—
And that he calls for drink, I'll have prepar'd
160   him
A chalice for the nonce;° whereon but sipping,
If he by chance escape your venom'd stuck,°
Our purpose may hold there. But stay, what
    noise?

              [Enter QUEEN.]
How now, sweet queen!
165 QUEEN. One woe doth tread upon another's heel,
So fast they follow. Your sister's drown'd,
    Laertes.
LAERTES. Drown'd! O, where?

QUEEN. There is a willow grows aslant a brook,
That shows his hoar° leaves in the glassy stream.
There with fantastic garlands did she come   170
Of crowflowers, nettles, daisies, and long
    purples,
That liberal° shepherds give a grosser name,
But our cold maids do dead men's fingers call
    them.
There on the pendent boughs her coronet°
    weeds
Clambering to hang, an envious sliver° broke,   175
When down her weedy trophies and herself
Fell in the weeping brook. Her clothes spread
    wide,
And mermaid-like a while they bore her up,
Which time she chanted snatches of old tunes
As one incapable of her own distress,   180
Or like a creature native and indu'd
Unto that element.° But long it could not be
Till that her garments, heavy with their drink,
Pull'd the poor wretch from her melodious lay°
To muddy death.
LAERTES.   Alas, then she is drown'd!   185
QUEEN. Drown'd, drown'd.
LAERTES. Too much of water hast thou, poor
    Ophelia,
And therefore I forbid my tears. But yet
It is our trick.° Nature her custom holds,
Let shame say what it will. When these are
    gone,   190
The woman° will be out. Adieu, my lord.
I have a speech of fire that fain would blaze,
But that this folly douts° it.   [Exit]
KING.   Let's follow, Gertrude.
How much I had to do to calm his rage!
Now fear I this will give it start again;   195
Therefore let's follow.   [Exeunt]

---

unbated unblunted   pass of practice treacherous thrust
unction poison   mountebank quack doctor
cataplasm poultice   simples herbs   that so that
shape purpose   drift intention
blast in proof "blow up in our faces"
chalice . . . nonce cup for the occasion   stuck thrust

hoar gray   liberal loose-talking
coronet weeds crown of flowers
envious sliver malicious bough
native . . . element born to live in the water
lay song   trick way   woman womanly weakness
douts puts out

ACT V

SCENE i
A churchyard.

[*Enter two* CLOWNS, *with spades and pickaxes.*]
FIRST CLOWN. Is she to be buried in Christian burial
that wilfully seeks her own salvation?
SECOND CLOWN. I tell thee she is, and therefore
make her grave straight. The crowner° hath sat
5 on her, and finds it Christian burial.
FIRST CLOWN. How can that be, unless she drowned
herself in her own defense?
SECOND CLOWN. Why, 'tis found so.
FIRST CLOWN. It must be *se offendendo*.° It cannot
10 be else. For here lies the point: if I drown myself
wittingly, it argues an act, and an act hath three
branches; it is, to act, to do, and to perform.
Argal,° she drowned herself wittingly.
SECOND CLOWN. Nay, but hear you, goodman
15 delver.
FIRST CLOWN. Give me leave. Here lies the water;
good. Here stands the man; good. If the man go
to this water and drown himself, it is will he,
nill he, he goes; mark you that. But if the water
20 come to him and drown him, he drowns not
himself. Argal, he that is not guilty of his own
death shortens not his own life.
SECOND CLOWN. But is this law?
FIRST CLOWN. Aye, marry, is 't; crowner's quest°
25 law.
SECOND CLOWN. Will you ha' the truth in 't? If this
had not been a gentlewoman, she should have
been buried out o' Christian burial.
FIRST CLOWN. Why, there thou say'st, and the more
30 pity that great folk should have countenance° in
this world to drown or hang themselves, more
than their even° Christian. Come, my spade.
There is no ancient gentlemen but gardeners,
ditchers, and gravemakers. They hold up
35 Adam's profession.
SECOND CLOWN. Was he a gentleman?
FIRST CLOWN. A' was the first that ever bore arms.
SECOND CLOWN. Why, he had none.

FIRST CLOWN. What, art a heathen? How dost thou
understand the Scripture? The Scripture says 40
Adam digged. Could he dig without arms? I'll
put another question to thee. If thou answerest
me not to the purpose, confess thyself—
SECOND CLOWN. Go to.
FIRST CLOWN. What is he that builds stronger than 45
either the mason, the shipwright, or the carpenter?
SECOND CLOWN. The gallows-maker; for that
frame outlives a thousand tenants.
FIRST CLOWN. I like thy wit well, in good faith. The
gallows does well, but how does it well? It does 50
well to those that do ill. Now, thou dost ill to
say the gallows is built stronger than the
church. Argal, the gallows may do well to thee.
To 't again, come.
SECOND CLOWN. "Who builds stronger than a 55
mason, a shipwright, or a carpenter?"
FIRST CLOWN. Aye, tell me that, and unyoke.°
SECOND CLOWN. Marry, now I can tell.
FIRST CLOWN. To 't.
SECOND CLOWN. Mass,° I cannot tell. 60
[*Enter* HAMLET *and* HORATIO, *afar off.*]
FIRST CLOWN. Cudgel thy brains no more about it,
for your dull ass will not mend his pace with
beating, and when you are asked this question
next, say "a gravemaker." The houses that he
makes last till doomsday. Go, get thee to 65
Yaughan;° fetch me a stoup of liquor.
[*Exit* SECOND CLOWN.]
[*He digs, and sings.*]

In youth, when I did love, did love,
   Methought it was very sweet,
To contract,° O, the time, for-a my behoove,°
   O, methought there-a was nothing-a meet. 70

HAMLET. Has this fellow no feeling of his business,
that he sings at gravemaking?
HORATIO. Custom hath made it in him a property
of easiness.°
HAMLET. 'Tis e'en so. The hand of little employ- 75
ment hath the daintier sense.°

crowner coroner
se offendendo First Clown's error for *se defendendo*,
   self-defense
Argal i.e., *ergo*, therefore
quest inquest   *countenance* special privilege
even fellow

unyoke have done with it   *Mass* by the mass
Yaughan presumably an alehouse keeper
contract shorten   *behoove* advantage
property of easiness i.e., a casual thing
hath . . . sense i.e., is more sensitive on such matters

Hamlet & mortality

FIRST CLOWN.

> [*Sings*] But age, with his stealing steps,
>   Hath claw'd me in his clutch,
>   And hath shipped me intil° the land,
> 80   As if I had never been such.

[*Throws up a skull.*]

HAMLET. That skull had a tongue in it, and could sing once. How the knave jowls it to the ground, as if it were Cain's jawbone, that did the first murder! It might be the pate of a politician, 85 which this ass now o'erreaches;° one that would circumvent God, might it not?

HORATIO. It might, my lord.

HAMLET. Or of a courtier, which could say "Good morrow, sweet lord! How dost thou, sweet 90 lord?" This might be my lord such-a-one that praised my lord such-a-one's horse when he meant to beg it, might it not?

HORATIO. Aye, my lord.

HAMLET. Why, e'en so. And now my Lady Worm's, 95 chapless,° and knocked about the mazzard° with a sexton's spade. Here's a fine revolution,° an we had the trick to see 't. Did these bones cost no more the breeding but to play at loggats° with 'em? Mine ache to think on 't.

FIRST CLOWN.

> 100   [*Sings*] A pickaxe and a spade, a spade,
>   For and a shrouding sheet.
>   O, a pit of clay for to be made
>   For such a guest is meet.

[*Throws up another skull.*]

HAMLET. There's another: why may not that be the 105 skull of a lawyer? Where be his quiddities now, his quillets,° his cases, his tenures, and his tricks? Why does he suffer this rude knave now to knock him about the sconce with a dirty shovel, and will not tell him of his action of 110 battery? Hum! This fellow might be in 's time a great buyer of land, with his statutes, his recognizances, his fines, his double vouchers, his recoveries. Is this the fine of his fines and the recovery of his recoveries, to have his fine pate 115 full of fine dirt? Will his vouchers vouch him no more of his purchases, and double ones too, than the length and breadth of a pair of indentures? The very conveyances of his lands will hardly lie in this box, and must the inheritor 120 himself have no more, ha?

HORATIO. Not a jot more, my lord.

HAMLET. Is not parchment made of sheepskins?

HORATIO. Aye, my lord, and of calfskins too.

HAMLET. They are sheep and calves which seek out assurance in that. I will speak to this fellow. 125 Whose grave's this, sirrah?

FIRST CLOWN. Mine, sir.

> [*Sings*] O, a pit of clay for to be made
>   For such a guest is meet.

HAMLET. I think it be thine indeed, for thou liest 130 in 't.

FIRST CLOWN. You lie out on 't, sir, and therefore 'tis not yours. For my part, I do not lie in 't, and yet it is mine.

HAMLET. Thou dost lie in 't, to be in 't and say it is 135 thine. 'Tis for the dead, not for the quick;° therefore thou liest.

FIRST CLOWN. 'Tis a quick° lie, sir; 'twill away again, from me to you.

HAMLET. What man dost thou dig it for? 140

FIRST CLOWN. For no man, sir.

HAMLET. What woman then?

FIRST CLOWN. For none, neither.

HAMLET. Who is to be buried in 't?

FIRST CLOWN. One that was a woman, sir; but, rest 145 her soul, she's dead.

HAMLET. How absolute the knave is! We must speak by the card,° or equivocation will undo us. By the Lord, Horatio, this three years I have taken note of it, the age is grown so picked 150 that the toe of the peasant comes so near the heel of the courtier, he galls his kibe.° How long hast thou been a gravemaker?

FIRST CLOWN. Of all the days i' the year, I came to 't that day that our last king Hamlet o'ercame 155 Fortinbras.

HAMLET. How long is that since?

FIRST CLOWN. Cannot you tell that? Every fool can tell that. It was that very day that young Hamlet was born—he that is mad and sent into England. 160

HAMLET. Aye, marry, why was he sent into England?

FIRST CLOWN. Why, because a' was mad. A' shall recover his wits there; or, if a' do not, 'tis no great matter there. 165

HAMLET. Why?

---

quick living

by the card according to the fine points on a mariner's compass; hence, precisely

age . . . kibe the times have become so refined that the peasant follows close enough behind the courtier to chafe his sore heel; i.e., a social revolution has been occurring

---

intil into   *o'erreaches* lords it over
chapless jawless   *mazzard* head
revolution turnabout   *loggats* ten-pins
quiddities . . . quillets subtle arguments and quibbles (the following are all law terms)

EngRoad

FIRST CLOWN. 'Twill not be seen in him there;
there the men are as mad as he.

HAMLET. How came he mad?

170 FIRST CLOWN. Very strangely, they say.

HAMLET. How "strangely"?

FIRST CLOWN. Faith, e'en with losing his wits.

HAMLET. Upon what ground?

FIRST CLOWN. Why, here in Denmark. I have been
175 sexton here, man and boy, thirty years.

HAMLET. How long will a man lie i' the earth ere
he rot?

FIRST CLOWN. I' faith, if a' be not rotten before a'
die—as we have many pocky corses° nowadays
180 that will scarce hold the laying in—a' will last
you some eight year or nine year. A tanner will
last you nine year.

HAMLET. Why he more than another?

FIRST CLOWN. Why, sir his hide is so tanned with
185 his trade that a' will keep out water a great
while, and your water is a sore decayer of your
whoreson° dead body. Here's a skull now. This
skull has lain in the earth three and twenty
years.

190 HAMLET. Whose was it?

FIRST CLOWN. A whoreson mad fellow's it was.
Whose do you think it was?

HAMLET. Nay, I know not.

FIRST CLOWN. A pestilence on him for a mad
195 rogue! A' poured a flagon of Rhenish° on my
head once. This same skull, sir, was Yorick's
skull, the king's jester.

HAMLET. This?

FIRST CLOWN. E'en that.

200 HAMLET. Let me see. [Takes the skull] Alas, poor
Yorick! I knew him, Horatio—a fellow of infinite jest, of most excellent fancy. He hath borne
me on his back a thousand times; and now how
abhorred in my imagination it is! My gorge rises
205 at it.° Here hung those lips that I have kissed I
know not how oft. Where be your gibes now?
Your gambols? Your songs? Your flashes of
merriment that were wont to set the table on a
roar? Not one now to mock your own grinning?
210 Quite chopfallen?° Now get you to my lady's
chamber, and tell her, let her paint an inch
thick, to this favor° she must come. Make her
laugh at that. Prithee, Horatio, tell me one
thing.

215 HORATIO. What's that, my lord?

HAMLET. Dost thou think Alexander looked o' this
fashion i' the earth?

HORATIO. E'en so.

HAMLET. And smelt so? Pah!

[Puts down the skull.]

HORATIO. E'en so, my lord.   220

HAMLET. To what base uses we may return,
Horatio! Why may not imagination trace the
noble dust of Alexander, till he find it stopping a
bunghole?°

HORATIO. 'Twere to consider too curiously,° to   225
consider so.

HAMLET. No, faith, not a jot, but to follow him
thither with modesty enough and likelihood to
lead it, as thus: Alexander died, Alexander was
buried, Alexander returneth into dust; the dust 230
is earth; of earth we make loam; and why of
that loam, whereto he was converted, might
they not stop a beer barrel?

Imperious Cæsar, dead and turn'd to clay,
Might stop a hole to keep the wind away.   235
O, that that earth, which kept the world in awe
Should patch a wall t' expel the winter's flaw!

But soft! But soft! Aside. Here comes the king.
[Enter PRIESTS, &c. in procession; the corpse of
Ophelia, LAERTES and MOURNERS following;
KING, QUEEN, their trains, &c.]
The queen, the courtiers. Who is this they
follow,
And with such maimed rites? This doth betoken 240
The corse they follow did with desperate hand
Fordo it° own life. 'Twas of some estate.°
Couch° we awhile, and mark.

[Retiring with HORATIO.]

LAERTES. What ceremony else?

HAMLET. This is Laertes, a very noble youth. Mark. 245

LAERTES. What ceremony else?

FIRST PRIEST. Her obsequies have been as far
enlarg'd
As we have warranty. Her death was doubtful,
And, but that great command o'ersways the
order,°
She should in ground unsanctified have lodg'd   250
Till the last trumpet; for charitable prayers,
Shards,° flints, and pebbles should be thrown on
her.
Yet here she is allow'd her virgin crants,°
Her maiden strewments, and the bringing home
Of bell and burial.°   255

---

pocky corses corpses rotten with syphilis
whoreson a frequent and emphatic term of abuse
Rhenish Rhine wine   My . . . it i.e., I feel nauseated
chopfallen literally jaw-fallen, hence, downcast
favor facial appearance

bunghole hole in a beer barrel   curiously inventively
Fordo it destroy its   some estate high rank
Couch hide   order i.e., church-prescribed disposition
Shards pieces of broken pots   crants wreaths
bringing . . . burial the funeral procession to the church

[handwritten at top: Hamlet acts — See how inappropriate!]

LAERTES. Must there no more be done?

FIRST PRIEST.   No more be done.
  We should profane the service of the dead
  To sing a requiem and such rest to her
  As to peace-parted souls.

LAERTES.   Lay her i' th' earth,
260 And from her fair and unpolluted flesh
  May violets spring! I tell thee, churlish priest,
  A minist'ring angel shall my sister be
  When thou liest howling.°

HAMLET.   What, the fair Ophelia!

QUEEN. [Scattering flowers] Sweets to the sweet:
  farewell!
  I hop'd thou shouldst have been my Hamlet's
265 wife;
  I thought thy bride bed to have deck'd, sweet
  maid,
  And not have strew'd thy grave.

LAERTES.   O, treble woe
  Fall ten times treble on that cursed head
  Whose wicked deed thy most ingenious° sense
270 Depriv'd thee of! Hold off the earth a while,
  Till I have caught her once more in mine arms:
               [Leaps into the grave.]
  Now pile your dust upon the quick and dead,
  Till of this flat a mountain you have made
  T' o'ertop old Pelion or the skyish head
  Of blue Olympus.°

275 HAMLET. [Advancing] What is he whose grief
  Bears such an emphasis? Whose phrase of sorrow
  Conjures the wand'ring stars and makes them
  stand
  Like wonder-wounded hearers? This is I,
  Hamlet the Dane.   [Leaps into the grave.]

LAERTES. The devil take thy soul!
               [Grappling with him.]

280 HAMLET.   Thou pray'st not well.
  I prithee, take thy fingers from my throat;
  For though I am not splenitive° and rash,
  Yet have I in me something dangerous
  Which let thy wisdom fear. Hold off thy hand.

KING. Pluck them asunder.

QUEEN.   Hamlet, Hamlet!

285 ALL.   Gentlemen—

HORATIO. Good my lord, be quiet.
    [The ATTENDANTS part them, and they come
           out of the grave.]

HAMLET. Why, I will fight with him upon this
  theme
  Until my eyelids will no longer wag.

QUEEN. O my son, what theme?

[handwritten left margin: H. asserts himself for 1st time / 1st time to threaten anyone]

HAMLET. I lov'd Ophelia. Forty thousand brothers 290
  Could not with all their quantity of love
  Make up my sum. What wilt thou do for her?

KING. O, he is mad, Laertes.

QUEEN. For love of God, forbear° him.

HAMLET. 'Swounds, show me what thou 'lt do. 295
  Woo 't° weep? Woo 't fight? Woo 't fast? Woo 't
  tear thyself?
  Woo 't drink up eisel?° Eat a crocodile?
  I'll do 't. Dost thou come here to whine?
  To outface me with leaping in her grave?
  Be buried quick° with her, and so will I. 300
  And if thou prate of mountains, let them throw
  Millions of acres on us till our ground,
  Singeing his pate against the burning zone,°
  Make Ossa° like a wart! Nay, an thou 'lt mouth,
  I'll rant as well as thou.

QUEEN.   This is mere madness; 305
  And thus a while the fit will work on him.
  Anon, as patient as the female dove
  When that her golden couplets are disclos'd,°
  His silence will sit drooping.

HAMLET.   Hear you, sir.
  What is the reason that you use me thus? 310
  I lov'd you ever. But it is no matter.
  Let Hercules himself do what he may,
  The cat will mew, and dog will have his day.
                [Exit]

KING. I pray thee, good Horatio, wait upon him.
             [Exit HORATIO.]
  [To LAERTES] Strengthen your patience in our
  last night's speech; 315
  We'll put the matter to the present push.°
  Good Gertrude, set some watch over your son.
  This grave shall have a living monument.
  An hour of quiet shortly shall we see;
  Till then, in patience our proceeding be. 320
                [Exeunt]

SCENE ii
A hall in the castle.

[Enter HAMLET and HORATIO.]

HAMLET. So much for this, sir. Now shall you see
  the other.
  You do remember all the circumstance?

HORATIO. Remember it, my lord!

---

liest howling i.e., in hell   ingenious lively
Pelion . . . Olympus mountain peaks in Thessaly
splenitive hot-headed

forbear have patience with
Woo 't wilt thou   eisel vinegar
quick alive   burning zone sun's sphere
Ossa mountain in Thessaly
golden . . . disclos'd young are hatched
present push immediate trial

HAMLET. Sir, in my heart there was a kind of
    fighting
5   That would not let me sleep. Methought I lay
    Worse than the mutines in the bilboes.° Rashly—
    And prais'd be rashness for it; let us know,
    Our indiscretion sometime serves us well
    When our deep plots do pall,° and that should
        learn° us
10 There's a divinity that shapes our ends,
    Rough-hew them how we will—
HORATIO.   That is most certain.
HAMLET. Up from my cabin,
    My sea-gown scarf'd about me, in the dark
    Grop'd I to find out them; had my desire,
15 Finger'd their packet, and in fine withdrew
    To mine own room again, making so bold,
    My fears forgetting manners, to unseal
    Their grand commission; where I found,
        Horatio—
    O royal knavery!—an exact command,
20 Larded° with many several sorts of reasons
    Importing Denmark's health and England's too,
    With, ho! such bugs and goblins in my life,°
    That, on the supervise,° no leisure bated,
    No, not to stay the grinding of the axe,
    My head should be struck off.
25 HORATIO.   Is 't possible?
HAMLET. Here's the commission. Read it at more
        leisure.
    But wilt thou hear now how I did proceed?
HORATIO. I beseech you.
HAMLET. Being thus benetted round with villainies,
30 Or° I could make a prologue to my brains
    They had begun the play. I sat me down,
    Devis'd a new commission, wrote it fair.
    I once did hold it, as our statists° do,
    A baseness to write fair, and labor'd much
35 How to forget that learning; but, sir, now
    It did me yeoman's service. Wilt thou know
    Th' effect of what I wrote?
HORATIO.   Aye, good my lord.
HAMLET. An earnest conjuration from the king—
    As England was his faithful tributary,
    As love between them like the palm might
40   flourish,
    As peace should still her wheaten garland wear
    And stand a comma 'tween their amities,
    And many suchlike "As'' es of great charge°—
    That on the view and knowing of these contents,

Without debatement further, more or less,   45
He should the bearers put to sudden death,
Not shriving time allow'd.
HORATIO.   How was this seal'd?
HAMLET. Why, even in that was heaven ordinant.°
    I had my father's signet in my purse,
    Which was the model of that Danish seal—   50
    Folded the writ up in the form of th' other,
    Subscrib'd° it, gave 't th' impression, plac'd it
        safely,
    The changeling° never known. Now, the next
        day
    Was our sea fight, and what to this was sequent
    Thou know'st already.   55
HORATIO. So Guildenstern and Rosencrantz go to 't.
HAMLET. Why, man, they did make love to this
        employment.
    They are not near my conscience; their defeat°
    Does by their own insinuation° grow.
    'Tis dangerous when the baser nature comes   60
    Between the pass and fell° incensed points
    Of mighty opposites.
HORATIO.   Why, what a king is this!
HAMLET. Does it not, thinks't thee, stand me now
        upon°—
    He that hath kill'd my king and whor'd my
        mother,
    Popp'd in between th' election and my hopes,   65
    Thrown out his angle for my proper° life,
    And with such cozenage°—is 't not perfect
        conscience
    To quit° him with this arm? And is 't not to be
        damn'd
    To let this canker of our nature come
    In further evil?   70
HORATIO. It must be shortly known to him from
        England
    What is the issue of the business there.
HAMLET. It will be short. The interim is mine.
    And a man's life's no more than to say "One."
    But I am very sorry, good Horatio,   75
    That to Laertes I forgot myself;
    For by the image of my cause I see
    The portraiture of his. I'll court his favors.
    But, sure, the bravery° of his grief did put me
    Into a towering passion.
HORATIO.   Peace! Who comes here?   80
        [Enter OSRIC.]

---

mutines . . . bilboes mutineers in their shackles
pall fail   learn teach   Larded garnished
such . . . life such dangers while I lived
supervise first reading   Or ere
statists statesmen   great charge i.e., important sound

ordinant providential   subscrib'd signed
changeling substitute   defeat destruction
insinuation interference   pass . . . fell thrust . . . fierce
stand . . . upon is it not my duty   proper own
cozenage deception   quit requite
bravery ostentation

OSRIC. Your lordship is right welcome back to Denmark.

HAMLET. I humbly thank you, sir. Dost know this waterfly?

HORATIO. No, my good lord.

85 HAMLET. Thy state is the more gracious, for 'tis a vice to know him. He hath much land, and fertile. Let a beast be lord of beasts, and his crib shall stand at the king's mess. 'Tis a chough, but, as I say, spacious in the possession of dirt.°

OSRIC. Sweet lord, if your lordship were at leisure,
90 I should impart a thing to you from his majesty.

HAMLET. I will receive it, sir, with all diligence of spirit. Put your bonnet to his right use; 'tis for the head.

OSRIC. I thank your lordship, it is very hot.

95 HAMLET. No, believe me, 'tis very cold; the wind is northerly.

OSRIC. It is indifferent° cold, my lord, indeed.

HAMLET. But yet methinks it is very sultry and hot for my complexion—

100 OSRIC. Exceedingly, my lord; it is very sultry, as 'twere—I cannot tell how. But, my lord, his majesty bade me signify to you that he has laid a great wager on your head. Sir, this is the matter—

105 HAMLET. I beseech you, remember—

[HAMLET *moves him to put on his hat.*]

OSRIC. Nay, good my lord; for mine ease, in good faith. Sir, here is newly come to court Laertes; believe me, an absolute gentleman, full of most excellent differences,° of very soft society and
110 great showing. Indeed, to speak feelingly of him, he is the card or calendar of gentry,° for you shall find in him the continent of what part a gentleman would see.°

HAMLET. Sir, his definement suffers no perdition
115 in you, though, I know, to divide him inventorially would dizzy the arithmetic of memory, and yet but yaw neither, in respect of his quick sail. But in the verity of extolment, I take him to be a soul of great article, and his infusion of
120 such dearth and rareness as, to make true diction of him, his semblabale is his mirror, and who else would trace him, his umbrage, nothing more.°

OSRIC. Your lordship speaks most infallibly of him.

HAMLET. The concernancy,° sir? Why do we wrap 125 the gentleman in our more rawer breath?°

OSRIC. Sir?

HORATIO. Is 't not possible to understand in another tongue? You will do 't, sir, really.

HAMLET. What imports the nomination of this 130 gentleman?°

OSRIC. Of Laertes?

HORATIO. His purse is empty already; all's golden words are spent.

HAMLET. Of him, sir. 135

OSRIC. I know you are not ignorant—

HAMLET. I would you did, sir; yet, in faith, if you did, it would not much approve° me. Well, sir?

OSRIC. You are not ignorant of what excellence Laertes is— 140

HAMLET. I dare not confess that, lest I should compare with him in excellence; but to know a man well were to know himself.°

OSRIC. I mean, sir, for his weapon; but in the imputation° laid on him by them,° in his meed° 145 he's unfellowed.

HAMLET. What's his weapon?

OSRIC. Rapier and dagger.

HAMLET. That's two of his weapons.° But, well.

OSRIC. The king, sir, hath wagered with him six 150 Barbary horses, against the which he has imponed,° as I take it, six French rapiers and poniards, with their assigns,° as girdle, hanger,° and so. Three of the carriages, in faith, are very dear to fancy,° very responsive° to the hilts, most 155 delicate carriages, and of very liberal conceit.°

HAMLET. What call you the carriages?

HORATIO. I knew you must be edified by the margent° ere you had done.

OSRIC. The carriages, sir, are the hangers. 160

HAMLET. The phrase would be more germane to the matter if we could carry a cannon by our sides. I would it might be hangers till then. But, on: six Barbary horses against six French

---

spacious . . . dirt the owner of much land; i.e., rich
indifferent moderately   *differences* exquisite qualities
card . . . gentry model of gentlemanliness
continent . . . see embodiment of all parts to be sought in a gentleman
Sir . . . more (throughout the speech Hamlet out-Osrics Osric in the use of extravagant diction that grows more outrageous as it continues)

concernancy what's the point of all this
Why . . . breath how dare we discuss the gentleman in our crude language
What . . . gentleman what is the point of mentioning this gentleman
approve commend
himself oneself   *imputation* reputation
them i.e., his weapons   *meed* deserving
That's . . . weapons (Osric has affectedly used the singular for the plural form)
imponed staked down   *assigns* appurtenances
girdle, hanger belt, strap
dear to fancy fancifully designed
responsive well suited
liberal conceit elaborate design
margent marginal note

Hamlet & murder (handwritten annotation)

165 swords, their assigns, and three liberal-con-
ceited carriages; that's the French bet against the
Danish. Why is this "imponed," as you call it?

Osric. The king, sir, hath laid, sir, that in a dozen
passes between yourself and him, he shall not
170 exceed you three hits. He hath laid on twelve for
nine. And it would come to immediate trial if
your lordship would vouchsafe the answer.

Hamlet. How if I answer no?

Osric. I mean, my lord, the opposition of your
175 person in trial.

Hamlet. Sir, I will walk here in the hall. If it please
his majesty, it is the breathing° time of day with
me. Let the foils be brought, the gentleman
willing, and the king hold his purpose, I will
180 win for him an I can. If not, I will gain nothing
but my shame and the odd hits.

Osric. Shall I redeliver you e'en so?

Hamlet. To this effect, sir, after what flourish your
nature will.°

185 Osric. I commend my duty to your lordship.

Hamlet. Yours, yours. [*Exit* Osric] He does well to
commend it himself; there are no tongues
else for 's turn.

Horatio. This lapwing° runs away with the shell
190 on his head.

Hamlet. He did comply with° his dug before he
sucked it. Thus has he—and many more of the
same breed that I know the drossy° age dotes
on—only got the tune of the time and outward
195 habit of encounter, a kind of yesty collection°
which carries them through and through the
most fann'd and winnowed° opinions; and do
but blow them to their trial, the bubbles are
out.

[*Enter a* Lord.]

200 Lord. My lord, his majesty commended him to
you by young Osric, who brings back to him
that you attend him in the hall. He sends to
know if your pleasure hold to play with Laertes,
or that you will take longer time.

205 Hamlet. I am constant to my purposes; they follow the king's pleasure. If his fitness speaks,
mine is ready, now or whensoever, provided I be
so able as now.

Lord. The king and queen and all are coming
210 down.

Hamlet. In happy time.

Lord. The queen desires you to use some gentle
entertainment° to Laertes before you fall to play.

Hamlet. She well instructs me. [*Exit* Lord.]

Horatio. You will lose this wager, my lord. 215

Hamlet. I do not think so. Since he went into
France, I have been in continual practice; I shall
win at the odds. But thou wouldst not think
how ill all's here about my heart. But it is no
matter. 220

Horatio. Nay, good my lord—

Hamlet. It is but foolery; but it is such a kind of
gaingiving° as would perhaps trouble a woman.

Horatio. If your mind dislike anything, obey it. I
will forestall their repair hither and say you are 225
not fit.

Hamlet. Not a whit; we defy augury. There's a
special providence in the fall of a sparrow.° If it
be now, 'tis not to come; if it be not to come, it
will be now; if it be not now, yet it will come: 230
the readiness is all. Since no man has aught of
what he leaves, what is 't to leave betimes?
Let be.

[*Enter* King, Queen, Laertes, *and* Lords, Osric
and other Attendants *with foils and gauntlets;
a table and flagons of wine on it.*]

King. Come, Hamlet, come, and take this hand
from me.

[*The* King *puts* Laertes' *hand into* Hamlet's]

Hamlet. Give me your pardon, sir. I've done you
wrong, 235
But pardon 't as you are a gentleman.
This presence° knows,
And you must needs have heard, how I am
punish'd
With sore distraction. What I have done
That might your nature, honor, and exception 240
Roughly awake, I here proclaim was madness.
Was 't Hamlet wrong'd Laertes? Never Hamlet.
If Hamlet from himself be ta'en away,
And when he's not himself does wrong Laertes,
Then Hamlet does it not, Hamlet denies it. 245
Who does it then? His madness. If 't be so,
Hamlet is of the faction that is wrong'd;
His madness is poor Hamlet's enemy.
Sir, in this audience
Let my disclaiming from a purpos'd evil 250
Free me so far in your most generous thoughts
That I have shot mine arrow o'er the house
And hurt my brother.

---

breathing exercising
after . . . will according to what elaborate phrasing you
like
lapwing the plover, which dashes about as soon as it is
hatched
comply with use compliments   *drossy*
yesty collection frothy vocabulary
fann'd and winnowed refined (harvest metaphor)

gentle entertainment i.e., conciliatory words
gaingiving misgiving
fall . . . sparrow ". . . one of them shall not fall to the
ground without your Father" (see Matthew 10:29)
presence i.e., the Danish court

LAERTES.   I am satisfied in nature,
　　Whose motive, in this case, should stir me most
255　To my revenge. But in my terms of honor°
　　I stand aloof and will no reconcilement
　　Till by some elder masters of known honor
　　I have a voice and precedent of peace
　　To keep my name ungor'd.° But till that time
260　I do receive your offer'd love like love
　　And will not wrong it.
HAMLET.   I embrace it freely,
　　And will this brother's wager frankly play.
　　Give us the foils. Come on.
LAERTES.   Come, one for me.
HAMLET. I'll be your foil, Laertes. In mine ignorance
265　Your skill shall, like a star i' the darkest night,
　　Stick fiery off° indeed.
LAERTES.   You mock me, sir.
HAMLET. No, by this hand.
KING. Give them the foils, young Osric. Cousin
　　Hamlet,
　　You know the wager?
HAMLET.   Very well, my lord.
270　Your grace has laid the odds o' the weaker side.
KING. I do not fear it; I have seen you both.
　　But since he is better'd,° we have therefore odds.
LAERTES. This is too heavy; let me see another.
HAMLET. This likes me well. These foils have all a
　　length?   [They prepare to play.]
275 OSRIC. Aye, my good lord.
KING. Set me the stoups of wine upon that table.
　　If Hamlet give the first or second hit,
　　Or quit° in answer of the third exchange,
　　Let all the battlements their ordnance fire.
280　The king shall drink to Hamlet's better breath,
　　And in the cup an union° shall he throw,
　　Richer than that which four successive kings
　　In Denmark's crown have worn. Give me the
　　cups,
　　And let the kettle to the trumpet speak,°
285　The trumpet to the cannoneer without,
　　The cannons to the heavens, the heaven to earth,
　　"Now the king drinks to Hamlet." Come,
　　begin;
　　And you, the judges, bear a wary eye.
HAMLET. Come on, sir.
LAERTES.   Come, my lord.
　　　　　　　　　　　　　　[They play.]
HAMLET.   One.

---

in nature . . . in . . . honor in my natural feelings as
　contrasted with my position as a man of honor
To . . . ungor'd i.e., that my reputation will not be
　blemished
stick . . . off stand out　　*better'd* improved
quit i.e., score a hit　　*union* pearl
kettle . . . speak kettledrum give the signal

LAERTES.   No.
HAMLET.   Judgment.
OSRIC. A hit, a very palpable hit.
LAERTES.   Well; again.   290
KING. Stay; give me drink. Hamlet, this pearl is
　　thine;
　　Here's to thy health.
　　　　[Trumpets sound, and cannon shot off within.]
　　　　　　　　　　　　　Give him the cup.
HAMLET. I'll play this bout first; set it by awhile.
　　Come. [They play] Another hit; what say you?
LAERTES. A touch, a touch, I do confess.   295
KING. Our son shall win.
QUEEN.   He's fat° and scant of breath.
　　Here, Hamlet, take my napkin, rub thy brows.
　　The queen carouses to thy fortune, Hamlet.
HAMLET. Good madam!
KING.   Gertrude, do not drink.
QUEEN. I will, my lord; I pray you, pardon me.   300
KING. [Aside] It is the poison'd cup; it is too late.
HAMLET. I dare not drink yet, madam; by and by.
QUEEN. Come, let me wipe thy face.
LAERTES. My lord, I'll hit him now.
KING.   I do not think 't.
LAERTES. [Aside] And yet it is almost against my
　　conscience.°   305
HAMLET. Come, for the third, Laertes. You but
　　dally.
　　I pray you, pass with your best violence;
　　I am afeard you make a wanton° of me.
LAERTES. Say you so? Come on.   [They play.]
OSRIC. Nothing, neither way.   310
LAERTES. Have at you now!°
　　　　[LAERTES wounds HAMLET; then, in scuffling,
　　　　　they change rapiers, and HAMLET wounds
　　　　　　　　　　LAERTES.]
KING.   Part them; they are incens'd.
HAMLET. Nay, come, again.   [The QUEEN falls.]
OSRIC.   Look to the queen there, ho!
HORATIO. They bleed on both sides. How is it, my
　　lord?
OSRIC. How is 't, Laertes?
LAERTES. Why, as a woodcock to mine own
　　springe, Osric;   315
　　I am justly kill'd with mine own treachery.
HAMLET. How does the queen?
KING.   She swounds to see them bleed.
QUEEN. No, no, the drink, the drink—O my dear
　　Hamlet—
　　The drink, the drink! I am poison'd.   [Dies.]

---

fat i.e., greasy from perspiration
And yet . . . conscience i.e., to use the "pass of practice,"
　or treacherous thrust
wanton spoiled child
Have . . . now i.e., while Hamlet's back is turned

320 HAMLET. O villainy! Ho! Let the door be lock'd.
Treachery! Seek it out.   [LAERTES *falls*.]
LAERTES. It is here, Hamlet. Hamlet, thou art
slain;
No medicine in the world can do thee good.
In thee there is not half an hour of life.
325 The treacherous instrument is in thy hand,
Unbated and envenom'd. The foul practice
Hath turn'd itself on me; lo, here I lie,
Never to rise again. Thy mother's poison'd.
I can no more. The king, the king's to blame.
330 HAMLET. The point envenom'd too!
Then, venom, to thy work.   [Stabs the KING.]
ALL. Treason! Treason!
KING. O, yet defend me, friends; I am but hurt.
HAMLET. Here, thou incestuous, murderous,
damned Dane,
335 Drink off this potion. Is thy union here?
Follow my mother.   [KING *dies*.]
LAERTES.   He is justly serv'd;
It is a poison temper'd° by himself.
Exchange forgiveness with me, noble Hamlet.
Mine and my father's death come not upon thee,
340 Nor thine on me!   [*Dies*.]
HAMLET. Heaven make thee free of it! I follow
thee.
I am dead, Horatio. Wretched queen, adieu!
You that look pale and tremble at this chance,
That are but mutes or audience to this act,
345 Had I but time—as this fell° sergeant, death,
Is strict in his arrest—O, I could tell you—
But let it be. Horatio, I am dead;
Thou liv'st. Report me and my cause aright
To the unsatisfied.°
HORATIO.   Never believe it.
350 I am more an antique Roman° than a Dane;
Here's yet some liquor left.
HAMLET.   As th'art a man,
Give me the cup. Let go; by heaven, I'll ha't.
O good Horatio, what a wounded name,
Things standing thus unknown, shall live be-
hind me!
355 If thou didst ever hold me in thy heart,
Absent thee from felicity awhile,
And in this harsh world draw thy breath in
pain
To tell my story. [*March afar off, and shot within*.]
What warlike noise is this?
OSRIC. Young Fortinbras, with conquest come from
Poland,

To the ambassadors of England gives   360
This warlike volley.
HAMLET.   O, I die, Horatio.
The potent poison quite o'er-crows° my spirit.
I cannot live to hear the news from England;
But I do prophesy th' election lights
On Fortinbras. He has my dying voice;   365
So tell him, with the occurrents, more and less,°
Which have solicited.° The rest is silence.
                                          [*Dies*.]
HORATIO. Now cracks a noble heart. Good night,
sweet prince,
And flights of angels sing thee to thy rest!
                                   [*March within*.]
Why does the drum come hither?   370
[*Enter* FORTINBRAS, *and the* ENGLISH
AMBASSADORS, *with drum, colors, and*
ATTENDANTS.]
FORTINBRAS. Where is this sight?
HORATIO.   What is it you would see?
If aught of woe or wonder, cease your search.
FORTINBRAS. This quarry cries on havoc.° O proud
death,
What feast is toward° in thine eternal cell,
That thou so many princes at a shot   375
So bloodily hast struck?
FIRST AMBASSADOR.   The sight is dismal,
And our affairs from England come too late.
The ears are senseless that should give us hearing
To tell him his commandment is fulfill'd,
That Rosencrantz and Guildenstern are dead. 380
Where should we have our thanks?
HORATIO.   Not from his mouth,
Had it th' ability of life to thank you.
He never gave commandment for their death.
But since, so jump upon this bloody question,°
You from the Polack wars and you from England 385
Are here arriv'd, give order that these bodies
High on a stage° be placed to the view;
And let me speak to th' yet unknowing world
How these things came about. So shall you hear
Of carnal, bloody, and unnatural acts,   390
Of accidental judgments,° casual° slaughters,
Of deaths put on° by cunning and forc'd cause,°
And, in this upshot, purposes mistook

---

temper'd prepared   *fell* cruel
the unsatisfied i.e., all of Denmark, which remains
   ignorant of what has happened
antique Roman to whom suicide, in dire circumstances,
   was honorable (see Brutus, Antony)

o'er-crows overwhelms
occurrents . . . less occurrences, great and small
solicited required my action
This . . . havoc this pile of bodies (like game) speaks of
   slaughter
toward in the offing
jump . . . question opportunely . . . matter
stage platform   *judgments* retributions, dooms
casual incidental   *put on* instigated
forc'd cause necessity

Fall'n on th' inventors' heads. All this can I
Truly deliver.

395 FORTINBRAS.   Let us haste to hear it,
And call the noblest to the audience.
For me, with sorrow I embrace my fortune.
I have some rights of memory° in this kingdom,
Which now to claim my vantage° doth invite
me.

400 HORATIO. Of that I shall have also cause to speak,
And from his mouth whose voice will draw on
more.°
But let this same be presently perform'd,
Even while men's minds are wild, lest more
mischance

On plots and errors happen.

FORTINBRAS.   Let four captains
Bear Hamlet, like a soldier, to the stage;   405
For he was likely, had he been put on,°
To have prov'd most royally. And for his
passage,°
The soldiers' music and the rites of war
Speak° loudly for him.
Take up the bodies. Such a sight as this   410
Becomes the field, but here shows much amiss.
Go, bid the soldiers shoot.

[*A dead march. Exeunt, bearing off the bodies;
after which a peal of ordnance is shot off.*]

*a tale, told by an idiot,
full of sound & fury,
signifying nothing*

---

rights of memory   ancient rights (now valid since the
   Danish royal family has been extinguished)
vantage   advantage (by possession)
draw on more   win more favorable voices

put on   i.e., the throne   passage   passing (death)
Speak   (imperative voice)

AFTERWORD

"This is that Hamlet the Dane," wrote Hazlitt, "whom we read of in our youth." And he goes on, "Hamlet is a name; his speeches and sayings but the idle coinage of the poet's brain. What, then, are they not real? They are as real as our own thoughts. Their reality is in the reader's mind. It is *we* who are Hamlet."

Hamlet was first in the surge of tremendous tragedies that Shakespeare wrote during a period of about five years, between 1601–1602 and 1605–1606. Critics have remarked that it lacks the sheer technical perfection of *Othello*, falls below the towering sublimity of *King Lear*, and probably never once achieves the degree of spellbinding poetic–dramatic intensity that characterizes so much of *Macbeth*. Yet Hazlitt no doubt struck the right key: the world has taken *Hamlet* the play and Hamlet the hero to its heart in a manner and to a degree unmatched by any other tragedy or tragic hero. *Hamlet* stands alone and unique in this respect. It is almost certainly the one play of Shakespeare's that the greatest number of knowledgeable readers and theatergoers would choose to save if from some catastrophic cause it should become necessary to give up all but one. We cannot know, of course, but we may imagine that this play was Shakespeare's favorite, too, that in a very profound way it may have been "special" for him—the whole work serving as a gigantic frame into which he could pour literally all he had felt, thought, and experienced of life and the world. To say so much, however, is not to suggest for one moment that *Hamlet* is in any sense autobiographical or personal; Shakespeare himself is presumably no more to be identified in person with Hamlet's philosophical observations than with Richard III's or King John's, to name a pair of least-likely candidates. Like all the other plays, *Hamlet* is thoroughly *dramatic*, hence impersonal. Yet it, to a greater extent than any of the others, gives an impression of being such a work as one would write who never intended to write, or would never be able to write, another masterpiece. We hear sometimes of the one-novel novelist, the author who produces a single world-shaking work into which he pours all that he has to say, drains himself, and never writes anything of importance again. *Hamlet* leaves the impression of being such a one-play achievement, but by a dramatist who created some thirty-seven plays in all, a dozen of which, at least, might appropriately vie for top place. It would be critically absurd to try to prove that *Hamlet*, or any one of the others, deserves to be called the greatest of the greater tragedies; at the artistic elevation that is represented by these masterpieces, the individual must, in the last analysis, choose for himself.

Yet it is a fact that far more has been written of *Hamlet* and Hamlet than of any other play and hero in history. Scholars, critics, and earnest general readers have been studying the play with rising intensity during the past three centuries, and there is no present hint that they will not go right on doing so for many generations to come. In our own time no month passes without someone's publishing a new book, chapter, or essay that endeavors to pluck out the heart of the Hamlet mystery. No theatrical season passes in the civilized world without presenting some established or aspiring actor brooding anew whether it is better to be or not to be and, holding up the chapfallen skull of Yorick, the friend and jester of Hamlet's childhood, demanding of Horatio, "Dost thou think Alexander looked o' this fashion i' th' earth?" No other drama in the world's literature even approaches *Hamlet* in the number and variety of such testimonials to its widespread and perennial popularity.

For over a century it has been axiomatic that the crowning jewel of an actor's career is a distinguished performance in the role of Hamlet; famed comedians have been quoted as saying that what they really wanted, at last, was to play Hamlet. Richard Burbage was the first great Hamlet, with Shakespeare himself, according to Nicholas Rowe, Shakespeare's first editor-biographer, acting the part of the Ghost. (What a souvenir playbill *that* would have made!) After the Restoration of 1660 Thomas Betterton was the great Hamlet, acting the part repeatedly over a long period of years; Pepys saw Betterton in the role again and again and liked him more each time. The eighteenth century, though it butchered the acting texts of the play, saw a notable succession of famous actors in the part, headed, of course, by David Garrick. Garrick was followed by John Philip Kemble, who in turn was succeeded early in the nineteenth century by a young and fiery rival, Edmund Kean. During the nineteenth century, borne aloft on the wings of the high-flying romantic critics, *Hamlet* reached a zenith of fame and popularity as a stage play—despite the fact that the greater critics disliked actors and loathed their performances in Shakespearean roles. Booth, Macready, Phelps, Forbes-Robertson, and Irving all achieved or extended their distinction in the part. The twentieth century, of course, has witnessed countless performances of *Hamlet* and has already contributed its quota of noteworthy actors. John Barrymore, the first American since Edwin Booth to win plaudits for his Hamlet in London, was the great Hamlet of the 1920's. More recently John Gielgud, Maurice Evans, Laurence Olivier, and Richard Burton have contributed strongly contrasting and popular Hamlets. Even actresses, no less than comedians, have always aspired to play Hamlet; Judith Anderson, the most recent of three distinguished actresses to essay the role of the prince, has performed with some success in America. *Hamlet* has been produced not only as a motion picture but as television fare. The filmed Olivier *Hamlet*, for all its Freudian slips and knots, has become a classic and has probably been seen by more people than ever saw the play in the centuries preceding ours. The Christopher Plummer *Hamlet* on television conferred distinction upon that medium.

What is in *Hamlet* that sets it apart even from its own peers—*Othello*, *King Lear*, and *Macbeth*? It is today a much overused word, applied more often than deserved, but here it seems right and even indispensable: Prince Hamlet is possessed of a rare *charisma* unmatched by that of any other fictional hero of any time. Even Ulysses runs a very poor second. His is indeed, in Ophelia's distraught words, "The courtier's, soldier's, scholar's eye, tongue, sword"; he is indeed

> The expectancy and rose of the fair state,
> The glass of fashion and the mold of form,
> The observ'd of all observers. . . .

But there is more: at the center of this personal magnetism, this power of fascination that has attached the hearts and minds of audiences for many generations, is an inexpressibly romantic mystery which tempts us to probe and to keep probing for the secret that always lies just a little deeper than we can reach.

Why does Hamlet delay? This is the secret that all critics would unlock if they could; it is the essence of the "Hamlet mystery." Yet it was a question that did not much trouble anyone until the very end of the eighteenth and beginning of the nineteenth century, when the critical remarks of Goethe, Schlegel, and Coleridge seem almost to have invented a new and fantastically romantic figure, a Hamlet destined to grow far beyond the confines of his niche as a mere revenge-hero of a revenge play. "There is an oak-tree planted in a costly jar," wrote Goethe in 1795, "which should have borne only pleasant flowers in its bosom; the roots expand, the jar is shivered." To Goethe, Hamlet was "A lovely, pure and most moral nature," which "without the strength of nerve which forms a hero sinks beneath a burden which it cannot bear and must not cast away. . . . Impossibilities have been required of him; not in themselves impossibilities, but such for him." Goethe created the "sentimental Hamlet," as A. C. Bradley has called this view, who is too delicate to carry out so gross a task as revenge. Coleridge, shortly afterward, attributed the character of Hamlet to "Shakespeare's deep and accurate science in mental philosophy." Hamlet, he remarked, "has been the darling of every country in which the literature of England is fostered" because his character is intimately related to "the common fundamental laws of our nature." In Hamlet, he continues, the balance between attention to real objects and meditation on the workings of our own minds is disturbed: "Hence we see a great . . . intellectual activity, and a proportionate aversion to real action. . . . Hamlet is brave and careless of death, but he vacillates from sensibility, and procrastinates from thought, and loses the power of action in the energy of resolve."

From Goethe and Coleridge, thus, the drive of critics to pluck out the heart of Hamlet's mystery, to identify the cause of his delay, and to label his "tragic flaw" received its greatest impetus, the current of which flows as vigorously as ever to this day. *Hamlet* criticism fills not only many volumes but whole library rooms, and the bulk of it is ultimately concerned—however it may be disguised by statements of more limited purposes—with explaining Hamlet's failure to accomplish speedily what he so boldly promised the Ghost to deal with in short order:

> Haste me to know't, that I with wings as swift
> As meditation or the thoughts of love
> May sweep to my revenge.

Answers have been nearly as numerous as critics. Some have found the hero too much debilitated by the disease of melancholy to get on with his assignment. Some have found him lacking in power of will. Some have argued that he has Christian scruples of such force as to prevent his taking non-Christian vengeance. Some have said that physical obstacles prevent him from getting at the King. Many have said that he is, in one or another manner, psychologically unfitted for the task of revenge. Some have said that he is not perfectly certain of his uncle's guilt, and that even after he becomes certain, he uses uncertainty as an excuse for not acting, all his "drive" being consumed in rationalization. Some have said that his entire situation is so complex that his mind is incapable of solving his problem. (Thus, in general, speaks the twentieth century, which identifies Hamlet's problem with its own insoluble complexities.) Some have said that he did not in fact love his father and, therefore, cannot bring himself to avenge the murder. Some (the Freudians) have found him afflicted with a version of the Oedipus complex; he resented his own father, and his sense of guilt prevents his acting against his uncle-stepfather. Some (most notably T. S. Eliot) have said that the fault is not Hamlet's alone, but Shakespeare's, who took on an impossible task in attempting to adapt to new purposes the "intractable materials" of his source. Some (most notably G. Wilson Knight) have insisted that "Hamlet's soul is sick," incapacitating him for action. Most, with broad or subtle variations, have followed the main Coleridgean argument, that Hamlet's special mental imbalance commits him rather to think than to act. Virtually all, in any event, have based their arguments on a single basic assumption, that one thing or another, somehow, is "wrong" with Hamlet and prevents him from sweeping to his revenge.

If the character of Hamlet is the first reason for the unique fame of the play, it is nevertheless not the only reason. If we could weigh and balance such ingredients quantitatively, we would probably find that *Hamlet* contains more of the elements that make all of Shakespeare's plays remarkable than does any other play. Its array of major characters in addition to the hero—Claudius, Gertrude, Polonius, Laertes, Ophelia,

If he had acted, there would be no play! His inaction & is the dramatic essence of our realization of "become" Hamlet

418

Horatio—is second in distinction to no other *dramatis personae* in drama. Among the tragedies *Hamlet* is fullest and most varied in comic elements: Hamlet himself is a superb comedian, one of the best in the world, either with his "antic disposition" on or with it off; Polonius ranks as a comic personage with the very greatest of those who populate the histories and the comedies—with Falstaff, Bottom, Malvolio, Dogberry, and the professional jesters. Comic incidents abound in the play, from beginning to end: Polonius with Reynaldo, Hamlet with Rosencrantz and Guildenstern, the Gravediggers alone and with Hamlet. Yet perhaps the finest use is made of the comic when it occurs quite spontaneously—in short, quick flashes during moments of high tension, as in Hamlet's ironic wit flashes or Horatio's wry understatements: "There needs no ghost, my lord, come from the grave/ To tell us this."

But tension itself, certainly, accounts for much of the play's power to hold audience and reader. The conflict between Claudius and Hamlet is the basis of this tension. It begins with the first appearance of both upon the stage, with Hamlet's double-edged first remark, "A little more than kin and less than kind," and does not cease until Hamlet is stricken and the King dead. As the play progresses, this conflict emerges more and more from its hiding place behind dark "asides" and darker ironies, though the mock game is continued by both Hamlet and Claudius into the last deadly encounter, which is almost grotesquely euphemized by each as a mere "fencing match." What keeps the tension so tightly drawn throughout is the fact that Hamlet and Claudius are evenly matched—infinitely more evenly than, for example, Iago and Othello. Hamlet's own words succinctly and precisely define the whole action, the whole play: it is a battle of "mighty opposites."

Finally, what cements all the other elements together and contributes the ultimate touch of greatness to *Hamlet* is its poetry. *Hamlet* is the most quoted of all the plays, and with good reason. Matthew Arnold, in his list of "touchstones" by which to recognize the finest poetry, that which has the quality of "high seriousness," chose one brief passage from Hamlet's dying speech to Horatio:

> Absent thee from felicity awhile,
> And in this harsh world draw thy breath in pain
> To tell my story.

Had he wished to illustrate more abundantly, Arnold might equally well have chosen any of fifty other passages in the play. Many of Hamlet's speeches have a lyric quality that is reminiscent of the lyricism of *Romeo and Juliet*, for indeed the sounds of this play hark back to the earlier period rather than forward to the time of *Macbeth*. Even so, the sounds of the earlier play are mainly from the higher registers, whereas those of *Hamlet* are full-throated, tending to be resonant and deep. The four soliloquies of the hero, in particular, make a vibrant and rich sound. But not only Hamlet speaks the great poetry of the play; Shakespeare spreads the gift of gorgeous sound and brilliant imagery around among them all: the King attempting to pray; Gertrude in the opening scene with her son and, later, in the boudoir scene; Ophelia describing the supposed fall of Hamlet's mind, "Like sweet bells jangled, out of tune and harsh"; Laertes beholding his mad sister: "O rose of May!/ Dear maid, kind sister, sweet Ophelia!" But in fact poetry pervades the play and is everywhere, and even Polonius is given his share of it:

> Set your entreatments at a higher rate
> Than a command to parley. For Lord Hamlet,
> Believe so much in him that he is young,

And with a larger tether may he walk
Than may be given you. In few, Ophelia,
Do not believe his vows, for they are brokers
Not of that dye which their investments show. . . .

Polonius could never be accused of lyricism; but his images are sharp, true to the argument that they illuminate, and so abundant that what is nonimagistic in the lines serves only to furnish the necessary grammatical links between them. All in all, the music of Hamlet is music for a full orchestra, with sounds for every instrument; and in this vital respect the music is especially appropriate to this play, which offers abundance and variety to every sort of dramatic taste, serving not only caviar for the judicious few but a complete range of what-you-will to gratify the palates of those who stepped into Shakespeare's theater and stood in the pit at a penny apiece. The action and the music alike, thus, are filled with "God's plenty."

From the very fact of its enormous and long popularity, the task of reading the play, for the modern reader, has become peculiarly difficult. Possibly even more than any other play of Shakespeare's, Hamlet needs to be read with an open mind; yet such is its fame that severely limiting preconceptions infect the minds even of very young readers and condition them in advance to assume that one or another interpretation is "right." Even those who have neither read the play nor seen it on stage, screen, or television have heard of the "melancholy Dane," and by that adjective alone have already received a slanting of their view. Who has not heard of "To be or not to be," Yorick's skull, and the hero's famed habit of procrastination? And to have heard only so much is to have had the mind's openness compromised in advance, if ever so little. Everyone knows that "Something is rotten in the state of Denmark," even without being aware that the line is from Hamlet. The Olivier film, magnificent as it is in important ways, drastically closes the spectator's mind with its initial pronouncement: "This is the story of a man who could not make up his mind." Possibly the very fame of Hamlet, abetted by critics, theatrical producers, and teachers, has made it impossible for any but small children to read the play with wide-open and uncommitted minds. This fact does not diminish the desirability of striving to keep one's mind open as wide as possible through not only the first reading but the second, the third, the fourth, and beyond, to resist the temptation to seize upon a quick answer to what is "wrong" with Hamlet that causes his "delay." Perhaps, indeed, there is *nothing* wrong with him, and perhaps he does not delay at all in the sense that is implied by "procrastination." For most masterpieces of literature the best advice is to read them and read them and read them until one certainly understands them; for Hamlet perhaps the best advice is to read it and read it and read it until one is convinced that he does *not* understand it and is no longer sure that what he thought to be right is so. The best way to approach Hamlet is not with answers but with questions, and to leave them unanswered as long as possible.

A NOTE ON THE COMPOSITION OF THE PLAY

Hamlet was very probably written in 1601–1602 and first performed early in 1602. It was first published in 1603. The story comes ultimately from Saxo Grammaticus's *Historiae Danicae* (about 1200); but a French version by Belleforest in his *Histoires Tragiques* (1576), and very possibly an earlier English dramatic version, were known to Shakespeare.

Measure for Measure

DRAMATIS PERSONÆ

VINCENTIO   *the Duke*
ANGELO   *Deputy*
ESCALUS   *an ancient Lord*
CLAUDIO   *a young gentleman*
LUCIO   *a fantastic*
TWO OTHER GENTLEMEN
PROVOST
THOMAS ⎱
PETER   ⎰ *two friars*
A JUSTICE
VARRIUS
ELBOW   *a simple constable*

FROTH   *a foolish gentleman*
POMPEY   *servant to Mistress Overdone*
ABHORSON   *an executioner*
BARNARDINE   *a dissolute prisoner*
ISABELLA   *sister to Claudio*
MARIANA   *betrothed to Angelo*
JULIET   *beloved of Claudio*
FRANCISCA   *a nun*
MISTRESS OVERDONE   *a bawd*
LORDS, OFFICERS, CITIZENS, BOY, *and* ATTENDANTS

SCENE: *Vienna.*

ACT I

SCENE i
An apartment in the DUKE's *palace.*

[*Enter* DUKE, ESCALUS, LORDS *and* ATTENDANTS.]
DUKE. Escalus.
ESCALUS. My lord.
DUKE. Of government the properties to unfold°
  Would seem in me t' affect speech and discourse,
5 Since I am put to know that your own science°
  Exceeds, in that, the lists° of all advice
  My strength can give you. Then no more re-
    mains
  But that to your sufficiency . . . . . .
  . . . . .as° your worth is able,

And let them work. The nature of our people, 10
Our city's institutions, and the terms
For common justice, you're as pregnant° in
As art and practice hath enriched any
That we remember. There is our commission,
From which we would not have you warp.° Call
  hither, 15
I say, bid come before us Angelo.
              [*Exit an* ATTENDANT.]
What figure of us think you he will bear?°
For you must know, we have with special soul°
Elected him our absence to supply,
Lent him our terror,° dress'd him with our love, 20

Of . . . unfold   to discourse upon the proper business of
  government
science knowledge   *lists* limits
sufficiency . . . as (two half lines are apparently omitted;
  no suggested readings are worth mention)

pregnant well versed   *warp* deviate
What . . . bear how will he conduct himself in the role
  of duke
special soul profoundest sentiments
terror i.e., "the dread and fear of kings" (*Merchant of
  Venice*, IV, i)

And given his deputation all the organs
Of our own power. What think you of it?
ESCALUS. If any in Vienna be of worth
  To undergo such ample grace and honor,
  It is Lord Angelo.
25 DUKE.   Look where he comes.
        [*Enter* ANGELO.]
ANGELO. Always obedient to your Grace's will,
  I come to know your pleasure.
DUKE.   Angelo,
  There is a kind of character in thy life
  That to th' observer doth thy history
30 Fully unfold. Thyself and thy belongings
  Are not thine own so proper° as to waste
  Thyself upon thy virtues, they on thee.
  Heaven doth with us as we with torches do,
  Not light them for themselves; for if our virtues
35 Did not go forth of us, 'twere all alike
  As if we had them not. Spirits are not finely
    touch'd
  But to fine issues; nor Nature never lends
  The smallest scruple° of her excellence
  But like a thrifty goddess she determines
40 Herself the glory of a creditor,
  Both thanks and use.° But I do bend° my speech
  To one that can my part in him advertise.°
  Hold° therefore, Angelo:
  In our remove° be thou at full ourself;
45 Mortality° and mercy in Vienna
  Live in thy tongue and heart. Old Escalus,
  Though first in question,° is thy secondary.
  Take thy commission.
ANGELO.   Now, good my lord,
  Let there be some more test made of my metal
50 Before so noble and so great a figure
  Be stamp'd° upon it.
DUKE.   No more evasion.
  We have with a leaven'd° and prepared choice
  Proceeded to you; therefore take your honors.
  Our haste from hence is of so quick condition°
55 That it prefers itself,° and leaves unquestion'd°
  Matters of needful value. We shall write to you,
  As time and our concernings shall importune,
  How it goes with us, and do look to know
  What doth befall you here. So fare you well.

To the hopeful execution do I leave you   60
  Of your commissions.
ANGELO.   Yet give leave, my lord,
  That we may bring you something on the way.
DUKE. My haste may not admit it,
  Nor need you, on mine honor, have to do
  With any scruple.° Your scope is as mine own,   65
  So to enforce or qualify the laws
  As to your soul seems good. Give me your hand.
  I'll privily away. I love the people,
  But do not like to stage me to their eyes.
  Though it do well, I do not relish well   70
  Their loud applause and Aves° vehement;
  Nor do I think the man of safe discretion
  That does affect° it. Once more, fare you well.
ANGELO. The heavens give safety to your purposes!
ESCALUS. Lead forth and bring you back in happi-
    ness!   75
DUKE. I thank you. Fare you well.   [*Exit*]
ESCALUS. I shall desire you, sir, to give me leave
  To have free speech with you, and it concerns
    me
  To look into the bottom of my place.°
  A power I have, but of what strength and nature 80
  I am not yet instructed.
ANGELO. 'Tis so with me. Let us withdraw to-
    gether,
  And we may soon our satisfaction have
  Touching that point.
ESCALUS.   I'll wait upon your honor.
                                        [*Exeunt*]

SCENE ii
A street.

[*Enter* LUCIO *and two* GENTLEMEN.]
LUCIO. If the Duke, with the other dukes, come
  not to composition° with the King of Hungary,
  why then all the dukes fall upon the king.
FIRST GENTLEMAN. Heaven grant us its peace, but
  not the King of Hungary's!   5
SECOND GENTLEMAN. Amen.
LUCIO. Thou concludest like the sanctimonious
  pirate that went to sea with the Ten Command-
  ments, but scraped one out of the table.
SECOND GENTLEMAN. "Thou shalt not steal"?   10
LUCIO. Aye, that he razed.
FIRST GENTLEMAN. Why, 'twas a commandment to
  command the captain and all the rest from their

---

proper exclusively   scruple particle   use interest
bend direct   advertise display to advantage
Hold i.e., take formal cognizance   remove absence
Mortality i.e., life and death
first in question i.e., of highest seniority
metal . . . stamp'd with obvious play on coinage
leaven'd well fermented, actively considered
of . . . condition i.e., urgent
prefers itself takes first priority
unquestion'd unresolved

scruple detail   Aves salutations   affect relish
To look . . . place explore the limits of my authority
composition agreement

15
functions.° They put forth to steal. There's not a soldier of us all that in the thanksgiving before meat do relish the petition well that prays for peace.

SECOND GENTLEMAN. I never heard any soldier dislike it.

20
LUCIO. I believe thee, for I think thou never wast where grace was said.

SECOND GENTLEMAN. No? A dozen times at least.

FIRST GENTLEMAN. What, in meter?

LUCIO. In any proportion° or in any language.

25
FIRST GENTLEMAN. I think or in any religion.

LUCIO. Aye, why not? Grace is grace, despite of all controversy. As, for example, thou thyself art a wicked villain, despite of all grace.

FIRST GENTLEMAN. Well, there went but a pair of
30
shears between us.°

LUCIO. I grant, as there may between the lists and the velvet.° Thou art the list.

FIRST GENTLEMAN. And thou the velvet. Thou art good velvet; thou'rt a three-piled° piece, I
35
warrant thee. I had as lief be a list of an English kersey° as be piled as thou art piled, for a French velvet. Do I speak feelingly now?°

LUCIO. I think thou dost, and indeed with most painful feeling of thy speech. I will, out of thine
40
own confession, learn to begin thy health°— but, whilst I live, forget to drink after thee.°

FIRST GENTLEMAN. I think I have done myself wrong, have I not?

SECOND GENTLEMAN. Yes, that thou hast, whether
45
thou art tainted or free.

LUCIO. Behold, behold, where Madam Mitigation comes! I have purchased as many diseases under her roof as come to—

SECOND GENTLEMAN. To what, I pray?

50
LUCIO. Judge.

SECOND GENTLEMAN. To three thousand dolors° a year.

FIRST GENTLEMAN. Aye, and more.

LUCIO. A French crown° more.

55
FIRST GENTLEMAN. Thou art always figuring diseases in me, but thou art full of error. I am sound.

LUCIO. Nay, not as one would say, healthy; but so sound as things that are hollow. Thy bones are hollow; impiety has made a feast of thee.

[*Enter* MISTRESS OVERDONE.]

FIRST GENTLEMAN. How now! Which of your hips
60
has the most profound sciatica?°

MISTRESS OVERDONE. Well, well, there's one yonder arrested and carried to prison was worth five thousand of you all.

SECOND GENTLEMAN. Who's that, I pray thee?
65

MISTRESS OVERDONE. Marry, sir, that's Claudio, Signior Claudio.

FIRST GENTLEMAN. Claudio to prison? 'Tis not so.

MISTRESS OVERDONE. Nay, but I know 'tis so. I saw him arrested, saw him carried away, and, which
70
is more, within these three days his head to be chopped off.

LUCIO. But after all this fooling I would not have it so. Art thou sure of this?

MISTRESS OVERDONE. I am too sure of it. And it is
75
for getting Madam Julietta with child.

LUCIO. Believe me, this may be. He promised to meet me two hours since, and he was ever precise in promise-keeping.

SECOND GENTLEMAN. Besides, you know, it draws
80
something near to the speech we had to such a purpose.

FIRST GENTLEMAN. But most of all agreeing with the proclamation.

LUCIO. Away! Let's go learn the truth of it.
85

[*Exeunt* LUCIO *and* GENTLEMEN.]

MISTRESS OVERDONE. Thus, what with the war, what with the sweat,° what with the gallows, and what with poverty, I am custom-shrunk.°

[*Enter* POMPEY.]

How now! What's the news with you?

POMPEY. Yonder man is carried to prison.
90

MISTRESS OVERDONE. Well, what has he done?

POMPEY. A woman.

MISTRESS OVERDONE. But what's his offense?

POMPEY. Groping for trouts in a peculiar° river.

MISTRESS OVERDONE. What, is there a maid with
95
child by him?

POMPEY. No, but there's a woman with maid by him. You have not heard of the proclamation, have you?

MISTRESS OVERDONE. What proclamation, man?
100

POMPEY. All houses° in the suburbs of Vienna must be plucked down.

MISTRESS OVERDONE. And what shall become of those in the city?

---

functions i.e., proper business   *proportion* length
there . . . us i.e., we're essentially alike
between . . . velvet i.e., between the worthless border and the rich material
three-piled i.e., of triple nap, the best velvet (with following pun on *piled – peeled*, bald from the "French disease," syphilis)
kersey heavy woolen cloth
Do I . . . now i.e., do I "get to you" now
begin thy health be first to drink to your health
forget . . . thee i.e., for fear of syphilis
dolors (with pun on *dollars*)
French crown with pun, bald head from syphilis

sciatica i.e., as a symptom of venereal disease
sweat sweating sickness (phase of the plague)
custom-shrunk losing business   *peculiar* private
houses brothels

105 POMPEY. They shall stand for seed. They had gone
down too, but that a wise burgher put in for
them.

MISTRESS OVERDONE. But shall all our houses of
resort in the suburbs be pulled down?

110 POMPEY. To the ground, mistress.

MISTRESS OVERDONE. Why, here's a change indeed
in the commonwealth! What shall become of
me?

POMPEY. Come, fear not you. Good counselors

115 lack no clients. Though you change your place,
you need not change your trade; I'll be your
tapster° still. Courage! There will be pity taken
on you. You that have worn your eyes almost
out in the service, you will be considered.

120 MISTRESS OVERDONE. What's to do here, Thomas
tapster? Let's withdraw.

POMPEY. Here comes Signior Claudio, led by the
provost° to prison; and there's Madam Juliet.

[*Exeunt*]

[*Enter* PROVOST, CLAUDIO, JULIET, *and* OFFICERS.]

CLAUDIO. Fellow, why dost thou show me thus to
the world?

125 Bear me to prison where I am committed.

PROVOST. I do it not in evil disposition,
But from Lord Angelo by special charge.

CLAUDIO. Thus can the demigod Authority
Make us pay down° for our offense by weight

130 The words of heaven. On whom it will, it will;
On whom it will not, so. Yet still 'tis just.°

[*Re-enter* LUCIO *and two* GENTLEMEN.]

LUCIO. Why, how now, Claudio! Whence comes
this restraint?

CLAUDIO. From too much liberty, my Lucio,
liberty.

As surfeit is the father of much fast,

135 So every scope° by the immoderate use
Turns to restraint. Our natures do pursue,
Like rats that ravin down their proper bane,°
A thirsty evil; and when we drink we die.

LUCIO. If I could speak so wisely under an arrest, I

140 would send for certain of my creditors. And
yet, to say the truth, I had as lief have the
foppery° of freedom as the morality of imprisonment. What's thy offense, Claudio?

CLAUDIO. What but to speak of would offend again.

145 LUCIO. What, is't murder?

CLAUDIO. No.

LUCIO. Lechery?

CLAUDIO. Call it so.

PROVOST. Away, sir! You must go.

CLAUDIO. One word, good friend. Lucio, a word
with you.   150

LUCIO. A hundred, if they'll do you any good.
Is lechery so look'd after?°

CLAUDIO. Thus stands it with me. Upon a true
contract°

I got possession of Julietta's bed.
You know the lady; she is fast my wife,   155
Save that we do the denunciation° lack
Of outward order. This we came not to,
Only for propagation° of a dower
Remaining in the coffer of her friends,°
From whom we thought it meet to hide our
love   160
Till time had made them for us.° But it chances
The stealth of our most mutual entertainment
With character too gross is writ on Juliet.

LUCIO. With child, perhaps?

CLAUDIO.   Unhappily, even so.
And the new Deputy now for the Duke—   165
Whether it be the fault and glimpse of newness,°
Or whether that the body public be
A horse whereon the governor doth ride,
Who, newly in the seat, that it may know
He can command, lets it straight feel the spur— 170
Whether the tyranny be in his place,
Or in his eminence that fills it up,
I stagger in.° But this new governor
Awakes me° all th' enrolled° penalties
Which have, like unscour'd armor, hung by the
wall   175
So long that nineteen zodiacs° have gone round
And none of them been worn; and, for a name,°
Now puts the drowsy and neglected act
Freshly on me. 'Tis surely for a name.

LUCIO. I warrant it is, and thy head stands so   180
tickle° on thy shoulders that a milkmaid, if she
be in love, may sigh it off. Send after the Duke
and appeal to him.

CLAUDIO. I have done so, but he's not to be found.

---

tapster pimp   *provost* prison-keeper
Make us . . . just (probable omission of a line or two)
pay down pay strictly
On whom . . . just (see Romans 9:15: "I will have mercy
  on whom I will have mercy")
scope freedom
ravin . . . bane devour what is poisonous to them
foppery folly

look'd after kept under surveillance
true contract legal betrothal
denunciation publication of marriage banns by the
  church
propagation increase   *friends* relatives
made . . . us (presumably) disposed them favorably
fault . . . newness i.e., the fault of having newly had a
  taste of authority
stagger in i.e., am incapable of determining
Awakes me awakes (the ethical dative *me* has no force)
enrolled duly recorded   *zodiacs* years
name example, precedent   *tickle* precariously

185   I prithee, Lucio, do me this kind service.
  This day my sister should the cloister enter
  And there receive her approbation.°
  Acquaint her with the danger of my state;
  Implore her, in my voice, that she make friends
190   To the strict deputy; bid herself assay° him.
  I have great hope in that, for in her youth
  There is a prone and speechless dialect°
  Such as move men. Beside, she hath prosperous art
  When she will play with reason and discourse,
195   And well she can persuade.
  LUCIO. I pray she may, as well for the encouragement of the like, which else would stand under grievous imposition, as for the enjoying of thy life, who I would be sorry should be thus
200 foolishly lost at a game of tick-tack.° I'll to her.
  CLAUDIO. I thank you, good friend Lucio.
  LUCIO. Within two hours.
  CLAUDIO. Come, officer, away!   [Exeunt]

SCENE iii
A monastery.

[Enter DUKE and FRIAR THOMAS.]
DUKE. No, holy father, throw away that thought.
  Believe not that the dribbling dart° of love
  Can pierce a complete bosom.°Why I desire thee
  To give me secret harbor hath a purpose
5   More grave and wrinkled than the aims and ends
  Of burning youth.
  FRIAR THOMAS.   May your grace speak of it?
  DUKE. My holy sir, none better knows than you
  How I have ever lov'd the life remov'd
  And held in idle price to haunt assemblies
  Where youth and cost and witless bravery°
10   keeps.
  I have deliver'd to Lord Angelo,
  A man of stricture° and firm abstinence,
  My absolute power and place here in Vienna,
  And he supposes me travel'd to Poland—
15   For so I have strew'd it in the common ear,
  And so it is receiv'd. Now, pious sir,
  You will demand of me why I do this.
  FRIAR THOMAS. Gladly, my lord.

DUKE. We have strict statutes and most biting laws,
  The needful bits and curbs to headstrong weeds, 20
  Which for this fourteen years we have let slip,
  Even like an o'ergrown lion in a cave,
  That goes not out to prey. Now, as fond fathers,
  Having bound up the threat'ning twigs of birch,
  Only to stick it in their children's sight 25
  For terror, not to use, in time the rod
  Becomes more mock'd than fear'd, so our decrees,
  Dead to infliction,° to themselves are dead,
  And liberty plucks justice by the nose,
  The baby beats the nurse, and quite athwart 30
  Goes all decorum.
  FRIAR THOMAS.   It rested in your Grace
  T' unloose this tied-up justice when you pleas'd.
  And it in you more dreadful would have seem'd
  Than in Lord Angelo.
  DUKE.   I do fear, too dreadful.
  Sith° 'twas my fault to give the people scope,° 35
  'Twould be my tyranny to strike and gall them
  For what I bid them do. For we bid this be done
  When evil deeds have their permissive pass
  And not the punishment. Therefore, indeed, my father,
  I have on Angelo impos'd the office, 40
  Who may, in th' ambush of my name, strike home,
  And yet my nature never in the fight
  To do it slander.° And to behold his sway,
  I will, as 'twere a brother of your order,
  Visit both prince and people. Therefore, I prithee, 45
  Supply me with the habit, and instruct me
  How I may formally in person bear me
  Like a true friar. Moe° reasons for this action
  At our more leisure shall I render you;
  Only, this one: Lord Angelo is precise, 50
  Stands at a guard with envy,° scarce confesses
  That his blood flows or that his appetite
  Is more to bread than stone. Hence shall we see,
  If power change purpose, what our seemers be.
              [Exeunt]

---

approbation novitiate   *assay* attempt
prone . . . dialect i.e., a silent, latent communicative force
tick-tack a game like backgammon (here used figuratively)
dribbling dart powerless arrow
complete fully armored   *bravery* finery
stricture strictness

infliction enforcement
Sith since   *scope* freedom
To . . . slander i.e., to reflect on me   *Moe* more
at . . . envy on guard against malice

SCENE iv
A nunnery.

[*Enter* ISABELLA *and* FRANCISCA.]

ISABELLA. And have you nuns no farther privileges?

FRANCISCA. Are not these large enough?

ISABELLA. Yes, truly. I speak not as desiring more,
But rather wishing a more strict restraint

5 Upon the sisterhood, the votarists of Saint Clare.°

LUCIO. [*Within*] Ho! Peace be in this place!

ISABELLA.   Who's that which calls?

FRANCISCA. It is a man's voice. Gentle Isabella,
Turn you the key and know his business of him.
You may, I may not; you are yet unsworn.
When you have vow'd, you must not speak with

10 men
But in the presence of the prioress.
Then, if you speak, you must not show your
face;
Or, if you show your face, you must not speak.
He calls again. I pray you, answer him.   [*Exit*]

ISABELLA. Peace and prosperity! Who is't that
15 calls?

[*Enter* LUCIO.]

LUCIO. Hail, virgin, if you be, as those cheek roses
Proclaim you are no less! Can you so stead me
As bring me to the sight of Isabella,
A novice of this place, and the fair sister

20 To her unhappy brother Claudio?

ISABELLA. Why "her unhappy brother"? Let me
ask
The rather for I now must make you know
I am that Isabella and his sister.

LUCIO. Gentle and fair, your brother kindly
greets you.

25 Not to be weary with you, he's in prison.

ISABELLA. Woe me! For what?

LUCIO. For that which, if myself might be his
judge,
He should receive his punishment in thanks.
He hath got his friend with child.

ISABELLA. Sir, make me not your story.°

30 LUCIO.   It is true.
I would not—though 'tis my familiar sin
With maids to seem the lapwing,° and to jest,
Tongue far from heart—play with all virgins so.
I hold you as a thing enskied and sainted;

35 By your renouncement, an immortal spirit,
And to be talk'd with in sincerity,

As with a saint.

ISABELLA. You do blaspheme the good in mocking
me.

LUCIO. Do not believe it. Fewness and truth,° 'tis
thus:
Your brother and his lover have embrac'd.   40
As those that feed grow full—as blossoming
time,
That from the seedness° the bare fallow brings
To teeming foison°—even so her plenteous
womb
Expresseth his full tilth° and husbandry.

ISABELLA. Some one with child by him? My cousin
Juliet?   45

LUCIO. Is she your cousin?

ISABELLA. Adoptedly, as school maids change their
names
By vain, though apt, affection.

LUCIO.   She it is.

ISABELLA. O, let him marry her.

LUCIO.   This is the point.
The duke is very strangely gone from hence—   50
Bore many gentlemen, myself being one,
In hand and hope of action.° But we do learn
By those that know the very nerves of state,
His givings-out were of an infinite distance
From his true-meant design. Upon his place,   55
And with full line of his authority,
Governs Lord Angelo—a man whose blood
Is very snow-broth, one who never feels
The wanton stings and motions of the sense,
But doth rebate° and blunt his natural edge   60
With profits of the mind, study and fast.
He—to give fear to use and liberty,°
Which have for long run by the hideous law
As mice by lions—hath pick'd out an act
Under whose heavy sense° your brother's life   65
Falls into forfeit. He arrests him on it
And follows close the rigor of the statute
To make him an example. All hope is gone
Unless you have the grace by your fair prayer
To soften Angelo. And that's my pith of business 70
'Twixt you and your poor brother.

ISABELLA. Doth he so seek his life?

LUCIO.   Has censur'd° him
Already, and, as I hear, the provost hath
A warrant for his execution.

Saint Clare of Assisi (a particularly strict order)
make . . . story don't jest with me
seem the lapwing deceive, mislead, as the lapwing draws
  intruders away from her nest by pretending injury

Fewness and truth in brief and in truth
seedness seeding   *foison* harvest   *tilth* tillage
Bore . . . action deluded . . . with hope of (military)
  action
rebate abate
use and liberty customary practice of licentiousness
heavy sense severe application   *censur'd* sentenced

75 ISABELLA. Alas! What poor ability's in me
     To do him good?
LUCIO.   Assay° the power you have.
ISABELLA. My power? Alas, I doubt—
LUCIO.   Our doubts are traitors,
     And make us lose the good we oft might win
     By fearing to attempt. Go to Lord Angelo
80   And let him learn to know, when maidens sue,
     Men give like gods; but when they weep and
        kneel,
     All their petitions are as freely theirs

As they themselves would owe them.°
ISABELLA. I'll see what I can do.
LUCIO.   But speedily.
ISABELLA. I will about it straight,   85
     No longer staying but to give the Mother
     Notice of my affair. I humbly thank you.
     Commend me to my brother. Soon at night
     I'll send him certain word of my success.
LUCIO. I take my leave of you.
ISABELLA.   Good sir, adieu.   90

                              [*Exeunt*]

Assay try

would owe them had them to give

A C T I I

SCENE i
A hall in ANGELO's *house.*

[*Enter* ANGELO, ESCALUS, *and a* JUSTICE, PROVOST,
   OFFICERS, *and other* ATTENDANTS, *behind.*]
ANGELO. We must not make a scarecrow of the
     law,
   Setting it up to fear° the birds of prey,
   And let it keep one shape till custom make it
   Their perch, and not their terror.
ESCALUS.   Aye, but yet
5   Let us be keen, and rather cut a little
   Than fall° and bruise to death. Alas, this gentle-
      man,
   Whom I would save, had a most noble father!
   Let but your honor know,
   Whom I believe to be most strait in virtue,
10   That, in the working of your own affections,°
   Had time coher'd with place or place with
      wishing,
   Or that the resolute acting of your blood
   Could have attain'd th' effect of your own
      purpose,
   Whether you had not sometime in your life
15   Err'd in this point which now you censure him,
   And pull'd the law upon you.
   ANGELO. 'Tis one thing to be tempted, Escalus,
     Another thing to fall. I not deny,
     The jury, passing on the prisoner's life,
20   May in the sworn twelve have a thief or two
     Guiltier than him they try. What's open made
        to justice,

That justice seizes. What knows the laws
That thieves do pass on thieves?° 'Tis very
   pregnant,°
The jewel that we find, we stoop and take't
Because we see it; but what we do not see   25
We tread upon and never think of it.
You may not so extenuate his offense
For° I have had such faults; but rather tell me,
When I, that censure him, do so offend,
Let mine own judgment pattern out my death,   30
And nothing come in partial.° Sir, he must die.
ESCALUS. Be it as your wisdom will.
ANGELO.   Where is the provost?
PROVOST. Here, if it like your honor.
ANGELO.   See that Claudio
   Be executed by nine tomorrow morning.
   Bring him his confessor, let him be prepar'd,   35
   For that's the utmost of his pilgrimage.
                              [*Exit* PROVOST.]
ESCALUS. [*Aside*] Well, heaven forgive him! And
      forgive us all!
   Some rise by sin, and some by virtue fall.
   Some run from brakes of ice° and answer none,
   And some condemned for a fault alone.   40
      [*Enter* ELBOW, *and* OFFICERS *with* FROTH
                  and POMPEY.]
ELBOW. Come, bring them away. If these be good
   people in a commonweal that do nothing but

fear frighten   *fall* fell (like a tree)
affections passions

What knows . . . thieves i.e., the law, as an impersonal
   entity, takes no cognizance of the fact that thieves may
   sometimes serve as jurors
pregnant evident   *For* because
come in partial no partiality be shown
brakes of ice (probably *ice* should be *vice*, hence thickets
   of vice, multiple crimes)

use their abuses in common houses,° I know no
law. Bring them away.

ANGELO. How now, sir! What's your name? And
what's the matter?

ELBOW. If it please your honor, I am the poor
Duke's constable,° and my name is Elbow. I do
lean upon justice, sir, and do bring in here
before your good honor two notorious benefactors.

ANGELO. Benefactors? Well. What benefactors are
they? Are they not malefactors?

ELBOW. If it please your honor, I know not well
what they are. But precise° villains they are, that
I am sure of, and void of all profanation° in the
world that good Christians ought to have.

ESCALUS. This comes off well; here's a wise officer.

ANGELO. Go to. What quality° are they of? Elbow
is your name? Why dost thou not speak, Elbow?

POMPEY. He cannot, sir; he's out at elbow.

ANGELO. What are you, sir?

ELBOW. He, sir! A tapster, sir, parcel-bawd,° one
that serves a bad woman, whose house, sir, was,
as they say, plucked down in the suburbs. And
now she professes a hothouse,° which, I think, is
a very ill house too.

ESCALUS. How know you that?

ELBOW. My wife, sir, whom I detest° before
heaven and your honor—

ESCALUS. How? Thy wife?

ELBOW. Aye, sir, whom, I thank heaven, is an
honest woman—

ESCALUS. Dost thou detest her therefore?

ELBOW. I say, sir, I will detest myself also, as well
as she, that this house, if it be not a bawd's
house, it is pity of her life, for it is a naughty°
house.

ESCALUS. How dost thou know that, constable?

ELBOW. Marry, sir, by my wife, who, if she had
been a woman cardinally° given, might have
been accused in fornication, adultery, and all
uncleanliness there.

ESCALUS. By the woman's means?°

ELBOW. Aye, sir, by Mistress Overdone's means.
But as she spit in his face, so she defied him.

POMPEY. Sir, if it please your honor, this is not so.

ELBOW. Prove it before these varlets here, thou
honorable man. Prove it.

ESCALUS. Do you hear how he misplaces?

POMPEY. Sir, she came in great with child, and longing, saving your honor's reverence, for stewed
prunes.° Sir, we had but two in the house,
which at that very distant time stood, as it were,
in a fruit-dish, a dish of some threepence. Your
honors have seen such dishes. They are not
China dishes, but very good dishes—

ESCALUS. Go to, go to. No matter for the dish, sir.

POMPEY. No, indeed, sir, not of a pin; you are
therein in the right. But to the point. As I say,
this Mistress Elbow, being, as I say, with child,
and being great-bellied, and longing, as I said,
for prunes, and having but two in the dish, as I
said, Master Froth here, this very man, having
eaten the rest, as I said, and, as I say, paying for
them very honestly; for, as you know, Master
Froth, I could not give you threepence again.

FROTH. No, indeed.

POMPEY. Very well. You being then, if you be
remembered, cracking the stones of the foresaid
prunes—

FROTH. Aye, so I did indeed.

POMPEY. Why, very well. I telling you then, if you
be remembered, that such a one and such a one
were past cure of the thing you wot° of, unless
they kept very good diet, as I told you—

FROTH. All this is true.

POMPEY. Why, very well, then—

ESCALUS. Come, you are a tedious fool. To the
purpose. What was done to Elbow's wife that he
hath cause to complain of? Come me to what
was done to her.

POMPEY. Sir, your honor cannot come to that yet.

ESCALUS. No, sir, nor I mean it not.

POMPEY. Sir, but you shall come to it, by your
honor's leave. And, I beseech you, look into
Master Froth here, sir—a man of fourscore
pound a year, whose father died at Hallowmas.°
Was't not at Hallowmas, Master Froth?

FROTH. All-hallond eve.°

POMPEY. Why, very well. I hope here be truths.
He, sir, sitting, as I say, in a lower chair, sir—
'twas in the Bunch of Grapes,° where, indeed,
you have a delight to sit, have you not?

FROTH. I have so, because it is an open room, and
good for winter.

common houses brothels
poor . . . constable i.e., Duke's poor constable; a modest
  example of Elbowism
precise possibly unmistakable; (another Elbowism)
profanation blunder for profession (of faith)
quality occupation   parcel-bawd part-time pimp
hothouse bathhouse   detest blunder for protest
naughty wicked
cardinally blunder for carnally
woman's means i.e., Pompey the pimp

stewed prunes (for uncertainly known reasons frequently
  identified as brothel fare)
wot know   Hallowmas All Saints' Day, November 1
All-hallond eve Hallowe'en, October 31
Bunch of Grapes name of a room

POMPEY. Why, very well, then. I hope here be truths.

ANGELO. This will last out a night in Russia,
When nights are longest there. I'll take my leave
140   And leave you to the hearing of the cause,
Hoping you'll find good cause to whip them all.

ESCALUS. I think no less. Good morrow to your
lordship.   [*Exit* ANGELO.]
Now, sir, come on. What was done to Elbow's
wife, once more?

145   POMPEY. Once, sir? There was nothing done to her
once.

ELBOW. I beseech you, sir, ask him what this man
did to my wife.

POMPEY. I beseech your honor, ask me.

150   ESCALUS. Well, sir, what did this gentleman to her?

POMPEY. I beseech you, sir, look in this gentleman's
face. Good Master Froth, look upon his honor;
'tis for a good purpose. Doth your honor mark
his face?

155   ESCALUS. Aye, sir, very well.

POMPEY. Nay, I beseech you, mark it well.

ESCALUS. Well, I do so.

POMPEY. Doth your honor see any harm in his face?

ESCALUS. Why, no.

160   POMPEY. I'll be supposed° upon a book, his face is
the worst thing about him. Good, then. If his
face be the worst thing about him, how could
Master Froth do the constable's wife any harm?
I would know that of your honor.

165   ESCALUS. He's in the right. Constable, what say
you to it?

ELBOW. First, an it like you, the house is a re-
spected° house; next, this is a respected fellow;
and his mistress is a respected woman.

170   POMPEY. By this hand, sir, his wife is a more respected person than any of us all.

ELBOW. Varlet, thou liest; thou liest, wicked varlet!
The time is yet to come that she was ever respected with man, woman, or child.

175   POMPEY. Sir, she was respected with him before he
married with her.

ESCALUS. Which is the wiser here? Justice or
Iniquity? Is this true?

ELBOW. O thou caitiff! O thou varlet! O thou
180   wicked Hannibal!° I respected with her before I
was married to her! If ever I was respected with
her, or she with me, let not your worship think
me the poor Duke's officer. Prove this, thou
wicked Hannibal, or I'll have mine action of
185   battery on thee.

ESCALUS. If he took you a box o' th' ear, you might
have your action of slander too.

ELBOW. Marry, I thank your good worship for it.
What is't your worship's pleasure I shall do
with this wicked caitiff?   190

ESCALUS. Truly, officer, because he hath some
offenses in him that thou wouldst discover° if
thou couldst, let him continue in his courses
till thou knowest what they are.

ELBOW. Marry, I thank your worship for it. Thou   195
seest, thou wicked varlet, now, what's come
upon thee. Thou art to continue now, thou
varlet; thou art to continue.

ESCALUS. Where were you born, friend?

FROTH. Here in Vienna, sir.   200

ESCALUS. Are you of fourscore pounds a year?

FROTH. Yes, an't please you, sir.

ESCALUS. So. What trade are you of, sir?

POMPEY. A tapster, a poor widow's tapster.

ESCALUS. Your mistress' name?   205

POMPEY. Mistress Overdone.

ESCALUS. Hath she had any more than one husband?

POMPEY. Nine, sir. Overdone by the last.

ESCALUS. Nine! Come hither to me, Master Froth.   210
Master Froth, I would not have you acquainted
with tapsters. They will draw° you, Master
Froth, and you will hang them. Get you gone,
and let me hear no more of you.

FROTH. I thank your worship. For mine own part,   215
I never come into any room in a taphouse, but
I am drawn in.

ESCALUS. Well, no more of it, Master Froth. Farewell. [*Exit* FROTH] Come you hither to me,
Master tapster. What's your name, Master   220
tapster?

POMPEY. Pompey.

ESCALUS. What else?

POMPEY. Bum, sir.

ESCALUS. Troth, and your bum is the greatest thing   225
about you; so that, in the beastliest sense, you
are Pompey the Great. Pompey, you are partly a
bawd, Pompey, howsoever you color it in being
a tapster, are you not? Come, tell me true. It
shall be the better for you.   230

POMPEY. Truly, sir, I am a poor fellow that would
live.

ESCALUS. How would you live, Pompey? By being
a bawd? What do you think of the trade, Pompey? Is it a lawful trade?   235

POMPEY. If the law would allow it, sir.

---

supposed   blunder for *deposed*, sworn
respected   blunder for *suspected*
Hannibal   presumably *cannibal*

discover   reveal
draw   i.e., as ale from a keg; but also allusion to *hang,
draw, and quarter*

ESCALUS. But the law will not allow it, Pompey,
   nor it shall not be allowed in Vienna.

POMPEY. Does your worship mean to geld and
240 splay all the youth of the city?

ESCALUS. No, Pompey.

POMPEY. Truly, sir, in my poor opinion, they will
   to 't, then. If your worship will take order for the
   drabs and the knaves, you need not to fear the
245 bawds.

ESCALUS. There are pretty orders beginning, I can
   tell you. It is but heading °and hanging.

POMPEY. If you head and hang all that offend that
   way but for ten year together, you'll be glad to
250 give out a commission for more heads. If this
   law hold in Vienna ten year, I'll rent the fairest
   house in it after° threepence a bay.° If you live to
   see this come to pass, say Pompey told you so.

ESCALUS. Thank you, good Pompey; and, in re-
255 quital of your prophecy, hark you. I advise you,
   let me not find you before me again upon any
   complaint whatsoever—no, not for dwelling
   where you do. If I do, Pompey, I shall beat you
   to your tent and prove a shrewd Cæsar to you.°
260 In plain dealing, Pompey, I shall have you
   whipt. So, for this time, Pompey, fare you well.

POMPEY. I thank your worship for your good
   counsel. [Aside] But I shall follow it as the flesh
   and fortune shall better determine.
265 Whip me? No, no. Let carman° whip his jade.°
   The valiant heart's not whipt out of his trade.
                                             [Exit]

ESCALUS. Come hither to me, Master Elbow; come
   hither, Master constable. How long have you
   been in this place of constable?
270 ELBOW. Seven year and a half, sir.

ESCALUS. I thought, by your readiness in the office,
   you had continued in it some time. You say
   seven years together?

ELBOW. And a half, sir.
275 ESCALUS. Alas, it hath been great pains to you.
   They do you wrong to put you° so oft upon 't.
   Are there not men in your ward sufficient to
   serve it?

ELBOW. Faith, sir, few of any wit in such matters.
280 As they are chosen, they are glad to choose me
   for them. I do it for some piece of money, and
   go through with all.

ESCALUS. Look you bring me in the names of some
   six or seven, the most sufficient of your parish.

ELBOW. To your worship's house, sir?   285

ESCALUS. To my house. Fare you well. [Exit ELBOW.]
   What's o'clock, think you?

JUSTICE. Eleven, sir.

ESCALUS. I pray you home to dinner with me.

JUSTICE. I humbly thank you.   290

ESCALUS. It grieves me for the death of Claudio.
   But there's no remedy.

JUSTICE. Lord Angelo is severe.

ESCALUS.   It is but needful.
   Mercy is not itself that oft looks so.
   Pardon is still° the nurse of second woe.   295
   But yet—poor Claudio! There is no remedy.
   Come, sir.   [Exeunt]

SCENE ii
Another room in the same.

[Enter PROVOST and a SERVANT.]

SERVANT. He's hearing of a cause. He will come
   straight.
   I'll tell him of you.

PROVOST.   Pray you, do. [Exit SERVANT.] I'll know
   His pleasure; may be he will relent. Alas,
   He hath but as offended in a dream!
   All sects,° all ages smack of this vice. And he   5
   To die for 't!
                      [Enter ANGELO.]

ANGELO.   Now what's the matter, provost?

PROVOST. Is it your will Claudio shall die tomorrow?

ANGELO. Did not I tell thee yea? Hadst thou not
   order?
   Why dost thou ask again?

PROVOST.   Lest I might be too rash.
   Under your good correction,° I have seen   10
   When, after execution, judgment hath
   Repented o'er his doom.

ANGELO.   Go to; let that be mine.
   Do you your office, or give up your place,
   And you shall well be spar'd.

PROVOST.   I crave your honor's pardon.
   What shall be done, sir, with the groaning
   Juliet?   15
   She's very near her hour.

ANGELO.   Dispose of her
   To some more fitter place, and that with speed.
                      [Re-enter SERVANT.]

SERVANT. Here is the sister of the man condemn'd
   Desires access to you.

ANGELO.   Hath he a sister?

---

heading beheading   *after* for
bay i.e., the space lying under one gable
beat . . . to you i.e., as Julius Caesar drove Pompey into
   Egypt, where he was murdered
carman cartman   *jade* nag
to put you choose you for the office

still always   *sects* classes
Under . . . correction by your pardon

20 PROVOST. Aye, my good lord, a very virtuous maid
    And to be shortly of a sisterhood,
    If not already.
ANGELO.   Well, let her be admitted.
                      [*Exit* SERVANT.]
    See you the fornicatress be remov'd.
    Let her have needful but not lavish means.
    There shall be order for 't.
            [*Enter* ISABELLA *and* LUCIO.]
25 PROVOST.   God save your honor!
ANGELO. Stay a little while. [*To* ISABELLA] You're
    welcome. What's your will?
ISABELLA. I am a woeful suitor to your honor,
    Please but your honor hear me.
ANGELO.   Well what's your suit?
ISABELLA. There is a vice that most I do abhor
30   And most desire should meet the blow of justice,
    For which I would not plead but that I must,
    For which I must not plead, but that I am
    At war 'twixt will and will not.
ANGELO.   Well, the matter?
ISABELLA. I have a brother is condemn'd to die.
35   I do beseech you, let it be his fault,°
    And not my brother.
PROVOST. [*Aside*] Heaven give thee moving graces!
ANGELO. Condemn the fault, and not the actor of
    it?
    Why, every fault's condemn'd ere it be done.
    Mine were the very cipher of a function,°
40   To fine the faults whose fine stands in record
    And let go by the actor.
ISABELLA.   O just but severe law!
    I had a brother, then.—Heaven keep your
    honor!
LUCIO. [*Aside to* ISABELLA] Give 't not o'er so. To
    him again. Entreat him.
    Kneel down before him, hang upon his gown.
45   You are too cold; if you should need a pin,
    You could not with more tame a tongue desire
    it.
    To him, I say!
ISABELLA. Must he needs die?
ANGELO.   Maiden, no remedy.
ISABELLA. Yes, I do think that you might pardon
    him,
    And neither heaven nor man grieve at the
50   mercy.
ANGELO. I will not do 't.
ISABELLA.   But can you, if you would?
ANGELO. Look, what I will not, that I cannot do.
ISABELLA. But might you do 't, and do the world no
    wrong,

If so your heart were touch'd with that remorse°
    As mine is to him?
ANGELO.   He's sentenc'd; 'tis too late. 55
LUCIO. [*Aside to* ISABELLA] You are too cold.
ISABELLA. Too late? Why, no. I, that do speak a
    word,
    May call it back again. Well, believe this:
    No ceremony that to great ones 'longs,
    Not the king's crown nor the deputed sword, 60
    The marshal's truncheon° nor the judge's robe,
    Become them with one half so good a grace
    As mercy does.
    If he had been as you, and you as he,
    You would have slipt like him; but he, like you, 65
    Would not have been so stern.
ANGELO.   Pray you, be gone.
ISABELLA. I would to heaven I had your potency,
    And you were Isabel! Should it then be thus?
    No, I would tell what 'twere to be a judge,
    And what a prisoner.
LUCIO. [*Aside to* ISABELLA] Aye, touch him; there's
    the vein. 70
ANGELO. Your brother is a forfeit of the law,
    And you but waste your words.
ISABELLA.   Alas, alas!
    Why, all the souls that were were forfeit once,
    And He that might the vantage best have took
    Found out the remedy. How would you be 75
    If He, which is the top of judgment, should
    But judge you as you are? O, think on that,
    And mercy then will breathe within your lips
    Like man new made.
ANGELO.   Be you content, fair maid.
    It is the law, not I, condemn your brother. 80
    Were he my kinsman, brother, or my son,
    It should be thus with him. He must die to-
    morrow.
ISABELLA. Tomorrow! O, that's sudden! Spare him,
    spare him!
    He's not prepar'd for death. Even for our kit-
    chens
    We kill the fowl of season.° Shall we serve
    heaven 85
    With less respect than we do minister
    To our gross selves? Good, good my lord, be-
    think you.
    Who is it that hath died for this offense?
    There's many have committed it.
LUCIO. [*Aside to* ISABELLA]   Aye, well said.
ANGELO. The law hath not been dead, though it
    hath slept. 90
    Those many had not dar'd to do that evil

---

let . . . fault i.e., punish the fault and not the doer
function office

remorse pity   *truncheon* staff of office
of season that is in season

If but the first that did th' edict infringe
Had answer'd for his deed. Now 'tis awake,
Takes note of what is done, and, like a prophet,
95   Looks in a glass that shows what future evils,
Either now or by remissness new-conceiv'd,
And so in progress to be hatch'd and born,
Are now to have no successive degrees,°
But, ere they live, to end.

ISABELLA.   Yet show some pity.
100 ANGELO. I show it most of all when I show justice,
For then I pity those I do not know,
Which a dismiss'd offense would after gall,°
And do him right that, answering one foul
      wrong,
Lives not to act another. Be satisfied.
105 Your brother dies tomorrow. Be content.

ISABELLA. So you must be the first that gives his
      sentence,
And he, that suffers. O, it is excellent
To have a giant's strength, but it is tyrannous
To use it like a giant.

LUCIO. [Aside to ISABELLA] That's well said.
110 ISABELLA. Could great men thunder
As Jove himself does, Jove would ne'er be quiet,
For every pelting,° petty officer
Would use his heaven for thunder,
Nothing but thunder! Merciful Heaven,
115 Thou rather with thy sharp and sulphurous bolt
Split'st the unwedgeable and gnarled oak
Than the soft myrtle. But man, proud man,
Drest in a little brief authority,
Most ignorant of what he's most assur'd,
120 His glassy essence,° like an angry ape,
Plays such fantastic tricks before high heaven
As make the angels weep—who, with our
      spleens,°
Would all themselves laugh mortal.

LUCIO. [Aside to ISABELLA] O, to him, to him, wench!
      He will relent.
He's coming; I perceive 't.
125 PROVOST. [Aside]   Pray heaven she win him!

ISABELLA. We cannot weigh our brother with our-
      self.
Great men may jest with saints—'tis wit in them,
But in the less foul profanation.

LUCIO. Thou'rt i' the right, girl; more o' that.
130 ISABELLA. That in the captain's but a choleric° word,
Which in the soldier is flat blasphemy.

LUCIO. [Aside to ISABELLA] Art avis'd° o' that? More
      on 't.

ANGELO. Why do you put these sayings upon me?

ISABELLA. Because authority, though it err like
      others,
Hath yet a kind of medicine in itself   135
That skins the vice o' the top. Go to your bosom;
Knock there, and ask your heart what it doth
      know
That's like my brother's fault. If it confess
A natural guiltiness such as is his,
Let it not sound a thought upon your tongue   140
Against my brother's life.

ANGELO. [Aside]   She speaks, and 'tis
Such sense that my sense breeds with it. Fare
      you well.

ISABELLA. Gentle my lord, turn back.

ANGELO. I will bethink me. Come again tomorrow.

ISABELLA. Hark how I'll bribe you. Good my lord,
      turn back.   145

ANGELO. How? Bribe me?

ISABELLA. Aye, with such gifts that heaven shall
      share with you.

LUCIO. [Aside to ISABELLA] You had marr'd all else.

ISABELLA. Not with fond sicles° of the tested gold,
Or stones whose rates are either rich or poor   150
As fancy values them, but with true prayers
That shall be up at heaven and enter there
Ere sunrise, prayers from preserved souls,
From fasting maids whose minds are dedicate
To nothing temporal.

ANGELO.   Well, come to me tomorrow. 155

LUCIO. [Aside to ISABELLA] Go to; 'tis well. Away!

ISABELLA. Heaven keep your honor safe!

ANGELO. [Aside]   Amen.
For I am that way going to temptation,
Where prayers cross.°

ISABELLA.   At what hour tomorrow
Shall I attend your lordship?

ANGELO.   At any time 'fore noon. 160

ISABELLA. 'Save your honor!
            [Exeunt ISABELLA, LUCIO, and PROVOST.]

ANGELO.   From thee—even from thy virtue!
What's this, what's this? Is this her fault or mine?
The tempter or the tempted, who sins most?
Ha!
Not she; nor doth she tempt. But it is I   165
That, lying by the violet in the sun,
Do as the carrion does,° not as the flower,
Corrupt with virtuous season.° Can it be
That modesty may more betray our sense

---

successive degrees descendants
after gall afterward injure   pelting paltry
glassy essence i.e., insubstantial, transitory being
spleens seat of the emotions   choleric angry
avis'd advised

fond sicles foolish (i.e., foolishly valued) shekels
cross i.e., conflict with baser impulses
Do . . . does i.e., rot
virtuous season i.e., the summer sun's strength

170 Than woman's lightness? Having waste ground
      enough,
   Shall we desire to raze the sanctuary,
   And pitch our evils there? O, fie, fie, fie!
   What dost thou, or what art thou, Angelo?
   Dost thou desire her foully for those things
175 That make her good? O, let her brother live.
   Thieves for their robbery have authority
   When judges steal themselves. What, do I love
      her,
   That I desire to hear her speak again,
   And feast upon her eyes? What is't I dream on?
180 O cunning enemy, that to catch a saint
   With saints dost bait thy hook! Most dangerous
   Is that temptation that doth goad us on
   To sin in loving virtue. Never could the strum-
      pet,
   With all her double vigor, art and nature,
185 Once stir my temper; but this virtuous maid
   Subdues me quite. Ever till now,
   When men were fond,° I smil'd and wonder'd
      how.   [Exit]

SCENE iii
A room in a prison.

[Enter, severally, Duke disguised as a friar, and
   Provost.]

Duke. Hail to you, Provost! So I think you are.
Provost. I am the provost. What's your will, good
   friar?
Duke. Bound by my charity and my blest order,
   I come to visit the afflicted spirits
5   Here in the prison. Do me the common right
   To let me see them and to make me know
   The nature of their crimes, that I may minister
   To them accordingly.
Provost. I would do more than that, if more were
   needful.
            [Enter Juliet.]
10 Look, here comes one, a gentlewoman of mine,
   Who, falling in the flaws of her own youth,
   Hath blister'd her report.° She is with child,
   And he that got it, sentenc'd—a young man
   More fit to do another such offense
15   Than die for this.
Duke. When must he die?
Provost.   As I do think, tomorrow.
   I have provided for you. Stay awhile,
                            [To Juliet.]
   And you shall be conducted.
Duke. Repent you, fair one, of the sin you carry?

fond foolishly doting   report reputation

Juliet. I do, and bear the shame most patiently. 20
Duke. I'll teach you how you shall arraign your
   conscience
   And try your penitence, if it be sound
   Or hollowly put on.
Juliet.   I'll gladly learn.
Duke. Love you the man that wrong'd you?
Juliet. Yes, as I love the woman that wrong'd him. 25
Duke. So, then, it seems your most offenseful act
   Was mutually committed?
Juliet.   Mutually.
Duke. Then was your sin of heavier kind than his.
Juliet. I do confess it, and repent it, father.
Duke. 'Tis meet so, daughter. But lest you do
   repent   30
   As that° the sin hath brought you to this shame,
   Which sorrow is always toward ourselves, not
      heaven,
   Showing we would not spare heaven as° we love
      it,
   But as we stand in fear—
Juliet. I do repent me as it is an evil,   35
   And take the shame with joy.
Duke.   There rest.
   Your partner, as I hear, must die tomorrow,
   And I am going with instruction to him.
   Grace go with you, Benedicite!°   [Exit]
Juliet. Must die tomorrow! O injurious love,   40
   That respites me a life whose very comfort
   Is still a dying horror!°
Provost.   'Tis pity of him.
                            [Exeunt]

SCENE iv
A room in Angelo's house.

[Enter Angelo.]

Angelo. When I would pray and think, I think
   and pray
   To several subjects.° Heaven hath my empty
      words,
   Whilst my invention,° hearing not my tongue,
   Anchors on Isabel: heaven in my mouth,
   As if I did but only chew his name,   5
   And in my heart the strong and swelling evil

As that because
spare . . . as avoid grieving heaven because
Benedicite bless you
O . . . horror (never explained to entire satisfaction; but
   Juliet blames "love," which, though it tendered her a
   child which is her comfort, yet that very comfort will
   always remain a reminder of Claudio's death)
several subjects discrepant purposes
invention imagination

Of my conception. The state,° whereon I studied,
Is like a good thing, being often read,
Grown fear'd° and tedious; yea, my gravity,
Wherein—let no man hear me—I take pride,
Could I with boot° change for an idle plume
Which the air beats for vain.° O place, O form,
How often dost thou with thy case,° thy habit,
Wrench awe from fools and tie the wiser souls
To thy false seeming! Blood,° thou art blood.
Let's write good angel on the devil's horn;
'Tis not the devil's crest.°

[*Enter a* SERVANT.]

How now! Who's there?

SERVANT. One Isabel, a sister, desires access to you.

ANGELO. Teach her the way. O heavens!
Why does my blood thus muster to my heart,
Making both it unable for itself
And dispossessing all my other parts
Of necessary fitness?
So play the foolish throngs with one that swoons—
Come all to help him, and so stop the air
By which he should revive. And even so
The general subject° to a well-wish'd king
Quit their own part, and in obsequious fondness
Crowd to his presence, where their untaught love
Must needs appear offense.

[*Enter* ISABELLA.]

How now, fair maid?

ISABELLA. I am come to know your pleasure.

ANGELO. That you might know it would much better please me
Than to demand what 'tis.° Your brother cannot live.

ISABELLA. Even so.—Heaven keep your honor!

ANGELO. Yet may he live awhile; and, it may be,
As long as you or I. Yet he must die.

ISABELLA. Under your sentence?

ANGELO. Yea.

ISABELLA. When, I beseech you?—that in his reprieve,

Longer or shorter, he may be so fitted°
That his soul sicken not.

ANGELO. Ha! Fie, these filthy vices! It were as good
To pardon him that hath from nature stolen
A man already made as to remit
Their saucy sweetness° that do coin heaven's image
In stamps° that are forbid. 'Tis all as easy
Falsely to take away a life true made
As to put metal in restrained° means
To make a false one.

ISABELLA. 'Tis set down so in heaven, but not in earth.

ANGELO. Say you so? Then I shall pose° you quickly.
Which had you rather—that the most just law
Now took your brother's life, or, to redeem him,
Give up your body to such sweet uncleanness
As she that he hath stain'd?

ISABELLA. Sir, believe this:
I had rather give my body than my soul.

ANGELO. I talk not of your soul. Our compell'd sins
Stand more for number than for accompt.°

ISABELLA. How say you?

ANGELO. Nay, I'll not warrant that, for I can speak
Against the thing I say. Answer to this:
I, now the voice of the recorded law,
Pronounce a sentence on your brother's life;
Might there not be a charity in sin
To save this brother's life?

ISABELLA. Please you to do't,
I'll take it as a peril to my soul,
It is no sin at all, but charity.

ANGELO. Pleas'd you to do't at peril of your soul,
Were equal poise° of sin and charity.

ISABELLA. That I do beg his life, if it be sin,
Heaven let me bear it! You granting of my suit,
If that be sin, I'll make it my morn prayer
To have it added to the faults of mine,
And nothing of your answer.

ANGELO. Nay, but hear me.
Your sense pursues not mine. Either you are ignorant,
Or seem so, craftily; and that's not good.

ISABELLA. Let me be ignorant, and in nothing good,
But graciously to know I am no better.

ANGELO. Thus wisdom wishes to appear most bright

state statecraft
fear'd (often emended to *sear'd,* dry)
boot advantage
air . . . vain which beats the air for vanity
case outward form   *Blood* passion
Let's . . . crest i.e., though we brand the devil's horn
(which is his most unmistakable mark of identification)
with the name of good angel, he is the devil still (with
verbal play on *Angelo* making the parallel between the
deputy and the devil)
general subject common subjects
That . . . 'tis (possibly spoken aside, with obvious play on
the unconscious sexual connotation of the preceding
line)

fitted i.e., for death
remit . . . sweetness pardon their licentious pleasures
stamps i.e., the dies for stamping coins
restrained forbidden
pose you i.e., pose a hypothetical problem
accompt judgment, final reckoning   *poise* balance

When it doth tax° itself, as these black masks
80 Proclaim an enshield° beauty ten times louder
Than beauty could, display'd. But mark me.
To be received plain, I'll speak more gross:
Your brother is to die.

ISABELLA. So.

85 ANGELO. And his offense is so, as it appears,
Accountant° to the law upon that pain.°

ISABELLA. True.

ANGELO. Admit no other way to save his life—
As I subscribe not that, nor any other,
90 But in the loss of question°—that you, his sister,
Finding yourself desir'd of such a person,
Whose credit with the judge, or own great place,
Could fetch your brother from the manacles
Of the all-building° law, and that there were
95 No earthly mean to save him but that either
You must lay down the treasures of your body
To this suppos'd° or else to let him suffer.
What would you do?

ISABELLA. As much for my poor brother as myself.
100 That is, were I under the terms of death,
Th' impression of keen whips I'd wear as rubies
And strip myself to death as to a bed
That longing have been sick for, ere I'd yield
My body up to shame.

ANGELO.   Then must your brother die.

105 ISABELLA. And 'twere the cheaper way.
Better it were a brother died at once
Than that a sister, by redeeming him,
Should die forever.

ANGELO. Were not you, then, as cruel as the sentence
110 That you have slander'd so?

ISABELLA. Ignomy in ransom° and free pardon
Are of two houses. Lawful mercy
Is nothing kin to foul redemption.

ANGELO. You seem'd of late to make the law a
tyrant,
115 And rather prov'd the sliding of your brother
A merriment than a vice.

ISABELLA. O, pardon me, my lord. It oft falls out,
To have what we would have, we speak not
what we mean.
I something° do excuse the thing I hate
120 For his advantage that I dearly love.

ANGELO. We are all frail.

ISABELLA.   Else let my brother die,
If not a feodary° but only he
Owe and succeed thy weakness.°

ANGELO. Nay, women are frail too.

ISABELLA. Aye, as the glasses where they view
themselves,   125
Which are as easy broke as they make forms.°
Women! Help, heaven! Men their creation mar
In profiting by them. Nay, call us ten times frail,
For we are soft as our complexions are,
And credulous° to false prints.

ANGELO.   I think it well,   130
And from this testimony of your own sex—
Since, I suppose, we are made to be no stronger
Than faults may shake our frames—let me be
bold.
I do arrest your words.° Be that you are,
That is, a woman; if you be more, you're none;   135
If you be one—as you are well express'd
By all external warrants—show it now
By putting on the destin'd livery.°

ISABELLA. I have no tongue but one. Gentle my
lord,
Let me entreat you speak the former language.   140

ANGELO. Plainly conceive, I love you.

ISABELLA. My brother did love Juliet,
And you tell me that he shall die for it.

ANGELO. He shall not, Isabel, if you give me love.

ISABELLA. I know your virtue hath a license in't,   145
Which seems a little fouler than it is,
To pluck on others.

ANGELO.   Believe me, on mine honor,
My words express my purpose.

ISABELLA. Ha! Little honor to be much believ'd,
And most pernicious purpose! Seeming, seem-
ing!   150
I will proclaim thee, Angelo; look for't.
Sign me a present pardon for my brother,
Or with an outstretch'd throat I'll tell the world
aloud
What man thou art.

ANGELO.   Who will believe thee, Isabel?
My unsoil'd name, th' austereness of my life,   155
My vouch against you, and my place i' the state
Will so your accusation overweigh
That you shall stifle in your own report
And smell of calumny. I have begun,
And now I give my sensual race the rein.   160
Fit thy consent to my sharp appetite.

---

tax castigate   *enshield* hidden   *Accountant* due
pain penalty
As I . . . question i.e., I do not commit myself one way or
   another except in the interest of the hypothetical case
all-building (possibly an error for *all-binding*)
suppos'd i.e., hypothetical person
Ignomy in ransom ignominious ransom
something somewhat

feodary accomplice
Else . . . weakness let my brother die for his weakness if
   it is not true that (as you say) we are all frail
forms images   *credulous* susceptible
I do . . . words I take you at your word
By . . . livery i.e., act like the woman you are

Lay by all nicety and prolixious° blushes
That banish what they sue for. Redeem thy
      brother
By yielding up thy body to my will—
165 Or else he must not only die the death,
But thy unkindness shall his death draw out
To ling'ring suff'rance.° Answer me tomorrow,
Or by th' affection° that now guides me most
I'll prove a tyrant to him. As for you,
170 Say what you can, my false o'erweighs your true.
                                                    [Exit]
ISABELLA. To whom should I complain? Did I tell
      this,
Who would believe me? O perilous mouths
That bear in them one and the self-same tongue

prolixious gratuitous   suff'rance suffering
affection passion

Either of condemnation or approof,°
Bidding the law make court'sy to their will,   175
Hooking both right and wrong to th' appetite,
To follow as it draws! I'll to my brother.
Though he hath fall'n by prompture of the
      blood,
Yet hath he in him such a mind of honor
That had he twenty heads to tender down   180
On twenty bloody blocks he'd yield them up
Before his sister should her body stoop
To such abhorr'd pollution.
Then, Isabel, live chaste, and, brother, die:
More than our brother is our chastity.   185
I'll tell him yet of Angelo's request,
And fit his mind to death, for his soul's rest.
                                                    [Exit]

approof approval

ACT III

SCENE i
A room in the prison.

[Enter DUKE disguised as before, CLAUDIO, and
PROVOST.]
DUKE. So, then, you hope of pardon from Lord
      Angelo?
CLAUDIO. The miserable have no other medicine
      But only hope.
I've hope to live, and am prepar'd to die.
5 DUKE. Be absolute for° death; either death or life
Shall thereby be the sweeter. Reason thus with
      life:
If I do lose thee, I do lose a thing
That none but fools would keep. A breath thou
      art,
Servile to all the skyey° influences
10 That dost this habitation where thou keep'st
Hourly afflict. Merely,° thou art death's fool,
For him thou labor'st by thy flight to shun
And yet runn'st toward him still. Thou art not
      noble,
For all th' accommodations° that thou bear'st
Are nurs'd by baseness. Thou'rt by no means
15   valiant,
For thou dost fear the soft and tender fork

Be . . . for expect absolutely   skyey planetary
Merely purely
accommodations conveniences, niceties

Of a poor worm.° Thy best of rest is sleep,
And that thou oft provok'st, yet grossly fear'st
Thy death, which is no more. Thou'rt not thyself,
For thou exist'st on many a thousand grains   20
That issue out of dust. Happy thou'rt not,
For what thou has not, still thou striv'st to get,
And what thou hast, forget'st. Thou art not cer-
      tain,°
For thy complexion° shifts to strange effects,
After the moon. If thou art rich, thou'rt poor,   25
For like an ass whose back with ingots bows,
Thou bear'st thy heavy riches but a journey,
And death unloads thee. Friend hast thou none,
For thine own bowels,° which do call thee sire,
The mere effusion of thy proper° loins,   30
Do curse the gout, serpigo,° and the rheum°
For ending thee no sooner. Thou hast nor youth
      nor age,
But, as it were, an after-dinner's sleep
Dreaming on both; for all thy blessed youth
Becomes as aged, and doth beg the alms   35
Of palsied eld;° and when thou'rt old and rich,
Thou'st neither heat, affection, limb, nor beauty
To make thy riches pleasant. What's yet in this

fork . . . worm forked tongue of a snake
certain constant
complexion physiological make-up; temperament
bowels offspring   proper own
serpigo skin eruption   rheum cold (in the head)
Of . . . eld due to old age

That bears the name of life? Yet in this life
40 Lie hid moe thousand deaths. Yet death we fear,
    That makes these odds all even.
CLAUDIO.   I humbly thank you.
    To sue to live, I find I seek to die;
    And, seeking death, find life. Let it come on.
ISABELLA. [*Within*] What, ho! Peace here; grace and
        good company!
PROVOST. Who's there? Come in. The wish de-
45   serves a welcome.
DUKE. Dear sir, ere long I'll visit you again.
CLAUDIO. Most holy sir, I thank you.
            [*Enter* ISABELLA.]
ISABELLA. My business is a word or two with
        Claudio.
PROVOST. And very welcome. Look, signior, here's
        your sister.
50 DUKE. Provost, a word with you.
PROVOST. As many as you please.
DUKE. Bring me to hear them speak where I may
        be conceal'd.   [*Exeunt* DUKE *and* PROVOST.]
CLAUDIO. Now, sister, what's the comfort?
ISABELLA.   Why,
    As all comforts are, most good, most good in-
        deed.
55 Lord Angelo, having affairs to heaven,
    Intends you for his swift ambassador,
    Where you shall be an everlasting leiger.°
    Therefore your best appointment make with
        speed;
    Tomorrow you set on.
CLAUDIO.   Is there no remedy?
60 ISABELLA. None but such remedy as, to save a head,
    To cleave a heart in twain.
CLAUDIO.   But is there any?
ISABELLA. Yes, brother, you may live.
    There is a dev'lish mercy in the judge,
    If you'll implore it, that will free your life,
    But fetter you till death.
65 CLAUDIO.   Perpetual durance?
ISABELLA. Aye, just°—perpetual durance, a re-
        straint,
    Though all the world's vastidity° you had,
    To a determin'd scope.
CLAUDIO.   But in what nature?
ISABELLA. In such a one as, you consenting to't,
    Would bark° your honor from that trunk you
70   bear
    And leave you naked.
CLAUDIO.   Let me know the point.
ISABELLA. O, I do fear thee, Claudio, and I quake,

Lest thou a fev'rous life shouldst entertain
And six or seven winters more respect
Than a perpetual honor. Dar'st thou die?   75
The sense of death is most in apprehension,
And the poor beetle that we tread upon,
In corp'ral suff'rance° finds a pang as great
As when a giant dies.
CLAUDIO.   Why give you me this shame?
    Think you I can a resolution fetch°
    From flow'ry tenderness? If I must die,   80
    I will encounter darkness as a bride
    And hug it in mine arms.
ISABELLA. There spake my brother; there my
        father's grave
    Did utter forth a voice. Yes, thou must die.
    Thou art too noble to conserve a life   85
    In base appliances.° This outward-sainted
        deputy,
    Whose settled° visage and deliberate word
    Nips youth i' the head, and follies doth emmew
    As falcon doth the fowl,° is yet a devil.
    His filth within being cast,° he would appear   90
    A pond as deep as hell.
CLAUDIO.   The prenzie° Angelo!
ISABELLA. O, 'tis the cunning livery of hell,
    The damned'st body to invest° and cover
    In prenzie guards!° Dost thou think, Claudio?—
    If I would yield him my virginity,   95
    Thou mightst be freed.
CLAUDIO.   O heavens! It cannot be.
ISABELLA. Yes, he would give't thee, from this rank
        offense,
    So to offend him still.° This night's the time
    That I should do what I abhor to name,
    Or else thou diest tomorrow.
CLAUDIO.   Thou shalt not do't. 100
ISABELLA. O, were it but my life,
    I'd throw it down for your deliverance
    As frankly as a pin.
CLAUDIO.   Thanks, dear Isabel.
ISABELLA. Be ready, Claudio, for your death tomor-
        row.

corp'ral suff'rance bodily suffering
resolution fetch find strength
In . . . appliances by base means
settled solemn
follies . . . fowl keeps frivolous pleasures mewed up
    (cooped up) as fear of the falcon keeps the fowl in its
    coop
cast vomited up
prenzie (of uncertain meaning, possibly a misprint;
    precise, *prim*, and *proxy* are among replacements
    suggested)
invest clothe   *guards* trimmings
he . . . still in return for my sin he would grant you
    freedom to go on sinning

leiger permanent ambassador   *just* exactly
vastidity vastness   *To . . . scope* for your allotted range
bark strip

105 CLAUDIO. Yes. Has he affections° in him
        That thus can make him bite the law by the
            nose,
        When he would force° it? Sure, it is no sin,
        Or of the deadly seven it is the least.
    ISABELLA. Which is the least?
110 CLAUDIO. If it were damnable, he being so wise,
        Why would he for the momentary trick
        Be perdurably fin'd?°—O Isabel!
    ISABELLA. What says my brother?
    CLAUDIO.   Death is a fearful thing.
    ISABELLA. And shamed life a hateful.
    CLAUDIO. Aye, but to die, and go we know not
115   where;
        To lie in cold obstruction° and to rot;
        This sensible warm motion to become
        A kneaded clod, and the delighted° spirit
        To bathe in fiery floods, or to reside
120   In thrilling region of thick-ribbed ice;
        To be imprison'd in the viewless° winds
        And blown with restless violence round about
        The pendent° world; or to be worse than worst
        Of those that lawless and incertain thought
125   Imagine howling. 'Tis too horrible!
        The weariest and most loathed worldly life
        That age, ache, penury, and imprisonment
        Can lay on nature is a paradise
        To what we fear of death.
    ISABELLA. Alas, alas!
130 CLAUDIO.   Sweet sister, let me live.
        What sin you do to save a brother's life,
        Nature dispenses with° the deed so far
        That it becomes a virtue.
    ISABELLA.   O you beast!
        O faithless coward! O dishonest wretch!
135   Wilt thou be made a man out of my vice?
        Is't not a kind of incest, to take life
        From thine own sister's shame? What should I
            think?
        Heaven shield° my mother play'd my father
            fair!
        For such a warped slip of wilderness°
140   Ne'er issu'd from his blood. Take my defiance!
        Die, perish! Might but my bending down
        Reprieve thee from thy fate, it should proceed.
        I'll pray a thousand prayers for thy death,
        No word to save thee.

CLAUDIO. Nay, hear me, Isabel.
ISABELLA.   O, fie, fie, fie!   145
    Thy sin's not accidental, but a trade.°
    Mercy to thee would prove itself a bawd.
    'Tis best that thou diest quickly.
CLAUDIO.   O, hear me, Isabella!
                [Re-enter DUKE.]
DUKE. Vouchsafe a word, young sister, but one
        word.
ISABELLA. What is your will?   150
DUKE. Might you dispense with your leisure, I
    would by and by have some speech with you.
    The satisfaction I would require is likewise your
    own benefit.
ISABELLA. I have no superfluous leisure; my stay   155
    must be stolen out of other affairs. But I will
    attend you awhile.   [Walks apart]
DUKE. Son, I have overheard what hath passed be-
    tween you and your sister. Angelo had never the
    purpose to corrupt her; only he hath made an   160
    assay of her virtue to practice his judgment with
    the disposition of natures.° She, having the truth
    of honor in her, hath made him that gracious
    denial which he is most glad to receive. I am con-
    fessor to Angelo, and I know this to be true;   165
    therefore prepare yourself to death. Do not
    satisfy your resolution with hopes that are
    fallible.° Tomorrow you must die; go to your
    knees, and make ready.
CLAUDIO. Let me ask my sister pardon. I am so out 170
    of love with life that I will sue to be rid of it.
DUKE. Hold you there. Farewell. [Exit CLAUDIO]
    Provost, a word with you!
                [Re-enter PROVOST.]
PROVOST. What's your will, father?
DUKE. That now you are come, you will be gone.   175
    Leave me awhile with the maid. My mind
    promises with my habit no loss shall touch her
    by my company.
PROVOST. In good time.
            [Exit PROVOST. ISABELLA comes forward.]
DUKE. The hand that hath made you fair hath   180
    made you good. The goodness that is cheap in
    beauty makes beauty brief in goodness; but
    grace, being the soul of your complexion,° shall
    keep the body of it ever fair. The assault that
    Angelo hath made to you, fortune hath con-   185
    veyed to my understanding; and, but that frailty
    hath examples for his falling, I should wonder at

affections passions   *force* enforce
perdurably fin'd eternally punished
obstruction immovableness
delighted capable of being delighted
viewless invisible   *pendent* suspended (in space)
dispenses with grants dispensation for   *shield* forbid
warped . . . wilderness reversion of the graft to the wild
    stock (horticultural image)

trade i.e., habitual way
practice . . . natures test his own ability to judge character
satisfy . . . fallible sustain your courage with false hopes
complexion character (with play on modern sense of the
    word)

Angelo. How will you do to content this substitute, and to save your brother?

190 ISABELLA. I am now going to resolve him.° I had rather my brother die by the law than my son should be unlawfully born. But, O, how much is the good Duke deceived in Angelo! If ever he return and I can speak to him, I will open my
195 lips in vain, or discover° his government.

DUKE. That shall not be much amiss. Yet, as the matter now stands, he will avoid your accusation; he made trial of you only. Therefore fasten your ear on my advisings. To the love I have in
200 doing good a remedy presents itself. I do make myself believe that you may most uprighteously do a poor wronged lady a merited benefit, redeem your brother from the angry law, do no stain to your own gracious person, and much
205 please the absent Duke, if peradventure he shall ever return to have hearing of this business.

ISABELLA. Let me hear you speak farther. I have spirit to do anything that appears not foul in the truth of my spirit.

210 DUKE. Virtue is bold, and goodness never fearful. Have you not heard speak of Mariana, the sister of Frederick, the great soldier who miscarried at sea?

ISABELLA. I have heard of the lady, and good words
215 went with her name.

DUKE. She should this Angelo have married, was affianced to her by oath, and the nuptial appointed—between which time of the contract and limit of the solemnity° her brother Frede-
220 rick was wrecked at sea, having in that perished vessel the dowry of his sister. But mark how heavily this befell to the poor gentlewoman. There she lost a noble and renowned brother, in his love toward her ever most kind and natural;
225 with him, the portion and sinew of her fortune, her marriage dowry; with both, her combinate° husband, this well-seeming Angelo.

ISABELLA. Can this be so? Did Angelo so leave her?

DUKE. Left her in her tears and dried not one of
230 them with his comfort, swallowed his vows whole, pretending in her discoveries of dishonor; in few, bestowed her on her own lamentation, which she yet wears for his sake, and he, a marble to her tears, is washed with them but relents
235 not.

ISABELLA. What a merit were it in death to take this poor maid from the world! What corruption in this life, that it will let this man live! But how out of this can she avail?

DUKE. It is a rupture that you may easily heal, and 240 the cure of it not only saves your brother but keeps you from dishonor in doing it.

ISABELLA. Show me how, good father.

DUKE. This forenamed maid hath yet in her the continuance of her first affection. His unjust un- 245 kindness, that in all reason should have quenched her love, hath, like an impediment in the current, made it more violent and unruly. Go you to Angelo. Answer his requiring with a plausible obedience; agree with his demands to the point; 250 only refer yourself to this advantage:° first, that your stay with him may not be long, that the time may have all shadow and silence in it, and the place answer to convenience. This being granted in course—and now follows all—we 255 shall advise this wronged maid to stead up your appointment,° go in your place. If the encounter acknowledge itself hereafter, it may compel him to her recompense. And here, by this, is your brother saved, your honor untainted, the poor 260 Mariana advantaged, and the corrupt Deputy scaled.° The maid will I frame° and make fit for his attempt. If you think well to carry this as you may, the doubleness of the benefit defends the deceit from reproof. What think you of it? 265

ISABELLA. The image of it gives me content already, and I trust it will grow to a most prosperous perfection.

DUKE. It lies much in your holding up. Haste you speedily to Angelo. If for this night he entreat 270 you to his bed, give him promise of satisfaction. I will presently° to Saint Luke's; there, at the moated grange,° resides this dejected Mariana. At that place call upon me; and dispatch with° Angelo, that it may be quickly. 275

ISABELLA. I thank you for this comfort. Fare you well, good father.   [Exeunt severally.]

---

refer . . . advantage   make requirement of the following conditions
stead . . . appointment   keep the appointment in your place
scaled   placed in the scales for judgment
frame   prepare   presently   immediately
moated grange   farmhouse surrounded by a moat
dispatch with   come to an agreement with

---

resolve him   give him my answer   discover   expose
limit . . . solemnity   date of the wedding
combinate   affianced

SCENE ii
The street before the prison.

[*Enter, on one side,* DUKE *disguised as before; on the other,* ELBOW, *and* OFFICERS *with* POMPEY.]

ELBOW. Nay, if there be no remedy for it but that you will needs buy and sell men and women like beasts, we shall have all the world drink brown and white bastard.°

5 DUKE. O heavens! What stuff is here?

POMPEY. 'Twas never merry world since, of two usuries, the merriest° was put down and the worser° allowed by order of law a furred gown to keep him warm—and furred with fox and

10 lambskins too, to signify that craft, being richer than innocency, stands for the facing.°

ELBOW. Come your way, sir. 'Bless you, good father friar.

DUKE. And you, good brother father. What offense

15 hath this man made you, sir?

ELBOW. Marry, sir, he hath offended the law. And, sir, we take him to be a thief too, sir, for we have found upon him, sir, a strange picklock which we have sent to the Deputy.

20 DUKE. Fie, sirrah! A bawd, a wicked bawd!
The evil that thou causest to be done,
That is thy means to live. Do thou but think
What 'tis to cram a maw or clothe a back
From such a filthy vice. Say to thyself,

25 "From their abominable and beastly touches
I drink, I eat, array myself, and live."
Canst thou believe thy living is a life,
So stinkingly depending? Go mend, go mend.

POMPEY. Indeed, it does stink in some sort, sir; but

30 yet, sir, I would prove—

DUKE. Nay, if the devil have given thee proofs for sin,
Thou wilt prove his. Take him to prison, officer.
Correction and instruction must both work
Ere this rude beast will profit.

35 ELBOW. He must before the Deputy, sir; he has given him warning. The Deputy cannot abide a whoremaster. If he be a whoremonger, and comes before him, he were as good go a mile on his errand.°

40 DUKE. That we were all, as some would seem to be,
From our faults, as faults from seeming, free!

ELBOW. His neck will come to your waist—a cord, sir.°

POMPEY. I spy comfort; I cry bail. Here's a gentleman and a friend of mine.   45

[*Enter* LUCIO.]

LUCIO. How now, noble Pompey! What, at the wheels of Cæsar?° Art thou led in triumph? What, is there none of Pygmalion's images,° newly made woman, to be had now, for putting the hand in the pocket and extracting it clut-   50 ched?° What reply, ha? What sayest thou to this tune, matter and method? Is't not drowned i' the last rain, ha? What sayest thou, Trot?° Is the world as it was, man? Which is the way? Is it sad, and few words? Or how? The trick of it?°   55

DUKE. Still thus, and thus; still worse!

LUCIO. How doth my dear morsel, thy mistress? Procures she still, ha?

POMPEY. Troth, sir, she hath eaten up all her beef, and she is herself in the tub.°   60

LUCIO. Why, 'tis good, it is the right of it, it must be so. Ever your fresh whore and your powdered bawd. An unshunned consequence; it must be so. Art going to prison, Pompey?

POMPEY. Yes, faith, sir.   65

LUCIO. Why, 'tis not amiss, Pompey. Farewell. Go say I sent thee thither. For debt, Pompey? Or how?

ELBOW. For being a bawd, for being a bawd.

LUCIO. Well, then, imprison him. If imprisonment   70 be the due of a bawd, why, 'tis his right. Bawd is he doubtless, and of antiquity too—bawd-born. Farewell, good Pompey. Commend me to the prison, Pompey. You will turn good husband now, Pompey; you will keep the house.°   75

POMPEY. I hope, sir, your good worship will be my bail.

LUCIO. No, indeed, will I not, Pompey; it is not the wear.° I will pray, Pompey, to increase your bondage. If you take it not patiently, why, your   80

His neck . . . sir (allusion to the friar's hempen rope about his waist, suitable also for hanging Pompey)
wheels of Caesar who defeated Pompey
Pygmalion's images (Pygmalion's statue was given life by Aphrodite)
clutched i.e., holding the prostitute's fee
Trot appropriate nickname for a busy pimp
What reply . . . trick of it (Lucio exhibits a range of contemporary slang and catch phrases, at the level of "Twenty-three skiddoo")
in the tub tub for corning beef; but also for boiling out venereal diseases
husband . . . house i.e., a good housekeeper because he will "keep the house"—stay locked in
wear fashion

---

bastard sweet Spanish wine
merriest i.e., prostitution   *worser* moneylending
stands . . . facing can afford the trimming
go . . . errand i.e., is as good as lost

mettle is the more. Adieu, trusty Pompey.
'Bless you, friar.

DUKE. And you.

LUCIO. Does Bridget paint still, Pompey, ha?

85 ELBOW. Come your ways, sir. Come.

POMPEY. You will not bail me, then, sir?

LUCIO. Then, Pompey, nor now. What news
abroad, friar? What news?

ELBOW. Come your ways, sir. Come.

90 LUCIO. Go to kennel, Pompey; go. [*Exeunt* ELBOW,
POMPEY, *and* OFFICERS] What news, friar, of the
Duke?

DUKE. I know none. Can you tell me of any?

LUCIO. Some say he is with the Emperor of Russia;
95 other some, he is in Rome. But where is he,
think you?

DUKE. I know not where; but wheresoever, I wish
him well.

LUCIO. It was a mad fantastical trick of him to steal
100 from the state and usurp the beggary he was
never born to. Lord Angelo dukes it well in his
absence. He puts transgression to't.

DUKE. He does well in't.

LUCIO. A little more lenity to lechery would do no
105 harm in him. Something too crabbed that way,
friar.

DUKE. It is too general a vice, and severity must
cure it.

LUCIO. Yes, in good sooth, the vice is of a great kin-
110 dred; it is well allied. But it is impossible to
extirp° it quite, friar, till eating and drinking be
put down. They say this Angelo was not made
by man and woman after this downright way of
creation. Is it true, think you?

115 DUKE. How should he be made, then?

LUCIO. Some report a sea maid spawned him;
some, that he was begot between two stock-
fishes. But it is certain that when he makes water
his urine is congealed ice. That I know to be true.
120 And he is a motion generative;° that's infallible.

DUKE. You are pleasant, sir, and speak apace.

LUCIO. Why, what a ruthless thing is this in him,
for the rebellion of a codpiece° to take away the
life of a man! Would the Duke that is absent
125 have done this? Ere he would have hanged a
man for the getting a hundred bastards, he
would have paid for the nursing a thousand. He
had some feeling of the sport. He knew the service, and that instructed him to mercy.

130 DUKE. I never heard the absent Duke much detected for° women. He was not inclined that way.

LUCIO. O, sir, you are deceived.

DUKE. 'Tis not possible.

LUCIO. Who, not the Duke? Yes, your beggar of
fifty,° and his use° was to put a ducat in her clack- 135
dish.° The Duke had crotchets° in him. He would
be drunk too—that let me inform you.

DUKE. You do him wrong, surely.

LUCIO. Sir, I was an inward° of his. A shy fellow was
the Duke. And I believe I know the cause of his 140
withdrawing.

DUKE. What, I prithee, might be the cause?

LUCIO. No, pardon; 'tis a secret must be locked
within the teeth and the lips. But this I can let
you understand. The greater file° of the subject 145
held the Duke to be wise.

DUKE. Wise! Why, no question but he was.

LUCIO. A very superficial, ignorant, unweighing
fellow.

DUKE. Either this is envy in you, folly, or mistaking. 150
The very stream of his life and the business he
hath helmed° must, upon a warranted need,°
give him a better proclamation. Let him be but
testimonied in his own bringings-forth,° and he
shall appear to the envious a scholar, a states- 155
man, and a soldier. Therefore you speak unskilfully;° or if your knowledge be more, it is much
darkened in your malice.

LUCIO. Sir, I know him, and I love him.

DUKE. Love talks with better knowledge, and 160
knowledge with dearer love.

LUCIO. Come, sir, I know what I know.

DUKE. I can hardly believe that, since you know not
what you speak. But if ever the Duke return, as
our prayers are he may, let me desire you to 165
make your answer before him. If it be honest you
have spoke, you have courage to maintain it. I
am bound to call upon you. And, I pray you,
your name?

LUCIO. Sir, my name is Lucio, well known to the 170
Duke.

DUKE. He shall know you better, sir, if I may live to
report you.

LUCIO. I fear you not.

DUKE. O, you hope the Duke will return no more, 175
or you imagine me too unhurtful an opposite.°
But, indeed, I can do you little harm; you'll forswear this again.

---

your . . . fifty i.e., even with an old beggarwoman
use custom
clack-dish covered alms-dish, rattled to draw attention
crotchets eccentricities   *inward* buddy
greater file majority   *helmed* steered
upon . . . need if called for
bringings-forth accomplishments
unskilfully unknowledgeably   *opposite* opponent

---

extirp extirpate, root out
motion generative puppet with powers of procreation
for . . . codpiece i.e., because his lust took control of him
detected for accused of

LUCIO. I'll be hanged first. Thou art deceived in
180 me, friar. But no more of this. Canst thou tell if
Claudio die tomorrow or no?

DUKE. Why should he die, sir?

LUCIO. Why? For filling a bottle with a tun-dish.°
I would the Duke we talk of were returned
185 again. This ungenitured° agent will unpeople the
province with continency. Sparrows must not
build in his house-eaves, because they are
lecherous. The Duke yet would have dark deeds
darkly answered;° he would never bring them to
190 light. Would he were returned! Marry, this
Claudio is condemned for untrussing.° Farewell,
good friar. I prithee, pray for me. The Duke, I
say to thee again, would eat mutton on Fridays.°
He's not past it yet, and I say to thee, he would
195 mouth with a beggar though she smelt brown
bread and garlic. Say that I said so. Farewell.
[Exit]

DUKE. No might nor greatness in mortality°
Can censure 'scape; back-wounding calumny
The whitest virtue strikes. What king so strong
200 Can tie the gall up in the sland'rous tongue?
But who comes here?
[Enter ESCALUS, PROVOST, and OFFICERS with
MISTRESS OVERDONE.]

ESCALUS. Go. Away with her to prison!

MISTRESS OVERDONE. Good my lord, be good to me.
Your honor is accounted a merciful man, good
205 my lord.

ESCALUS. Double and treble admonition, and still
forfeit in the same kind!° This would make
mercy swear and play the tyrant.

PROVOST. A bawd of eleven years' continuance,
210 may it please your honor.

MISTRESS OVERDONE. My lord, this is one Lucio's
information against me. Mistress Kate Keep-
down was with child by him in the Duke's time.
He promised her marriage. His child is a year and
215 a quarter old, come Philip and Jacob.° I have
kept it myself. And see how he goes about to
abuse me!

ESCALUS. That fellow is a fellow of much license.
Let him be called before us. Away with her to
220 prison! Go to; no more words. [Exeunt OFFICERS
with MISTRESS OVERDONE] Provost, my brother
Angelo will not be altered; Claudio must die

tomorrow. Let him be furnished with divines
and have all charitable preparation. If my
brother wrought by° my pity, it should not be 225
so with him.

PROVOST. So please you, this friar hath been with
him and advised him for the entertainment of
death.

ESCALUS. Good even, good father. 230

DUKE. Bliss and goodness on you!

ESCALUS. Of whence are you?

DUKE. Not of this country, though my chance is
now
To use it for my time.° I am a brother
Of gracious order, late come from the See° 235
In special business from his Holiness.

ESCALUS. What news abroad i' the world?

DUKE. None but that there is so great a fever on
goodness that the dissolution of it° must cure it.
Novelty is only in request, and it is as dangerous° 240
to be aged in any kind of course as it is virtuous
to be constant in any undertaking. There is
scarce truth enough alive to make societies
secure, but security enough to make fellowships
accurst.° Much upon this riddle runs the wisdom 245
of the world. This news is old enough, yet it is
every day's news. I pray you, sir, of what disposition was the Duke?

ESCALUS. One that, above all other strifes, conten-
ded especially to know himself. 250

DUKE. What pleasure was he given to?

ESCALUS. Rather rejoicing to see another merry
than merry at anything which professed to make
him rejoice. A gentleman of all temperance. But
leave we him to his events, with a prayer they 255
may prove prosperous, and let me desire to
know how you find Claudio prepared. I am
made to understand that you have lent him
visitation.

DUKE. He professes to have received no sinister 260
measure° from his judge, but most willingly
humbles himself to the determination of justice.
Yet had he framed to himself, by the instruction
of his frailty, many deceiving promises of life,
which I, by my good leisure, have discredited to 265
him. And now is he resolved to die.

---

tun-dish funnel; with obvious figurative connotation
ungenitured sexless   darkly answered kept secret
untrussing unfastening his breeches
eat . . . Fridays i.e., violate a fasting day; but also,
  patronize a prostitute (mutton)
mortality mortal life
forfeit . . . king guilty of the same offense
Philip . . . Jacob St. Philip's and St. James' day, May 1

wrought by acted according to
To . . . time i.e., to spend some time here
See i.e., the Holy See of Rome
dissolution . . . it only the death of goodness will cure its
  fever
it is . . . dangerous it is as dangerous to be constant in
  anything as it is virtuous to be so
but . . . accurst such are the demands for (legal) surety
  that the bonds of friendship are blasted
sinister measure unjust judgment

ESCALUS. You have paid the heavens your function
   and the prisoner the very debt of your calling. I
   have labored for the poor gentleman to the
270   extremest shore of my modesty.° But my
   brother justice have I found so severe that he
   hath forced me to tell him he is indeed Justice.
DUKE. If his own life answer the straitness of his
   proceeding, it shall become him well; wherein if
275   he chance to fail, he hath sentenced himself.
ESCALUS. I am going to visit the prisoner. Fare you
   well.
DUKE. Peace be with you!

            [*Exeunt* ESCALUS *and* PROVOST.]
   He who the sword of heaven will bear
280   Should be as holy as severe;
   Pattern in himself to know,°
   Grace to stand and virtue go,°

More nor less to others paying
Than by self-offenses weighing.
Shame to him whose cruel striking   285
Kills for faults of his own liking!
Twice treble shame on Angelo,
To weed my vice and let his grow!
O, what may man within him hide,
Though angel on the outward side!   290
How may likeness made in crimes,
Making practice on the times,
To draw with idle spiders' strings
Most pond'rous and substantial things!°
Craft against vice I must apply.   295
With Angelo tonight shall lie
His old betrothed but despis'd;
So disguise shall, by the disguis'd,
Pay with falsehood false exacting,
And perform an old contracting.°   [*Exit*]   300

---

modesty   sense of propriety
Pattern . . . know   i.e., live up to the conduct that he
   requires of others
go   to proceed

How . . . things   (an unexplained and possibly corrupt
   passage)
old contracting   i.e., of Angelo and Mariana (III, i, 216ff.)

ACT IV

SCENE i
The moated grange at ST. LUKE'S.

[*Enter* MARIANA *and a* BOY.]
BOY.

[*Sings*] Take, O take those lips away,
    That so sweetly were forsworn,
   And those eyes, the break of day,
    Lights that do mislead the morn.
5   But my kisses bring again, bring again,
    Seals of love, but seal'd in vain, seal'd in vain.

MARIANA. Break off thy song and haste thee quick
   away.
   Here comes a man of comfort, whose advice
   Hath often still'd my brawling° discontent.
                  [*Exit* BOY.]
      [*Enter* DUKE *disguised as before.*]
10   I cry you mercy, sir, and well could wish
   You had not found me here so musical.
   Let me excuse me, and believe me so,
   My mirth it much displeas'd, but pleas'd my
   woe.
DUKE. 'Tis good, though music oft hath such a
   charm

To make bad good and good provoke to harm.   15
   I pray you tell me, hath anybody inquired for me
   here today? Much upon this time have I pro-
   mised here to meet.
MARIANA. You have not been inquired after. I
   have sat here all day.   20
            [*Enter* ISABELLA.]
DUKE. I do constantly believe you. The time is
   come even now. I shall crave your forbearance a
   little. May be I will call upon you anon, for some
   advantage to yourself.
MARIANA. I am always bound to you.   [*Exit*]   25
DUKE. Very well met, and well come.
   What is the news from this good Deputy?
ISABELLA. He hath a garden circummur'd° with
   brick,
   Whose western side is with a vineyard back'd.
   And to that vineyard is a planched° gate   30
   That makes his opening with this bigger key.
   This other doth command a little door
   Which from the vineyard to the garden leads.
   There have I made my promise
   Upon the heavy middle of the night   35
   To call upon him.

---

brawling   tumultuous

circummur'd   walled around   *planched*   planked

DUKE. But shall you on your knowledge find this
    way?

ISABELLA. I have ta'en a due and wary note upon 't.
    With whisp'ring and most guilty diligence,
40   In action all of precept,° he did show me
    The way twice o'er.

DUKE.   Are there no other tokens
    Between you 'greed concerning her observance?

ISABELLA. No, none, but only a repair i' the dark,
    And that I have possess'd him my most stay
45   Can be but brief; for I have made him know
    I have a servant comes with me along
    That stays upon me, whose persuasion is
    I come about my brother.

DUKE.   'Tis well borne up.
    I have not yet made known to Mariana
50   A word of this. What, ho! Within! Come forth!

        [Re-enter MARIANA.]
    I pray you, be acquainted with this maid.
    She comes to do you good.

ISABELLA.   I do desire the like.

DUKE. Do you persuade yourself that I respect you?

MARIANA. Good friar, I know you do, and have
    found it.

DUKE. Take, then, this your companion by the
55   hand,
    Who hath a story ready for your ear.
    I shall attend your leisure. But make haste;
    The vaporous night approaches.

MARIANA. Will't please you walk aside?

        [Exeunt MARIANA and ISABELLA.]

60 DUKE. O place and greatness, millions of false eyes
    Are stuck° upon thee! Volumes of report
    Run with these false and most contrarious
    quests°
    Upon thy doings! Thousand escapes° of wit
    Make thee the father of their idle dreams
    And rack thee° in their fancies!

        [Re-enter MARIANA and ISABELLA.]
65   Welcome. How agreed?

ISABELLA. She'll take the enterprise upon her,
    father,
    If you advise it.

DUKE.   It is not my consent,
    But my entreaty too.

ISABELLA.   Little have you to say
    When you depart from him, but, soft and low,
    "Remember now my brother."

70 MARIANA.   Fear me not.

DUKE. Nor, gentle daughter, fear you not at all.

In . . . precept with instructive actions
stuck fixed   *quests* pursuits (a hunting image)
escapes sallies
rack thee stretch you on the rack

He is your husband on a pre-contract.
To bring you thus together 'tis no sin,
Sith° that the justice of your title to him
Doth flourish° the deceit. Come, let us go.   75
Our corn's to reap, for yet our tithe's to sow.°

        [Exeunt]

SCENE ii
A room in the prison.

[Enter PROVOST and POMPEY.]

PROVOST. Come hither, sirrah. Can you cut off a
    man's head?

POMPEY. If the man be a bachelor, sir, I can, but if
    he be a married man, he's his wife's head, and I
    can never cut off a woman's head.   5

PROVOST. Come, sir, leave me your snatches° and
    yield me a direct answer. Tomorrow morning
    are to die Claudio and Barnardine. Here is in our
    prison a common executioner, who in his office
    lacks a helper. If you will take it on you to assist   10
    him, it shall redeem you from your gyves;° if not,
    you shall have your full time of imprisonment,
    and your deliverance with an unpitied whipping,
    for you have been a notorious bawd.

POMPEY. Sir, I have been an unlawful bawd time   15
    out of mind; but yet I will content to be a lawful
    hangman. I would be glad to receive some in-
    struction from my fellow partner.

PROVOST. What, ho! Abhorson! Where's Abhor-
    son, there?   20

        [Enter ABHORSON.]

ABHORSON. Do you call, sir?

PROVOST. Sirrah, here's a fellow will help you to-
    morrow in your execution. If you think it meet,
    compound° with him by the year and let him
    abide here with you; if not, use him for the   25
    present and dismiss him. He cannot plead his
    estimation° with you; he hath been a bawd.

ABHORSON. A bawd, sir? Fie upon him! He will dis-
    credit our mystery.°

PROVOST. Go to, sir, you weigh equally;° a feather   30
    will turn the scale.   *[Exit]*

POMPEY. Pray, sir, by your good favor—for surely,
    sir, a good favor° you have, but that you have a

Sith since   *flourish* embellish
tithe's to sow our tithe (tenth part of the corn) is yet to
    be sowed
snatches cracks   *gyves* fetters
compound agree to terms   *estimation* reputation
mystery trade
weigh equally i.e., a bawd is no worse than an
    executioner
favor face (with obvious pun)

35 hanging look—do you call, sir, your occupation
a mystery?

ABHORSON. Aye, sir, a mystery.

POMPEY. Painting, sir, I have heard say, is a mystery,
and your whores, sir, being members of my
occupation, using painting, do prove my occupa-
40 tion a mystery. But what mystery there should
be in hanging, if I should be hanged, I cannot
imagine.

ABHORSON. Sir, it is a mystery.

POMPEY. Proof?

45 ABHORSON. Every true° man's apparel fits your
thief. If it be too little for your thief, your true
man thinks it big enough; if it be too big for your
thief, your thief thinks it little enough. So every
man's apparel fits your thief.

[Re-enter PROVOST.]

50 PROVOST. Are you agreed?

POMPEY. Sir, I will serve him, for I do find your
hangman is a more penitent trade than your
bawd. He doth oftener ask forgiveness.°

PROVOST. You, sirrah, provide your block and your
55 axe tomorrow four o'clock.

ABHORSON. Come on, bawd, I will instruct thee in
my trade. Follow.

POMPEY. I do desire to learn, sir, and I hope, if you
have occasion to use me for your own turn, you
60 shall find me yare;° for, truly, sir, for your kindness I owe you a good turn.

PROVOST. Call hither Barnardine and Claudio.

[Exeunt POMPEY and ABHORSON.]

The one has my pity, not a jot the other,
Being a murderer, though he were my brother.

[Enter CLAUDIO.]

65 Look, here's the warrant, Claudio, for thy death.
'Tis now dead midnight, and by eight tomorrow
Thou must be made immortal. Where's Barnar-
dine?

CLAUDIO. As fast lock'd up in sleep as guiltless
labor
When it lies starkly in the traveler's bones.
He will not wake.

70 PROVOST.   Who can do good on him?
Well, go, prepare yourself. [Knocking within] But
hark, what noise?—
Heaven give your spirits comfort! [Exit CLAUDIO]
By and by.—
I hope it is some pardon or reprieve
For the most gentle Claudio.

[Enter DUKE disguised as before.]
          Welcome, father.

true honest
ask forgiveness   hangmen customarily asked their victims'
forgiveness
yare quick, ready

DUKE. The best and wholesomest spirits of the
night   75
Envelop you, good Provost! Who call'd here of
late?

PROVOST. None, since the curfew rung.

DUKE. Not Isabel?

PROVOST.   No.

DUKE.   They will, then, ere 't be long.

PROVOST. What comfort is for Claudio?

DUKE. There's some in hope.

PROVOST.   It is a bitter deputy.   80

DUKE. Not so, not so; his life is parallel'd
Even with the stroke and line of his great justice.
He doth with holy abstinence subdue
That in himself which he spurs on his power
To qualify in others. Were he meal'd° with that   85
Which he corrects, then were he tyrannous;
But this being so, he's just.   [Knocking within.]
                    Now are they come.

[Exit PROVOST.]
This is a gentle provost. Seldom when
The steeled jailer is the friend of men.

[Knocking within.]
How now! What noise? That spirit's possess'd
with haste   90
That wounds th' unsisting postern° with these
strokes.

[Re-enter PROVOST.]

PROVOST. There he must stay until the officer
Arise to let him in. He is call'd up.

DUKE. Have you no countermand for Claudio yet,
But he must die tomorrow?

PROVOST.   None, sir, none.   95

DUKE. As near the dawning, provost, as it is,
You shall hear more ere morning.

PROVOST.   Happily
You something know; yet I believe there comes
No countermand. No such example have we.
Besides, upon the very siege° of justice   100
Lord Angelo hath to the public ear
Profess'd the contrary.

[Enter a MESSENGER.]
                    This is his lordship's man.

DUKE. And here comes Claudio's pardon.

MESSENGER. [Giving a paper] My lord hath sent you
this note, and by me this further charge that you   105
swerve not from the smallest article of it,
neither in time, matter, or other circumstance.
Good morrow; for, as I take it, it is almost day.

PROVOST. I shall obey him.   [Exit MESSENGER.]

DUKE. [Aside] This is his pardon, purchas'd by   110
such sin

meal'd tainted   unsisting postern unresisting gate
siege seat

445

For which the pardoner himself is in.
Hence hath offense his quick celerity,
When it is borne in high authority.
When vice makes mercy, mercy's so extended
115 That for the fault's love is th' offender friended.
Now, sir, what news?
PROVOST. I told you. Lord Angelo, belike thinking
me remiss in mine office, awakens me with this
unwonted putting-on—methinks strangely, for
120 he hath not used it before.
DUKE. Pray you, let's hear.
PROVOST.

[Reads] Whatsoever you may hear to the
contrary, let Claudio be executed by four of the
clock, and in the afternoon Barnardine. For my
125 better satisfaction, let me have Claudio's head
sent me by five. Let this be duly performed,
with a thought that more depends on it than
we must yet deliver. Thus fail not to do your
office, as you will answer it at your peril.

130 What say you to this, sir?
DUKE. What is that Barnardine who is to be
executed in the afternoon?
PROVOST. A Bohemian born, but here nursed up
135 and bred; one that is a prisoner nine years old.°
DUKE. How came it that the absent Duke had not
either delivered him to his liberty or executed
him? I have heard it was ever his manner to do
so.
140 PROVOST. His friends still wrought reprieves for
him. And, indeed, his fact,° till now in the
government of Lord Angelo, came not to an
undoubtful proof.
DUKE. It is now apparent?
PROVOST. Most manifest, and not denied by him-
145 self.
DUKE. Hath he borne himself penitently in prison?
How seems he to be touched?
PROVOST. A man that apprehends death no more
dreadfully but as a drunken sleep—careless,
150 reckless, and fearless of what's past, present, or
to come, insensible of mortality, and desperately
mortal.°
DUKE. He wants advice.
PROVOST. He will hear none. He hath evermore
155 had the liberty of the prison. Give him leave to
escape hence, he would not. Drunk many times
a day, if not many days entirely drunk. We have
very oft awaked him, as if to carry him to execution, and showed him a seeming warrant for it.
160 It hath not moved him at all.

nine . . . old   i.e., nine years a prisoner
fact   crime
desperately mortal   i.e., beyond hope of salvation

DUKE. More of him anon. There is written in your
brow, provost, honesty and constancy. If I read
it not truly, my ancient skill beguiles me; but,
in the boldness of my cunning, I will lay myself
in hazard. Claudio, whom here you have 165
warrant to execute, is no greater forfeit to the
law than Angelo who hath sentenced him. To
make you understand this in a manifested
effect, I crave but four days' respite, for the
which you are to do me both a present and a 170
dangerous courtesy.
PROVOST. Pray, sir, in what?
DUKE. In the delaying death.
PROVOST. Alack, how may I do it, having the hour
limited, and an express command, under 175
penalty, to deliver his head in the view of
Angelo? I may make my case as Claudio's, to
cross this in the smallest.
DUKE. By the vow of mine order I warrant you, if
my instructions may be your guide. Let this 180
Barnardine be this morning executed and his
head borne to Angelo.
PROVOST. Angelo hath seen them both and will
discover the favor.°
DUKE. O, death's a great disguiser, and you may 185
add to it. Shave the head and tie the beard, and
say it was the desire of the penitent to be so
bared before his death. You know the course is
common. If anything fall to you upon this, more
than thanks and good fortune, by the Saint 190
whom I profess, I will plead against it with my
life.
PROVOST. Pardon me, good father; it is against my
oath.
DUKE. Were you sworn to the Duke, or to the 195
Deputy?
PROVOST. To him, and to his substitutes.
DUKE. You will think you have made no offense if
the Duke avouch the justice of your dealing?
PROVOST. But what likelihood is in that? 200
DUKE. Not a resemblance,° but a certainty. Yet
since I see you fearful, that neither my coat,
integrity, nor persuasion can with ease attempt
you, I will go further than I meant, to pluck all
fears out of you. Look you, sir, here is the hand 205
and seal of the Duke. You know the character, I
doubt not, and the signet is not strange to you.
PROVOST. I know them both.
DUKE. The contents of this is the return of the
Duke. You shall anon over-read it at your 210
pleasure, where you shall find within these two
days he will be here. This is a thing that Angelo
knows not, for he this very day receives letters

favor   face   resemblance   probability

215 of strange tenor—perchance of the Duke's
death, perchance entering into some monastery,
but, by chance, nothing of what is writ. Look, the
unfolding star° calls up the shepherd. Put not
yourself into amazement how these things
should be. All difficulties are but easy when
220 they are known. Call your executioner, and off
with Barnardine's head. I will give him a present
shrift and advise him for a better place. Yet you
are amazed; but this° shall absolutely resolve
you. Come away; it is almost clear dawn.

[*Exeunt*]

SCENE iii
Another room in the same.

[*Enter* POMPEY.]

POMPEY. I am as well acquainted here as I was in
our house of profession. One would think it
were Mistress Overdone's own house, for here
be many of her old customers. First, here's
5 young Master Rash; he's in for a commodity° of
brown paper and old ginger, nine-score and
seventeen pounds, of which he made five
marks,° ready money. Marry, then ginger was
not much in request, for the old women were all
10 dead.° Then is there here one Master Caper, at
the suit of Master Three-pile the mercer, for
some four suits of peach-colored satin, which
now peaches° him a beggar. Then have we here
young Dizzy, and young Master Deep-vow, and
15 Master Copper-spur, and Master Starve-lackey
the rapier and dagger man, and young Drop-
heir that killed lusty Pudding, and Master
Forthlight the tilter,° and brave Master Shooty
the great traveler, and wild Half-can that
20 stabbed Pots, and I think forty more—all great
doers in our trade, and are now "for the Lord's
sake."°

[*Enter* ABHORSON.]

ABHORSON. Sirrah, bring Barnardine hither.
POMPEY. Master Barnardine! You must rise and
25 be hanged, Master Barnardine!
ABHORSON. What, ho, Barnardine!

BARNARDINE. [*Within*] A pox o' your throats! Who
makes that noise there? What are you?
POMPEY. Your friends, sir, the hangman. You must
30 be so good, sir, to rise and be put to death.
BARNARDINE. [*Within*] Away, you rogue, away!
I am sleepy.
ABHORSON. Tell him he must awake, and that
quickly too.
35 POMPEY. Pray, Master Barnardine, awake till you
are executed, and sleep afterwards.
ABHORSON. Go in to him and fetch him out.
POMPEY. He is coming, sir, he is coming; I hear his
straw rustle.
40 ABHORSON. Is the axe upon the block, sirrah?
POMPEY. Very ready, sir.

[*Enter* BARNARDINE.]

BARNARDINE. How now, Abhorson? What's the
news with you?
ABHORSON. Truly, sir, I would desire you to clap
45 into your prayers; for, look you, the warrant's
come.
BARNARDINE. You rogue, I have been drinking all
night; I am not fitted for 't.
POMPEY. O, the better, sir; for he that drinks all
50 night and is hanged betimes in the morning may
sleep the sounder all the next day.
ABHORSON. Look you, sir, here comes your ghostly°
father. Do we jest now, think you?

[*Enter* DUKE *disguised as before.*]

DUKE. Sir, induced by my charity, and hearing
55 how hastily you are to depart, I am come to
advise you, comfort you, and pray with you.
BARNARDINE. Friar, not I. I have been drinking
hard all night. I will have more time to prepare
me, or they shall beat out my brains with
60 billets.° I will not consent to die this day, that's
certain.
DUKE. O, sir, you must, and therefore I beseech
you
Look forward on the journey you shall go.
65 BARNARDINE. I swear I will not die today for any
man's persuasion.
DUKE. But hear you.
BARNARDINE. Not a word. If you have anything to
say to me, come to my ward, for thence will not
70 I today   [*Exit*]
DUKE. Unfit to live or die. O gravel heart!
After him, fellows; bring him to the block.

[*Exeunt* ABHORSON *and* POMPEY.]
[*Enter* PROVOST.]

PROVOST. Now, sir, how do you find the prisoner?
DUKE. A creature unprepar'd, unmeet for death,
75 And to transport him in the mind he is

---

unfolding star morning star
this i.e., the letter
commodity quantity (with possible reference to
 moneylenders' practice of evading usury laws by
 including goods with money lent and charging
 interest on the total)
mark about two thirds of a pound
ginger . . . dead ginger was used as a medicine
peaches proclaims
tilter fencer   *for . . . sake* the prisoners' plea for alms

ghostly spiritual   *billets* blocks of wood

Were damnable.

PROVOST.   Here in the prison, father,
There died this morning of a cruel fever
One Ragozine, a most notorious pirate,
A man of Claudio's years, his beard and head
80 Just of his color. What if we do omit
This reprobate till he were well inclin'd,
And satisfy the Deputy with the visage
Of Ragozine, more like to Claudio?

DUKE. O, 'tis an accident that heaven provides!
85 Dispatch it presently;° the hour draws on
Prefix'd by Angelo. See this be done
And sent according to command, whiles I
Persuade this rude wretch willingly to die.

PROVOST. This shall be done, good father
presently.
90 But Barnardine must die this afternoon.
And how shall we continue Claudio,
To save me from the danger that might come
If he were known alive?

DUKE.   Let this be done.
Put them in secret holds, both Barnardine
95 And Claudio.
Ere twice the sun hath made his journal°
greeting
To th' under generation,° you shall find
Your safety manifested.

PROVOST. I am your free dependant.°

DUKE. Quick, dispatch, and send the head to
100   Angelo.   [Exit PROVOST.]
Now will I write letters to Angelo—
The provost, he shall bear them—whose
contents
Shall witness to him I am near at home,
And that, by great injunctions, I am bound
105 To enter publicly. Him I'll desire
To meet me at the consecrated fount
A league below the city; and from thence,
By cold gradation and well-balanc'd form,°
We shall proceed with Angelo.

                        [Re-enter PROVOST.]
110 PROVOST. Here is the head; I'll carry it myself.

DUKE. Convenient is it. Make a swift return,
For I would commune with you of such things
That want no ear but yours.

PROVOST.   I'll make all speed.
                                              [Exit]

ISABELLA. [Within] Peace, ho, be here!
115 DUKE. The tongue of Isabel. She's come to know
If yet her brother's pardon be come hither.

But I will keep her ignorant of her good,
To make her heavenly comforts of despair
When it is least expected.

                    [Enter ISABELLA.]

ISABELLA.   Ho, by your leave!

DUKE. Good morning to you, fair and gracious
daughter.   120

ISABELLA. The better, given me by so holy a man.
Hath yet the Deputy sent my brother's pardon?

DUKE. He hath releas'd him, Isabel, from the
world.
His head is off and sent to Angelo.

ISABELLA. Nay, but it is not so.   125

DUKE. It is no other. Show your wisdom, daughter,
In your close patience.°

ISABELLA. O, I will to him and pluck out his eyes!

DUKE. You shall not be admitted to his sight.

ISABELLA. Unhappy Claudio! Wretched Isabel!   130
Injurious world! Most damned Angelo!

DUKE. This nor hurts him nor profits you a jot.
Forbear it therefore; give your cause to heaven.
Mark what I say, which you shall find
By every syllable a faithful verity.   135
The Duke comes home tomorrow—nay, dry
your eyes;
One of our covent, and his confessor,
Gives me this instance.° Already he hath carried
Notice to Escalus and Angelo,
Who do prepare to meet him at the gates,   140
There to give up their power. If you can, pace
your wisdom
In that good path that I would wish it go,
And you shall have your bosom° on this wretch,
Grace of the Duke, revenges to your heart,
And general honor.

ISABELLA.   I am directed by you.   145

DUKE. This letter, then, to Friar Peter give;
'Tis that he sent me of the Duke's return.
Say, by this token, I desire his company
At Mariana's house tonight. Her cause and yours
I'll perfect him withal, and he shall bring you   150
Before the Duke, and to the head of Angelo
Accuse him home and home.° For my poor self,
I am combined° by a sacred vow,
And shall be absent. Wend you with this letter.
Command these fretting waters from your eyes   155
With a light heart; trust not my holy order
If I pervert your course.—Who's here?

                        [Enter LUCIO.]

LUCIO. Good even, Friar. Where's the provost?

---

presently immediately   journal daily
under generation the Antipodes
your free dependant entirely at your service
cold . . . form deliberate and formal steps

close patience silent restraint   instance information
have . . . bosom i.e., gain the satisfaction that your heart
  desires
home and home through and through
combined bound

DUKE. Not within, sir.

160 LUCIO. O pretty Isabella, I am pale at mine heart
to see thine eyes so red. Thou must be patient.
I am fain to dine and sup with water and bran;
I dare not for my head fill my belly; one fruitful
meal would set me to't. But they say the Duke
165 will be here tomorrow. By my troth, Isabel, I
loved thy brother. If the old fantastical Duke of
dark corners had been at home, he had lived.
                                [*Exit* ISABELLA.]

DUKE. Sir, the Duke is marvelous little beholding
to your reports; but the best is, he lives not in
170 them.

LUCIO. Friar, thou knowest not the Duke so well as
I do. He's a better woodman° than thou takest
him for.

DUKE. Well, you'll answer this one day. Fare ye
175 well.

LUCIO. Nay, tarry; I'll go along with thee. I can
tell thee pretty tales of the Duke.

DUKE. You have told me too many of him already,
sir, if they be true; if not true, none were
180 enough.

LUCIO. I was once before him for getting a wench
with child.

DUKE. Did you such a thing?

LUCIO. Yes, marry, did I. But I was fain to for-
185 swear it; they would else have married me to
the rotten medlar.°

DUKE. Sir, your company is fairer than honest.
Rest you well.

LUCIO. By my troth, I'll go with thee to the lane's
190 end. If bawdy talk offend you, we'll have very
little of it. Nay, friar, I am a kind of burr; I shall
stick.   [*Exeunt*]

SCENE iv
A room in ANGELO's *house.*

[*Enter* ANGELO *and* ESCALUS.]

ESCALUS. Every letter he hath writ hath disvouched
other.

ANGELO. In most uneven and distracted manner.
His actions show much like to madness. Pray
5 heaven his wisdom be not tainted! And why
meet him at the gates and redeliver our authorities there?

ESCALUS. I guess not.

ANGELO. And why should we proclaim it in an
10 hour before his entering that if any crave re-

dress of injustice, they should exhibit their
petitions in the street?

ESCALUS. He shows his reason for that: to have a
dispatch of complaints, and to deliver us from
devices° hereafter, which shall then have no 15
power to stand against us.

ANGELO. Well, I beseech you, let it be proclaimed
betimes i' the morn. I'll call you at your house.
Give notice to such men of sort and suit° as are
to meet him. 20

ESCALUS. I shall, sir. Fare you well.

ANGELO. Good night.   [*Exit* ESCALUS.]
This deed unshapes° me quite, makes me un-
pregnant°
And dull to all proceedings. A deflower'd maid!
And by an eminent body that enforc'd 25
The law against it! But that her tender shame
Will not proclaim against her maiden loss,°
How might she tongue me! Yet reason dares
her no;
For my authority bears a credent bulk°
That no particular scandal once can touch 30
But it confounds the breather. He should have
liv'd,
Save that his riotous youth, with dangerous
sense,°
Might in the times to come have ta'en revenge
By so receiving a dishonor'd life
With ransom of such shame. Would yet he had
liv'd! 35
Alack, when once our grace we have forgot,
Nothing goes right. We would, and we would
not.   [*Exit*]

SCENE v
Fields without the town.

[*Enter* DUKE *in his own habit, and* FRIAR PETER.]

DUKE. These letters at fit time deliver me.°
                              [*Giving letters.*]
The provost knows our purpose and our plot.
The matter being afoot, keep your instruction
And hold you ever to our special drift,
Though sometimes you do blench° from this to
that, 5
As cause doth minister. Go call at Flavius'
house
And tell him where I stay. Give the like notice

woodman   hunter (of women)
medlar   applelike fruit that turns mushy

devices   libelous plots   sort and suit   place and rank
unshapes   confounds   unpregnant   inept, indifferent
maiden loss   of maidenhood
credent bulk   weight of credibility   sense   passion
me   for me   blench   turn aside

To Valentius, Rowland, and to Crassus,
And bid them bring the trumpets to the gate;
But send me Flavius first.

10 FRIAR PETER.   It shall be speeded well.
                                          [*Exit*]

                    [*Enter* VARRIUS.]

DUKE. I thank thee, Varrius; thou hast made good
    haste.
    Come, we will walk. There's other of our
        friends
    Will greet us here anon, my gentle Varrius.
                                          [*Exeunt*]

                 SCENE vi
         Street near the city gate.

         [*Enter* ISABELLA *and* MARIANA.]

ISABELLA. To speak so indirectly I am loath.
    I would say the truth; but to accuse him so,
    That is your part. Yet I am advis'd to do it—

He says, to veil full purpose.
MARIANA.   Be rul'd by him.
ISABELLA. Besides, he tells me that if peradventure   5
    He speak against me on the adverse side,
    I should not think it strange, for 'tis a physic
    That's bitter to sweet end.
MARIANA. I would Friar Peter—
ISABELLA.   O, peace! The friar is come.
                    [*Enter* FRIAR PETER.]
FRIAR PETER. Come, I have found you out a stand°
    most fit   10
    Where you may have such vantage° on the Duke
    He shall not pass you. Twice have the trumpets
        sounded;
    The generous and gravest citizens
    Have hent° the gates, and very near upon
    The Duke is entering. Therefore, hence, away!   15
                                          [*Exeunt*]

---

stand position   *vantage* advantageous position
hent taken positions at

                    A C T   V

                 SCENE i
             The city-gate.

[MARIANA *veiled,* ISABELLA, *and* FRIAR PETER, *at
    their stand. Enter* DUKE, VARRIUS, LORDS,
    ANGELO, ESCALUS, LUCIO, PROVOST, OFFICERS,
    and CITIZENS, *at several doors.*]

DUKE. My very worthy cousin,° fairly met!
    Our old and faithful friend, we are glad to see
        you.
ANGELO *and* ESCALUS. Happy return be to your
    royal Grace!
DUKE. Many and hearty thankings to you both.
5   We have made inquiry of you, and we hear
    Such goodness of your justice that our soul
    Cannot but yield you forth to public thanks,
    Forerunning more requital.
ANGELO.   You make my bonds still greater.
DUKE. O, your desert speaks loud, and I should
    wrong it
10   To lock it in the wards of covert bosom
    When it deserves, with characters° of brass,
    A forted residence 'gainst the tooth of time

And razure of oblivion. Give me your hand
And let the subject see, to make them know
That outward courtesies would fain proclaim   15
Favors that keep within. Come, Escalus,
You must walk by us on our other hand.
And good supporters are you.
        [FRIAR PETER *and* ISABELLA *come forward.*]
FRIAR PETER. Now is your time. Speak loud, and
    kneel before him.
ISABELLA. Justice, O royal Duke! Vail your regard°   20
    Upon a wrong'd—I would fain have said, a
        maid!
    O worthy prince, dishonor not your eye
    By throwing it on any other object
    Till you have heard me in my true complaint
    And given me justice, justice, justice, justice!   25
DUKE. Relate your wrongs. In what? By whom? Be
    brief.
    Here is Lord Angelo shall give you justice.
    Reveal yourself to him.
ISABELLA.   O worthy Duke,
    You bid me seek redemption of the devil.
    Hear me yourself, for that which I must speak   30
    Must either punish me, not being believ'd,

---

cousin (here marking respect, not kinship)
characters letters

Vail . . . regard look down

                      450

Or wring redress from you. Hear me, O hear me,
    hear!
ANGELO. My lord, her wits, I fear me, are not firm.
    She hath been a suitor to me for her brother
    Cut off by course of justice—
35 ISABELLA.   By course of justice!
ANGELO. And she will speak most bitterly and
    strange.
ISABELLA. Most strange, but yet most truly, will I
    speak.
    That Angelo's forsworn, is it not strange?
    That Angelo's a murderer, is't not strange?
40   That Angelo is an adulterous thief,
    An hypocrite, a virgin-violator,
    Is it not strange and strange?
DUKE.   Nay, it is ten times strange.
ISABELLA. It is not truer he is Angelo
    Than this is all as true as it is strange.
45   Nay, it is ten times true; for truth is truth
    To th' end of reckoning.
DUKE.   Away with her!—Poor soul,
    She speaks this in th' infirmity of sense.
ISABELLA. O prince, I conjure thee, as thou be-
    liev'st
    There is another comfort than this world,
50   That thou neglect me not, with that opinion
    That I am touch'd with madness! Make not im-
    possible
    That which but seems unlike. 'Tis not impossible
    But one, the wicked'st caitiff° on the ground,
    May seem as shy, as grave, as just, as absolute°
55   As Angelo; even so may Angelo,
    In all his dressings, caracts,° titles, forms,
    Be an arch-villain. Believe it, royal prince.
    If he be less, he's nothing; but he's more,
    Had I more name for badness.
DUKE.   By mine honesty,
60   If she be mad—as I believe no other—
    Her madness hath the oddest frame of sense,
    Such a dependency of thing on thing,
    As e'er I heard in madness.
ISABELLA.   O gracious Duke,
    Harp not on that, nor do not banish reason
65   For inequality, but let your reason serve
    To make the truth appear where it seems hid,
    And hide the false seems true.
DUKE.   Many that are not mad
    Have, sure, more lack of reason. What would
    you say?
ISABELLA. I am the sister of one Claudio,
70   Condemn'd upon the act of fornication
    To lose his head—condemn'd by Angelo.

I, in probation of a sisterhood,
    Was sent to by my brother; one Lucio
    As then the messenger—
LUCIO.   That's I, an't like your Grace.
    I came to her from Claudio, and desir'd her   75
    To try her gracious fortune with Lord Angelo
    For her poor brother's pardon.
ISABELLA.   That's he indeed.
DUKE. You were not bid to speak.
LUCIO.   No, my good lord,
    Nor wish'd to hold my peace.
DUKE.   I wish you now, then;
    Pray you, take note of it. And when you have   80
    A business for yourself, pray heaven you then
    Be perfect.
LUCIO.   I warrant your honor.
DUKE. The warrant's for yourself; take heed to't.
ISABELLA. This gentleman told somewhat of my
    tale—
LUCIO. Right.   85
DUKE. It may be right, but you are i' the wrong
    To speak before your time. Proceed.
ISABELLA.   I went
    To this pernicious caitiff Deputy—
DUKE. That's somewhat madly spoken.
ISABELLA.   Pardon it;
    The phrase is to° the matter.   90
DUKE. Mended again. The matter—proceed.
ISABELLA. In brief—to set the needless process by
    How I persuaded, how I pray'd, and kneel'd,
    How he refell'd° me, and how I replied—
    For this was of much length—the vile conclusion   95
    I now begin with grief and shame to utter.
    He would not, but by gift of my chaste body
    To his concupiscible° intemperate lust,
    Release my brother; and, after much debate-
    ment,
    My sisterly remorse° confutes mine honor,   100
    And I did yield to him. But the next morn be-
    times,
    His purpose surfeiting, he sends a warrant
    For my poor brother's head.
DUKE.   This is most likely!
ISABELLA. O, that it were as like as it is true!
DUKE. By heaven, fond wretch, thou know'st not
    what thou speak'st,
    Or else thou art suborn'd against his honor   105
    In hateful practice.° First, his integrity
    Stands without blemish. Next, it imports no
    reason
    That with such vehemency he should pursue

---

caitiff wretch   *absolute* perfect
caracts distinctive qualities

to appropriate to   *refell'd* refused
concupiscible sensual   *remorse* compassion
practice plot

110 Faults proper to himself.° If he had so offended,
He would have weigh'd thy brother by himself,
And not have cut him off. Some one hath set
    you on.
Confess the truth, and say by whose advice
Thou cam'st here to complain.

ISABELLA.   And is this all?
115 Then, O you blessed ministers above,
Keep me in patience, and with ripen'd time
Unfold the evil which is here wrapt up
In countenance!°—Heaven shield your Grace
    from woe,
As I, thus wrong'd, hence unbelieved go!

120 DUKE. I know you'd fain be gone.—An officer!
To prison with her!—Shall we thus permit
A blasting and a scandalous breath to fall
On him so near us? This needs must be a
    practice.
Who knew of your intent and coming hither?

ISABELLA. One that I would were here, Friar
125   Lodowick.

DUKE. A ghostly father, belike. Who knows that
    Lodowick?

LUCIO. My lord, I know him; 'tis a meddling friar.
I do not like the man. Had he been lay, my lord,
For certain words he spake against your Grace
130 In your retirement, I had swing'd° him soundly.

DUKE. Words against me! This's a good friar,
    belike!
And to set on this wretched woman here
Against our substitute! Let this friar be found.

LUCIO. But yesternight, my lord, she and that friar,
135 I saw them at the prison. A saucy friar,
A very scurvy fellow.

FRIAR PETER. Bless'd be your royal Grace!
I have stood by, my lord, and I have heard
Your royal ear abus'd. First hath this woman
140 Most wrongfully accus'd your substitute,
Who is as free from touch or soil with her
As she from one ungot.°

DUKE.   We did believe no less.
Know you that Friar Lodowick that she speaks
    of?

FRIAR PETER. I know him for a man divine and
    holy,
145 Not scurvy, nor a temporary meddler,°
As he's reported by this gentleman;
And, on my trust, a man that never yet
Did, as he vouches, misreport your Grace.

LUCIO. My lord, most villainously. Believe it.

FRIAR PETER. Well, he in time may come to clear
    himself,
150 But at this instant he is sick, my lord,
Of a strange fever. Upon his mere request—
Being come to knowledge that there was
    complaint
Intended 'gainst Lord Angelo—came I hither
To speak, as from his mouth, what he doth
    know
155 Is true and false, and what he with his oath
And all probation° will make up full clear
Whensoever he's convented.° First, for this
    woman,
To justify this worthy nobleman,
160 So vulgarly and personally accus'd,
Her shall you hear disproved to her eyes,
Till she herself confess it.

DUKE.   Good friar, let's hear it.
[ISABELLA is carried off guarded; and MARIANA
                                    comes forward.]
Do you not smile at this, Lord Angelo?—
O heaven, the vanity of wretched fools!—
165 Give us some seats. Come, cousin Angelo;
In this I'll be impartial. Be you judge
Of your own cause. Is this the witness, friar?
First let her show her face, and after speak.

MARIANA. Pardon, my lord; I will not show my
    face
170 Until my husband bid me.

DUKE. What, are you married?

MARIANA. No, my lord.

DUKE. Are you a maid?

MARIANA. No, my lord.

DUKE. A widow, then?   175

MARIANA. Neither, my lord.

DUKE. Why, you are nothing, then—neither maid,
    widow, nor wife?

LUCIO. My lord, she may be a punk;° for many of
    them are neither maid, widow, nor wife.   180

DUKE. Silence that fellow. I would he had some
    cause
To prattle for himself.

LUCIO. Well, my lord.

MARIANA. My lord, I do confess I ne'er was mar-
    ried,
And I confess, besides, I am no maid.   185
I have known my husband; yet my husband
Knows not that ever he knew me.

LUCIO. He was drunk, then, my lord. It can be no
    better.

DUKE. For the benefit of silence, would thou wert
    so too!

---

pursue ... himself persecute crimes of which he is
    himself guilty
wrapt ... countenance concealed by favoritism
swing'd beaten   ungot unborn
temporary meddler meddler in temporal matters

probation proof   convented summoned
punk prostitute

190 LUCIO. Well, my lord.
DUKE. This is no witness for Lord Angelo.
MARIANA. Now I come to't, my lord.
   She that accuses him of fornication,
   In self-same manner doth accuse my husband,
195   And charges him, my lord, with such a time
   When I'll depose I had him in mine arms
   With all th' effect of love.
ANGELO. Charges she moe° than me?
MARIANA.   Not that I know.
DUKE. No? You say your husband.
200 MARIANA. Why, just, my lord, and that is Angelo,
   Who thinks he knows that he ne'er knew my
      body,
   But knows he thinks that he knows Isabel's.
ANGELO. This is a strange abuse. Let's see thy face.
MARIANA. My husband bids me; now I will un-
      mask.   [Unveiling.]
205   This is that face, thou cruel Angelo,
   Which once thou swor'st was worth the looking
      on.
   This is the hand which, with a vow'd contract,
   Was fast belock'd in thine. This is the body
   That took away the match from Isabel
210   And did supply thee at thy garden-house
   In her imagin'd person.
DUKE.   Know you this woman?
LUCIO. Carnally, she says.
DUKE.   Sirrah, no more!
LUCIO. Enough, my lord.
ANGELO. My lord, I must confess I know this
      woman,
   And five years since there was some speech of
215   marriage
   Betwixt myself and her, which was broke off,
   Partly for that her promised proportions°
   Came short of composition, but in chief
   For that her reputation was disvalu'd
220   In levity. Since which time of five years
   I never spake with her, saw her, nor heard from
      her,
   Upon my faith and honor.
MARIANA.   Noble prince,
   As there comes light from heaven and words
      from breath,
   As there is sense in truth and truth in virtue,
225   I am affianc'd this man's wife as strongly
   As words could make up vows. And, my good
      lord,
   But Tuesday night last gone in's garden-house
   He knew me as a wife. As this is true,
   Let me in safety raise me from my knees,
230   Or else forever be confixed° here

A marble monument!
ANGELO.   I did but smile till now.
   Now, good my lord, give me the scope of justice.
   My patience here is touch'd. I do perceive
   These poor informal° women are no more
   But instruments of some more mightier mem-
      ber   235
   That sets them on. Let me have way, my lord,
   To find this practice out.
DUKE.   Aye, with my heart,
   And punish them unto your height of pleasure.
   Thou foolish friar, and thou pernicious woman,
   Compact° with her that's gone, think'st thou
      thy oaths,   240
   Though they would swear down each particular
      saint,
   Were testimonies 'gainst his worth and credit
   That's seal'd in approbation?° You, Lord Escalus,
   Sit with my cousin; lend him your kind pains
   To find out this abuse, whence 'tis deriv'd.   245
   There is another friar that set them on;
   Let him be sent for.
FRIAR PETER. Would he were here, my lord! For
      he, indeed,
   Hath set the women on to this complaint.
   Your provost knows the place where he abides, 250
   And he may fetch him.
DUKE.   Go, do it instantly.
                              [Exit PROVOST.]
   And you, my noble and well-warranted cousin,
   Whom it concerns to hear this matter forth,
   Do with your injuries as seems you best
   In any chastisement. I for a while   255
   Will leave you. But stir not you till you have
   Well determin'd upon these slanderers.
ESCALUS. My lord, we'll do it throughly.° [Exit
   DUKE] Signior Lucio, did not you say you knew
   that Friar Lodowick to be a dishonest person? 260
LUCIO. "Cucullus non facit monachum"°—honest in
   nothing but in his clothes; and one that hath
   spoke most villainous speeches of the Duke.
ESCALUS. We shall entreat you to abide here till
   he come, and enforce° them against him. We   265
   shall find this friar a notable fellow.
LUCIO. As any in Vienna, on my word.
ESCALUS. Call that same Isabel here once again. I
   would speak with her. [Exit an ATTENDANT]
   Pray you, my lord, give me leave to question;   270
   you shall see how I'll handle her.

---

informal deranged   Compact leagued
seal'd in approbation of proven integrity
throughly thoroughly
Cucullus . . . monachum a cowl does not make a monk
enforce charge

---

moe more   proportions dowry   confixed fixed

LUCIO. Not better than he, by her own report.

ESCALUS. Say you?

LUCIO. Marry, sir, I think if you handled her
275 privately she would sooner confess. Perchance,
publicly, she'll be ashamed.

ESCALUS. I will go darkly to work with her.

LUCIO. That's the way, for women are light at
midnight.

[*Re-enter* OFFICERS *with* ISABELLA; *and* PROVOST
with the DUKE *in his friar's habit.*]

280 ESCALUS. Come on, mistress. Here's a gentlewoman denies all that you have said.

LUCIO. My lord, here comes the rascal I spoke of,
here with the provost.

ESCALUS. In very good time. Speak not you to him
285 till we call upon you.

LUCIO. Mum.

ESCALUS. Come, sir. Did you set these women on
to slander Lord Angelo? They have confessed
you did.

290 DUKE. 'Tis false.

ESCALUS. How! Know you where you are?

DUKE. Respect to your great place! And let the
devil
Be sometime honor'd for his burning throne!
Where is the Duke? 'Tis he should hear me
speak.

ESCALUS. The Duke's in us, and we will hear you
295 speak.
Look you speak justly.

DUKE. Boldly, at least. But, O, poor souls,
Come you to seek the lamb here of the fox?
Good night to your redress! Is the Duke gone?
300 Then is your cause gone too. The Duke's unjust
Thus to retort° your manifest appeal
And put your trial in the villain's mouth
Which here you come t' accuse.

LUCIO. This is the rascal; this is he I spoke of.

ESCALUS. Why, thou unrev'rend and unhallow'd
305 friar,
Is't not enough thou hast suborn'd these women
T' accuse this worthy man, but, in foul mouth,
And in the witness of his proper° ear,
To call him villain? And then to glance from
him
310 To the Duke himself, to tax him with injustice?
Take him hence; to the rack with him! We'll
touse° you
Joint by joint, but we will know his purpose.
What, "unjust"!

DUKE.   Be not so hot. The Duke
Dare no more stretch this finger of mine than he
315 Dare rack his own. His subject am I not,

Nor here provincial. My business in this state
Made me a looker-on here in Vienna,
Where I have seen corruption boil and bubble
Till it o'er-run the stew;° laws for all faults,
But faults so countenanc'd that the strong
statutes   320
Stand like the forfeits° in a barber's shop,
As much in mock as mark.°

ESCALUS. Slander to the state! Away with him to
prison!

ANGELO. What can you vouch against him, Signior
Lucio?
Is this the man that you did tell us of?   325

LUCIO. 'Tis he, my lord. Come hither, goodman
baldpate. Do you know me?

DUKE. I remember you, sir, by the sound of your
voice. I met you at the prison, in the absence of
the Duke.   330

LUCIO. O, did you so? And do you remember what
you said of the Duke?

DUKE. Most notedly, sir.

LUCIO. Do you so, sir? And was the Duke a flesh-
monger, a fool, and a coward, as you then 335
reported him to be?

DUKE. You must, sir, change persons with me ere
you make that my report. You, indeed, spoke so
of him, and much more, much worse.

LUCIO. O thou damnable fellow! Did not I pluck 340
thee by the nose for thy speeches?

DUKE. I protest I love the Duke as I love myself.

ANGELO. Hark, how the villain would close° now,
after his treasonable abuses!

ESCALUS. Such a fellow is not to be talked withal. 345
Away with him to prison! Where is the provost?
Away with him to prison! Lay bolts enough upon
him. Let him speak no more. Away with those
giglets° too, and with the other confederate
companion!   350

DUKE. [*To the* PROVOST] Stay, sir. Stay awhile.

ANGELO. What, resists he? Help him, Lucio.

LUCIO. Come, sir; come, sir; come, sir; foh, sir!
Why, you bald-pated, lying rascal, you must be
hooded, must you? Show your knave's visage, 355
with a pox to you! Show your sheep-biting° face,
and be hanged an hour! Will't not off?

[*Pulls off the friar's hood, and discovers the Duke.*]

DUKE. Thou art the first knave that e'er mad'st a
Duke.
First, Provost, let me bail these gentle three.

stew pot (with pun, brothel)
forfeits teeth extracted and displayed (barbers served
also as dentists)
mock as mark jest as advertisement
close come to terms   *giglets* wanton women
sheep-biting i.e., sneaking, nipping

retort reject   *proper* own   *touse* rend

[*To* Lucio] Sneak not away, sir, for the friar and
360 you
       Must have a word anon. Lay hold on him.
Lucio. This may prove worse than hanging.
Duke. [*To* Escalus] What you have spoke I pardon.
       Sit you down.
       We'll borrow place of him. [*To* Angelo] Sir, by
       your leave.
365 Hast thou or word, or wit, or impudence,
       That yet can do thee office? If thou hast,
       Rely upon it till my tale be heard,
       And hold no longer out.
Angelo.   O my dread lord,
       I should be guiltier than my guiltiness
370 To think I can be undiscernible
       When I perceive your Grace, like power divine,
       Hath look'd upon my passes. Then, good Prince,
       No longer session hold upon my shame,
       But let my trial be mine own confession.
375 Immediate sentence then, and sequent death,
       Is all the grace I beg.
Duke.   Come hither, Mariana.
       Say, wast thou e'er contracted to this woman?
Angelo. I was, my lord.
Duke. Go take her hence and marry her instantly.
380 Do you the office, friar, which consummate,
       Return him here again. Go with him, Provost.
       [*Exeunt* Angelo, Mariana, Friar Peter *and*
                    Provost.]
Escalus. My lord, I am more amaz'd at his dis-
       honor
       Than at the strangeness of it.
Duke.   Come hither, Isabel.
       Your friar is now your prince. As I was then
385 Advertising and holy° to your business,
       Not changing heart with habit, I am still
       Attorney'd° at your service.
Isabella.   O, give me pardon
       That I, your vassal, have employ'd and pain'd
       Your unknown sovereignty!
Duke   You are pardon'd, Isabel,
390 And now, dear maid, be you as free to us.
       Your brother's death, I know, sits at your heart,
       And you may marvel why I obscur'd myself,
       Lab'ring to save his life, and would not rather
       Make rash remonstrance of my hidden power
395 Than let him so be lost. O most kind maid,
       It was the swift celerity of his death,
       Which I did think with slower foot came on,
       That brain'd my purpose. But peace be with
       him!
       That life is better life, past fearing death,

Than that which lives to fear. Make it your com-
       fort,   400
       So happy is your brother.
Isabella.   I do, my lord.
       Re-enter Angelo, Mariana, Friar Peter, *and*
                    Provost]
Duke. For this new-married man approaching
       here,
       Whose salt° imagination yet hath wrong'd
       Your well-defended honor, you must pardon
       For Mariana's sake. But as he adjudg'd your
       brother—   405
       Being criminal, in double violation
       Of sacred chastity and of promise-breach
       Thereon dependent, for your brother's life—
       The very mercy of the law cries out
       Most audible, even from his proper tongue,   410
       "An Angelo for Claudio, death for death!"
       Haste still pays haste, and leisure answers
       leisure;
       Like doth quit° like, and Measure still For
       Measure.
       Then, Angelo, thy fault's thus manifested,
       Which, though thou wouldst deny, denies thee
       vantage.   415
       We do condemn thee to the very block
       Where Claudio stoop'd to death, and with like
       haste.
       Away with him!
Mariana.   O my most gracious lord,
       I hope you will not mock me with a husband.
Duke. It is your husband mock'd you with a hus-
       band.   420
       Consenting to the safeguard of your honor,
       I thought your marriage fit; else imputation,°
       For that he knew you, might reproach your life
       And choke your good to come. For his posses-
       sions,
       Although by confiscation they are ours,   425
       We do instate and widow you withal
       To buy you a better husband.
Mariana.   O my dear lord,
       I crave no other, nor no better man.
Duke. Never crave him; we are definitive.
Mariana. Gentle my liege—   [*Kneeling.*]
Duke.   You do but lose your labor. 430
       Away with him to death! [*To* Lucio] Now, sir, to
       you.
Mariana. O my good lord! Sweet Isabel, take my
       part;
       Lend me your knees, and all my life to come
       I'll lend you all my life to do you service.

Advertising and holy attentive and devoted
Attorney'd retained as advocate

salt lustful   quit repay
imputation slander

435 DUKE. Against all sense you do importune her.
Should she kneel down in mercy of this fact,
Her brother's ghost his paved bed would break
And take her hence in horror.
MARIANA.   Isabel,
Sweet Isabel, do yet but kneel by me;
440 Hold up your hands, say nothing, I'll speak all.
They say best men are moulded out of faults,
And, for the most, become much more the
better
For being a little bad. So may my husband.
O Isabel, will you not lend a knee?
DUKE. He dies for Claudio's death.
445 ISABELLA.   Most bounteous sir, [*Kneeling.*]
Look, if it please you, on this man condemn'd
As if my brother liv'd. I partly think
A due sincerity govern'd his deeds
Till he did look on me. Since it is so,
450 Let him not die. My brother had but justice
In that he did the thing for which he died.
For Angelo,
His act did not o'ertake his bad intent,
And must be buried but as an intent
That perish'd by the way. Thoughts are no sub-
455 jects°—
Intents, but merely thoughts.
MARIANA.   Merely, my lord.
DUKE. Your suit's unprofitable; stand up, I say.
I have bethought me of another fault.
Provost, how came it Claudio was beheaded
At an unusual hour?
460 PROVOST.   It was commanded so.
DUKE. Had you a special warrant for the deed?
PROVOST. No, my good lord; it was by private
message.
DUKE. For which I do discharge you of your office.
Give up your keys.
PROVOST.   Pardon me, noble lord.
465 I thought it was a fault but knew it not,
Yet did repent me after more advice.
For testimony whereof, one in the prison
That should by private order else have died,
I have reserv'd alive.
DUKE.   What's he?
470 PROVOST.   His name is Barnardine.
DUKE. I would thou hadst done so by Claudio.
Go fetch him hither; let me look upon him.
[*Exit* PROVOST.]
ESCALUS. I am sorry one so learned and so wise
As you, Lord Angelo, have still appear'd,
475 Should slip so grossly both in the heat of blood
And lack of temper'd judgment afterward.
ANGELO. I am sorry that such sorrow I procure.

subjects i.e., punishable acts

And so deep sticks it in my penitent heart
That I crave death more willingly than mercy;
'Tis my deserving, and I do entreat it.   480
[*Re-enter* PROVOST, *with* BARNARDINE, CLAUDIO
muffled, and JULIET.]
DUKE. Which is that Barnardine?
PROVOST.   This, my lord.
DUKE. There was a friar told me of this man.
Sirrah, thou art said to have a stubborn soul
That apprehends no further than this world,
And squar'st thy life according. Thou'rt con-
demn'd.   485
But, for those earthly faults, I quit° them all,
And pray thee take this mercy to provide
For better times to come. Friar, advise him;
I leave him to your hand. What muffled fellow's
that?
PROVOST. This is another prisoner that I sav'd,   490
Who should have died when Claudio lost his
head—
As like almost to Claudio as himself.
[*Unmuffles* CLAUDIO.]
DUKE. [*To* ISABELLA] If he be like your brother, for
his sake
Is he pardon'd; and, for your lovely sake,
Give me your hand and say you will be mine.   495
He is my brother too: but fitter time for that.
By this Lord Angelo perceives he's safe;
Methinks I see a quick'ning in his eye.
Well, Angelo, your evil quits° you well.
Look that you love your wife; her worth worth
yours.   500
I find an apt remission° in myself;
And yet here's one in place I cannot pardon.
[*To* LUCIO] You, sirrah, that knew me for a fool,
a coward,
One all of luxury,° an ass, a madman,
Wherein have I deserved so of you,   505
That you extol me thus?
LUCIO. 'Faith, my lord, I spoke it but according to
the trick.° If you will hang me for it, you may;
but I had rather it would please you I might be
whipt.   510
DUKE. Whipt first, sir, and hang'd after.
Proclaim it, Provost, round about the city,
If any woman wrong'd by this lewd fellow—
As I have heard him swear himself there's one
Whom he begot with child—let her appear,   515
And he shall marry her. The nuptial finish'd,
Let him be whipt and hang'd.
LUCIO. I beseech your highness, do not marry me

quit forgive   *quits* repays
remission aptness to pardon   *luxury* lechery
according . . . trick i.e., as mere chatter

to a whore. Your highness said even now I made
520   you a Duke. Good my lord, do not recompense
me in making me a cuckold.
Duke. Upon mine honor, thou shalt marry her.
Thy slanders I forgive, and therewithal
Remit thy other forfeits.°—Take him to prison,
525   And see our pleasure herein executed.
Lucio. Marrying a punk, my lord, is pressing to
death, whipping, and hanging.
Duke. Slandering a prince deserves it.
                    [*Exeunt* OFFICERS *with* LUCIO.]
She, Claudio, that you wrong'd, look you
restore.°
530   Joy to you, Mariana! Love her, Angelo.
I have confess'd her, and I know her virtue.

Thanks, good friend Escalus, for thy much
goodness.
There's more behind° that is more gratulate.°
Thanks, Provost, for thy care and secrecy.
We shall employ thee in a worthier place.   535
Forgive him, Angelo, that brought you home
The head of Ragozine for Claudio's.
Th' offense pardons itself. Dear Isabel,
I have a motion° much imports your good,
Whereto if you'll a willing ear incline,   540
What's mine is yours, and what is yours is mine.
So bring us to our palace, where we'll show
What's yet behind that's meet you all should
know.   [*Exeunt*]

---

forfeits penalties   *restore* i.e., by marriage

behind yet to come   *gratulate* gratifying (substantial)
motion proposal

AFTERWORD

Written in the middle of the eight or nine years that produced the great tragedies, *Measure for Measure* itself verges briefly on tragedy; in the words of one modern editor, "In no other comedy of Shakespeare is there quite the same sense of tragedy averted." Earlier, in fact, *The Merchant of Venice* flirted with tragedy when Shylock, during successive scenes, moved ominously nearer to obtaining his pound of flesh. For that matter, *Much Ado About Nothing,* in its painful scene at the center, pauses at the brink and raises the spectre of a new *Romeo and Juliet* wherein Hero will perish of grief or shock and afterward a repentant Claudio will surely (one may hope) kill himself. But actual disaster is really unthinkable in either play, as it is in all the "happy comedies," where the general atmosphere or "climate" is reassuringly wholesome, benign, and healing; if we should take any momentarily perilous situation in these plays so seriously that we anticipate the occurrence of some irremediable ill, then we have somehow misread them, mistaken their spirit, and need to review the Clown's casual admonition that ends *Twelfth Night*: ". . . that's all one, our play is done,/ And we'll strive to please you every day."

Moreover, we should not neglect this reminder in considering *Measure for Measure.* But here the world, like the worlds of *All's Well That Ends Well* and *Troilus and Cressida,* its nontragic contemporaries (though indeed *Troilus* is often classed as tragedy), is one in which something like the catastrophe of tragedy might take place—might, that is to say, were there no Duke Vincentio. Once the Duke has learned, and he learns early, of Claudio's plight and Angelo's malfeasance in office, the possibility of catastrophe vanishes and the parallel with tragedy abruptly ends. Nevertheless, both before and after the Duke learns of Claudio's peril, the world of *Measure for Measure* is dark and ugly, its atmosphere unhealthful, its inhabitants (with the obvious exceptions) as repugnant as their environment. Most notably in this play Shakespeare has anticipated the grime of a modern metropolis in its least attractive districts of tenderloin and prison; this Vienna is hardly the Vienna of a Strauss waltz. In an early comedy, Lucio might have been a Gratiano (of Venice and *The Merchant*), bawdy, loud, irrepressible, but withal innocent and healthy. But this Lucio's talk is now limited to brothels and venereal disease; he jests scurrilously, finding it preposterous that Claudio should lose his life because of "a game of tick-tack" and "For filling a bottle with a tun-dish." He reports that the absent Duke "would mouth with a beggar, though she smelt brown bread and garlic," and in the same cynically garrulous vein runs on habitually. Yet Lucio is among the more delightful of the denizens met by the Duke during his secret time as "looker-on" in sinful Vienna, where he sees "corruption boil and bubble/ Till it o'errun the stew." Lucio (like the pimp Pompey and, more limitedly, the executioner Abhorson) renders the play a vital service, for at the same time that his ribald chatter faithfully reflects the decay of the city it also casts a comic lightness over what would otherwise show as unrelievedly ugly. Hence, while the world of *Measure for Measure* is quite devoid of that shining quality that makes the worlds of the romantic comedies so memorably luminescent, its grime and grimness are short of total.

Measure for Measure is conventionally classed as a "dark comedy," a "tragicomedy," a "problem play," and doubtless there is as good cause to name it one as the other; for dark it is, in both setting and action, and tragic it briefly threatens to become. But *problem* may be the last, best word for it. It is quite true that all Shakespeare's plays are in a broad sense problem plays, for even a light fantasy-farce like *A Midsummer Night's Dream* poses a double problem to be worked out in course of the action, that of two young men loving Hermia and none loving Helena, and that of the fairy queen and king; and of course every tragedy revolves about a problem or problems. But in reference to *Measure or Measure* the term applies more narrowly and serves to distinguish this play from most others and in fact to place it in rare and special company—for example, with the tragedy of *Coriolanus*, which few can study without recognizing that there Shakespeare "had something on his mind," a political dilemma of aristocratic and democratic rule. In that play, though the problem is worked out in the usual dramatic terms of characters and action, one's impression grows, especially during the frequent scenes of political debate, that the problem is primary and the characters and incidents secondary, so that Coriolanus and his affairs seem to exist to illustrate an issue.

Coriolanus represents the extreme instance of Shakespeare's reversing his usual way, which is to put characters and their story first and to make any philosophical issue at most subordinate and more often merely incidental. The degree to which *Measure for Measure* also represents a reversal is one of the critical questions about the play. That at least to a limited extent its characters and their actions perform in the service of various but closely related issues—moral right and wrong, liberty and license, sin and salvation, justice and mercy—few will deny. The central problem—what, exactly, it was that was "on Shakespeare's mind"—is by no means as clearly identified as in *Coriolanus*; it appears rather to embrace a core of basic human dilemmas. It is probably therefore that twentieth-century critics, in particular, have advanced sundry and diverse interpretations: *Measure for Measure* is essentially a morality play wherein vices and virtues struggle for man's soul; it argues the Christian doctrine of the atonement; the Duke is a Christ figure, and it is all "a parable, like the Parables of Jesus." It is widely accepted as "profoundly Christian"; names are symbolic: Angelo suggests angel, and Satan, the fallen angel; Mariana is Mary and Anne, Virgin and Mother. The Duke's use of the bed-trick to deceive Angelo is "the Divine Spirit fighting the Devil with his own weapons." (But keenly instructive, at this point, is an essay by the editor of the Yale edition of the play, "*Measure for Measure* as a Measure for Critics," wherein are examined ways in which the play tempts overly earnest interpreters to indulge their personal biases with laughable results.)

And indeed to stress too much the didactic pretensions of the play is to risk disparaging it as dramatic entertainment; it is, after all, a stage play and is not to be examined like a sermon. We denigrate the dramatic force and human validity of the principal characters, and the secondary ones as well, if we exaggerate their functions as symbolic figures in the services of parable. The truth is that *Measure for Measure* is not only a stage play but a superb one that "acts" better than it reads. It moves briskly forward, compressing a considerable period into what seems, in the theater, only what time is needed for acting. Individual scenes, virtually with no exceptions, like the total structure, are shrewdly devised and are so arranged that they rush toward the denouement very much as *Othello* (which may have been written in the same year) rushes to its catastrophe. During the rare occasions when an interval is necessary in order to allow some action time to ripen, Shakespeare trots in his chattering Lucio (or Elbow, Pompey, Froth, Abhorson, Barnardine) to fill the gap, and waiting becomes sheer delight. Nor is the denouement toward which the forward movement presses disappointing. It has been remarked with some truth that in certain plays Shakespeare seems to have written all his foregoing action for the sake of a sensational denouement, as, for example, in *The Winter's Tale*, where the "statue" of long-supposed-dead Hermione grows warm, breathes, and steps down from its dais. In *Measure for Measure* the comparable instant, which as something calculated to take the breath away is certainly second only to that in *The Winter's Tale*, occurs when Lucio, all the while erupting with scurrilous epithets, snatches off the friar's hood and reveals the face of the almighty Duke, the effect of whose countenance awes Angelo "like power divine."

If the stagecraft is more sensational than we might expect were the primary intent that of parable, so are the main characters more fully realized human individuals than are required when they serve as the puppets of an overriding philosophical rather than dramatic purpose. The Duke, Isabella, and Angelo arouse interest for themselves, whatever symbolic roles they may be alleged to play. One evidence of their dramatic validity is the diversity of critical reaction that they continue to inspire. At one extreme the Duke is taken for a Christ figure, but at the other he is taken for a charlatan who likes to engage in tricks, a coward who evades his ducal responsibilities, leaving his own dirty work to be carried out by Angelo, a showman who relishes his masquerade in the friar's robes. Indeed he does seem to be in league with Shakespeare in building and prolonging the suspenseful effects that lead to the spectacular denouement.

The Duke is explicit about his motives in giving the reins of office to Angelo while he himself remains a secret "looker-on" in Vienna. Perhaps he is even too explicit and the reasons he gives too numerous, so that we can never be quite sure of the true reason. In this respect, if no other, he reminds us of Iago, who cites so many causes for his ruinous campaign against Othello that we suspect them all, and may even, with Coleridge, end by declaring him a "motiveless malignity." Is the Duke a "motiveless benignity"? He lies when he speaks to Angelo and Escalus of his "remove" from Vienna, and he acknowledges the lie when he tells Friar Thomas that he has "strew'd it in the common ear" that he will travel in Poland. Does he lie also to Friar Thomas in stating that he wishes Angelo to enforce laws that "we have let slip," so that his own image will not suffer by the enforcement? Does he come nearer the truth when he confides doubt about Angelo's true character?

> Moe reasons for this action
> At our more leisure shall I render you;
> Only, this one: Lord Angelo is precise,
> Stands at a guard with envy, scarce confesses
> That his blood flows or that his appetite
> Is more to bread than stone; hence shall we see,
> If power change purpose, what our seemers be.

Is it for this, really—to flush out Angelo's suspected hypocrisy? Or does the true reason lie among the "Moe reasons" that we never hear of again? There are many "Moe questions" to be raised about the Duke himself, and one is whether any of his motives do him much credit, regardless of the ultimate good that his long masquerade achieves. Must we settle finally for the opinion of one of Shakespeare's greatest modern editors that, "The Duke is created for the sake of the plot; without his shiftiness, his scheming, and his falsehoods there would be no story running through five acts"? But is not *Measure for Measure*, then, a desperately bad play if the actions of its central character can be accounted for only on grounds of dramatic expediency? Certainly the Duke is no Hamlet, wholly deserving centuries of earnest probing in an effort to pluck out the heart of his mystery; but, like Hamlet, he inspires many and diverse questions, and, like Hamlet, he is a superb stage figure.

Isabella's character confronts the interpreter with much less of a problem. Her qualities are delineated sharply, with few ambiguities. We know well enough what she is, and it is mainly in liking or disliking what she is that we differ. Hazlitt's pronouncement on her "rigid chastity" is mild in comparison to some later verdicts; and twentieth-century undergraduates frequently vie with one another in search of harsh epithets to denote her alleged prudishness and insensitivity. Best proof of Shakespeare's success with

Isabella is that she almost invariably provokes readers to some kind of potent response. Students who have remained at best politely respectful and at worst yawningly indifferent to romantic heroines like Viola, Rosalind, Bassanio's Portia, and even the sparkling Beatrice come suddenly alive with genuine feeling for Isabella, one way or the other. Within the play itself Isabella's native gift for affecting others is noteworthy. The dissolute and scurrilous Lucio claims to hold her "as a thing enskied and sainted," to be conversed with "As with a saint"—but then he goes on to talk bawdily in her presence. Claudio speaks of her "prone and speechless dialect"—a silent communicative force more persuasive than words—by which she may move Angelo. And indeed it is Isabella's main problem that her "prone and speechless dialect" communicates somewhat too well, for it shortly brings the blood of Angelo—"a man/ Whose blood is very snow-broth"—to a boil. And, finally, Isabella's special, and ardently suppressed, quality communicates itself to the Duke himself. It is one of the play's ambiguities that we cannot identify the moment when his interest in her begins to grow more personal than professional; in any event, his proposal comes without warning and must represent the briefest courtship in the Shakespeare canon: "Give me your hand and say you will be mine." Thus with a single line Shakespeare dispatches the entire matter of love with which the romantic comedies are concerned during five acts.

But the best of Isabella's characterization is the record it presents of her transformation from frigid "saint" to warm (or at least no longer quite icy) and compassionate human being. By and large the heroes and heroines of the comedies, unlike those of the tragedies, do not "grow." But Isabella grows. When we first meet her, she is wishing "a more strict restraint" upon the sisterhood of the nunnery, though to the layman it may appear that certain of the rules are already strict enough:

> When you have vow'd, you must not speak with men
> But in the presence of the prioress;
> Then, if you speak, you must not show your face,
> Or, if you show your face, you must not speak.

(Very, very timidly one might question the significance of Isabella's wish for stricter rules: can it possibly be that she is aware of and fearful of that within her—call it a "prone and speechless dialect"—which is later manifest in the heating of Angelo's blood? Does she *need* a nunnery's protection from herself, and the tighter its rules, the better?) Her initial coldness shows in her first talk with Angelo, and Lucio twice admonishes her, "You are too cold!" Her chilly summation of the principle on which she rejects Angelo's proposition is the most-quoted utterance repeated by critics who dislike her: "More than our brother is our chastity." Yet it is not her rejection of Angelo per se that most readers condemn; it is her unbridled outburst at Claudio's plea to be saved at her expense: "Die, perish! Might but my bending down/ Reprieve thee from thy fate, it should proceed."

The Duke overhears her outburst, and perhaps we are to assume that at this point the re-education of her humanity becomes part of his obscure purposes. In any event Isabella's transformation begins here and proceeds under his management—indeed, with something like the "cold gradation and well-balanc'd form" that, later, he uses in disciplining his erring deputy—toward her eventual demonstration of a newly won humanity. It is noteworthy that the Duke is too shrewd to demand compassion from her all at once. When he asks her to help restore the fortunes of the "poor wronged lady," Mariana, he points out the grosser advantages she stands to gain also: "by this is your brother saved, your honor untainted, the poor Mariana advantaged, the corrupt deputy scaled." Thus in the beginning we may assume that a large share of her motive is the desire for revenge on Angelo and a much smaller share is her desire to aid Mariana. But, however slight, this concern for the plight of another than herself *is* a beginning; and after prolonged trial the re-education of Isabella culminates in her going to her knees (admittedly after some strong prompting by both the Duke and Mariana) to beg mercy for the man who, as the Duke has continued to make her suppose, has executed her brother. It would be hard to imagine that the Isabella whom we first heard expressing a wish that the nunnery rules were more strict would have gone to her knees in behalf of an Angelo. In doing so at last, she proves that her humanity has been enlarged and earns her reward: "Give me your hand and say you will be mine."

Angelo, to come finally to the "fallen angel" whose role many star actors during three centuries have preferred to play, is one of Shakespeare's finest studies of the "seemer," a type of erring mortal in the devious workings of whose psyche Shakespeare was interested throughout his career. The role of the seemer is writ largest with Iago, whose "I am not what I am" might stand as the motto of all; but it is difficult to identify one play of Shakespeare's that fails to exhibit at least one seemer. All the heroines who don male garb and go a-masquerading are seemers—innocent ones, to be sure, but seemers are not all bad. The Macbeths are seemers; so is Claudius, whose skill in the craft probably stands next to Iago's; so, for that matter, is Hamlet, with his "antic disposition" on; so are the modestly endowed Claudio and Hero of *Much Ado*, in deceiving Benedick and Beatrice into giving in to love. Seemers are often villains, but obviously they need not be so: Duke Vincentio, whose machinations are strictly benevolent, is a master seemer as Friar Lodowick.

Angelo is unique among the seemers in at least one way: he is the "seemer-in-spite-of-himself." The large question about him is whether he was natively a hypocrite or indeed truly what he "seemed" to others until the subtle force of Isabella's person wrought a drastic transformation in his nature (one which strangely parallels that which Isabella more gradually experiences). Angelo does not succumb easily or willingly; the soliloquy that closes Act II, scene ii marks a soul in torment, and there is never a moment afterward when he does not deplore the wrongness of his own duplicity. Perhaps we should in fact take him for what he seems to be at the outset, and not for what he seems to be after his passions have been aroused by Isabella's unconscious assault. Once he has given his "sensual race the rein," his indulgence remains repugnant to him, and he embraces the Duke's expected doom as a welcome relief:

> . . . let my trial be mine own confession.
> Immediate sentence, then, and sequent death
> Is all the grace I beg.

As much as the Duke and Isabella, Angelo has served as a "measure for critics," not all of whom have been as ready as Isabella to extend him mercy. Coleridge, for one, who found the comic parts of this play "disgusting" and the tragic ones "horrible," could not forgive the pardon accorded Angelo, but found it "degrading to the character of woman."

Hardin Craig, pre-eminent American scholar and editor of Shakespeare, as late as 1951 pronounced *Measure for Measure* "one of Shakespeare's worst plays." But for our century generally its vexing problems, psychological, moral, religious, political, as well as artistic, hold a special fascination. The play leaves inviting space for debate on the perennially vital issues it raises, and if that is a fault, it is also a fault of *Hamlet*. In our time at least Shakespeare seems most exciting when he raises large questions and neither commits himself to nor allows reasonable readers to impose absolute answers. But what is devoutly to be wished is that our century, in its zeal for symbolic meanings and compulsion to erect elaborate structures of interpretation, does not, for the general public, destroy the play as a play. For a stage play it is, as every able performance attests, and no treatise.

Indeed (parenthetically and very modestly), may we not even hazard the suggestion that the play is not only a stage play but somewhat lighter than it is usually taken to be? There are moments when, if events are seen just a shade differently, the situation appears to border on high comedy. Is there not something deliciously comic in the plight of the prudish young novice who had wished the nunnery rules more strict, when her "prone and speechless dialect" awakens the latent beast in a man thought by all, himself included, to be immune to passion? Is there a lurking "in" joke between dramatist and cast when Angelo, eying the boy actor playing Isabella—whose padding has perhaps been a trifle exaggerated—says, "Be that you are,/ That is, a woman . . ./ If you be one, as you are well express'd/ By all external warrants . . ."? (On the modern stage any robust actress easily points up the implication, perhaps at the root of Isabella's problem, of Angelo's otherwise seemingly gratuitous remark.) Is there nothing comic in the fact that all the while that Isabella's earnestly intellectual arguments with the deputy are pointed in one direction, her whole physical being is arguing in quite another? She is a devout young lady whose person, vexingly to her, argues against and more effectively than her cold logic. Is it to strain too far to imagine that the spirit of high comedy hovers over the situation when, outraged by Angelo's indecent proposal (angry with herself too, perhaps), Isabella rushes to Claudio, counting positively on his honor and brotherly feeling—only to hear him almost instantly begin to argue that because the all-wise Angelo himself offers to participate in a forbidden assignation, the sin cannot really be all bad? In any event the comic spirit cannot be far off at the end, when the Duke, who has had four acts in which to eye Isabella without saying anything to the purpose, abruptly makes his own proposal to her—one that she does not rebut, for indeed she speaks not another word, as if her spirit may be tired of fighting the losing battle against her own physical attractions.

These unorthodox suggestions that Shakespeare's tongue may sometimes have been in his cheek in *Measure for Measure*—as indeed it often is elsewhere, even in the most strenuous moments of tragedy—may be worth entertaining for no more than a single instant; but at their very best they may help counteract the twentieth-century zeal to take *Measure for Measure* much too seriously. "For the rain," quoth Feste, "it raineth every day."

A NOTE ON THE COMPOSITION OF THE PLAY

It is generally agreed that *Measure for Measure* was written in 1604, or possibly 1603–1604. In any event a first performance is recorded on December 26, 1604. It was not published until the Folio of 1623. The immediate source was a play by George Whetstone, *Promos and Cassandra* (1578), which in its turn was based on a tale of Giraldi Cinthio's included in his *Hundred Tales* (1565).

Othello

DRAMATIS PERSONÆ

DUKE OF VENICE
BRABANTIO *a senator*
OTHER SENATORS
GRATIANO *brother to Brabantio*
LODOVICO *kinsman to Brabantio*
OTHELLO *a noble Moor in the service of the Venetian state*
CASSIO *his lieutenant*
IAGO *his ancient*
MONTANO *Othello's predecessor in the government of Cyprus*

RODERIGO *a Venetian gentleman*
CLOWN *servant to Othello*
DESDEMONA *daughter to Brabantio and wife to Othello*
EMILIA *wife to Iago*
BIANCA *mistress to Cassio*
SAILOR, MESSENGER, HERALD, OFFICERS, GENTLEMEN, MUSICIANS, *and* ATTENDANTS

SCENE: *Venice; a seaport in Cyprus*

ACT I

SCENE i
Venice. A street.

[*Enter* RODERIGO *and* IAGO.]

RODERIGO. Tush, never tell me. I take it much unkindly
That thou, Iago, who hast had my purse
As if the strings were thine, shouldst know of this.

IAGO. 'Sblood,° but you will not hear me.
5   If ever I did dream of such a matter,
Abhor me.

RODERIGO. Thou told'st me thou didst hold him in thy hate.

IAGO. Despise me if I do not. Three great ones of the city,
In personal suit to make me his lieutenant,
10   Off-capp'd to him. And, by the faith of man,
I know my price: I am worth no worse a place.

But he, as loving his own pride and purposes,
Evades them, with a bombast circumstance°
Horribly stuff'd with epithets of war,
And, in conclusion,   15
Nonsuits° my mediators; for, "Certes," says he,
"I have already chose my officer."
And what was he?
Forsooth, a great arithmetician,°
One Michael Cassio, a Florentine,   20
A fellow almost damn'd in a fair wife,°
That never set a squadron in the field,
Nor the division of a battle knows
More than a spinster—unless the bookish theoric,
Wherein the toged consuls can propose   25

---

bombast circumstance elaborate excuse; empty words
Nonsuits overrules   *arithmetician* mere theoretician
almost . . . wife (possibly Shakespeare's slip; Cassio has no wife in the play but had in Cinthio's version that was Shakespeare's source; to be married to "a fair wife" is to risk being cuckolded)

'Sblood by God's blood

As masterly as he.° Mere prattle without prac-
tice
Is all his soldiership. But he, sir, had the elec-
tion,°
And I, of whom his eyes° had seen the proof
At Rhodes, at Cyprus, and on other grounds
Christian and heathen, must be be-lee'd and
30   calm'd°
By debitor and creditor.° This counter-caster,°
He, in good time, must his lieutenant be,
And I—God bless the mark!—his Moorship's
ancient.°
RODERIGO. By heaven, I rather would have been
his hangman.
IAGO. Why, there's no remedy; 'tis the curse of
35   service.
Preferment goes by letter and affection,°
And not by old gradation,° where each second
Stood heir to the first. Now, sir, be judge your-
self
Whether I in any just term am affin'd°
To love the Moor.
40 RODERIGO.   I would not follow him then.
IAGO. O, sir, content you.
I follow him to serve my turn upon him.
We cannot all be masters, nor all masters
Cannot be truly follow'd. You shall mark
45 Many a duteous and knee-crooking knave
That, doting on his own obsequious bondage,
Wears out his time, much like his master's ass,
For naught but provender, and when he's old,
cashier'd.°
Whip me such honest knaves.° Others there are
50 Who, trimm'd in forms and visages° of duty,
Keep yet their hearts attending on themselves,
And throwing but shows of service on their
lords
Do well thrive by them, and when they have
lin'd their coats,
Do themselves homage. These fellows have
some soul,
55 And such a one do I profess myself. For, sir,
It is as sure as you are Roderigo,

That never . . . as he (Iago heaps scorn on Cassio as a
    student of war rather than an experienced warrior)
had the election   won the appointment
his eyes   i.e., Othello's eyes
be-lee'd and calm'd   left stranded and windless, like a
    ship, by this *debitor and creditor* Cassio
counter-caster   the "arithmetician," bookkeeper Cassio
ancient   ensign (third officer)
letter and affection   i.e., "pull"
old gradation   seniority   *affin'd*   duty-bound
cashier'd   turned out
whip . . . knaves   let such fellows be whipped
forms and visages   appearances

Were I the Moor, I would not be Iago.
In following him, I follow but myself.
Heaven is my judge, not I for love and duty,
But seeming so, for my peculiar° end.   60
For when my outward action doth demonstrate
The native act and figure of my heart°
In compliment extern,° 'tis not long after
But I will wear my heart upon my sleeve
For daws to peck at. I am not what I am.   65
RODERIGO. What a full fortune does the thick-lips
owe,°
If he can carry 't thus!°
IAGO.   Call up her father.
Rouse him, make after him, poison his delight,
Proclaim him in the streets, incense her kins-
men,
And, though he in a fertile climate dwell,   70
Plague him with flies. Though that his joy be
joy,
Yet throw such changes of vexation on 't
As it may lose some color.
RODERIGO. Here is her father's house. I'll call
aloud.
IAGO. Do, with like timorous° accent and dire yell   75
As when, by night and negligence, the fire
Is spied in populous cities.
RODERIGO. What ho, Brabantio! Signior Brabantio,
ho!
IAGO. Awake! What ho, Brabantio! Thieves!
Thieves! Thieves!
Look to your house, your daughter, and your
bags!   80
Thieves! Thieves!
    [BRABANTIO *appears above, at a window.*]
BRABANTIO. What is the reason of this terrible
summons?
What is the matter there?
RODERIGO. Signior, is all your family within?
IAGO. Are your doors lock'd?
BRABANTIO.   Why, wherefore ask you this?   85
IAGO. 'Zounds,° sir, you're robb'd. For shame, put
on your gown.
Your heart is burst, you have lost half your soul.
Even now, now, very now, an old black ram
Is tupping your white ewe. Arise, arise!
Awake the snorting citizens with the bell,   90
Or else the devil will make a grandsire of you.
Arise, I say!
BRABANTIO.   What, have you lost your wits?

peculiar   personal
The native . . . heart   my real feelings
compliment extern   external show   *owe*   own, have
carry 't thus   get away with it   *timorous*   terrifying
'Zounds   by God's wounds

465

RODERIGO. Most reverend signior, do you know my
    voice?

BRABANTIO. Not I. What are you?

RODERIGO. My name is Roderigo.

95 BRABINTIO.   The worser welcome.
    I have charg'd thee not to haunt about my
        doors.
    In honest plainness thou hast heard me say
    My daughter is not for thee; and now, in
        madness,
    Being full of supper and distemp'ring draughts,°
100 Upon malicious bravery,° dost thou come
    To start° my quiet.

RODERIGO. Sir, sir, sir—

BRABANTIO.   But thou must needs be sure
    My spirit and my place have in them power
    To make this bitter to thee.

RODERIGO.   Patience, good sir.

BRABANTIO. What tell'st thou me of robbing? This
105   is Venice;
    My house is not a grange.°

RODERIGO.   Most grave Brabantio,
    In simple and pure soul I come to you.

IAGO. 'Zounds, sir, you are one of those that will
    not serve God if the devil bid you. Because we
110 come to do you service and you think we are
    ruffians, you'll have your daughter covered with
    a Barbary° horse. You'll have your nephews°
    neigh to you. You'll have coursers for cousins,
    and gennets for germans.°

115 BRABANTIO. What profane wretch art thou?

IAGO. I am one, sir, that comes to tell you your
    daughter and the Moor are now making the
    beast with two backs.

BRABANTIO. Thou art a villain.

IAGO.   You are a—senator.

BRABANTIO. This thou shalt answer. I know thee,
120   Roderigo.

RODERIGO. Sir, I will answer anything. But, I
    beseech you,
    If't be your pleasure and most wise consent,
    As partly I find it is, that your fair daughter,
    At this odd-even° and dull watch o' the night,
125 Transported with no worse nor better guard
    But with a knave of common hire, a gondolier,
    To the gross clasps of a lascivious Moor—
    If this be known to you, and your allowance,
    We then have done you bold and saucy wrongs.
130 But if you know not this, my manners tell me

We have your wrong rebuke. Do not believe
That, from° the sense of all civility,
I thus would play and trifle with your reverence.
Your daughter, if you have not given her leave,
I say again, hath made a gross revolt,   135
Tying her duty, beauty, wit, and fortunes
In an extravagant and wheeling° stranger
Of here and everywhere. Straight satisfy your-
    self.
If she be in her chamber or your house,
Let loose on me the justice of the state   140
For thus deluding you.

BRABANTIO.   Strike on the tinder, ho!
    Give me a taper! Call up all my people!
    This accident° is not unlike my dream.
    Belief of it oppresses me already.
    Light, I say! Light!   [Exit above]

IAGO.   Farewell, for I must leave you.   145
    It seems not meet, nor wholesome to my
        place,°
    To be produc'd—as, if I stay, I shall—
    Against the Moor. For I do know, the state,
    However this may gall him with some check,
    Cannot with safety cast° him; for he's embark'd   150
    With such loud reason° to the Cyprus wars,
    Which even now stand in act,° that, for their
        souls,
    Another of his fathom they have none
    To lead their business. In which regard,
    Though I do hate him as I do hell pains,   155
    Yet for necessity of present life,
    I must show out a flag and sign of love,
    Which is indeed but sign. That you shall surely
        find him,
    Lead to the Sagittar° the raised search,
    And there will I be with him. So farewell.   160
                                            [Exit]
[Enter, below, BRABANTIO, in his nightgown, and
        SERVANTS with torches.]

BRABANTIO. It is too true an evil. Gone she is,
    And what's to come of my despised time
    Is naught but bitterness. Now, Roderigo,
    Where didst thou see her? O unhappy girl!
    With the Moor, say'st thou? Who would be a
        father!   165
    How didst thou know 'twas she? O, she deceives
        me

---

distempering draughts drink   *bravery* bravado
start startle   *grange* outlying farmhouse
Barbary Arabian, i.e., Moorish
nephews grandchildren   *germans* blood relatives
odd-even toss-up, whether night or morning

from contrary to
extravagant and wheeling i.e., frequently moving about
    from post to post
accident event   *place* office   *cast* dismiss
loud reason compelling necessity
stand in act have begun
Sagittar Othello's lodging place

Past thought! What said she to you? Get more
 tapers.
Raise all my kindred. Are they married, think
 you?
RODERIGO. Truly, I think they are.
BRABANTIO. O heaven! How got she out? O treason
170 of the blood!
Fathers, from hence trust not your daughters'
 minds
By what you see them act. Is there not charms
By which the property° of youth and maidhood
May be abus'd? Have you not read, Roderigo,
Of some such thing?
175 RODERIGO.   Yes, sir, I have indeed.
BRABANTIO. Call up my brother. O, would you had
 had her!
Some one way, some another. Do you know
Where we may apprehend her and the Moor?
RODERIGO. I think I can discover him, if you please
180 To get good guard and go along with me.
BRABANTIO. Pray you, lead on. At every house I'll
 call;
I may command at most. Get weapons, ho!
And raise some special officers of night.
On, good Roderigo; I'll deserve your pains.°
                                        [*Exeunt*]

SCENE ii
Another street.

[*Enter* OTHELLO, IAGO, *and* ATTENDANTS *with*
torches.]
IAGO. Though in the trade of war I have slain men,
Yet do I hold it very stuff o' the conscience
To do no contriv'd murder. I lack iniquity
Sometimes to do me service. Nine or ten times
I had thought to have yerk'd° him here under
5 the ribs.
OTHELLO. 'Tis better as it is.
IAGO.   Nay, but he prated
And spoke such scurvy and provoking terms
Against your honor,
That, with the little godliness I have,
10 I did full hard forbear him. But I pray you, sir,
Are you fast married? Be assur'd of this,
That the magnifico° is much belov'd,
And hath in his effect a voice potential
As double as the duke's.° He will divorce you

Or put upon you what restraint and grievance 15
The law, with all his might to enforce it on,
Will give him cable.°
OTHELLO.   Let him do his spite.
My services which I have done the signiory°
Shall out-tongue his complaints. 'Tis yet to
 know°—
Which, when I know that boasting is an honor, 20
I shall promulgate—I fetch my life and being
From men of royal siege,° and my demerits°
May speak unbonneted° to as proud a fortune
As this that I have reach'd. For know, Iago,
But that I love the gentle Desdemona, 25
I would not my unhoused free condition
Put into circumscription and confine°
For the sea's worth. But, look! What lights come
 yond?
IAGO. Those are the raised father and his friends.
You were best go in.
OTHELLO.   Not I; I must be found. 30
My parts, my title, and my perfect soul°
Shall manifest me rightly. Is it they?
IAGO. By Janus,° I think no.
[*Enter* CASSIO, *and certain* OFFICERS *with torches.*]
OTHELLO. The servants of the duke, and my
 lieutenant.
The goodness of the night upon you, friends! 35
What is the news?
CASSIO.   The duke does greet you, general,
And he requires your haste-posthaste ap-
 pearance,
Even on the instant.
OTHELLO.   What is the matter, think you?
CASSIO. Something from Cyprus, as I may divine.
It is a business of some heat.° The galleys 40
Have sent a dozen sequent° messengers
This very night at one another's heels;
And many of the consuls, rais'd and met,
Are at the duke's already. You have been hotly
 call'd for,
When, being not at your lodging to be found, 45
The senate hath sent about three several quests
To search you out.
OTHELLO.   'Tis well I am found by you.
I will but spend a word here in the house,
And go with you.   [*Exit*]
CASSIO.   Ancient, what makes he here?

property true nature
deserve your pains reward you   *yerk'd* stabbed
magnifico nobleman
voice . . . duke's doubly powerful, like the duke's

cable scope   *signiory* governing body
yet to know yet to be made known
siege seat, i.e., rank   *demerits* merits
unbonneted on even terms   *confine* confinement
parts . . . soul merits, place, and unblemished
 character
Janus two-faced god
heat urgency   *sequent* successive

IAGO. Faith, he tonight hath boarded a land
50   carrack.°
    If it prove lawful prize, he's made forever.
CASSIO. I do not understand.
IAGO.   He's married.
CASSIO.   To who?
            [Re-enter OTHELLO.]
IAGO. Marry,° to—Come, captain, will you go?
OTHELLO.   Have with you.
CASSIO. Here comes another troop to seek for you.
55 IAGO. It is Brabantio. General, be advis'd.
    He comes to bad intent.
        [Enter BRABANTIO, RODERIGO, and OFFICERS with
                torches and weapons.]
OTHELLO.   Holla! Stand there!
RODERIGO. Signior, it is the Moor.
BRABANTIO.   Down with him, thief!
                [They draw on both sides.]
IAGO. You, Roderigo! Come, sir, I am for you.
OTHELLO. Keep up your bright swords, for the
    dew will rust them.
    Good signior, you shall more command with
60   years
    Than with your weapons.
BRABANTIO. O thou foul thief, where hast thou
    stow'd my daughter?
    Damn'd as thou art, thou hast enchanted her;
    For I'll refer me to all things of sense,
65 If she in chains of magic were not bound,
    Whether a maid so tender, fair, and happy,
    So opposite to marriage that she shunn'd
    The wealthy curled darlings of our nation,
    Would ever have, t' incur a general mock,°
70 Run from her guardage° to the sooty bosom
    Of such a thing as thou, to fear, not to delight.
    Judge me the world, if 'tis not gross in sense°
    That thou hast practic'd on her with foul
        charms,
    Abus'd her delicate youth with drugs or min-
        erals
75 That weaken motion.° I'll have 't disputed on;
    'Tis probable, and palpable to thinking.
    I therefore apprehend and do attach thee
    For an abuser of the world, a practicer
    Of arts inhibited and out of warrant.°
80 Lay hold upon him. If he do resist,
    Subdue him at his peril.
OTHELLO.   Hold your hands,
    Both you of my inclining and the rest.

Were it my cue to fight, I should have known it
Without a prompter. Where will you that I go
To answer this your charge?
BRABANTIO.   To prison, till fit time   85
Of law and course of direct session°
Call thee to answer.
OTHELLO.   What if I do obey?
How may the duke be therewith satisfied,
Whose messengers are here about my side
Upon some present business of the state   90
To bring me to him?
FIRST OFFICER.   'Tis true, most worthy signior.
The duke's in council, and your noble self,
I am sure, is sent for.
BRABANTIO.   How! The duke in council!
In this time of the night! Bring him away.
Mine's not an idle cause: the duke himself,   95
Or any of my brothers of the state,
Cannot but feel this wrong as 'twere their own;
For if such actions may have passage free,
Bond-slaves and pagans shall our statesmen be.
                                          [Exeunt]

                    SCENE iii
                A council chamber.

        [*The* DUKE *and* SENATORS *sitting at a table;*
                    OFFICERS *attending.*]
DUKE. There is no composition in these news
    That gives them credit.
FIRST SENATOR.   Indeed they are disproportion'd;
    My letters say a hundred and seven galleys.
DUKE. And mine, a hundred and forty.
SECOND SENATOR.   And mine, two hundred.
    But though they jump° not on a just° account— 5
    As in these cases, where the aim° reports,
    'Tis oft with difference—yet do they all confirm
    A Turkish fleet, and bearing up to Cyprus.
DUKE. Nay, it is possible enough to judgment.
    I do not so secure me in the error,   10
    But the main article I do approve
    In fearful sense.°
SAILOR. [*Within*] What, ho! What, ho! What, ho!
FIRST OFFICER. A messenger from the galleys.
                [*Enter* SAILOR.]
DUKE.   Now, what's the business?
SAILOR. The Turkish preparation makes for Rhodes.

---

carrack treasure ship
Marry by the Virgin Mary (with pun)
general mock public disgrace   *guardage* i.e., home
gross in sense all too obvious
weaken motion destroy the will
arts . . . warrant prohibited and illegal (black arts)

course . . . session in due course (no special treatment)
composition consistency   *jump* agree   *just* exact
aim estimate
I do . . . sense I am not so much reassured by the
    discrepant reports but that I do believe, fearfully, the
    general purport

15   So was I bid report here to the state
      By Signior Angelo.
    Duke. How say you by this change?
    First Senator.   This cannot be,
      By no assay of reason. 'Tis a pageant°
      To keep us in false gaze, when we consider
20   Th' importancy of Cyprus to the Turk;
      And let ourselves again but understand
      That as it more concerns the Turk than Rhodes,
      So may he with more facile question bear it,°
      For that it stands not in such warlike brace,°
25   But altogether lacks th' abilities
      That Rhodes is dress'd in. If we make thought of
      this,
      We must not think the Turk is so unskilful
      To leave that latest which concerns him first,
      Neglecting an attempt of ease and gain
30   To wake and wage° a danger profitless.
    Duke. Nay, in all confidence, he's not for Rhodes.
    First Officer. Here is more news.

                [Enter a MESSENGER.]

    Messenger. The Ottomites, reverend and gracious,
      Steering with due course toward the isle of
      Rhodes,
35   Have there injointed them with an after fleet.
    First Senator. Aye, so I thought. How many, as
      you guess?
    Messenger. Of thirty sail. And now they do re-stem°
      Their backward course, bearing with frank
      appearance
      Their purposes toward Cyprus. Signior Mon-
      tano,
40   Your trusty and most valiant servitor,
      With his free duty° recommends you thus,
      And prays you to believe him.
    Duke. 'Tis certain then for Cyprus.
      Marcus Luccicos, is not he in town?
45   First Senator. He's now in Florence.
    Duke. Write from us to him, post-posthaste
      dispatch.
    First Senator. Here comes Brabantio and the
      valiant Moor.

      [Enter BRABANTIO, OTHELLO, IAGO, RODERIGO,
            and OFFICERS.]

    Duke. Valiant Othello, we must straight employ
      you
      Against the general enemy Ottoman.
      [To BRABANTIO] I did not see you; welcome,
50   gentle signior.

We lack'd your counsel and your help tonight.
Brabantio. So did I yours. Good your grace,
    pardon me;
    Neither my place nor aught I heard of business
    Hath rais'd me from my bed, nor doth the
    general care
    Take hold on me. For my particular grief   55
    Is of so flood-gate and o'erbearing nature
    That it engluts and swallows other sorrows,
    And it is still itself.
Duke   Why, what's the matter?
Brabantio. My daughter! O, my daughter!
All.   Dead?
Brabantio.   Aye, to me.
    She is abus'd, stol'n from me, and corrupted   60
    By spells and medicines bought of mounte-
    banks;
    For nature so preposterously to err,
    Being not deficient, blind, or lame of sense,
    Sans° witchcraft could not.
Duke. Whoe'er he be that in this foul proceeding   65
    Hath thus beguil'd your daughter of herself
    And you of her, the bloody book of law
    You shall yourself read in the bitter letter
    After your own sense,° yea, though our proper°
    son
    Stood in your action.
Brabantio.   Humbly I thank your grace.   70
    Here is the man, this Moor, whom now, it
    seems,
    Your special mandate for the state affairs
    Hath hither brought.
All.   We are very sorry for 't.
Duke. [To OTHELLO] What in your own part can
    you say to this?
Brabantio. Nothing but this is so.   75
Othello. Most potent, grave, and reverend
    signiors,
    My very noble and approv'd° good masters,
    That I have ta'en away this old man's daughter,
    It is most true; true, I have married her.
    The very head and front of my offending   80
    Hath this extent, no more. Rude am I in my
    speech,
    And little blest with the soft phrase of peace;
    For since these arms of mine had seven years'
    pith,°
    Till now some nine moons wasted, they have
    us'd
    Their dearest action in the tented field,   85

---

pageant (false) show
with . . . bear it more easily conquer it
warlike brace state of preparedness
wage and wage initiate and carry out
restem retrace   free duty expressions of respect

Sans without
the bloody . . . sense i.e., you may choose what penalty
  you will
proper own   approv'd proven   pith strength

And little of this great world can I speak
More than pertains to feats of broil and battle;
And therefore little shall I grace my cause
In speaking for myself. Yet, by your gracious
   patience,
90 I will a round° unvarnish'd tale deliver
Of my whole course of love: what drugs, what
   charms,
What conjuration, and what mighty magic—
For such proceeding I am charg'd withal—
I won his daughter.
BRABANTIO.   A maiden never bold,
95 Of spirit so still and quiet that her motion°
Blush'd at herself, and she—in spite of nature,
Of years, of country, credit, everything—
To fall in love with what she fear'd to look on!
It is a judgment maim'd and most imperfect
100 That will confess perfection so could err
Against all rules of nature, and must be driven
To find out practices of cunning hell
Why this should be. I therefore vouch again
That with some mixtures powerful o'er the
   blood,
105 Or with some dram conjur'd to this effect,
He wrought upon her.
DUKE.   To vouch this is no proof
Without more certain and more overt test
Than these thin habits and poor likelihoods
Of modern seeming° do prefer against him.
110 FIRST SENATOR. But, Othello, speak.
Did you by indirect and forced° courses
Subdue and poison this young maid's affections?
Or came it by request, and such fair question
As soul to soul affordeth?
OTHELLO.   I do beseech you,
115 Send for the lady to the Sagittar
And let her speak of me before her father.
If you do find me foul in her report,
The trust, the office I do hold of you,
Not only take away, but let your sentence
Even fall upon my life.
120 DUKE.   Fetch Desdemona hither.
OTHELLO. Ancient, conduct them; you best know
   the place.
          [Exeunt IAGO and ATTENDANTS.]
And till she come, as truly as to heaven
I do confess the vices of my blood,
So justly to your grave ears I'll present
125 How I did thrive in this fair lady's love
And she in mine.
DUKE. Say it, Othello.

OTHELLO. Her father lov'd me, oft invited me,
Still° question'd me the story of my life
From year to year, the battles, sieges, fortunes   130
That I have pass'd.
I ran it through, even from my boyish days
To the very moment that he bade me tell it:
Wherein I spake of most disastrous chances,
Of moving accidents by flood and field,   135
Of hair-breadth 'scapes i' th' imminent deadly
   breach,
Of being taken by th' insolent foe
And sold to slavery, of my redemption thence
And portance° in my travel's history,
Wherein of antres° vast and deserts idle,°   140
Rough quarries, rocks, and hills whose heads
   touch heaven
It was my hint° to speak—such was the process;
And of the cannibals that each other eat,
The anthropophagi,° and men whose heads
Do grow beneath their shoulders. This to hear   145
Would Desdemona seriously incline.
But still the house affairs would draw her thence,
Which ever as she could with haste dispatch,
She'd come again and with a greedy ear
Devour up my discourse, which I observing   150
Took once a pliant hour and found good means
To draw from her a prayer of earnest heart
That I would all my pilgrimage dilate,
Whereof by parcels she had something heard
But not intentively.° I did consent,   155
And often did beguile her of her tears
When I did speak of some distressful stroke
That my youth suffer'd. My story being done,
She gave me for my pains a world of sighs.
She swore, in faith, 'twas strange, 'twas passing°
   strange,   160
'Twas pitiful, 'twas wondrous pitiful;
She wish'd she had not heard it, yet she wish'd
That heaven had made her° such a man. She
   thank'd me
And bade me, if I had a friend that lov'd her,
I should but teach him how to tell my story,   165
And that would woo her. Upon this hint° I spake.
She lov'd me for the dangers I had pass'd,
And I lov'd her that she did pity them.
This only is the witchcraft I have us'd.
Here comes the lady; let her witness it.   170
     [Enter DESDEMONA, IAGO, and ATTENDANTS.]
DUKE. I think this tale would win my daughter too.
Good Brabantio,

---

round plain   *motion* emotion
modern seeming insignificant evidence
forced contrived

Still always   *portance* personal bearing
antres caverns   *idle* empty   *hint* occasion
anthropophagi man-eaters   *intentively* uninterruptedly
passing surpassing   *her* for her   *hint* cue

Take up this mangled matter at the best.°
Men do their broken weapons rather use
Than their bare hands.

175 BRABANTIO.   I pray you, hear her speak.
If she confess that she was half the wooer,
Destruction on my head if my bad blame
Light on the man! Come hither, gentle mistress.
Do you perceive in all this noble company
Where most you owe obedience?

180 DESDEMONA.   My noble father,
I do perceive here a divided duty.
To you I am bound for life and education;
My life and education both do learn me
How to respect you. You are the lord of duty.
I am hitherto your daughter. But here's my
185   husband,
And so much duty as my mother show'd
To you, preferring you before her father,
So much I challenge that I may profess
Due to the Moor my lord.

BRABANTIO.   God be with you! I have done.
190 Please it your grace, on to the state of affairs.
I had rather to adopt a child than get° it.
Come hither, Moor.
I here do give thee that with all my heart
Which, but thou hast already, with all my heart
195 I would keep from thee. For your sake, jewel,
I am glad at soul I have no other child;
For thy escape would teach me tyranny,
To hang clogs on them. I have done, my lord.

DUKE. Let me speak like yourself, and lay a sen-
    tence
200 Which, as a grise° or step, may help these lovers
Into your favor.
When remedies are past, the griefs are ended
By seeing the worst, which late on hopes de-
    pended.
To mourn a mischief that is past and gone
205 Is the next way to draw new mischief on.
What cannot be preserv'd when fortune takes,
Patience her injury a mockery makes.
The robb'd that smiles steals something from
    the thief;
He robs himself that spends a bootless° grief.

210 BRABANTIO. So let the Turk of Cyprus us beguile—
We lose it not so long as we can smile!
He bears the sentence well that nothing bears
But the free comfort which from thence he
    hears;
But he bears both the sentence and the sorrow,
215 That, to pay grief, must of poor patience borrow.
These sentences, to sugar or to gall,

Being strong on both sides, are equivocal.
But words are words; I never yet did hear
That the bruis'd heart was pierced° through the
    ear.
I humbly beseech you, proceed to the affairs of
    state.   220

DUKE. The Turk with a most mighty preparation
makes for Cyprus. Othello, the fortitude of the
place is best known to you, and though we have
there a substitute of most allowed° sufficiency,
yet opinion, a sovereign mistress of effects,°   225
throws a more safer voice on you. You must
therefore be content to slubber° the gloss of
your new fortunes with this more stubborn and
boisterous expedition.

OTHELLO. The tyrant custom, most grave senators, 230
Hath made the flinty and steel couch of war
My thrice-driven° bed of down. I do agnize°
A natural and prompt alacrity
I find in hardness, and do undertake
These present wars against the Ottomites.   235
Most humbly therefore bending to your state,
I crave fit disposition for my wife,
Due reference of place and exhibition,
With such accommodation and besort°
As levels with her breeding.

DUKE.   If you please,   240
Be 't at her father's.

BRABANTIO.   I'll not have it so.

OTHELLO. Nor I.

DESDEMONA.   Nor I. I would not there reside,
To put my father in impatient thoughts
By being in his eye. Most gracious duke,
To my unfolding° lend your prosperous° ear,   245
And let me find a charter° in your voice
T' assist my simpleness.

DUKE.   What would you, Desdemona?

DESDEMONA. That I did love the Moor to live with
    him,
My downright violence and storm of fortunes°
May trumpet to the world. My heart's subdu'd   250
Even to the very quality of my lord.
I saw Othello's visage in his mind,
And to his honors and his valiant parts

---

pierced reached   *allowed* acknowledged
opinion . . . effects public opinion, which directs our
    actions
slubber besmear
thrice-driven thrice-sifted   *agnize* acknowledge
Due . . . besort suitable assignment of lodgings, monetary
    allowance, and appropriate attendants
unfolding proposal   *prosperous* favorable
charter authorization
downright . . . fortunes i.e., in taking the bull by the
    horns, eloping with Othello

Take . . . best make the best of the situation
get beget   *grise* degree   *bootless* fruitless

471

Did I my soul and fortunes consecrate.

255 So that, dear lords, if I be left behind,
A moth of peace, and he go to the war,
The rites for which I love him are bereft me,
And I a heavy interim shall support
By his dear absence. Let me go with him.

260 OTHELLO. Let her have your voices.
Vouch with me, heaven, I therefore beg it not
To please the palate of my appetite,
Nor to comply with heat—the young affects°
In me defunct—and proper° satisfaction,

265 But to be free and bounteous to her mind.
And heaven defend° your good souls that you
think
I will your serious and great business scant
For she is with me. No, when light-wing'd toys
Of feather'd Cupid seel° with wanton dulness

270 My speculative and offic'd instruments,°
That my disports corrupt and taint my business,
Let housewives make a skillet of my helm,
And all indign° and base adversities
Make head against my estimation!°

275 DUKE. Be it as you shall privately determine,
Either for her stay or going. Th' affair cries
haste,
And speed must answer 't; you must hence
tonight.

DESDEMONA. Tonight, my lord?

DUKE.   This night.

OTHELLO.   With all my heart.

DUKE. At nine i' the morning here we'll meet
again.

280 Othello, leave some officer behind,
And he shall our commission bring to you
With such things else of quality and respect
As doth import° you.

OTHELLO.   So please your grace, my ancient.
A man he is of honesty and trust.

285 To his conveyance I assign my wife,
With what else needful your good grace shall
think
To be sent after me.

DUKE.   Let it be so.
Good night to everyone. [To BRABANTIO] And,
noble signior,
If virtue no delighted° beauty lack,

290 Your son-in-law is far more fair than black.

FIRST SENATOR. Adieu, brave Moor. Use Desdemona well.

BRABANTIO. Look to her, Moor, if thou hast eyes to
see.
She has deceiv'd her father, and may thee.
                    [Exeunt DUKE, SENATORS, OFFICERS, &c.]

OTHELLO. My life upon her faith! Honest Iago,
My Desdemona must I leave to thee.   295
I prithee, let thy wife attend on her,
And bring them after in the best advantage.
Come, Desdemona; I have but an hour
Of love, of worldly matters, and direction
To spend with thee. We must obey the time.   300
                    [Exeunt OTHELLO and DESDEMONA.]

RODERIGO. Iago!

IAGO. What say'st thou, noble heart?

RODERIGO. What will I do, think'st thou?

IAGO. Why, go to bed and sleep.

RODERIGO. I will incontinently° drown myself.   305

IAGO. If thou dost, I shall never love thee after.
Why, thou silly gentleman!

RODERIGO. It is silliness to live when to live is
torment; and then have we a prescription to
die when death is our physician.   310

IAGO. O villainous! I have looked upon the world
for four times seven years, and since I could
distinguish betwixt a benefit and an injury, I
never found man that knew how to love himself. Ere I would say I would drown myself for 315
the love of a guinea hen, I would change my
humanity with a baboon.

RODERIGO. What should I do? I confess it is my
shame to be so fond, but it is not in my virtue to
amend it.   320

IAGO. Virtue! A fig! 'Tis in ourselves that we are
thus or thus. Our bodies are gardens, to the
which our wills are gardeners, so that if we will
plant nettles or sow lettuce, set hyssop and
weed up thyme, supply it with one gender of 325
herbs or distract it with many, either to have it
sterile with idleness or manured with industry,
why, the power and corrigible authority of this
lies in our wills. If the balance of our lives had
not one scale of reason to poise another of 330
sensuality, the blood and baseness of our
natures would conduct us to most preposterous
conclusions. But we have reason to cool our
raging motions,° our carnal stings, our unbitted°
lusts, whereof I take this that you call love to be 335
a sect or scion.

RODERIGO. It cannot be.

IAGO. It is merely a lust of the blood and a permission of the will. Come, be a man. Drown
thyself! Drown cats and blind puppies. I have 340

---

young affects youthful passions   *proper* my own
defend forbid   *seel* cover over
speculative . . . instruments eyes and mental faculties
indign shameful
Make . . . estimation assault my reputation
import concern   *delighted* delightful

incontinently immediately
motions impulses   *unbitted* unbridled

professed me thy friend, and I confess me knit to
thy deserving with cables of perdurable tough-
ness. I could never better stead thee than now.
Put money in thy purse; follow thou the wars;
345   defeat thy favor° with an usurped beard; I say,
put money in thy purse. It cannot be that
Desdemona should long continue her love to
the Moor—put money in thy purse—nor he his
to her. It was a violent commencement, and
350   thou shalt see an answerable sequestration;°
put but money in thy purse. These Moors are
changeable in their wills; fill thy purse with
money. The food that to him now is as luscious
as locusts° shall be to him shortly as bitter as
355   coloquintida.° She must change for youth.
When she is sated with his body, she will find the
error of her choice. She must have change, she
must; therefore put money in thy purse. If thou
wilt needs damn thyself, do it a more delicate
360   way than drowning. Make all the money thou
canst. If sanctimony and a frail vow betwixt an
erring° barbarian and a supersubtle Venetian
be not too hard for my wits and all the tribe of
hell, thou shalt enjoy her; therefore make
365   money. A pox of drowning thyself! It is clean
out of the way. Seek thou rather to be hanged in
compassing thy joy than to be drowned and go
without her.

RODERIGO. Wilt thou be fast to my hopes if I
370   depend on the issue?

IAGO. Thou art sure of me. Go, make money. I
have told thee often, and I re-tell thee again and
again, I hate the Moor. My cause is hearted;°
thine hath no less reason. Let us be conjunctive
375   in our revenge against him. If thou canst cuckold

him, thou dost thyself a pleasure, me a sport.
There are many events in the womb of time
which will be delivered. Traverse. Go. Provide
thy money. We will have more of this tomor-
row. Adieu.   380

RODERIGO. Where shall we meet i' the morning?

IAGO. At my lodging.

RODERIGO. I'll be with thee betimes.

IAGO. Go to, farewell. Do you hear, Roderigo?

RODERIGO. What say you?   385

IAGO. No more of drowning, do you hear?

RODERIGO. I am changed. I'll go sell all my land.
                                              [Exit]

IAGO. Thus do I ever make my fool my purse;
   For I mine own gain'd knowledge should
      profane
   If I would time expend with such a snipe   390
   But for my sport and profit. I hate the Moor,
   And it is thought abroad that 'twixt my sheets
   He has done my office. I know not if 't be true,
   But I for mere suspicion in that kind
   Will do as if for surety. He holds me well;   395
   The better shall my purpose work on him.
   Cassio's a proper° man. Let me see now:
   To get his place, and to plume up my will
   In double knavery. How, how? Let's see:
   After some time, t' abuse Othello's ear   400
   That he is too familiar with his wife.
   He hath a person and a smooth dispose°
   To be suspected, fram'd to make women false.
   The Moor is of a free and open nature,
   That thinks men honest that but seem to be so, 405
   And will as tenderly be led by the nose
   As asses are.
   I have 't. It is engender'd. Hell and night
   Must bring this monstrous birth to the world's
      light.   [Exit]

defeat thy favor   change your face
answerable sequestration   corresponding conclusion
locusts   sweet fruit   coloquintida   bitter drug
erring   wandering   hearted   deep-seated

proper   handsome   dispose   manner

A C T   I I

SCENE i
*A seaport in Cyprus. An open place near the
quay.*

[*Enter* MONTANO *and two* GENTLEMEN.]

MONTANO. What from the cape can you discern at
sea?

FIRST GENTLEMAN. Nothing at all. It is a high-
wrought flood.

I cannot, 'twixt the heaven and the main,
   Descry a sail.

MONTANO. Methinks the wind hath spoke aloud at
   land;   5
   A fuller blast ne'er shook our battlements.
   If it hath ruffian'd so upon the sea,
   What ribs of oak, when mountains melt on
      them,
   Can hold the mortise? What shall we hear of this?

SECOND GENTLEMAN. A segregation° of the Turkish
10   fleet.
      For do but stand upon the foaming shore,
      The chidden billow seems to pelt the clouds;
      The wind-shak'd surge, with high and mon-
          strous main,
      Seems to cast water on the burning Bear°
15   And quench the guards of th' ever-fixed pole.°
      I never did like molestation° view
      On the enchafed flood.
    MONTANO.   If that the Turkish fleet
      Be not enshelter'd and embay'd, they are
          drown'd;
      It is impossible to bear it out.
              [Enter a THIRD GENTLEMAN.]
20 THIRD GENTLEMAN. News, lads! Our wars are done.
      The desperate tempest hath so bang'd the Turks
      That their designment halts.° A noble ship of
          Venice
      Hath seen a grievous wreck and sufferance
      On most part of their fleet.
    MONTANO. How! Is this true?
25 THIRD GENTLEMAN.   The ship is here put in,
      A Veronesa. Michael Cassio,
      Lieutenant to the warlike Moor Othello,
      Is come on shore, the Moor himself at sea,
      And is in full commission here for Cyprus.
30 MONTANO. I am glad on 't; 'tis a worthy governor.
    THIRD GENTLEMAN. But this same Cassio, though
          he speak of comfort
      Touching the Turkish loss, yet he looks sadly
      And prays the Moor be safe, for they were
          parted
      With foul and violent tempest.
    MONTANO.   Pray heavens he be,
      For I have serv'd him, and the man commands
35   Like a full° soldier. Let's to the seaside, ho!
      As well to see the vessel that's come in
      As to throw out our eyes for brave Othello,
      Even till we make the main and th' aerial blue
      An indistinct regard.°
    THIRD GENTLEMAN.   Come, let's do so,
40   For every minute is expectancy
      Of more arrivance.
              [Enter CASSIO.]
    CASSIO. Thanks, you the valiant of this warlike isle,
      That so approve the Moor! O, let the heavens
      Give him defense against the elements,
45   For I have lost him on a dangerous sea.
    MONTANO. Is he well shipp'd?

CASSIO. His bark is stoutly timber'd, and his pilot
      Of very expert and approv'd allowance;°
      Therefore my hopes, not surfeited to death,
      Stand in bold cure.°   50
              [A cry within: "A sail, a sail, a sail!"]
              [Enter a FOURTH GENTLEMAN.]
    CASSIO. What noise?
    FOURTH GENTLEMAN. The town is empty. On the
          brow o' the sea
      Stand ranks of people, and they cry "A sail!"
    CASSIO. My hopes do shape him for the governor.
              [Guns heard.]
    SECOND GENTLEMAN. They do discharge their shot
          of courtesy—   55
      Our friends at least.
    CASSIO.   I pray you, sir, go forth,
      And give us truth who 'tis that is arriv'd.
    SECOND GENTLEMAN. I shall.   [Exit]
    MONTANO. But, good lieutenant, is your general
          wiv'd?
    CASSIO. Most fortunately. He hath achiev'd a maid   60
      That paragons° description and wild fame,°
      One that excels the quirks of blazoning pens,°
      And in th' essential vesture of creation
      Does tire the ingener.°
              [Re-enter SECOND GENTLEMAN.]
                          How now! Who has put in?
    SECOND GENTLEMAN. 'Tis one Iago, ancient to the
          general.   65
    CASSIO. He has had most favorable and happy
          speed.
      Tempests themselves, high seas, and howling
          winds,
      The gutter'd rocks, and congregated sands,
      Traitors ensteep'd to clog the guiltless keel,
      As having sense of beauty, do omit   70
      Their mortal natures, letting go safely by
      The divine Desdemona.
    MONTANO.   What is she?
    CASSIO. She that I spake of, our great captain's
          captain,
      Left in the conduct of the bold Iago,
      Whose footing here anticipates our thoughts   75
      A se'nnight's speed. Great Jove, Othello guard,
      And swell his sail with thine own powerful
          breath,
      That he may bless this bay with his tall ship,
      Make love's quick pants in Desdemona's arms,
      Give renew'd fire to our extinct spirits,   80

---

segregation dispersion   Bear the constellation
pole the Pole Star   molestation disturbance
designment halts enterprise is lamed
full complete   indistinct regard indistinguishable

approv'd allowance   proven reputation
Stand . . . cure expect recovery   paragons surpasses
wild fame extravagant report
quirks . . . pens i.e., ingenious efforts of poets
tire the ingener weary the inventive describer

And bring all Cyprus comfort.
    [*Enter* Desdemona, Emilia, Iago, Roderigo,
          and Attendants.]
                    O, behold,
The riches of the ship is come on shore!
Ye men of Cyprus, let her have your knees.
Hail to thee, lady! And the grace of heaven,
85   Before, behind thee, and on every hand,
Enwheel thee round!
Desdemona.   I thank you, valiant Cassio.
What tidings can you tell me of my lord?
Cassio. He is not yet arriv'd, nor know I aught
But that he's well and will be shortly here.
90   Desdemona. O, but I fear—how lost you company?
Cassio. The great contention of the sea and skies
Parted our fellowship—but, hark! A sail.
    [*A cry within:* "A sail, a sail!" *Guns heard.*]
Second Gentleman. They give their greeting to the
citadel.
This likewise is a friend.
Cassio.   See for the news.
                    [*Exit* Gentleman.]
Good ancient, you are welcome. [*To* Emilia]
95   Welcome, mistress.
Let it not gall your patience, good Iago,
That I extend° my manners; 'tis my breeding
That gives me this bold show of courtesy.
                    [*Kissing her.*]
Iago. Sir, would she give you so much of her lips
100   As of her tongue she oft bestows on me,
You'd have enough.
Desdemona.   Alas, she has no speech.
Iago. In faith, too much—
I find it still when I have list to sleep.
Marry, before your ladyship, I grant
105   She puts her tongue a little in her heart
And chides with thinking.
Emilia. You have little cause to say so.
Iago. Come on, come on; you are pictures° out of
doors,
Bells° in your parlors, wildcats° in your kitchens,
110   Saints in your injuries, devils being offended,
Players in your housewifery, and housewives in
your beds.
Desdemona. O, fie upon thee, slanderer!
Iago. Nay, it is true, or else I am a Turk.
You rise to play, and go to bed to work.
Emilia. You shall not write my praise.
115   Iago.   No, let me not.
Desdemona. What wouldst thou write of me, if
thou shouldst praise me?
Iago. O gentle lady, do not put me to 't;

For I am nothing if not critical.
Desdemona. Come on, assay. There's one gone to
the harbor?   120
Iago. Aye, madam.
Desdemona. I am not merry, but I do beguile
The thing I am by seeming otherwise.
Come, how wouldst thou praise me?
Iago. I am about it; but indeed my invention   125
Comes from my pate as birdlime° does from
frieze;°
It plucks out brains and all. But my Muse labors,
And thus she is deliver'd:
If she be fair and wise, fairness and wit,
The one's for use, the other useth it.   130
Desdemona. Well prais'd! How if she be black and
witty?
Iago. If she be black, and thereto have a wit,
She'll find a white that shall her blackness fit.
Desdemona. Worse and worse.
Emilia. How if fair and foolish?   135
Iago. She never yet was foolish that was fair,
For even her folly help'd her to an heir.
Desdemona. These are old fond paradoxes to
make fools laugh i' th' alehouse. What miserable
praise hast thou for her that's foul and foolish? 140
Iago. There's none so foul, and foolish thereunto,
But does foul pranks which fair and wise ones do.
Desdemona. O heavy ignorance! Thou praisest the
worst best. But what praise couldst thou bestow
on a deserving woman indeed, one that in the 145
authority of her merit did justly put on the
vouch° of very malice itself?
Iago. She that was ever fair and never proud,
Had tongue at will and yet was never loud,
Never lack'd gold and yet went never gay,   150
Fled from her wish and yet said "Now I may;"
She that, being anger'd, her revenge being nigh,
Bade her wrong stay and her displeasure fly;
She that in wisdom never was so frail
To change the cod's head for the salmon's tail;° 155
She that could think and ne'er disclose her mind,
See suitors following and not look behind:
She was a wight,° if ever such wight were—
Desdemona. To do what?
Iago. To suckle fools and chronicle small beer.° 160
Desdemona. O most lame and impotent con-
clusion! Do not learn of him, Emilia, though he
be thy husband. How say you, Cassio? Is he not a
most profane and liberal counselor?

---

extend stretch   *pictures* i.e., painted
Bells i.e., ever jangling   *wildcats* i.e., rambunctious

birdlime sticky substance   *frieze* woolen material
put . . . vouch win the favorable testimony
cod's . . . tail i.e., the more valuable for the less
wight person
chronicle . . . beer i.e., manage trivialities

165 CASSIO. He speaks home, madam. You may relish
    him more in the soldier than in the scholar.
    IAGO. [*Aside*] He takes her by the palm. Aye, well
    said, whisper. With as little a web as this will I
    ensnare as great a fly as Cassio. Aye, smile upon
170 her, do; I will gyve° thee in thine own courtship.°
    You say true; 'tis so, indeed. If such tricks as
    these strip you out of your lieutenantry, it had
    been better you had not kissed your three
    fingers so oft, which now again you are most
175 apt to play the sir in. Very good; well kissed!
    An excellent courtesy! 'Tis so, indeed. Yet
    again your fingers to your lips? Would they were
    clyster pipes° for your sake!—[*Trumpet within*]
    The Moor! I know his trumpet.
180 CASSIO. 'Tis truly so.
    DESDEMONA. Let's meet him and receive him.
    CASSIO. Lo, where he comes!
            [*Enter* OTHELLO *and* ATTENDANTS.]
    OTHELLO. O my fair warrior!
    DESDEMONA.   My dear Othello!
    OTHELLO. It gives me wonder great as my content
185 To see you here before me. O my soul's joy!
    If after every tempest come such calms,
    May the winds blow till they have waken'd
        death!
    And let the lab'ring bark climb hills of seas
    Olympus-high and duck again as low
190 As hell's from heaven! If it were now to die,
    'Twere now to be most happy, for I fear
    My soul hath her content so absolute
    That not another comfort like to this
    Succeeds in unknown fate.
    DESDEMONA.   The heavens forbid
195 But that our loves and comforts should increase,
    Even as our days do grow!
    OTHELLO.   Amen to that, sweet powers!
    I cannot speak enough of this content.
    It stops me here; it is too much of joy.
    And this, and this, the greatest discords be
                                    [*Kissing her.*]
    That e'er our hearts shall make!
200 IAGO.   [*Aside*] O, you are well tun'd now!
    But I'll set down the pegs° that make this music,
    As honest as I am.
    OTHELLO.   Come, let us to the castle.
    News, friends. Our wars are done; the Turks
        are drown'd.
    How does my old acquaintance of this isle?
205 Honey, you shall be well desir'd in Cyprus;

I have found great love amongst them. O my
    sweet,
I prattle out of fashion, and I dote
In mine own comforts. I prithee, good Iago,
Go to the bay and disembark my coffers.
Bring thou the master to the citadel;   210
He is a good one, and his worthiness
Does challenge much respect. Come, Desde-
    mona,
Once more well met at Cyprus.
        [*Exeunt all but* IAGO *and* RODERIGO.]
IAGO. Do thou meet me presently at the harbor.
Come hither. If thou be'st valiant—as, they say, 215
base men being in love have then a nobility in
their natures more than is native to them—
list me. The lieutenant tonight watches on the
court of guard. First, I must tell thee this:
Desdemona is directly in love with him.   220
RODERIGO. With him! Why, 'tis not possible.
IAGO. Lay thy finger thus,° and let thy soul be
instructed. Mark me with what violence she
first loved the Moor but for bragging and telling
her fantastical lies. And will she love him still for 225
prating? Let not thy discreet heart think it. Her
eye must be fed, and what delight shall she
have to look on the devil? When the blood is
made dull with the act of sport, there should be,
again to inflame it and to give satiety a fresh   230
appetite, loveliness in favor,° sympathy in years,
manners, and beauties, all which the Moor is
defective in. Now, for want of these required
conveniences, her delicate tenderness will find
itself abused, begin to heave the gorge, disrelish 235
and abhor the Moor; very nature will instruct
her in it and compel her to some second choice.
Now, sir, this granted—as it is a most pregnant°
and unforced position—who stands so eminently in the degree of this fortune as Cassio   240
does? A knave very voluble, no further con-
scionable° than in putting on the mere form of
civil and humane seeming for the better compassing of his salt° and most hidden loose affection? Why, none; why, none. A slipper° and   245
subtle knave, a finder-out of occasions, that has
an eye can stamp and counterfeit advantages,°
though true advantage never present itself. A
devilish knave! Besides, the knave is handsome,
young, and hath all those requisites in him that   250
folly and green minds look after. A pestilent

---

gyve fetter   courtship courtly manners
clyster pipes i.e., for giving enemas or douches
set . . . pegs i.e., untune the strings

Lay . . . thus i.e., keep silent   favor face
pregnant natural
conscionable guided by conscience   salt lustful
slipper slick   advantages opportunities

complete knave, and the woman hath found him° already.

255 RODERIGO. I cannot believe that in her; she's full of most blest condition.

IAGO. Blest fig's end!° The wine she drinks is made of grapes.° If she had been blest, she would never have loved the Moor. Blest pud-
260 ding! Didst thou not see her paddle with the palm of his hand? Didst not mark that?

RODERIGO. Yes, that I did, but that was but courtesy.

IAGO. Lechery, by this hand, an index and obscure prologue to the history of lust and foul thoughts. They met so near with their lips that their
265 breaths embraced together. Villainous thoughts, Roderigo! When these mutualities° so marshal the way, hard at hand comes the master and main exercise, the incorporate conclusion.° Pish! But, sir, be you ruled by me. I have brought
270 you from Venice. Watch you tonight. For the command, I'll lay 't upon you. Cassio knows you not. I'll not be far from you. Do you find some occasion to anger Cassio, either by speaking too loud, or tainting° his discipline, or from what
275 other course you please, which the time shall more favorably minister.

RODERIGO. Well.

IAGO. Sir, he is rash and very sudden in choler,° and haply° may strike at you. Provoke him,
280 that he may; for even out of that will I cause these of Cyprus to mutiny, whose qualification° shall come into no true taste again but by the displanting of Cassio. So shall you have a shorter journey to your desires by the means I shall
285 then have to prefer° them, and the impediment most profitably removed, without the which there were no expectation of our prosperity.

RODERIGO. I will do this if I can bring it to any opportunity.

290 IAGO. I warrant thee. Meet me by and by at the citadel. I must fetch his necessaries ashore. Farewell.

RODERIGO. Adieu.   [Exit]

IAGO. That Cassio loves her, I do well believ't.
295 That she loves him, 'tis apt and of great credit. The Moor, howbeit that I endure him not, Is of a constant, loving, noble nature, And I dare think he'll prove to Desdemona

A most dear husband. Now, I do love her too, 300
Not out of absolute lust, though peradventure
I stand accountant for as great a sin,
But partly led to diet° my revenge
For that I do suspect the lusty Moor
Hath leap'd into my seat: the thought whereof
Doth like a poisonous mineral gnaw my in- 305
    wards,
And nothing can or shall content my soul
Till I am even'd with him, wife for wife;
Or failing so, yet that I put the Moor
At least into a jealousy so strong
That judgment cannot cure. Which thing to do, 310
If this poor trash of Venice, whom I trash°
For his quick hunting, stand the putting-on,
I'll have our Michael Cassio on the hip,°
Abuse him to the Moor in the rank garb°—
For I fear Cassio with my nightcap too— 315
Make the Moor thank me, love me, and reward
    me
For making him egregiously an ass
And practicing upon his peace and quiet
Even to madness. 'Tis here, but yet confus'd.
Knavery's plain face is never seen till us'd. 320
                            [Exit]

SCENE ii
A street.

[Enter a HERALD with a proclamation; PEOPLE following.]

HERALD. It is Othello's pleasure, our noble and valiant general, that upon certain tidings now arrived, importing the mere perdition° of the Turkish fleet, every man put himself into triumph°—some to dance, some to make 5 bonfires, each man to what sport and revels his addiction leads him. For, besides these beneficial news, it is the celebration of his nuptial. So much was his pleasure should be proclaimed. All offices are open, and there is full liberty of 10 feasting from this present hour of five till the bell have told eleven. Heaven bless the isle of Cyprus and our noble general Othello!

                            [Exeunt]

found him perceived what he is
Blest fig's end rubbish!
wine . . . grapes i.e., she is only human
mutualities shared impulses
incorporate conclusion bodily consummation
tainting disparaging   *choler* anger   *haply* perhaps
qualification satisfaction   *prefer* forward

diet feed
trash . . . trash rubbish . . . slow down (hounds that outdistance the pack are "trashed" with added weights)
on the hip i.e., "over a barrel"
rank garb foul manner
mere perdition complete ruination
triumph celebration

SCENE iii
A hall in the castle.

[*Enter* OTHELLO, DESDEMONA, CASSIO, *and*
ATTENDANTS.]

OTHELLO. Good Michael, look you to the guard
  tonight.
  Let's teach ourselves that honorable stop,
  Not to outsport discretion.
CASSIO. Iago hath direction what to do,
5 But notwithstanding with my personal eye
  Will I look to 't.
OTHELLO.   Iago is most honest.
  Michael, good night. Tomorrow with your
    earliest
  Let me have speech with you. Come, my dear
    love,
  The purchase made, the fruits are to ensue;
10 That profit's yet to come 'tween me and you.
  Good night.
  [*Exeunt* OTHELLO, DESDEMONA, *and* ATTENDANTS.]
          [*Enter* IAGO.]
CASSIO. Welcome, Iago. We must to the watch.
IAGO. Not this hour, lieutenant; 'tis not yet ten o'
  the clock. Our general cast° us thus early for the
15 love of his Desdemona, who let us not therefore
  blame. He hath not yet made wanton the night
  with her, and she is sport for Jove.
CASSIO. She's a most exquisite lady.
IAGO. And, I'll warrant her, full of game.
20 CASSIO. Indeed she's a most fresh and delicate
  creature.
IAGO. What an eye she has! Methinks it sounds a
  parley to provocation.°
CASSIO. An inviting eye, and yet methinks right
25 modest.
IAGO. And when she speaks, is it not an alarum° to
  love?
CASSIO. She is indeed perfection.
IAGO. Well, happiness to their sheets! Come,
30 lieutenant, I have a stoup of wine, and here
  without are a brace of Cyprus gallants that
  would fain have a measure to the health of
  black Othello.
CASSIO. Not tonight, good Iago. I have very poor
35 and unhappy brains for drinking. I could well
  wish courtesy would invent some other custom
  of entertainment.
IAGO. O, they are our friends. But one cup. I'll
  drink for you.

CASSIO. I have drunk but one cup tonight, and that 40
  was craftily qualified° too, and behold what
  innovation it makes here. I am unfortunate in
  the infirmity and dare not task my weakness
  with any more.
IAGO. What, man! 'Tis a night of revels. The 45
  gallants desire it.
CASSIO. Where are they?
IAGO. Here at the door; I pray you, call them in.
CASSIO. I'll do 't, but it dislikes me.   [*Exit*
IAGO. If I can fasten but one cup upon him, 50
  With that which he hath drunk tonight already,
  He'll be as full of quarrel and offense
  As my young mistress' dog. Now my sick fool
    Roderigo,
  Whom love hath turn'd almost the wrong side
    out,
  To Desdemona hath tonight carous'd 55
  Potations pottle-deep;° and he's to watch.
  Three lads of Cyprus, noble swelling spirits
  That hold their honors in a wary distance,
  The very elements of this warlike isle,
  Have I tonight fluster'd with flowing cups, 60
  And they watch too. Now, 'mongst this flock of
    drunkards,
  Am I to put our Cassio in some action
  That may offend the isle. But here they come.
  If consequence do but approve° my dream,
  My boat sails freely, both with wind and stream. 65
    [*Re-enter* CASSIO; *with him* MONTANO *and*
    GENTLEMEN; SERVANTS *following with wine.*]
CASSIO. 'Fore God, they have given me a rouse°
  already.
MONTANO. Good faith, a little one; not past a pint,
  as I am a soldier.
IAGO. Some wine, ho! 70

[*Sings*]   And let me the canakin° clink, clink,
        And let me the canakin clink.
          A soldier's a man,
          A life's but a span;
        Why then let a soldier drink. 75

  Some wine, boys!
CASSIO. 'Fore God, an excellent song.
IAGO. I learned it in England, where indeed they
  are most potent in potting. Your Dane, your
  German, and your swag-bellied Hollander— 80
  drink, ho!—are nothing to your English.
CASSIO. Is your Englishman so expert in his
  drinking?
IAGO. Why, he drinks you with facility your Dane

---

cast dismissed
parley to provocation invitation to encounter
alarum trumpet call

qualified diluted   *pottle-deep* to the bottom
consequence . . . approve what follows will only confirm
rouse large drink   *canakin* drinking vessel

85 dead drunk; he swears not to overthrow your
Almain;° he gives your Hollander a vomit ere
the next pottle can be filled.

CASSIO. To the health of our general!

MONTANO. I am for it, lieutenant, and I'll do you
90   justice.

IAGO. O sweet England!

[Sings]   King Stephen was a worthy peer,
        His breeches cost him but a crown;
       He held them sixpence all too dear,
95   With that he call'd the tailor lown.°

       He was a wight of high renown,
        And thou art but of low degree.
       'Tis pride that pulls the country down;
        Then take thine auld cloak about thee.

100   Some wine, ho!

CASSIO. Why, this is a more exquisite song than the
other.

IAGO. Will you hear 't again?

CASSIO. No, for I hold him to be unworthy of his
105   place that does those things. Well, God's above
all, and there be souls must be saved and there
be souls must not be saved.

IAGO. It's true, good lieutenant.

CASSIO. For mine own part—no offense to the
110   general, nor any man of quality—I hope to be
saved.

IAGO. And so do I too, lieutenant.

CASSIO. Aye, but, by your leave, not before me; the
lieutenant is to be saved before the ancient.
115   Let's have no more of this; let's to our affairs.
God forgive us our sins! Gentlemen, let's look
to our business. Do not think, gentlemen, I am
drunk. This is my ancient, this is my right hand,
and this is my left. I am not drunk now; I can
120   stand well enough and speak well enough.

ALL. Excellent well.

CASSIO. Why, very well then; you must not think
then that I am drunk.   [Exit]

MONTANO. To the platform, masters. Come, let's
125   set the watch.

IAGO. You see this fellow that is gone before.
He is a soldier fit to stand by Cæsar
And give direction. And do but see his vice.
'Tis to his virtue a just equinox,°
130   The one as long as th'other. 'Tis pity of him.
I fear the trust Othello puts him in
On some odd time of his infirmity
Will shake this island.

MONTANO.   But is he often thus?

IAGO. 'Tis evermore the prologue to his sleep.
He'll watch the horologe a double set°   135
If drink rock not his cradle.

MONTANO.   It were well
The general were put in mind of it.
Perhaps he sees it not, or his good nature
Prizes the virtue that appears in Cassio
And looks not on his evils. Is not this true?   140
               [Enter RODERIGO.]

IAGO. [Aside to him] How now, Roderigo!
I pray you, after the lieutenant. Go.
                 [Exit RODERIGO.]

MONTANO. And 'tis great pity that the noble Moor
Should hazard such a place as his own second
With one of an ingraft infirmity.   145
It were an honest action to say
So to the Moor.

IAGO.   Not I, for this fair island.
I do love Cassio well, and would do much
To cure him of this evil. But, hark! What noise?
        [A cry within: "Help! help!"]
   [Re-enter CASSIO, driving in RODERIGO.]

CASSIO. 'Zounds! You rogue! You rascal!   150

MONTANO. What's the matter, lieutenant?

CASSIO. A knave teach me my duty! But I'll beat
the knave into a wicker bottle.

RODERIGO. Beat me!

CASSIO. Dost thou prate, rogue?   155
                [Striking RODERIGO.]

MONTANO. Nay, good lieutenant; I pray you, sir,
hold your hand.

CASSIO. Let me go, sir, or I'll knock you o'er the
mazzard.°

MONTANO. Come, come, you're drunk.   160

CASSIO. Drunk!   [They fight.]

IAGO. [Aside to RODERIGO] Away, I say; go out, and
cry a mutiny.   [Exit RODERIGO.]
Nay, good lieutenant! God's will, gentlemen!
Help, ho!—Lieutenant—sir—Montano—sir—
Help, masters!—Here's a goodly watch indeed! 165
                [A bell rings.]
Who's that that rings the bell?—Diablo, ho!
The town will rise. God's will, lieutenant, hold,
You will be sham'd forever.
    [Re-enter OTHELLO and ATTENDANTS.]

OTHELLO.   What is the matter here?

MONTANO. 'Zounds, I bleed still, I am hurt to the
death.   [Faints.]

OTHELLO. Hold, for your lives!   170

IAGO. Hold, ho! Lieutenant—sir—Montano—
gentlemen—
Have you forgot all sense of place and duty?

Almain German   lown lout
just equinox exact equivalent

horologe . . . set the clock twice around
mazzard head

Hold! The general speaks to you. Hold, hold, for
     shame!
OTHELLO. Why, how now, ho! From whence
     ariseth this?
175 Are we turn'd Turks, and to ourselves do that
     Which heaven hath forbid the Ottomites?
     For Christian shame, put by this barbarous
        brawl.
     He that stirs next to carve for his own rage°
     Holds his soul light; he dies upon his motion.
180 Silence that dreadful bell. It frights the isle
     From her propriety. What is the matter,
        masters?
     Honest Iago, that look'st dead with grieving,
     Speak, who began this? On thy love, I charge
        thee.
IAGO. I do not know. Friends all but now, even now,
185 In quarter and in terms like bride and groom
     Devesting them for bed, and then, but now,
     As if some planet had unwitted men,
     Swords out, and tilting one at other's breast
     In opposition bloody. I cannot speak
190 Any beginning to this peevish odds,°
     And would in action glorious I had lost
     Those legs that brought me to a part of it!
OTHELLO. How comes it, Michael, you are thus
     forgot?°
CASSIO. I pray you, pardon me. I cannot speak.
OTHELLO. Worthy Montano, you were wont be
195   civil.
     The gravity and stillness of your youth
     The world hath noted, and your name is great
     In mouths of wisest censure. What's the matter,
     That you unlace your reputation thus,
200 And spend your rich opinion° for the name
     Of a night-brawler? Give me answer to it.
MONTANO. Worthy Othello, I am hurt to danger.
     Your officer, Iago, can inform you—
     While I spare speech, which something now
        offends me—
205 Of all that I do know. Nor know I aught
     By me that's said or done amiss this night,
     Unless self-charity be sometimes a vice,
     And to defend ourselves it be a sin
     When violence assails us.
OTHELLO.   Now, by heaven,
210 My blood begins my safer guides to rule,
     And passion, having my best judgment collied,°
     Assays to lead the way. If I once stir,
     Or do but lift this arm, the best of you

Shall sink in my rebuke. Give me to know
How this foul rout began, who set it on,   215
And he that is approv'd° in this offense,
Though he had twinn'd with me, both at a
   birth,
Shall lose me. What! In a town of war,
Yet wild, the people's hearts brimful of fear,
To manage° private and domestic quarrel,   220
In night, and on the court and guard of safety!
'Tis monstrous. Iago, who began 't?
MONTANO. If partially affin'd,° or leagu'd in office,
Thou dost deliver more or less than truth,
Thou art no soldier.
IAGO.   Touch me not so near.   225
I had rather have this tongue cut from my
   mouth
Than it should do offense to Michael Cassio;
Yet, I persuade myself, to speak the truth
Shall nothing wrong him. Thus it is, general.
Montano and myself being in speech,   230
There comes a fellow crying out for help,
And Cassio following him with determin'd
   sword
To execute upon him. Sir, this gentleman
Steps in to Cassio and entreats his pause.
Myself the crying fellow did pursue,   235
Lest by his clamor—as it so fell out—
The town might fall in fright. He, swift of foot,
Outran my purpose, and I return'd the rather
For that I heard the clink and fall of swords
And Cassio high in oath, which till tonight   240
I ne'er might say before. When I came back—
For this was brief—I found them close together,
At blow and thrust, even as again they were
When you yourself did part them.
More of this matter cannot I report.   245
But men are men; the best sometimes forget.
Though Cassio did some little wrong to him,
As men in rage strike those that wish them best,
Yet surely Cassio, I believe, receiv'd
From him that fled some strange indignity   250
Which patience could not pass.
OTHELLO.   I know, Iago,
Thy honesty and love doth mince this matter,
Making it light to Cassio. Cassio, I love thee.
But never more be officer of mine.
     [Re-enter DESDEMONA, attended.]
Look, if my gentle love be not rais'd up!   255
I'll make thee an example.
DESDEMONA.   What's the matter?
OTHELLO. All's well now, sweeting; come away to
   bed.

carve . . . rage indulge his own anger   odds quarrel
are . . . forgot have so forgotten yourself
spend . . . opinion waste your good name
collied blackened (as with coal dust)

approv'd found guilty   manage carry on
partially affin'd bound by partisanship

Sir, for your hurts, myself will be your surgeon
                              [*To* Montano, *who is led off.*]
Lead him off.
260   Iago, look with care about the town,
And silence those whom this vile brawl distracted.
Come, Desdemona: 'tis the soldiers' life
To have their balmy slumbers wak'd with strife.
                              [*Exeunt all but* Iago *and* Cassio.]
Iago. What, are you hurt, lieutenant?
265   Cassio. Aye, past all surgery.
Iago. Marry, heaven forbid!
Cassio. Reputation, reputation, reputation! O, I
have lost my reputation! I have lost the immortal part of myself, and what remains is
270   bestial. My reputation, Iago, my reputation!
Iago. As I am an honest man, I thought you had
received some bodily wound; there is more
sense in that than in reputation. Reputation is an
idle and most false imposition, oft got without
275   merit and lost without deserving. You have lost
no reputation at all, unless you repute yourself
such a loser. What, man! There are ways to
recover the general again. You are but now
cast in his mood, a punishment more in policy
280   than in malice, even so as one would beat his
offenseless dog to affright an imperious lion.
Sue to him again, and he's yours.
Cassio. I will rather sue to be despised than to
deceive so good a commander with so slight, so
285   drunken, and so indiscreet an officer. Drunk?
And speak parrot?° And squabble? Swagger?
Swear? And discourse fustian° with one's own
shadow? O thou invisible spirit of wine, if thou
hast no name to be known by, let us call thee
devil!
290   Iago. What was he that you followed with your
sword? What had he done to you?
Cassio. I know not.
Iago. Is 't possible?
Cassio. I remember a mass of things, but nothing
295   distinctly; a quarrel, but nothing wherefore. O
God, that men should put an enemy in their
mouths to steal away their brains! That we
should, with joy, pleasance, revel, and applause,
transform ourselves into beasts!
300   Iago. Why, but you are now well enough. How
came you thus recovered?
Cassio. It hath pleased the devil drunkenness to
give place to the devil wrath. One unperfectness
shows me another, to make me frankly despise
305   myself.

speak parrot   jabber
discourse fustian   speak mere stuff

Iago. Come, you are too severe a moraler. As the
time, the place, and the condition of this country
stands, I could heartily wish this had not befallen. But since it is as it is, mend it for your
own good.   310
Cassio. I will ask him for my place again; he shall
tell me I am a drunkard! Had I as many mouths
as Hydra,° such an answer would stop them all.
To be now a sensible man, by and by a fool, and
presently a beast! O strange! Every inordinate   315
cup is unblest, and the ingredient is a devil.
Iago. Come, come, good wine is a good familiar
creature if it be well used. Exclaim no more
against it. And, good lieutenant, I think you
think I love you.   320
Cassio. I have well approved it, sir. I drunk!
Iago. You or any man living may be drunk at some
time, man. I'll tell you what you shall do. Our
general's wife is now the general. I may say so in
this respect, for that he hath devoted and given   325
up himself to the contemplation, mark, and
denotement of her parts and graces. Confess
yourself freely to her; importune her help to
put you in your place again. She is of so free, so
kind, so apt,° so blessed a disposition, she holds   330
it a vice in her goodness not to do more than she
is requested. This broken joint between you
and her husband entreat her to splinter,° and,
my fortunes against any lay° worth naming,
this crack of your love shall grow stronger than   335
it was before.
Cassio. You advise me well.
Iago. I protest, in the sincerity of love and honest
kindness.
Cassio. I think it freely, and betimes in the morn-   340
ing I will beseech the virtuous Desdemona to
undertake for me. I am desperate of my fortunes
if they check me here.
Iago. You are in the right. Good night, lieutenant;
I must to the watch.   345
Cassio. Good night, honest Iago.   [*Exit*]
Iago. And what's he then that says I play the
villain,
When this advice is free I give and honest,
Probal° to thinking, and indeed the course
To win the Moor again? For 'tis most easy   350
Th' inclining Desdemona to subdue
In any honest suit. She's fram'd as fruitful°
As the free elements.° And then for her
To win the Moor, were 't to renounce his
baptism,

Hydra   many-headed monster slain by Hercules
apt   ready   *splinter*   splint   *lay*   wager
probal   probable   *fruitful*   generous
free elements   i.e., air

355 All seals and symbols of redeemed sin,
His soul is so enfetter'd to her love,
That she may make, unmake, do what she list,
Even as her appetite shall play the god
With his weak function.° How am I then a
villain
360 To counsel Cassio to this parallel course,
Directly to his good? Divinity of hell!
When devils will the blackest sins put on,
They do suggest at first with heavenly shows,
As I do now; for whiles this honest fool
365 Plies Desdemona to repair his fortunes,
And she for him pleads strongly to the Moor,
I'll pour this pestilence into his ear,
That she repeals° him for her body's lust;
And by how much she strives to do him good,
370 She shall undo her credit with the Moor.
So will I turn her virtue into pitch,
And out of her own goodness make the net
That shall enmesh them all.
            [Enter RODERIGO.]
                    How now, Roderigo!
RODERIGO. I do follow here in the chase, not like a
375 hound that hunts, but one that fills up the cry.°
My money is almost spent, I have been tonight
exceedingly well cudgeled, and I think the issue

will be, I shall have so much experience for my
pains, and so, with no money at all and a little
more wit, return again to Venice.   380
IAGO. How poor are they that have not patience!
What wound did ever heal but by degrees?
Thou know'st we work by wit and not by
witchcraft,
And wit depends on dilatory time.
Does 't not go well? Cassio hath beaten thee,   385
And thou by that small hurt hast cashier'd
Cassio.
Though other things grow fair against the sun,
Yet fruits that blossom first will first be ripe.
Content thyself awhile. By the mass, 'tis morn-
ing;
Pleasure and action make the hours seem short.   390
Retire thee; go where thou art billeted.
Away, I say; thou shalt know more hereafter.
Nay, get thee gone. [Exit RODERIGO] Two things
are to be done:
My wife must move for Cassio to her mistress—
I'll set her on;   395
Myself the while to draw the Moor apart,
And bring him jump° when he may Cassio find
Soliciting his wife. Aye, that's the way;
Dull not device by coldness and delay.   [Exit]

weak function sexual inadequacy (cf. I, iii, 263–264)
repeals recalls   cry common pack

jump exactly at the right time and place

A C T   I I I

SCENE i
Before the castle.

[Enter CASSIO *and some* MUSICIANS.]
CASSIO. Masters, play here. I will content your
pains.
Something that's brief, and bid "Good mor-
row, general."   [Music.]
            [Enter CLOWN.]
CLOWN. Why, masters, have your instruments
been in Naples, that they speak i' the nose thus?°
5 FIRST MUSICIAN. How, sir, how?
CLOWN. Are these, I pray you, wind instruments?
FIRST MUSICIAN. Aye, marry, are they, sir.
CLOWN. O, thereby hangs a tail.
FIRST MUSICIAN. Whereby hangs a tale, sir?

speak . . . thus (obscure reference to Naples' notoriety as
    a venereal disease center)

CLOWN. Marry, sir, by many a wind instrument°   10
that I know. But, masters, here's money for you,
and the general so likes your music that he
desires you, for love's sake, to make no more
noise with it.
FIRST MUSICIAN. Well, sir, we will not.   15
CLOWN. If you have any music that may not be
heard, to 't again. But, as they say, to hear music
the general does not greatly care.
FIRST MUSICIAN. We have none such, sir.
CLOWN. Then put up your pipes in your bag, for   20
I'll away. Go, vanish into air, away!
                    [Exeunt MUSICIANS.]
CASSIO. Dost thou hear, my honest friend?
CLOWN. No, I hear not your honest friend; I hear
you.

tail . . . tale . . . wind instrument (a gross and obvious
    jest)

CASSIO. Prithee, keep up thy quillets.° There's a
25 poor piece of gold for thee. If the gentlewoman
    that attends the general's wife be stirring, tell
    her there's one Cassio entreats her a little favor
    of speech. Wilt thou do this?
CLOWN. She is stirring, sir. If she will stir hither, I
30 shall seem to notify unto her.
CASSIO. Do, good my friend.   [Exit CLOWN.]
                    [Enter IAGO.]
                              In happy time, Iago.
IAGO. You have not been abed, then?
CASSIO. Why, no, the day had broke
    Before we parted. I have made bold, Iago,
35 To send in to your wife. My suit to her
    Is that she will to virtuous Desdemona
    Procure me some access.
IAGO.   I'll send her to you presently,
    And I'll devise a mean to draw the Moor
    Out of the way, that your converse and business
40 May be more free.
CASSIO. I humbly thank you for 't. [Exit IAGO] I
       never knew
    A Florentine° more kind and honest.
                    [Enter EMILIA.]
EMILIA. Good morrow, good lieutenant. I am sorry
    For your displeasure, but all will sure be well.
45 The general and his wife are talking of it,
    And she speaks for you stoutly. The Moor
       replies
    That he you hurt is of great fame in Cyprus
    And great affinity,° and that in wholesome
       wisdom
    He might not but refuse you. But he protests he
       loves you
50 And needs no other suitor but his likings
    To take the safest occasion by the front
    To bring you in again.
CASSIO.   Yet, I beseech you,
    If you think fit, or that it may be done,
    Give me advantage of some brief discourse
    With Desdemona alone.
55 EMILIA.   Pray you, come in.
    I will bestow you where you shall have time
    To speak your bosom freely.
CASSIO.   I am much bound to you.
                                        [Exeunt]

SCENE ii
A room in the castle.

[Enter OTHELLO, IAGO, and GENTLEMEN.]
OTHELLO. These letters give, Iago, to the pilot,
    And by him do my duties to the senate.
    That done, I will be walking on the works.°
    Repair there to me.
IAGO.   Well, my good lord, I'll do 't.
OTHELLO. This fortification, gentlemen, shall we
       see 't?   5
GENTLEMAN. We'll wait upon your lordship.
                                        [Exeunt]

SCENE iii
The garden of the castle.

[Enter DESDEMONA, CASSIO, and EMILIA.]
DESDEMONA. Be thou assur'd, good Cassio, I will do
    All my abilities in thy behalf.
EMILIA. Good madam, do. I warrant it grieves my
       husband
    As if the case were his.
DESDEMONA. O, that's an honest fellow. Do not
       doubt, Cassio,   5
    But I will have my lord and you again
    As friendly as you were.
CASSIO.   Bounteous madam,
    Whatever shall become of Michael Cassio,
    He's never anything but your true servant.
DESDEMONA. I know 't. I thank you. You do love
       my lord,   10
    You have known him long, and be you well as-
       sur'd
    He shall in strangeness stand no farther off
    Than in a politic distance.°
CASSIO.   Aye, but, lady,
    That policy may either last so long,
    Or feed upon such nice° and waterish diet,   15
    Or breed itself so out of circumstance,°
    That, I being absent and my place supplied,
    My general will forget my love and service.
DESDEMONA. Do not doubt° that. Before Emilia
       here
    I give thee warrant of thy place. Assure thee,   20
    If I do vow a friendship, I'll perform it

works fortifications
politic distance   such distance as appearance (politics)
   requires
nice finicky
breed . . . circumstance i.e., grow to so large dimension
doubt fear

quillets quibbles, witticisms
Florentine i.e., this Venetian is as kind as a Florentine
affinity family connections

To the last article. My lord shall never rest;
I'll watch him tame° and talk him out of
    patience;
His bed shall seem a school, his board a shrift.°
25 I'll intermingle everything he does
With Cassio's suit. Therefore be merry, Cassio,
For thy solicitor shall rather die
Than give thy cause away.
            [*Enter* OTHELLO *and* IAGO, *at a distance.*]
EMILIA. Madam, here comes my lord.
30 CASSIO. Madam, I'll take my leave.
DESDEMONA. Nay, stay and hear me speak.
CASSIO. Madam, not now. I am very ill at ease,
    Unfit for mine own purposes.
DESDEMONA. Well, do your discretion.
                                    [*Exit* CASSIO.]
35 IAGO. Ha! I like not that.
OTHELLO. What dost thou say?
IAGO. Nothing, my lord. Or if—I know not what.
OTHELLO. Was not that Cassio parted from my
    wife?
IAGO. Cassio, my lord! No, sure, I cannot think it,
40 That he would steal away so guilty-like,
    Seeing you coming.
OTHELLO.   I do believe 'twas he.
DESDEMONA. How now, my lord!
    I have been talking with a suitor here,
    A man that languishes in your displeasure.
45 OTHELLO. Who is 't you mean?
DESDEMONA. Why, your lieutenant, Cassio. Good
    my lord,
    If I have any grace or power to move you,
    His present reconciliation take;
    For if he be not one that truly loves you,
50 That errs in ignorance and not in cunning,
    I have no judgment in an honest face.
    I prithee, call him back.
OTHELLO.   Went he hence now?
DESDEMONA. Aye, sooth, so humbled
    That he hath left part of his grief with me
55 To suffer with him. Good love, call him back.
OTHELLO. Not now, sweet Desdemona; some
    other time.
DESDEMONA. But shall 't be shortly?
OTHELLO.   The sooner, sweet, for you.
DESDEMONA. Shall 't be tonight at supper?
OTHELLO.   No, not tonight.
DESDEMONA. Tomorrow dinner then?
OTHELLO.   I shall not dine at home;
60 I meet the captains at the citadel.
DESDEMONA. Why then tomorrow night or Tues-
    day morn,

On Tuesday noon, or night, on Wednesday
    morn.
I prithee, name the time, but let it not
Exceed three days. In faith, he's penitent,
And yet his trespass, in our common reason— 65
Save that, they say, the wars must make
    examples
Out of their best—is not almost a fault
T' incur a private check. When shall he come?
Tell me, Othello. I wonder in my soul
What you would ask me that I should deny, 70
Or stand so mamm'ring° on. What! Michael
    Cassio,
That came a-wooing with you, and so many a
    time
When I have spoke of you dispraisingly
Hath ta'en your part; to have so much to do
To bring him in! Trust me, I could do much— 75
OTHELLO. Prithee, no more. Let him come when
    he will;
I will deny thee nothing.
DESDEMONA.   Why, this is not a boon.
'Tis as I should entreat you wear your gloves,
Or feed on nourishing dishes, or keep you warm,
Or sue to you to do a peculiar° profit 80
To your own person. Nay, when I have a suit
Wherein I mean to touch° your love indeed,
It shall be full of poise° and difficult weight,
And fearful to be granted.
OTHELLO.   I will deny thee nothing.
Whereon, I do beseech thee, grant me this, 85
To leave me but a little to myself.
DESDEMONA. Shall I deny you? No. Farewell, my
    lord.
OTHELLO. Farewell, my Desdemona. I'll come to
    thee straight.
DESDEMONA. Emilia, come. Be as your fancies teach
    you;
Whate'er you be, I am obedient. 90
                [*Exeunt* DESDEMONA *and* EMILIA.]
OTHELLO. Excellent wretch! Perdition catch my
    soul
But I do love thee! And when I love thee not,
Chaos is come again.
IAGO. My noble lord—
OTHELLO.   What dost thou say, Iago?
IAGO. Did Michael Cassio, when you woo'd my
    lady, 95
Know of your love?
OTHELLO. He did, from first to last. Why dost thou
    ask?

---

watch him tame keep him awake until he gives in
shrift place of confession

mamm'ring hesitating   *peculiar* special
touch test, place demands on
full of poise precisely balanced, difficult to decide

IAGO. But for a satisfaction of my thought,
  No further harm.
OTHELLO.   Why of thy thought, Iago?
IAGO. I did not think he had been acquainted with
100   her.
OTHELLO. O, yes, and went between us very oft.
IAGO. Indeed!
OTHELLO. Indeed! Aye, indeed. Discern'st thou
    aught in that?
    Is he not honest?
105 IAGO. Honest, my lord!
OTHELLO. Honest! Aye, honest.
IAGO. My lord, for aught I know.
OTHELLO. What dost thou think?
IAGO. Think, my lord!
OTHELLO. Think, my lord! By heaven, he echoes
110   me,
    As if there were some monster in his thought
    Too hideous to be shown. Thou dost mean some-
      thing.
    I heard thee say even now thou lik'st not that,
    When Cassio left my wife. What didst not like?
115   And when I told thee he was of my counsel
    In my whole course of wooing, thou criedst
      "Indeed!"
    And didst contract and purse thy brow together
    As if thou then hadst shut up in thy brain
    Some horrible conceit.° If thou dost love me,
120   Show me thy thought.
IAGO. My lord, you know I love you.
OTHELLO.   I think thou dost,
    And for I know thou'rt full of love and honesty
    And weigh'st thy words before thou giv'st them
      breath,
    Therefore these stops of thine fright me the
      more.
125   For such things in a false disloyal knave
    Are tricks of custom;° but in a man that's just
    They're close dilations,° working from the heart,
    That passion cannot rule.
IAGO.   For Michael Cassio,
    I dare be sworn I think that he is honest.
OTHELLO. I think so too.
130 IAGO.   Men should be what they seem,
    Or those that be not, would they might seem
      none!
OTHELLO. Certain, men should be what they seem.
IAGO. Why, then, I think Cassio's an honest man.
OTHELLO. Nay, yet there's more in this.
135   I prithee, speak to me as to thy thinkings,
    As thou dost ruminate, and give thy worst of
      thoughts

The worst of words.
IAGO.   Good my lord, pardon me.
    Though I am bound to every act of duty,
    I am not bound to that all slaves are free to.
    Utter my thoughts? Why, say they are vile and
      false,   140
    As where's that palace whereinto foul things
    Sometimes intrude not? Who has a breast so
      pure,
    But some uncleanly apprehensions
    Keep leets° and law days, and in session sit
    With meditations lawful?   145
OTHELLO. Thou dost conspire against thy friend,
      Iago,
    If thou but think'st him wrong'd and mak'st his
      ear
    A stranger to thy thoughts.
IAGO.   I do beseech you—
    Though I perchance am vicious in my guess,
    As, I confess, it is my nature's plague   150
    To spy into abuses, and oft my jealousy°
    Shapes faults that are not—that your wisdom
      yet,
    From one that so imperfectly conceits,°
    Would take no notice, nor build yourself a
      trouble
    Out of his scattering and unsure observance.   155
    It were not for your quiet nor your good,
    Nor for my manhood, or wisdom,
    To let you know my thoughts.
OTHELLO.   What dost thou mean?
IAGO. Good name in man and woman, dear my
      lord,
    Is the immediate jewel of their souls.   160
    Who steals my purse steals trash; 'tis something,
      nothing;
    'Twas mine, 'tis his, and has been slave to thou-
      sands.
    But he that filches from me my good name
    Robs me of that which not enriches him
    And makes me poor indeed.   165
OTHELLO. By heaven, I'll know thy thoughts.
IAGO. You cannot if my heart were in your hand,
    Nor shall not, whilst 'tis in my custody.
OTHELLO. Ha!
IAGO.   O, beware, my lord, of jealousy.
    It is the green-eyed monster, which doth mock   170
    The meat it feeds on. That cuckold lives in bliss
    Who, certain of his fate, loves not his wronger;
    But, O, what damned minutes tells° he o'er
    Who dotes, yet doubts, suspects, yet strongly
      loves!

---

conceit idea   *tricks of custom*   usual tricks
close dilations revealed secrets

keep leets hold courts   *jealousy* suspicion
conceits imagines   *tells* counts

175 OTHELLO. O misery!
  IAGO. Poor and content is rich, and rich enough;
    But riches fineless° is as poor as winter
    To him that ever fears he shall be poor.
    Good heaven, the souls of all my tribe defend
    From jealousy!
180 OTHELLO.   Why, why is this?
    Think'st thou I'd make a life of jealousy,
    To follow still the changes of the moon
    With fresh suspicions? No, to be once in doubt
    Is once to be resolv'd. Exchange me for a goat
185   When I shall turn the business of my soul
    To such exsufflicate° and blown surmises,
    Matching thy inference. 'Tis not to make me
      jealous
    To say my wife is fair, feeds well, loves com-
      pany,
    Is free of speech, sings, plays, and dances well.
190   Where virtue is, these are more virtuous.
    Nor from mine own weak merits will I draw
    The smallest fear or doubt of her revolt;
    For she had eyes, and chose me. No, Iago.
    I'll see before I doubt; when I doubt, prove;
195   And on the proof, there is no more but this—
    Away at once with love or jealousy!
  IAGO. I am glad of it, for now I shall have reason
    To show the love and duty that I bear you
    With franker spirit. Therefore, as I am bound,
200   Receive it from me. I speak not yet of proof.
    Look to your wife. Observe her well with Cassio.
    Wear your eye thus, not jealous nor secure.
    I would not have your free and noble nature
    Out of self-bounty° be abus'd; look to 't.
205   I know our country° disposition well.
    In Venice they do let heaven see the pranks
    They dare not show their husbands; their con-
      science
    Is not to leave 't undone, but keep 't unknown.
  OTHELLO. Dost thou say so?
210 IAGO. She did deceive her father, marrying you,
    And when she seem'd to shake and fear your
      looks,
    She lov'd them most.
  OTHELLO.   And so she did.
  IAGO.   Why, go to then.
    She that so young could give out such a seeming,
    To seel her father's eyes up close as oak°—
    He thought 'twas witchcraft. But I am much to
215   blame;
    I humbly do beseech you of your pardon
    For too much loving you.

OTHELLO.   I am bound to thee forever.
IAGO. I see this hath a little dash'd your spirits.
OTHELLO. Not a jot, not a jot.
IAGO.   I' faith, I fear it has.
    I hope you will consider what is spoke   220
    Comes from my love; but I do see you're
      mov'd.
    I am to pray you not to strain my speech
    To grosser issues nor to larger reach°
    Than to suspicion.
OTHELLO. I will not.
IAGO.   Should you do so, my lord,   225
    My speech should fall into such vile success
    As my thoughts aim not at. Cassio's my worthy
      friend—
    My lord, I see you're mov'd.
OTHELLO.   No, not much mov'd.
    I do not think but Desdemona's honest.
IAGO. Long live she so! And long live you to think
    so!   230
OTHELLO. And yet, how nature erring from itself—
IAGO. Aye, there's the point. As—to be bold with
    you—
    Not to affect° many proposed matches
    Of her own clime, complexion, and degree,
    Whereto we see in all things nature tends—   235
    Foh! One may smell in such, a will most rank,°
    Foul disproportion,° thoughts unnatural.
    But pardon me: I do not in position°
    Distinctly speak of her, though I may fear
    Her will, recoiling to her better judgment,   240
    May fall to match you with her country forms,°
    And happily° repent.
OTHELLO.   Farewell, farewell.
    If more thou dost perceive, let me know more.
    Set on thy wife to observe. Leave me, Iago.
IAGO. [Going] My lord, I take my leave.   245
OTHELLO. Why did I marry? This honest creature
    doubtless
    Sees and knows more, much more, than he un-
    folds.
IAGO. [Returning] My lord, I would I might entreat
    your honor
    To scan this thing no further. Leave it to time.
    Though it be fit that Cassio have his place,   250
    For sure he fills it up with great ability,
    Yet, if you please to hold him off awhile,
    You shall by that perceive him and his means.
    Note if your lady strain his entertainment

---

fineless unlimited   *exsufflicate* insubstantial
self-bounty innate generosity   *country* country's
close as oak tight as oakum

grosser . . . reach worse and sure conclusions
affect incline toward   *rank* lustful
disproportion abnormality   *in position* categorically
fall . . . forms fall to comparing you with Venetians
   (i.e., white men)
happily haply, perhaps

255 With any strong or vehement importunity;
Much will be seen in that. In the meantime,
Let me be thought too busy in my fears—
As worthy cause I have to fear I am—
And hold her free,° I do beseech your honor.

260 OTHELLO. Fear not my government.°

IAGO. I once more take my leave.   [*Exit*]

OTHELLO. This fellow's of exceeding honesty,
And knows all qualities, with a learned spirit,
Of human dealings. If I do prove her haggard,°
Though that her jesses° were my dear heart-
265   strings,
I'd whistle her off and let her down the wind
To prey at fortune.° Haply, for I am black
And have not those soft parts of conversation
That chamberers° have, or for I am declin'd
270 Into the vale of years—yet that's not much—
She's gone. I am abus'd, and my relief
Must be to loathe her. O curse of marriage,
That we can call these delicate creatures ours,
And not their appetites! I had rather be a toad
275 And live upon the vapor of a dungeon
Than keep a corner in the thing I love
For others' uses. Yet 'tis the plague of great ones;
Prerogativ'd are they less than the base.
'Tis destiny unshunnable, like death.
280 Even then this forked plague° is fated to us
When we do quicken.° Desdemona comes.

    [*Re-enter* DESDEMONA *and* EMILIA]

If she be false, O, then heaven mocks itself!
I'll not believe 't.

DESDEMONA.   How now, my dear Othello!
Your dinner and the generous islanders
285 By you invited do attend your presence.

OTHELLO. I am to blame.

DESDEMONA.   Why do you speak so faintly?
Are you not well?

OTHELLO. I have a pain upon my forehead here.

DESDEMONA. Faith, that's with watching;° 'twill
    away again.
290 Let me but bind it hard, within this hour
It will be well.

OTHELLO.   Your napkin is too little.

[*He puts the handkerchief from him; and she drops it.*]
    Let it alone. Come, I'll go in with you.

DESDEMONA. I am very sorry that you are not well.
        [*Exeunt* OTHELLO *and* DESDEMONA.]

EMILIA. I am glad I have found this napkin.
295 This was her first remembrance from the Moor.

My wayward husband hath a hundred times
Woo'd me to steal it; but she so loves the token,
For he conjur'd her she should ever keep it,
That she reserves it evermore about her
To kiss and talk to. I'll have the work ta'en out° 300
And give 't Iago. What he will do with it
Heaven knows, not I;
I nothing but to please his fantasy.

        [*Re-enter* IAGO.]

IAGO. How now! What do you here alone?

EMILIA. Do not you chide; I have a thing for you. 305

IAGO. A thing for me? It is a common thing—

EMILIA. Ha!

IAGO. To have a foolish wife.

EMILIA. O, is that all? What will you give me now
For that same handkerchief?

IAGO.   What handkerchief? 310

EMILIA. What handkerchief!
Why, that the Moor first gave to Desdemona;
That which so often you did bid me steal.

IAGO. Hast stol'n it from her?

EMILIA. No, faith; she let it drop by negligence, 315
And, to th' advantage,° I being here took 't up.
Look, here it is.

IAGO.   A good wench; give it me.

EMILIA. What will you do with 't, that you have
    been so earnest
To have me filch it?

IAGO. [*Snatching it*] Why, what's that to you?

EMILIA. If 't be not for some purpose of import, 320
Give 't me again. Poor lady, she'll run mad
When she shall lack it.

IAGO. Be not acknown° on 't; I have use for it.
Go, leave me.   [*Exit* EMILIA.]
I will in Cassio's lodging lose this napkin, 325
And let him find it. Trifles light as air
Are to the jealous confirmations strong
As proofs of holy writ. This may do something.
The Moor already changes with my poison.
Dangerous conceits are in their natures poisons, 330
Which at the first are scarce found to distaste,
But with a little act° upon the blood,
Burn like the mines of sulphur. I did say so—
Look where he comes!

        [*Re-enter* OTHELLO.]

                    Not poppy nor mandragora
Nor all the drowsy syrups of the world 335
Shall ever medicine thee to that sweet sleep
Which thou ow'dst yesterday.

OTHELLO.   Ha! Ha! False to me?

---

free innocent   *government* i.e., how I will handle it
haggard wild (i.e., a female hawk)   *jesses* fastenings
whistle . . . fortune release her to pursue what she will
chamberers gallants
forked plague cuckoldry   *do quicken* are born
watching staying awake

work ta'en out the pattern copied
to th' advantage seizing the opportunity
not acknown ignorant
with a little act given a little time to operate

IAGO. Why, how now, general! No more of that.

OTHELLO. Avaunt! Be gone! Thou hast set me on
the rack.

340 I swear 'tis better to be much abus'd
Than but to know 't a little.

IAGO.   How now, my lord!

OTHELLO. What sense had I of her stol'n hours of
lust?

I saw 't not, thought it not, it harm'd not me.

I slept the next night well, was free and merry;

345 I found not Cassio's kisses on her lips.

He that is robb'd, not wanting° what is stol'n,

Let him not know 't and he's not robb'd at all.

IAGO. I am sorry to hear this.

OTHELLO. I had been happy if the general camp,

350 Pioners° and all, had tasted her sweet body,

So I had nothing known. O, now forever

Farewell the tranquil mind! Farewell content!

Farewell the plumed troop and the big wars

That make ambition virtue! O, farewell,

Farewell the neighing steed and the shrill

355 trump,

The spirit-stirring drum, th' ear-piercing fife,

The royal banner and all quality,

Pride, pomp, and circumstance of glorious war!

And, O you mortal engines whose rude throats

360 Th' immortal Jove's dread clamors counterfeit,

Farewell! Othello's occupation's gone!

IAGO. Is 't possible, my lord?

OTHELLO. Villain, be sure thou prove my love a
whore.

Be sure of it. Give me the ocular proof,

365 Or, by the worth of man's eternal soul,

Thou hadst been better have been born a dog

Than answer my wak'd wrath!

IAGO.   Is 't come to this?

OTHELLO. Make me to see 't, or at the least so
prove it

That the probation° bear no hinge nor loop

370 To hang a doubt on, or woe upon thy life!

IAGO. My noble lord—

OTHELLO. If thou dost slander her and torture me,

Never pray more. Abandon all remorse,

On horror's head horrors accumulate,

Do deeds to make heaven weep, all earth

375 amaz'd.

For nothing canst thou to damnation add

Greater than that.

IAGO.   O grace! O heaven defend me!

Are you a man? Have you a soul or sense?

God be wi' you; take mine office. O wretched
fool,

That liv'st to make thine honesty a vice!   380

O monstrous world! Take note, take note, O
world:

To be direct and honest is not safe.

I thank you for this profit, and from hence

I'll love no friend sith love breeds such offense.

OTHELLO. Nay, stay. Thou shouldst be honest.   385

IAGO. I should be wise; for honesty's a fool,

And loses that it works for.

OTHELLO.   By the world,

I think my wife be honest, and think she is not;

I think that thou art just, and think thou art not.

I'll have some proof. Her name, that was as
fresh   390

As Dian's° visage, is now begrim'd and black

As mine own face. If there be cords, or knives,

Poison, or fire, or suffocating streams,

I'll not endure it. Would I were satisfied!

IAGO. I see, sir, you are eaten up with passion.   395

I do repent me that I put it to you.

You would be satisfied?

OTHELLO.   Would! Nay, I will.

IAGO. And may. But, how? How satisfied, my lord?

Would you, the supervisor,° grossly gape on?

Behold her topp'd?

OTHELLO.   Death and damnation! O!   400

IAGO. It were a tedious difficulty, I think,

To bring them to that prospect.° Damn them
then,

If ever mortal eyes do see them bolster°

More than their own! What then? How then?

What shall I say? Where's satisfaction?   405

It is impossible you should see this,

Were they as prime as goats, as hot as monkeys,

As salt as wolves in pride,° and fools as gross

As ignorance made drunk. But yet, I say,

If imputation and strong circumstances,   410

Which lead directly to the door of truth,

Will give you satisfaction, you may have 't.

OTHELLO. Give me a living reason° she's disloyal.

IAGO. I do not like the office,

But sith I am enter'd in this cause so far,   415

Prick'd to 't by foolish honesty and love,

I will go on. I lay with Cassio lately,

And being troubled with a raging tooth,

I could not sleep.

There are a kind of men so loose of soul   420

That in their sleeps will mutter their affairs.

---

wanting lacking
pioners the lowliest rank of soldiers, mere "diggers" of
  mines and trenches
probation proof

Dian's Diana's (goddess of chastity)
supervisor onlooker   prospect spectacle
bolster lie together   pride heat
living reason actual proof

One of this kind is Cassio.
In sleep I heard him say, "Sweet Desdemona,
Let us be wary, let us hide our loves."
And then, sir, would he gripe and wring my
425   hand,
Cry "O sweet creature!" and then kiss me hard,
As if he pluck'd up kisses by the roots
That grew upon my lips, then laid his leg
Over my thigh, and sigh'd and kiss'd, and then
430   Cried "Cursed fate that gave thee to the Moor!"
OTHELLO. O monstrous! Monstrous!
IAGO.   Nay, this was but his dream.
OTHELLO. But this denoted a foregone conclusion.°
'Tis a shrewd doubt,° though it be but a dream.
IAGO. And this may help to thicken other proofs
That do demonstrate thinly.
435 OTHELLO.   I'll tear her all to pieces.
IAGO. Nay, but be wise. Yet we see nothing done;
She may be honest yet. Tell me but this:
Have you not sometimes seen a handkerchief
Spotted with strawberries in your wife's hand?
440 OTHELLO. I gave her such a one; 'twas my first gift.
IAGO. I know not that. But such a handkerchief—
I am sure it was your wife's—did I today
See Cassio wipe his beard with.
OTHELLO.   If it be that—
IAGO. If it be that, or any that was hers,
445   It speaks against her with the other proofs.
OTHELLO. O, that the slave had forty thousand
lives!
One is too poor, too weak for my revenge.
Now do I see 'tis true. Look here, Iago.
All my fond love thus do I blow to heaven:
450   'Tis gone.
Arise, black vengeance, from thy hollow cell!
Yield up, O love, thy crown and hearted throne
To tyrannous hate! Swell, bosom, with thy
fraught,°
For 'tis of aspics'° tongues!
IAGO.   Yet be content.
455 OTHELLO. O, blood, blood, blood!
IAGO. Patience, I say; your mind perhaps may
change.
OTHELLO. Never, Iago. Like to the Pontic sea,°
Whose icy current and compulsive course
Ne'er feels retiring ebb, but keeps due on
460   To the Propontic and the Hellespont,
Even so my bloody thoughts, with violent pace,
Shall ne'er look back, ne'er ebb to humble love,
Till that a capable and a wide° revenge

foregone conclusion previous actuality
shrewd doubt sharp (cause of) suspicion
fraught freight, burden   *aspics'* asps'
Pontic sea Black Sea
capable and wide all-encompassing

Swallow them up. Now, by yond marble heaven,
In the due reverence of a sacred vow   [*Kneels.*] 465
I here engage my words.
IAGO.   Do not rise yet.
                                          [*Kneels.*]
Witness, you ever-burning lights above,
You elements that clip° us round about,
Witness that here Iago doth give up
The execution of his wit, hands, heart   470
To wrong'd Othello's service! Let him com-
mand,
And to obey shall be in me remorse,°
What bloody business ever.   [*They rise.*]
OTHELLO.   I greet thy love,
Not with vain thanks, but with acceptance
bounteous,
And will upon the instant put thee to 't.   475
Within these three days let me hear thee say
That Cassio's not alive.
IAGO. My friend is dead; 'tis done at your request.
But let her live.
OTHELLO.   Damn her, lewd minx! O, damn her!
Come, go with me apart; I will withdraw   480
To furnish me with some swift means of death
For the fair devil. Now art thou my lieutenant.
IAGO. I am your own forever.   [*Exeunt*]

SCENE iv
Before the castle.

[*Enter* DESDEMONA, EMILIA, *and* CLOWN.]
DESDEMONA. Do you know, sirrah, where Lieu-
tenant Cassio lies?
CLOWN. I dare not say he lies anywhere.
DESDEMONA. Why, man?
CLOWN. He's a soldier, and for one to say a soldier 5
lies is stabbing.
DESDEMONA. Go to, where lodges he?
CLOWN. To tell you where he lodges is to tell you
where I lie.
DESDEMONA. Can anything be made of this?   10
CLOWN. I know not where he lodges, and for me to
devise a lodging and say he lies here or he lies
there were to lie in mine own throat.
DESDEMONA. Can you inquire him out and be
edified° by report?   15
CLOWN. I will catechize the world for him; that is,
make questions and by them answer.
DESDEMONA. Seek him, bid him come hither. Tell
him I have moved my lord on his behalf and
hope all will be well.   20

clip embrace   *remorse* solemn duty
edified enlightened (Desdemona speaks mockingly)

CLOWN. To do this is within the compass of man's wit, and therefore I will attempt the doing it.

                                      [Exit]

DESDEMONA. Where should I lose that handkerchief, Emilia?

EMILIA. I know not, madam.

DESDEMONA. Believe me, I had rather have lost my purse

25   Full of crusadoes.° And, but my noble Moor
Is true of mind and made of no such baseness
As jealous creatures are, it were enough
To put him to ill thinking.

EMILIA.   Is he not jealous?

DESDEMONA. Who, he? I think the sun where he

30   was born
Drew all such humors° from him.

EMILIA.   Look, where he comes.

DESDEMONA. I will not leave him now till Cassio
Be call'd to him.

            [Enter OTHELLO.]
               How is 't with you, my lord?

OTHELLO. Well, my good lady. [Aside] O, hardness to dissemble!
How do you, Desdemona?

35 DESDEMONA.   Well, my good lord.

OTHELLO. Give me your hand. This hand is moist,° my lady.

DESDEMONA. It yet has felt no age nor known no sorrow.

OTHELLO. This argues fruitfulness and liberal heart.
Hot, hot, and moist: this hand of yours requires

40   A sequester° from liberty, fasting and prayer,
Much castigation, exercise devout;
For here's a young and sweating devil here,
That commonly rebels. 'Tis a good hand,
A frank one.

DESDEMONA.   You may, indeed, say so,

45   For 'twas that hand that gave away my heart.

OTHELLO. A liberal hand. The hearts of old gave hands,
But our new heraldry is hands, not hearts.°

DESDEMONA. I cannot speak of this. Come now, your promise.

OTHELLO. What promise, chuck?°

DESDEMONA. I have sent to bid Cassio come speak

50   with you.

OTHELLO. I have a salt and sorry rheum° offends me;
Lend me thy handkerchief.

DESDEMONA. Here, my lord.

OTHELLO. That which I gave you.

DESDEMONA. I have it not about me.   55

OTHELLO. Not?

DESDEMONA. No, indeed, my lord.

OTHELLO. That's a fault. That handkerchief
Did an Egyptian to my mother give.
She was a charmer,° and could almost read   60
The thoughts of people. She told her, while she kept it,
'Twould make her amiable and subdue my father
Entirely to her love; but if she lost it
Or made a gift of it, my father's eye
Should hold her loathly and his spirits should hunt   65
After new fancies. She dying gave it me,
And bid me, when my fate would have me wive,
To give it her. I did so. And take heed on 't;
Make it a darling like your precious eye.
To lose 't or give 't away were such perdition   70
As nothing else could match.

DESDEMONA.   Is 't possible?

OTHELLO. 'Tis true: there's magic in the web of it.
A sibyl,° that had number'd in the world
The sun to course two hundred compasses,
In her prophetic fury sew'd the work.   75
The worms were hallow'd that did breed the silk,
And it was dy'd in mummy° which the skilful
Conserv'd of maidens' hearts.

DESDEMONA.   Indeed! Is 't true?

OTHELLO. Most veritable; therefore look to 't well.

DESDEMONA. Then would to God that I had never seen 't!   80

OTHELLO. Ha! Wherefore?

DESDEMONA. Why do you speak so startingly and rash?

OTHELLO. Is 't lost? Is 't gone? Speak, is it out o' the way?

DESDEMONA. Heaven bless us!

OTHELLO. Say you?   85

DESDEMONA. It is not lost. But what an if it were?

OTHELLO. How!

DESDEMONA. I say, it is not lost.

OTHELLO. Fetch 't, let me see it.

DESDEMONA. Why, so I can, sir, but I will not now.   90

---

crusadoes Portuguese coins   humors moods
moist i.e., indicative of a lustful inclination
sequester separation
The hearts . . . hearts formerly, love accompanied the
    giving of hands, but the modern fashion is to give
    hands without love
chuck a familiar term of endearment (here used
    contemptuously)

salt . . . rheum i.e., runny nose (or eyes)
charmer magician
sibyl prophetess
mummy drug concocted from mummified flesh

This is a trick to put me from my suit.
Pray you, let Cassio be receiv'd again.

OTHELLO. Fetch me the handkerchief. My mind
    misgives.

DESDEMONA. Come, come.

95   You'll never meet a more sufficient man.

OTHELLO. The handkerchief!

DESDEMONA.   I pray, talk me of Cassio.

OTHELLO. The handkerchief!

DESDEMONA.   A man that all his time
    Hath founded his good fortunes on your love,
    Shar'd dangers with you—

100   OTHELLO. The handkerchief!

DESDEMONA. In sooth, you are to blame.

OTHELLO. Away!   [Exit]

EMILIA. Is not this man jealous?

DESDEMONA. I ne'er saw this before.

105   Sure there's some wonder in this handkerchief.
    I am most unhappy in the loss of it.

EMILIA. 'Tis not a year or two shows us a man.
    They are all but stomachs and we all but food;
    They eat us hungerly, and when they are full

110   They belch us. Look you, Cassio and my husband.
              [Enter CASSIO and IAGO.]

IAGO. There is no other way; 'tis she must do 't.
    And, lo, the happiness! Go and importune her.

DESDEMONA. How now, good Cassio! What's the
    news with you?

CASSIO. Madam, my former suit. I do beseech you

115   That by your virtuous means I may again
    Exist, and be a member of his love
    Whom I with all the office of my heart
    Entirely honor. I would not be delay'd.
    If my offense be of such mortal kind

120   That nor my service past nor present sorrows
    Nor purpos'd merit in futurity
    Can ransom me into his love again,
    But to know so must be my benefit.
    So shall I clothe me in a forc'd content

125   And shut myself up in some other course
    To fortune's alms.

DESDEMONA.   Alas, thrice-gentle Cassio!
    My advocation is not now in tune.
    My lord is not my lord, nor should I know him
    Were he in favor° as in humor alter'd.

130   So help me every spirit sanctified,
    As I have spoken for you all my best
    And stood within the blank° of his displeasure
    For my free speech! You must awhile be patient.
    What I can do I will, and more I will

135   Than for myself I dare. Let that suffice you.

IAGO. Is my lord angry?

EMILIA.   He went hence but now,

And certainly in strange unquietnes[s]

IAGO. Can he be angry? I have seen th[e]
    When it hath blown his ranks into
    And, like the devil, from his very ar[m]
    Puff'd his own brother; and can he be angry?
    Something of moment then. I will go meet him.
    There's matter in 't indeed if he be angry.

DESDEMONA. I prithee, do so.   [Exit IAGO.]
             Something sure of state,
    Either from Venice or some unhatch'd practice°   145
    Made demonstrable° here in Cyprus to him,
    Hath puddled his clear spirit; and in such cases
    Men's natures wrangle with inferior things,
    Though great ones are their object. 'Tis even so;
    For let our finger ache, and it indues°   150
    Our other healthful members even to that sense
    Of pain. Nay, we must think men are not gods,
    Nor of them look for such observancy°
    As fits the bridal. Beshrew me much, Emilia,
    I was, unhandsome warrior as I am,   155
    Arraigning his unkindness with my soul.
    But now I find I had suborn'd° the witness,
    And he's indicted falsely.

EMILIA. Pray heaven it be state matters, as you
    think,
    And no conception nor no jealous toy   160
    Concerning you.

DESDEMONA. Alas the day, I never gave him cause!

EMILIA. But jealous souls will not be answer'd so;
    They are not ever jealous for the cause,
    But jealous for they are jealous. 'Tis a monster   165
    Begot upon itself, born on itself.

DESDEMONA. Heaven keep that monster from
    Othello's mind!

EMILIA. Lady, amen.

DESDEMONA. I will go seek him. Cassio, walk here-
    about.
    If I do find him fit, I'll move your suit   170
    And seek to effect it to my uttermost.

CASSIO. I humbly thank your ladyship.
        [Exeunt DESDEMONA and EMILIA.]
                [Enter BIANCA.]

BIANCA. Save you, friend Cassio!

CASSIO.   What make you from home?
    How is it with you, my most fair Bianca?
    I' faith, sweet love, I was coming to your house.   175

BIANCA. And I was going to your lodging, Cassio.
    What, keep a week away? Seven days and nights?
    Eight score eight hours? And lovers' absent
    hours,
    More tedious than the dial eight score times?

---

favor countenance   blank center

unhatch'd practice undisclosed plot
demonstrable exposed   indues induces
observancy attention   suborn'd corrupted

O weary reck'ning!

CASSIO.   Pardon me, Bianca.
I have this while with leaden thoughts been
   press'd;
But I shall in a more convenient time
Strike off this score of absence. Sweet Bianca,
         [*Giving her* DESDEMONA'S *handkerchief.*
Take me this work out.

BIANCA.   O Cassio, whence came this?
185 This is some token from a newer friend.
To the felt absence now I feel a cause.
Is 't come to this? Well, well.

CASSIO.   Go to, woman!
Throw your vile guesses in the devil's teeth,
From whence you have them. You are jealous
   now
That this is from some mistress, some remem-
190   brance.
No, by my faith, Bianca.

BIANCA.   Why, whose is it?

CASSIO. I know not, sweet. I found it in my chamber.

I like the work well. Ere it be demanded—
As like enough it will—I'd have it copied.
Take it, and do 't, and leave me for this time.   195

BIANCA. Leave you! Wherefore?

CASSIO. I do attend here on the general,
And think it no addition,° nor my wish,
To have him see me woman'd.

BIANCA.   Why, I pray you?

CASSIO. Not that I love you not.

BIANCA.   But that you do not love me.   200
I pray you, bring me on the way a little,
And say if I shall see you soon at night.

CASSIO. 'Tis but a little way that I can bring you,
For I attend here. But I'll see you soon.

BIANCA. 'Tis very good; I must be circumstanc'd.°   205
                                    [*Exeunt*]

addition advantage
circumstanc'd made the loser by circumstances

ACT IV

SCENE i
Cyprus. Before the castle.

[*Enter* OTHELLO *and* IAGO.]

IAGO. Will you think so?

OTHELLO.   Think so, Iago!

IAGO.   What,
To kiss in private?

OTHELLO.   An unauthoriz'd kiss.

IAGO. Or to be naked with her friend in bed
An hour or more, not meaning any harm?

5 OTHELLO. Naked in bed, Iago, and not mean harm!
It is hypocrisy against the devil.°
They that mean virtuously and yet do so,
The devil their virtue tempts and they tempt
   heaven.

IAGO. So they do nothing, 'tis a venial slip.
10 But if I give my wife a handkerchief—

OTHELLO. What then?

IAGO. Why, then, 'tis hers, my lord, and being hers,
She may, I think, bestow 't on any man.

OTHELLO. She is protectress of her honor too.
15   May she give that?

IAGO. Her honor is an essence that's not seen;

They have it very oft that have it not.
But for the handkerchief—

OTHELLO. By heaven, I would most gladly have
   forgot it.
Thou said'st—O, it comes o'er my memory   20
As doth the raven o'er the infected house,
Boding to all—he had my handkerchief.

IAGO. Aye, what of that?

OTHELLO.   That's not so good now.

IAGO.   What
If I had said I had seen him do you wrong?
Or heard him say—as knaves be such abroad,   25
Who having, by their own importunate suit,
Or voluntary dotage of some mistress,
Convinced or supplied them,° cannot choose
But they must blab—

OTHELLO.   Hath he said anything?

IAGO. He hath, my lord. But be you well assur'd,   30
No more than he'll unswear.

OTHELLO.   What hath he said?

IAGO. Faith, that he did—I know not what he did.

OTHELLO. What? What?

IAGO. Lie—

hypocrisy . . . devil i.e., appearing evil and meaning well

Convinced or supplied persuaded the one or gratified the
other

OTHELLO. With her?

IAGO.   With her, on her; what you will.

35 OTHELLO. Lie with her! Lie on her!—We say lie on
her, when they belie her.—Lie with her!
'Zounds, that's fulsome! Handkerchief—con-
fessions—handkerchief!—To confess, and be
hanged for his labor; first, to be hanged, and
40 then to confess. I tremble at it. Nature would
not invest herself in such shadowing passion
without some instruction.° It is not words that
shakes me thus. Pish! Noses, ears, and lips. Is 't
possible?—Confess?—Handkerchief?—O devil!
                    [Falls in a trance.]

45 IAGO. Work on,
My medicine, work! Thus credulous fools are
caught,
And many worthy and chaste dames even thus,
All guiltless, meet reproach. What, ho! My lord!
My lord, I say! Othello!
                    [Enter CASSIO.]
                    How now, Cassio!

50 CASSIO. What's the matter?

IAGO. My lord is fall'n into an epilepsy.
This is his second fit; he had one yesterday.

CASSIO. Rub him about the temples.

IAGO.   No, forbear;
The lethargy° must have his quiet course.
55 If not, he foams at mouth, and by and by
Breaks out to savage madness. Look, he stirs.
Do you withdraw yourself a little while;
He will recover straight. When he is gone,
I would on great occasion speak with you.
                    [Exit CASSIO.]
60 How is it, general? Have you not hurt your head?

OTHELLO. Dost thou mock me?

IAGO.   I mock you! No, by heaven.
Would you would bear your fortune like a man!

OTHELLO. A horned man's a monster and a beast.

IAGO. There's many a beast then in a populous city,
65 And many a civil° monster.

OTHELLO. Did he confess it?

IAGO.   Good sir, be a man.
Think every bearded fellow that's but yok'd
May draw with you.° There's millions now alive
That nightly lie in those unproper° beds
Which they dare swear peculiar.° Your case is
better.
70 O, 'tis the spite of hell, the fiend's arch-mock,

To lip a wanton in a secure couch
And to suppose her chaste! No, let me know,
And knowing what I am, I know what she shall
be.

OTHELLO. O, thou art wise; 'tis certain.

IAGO.   Stand you awhile apart;   75
Confine yourself but in a patient list.°
Whilst you were here o'erwhelmed with your
grief—
A passion most unsuiting such a man—
Cassio came hither. I shifted him away
And laid good 'scuse upon your ecstasy,°   80
Bade him anon return and here speak with me,
The which he promis'd. Do but encave° yourself,
And mark the fleers, the gibes, and notable
scorns
That dwell in every region of his face;
For I will make him tell the tale anew,   85
Where, how, how oft, how long ago, and when
He hath and is again to cope° your wife.
I say, but mark his gesture. Marry, patience,
Or I shall say you are all in all in spleen,°
And nothing of a man.

OTHELLO.   Dost thou hear, Iago?   90
I will be found most cunning in my patience;
But—dost thou hear?—most bloody.

IAGO.   That's not amiss;
But yet keep time° in all. Will you withdraw?
                    [OTHELLO retires.]
Now will I question Cassio of Bianca,
A housewife° that by selling her desires   95
Buys herself bread and clothes. It is a creature
That dotes on Cassio, as 'tis the strumpet's
plague
To beguile many and be beguil'd by one.
He, when he hears of her, cannot refrain
From the excess of laughter. Here he comes.   100
                    [Re-enter CASSIO.]
As he shall smile, Othello shall go mad,
And his unbookish° jealousy must construe
Poor Cassio's smiles, gestures, and light be-
havior
Quite in the wrong. How do you now, lieu-
tenant?

CASSIO. The worser that you give me the addition°   105
Whose want even kills me.

IAGO. Ply Desdemona well, and you are sure on 't.
Now, if this suit lay in Bianca's power,
How quickly should you speed!

Nature . . . instruction i.e., my imagination would not be
  so overwrought without substantial cause
lethargy fit   civil civilized
Think . . . you i.e., consider that every married man
  shares the same fate as you
unproper i.e., not belonging to the husband alone
peculiar belonging to the husband alone

patient list the bounds of patience   ecstasy fit
encave hide   cope encounter
all . . . spleen possessed by uncontrolled passions
keep time keep self-control   housewife hussy
unbookish unadvised   addition title (lieutenant)

CASSIO.   Alas, poor caitiff!°
110 OTHELLO. Look, how he laughs already!
     IAGO. I never knew a woman love man so.
     CASSIO. Alas, poor rogue! I think, i' faith, she loves
        me.
     OTHELLO. Now he denies it faintly and laughs it
        out.
     IAGO. Do you hear, Cassio?
     OTHELLO.   Now he importunes him
115   To tell it o'er. Go to; well said, well said
     IAGO. She gives it out that you shall marry her.
        Do you intend it?
     CASSIO. Ha, ha, ha!
     OTHELLO. Do you triumph, Roman?° Do you
        triumph?
120 CASSIO. I marry her! What, a customer!° I prithee,
        bear some charity to my wit. Do not think it so
        unwholesome. Ha, ha, ha!
     OTHELLO. So, so, so, so. They laugh that win.
     IAGO. Faith, the cry goes that you shall marry her.
125 CASSIO. Prithee, say true.
     IAGO. I am a very villain else.
     OTHELLO. Have you scored me? Well.
     CASSIO. This is the monkey's own giving out. She is
        persuaded I will marry her, out of her own love
130   and flattery, not out of my promise.
     OTHELLO. Iago beckons me; now he begins the
        story.
     CASSIO. She was here even now. She haunts me in
        every place. I was the other day talking on the
135   sea bank with certain Venetians, and thither
        comes the bauble,° and, by this hand, she falls
        me thus about my neck—
     OTHELLO. Crying "O dear Cassio!" as it were: his
        gesture imports it.
140 CASSIO. So hangs and lolls and weeps upon me, so
        hales and pulls me. Ha, ha, ha!
     OTHELLO. Now he tells how she plucked him to
        my chamber. O, I see that nose of yours, but not
        that dog I shall throw it to.
145 CASSIO. Well, I must leave her company.
     IAGO. Before me! Look, where she comes.
     CASSIO. 'Tis such another fitchew!° Marry, a per-
        fumed one.
                    [Enter BIANCA.]
     What do you mean by this haunting of me?
150 BIANCA. Let the devil and his dam haunt you! What
        did you mean by that same handkerchief you
        gave me even now? I was a fine fool to take it. I

must take out the work? A likely piece of work,
that you should find it in your chamber, and
not know who left it there! This is some minx's   155
token, and I must take out the work? There.
Give it your hobbyhorse. Wheresoever you had
it, I'll take out no work on 't.
CASSIO. How now, my sweet Bianca! How now!
   How now!   160
OTHELLO. By heaven, that should be my handker-
   chief!
BIANCA. An you'll come to supper tonight, you
   may; an you will not, come when you are next
   prepared for.°   [Exit]   165
IAGO. After her, after her.
CASSIO. Faith, I must. She'll rail i' the street else.
IAGO. Will you sup there?
CASSIO. Faith, I intend so.
IAGO. Well, I may chance to see you, for I would   170
   very fain speak with you.
CASSIO. Prithee, come. Will you?
IAGO. Go to; say no more.   [Exit CASSIO.]
OTHELLO. [Advancing] How shall I murder him,
   Iago?   175
IAGO. Did you perceive how he laughed at his vice?
OTHELLO. O Iago!
IAGO. And did you see the handkerchief?
OTHELLO. Was that mine?
IAGO. Yours, by this hand. And to see how he   180
   prizes the foolish woman your wife! She gave it
   him, and he hath given it his whore.
OTHELLO. I would have him nine years a-killing. A
   fine woman! A fair woman! A sweet woman!
IAGO. Nay, you must forget that.   185
OTHELLO. Aye, let her rot, and perish, and be
   damned tonight, for she shall not live. No, my
   heart is turned to stone. I strike it, and it hurts
   my hand. O, the world hath not a sweeter
   creature. She might lie by an emperor's side and 190
   command him tasks.
IAGO. Nay, that's not your way.
OTHELLO. Hang her! I do but say what she is. So
   delicate with her needle; an admirable musician.
   O, she will sing the savageness out of a bear. Of 195
   so high and plenteous wit and invention°—
IAGO. She's the worse for all this.
OTHELLO. O, a thousand thousand times. And
   then, of so gentle a condition!°
IAGO. Aye, too gentle.   200
OTHELLO. Nay, that's certain. But yet the pity of it,
   Iago!
   O Iago, the pity of it, Iago!

caitiff wretch
triumph, Roman i.e., make a triumphal show, like the
  Romans
customer seller (here, prostitute)
bauble plaything
fitchew polecat (symbolic of lust, like the goat and minx)

next prepared for i.e., never
wit and invention intelligence and imagination
gentle a condition noble of birth and impulse

IAGO. If you are so fond over her iniquity, give her
patent° to offend; for, if it touch not you, it
205　comes near nobody.

OTHELLO. I will chop her into messes.° Cuckold
me!

IAGO. O, 'tis foul in her.

OTHELLO. With mine officer!

210　IAGO. That's fouler.

OTHELLO. Get me some poison, Iago, this night. I'll
not expostulate with her, lest her body and
beauty unprovide my mind again. This night,
Iago.

215　IAGO. Do it not with poison. Strangle her in her
bed, even the bed she hath contaminated.

OTHELLO. Good, good. The justice of it pleases.
Very good.

IAGO. And for Cassio, let me be his undertaker.°
You shall hear more by midnight.

OTHELLO. Excellent good. [*A trumpet within*] What
220　trumpet is that same?

IAGO. Something from Venice, sure. 'Tis Lodovico
Come from the duke. And, see, your wife is with
him.

[*Enter* LODOVICO, DESDEMONA, *and* ATTENDANTS.]

LODOVICO. God save the worthy general!

OTHELLO.　　　　　　　　With all my heart, sir.

LODOVICO. The duke and senators of Venice greet
you.　　　　　　　　　[*Gives him a letter.*]

225　OTHELLO. I kiss the instrument of their pleasures.
[*Opens the letter, and reads.*]

DESDEMONA. And what's the news, good cousin
Lodovico?

IAGO. I am very glad to see you, signior.
Welcome to Cyprus.

LODOVICO. I thank you. How does Lieutenant
Cassio?

230　IAGO. Lives, sir.

DESDEMONA. Cousin, there's fall'n between him
and my lord
An unkind breach. But you shall make all well.

OTHELLO. Are you sure of that?

DESDEMONA. My lord?

235　OTHELLO. [*Reads*] "This fail you not to do, as you
will—"

LODOVICO. He did not call; he's busy in the paper.
Is there division 'twixt my lord and Cassio?

DESDEMONA. A most unhappy one. I would do
much

240　To atone them, for the love I bear to Cassio.

OTHELLO. Fire and brimstone!

DESDEMONA. My lord?

OTHELLO. Are you wise?

DESDEMONA. What, is he angry?

LODOVICO.　　　　　May be the letter mov'd him,
For, as I think, they do command him home,　245
Deputing Cassio in his government.

DESDEMONA. By my troth, I am glad on 't.

OTHELLO.　　　　　　　　　　Indeed!

DESDEMONA.　　　　　　　　　　My lord?

OTHELLO. I am glad to see you mad.°

DESDEMONA.　　　　　　Why, sweet Othello?

OTHELLO. Devil!　　　　　　　[*Striking her.*]

DESDEMONA. I have not deserv'd this.　　　　　250

LODOVICO. My lord, this would not be believ'd in
Venice,
Though I should swear I saw 't. 'Tis very much.
Make her amends; she weeps.

OTHELLO.　　　　　　　　O devil, devil!
If that the earth could teem with° woman's
tears,
Each drop she falls would prove a crocodile.°　255
Out of my sight!

DESDEMONA.　　　　I will not stay to offend you.
[*Going.*]

LODOVICO. Truly, an obedient lady.
I do beseech your lordship, call her back.

OTHELLO. Mistress!

DESDEMONA. My lord?　　　　　　　　　　260

OTHELLO. What would you with her, sir?

LODOVICO.　　　　　　　Who, I, my lord?

OTHELLO. Aye, you did wish that I would make her
turn.
Sir, she can turn and turn, and yet go on,
And turn again; and she can weep, sir, weep;
And she's obedient, as you say, obedient,　　265
Very obedient. Proceed you in your tears.
Concerning this, sir—O well-painted passion!—
I am commanded home. Get you away;
I'll send for you anon. Sir, I obey the mandate,
And will return to Venice. Hence, avaunt!　　270
[*Exit* DESDEMONA.]
Cassio shall have my place. And, sir, tonight
I do entreat that we may sup together.
You are welcome, sir, to Cyprus. Goats and
monkeys!　　　　　　　　　　[*Exit*]

LODOVICO. Is this the noble Moor whom our full
senate
Call all in all sufficient? This the nature　　275
Whom passion could not shake? Whose solid
virtue
The shot of accident nor dart of chance

I am . . . mad (possibly corrupt reading for *glad to see you glad*)
teem with conceive by
would . . . crocodile i.e., her false tears would breed monsters

patent license　　*messes* food portions
undertaker i.e., one who undertakes to deal with him

Could neither graze nor pierce?

IAGO.   He is much chang'd.

LODOVICO. Are his wits safe? Is he not light of
    brain?

IAGO. He's that he is. I may not breathe my
280   censure°
    What he might be. If what he might he is not,
    I would to heaven he were!

LODOVICO.   What, strike his wife!

IAGO. Faith, that was not so well; yet would I
    knew
    That stroke would prove the worst!

LODOVICO.   Is it his use?
285   Or did the letter work upon his blood
    And new create this fault?

IAGO.   Alas, alas!
    It is not honesty in me to speak
    What I have seen and known. You shall observe
    him,
    And his own courses will denote him so
290   That I may save my speech. Do but go after,
    And mark how he continues.

LODOVICO. I am sorry that I am deceiv'd in him.

                            [*Exeunt*]

SCENE ii

A room in the castle.

[*Enter* OTHELLO *and* EMILIA.]

OTHELLO. You have seen nothing, then?

EMILIA. Nor ever heard, nor ever did suspect.

OTHELLO. Yes, you have seen Cassio and she
    together.

EMILIA. But then I saw no harm, and then I heard
    Each syllable that breath made up between
5   them.

OTHELLO. What, did they never whisper?

EMILIA.   Never, my lord.

OTHELLO. Nor send you out o' the way?

EMILIA. Never.

OTHELLO. To fetch her fan, her gloves, her mask,
    nor nothing?

10 EMILIA. Never, my lord.

OTHELLO. That's strange.

EMILIA. I durst, my lord, to wager she is honest,
    Lay down my soul at stake. If you think other,
    Remove your thought; it doth abuse your
    bosom.
15   If any wretch have put this in your head,
    Let heaven requite it with the serpent's curse!°
    For if she be not honest, chaste, and true,

There's no man happy; the purest of their wives
Is foul as slander.

OTHELLO.   Bid her come hither. Go.

                      [*Exit* EMILIA.]

She says enough; yet she's a simple bawd   20
That cannot say as much. This is a subtle whore,
A closet lock and key of villainous secrets.
And yet she'll kneel and pray; I have seen her
    do 't.

      [*Enter* DESDEMONA *with* EMILIA.]

DESDEMONA. My lord, what is your will?

OTHELLO.   Pray, chuck, come hither.

DESDEMONA. What is your pleasure?

OTHELLO.   Let me see your eyes;   25
    Look in my face.

DESDEMONA.   What horrible fancy's this?

OTHELLO. [*To* EMILIA] Some of your function,°
    mistress:
    Leave procreants alone and shut the door;
    Cough, or cry hem, if anybody come.
    Your mystery,° your mystery. Nay, dispatch.   30

                    [*Exit* EMILIA.]

DESDEMONA. Upon my knees, what doth your
    speech import?
    I understand a fury in your words,
    But not the words.

OTHELLO. Why, what art thou?

DESDEMONA. Your wife, my lord, your true and
    loyal wife.   35

OTHELLO. Come, swear it, damn thyself,
    Lest, being like one of heaven, the devils them-
    selves
    Should fear to seize thee. Therefore be double-
    damn'd;
    Swear thou art honest.

DESDEMONA.   Heaven doth truly know it.

OTHELLO. Heaven truly knows that thou art false
    as hell.   40

DESDEMONA. To whom, my lord? With whom?
    How am I false?

OTHELLO. O Desdemona! Away! Away! Away!

DESDEMONA. Alas the heavy day! Why do you
    weep?
    Am I the motive of these tears, my lord?
    If haply you my father do suspect   45
    An instrument of this your calling back,
    Lay not your blame on me. If you have lost him,
    Why, I have lost him too.

OTHELLO.   Had it pleas'd heaven
    To try me with affliction, had they rain'd
    All kind of sores and shames on my bare head, 50

---

censure judgment   *use* custom
serpent's curse i.e., God's curse laid upon Satan

Some . . . function i.e., perform your service (as brothel
  keeper)
mystery trade

Steep'd me in poverty to the very lips,
Given to captivity me and my utmost hopes,
I should have found in some place of my soul
A drop of patience. But, alas, to make me
55 A fixed figure for the time of scorn
To point his slow unmoving finger at!
Yet could I bear that too, well, very well.
But there, where I have garner'd up my heart,
Where either I must live or bear no life,
60 The fountain from the which my current runs,
Or else dries up—to be discarded thence,
Or keep it as a cistern for foul toads
To knot and gender° in! Turn thy complexion there,
Patience, thou young and rose-lipp'd cherubin,
65 Aye, there, look grim as hell!
DESDEMONA. I hope my noble lord esteems me honest.
OTHELLO. O, aye, as summer flies are in the shambles,°
That quicken even with blowing.° O thou weed,
Who art so lovely fair and smell'st so sweet
That the sense aches at thee, would thou hadst
70 ne'er been born!
DESDEMONA. Alas, what ignorant sin have I committed?
OTHELLO. Was this fair paper, this most goodly book,
Made to write "whore" upon? What committed!
Committed! O thou public commoner!°
75 I should make very forges of my cheeks,
That would to cinders burn up modesty,
Did I but speak thy deeds. What committed!
Heaven stops the nose at it, and the moon winks.
The bawdy wind, that kisses all it meets,
80 Is hush'd within the hollow mine of earth
And will not hear it. What committed!
Impudent strumpet!
DESDEMONA.   By heaven, you do me wrong.
OTHELLO. Are not you a strumpet?
DESDEMONA.   No, as I am a Christian.
If to preserve this vessel for my lord
85 From any other foul unlawful touch
Be not to be a strumpet, I am none.
OTHELLO. What, not a whore?
DESDEMONA.   No, as I shall be sav'd.
OTHELLO. Is 't possible?
DESDEMONA. O, heaven forgive us!
OTHELLO.   I cry you mercy then;

I took you for that cunning whore of Venice   90
That married with Othello. [*Raising his voice*]
You, mistress,
That have the office opposite to Saint Peter,
And keep the gate of hell!
          [*Re-enter* EMILIA.]
                    You, you, aye, you!
We have done our course; there's money for your pains.
I pray you, turn the key, and keep our counsel.   95
                    [*Exit*]
EMILIA. Alas, what does this gentleman conceive?
How do you, madam? How do you, my good lady?
DESDEMONA. Faith, half asleep.
EMILIA. Good madam, what's the matter with my lord?
DESDEMONA. With who?   100
EMILIA. Why, with my lord, madam.
DESDEMONA. Who is thy lord?
EMILIA.   He that is yours, sweet lady.
DESDEMONA. I have none. Do not talk to me, Emilia;
I cannot weep, nor answer have I none
But what should go by water.° Prithee, tonight   105
Lay on my bed my wedding sheets: remember,
And call thy husband hither.
EMILIA.   Here's a change indeed! [*Exit*]
DESDEMONA. 'Tis meet I should be us'd so, very meet.
How have I been behav'd, that he might stick
The small'st opinion on my greatest abuse?°   110
          [*Re-enter* EMILIA *with* IAGO.]
IAGO. What is your pleasure, madam? How is 't with you?
DESDEMONA. I cannot tell. Those that do teach young babes
Do it with gentle means and easy tasks.
He might have chid me so; for, in good faith,
I am a child to chiding.
IAGO.   What's the matter, lady?   115
EMILIA. Alas, Iago, my lord hath so bewhor'd her,
Thrown such despite and heavy terms upon her,
As true hearts cannot bear.
DESDEMONA. Am I that name, Iago?
IAGO.   What name, fair lady?
DESDEMONA. Such as she says my lord did say I was.   120
EMILIA. He call'd her whore. A beggar in his drink
Could not have laid such terms upon his callet.°

---

knot and gender procreate   shambles slaughterhouse
quicken . . . blowing come alive as soon as the eggs are laid
public commoner common prostitute

water tears
stick . . . abuse i.e., think ill of even my worst fault
callet slut

IAGO. Why did he so?

DESDEMONA. I do not know. I am sure I am none such.

125 IAGO. Do not weep, do not weep. Alas the day!

EMILIA. Hath she forsook so many noble matches?
Her father? And her country? And her friends?
To be call'd whore? Would it not make one weep?

DESDEMONA. It is my wretched fortune.

IAGO.   Beshrew him for 't!
How comes this trick upon him?

130 DESDEMONA.   Nay, heaven doth know.

EMILIA. I will be hang'd, if some eternal villain,
Some busy and insinuating rogue,
Some cogging, cozening° slave, to get some office,
Have not devis'd this slander. I'll be hang'd else.

135 IAGO. Fie, there is no such man; it is impossible.

DESDEMONA. If any such there be, heaven pardon him!

EMILIA. A halter° pardon him! And hell gnaw his bones!
Why should he call her whore? Who keeps her company?
What place? What time? What form? What likelihood?
The Moor's abus'd by some most villainous
140 knave,
Some base notorious knave, some scurvy fellow.
O heaven, that such companions° thou' dst unfold,°
And put in every honest hand a whip
To lash the rascals naked through the world
Even from the east to the west!

145 IAGO.   Speak within door.

EMILIA. O, fie upon them! Some such squire he was
That turn'd your wit the seamy side without,
And made you to suspect me with the Moor.

IAGO. You are a fool; go to.

DESDEMONA.   O good Iago,
150 What shall I do to win my lord again?
Good friend, go to him, for, by this light of heaven,
I know not how I lost him. Here I kneel.
If e'er my will did trespass 'gainst his love
Either in discourse of thought or actual deed,
155 Or that mine eyes, mine ears, or any sense
Delight them in any other form,
Or that I do not yet, and ever did,
And ever will, though he do shake me off

To beggarly divorcement, love him dearly,
Comfort forswear me! Unkindness may do much,   160
And his unkindness may defeat° my life,
But never taint my love. I cannot say "whore":
It doth abhor me now I speak the word.
To do the act that might th' addition earn,
Not the world's mass of vanity° could make me.   165

IAGO. I pray you, be content; 'tis but his humor.°
The business of the state does him offense,
And he does chide with you.

DESDEMONA. If 'twere no other—

IAGO.   'Tis but so, I warrant.   [Trumpets.]
Hark, how these instruments summon to supper!   170
The messengers of Venice stay the meat.°
Go in, and weep not; all things shall be well.
                    [Exeunt DESDEMONA and EMILIA.]
                    [Enter RODERIGO.]
How now, Roderigo!

RODERIGO. I do not find that thou deal'st justly with me.

IAGO. What in the contrary?   175

RODERIGO. Every day thou daffest me with some device,° Iago, and rather, as it seems to me now, keepest from me all conveniency° than suppliest me with the least advantage of hope. I will indeed no longer endure it, nor am I yet per-   180 suaded to put up in peace what already I have foolishly suffered.

IAGO. Will you hear me, Roderigo?

RODERIGO. Faith, I have heard too much, for your words and performances are no kin together.   185

IAGO. You charge me most unjustly.

RODERIGO. With naught but truth. I have wasted myself out of my means. The jewels you have had from me to deliver to Desdemona would half have corrupted a votarist.° You have told   190 me she hath received them and returned me expectations and comforts of sudden respect° and acquaintance, but I find none.

IAGO. Well, go to. Very well.

RODERIGO. Very well, go to! I cannot go to, man,   195 nor 'tis not very well. By this hand, I say 'tis very scurvy, and begin to find myself fopped° in it.

IAGO. Very well.

RODERIGO. I tell you 'tis not very well. I will make myself known to Desdemona. If she will return   200 me my jewels, I will give over my suit and

cogging, cozening cheating, deceiving
halter noose   companions knaves
unfold disclose

defeat destroy   vanity worldly treasures
humor mood   stay the meat await supper
daffest . . . device put me off with some trick
conveniency opportunity   votarist nun
respect attention   fopped gulled

repent my unlawful solicitation; if not, assure
yourself I will seek satisfaction of you.

IAGO. You have said now?

RODERIGO. Aye, and said nothing but what I
205 protest intendment of doing.

IAGO. Why, now I see there's mettle in thee, and
even from this instant do build on thee a better
opinion than ever before. Give me thy hand,
Roderigo. Thou hast taken against me a most
210 just exception. But yet, I protest, I have dealt
most directly in thy affair.

RODERIGO. It hath not appeared.

IAGO. I grant indeed it hath not appeared, and your
suspicion is not without wit and judgment. But,
215 Roderigo, if thou hast that in thee indeed which I
have greater reason to believe now than ever—I
mean purpose, courage, and valor—this night
show it. If thou the next night following enjoy
not Desdemona, take me from this world with
220 treachery and devise engines° for my life.

RODERIGO. Well, what is it? Is it within reason and
compass?

IAGO. Sir, there is especial commission come from
Venice to depute Cassio in Othello's place.

225 RODERIGO. Is that true? Why, then Othello and
Desdemona return again to Venice.

IAGO. O, no. He goes into Mauritania, and takes
away with him the fair Desdemona, unless his
abode be lingered here by some accident—
230 wherein none can be so determinate° as the
removing of Cassio.

RODERIGO. How do you mean, removing of him?

IAGO. Why, by making him uncapable of Othello's
place. Knocking out his brains.

235 RODERIGO. And that you would have me to do?

IAGO. Aye, if you dare do yourself a profit and a
right. He sups tonight with a harlotry, and
thither will I go to him. He knows not yet of his
honorable fortune. If you will watch his going
240 thence, which I will fashion to fall out between
twelve and one, you may take him at your
pleasure. I will be near to second your attempt,
and he shall fall between us. Come, stand not
amazed at it, but go along with me. I will show
245 you such a necessity in his death that you shall
think yourself bound to put it on him. It is now
high suppertime, and the night grows to waste.
About it.

RODERIGO. I will hear further reason for this.

250 IAGO. And you shall be satisfied.   [*Exeunt*]

SCENE iii
Another room in the castle.

[*Enter* OTHELLO, LODOVICO, DESDEMONA,
EMILIA, *and* ATTENDANTS.]

LODOVICO. I do beseech you, sir, trouble yourself
no further.

OTHELLO. O, pardon me. 'Twill do me good to
walk.

LODOVICO. Madam, good night. I humbly thank
your ladyship.

DESDEMONA. Your honor is most welcome.

OTHELLO.   Will you walk, sir?
O—Desdemona—   5

DESDEMONA. My lord?

OTHELLO. Get you to bed on the instant; I will be
returned forthwith. Dismiss your attendant
there. Look it be done.

DESDEMONA. I will, my lord.   10

[*Exeunt* OTHELLO, LODOVICO, *and* ATTENDANTS.]

EMILIA. How goes it now? He looks gentler than he
did.

DESDEMONA. He says he will return incontinent.°
He hath commanded me to go to bed,
And bade me to dismiss you.

EMILIA.   Dismiss me!

DESDEMONA. It was his bidding. Therefore, good
Emilia,   15
Give me my nightly wearing, and adieu.
We must not now displease him.

EMILIA. I would you had never seen him!

DESDEMONA. So would not I. My love doth so
approve him,
That even his stubbornness, his checks, his
frowns—   20
Prithee, unpin me—have grace and favor in
them.

EMILIA. I have laid those sheets you bade me on the
bed.

DESDEMONA. All's one. Good faith, how foolish are
our minds!
If I do die before thee, prithee, shroud me
In one of those same sheets.

EMILIA.   Come, come, you talk.   25

DESDEMONA. My mother had a maid call'd Bar-
bary.
She was in love, and he she lov'd prov'd mad
And did forsake her. She had a song of "wil-
low"—
An old thing 'twas, but it express'd her fortune,
And she died singing it. That song tonight   30

---

devise engines lay plots *determinate* effective   *incontinent* immediately

Will not go from my mind. I have much to do
But to go hang my head all at one side
And sing it like poor Barbary. Prithee, dispatch.
EMILIA. Shall I go fetch your nightgown?
DESDEMONA.   No, unpin me here.
35   This Lodovico is a proper° man.
EMILIA. A very handsome man.
DESDEMONA. He speaks well.
EMILIA. I know a lady in Venice would have walked
    barefoot to Palestine for a touch of his nether lip.
DESDEMONA.

40   [Singing] The poor soul sat sighing by a sycamore tree,
        Sing all a green willow;
    Her hand on her bosom, her head on her knee.
        Sing willow, willow, willow.
    The fresh streams ran by her, and murmur'd her
        moans;
45   Sing willow, willow, willow.
    Her salt tears fell from her, and soften'd the stones—

        Lay by these—

    [Singing] Sing willow, willow, willow.

        Prithee, hie thee; he'll come anon—

50   [Singing] Sing all a green willow must be my garland.
        Let nobody blame him; his scorn I approve—

        Nay, that's not next. Hark! Who is 't that
            knocks?
EMILIA. It's the wind.
DESDEMONA.

    [Singing] I call'd my love false love; but what said he
        then?
55   Sing willow, willow, willow.
    If I court moe women, you'll couch with moe men.

        So get thee gone; good night. Mine eyes do itch.
        Doth that bode weeping?
EMILIA.   'Tis neither here nor there.
DESDEMONA. I have heard it said so. O, these men,
    these men!
60   Dost thou in conscience think—tell me, Emilia—
    That there be women do abuse their husbands
    In such gross kind?
EMILIA.   There be some such, no question.
DESDEMONA. Wouldst thou do such a deed for all
    the world?
EMILIA. Why, would not you?
DESDEMONA.   No, by this heavenly light!
65   EMILIA. Nor I neither by this heavenly light. I
    might do 't as well i' the dark.
DESDEMONA. Wouldst thou do such a deed for all
    the world?

    proper   handsome

EMILIA. The world's a huge thing. It is a great
    price
    For a small vice.
DESDEMONA.   In troth, I think thou wouldst not.
EMILIA. In troth, I think I should, and undo 't   70
    when I had done. Marry, I would not do such a
    thing for a joint-ring,° nor for measures of lawn,
    nor for gowns, petticoats, nor caps, nor any petty
    exhibition; but, for the whole world—why,
    who would not make her husband a cuckold to   75
    make him a monarch? I should venture purga-
    tory for 't.
DESDEMONA. Beshrew me if I would do such a
    wrong
    For the whole world.
EMILIA. Why, the wrong is but a wrong i' the   80
    world, and having the world for your labor, 'tis a
    wrong in your own world, and you might
    quickly make it right.
DESDEMONA. I do not think there is any such
    woman.   85
EMILIA. Yes, a dozen; and as many to the vantage°
    as would store the world they played for.
    But I do think it is their husbands' faults
    If wives do fall. Say that they slack their duties
    And pour our treasures into foreign° laps,   90
    Or else break out in peevish jealousies,
    Throwing restraint upon us, or say they strike
        us,
    Or scant our former having in despite,
    Why, we have galls, and though we have some
        grace,
    Yet have we some revenge. Let husbands know   95
    Their wives have sense like them; they see and
        smell
    And have their palates both for sweet and sour,
    As husbands have. What is it that they do
    When they change us for others? Is it sport?
    I think it is. And doth affection° breed it?   100
    I think it doth. Is 't frailty that thus errs?
    It is so too. And have not we affections,
    Desires for sport, and frailty, as men have?
    Then let them use us well. Else let them know
    The ills we do, their ills instruct us so.   105
DESDEMONA. Good night, good night. Heaven me
    such uses° send,
    Not to pick bad from bad, but by bad mend!°
                                            [Exeunt]

joint-ring   one made of separable halves
to the vantage   in addition
foreign   i.e., other women's
affection   desire   uses   practices
Not to . . . mend   i.e., not to accept the bad as my own
    way, but to improve by its example

A C T   V

SCENE i
Cyprus. A street.

[*Enter* Iago *and* Roderigo.]

Iago. Here, stand behind this bulk;° straight will
    he come.
    Wear thy good rapier bare, and put it home.
    Quick, quick; fear nothing; I'll be at thy elbow.
    It makes us, or it mars us; think on that,

5   And fix most firm thy resolution.
Roderigo. Be near at hand; I may miscarry in 't.
Iago. Here, at thy hand. Be bold, and take thy
    stand.   [*Retires.*]
Roderigo. I have no great devotion to the deed,
    And yet he hath given me satisfying reasons.

10   'Tis but a man gone. Forth, my sword. He dies.
Iago. I have rubb'd this young quat° almost to the
    sense,
    And he grows angry. Now, whether he kill
    Cassio,
    Or Cassio him, or each do kill the other,
    Every way makes my gain. Live Roderigo,

15   He calls me to a restitution large
    Of gold and jewels that I bobb'd from him
    As gifts to Desdemona.
    It must not be. If Cassio do remain,
    He hath a daily beauty in his life

20   That makes me ugly, and besides, the Moor
    May unfold me to him; there stand I in much
    peril.
    No, he must die. Be 't so. I hear him coming.

[*Enter* Cassio.]

Roderigo. I know his gait; 'tis he. Villain, thou
    diest!   [*Makes a pass at* Cassio.]
Cassio. That thrust had been mine enemy indeed,

25   But that my coat is better than thou know'st.
    I will make proof of thine.

         [*Draws, and wounds* Roderigo.]

Roderigo.   O, I am slain!

[Iago *from behind wounds* Cassio *in the leg, and
         exit.*]

Cassio. I am maim'd for ever. Help, ho! Murder!
    Murder!   [*Falls.*]

[*Enter* Othello.]

Othello. The voice of Cassio. Iago keeps his word.
Roderigo. O, villain that I am!
Othello.   It is even so.

Cassio. O, help, ho! Light! A surgeon!   30
Othello. 'Tis he. O brave Iago, honest and just,
    That hast such noble sense of thy friend's wrong!
    Thou teachest me. Minion,° your dear lies dead,
    And your unblest fate hies. Strumpet, I come!
    Forth of my heart those charms, thine eyes, are
    blotted;   35
    Thy bed lust-stain'd shall with lust's blood be
    spotted.   [*Exit*]

[*Enter* Lodovico *and* Gratiano.]

Cassio. What, ho! No watch? No passage?°
    Murder! Murder!
Gratiano. 'Tis some mischance; the cry is very
    direful.
Cassio. O, help!
Lodovico. Hark!   40
Roderigo. O wretched villain!
Lodovico. Two or three groan. It is a heavy night.
    These may be counterfeits. Let's think 't unsafe
    To come in to the cry without more help.
Roderigo. Nobody come? Then shall I bleed to
    death.   45
Lodovico. Hark!

[*Re-enter* Iago, *with a light.*]

Gratiano. Here's one comes in his shirt, with light
    and weapons.
Iago. Who's there? Whose noise is this that cries
    on murder?
Lodovico. We do not know.
Iago.   Did not you hear a cry?
Cassio. Here, here! For heaven's sake, help me!
Iago.   What's the matter?   50
Gratiano. This is Othello's ancient, as I take it.
Lodovico. The same indeed, a very valiant fellow.
Iago. What are you here that cry so grievously?
Cassio. Iago? O, I am spoil'd, undone by villains!
    Give me some help.   55
Iago. O me, lieutenant! What villains have done
    this?
Cassio. I think that one of them is hereabout,
    And cannot make away.
Iago.   O treacherous villains!
    What are you there? Come in and give some
    help.

         [*To* Lodovico *and* Gratiano.]

Roderigo. O, help me here!   60
Cassio. That's one of them.

---

bulk projecting wall   *quat* pimple   *Minion* darling (in contempt)   *passage* passersby

IAGO.   O murd'rous slave! O villain!
                    [Stabs RODERIGO.]
RODERIGO. O damn'd Iago! O inhuman dog!
IAGO. Kill men i' the dark! Where be these bloody
    thieves?
    How silent is this town! Ho! Murder! Murder!
65   What may you be? Are you of good or evil?
LODOVICO. As you shall prove us, praise° us.
IAGO. Signior Lodovico?
LODOVICO. He, sir.
IAGO. I cry you mercy. Here's Cassio hurt by
    villains.
70 GRATIANO. Cassio!
IAGO. How is 't, brother?
CASSIO. My leg is cut in two.
IAGO.   Marry, heaven forbid!
    Light, gentlemen. I'll bind it with my shirt.
                    [Enter BIANCA.]
BIANCA. What is the matter, ho? Who is 't that
    cried?
75 IAGO. Who is 't that cried!
BIANCA. O my dear Cassio! My sweet Cassio!
    O Cassio, Cassio, Cassio!
IAGO. O notable strumpet! Cassio, may you suspect
    Who they should be that have thus mangled
    you?
80 CASSIO. No.
GRATIANO. I am sorry to find you thus. I have been
    to seek you.
IAGO. Lend me a garter. So. O, for a chair,
    To bear him easily hence!
BIANCA. Alas, he faints! O Cassio, Cassio, Cassio!
85 IAGO. Gentlemen all, I do suspect this trash
    To be a party in this injury.
    Patience awhile, good Cassio. Come, come,
    Lend me a light. Know we this face or no?
    Alas, my friend and my dear countryman
90   Roderigo? No—yes, sure. O heaven! Roderigo.
GRATIANO. What, of Venice?
IAGO. Even he, sir. Did you know him?
GRATIANO.   Know him! Aye.
IAGO. Signior Gratiano? I cry you gentle pardon.
    These bloody accidents must excuse my man-
    ners,
    That so neglected you.
95 GRATIANO.   I am glad to see you.
IAGO. How do you, Cassio? O, a chair, a chair!
GRATIANO. Roderigo!
IAGO. He, he, 'tis he. [A chair brought in] O, that's
    well said; the chair.
    Some good man bear him carefully from hence;
    I'll fetch the general's surgeon. [To BIANCA] For
100   you, mistress,

Save you your labor. He that lies slain here,
    Cassio,
    Was my dear friend. What malice was between
    you?
CASSIO. None in the world; nor do I know the man.
IAGO. [To BIANCA] What, look you pale? O, bear
    him out o' th' air.
                    [CASSIO and RODERIGO are borne off.]
    Stay you, good gentlemen. Look you pale,
    mistress?
    Do you perceive the gastness of her eye?   105
    Nay, if you stare, we shall hear more anon.
    Behold her well; I pray you, look upon her.
    Do you see, gentlemen? Nay, guiltiness will
    speak,
    Though tongues were out of use.   110
                    [Enter EMILIA.]
EMILIA. 'Las, what's the matter? What's the mat-
    ter, husband?
IAGO. Cassio hath here been set on in the dark
    By Roderigo, and fellows that are 'scap'd.
    He's almost slain, and Roderigo dead.
EMILIA. Alas, good gentleman! Alas, good Cassio!   115
IAGO. This is the fruit of whoring. Prithee,
    Emilia,
    Go know of Cassio where he supp'd tonight.
    What, do you shake at that?
BIANCA. He supp'd at my house, but I therefore
    shake not.
IAGO. O, did he so? I charge you, go with me.   120
EMILIA. Fie, fie upon thee, strumpet!
BIANCA. I am no strumpet, but of life as honest
    As you that thus abuse me.
EMILIA.   As I! Foh! Fie upon thee!
IAGO. Kind gentlemen, let's go see poor Cassio
    dress'd.
    Come, mistress, you must tell 's another tale.   125
    Emilia, run you to the citadel
    And tell my lord and lady what hath happ'd!
    Will you go on, I pray? [Aside] This is the night
    That either makes me or fordoes me quite.°
                    [Exeunt]

SCENE ii
A bedchamber in the castle: DESDEMONA *in
bed asleep; a light burning.*

[Enter OTHELLO.]
OTHELLO. It is the cause, it is the cause, my soul.
    Let me not name it to you, you chaste stars!
    It is the cause. Yet I'll not shed her blood,
    Nor scar that whiter skin of hers than snow

praise appraise (i.e., identify)

fordoes me quite ruins me

5 And smooth as monumental alabaster.
Yet she must die, else she'll betray more men.
Put out the light, and then put out the light.
If I quench thee, thou flaming minister,
I can again thy former light restore,
10 Should I repent me; but once put out thy light,
Thou cunning'st pattern of excelling nature,
I know not where is that Promethean heat°
That can thy light relume. When I have pluck'd
the rose,
I cannot give it vital growth again;
15 It must needs wither. I'll smell it on the tree.
[*Kissing her.*]
Ah, balmy breath, that doth almost persuade
Justice to break her sword! One more, one more.
Be thus when thou art dead, and I will kill thee
And love thee after. One more, and this the last.
20 So sweet was ne'er so fatal. I must weep,
But they are cruel tears. This sorrow's heavenly;
It strikes where it doth love. She wakes.
DESDEMONA. Who's there? Othello?
OTHELLO. Aye, Desdemona.
DESDEMONA. Will you come to bed, my lord?
OTHELLO. Have you pray'd tonight, Desdemona?
25 DESDEMONA. Aye, my lord.
OTHELLO. If you bethink yourself of any crime
Unreconcil'd as yet to heaven and grace,
Solicit for it straight.
DESDEMONA. Alas, my lord, what may you mean
by that?
30 OTHELLO. Well, do it, and be brief; I will walk by.
I would not kill thy unprepared spirit.
No, heaven forfend! I would not kill thy soul.
DESDEMONA. Talk you of killing?
OTHELLO. Aye, I do.
35 DESDEMONA. Then heaven have mercy on me!
OTHELLO. Amen, with all my heart!
DESDEMONA. If you say so, I hope you will not kill
me.
OTHELLO. Hum!
DESDEMONA. And yet I fear you, for you are fatal
then
When your eyes roll so. Why I should fear I
40 know not,
Since guiltiness I know not; but yet I feel I fear.
OTHELLO. Think on thy sins.
DESDEMONA. They are loves I bear to you.
OTHELLO. Aye, and for that thou diest.
DESDEMONA. That death's unnatural that kills for
loving.
Alas, why gnaw you so your nether lip?
45 Some bloody passion shakes your very frame.

These are portents; but yet I hope, I hope,
They do not point on me.
OTHELLO. Peace, and be still!
DESDEMONA. I will so. What's the matter?
OTHELLO. That handkerchief which I so lov'd and
gave thee,
Thou gav'st to Cassio.
DESDEMONA. No, by my life and soul! 50
Send for the man, and ask him.
OTHELLO. Sweet soul, take heed,
Take heed of perjury; thou'rt on thy deathbed.
DESDEMONA. Aye, but not yet to die.
OTHELLO. Yes, presently.°
Therefore confess thee freely of thy sin;
For to deny each article with oath 55
Cannot remove nor choke the strong conception
That I do groan withal. Thou art to die.
DESDEMONA. Then Lord have mercy on me!
OTHELLO. I say, amen.
DESDEMONA. And have you mercy too! I never did
Offend you in my life, never lov'd Cassio 60
But with such general warranty of heaven
As I might love. I never gave him token.
OTHELLO. By heaven, I saw my handkerchief in 's
hand.
O perjur'd woman! Thou dost stone my heart,
And mak'st me call what I intend to do 65
A murder, which I thought a sacrifice.
I saw the handkerchief.
DESDEMONA. He found it, then.
I never gave it him. Send for him hither;
Let him confess a truth.
OTHELLO. He hath confess'd.
DESDEMONA. What, my lord? 70
OTHELLO. That he hath us'd thee.
DESDEMONA. How? Unlawfully?
OTHELLO. Aye.
DESDEMONA. He will not say so.
OTHELLO. No, his mouth is stopp'd.
Honest Iago hath ta'en order for° 't.
DESDEMONA. O, my fear interprets! What, is he
dead? 75
OTHELLO. Had all his hairs been lives, my great
revenge
Had stomach for them all.
DESDEMONA. Alas, he is betray'd, and I undone!
OTHELLO. Out, strumpet! Weep'st thou for him to
my face?
DESDEMONA. O, banish me, my lord, but kill me
not! 80
OTHELLO. Down, strumpet!
DESDEMONA. Kill me tomorrow; let me live to-
night!

Promethean heat divine fire (Prometheus stole fire from heaven for man)

presently immediately   *ta'en order for* taken care of

OTHELLO. Nay, if you strive—

DESDEMONA. But half an hour!

OTHELLO.   Being done, there is no pause.°

DESDEMONA. But while I say one prayer!

85 OTHELLO.   It is too late. [*He stifles her.*]

EMILIA. [*Within*] My lord, my lord! What, ho! My
   lord, my lord!

OTHELLO. What noise is this? Not dead? Not yet
   quite dead?
   I that am cruel am yet merciful;
   I would not have thee linger in thy pain.
   So, so.

EMILIA. [*Within*] What, ho! My lord, my lord!

90 OTHELLO.   Who's there?

EMILIA. [*Within*] O, good my lord, I would speak a
   word with you!

OTHELLO. Yes, 'tis Emilia. By and by. She's dead.
   'Tis like she comes to speak of Cassio's death—
   The noise was high. Ha! No more moving?
   Still as the grave. Shall she come in? Were 't

95 good?
   I think she stirs again. No. What's best to do?
   If she come in, she'll sure speak to my wife.
   My wife! My wife! What wife? I have no wife.
   O, insupportable! O heavy hour!

100 Methinks it should be now a huge eclipse
   Of sun and moon, and that th' affrighted globe
   Should yawn at alteration.°

EMILIA.   [*Within*] I do beseech you
   That I may speak with you, O, good my lord!

OTHELLO. I had forgot thee. O, come in, Emilia.

105 Soft; by and by. Let me the curtains draw.
   Where art thou?   [*Unlocks the door.*]

                [*Enter* EMILIA.]
                What's the matter with thee now?

EMILIA. O, my good lord, yonder's foul murders
   done!

OTHELLO. What, now?

EMILIA. But now, my lord.

110 OTHELLO. It is the very error of the moon.°
   She comes more nearer earth than she was wont
   And makes men mad.

EMILIA. Cassio, my lord, hath kill'd a young
   Venetian
   Call'd Roderigo.

OTHELLO.   Roderigo kill'd!
   And Cassio kill'd!

115 EMILIA.   No, Cassio is not kill'd.

OTHELLO. Not Cassio kill'd! Then murder's out of
   tune,
   And sweet revenge grows harsh.

DESDEMONA. O, falsely, falsely murder'd!

EMILIA.   Alas, what cry is that?

OTHELLO. That! What?

EMILIA. Out, and alas! That was my lady's voice.   120
   Help! Help, ho! Help! O lady, speak again!
   Sweet Desdemona! O sweet mistress, speak!

DESDEMONA. A guiltless death I die.

EMILIA. O, who hath done this deed?

DESDEMONA. Nobody; I myself. Farewell.   125
   Commend me to my kind lord. O, farewell!
                              [*Dies.*]

OTHELLO. Why, how should she be murder'd?

EMILIA.   Alas, who knows?

OTHELLO. You heard her say herself, it was not I.

EMILIA. She said so. I must needs report the truth.

OTHELLO. She's like a liar gone to burning hell.   130
   'Twas I that kill'd her.

EMILIA.   O, the more angel she,
   And you the blacker devil!

OTHELLO. She turn'd to folly,° and she was a whore.

EMILIA. Thou dost belie her, and thou art a devil.

OTHELLO. She was false as water.°

EMILIA.   Thou art rash as fire, to say   135
   That she was false. O, she was heavenly true!

OTHELLO. Cassio did top her; ask thy husband else.
   O, I were damn'd beneath all depth in hell
   But that I did proceed upon just grounds
   To this extremity. Thy husband knew it all.   140

EMILIA. My husband!

OTHELLO. Thy husband.

EMILIA. That she was false to wedlock?

OTHELLO. Aye, with Cassio. Nay, had she been
   true,
   If heaven would make me such another world   145
   Of one entire and perfect chrysolite,°
   I'd not have sold her for it.

EMILIA. My husband!

OTHELLO.   Aye, 'twas he that told me first.
   An honest man he is, and hates the slime
   That sticks on filthy deeds.

EMILIA.   My husband!   150

OTHELLO. What needs this iteration, woman? I say
   thy husband.

EMILIA. O mistress, villainy hath made mocks
   with° love!
   My husband say that she was false!

OTHELLO.   He, woman.
   I say thy husband. Dost understand the word?
   My friend, thy husband, honest, honest Iago.   155

EMILIA. If he say so, may his pernicious soul
   Rot half a grain a day! He lies to the heart.

Being . . . pause i.e., what has begun cannot be stopped
yawn at alteration split open for what has happened
error . . . moon deviation from its course (causing earthly
   aberrations)

folly unchastity
false as water i.e., assuming any shape
chrysolite precious stone   *made mocks with* mocked

She was too fond of her most filthy bargain.
OTHELLO. Ha!
160 EMILIA. Do thy worst.
This deed of thine is no more worthy heaven
Than thou wast worthy her.
OTHELLO.   Peace, you were best.
EMILIA. Thou hast not half that power to do me harm
As I have to be hurt. O gull! O dolt!
165 As ignorant as dirt! Thou hast done a deed—
I care not for thy sword; I'll make thee known
Though I lost twenty lives. Help! Help, ho! Help!
The Moor hath kill'd my mistress! Murder! Murder!
[Enter MONTANO, GRATIANO, IAGO, and others.]
MONTANO. What is the matter? How now, general!
170 EMILIA. O, are you come, Iago? You have done well,
That men must lay their murders on your neck.
GRATIANO. What is the matter?
EMILIA. Disprove this villain, if thou be'st a man.
He says thou told'st him that his wife was false.
175 I know thou didst not; thou'rt not such a villain.
Speak, for my heart is full.
IAGO. I told him what I thought, and told no more
Than what he found himself was apt and true.
EMILIA. But did you ever tell him she was false?
180 IAGO. I did.
EMILIA. You told a lie, an odious, damned lie,
Upon my soul, a lie, a wicked lie!
She false with Cassio! Did you say with Cassio?
IAGO. With Cassio, mistress. Go to, charm° your tongue.
EMILIA. I will not charm my tongue. I am bound to
185 speak.
My mistress here lies murder'd in her bed—
ALL. O heavens forfend!
EMILIA. And your reports have set the murder on.
OTHELLO. Nay, stare not, masters. It is true indeed.
190 GRATIANO. 'Tis a strange truth.
MONTANO. O monstrous act!
EMILIA.   Villainy, villainy, villainy!
I think upon 't. I think I smell 't. O villainy!
I thought so then. I'll kill myself for grief.
O villainy, villainy!
IAGO. What, are you mad? I charge you, get you
195 home.
EMILIA. Good gentlemen, let me have leave to speak.
'Tis proper I obey him, but not now.
Perchance, Iago, I will ne'er go home.
OTHELLO. O! O! O!   [Falling on the bed.]

EMILIA.   Nay, lay thee down and roar;
For thou hast kill'd the sweetest innocent   200
That e'er did lift up eye.
OTHELLO.   [Rising] O, she was foul!
I scarce did know you, uncle. There lies your niece,
Whose breath indeed these hands have newly stopp'd.
I know this act shows horrible and grim.
GRATIANO. Poor Desdemona! I am glad thy father's dead.   205
Thy match was mortal to him, and pure grief
Shore his old thread in twain. Did he live now,
This sight would make him do a desperate turn,
Yea, curse his better angel from his side
And fall to reprobation.°   210
OTHELLO. 'Tis pitiful. But yet Iago knows
That she with Cassio hath the act of shame
A thousand times committed. Cassio confess'd it,
And she did gratify his amorous works
With that recognizance and pledge of love   215
Which I first gave her; I saw it in his hand.
It was a handkerchief, an antique token
My father gave my mother.
EMILIA. O heaven! O heavenly powers!
IAGO. 'Zounds! Hold your peace.
EMILIA.   'Twill out, 'twill out. I peace!   220
No, I will speak as liberal as the north.°
Let heaven and men and devils, let them all,
All, all cry shame against me, yet I'll speak.
IAGO. Be wise, and get you home.
EMILIA.   I will not.
[IAGO offers to stab EMILIA.]
GRATIANO.   Fie!
Your sword upon a woman!   225
EMILIA. O thou dull Moor! That handkerchief thou speak'st of
I found by fortune and did give my husband,
For often with a solemn earnestness,
More than indeed belong'd to such a trifle,
He begg'd of me to steal it.
IAGO.   Villainous whore!   230
EMILIA. She give it Cassio! No, alas, I found it,
And I did give 't my husband.
IAGO.   Filth, thou liest!
EMILIA. By heaven, I do not, I do not, gentlemen.
O murd'rous coxcomb! What should such a fool
Do with so good a wife?
OTHELLO.   Are there no stones° in heaven   235
But what serve for the thunder? Precious villain!
[He runs at IAGO. IAGO, from behind, stabs EMILIA, and exit.]

charm subdue

reprobation damnation   north north wind
stones thunderbolts

GRATIANO. The woman falls. Sure, he hath kill'd
   his wife.
EMILIA. Aye, aye. O, lay me by my mistress' side.
GRATIANO. He's gone, but his wife's kill'd.
MONTANO. 'Tis a notorious villain. Take you this
240   weapon,
   Which I have here recover'd from the Moor.
   Come, guard the door without; let him not
   pass,
   But kill him rather. I'll after that same villain,
   For 'tis a damned slave.
            [*Exeunt all but* OTHELLO *and* EMILIA.]
OTHELLO.   I am not valiant neither,
245   But every puny whipster° gets my sword.
   But why should honor outlive honesty?°
   Let it go all.
EMILIA.   What did thy song bode, lady?
   Hark, canst thou hear me? I will play the swan,
   And die in music.°

         [*Singing*] Willow, willow, willow.

250   Moor, she was chaste; she lov'd thee, cruel Moor.
   So come my soul to bliss as I speak true.
   So speaking as I think, I die, I die.   [*Dies.*]
OTHELLO. I have another weapon in this chamber;
   It is a sword of Spain, the ice-brook's temper.°—
255   O, here it is. Uncle, I must come forth.
GRATIANO. [*Within*] If thou attempt it, it will cost
   thee dear.
   Thou hast no weapon, and perforce must suffer.
OTHELLO. Look in upon me then, and speak with
   me,
   Or, naked as I am, I will assault thee.
            [*Re-enter* GRATIANO.]
GRATIANO. What is the matter?
260 OTHELLO.   Behold, I have a weapon;
   A better never did itself sustain
   Upon a soldier's thigh. I have seen the day
   That with this little arm and this good sword
   I have made my way through more impedi-
   ments
   Than twenty times your stop. But, O vain
265   boast!
   Who can control his fate? 'Tis not so now.
   Be not afraid, though you do see me weapon'd.
   Here is my journey's end, here is my butt°
   And very sea-mark° of my utmost sail.
270   Do you go back dismay'd? 'Tis a lost° fear.

whipster stripling
honor . . . honesty i.e., reputation outlive true honor
swan . . . music i.e., by report, swans sing only at their
   death
ice-brook's temper tempered in ice water
butt destination   *sea-mark* utmost limit
lost wasted

Man but a rush against Othello's breast,
   And he retires. Where should Othello go?
   Now, how dost thou look now? O ill-starr'd
   wench!
   Pale as thy smock! When we shall meet at
   compt,°
   This look of thine will hurl my soul from
   heaven,   275
   And fiends will snatch at it. Cold, cold, my girl,
   Even like thy chastity. O cursed slave!
   Whip me, ye devils,
   From the possession of this heavenly sight!
   Blow me about in winds! Roast me in sulphur! 280
   Wash me in steep-down gulfs of liquid fire!
   O Desdemona! Desdemona! Dead!
   O! O! O!
[*Enter* LODOVICO, MONTANO, CASSIO *carried in a*
   chair, and OFFICERS *with* IAGO, *prisoner*.]
LODOVICO. Where is this rash and most unfortu-
   nate man?
OTHELLO. That's he that was Othello. Here I am. 285
LODOVICO. Where is that viper? Bring the villain
   forth.
OTHELLO. I look down towards his feet; but that's a
   fable.°
   If that thou be'st a devil, I cannot kill thee.
                              [*Wounds* IAGO.]
LODOVICO. Wrench his sword from him.
IAGO.   I bleed, sir, but not kill'd.
OTHELLO. I am not sorry neither. I'd have thee
   live;   290
   For, in my sense, 'tis happiness to die.
LODOVICO. O thou Othello, that wert once so
   good,
   Fall'n in the practice of a damned slave,
   What shall be said to thee?
OTHELLO.   Why, anything.
   An honorable murderer, if you will;   295
   For naught did I in hate, but all in honor.
LODOVICO. This wretch hath part confess'd his
   villainy.
   Did you and he consent in Cassio's death?
OTHELLO. Aye.
CASSIO. Dear general, I never gave you cause.   300
OTHELLO. I do believe it, and I ask your pardon.
   Will you, I pray, demand that demi-devil
   Why he hath thus ensnar'd my soul and body?
IAGO. Demand me nothing; what you know, you
   know.
   From this time forth I never will speak word. 305
LODOVICO. What, not to pray?
GRATIANO.   Torments will ope your lips.

at compt i.e., Judgment Day
I look . . . fable i.e., that the Devil's feet were cloven

OTHELLO. Well, thou dost best.

LODOVICO. Sir, you shall understand what hath befall'n,
  Which, as I think, you know not. Here is a letter
310 Found in the pocket of the slain Roderigo,
  And here another. The one of them imports
  The death of Cassio to be undertook
  By Roderigo.

OTHELLO. O villain!

CASSIO.   Most heathenish and most gross!

315 LODOVICO. Now here's another discontented paper
  Found in his pocket too, and this, it seems,
  Roderigo meant to have sent this damned villain,
  But that, belike, Iago in the interim
  Came in and satisfied him.°

OTHELLO.   O the pernicious caitiff!
320 How came you, Cassio, by that handkerchief
  That was my wife's?

CASSIO.   I found it in my chamber,
  And he himself confess'd but even now
  That there he dropp'd it for a special purpose
  Which wrought to his desire.

OTHELLO.   O fool! Fool! Fool!

325 CASSIO. There is besides in Roderigo's letter
  How he upbraids Iago that he made him
  Brave° me upon the watch, whereon it came
  That I was cast.° And even but now he spake
  After long seeming dead, Iago hurt him,
330 Iago set him on.

LODOVICO. You must forsake this room and go with us.
  Your power and your command is taken off,
  And Cassio rules in Cyprus. For this slave,
  If there be any cunning cruelty
335 That can torment him much and hold him long,
  It shall be his. You shall close prisoner rest
  Till that the nature of your fault be known
  To the Venetian state. Come, bring away.

OTHELLO. Soft you, a word or two before you go.
  I have done the state some service, and they
340 know 't.

No more of that. I pray you, in your letters,
  When you shall these unlucky deeds relate,
  Speak of me as I am; nothing extenuate,
  Nor set down aught in malice. Then must you speak
  Of one that lov'd not wisely but too well;   345
  Of one not easily jealous, but, being wrought,
  Perplex'd in the extreme; of one whose hand,
  Like the base° Indian, threw a pearl away
  Richer than all his tribe; of one whose subdu'd eyes,
  Albeit unused to the melting mood,   350
  Drop tears as fast as the Arabian trees
  Their med'cinable gum. Set you down this,
  And say besides that in Aleppo once,
  Where a malignant and a turban'd Turk
  Beat a Venetian and traduc'd the state,   355
  I took by the throat the circumcised dog
  And smote him, thus.   [Stabs himself.]

LODOVICO. O bloody period!°

GRATIANO.   All that's spoke is marr'd.

OTHELLO. I kiss'd thee ere I kill'd thee: no way but this,
  Killing myself, to die upon a kiss.   360
                    [Falls on the bed, and dies.]

CASSIO. This did I fear, but thought he had no weapon;
  For he was great of heart.

LODOVICO.   [To IAGO] O Spartan° dog,
  More fell° than anguish, hunger, or the sea!
  Look on the tragic loading of this bed:
  This is thy work. The object poisons sight;   365
  Let it be hid. Gratiano, keep the house,
  And seize upon the fortunes of the Moor,
  For they succeed on you. To you, lord governor,
  Remains the censure° of this hellish villain,
  The time, the place, the torture.   370
  O, enforce it!
  Myself will straight aboard, and to the state
  This heavy act with heavy heart relate.

                    [Exeunt]

Othello — too much pride

---

satisfied i.e., killed   *Brave* challenge
cast dismissed

base i.e., ignorant, unknowing   *period* end-stop
Spartan i.e., hardened   *fell* cruel
censure judgment

AFTERWORD

For the plot of the second of his four supreme tragedies, Shakespeare turned to a tawdry little Italian tale of passion, intrigue, murder, and revenge, a tale that most modern readers would find revolting. In it a certain Ensign, carnally attracted to one "Disdemona," the wife of a Moor, and jealous of a certain Captain under the Moor's command, devises a revenge meant to destroy both the Captain and the Moor's faith in his wife. Ugly event thereafter follows ugly event. The Ensign, on a dark night, attacks the Captain and with one blow cuts off his right leg. Having aroused the Moor to a bestial fury of jealousy, chiefly by villainous use of a rare handkerchief that he has stolen from Disdemona, the Ensign, together with the Moor, next plots the death of the innocent wife. They talk of poisons and daggers, but finally agree on a plan to beat Disdemona to death with sandbags and then to pull down upon her body the ceiling of the Moor's lodging so that her death will appear to have been accidental. The brutal beating and murder are narrated realistically. Afterward, in due time, Moor and Ensign come to hate and distrust each other; ultimately apprehended, each is tortured and dies a violent death.

Shakespeare's artistic achievement in *Othello* is best measured by the degree to which he transformed the effects of this mean little story of essentially brutal persons and events to accommodate the dignity, stature, and cathartic force of tragedy.

It is possible, even so, to find critics, general readers, and theatrical spectators who prefer to deny that he wholly succeeded. One Thomas Rymer, in 1693, belittled *Othello* as "the tragedy of the handkerchief," and found no redeeming qualities whatsoever in it. Dr. Johnson found good things in the play but was basically offended by it, and other critics almost as famous have echoed Johnson's reaction. General readers regularly find it difficult to forgive Othello, at the moment, for killing his innocent wife, and spectators have been known to protest vocally; "a very pretty lady that sat by me called out," wrote Pepys, "to see Desdemona smothered." Sir Arthur Quiller-Couch records that during a London performance an acquaintance of his stood up and shouted, "Oh, you great black fool! Can't you *see*?" And there is yet another report of a military officer who stood up and shot the actor of Othello just in time to prevent the fatal act. But these are testimonials rather to the force of the play than to any serious flaw.

It was never Shakespeare's practice as dramatist to "pull his punches," and much of the intolerably strong stuff of the Italian tale survives unchanged, or modified for dramatic reasons but still harsh. True, Othello does not sandbag his wife and then pull down the ceiling upon the body, but he does smother her, an unpleasant action that some directors hide behind a curtain. Iago does not cut Cassio's leg clean off at a stroke, but he wounds him viciously in the thigh; and, marking Shakespeare's own contribution to the original savagery of the story, Iago stabs Roderigo to death as he lies in the street crying for help. In Shakespeare, too, we sometimes catch a glimpse of something natively brutish that lies deep in Othello's character and is revealed only when, in his rage, the veneer of civilization peels away. "O, I see that nose of yours, but not that dog I shall throw it to," he mutters as he eavesdrops on Cassio and Iago; again, in his first fury at Desdemona: "I'll chop her into messes." By such details, far from "prettying up" the original, Shakespeare has occasionally accentuated its unsavoriness.

Had he done only this, of course, *Othello* would be no tragedy, but a melodrama depicting a tawdry domestic case of wrangling and murder such as occurs in any city on a Saturday night and is written up from police reports for the Sunday newspaper. But from his hands *Othello* emerges not only as legitimate tragedy but as one of the greatest half dozen in the world's literature. For even while retaining much of what makes the tale revolting, Shakespeare manages, by his art, to invest the whole with dignity, importance, and even beauty—in short, to give it permanence. What was insignificant and ugly in the source is in the tragedy not so much omitted or glossed over as it is probed for meaning. It is as if, in taking up the grubby affair of an Ensign, a Moor, a runaway girl, and a Captain of troops, Shakespeare had said to himself, "More is here than meets the eye," and had set out to find the heart of it. "I pray you in your letters," says Othello at last,

> When you shall these unlucky deeds relate,
> Speak of me as I am. Nothing extenuate,
> Nor set down aught in malice. Then must you speak
> Of one that lov'd not wisely, but too well;
> Of one not easily jealous, but, being wrought,
> Perplex'd in the extreme . . .

Dying, Othello gives this charge to the surviving officials on Cyprus; but it is Shakespeare who, in writing the tragedy, actually fulfils the request.

In transforming the Italian tale into a moving tragedy, the dramatist, now at the very zenith of his powers, combined his best talents for characterization, plotting, and poetry. It is noteworthy that in the source the characters, except for "Disdemona," do not even have names. Shakespeare's Othello, Iago, Desdemona, Emilia, and Cassio, with others, not only bear names but are shrewdly revealed human beings. None of them, even the wretched Roderigo, can be summed up in a phrase; they must be seen at full length, as they are shown in the play itself. As always with Shakespeare, their characters are mainly delineated in action, in their responses to situations that confront them, or, as in the case of Iago, situations that they themselves make. In this play especially, plot is not only inseparable from character, it is the *result* of character. *Othello* has rightly been called the most nearly flawless, technically, of the supreme tragedies. It is more tightly constructed than *Hamlet*, *King Lear*, or even *Macbeth*, and more than any other it creates the illusion of growing from within (Coleridge's "organic unity") rather than being shaped from without. No doubt this latter effect derives mainly from the fact that Iago himself simultaneously creates and directs both his own and Shakespeare's plot. It is he who conceives the action and sets it moving, and under his hand it grows, whirls, turns violent, and ultimately escapes his hand altogether.

Why Iago starts it at all is the central question of *Othello*, much as the hero's "delay" is the question of *Hamlet*. A dozen times Iago directly states motives, but few critics have taken him at his word. The most famous utterance upon this question was Coleridge's, that Iago's alacrity in speaking about his motives is "the motive hunting of a motiveless malignity." Is he indeed merely malignant by nature, drawing his pleasure out of doing evil, as Jaques of *As You Like It* sucks *his* joy from melancholy? Is he psychopathic, an egomaniac, and in the end, as one critic put it, a "silent, glaring madman"? Or is he, as Othello finally implies, looking at Iago's feet to see whether they are cloven, the devil himself? Or is there something that yet defies analysis after nearly four hundred years, hinted but not revealed in his own categorical statement: "I am not what I am."

Motiveless or not, Iago proves himself the master engineer, constructing and directing his evil campaign with fantastic skill, taking advantage of precisely those qualities in the persons around him that make them vulnerable. We should underestimate the tragedy badly if we thought it represented only the gulling of an easily gulled, simple Moor by an ordinary villain. For Iago deceives all other principal persons at Venice and on Cyprus as wholly as he deceives Othello. To all others he is "honest Iago," and never more so than during the very moments when he is most insidiously playing the villain. Preying on

Roderigo's vain passion for Desdemona, he has long had the use of his victim's purse. Recognizing Cassio's rather flamboyantly elegant manner with ladies, he takes advantage of precisely that characteristic in weaving the net that enmeshes them all. Similarly, he seizes upon the notably chaste and noble generosity that peculiarly distinguishes Desdemona and uses it for her ruin. Emilia, his own wife, for all her superior worldly wisdom, he has deceived utterly about himself during all the years of their marriage, for in the end it is she who finds it most incredible that her husband was capable of villainy: "*My* husband?" she repeatedly cries, "*My* husband?"

Thus he finds the needed bits and pieces for his design in the qualities of those around him and in occasions as they arise. Nor is he less shrewd in identifying exactly that in Othello that is most susceptible to undermining. Othello is of an alien culture, proud and all-sufficient in war, but deeply insecure in his new role as husband to a pure white and lovely Venetian aristocrat, and it is through this chink of insecurity that Iago insinuates the fatal wedge. Iago's importance to the tragedy, as prime instigator and guiding genius of the entire action, can hardly be overestimated, and the fact poses the question whether, in that case, *Othello* is not an imperfect example of Shakespearean tragedy. As we generally define such tragedy, the protagonist (hero) is the author of his own destruction, his own nature having driven him inevitably upon catastrophe. Thus, in *Julius Caesar*, Brutus, though mightily influenced by Cassius in the decision to assassinate Caesar, thereafter makes his fatal decisions alone and makes them because, being Brutus, he cannot make different ones; he is ruled by his conception of honor and duty. Hence it is, finally, Brutus and not Cassius who is responsible for the hero's fate. With some reflection, it appears that the case of Othello is nearest that of Brutus; no other tragic heroes of Shakespeare's bear quite the same relation to each other. Othello, though thrust into a situation devised by Iago, makes the decisions that his own nature dictates. Othello is as much dedicated to the principle of justice as Brutus is to the idea of honor. When it appears to him that Cassio has failed his responsibility as captain of the nightwatch on Cyprus, he forthwith sacks Cassio. When it appears to him that Desdemona has abdicated her place as his faithful wife, he executes her—not, indeed, in a jealous fit, but in spite of personal feeling, as an act of justice, "lest she betray more men." Once before, at Aleppo, he had seized by the throat and smote to death "a malignant and a turban'd Turk" who had beaten a Venetian and "traduc'd the state." And exactly so, when it appears to him that he has betrayed his own responsibilities, he kills himself. Thus all the decisions are ultimately his own and are made because, being as he is, he could make no others. Iago's "contribution" to the tragedy was only to place him in the situations in which the fatal decisions were made, as Cassius did Brutus.

Finally, much of the power that is in *Othello*, building its great cumulative force and elevating it from scandalous tale to high tragedy, derives from the language of the play. Not as lyrical as *Romeo and Juliet*, as richly resonant as *Hamlet's* great passages, as thunderous as *King Lear*, or as spellbinding as *Macbeth*, *Othello* nevertheless contains some of Shakespeare's most potent dramatic verse. Whether eloquently soaring, as when Othello describes for the Senators the manner of his wooing; sharp with sarcastic thrusts or saturated with physical images, as when Iago blackens Othello's vision of his chaste white bride; or hauntingly pitiful, as when Desdemona talks with Emilia and sings of poor Barbary in her last hour—the poetic language is invariably compelling, always "right" for occasion, matter, and speaker.

The combination of immediately exciting theatrical figures (most notably Iago), swift action, tight plot, and dramatically potent verse is doubtless responsible for *Othello's* record as a successful stage play. History suggests that to this day new productions of *Othello* stand a better chance of being "hits" than do those of any other Shakespearean tragedy. From Shakespeare's own Burbage to our century's Paul Robeson, Olivier, and others, the most distinguished actors of England and America have played the role of the hero, or of the villain, and some have alternated in these roles.

A NOTE ON THE COMPOSITION OF THE PLAY

We have it on good authority that *Othello* was written in 1604 and first acted in that year. It was first printed in the Quarto of 1622 and reprinted in the First Folio, 1623. The source is a tale in Giraldi Cinthio's collection called *Hecatommithi* (1565).

King Lear

DRAMATIS PERSONÆ

LEAR   *King of Britain*
KING OF FRANCE
DUKE OF BURGUNDY
DUKE OF CORNWALL
DUKE OF ALBANY
EARL OF KENT
EARL OF GLOUCESTER
EDGAR   *son to Gloucester*
EDMUND   *bastard son to Gloucester*
CURAN   *a courtier*
OLD MAN   *tenant to Gloucester*
DOCTOR

FOOL
OSWALD   *steward to Goneril*
A CAPTAIN   *employed by Edmund*
GENTLEMAN   *attendant on Cordelia*
HERALD
SERVANTS   *to Cornwall*
GONERIL ⎫
REGAN   ⎬ *daughters to Lear*
CORDELIA ⎭
KNIGHTS   *of Lear's train*, CAPTAINS, MESSENGERS,
   SOLDIERS, *and* ATTENDANTS
SCENE: *Britain*

ACT I

[handwritten: Sub plot] *[handwritten: another stupid parent]*

SCENE i
KING LEAR'S *palace.*

[*Enter* KENT, GLOUCESTER, *and* EDMUND.]
KENT. I thought the king had more affected° the
   Duke of Albany than Cornwall.
GLOUCESTER. It did always seem so to us. But now,
   in the division of the kingdom, it appears not
5 which of the dukes he values most, for equalities
   are so weighed that curiosity in neither can make
   choice of either's moiety.°
KENT. Is not this your son, my lord?
GLOUCESTER. His breeding, sir, hath been at my
10   charge. I have so often blushed to acknowledge
   him that now I am brazed° to it.

KENT. I cannot conceive° you.
GLOUCESTER. Sir, this young fellow's mother
   could; whereupon she grew round-wombed,
   and had indeed, sir, a son for her cradle ere she   15
   had a husband for her bed. Do you smell a
   fault?
KENT. I cannot wish the fault undone, the issue of it
   being so proper.°
GLOUCESTER. But I have, sir, a son by order of law,   20
   some year elder than this, who yet is no dearer
   in my account. Though this knave came some-
   thing° saucily into the world before he was sent
   for, yet was his mother fair; there was good
   sport at his making, and the whoreson° must   25
   be acknowledged. Do you know this noble
   gentleman, Edmund?

affected   favored
equalities . . . moiety   shares are so evenly balanced that
   scrutiny cannot choose between the portions
brazed   brassed; hence, hardened

conceive   understand
issue . . . proper   result . . . handsome
something   somewhat   *whoreson*   bastard

EDMUND. No, my lord.

GLOUCESTER. My lord of Kent. Remember him
30   hereafter as my honorable friend.

EDMUND. My services to your lordship.

KENT. I must love you, and sue to know you
better.

EDMUND. Sir, I shall study deserving.

35   GLOUCESTER. He hath been out° nine years, and
away he shall again. The king is coming.

[*Sennet.° Enter one bearing a coronet,* KING LEAR,
CORNWALL, ALBANY, GONERIL, REGAN,
CORDELIA, *and* ATTENDANTS.]

LEAR. Attend the lords of France and Burgundy,
Gloucester.

GLOUCESTER. I shall, my liege.

[*Exeunt* GLOUCESTER *and* EDMUND.]

LEAR. Meantime we shall express our darker
purpose.°

Give me the map there. Know we have divided
40   In three our kingdom, and 'tis our fast intent
To shake all cares and business from our age,
Conferring them on younger strengths, while
we
Unburden'd crawl toward death. Our son of
Cornwall,
And you, our no less loving son° of Albany,
45   We have this hour a constant will to publish
Our daughters' several° dowers, that° future
strife
May be prevented now. The princes, France and
Burgundy,
Great rivals in our youngest daughter's love,
Long in our court have made their amorous
sojourn,
50   And here are to be answer'd. Tell me, my
daughters,
Since now we will divest us both of rule,
Interest of territory, cares of state,
Which of you shall we say doth love us most,
That we our largest bounty may extend
55   Where nature doth with merit challenge?
Goneril,°
Our eldest-born, speak first.

GONERIL. Sir, I love you more than words can
wield° the matter,
Dearer than eyesight, space, and liberty,

Beyond what can be valu'd, rich or rare,
No less than life, with grace, health, beauty,   60
honor,
As much as child e'er lov'd or father found—
A love that makes breath poor and speech
unable.
Beyond all manner of so much I love you.

CORDELIA. [*Aside*] What shall Cordelia do? Love,
and be silent.

LEAR. Of all these bounds, even from this line to
this,
With shadowy forests and with champains
rich'd,°
With plenteous rivers and wide-skirted meads,°
We make thee lady. To thine and Albany's
issue
Be this perpetual. What says our second daugh-
ter,
Our dearest Regan, wife to Cornwall? Speak.   70

REGAN. I am made of that self° metal as my sister,
And prize me at her worth. In my true heart
I find she names my very deed° of love;
Only she comes too short, that° I profess
Myself an enemy to all other joys   75
Which the most precious square° of sense
possesses,
And find I am alone felicitate°
In your dear highness' love.

CORDELIA.   [*Aside*] Then poor Cordelia!
And yet not so, since I am sure my love's
More ponderous° than my tongue.   80

LEAR. To thee and thine hereditary ever
Remain this ample third of our fair kingdom,
No less in space, validity,° and pleasure
Than that conferr'd on Goneril. Now, our joy,
Although the last, not least, to whose young love   85
The vines of France and milk of Burgundy
Strive to be interess'd,° what can you say to
draw
A third more opulent than your sisters? Speak.

CORDELIA. Nothing, my lord.

LEAR. Nothing!   90

CORDELIA. Nothing.

LEAR. Nothing will come of nothing. Speak again.

CORDELIA. Unhappy that I am, I cannot heave
My heart into my mouth. I love your majesty
According to my bond; nor more nor less.   95

LEAR. How, how, Cordelia! Mend your speech a
little,

out away for training or military service
Sennet flourish of trumpets
our . . . purpose our hidden purpose; Lear uses the royal
plural
son . . . son son-in-law   *several* separate
that so that
That . . . challenge so that I can give most to the one
whose natural affection and desert are greatest
wield express

champains rich'd plains made rich
wide-skirted meads extensive meadows   *self* selfsame
very deed actuality   *that* in that   *square* area
felicitate made happy   *ponderous* weighty
validity value   *interess'd* joined

Lest it may mar your fortunes.

CORDELIA.   Good my lord,
You have begot me, bred me, lov'd me. I
100 Return those duties back as are right fit,
Obey you, love you, and most honor you.
Why have my sisters husbands, if they say
They love you all? Haply,° when I shall wed,
That lord whose hand must take my plight°
    shall carry
105 Half my love with him, half my care and duty.
Sure, I shall never marry like my sisters,
To love my father all.

LEAR. But goes thy heart with this?

CORDELIA.   Aye, good my lord.

LEAR. So young, and so untender?

110 CORDELIA. So young, my lord, and true.

LEAR. Let it be so; thy truth then be thy dower.
For, by the sacred radiance of the sun,
The mysteries of Hecate,° and the night,
By all the operation of the orbs°
115 From whom we do exist and cease to be,
Here I disclaim all my paternal care,
Propinquity, and property of blood,°
And as a stranger to my heart and me
Hold thee from this forever. The barbarous
    Scythian,°
120 Or he that makes his generation° messes
To gorge his appetite, shall to my bosom
Be as well neighbor'd, pitied, and reliev'd
As thou my sometime° daughter.

KENT.   Good my liege—

LEAR. Peace, Kent!
125 Come not between the dragon and his wrath.
I lov'd her most, and thought to set my rest
On her kind nursery.° Hence, and avoid my
    sight!
So be my grave my peace, as here I give
Her father's heart from her! Call France. Who
    stirs?
130 Call Burgundy. Cornwall and Albany,
With my two daughters' dowers digest this
    third.
Let pride, which she calls plainness,° marry her.
I do invest you jointly with my power,
Pre-eminence,° and all the large effects

That troop with majesty. Ourself, by monthly
    course,   135
With reservation of an hundred knights
By you to be sustain'd, shall our abode
Make with you by due turns. Only we still re-
    tain
The name and all th' additions° to a king.
The sway,° revenue, execution of the rest,   140
Beloved sons, be yours. Which to confirm,
This coronet part betwixt you.

KENT.   Royal Lear,
Whom I have ever honor'd as my king,
Lov'd as my father, as my master follow'd,
As my great patron thought on in my prayers— 145

LEAR. The bow is bent and drawn; make from the
    shaft.

KENT. Let it fall rather, though the fork° invade
The region of my heart. Be Kent unmannerly
When Lear is mad. What wouldst thou do, old
    man?
Think'st thou that duty shall have dread to speak, 150
When power to flattery bows? To plainness
    honor's bound
When majesty stoops to folly. Reverse thy doom,
And in thy best consideration check
This hideous rashness. Answer my life my judg-
    ment,°
Thy youngest daughter does not love thee least, 155
Nor are those empty-hearted whose low sound
Reverbs no hollowness.

LEAR.   Kent, on thy life, no more.

KENT. My life I never held but as a pawn
To wage against thy enemies, nor fear to lose it,
Thy safety being the motive.

LEAR.   Out of my sight!   160

KENT. See better, Lear, and let me still remain
The true blank° of thine eye.

LEAR. Now, by Apollo—

KENT.   Now, by Apollo, king,
Thou swear'st thy gods in vain.

LEAR.   O, vassal! Miscreant!
    [Laying his hand on his sword.]

ALBANY and CORNWALL. Dear sir, forbear.   165

KENT. Do.
Kill thy physician, and the fee bestow
Upon the foul disease. Revoke thy doom,
Or, whilst I can vent clamor from my throat,
I'll tell thee thou dost evil.

LEAR.   Hear me, recreant!   170
On thy allegiance, hear me!

Haply perhaps   plight betrothal pledge
Hecate goddess of witchcraft
operation . . . orbs influences of the planets and stars
Propinquity . . . blood relationship and claims to kinship
Scythian inhabitants of Scythia, classical examples of
    savagery
generation offspring   sometime former
nursery nursing   plainness plain speech
Pre-eminence authority

Only . . . additions I shall retain only the name and titles
    of honor
sway rule   fork forked head, barb
Answer . . . judgment I stake my life on my judgment
Reverbs reverberates   blank target, bull's-eye

Since thou hast sought to make us break our
   vow,
Which we durst never yet, and with strain'd°
   pride
To come between our sentence and our power,
175 Which nor our nature nor° our place can bear,
Our potency made good,° take thy reward.
Five days we do allot thee, for provision
To shield thee from diseases of the world,
And on the sixth to turn thy hated back
Upon our kingdom. If on the tenth day follow-
180   ing
Thy banish'd trunk be found in our dominions,
The moment is thy death. Away! By Jupiter,
This shall not be revok'd.
KENT. Fare thee well, king. Sith° thus thou wilt
   appear,
185 Freedom lives hence, and banishment is here.
[To CORDELIA] The gods to their dear shelter
   take thee, maid,
That justly think'st and hast most rightly said!
[To REGAN and GONERIL] And your large speeches
   may your deeds approve,°
That good effects may spring from words of love.
190 Thus Kent, O princes, bids you all adieu.
He'll shape his old course° in a country new.
                              [Exit]
[Flourish. Re-enter GLOUCESTER, with FRANCE,
   BURGUNDY, and ATTENDANTS.]
GLOUCESTER. Here's France and Burgundy, my
   noble lord.
LEAR. My lord of Burgundy,
We first address towards you, who with this king
195 Hath rival'd for our daughter. What, in the least,
Will you require in present° dower with her,
Or cease your quest of love?
BURGUNDY.   Most royal majesty,
I crave no more than what your highness offer'd,
Nor will you tender less.
LEAR.   Right noble Burgundy,
200 When she was dear to us, we did hold her so.
But now her price is fall'n. Sir, there she stands.
If aught within that little-seeming substance,
Or all of it, with our displeasure piec'd,°
And nothing more, may fitly like your grace,
She's there, and she is yours.
205 BURGUNDY.   I know no answer.
LEAR. Will you, with those infirmities she owes,°
Unfriended, new adopted to our hate,

Dower'd with our curse and stranger'd wi
   oath,
Take her, or leave her?
BURGUNDY.   Pardon me, royal sir;
Election makes not up° on such conditions.   210
LEAR. Then leave her, sir; for, by the power that
   made me,
I tell you all her wealth. [To FRANCE] For you,
   great king,
I would not from your love make such a stray°
To match you where I hate. Therefore beseech
   you
T'avert your liking a more worthier way   215
Than on a wretch whom nature is asham'd
Almost t'acknowledge hers.
FRANCE.   This is most strange,
That she, that even but now was your best
   object,
The argument° of your praise, balm of your age,
Most best, most dearest, should in this trice of
   time   220
Commit a thing so monstrous to° dismantle
So many folds of favor. Sure, her offense
Must be of such unnatural degree
That monsters° it, or your fore-vouch'd affection
Fall'n into taint. Which to believe of her   225
Must be a faith that reason without miracle
Could never plant in me.°
CORDELIA.   I yet beseech your majesty—
If for I want° that glib and oily art
To speak and purpose not, since what I well
   intend
I'll do 't before I speak—that you make known   230
It is no vicious blot, murder, or foulness,
No unchaste action, or dishonor'd step
That hath depriv'd me of your grace and favor;
But even for want of that for which I am richer,
A still-soliciting° eye, and such a tongue   235
As I am glad I have not, though not to have it
Hath lost me in your liking.
LEAR.   Better thou
Hadst not been born than not t'have pleas'd me
   better.
FRANCE. Is it but this? A tardiness in nature°
Which often leaves the history unspoke   240
That it intends to do? My lord of Burgundy,
What say you to the lady? Love's not love
When it is mingled with regards that stand

---

strain'd excessive   nor . . . nor neither . . . nor
Our . . . good my power being thus asserted
Sith since   approve prove
shape . . . course continue in his (honest) ways
present immediate   piec'd added
owes possesses

Election . . . up it is impossible to decide
stray deviation   argument subject   to as to
monsters makes a monster of
Which . . . me reason could not establish such a belief
  in me except by a miracle   for I want because I lack
still-soliciting ever-greedy
tardiness in nature reticent nature

Into Prose   *lucar Fleyly*

Aloof from th' entire point.° Will you have her?
She is herself a dowry.

245 BURGUNDY.   Royal Lear,
Give but that portion which yourself propos'd,
And here I take Cordelia by the hand,
Duchess of Burgundy.

LEAR. Nothing. I have sworn; I am firm.

BURGUNDY. I am sorry, then, you have so lost a
250   father
That you must lose a husband.

CORDELIA.   Peace be with Burgundy!
Since that respects° of fortune are his love,
I shall not be his wife.

FRANCE. Fairest Cordelia, that art most rich being
poor,
255   Most choice forsaken, and most lov'd despis'd,
Thee and thy virtues here I seize upon,
Be it lawful I take up what's cast away.
Gods, gods! 'Tis strange that from their cold'st
neglect
My love should kindle to inflam'd respect.°
Thy dowerless daughter, king, thrown to my
260   chance,
Is queen of us, of ours, and our fair France.
Not all the dukes of waterish Burgundy
Can buy this unpriz'd precious maid of me.
Bid them farewell, Cordelia, though unkind.
265   Thou losest here, a better where to find.

LEAR. Thou hast her, France. Let her be thine, for
we
Have no such daughter, nor shall ever see
That face of hers again. Therefore be gone
Without our grace, our love, our benison.
270   Come, noble Burgundy.
       [*Flourish. Exeunt all but* FRANCE, GONERIL,
            REGAN, *and* CORDELIA.]

FRANCE. Bid farewell to your sisters.

CORDELIA. The jewels of our father, with wash'd°
eyes
Cordelia leaves you. I know you what you are,
And, like a sister, am most loath to call
Your faults as they are nam'd. Use well our
275   father.
To your professed bosoms I commit him.
But yet, alas, stood I within his grace,
I would prefer° him to a better place.
So farewell to you both.

REGAN. Prescribe not us our duties.

280 GONERIL.   Let your study

Be to content your lord, who hath receiv'd you
At fortune's alms.° You have obedience scanted,
And well are worth the want that you have
wanted.°

CORDELIA. Time shall unfold what plaited° cun-
ning hides:
Who cover faults, at last shame them derides.   285
Well may you prosper!

FRANCE.   Come, my fair Cordelia.
         [*Exeunt* FRANCE *and* CORDELIA.]

GONERIL. Sister, it is not a little I have to say of what
most nearly appertains to us both. I think our
father will hence tonight.

REGAN. That's most certain, and with you. Next   290
month with us.

GONERIL. You see how full of changes his age is. The
observation we have made of it hath not been
little. He always loved our sister most, and with
what poor judgment he hath now cast her off   295
appears too grossly.

REGAN. 'Tis the infirmity of his age. Yet he hath
ever but slenderly known himself.

GONERIL. The best and soundest of his time hath
been but rash. Then must we look to receive from   300
his age, not alone the imperfections of long in-
grafted° condition, but therewithal the unruly
waywardness that infirm and choleric° years
bring with them.

REGAN. Such unconstant starts° are we like to have   305
from him as this of Kent's banishment.

GONERIL. There is further compliment° of leave-
taking between France and him. Pray you, let's
hit together.° If our father carry authority with
such dispositions as he bears, this last surrender   310
of his will but offend us.

REGAN. We shall further think on 't.

GONERIL. We must do something, and i' the heat.°
                                   [*Exeunt*]

SCENE ii
The EARL OF GLOUCESTER'S *castle.*

[*Enter* EDMUND, *with a letter.*]

EDMUND. Thou, nature, art my goddess; to thy
law
My services are bound. Wherefore should I
Stand in the plague of° custom and permit

---

regards . . . point i.e., considerations of dowry that are
   irrelevant to love
respects considerations
inflam'd respect ardent regard
wash'd i.e., clear-sighted from weeping
prefer recommend

At . . . alms i.e., like a beggar
worth . . . wanted deserve to be denied what you have
   denied
plaited i.e., pleated, hiding within folds
ingrafted ingrown   *choleric* ill-tempered
unconstant starts unpredictable outbursts
compliment formality   *hit together* agree
i' the heat quickly   *Stand . . . of* be plagued by

Edmund's soliloquy   He plays on Gloucester character   Prose (handwritten)

The curiosity° of nations to deprive me
For that° I am some twelve or fourteen moon-
5   shines
Lag of° a brother? Why bastard? Wherefore
      base,
When my dimensions are as well compact,°
My mind as generous,° and my shape as true
As honest madam's issue? Why brand they us
10   With base? With baseness? Bastardy? Base, base?
Who in the lusty stealth° of nature take
More composition° and fierce quality
Than doth, within a dull, stale, tired bed,
Go to the creating a whole tribe of fops,°
15   Got° 'tween asleep and wake? Well then,
Legitimate Edgar, I must have your land.
Our father's love is to the bastard Edmund
As to the legitimate. Fine word, "legitimate"!
Well, my legitimate, if this letter speed°
20   And my invention° thrive, Edmund the base
Shall top the legitimate. I grow; I prosper.
Now, gods, stand up for bastards!
                      [*Enter* GLOUCESTER.]
GLOUCESTER. Kent banish'd thus! And France in
      choler parted!°
And the king gone tonight! Subscrib'd° his
      power!
25   Confin'd to exhibition!° All this done
Upon the gad!° Edmund, how now! What news?
EDMUND. So please your lordship, none.
                      [*Putting up the letter.*]
GLOUCESTER. Why so earnestly seek you to put up
      that letter?
EDMUND. I know no news, my lord.
30   GLOUCESTER. What paper were you reading?
EDMUND. Nothing, my lord.   *echo of Cord.* (handwritten)
GLOUCESTER. No? What needed then that terrible
      dispatch of it into your pocket? The quality of
      nothing hath not such need to hide itself. Let's
35   see. Come, if it be nothing, I shall not need
      spectacles.
EDMUND. I beseech you, sir, pardon me. It is a letter
      from my brother, that I have not all o'erread;
      and for so much as I have perused, I find it not
40   fit for your o'erlooking.
GLOUCESTER. Give me the letter, sir.

EDMUND. I shall offend, either to detain or give it.
      The contents, as in part I understand them, are
      to blame.
GLOUCESTER. Let's see, let's see.   45
EDMUND. I hope, for my brother's justification, he
      wrote this but as an essay or taste of my virtue.
GLOUCESTER.
   [*Reads*] This policy and reverence of age° makes
   the world bitter to the best of our times;° keeps
   our fortunes from us till our oldness cannot   50
   relish them. I begin to find an idle and fond°
   bondage in the oppression of aged tyranny,
   who sways° not as it hath power but as it is
   suffered. Come to me, that of this I may speak
   more. If our father would sleep till I waked   55
   him, you should enjoy half his revenue forever
   and live the beloved of your brother,   EDGAR.

Hum! Conspiracy!—"Sleep till I waked him,
you should enjoy half his revenue!"—My son
Edgar! Had he a hand to write this? A heart and   60
brain to breed it in? When came this to you?
Who brought it?
EDMUND. It was not brought me, my lord; there's
the cunning of it. I found it thrown in at the casement of my closet.   65
GLOUCESTER. You know the character° to be your
brother's?
EDMUND. If the matter were good, my lord, I durst
swear it were his; but, in respect of that,° I
would fain think it were not.   70
GLOUCESTER. It is his.
EDMUND. It is his hand, my lord, but I hope his
heart is not in the contents.
GLOUCESTER. Hath he never heretofore sounded
you° in this business?   75
EDMUND. Never, my lord. But I have heard him oft
maintain it to be fit that, sons at perfect age and
fathers declining, the father should be as ward to
the son, and the son manage his revenue.
GLOUCESTER. O villain, villain! His very opinion in   80
the letter! Abhorred villain! Unnatural, detested, brutish villain! Worse than brutish! Go,
sirrah, seek him; aye, apprehend him. Abominable villain! Where is he?
EDMUND. I do not well know, my lord. If it shall   85
please you to suspend your indignation against
my brother till you can derive from him better
testimony of his intent, you should run a certain°
course; where,° if you violently proceed against

11 to Lear plot (handwritten)

---

curiosity   conventional fine distinctions
For that   because   *Lag of* i.e., born later than
compact   composed   *generous*   noble
lusty stealth   vigorous secrecy
composition   blending of elements
fops fools   *Got* begotten   *speed*   succeed
invention   trick, device
in choler parted   gone in anger   *Subscrib'd*   surrendered
Confin'd to exhibition   reduced to an allowance
Upon the gad   i.e., suddenly, on the spur

This . . . age   this custom of revering age
best . . . times i.e., to youth   *fond*   foolish
sways   rules   *character*   hand
in . . . that i.e., in view of its contents
sounded you   sounded you out   *certain*   safe
where   whereas

90 him, mistaking his purpose, it would make a great gap° in your own honor and shake in pieces the heart of his obedience. I dare pawn down my life for him that he hath wrote this to feel° my affection to your honor and to no other 95 pretense of danger.°

GLOUCESTER. Think you so?

EDMUND. If your honor judge it meet,° I will place you where you shall hear us confer of this and by an auricular assurance have your satisfaction, and 100 that without any further delay than this very evening.

GLOUCESTER. He cannot be such a monster—

EDMUND. Nor is not, sure.

GLOUCESTER. To his father that so tenderly and 105 entirely loves him. Heaven and earth! Edmund, seek him out; wind me° into him, I pray you. Frame the business after your own wisdom. I would unstate myself to be in a due resolution.°

EDMUND. I will seek him, sir, presently,° convey° 110 the business as I shall find means, and acquaint you withal.°

GLOUCESTER. These late eclipses in the sun and moon portend no good to us. Though the wisdom of nature° can reason it thus and thus, yet 115 nature finds itself scourged by the sequent° effects: love cools, friendship falls off, brothers divide; in cities, mutinies; in countries, discord; in palaces, treason; and the bond cracked 'twixt son and father. This villain of mine comes under 120 the prediction;° there's son against father. The king falls from bias of nature;° there's father against child. We have seen the best of our time. Machinations, hollowness, treachery, and all ruinous disorders follow us disquietly to our 125 graves. Find out this villain, Edmund; it shall lose thee nothing. Do it carefully. And the noble and true-hearted Kent banished! His offense, honesty! 'Tis strange. [Exit]

EDMUND. This is the excellent foppery° of the 130 world, that when we are sick in fortune—often the surfeit° of our own behavior—we make guilty of our disasters the sun, the moon, and the stars, as if we were villains by necessity, fools by heavenly compulsion, knaves, thieves, and

treachers by spherical predominance,° drun- 135 kards, liars, and adulterers by an enforced obedience of planetary influence, and all that we are evil in, by a divine thrusting on. An admirable evasion of whoremaster man, to lay his goatish disposition to the charge of a star! My 140 father compounded with my mother under the dragon's tail, and my nativity was under Ursa major,° so that it follows I am rough and lecherous. Tut, I should have been that I am had the maidenliest star in the firmament twinkled on 145 my bastardizing. Edgar—

[Enter EDGAR.]

And pat he comes like the catastrophe° of the old comedy. My cue is villainous melancholy, with a sigh like Tom o' Bedlam.° O, these eclipses do portend these divisions! Fa, sol, la, mi. 150

EDGAR. How now, brother Edmund! What serious contemplation are you in?

EDMUND. I am thinking, brother, of a prediction I read this other day, what should follow these eclipses. 155

EDGAR. Do you busy yourself about that?

EDMUND. I promise you, the effects he writ of succeed° unhappily—as of unnaturalness between the child and the parent; death, dearth, dissolutions of ancient amities; divisions in state, 160 menaces and maledictions against king and nobles; needless diffidences, banishment of friends, dissipation of cohorts, nuptial breaches, and I know not what.

EDGAR. How long have you been a sectary astrono- 165 mical?°

EDMUND. Come, come. When saw you my father last?

EDGAR. Why, the night gone by.

EDMUND. Spake you with him? 170

EDGAR. Aye, two hours together.

EDMUND. Parted you in good terms? Found you no displeasure in him by word or countenance?

EDGAR. None at all.

EDMUND. Bethink yourself wherein you may have 175 offended him, and at my entreaty forbear his presence till some little time hath qualified the heat of his displeasure, which at this instant so

gap fault   feel feel out
pretense of danger dangerous intent
meet fitting   wind me worm your way
unstate . . . resolution give my all to resolve the question
presently immediately   convey manage
withal with it   widsom of nature human knowledge
sequent subsequent
comes . . . prediction accords with the general tendency
bias of nature i.e., tendency of his own nature
foppery foolishness   surfeit result of excess

treachers . . . predominance traitors by influence of the stars
dragon's . . . major the constellation Draco's tail . . the Great Bear
catastrophe denouement
Tom o' Bedlam common name for a begging lunatic from London's madhouse, Bethlehem Hospital
succeed follow one another
sectary astronomical devotee of astrology

theme of disguise

rageth in him that with the mischief of your per-
180 son it would scarcely allay.°
EDGAR. Some villain hath done me wrong.
EDMUND. That's my fear. I pray you, have a continent forbearance° till the speed of his rage goes
slower, and, as I say, retire with me to my
185 lodging, from whence I will fitly bring you to
hear my lord speak. Pray ye, go; there's my key.
If you do stir abroad, go armed.
EDGAR. Armed, brother!
EDMUND. Brother, I advise you to the best. Go
190 armed. I am no honest man if there be any good
meaning towards you. I have told you what I
have seen and heard, but faintly, nothing like the
image and horror of it. Pray you, away.
EDGAR. Shall I hear from you anon?
195 EDMUND. I do serve you in this business.

                              [*Exit* EDGAR.]

A credulous father and a brother noble,
Whose nature is so far from doing harms
That he suspects none, on whose foolish honesty
My practices° ride easy. I see the business.
200 Let me, if not by birth, have lands by wit.
All with me's meet° that I can fashion fit.

                                        [*Exit*]

SCENE iii
The DUKE OF ALBANY's *palace.*

[*Enter* GONERIL *and* OSWALD, *her steward.*]
GONERIL. Did my father strike my gentleman for
chiding of his fool?
OSWALD. Yes, madam.
GONERIL. By day and night he wrongs me. Every
hour
He flashes into one gross crime or other
5   That sets us all at odds. I'll not endure it.
His knights grow riotous, and himself upbraids
us
On every trifle. When he returns from hunting,
I will not speak with him; say I am sick.
If you come slack of former services,
10   You shall do well; the fault of it I'll answer.
OSWALD. He's coming, madam; I hear him.
                                    [*Horns within.*]
GONERIL. Put on what weary negligence you
please,
You and your fellows. I'd have it come to ques-
tion.°

If he distaste it, let him to our sister,
Whose mind and mine, I know, in that are one, 15
Not to be overrul'd. Idle old man,
That still would manage those authorities
That he hath given away! Now, by my life,
Old fools are babes again, and must be us'd
With checks as flatteries, when they are seen
abus'd.°   20
Remember what I tell you.
OSWALD.   Very well, madam.
GONERIL. And let his knights have colder looks
among you.
What grows of it, no matter. Advise your fellows
so.
I would breed from hence occasions, and I shall,
That I may speak. I'll write straight to my sister 25
To hold my very course. Prepare for dinner.

                                        [*Exeunt*]

SCENE iv
A hall in the same.

[*Enter* KENT, *disguised.*]
KENT. If but as well I other accents borrow
That can my speech defuse,° my good intent
May carry through itself to that full issue
For which I raz'd my likeness.° Now, banish'd
Kent,
If thou canst serve where thou dost stand con-
demn'd,   5
So may it come thy master whom thou lov'st
Shall find thee full of labors.
       [*Horns within. Enter* LEAR, KNIGHTS, *and*
                        ATTENDANTS.]
LEAR. Let me not stay a jot for dinner; go get it
ready. [*Exit an* ATTENDANT] How now! What art
thou?   10
KENT. A man, sir.
LEAR. What dost thou profess? What wouldst thou
with us?
KENT. I do profess to be no less than I seem: to
serve him truly that will put me in trust, to love 15
him that is honest, to converse with him that is
wise and says little, to fear judgment,° to fight
when I cannot choose, and to eat no fish.°
LEAR. What art thou?
KENT. A very honest-hearted fellow, and as poor as 20
the king.

with ... allay even injury done to you would scarcely
   allay it
have ... forbearance exercise self-control
practices plots   *All's ... meet* "anything goes"
come to question brought to a head

With ... abus'd with restraints instead of flattery when
   they get out of hand
defuse disguise
raz'd my likeness erased my former appearance
judgment i.e., God's judgment
to ... fish i.e., I am not a Catholic

Fool is fond of Cordelia

LEAR. If thou be as poor for a subject as he is for a king, thou art poor enough. What wouldst thou?

KENT. Service.

25 LEAR. Who wouldst thou serve?

KENT. You.

LEAR. Dost thou know me, fellow?

KENT. No, sir, but you have that in your countenance which I would fain call master.

30 LEAR. What's that?

KENT. Authority.

LEAR. What services canst thou do?

KENT. I can keep honest counsel, ride, run, mar a curious tale in telling it,° and deliver a plain
35 message bluntly. That which ordinary men are fit for, I am qualified in, and the best of me is diligence.

LEAR. How old art thou?

48

KENT. Not so young, sir, to love a woman for sing-
40 ing, nor so old to dote on her for anything. I have years on my back forty eight.

LEAR. Follow me; thou shalt serve me. If I like thee no worse after dinner, I will not part from thee yet. Dinner, ho, dinner! Where's my knave?°
45 My fool? Go you, and call my fool hither.

[*Exit an* ATTENDANT.]
[*Enter* OSWALD.]

You, you, sirrah, where's my daughter?

OSWALD. So please you—   [*Exit*]

LEAR. What says the fellow there? Call the clot-
poll° back. [*Exit a* KNIGHT] Where's my fool, ho?
50 I think the world's asleep.

[*Re-enter* KNIGHT.]

How now! Where's that mongrel?

KNIGHT. He says, my lord, your daughter is not well.

LEAR. Why came not the slave back to me when I
55 called him?

KNIGHT. Sir, he answered me in the roundest° manner, he would not.

LEAR. He would not!

KNIGHT. My lord, I know not what the matter is,
60 but to my judgment, your highness is not enter-
tained with that ceremonious affection as you were wont. There's a great abatement of kindness appears as well in the general dependants as in the duke himself also and your daughter.

65 LEAR. Ha! Sayest thou so?

KNIGHT. I beseech you, pardon me, my lord, if I be mistaken; for my duty cannot be silent when I think your highness wronged.

LEAR. Thou but rememberest° me of mine own conception. I have perceived a most faint neglect
70 of late, which I have rather blamed as mine own jealous curiosity° than as a very pretense° and purpose of unkindness. I will look further into 't. But where's my fool? I have not seen him this
75 two days.

KNIGHT. Since my young lady's going into France, sir, the fool hath much pined away.

LEAR. No more of that; I have noted it well. Go you, and tell my daughter I would speak with
80 her. [*Exit an* ATTENDANT] Go you, call hither my fool.   [*Exit an* ATTENDANT.]

[*Re-enter* OSWALD.]

O, you sir, you, come you hither, sir. Who am I, sir?

OSWALD. My lady's father.

85 LEAR. My lady's father! My lord's knave. You whoreson dog! You slave! You cur!

OSWALD. I am none of these, my lord. I beseech your pardon.

LEAR. Do you bandy looks with me, you rascal?

[*Striking him.*]

90 OSWALD. I'll not be struck, my lord.

KENT. Nor tripped neither, you base football player.   [*Tripping up his heels.*]

LEAR. I thank thee, fellow; thou servest me, and I'll love thee.

95 KENT. Come, sir, arise, away! I'll teach you dif-
ferences.° Away, away! If you will measure your lubber's length again, tarry. But away! Go to; have you wisdom? So.   [*Pushes* OSWALD *out.*]

LEAR. Now, my friendly knave, I thank thee.
100 There's earnest° of thy service.

[*Giving* KENT *money.*]
[*Enter* FOOL.]

FOOL. Let me hire him too. Here's my coxcomb.°

[*Offering* KENT *his cap.*]

LEAR. How now, my pretty knave! How dost thou?

FOOL. Sirrah, you were best take my coxcomb.

KENT. Why, fool?

105 FOOL. Why, for taking one's part that's out of favor. Nay, an thou canst not smile as the wind sits,° thou'lt catch cold shortly. There, take my coxcomb. Why, this fellow hath banished two on 's° daughters, and done the third a blessing against his will. If thou follow him, thou must
110

---

rememberest remindest
jealous curiosity tendency to be overly suspicious
pretense intention
differences distinctions of rank
earnest token payment   *coxcomb* jester's cap
an . . . sits if you can't shift with the wind (i.e., stay
   "in" with the right people)
on 's of his

---

mar . . . it i.e., mar its extravagant language by putting
   it plainly
knave boy   *clotpoll* blockhead
roundest most direct

the wise fool

needs wear my coxcomb. How now, nuncle!°
  Would I had two coxcombs and two daughters!
LEAR. Why, my boy?
FOOL. If I gave them all my living, I'd keep my
115 coxcombs myself. There's mine; beg another of
  thy daughters.
LEAR. Take heed, sirrah; the whip.
FOOL. Truth's a dog must to kennel; he must be
  whipped out, when Lady the brach° may stand
120 by the fire and stink.
LEAR. A pestilent gall to me!
FOOL. Sirrah, I'll teach thee a speech.
LEAR. Do.
FOOL. Mark it, nuncle:

125   Have more than thou showest,
       Speak less than thou knowest,
       Lend less than thou owest,
       Ride more than thou goest,°
       Learn more than thou trowest,°
130   Set less than thou throwest;°
       Leave thy drink and thy whore,
       And keep in-a-door,
       And thou shalt have more
       Than two tens to a score.

135 KENT. This is nothing, fool.
FOOL. Then 'tis like the breath of an unfee'd
  lawyer—you gave me nothing for 't. Can you
  make no use of nothing, nuncle?
LEAR. Why, no, boy; nothing can be made out of
140 nothing.
FOOL. [*To* KENT] Prithee, tell him, so much the
  rent of his land comes to. He will not believe a
  fool.
LEAR. A bitter fool!
145 FOOL. Dost thou know the difference, my boy,
  between a bitter fool and a sweet fool?
LEAR. No, lad; teach me.
FOOL.

       That lord that counsel'd thee
         To give away thy land,
150   Come place him here by me;
         Do thou for him stand.
       The sweet and bitter fool
         Will presently° appear;
       The one in motley° here,
155   The other found out there.

LEAR. Dost thou call me fool, boy?
FOOL. All thy other titles thou hast given away;
  that thou wast born with.

KENT. This is not altogether fool, my lord.
FOOL. No, faith, lords and great men will not let   160
  me. If I had a monopoly out, they would have
  part on 't; and ladies too, they will not let me
  have all the fool to myself, they'll be snatching.
  Give me an egg, nuncle, and I'll give thee two
  crowns.   165
LEAR. What two crowns shall they be?
FOOL. Why, after I have cut the egg in the middle
  and eat up the meat, the two crowns of the egg.
  When thou clovest thy crown i' the middle and
  gavest away both parts, thou borest thine ass on   170
  thy back o'er the dirt. Thou hadst little wit in thy
  bald crown when thou gavest thy golden one
  away. If I speak like myself in this, let him be
  whipped that first finds it so.

  [*Singing*] Fools had ne'er less wit in a year,   175
       For wise men are grown foppish,°
     And know not how their wits to wear,
       Their manners are so apish.

LEAR. When were you wont to be so full of songs,
  sirrah?   180
FOOL. I have used it, nuncle, ever since thou madest
  thy daughters thy mother. For when thou gavest
  them the rod and puttest down thine own
  breeches,

  [*Singing*] Then they for sudden joy did weep,   185
       And I for sorrow sung,
     That such a king should play bo-peep,
       And go the fools among.

  Prithee, nuncle, keep a schoolmaster that can
  teach thy fool to lie. I would fain learn to lie.   190
LEAR. An you lie, sirrah, we'll have you whipped.
FOOL. I marvel what kin thou and thy daughters
  are. They'll have me whipped for speaking true,
  thou'lt have me whipped for lying, and sometimes I am whipped for holding my peace. I had   195
  rather be any kind o' thing than a fool. And yet I
  would not be thee, nuncle; thou hast pared thy
  wit o' both sides and left nothing i' the middle.
  Here comes one o' the parings.
             [*Enter* GONERIL.]
LEAR. How now, daughter! What makes that   200
  frontlet° on? Methinks you are too much of late
  i' the frown.
FOOL. Thou wast a pretty fellow when thou hadst
  no need to care for her frowning; now thou art
  an O without a figure. I am better than thou art   205
  now; I am a fool, thou art nothing. [*To* GONERIL]

---

nuncle uncle   brach bitch
goest walkest   trowest believest
Set . . . throwest risk less than you play to win
presently immediately   motley fool's costume

foppish foolish
frontlet forehead-band; hence, frown

Yes, forsooth, I will hold my tongue; so your
face bids me, though you say nothing.

210
     Mum, mum,
     He that keeps nor crust nor crumb,
     Weary of all, shall want some.

[*Pointing to* LEAR] That's a shealed peascod.°
GONERIL. Not only, sir, this your all-licens'd fool,
  But other of your insolent retinue
215 Do hourly carp and quarrel, breaking forth
  In rank° and not to be endured riots. Sir,
  I had thought, by making this well known unto
    you,
  To have found a safe° redress, but now grow
    fearful,
  By what yourself too late have spoke and done,
220 That you protect this course and put it on
  By your allowance;° which if you should, the
    fault
  Would not 'scape censure nor the redresses
    sleep
  Which, in the tender° of a wholesome weal,°
  Might in their working do you that offense
225 Which else were shame, that then necessity
  Will call discreet proceeding.°
FOOL. For, you know, nuncle,

  The hedge-sparrow fed the cuckoo° so long,
  That it had it head bit off by it° young.

  So out went the candle, and we were left dark-
230   ling.°
LEAR. Are you our daughter?
GONERIL. Come, sir,
  I would you would make use of that good wis-
    dom
  Whereof I know you are fraught,° and put away
235 These dispositions that of late transform you
  From what you rightly are.
FOOL. May not an ass know when the cart draws
  the horse?
  Whoop, Jug!° I love thee.
LEAR. Doth any here know me? This is not Lear.
  Doth Lear walk thus? Speak thus? Where are his
240   eyes?

Either his notion° weakens, his discernings
  Are lethargied—Ha! Waking? 'Tis not so.
  Who is it that can tell me who I am?
FOOL. Lear's shadow.
LEAR. I would learn that; for, by the marks of 245
  sovereignty, knowledge, and reason, I should be
  false persuaded I had daughters.
FOOL. Which they will make an obedient father.
LEAR. Your name, fair gentlewoman?
GONERIL. This admiration,° sir, is much o' the
  savor   250
  Of other your new pranks. I do beseech you
  To understand my purposes aright.
  As you are old and reverend, should be wise.
  Here do you keep a hundred knights and squires,
  Men so disorder'd, so debosh'd° and bold,   255
  That this our court, infected with their manners,
  Shows like a riotous inn. Epicurism° and lust
  Make it more like a tavern or a brothel
  Than a grac'd palace. The shame itself doth
    speak
  For instant remedy. Be then desir'd   260
  By her that else will take the thing she begs,
  A little to disquantity your train,
  And the remainder that shall still depend,
  To be such men as may besort° your age,
  Which know themselves and you.
LEAR.   Darkness and devils! 265
  Saddle my horses; call my train together.
  Degenerate bastard! I'll not trouble thee.
  Yet have I left a daughter.
GONERIL. You strike my people, and your dis-
  order'd rabble
  Make servants of their betters.   270
          [*Enter* ALBANY.]
LEAR. Woe, that too late repents—[*To* ALBANY] O,
  sir, are you come?
  Is it your will? Speak, sir.—Prepare my horses.
  Ingratitude, thou marble-hearted fiend,
  More hideous when thou show'st thee in a child
  Than the sea monster!
ALBANY.   Pray, sir, be patient. 275
LEAR. [*To* GONERIL] Detested kite!° Thou liest.
  My train are men of choice and rarest parts,
  That all particulars of duty know,
  And in the most exact regard support
  The worships° of their name. O most small fault, 280
  How ugly didst thou in Cordelia show!
  That, like an engine, wrench'd my frame of
    nature

shealed peascod shelled peapod   *rank* gross
safe sure
put . . . allowance encourage it by your laxity
tender care   *weal* state
Which . . . proceeding which in other circumstances
  would appear shameful but in these will be
  considered appropriate
hedge-sparrow . . . cuckoo (the cuckoo lays its eggs in
  other birds' nests)
it its   *darkling* in the dark
fraught laden
Whoop, Jug (scrap from a popular song)

notion understanding
admiration i.e., pretended amazement
debosh'd debauched   *Epicurism* riotous living
besort befit   *kite* scavenging hawk
worships dignities

weak Albany

From the fix'd place, drew from my heart all
  love,
And added to the gall. O Lear, Lear, Lear!
285 Beat at this gate that let thy folly in
                                    [*Striking his head.*]
  And thy dear judgment out! Go, go, my people.
ALBANY. My lord, I am guiltless, as I am ignorant
  Of what hath mov'd you.
LEAR.   It may be so, my lord.
  Hear, nature, hear; dear goddess, hear!
290 Suspend thy purpose, if thou didst intend
  To make this creature fruitful.
  Into her womb convey sterility.
  Dry up in her the organs of increase,
  And from her derogate° body never spring
295 A babe to honor her! If she must teem,°
  Create her child of spleen,° that it may live
  And be a thwart disnatur'd torment to her.
  Let it stamp wrinkles in her brow of youth,
  With cadent° tears fret° channels in her cheeks;
300 Turn all her mother's pains and benefits
  To laughter and contempt, that she may feel
  How sharper than a serpent's tooth it is
  To have a thankless child! Away, away! [*Exit*]
ALBANY. Now, gods that we adore, whereof comes
  this?
305 GONERIL. Never afflict yourself to know the cause,
  But let his disposition have that scope
  That dotage gives it.
              [*Re-enter* LEAR.]
LEAR. What, fifty of my followers at a clap!
  Within a fortnight!
ALBANY.   What's the matter, sir?
LEAR. I'll tell thee. [*To* GONERIL] Life and death! I
310 am asham'd
  That thou hast power to shake my manhood
  thus,
  That these hot tears, which break from me per-
  force,°
  Should make thee worth them. Blasts and fogs
  upon thee!
  Th' untented° woundings of a father's curse
315 Pierce every sense about thee! Old fond eyes,
  Beweep this cause again, I'll pluck ye out
  And cast you with the waters that you lose
  To temper clay. Yea, is it come to this?
  Let it be so. Yet have I left a daughter,
320 Who, I am sure, is kind and comfortable.°
  When she shall hear this of thee, with her nails
  She'll flay thy wolvish visage. Thou shalt find

derogate degenerate   teem reproduce
spleen ill-temper
thwart disnatur'd perverse, unnatural
cadent falling   fret trench   perforce by force
untented uncleanable   comfortable comforting

That I'll resume the shape which thou dost
  think
  I have cast off forever. Thou shalt, I warrant thee.
              [*Exeunt* LEAR, KENT, *and* ATTENDANTS.]
GONERIL. Do you mark that, my lord?   325
ALBANY. I cannot be so partial, Goneril,
  To the great love I bear you—
GONERIL. Pray you, content. What, Oswald, ho!
  [*To the* FOOL] You, sir, more knave than fool,
  after your master.
FOOL. Nuncle Lear, nuncle Lear, tarry. Take the 330
  fool with thee.

              A fox, when one has caught her,
              And such a daughter,
              Should sure to the slaughter,
              If my cap would buy a halter.°   335
              So the fool follows after.
                                    [*Exit*]
GONERIL. This man hath had good counsel. A hun-
  dred knights!
  'Tis politic and safe to let him keep
  At point° a hundred knights! Yes, that on every
  dream,
  Each buzz, each fancy, each complaint, dislike, 340
  He may enguard° his dotage with their powers
  And hold our lives in mercy. Oswald, I say!
ALBANY. Well, you may fear too far.
GONERIL.   Safer than trust too far.
  Let me still° take away the harms I fear,
  Not fear still to be taken. I know his heart.   345
  What he hath utter'd I have writ my sister.
  If she sustain him and his hundred knights,
  When I have show'd th' unfitness—
              [*Re-enter* OSWALD.]
                              How now, Oswald!
  What, have you writ that letter to my sister?
OSWALD. Yes, madam.   350
GONERIL. Take you some company, and away to
  horse.
  Inform her full of my particular fear,
  And thereto add such reasons of your own
  As may compact° it more. Get you gone,
  And hasten your return. [*Exit* OSWALD] No, no,
  my lord,   355
  This milky gentleness and course of yours
  Though I condemn not, yet, under pardon,
  You are much more atask'd° for want of wisdom
  Than prais'd for harmful mildness.
ALBANY. How far your eyes may pierce I cannot tell. 360
  Striving to better, oft we mar what's well.
GONERIL. Nay, then—
ALBANY. Well, well; th' event.°   [*Exeunt*]

halter noose   At point in arms   enguard safeguard
still always   compact weight   atask'd censured
event outcome

SCENE v
Court before the same.

[*Enter* LEAR, KENT, *and* FOOL.]

LEAR. Go you before to Gloucester with these
letters. Acquaint my daughter no further with
anything you know than comes from her demand out of the letter. If your diligence be not
5   speedy, I shall be there afore you.

KENT. I will not sleep, my lord, till I have delivered
your letter.   [*Exit*]

FOOL. If a man's brains were in 's heels, were 't not
in danger of kibes?°

10   LEAR. Aye, boy.

FOOL. Then, I prithee, be merry; thy wit shall
ne'er go slipshod.°

LEAR. Ha, ha, ha!

FOOL. Shalt see thy other daughter will use thee
15   kindly;° for though she's as like this as a crab's°
like an apple, yet I can tell what I can tell.

LEAR. Why, what canst thou tell, my boy?

FOOL. She will taste as like this as a crab does to a
crab. Thou canst tell why one's nose stands i' the
20   middle on 's° face?

LEAR. No.

FOOL. Why, to keep one's eyes of either side 's nose,
that what a man cannot smell out he may spy
into.

25   LEAR. I did her wrong—

FOOL. Canst tell how an oyster makes his shell?

LEAR. No.

FOOL. Nor I neither. But I can tell why a snail has a
house.

LEAR. Why?   30

FOOL. Why, to put 's head in, not to give it away to
his daughters and leave his horns° without a
case.

LEAR. I will forget my nature.—So kind a father!—
Be my horses ready?   35

FOOL. Thy asses are gone about 'em. The reason
why the seven stars are no more than seven is a
pretty reason.

LEAR. Because they are not eight?

FOOL. Yes, indeed. Thou wouldst make a good   40
fool.

LEAR. To take 't again perforce! Monster ingratitude!

FOOL. If thou wert my fool, nuncle, I'd have thee
beaten for being old before thy time.   45

LEAR. How's that?

FOOL. Thou shouldst not have been old till thou
hadst been wise.

LEAR. O, let me not be mad, not mad, sweet
heaven!
Keep me in temper. I would not be mad!   50
[*Enter* GENTLEMAN.]
How now! Are the horses ready?

GENTLEMAN. Ready, my lord.

LEAR. Come, boy.

FOOL. She that's a maid now and laughs at my
departure
Shall not be a maid long, unless things be cut
shorter.°   [*Exeunt*] 55

kibes chilblains   *slipshod* in slippers
kindly according to her kind (nature)   *crab* crabapple
on 's of his

horns i.e., with implication that Lear wears a
cuckold's horns
She . . . shorter (an indecent and irrelevant jest directed
to the audience)

ACT II

SCENE i
The EARL OF GLOUCESTER's *castle*

[*Enter* EDMUND *and* CURAN, *meeting.*]

EDMUND. Save thee, Curan.

CURAN. And you, sir. I have been with your father
and given him notice that the Duke of Cornwall
and Regan his duchess will be here with him this
5   night.

EDMUND. How comes that?

CURAN. Nay, I know not. You have heard of the
news abroad, I mean the whispered ones, for
they are yet but ear-kissing arguments?°

EDMUND. Not I. Pray you, what are they?   10

CURAN. Have you heard of no likely wars toward,°
'twixt the Dukes of Cornwall and Albany?

EDMUND. Not a word.

CURAN. You may do then in time. Fare you well,
sir.   [*Exit*]

ear-kissing arguments whispered rumors
toward in the making

EDMUND. The duke be here tonight? The better!
15   Best!
This weaves itself perforce into my business.
My father hath set guard to take my brother,
And I have one thing, of a queasy question,°
Which I must act. Briefness and fortune, work!
20 Brother, a word, descend. Brother, I say!
              [*Enter* EDGAR.]
My father watches. O sir, fly this place;
Intelligence is given where you are hid.
You have now the good advantage of the night.
Have you not spoken 'gainst the Duke of Corn-
    wall?
25 He's coming hither, now, i' the night, i' the haste,
And Regan with him. Have you nothing said
Upon his party 'gainst° the Duke of Albany?
Advise yourself.
EDGAR.   I am sure on 't, not a word.
EDMUND. I hear my father coming. Pardon me.
30 In cunning° I must draw my sword upon you.
Draw. Seem to defend yourself. Now quit you
    well.°
Yield! Come before my father. Light, ho,
    here!—
Fly, brother.—Torches, torches! So farewell.
                        [*Exit* EDGAR.]
Some blood drawn on me would beget opinion°
                        [*Wounds his arm.*]
Of my more fierce endeavor. I have seen drun-
35   kards
Do more than this in sport. Father, father!
Stop, stop! No help?
[*Enter* GLOUCESTER, *and* SERVANTS *with torches.*]
GLOUCESTER. Now, Edmund, where's the villain?
EDMUND. Here stood he in the dark, his sharp
    sword out,
Mumbling of wicked charms, conjuring the
40   moon
To stand 's auspicious mistress.°
GLOUCESTER.   But where is he?
EDMUND. Look, sir, I bleed.
GLOUCESTER.   Where is the villain, Edmund?
EDMUND. Fled this way, sir. When by no means he
    could—
GLOUCESTER. Pursue him, ho!—Go after.
                    [*Exeunt some* SERVANTS.]
                  "By no means" what?
EDMUND. Persuade me to the murder of your lord-
45   ship,

of . . . question i.e., of ticklish nature
Upon . . . 'gainst concerning his opposition to
In cunning i.e., to make a show
quit . . . well acquit yourself well; put up a fight
beget opinion give persuasive evidence
To . . . mistress i.e., to exercise her favorable influence

But that I told him the revenging gods
'Gainst parricides did all their thunders bend,
Spoke with how manifold and strong a bond
The child was bound to the father. Sir, in fine,°
Seeing how loathly opposite I stood   50
To his unnatural purpose, in fell° motion
With his prepared° sword he charges home
My unprovided body, lanc'd mine arm.
But when he saw my best alarum'd° spirits
Bold in the quarrel's right, rous'd to th'encoun-
    ter,   55
Or whether gasted° by the noise I made,
Full suddenly he fled.
GLOUCESTER.   Let him fly far.
Not in this land shall he remain uncaught;
And found—dispatch.° The noble duke my
    master,
My worthy arch° and patron, comes tonight.   60
By his authority I will proclaim it,
That he which finds him shall deserve our
    thanks,
Bringing the murd'rous caitiff° to the stake;°
He that conceals him, death.
EDMUND. When I dissuaded him from his intent   65
And found him pight° to do it, with curst° speech
I threaten'd to discover° him. He replied,
"Thou unpossessing bastard! Dost thou think,
If I would stand against thee, could the reposal
Of any trust, virtue, or worth in thee   70
Make thy words faith'd?° No. What I should
    deny—
As this I would, aye, though thou didst produce
My very character°—I'd turn it all
To thy suggestion, plot, and damned practice,
And thou must make a dullard of the world   75
If they not thought° the profits of my death
Were very pregnant and potential spurs
To make thee seek it."
GLOUCESTER.   Strong and fasten'd° villain!
Would he deny his letter? I never got° him.
                        [*Tucket° within.*]
Hark, the duke's trumpets! I know not why he
    comes.   80
All ports I'll bar. The villain shall not 'scape;
The duke must grant me that. Besides, his pic-
    ture

in fine in sum   fell savage   prepared drawn
alarum'd aroused
gasted made aghast   dispatch i.e., kill
arch support   caitiff wretch
stake literally, the place of execution; figuratively, to be
    tied to the stake for burning
pight determined   curst bitter   discover expose
faith'd believed   character handwriting
not thought did not think   fasten'd confirmed
got begot   Tucket trumpet call

I will send far and near, that all the kingdom
May have due note of him. And of my land,
Loyal and natural boy, I'll work the means
To make thee capable.°

[_Enter_ CORNWALL, REGAN, _and_ ATTENDANTS.]

CORNWALL. How now, my noble friend! Since I
came hither,
Which I can call but now, I have heard strange
news.

REGAN. If it be true, all vengeance comes too short
Which can pursue th' offender. How dost, my
lord?

GLOUCESTER. O, madam, my old heart is crack'd, is
crack'd!

REGAN. What, did my father's godson seek your life?
He whom my father nam'd? Your Edgar?

GLOUCESTER. O, lady, lady, shame would have it
hid!

REGAN. Was he not companion with the riotous
knights
That tend upon my father?

GLOUCESTER. I know not, madam. 'Tis too bad, too
bad.

EDMUND. Yes, madam, he was of that consort.°

REGAN. No marvel then, though he were ill affec-
ted.°
'Tis they have put him on the old man's death,
To have the waste and spoil of his revenues.°
I have this present evening from my sister
Been well inform'd of them, and with such
cautions
That if they come to sojourn at my house,
I'll not be there.

CORNWALL.   Nor I, assure thee, Regan.
Edmund, I hear that you have shown your
father
A childlike office.°

EDMUND.   'Twas my duty, sir.

GLOUCESTER. He did bewray his practice° and
receiv'd
This hurt you see, striving to apprehend him.

CORNWALL. Is he pursu'd?

GLOUCESTER.   Aye, my good lord.

CORNWALL. If he be taken, he shall never more
Be fear'd of doing harm. Make your own purpose,
How in my strength you please.° For you, Edmund,

Whose virtue and obedience doth this instant
So much commend itself, you shall be ours.
Natures of such deep trust° we shall much need.
You we first seize on.

EDMUND.   I shall serve you, sir,
Truly, however else.

GLOUCESTER.   For him I thank your grace.

CORNWALL. You know not why we came to visit
you—

REGAN. Thus out of season, threading dark-ey'd
night.
Occasions, noble Gloucester, of some poise,°
Wherein we must have use of your advice.
Our father he hath writ, so hath our sister,
Of differences which I best thought it fit
To answer from° our home; the several mes-
sengers
From hence attend dispatch.° Our good old
friend,
Lay comforts to your bosom, and bestow
Your needful counsel to our business,
Which craves the instant use.°

GLOUCESTER.   I serve you, madam.
Your graces are right welcome.

[_Flourish. Exeunt._]

SCENE ii

Before GLOUCESTER'S _castle._

[_Enter_ KENT _and_ OSWALD, _severally._]

OSWALD. Good dawning to thee, friend. Art of this
house?

KENT. Aye.

OSWALD. Where may we set our horses?

KENT. I' the mire.

OSWALD. Prithee, if thou lovest me, tell me.

KENT. I love thee not.

OSWALD. Why then I care not for thee.

KENT. If I had thee in Lipsbury pinfold,° I would
make thee care for me.

OSWALD. Why dost thou use me thus? I know thee
not.

KENT. Fellow, I know thee.

OSWALD. What dost thou know me for?

---

capable legally qualified to inherit   _consort_ retinue
though . . . affected that he was evilly inclined
revenues (accent on second syllable)
childlike office service appropriate to a son
He . . . practice i.e., Edmund exposed Edgar's plot
Make . . . please choose for yourself what powers of
mine you please

of . . . trust so trustworthy
poise weight, importance
from away from
attend dispatch wait to be sent back
craves . . . use has immediate need of it (your counsel)
Lipsbury pinfold (an obscure reference; a pinfold is a pen
for impounding stray animals)

Kent's temper — like Hotspur

KENT. A knave, a rascal, an eater of broken meats,°
   a base, proud, shallow, beggarly, three-suited,
15 hundred-pound, filthy, worsted-stocking knave;
   a lily-livered, action-taking knave; a whoreson,
   glass-gazing, superserviceable, finical rogue; one-
   trunk-inheriting slave; one that wouldst be a
   bawd in way of good service, and art nothing but
20 the composition of a knave, beggar, coward,
   pander, and the son and heir of a mongrel bitch.
   One whom I will beat into clamorous whining,
   if thou deniest the least syllable of thy addition.°
OSWALD. Why, what a monstrous fellow art thou,
25 thus to rail on one that is neither known of thee
   nor knows thee!
KENT. What a brazen-faced varlet art thou to deny
   thou knowest me! Is it two days ago since I
   tripped up thy heels and beat thee before the
30 king? Draw, you rogue, for, though it be night,
   yet the moon shines. I'll make a sop o' the moon-
   shine° of you. Draw, you whoreson cullionly
   barber-monger,° draw.   [*Drawing his sword.*]
OSWALD. Away! I have nothing to do with thee.
35 KENT. Draw, you rascal. You come with letters
   against the king, and take Vanity the puppet's
   part° against the royalty of her father. Draw,
   you rogue, or I'll so carbonado' your shanks—
   draw, you rascal. Come your ways.°
40 OSWALD. Help, ho! Murder! Help!
KENT. Strike, you slave. Stand, rogue. Stand, you
   neat° slave, strike.   [*Beating him.*]
OSWALD. Help, ho! Murder! Murder!
[*Enter* EDMUND, *with his rapier drawn,* CORNWALL,
   REGAN, GLOUCESTER, *and* SERVANTS.]
EDMUND. How now! What's the matter?
                                    [*Parting them.*]
45 KENT. With you,° goodman boy,° an° you please.
   Come, I'll flesh you;° come on, young master.

GLOUCESTER. Weapons! Arms! What's the matter
   here?
CORNWALL. Keep peace, upon your lives.
   He dies that strikes again. What is the matter? 50
REGAN. The messengers from our sister and the
   king.
CORNWALL. What is your difference? Speak.
OSWALD. I am scarce in breath, my lord.
KENT. No marvel, you have so bestirred your 55
   valor. You cowardly rascal, nature disclaims in°
   thee. A tailor made thee.
CORNWALL. Thou art a strange fellow. A tailor
   make a man?
KENT. Aye, a tailor, sir. A stone-cutter or a painter 60
   could not have made him so ill, though he had
   been but two hours at the trade.
CORNWALL. Speak yet, how grew your quarrel?
OSWALD. This ancient ruffian, sir, whose life I have
   spared at suit of his gray beard— 65
KENT. Thou whoreson zed! Thou unnecessary
   letter!° My lord, if you will give me leave, I will
   tread this unbolted° villain into mortar, and
   daub the walls of a jakes° with him. Spare my
   gray beard, you wagtail?° 70
CORNWALL. Peace, sirrah!
   You beastly knave, know you no reverence?
KENT. Yes, sir, but anger hath a privilege.
CORNWALL. Why art thou angry?
KENT. That such a slave as this should wear a
   sword, 75
   Who wears no honesty. Such smiling rogues as
   these,
   Like rats, oft bite the holy cords° atwain
   Which are too intrinse° t'unloose, smooth°
   every passion
   That in the natures of their lords rebel,
   Bring oil to fire, snow to their colder moods, 80
   Renege,° affirm, and turn their halcyon beaks°
   With every gale and vary° of their masters,
   Knowing naught, like dogs, but following.
   A plague upon your epileptic visage!
   Smile you my speeches° as I were a fool? 85
   Goose, if I had you upon Sarum° plain,

broken meats scraps (in what follows, Kent cites Oswald
   as thoroughly contemptible, a servant who would pass
   as a gentleman, but is worth only a hundred pounds,
   wears worsted instead of silk, is white-livered, runs to
   the law rather than face his enemy, fawns to his
   superiors, owns only what can go into a single trunk,
   would turn pimp to serve his master, and comes of
   extremely low parentage)
addition i.e., the titles I have given you
sop . . . moonshine i.e., filled with holes like a sponge
   that will soak up the moonlight
cullionly barber-monger low-down barbershop patron;
   i.e., effeminate lout
Vanity . . . part vanity was represented as a vice-
   character in medieval drama; here, Goneril is signified
carbonado slash, score, like a steak before broiling
Come . . . ways move along   *neat* fancy-dressed
With you the quarrel (matter) is with you
goodman boy (a term of contempt, especially to a
   nobleman)
an if   *flesh you* introduce you to swordplay

disclaims in denies having had any part in
zed . . . letter the letter *z* which can be replaced by *s*
   and is therefore superfluous
unbolted unsifted (a grain-chaff metaphor)
jakes privy   *wagtail* small, cocky bird
holy cords i.e., as of kinship, marriage
intrinse intrinsic   *smooth* cater to   *Renege* deny
halcyon beaks kingfisher beaks, which when hung up
   were said to turn like weathervanes   *vary* shift
epileptic . . . speeches i.e., Oswald is wearing a fixed,
   frozen smile
Sarum Salisbury, noted for geese

I'd drive ye cackling home to Camelot.°
CORNWALL. What, art thou mad, old fellow?
GLOUCESTER. How fell you out? Say that.
90 KENT. No contraries hold more antipathy
   Than I and such a knave.
CORNWALL. Why dost thou call him knave? What
   is his fault?
KENT. His countenance likes me not.°
CORNWALL. No more perchance does mine, nor his,
   nor hers.
95 KENT. Sir, 'tis my occupation to be plain.
   I have seen better faces in my time
   Than stands on any shoulder that I see
   Before me at this instant.
CORNWALL.   This is some fellow
   Who, having been prais'd for bluntness, doth
   affect
100 A saucy roughness and constrains the garb°
   Quite from his° nature. He cannot flatter, he—
   An honest mind and plain—he must speak
   truth!
   An they will take it, so; if not, he's plain.
   These kind of knaves I know, which in this plain-
   ness
105 Harbor more craft and more corrupter ends
   Than twenty silly ducking observants°
   That stretch their duties nicely.°
KENT. Sir, in good faith, in sincere verity,
   Under th' allowance of your great aspect,°
110 Whose influence,° like the wreath of radiant fire
   On flickering Phœbus' front—°
CORNWALL.   What mean'st by this?
KENT. To go out of my dialect, which you discom-
   mend so much. I know, sir, I am no flatterer. He
   that beguiled you in a plain accent was a plain
115 knave, which, for my part, I will not be, though
   I should win your displeasure to entreat me
   to't.°
CORNWALL. What was th' offense you gave him?
OSWALD. I never gave him any.
120 It pleas'd the king his master very late

To strike at me, upon his misconstruction;°
When he, conjunct,° and flattering his dis-
   pleasure,
Tripp'd me behind; being down, insulted, rail'd,
And put upon him such a deal of man°
That worthied° him, got praises of the king   125
For him attempting who was self-subdu'd,°
And in the fleshment of° this dread exploit
Drew on me here again.
KENT.   None of these rogues and cowards
   But Ajax is their fool.°
CORNWALL.   Fetch forth the stocks!
   You stubborn ancient knave, you reverend brag-
   gart,   130
   We'll teach you—
KENT.   Sir, I am too old to learn.
   Call not your stocks for me: I serve the king,
   On whose employment I was sent to you.
   You shall do small respect, show too bold malice
   Against the grace and person of my master,   135
   Stocking his messenger.
CORNWALL. Fetch forth the stocks! As I have life
   and honor,
   There shall he sit till noon.
REGAN. Till noon! Till night, my lord, and all
   night too.
KENT. Why, madam, if I were your father's dog,   140
   You should not use me so.
REGAN.   Sir, being his knave, I will.
CORNWALL. This is a fellow of the self-same color°
   Our sister speaks of. Come, bring away the
   stocks!   [Stocks brought out.]
GLOUCESTER. Let me beseech your grace not to do
   so.
   His fault is much, and the good king his master   145
   Will check him for 't. Your purpos'd low correc-
   tion
   Is such as basest and contemned'st wretches
   For pilferings and most common trespasses
   Are punish'd with. The king must take it ill,
   That he, so slightly valu'd in his messenger,   150
   Should have him thus restrain'd.
CORNWALL.   I'll answer° that.
REGAN. My sister may receive it much more worse
   To have her gentleman abus'd, assaulted,
   For following her affairs. Put in his legs.
                    [KENT is put in the stocks.]

Camelot King Arthur's legendary seat (uncertain
   relevance here; Kent possibly misleadingly identifying
   his own locality)
His . . . not i.e., I can't stand his face
constrains the garb forces (overdoes) the manner
his its   observants i.e., of petty formalities
nicely obsequiously
aspect appearance, countenance (but normally applied
   to a planet)
influence i.e., as planetary force exerted on human
   affairs
Sir . . . front (Kent parodies the affected speech of the
   courtier)
Phoebus' front the face of the sun
win . . . to't win your displeasure by refusing when you
   entreat me (to be a knave)

misconstruction misunderstanding
conjunct i.e., siding with the king   man manliness
worthied made him look good
was self-subdu'd showed self-restraint
in . . . of inflamed by the first success of
Ajax . . . fool Ajax (heroic Greek and rival of
   Achilles) is as nothing beside them
color ilk   answer answer for

[handwritten: Kent is Stoical, philosophical   disguise]

155 Come, my good lord, away.
     [Exeunt all but GLOUCESTER *and* KENT.*]*
GLOUCESTER. I am sorry for thee, friend; 'tis the
 duke's pleasure,
 Whose disposition, all the world well knows,
 Will not be rubb'd nor stopp'd. I'll entreat for
 thee.
KENT. Pray, do not, sir. I have watch'd° and
 travel'd hard;
160 Some time I shall sleep out, the rest I'll whistle.
 A good man's fortune may grow out at heels.°
 Give you good morrow!
GLOUCESTER. The duke's to blame in this; 'twill be
 ill taken.   *[Exit]*
KENT. Good king, that must approve the common
 saw,°
165 Thou out of heaven's benediction com'st
 To the warm sun!°
 Approach, thou beacon to this under globe,
 That by thy comfortable beams I may
 Peruse this letter! Nothing almost sees miracles
170 But misery.° I know 'tis from Cordelia,
 Who hath most fortunately been inform'd
 Of my obscured° course, *[Reads]* ". . . *and shall*
  find time
 From this enormous state, seeking to give
 Losses their remedies." All weary and o'er-watch'd,
175 Take vantage,° heavy eyes, not to behold
 This shameful lodging.
 Fortune, good night. Smile once more; turn thy
  wheel!   *[Sleeps.]*

SCENE iii
A wood.

[Enter EDGAR.*]*
EDGAR. I heard myself proclaim'd,
 And by the happy hollow of a tree
 Escap'd the hunt. No port is free; no place
 That guard and most unusual vigilance
5 Does not attend my taking.° Whiles I may 'scape
 I will preserve myself, and am bethought°
 To take the basest and most poorest shape
 That ever penury in contempt of man
 Brought near to beast. My face I'll grime with
  filth,

watch'd stayed awake
A good . . . heels i.e., it is no disgrace to suffer hardships
approve . . . saw prove the common saying true
Thou . . . sun i.e., your fortunes turn from better to
 worse
Nothing . . . misery only misery can count on miracles
obscured disguised *vantage* advantage
attend my taking await my apprehension
am bethought have in mind

Blanket my loins, elf° all my hair in knots, 10
And with presented° nakedness outface°
The winds and persecutions of the sky.
The country gives me proof° and precedent
Of Bedlam° beggars, who with roaring voices
Strike in° their numb'd and mortified° bare
 arms   15
Pins, wooden pricks, nails, sprigs of rosemary;
And with this horrible object,° from low farms,
Poor pelting° villages, sheepcotes, and mills,
Sometime with lunatic bans,° sometime with
 prayers,
Enforce their charity. Poor Turlygod! Poor
 Tom!°   20
That's something yet. Edgar I nothing am.°
           [Exit]

SCENE iv
Before GLOUCESTER's *castle.*
KENT *in the stocks.*

[Enter LEAR, FOOL, *and* GENTLEMAN.*]*
LEAR. 'Tis strange that they should so depart from
 home
 And not send back my messenger.
GENTLEMAN.   As I learn'd,
 The night before there was no purpose in them
 Of this remove.°
KENT.   Hail to thee, noble master!
LEAR. Ha!
 Mak'st thou this shame thy pastime?
KENT.   No, my lord. 5
FOOL. Ha, ha! He wears cruel° garters. Horses are
 tied by the heads, dogs and bears by the neck,
 monkeys by the loins, and men by the legs.
 When a man's overlusty° at legs, then he wears
 wooden nether-stocks.°   10
LEAR. What's he that hath so much thy place mis-
 took
 To set thee here?
KENT.   It is both he and she,
 Your son and daughter.

elf tangle, as elves were reported to do
presented i.e., to the elements *outface* dare
proof example *Bedlam* (see I, ii, 149n)
Strike in stick into *mortified* deadened to pain
object spectacle *pelting* paltry *bans* curses
Turlygod . . . Tom lunatic names
That's . . . am i.e., as Tom I can survive; as Edgar I am
 doomed
there . . . remove they had no intention of leaving
Mak'st . . . pastime are you doing this for fun
cruel with pun on *crewel* worsted
overlusty too active *nether-stocks* stockings

stichomythia

LEAR. No.
15 KENT. Yes.
LEAR. No, I say.
KENT. I say, yea.
LEAR. No, no, they would not.
KENT. Yes, they have.
20 LEAR. By Jupiter, I swear, no.
KENT. By Juno, I swear, aye.
LEAR.   They durst not do 't.
They could not, would not do 't. 'Tis worse than murder
To do upon respect° such violent outrage.
Resolve me with all modest° haste which way
25 Thou mightst deserve or they impose this usage,
Coming from us.°
KENT.   My lord, when at their home
I did commend your highness' letters to them,
Ere I was risen from the place that show'd
My duty kneeling, came there a reeking post,°
30 Stew'd in his haste, half breathless, panting forth
From Goneril his mistress salutations;
Deliver'd letters, spite of intermission,°
Which presently° they read. On whose contents
They summon'd up their meiny,° straight took horse,
35 Commanded me to follow and attend
The leisure of their answer, gave me cold looks.
And meeting here the other messenger,
Whose welcome, I perceiv'd, had poison'd mine—
Being the very fellow that of late
40 Display'd° so saucily against your highness—
Having more man than wit about me, drew.
He rais'd the house with loud and coward cries.
Your son and daughter found this trespass worth
The shame which here it suffers.
45 FOOL. Winter's not gone yet if the wild geese fly that way.

        Fathers that wear rags
          Do make their children blind;°
        But fathers that bear bags°
50   Shall see their children kind.
        Fortune, that arrant whore,
        Ne'er turns the key to the poor.

But, for all this, thou shalt have as many dolors°
for thy daughters as thou canst tell° in a year.
LEAR. O, how this mother swells up toward my heart!   55
Hysterica passio,° down, thou climbing sorrow,
Thy element's° below! Where is this daughter?
KENT. With the earl, sir, here within.
LEAR. Follow me not; stay here.   [Exit]
GENTLEMAN. Made you no more offense but what you speak of?   60
KENT. None.
How chance the king comes with so small a train?
FOOL. An thou hadst been set i' the stocks for that question, thou hadst well deserved it.
KENT. Why, fool?   65
FOOL. We'll set thee to school to an ant, to teach thee there's no laboring i' the winter. All that follow their noses are led by their eyes but blind men, and there's not a nose among twenty but can smell him that's stinking. Let go thy hold   70 when a great wheel runs down a hill, lest it break thy neck with following it; but the great one that goes up the hill, let him draw thee after. When a wise man gives thee better counsel, give me mine again. I would have none but knaves   75 follow it, since a fool gives it.

        That sir which serves and seeks for gain,
          And follows but for form,
        Will pack° when it begins to rain,
          And leave thee in the storm.   80

        But I will tarry, the fool will stay,
          And let the wise man fly.
        The knave turns fool that runs away,
          The fool no knave, perdy.°

KENT. Where learned you this, fool?   85
FOOL. Not i' the stocks, fool.
        [Re-enter LEAR, with GLOUCESTER.]
LEAR. Deny to speak with me? They are sick? They are weary?
They have travel'd all the night? Mere fetches;°
The images of revolt and flying off.
Fetch me a better answer.
GLOUCESTER.   My dear lord,   90
You know the fiery quality of the duke,
How unremovable and fix'd he is
In his own course.

---

upon respect   against a place of respect (as king and father)
modest   suitable
Coming from us   i.e., as king's messenger
reeking post   sweating messenger
spite of intermission   in spite of the fact that he was interrupting
presently   immediately   meiny   retinue
Display'd   conducted himself
blind   i.e., to the fathers' needs   bags   money-bags

dolors   griefs (with pun on "dollars")   tell   count
mother . . . Hysterica passio   popular and medical terms for the same phenomenon, hysteria, with a feeling of suffocation
element's   place is
pack   run out   perdy   corruption of par Dieu
fetches   excuses

LEAR. Vengeance! Plague! Death! Confusion!
Fiery? What quality? Why, Gloucester, Glouces-
95   ter,
I'd speak with the Duke of Cornwall and his
        wife.
GLOUCESTER. Well, my good lord, I have inform'd
        them so.
LEAR. Inform'd them! Dost thou understand me,
        man?
GLOUCESTER. Aye, my good lord.
LEAR. The king would speak with Cornwall; the
100   dear father
Would with his daughter speak, commands her
        service.
Are they inform'd of this? My breath and blood!
"Fiery"? "The fiery duke"? Tell the hot duke
        that—
No, but not yet; may be he is not well.
105 Infirmity doth still neglect all office
Whereto our health is bound.° We are not our-
        selves
When nature being oppress'd commands the
        mind
To suffer with the body. I'll forbear,
And am fall'n out with my more headier° will
110 To take the indispos'd and sickly fit
For the sound man. [Looking on KENT] Death on
        my state! Wherefore
Should he sit here? This act persuades me
That this remotion° of the duke and her
Is practice° only. Give me my servant forth.
115 Go tell the duke and's wife I'd speak with them,
Now, presently. Bid them come forth and hear
        me,
Or at their chamber door I'll beat the drum
Till it cry sleep to death.
GLOUCESTER. I would have all well betwixt you.
                                    [Exit]
120 LEAR. O me, my heart, my rising heart! But down!
FOOL. Cry to it, nuncle, as the cockney did to the
eels when she put 'em i' the paste° alive; she
knapped° 'em o' the coxcombs with a stick, and
cried "Down, wantons, down!" 'Twas her
125 brother that, in pure kindness to his horse,
buttered his hay.
        [Re-enter GLOUCESTER, with CORNWALL, REGAN,
                and SERVANTS.]
LEAR. Good morrow to you both.
CORNWALL.   Hail to your grace!
                            [KENT is set at liberty.]

REGAN. I am glad to see your highness.
LEAR. Regan, I think you are. I know what reason
I have to think so. If thou shouldst not be glad,   130
I would divorce me from thy mother's tomb,
Sepulchring an adultress. [To KENT] O, are you
        free?
Some other time for that. Beloved Regan,
Thy sister's naught.° O Regan, she hath tied
Sharp-tooth'd unkindness, like a vulture, here.   135
                            [Points to his heart.]
I can scarce speak to thee; thou'lt not believe
With how deprav'd a quality—O Regan!
REGAN. I pray you, sir, take patience. I have hope
You less know how to value her desert
Than she to scant her duty.
LEAR.   Say, how is that?   140
REGAN. I cannot think my sister in the least
Would fail her obligation. If, sir, perchance
She have restrain'd the riots of your followers,
'Tis on such ground and to such wholesome end
As clears her from all blame.   145
LEAR. My curses on her!
REGAN.   O, sir, you are old.
Nature in you stands on the very verge
Of her confine.° You should be rul'd and led
By some discretion that discerns your state
Better than you yourself. Therefore I pray you   150
That to our sister you do make return.
Say you have wrong'd her, sir.
LEAR.   Ask her forgiveness?
Do you but mark how this becomes the house:
[Kneeling] "Dear daughter, I confess that I am
        old.
Age is unnecessary. On my knees I beg   155
That you'll vouchsafe me raiment, bed, and
        food."
REGAN. Good sir, no more; these are unsightly
        tricks.
Return you to my sister.
LEAR.   [Rising] Never, Regan.
She hath abated me of half my train,
Look'd black upon me, struck me with her
        tongue,   160
Most serpent-like, upon the very heart.
All the stor'd vengeances of heaven fall
On her ingrateful top! Strike her young bones,
You taking° airs, with lameness.
CORNWALL.   Fie, sir, fie!
LEAR. You nimble lightnings, dart your blinding
        flames   165
Into her scornful eyes. Infect her beauty,

Infirmity . . . bound sickness is privileged to neglect duty
  that we are obliged to perform when in health
headier impatient, headstrong   *take* mistake
sound healthy   *remotion* removal, departure
practice plot   *paste* pastry   *knapped* rapped

naught wicked   *confine* domain
taking pestilential

You fen-suck'd° fogs, drawn by the powerful sun
To fall and blast her pride.
REGAN. O the blest gods! So will you wish on me
170   When the rash mood is on.
LEAR. No, Regan, thou shalt never have my curse.
Thy tender-hefted° nature shall not give
Thee o'er to harshness. Her eyes are fierce, but thine
Do comfort and not burn. 'Tis not in thee
175   To grudge my pleasures, to cut off my train,
To bandy hasty words, to scant my sizes,°
And in conclusion to oppose the bolt
Against my coming in. Thou better know'st
The offices of nature, bond of childhood,
180   Effects of courtesy, dues of gratitude.
Thy half o' the kingdom hast thou not forgot,
Wherein I thee endow'd.
REGAN.   Good sir, to the purpose.
LEAR. Who put my man i' the stocks?
                              [Tucket within.]
CORNWALL.   What trumpet's that?
REGAN. I know 't; my sister's. This approves° her letter,
That she would soon be here.
             [Enter OSWALD.]
185   Is your lady come?
LEAR. This is a slave whose easy-borrow'd pride
Dwells in the fickle grace of her he follows.
Out, varlet, from my sight!
CORNWALL.   What means your grace?
LEAR. Who stock'd my servant? Regan, I have good hope
Thou didst not know on 't. Who comes here?
             [Enter GONERIL.]
190   O heavens,
If you do love old men, if your sweet sway
Allow° obedience, if yourselves are old,
Make it your cause; send down, and take my part!
[To GONERIL] Art not asham'd to look upon this beard?
195   O Regan, wilt thou take her by the hand?
GONERIL. Why not by the hand, sir? How have I offended?
All's not offense that indiscretion finds
And dotage terms so.
LEAR.   O sides, you are too tough.°
Will you yet hold? How came my man i' the stocks?

CORNWALL. I set him there, sir, but his own dis-
orders   200
Deserv'd much less advancement.
LEAR.   You! Did you?
REGAN. I pray you, father, being weak, seem so.
If, till the expiration of your month,
You will return and sojourn with my sister,
Dismissing half your train, come then to me.   205
I am now from home and out of that provision
Which shall be needful for your entertainment.
LEAR. Return to her, and fifty men dismiss'd?
No, rather I abjure all roofs, and choose
To wage° against the enmity o' th' air,   210
To be a comrade with the wolf and owl—
Necessity's sharp pinch!° Return with her?
Why, the hot-blooded France, that dowerless took
Our youngest born, I could as well be brought
To knee his throne, and, squire-like,° pension beg   215
To keep base life afoot. Return with her?
Persuade me rather to be slave and sumpter°
To this detested groom.   [Pointing at OSWALD.]
GONERIL.   At your choice, sir.
LEAR. I prithee, daughter, do not make me mad.
I will not trouble thee, my child. Farewell.   220
We'll no more meet, no more see one another.
But yet thou art my flesh, my blood, my daugh-
ter;
Or rather a disease that's in my flesh,
Which I must needs call mine. Thou art a boil,
A plague-sore, an embossed carbuncle°   225
In my corrupted blood. But I'll not chide thee;
Let shame come when it will, I do not call it.
I do not bid the thunder-bearer° shoot,°
Nor tell tales of thee to high-judging Jove.
Mend° when thou canst; be better at thy leisure. 230
I can be patient; I can stay with Regan,
I and my hundred knights.
REGAN.   Not altogether so.
I look'd not for you yet, nor am provided
For your fit welcome. Give ear, sir, to my sister;
For those that mingle reason with your passion°   235
Must be content to think you old, and so—
But she knows what she does.
LEAR.   Is this well spoken?
REGAN. I dare avouch it, sir. What, fifty followers?

---

fen-suck'd drawn up from swamps
tender-hefted sensitive, responsive   *sizes* allowances
approves confirms
Allow approve of
O sides . . . tough i.e., they should burst with passion

wage wage war
Necessity's . . . pinch i.e., to feel the pains of neediness
squire-like servantlike   *sumpter* packhorse
embossed carbuncle boil that has come to a head
thunder-bearer Jove   *shoot* i.e., hurl thunderbolts
Mend improve
mingle . . . passion use their reason in understanding
   your passion

Storm coming up

Is it not well? What should you need of more?
Yea, or so many, sith that both charge and danger
240 Speak 'gainst so great a number? How in one house
Should many people under two commands
Hold amity? 'Tis hard, almost impossible.
GONERIL. Why might not you, my lord, receive attendance
245 From those that she calls servants or from mine?
REGAN. Why not, my lord? If then they chanc'd to slack you,
We could control them. If you will come to me,
For now I spy a danger, I entreat you
To bring but five and twenty. To no more
250 Will I give place or notice.
LEAR. I gave you all—
REGAN.   And in good time you gave it.
LEAR. Made you my guardians, my depositaries,°
But kept a reservation to be follow'd
With such a number. What, must I come to you
255 With five and twenty, Regan? Said you so?
REGAN. And speak 't again, my lord; no more with me.
LEAR. Those wicked creatures yet do look well-favor'd,°
When others are more wicked. Not being the worst
Stands in some rank of praise. [*To* GONERIL] I'll go with thee.
260 Thy fifty yet doth double five and twenty,
And thou art twice her love.
GONERIL.   Hear me, my lord.
What need you five and twenty, ten, or five,
To follow in a house where twice so many
Have a command to tend you?
REGAN.   What need one?
265 LEAR. O, reason not the need. Our basest beggars
Are in the poorest thing superfluous.
Allow not nature more than nature needs,
Man's life's as cheap as beast's. Thou art a lady;
If only to go warm were gorgeous,
Why, nature needs not what thou gorgeous
270 wear'st,
Which scarcely keeps thee warm. But for true need—
You heavens, give me that patience, patience I need!
You see me here, you gods, a poor old man,
As full of grief as age, wretched in both.
275 If it be you that stirs these daughters' hearts
Against their father, fool me not so much

To bear it tamely;° touch me with noble anger,
And let not women's weapons, waterdrops,
Stain my man's cheeks! No, you unnatural hags,
280 I will have such revenges on you both
That all the world shall—I will do such things—
What they are, yet I know not, but they shall be
The terrors of the earth. You think I'll weep.
No, I'll not weep.
285 I have full cause of weeping, but this heart
Shall break into a hundred thousand flaws°
Or ere I'll weep. O fool, I shall go mad!
[*Exeunt* LEAR, GLOUCESTER, KENT, *and* FOOL.]
CORNWALL. Let us withdraw; 'twill be a storm.
[*Storm and tempest.*]
REGAN. This house is little. The old man and his people
290 Cannot be well bestow'd.
GONERIL. 'Tis his own blame. Hath put himself from rest,
And must needs taste his folly.
REGAN. For his particular,° I'll receive him gladly,
But not one follower.
GONERIL.   So am I purpos'd.
295 Where is my lord of Gloucester?
CORNWALL. Follow'd the old man forth.—He is return'd.
[*Re-enter* GLOUCESTER.]
GLOUCESTER. The king is in high rage.
CORNWALL.   Whither is he going?
GLOUCESTER. He calls to horse, but will I know not whither.
CORNWALL. 'Tis best to give him way; he leads himself.
GONERIL. My lord, entreat him by no means to stay.
300
GLOUCESTER. Alack, the night comes on, and the bleak winds
Do sorely ruffle.° For many miles about
There's scarce a bush.
REGAN.   O, sir, to wilful men
The injuries that they themselves procure
Must be their schoolmasters. Shut up your doors. 305
He is attended with a desperate train,
And what they may incense him to, being apt
To have his ear abus'd,° wisdom bids fear.
CORNWALL. Shut up your doors, my lord; 'tis a wild night.
My Regan counsels well. Come out o' the storm. 310
[*Exeunt*]

fool . . . tamely do not make me such a weakling that I bear it without defiance
flaws pieces   *his particular* himself alone
ruffle rage   *abus'd* deceived

depositaries trustees   *well-favor'd* attractive

*dissension in
kingdom*   *Lear & storm*

ACT III

SCENE i
A heath.

[*Storm still. Enter* KENT *and a* GENTLEMAN,
meeting.]

KENT. Who's there, besides foul weather?
GENTLEMAN. One minded like the weather, most
  unquietly.
KENT. I know you. Where's the king?
GENTLEMAN. Contending with the fretful elements.
5   Bids the wind blow the earth into the sea
     Or swell the curled waters 'bove the main,°
     That things might change or cease; tears his
       white hair,
     Which the impetuous blasts, with eyeless rage,
     Catch in their fury and make nothing of;
10   Strives in his little world of man° t' outscorn
     The to-and-fro-conflicting wind and rain.
     This night, wherein the cub-drawn bear would
       couch,°
     The lion and the belly-pinched wolf
     Keep their fur dry, unbonneted he runs
     And bids what will take all.°
15 KENT.   But who is with him?
GENTLEMAN. None but the fool, who labors to out-
     jest
     His heart-struck injuries.
KENT.   Sir, I do know you,
     And dare, upon the warrant of my note,°
     Commend a dear° thing to you. There is division,
20 • Although as yet the face of it be cover'd
     With mutual cunning, 'twixt Albany and Corn-
       wall,
     Who have—as who have not, that their great
       stars
     Thron'd and set high?°—servants, who seem no
       less,
     Which are to France the spies and speculations°

---

main mainland
his . . . man allusion to the Elizabethan idea of man as a
  little world (microcosm) which reproduced within
  itself the universe (macrocosm)
cub-drawn . . . couch i.e., though drained dry (and
  hungry) would prefer to remain in the cave
bids . . . all risks all (gambling metaphor)
warrant . . . note assurance of my knowledge
dear i.e., of great importance (and secrecy)
that . . . high whom fate has placed in high position
speculations informers

Intelligent of our state. What hath been seen,   25
Either in snuffs° and packings° of the dukes
Or the hard rein which both of them have borne
Against the old king, or something deeper,
Whereof perchance these are but furnishings—
But true it is, from France there comes a power   30
Into this scatter'd° kingdom, who already,
Wise in our negligence, have secret feet
In some of our best ports and are at point
To show their open banner. Now to you.
If on my credit you dare build so far   35
To make your speed to Dover, you shall find
Some that will thank you, making° just report
Of how unnatural and bemadding sorrow
The king hath cause to plain.°
I am a gentleman of blood and breeding,   40
And from some knowledge and assurance offer
This office to you.
GENTLEMAN. I will talk further with you.
KENT.   No, do not.
  For confirmation that I am much more
  Than my out-wall, open this purse and take   45
  What it contains. If you shall see Cordelia—
  As fear not but you shall—show her this ring,
  And she will tell you who your fellow is
  That yet you do not know. Fie on this storm!
  I will go seek the king.
GENTLEMAN.   Give me your hand.   50
  Have you no more to say?
KENT. Few words, but, to effect,° more than all
    yet;
  That when we have found the king—in which
    your pain
  That way, I'll this—he that first lights on him
  Holla the other.   [*Exeunt severally.*] 55

SCENE ii
Another part of the heath. Storm still.

[*Enter* LEAR *and* FOOL.]
LEAR. Blow, winds, and crack your cheeks! Rage!
    Blow!
  You cataracts and hurricanoes,° spout

---

snuffs quarrels   *packings* plottings
furnishings outward shows   *scatter'd* divided
making for making   *plain* complain
to effect in importance   *hurricanoes* waterspouts

Till you have drench'd our steeples, drown'd the
   cocks!°
You sulphurous and thought-executing fires,°
5 Vaunt-couriers° to oak-cleaving thunderbolts,
Singe my white head! And thou, all-shaking
   thunder,
Smite flat the thick rotundity o' the world!
Crack nature's moulds, all germens° spill at once
That make ingrateful man!
10 FOOL. O nuncle, court holy-water° in a dry house is
   better than this rainwater out o' doors. Good
   nuncle, in, and ask thy daughters' blessing.
   Here's a night pities neither wise man nor fool.
LEAR. Rumble thy bellyful! Spit, fire! Spout, rain!
15 Nor rain, wind, thunder fire are my daughters.
I tax not you, you elements, with unkindness—
I never gave you kingdom, call'd you children;
You owe me no subscription.° Then let fall
Your horrible pleasure; here I stand, your slave,
20 A poor, infirm, weak, and despis'd old man.
But yet I call you servile ministers
That have with two pernicious daughters join'd
Your high-engender'd battles° 'gainst a head
So old and white as this. O! O! 'Tis foul!
25 FOOL. He that has a house to put 's head in has a
   good headpiece.

         The cod-piece that will house
            Before the head has any,
         The head and he shall louse;
30   So beggars marry many.°
         The man that makes his toe
            What he his heart should make
         Shall of a corn cry woe,
         And turn his sleep to wake.

35 For there was never yet fair woman but she
   made mouths in a glass.°
LEAR. No, I will be the pattern of all patience. *echoe of Cordelia*
   I will say nothing.
         [Enter KENT.]
KENT. Who's there?
40 FOOL. Marry, here's grace and a cod-piece; that's a
   wise man and a fool.
KENT. Alas, sir, are you here! Things that love
   night

Love not such nights as these. The wrathful
   skies
Gallow° the very wanderers of the dark
And make them keep their caves. Since I was
   man,   45
Such sheets of fire, such bursts of horrid thunder,
Such groans of roaring wind and rain, I never
Remember to have heard. Man's nature cannot
   carry°
Th' affliction nor the fear.
LEAR.   Let the great gods
That keep this dreadful pudder° o'er our heads   50
Find out their enemies now. Tremble, thou
   wretch
That hast within thee undivulged crimes
Unwhipp'd of° justice. Hide thee, thou bloody
   hand,
Thou perjur'd,° and thou simular man° of virtue
That art incestuous. Caitiff,° to pieces shake,   55
That under covert and convenient seeming°
Hast practic'd on man's life. Close pent-up guilts,
Rive° your concealing continents° and cry
These dreadful summoners grace.° I am a man   *Paper ? Topic*
More sinn'd against than sinning.
KENT.   Alack, bareheaded!   60
Gracious my lord, hard by here is a hovel.
Some friendship will it lend you 'gainst the tem-
   pest.
Repose you there, while I to this hard house—
More harder than the stones whereof 'tis rais'd—
Which even but now, demanding after you,   65
Denied me to come in, return and force
Their scanted courtesy.
LEAR.   My wits begin to turn.
Come on, my boy. How dost, my boy? Art cold?
I am cold myself. Where is this straw, my fellow?
The art of our necessities° is strange,   70
That can make vile things precious. Come, your
   hovel.
Poor fool and knave, I have one part in my heart
That's sorry yet for thee.
FOOL.

[Singing] He that has and a little tiny wit—
         With hey, ho, the wind and the rain—   75
         Must make content with his fortune fit,
         For the rain it raineth every day.

LEAR. True, my good boy, Come, bring us to this
   hovel.   [Exeunt LEAR and KENT.]

cocks weathercocks
thought-executing fires presumably lightning flashes
   swift as thought
vaunt-couriers forerunners   *germens* basic seeds of life
court holy-water i.e., flattery used by fawning courtiers
subscription allegiance as subjects
high-engender'd battles forces engendered in the heavens
The . . . many i.e., copulation before one has a house to
   put his head in results in beggary; thus many beggars
   marry
made . . . glass primped before a mirror

Gallow appall   *carry* bear   *pudder* uproar
of by   *perjur'd* perjurer   *simular man* pretender
Caitiff wretch
covert . . . seeming secret and easy hypocrisy
Rive split   *continents* containers   *grace* mercy
The art . . . necessities the power of necessity

FOOL. This is a brave° night to cool a courtesan. I'll
80   speak a prophecy ere I go:

    When priests are more in word than matter,
    When brewers mar their malt with water,
    When nobles are their tailors' tutors,
    No heretics burn'd, but wenches' suitors,
85 When every case in law is right,
    No squire in debt, nor no poor knight,
    When slanders do not live in tongues,
    Nor cutpurses come not to throngs,
    When usurers tell their gold i' the field,°
90 And bawds and whores do churches build—
    Then shall the realm of Albion°
    Come to great confusion.
    Then comes the time, who live to see't,
    That going shall be us'd° with feet.

95   This prophecy Merlin shall make, for I live be-
    fore his time.°   [*Exit*]

SCENE iii
GLOUCESTER'S *castle*.

[*Enter* GLOUCESTER *and* EDMUND.]

GLOUCESTER. Alack, alack, Edmund, I like not this
unnatural dealing. When I desired their leave
that I might pity him, they took from me the
use of mine own house, charged me, on pain of
5 their perpetual displeasure, neither to speak of
him, entreat for him, nor any way sustain him.

EDMUND. Most savage and unnatural!

GLOUCESTER. Go to; say you nothing. There's a division betwixt the dukes, and a worse matter than
10 that. I have received a letter this night; 'tis dangerous to be spoken. I have locked the letter in
my closet. These injuries the king now bears
will be revenged home.° There is part of a
power already footed. We must incline to the
15 king. I will seek him and privily relieve him. Go
you and maintain talk with the duke, that my
charity be not of him perceived. If he ask for me,
I am ill and gone to bed. Though I die for it, as
no less is threatened me, the king my old
20 master must be relieved. There is some strange
thing toward, Edmund; pray you, be careful.
                         [*Exit*]

EDMUND. This courtesy forbid thee° shall the duke
Instantly know, and of that letter too.
This seems a fair deserving° and must draw me

That which my father loses—no less than all.   25
The younger rises when the old doth fall. [*Exit*]

SCENE iv
The heath. Before a hovel.

[*Enter* LEAR, KENT, *and* FOOL.]

KENT. Here is the place, my lord. Good my lord,
  enter.
  The tyranny of th' open night's too rough
  For nature to endure.   [*Storm still.*]

LEAR.   Let me alone.

KENT. Good my lord, enter here.

LEAR.   Wilt break my heart?

KENT. I had rather break mine own. Good my   5
  lord, enter.

LEAR. Thou think'st 'tis much that this contentious
  storm
  Invades us to the skin. So 'tis to thee.
  But where the greater malady is fix'd,
  The lesser is scarce felt. Thou'dst shun a bear,
  But if thy flight lay toward the raging sea   10
  Thou'dst meet the bear i' the mouth. When the
    mind's free,°
  The body's delicate.° The tempest in my mind
  Doth from my senses take all feeling else
  Save what beats there. Filial ingratitude!
  Is it not as this mouth should tear this hand   15
  For lifting food to 't? But I will punish home.°
  No, I will weep no more. In such a night
  To shut me out! Pour on; I will endure.
  In such a night as this! O Regan, Goneril!
  Your old kind father, whose frank heart gave
    all—   20
  O, that way madness lies; let me shun that.
  No more of that.

KENT.   Good my lord, enter here.

LEAR. Prithee, go in thyself; seek thine own ease.
  This tempest will not give me leave to ponder
  On things would hurt me more. But I'll go in.   25
  [*To the* FOOL] In, boy; go first. You houseless
    poverty—
  Nay, get thee in. I'll pray, and then I'll sleep.
                     [FOOL *goes in.*]
  Poor naked wretches, wheresoe'er you are,
  That bide the pelting of this pitiless storm,
  How shall your houseless heads and unfed sides,   30
  Your loop'd and window'd° raggedness, defend
    you
  From seasons such as these? O, I have ta'en

---

brave fine   tell . . . field count their money openly
Albion England   going . . . us'd walking . . . done
This . . . time (a gratuitous and self-conscious
  anachronism by the Fool)
home thoroughly   courtesy . . . thee i.e., to Lear
fair deserving i.e., worthy of reward

free untroubled   delicate overly sensitive
home to the limit
loop'd and window'd filled with holes

Lear: "edercentras" (handwritten)
Lear slipping into madness (handwritten)

Too little care of this! Take physic, pomp;°
Expose thyself to feel what wretches feel,
35 That thou mayst shake the superflux° to them
And show the heavens more just.
EDGAR. [*Within*] Fathom and half, fathom and
half! Poor Tom!
        [*The* FOOL *runs out from the hovel.*]
FOOL. Come not in here, nuncle, here's a spirit.
Help me, help me!
40 KENT. Give me thy hand. Who's there?
FOOL. A spirit, a spirit. He says his name's poor
Tom.
KENT. What art thou that dost grumble there i' the
straw?
Come forth.
      [*Enter* EDGAR *disguised as a madman.*]
45 EDGAR. Away! The foul fiend follows me!
Through the sharp hawthorn blows the cold
wind.
Hum! Go to thy cold bed and warm thee.
LEAR. Hast thou given all to thy two daughters?
And art thou come to this?
50 EDGAR. Who gives anything to poor Tom? Whom
the foul fiend hath led through fire and through
flame, through ford and whirlpool, o'er bog and
quagmire, that hath laid knives under his pillow
and halters° in his pew, set ratsbane° by his
55 porridge, made him proud of heart, to ride on a
bay trotting-horse over four-inched° bridges,
to course° his own shadow for a traitor. Bless thy
five wits! Tom's a-cold. O, do de, do de, do de.
Bless thee from whirlwinds, star-blasting, and
60 taking!° Do poor Tom some charity, whom the
foul fiend vexes. There could I have him now,
and there, and there again, and there.
              [*Storm still.*]
LEAR. What, have his daughters brought him to
this pass?
Couldst thou save nothing? Didst thou give them
all?
65 FOOL. Nay, he reserved a blanket, else we had been
all shamed.
LEAR. Now, all the plagues that in the pendulous°
air
Hang fated o'er men's faults light on thy
daughters!
KENT. He hath no daughters, sir.
LEAR. Death, traitor! Nothing could have subdu'd
70 nature

Take . . . pomp try this medicine yourselves, great ones
shake the superflux distribute what is superfluous
halters hangman's nooses   *ratsbane* rat poison
four-inched i.e., dangerous   *course* pursue
star-blasting, and taking injurious influences of planets,
   and fairies
pendulous overhanging, ominous

To such a lowness but his unkind daughters.
Is it the fashion that discarded fathers
Should have thus little mercy on their flesh?
Judicious punishment! 'Twas this flesh begot
Those pelican° daughters. 75
EDGAR.
    Pillicock sat on Pillicock hill.
    Halloo, halloo, loo, loo!°
FOOL. This cold night will turn us all to fools and
madmen.
EDGAR. Take heed o' the foul fiend. Obey thy 80
parents, keep thy word justly, swear not,
commit not with man's sworn spouse, set not
thy sweet heart on proud array. Tom's a-cold.
LEAR. What hast thou been?
EDGAR. A servingman, proud in heart and mind, 85
that curled my hair, wore gloves in my cap,
served the lust of my mistress' heart and did the
act of darkness with her, swore as many oaths
as I spake words and broke them in the sweet
face of heaven. One that slept in the contriving 90
of lust and waked to do it. Wine loved I deeply,
dice dearly, and in woman out-paramoured the
Turk. False of heart, light of ear, bloody of hand,
hog in sloth, fox in stealth, wolf in greediness,
dog in madness, lion in prey. Let not the creak- 95
ing of shoes nor the rustling of silks betray thy
poor heart to woman. Keep thy foot out of
brothels, thy hand out of plackets,° thy pen from
lenders' books, and defy the foul fiend.

Still through the hawthorn blows the cold wind. 100
Says suum, mun, ha, no, nonny.
Dolphin my boy, my boy, sessa! Let him trot by.

              [*Storm still.*]
LEAR. Why, thou wert better in thy grave than to
answer with thy uncovered body this extremity
of the skies. Is man no more than this? Consider 105
him well. Thou owest the worm no silk, the
beast no hide, the sheep no wool, the cat no
perfume. Ha! Here's three on's° are sophisticated.° Thou art the thing itself: unaccom-
modated° man is no more but such a poor, bare, 110
forked animal as thou art. Off, off, you lendings!
Come, unbutton here.   [*Tearing off his clothes.*]
FOOL. Prithee, nuncle, be contented. 'Tis a
naughty° night to swim in. Now a little fire in a

pelican young pelicans were thought to feed on their
   parents' blood
Pillicock . . . loo nursery rhyme, presumably suggested
   by "pelican"
plackets slits in petticoats   *on 's* of us
sophisticated since, unlike Tom, they are adorned with
   silk and wool
unaccommodated naked   *naughty* foul

115 wild field were like an old lecher's heart, a small
spark, all the rest on's° body cold. Look, here
comes a walking fire.

        [Enter GLOUCESTER, *with a torch.]*
EDGAR. This is the foul fiend Flibbertigibbet. He
begins at curfew and walks till the first cock; he
120 gives the web and the pin,° squints the eye and
makes the harelip, mildews the white wheat,
and hurts the poor creature of earth.

      Swithold footed thrice the 'old;°
      He met the nightmare and her nine-fold.°
125   Bid her alight,
        And her troth plight,
      And aroint thee, witch, aroint° thee!

KENT. How fares your grace?
LEAR. What's he?
130 KENT. Who's there? What is 't you seek?
GLOUCESTER. What are you there? Your names?
EDGAR. Poor Tom, that eats the swimming frog,
the toad, the tadpole, the wall newt, and the
water; that in the fury of his heart, when the
135 foul fiend rages, eats cow dung for sallets,°
swallows the old rat and the ditch-dog,° drinks
the green mantle of the standing pool; who is
whipped from tithing to tithing,° and stock-
punished, and imprisoned; who hath had three
140 suits to his back, six shirts to his body, horse to
ride and weapon to wear.

      But mice and rats and such small deer°
      Have been Tom's food for seven long year.

Beware my follower. Peace, Smulkin;° peace,
thou fiend!
GLOUCESTER. What, hath your grace no better
145 company?
EDGAR. The prince of darkness is a gentleman.
Modo he's call'd, and Mahu.
GLOUCESTER. Our flesh and blood is grown so vile,
my lord,
That it doth hate what gets° it.
EDGAR. Poor Tom's a-cold.
GLOUCESTER. Go in with me. My duty cannot
150 suffer
To obey in all your daughters' hard commands.
Though their injunction be to bar my doors

And let this tyrannous night take hold upon
   you,
Yet have I ventur'd to come seek you out
And bring you where both fire and food is
   ready.   155
LEAR. First let me talk with this philosopher.
What is the cause of thunder?
KENT. Good my lord, take his offer; go into the
house.
LEAR. I'll talk a word with this same learned
Theban.°
What is your study?   160
EDGAR. How to prevent the fiend and to kill
vermin.
LEAR. Let me ask you one word in private.
KENT. Importune him once more to go, my lord.
His wits begin t' unsettle.
GLOUCESTER.   Canst thou blame him?
                           [Storm still.]
His daughters seek his death. Ah, that good
   Kent!   165
He said it would be thus, poor banish'd man!
Thou say'st the king grows mad; I'll tell thee,
   friend.
I am almost mad myself. I had a son,
Now outlaw'd from my blood; he sought my
   life,
But lately, very late. I lov'd him, friend,   170
No father his son dearer. Truth to tell thee,
The grief hath craz'd my wits. What a night's
   this!
I do beseech your grace—
LEAR.   O, cry you mercy, sir.
Noble philosopher, your company.
EDGAR. Tom's a-cold.   175
GLOUCESTER. In, fellow, there, into the hovel.
Keep thee warm.
LEAR. Come, let's in all.
KENT.   This way, my lord.
LEAR.   With him;
I will keep still with my philosopher.
KENT. Good my lord, soothe him; let him take the
fellow.
GLOUCESTER. Take him you on.   180
KENT. Sirrah, come on; go along with us.
LEAR. Come, good Athenian.
GLOUCESTER. No words, no words. Hush.
EDGAR. Child Rowland° to the dark tower came.
His word was still "Fie, foh, and fum,   185
I smell the blood of a British man."

                        [Exeunt]

---

on 's of his   *web . . . pin* eye diseases
Swithold . . . 'old St. Withold walked thrice over the
  wold (upland)
nine-fold nine offspring   *aroint* be gone
sallets salads   *ditch-dog* drowned dog
tithing parish (ten families)   *deer* small animals
Smulkin one of Tom's several attendant fiends
gets begets

Theban i.e., philosopher; so also "Athenian" in line 182
Child Rowland the hero Roland of the Charlemagne
  legends ("Child" is an aspirant to knighthood; see
  Browning's poem based on this line)

*Lear is mad
Edgar pretends madness   the mock trial*

SCENE v
GLOUCESTER's *castle.*

[*Enter* CORNWALL *and* EDMUND.]

CORNWALL. I will have my revenge ere I depart his
    house.

EDMUND. How, my lord, I may be censured, that
    nature° thus gives way to loyalty, something
5   fears° me to think of.

CORNWALL. I now perceive it was not altogether
    your brother's evil disposition made him seek
    his death, but a provoking merit, set a-work by
    a reprovable badness in himself.°

10 EDMUND. How malicious is my fortune, that I must
    repent to be just! This is the letter he spoke of,
    which approves him an intelligent party° to the
    advantages of France. O heavens! That this
    treason were not, or not I the detector!

15 CORNWALL. Go with me to the duchess.

EDMUND. If the matter of this paper be certain, you
    have mighty business in hand.

CORNWALL. True or false, it hath made thee earl of
    Gloucester. Seek out where thy father is, that he
20 may be ready for our apprehension.

EDMUND. [*Aside*] If I find him comforting the king,
    it will stuff his suspicion more fully.—I will
    persever° in my course of loyalty, though the
    conflict be sore between that and my blood.

25 CORNWALL. I will lay trust upon thee, and thou
    shalt find a dearer father in my love.

                                    [*Exeunt*]

SCENE vi
A chamber in a farmhouse adjoining the castle.

[*Enter* GLOUCESTER, LEAR, KENT, FOOL, *and*
    EDGAR.]

GLOUCESTER. Here is better than the open air;
    take it thankfully. I will piece out the comfort
    with what addition I can. I will not be long
    from you.

5   KENT. All the power of his wits have given way to
    his impatience. The gods reward your kindness!
                        [*Exit* GLOUCESTER.]

EDGAR. Frateretto calls me, and tells me Nero is an
    angler in the lake of darkness.° Pray, innocent,
    and beware the foul fiend.

---

nature natural feeling
something fears somewhat frightens
in himself i.e., in Gloucester   *intelligent party* spy
persever persevere
Frateretto . . . darkness (yet another fiend brings Tom
    news from Hades)

FOOL. Prithee, nuncle, tell me whether a madman   10
    be a gentleman or a yeoman.°

LEAR. A king, a king!

FOOL. No, he's a yeoman that has a gentleman to
    his son, for he's a mad yeoman that sees his son a
    gentleman before him.   15

LEAR. To have a thousand with red burning spits
    Come hissing in upon 'em—

EDGAR. The foul fiend bites my back.

FOOL. He's mad that trusts in the tameness of a
    wolf, a horse's health, a boy's love, or a whore's   20
    oath.

LEAR. It shall be done; I will arraign them straight.
    [*To* EDGAR] Come, sit thou here, most learned
        justicer.
    [*To the* FOOL] Thou, sapient sir, sit here. Now,
        you she foxes!°

EDGAR. Look, where he stands and glares! Want'st   25
    thou° eyes at trial, madam?

        Come o'er the bourn,° Bessy, to me.

FOOL.

        Her boat hath a leak,
        And she must not speak
        Why she dares not come over to thee.   30

EDGAR. The foul fiend haunts poor Tom in the
    voice of a nightingale. Hopdance cries in Tom's
    belly for two white herring. Croak not, black
    angel; I have no food for thee.

KENT. How do you, sir? Stand you not so amaz'd: 35
    Will you lie down and rest upon the cushions?

LEAR. I'll see their trial first. Bring in the evidence.
    [*To* EDGAR] Thou robed man of justice, take thy
        place.
    [*To the* FOOL] And thou, his yoke-fellow of
        equity,°
    Bench by his side. [*To* KENT] You are o' the com-
        mission;   40
    Sit you too.

EDGAR. Let us deal justly.

        Sleep'st or wak'st thou, jolly shepherd?
            Thy sheep be in the corn;
        And for one blast of thy minikin° mouth,   45
            Thy sheep shall take no harm.

    Purr! The cat is gray.

LEAR. Arraign her first; 'tis Goneril. I here take
    my oath before this honorable assembly, she
    kicked the poor king her father.   50

---

yeoman farmer
she foxes i.e., Goneril and Regan
Want'st thou do you lack   *bourn* brook
yoke-fellow of equity associate judge   *minikin* dainty

FOOL. Come hither, mistress. Is your name
   Goneril?

LEAR. She cannot deny it.

FOOL. Cry you mercy, I took you for a joint-stool.°

LEAR. And here's another, whose warp'd looks
   proclaim

55 What store her heart is made on.° Stop her there!
   Arms, arms, sword, fire! Corruption in the place!
   False justicer, why hast thou let her 'scape?

EDGAR. Bless thy five wits!

KENT. O pity! Sir, where is the patience now,

60 That you so oft have boasted to retain?

EDGAR. [Aside] My tears begin to take his part so
   much,
   They'll mar my counterfeiting.

LEAR. The little dogs and all,
   Tray, Blanch, and Sweetheart, see, they bark at
   me.

65 EDGAR. Tom will throw his head at them. Avaunt,
   you curs!

     Be thy mouth or black or° white,
     Tooth that poisons if it bite;
     Mastiff, greyhound, mongrel grim,
70   Hound or spaniel, brach° or lym,°
     Or bobtail tike or trundle-tail,°
     Tom will make them weep and wail.
     For, with throwing thus my head,
     Dogs leap the hatch, and all are fled.

75 Do de, de de. Sessa!° Come, march to wakes and
   fairs and market-towns. Poor Tom, thy horn° is
   dry.

LEAR. Then let them anatomize Regan; see what
   breeds about her heart. Is there any cause in
80 nature that makes these hard hearts? [To
   EDGAR] You, sir, I entertain for one of my
   hundred; only I do not like the fashion of your
   garments. You will say they are Persian° attire;
   but let them be changed.

KENT. Now, good my lord, lie here and rest
85 awhile.

LEAR. Make no noise, make no noise. Draw the
   curtains.
   So, so, so. We'll go to supper i' the morning.
   So, so, so.

FOOL. And I'll go to bed at noon.
       [Re-enter GLOUCESTER.]

GLOUCESTER. Come hither, friend. Where is the
   king my master?

KENT. Here, sir; but trouble him not. His wits are
   gone.   90

GLOUCESTER. Good friend, I prithee, take him in
   thy arms.
   I have o'erheard a plot of death upon him.
   There is a litter ready; lay him in 't
   And drive toward Dover, friend, where thou
   shalt meet
   Both welcome and protection. Take up thy
   master.   95
   If thou shouldst dally half an hour, his life,
   With thine and all that offer to defend him,
   Stand in assured loss. Take up, take up,
   And follow me, that will to some provision
   Give thee quick conduct.

KENT.   Oppressed nature sleeps. 100
   This rest might yet have balm'd thy broken
   sinews,
   Which, if convenience will not allow,
   Stand in hard cure. [To the FOOL] Come, help to
   bear thy master;
   Thou must not stay behind.

GLOUCESTER.   Come, come, away.
             [Exeunt all but EDGAR.]

EDGAR. When we our betters see bearing our woes, 105
   We scarcely think our miseries our foes.
   Who alone suffers suffers most i' the mind,
   Leaving free° things and happy shows° behind.
   But then the mind much suff'rance doth
   o'erskip
   When grief hath mates, and bearing fellow-
   ship.°   110
   How light and portable my pain seems now
   When that which makes me bend makes the
   king bow.
   He childed as I father'd! Tom, away!
   Mark the high noises,° and thyself bewray°
   When false opinion, whose wrong thought
   defiles thee,   115
   In thy just proof repeals and reconciles thee.°
   What° will hap more tonight, safe 'scape the
   king!
   Lurk, lurk.   [Exit]

---

joint-stool (Goneril's stand-in at the "trial")   *on* of
or . . . or either . . . or   *brach* bitch
lym bloodhound
bobtail . . . trundle-tail short-tailed or curly-tailed cur
Sessa be gone   *horn* begging-cup
Persian i.e., rich

free carefree   *shows* scenes
the mind . . . fellowship the mind avoids much suffering
   when misery has company
Mark . . . noises heed what is occurring in high places
bewray reveal   *In . . . thee* upon proof of your
   innocence, recalls you from banishment and reconciles
   you to your father
What whatever

SCENE vii
GLOUCESTER's *castle.*

[*Enter* CORNWALL, REGAN, GONERIL, EDMUND,
and SERVANTS.]

CORNWALL. Post speedily to my lord your husband.
Show him this letter. The army of France is
landed. Seek out the traitor Gloucester.
                    [*Exeunt some of the* SERVANTS.]

REGAN. Hang him instantly.

5 GONERIL. Pluck out his eyes.

CORNWALL. Leave him to my displeasure. Edmund,
keep you our sister company. The revenges we
are bound to take upon your traitorous father
are not fit for your beholding. Advise the duke,
10 where you are going, to a most festinate°
preparation. We are bound to the like. Our
posts shall be swift and intelligent° betwixt us.
Farewell, dear sister. Farewell, my lord of
Gloucester.
                    [*Enter* OSWALD.]
15 How now! Where's the king?

OSWALD. My lord of Gloucester hath convey'd
him hence.
Some five or six and thirty of his knights,
Hot questrists° after him, met him at gate;
Who, with some other of the lord's dependants,
Are gone with him toward Dover, where they
20 boast
To have well-armed friends.

CORNWALL.   Get horses for your mistress.

GONERIL. Farewell, sweet lord, and sister.

CORNWALL. Edmund, farewell.
                    [*Exeunt* GONERIL, EDMUND, *and* OSWALD.]
                    Go seek the traitor Gloucester.
Pinion him like a thief. Bring him before us.
                    [*Exeunt other* SERVANTS.]
25 Though well we may not pass upon his life
Without the form of justice, yet our power
Shall do a court'sy to our wrath, which men
May blame but not control. Who's there? The
traitor?
                    [*Enter* GLOUCESTER, *brought in by two or three.*]

REGAN. Ingrateful fox! 'Tis he.

30 CORNWALL. Bind fast his corky° arms.

GLOUCESTER. What mean your graces? Good my
friends, consider
You are my guests. Do me no foul play, friends.

CORNWALL. Bind him, I say.
                    [SERVANTS *bind him.*]

REGAN.   Hard, hard. O filthy traitor!

---

festinate speedy   *intelligent* informative
questrists seekers   *corky* i.e., pithy, from age

GLOUCESTER. Unmerciful lady as you are, I'm
none.

CORNWALL. To this chair bind him. Villain, thou
shalt find—   [REGAN *plucks his beard.*] 35

GLOUCESTER. By the kind gods, 'tis most ignobly
done
To pluck me by the beard.

REGAN. So white, and such a traitor!

GLOUCESTER.   Naughty° lady,
These hairs which thou dost ravish from my
chin
Will quicken° and accuse thee. I am your host. 40
With robbers' hands my hospitable favors
You should not ruffle thus. What will you do?

CORNWALL. Come, sir, what letters had you late
from France?

REGAN. Be simple answer'd, for we know the
truth.

CORNWALL. And what confederacy have you with
the traitors   45
Late footed in the kingdom?

REGAN. To whose hands have you sent the lunatic
king?
Speak.

GLOUCESTER. I have a letter guessingly set down,
Which came from one that's of a neutral heart, 50
And not from one oppos'd.

CORNWALL.   Cunning.

REGAN.   And false.

CORNWALL. Where hast thou sent the king?

GLOUCESTER.   To Dover.

REGAN. Wherefore to Dover? Wast thou not
charg'd at peril—

CORNWALL. Wherefore to Dover? Let him first
answer that.

GLOUCESTER. I am tied to the stake,° and I must
stand the course.   55

REGAN. Wherefore to Dover, sir?

GLOUCESTER. Because I would not see thy cruel
nails
Pluck out his poor old eyes, nor thy fierce sister
In his anointed° flesh stick boarish fangs.
The sea, with such a storm as his bare head 60
In hell-black night endur'd, would have buoy'd
up
And quench'd the stelled° fires.
Yet, poor old heart, he holp° the heavens to
rain.
If wolves had at thy gate howl'd that stern time,

Naughty wicked   *quicken* come to life
tied . . . stake like a bear in the sport of bear-baiting
anointed with holy oil, as king, making his person
   sacred
stelled starry   *holp* helped

65 Thou shouldst have said, "Good porter, turn the
key,"
All cruels else subscrib'd.° But I shall see
The winged vengeance overtake such children.
CORNWALL. See 't shalt thou never. Fellows, hold
the chair.
Upon these eyes of thine I'll set my foot.
GLOUCESTER. He that will think to live till he be
70 old,
Give me some help!—O cruel! O you gods!
REGAN. One side will mock another; th' other too.
CORNWALL. If you see vengeance—
FIRST SERVANT.   Hold your hand, my lord.
I have serv'd you ever since I was a child,
75 But better service have I never done you
Than now to bid you hold.
REGAN.   How now, you dog!
FIRST SERVANT. If you did wear a beard upon your
chin,
I'd shake it on this quarrel. What do you mean?
CORNWALL. My villain!
    [*They draw and fight; Cornwall is wounded.*]
FIRST SERVANT. Nay, then, come on, and take the
80 chance of anger.
REGAN. Give me thy sword. A peasant stand up
thus!
    [*Takes a sword and runs at him behind.*]
FIRST SERVANT. O, I am slain! My lord, you have
one eye left
To see some mischief on him. O!   [*Dies.*]
CORNWALL. Lest it see more, prevent it. Out, vile
jelly!
85 Where is thy lustre now?

All ... subscrib'd all other considerations of cruelty laid
aside

GLOUCESTER. All dark and comfortless. Where's
my Edmund?
Edmund, enkindle all the sparks of nature
To quit° this horrid act.
REGAN.   Out, treacherous villain!
Thou call'st on him that hates thee. It was he
That made th' overture of thy treasons to us, 90
Who is too good to pity thee.
GLOUCESTER. O my follies! Then Edgar was abus'd.
Kind gods, forgive me that, and prosper him!
REGAN. Go thrust him out at gates and let him
smell
His way to Dover. [*Exit one with* GLOUCESTER]
How is 't, my lord? How look you? 95
CORNWALL. I have receiv'd a hurt. Follow me, lady.
Turn out that eyeless villain. Throw this slave
Upon the dunghill. Regan, I bleed apace.
Untimely comes this hurt. Give me your arm.
    [*Exit* CORNWALL, *led by* REGAN.]
SECOND SERVANT. I'll never care what wickedness
I do 100
If this man come to good.
THIRD SERVANT.   If she live long,
And in the end meet the old course of death,
Women will all turn monsters.
SECOND SERVANT. Let's follow the old earl and get
the Bedlam
To lead him where he would. His roguish
madness 105
Allows itself to anything.
THIRD SERVANT. Go thou. I'll fetch some flax and
whites of eggs
T' apply to's bleeding face. Now heaven help
him!
    [*Exeunt severally.*]

quit requite   *The Servants abandon the Cornwalls*

ACT IV

SCENE i
The heath.

[*Enter* EDGAR.]
EDGAR. Yet better thus, and known to be con-
temn'd,
Than still contemn'd and flatter'd. To be worst,
The lowest and most dejected thing of fortune,
Stands still in esperance, lives not in fear.
5 The lamentable change is from the best;

The worst returns to laughter.° Welcome then,
Thou unsubstantial air that I embrace!
The wretch that thou hast blown unto the
worst

Yet ... laughter better to be thus (beggarly) and be
conscious of being despised than to be always despised
yet flattered. To be at the very bottom of fortune is to
have hope and not fear falling further; the change to be
lamented is that from good to bad, for if one is already
at the worst he can go only toward better

A Gloucester's pessimism [handwritten]

Gloucester learning [handwritten]

Owes nothing to thy blasts. But who comes
here?
[*Enter* GLOUCESTER, *led by an* OLD MAN.]

10   My father, poorly led? World, world, O world!
But that thy strange mutations make us hate
thee,
Life would not yield to age.°

OLD MAN. O, my good lord, I have been your
tenant and your father's tenant these fourscore
15   years.

GLOUCESTER. Away, get thee away, good friend,
be gone.
Thy comforts can do me no good at all;
Thee they may hurt.

OLD MAN. Alack, sir, you cannot see your way.

GLOUCESTER. I have no way and therefore want° no
20   eyes.
I stumbled when I saw. Full oft 'tis seen,
Our means secure us, and our mere defects
Prove our commodities.° Ah, dear son Edgar,
The food of thy abused father's wrath!
25   Might I but live to see thee in my touch,
I'd say I had eyes again!

OLD MAN.   How now! Who's there?

EDGAR. [*Aside*] O gods! Who is 't can say "I am at
the worst"?
I am worse than e'er I was.

OLD MAN.   'Tis poor mad Tom.

EDGAR. [*Aside*] And worse I may be yet. The worst
is not
30   So long as we can say "This is the worst."

OLD MAN. Fellow, where goest?

GLOUCESTER.   Is it a beggarman?

OLD MAN. Madman and beggar too.

GLOUCESTER. He has some reason,° else he could
not beg.
I' the last night's storm I such a fellow saw,
35   Which made me think a man a worm. My son
Came then into my mind, and yet my mind
Was then scarce friends with him. I have heard
more since.
As flies to wanton boys are we to the gods;
They kill us for their sport.

EDGAR.   [*Aside*] How should this be?
40   Bad is the trade that must play fool to sorrow,
Ang'ring itself and others.° Bless thee, master!

But . . . age the only thing that makes us content to
  grow old is that the world's strange vicissitudes make
  us hate living
want need
Our . . . commodities our prosperity makes us overly
  secure, and our lacks prove advantages
reason i.e., powers of   *wanton* sportive
Bad . . . others i.e., it is a bad business that I must
  continue playing my mad role to my miserable
  father—a role vexing to itself and to others

GLOUCESTER. Is that the naked fellow?

OLD MAN.   Aye, my lord.

GLOUCESTER. Then, prithee, get thee gone. If for my
sake
Thou wilt o'ertake us hence a mile or twain
I' the way toward Dover, do it for ancient love; 45
And bring some covering for this naked soul,
Who I'll entreat to lead me.

OLD MAN.   Alack, sir, he is mad.

GLOUCESTER. 'Tis the times' plague, when madmen
lead the blind.
Do as I bid thee, or rather do thy pleasure;
Above the rest, be gone. 50

OLD MAN. I'll bring him the best 'parel that I have,
Come on 't° what will.   [*Exit*]

GLOUCESTER. Sirrah, naked fellow—

EDGAR. Poor Tom's a-cold. [*Aside*] I cannot daub it°
further.

GLOUCESTER. Come hither, fellow. 55

EDGAR. [*Aside*] And yet I must.—Bless thy sweet
eyes, they bleed.

GLOUCESTER. Know'st thou the way to Dover?

EDGAR. Both stile and gate, horseway and foot-
path. Poor Tom hath been scared out of his good
wits. Bless thee, good man's son, from the foul 60
fiend! Five fiends have been in poor Tom at
once—of lust, as Obidicut; Hobbididence, prince
of dumbness; Mahu, of stealing; Modo, of
murder; Flibbertigibbet, of mopping and
mowing,° who since possesses° chambermaids 65
and waiting-women. So, bless thee, master!

GLOUCESTER. Here, take this purse, thou whom the
heavens' plagues
Have humbled to all strokes.° That I am
wretched
Makes thee the happier. Heavens, deal so still!
Let the superfluous and lust-dieted man, 70
That slaves your ordinance,° that will not see
Because he doth not feel, feel your power
quickly.
So distribution should undo excess
And each man have enough. Dost thou know
Dover?

EDGAR. Aye, master. 75

GLOUCESTER. There is a cliff whose high and bend-
ing head
Looks fearfully in the confined deep.
Bring me but to the very brim of it,
And I'll repair the misery thou dost bear

on 't of it   *daub it* dissemble it
mopping and mowing making faces   *possesses* afflicts
humbled . . . strokes reduced to complete resignation
slaves . . . ordinance treats contemptuously your
  commandment (to share)

Goneril's "treason"

Albany is now active

80 With something rich about me. From that place
I shall no leading need.
EDGAR. Give me thy arm.
Poor Tom shall lead thee. [*Exeunt*]

SCENE ii

Before the DUKE OF ALBANY's *palace.*

[*Enter* GONERIL *and* EDMUND.]
GONERIL. Welcome, my lord. I marvel our mild
husband
Not met us on the way.
[*Enter* OSWALD.]
Now, where's your master?
OSWALD. Madam, within, but never man so
chang'd.
I told him of the army that was landed;
5 He smiled at it. I told him you were coming;
His answer was, "The worse." Of Gloucester's
treachery
And of the loyal service of his son
When I inform'd him, then he call'd me sot
And told me I had turn'd the wrong side out.
What most he should dislike seems pleasant to
10 him;
What like, offensive.
GONERIL. [*To* EDMUND] Then shall you go no
further.
It is the cowish° terror of his spirit,
That dares not undertake. He'll not feel wrongs
Which tie him to an answer.° Our wishes on the
way
May prove effects.° Back, Edmund, to my
15 brother;
Hasten his musters and conduct his powers.
I must change° arms at home and give the
distaff°
Into my husband's hands. This trusty servant
Shall pass between us. Ere long you are like to
hear,
20 If you dare venture in your own behalf,
A mistress's command. Wear this; spare speech.
[*Giving a favor.*]
Decline your head. This kiss, if it durst speak,
Would stretch thy spirits up into the air.
Conceive,° and fare thee well.

EDMUND. Yours in the ranks of death.
GONERIL. My most dear Gloucester! 25
[*Exit* EDMUND.]
O, the difference of man and man!
To thee a woman's services are due.
My fool° usurps my body.
OSWALD. Madam, here comes my lord.
[*Exit*]
[*Enter* ALBANY.]
GONERIL. I have been worth the whistle.°
ALBANY. O Goneril!
You are not worth the dust which the rude wind 30
Blows in your face. I fear your disposition.
That nature which contemns it° origin
Cannot be border'd certain in itself.°
She that herself will sliver and disbranch
From her material sap, perforce must wither 35
And come to deadly use.°
GONERIL. No more; the text is foolish.
ALBANY. Wisdom and goodness to the vile seem
vile;
Filths savor but themselves. What have you
done?
Tigers, not daughters, what have you per-
form'd? 40
A father and a gracious aged man
Whose reverence even the head-lugg'd° bear
would lick,
Most barbarous, most degenerate,° have you
madded.
Could my good brother° suffer you to do it?
A man, a prince, by him so benefited! 45
If that the heavens do not their visible spirits
Send quickly down to tame these vile offenses,
It will come:
Humanity must perforce prey on itself
Like monsters of the deep.
GONERIL. Milk-liver'd man! 50
That bear'st a cheek for blows, a head for
wrongs,
Who hast not in thy brows an eye discerning
Thine honor from thy suffering;° that not
know'st

cowish cowardly
tie . . . answer oblige him to retaliate
Our . . . effects our expressed hopes as we rode along
  may become realities
change exchange distaff i.e., woman's work
Conceive understand

fool i.e., husband
I . . . whistle i.e., unlike a common cur that is
  traditionally "not worth a whistle" (Goneril feigns
  anger at Albany's failure to greet her)
contemns it despises its
border'd . . . itself itself be counted on for stability
deadly use i.e., as firewood
head-lugg'd chained by the head; hence, enraged
barbarous . . . degenerate barbarously . . . degenerately
brother brother-in-law
discerning . . . suffering distinguishing between what
  honor should bear and what it should balk at

Fools do those villains pity° who are punish'd
Ere they have done their mischief. Where's thy
55   drum?°
France spreads his banners in our noiseless°
    land,
With plumed helm thy state begins to threat,°
Whiles thou, a moral° fool, sit'st still and cri'st
"Alack, why does he so?"
ALBANY.   See thyself, devil!
60   Proper deformity seems not in the fiend
So horrid as in woman.°
GONERIL.   O vain fool!
ALBANY. Thou changed and self-cover'd thing, for
    shame,
Be-monster not thy feature.° Were 't my fitness
To let these hands obey my blood,
65   They are apt enough to dislocate and tear
Thy flesh and bones. Howe'er thou art a fiend,
A woman's shape doth shield thee.
GONERIL. Marry, your manhood! Mew!
            [Enter a MESSENGER.]
ALBANY. What news?
MESSENGER. O, my good lord, the Duke of Corn-
70   wall's dead,
Slain by his servant, going to put out
The other eye of Gloucester.
ALBANY.   Gloucester's eyes!
MESSENGER. A servant that he bred, thrill'd with
    remorse,°
Oppos'd against the act, bending his sword
75   To his great master, who thereat enrag'd
Flew on him and amongst them fell'd him dead,
But not without that harmful stroke which
    since
Hath pluck'd him after.
ALBANY.   This shows you are above,
You justicers, that these our nether° crimes
80   So speedily can venge! But, O poor Gloucester!
Lost he his other eye?
MESSENGER.   Both, both, my lord.
This letter, madam, craves a speedy answer.
'Tis from your sister.
GONERIL.   [Aside] One way I like this well.
But being widow, and my Gloucester with her,
85   May all the building in my fancy pluck

Upon my hateful life. Another way,
The news is not so tart.—I'll read and answer.
                            [Exit]
ALBANY. Where was his son when they did take his
    eyes?
MESSENGER. Come with my lady hither.
ALBANY.   He is not here.
MESSENGER. No, my good lord; I met him back
    again.   90
ALBANY. Knows he the wickedness?
MESSENGER. Aye, my good lord; 'twas he inform'd
    against him
And quit the house on purpose that their
    punishment
Might have the freer course.
ALBANY.   Gloucester, I live
To thank thee for the love thou show'dst the
    king,   95
And to revenge thine eyes. Come hither, friend.
Tell me what more thou know'st.   [Exeunt]

SCENE iii
The French camp near Dover.

[Enter KENT and a GENTLEMAN.]
KENT. Why the King of France is so suddenly gone
back, know you the reason?
GENTLEMAN. Something he left imperfect in the
state which since his coming forth is thought of,
which imports to the kingdom so much fear   5
and danger that his personal return was most
required and necessary.
KENT. Who hath he left behind him general?
GENTLEMAN. The Marshal of France, Monsieur La
Far.   10
KENT. Did your letters pierce the queen to any
demonstration of grief?
GENTLEMAN. Aye, sir. She took them, read them in
    my presence,
And now and then an ample tear trill'd down
Her delicate cheek. It seem'd she was a queen   15
Over her passion, who° most rebel-like
Sought to be king o'er her.
KENT.   O, then it mov'd her.
GENTLEMAN. Not to a rage. Patience and sorrow
    strove
Who should express her goodliest. You have seen
Sunshine and rain at once. Her smiles and tears   20
Were like, a better way.° Those happy smilets
That play'd on her ripe lip seem'd not to know
What guests were in her eyes, which parted
    thence

Fools . . . pity   only fools pity those villains (i.e., "good
    guys finish last")
drum military preparation   noiseless unreplying
threat threaten   moral moralizing
Proper . . . woman   ugliness is less horrid in the devil
    than in a woman
Thou . . . feature   i.e., thou fiend in woman's guise, do
    not make yourself even more hideous
fitness i.e., in my nature
thrill'd . . . remorse   pierced by compassion
nether earthly, here below

who which   a . . . way but more impressive

As pearls from diamonds dropp'd. In brief,
25 Sorrow would be a rarity most belov'd,
    If all could so become it.
    KENT.   Made she no verbal question?
    GENTLEMAN. Faith, once or twice she heav'd the
        name of "father"
    Pantingly forth, as if it press'd her heart;
    Cried "Sisters! Sisters! Shame of ladies! Sisters!
    Kent! Father! Sisters! What, i' the storm? i' the
30   night?
    Let pity not be believ'd!" There she shook
    The holy water from her heavenly eyes,
    And clamor moisten'd.° Then away she started
    To deal with grief alone.
    KENT.   It is the stars,
35 The stars above us, govern our conditions;
    Else° one self° mate and mate could not beget
    Such different issues. You spoke not with her
        since?
    GENTLEMAN. No.
    KENT. Was this before the king return'd?
    GENTLEMAN.   No, since.
    KENT. Well, sir, the poor distressed Lear's i' the
40   town,
    Who sometime in his better tune° remembers
    What we are come about, and by no means
    Will yield to see his daughter.
    GENTLEMAN.   Why, good sir?
    KENT. A sovereign shame so elbows him—his own
        unkindness
    That stripp'd her from his benediction, turn'd
45   her
    To foreign casualties,° gave her dear rights
    To his dog-hearted daughters. These things
        sting
    His mind so venomously that burning shame
    Detains him from Cordelia.
    GENTLEMAN.   Alack, poor gentleman!
    KENT. Of Albany's and Cornwall's powers you
50   heard not?
    GENTLEMAN. 'Tis so; they are afoot.
    KENT. Well, sir, I'll bring you to our master Lear
    And leave you to attend him. Some dear cause
    Will in concealment wrap me up awhile.
55 When I am known aright, you shall not grieve
    Lending me this acquaintance. I pray you, go
    Along with me.   [Exeunt]

SCENE iv
The same. A tent.

[*Enter, with drum and colors,* CORDELIA, DOCTOR,
    and SOLDIERS.]

CORDELIA. Alack, 'tis he. Why, he was met even
    now
As mad as the vex'd sea, singing aloud,
Crown'd with rank fumiter and furrow-weeds,
With burdocks, hemlock, nettles, cuckoo
    flowers,
Darnel,° and all the idle weeds that grow   5
In our sustaining corn.° A century° send forth.
Search every acre in the high-grown field,
And bring him to our eye. [*Exit an* OFFICER]
    What can man's wisdom
In the restoring his bereaved sense?
He that helps him take all my outward worth.   10
DOCTOR. There is means, madam.
    Our foster nurse of nature is repose,
    The which he lacks. That to provoke in him,
    Are many simples operative,° whose power
    Will close the eye of anguish.
CORDELIA.   All blest secrets,   15
All you unpublish'd virtues° of the earth,
Spring with my tears! Be aidant and remediate°
In the good man's distress! Seek, seek for him,
Lest his ungovern'd rage dissolve the life
That wants° the means to lead° it.
                    [*Enter a* MESSENGER.]
MESSENGER.   News, madam.   20
    The British powers are marching hitherward.
CORDELIA. 'Tis known before; our preparation
    stands
In expectation of them. O dear father,
It is thy business that I go about;
Therefore great France   25
My mourning and important° tears hath pitied.
No blown° ambition doth our arms incite,
But love, dear love, and our ag'd father's right.
Soon may I hear and see him!   [*Exeunt*]

And . . . moisten'd her tears wet her cries of
    lamentation
Else otherwise   *self* selfsame
better tune saner moments
casualties chances, fortunes

fumiter . . . Darnel varieties of weeds and wild-flowers
sustaining corn life-sustaining grain
century one hundred men
simples operative herbs effective
unpublish'd virtues unknown strengths
remediate remedial   *wants* lacks   *lead* guide
important importunate   *blown* puffed up

[handwritten: now Regan is after Edmund]

SCENE v
GLOUCESTER'S *castle.*

[*Enter* REGAN *and* OSWALD.]

REGAN. But are my brother's powers set forth?
OSWALD.   Aye, madam.
REGAN. Himself in person there?
OSWALD.   Madam, with much ado.
  Your sister is the better soldier.
REGAN. Lord Edmund spake not with your lord at
  home?
5 OSWALD. No, madam.
REGAN. What might import my sister's letter to
  him?
OSWALD. I know not, lady.
REGAN. Faith, he is posted hence on serious matter.
  It was great ignorance, Gloucester's eyes being
  out,
10 To let him live. Where he arrives he moves
  All hearts against us. Edmund, I think, is gone,
  In pity of his misery, to dispatch
  His nighted° life; moreover, to descry
  The strength o' th' enemy.
OSWALD. I must needs after him, madam, with my
15 letter.
REGAN. Our troops set forth tomorrow. Stay with
  us;
  The ways are dangerous.
OSWALD.   I may not, madam.
  My lady charg'd my duty° in this business.
REGAN. Why should she write to Edmund? Might
  not you
20 Transport her purposes by word? Belike,
  Something—I know not what. I'll love thee
  much—
  Let me unseal the letter.
OSWALD.   Madam, I had rather—
REGAN. I know your lady does not love her hus-
  band,
  I am sure of that. And at her late being here
  She gave strange œillades° and most speaking
25 looks
  To noble Edmund. I know you are of her
  bosom.°
OSWALD. I, madam?
REGAN. I speak in understanding.° You are; I
  know 't.
  Therefore I do advise you, take this note:°

nighted benighted (eyeless)
charg'd my duty formally ordered me
œillades amorous glances
of her bosom in her confidence
in understanding knowingly
take this note note what I say

My lord is dead, Edmund and I have talk'd,   30
And more convenient is he for my hand
Than for your lady's. You may gather more.
If you do find him, pray you, give him this;°
And when your mistress hears thus much from
  you,
I pray, desire her call her wisdom to her.   35
So, fare you well.
If you do chance to hear of that blind traitor,
Preferment° falls on him that cuts him off.
OSWALD. Would I could meet him, madam! I
  should show
  What party I do follow.
REGAN.   Fare thee well.   40

[*Exeunt*]

SCENE vi
Fields near Dover.

[*Enter* GLOUCESTER, *and* EDGAR *dressed like a
  peasant.*]

GLOUCESTER. When shall I come to the top of
  that same hill?
EDGAR. You do climb up it now. Look, how we
  labor.
GLOUCESTER. Methinks the ground is even.
EDGAR.   Horrible steep.
  Hark, do you hear the sea?
GLOUCESTER.   No, truly.
EDGAR. Why then your other senses grow im-
  perfect   5
  By your eyes' anguish.
GLOUCESTER.   So may it be indeed.
  Methinks thy voice is alter'd, and thou speak'st
  In better phrase and matter than thou didst.
EDGAR. You're much deceiv'd. In nothing am I
  chang'd
  But in my garments.
GLOUCESTER.   Methinks you're better spoken.   10
EDGAR. Come on, sir. Here's the place. Stand still.
  How fearful
  And dizzy 'tis to cast one's eyes so low!
  The crows and choughs that wing the midway
  air
  Show scarce so gross as beetles. Half way down
  Hangs one that gathers samphire, dreadful
  trade!   15
  Methinks he seems no bigger than his head.
  The fishermen that walk upon the beach
  Appear like mice, and yond tall anchoring bark
  Diminish'd to her cock;° her cock, a buoy

this this word   *Preferment* advancement
cock small boat (cockboat)

547

Almost too small for sight. The murmuring
20   surge
That on th' unnumber'd idle pebbles chafes
Cannot be heard so high. I'll look no more,
Lest my brain turn and the deficient sight
Topple° down headlong.
GLOUCESTER.   Set me where you stand.
EDGAR. Give me your hand. You are now within a
25   foot
Of th' extreme verge. For all beneath the moon
Would I not leap upright.
GLOUCESTER.   Let go my hand.
Here, friend, 's another purse, in it a jewel
Well worth a poor man's taking. Fairies° and
gods
30 Prosper it with thee! Go thou further off.
Bid me farewell, and let me hear thee going.
EDGAR. Now fare you well, good sir.
GLOUCESTER.   With all my heart.
EDGAR. Why I do trifle thus with his despair°
Is done to cure it.
GLOUCESTER.   [Kneeling] O you mighty gods!
35 This world I do renounce, and in your sights
Shake patiently my great affliction off.
If I could bear it longer and not fall
To quarrel with your great opposeless wills,
My snuff and loathed part of nature should
40 Burn itself out.° If Edgar live, O bless him!
Now, fellow, fare thee well.   [He falls forward.]
EDGAR.   Gone, sir. Farewell.—
And yet I know not how conceit may rob
The treasury of life, when life itself
Yields to the theft.° Had he been where he
thought,
45 By this had thought been past.—Alive or dead?
Ho, you sir! Friend! Hear you, sir! Speak!—
Thus might he pass° indeed. Yet he revives.—
What are you, sir?
GLOUCESTER.   Away, and let me die.
EDGAR. Hadst thou been aught but gossamer,
feathers, air,
50 So many fathom down precipitating,
Thou'dst shiver'd like an egg. But thou dost
breathe,
Hast heavy substance, bleed'st not, speak'st, art
sound.

Ten masts at each° make not the altitude
Which thou hast perpendicularly fell.
Thy life's a miracle. Speak yet again.   55
GLOUCESTER. But have I fall'n, or no?
EDGAR. From the dread summit of this chalky
bourn.°
Look up a-height. The shrill-gorg'd° lark so far
Cannot be seen or heard. Do but look up.
GLOUCESTER. Alack, I have no eyes.   60
Is wretchedness depriv'd that benefit,
To end itself by death? 'Twas yet some comfort,
When misery could beguile° the tyrant's rage
And frustrate his proud will.
EDGAR.   Give me your arm.
Up. So. How is 't? Feel you your legs? You stand. 65
GLOUCESTER. Too well, too well.
EDGAR.   This above all strangeness.
Upon the crown o' the cliff, what thing was that
Which parted from you?
GLOUCESTER.   A poor unfortunate beggar.
EDGAR. As I stood here below, methought his eyes
Were two full moons. He had a thousand noses, 70
Horns whelk'd° and waved like th' enridged°
sea.
It was some fiend. Therefore, thou happy
father,
Think that the clearest gods, who make them
honors
Of men's impossibilities,° have preserv'd thee.
GLOUCESTER. I do remember now. Henceforth I'll
bear   75
Affliction till it do cry out itself
"Enough, enough," and die. That thing you
speak of,
I took it for a man; often 'twould say
"The fiend, the fiend." He led me to that place.
EDGAR. Bear free and patient thoughts. But who
comes here?   80
[Enter LEAR, fantastically dressed with wild
flowers.]
The safer sense will n'er accommodate
His master thus.°
LEAR. No, they cannot touch me for coining;° I am
the king himself.
EDGAR. O thou side-piercing sight!   85
LEAR. Nature's above art in that respect. There's

---

deficient . . . Topple dizziness cause me to topple
Fairies (traditional guardians of treasure)
trifle . . . despair (spoken aside; by making Gloucester
   think he has leaped from Dover Cliff and
   miraculously survived, Edgar hopes to restore him)
My . . . out I would live out the smoking (as a snuffed
   candle) and hated remainder of my life
I . . . theft I do not know but that imagination (of
   falling) may kill him, when he so welcomes death
pass die

at each end to end   bourn boundary
shrill-gorg'd shrill-throated   beguile cheat
whelk'd knobby   enridged wavy
the clearest . . . impossibilities the most glorious gods,
   who make honor for themselves by feats impossible to
   men
The safer . . . thus a sane mind would never dress (the
   body) thus
touch . . . coining arrest me for minting coins

appearance/reality   *Lear—misanthropy*   *Lear's insight into guilt*   *CCf Hamlet*

your press-money.° That fellow handles his
bow like a crow-keeper;° draw me a clothier's
yard. Look, look, a mouse! Peace, peace; this
90 piece of toasted cheese will do't. There's my
gauntlet; I'll prove it° on a giant. Bring up the
brown bills.° O, well flown, bird! I' the clout, i'
the clout.° Hewgh! Give the word.°

EDGAR. Sweet marjoram.°

95 LEAR. Pass.

GLOUCESTER. I know that voice.

LEAR. Ha! Goneril, with a white beard! They
flattered me like a dog, and told me I had white
hairs in my beard ere the black ones were there.
100 To say "aye" and "no" to everything that I
said! "Aye" and "no" too was no good divinity.°
When the rain came to wet me once and the
wind to make me chatter, when the thunder
would not peace at my bidding, there I found
105 'em, there I smelt 'em out. Go to, they are not
men o' their words. They told me I was everything. 'Tis a lie, I am not ague-proof.°

GLOUCESTER. The trick of that voice I do well
remember.
Is't not the king?

LEAR.   Aye, every inch a king.
110 When I do stare, see how the subject quakes.
I pardon that man's life. What was thy cause?
Adultery?
Thou shalt not die. Die for adultery! No.
The wren goes to't, and the small gilded fly
115 Does lecher in my sight.
Let copulation thrive, for Gloucester's bastard
son   *deception*
Was kinder to his father than my daughters
Got 'tween the lawful sheets.
To't, luxury,° pell-mell! For I lack soldiers.
120 Behold yond simpering dame,
Whose face between her forks presages snow,°
That minces virtue and does shake the head
To hear of pleasure's name:
The fitchew° nor the soiled horse° goes to't
125 With a more riotous appetite.

Down from the waist they are Centaurs,°
Though women all above.
But° to the girdle do the gods inherit;°
Beneath is all the fiends'.
There's hell, there's darkness, there's the sul- 130
phurous pit, burning, scalding, stench, con-
sumption. Fie, fie, fie! Pah, pah! Give me an
ounce of civet,° good apothecary, to sweeten my
imagination. There's money for thee.

GLOUCESTER. O, let me kiss that hand!   135

LEAR. Let me wipe it first; it smells of mortality.

GLOUCESTER. O ruin'd piece of nature! This great
world
Shall so wear out to naught. Dost thou know
me?

LEAR. I remember thine eyes well enough. Dost
thou squiny° at me? No, do thy worst, blind 140
Cupid; I'll not love. Read thou this challenge;
mark but the penning on 't.

GLOUCESTER. Were all the letters suns, I could not
see one.

EDGAR. I would not take this from report. It is,
And my heart breaks at it.   145

LEAR. Read.

GLOUCESTER. What, with the case° of eyes?

LEAR. O, ho, are you there with me? No eyes in
your head, nor no money in your purse? Your
eyes are in a heavy case,° your purse in a light. 150
Yet you see how this world goes.

GLOUCESTER. I see it feelingly.

LEAR. What, art mad? A man may see how this
world goes with no eyes. Look with thine ears.
See how yond justice rails upon yond simple 155
thief. Hark, in thine ear. Change places, and,
handy-dandy,° which is the justice, which is the
thief? Thou hast seen a farmer's dog bark at a
beggar?

GLOUCESTER. Aye, sir.   160

LEAR. And the creature run from the cur? There
thou mightst behold the great image of authority: a dog's obeyed in office.
Thou rascal beadle,° hold thy bloody hand!
Why dost thou lash that whore? Strip thine own
back;   165
Thou hotly lust'st to use her in that kind
For which thou whip'st her. The usurer hangs
the cozener.°

---

press-money money paid to a new recruit for signing up
crowkeeper i.e., a living scarecrow
prove it stand to it   *brown bills* soldiers carrying
halberds
clout target
Nature's . . . word (Lear's speech is now completely
incoherent, but with passing flashes of sense)
marjoram healing herb
no . . . divinity not good theology (see Matthew 5:37)
ague-proof immune to chills   *luxury* lechery
Whose . . . snow whose (cold) demeanor feigns
disinterest in sexuality
fitchew the polecat (notoriously lecherous)
soiled horse i.e., pastured in fresh grass

Centaurs mythological beasts, half man–half horse,
symbolical of lust   *But* only   *inherit* rule
civet perfume derived from the musk sac of civet cats
squiny squint   *case* sockets   *heavy case* sad plight
handy-dandy as in the child's game: "Which hand?"
beadle constable
The usurer . . . cozener the worse offender hangs the
petty cheat

Through tatter'd clothes small vices do appear;
Robes and furr'd gowns hide all. Plate sin with gold,

170 And the strong lance of justice hurtless breaks;
Arm it in rags, a pigmy's straw does pierce it.
None does offend, none, I say, none. I'll able°
'em.
Take that of me, my friend, who have the power
To seal th' accuser's lips. Get thee glass eyes,

175 And, like a scurvy politician, seem
To see the things thou dost not.
Now, now, now, now. Pull off my boots.
Harder, harder; so.
EDGAR. O, matter and impertinency° mix'd!
Reason in madness!
LEAR. If thou wilt weep my fortunes, take my

180 eyes.
I know thee well enough; thy name is
Gloucester.
Thou must be patient. We came crying hither;
Thou know'st the first time that we smell the air,
We wawl and cry. I will preach to thee. Mark.

185 GLOUCESTER. Alack, alack the day!
LEAR. When we are born, we cry that we are come
To this great stage of fools. This 's a good block.°
It were a delicate stratagem to shoe
A troop of horse with felt.° I'll put 't in proof.°

190 And when I have stol'n upon these sons-in-law,
Then, kill, kill, kill, kill, kill, kill!
[Enter a GENTLEMAN, with ATTENDANTS.]
GENTLEMAN. O, here he is. Lay hand upon him.
Sir,
Your most dear daughter—
LEAR. No rescue? What, a prisoner? I am even

195 The natural fool of fortune.° Use me well;
You shall have ransom. Let me have a surgeon;
I am cut to the brains.
GENTLEMAN.   You shall have anything.
LEAR. No seconds? All myself?
Why, this would make a man a man of salt,

200 To use his eyes for garden waterpots,
Aye, and laying autumn's dust.
GENTLEMAN. Good sir—
LEAR. I will die bravely, like a smug bridegroom.
What!
I will be jovial. Come, come; I am a king,

205 My masters, know you that?

GENTLEMAN. You are a royal one, and we obey you.
LEAR. Then there's life in 't. Nay, an you get it, you
shall get it by running. Sa, sa, sa, sa.
[Exit running; ATTENDANTS follow.]
GENTLEMAN. A sight most pitiful in the meanest
wretch,
Past speaking of in a king! Thou hast one
daughter   210
Who redeems nature from the general curse
Which twain have brought her to.
EDGAR. Hail, gentle sir.
GENTLEMAN.   Sir, speed° you. What's your will?
EDGAR. Do you hear aught, sir, of a battle toward?
GENTLEMAN. Most sure and vulgar.° Everyone
hears that   215
Which can distinguish sound.
EDGAR.   But, by your favor,
How near's the other army?
GENTLEMAN. Near and on speedy foot; the main
descry
Stands on the hourly thought.°
EDGAR.   I thank you, sir; that's all.
GENTLEMAN. Though that the queen on special
cause is here,   220
Her army is mov'd on.
EDGAR.   I thank you, sir.
[Exit GENTLEMAN.]
GLOUCESTER. You ever-gentle gods, take my
breath from me;
Let not my worser spirit tempt me again
To die before you please!
EDGAR.   Well pray you, father.
GLOUCESTER. Now, good sir, what are you?   225
EDGAR. A most poor man, made tame to fortune's
blows,
Who, by the art of known and feeling sorrows,°
Am pregnant to° good pity. Give me your hand;
I'll lead you to some biding.°
GLOUCESTER.   Hearty thanks.
The bounty and the benison of heaven   230
To boot,° and boot!
[Enter OSWALD.]
OSWALD.   A proclaim'd prize!° Most happy!
That eyeless head of thine was first fram'd flesh
To raise my fortunes. Thou old unhappy traitor,
Briefly thyself remember. The sword is out
That must destroy thee.

---

able license
matter and impertinency sense and nonsense
block hat   *felt* (suggested by *felt hat*)
put . . . proof try it
The . . . fortune born to be used like a toy by fortune

speed prosper   *vulgar* commonly known
the main . . . thought the main force is expected to
appear at any hour
by . . . sorrows from the experience of known and
heartfelt sorrows
pregnant to capable of   *biding* biding place
To boot in addition
proclaim'd prize (cf. IV, v, 37–38)

235 GLOUCESTER.   Now let thy friendly hand
Put strength enough to 't.   [EDGAR *interposes.*]
OSWALD.   Wherefore, bold peasant,
Dar'st thou support a publish'd traitor? Hence!
Lest that th' infection of his fortune take
Like hold on thee. Let go his arm.
EDGAR. Chill° not let go, zir, without vurther
240   'casion.°
OSWALD. Let go, slave, or thou diest!
EDGAR. Good gentleman, go your gait,° and let
poor volk pass. An chud ha' been zwaggered
out° of my life, 'twould not ha' been zo long as
245 'tis by a vortnight. Nay, come not near th' old
man; keep out, che vor ye,° or I'se try whether
your costard or my ballow° be the harder. Chill
be plain with you.
OSWALD. Out, dunghill!   [*They fight.*]
250 EDGAR. Chill pick° your teeth, zir. Come; no
matter vor your foins.°   [OSWALD *falls.*]
OSWALD. Slave, thou hast slain me. Villain, take
my purse.
If ever thou wilt thrive, bury my body,
And give the letters which thou find'st about me
255 To Edmund Earl of Gloucester. Seek him out
Upon the British party. O, untimely death!
Death!   [*Dies.*]
EDGAR. I know thee well. A serviceable° villain,
As duteous to the vices of thy mistress
As badness would desire.
260 GLOUCESTER.   What, is he dead?
EDGAR. Sit you down, father; rest you.
Let's see these pockets. The letters that he
speaks of
May be my friends. He's dead; I am only sorry
He had no other deathsman. Let us see.
265 Leave,° gentle wax, and, manners, blame us not.
To know our enemies' minds, we'd rip their
hearts;
Their papers, is more lawful.

[*Reads*] Let our reciprocal vows be remembered. You have many opportunities to cut him
270 off. If your will want not, time and place will be
fruitfully offered. There is nothing done, if he
return the conqueror: then am I the prisoner,
and his bed my jail. From the loathed warmth
whereof deliver me, and supply the place for
275 your labor.

Your—wife, so I would say—affectionate
servant,   GONERIL.
O undistinguish'd° space of woman's will!
A plot upon her virtuous husband's life,
And the exchange° my brother! Here in the
sands   280
Thee I'll rake up,° the post unsanctified°
Of murderous lechers, and in the mature time
With this ungracious paper strike the sight
Of the death-practic'd duke. For him 'tis well
That of thy death and business I can tell.   285
GLOUCESTER. The king is mad. How stiff° is my vile
sense,°
That I stand up and have ingenious° feeling
Of my huge sorrows! Better I were distract.°
So should my thoughts be sever'd from my
griefs,
And woes by wrong imaginations lose   290
The knowledge of themselves.   [*Drum afar off.*]
EDGAR.   Give me your hand.
Far off, methinks, I hear the beaten drum.
Come, father, I'll bestow you with a friend.
        [*Exeunt*]

SCENE vii
A tent in the French camp.
LEAR *on a bed asleep, soft music playing;*
GENTLEMAN, *and others attending.*

[*Enter* CORDELIA, KENT, *and* DOCTOR.]
CORDELIA. O thou good Kent, how shall I live and
work
To match thy goodness? My life will be too
short
And every measure fail me.
KENT. To be acknowledg'd, madam, is o'erpaid.   5
All my reports go with the modest truth,
Nor more nor clipp'd,° but so.
CORDELIA.   Be better suited.
These weeds° are memories of those worser
hours.
I prithee, put them off.
KENT.   Pardon me, dear madam;
Yet to be known shortens my made intent.°

Chill I'll (here Edgar assumes a new character as a
   Somersetshire peasant)
vurther 'casion further occasion   *gait* way
An . . . out if I could have been swaggered out
che vor ye I warn you
costard . . . ballow head . . . cudgel
pick i.e., knock out   *foins* thrusts
serviceable i.e., as a "tool"   *Leave* "by your leave"

undistinguish'd boundless   *exchange* replacement
rake up rake over (bury)
post unsanctified unholy messenger   *stiff* stubborn
vile sense cursed sensibility
ingenious sharp, painful   *distract* mad
All . . . clipp'd may all reports of me tell the simple
   truth, neither exaggerated nor diminished
weeds garments
shortens . . . intent stops short of my purpose

80 ✗

10   My boon I make it that you know me not
      Till time and I think meet.
      CORDELIA. Then be 't so, my good lord. [*To the*
          DOCTOR] How does the king?
      DOCTOR. Madam, sleeps still.
      CORDELIA. O you kind gods,
15   Cure this great breach in his abused nature!
      Th' untun'd and jarring senses, O, wind up
      Of this child-changed° father!
      DOCTOR.   So please your majesty
      That we may wake the king. He hath slept long.
      CORDELIA. Be govern'd by your knowledge, and
          proceed
20   I' the sway° of your own will. Is he array'd?
      GENTLEMAN. Aye, madam; in the heaviness of his
          sleep
      We put fresh garments on him.
      DOCTOR. Be by, good madam, when we do awake
          him;
      I doubt not of his temperance.°
      CORDELIA.   Very well.
      DOCTOR. Please you, draw near. Louder the music 80 ✗
25   there!
      CORDELIA. O my dear father! Restoration hang
      Thy medicine on my lips, and let this kiss
      Repair those violent harms that my two sisters
      Have in thy reverence made!
      KENT.   Kind and dear princess!
      CORDELIA. Had you not been their father, these
30   white flakes°
      Had challeng'd° pity of them. Was this a face
      To be oppos'd against the warring winds?
      To stand against the deep dread-bolted thunder?
      In the most terrible and nimble stroke
      Of quick cross lightning? To watch—poor
35   perdu!°—
✓   With this thin helm? Mine enemy's dog,
      Through he had bit me, should have stood that
          night
      Against my fire; and wast thou fain, poor
          father,
      To hovel thee with swine and rogues forlorn
40   In short and musty straw? Alack, alack!
      'Tis wonder that thy life and wits at once
      Had not concluded all. He wakes; speak to him.
      DOCTOR. Madam, do you; 'tis fittest.
      CORDELIA. How does my royal lord? How fares
          your majesty?

LEAR. You do me wrong to take me out o' the
      grave.   45
      Thou art a soul in bliss; but I am bound
      Upon a wheel of fire, that° mine own tears
      Do scald like molten lead.
      CORDELIA.   Sir, do you know me?
      LEAR. You are a spirit, I know. When did you die?
      CORDELIA. Still, still, far wide!°   50
      DOCTOR. He's scarce awake. Let him alone awhile.
      LEAR. Where have I been? Where am I? Fair day-
          light?
      I am mightily abus'd. I should e'en die with pity
      To see another thus. I know not what to say.
      I will not swear these are my hands. Let's see;   55
      I feel this pin prick. Would I were assur'd
      Of my condition!
      CORDELIA.   O, look upon me, sir,
      And hold your hands in benediction o'er me.
      No, sir, you must not kneel.
      LEAR.   Pray do not mock me.
      I am a very foolish fond old man,   60
      Fourscore and upward, not an hour more nor
          less;
      And, to deal plainly,
      I fear I am not in my perfect mind.
      Methinks I should know you and know this
          man.
      Yet I am doubtful, for I am mainly° ignorant   65
      What place this is, and all the skill I have
      Remembers not these garments, nor I know
          not
      Where I did lodge last night. Do not laugh at
          me;
      For, as I am a man, I think this lady
      To be my child Cordelia.
      CORDELIA.   And so I am, I am.   70
      LEAR. Be your tears wet? Yes, faith. I pray, weep
          not.
      If you have poison for me, I will drink it.
      I know you do not love me; for your sisters
      Have, as I do remember, done me wrong.
      You have some cause, they have not.
      CORDELIA.   No cause, no cause. 75
      LEAR. Am I in France?
      KENT.   In your own kingdom, sir.
      LEAR. Do not abuse me.
      DOCTOR. Be comforted, good madam. The great
          rage,
      You see, is kill'd in him; and yet it is danger
      To make him even o'er° the time he has lost.   80
      Desire him to go in; trouble him no more
      Till further settling.

---

child-changed exchanged with a child (Lear's mind has
    been reduced to that of a child)
sway rule   *temperance* sanity   *flakes* hairs
challeng'd claimed
perdu lost one; with special military application, a lone,
    exposed sentry

that so that   *wide* i.e., of the mark (sanity)
mainly wholly   *even o'er* fill in

CORDELIA. Will 't please your highness walk?

LEAR. You must bear with me. Pray you now,
85 forget and forgive: I am old and foolish.

    [Exeunt all but KENT *and* GENTLEMAN.]*

GENTLEMAN. Holds it true, sir, that the Duke of
    Cornwall was so slain?

KENT. Most certain, sir.

GENTLEMAN. Who is conductor of his people?

90 KENT. As 'tis said, the bastard son of Gloucester.

GENTLEMAN. They say Edgar, his banish'd son, is
    with the Earl of Kent in Germany.

KENT. Report is changeable. 'Tis time to look
about; the powers of the kingdom approach
apace.   95

GENTLEMAN. The arbitrement° is like to be bloody.
    Fare you well, sir.   *[Exit]*

KENT. My point and period will be throughly
    wrought,°
    Or well or° ill, as this day's battle's fought.

                                             [Exit]

arbitrement decision
My . . . wrought the end of my affairs will be thoroughly
    worked out   *Or . . . or* either . . . or

ACT V

SCENE i
The British camp near Dover.

[Enter, with drum and colors, EDMUND, REGAN,
        GENTLEMEN, *and* SOLDIERS.]*

EDMUND. Know of the duke if his last purpose hold,
    Or whether since he is advis'd by aught
    To change the course. He's full of alteration
    And self-reproving. Bring his constant pleasure.°

            [To a GENTLEMAN, *who goes out.]*

5 REGAN. Our sister's man is certainly miscarried.

EDMUND. 'Tis to be doubted,° madam.

REGAN.   Now, sweet lord,
    You know the goodness I intend upon you.
    Tell me, but truly, but then speak the truth,
    Do you not love my sister?

EDMUND.   In honor'd° love.

REGAN. But have you never found my brother's
10   way
    To the forfended° place?

EDMUND.   That thought abuses you.

REGAN. I am doubtful° that you have been con-
    junct
    And bosom'd° with her, as far as we call hers.°

EDMUND. No, by mine honor, madam.

15 REGAN. I never shall endure her. Dear my lord,
    Be not familiar with her.

EDMUND.   Fear me not.—
    She and the duke her husband!

    [Enter, with drum and colors, ALBANY, GONERIL,
            and SOLDIERS.]*

GONERIL. *[Aside]* I had rather lose the battle than
    that sister
    Should loosen him and me.

ALBANY. Our very loving sister, well be-met.   20
    Sir, this I hear: the king is come to his daughter
    With others whom the rigor° of our state
    Forc'd to cry out. Where I could not be honest,
    I never yet was valiant. For this business,
    It toucheth us as France invades our land,   25
    Not bolds the king, with others whom, I fear,
    Most just and heavy causes make oppose.°

EDMUND. Sir, you speak nobly.

REGAN.   Why is this reason'd?

GONERIL. Combine together 'gainst the enemy;
    For these domestic and particular broils   30
    Are not the question here.

ALBANY.   Let's then determine
    With th' ancient of war° on our proceedings.

EDMUND. I shall attend you presently at your tent.

REGAN. Sister, you'll go with us?

GONERIL. No.   35

REGAN. 'Tis most convenient; pray you, go with us.

GONERIL. *[Aside]* O, ho, I know the riddle.—I will
    go.

    [As they are going out, enter EDGAR *disguised.]*

EDGAR. If e'er your grace had speech with man so
    poor,
    Hear me one word.

ALBANY.   I'll overtake you. Speak.

        [Exeunt all but ALBANY *and* EDGAR.]*

rigor severity
For . . . oppose as for this business, it concerns us
    because France invades our land, not because he
    encourages the king and others who, I fear, have good
    cause to oppose us
th' ancient of war the military professionals

constant pleasure settled resolve   *doubted* suspected
honor'd honorable   *forfended* forbidden
am doubtful suspect   *conjunct and bosom'd* intimate
as . . . hers i.e., to the limit

40 EDGAR. Before you fight the battle, ope this letter.
   If you have victory, let the trumpet sound
   For him that brought it. Wretched though I
     seem,
   I can produce a champion that will prove
   What is avouched there. If you miscarry,
45 Your business of the world hath so an end,
   And machination ceases. Fortune love you!
ALBANY. Stay till I have read the letter.
EDGAR.   I was forbid it.
   When time shall serve,° let but the herald cry,
   And I'll appear again.
ALBANY. Why, fare thee well. I will o'erlook thy
50   paper.   [Exit EDGAR.]
          [Re-enter EDMUND.]
EDMUND. The enemy's in view. Draw up your
     powers.
   Here is the guess of their true strength and
     forces
   By diligent discovery;° but your haste
   Is now urg'd on you.
ALBANY.   We will greet the time.°
                                    [Exit]
EDMUND. To both these sisters have I sworn my
55   love,
   Each jealous° of the other as the stung
   Are of the adder. Which of them shall I take?
   Both? One? Or neither? Neither can be enjoy'd
   If both remain alive. To take the widow
60 Exasperates, makes mad her sister Goneril;
   And hardly shall I carry out my side,°
   Her husband being alive. Now then we'll use
   His countenance for the battle, which being
     done,
   Let her who would be rid of him devise
65 His speedy taking off. As for the mercy
   Which he intends to Lear and to Cordelia,
   The battle done and they within our power,
   Shall never see his pardon; for my state
   Stands on me to defend, not to debate.°   [Exit]

SCENE ii
A field between the two camps.

[Alarum within. Enter, with drum and colors,
LEAR, CORDELIA, and SOLDIERS, over the stage;
and exeunt. Enter EDGAR and GLOUCESTER.]
EDGAR. Here, father, take the shadow of this tree
   For your good host; pray that the right may
     thrive.
   If ever I return to you again,
   I'll bring you comfort.
GLOUCESTER.   Grace go with you, sir!
                                [Exit EDGAR.]
[Alarum and retreat within. Re-enter EDGAR.]
EDGAR. Away, old man. Give me thy hand. Away!   5
   King Lear hath lost, he and his daughter ta'en.
   Give me thy hand. Come on.
GLOUCESTER. No further, sir; a man may rot even
     here.
EDGAR. What, in ill thoughts again? Men must en-
     dure
   Their going hence even as their coming hither.   10
   Ripeness is all.° Come on.
GLOUCESTER.   And that's true too.
                                    [Exeunt]

See Hamlet V-ii-230 (p. 412)

SCENE iii
The British camp near Dover.

[Enter, in conquest, with drum and colors, EDMUND;
LEAR and CORDELIA, as prisoners; CAPTAIN,
SOLDIERS, &c.]
EDMUND. Some officers take them away. Good
     guard,
   Until their greater pleasures° first be known
   That are to censure them.
CORDELIA.   We are not the first
   Who with best meaning° have incurr'd the
     worst.
   For thee, oppressed king, am I cast down;°   5
   Myself could else out-frown false fortune's
     frown.
   Shall we not see these daughters and these sis-
     ters?
LEAR. No, no, no, no! Come, let's away to prison.
   We two alone will sing like birds i' the cage.
   When thou dost ask me blessing, I'll kneel down   10
   And ask of thee forgiveness. So we'll live,
   And pray, and sing, and tell old tales, and laugh

When . . . serve at the appropriate moment
By . . . discovery arrived at by diligent spying
greet the time i.e., be ready   jealous suspicious
carry . . . side succeed with her
for . . . debate for my fortune requires me to act, not
  argue

Ripeness is all readiness (for death) is all
their . . . pleasures i.e. the wishes of my superiors
meaning intentions   cast down dejected

Lear's joy, Kent

puarded as F2.

At gilded butterflies,° and hear poor rogues
Talk of court news. And we'll talk with them
   too—
15   Who loses and who wins, who's in, who's out,
And take upon's the mystery of things
As if we were God's spies. And we'll wear out,
In a wall'd prison, packs and sects of great ones
That ebb and flow by the moon.
EDMUND.   Take them away.
20   LEAR. Upon such sacrifices,° my Cordelia,
The gods themselves throw incense. Have I
   caught thee?
He that parts us shall bring a brand° from
   heaven,
And fire us hence like foxes.° Wipe thine eyes;
The goodyears° shall devour them, flesh and fell,
Ere they shall make us weep. We'll see 'em
25   starve first.
Come.   [*Exeunt* LEAR *and* CORDELIA, *guarded.*]
EDMUND. Come hither, captain; hark.
Take thou this note; go follow them to prison.
One step I have advanc'd thee; if thou dost
30   As this instructs thee, thou dost make thy way
To noble fortunes. Know thou this, that men
Are as the time is. To be tender-minded
Does not become a sword. Thy great employ-
   ment
Will not bear question;° either say thou'lt do 't,
Or thrive by other means.
35   CAPTAIN.   I'll do't, my lord.
EDMUND. About it, and write happy° when thou'st
   done.
Mark; I say, instantly, and carry it so
As I have set it down.
CAPTAIN. I cannot draw a cart, nor eat dried oats;
40   If it be man's work, I'll do 't.   [*Exit*]
[*Flourish. Enter* ALBANY, GONERIL, REGAN, *another*
         CAPTAIN, *and* SOLDIERS.]
ALBANY. Sir, you have shown today your valiant
   strain,
And fortune led you well. You have the captives
That were the opposites of° this day's strife.
We do require them of you, so to use them

As we shall find their merits and our safety   45
May equally determine.
EDMUND.   Sir, I thought it fit
To send the old and miserable king
To some retention and appointed guard,
Whose° age has charms in it, whose title more,
To pluck the common bosom° on his side   50
And turn our impress'd lances° in our eyes
Which do command them. With him I sent the
   queen,
My reason all the same; and they are ready
Tomorrow or at further space t'appear
Where you shall hold your session. At this time 55
We sweat and bleed. The friend hath lost his
   friend,
And the best quarrels,° in the heat, are curs'd
By those that feel their sharpness.
The question of Cordelia and her father
Requires a fitter place.
ALBANY.   Sir, by your patience,   60
I hold you but a subject of this war,
Not as a brother.
REGAN.   That's as we list to grace° him.
Methinks our pleasure might have been de-
   manded
Ere you had spoke so far. He led our powers,
Bore the commission of my place and person,   65
The which immediacy° may well stand up
And call itself your brother.
GONERIL.   Not so hot.
In his own grace he doth exalt himself
More than in your addition.°
REGAN.   In my rights,
By me invested, he compeers° the best.   70
GONERIL. That were the most, if he should husband
   you.
REGAN. Jesters do oft prove prophets.
GONERIL.   Holla, holla!
That eye that told you so look'd but a-squint.
REGAN. Lady, I am not well, else I should answer
From a full-flowing stomach.° General,   75
Take thou my soldiers, prisoners, patrimony;°
Dispose of them, of me; the walls are thine.°
Witness the world that I create thee here
My lord and master.
GONERIL.   Mean you to enjoy him?

---

gilded butterflies foppish courtiers
such sacrifices i.e., as we are   *brand* firebrand
fire . . . foxes i.e., only fire and smoke will drive foxes
   from their holes; to separate Lear and his daughter
   heavenly fire will be needed
goodyears (a term of uncertain origin, taken as
   signifying some malign force; but conceivably Lear
   means that the years that are good to himself and
   Cordelia will destroy their enemies, echoing lines
   17–19 above)
question discussion
write happy call yourself a happy (fortunate) man
opposites of opponents in

Whose i.e., Lear's   *pluck . . . bosom* win the people
impress'd lances drafted warriors
best quarrels worthiest causes
list to grace please to honor
immediacy immediate status
your addition titles conferred by you
compeers stands the peer of   *stomach* anger
patrimony inheritance
the . . . thine i.e., you have captured the city (myself)

80 ALBANY. The let-alone lies not in your good will.°
 EDMUND. Nor in thine, lord.
ALBANY.   Half-blooded fellow, yes.
REGAN. [To EDMUND] Let the drum strike, and
    prove my title thine.
ALBANY. Stay yet; hear reason. Edmund, I arrest
    thee
    On capital treason, and in thine attaint°
    This gilded serpent [pointing to GONERIL]. For
85 your claim, fair sister,
    I bar it in the interest of my wife.
    'Tis she is sub-contracted to this lord,
    And I, her husband, contradict your bans.°
    If you will marry, make your loves to me;
    My lady is bespoke.
90 GONERIL.   An interlude!°
ALBANY. Thou art arm'd, Gloucester. Let the trum-
    pet sound.
    If none appear to prove upon thy person
    Thy heinous, manifest, and many treasons,
    There is my pledge [throwing down a glove]. I'll
    prove it on thy heart,
95 Ere I taste bread, thou art in nothing less
    Than I have here proclaim'd thee.
REGAN.   Sick, O, sick!
GONERIL. [Aside] If not, I'll ne'er trust medicine.
EDMUND. [Throwing down a glove] There's my ex-
    change. What in the world he is
    That names me traitor, villain-like he lies.
100 Call by thy trumpet. He that dares approach,
    On him, on you—who not?—I will maintain
    My truth and honor firmly.
ALBANY. A herald, ho!
EDMUND.   A herald, ho, a herald!
ALBANY. Trust to thy single virtue;° for thy soldiers,
105 All levied in my name, have in my name
    Took their discharge.
REGAN.   My sickness grows upon me.
ALBANY. She is not well; convey her to my tent.
                              [Exit REGAN, led.]
                      [Enter a HERALD.]
    Come hither, herald.—Let the trumpet sound.—
    And read out this.
110 CAPTAIN. Sound, trumpet!   [A trumpet sounds.]
HERALD.

    [Reads] If any man of quality or degree°
    within the lists of the army will maintain upon

Edmund, supposed Earl of Gloucester, that he
is a manifold traitor, let him appear by the
third sound of the trumpet. He is bold in his   115
defense.

EDMUND. Sound!   [First trumpet.]
HERALD. Again!   [Second trumpet.]
HERALD. Again!   [Third trumpet.]
                    [Trumpet answers within.]
      [Enter EDGAR, at the third sound, armed with a
              trumpet before him.°]
ALBANY. Ask him his purposes, why he appears   120
    Upon this call o' the trumpet.
HERALD.   What are you?
    Your name, your quality, and why you answer
    This present summons?
EDGAR.   Know my name is lost,
    By treason's tooth bare-gnawn and canker-bit.°
    Yet am I noble as the adversary   125
    I come to cope.°
ALBANY.   Which is that adversary?
EDGAR. What's he that speaks for Edmund, Earl of
    Gloucester?
EDMUND. Himself. What say'st thou to him?
EDGAR.   Draw thy sword,
    That if my speech offend a noble heart,
    Thy arm may do thee justice. Here is mine.   130
    Behold, it is the privilege of mine honors,
    My oath, and my profession. I protest,
    Maugre° thy strength, youth, place, and emi-
    nence,
    Despite thy victor sword and fire-new° fortune,
    Thy valor and thy heart, thou art a traitor,   135
    False to thy gods, thy brother, and thy father,
    Conspirant 'gainst this high illustrious prince,
    And from th' extremest upward of thy head
    To the descent and dust below thy foot,
    A most toad-spotted° traitor. Say thou "No,"   140
    This sword, this arm, and my best spirits are
    bent
    To prove upon thy heart, whereto I speak,
    Thou liest.
EDMUND. In wisdom I should ask thy name,
    But since thy outside looks so fair and warlike   145
    And that thy tongue some say° of breeding
    breathes,
    What safe and nicely° I might well delay
    By rule of knighthood, I disdain and spurn.
    Back do I toss these treasons to thy head,

The let-alone . . . good will   the "say so" is not yours
in thine attaint   impeached along with you
bans   public notice of intention to marry
interlude   incidental comedy
in nothing less   i.e., no less in villainy
single virtue   your own valor only
quality or degree   noble birth

trumpet before him   trumpeter preceding him
canker-bit   worm-bitten   cope   cope with
Maugre   in spite of   fire-new   freshly minted
toad-spotted   venomous
some say   some sign
nicely   i.e. by standing on the fine points

150 With the hell-hated lie o'erwhelm thy heart,
Which° for they yet glance by and scarcely
    bruise,
This sword of mine shall give them instant way
Where they shall rest forever. Trumpets, speak!
    [*Alarums. They fight.* EDMUND *falls.*]
ALBANY. Save him, save him!
GONERIL.   This is practice,° Gloucester.
By the law of arms thou wast not bound to
155   answer
An unknown opposite; thou art not vanquish'd,
But cozen'd° and beguil'd.
ALBANY.   Shut your mouth, dame,
Or with this paper° shall I stop it. Hold, sir,
Thou° worse than any name, read thine own
    evil.
160 No tearing, lady; I perceive you know it.
GONERIL. Say if I do? The laws are mine, not thine.
Who can arraign me for 't?
ALBANY.   Most monstrous!
Know'st thou this paper?
GONERIL.   Ask me not what I know.
                    [*Exit*]
ALBANY. Go after her. She's desperate; govern° her.
EDMUND. What you have charg'd me with, that
165   have I done,
And more, much more; the time will bring it
    out.
'Tis past, and so am I. But what art thou
That hast this fortune° on me? If thou 'rt noble,
I do forgive thee.
EDGAR.   Let's exchange charity.
170 I am no less in blood than thou art, Edmund;
If more, the more thou 'st wrong'd me.
My name is Edgar, and thy father's son.
The gods are just, and of our pleasant vices
Make instruments to plague us:
175 The dark and vicious place where thee he got
Cost him his eyes.
EDMUND.   Thou hast spoken right, 'tis true;
The wheel° is come full circle; I am here.
ALBANY. Methought thy very gait did prophesy
A royal nobleness. I must embrace thee.
180 Let sorrow split my heart if ever I
Did hate thee or thy father!
EDGAR.   Worthy prince, I know't.
ALBANY. Where have you hid yourself?
How have you known the miseries of your
    father?

EDGAR. By nursing them, my lord. List a brief tale,
And when 'tis told, O, that my heart would
    burst!   185
The bloody proclamation to escape
That follow'd me so near—O, our lives' sweet-
    ness!
That we the pain of death would hourly die
Rather than die at once!—taught me to shift
Into a madman's rags, t'assume a semblance   190
That very dogs disdain'd. And in this habit
Met I my father with his bleeding rings,°
Their precious stones new lost; became his
    guide,
Led him, begg'd for him, sav'd him from des-
    pair.
Never—O fault!—reveal'd myself unto him,   195
Until some half-hour past, when I was arm'd.°
Not sure, though hoping, of this good success,
I ask'd his blessing, and from first to last
Told him my pilgrimage. But his flaw'd heart—
Alack, too weak the conflict to support!—   200
'Twixt two extremes of passion, joy and grief,
Burst smilingly.
EDMUND.   This speech of yours hath mov'd me,
And shall perchance do good. But speak you on;
You look as you had something more to say.
ALBANY. If there be more, more woeful, hold it in,   205
For I am almost ready to dissolve,
Hearing of this.
EDGAR.   This would have seem'd a period
To such as love not sorrow; but another,
To amplify too much, would make much more,
And top extremity.°   210
Whilst I was big° in clamor, came there in a man
Who, having seen me in my worst estate,°
Shunn'd my abhorr'd society, but then, finding
Who 'twas that so endur'd, with his strong arms
He fasten'd on my neck and bellow'd out   215
As he'd burst heaven; threw him on my father,
Told the most piteous tale of Lear and him
That ever ear receiv'd, which in recounting
His grief grew puissant, and the strings of life
Began to crack. Twice then the trumpets soun-
    ded,   220
And there I left him tranc'd.
ALBANY.   But who was this?
EDGAR. Kent, sir, the banish'd Kent, who in dis-
    guise
Follow'd his enemy king and did him service
Improper for a slave.

Which the accusations of treason   *practice* trickery
cozen'd cheated
this paper i.e., Goneril's love letter to Edmund
Thou i.e., Goneril   *govern* restrain
hast this fortune have gained this victory
wheel Fortune's wheel

rings sockets   *arm'd* for the combat with Edmund
another . . . extremity another such story, elaborated too
    much, would exceed the limits of endurance
big loud   *estate* condition (as Tom)

[*Enter a* Gentleman, *with a bloody knife.*]

GENTLEMAN. Help, help, O, help!

EDGAR.   What kind of help?

225 ALBANY.   Speak, man.

EDGAR. What means this bloody knife?

GENTLEMAN.   'Tis hot, it smokes.°
   It came even from the heart of—O, she's dead!

ALBANY. Who dead? Speak, man.

GENTLEMAN. Your lady, sir, your lady. And her
   sister

230 By her is poison'd; she hath confess'd it.

EDMUND. I was contracted to them both. All three
   Now marry in an instant.

EDGAR.   Here comes Kent.

ALBANY. Produce the bodies, be they alive or dead.
                        [*Exit* GENTLEMAN.]
   This judgment of the heavens, that makes us
     tremble,
   Touches us not with pity.
                [*Enter* KENT.]
                     O, is this he?

235 The time will not allow the compliment°
   Which very manners urges.

KENT.   I am come
   To bid my king and master aye° goodnight.
   Is he not here?

ALBANY.   Great thing of us forgot!
   Speak, Edmund, where's the king? And where's
     Cordelia?

240 See'st thou this object, Kent?

[*The bodies of* GONERIL *and* REGAN *are brought in.*]

KENT. Alack, why thus?

EDMUND.   <u>Yet Edmund was belov'd.</u>
   The one the other poison'd for my sake,
   And after slew herself.

ALBANY. Even so. Cover their faces.

245 EDMUND. I pant for life. <u>Some good I mean</u> to do,
   Despite of mine own nature. Quickly send,
   Be brief in it, to the castle; for my writ
   Is on the life of Lear and on Cordelia.
   Nay, send in time.

ALBANY.   Run, run, O, run!

EDGAR. To who, my lord? Who hath the office?

250 Send
   Thy token of reprieve.

EDMUND. Well thought on. Take my sword,
   Give it the captain.

ALBANY.   Haste thee, for thy life.
                       [*Exit* EDGAR.]

EDMUND. He hath commission from thy wife and
   me

255 To hang Cordelia in the prison, and
   To lay the blame upon her own despair,

That she fordid° herself.

ALBANY. The gods defend her! Bear him hence
   awhile.   [EDMUND *is borne off.*]

[*Re-enter* LEAR, *with* CORDELIA *dead in his arms;*
    EDGAR, CAPTAIN, *and others following.*]

LEAR. Howl, howl, howl, howl! O, you are men of
   stones.
   Had I your tongues and eyes, I'd use them so   260
   That heaven's vault should crack. She's gone for-
     ever!
   I know when one is dead and when one lives.
   She's dead as earth. Lend me a looking-glass;
   If that her breath will mist or stain the stone,°
   Why, then she lives.

KENT.   Is this the promis'd end?°   265

EDGAR. Or image of that horror?

ALBANY.   Fall and cease.°

LEAR. This feather stirs; she lives. If it be so,
   It is a chance which does redeem all sorrows
   That ever I have felt.

KENT.   [*Kneeling*] O my good master!

LEAR. Prithee, away.

EDGAR.   'Tis noble Kent, your friend.   270

LEAR. A plague upon you, murderers, traitors all!
   I might have sav'd her; now she's gone forever!
   Cordelia, Cordelia! Stay a little. Ha!
   What is 't thou say'st? Her voice was ever soft,
   Gentle and low, an excellent thing in woman.   275
   I kill'd the slave that was a-hanging thee.

CAPTAIN. 'Tis true, my lords, he did.

LEAR.   Did I not, fellow?
   I have seen the day, with my good biting fal-
     chion,°
   I would have made them skip. I am old now,
   And these same crosses spoil° me. Who are you?   280
   Mine eyes are not o' the best. I'll tell you straight.

KENT. If fortune brag of two° she lov'd and hated,
   One of them we behold.

LEAR. This is a dull sight. Are you not Kent?

KENT.   The same,
   Your servant Kent. Where is your servant Caius?°   285

LEAR. He's a good fellow, I can tell you that;
   He'll strike, and quickly too. He's dead and
     rotten.

KENT. No, my good lord; I am the very man—

LEAR. I'll see that straight.°

---

smokes steams   *compliment* ceremony   *aye* forever

fordid destroyed   *stone* glass
promis'd end doomsday
Fall and cease let all things come to an end
falchion curved sword
crosses spoil afflictions weaken
two i.e., Lear and some nameless other sufferer
Caius i.e., Kent's name in disguise, not elsewhere
   mentioned
I'll . . . straight I'll understand that in a moment

290 KENT. That from your first of difference and decay
      Have follow'd your sad steps.
    LEAR.   You are welcome hither.
    KENT. Nor no man else.° All's cheerless, dark and
      deadly.
      Your eldest daughters have fordone° themselves,
      And desperately are dead.
    LEAR.   Aye, so I think.
295 ALBANY. He knows not what he says, and vain is it
      That we present us to him.
    EDGAR.   Very bootless.°
                [Enter a CAPTAIN.]
    CAPTAIN. Edmund is dead, my lord.
    ALBANY.   That's but a trifle here.
      You lords and noble friends, know our intent.
      What comfort to this great decay° may come
300   Shall be applied. For us, we will resign,
      During the life of this old majesty,
      To him our absolute power.
                      [To EDGAR and KENT.]
      You, to your rights,
      With boot,° and such addition° as your honors
305   Have more than merited. All friends shall taste
      The wages of their virtue, and all foes
      The cup of their deservings. O, see, see!
    LEAR. And my poor fool° is hang'd! No, no, no life!
      Why should a dog, a horse, a rat have life,
      And thou no breath at all? Thou'lt come no
310   more,

Never, never, never, never, never!
Pray you, undo this button; thank you, sir.
Do you see this? Look on her, look, her lips,
Look there, look there!   [Dies.]
EDGAR.   He faints. My lord, my lord!
KENT. Break, heart; I prithee, break!
EDGAR.   Look up, my lord. 315
KENT. Vex not his ghost. O, let him pass! He hates
  him
  That would upon the rack° of this tough world
  Stretch him out longer.
EDGAR.   He is gone indeed.
KENT. The wonder is he hath endur'd so long.
  He but usurp'd his life.°   320
ALBANY. Bear them from hence. Our present
  business
  Is general woe. [To KENT and EDGAR] Friends of
    my soul, you twain
  Rule in this realm and the gor'd state sustain.
KENT. I have a journey, sir, shortly to go;
  My master calls me. I must not say no.   325
ALBANY. The weight of this sad time we must
  obey,°
  Speak what we feel, not what we ought to say.   ☆
  The oldest hath borne most. We that are young
  Shall never see so much, nor live so long.
                [Exeunt, with a dead march.]

Nor . . . else   neither I nor anyone can be welcome at
  such a time as this   fordone   destroyed
bootless   useless   this . . . decay   i.e., Lear
boot   increase   addition   titles
poor fool   Cordelia (a term of endearment)

rack   infamous device of torture which stretched and
  broke the body
usurp'd his life   i.e., death rightfully possessed it before
obey   yield to

AFTERWORD

When William Hazlitt, in the course of his discussions of Shakespeare's plays, came at last to *King Lear*, he expressed regret that he could not pass it by without a word, so inadequate did he feel to do it justice.

It is impossible to tabulate the opinions of general readers and theatergoers on the question, but it may be asserted confidently that more Shakespearean critics, scholars, and editors have identified *King Lear* as Shakespeare's greatest work than have so distinguished any other single play. Hazlitt, speaking for the Romantics, called it "the best of all Shakespeare's plays, for it is the one in which he was the most in earnest." Bradley, at the opening of the twentieth century, agreed that *King Lear* is Shakespeare's "greatest work," but denied Hazlitt's nomination of it as the best "of his plays," for its appeal "is made not so much to dramatic perception as to a rarer and more strictly poetic kind of imagination." It is, said Bradley, "too huge for the stage." In the middle of the twentieth century, Hardin Craig, only slightly less categorically than Hazlitt and Bradley, named *King Lear* as "possibly the greatest of Shakespeare's tragedies."

The issue between Hazlitt and Bradley has particular relevance for any discussion of *King Lear*, which has never rivalled *Hamlet* for popularity on the stage, or, for that matter, *Othello* or *Macbeth*. Bradley speaks accurately of its "comparative unpopularity" in the theater, which he ascribes only partly to "the extreme painfulness of the catastrophe" and to certain "dramatic defects." In the main, he says, its partial failure as theater is due to the fact that there is "something in its very essence which is at war with the senses, and demands a purely imaginative realisation."

Far the most famous utterance on this precise issue of *King Lear*'s fitness or unfitness for the stage is that of Charles Lamb, who, it must in fairness be acknowledged, found it hard to accept *any* of Shakespeare's plays as suited for "representation." Right or wrong, and certainly his view is regarded today with little favor, Lamb's remarks so illuminate and do such credit to the magnitude of this tragedy, and to so many of its unique qualities, that they require quoting at length here. "To see Lear acted," wrote the angry Lamb,

—to see an old man tottering about the stage with a walking-stick, turned out of doors by his daughters in a rainy night, has nothing in it but what is painful and disgusting. We want to take him into shelter and relieve him. That is all the feeling which the acting of Lear ever produced in me. But the Lear of Shakespeare cannot be acted. The contemptible machinery by which they mimic the storm which he goes out in, is not more inadequate to represent the horrors of the real elements, than any actor can be to represent Lear: they might more easily propose to personate the Satan of Milton upon a stage, or one of Michael Angelo's terrible figures. The greatness of Lear is not in corporal dimension, but in intellectual: the explosions of his passion are terrible as a volcano; they are storms turning up and disclosing to the bottom that sea, his mind, with all its vast riches. It is his mind which is laid bare. This case of flesh and blood seems too insignificant to be thought on. . . . On the stage we see nothing but corporal infirmities and weakness, the impotence of rage. While we read it, we see not Lear, but we are Lear: we are in his mind, we are sustained by a grandeur which baffles the malice of daughters and storms. . . . What have looks, or tones, to do with that sublime identification of his age with that of the heavens themselves. . . . What gesture shall we appropriate to this? What has the voice or the eye to do with such things? But the play is beyond art. . . .

The modern theater, equipped with mechanical devices for creating whatever effects of sight and sound are desired, is physically far less limited than the London theater where Lamb saw *Lear* and denounced the "contemptible machinery by which they mimic the storm." And today's filming technology removes literally all the physical limitations that once were formidable barriers to representation of such universal paroxysms as the text of *King Lear* demands that we envisage. But removal of physical limitations does not solve all the problems, and Lamb's judgment, along with Bradley's cryptic statement that *Lear* is "too huge for the stage," still poses a valid question; indeed, perhaps the modern theater, with its sophisticated facilities, is at the greater disadvantage.

For what *King Lear* requires of the imagination is akin to what is demanded by folk tale, from which the main story derives. Its primary quality is that of unreality. Partially excepting the stalwart Kent, the base tool Oswald, and the solid "norm" of the play, Albany—whose true position, however, as the bulwark of sanity, is left ambiguous until Act V—all the figures of the tragedy are creatures of unreality. They look not back to earlier notably substantial and realistic characterizations, but forward to strange and wild inhabitants of the late romances, like incestuous Antiochus and his daughter, and Cleon and Dionyza, of *Pericles*; Cymbeline's vicious queen and to a degree Cymbeline himself, and Belarius and the two wild young princes, of *Cymbeline*; and virtually all the residents who inhabit Sicilia and Bohemia in *The Winter's Tale*. *Antony and Cleopatra* and *Coriolanus*, the last tragedies before these romances, contain no such characters; but *Macbeth* and *Timon of Athens*, which also intervene before the romances, include persons and moments that are reminiscent of the quality of unreality that predominates in *King Lear*.

The mind's eye, to which *King Lear* is addressed, deals easily if not involuntarily with the principal figures and incidents of the play. Although the modern theater can re-create realistically the effects that the machinery of Lamb's day could not, in a sense the modern theater may do the greater disservice to *Lear*, for the unreal, when it is rendered "realistic" becomes intolerable, or, in any event, false to its nature. Hazlitt, speaking of *A Midsummer Night's Dream*, observed that the imagination, left to its own devices, can manage anything, and thus "Bottom's head, in the play (i.e., the text), is a fantastic illusion, produced by magic spells." But, he goes on, "on the stage it is an ass's head, and nothing more; certainly a very strange costume for a gentleman to appear in." So, on the stage, at the height of the storm that is as much within his head as without, Lear is of necessity a pygmy of a man—whether the actor be Burbage, Betterton, Garrick, Kemble, Kean, Booth, Irving, Gielgud, Olivier, or Louis Calhern—howling forth language the dimensions of which satirize his own:

> Blow, winds, and crack your cheeks! Rage! Blow!
> You cataracts and hurricanoes, spout
> Till you have drench'd our steeples, drown'd the cocks!

Before the mind's eye, which is not limited by physical fact, the Lear who bellows these lines may tower forty feet high; the Fool at his elbow, who whimpers at the outburst,

> O Nuncle, court holy-water in a dry house is better than this rainwater out o' doors. Good nuncle, in, and ask thy daughter's blessing. Here's a night pities neither wise man nor fool.

may be whatever the imagination conceives, whether white, black, tall, short, solid, transparent, or even invisible. Before the mind's eye, the vicious daughters of Lear may be half woman, half serpent; they may sprout devil's horns and have cloven feet; when

561

they speak, their tongues may show themselves forked. But to represent them so on the stage—however skilfully, so that the effect is wholly realistic and convincing—is to confront the physical eye with a gross image like Hazlitt's Bottom: "an ass's head . . . a very strange costume for a gentleman to appear in."

Cordelia, as a creature of the mind's eye, is no more "real" than the youngest daughter in a folk-tale household that includes a stepmother, wholly wicked, two daughters, wholly wicked, and herself, wholly innocent—if, in this case, somewhat stubborn. Again, the mind's eye creates its free image of Cordelia, whereas a "great" Cordelia on the stage is, by Lamb's theory, a contradiction in terms. Along with Lear, the Fool, and the wicked daughters, she is a creature of unreality, best imagined, and rendered less potent and true by being rendered physically. By the same token, Edmund, Shakespeare's most glamorous villain, an Iago with charisma, in basic concept as much Renaissance Man as Hamlet is, is also a folk-tale creature, a creature of the mind. Whereas Iago fairly shouts to be seen in the flesh of a clever actor, Edmund appears best in the shifting, dark, mercurial shape that imagination alone can provide; "representation" does not magnify, but diminishes him. "My father compounded with my mother under the dragon's tail," he confides,

> . . . and my nativity was under Ursa Major, so that it follows I
> am rough and lecherous. Tut, I should have been that I am had
> the maidenliest star in the firmament twinkled on my bastardizing.

"Now, gods, stand up for bastards!" he cries in justification of his being and his villainy. Greedily coveted by both of Lear's serpent-daughters, one of whom poisons the other for his sake and then stabs herself in final frustration, Edmund belongs with them in the deep, dark recesses of the mind where evil inhabits. Edgar, beside him—admirably devoted to goodness and filial duty though he is—is a clod of mortality, well fitted for representation on the stage. In his proper character, that is to say, he is dull; but with his "antic disposition" on, in Hamlet's phrase, he is quite something else. Then he, too, belongs to the imagination and shows best on the screen of the mind's eye, where, like Lear, he can tower forty feet high at need, or can assume such shape as that he invents to deceive blind Gloucester, who supposes himself to have fallen from the summit of Dover Cliff. "Upon the crown o' the cliff," asks Edgar, "what thing was that/Which parted from you?"

> As I stood here below, methought his eyes
> Were two full moons. He had a thousand noses,
> Horns whelk'd and waved like th' enridged sea.
> It was some fiend. . . .

Mad Tom is pre-eminently a "stage lunatic," such as Shakespeare's age presumably liked to see, and saw repeatedly in the plays between 1590 and 1625. Even so, how much the whole play demands of the uninhibited imagination is epitomized in this incident: no such creature as Edgar describes *really* stood at the top of Dover Cliff; what stood there was Edgar himself, in his role of Mad Tom—a being that was itself only a creature of his mind; and of course Edgar *still* stands there, for Gloucester's fall, too, was only imaginary, like the existence of Mad Tom and the being of the new identity that Edgar, feigning to be at the bottom of the cliff, next takes on. Such things are best acted, no doubt, on the mind's private stage.

Like the principal characters, the incidents, movement, the very landscapes ("for many miles about/ There's scarce a bush") are marked by unreality. The opening scene alone will suffice to illustrate. Old Lear looms suddenly before us and abruptly, without prologue or apology, wholly in the manner of a folk-tale king, in a gigantic and incredible gesture, offers in effect to raffle off the largest portion of his kingdom to that one of three daughters who shall profess the largest affection for him. In turn the first two daughters, reeking of hypocrisy in every syllable, play their father's game with extravagant and transparent protestations of love—and, incredibly, are believed. And then the third daughter, for whose advantage the whole game is in fact being played, balks at the game of make-believe and thereby tops, in her uncompromising virtue, the folk-tale character of the two wicked sisters in their patent hypocrisy and of the old king in his towering pride. But there is more: the mercenary Burgundy, whom we instantly dislike, rejects the honest but dowerless maiden out of hand; but the great King of France—whom the mind's eye is free to picture, if it will, as nine feet tall, clothed in shining white armor, and even (so flexible and lightning-quick is imagination) astride a white charger of appropriate proportions—gathers her up and carries her off with a flourish and grace such as we expect of princes who have been changed back from frogs and who awaken sleeping beauties:

> . . . most rich, being poor,
> Most choice forsaken, and most lov'd despis'd,
> Thee and thy virtues here I seize upon . . .
> Thy dowerless daughter, king, thrown to my chance,
> Is queen of us, of ours, and our fair France.

It would be false to assert that the movement of the whole play matches the folk-tale character of this opening, but it is a fact that the impressions that remain longest to haunt the mind are of just this quality: Lear sweeping in, flamboyantly, with his hundred knights, which are cut to fifty, to twenty-five, to none, in the abrupt, unapologetic movements of wild tales and romances; Lear in the storm; the mad arraignment of the two she-foxes by the royal lunatic, the professional fool, the feigned Bedlamite—and the sane, speechless Kent ("you are o' the commission,/ Sit you too"); the eye-gouging, when Cornwall, too, for the first time reveals himself as a villain of folk-tale degree.

In 1680 Nahum Tate, a minor talent of giant pretensions, rewrote *King Lear* to suit the tastes of his time; and so well did he succeed that, with some variations, his text was acted by a succession of the greatest performers over a period of more than a hundred and fifty years: Betterton, Garrick, Spranger, Barry, Kemble, and even Kean (who, however, in order to show London his tragic brilliance in the final scene where Lear enters with dead Cordelia in his arms, discarded Tate's happy ending wherein Lear is restored to the throne and Edgar and Cordelia are married). Dr. Johnson himself preferred Tate's version on the grounds that Shakespeare did injustice to virtuous and innocent people: "I was many years ago so shocked by Cordelia's death, that I know not whether I ever endured to read again the last scenes of the play till I undertook to revise them as editor." But in fact Tate's version altered the play even more fundamentally than is implied by the shift to a happy ending, for it effectually destroyed the atmosphere of unreality, the folk-tale quality of characters and incidents, and transformed the whole to acceptable theatrical spectacle. Thus Tate, in a perverse sort of way, testified a century and a half before Lamb to the "unsuitability" of *King Lear* for the stage.

King Lear is the only one of the great tragedies to be provided with a double plot. Here are paralleled (and contrasted) the stories of Lear and Gloucester. Actually, the two plots become welded together at once, for Edmund enters Cornwall's service and quickly steps up his ambition beyond the original one of getting legitimate Edgar's estate. Soon, indeed, all the principal characters are involved in one way or another, or in multiple ways, with both plots. Edmund and Edgar in particular cross and recross from plot to plot. In the final scene, when Edgar challenges Edmund, the accusation is for "heinous, manifest, and many treasons" in the affairs of the kingdom, and not for private wrongs done within the Gloucester family. Nevertheless, the plots remain distinct insofar as each centers upon its single sufferer; thus the story of Gloucester remains just that to the end, regardless of the active participation of both his sons in Lear's story.

Coleridge asserted that "Edgar's assumed madness serves the great purpose of taking off part of the shock which would otherwise be caused by the true madness of Lear," but no doubt the main effect gained by combining the parallel tales within the frame of a single tragedy is that of intensification rather than alleviation, of hardening the final impact rather than softening it. The tragedies of the two men are parallel as well in origin as in their course and conclusion. Lear's self-centered vanity, his greed for flattery, his blind disregard of distinction between outward show and inner truth invite the evils that require only slight invitation to swarm over him. Gloucester's initial fault lay years before, when he begot Edmund out of wedlock, and Edgar is not above moralizing the point at the end of the play, while Edmund lies dying: "The dark and secret place where thee he got/ Cost him his eyes." Yet Gloucester, like Lear, is not blameless when the play opens, for he jests rather coarsely with Kent: "I cannot conceive you," says Kent, and Gloucester, perhaps with a nudge at Kent's ribs and a knowing wink, replies,

> Sir, this young fellow's mother could. Whereupon she grew
> round-wombed, and had indeed, sir, a son for her cradle
> ere she had a husband for her bed. Do you smell a fault?

Edmund's mother was fair, he adds, and there was "good sport at his making." What is more, Gloucester is at fault in the readiness with which he credits his bastard son's libels upon Edgar, even as is Lear in taking his daughters' flattery for truth. In a measure, at least, both men invite the ills that befall them.

Lear is first to perceive his error, and his initial reactions are characteristic of his nature as we first know him: he responds with arrogant fury because his pride has been offended, and, when fury proves unavailing, he falls into self-pity that briefly threatens to make him contemptible. But during the storm he begins to undergo a transformation. Suddenly, and perhaps even unexpectedly he expresses a limited concern for the misery of the wet, cold Fool: "Poor fool and knave, I have one part in my heart/ That's sorry yet for thee." It is perhaps the first nudge of compassion for another that he has ever felt. Soon he is moved to express a new-found compassion for sufferers in general:

> Poor naked wretches, whereso'er you are,
> That bide the pelting of this pitiless storm,
> How shall your houseless heads and unfed sides,
> Your loop'd and window'd raggedness, defend you
> From seasons such as these? O, I have ta'en
> Too little care of this.

Ultimately his ordeal of madness leads him not only to a larger sympathy but to a health of mind that was never his before. As for Gloucester, he too first undergoes a depression that borders on self-pity, ably diagnosed by Edgar, who cures him of it by the drastic method of making him suppose that he miraculously survives a leap from Dover Cliff. In comparatively short space Gloucester moves from a philosophy of negation ("As flies to wanton boys are we to the gods;/ They kill us for their sport") to one of acceptance and humility:

> You ever-gentle gods, take my breath from me;
> Let not my worser spirit tempt me again
> To die before you please.

Gloucester had no such deadly sins of selfish pride and vanity as Lear had, to be purged of; on the contrary, a noble generosity and care of others were always his; in the worst moments of his adversity he is more grieved for the demented king and the lost Edgar than for himself. It is thus through the contrasts as well as the similarities that the paralleled tales complement each other and contribute to the significance of a single, total tragedy that is almost too potent to be borne by either the reader or, Lamb to the contrary notwithstanding, the spectator in the theater.

In the end, what does this most terrible of Shakespeare's tragedies "mean"? After unspeakable suffering, Lear, Gloucester, and Cordelia are dead. We may gain some comfort by contemplating that in dying they have also cleansed the world of much evil—for Edmund, Cornwall, the bad daughters, and the intolerable Oswald are dead, too, and the world is well off without them. Good has not been wasted in vain, but has won its battle against evil, the ultimate theme of this tragedy, and of all Shakespearean tragedy. More cheeringly, we have seen both Lear and Gloucester grow in wisdom, in humility, and in human compassion through their dire experiences; for them, at least, suffering was the way to salvation.

A NOTE ON THE COMPOSITION OF THE PLAY

King Lear was written in 1605–1606 and was first performed in 1606. It was first published in quarto in 1608. The first account of the legend of King Lear was presented in the twelfth-century *Historia Regum Britanniae* by Geoffrey of Monmouth, but Shakespeare presumably drew principally on Holinshed's *Chronicles* and an anonymous play, *The True Chronicle History of King Leir*. For the secondary plot of Gloucester and his sons the source was an incident in Sidney's *Arcadia*. The name of Cordelia and the manner of her death were drawn from Spenser's *Faerie Queene*.

Macbeth

DRAMATIS PERSONÆ

DUNCAN *King of Scotland*
MALCOLM } *his sons*
DONALBAIN }
MACBETH
BANQUO
MACDUFF
LENNOX
ROSS } *noblemen of Scotland*
MENTEITH
ANGUS
CAITHNESS
FLEANCE *son to Banquo*
SIWARD *Earl of Northumberland, general of the English forces*
YOUNG SIWARD *his son*
SEYTON *an officer attending on Macbeth*

SON TO MACDUFF
AN ENGLISH DOCTOR
A SCOTTISH DOCTOR
A PORTER
AN OLD MAN
THREE MURDERERS
LADY MACBETH
LADY MACDUFF
A GENTLEWOMAN *attending on Lady Macbeth*
HECATE
WITCHES
APPARITIONS
LORDS, OFFICERS, SOLDIERS, ATTENDANTS, *and* MESSENGERS

SCENE: *Scotland; England.*

ACT I

SCENE i
An open place.

[*Thunder and lightning. Enter Three Witches.*]
FIRST WITCH. When shall we three meet again?
  In thunder, lightning, or in rain?
SECOND WITCH. When the hurlyburly's° done,
  When the battle's lost and won.
5 THIRD WITCH. That will be ere the set of sun.
FIRST WITCH. Where the place?
SECOND WITCH.   Upon the heath.
THIRD WITCH. There to meet with Macbeth.
FIRST WITCH. I come, Graymalkin.°

hurlyburly tumult
Graymalkin gray cat, the Witch's pet spirit

SECOND WITCH.   Paddock° calls.
THIRD WITCH.   Anon!
ALL. Fair is foul, and foul is fair.
  Hover through the fog and filthy air.   [*Exeunt*]   10

SCENE ii

[*Alarum within. Enter* KING [DUNCAN], MALCOLM, DONALBAIN, LENNOX, *with* ATTENDANTS, *meeting a bleeding* CAPTAIN.]
DUNCAN. What bloody man is that? He can report,
  As seemeth by his plight, of the revolt
  The newest state.

Paddock toad

MALCOLM.   This is the sergeant
    Who like a good and hardy soldier fought
5   'Gainst my captivity. Hail, brave friend!
    Say to the king the knowledge of the broil
    As thou didst leave it.
SERGEANT.   Doubtful it stood,
    As two spent swimmers that do cling together
    And choke their art.° The merciless Macdon-
        wald—
10 Worthy to be a rebel, for to that
    The multiplying villainies of nature
    Do swarm upon him—from the western isles
    Of kerns and gallowglasses° is supplied,
    And fortune, on his damned quarrel smiling,
15 Show'd like a rebel's whore. But all's too weak;
    For brave Macbeth—well he deserves that
        name—
    Disdaining fortune, with his brandish'd steel,
    Which smok'd with bloody execution,
    Like valor's minion° carved out his passage
20 Till he fac'd the slave,
    Which° ne'er shook hands nor bade farewell to
        him
    Till he unseam'd him from the nave to the
        chaps°
    And fix'd his head upon our battlements.
DUNCAN. O valiant cousin! Worthy gentleman!
25 SERGEANT. As whence the sun 'gins his reflection°
    Shipwrecking storms and direful thunders
        break,
    So from that spring whence comfort seem'd to
        come
    Discomfort swells. Mark, king of Scotland,
        mark:
    No sooner justice had, with valor arm'd,
    Compell'd these skipping kerns to trust their
30   heels,
    But the Norweyan lord,° surveying vantage,°
    With furbish'd arms and new supplies of men
    Began a fresh assault.
DUNCAN.   Dismay'd not this
    Our captains, Macbeth and Banquo?
SERGEANT.   Yes—
35 As sparrows eagles, or the hare the lion.
    If I say sooth, I must report they were

As cannons overcharg'd with double cracks,°
So they
Doubly redoubled strokes upon the foe.
Except° they meant to bathe in reeking wounds,   40
Or memorize another Golgotha,°
I cannot tell—
But I am faint; my gashes cry for help.
DUNCAN. So well thy words become thee as thy
    wounds;
    They smack of honor both. Go get him surgeons.   45
                [Exit SERGEANT, attended.]
    Who comes here?
                    [Enter ROSS.]
MALCOLM.   The worthy thane° of Ross.
LENNOX. What a haste looks through his eyes! So
    should he look
    That seems° to speak things strange.
ROSS.   God save the king!
DUNCAN. Whence cam'st thou, worthy thane?
ROSS.   From Fife, great king,
    Where the Norweyan banners flout the sky   50
    And fan our people cold.
    Norway himself, with terrible numbers,
    Assisted by that most disloyal traitor
    The thane of Cawdor, began a dismal conflict,
    Till that Bellona's° bridegroom,° lapp'd in
        proof,°   55
    Confronted him with self-comparisons,°
    Point against point, rebellious arm 'gainst arm,
    Curbing his lavish° spirit. And, to conclude,
    The victory fell on us.
DUNCAN.   Great happiness!
ROSS. That now   60
    Sweno, the Norways' king, craves composition.°
    Nor would we deign him burial of his men
    Till he disburs'd, at Saint Colme's inch,°
    Ten thousand dollars to our general use.
DUNCAN. No more that thane of Cawdor shall de-
    ceive   65
    Our bosom interest. Go pronounce his present
        death,
    And with his former title greet Macbeth.
ROSS. I'll see it done.
DUNCAN. What he hath lost, noble Macbeth hath
    won.   [Exeunt]

---

choke their art   prevent each other from swimming
western isles   Ireland and the Hebrides
kerns and gallowglasses   light infantry and armored
    soldiers
minion   darling   *Which* i.e., Macbeth
nave . . . chaps   navel . . . jaws
As whence . . . reflection   i.e., the East
Norweyan lord   Sweno, King of Norway
surveying vantage   i.e., seeing his chance

cracks   charges   *Except*   unless
memorize . . . Golgotha   make as memorable as Calvary
thane   earl   *seems*   i.e., seems ready
Bellona   goddess of war   *bridegroom*   i.e., Macbeth
lapp'd in proof   clad in armor
self-comparisons   i.e., equal skill
lavish   inflated, overconfident
composition   terms for surrender
Saint Colme's inch   Inchcomb Island, near Edinburgh

SCENE iii
A heath.

[*Thunder. Enter the* THREE WITCHES.]
FIRST WITCH. Where hast thou been, sister?
SECOND WITCH. Killing swine.
THIRD WITCH. Sister, where thou?
FIRST WITCH. A sailor's wife had chestnuts in her
 lap,
 And munch'd, and munch'd, and munch'd.
5 "Give me," quoth I.
 "Aroint° thee, witch!" the rump-fed ronyon°
  cries.
 Her husband's to Aleppo gone, master o' the
  Tiger.
 But in a sieve I'll thither sail,
 And like a rat without a tail
10 I'll do, I'll do, and I'll do.
SECOND WITCH. I'll give thee a wind.
FIRST WITCH. Thou'rt kind.
THIRD WITCH. And I another.
FIRST WITCH. I myself have all the other,°
15 And the very ports they blow,°
 All the quarters that they know
 I' the shipman's card.°
 I will drain him dry as hay.
 Sleep shall neither night nor day
20 Hang upon his pent-house lid.°
 He shall live a man forbid.
 Weary sev'nights nine times nine
 Shall he dwindle, peak, and pine.
 Though his bark cannot be lost,
25 Yet it shall be tempest-tost.
 Look what I have.
SECOND WITCH. Show me, show me.
FIRST WITCH. Here I have a pilot's thumb,
 Wreck'd as homeward he did come.
        [*Drum within.*]
30 THIRD WITCH. A drum, a drum!
 Macbeth doth come.
ALL. The weird sisters, hand in hand,
 Posters° of the sea and land,
 Thus do go about, about.
35 Thrice to thine, and thrice to mine,
 And thrice again, to make up nine.
 Peace! The charm's wound up.
   [*Enter* MACBETH *and* BANQUO.]
MACBETH. So foul and fair a day I have not seen.

Aroint begone *rump-fed ronyon* fat-rumped hag
other i.e., other winds
they blow i.e., toward which they blow
card compass dial *penthouse lid* eyelid
Posters posthaste riders

BANQUO. How far is 't call'd to Forres? What are
 these
 So wither'd, and so wild in their attire,   40
 That look not like th' inhabitants o' th' earth,
 And yet are on 't? Live you? Or are you aught
 That man may question? You seem to under-
  stand me,
 By each at once her choppy° finger laying
 Upon her skinny lips. You should be women, 45
 And yet your beards forbid me to interpret
 That you are so.
MACBETH.   Speak, if you can. What are you?
FIRST WITCH. All hail, Macbeth! Hail to thee, thane
 of Glamis!
SECOND WITCH. All hail, Macbeth! Hail to thee,
 thane of Cawdor!
THIRD WITCH. All hail, Macbeth, that shalt be king
 hereafter!   50
BANQUO. Good sir, why do you start, and seem to
 fear
 Things that do sound so fair? I' the name of
  truth,
 Are ye fantastical,° or that indeed
 Which outwardly ye show? My noble partner
 You greet with present grace and great predic-
  tion   55
 Of noble having and of royal hope,
 That he seems rapt withal.° To me you speak
  not.
 If you can look into the seeds of time,
 And say which grain will grow and which will
  not,
 Speak then to me, who neither beg nor fear 60
 Your favors nor your hate.
FIRST WITCH. Hail!
SECOND WITCH. Hail!
THIRD WITCH. Hail!
FIRST WITCH. Lesser than Macbeth, and greater. 65
SECOND WITCH. Not so happy, yet much happier.
THIRD WITCH. Thou shalt get° kings, though thou
 be none.
 So all hail, Macbeth and Banquo!
FIRST WITCH. Banquo and Macbeth, all hail!
MACBETH. Stay, you imperfect speakers, tell me
 more.   70
 By Sinel's° death I know I am thane of Glamis;
 But how of Cawdor? The thane of Cawdor lives,
 A prosperous gentleman. And to be king
 Stands not within the prospect of belief
 No more than to be Cawdor. Say from whence 75
 You owe this strange intelligence? Or why

---

choppy chapped *fantastical* imaginary
withal therewith *get* beget
Sinel Macbeth's father

Upon this blasted heath you stop our way
With such prophetic greeting? Speak, I charge
  you.   [Witches *vanish.*]
Banquo. The earth hath bubbles as the water has,
  And these are of them. Whither are they
80   vanish'd?
Macbeth. Into the air, and what seem'd corporal°
  melted
  As breath into the wind. Would they had stay'd!
Banquo. Were such things here as we do speak
  about?
  Or have we eaten on the insane root°
85   That takes the reason prisoner?
Macbeth. Your children shall be kings.
Banquo.   You shall be king.
Macbeth. And thane of Cawdor too. Went it not
  so?
Banquo. To the selfsame tune and words. Who's
  here?
            [*Enter* Ross *and* Angus.]
Ross. The king hath happily receiv'd, Macbeth,
90   The news of thy success, and when he reads
  Thy personal venture in the rebels' fight,
  His wonders and his praises do contend
  Which should be thine or his. Silenc'd° with that,
  In viewing o'er the rest o' the selfsame day,
95 He finds thee in the stout Norweyan ranks,
  Nothing afeard of what thyself didst make,
  Strange images of death. As thick as hail
  Came post with post, and every one did bear
  Thy praises in his kingdom's great defense
  And pour'd them down before him.
100 Angus.   We are sent
  To give thee, from our royal master, thanks;
  Only to herald thee into his sight,
  Not pay thee.
Ross. And for an earnest° of a greater honor,
  He bade me, from him, call thee thane of Caw-
105   dor.
  In which addition,° hail, most worthy thane!
  For it is thine.
Banquo.   What, can the devil speak true?
Macbeth. The thane of Cawdor lives. Why do you
  dress me
  In borrow'd robes?
Angus.   Who was the thane lives yet,
110   But under heavy judgment bears that life
  Which he deserves to lose. Whether he was com-
  bin'd
  With those of Norway, or did line° the rebel

With hidden help and vantage, or that with both
He labor'd in his country's wrack,° I know not,
But treasons capital, confess'd and prov'd,   115
Have overthrown him.
Macbeth. [*Aside*] Glamis, and thane of Cawdor:
  The greatest is behind.°—Thanks for your
  pains.—
  Do you not hope your children shall be kings,
  When those that gave the thane of Cawdor to
  me
  Promis'd no less to them?
Banquo.   That, trusted home,°   120
  Might yet enkindle you unto the crown,
  Besides the thane of Cawdor. But 'tis strange,
  And oftentimes, to win us to our harm,
  The instruments of darkness tell us truths,
  Win us with honest trifles, to betray's   125
  In deepest consequence.
  Cousins, a word, I pray you.
Macbeth.   [*Aside*] Two truths are told,
  As happy prologues to the swelling act
  Of the imperial theme.°—I thank you, gentle-
  men.—
  [*Aside*] This supernatural soliciting   130
  Cannot be ill, cannot be good. If ill,
  Why hath it given me earnest of success,
  Commencing in a truth? I am thane of Cawdor.
  If good, why do I yield to that suggestion
  Whose horrid image doth unfix my hair   135
  And make my seated heart knock at my ribs
  Against the use of nature?° Present fears
  Are less than horrible imaginings.
  My thought, whose murder yet is but fantastical,
  Shakes so my single state of man° that function° 140
  Is smother'd in surmise, and nothing is
  But what is not.
Banquo.   Look, how our partner's rapt.
Macbeth. [*Aside*] If chance will have me king, why,
  chance may crown me
  Without my stir.
Banquo.   New honors come upon him,
  Like our strange° garments, cleave not to their
  mould   145
  But with the aid of use.
Macbeth.   [*Aside*] Come what come may,
  Time and the hour runs through the roughest
  day.
Banquo. Worthy Macbeth, we stay upon your
  leisure.

wrack destruction   behind yet to come
home fully   imperial theme i.e., of the crown
Against . . . nature i.e., unnaturally
single . . . man allusion to the microcosm: man as
  miniature of the universe
function normal activity   strange unaccustomed

---

corporal substantial
insane root insanity-producing; hemlock
Silenc'd i.e., made speechless   *earnest* token
addition title   *line* reinforce

MACBETH. Give me your favor.° My dull brain was wrought
With things forgotten. Kind gentlemen, your pains
150 Are register'd where every day I turn
The leaf to read them. Let us toward the king.
Think upon what hath chanc'd, and at more time,
The interim having weigh'd it, let us speak
Our free hearts each to other.
155 BANQUO.   Very gladly.
MACBETH. Till then, enough. Come, friends.
                                              [Exeunt]

SCENE iv
Forres. The palace.

[*Flourish. Enter* DUNCAN, MALCOLM, DONALBAIN, LENNOX, *and* ATTENDANTS.]
DUNCAN. Is execution done on Cawdor? Are not
Those in commission yet return'd?
MALCOLM.   My liege,
They are not yet come back. But I have spoke
With one that saw him die, who did report
5 That very frankly he confess'd his treasons,
Implor'd your highness' pardon, and set forth
A deep repentance. Nothing in his life
Became him like the leaving it; he died
As one that had been studied in his death,
10 To throw away the dearest thing he ow'd°
As 'twere a careless trifle.
DUNCAN.   There's no art
To find the mind's construction° in his face.
He was a gentleman on whom I built
An absolute trust.
     [*Enter* MACBETH, BANQUO, ROSS, *and* ANGUS.]
                    O worthiest cousin!
15 The sin of my ingratitude even now
Was heavy on me. Thou art so far before,
That swiftest wing of recompense is slow
To overtake thee. Would thou hadst less deserv'd,
That the proportion both of thanks and payment
20 Might have been mine! Only I have left to say,
More is thy due than more than all can pay.
MACBETH. The service and the loyalty I owe,
In doing it, pays itself. Your highness' part
Is to receieve our duties, and our duties
Are to your throne and state children and servants
25 Which do but what they should by doing every thing

Give . . . favor I beg your pardon
ow'd owned   construction disposition

Safe toward° your love and hono'r.
DUNCAN.   Welcome hither.
I have begun to plant thee, and will labor
To make thee full of growing. Noble Banquo,
That hast no less deserv'd, nor must be known   30
No less to have done so, let me infold thee
And hold thee to my heart.
BANQUO.   There if I grow,
The harvest is your own.
DUNCAN.   My plenteous joys,
Wanton° in fulness, seek to hide themselves
In drops of sorrow. Sons, kinsmen, thanes,   35
And you whose places are the nearest, know
We will establish our estate° upon
Our eldest, Malcolm, whom we name hereafter
The Prince of Cumberland. Which honor must
Not unaccompanied invest him only,   40
But signs of nobleness, like stars, shall shine
On all deservers. From hence to Inverness,
And bind us further to you.
MACBETH. The rest is labor which is not used for you.°
I'll be myself the harbinger, and make joyful   45
The hearing of my wife with your approach;
So humbly take my leave.
DUNCAN.   My worthy Cawdor!
MACBETH. [*Aside*] The Prince of Cumberland! That is a step
On which I must fall down, or else o'erleap,
For in my way it lies. Stars, hide your fires;   50
Let not light see my black and deep desires.
The eye wink° at the hand; yet let that be
Which the eye fears, when it is done, to see.
                                              [*Exit*]
DUNCAN. True, worthy Banquo, he is full so valiant,
And in his commendations I am fed;   55
It is a banquet to me. Let's after him,
Whose care is gone before to bid us welcome.
It is a peerless kisman.   [*Flourish. Exeunt*]

SCENE v
Inverness. MACBETH'S *castle.*

[*Enter* LADY MACBETH, *reading a letter.*]
LADY MACBETH.

     They met me in the day of success, and I have
     learned by the perfectest report, they have
     more in them than mortal knowledge. When I

Safe toward to safeguard   *Wanton* uninhibited
establish our estate settle the kingdom on
The rest . . . you i.e., rest not used for you is labor
wink close, not see

burned in desire to question them further, they
made themselves air, into which they vanished.
Whiles I stood rapt in the wonder of it, came
missives from the king, who all-hailed me
Thane of Cawdor, by which title, before, these
weird sisters saluted me, and referred me to the
coming on of time, with Hail, king that shalt be!
This have I thought good to deliver thee, my
dearest partner of greatness, that thou mightst
not lose the dues of rejoicing by being ignorant
of what greatness is promised thee. Lay it to thy
heart, and farewell.

Glamis thou art, and Cawdor, and shalt be
What thou art promis'd. Yet do I fear thy
     nature;
It is too full o' the milk of human kindness°
To catch° the nearest way. Thou wouldst be
     great,
Art not without ambition, but without
The illness° should attend it. What thou wouldst
     highly,
That wouldst thou holily; wouldst not play
     false,
And yet wouldst wrongly win. Thou'dst have,
     great Glamis,
That which° cries "Thus thou must do, if thou
     have it,"
And that which° rather thou dost fear to do
Than wishest should be undone. Hie thee
     hither,
That I may pour my spirits in thine ear
And chastise with the valor of my tongue
All that impedes thee from the golden round,°
Which fate and metaphysical° aid doth seem
To have thee crown'd withal.
                    [Enter a MESSENGER.]
                              What is your tidings?
MESSENGER. The king comes here tonight.
LADY MACBETH.   Thou'rt mad to say it.
     Is not thy master with him? Who, were't so,
     Would have inform'd for preparation.
MESSENGER. So please you, it is true. Our thane is
     coming.
     One of my fellows had the speed of him,°
     Who, almost dead for breath, had scarcely
          more
     Than would make up his message.
LADY MACBETH.   Give him tending;
     He brings great news.   [Exit MESSENGER.]
                         The raven himself is hoarse

That croaks the fatal entrance of Duncan   40
Under my battlements. Come, you spirits
That tend on mortal thoughts, unsex me here,
And fill me, from the crown to the toe, top-full
Of direst cruelty! Make thick my blood,
Stop up th' access and passage to remorse,   45
That no compunctious visitings of nature
Shake my fell° purpose, nor keep peace between
Th' effect and it! Come to my woman's breasts,
And take° my milk for gall, you murd'ring
     ministers,
Wherever in your sightless° substances   50
You wait on° nature's mischief! Come, thick
     night,
And pall° thee in the dunnest smoke of hell,
That my keen knife see not the wound it makes,
Nor heaven peep through the blanket of the
     dark
To cry "Hold, hold!"
               [Enter MACBETH.]
                    Great Glamis! Worthy Cawdor!   55
Greater than both, by the all-hail hereafter!
Thy letters have transported me beyond
This ignorant present, and I feel now
The future in the instant.
MACBETH.   My dearest love,
     Duncan comes here tonight.
LADY MACBETH.   And when goes hence?   60
MACBETH. Tomorrow, as he purposes.
LADY MACBETH.   O, never
     Shall sun that tomorrow see!
     Your face, my thane, is as a book where men
     May read strange matters. To beguile° the time,
     Look like the time;° bear welcome in your eye,   65
     Your hand, your tongue. Look like the innocent
          flower,
     But be the serpent under 't. He that's coming
     Must be provided for. And you shall put
     This night's great business into my dispatch,
     Which shall to all our nights and days to come   70
     Give solely sovereign sway° and masterdom.
MACBETH. We will speak further.
LADY MACBETH.   Only look up clear;°
     To alter favor° ever° is to fear.
     Leave all the rest to me.   [Exeunt]

---

milk . . . kindness i.e., the soft part of humankind
catch take   illness evil taint
That which i.e., the crown   that which i.e., murder
round crown   metaphysical supernatural
had . . . him outran

fell cruel   take exchange
sightless invisible   wait on assist   pall envelop
beguile deceive
Look . . . time i.e., let your appearance fit the occasion
solely . . . sway absolute rule   clear innocently
favor facial expression   ever always

SCENE vi
Before Macbeth's *castle*.

[*Hautboys and torches. Enter* Duncan, Malcolm,
Donalbain, Banquo, Lennox, Macduff, Ross,
Angus, *and* Attendants.]
Duncan. This castle hath a pleasant seat; the air
Nimbly and sweetly recommends itself
Unto our gentle senses.
Banquo.   This guest of summer,
The temple-haunting martlet, does approve°
By his lov'd mansionry that the heaven's
5   breath
Smells wooingly here. No jutty, frieze,
Buttress, nor coign of vantage,° but this bird
Hath made his pendent bed and procreant
cradle.°
Where they most breed and haunt, I have
observ'd
The air is delicate.
                    [*Enter* Lady Macbeth.]
10 Duncan.   See, see, our honor'd hostess!
The love that follows us sometime is our
trouble,°
Which still we thank as love. Herein I teach you
How you shall bid God 'ild us° for your pains,
And thank us for your trouble.
Lady Macbeth.   All our service
15   In every point twice done and then done double
Were poor and single business to contend
Against those honors deep and broad wherewith
Your majesty loads our house. For those of old,
And the late dignities heap'd up to them,
We rest your hermits,°
20 Duncan.   Where's the thane of Cawdor?
We cours'd° him at the heels, and had a purpose
To be his purveyor.° But he rides well,
And his great love, sharp as his spur, hath holp
him
To his home before us. Fair and noble hostess,
We are your guest tonight.
25 Lady Macbeth.   Your servants ever
Have theirs, themselves, and what is theirs, in
compt,°
To make their audit at your highness' pleasure,
Still° to return your own.

Duncan.   Give me your hand;
Conduct me to mine host. We love him highly,
And shall continue our graces towards him.   30
By your leave, hostess.   [*Exeunt*]

SCENE vii
Macbeth's *castle*.

[*Hautboys and torches. Enter a* Sewer,° *and divers*
Servants *with dishes and service, and pass over
the stage. Then enter* Macbeth.]
Macbeth. If it were done when 'tis done, then
'twere well
It were done quickly. If th' assassination
Could trammel up° the consequence, and catch,
With his surcease,° success; that but this blow
Might be the be-all and the end-all here,   5
But here, upon this bank and shoal of time,
We'd jump° the life to come. But in these cases
We still have judgment here, that we but teach
Bloody instructions, which being taught return
To plague th' inventor. This even-handed
justice   10
Commends th' ingredients of our poison'd
chalice
To our own lips. He's here in double trust:
First, as I am his kinsman and his subject,
Strong both against the deed; then, as his host,
Who should against his murderer shut the door,   15
Not bear the knife myself. Besides, this Duncan
Hath borne his faculties° so meek, hath been
So clear in his great office, that his virtues
Will plead like angels, trumpet-tongu'd, against
The deep damnation of his taking-off,   20
And pity, like a naked new-born babe
Striding the blast,° or heaven's cherubin hors'd
Upon the sightless couriers° of the air,
Shall blow the horrid deed in every eye,
That° tears shall drown the wind. I have no spur 25
To prick the sides of my intent, but only
Vaulting ambition, which o'erleaps itself
And falls on th' other.°
                    [*Enter* Lady Macbeth.]
                    How now! What news?
Lady Macbeth. He has almost supp'd. Why have
you left the chamber?
Macbeth. Hath he ask'd for me?
Lady Macbeth.   Know you not he has?   30

---

approve prove   coign of vantage advantageous corner
procreant cradle breeding place
The love . . . trouble i.e., the love my subjects have for me
   sometimes puts them to trouble, which I always thank
   as love, not trouble
'ild us reward me   hermits i.e., to pray for you
cours'd chased   purveyor herald
in compt accountable, ready   Still always

---

sewer butler
trammel up enmesh, prevent
his surcease Duncan's death   jump risk
faculties powers   Striding the blast riding the wind
sightless couriers invisible messengers, i.e., the winds
That so that   other other side

MACBETH. We will proceed no further in this
   business.
He hath honor'd me of late, and I have bought°
Golden opinions from all sorts of people,
Which would be worn now in their newest
   gloss,
Not cast aside so soon.

35 LADY MACBETH.   Was the hope drunk
Wherein you dress'd yourself? Hath it slept
   since?
And wakes it now, to look so green and pale
At what it did so freely? From this time
Such I account thy love. Art thou afeard
40 To be the same in thine own act and valor
As thou art in desire? Wouldst thou have that
Which thou esteem'st the ornament of life,
And live a coward in thine own esteem,
Letting "I dare not" wait upon "I would,"
Like the poor cat i' th' adage?

45 MACBETH.   Prithee, peace.
I dare do all that may become a man;
Who dares do more is none.

LADY MACBETH.   What beast was 't then
That made your break this enterprise to me?
When you durst do it, then you were a man;
And, to be more than what you were, you
50   would
Be so much more the man. Nor time nor° place
Did then adhere,° and yet you would make both.
They have made themselves, and that their
   fitness now
Does unmake you. I have given suck, and know
55 How tender 'tis to love the babe that milks me.
I would, while it was smiling in my face,

Have pluck'd my nipple from his boneless gums
And dash'd the brains out, had I so sworn as you
Have done to this.
MACBETH.   If we should fail?
LADY MACBETH.   We fail!
But screw your courage to the sticking-place,   60
And we'll not fail. When Duncan is asleep—
Whereto the rather shall his day's hard journey
Soundly invite him—his two chamberlains
Will I with wine and wassail° so convince,
That memory, the warder of the brain,   65
Shall be a fume, and the receipt° of reason
A limbec° only. When in swinish sleep
Their drenched natures lie as in a death,
What cannot you and I perform upon
Th' unguarded Duncan? What not put upon   70
His spongy officers, who shall bear the guilt
Of our great quell?°
MACBETH.   Bring forth men-children only,
For thy undaunted mettle should compose
Nothing but males. Will it not be receiv'd,
When we have mark'd with blood those sleepy
   two   75
Of his own chamber, and us'd their very daggers,
That they have done 't?
LADY MACBETH.   Who dares receive it other,
As we shall make our griefs and clamor roar
Upon his death?
MACBETH.   I am settled, and bend up°
Each corporal° agent to this terrible feat.   80
Away, and mock the time with fairest show:
False face must hide what the false heart doth
   know.   [Exeunt]

---

bought earned
Nor . . . nor neither . . . nor   *adhere* suit

wassail carousing   *convince* subdue
receipt receptacle, i.e., the brain   *limbec* still
quell killing   *bend up* stiffen   *corporal* bodily

ACT II

SCENE i
Inverness. Court of MACBETH's *castle.*

[*Enter* BANQUO, *and* FLEANCE *bearing a torch
before him.*]
BANQUO. How goes the night, boy?
FLEANCE. The moon is down; I have not heard
   the clock.
BANQUO. And she goes down at twelve.
FLEANCE.   I take 't 'tis later, sir.

BANQUO. Hold, take my sword. There's husbandry°
   in heaven—
Their candles are all out. Take thee that too.   5
A heavy summons lies like lead upon me,
And yet I would not sleep. Merciful powers,
Restrain in me the cursed thoughts that nature
Gives way to in repose!
[*Enter* MACBETH, *and a* SERVANT *with a torch.*]

husbandry thrift

Give me my sword.

10   Who's there?

MACBETH.   A friend.

BANQUO.   What, sir, not yet at rest? The king's
   abed.

   He hath been in unusual pleasure, and
   Sent forth great largess to your offices.°

15   This diamond he greets your wife withal,
   By the name of most kind hostess, and shut up°
   In measureless content.

MACBETH.   Being unprepar'd,
   Our will became the servant to defect,°
   Which else should free° have wrought.

BANQUO.   All's well.

20   I dreamt last night of the three weird sisters.
   To you they have show'd some truth.

MACBETH.   I think not of them.
   Yet, when we can entreat an hour to serve,
   We would spend it in some words upon that
      business
   If you would grant the time.

BANQUO.   At your kind'st leisure.

MACBETH. If you shall cleave to my consent, when
25   'tis,°
   It shall make honor for you.

BANQUO.   So I lose none
   In seeking to augment it, but still keep
   My bosom franchis'd° and allegiance clear,
   I shall be counsel'd.

MACBETH.   Good repose the while!

30 BANQUO. Thanks, sir. The like to you!
                     [Exeunt BANQUO and FLEANCE.]

MACBETH. Go bid thy mistress, when my drink is
      ready,
   She strike upon the bell. Get thee to bed.
                              [Exit SERVANT.]
   Is this a dagger which I see before me,
   The handle toward my hand? Come, let me
      clutch thee.

35   I have thee not, and yet I see thee still.
   Art thou not, fatal vision, sensible
   To feeling as to sight? Or art thou but
   A dagger of the mind, a false creation
   Proceeding from the heat-oppressed brain?

40   I see thee yet, in form as palpable
   As this which now I draw.
   Thou marshal'st me the way that I was going,
   And such an instrument I was to use.
   Mine eyes are made the fools o' th' other senses,

45   Or else worth all the rest. I see thee still,

And on thy blade and dudgeon° gouts° of blood,
Which was not so before. There's no such thing:
It is the bloody business which informs°
Thus to mine eyes. Now o'er the one half-world
Nature seems dead, and wicked dreams abuse   50
The curtain'd sleep. Witchcraft celebrates
Pale Hecate's offerings, and wither'd murder,
Alarum'd by his sentinel, the wolf,
Whose howl's his watch, thus with his stealthy
      pace,
With Tarquin's° ravishing strides, towards his
      design   55
Moves like a ghost. Thou sure and firm-set
      earth,
Hear not my steps, which way they walk, for
      fear
Thy very stones prate of my whereabout
And take the present horror from the time,
Which now suits with it. Whiles I threat, he
      lives.—   60
Words to the heat of deeds too cold breath gives.
                              [A bell rings.]
I go, and it is done. The bell invites me.
Hear it not, Duncan, for it is a knell
That summons thee to heaven, or to hell.
                                        [Exit]

SCENE ii
The same.

[Enter LADY MACBETH.]

LADY MACBETH. That which hath made them
      drunk hath made me bold;
   What hath quench'd them hath given me fire.
      Hark! Peace!
   It was the owl that shriek'd, the fatal bellman,
   Which gives the stern'st good night. He is
      about it.
   The doors are open, and the surfeited grooms   5
   Do mock their charge with snores. I have
      drugg'd their possets,°
   That death and nature do contend about them,
   Whether they live or die.

MACBETH.   [Within] Who's there? What, ho!

LADY MACBETH. Alack, I am afraid they have
      awak'd
   And 'tis not done. Th' attempt and not the
      deed   10
   Confounds° us. Hark! I laid their daggers
      ready;

He could not miss 'em. Had he not resembled
My father as he slept, I had done 't.
                [*Enter* MACBETH.]
                                My husband!
MACBETH. I have done the deed. Didst thou not
    hear a noise?
LADY MACBETH. I heard the owl scream and the
15   crickets cry.
    Did not you speak?
MACBETH.   When?
LADY MACBETH.   Now.
MACBETH.   As I descended?
LADY MACBETH. Aye.
MACBETH. Hark!
    Who lies i' the second chamber?
LADY MACBETH.   Donalbain.
20 MACBETH. This is a sorry sight.
                [*Looking on his hands.*]
LADY MACBETH. A foolish thought, to say a sorry
    sight.
MACBETH. There's one did laugh in 's sleep, and
    one cried "Murder!"
    That they did wake each other. I stood and heard
    them.
    But they did say their prayers, and address'd
    them
    Again to sleep.
25 LADY MACBETH.   There are two lodg'd together.
MACBETH. One cried "God bless us!" and "Amen"
    the other,
    As they had seen me with these hangman's
    hands.°
    Listening their fear, I could not say "Amen,"
    When they did say "God bless us!"
30 LADY MACBETH. Consider it not so deeply.
MACBETH. But wherefore could not I pronounce
    "Amen"?
    I had most need of blessing, and "Amen"
    Stuck in my throat.
LADY MACBETH. These deeds must not be thought
    After these ways; so, it will make us mad.
MACBETH. Methought I heard a voice cry "Sleep
35   no more!
    Macbeth does murder sleep"—th' innocent
    sleep,
    Sleep that knits up the ravel'd sleave° of care,
    The death of each day's life, sore labor's bath,
    Balm of hurt minds, great nature's second°
    course,
    Chief nourisher in life's feast—
40 LADY MACBETH   What do you mean?

MACBETH. Still it cried "Sleep no more!" to all
    the house:
    "Glamis hath murder'd sleep, and therefore
    Cawdor
    Shall sleep no more. Macbeth shall sleep no
    more."
LADY MACBETH. Who was it that thus cried?
    Why, worthy thane,
    You do unbend your noble strength to think   45
    So brainsickly of things. Go get some water
    And wash this filthy witness from your hand.
    Why did you bring these daggers from the
    place?
    They must lie there. Go carry them, and smear
    The sleepy grooms with blood.
MACBETH.   I'll go no more.   50
    I am afraid to think what I have done;
    Look on 't again I dare not.
LADY MACBETH.   Infirm of purpose!
    Give me the daggers. The sleeping and the dead
    Are but as pictures: 'tis the eye of childhood
    That fears a painted devil. If he do bleed,   55
    I'll gild the faces of the grooms withal,
    For it must seem their guilt.
                [*Exit. Knocking within.*]
MACBETH.   Whence is that knocking?
    How is 't with me, when every noise appalls me?
    What hands are here? Ha! They pluck out mine
    eyes!
    Will all great Neptune's ocean wash this blood   60
    Clean from my hand? No; this my hand will
    rather
    The multitudinous seas incarnadine,°
    Making the green one red.
                [*Re-enter* LADY MACBETH.]
LADY MACBETH. My hands are of your color, but I
    shame
    To wear a heart so white. [*Knocking within*] I hear
    a knocking   65
    At the south entry. Retire we to our chamber.
    A little water clears us of this deed.
    How easy is it then! Your constancy
    Hath left you unattended.° [*Knocking within*]
    Hark! More knocking.
    Get on your nightgown, lest occasion call us   70
    And show us to be watchers.° Be not lost
    So poorly in your thoughts.
MACBETH. To know my deed, 'twere best not
    know myself.
                [*Knocking within.*]
    Wake Duncan with thy knocking! I would thou
    couldst!   [*Exeunt*]

hangman's hands   i.e., bloody (hangmen also
    disemboweled the victim)
sleave thread   *second* i.e., main

incarnadine make red
Your . . . unattended i.e., your wits have deserted you
watchers i.e., still up and about

SCENE iii
The same.

[*Enter a* PORTER. *Knocking within.*]
PORTER. Here's a knocking indeed! If a man were
porter of hellgate, he should have old° turning
the key. [*Knocking within*] Knock, knock, knock!
Who's there, i' the name of Beelzebub? Here's a
5 farmer that hanged himself on th' expectation of
plenty. Come in time; have napkins enow°
about you; here you'll sweat for 't. [*Knocking
within*] Knock, knock! Who's there, in th' other
devil's name? Faith, here's an equivocator that
10 could swear in both the scales against either
scale, who committed treason enough for God's
sake, yet could not equivocate to heaven. O,
come in, equivocator. [*Knocking within*] Knock,
knock, knock! Who's there? Faith, here's an
15 English tailor come hither for stealing out of a
French hose.° Come in, tailor; here you may
roast your goose.° [*Knocking within*] Knock,
knock; never at quiet! What are you? But this
place is too cold for hell. I'll devil-porter it no
20 further. I had thought to have let in some of all
professions that go the primrose way to the
everlasting bonfire. [*Knocking within*] Anon,
anon! I pray you, remember the porter.
[*Opens the gate.*]
[*Enter* MACDUFF *and* LENNOX.]
MACDUFF. Was it so late, friend, ere you went to
bed,
25 That you do lie so late?
PORTER. Faith, sir, we were carousing till the
second cock, and drink, sir, is a great provoker of
three things.
MACDUFF. What three things does drink especially
provoke?
30 PORTER. Marry, sir, nose-painting, sleep, and
urine. Lechery, sir, it provokes and unprovokes;
it provokes the desire, but it takes away the
performance: therefore much drink may be
said to be an equivocator with lechery. It makes
35 him and mars him; it sets him on and it takes
him off; it persuades him and disheartens him;
makes him stand to and not stand to; in conclusion, equivocates him in a sleep, and giving
him the lie, leaves him.
40 MACDUFF. I believe drink gave thee the lie° last
night.

old enough   *napkins enow* towels enough
French hose tight breeches
second cock 3 A.M.   *goose* pressing iron (with pun)
gave . . . lie laid you out (with pun)

PORTER. That it did, sir, i' the very throat on me.
But I requited him for his lie, and, I think,
being too strong for him, though he took up my
legs sometime, yet I made a shift to cast him.°   45
MACDUFF. Is thy master stirring?
[*Enter* MACBETH.]
Our knocking has awak'd him; here he comes.
LENNOX. Good morrow, noble sir.
MACBETH.   Good morrow both.
MACDUFF. Is the king stirring worthy thane?
MACBETH.   Not yet.
MACDUFF. He did command me to call timely on
him.   50
I have almost slipp'd the hour.
MACBETH.   I'll bring you to him.
MACDUFF. I know this is a joyful trouble to you,
But yet 'tis one.
MACBETH. The labor we delight in physics° pain.
This is the door.
MACDUFF.   I'll make so bold to call,   55
For 'tis my limited service.°   [*Exit*]
LENNOX. Goes the king hence today?
MACBETH.   He does; he did appoint so.
LENNOX. The night has been unruly. Where we
lay
Our chimneys were blown down, and, as they
say,
Lamentings heard i' th' air, strange screams of
death,·   60
And prophesying with accents terrible
Of dire combustion° and confus'd events
New hatch'd to the woeful time. The obscure
bird°
Clamor'd the livelong night. Some say the earth
Was feverous and did shake.
MACBETH.   'Twas a rough night.   65
LENNOX. My young remembrance cannot parallel
A fellow to it.
[*Re-enter* MACDUFF.]
MACDUFF. O horror, horror, horror! Tongue nor
heart
Cannot conceive nor name thee.
MACBETH *and* LENNOX.   What's the matter?
MACDUFF. Confusion now hath made his master-
piece.   70
Most sacrilegious murder hath broke ope
The Lord's anointed temple and stole thence
The life o' the building.
MACBETH.   What is 't you say? The life?
LENNOX. Mean you his majesty?
MACDUFF. Approach the chamber and destroy
your sight   75

made . . . him managed to throw (vomit) him (with pun)
physics cures   *limited service* assigned task
combustion uproar   *obscure bird* owl

With a new Gorgon.° Do not bid me speak;
See, and then speak yourselves.

> [*Exeunt* MACBETH *and* LENNOX.]
> Awake, awake!

Ring the alarum bell. Murder and treason!
Banquo and Donalbain! Malcolm! Awake!
80 Shake off this downy sleep, death's counterfeit,
And look on death itself! Up, up, and see
The great doom's image!° Malcolm! Banquo!
As from your graves rise up and walk like sprites
To countenance° this horror. Ring the bell.

> [*Bell rings.*]

> [*Enter* LADY MACBETH.]

85 LADY MACBETH. What's the business,
That such a hideous trumpet calls to parley
The sleepers of the house? Speak, speak!
MACDUFF. O gentle lady,
'Tis not for you to hear what I can speak.
90 The repetition, in a woman's ear,
Would murder as it fell.

> [*Enter* BANQUO.]

> O Banquo, Banquo!

Our royal master's murder'd.
LADY MACBETH.   Woe, alas!
What, in our house?
BANQUO.   Too cruel anywhere.
Dear Duff, I prithee, contradict thyself,
95 And say it is not so.

> [*Re-enter* MACBETH *and* LENNOX, *with* ROSS.]

MACBETH. Had I but died an hour before this
chance,
I had liv'd a blessed time; for from this instant
There's nothing serious in mortality.
All is but toys; renown and grace is dead;
100 The wine of life is drawn, and the mere lees°
Is left this vault° to brag of.

> [*Enter* MALCOLM *and* DONALBAIN.]

DONALBAIN. What is amiss?
MACBETH.   You are and do not know 't.
The spring, the head, the fountain of your
blood
Is stopp'd; the very source of it is stopp'd.
MACDUFF. Your royal father's murder'd.
105 MALCOLM.   O, by whom?
LENNOX. Those of his chamber, as it seem'd, had
done 't.
Their hands and faces were all badg'd with
blood;
So were their daggers, which unwip'd we found
Upon their pillows.

They star'd and were distracted; no man's life 110
Was to be trusted with them.
MACBETH. O, yet I do repent me of my fury
That I did kill them.
MACDUFF.   Wherefore did you so?
MACBETH. Who can be wise, amaz'd, temp'rate
and furious,
Loyal and neutral, in a moment? No man. 115
The expedition° of my violent love
Outrun the pauser, reason. Here lay Duncan,
His silver skin lac'd with his golden blood,
And his gash'd stabs look'd like a breach in
nature
For ruin's wasteful entrance; there, the mur-
derers, 120
Steep'd in the colors of their trade, their daggers
Unmannerly breech'd° with gore. Who could
refrain,
That had a heart to love, and in that heart
Courage to make 's love known?
LADY MACBETH.   Help me hence, ho!
MACDUFF. Look to the lady.
MALCOLM. [*Aside to* DONALBAIN] Why do we hold
our tongues, 125
That most may claim this argument° for ours?
DONALBAIN. [*Aside to* MALCOLM] What should be
spoken here, where our fate,
Hid in an auger hole,° may rush and seize us?
Let's away;
Our tears are not yet brew'd.
MALCOLM. [*Aside to* DONALBAIN] Nor our strong
sorrow 130
Upon the foot of motion.°
BANQUO.   Look to the lady.

> [LADY MACBETH *is carried out.*]

And when we have our naked frailties hid,°
That suffer in exposure, let us meet
And question this most bloody piece of work
To know it further. Fears and scruples° shake us. 135
In the great hand of God I stand, and thence
Against the undivulg'd pretense° I fight
Of treasonous malice.
MACDUFF.   And so do I.
ALL.   So all.
MACBETH. Let's briefly put on manly readiness,
And meet i' the hall together.
ALL.   Well contented. 140

> [*Exeunt all but* MALCOLM *and* DONALBAIN.]

Gorgon Medusa, sight of whom turned gazers to stone
doom's image image of Doomsday
countenance look on   *lees* dregs
vault world

expedition speed
breech'd clothed   *argument* subject of conversation
auger hole i.e., small, unpredictable place
Upon . . . motion set in action
naked frailties hid (1) dressed ourselves; (2) controlled
our emotions
scruples misgivings   *pretense* intents

MALCOLM. What will you do? Let's not consort
  with them.
    To show an unfelt sorrow is an office
    Which the false man does easy. I'll to England.
DONALBAIN. To Ireland, I; our separated fortune
145 Shall keep us both the safer. Where we are,
    There's daggers in men's smiles. The near in
    blood,
    The nearer bloody.
MALCOLM.   This murderous shaft that's shot
    Hath not yet lighted, and our safest way
    Is to avoid the aim. Therefore to horse,
150 And let us not be dainty of leave-taking,
    But shift° away. There's warrant in° that theft
    Which steals itself when there's no mercy left.
                                  [Exeunt]

SCENE iv
Outside MACBETH's castle.

[*Enter* ROSS *with an* OLD MAN.]

OLD MAN. Threescore and ten I can remember
  well,
    Within the volume of which time I have seen
    Hours dreadful and things strange, but this sore
    night
    Hath trifled former knowings.
ROSS.   Ah, good father,
    Thou seest, the heavens, as troubled with man's
5   act,
    Threaten his bloody stage. By the clock 'tis day,
    And yet dark night strangles the traveling
    lamp.°
    Is 't night's predominance, or the day's shame,
    That darkness does the face of earth entomb
    When living light should kiss it?
10 OLD MAN.   'Tis unnatural,
    Even like the deed that's done. On Tuesday last
    A falcon tow'ring in her pride of place
    Was by a mousing owl hawk'd at and kill'd.
ROSS. And Duncan's horses—a thing most strange
    and certain—

Beauteous and swift, the minions° of their race,   15
    Turn'd wild in nature, broke their stalls, flung
    out,
    Contending 'gainst obedience, as they would
    make
    War with mankind.
OLD MAN.   'Tis said they eat each other.
ROSS. They did so, to the amazement of mine eyes,
    That look'd upon 't.
          [*Enter* MACDUFF.]
               Here comes the good Macduff.   20
    How goes the world, sir, now?
MACDUFF.   Why, see you not?
ROSS. Is 't known who did this more than bloody
    deed?
MACDUFF. Those that Macbeth hath slain.
ROSS.   Alas, the day!
    What good could they pretend?
MACDUFF.   They were suborn'd.°
    Malcolm and Donalbain, the king's two sons,   25
    Are stol'n away and fled, which puts upon them
    Suspicion of the deed.
ROSS.   'Gainst nature still.
    Thriftless ambition, that wilt ravin up°
    Thine own life's means! Then 'tis most like
    The sovereignty will fall upon Macbeth.   30
MACDUFF. He is already nam'd, and gone to Scone
    To be invested.°
ROSS.   Where is Duncan's body?
MACDUFF. Carried to Colmekill,
    The sacred storehouse° of his predecessors
    And guardian of their bones.
ROSS.   Will you to Scone? 35
MACDUFF. No, cousin, I'll to Fife.
ROSS.   Well, I will thither.
MACDUFF. Well, may you see things well done
    there. Adieu!
    Lest our old robes sit easier than our new!
ROSS. Farewell, father.
OLD MAN. God's benison go with you, and with
    those   40
    That would make good of bad and friends of
    foes!   [*Exeunt*]

---

shift slip   *warrant in* justification for
traveling lamp i.e., the sun

minions darlings   *suborn'd* bribed
ravin up devour   *invested* crowned
storehouse tomb

ACT III

SCENE i
Forres. The palace.

[*Enter* BANQUO.]

BANQUO. Thou hast it now: king, Cawdor, Glamis, all,
     As the weird women promis'd, and I fear
     Thou play'dst most foully for 't. Yet it was said
     It should not stand in thy posterity,
5   But that myself should be the root and father
     Of many kings. If there come truth from them—
     As upon thee, Macbeth, their speeches shine—
     Why, by the verities on thee made good,
     May they not be my oracles as well
10   And set me up in hope? But hush, no more.
     [*Sennet sounded. Enter* MACBETH, *as king;* LADY
         MACBETH, *as queen;* LENNOX, ROSS, LORDS,
             LADIES, *and* ATTENDANTS.]
MACBETH. Here's our chief guest.
LADY MACBETH.   If he had been forgotten,
     It had been as a gap in our great feast,
     And all-thing° unbecoming.
MACBETH. Tonight we hold a solemn° supper, sir,
     And I'll request your presence.
15   BANQUO.   Let your highness
     Command upon me, to the which my duties
     Are with a most indissoluble tie
     Forever knit.
MACBETH. Ride you this afternoon?
BANQUO.   Aye, my good lord.
MACBETH. We should have else desir'd your good
20   advice,
     Which still° hath been both grave and pros-
         perous,
     In this day's council; but we'll take tomorrow.
     Is 't far you ride?
BANQUO. As far, my lord, as will fill up the time
     'Twixt this and supper. Go not my horse the
25   better,
     I must become a borrower of the night
     For a dark hour or twain.
MACBETH.   Fail not our feast.
BANQUO. My lord, I will not.
MACBETH. We hear our bloody cousins are be-
         stow'd
30   In England and in Ireland, not confessing

Their cruel parricide, filling their hearers
With strange invention. But of that tomorrow,
When therewithal we shall have cause of state
Craving us jointly. Hie you to horse. Adieu
Till you return at night. Goes Fleance with you?   35
BANQUO. Aye, my good lord. Our time does call
     upon 's.
MACBETH. I wish your horses swift and sure of foot,
     And so I do commend you to their backs.
     Farewell.   [*Exit* BANQUO.]
     Let every man be master of his time   40
     Till seven at night. To make society
     The sweeter welcome, we will keep ourself
     Till suppertime alone. While° then, God be
         with you!
         [*Exeunt all but* MACBETH *and an* ATTENDANT.]
     Sirrah, a word with you. Attend those men
     Our pleasure?   45
ATTENDANT. They are, my lord, without the palace
     gate.
MACBETH. Bring them before us.
                           [*Exit* ATTENDANT.]
                 To be thus is nothing;
     But to be safely thus! Our fears in Banquo
     Stick deep, and in his royalty of nature
     Reigns that which would be fear'd. 'Tis much he
         dares,   50
     And, to that dauntless temper of his mind,
     He hath a wisdom that doth guide his valor
     To act in safety. There is none but he
     Whose being I do fear, and under him
     My Genius is rebuk'd,° as it is said   55
     Mark Antony's was by Cæsar.° He chid the sisters
     When first they put the name of king upon me,
     And bade them speak to him; then prophet-like
     They hail'd him father to a line of kings.
     Upon my head they plac'd a fruitless crown   60
     And put a barren scepter in my gripe,
     Thence to be wrench'd with an unlineal hand,
     No son of mine succeeding. If 't be so,
     For Banquo's issue have I fil'd° my mind,
     For them the gracious Duncan have I murder'd, 65
     Put rancors° in the vessel of my peace

---

all-thing altogether   *solemn* formal (state)
still always

While until
Genius is rebuk'd guardian spirit is intimidated
Cæsar Octavius, not Julius (see *Antony and Cleopatra*,
     II, iii)
fil'd defiled   *rancors* bitter dregs

Only for them, and mine eternal jewel°
Given to the common enemy of man,
To make them kings, the seed of Banquo kings!
70 Rather than so, come fate into the list,°
And champion me to th' utterance!° Who's
there?
[*Re-enter* Attendant, *with* Two Murderers.]
Now go to the door, and stay there till we call.
[*Exit* Attendant.]
Was it not yesterday we spoke together?
First Murderer. It was, so please your highness.
Macbeth.   Well then, now
75 Have you consider'd of my speeches? Know
That it was he in the times past which held you
So under fortune, which you thought had been
Our innocent self. This I made good to you
In our last conference; pass'd in probation° with
you,
How you were borne in hand,° how cross'd, the
80 instruments,
Who wrought with them, and all things else that
might
To half a soul and to a notion craz'd
Say "Thus did Banquo."
First Murderer.   You made it known to us.
Macbeth. I did so, and went further, which is now
85 Our point of second meeting. Do you find
Your patience so predominant in your nature
That you can let this go? Are you so gospel'd°
To pray for this good man and for his issue,
Whose heavy hand hath bow'd you to the grave
✓ And beggar'd yours forever?
90 First Murderer.   We are men, my liege.
Macbeth. Aye, in the catalogue ye go for men,
As hounds and greyhounds, mongrels, spaniels,
curs,
Shoughs, waterrugs, and demiwolves are clept°
All by the name of dogs. The valu'd file°
95 Distinguishes the swift, the slow, the subtle,
The housekeeper, the hunter, every one
According to the gift which bounteous nature
Hath in him clos'd,° whereby he does receive
Particular addition° from the bill
100 That writes them all alike. And so of men.
Now if you have a station in the file
Not i' the worst rank of manhood, say it,
And I will put that business in your bosoms

Whose execution takes your enemy off,
Grapples you to the heart and love of us   105
Who wear our health but sickly in his life,
Which in his death were perfect.
Second Murderer.   I am one, my liege,
Whom the vile blows and buffets of the world
Have so incens'd that I am reckless what
I do to spite the world.
First Murderer.   And I another   110
So weary with disasters, tugg'd with fortune,
That I would set my life on any chance
To mend it or be rid on 't.
Macbeth.   Both of you
Know Banquo was your enemy.
Both Murderers.   True, my lord.
Macbeth. So is he mine, and in such bloody dis-
tance°   115
That every minute of his being thrusts
Against my near'st of life.° And though I could
With barefac'd power sweep him from my sight
And bid my will avouch° it, yet I must not,
For certain friends that are both his and mine,   120
Whose loves I may not drop, but wail his fall
Who I myself struck down. And thence it is
That I to your assistance do make love,
Masking the business from the common eye
For sundry weighty reasons.
Second Murderer.   We shall, my lord,   125
Perform what you command us.
First Murderer.   Though our lives—
Macbeth. Your spirits shine through you. Within
this hour at most
I will advise you where to plant yourselves,
Acquaint you with the perfect spy o' the time,°
The moment on 't;° for 't must be done tonight, 130
And something° from the palace—always
thought
That I require a clearness.° And with him—
To leave no rubs nor botches in the work—
Fleance his son, that keeps him company,
Whose absence is no less material to me   135
Than is his father's, must embrace the fate
Of that dark hour. Resolve yourselves apart.
I'll come to you anon.
Both Murderers.   We are resolv'd, my lord.
Macbeth. I'll call upon you straight. Abide within.
[*Exeunt* Murderers.]
It is concluded. Banquo, thy soul's flight,   140
If it find heaven, must find it out tonight. [*Exit*]

eternal jewel i.e., immortal soul
list place of combat   *utterance* uttermost
pass'd in probation gave proofs
borne in hand treated highhandedly
so gospel'd so cowed by Christian teachings
clept called   *valu'd file* qualitative ranking
clos'd enclosed; i.e., bred
Particular addition individual characteristic

distance difference, hostility
near'st of life innermost being   *avouch* condone
Acquaint . . . time advise you of the exact time
on 't of it   *something* somewhat
always . . . clearness always remembering that I require
to be in the clear

SCENE ii
The palace.

[*Enter* LADY MACBETH *and a* SERVANT.]

LADY MACBETH. Is Banquo gone from court?

SERVANT. Aye, madam, but returns again tonight.

LADY MACBETH. Say to the king I would attend his leisure
For a few words.

SERVANT.   Madam, I will.   [*Exit*]

LADY MACBETH.   Naught's had, all's spent,

5   Where our desire is got without content.
'Tis safer to be that which we destroy
Than by destruction dwell in doubtful joy.

[*Enter* MACBETH.]

How now, my lord! Why do you keep alone,
Of sorriest fancies your companions making,
Using those thoughts which should indeed have
10   died
With them they think on? Things without all
remedy
Should be without regard. What's done is done.

MACBETH. We have scotch'd° the snake, not kill'd
it.
She'll close° and be herself, whilst our poor
malice
15   Remains in danger of her former° tooth.
But let the frame of things disjoint,° both the
worlds suffer,
Ere we will eat our meal in fear and sleep
In the affliction of these terrible dreams
That shake us nightly. Better be with the dead,
20   Whom we, to gain our peace, have sent to peace,
Than on the torture of the mind to lie
In restless ecstasy. Duncan is in his grave;
After life's fitful fever he sleeps well.
Treason has done his worst. Nor° steel, nor
poison,
25   Malice domestic, foreign levy,° nothing
Can touch him further.

LADY MACBETH.   Come on,
Gentle my lord, sleek o'er your rugged looks;
Be bright and jovial among your guests tonight.

MACBETH. So shall I, love, and so, I pray, be you.
30   Let your remembrance apply to Banquo;
Present him eminence,° both with eye and
tongue.
Unsafe the while,° that we

Must lave our honors in these flattering streams
And make our faces vizards° to our hearts,
Disguising what they are.

LADY MACBETH.   You must leave this.   35

MACBETH. O, full of scorpions is my mind, dear
wife!
Thou know'st that Banquo, and his Fleance,
lives.

LADY MACBETH. But in them nature's copy's not
eterne.°

MACBETH. There's comfort yet; they are assailable.
Then be thou jocund. Ere the bat hath flown   40
His cloister'd flight, ere to black Hecate's sum-
mons
The shard-borne° beetle with his drowsy hums
Hath rung night's yawning peal, there shall be
done
A deed of dreadful note.

LADY MACBETH.   What's to be done?

MACBETH. Be innocent of the knowledge, dearest
chuck,   45
Till thou applaud the deed. Come, seeling°
night,
Scarf up the tender eye of pitiful day,
And with thy bloody and invisible hand
Cancel and tear to pieces that great bond
Which keeps me pale! Light thickens, and the
crow   50
Makes wing to the rooky° wood.
Good things of day begin to droop and drowse,
Whiles night's black agents to their preys do
rouse.
Thou marvel'st at my words. But hold thee still;
Things bad begun make strong themselves by
ill.   55
So, prithee, go with me.   [*Exeunt*]

SCENE iii
A park near the palace.

[*Enter* THREE MURDERERS.]

FIRST MURDERER. But who did bid thee join with
us?

THIRD MURDERER.   Macbeth.

SECOND MURDERER. He° needs not our mistrust,
since he delivers
Our offices° and what we have to do

---

scotch'd gashed   close heal over
former i.e., as before
frame . . . disjoint universe fall apart   Nor neither
foreign levy i.e., threats from abroad
Present him eminence i.e., make over him
Unsafe the while so insecure is the time

vizards masks
copy's . . . not eterne pattern is not perpetual; i.e., they
can be destroyed
shardborne i.e., borne on shellike wings
seeling sewing-shut   rooky i.e., full of rocks
He i.e., Third Murderer   offices duties

To the direction just.°
FIRST MURDERER.   Then stand with us.
The west yet glimmers with some streaks of
5   day.
Now spurs the lated° traveler apace
To gain the timely inn, and near approaches
The subject of our watch.
THIRD MURDERER.   Hark! I hear horses.
BANQUO. [Within] Give us a light there, ho!
SECOND MURDERER.   Then 'tis he. The rest
10 That are within the note of expectation
Already are i' the court.
FIRST MURDERER.   His horses go about.
THIRD MURDERER. Almost a mile. But he does
usually—
So all men do—from hence to the palace gate
Make it their walk.
SECOND MURDERER.   A light, a light!
    [Enter BANQUO and FLEANCE with a torch.]
THIRD MURDERER.   'Tis he.
15 FIRST MURDERER. Stand to 't.
BANQUO. It will rain tonight.
FIRST MURDERER.   Let it come down.
    [They set upon BANQUO.]
BANQUO. O, treachery! Fly, good Fleance, fly, fly,
    fly!
Thou mayst revenge. O slave!
    [Dies. FLEANCE escapes.]
THIRD MURDERER. Who did strike out the light?
FIRST MURDERER.   Was 't not the way?
THIRD MURDERER. There's but one down; the son
is fled.
20 SECOND MURDERER.   We have lost
Best half of our affair.
FIRST MURDERER. Well, let's away and say how
much is done.   [Exeunt]

SCENE iv
Hall in the palace.

[A banquet prepared. Enter MACBETH, LADY
MACBETH, ROSS, LENNOX, LORDS, and ATTENDANTS.]
MACBETH. You know your own degrees;° sit down.
At first
And last the hearty welcome.
LORDS.   Thanks to your majesty.
MACBETH. Ourself will mingle with society
And play the humble host.
5 Our hostess keeps her state,° but in best time
We will require her welcome.

LADY MACBETH. Pronounce it for me, sir, to all our
friends,
For my heart speaks they are welcome.
    [Enter FIRST MURDERER to the door.]
MACBETH. See, they encounter° thee with their
hearts' thanks;
Both sides are even.° Here I'll sit i' the midst. 10
Be large in mirth; anon we'll drink a measure
The table round. [Approaching the door] There's
blood upon thy face.
MURDERER. 'Tis Banquo's then.
MACBETH. 'Tis better thee without than he within.°
Is he dispatch'd? 15
MURDERER. My lord, his throat is cut; that I did for
him.
MACBETH. Thou art the best o' the cutthroats. Yet
he's good
That did the like for Fleance; if thou didst it,
Thou art the nonpareil.°
MURDERER.   Most royal sir,
Fleance is 'scap'd. 20
MACBETH. [Aside] Then comes my fit again. I had
else been perfect,
Whole as the marble, founded as the rock,
As broad and general as the casing° air.
But now I am cabin'd, cribb'd, confin'd, bound
in
To saucy doubts and fears.—But Banquo's safe? 25
MURDERER. Aye, my good lord. Safe in a ditch he
bides,
With twenty trenched gashes on his head,
The least a death to nature.
MACBETH.   Thanks for that.
[Aside] There the grown serpent lies; the worm
that's fled
Hath nature that in time will venom breed, 30
No teeth for the present. Get thee gone. Tomor-
row
We'll hear ourselves again.   [Exit MURDERER.]
LADY MACBETH.   My royal lord,
You do not give the cheer. The feast is sold
That is not often vouch'd, while 'tis a-making,
'Tis given with welcome.° To feed° were best at
home; 35
From° thence the sauce to meat is ceremony;
Meeting were bare without it.

encounter   greet
Both . . . even   i.e., hostess and guests have exchanged
  greetings
thee . . . within   outside of you than inside of him
nonpareil   unequalled one   casing   encasing
The feast . . . welcome   i.e., unless assurances of welcome
are frequently given during the feast, the effect is that
of eating at an inn
To feed   i.e., merely to feed   From   away from

To . . . just   in exact detail   lated   belated
degrees   ranks   keeps her state   remains on her throne

MACBETH.   Sweet remembrancer!
Now good digestion wait on° appetite,
And health on both!
LENNOX.   May 't please your highness sit.
　　　[The GHOST OF BANQUO enters, and sits in
　　　　MACBETH's place.]
MACBETH. Here had we now our country's honor
40　　roof'd,°
Were the grac'd person of our Banquo present—
Who may I rather challenge° for unkindness
Than pity for mischance!
ROSS.   His absence, sir,
Lays blame upon his promise. Please 't your
highness
45　To grace us with your royal company.
MACBETH. The table's full.
LENNOX.   Here is a place reserv'd, sir.
MACBETH. Where?
LENNOX. Here, my good lord. What is 't that moves
your highness?
MACBETH. Which of you have done this?
LORDS.   What, my good lord?
50　MACBETH. Thou canst not say I did it. Never shake
Thy gory locks at me.
ROSS. Gentlemen, rise. His highness is not well.
LADY MACBETH. Sit, worthy friends. My lord is
often thus,
And hath been from his youth. Pray you, keep
seat,
55　The fit is momentary; upon a thought
He will again be well. If much you note him,
You shall offend him and extend his passion.
Feed, and regard him not.—Are you a man?
MACBETH. Aye, and a bold one, that dare look on
that
Which might appall the devil.
60　LADY MACBETH.   O proper stuff!°
This is the very painting of your fear.
This is the air-drawn dagger which you said
Led you to Duncan. O, these flaws and starts,
Impostors to true fear, would well become
65　A woman's story at a winter's fire,
Authoriz'd° by her grandam. Shame itself!
Why do you make such faces? When all's done,
You look but on a stool.
MACBETH. Prithee, see there! Behold! Look! Lo!
How say you?
70　Why, what care I? If thou canst nod, speak too.
If charnel houses and our graves must send

Those that we bury back, our monuments
Shall be the maws of kites.°   [Exit GHOST.]
LADY MACBETH.   What, quite unmann'd in folly?
MACBETH. If I stand here, I saw him.
LADY MACBETH.   Fie, for shame!
MACBETH. Blood hath been shed ere now, i' th'
olden time,   75
Ere humane statute purg'd the gentle weal;°
Aye, and since too, murders have been per-
form'd
Too terrible for the ear. The time has been
That when the brains were out the man would
die,
And there an end; but now they rise again,   80
With twenty mortal murders on their crowns,
And push us from our stools. This is more
strange
Than such a murder is.
LADY MACBETH.   My worthy lord,
Your noble friends do lack you.
MACBETH.   I do forget.
Do not muse at me, my most worthy friends;   85
I have a strange infirmity, which is nothing
To those that know me. Come, love and health
to all.
Then I'll sit down. Give me some wine, fill full.
I drink to the general joy o' the whole table,
And to our dear friend Banquo, whom we miss;   90
Would he were here! To all and him we thirst,
And all to all.
LORDS.   Our duties, and the pledge.
　　　　[Re-enter GHOST.]
MACBETH. Avaunt,° and quit my sight! Let the
earth hide thee!
Thy bones are marrowless, thy blood is cold;
Thou hast no speculation° in those eyes   95
Which thou dost glare with.
LADY MACBETH.   Think of this, good peers,
But as a thing of custom,° 'tis no other,
Only it spoils the pleasure of the time.
MACBETH. What man dare, I dare.
Approach thou like the rugged Russian bear,   100
The arm'd rhinoceros, or the Hyrcan° tiger;
Take any shape but that, and my firm nerves
Shall never tremble. Or be alive again,
And dare me to the desert with thy sword;
If trembling I inhabit° then, protest me   105
The baby of a girl.° Hence, horrible shadow!

Unreal mockery, hence!   [*Exit* GHOST.]
                                      Why, so. Being gone,
I am a man again. Pray you, sit still.
LADY MACBETH. You have displac'd the mirth,
    broke the good meeting
With most admir'd° disorder.
110 MACBETH.   Can such things be,
And overcome° us like a summer's cloud,
Without our special wonder? You make me
    strange
Even to the disposition° that I owe,
When now I think you can behold such sights
115 And keep the natural ruby of your cheeks
When mine is blanch'd with fear.
ROSS.   What sights, my lord?
LADY MACBETH. I pray you, speak not; he grows
    worse and worse.
Question enrages him. At once, good night.
Stand not upon the order of your going,
But go at once.
120 LENNOX.   Good night, and better health
Attend his majesty!
LADY MACBETH.   A kind good night to all!
    [*Exeunt all but* MACBETH *and* LADY MACBETH.]
MACBETH. It will have blood. They say blood will
    have blood.
Stones have been known to move and trees to
    speak;
Augures and understood relations° have
By maggot pies° and choughs and rooks brought
125   forth°
The secret'st man of blood. What is the night?
LADY MACBETH. Almost at odds with morning,
    which is which.
MACBETH. How say'st thou that Macduff denies his
    person
At our great bidding?
LADY MACBETH.   Did you send to him, sir?
130 MACBETH. I hear it by the way,° but I will send.
There's not a one of them but in his house
I keep a servant fee'd.° I will tomorrow,
And betimes° I will, to the weird sisters.
More shall they speak, for now I am bent to
    know,
By the worst means, the worst. For mine own
135   good
All causes shall give way. I am in blood

Stepp'd in so far that should I wade no more,
Returning were as tedious as go o'er.
Strange things I have in head that will to hand,
Which must be acted ere they may be scann'd.   140
LADY MACBETH. You lack the season° of all natures,
    sleep.
MACBETH. Come, we'll to sleep. My strange and
    self-abuse°
Is the initiate fear that wants hard use.°
We are yet but young in deed.   [*Exeunt*]

SCENE V
A heath.

[*Thunder. Enter the* THREE WITCHES, *meeting*
    HECATE.]
FIRST WITCH. Why, how now, Hecate! You look
    angerly.
HECATE. Have I not reason, beldams° as you are,
    Saucy and overbold? How did you dare
    To trade and traffic with Macbeth
    In riddles and affairs of death,   5
    And I, the mistress of your charms,
    The close contriver of all harms,
    Was never call'd to bear my part
    Or show the glory of our art?
    And, which is worse, all you have done   10
    Hath been but for a wayward son,
    Spiteful and wrathful, who, as others do,
    Loves for his own ends, not for you.
    But make amends now. Get you gone,
    And at the pit of Acheron°   15
    Meet me i' the morning. Thither he
    Will come to know his destiny.
    Your vessels and your spells provide,
    Your charms and everything beside.
    I am for the air; this night I'll spend   20
    Unto a dismal and a fatal end.
    Great business must be wrought ere noon.
    Upon the corner of the moon
    There hangs a vaporous drop profound;
    I'll catch it ere it come to ground,   25
    And that distill'd by magic sleights
    Shall raise such artificial sprites
    As by the strength of their illusion
    Shall draw him on to his confusion.°
    He shall spurn fate, scorn death, and bear   30
    His hopes 'bove wisdom, grace, and fear.

---

admir'd wondered at   *overcome* come over
You . . . disposition you make me feel unacquainted
    with my own nature
Augures . . . relations omens and rightly interpreted
    significances
maggot pies magpies   *brought forth* exposed
by the way indirectly   *a servant fee'd* i.e., a spy
betimes early

season seasoning
strange and self-abuse unaccustomed and self-imposed
    torment
initiate . . . use beginner's misgivings that lacks experience
beldams hags   *Acheron* river of Hades
confusion destruction

And you all know security°
Is mortals' chiefest enemy.
          [*Music and a song within.*
                  "Come away, come away," *etc.*]
Hark! I am call'd; my little spirit, see,
35 Sits in a foggy cloud and stays for me.   [*Exit*]
First Witch. Come, let's make haste; she'll soon
      be back again.   [*Exeunt*]

                    SCENE vi
                Forres. The palace.

          [*Enter* Lennox *and another* Lord.]
Lennox. My former speeches have but hit your
      thoughts,
Which can interpret farther. Only I say
Things have been strangely borne.° The gracious
      Duncan
Was pitied of Macbeth. Marry,° he was dead.
5 And the right-valiant Banquo walk'd too late,
Whom, you may say, if 't please you, Fleance
      kill'd,
For Fleance fled. Men must not walk too late.
Who cannot want° the thought how monstrous
It was for Malcolm and for Donalbain
10 To kill their gracious father? Damned fact!
How it did grieve Macbeth! Did he not straight,
In pious rage, the two delinquents tear
That were the slaves of drink and thralls of
      sleep?
Was not that nobly done? Aye, and wisely too,
15 For 'twould have anger'd any heart alive
To hear the men deny 't. So that, I say,
He has borne all things well, and I do think
That, had he Duncan's sons under his key—
As, an 't please heaven, he shall not—they
      should find

What 'twere to kill a father; so should Fleance.   20
But, peace! For from° broad° words and 'cause
      he fail'd
His presence at the tyrant's feast, I hear
Macduff lives in disgrace. Sir, can you tell
Where he bestows himself?
Lord.   The son of Duncan,
From whom this tyrant holds the due of birth,   25
Lives in the English court, and is receiv'd
Of the most pious Edward with such grace
That the malevolence of fortune nothing
Takes from his high respect. Thither Macduff
Is gone to pray the holy king, upon his aid   30
To wake Northumberland and warlike Siward,
That by the help of these, with Him above
To ratify the work, we may again
Give to our tables meat, sleep to our nights,
Free from our feasts and banquets bloody
      knives,   35
Do faithful homage, and receive free honors—
All which we pine for now. And this report
Hath so exasperate the king that he
Prepares for some attempt of war.
Lennox.   Sent he to Macduff?
Lord. He did, and with an absolute "Sir, not I,"   40
The cloudy° messenger turns me° his back
And hums, as who should say "You'll rue the
      time
That clogs° me with this answer."
Lennox.   And that well might
Advise him to a caution to hold what distance
His wisdom can provide. Some holy angel   45
Fly to the court of England and unfold
His message ere he come, that a swift blessing
May soon return to this our suffering country
Under a hand accurs'd!
Lord.   I'll send my prayers with him.
                                          [*Exeunt*]

---

security overconfidence.   *borne* managed
Marry by the Virgin   *want* lack

For from because of   *broad* outspoken   *cloudy* surly
turns me turns   *clogs* burdens

ACT IV

SCENE i
A cavern. In the middle, a boiling cauldron.

[*Thunder. Enter the* THREE WITCHES.]
FIRST WITCH. Thrice the brinded° cat hath mew'd.
SECOND WITCH. Thrice and once the hedge-pig whin'd.
THIRD WITCH. Harpier° cries "'Tis time, 'tis time."
FIRST WITCH. Round about the cauldron go;
5   In the poison'd entrails throw.
    Toad, that under cold stone
    Days and nights has thirty-one
    Swelter'd° venom sleeping got,
    Boil thou first i' the charmed pot.
10 ALL. Double, double, toil and trouble;
    Fire burn and cauldron bubble.
    SECOND WITCH. Fillet of a fenny° snake,
    In the cauldron boil and bake;
    Eye of newt and toe of frog,
15 Wool of bat and tongue of dog,
    Adder's fork° and blind-worm's° sting,
    Lizard's leg and howlet's° wing,
    For a charm of powerful trouble,
    Like a hell-broth boil and bubble.
20 ALL. Double, double, toil and trouble;
    Fire burn and cauldron bubble.
    THIRD WITCH. Scale of dragon, tooth of wolf,
    Witches' mummy, maw and gulf°
    Of the ravin'd° salt-sea shark,
25 Root of hemlock digg'd i' the dark,
    Liver of blaspheming Jew,
    Gall of goat and slips of yew
    Sliver'd in the moon's eclipse,
    Nose of Turk and Tartar's lips,
30 Finger of birth-strangled babe
    Ditch-deliver'd by a drab,
    Make the gruel thick and slab.°
    Add thereto a tiger's chaudron,°
    For th' ingredients of our cauldron.
35 ALL. Double, double, toil and trouble;
    Fire burn and cauldron bubble.
    SECOND WITCH. Cool it with a baboon's blood;
    Then the charm is firm and good.

---

brinded striped
Harpier name of attendant spirit
Swelter'd sweated out   *fenny* i.e., of the fen (swamp)
fork tongue   *blind-worm's* lizard's
howlet's owlet's   *maw and gulf* belly and gullet
ravin'd ravenous   *slab* slablike   *chaudron* entrails

[*Enter* HECATE *to the* THREE WITCHES.]
HECATE. O, well done! I commend your pains,
    And everyone shall share i' the gains.   40
    And now about the cauldron sing
    Like elves and fairies in a ring,
    Enchanting all that you put in.
        [*Music and a song:* "Black Spirits," *etc.*]
                                    [HECATE *retires.*]
SECOND WITCH. By the pricking of my thumbs,
    Something wicked this way comes.   45
        Open, locks,
        Whoever knocks!
                [*Enter* MACBETH.]
MACBETH. How now, you secret, black, and mid-
        night hags!
    What is 't you do?
ALL.   A deed without a name.
MACBETH. I conjure you by that which you profess, 50
    Howe'er you come to know it, answer me.
    Though you untie the winds and let them fight
    Against the churches; though the yesty° waves
    Confound and swallow navigation up;
    Though bladed corn be lodg'd and trees blown
        down;   55
    Though castles topple on their warders' heads;
    Though palaces and pyramids do slope
    Their heads to their foundations; though the
        treasure
    Of nature's germens° tumble all together
    Even till destruction sicken,° answer me   60
    To what I ask you.
FIRST WITCH.   Speak.
SECOND WITCH.   Demand.
THIRD WITCH.   We'll answer.
FIRST WITCH. Say if thou'dst rather hear it from our
        mouths
    Or from our masters.
MACBETH.   Call 'em, let me see 'em.
FIRST WITCH. Pour in sow's blood, that hath eaten
    Her nine farrow; grease that's sweaten   65
    From the murderer's gibbet throw
    Into the flame.
ALL.   Come, high or low;
    Thyself and office deftly show!
    [*Thunder.* FIRST APPARITION: *an armed Head.*]
MACBETH. Tell me, thou unknown power—

---

yesty foamy   *germens* seeds   *sicken* is satiated

FIRST WITCH.   He knows thy thought.
70   Hear his speech, but say thou naught.
FIRST APPARITION. Macbeth! Macbeth! Macbeth!
       Beware Macduff;
       Beware the thane of Fife. Dismiss me. Enough.
                              [*Descends.*]
MACBETH. Whate'er thou art, for thy good caution
       thanks;
       Thou hast harp'd° my fear aright. But one word
       more—
FIRST WITCH. He will not be commanded. Here's
75   another,
       More potent than the first.
       [*Thunder.* SECOND APPARITION: *a bloody Child.*]
SECOND APPARITION. Macbeth! Macbeth! Macbeth!
MACBETH. Had I three ears, I'd hear thee.
SECOND APPARITION. Be bloody, bold, and resolute;
       laugh to scorn
80   The power of man, for none of woman born
       Shall harm Macbeth.   [*Descends.*]
MACBETH. Then live, Macduff. What need I fear of
       thee?
       But yet I'll make assurance double sure,
       And take a bond of fate.° Thou shalt not live,
85   That I may tell pale-hearted fear it lies,
       And sleep in spite of thunder.
       [*Thunder.* THIRD APPARITION: *a Child crowned,
              with a tree in his hand.*]
                              What is this,
       That rises like the issue of a king,
       And wears upon his baby brow the round°
       And top of sovereignty?
ALL.   Listen, but speak not to 't.
THIRD APPARITION. Be lion-mettled, proud, and
90   take no care
       Who chafes, who frets, or where conspirers are.
       Macbeth shall never vanquish'd be until
       Great Birnam wood to high Dunsinane hill
       Shall come against him.   [*Descends.*]
MACBETH.   That will never be.
95   Who can impress° the forest, bid the tree
       Unfix his earthbound root? Sweet bodements!°
       Good!
       Rebellion's head, rise never till the wood
       Of Birnam rise, and our high-plac'd Macbeth
       Shall live the lease of nature, pay his breath
100 To time and mortal custom. Yet my heart
       Throbs to know one thing. Tell me, if your art
       Can tell so much, shall Banquo's issue ever
       Reign in this kingdom?

ALL.   Seek to know no more.
MACBETH. I will be satisfied. Deny me this,
       And an eternal curse fall on you! Let me know.   105
       Why sinks that cauldron? And what noise is this?
                              [*Hautboys.*]
FIRST WITCH. Show!
SECOND WITCH. Show!
THIRD WITCH. Show!
ALL. Show his eyes, and grieve his heart;   110
       Come like shadows, so depart!
       [*A show of eight* KINGS, *the last with a glass in his
              hand;* BANQUO'S GHOST *following.*]
MACBETH. Thou art too like the spirit of Banquo.
       Down!
       Thy crown does sear mine eyeballs. And thy
       hair,
       Thou other gold-bound brow, is like the first.
       A third is like the former. Filthy hags!   115
       Why do you show me this? A fourth! Start, eyes!
       What, will the line stretch out to the crack of
       doom?
       Another yet! A seventh! I'll see no more.
       And yet the eighth appears, who bears a glass
       Which shows me many more; and some I see   120
       That twofold balls and treble scepters° carry.
       Horrible sight! Now I see 'tis true,
       For the blood-bolter'd Banquo smiles upon me
       And points at them for his. What, is this so?
FIRST WITCH. Aye, sir, all this is so. But why   125
       Stands Macbeth thus amazedly?
       Come, sisters, cheer we up his sprites,
       And show the best of our delights.
       I'll charm the air to give a sound,
       While you perform your antic round,°   130
       That this great king may kindly say
       Our duties did his welcome pay.
       [*Music. The* WITCHES *dance, and then vanish, with*
              HECATE.]
MACBETH. Where are they? Gone? Let this per-
       nicious hour
       Stand aye accursed in the calendar!
       Come in, without there!
                              [*Enter* LENNOX.]
LENNOX.   What's your grace's will?   135
MACBETH. Saw you the weird sisters?
LENNOX.   No, my lord.
MACBETH. Came they not by you?
LENNOX.   No indeed, my lord.
MACBETH. Infected be the air whereon they ride,
       And damn'd all those that trust them! I did hear
       The galloping of horse. Who was 't came by?   140

---

harp'd struck
take . . . fate require a guarantee (i.e., kill Macduff)
round crown   *impress* conscript
bodements omens

twofold . . . scepters i.e., for England, Ireland, Scotland,
   united under James I
antic round grotesque dance

LENNOX. 'Tis two or three, my lord, that bring you word
   Macduff is fled to England.
MACBETH.   Fled to England!
LENNOX. Aye, my good lord.
MACBETH. [*Aside*] Time, thou anticipat'st my dread exploits.
145   The flighty purpose never is o'ertook
   Unless the deed go with it. From this moment
   The very firstlings° of my heart shall be
   The firstlings of my hand. And even now,
   To crown my thoughts with acts, be it thought and done.
150   The castle of Macduff I will surprise,
   Seize upon Fife; give to the edge o' the sword
   His wife, his babes, and all unfortunate souls
   That trace him in his line. No boasting like a fool;
   This deed I'll do before this purpose cool.
   But no more sights!—Where are these gentle-
155   men?
   Come, bring me where they are.   [*Exeunt*]

SCENE ii
Fife. MACDUFF'S *castle.*

[*Enter* LADY MACDUFF, *her* SON, *and* ROSS.]
LADY MACDUFF. What had he done, to make him fly the land?
ROSS. You must have patience, madam.
LADY MACDUFF.   He had none.
   His flight was madness. When our actions do not,
   Our fears do make us traitors.
ROSS.   You know not
5   Whether it was his wisdom or his fear.
LADY MACDUFF. Wisdom! To leave his wife, to leave his babes,
   His mansion, and his titles in a place
   From whence himself does fly? He loves us not;
   He wants the natural touch. For the poor wren,
10   The most diminutive of birds, will fight,
   Her young ones in her nest, against the owl.
   All is the fear and nothing is the love;
   As little is the wisdom, where the flight
   So runs against all reason.
ROSS.   My dearest coz,
   I pray you, school yourself. But, for your hus-
15   band,
   He is noble, wise, judicious, and best knows
   The fits o' the season.° I dare not speak much further.

firstlings first impulses
fits . . . season quirks of the times

But cruel are the times, when we are traitors
And do not know ourselves; when we hold rumor
From what we fear,° yet know not what we fear,   20
But float upon a wild and violent sea
Each way and move.° I take my leave of you.
Shall not be long but I'll be here again.
Things at the worst will cease, or else climb up-
ward
To what they were before. My pretty cousin,   25
Blessing upon you!
LADY MACDUFF. Father'd he is, and yet he's father-less.
ROSS. I am so much a fool, should I stay longer,
   It would be my disgrace and your discomfort.
   I take my leave at once.   [*Exit*]
LADY MACDUFF.   Sirrah, your father's dead.   30
   And what will you do now? How will you live?
SON. As birds do, mother.
LADY MACDUFF.   What, with worms and flies?
SON. With what I get, I mean, and so do they.
LADY MACDUFF. Poor bird! Thou'dst never fear the net nor lime,°
   The pitfall nor the gin.°   35
SON. Why should I, mother? Poor birds they are not set for.
   My father is not dead, for all your saying.
LADY MACDUFF. Yes, he is dead. How wilt thou do for a father?
SON. Nay, how will you do for a husband?
LADY MACDUFF. Why, I can buy me twenty at any market.   40
SON. Then you'll buy 'em to sell again.
LADY MACDUFF. Thou speak'st with all thy wit, and yet, i' faith,
   With wit enough for thee.
SON. Was my father a traitor, mother?
LADY MACDUFF. Aye, that he was.   45
SON. What is a traitor?
LADY MACDUFF. Why, one that swears and lies.
SON. And be all traitors that do so?
LADY MACDUFF. Every one that does so is a traitor, and must be hanged.   50
SON. And must they all be hanged that swear and lie?
LADY MACDUFF. Every one.
SON. Who must hang them?
LADY MACDUFF. Why, the honest men.   55
SON. Then the liars and swearers are fools, for there are liars and swearers enow to beat the honest men and hang up them.

hold . . . fear catch at every rumor because of our fears
way and move i.e., hither and yon
lime birdlime   *gin* snare

LADY MACDUFF. Now, God help thee, poor mon-
60   key! But how wilt thou do for a father?
SON. If he were dead, you'd weep for him. If you
      would not, it were a good sign that I should
      quickly have a new father.
LADY MACDUFF. Poor prattler, how thou talk'st!
            [*Enter a* MESSENGER.]
MESSENGER. Bless you, fair dame! I am not to you
65   known,
      Though in your state of honor I am perfect.°
      I doubt° some danger does approach you nearly.
      If you will take a homely° man's advice,
      Be not found here; hence with your little ones.
70   To fright you thus, methinks I am too savage;
      To do worse to you were fell° cruelty,
      Which is too nigh your person. Heaven preserve
      you!
      I dare abide no longer.   [*Exit*]
LADY MACDUFF.   Whither should I fly?
      I have done no harm. But I remember now
75   I am in this earthly world, where to do harm
      Is often laudable, to do good sometime
    · Accounted dangerous folly. Why then, alas,
      Do I put up that womanly defense,
      To say I have done no harm?—What are these
      faces?
            [*Enter* MURDERERS.]
80 FIRST MURDERER. Where is your husband?
LADY MACDUFF. I hope in no place so unsanctified
      Where such as thou mayst find him.
FIRST MURDERER.   He's a traitor.
SON. Thou liest, thou shag-hair'd villain!
FIRST MURDERER.   What, you egg!
                        [*Stabbing him.*]
      Young fry° of treachery!
SON.   He has kill'd me, mother.
85   Run away, I pray you!   [*Dies.*]
        [*Exit* LADY MACDUFF, *crying* "Murder!"]
        [*Exeunt* MURDERERS, *following her.*]

SCENE iii
England. Before the KING'S *palace.*

[*Enter* MALCOLM *and* MACDUFF.]
MALCOLM. Let us seek out some desolate shade, and
      there
      Weep our sad bosoms empty.
MACDUFF.   Let us rather
      Hold fast the mortal sword, and like good men

Bestride our down-fall'n birthdom. Each new
      morn
New widows howl, new orphans cry, new sor-
      rows   5
Strike heaven on the face, that it resounds
As if it felt with Scotland and yell'd out
Like syllable of dolor.
MALCOLM.   What I believe, I'll wail;
      What know, believe; and what I can redress,
      As I shall find the time to friend,° I will.   10
      What you have spoke, it may be so perchance.
      This tyrant, whose sole° name blisters our
      tongues,
      Was once thought honest. You have lov'd him
      well;
      He hath not touch'd you yet. I am young; but
      something
      You may deserve of him through me, and wis-
      dom   15
      To offer up a weak, poor, innocent lamb
      T' appease an angry god.
MACDUFF. I am not treacherous.
MALCOLM.   But Macbeth is.
      A good and virtuous nature may recoil°
      In an imperial charge. But I shall crave your
      pardon;   20
      That which you are, my thoughts cannot trans-
      pose.
      Angels are bright still, though the brightest fell.
      Though all things foul would wear the brows of
      grace,
      Yet grace must still look so.°
MACDUFF.   I have lost my hopes.
MALCOLM. Perchance even there where I did find
      my doubts.   25
      Why in that rawness left you wife and child,
      Those precious motives, those strong knots of
      love,
      Without leave-taking? I pray you,
      Let not my jealousies° be your dishonors,
      But mine own safeties.° You may be rightly just, 30
      Whatever I shall think.
MACDUFF.   Bleed, bleed, poor country.
      Great tyranny, lay thou thy basis sure,
      For goodness dare not check thee. Wear thou thy
      wrongs;
      The title is affeer'd.° Fare thee well, lord.
      I would not be the villain that thou think'st   35
      For the whole space that's in the tyrant's grasp
      And the rich East to boot.

---

in . . . perfect I am well acquainted with your noble
      rank
doubt suspect   *homely* humble   *fell* savage
fry spawn

to friend favorable   *sole* mere   *recoil* be corrupted
so i.e., gracious   *jealousies* suspicions
safeties safeguards
affeer'd confirmed, made sure (with pun, *afear'd*)

MALCOLM.   Be not offended.
I speak not as in absolute fear of you.
I think our country sinks beneath the yoke;
40 It weeps, it bleeds, and each new day a gash
Is added to her wounds. I think withal°
There would be hands uplifted in my right,
And here from gracious England have I offer
Of goodly thousands. But for all this,
45 When I shall tread upon the tyrant's head,
Or wear it on my sword, yet my poor country
Shall have more vices than it had before,
More suffer and more sundry ways than ever,
By him that shall succeed.
MACDUFF.   What should he be?
50 MALCOLM. It is myself I mean, in whom I know
All the particulars of vice so grafted°
That, when they shall be open'd, black Macbeth
Will seem as pure as snow, and the poor state
Esteem him as a lamb, being compar'd
55 With my confineless harms.
MACDUFF.   Not in the legions
Of horrid hell can come a devil more damn'd
In evils to top Macbeth.
MALCOLM.   I grant him bloody,
Luxurious,° avaricious, false, deceitful,
Sudden, malicious, smacking of every sin
60 That has a name. But there's no bottom, none,
In my vulptuousness. Your wives, your daughters,
Your matrons, and your maids could not fill up
The cistern of my lust, and my desire
All continent impediments would o'erbear
65 That did oppose my will. Better Macbeth
Than such an one to reign.
MACDUFF.   Boundless intemperance
In nature is a tyranny; it hath been
Th' untimely emptying of the happy throne,
And fall of many kings. But fear not yet
70 To take upon you what is yours. You may
Convey° your pleasures in a spacious plenty,
And yet seem cold, the time you may so hoodwink.°
We have willing dames enough; there cannot be
That vulture in you, to devour so many
75 As will to greatness dedicate themselves,
Finding it so inclin'd.
MALCOLM.   With this there grows
In my most ill-compos'd affection° such
A stanchless° avarice that, were I king,

I should cut off the nobles for their lands,
Desire his jewels and this other's house; 80
And my more-having would be as a sauce
To make me hunger more, that I should forge
Quarrels unjust against the good and loyal,
Destroying them for wealth.
MACDUFF.   This avarice
Sticks deeper, grows with more pernicious root 85
Than summer-seeming lust, and it hath been
The sword° of our slain kings. Yet do not fear;
Scotland hath foisons° to fill up your will
Of your mere own. All these are portable,°
With other graces weigh'd. 90
MALCOLM. But I have none. The king-becoming graces,
As justice, verity, temperance, stableness,
Bounty, perseverance, mercy, lowliness,
Devotion, patience, courage, fortitude—
I have no relish° of them, but abound 95
In the division of each several° crime,
Acting it many ways. Nay, had I power, I should
Pour the sweet milk of concord into hell,
Uproar the universal peace, confound
All unity on earth.
MACDUFF.   O Scotland, Scotland! 100
MALCOLM. If such a one be fit to govern, speak.
I am as I have spoken.
MACDUFF.   Fit to govern!
No, not to live. O nation miserable!
With an untitled tyrant bloody-scepter'd,
When shalt thou see thy wholesome days again, 105
Since that the truest issue of thy throne
By his own interdiction° stands accurs'd,
And does blaspheme his breed? Thy royal father
Was a most sainted king. The queen that bore thee,
Oftener upon her knees than on her feet, 110
Died° every day she liv'd. Fare thee well!
These evils thou repeat'st upon thyself
Have banish'd me from Scotland. O my breast,
Thy hope ends here!
MALCOLM.   Macduff, this noble passion,
Child of integrity, hath from my soul 115
Wip'd the black scruples, reconcil'd my thoughts
To thy good truth and honor. Devilish Macbeth
By many of these trains° hath sought to win me
Into his power, and modest wisdom plucks me
From over-credulous haste. But God above 120
Deal between thee and me! For even now

---

withal besides   *grafted* engrafted, fixed
Luxurious lustful   *continent impediments* restraints
Convey carry on
the time . . . hoodwink   you may so deceive the public
affection disposition   *stanchless* unquenchable

sword i.e., ruination   *foisons* abundances
portable bearable   *relish* trace
division . . . several variations upon each separate
interdiction indictment
Died i.e., readied herself for Heaven
trains stratagems

I put myself to thy direction and
Unspeak mine own detraction; here abjure
The taints and blames I laid upon myself
125 For strangers to my nature. I am yet
Unknown to woman, never was forsworn,
Scarcely have coveted what was mine own,
At no time broke my faith, would not betray
The devil to his fellow, and delight
130 No less in truth than life. My first false speaking
Was this upon myself. What I am truly
Is thine and my poor country's to command,
Whither indeed, before thy here-approach,
Old Siward, with ten thousand warlike men,
135 Already at a point,° was setting forth.
Now we'll together, and the chance of goodness
Be like our warranted quarrel! Why are you
    silent?
MACDUFF. Such welcome and unwelcome things at
    once
'Tis hard to reconcile.
                    [Enter a DOCTOR.]
MALCOLM. Well, more anon. Comes the King
140   forth, I pray you?
DOCTOR. Aye, sir; there are a crew of wretched
    souls
That stay° his cure. Their malady convinces
The great assay of art;° but at his touch,
Such sanctity hath heaven given his hand,
They presently° amend.
145 MALCOLM.   I thank you, doctor.
                    [Exit DOCTOR.]
MACDUFF. What's the disease he means?
MALCOLM.   'Tis call'd the evil.°
A most miraculous work in this good King,
Which often, since my here-remain in England,
I have seen him do. How he solicits heaven,
Himself best knows. But strangely visited°
150   people,
All swoln and ulcerous, pitiful to the eye,
The mere despair of surgery, he cures,
Hanging a golden stamp° about their necks,
Put on with holy prayers. And 'tis spoken,
155 To the succeeding royalty he leaves
The healing benediction.° With this strange
    virtue
He hath a heavenly gift of prophecy,
And sundry blessings hang about his throne

That speak him full of grace.
                    [Enter ROSS.]
MACDUFF.   See, who comes here?
MALCOLM. My countryman, but yet I know him
    not.   160
MACDUFF. My ever gentle cousin, welcome hither.
MALCOLM. I know him now. Good God, betimes
    remove
The means that makes us strangers!
ROSS.   Sir, amen.
MACDUFF. Stands Scotland where it did?
ROSS.   Alas, poor country!
Almost afraid to know itself! It cannot   165
Be call'd our mother, but our grave, where
    nothing
But who knows nothing is once seen to smile;
Where sighs and groans and shrieks that rend
    the air
Are made, not mark'd; where violent sorrow
    seems
A modern ecstasy.° The dead man's knell   170
Is there scarce ask'd for who, and good men's
    lives
Expire before the flowers in their caps,
Dying or ere they sicken.
MACDUFF.   O, relation
Too nice,° and yet too true!
MALCOLM.   What's the newest grief?
ROSS. That of an hour's age doth hiss the speaker; 175
Each minute teems a new one.
MACDUFF.   How does my wife?
ROSS. Why, well.
MACDUFF.   And all my children?
ROSS.   Well too.
MACDUFF. The tyrant has not batter'd at their
    peace?
ROSS. No; they were well at peace when I did leave
    'em.
MACDUFF. Be not a niggard of your speech. How
    goes 't?   180
ROSS. When I came hither to transport the tidings,
Which I have heavily borne, there ran a rumor
Of many worthy fellows that were out,°
Which was to my belief witness'd° the rather
For that I saw the tyrant's power afoot.   185
Now is the time of help; your eye in Scotland
Would create soldiers, make our women fight,
To doff their dire distresses.
MALCOLM.   Be 't their comfort
We are coming thither. Gracious England hath
Lent us good Siward and ten thousand men—   190

at a point armed   stay await
convinces . . . art defeats the best attempts of medicine
presently immediately
evil scrofula   visited afflicted
stamp stamped medal
To the . . . benediction (Shakespeare's compliment to
    King James as inheritor of Edward the Confessor's
    gift)

modern ecstasy commonplace emotion
nice precisely detailed
out in arms   witness'd confirmed

An older and a better soldier none
That Christendom gives out.
Ross.   Would I could answer
This comfort with the like! But I have words
That would be howl'd out in the desert air,
Where hearing should not latch them.
195 MACDUFF.   What concern they?
The general cause? Or is it a fee-grief°
Due to some single breast?
Ross.   No mind that's honest
But in it shares some woe, though the main part
Pertains to you alone.
MACDUFF.   If it be mine,
200 Keep it not from me. Quickly let me have it.
Ross. Let not your ears despise my tongue forever,
Which shall possess them with the heaviest
sound
That ever yet they heard.
MACDUFF.   Hum! I guess at it.
Ross. Your castle is surpris'd, your wife and babes
205 Savagely slaughter'd. To relate the manner
Were, on the quarry° of these murder'd deer,
To add the death of you.
MALCOLM.   Merciful heaven!
What, man! Ne'er pull your hat upon your
brows;
Give sorrow words. The grief that does not
speak
Whispers the o'erfraught° heart, and bids it
210 break.
MACDUFF. My children too?
Ross.   Wife, children, servants, all
That could be found.
MACDUFF.   And I must be from thence!
My wife kill'd too?
Ross.   I have said.
MALCOLM.   Be comforted.

Let's make us medicines of our great revenge
To cure this deadly grief.   215
MACDUFF. He has no children. All my pretty ones?
Did you say all? O hell-kite! All?
What, all my pretty chickens and their dam
At one fell swoop?
MALCOLM. Dispute it like a man.
MACDUFF.   I shall do so,   220
But I must also feel it as a man.
I cannot but remember such things were
That were most precious to me. Did heaven
look on
And would not take their part? Sinful Macduff,
They were all struck for thee! Naught° that I am,   225
Not for their own demerits, but for mine,
Fell slaughter on their souls. Heaven rest them
now!
MALCOLM. Be this the whetstone of your sword. Let
grief
Convert to anger; blunt not the heart, enrage it.
MACDUFF. O, I could play the woman with mine
eyes,   230
And braggart with my tongue! But, gentle
heavens,
Cut short all intermission.° Front to front
Bring thou this fiend of Scotland and myself.
Within my sword's length set him. If he 'scape,
Heaven forgive him too!
MALCOLM.   This tune goes manly.   235
Come, go we to the king; our power is ready;
Our lack is nothing but our leave. Macbeth
Is ripe for shaking, and the powers above
Put on their instruments.° Receive what cheer
you may;
The night is long that never finds the day.   240
                              [Exeunt]

fee-grief private woe
quarry pile, heap   o'er-fraught overloaded

Naught wicked one   intermission interval
Put . . . instruments   send us forth as their agents

ACT V

SCENE i

Dunsinane. Anteroom in the castle.

[Enter a DOCTOR OF PHYSIC and a WAITING
GENTLEWOMAN.]
DOCTOR. I have two nights watched with you, but
can perceive no truth in your report. When was
it she last walked?

GENTLEWOMAN. Since his majesty went into the
field, I have seen her rise from her bed, throw   5
her nightgown upon her, unlock her closet, take
forth paper, fold it, write upon 't, read it, afterwards seal it, and again return to bed, yet all this
while in a most fast sleep.
DOCTOR. A great perturbation in nature, to re-   10
ceive at once the benefit of sleep and do the

effects of watching!° In this slumbery agitation, besides her walking and other actual performances, what, at any time, have you heard her
15 say?

GENTLEWOMAN. That, sir, which I will not report after her.

DOCTOR. You may to me, and 'tis most meet° you should.

20 GENTLEWOMAN. Neither to you nor anyone, having no witness to confirm my speech.

[*Enter* LADY MACBETH, *with a taper.*]

Lo you, here she comes! This is her very guise, and, upon my life, fast asleep. Observe her; stand close.

25 DOCTOR. How came she by that light?

GENTLEWOMAN. Why, it stood by her. She has light by her continually; 'tis her command.

DOCTOR. You see, her eyes are open.

GENTLEWOMAN. Aye, but their sense is shut.

30 DOCTOR. What is it she does now? Look how she rubs her hands.

GENTLEWOMAN. It is an accustomed action with her to seem thus washing her hands. I have known her continue in this a quarter of an hour.

35 LADY MACBETH. Yet here's a spot.

DOCTOR. Hark! She speaks. I will set down what comes from her, to satisfy my remembrance the more strongly.

LADY MACBETH. Out, damned spot! Out, I say!
40 One, two—why, then 'tis time to do 't. Hell is murky. Fie, my lord, fie! A soldier, and afeard? What need we fear who knows it, when none can call our power to account? Yet who would have thought the old man to have had so much
45 blood in him?

DOCTOR. Do you mark that?

LADY MACBETH. The thane of Fife had a wife; where is she now? What, will these hands ne'er be clean? No more o' that, my lord, no more o'
50 that. You mar all with this starting.

DOCTOR. Go to, go to; you have known what you should not.

GENTLEWOMAN. She has spoke what she should not, I am sure of that. Heaven knows what she has
55 known.

LADY MACBETH. Here's the smell of the blood still. All the perfumes of Arabia will not sweeten this little hand. Oh, oh, oh!

DOCTOR. What a sigh is there! The heart is sorely
60 charged.°

GENTLEWOMAN. I would not have such a heart in my bosom for the dignity of the whole body.

DOCTOR. Well, well, well—

GENTLEWOMAN. Pray God it be, sir.

DOCTOR. This disease is beyond my practice. Yet I 65
have known those which have walked in their sleep who have died holily in their beds.

LADY MACBETH. Wash your hands; put on your nightgown; look not so pale. I tell you yet again, Banquo's buried; he cannot come out on 's 70
grave.

DOCTOR. Even so?

LADY MACBETH. To bed, to bed; there's knocking at the gate. Come, come, come, come, give me your hand. What's done cannot be undone. To 75
bed, to bed, to bed.   [*Exit*]

DOCTOR. Will she go now to bed?

GENTLEWOMAN. Directly.

DOCTOR. Foul whisperings are abroad. Unnatural deeds
Do breed unnatural troubles. Infected minds 80
To their deaf pillows will discharge their secrets.
More needs she the divine than the physician.
God, God forgive us all! Look after her;
Remove from her the means of all annoyance,°
And still° keep eyes upon her. So good night. 85
My mind she has mated° and amaz'd my sight.
I think, but dare not speak.

GENTLEWOMAN.   Good night, good doctor.
[*Exeunt*]

SCENE ii
The country near Dunsinane.

[*Drum and colors. Enter* MENTEITH, CAITHNESS,
ANGUS, LENNOX, *and* SOLDIERS.]

MENTEITH. The English power is near, led on by Malcolm,
His uncle Siward, and the good Macduff.
Revenges burn in them, for their dear° causes
Would to the bleeding and the grim alarm°
Excite the mortified° man.

ANGUS.   Near Birnam wood 5
Shall we well meet them; that way are they coming.

CAITHNESS. Who knows if Donalbain be with his brother?

LENNOX. For certain, sir, he is not. I have a file
Of all the gentry. There is Siward's son,
And many unrough° youths that even now 10
Protest their first of manhood.

MENTEITH.   What does the tyrant?

---

do . . . watching perform the acts of one who is awake
meet proper   charged burdened

annoyance injury   still always
mated astonished   dear heartfelt
alarm call to battle   mortified dead
unrough smooth-faced, i.e., beardless

CAITHNESS. Great Dunsinane he strongly fortifies.
  Some say he's mad; others, that lesser hate him,
  Do call it valiant fury. But, for certain,
15 He cannot buckle his distemper'd cause
  Within the belt of rule.°
  ANGUS.   Now does he feel
  His secret murders sticking on his hands;
  Now minutely revolts upbraid his faith-breach,°
  Those he commands move only in command,
20 Nothing in love. Now does he feel his title
  Hang loose about him, like a giant's robe
  Upon a dwarfish thief.
  MENTEITH.   Who then shall blame
  His pester'd senses to recoil and start,
  When all that is within him does condemn
  Itself for being there?
25 CAITHNESS.   Well, march we on
  To give obedience where 'tis truly ow'd.
  Meet we the medicine of the sickly weal,°
  And with him pour we, in our country's purge,
  Each drop of us.
  LENNOX.   Or so much as it needs
  To dew the sovereign flower and drown the
30   weeds.
  Make we our march towards Birnam.
                                    [Exeunt, marching.]

                SCENE iii
        Dunsinane. A room in the castle.

  [Enter MACBETH, DOCTOR, and ATTENDANTS.]
  MACBETH. Bring me no more reports; let them fly
    all.
  Till Birnam wood remove to Dunsinane
  I cannot taint° with fear. What's the boy
    Malcolm?
  Was he not born of woman? The spirits that
    know
  All mortal consequences have pronounc'd me
5   thus:
  "Fear not, Macbeth; no man that's born of
    woman
  Shall e'er have power upon thee." Then fly,
    false thanes,
  And mingle with the English epicures.°
  The mind I sway by° and the heart I bear

Shall never sag with doubt nor shake with fear.   10
                  [Enter a SERVANT.]
  The devil damn thee black, thou cream-fac'd
    loon.
  Where got'st thou that goose look?
  SERVANT. There is ten thousand—
  MACBETH.   Geese, villain?
  SERVANT.   Soldiers, sir.
  MACBETH. Go prick thy face and over-red thy fear,
    Thou lily-liver'd boy. What soldiers, patch?°   15
    Death of thy soul! Those linen cheeks of thine
    Are counselors to fear. What soldiers, wheyface?
  SERVANT. The English force, so please you.
  MACBETH. Take thy face hence.   [Exit SERVANT.]
                    Seyton!—I am sick at heart,
    When I behold—Seyton, I say!—This push°   20
    Will cheer me ever, or disseat me now.
    I have liv'd long enough. My way of life
    Is fall'n into the sear,° the yellow leaf,
    And that which should accompany old age,
    As honor, love, obedience, troops of friends,   25
    I must not look to have; but, in their stead,
    Curses, not loud but deep, mouth-honor, breath,
    Which the poor heart would fain deny, and dare
      not.
  Seyton!
                  [Enter SEYTON.]
  SEYTON. What's your gracious pleasure?
  MACBETH.   What news more?   30
  SEYTON. All is confirm'd, my lord, which was
    reported.
  MACBETH. I'll fight till from my bones my flesh be
    hack'd.
  Give me my armor.
  SEYTON.   'Tis not needed yet.
  MACBETH. I'll put it on.
  Send out moe horses, skirr° the country round,   35
    Hang those that talk of fear. Give me mine
      armor.
  How does your patient, doctor?
  DOCTOR.   Not so sick, my lord,
    As she is troubled with thick-coming fancies
    That keep her from her rest.
  MACBETH.   Cure her of that.
    Canst thou not minister to a mind diseas'd,   40
    Pluck from the memory a rooted sorrow,
    Raze out the written troubles of the brain,
    And with some sweet oblivious° antidote
    Cleanse the stuff'd bosom of that perilous stuff
    Which weighs upon the heart?
  DOCTOR.   Therein the patient   45
    Must minister to himself.

---

buckle . . . rule keep his sick rage under control
upbraid his faith-breach call his disloyalty to account
medicine . . . weal i.e., Malcolm, the healer of the sick
  state
taint be tainted
epicures i.e., high living, unlike the Scots
sway by am ruled by

patch fool   push attack   sear withered
skirr scour   oblivious causing oblivion

MACBETH. Throw physic° to the dogs, I'll none of it.
Come, put mine armor on; give me my staff.
Seyton, send out. Doctor, the thanes fly from me.
Come, sir, dispatch. If thou couldst, doctor, cast°
50 The water of my land, find her disease,
And purge it to a sound and pristine health,
I would applaud thee to the very echo,
That should applaud again. Pull 't off, I say.
55 What rhubarb, senna, or what purgative drug
Would scour these English hence? Hear'st thou of them?
DOCTOR. Aye, my good lord; your royal preparation
Makes us hear something.
MACBETH.   Bring it after me.
I will not be afraid of death and bane°
60 Till Birnam forest come to Dunsinane.
DOCTOR. [Aside] Were I from Dunsinane away and clear,
Profit again should hardly draw me here.
[Exeunt]

SCENE iv
Country near Birnam wood.

[Drum and colors. Enter MALCOLM, old SIWARD
and his SON, MACDUFF, MENTEITH, CAITHNESS,
ANGUS, LENNOX, ROSS, and SOLDIERS, marching.]
MALCOLM. Cousins, I hope the days are near at hand
That chambers will be safe.
MENTEITH.   We doubt it nothing.
SIWARD. What wood is this before us?
MENTEITH.   The wood of Birnam.
MALCOLM. Let every soldier hew him down a bough
And bear 't before him. Thereby shall we shadow
5 The numbers of our host, and make discovery
Err in report of us.
SOLDIERS.   It shall be done.
SIWARD. We learn no other but the confident tyrant
Keeps still in Dunsinane, and will endure
Our setting down° before 't.
10 MALCOLM.   'Tis his main hope;
For where there is advantage to be given,°
Both more and less° have given him the revolt,
And none serve with him but constrained things

---

physic medicine   cast analyze   bane destruction
setting down laying siege
advantage . . . given opportunity is afforded
more and less   high and low ranks

Whose hearts are absent too.
MACDUFF.   Let our just censures
Attend the true event,° and put we on   15
Industrious soldiership.
SIWARD.   The time approaches
That will with due decision make us know
What we shall say we have and what we owe.°
Thoughts speculative their unsure hopes relate,
But certain issue strokes must arbitrate.   20
Towards which advance the war.
[Exeunt, marching.]

SCENE v
Dunsinane. Within the castle.

[Enter MACBETH, SEYTON, and SOLDIERS, with
drum and colors.]
MACBETH. Hang out our banners on the outward walls;
The cry is still "They come." Our castle's strength
Will laugh a siege to scorn. Here let them lie
Till famine and the ague eat them up.
Were they not forc'd° with those that should be ours,   5
We might have met them dareful, beard to beard,
And beat them backward home.
[A cry of women within.]
What is that noise?
SEYTON. It is the cry of women, my good lord.
[Exit]
MACBETH. I have almost forgot the taste of fears.
The time has been, my senses would have cool'd   10
To hear a night-shriek, and my fell° of hair
Would at a dismal treatise° rouse and stir
As life were in 't. I have supp'd full with horrors;
Direness, familiar to my slaughterous thoughts,
Cannot once start me.
[Re-enter SEYTON.]
Wherefore was that cry?   15
SEYTON. The queen, my lord, is dead.
MACBETH. She should have died hereafter;
There would have been a time for such a word.
Tomorrow, and tomorrow, and tomorrow
Creeps in this petty pace from day to day   20
To the last syllable of recorded time,

Let . . . event let us suspend our judgments until after
  the battle is over
What . . . owe what we claim to have and what we
  really have
forc'd reinforced   fell scalp
dismal treatise horror story

And all our yesterdays have lighted fools
The way to dusty death. Out, out, brief candle!
Life's but a walking shadow, a poor player
25 That struts and frets his hour upon the stage
And then is heard no more. It is a tale
Told by an idiot, full of sound and fury,
Signifying nothing.
                    [Enter a MESSENGER.]
Thou com'st to use thy tongue; thy story
    quickly.
30 MESSENGER. Gracious my lord,
    I should report that which I say I saw,
    But know not how to do it.
MACBETH.   Well, say, sir.
MESSENGER. As I did stand my watch upon the hill,
    I look'd toward Birnam, and anon, methought,
    The wood began to move.
35 MACBETH.   Liar and slave!
MESSENGER. Let me endure your wrath, if 't be not
    so.
    Within this three mile may you see it coming,
    I say, a moving grove.
MACBETH.   If thou speak'st false,
    Upon the next tree shalt thou hang alive,
40 Till famine cling° thee. If thy speech be sooth,
    I care not if thou dost for me as much.
    I pull in resolution,° and begin
    To doubt° th' equivocation of the fiend
    That lies like truth: "Fear not, till Birnam
        wood
45 Do come to Dunsinane." And now a wood
    Comes toward Dunsinane. Arm, arm, and out!
    If this which he avouches does appear,
    There is nor flying hence nor tarrying here.
    I 'gin to be aweary of the sun
50 And wish th' estate o' the world were now
        undone.
    Ring the alarum bell! Blow, wind! Come,
        wrack!°
    At least we'll die with harness° on our back.
                                        [Exeunt]

SCENE vi
Dunsinane. Before the castle.

[*Drum and colors. Enter* MALCOLM, *old* SIWARD,
    MACDUFF, *and their* ARMY, *with boughs.*]
MALCOLM. Now near enough; your leavy screens
    throw down,
    And show like those you are. You, worthy
        uncle,

Shall, with my cousin, your right noble son,
Lead our first battle.° Worthy Macduff and we
Shall take upon 's what else remains to do,   5
According to our order.°
SIWARD.   Fare you well.
    Do we but find the tyrant's power tonight,
    Let us be beaten if we cannot fight.
MACDUFF. Make all our trumpets speak; give them
    all breath,
    Those clamorous harbingers of blood and death.   10
                                        [Exeunt]

SCENE vii
Another part of the field.

[*Alarums. Enter* MACBETH.]
MACBETH. They have tied me to a stake; I cannot
    fly,
    But bearlike I must fight the course. What's he
    That was not born of woman? Such a one
    Am I to fear, or none.
                    [Enter YOUNG SIWARD.]
YOUNG SIWARD. What is thy name?
MACBETH.   Thou'lt be afraid to hear it.   5
YOUNG SIWARD. No, though thou call'st thyself a
    hotter name
    Than any is in hell.
MACBETH.   My name's Macbeth.
YOUNG SIWARD. The devil himself could not
    pronounce a title
    More hateful to mine ear.
MACBETH.   No, nor more fearful.
YOUNG SIWARD. Thou liest, abhorred tyrant; with
    my sword   10
    I'll prove the lie thou speak'st.
            [*They fight, and* YOUNG SIWARD *is slain.*]
MACBETH.   Thou wast born of woman.
    But swords I smile at, weapons laugh to scorn,
    Brandish'd by man that's of a woman born.
                                        [*Exit*]
            [*Alarums. Enter* MACDUFF.]
MACDUFF. That way the noise is. Tyrant, show thy
    face!
    If thou be'st slain and with no stroke of mine,   15
    My wife and children's ghosts will haunt me
        still.°
    I cannot strike at wretched kerns,° whose arms
    Are hir'd to bear their staves.° Either thou,
        Macbeth,
    Or else my sword, with an unbatter'd edge,

cling shrivel
pull in resolution rein in (my former) confidence
doubt suspect   *wrack* ruin   *harness* armor

battle battalion   *order* plan of battle
still always   *kerns* common foot soldiers
staves wooden spears

I sheathe again undeeded. There thou shouldst
20   be;
By this great clatter, one of greatest note
Seems bruited.° Let me find him, fortune!
And more I beg not.   [*Exit. Alarums.*]
         [*Enter* MALCOLM *and old* SIWARD.]
SIWARD. This way, my lord; the castle's gently
     render'd.°
25   The tyrant's people on both sides do fight,
The noble thanes do bravely in the war,
The day almost itself professes yours,
And little is to do.
MALCOLM.   We have met with foes
That strike beside us.
SIWARD.   Enter, sir, the castle.
                        [*Exeunt. Alarum.*]

                    SCENE viii
               Another part of the field.

                 [*Enter* MACBETH.]
MACBETH. Why should I play the Roman fool and
     die
On mine own sword? Whiles I see lives, the
     gashes
Do better upon them.
                 [*Enter* MACDUFF.]
MACDUFF.   Turn, hellhound, turn!
MACBETH. Of all men else I have avoided thee.
5   But get thee back; my soul is too much charg'd
With blood of thine already.
MACDUFF.   I have no words.
My voice is in my sword, thou bloodier villain
Than terms can give thee out!   [*They fight.*]
MACBETH.   Thou losest labor.
As easy mayst thou the intrenchant° air
10   With thy keen sword impress as make me bleed.
Let fall thy blade on vulnerable crests;
I bear a charmed life, which must not yield
To one of woman born.
MACDUFF.   Despair thy charm,
And let the angel whom thou still hast serv'd
15   Tell thee Macduff was from his mother's womb
Untimely ripp'd.
MACBETH. Accursed be that tongue that tells me
     so,
For it hath cow'd my better part of man!
And be these juggling fiends no more believ'd
20   That palter° with us in a double sense,
That keep the word of promise to our ear,
And break it to our hope. I'll not fight with thee.

MACDUFF. Then yield thee, coward,
And live to be the show and gaze o' the time.
We'll have thee, as our rarer monsters are,   25
Painted upon a pole, and underwrit,
"Here may you see the tyrant."
MACBETH.   I will not yield
To kiss the ground before young Malcolm's feet
And to be baited° with the rabble's curse.
Though Birnam wood be come to Dunsinane   30
And thou oppos'd being of no woman born,
Yet I will try the last. Before my body
I throw my warlike shield. Lay on, Macduff,
And damn'd be him that first cries "Hold,
     enough!"   [*Exeunt, fighting. Alarums.*]
[*Retreat. Flourish. Enter, with drum and colors,*
     MALCOLM, *old* SIWARD, ROSS, *the other* THANES,
               and SOLDIERS.]
MALCOLM. I would the friends we miss were safe
     arriv'd.   35
SIWARD. Some must go off.° And yet, by these I see,
So great a day as this is cheaply bought.
MALCOLM. Macduff is missing, and your noble
     son.
ROSS. Your son, my lord, has paid a soldier's debt.
He only liv'd but till he was a man,   40
The which no sooner had his prowess confirm'd
In the unshrinking station where he fought,
But like a man he died.
SIWARD.   Then he is dead?
ROSS. Aye, and brought off the field. Your cause of
     sorrow
Must not be measur'd by his worth, for then   45
It hath no end.
SIWARD.   Had he his hurts before?
ROSS. Aye, on the front.
SIWARD.   Why then, God's soldier be he!
Had I as many sons as I have hairs,°
I would not wish them to a fairer death.
And so his knell is knoll'd.
MALCOLM.   He's worth more sorrow,   50
And that I'll spend for him.
SIWARD.   He's worth no more.
They say he parted well and paid his score.
And so God be with him! Here comes newer
     comfort.
     [*Re-enter* MACDUFF, *with* MACBETH's *head.*]
MACDUFF. Hail, king! For so thou art. Behold
     where stands
Th' usurper's cursed head. The time is free.   55
I see thee compass'd with thy kingdom's pearl°

---

bruited noisily announced   *render'd* surrendered
intrenchant untrenchable   *palter* equivocate

baited i.e., bear-baited, chained and attacked by dogs
go off i.e., die   *hairs* (with pun)
compass'd . . . pearl surrounded by the nobility of the
     land

That speak my salutation in their minds,
Whose voices I desire aloud with mine:
Hail, King of Scotland!°

ALL.   Hail, King of Scotland!
                                          [*Flourish.*]

MALCOLM. We shall not spend a large expense of
60   time
Before we reckon with your several loves
And make us even with you. My thanes and
   kinsmen,
Henceforth be earls, the first that ever Scotland
In such an honor nam'd. What's more to do,

Which would be planted newly with the time,   65
As calling home our exil'd friends abroad
That fled the snares of watchful tyranny,
Producing forth the cruel ministers
Of this dead butcher and his fiendlike queen,
Who, as 'tis thought, by self and violent hands   70
Took off her life—this, and what needful else
That calls upon us, by the grace of Grace
We will perform in measure,° time, and place.
So thanks to all at once and to each one,
Whom we invite to see us crown'd at Scone.   75
                                     [*Flourish. Exeunt.*]

Hail . . . Scotland   (Shakespeare's compliment to King
James)

in measure   i.e., in full measure

AFTERWORD

The last, shortest, and most concentrated of Shakespeare's four supreme tragedies, with all of which it has much in common in its dramatic force, its penetrating characterization, its poetic power, its breadth and depth, *Macbeth* is at the same time strongly linked to the two major tragedies that immediately followed it, *Antony and Cleopatra* and *Coriolanus*. It is primarily in the character of the hero that the tragedy marks a notable shift from the earlier toward the final tragedies.

The heroes of all the earlier tragedies, including Brutus of *Julius Caesar*, are essentially good men, and most are distinguished examples of nobility and honor. Though Brutus assassinates "the foremost man of all the world," he does so selflessly, for what he firmly believes to be the good of his country: "Not that I loved Caesar less, but that I loved Rome more." Hamlet's nobility is beyond any reasonable question; he is concerned for both his own and Denmark's honor and reputation in the world, and the fact profoundly influences his conduct and contributes to his famous "delay." Othello commits an appalling act, the murder of his innocent wife, but he does so in spite of his personal emotions at the moment, in the mistaken conviction that it is a good and necessary act required by justice, "lest she betray moe men." Lear first appears as a foolish, vain, and selfish old man who has perhaps never experienced a genuine feeling of compassion for another human being; but he is constantly "every inch a king," comes to learn compassion, and ends his ordeal a wiser and better man. In each of these tragedies, evil (as distinct from some frailty or error of judgment) is represented as external to the hero, in the persons of others—Cassius in *Julius Caesar*, Claudius in *Hamlet*, Iago in *Othello*, Regan, Goneril, Edmund, and Cornwall in *King Lear*. Except for Cassius, all these are outright villains whose evil directly affects the hero and his actions, yet the hero's nature remains in itself as noble as before, uncorrupted and incorruptible.

For the moment overleaping Macbeth, we find in the last tragedies heroes whose innermost natures are at the least suspect, who, so to speak, carry their own "villain" inside themselves. The valiant Antony, famous warrior, magnanimous captain, world conqueror, and "triple pillar" of the Empire, turns his back squarely on the kind of honor that directs the decisions and actions of a Brutus or a Hamlet, immerses himself in the voluptuous pleasures of Egypt, and bids Rome—where duty lies—"in Tiber melt." Once, but briefly, he rouses himself from indulgence, returns to Rome, marries Caesar's sister to keep the peace, but almost immediately deserts her and hastens back to his "Egyptian dish," never to return. Coriolanus, like Antony a famous warrior, holds valor as the "chiefest virtue" of a man and yields to no man in his devotion to honor, but carries also in his nature an inflexible pride that stands just as high as his valor and is inextricably bound up with it. In these final tragedies, thus, though external villains, enemies, antagonists also participate in the action, the fatal evil is that which is contained within the heroes and is inseparable from their best virtues.

In the tragedy of *Macbeth* there is no villain at all, outside the hero. Of all Shakespeare's tragic protagonists, only Macbeth knowingly and deliberately plots and commits a wicked deed and embarks upon a wicked career. Brutus, to mention the perfect contrast, assassinates Caesar in the certainty that his country requires Caesar's death; but Macbeth kills Duncan in the certainty that it is a wicked act committed for selfish gain. Cassius tempts and misleads Brutus, but he does not corrupt his nature; Brutus follows Cassius in the belief that Cassius leads him toward good, not evil. The Witches and Lady Macbeth tempt and mislead Macbeth, but they also do corrupt him (for his nature already had a crack in it that admitted corruption) and he follows their lead knowing that it is toward evil. Hence if we blame these tempters we are justified in blaming them only secondarily; Macbeth himself makes the choice, and it is a particularly heinous one: to kill an old man, a good man, his house guest, his king to whom he has sworn allegiance, his generous benefactor—and to do so while the victim lies asleep in bed. The Witches, it should be observed, never once suggest murder, never suggest any means at all by which the promised crown is to be gained; Lady Macbeth suggests murder, but her husband has thought of it before she speaks to him. Thus murder is Macbeth's own idea, and it occurs to him because he is ambitious to be king. Though Lady Macbeth exhorts, shames, and fairly drives her husband on to the initial murder, besides proving an able accomplice with bloody daggers once the deed has been done, the fact diminishes not a whit the central guilt, which is Macbeth's alone.

So Macbeth, unlike the earlier tragic heroes, and like the final ones, carries his own "villain" within. Nevertheless, as is the case also with Antony and Coriolanus, the problem of defining his true character is a severe one and continues to be the subject of debate. On the one side stand critics who insist that the hero, besides being loyal and valiant in the highest degree on the field of battle—a fact to which the text gives ample testimony—is essentially a *good* man who is corrupted despite a strong moral sense and inner struggle against corruption, by the overwhelming combination of Fate, his wife, sudden and unexpected opportunity, and his swelling ambition. These critics, some of whose names are among those outstanding in Shakespeare criticism, can point to a good deal of evidence to support their views: to the early reports of other participants on Macbeth ("It is a peerless kinsman"), to the inward horror that he experiences and the air-drawn dagger that his imagination conjures up just before the murder, to the immediate revulsion and soul panic that affect him during the act of murder and afterward, to his expressed wish that the early callers who come knocking at the gate could indeed wake Duncan with their knocking, to his fits of conscience, when his mind is "full of scorpions" and he complains of "these terrible dreams/ That shake us nightly." Gradually, say these critics, his erstwhile moral fiber deteriorates: he can kill Banquo with less horror than Duncan (though the Ghost's arrival at the banquet shakes him badly); he can kill Lady Macduff and her children with no seeming pangs (though later he first refuses to fight Macduff because "My soul is too much charg'd/ With blood of thine already"); he becomes a tyrant, and, if we believe the report brought Malcolm in England, all Scotland is now filled "with sighs and groans and shrieks," and death has become so frequent that "The dead man's knell/ Is there scarce ask'd for who." And finally, when the shriek of women announces his wife's death, he can no longer feel emotion, for he is "supp'd full with horrors." Such, according to what is probably the majority view among critics of nearly three centuries, is the progress of Macbeth: from a basically good man, a moral man, through stages of corruption, revulsion, and unceasing pangs of conscience, to remorseless tyrant and wanton killer, and at last to an unfeeling lump, surfeited alike with murder and sorrow, not unlike the Second Murderer, hired to kill Banquo: "I am one, my liege,/ Whom the vile blows and buffets of the world/ Hath so incens'd that I am reckless what/ I do to spite the world."

But by another set of views Macbeth's history is no such thing. It is arguable that, martial valor, physical courage notwithstanding, Macbeth is not basically a good man at all, but a man of criminal mentality, either already corrupted or in any event corruptible, because he possesses a severely defective moral mechanism, or no moral sense at all. Fate, Witches, Lady Macbeth, opportunity, overreaching ambition, all combined, would never corrupt a Brutus or a Hamlet. Whether Macbeth had or had not already thought of killing Duncan or whether the Witches put the first idea of murder into his head are only academic questions: if he was not already corrupt, yet he was corruptible, and the difference is only one of degree. The strongest textual evidence of his bent toward, or his susceptibility to, immoral action is supplied by the crucial "If it were done" soliloquy (I, vii), wherein the prospective murderer raises the question of murder and then proceeds to talk himself out of killing Duncan, but not on moral grounds. Bluntly paraphrased, the soliloquy says that Macbeth would do the deed, risking the Hereafter with its possible punishment, if only he might be assured of escaping apprehension and punishment in this earthly life—"But here, upon this bank and shoal of time." But he finds the odds against avoiding earthly consequences too great to risk:

> . . . we but teach
> Bloody instructions, which, being taught, return
> To plague th' inventor.

Briefly he speaks of the impropriety of murdering a house guest, but it is no more than that, only an impropriety—socially, not morally, unacceptable. Finally, he appears to stand on the verge of reasoning that Duncan should not be killed because he is a *good* man and king, but then, grossly, he concludes that it is worse to kill a *good* man and king because in that case the repercussion will be greater throughout the land, and he will therefore be all the more likely to be run down, caught, and punished, for Duncan's virtues "Shall blow the horrid deed in every eye."

So says the soliloquy, which is composed of Macbeth's own words and proceeds from his own soul. He talks himself out of the murder, but not for moral reasons. Immediately afterward, he tells his wife, "We will proceed no further in this business." Lady Macbeth, who evidently knows her husband well, thereupon proceeds very quickly and efficiently (Act I, scene vii of *Macbeth* is one of the most economical scenes in Shakespeare) to talk him back into going on with the murder. However, she does so not by trying to overcome any "moral scruples" (she wastes no words on such nonsense), but by showing him *how they can do the deed and get away with it*. When she has outlined her simple plan, Macbeth, with a burst of renewed enthusiasm, agrees to do the deed. Taken together, the soliloquy and the brief interview with Lady Macbeth provide grim evidence for the view that Macbeth is a man who not only lacks moral conscience but has no understanding of what it is.

But even though it be a fact that he has no truly moral restraints before the murder, is it not true that immediately thereafter his conscience comes alive, so that he is tormented by remorse through all the events that follow? What of the "scorpions" that sting his mind, and the "dreams that shake us nightly"? Are not these unmistakable symptoms of a live conscience, of outraged moral sensibilities? No, say the critics who deny that Macbeth was ever a good man: these are rather the disturbances of one who lives in mortal terror that his crime will be exposed, that the crown will be torn from his head, and that, in any event, his heirs will not succeed to the throne. By this view, Macbeth's is not the story of a basically good man's swift moral deterioration, but the history of a crime and its consequences for one who lacked moral sense from the outset. According to this view, finally, Macbeth never does repent on moral grounds, never recognizes that he has done wrong—never, indeed, learns what "wrong" means. Rather, he learns only to regret that he could not "get away with it," and spitefully blames the Witches for having misinformed him: ". . . be these juggling fiends no more believ'd."

Shakespeare's presentation of Macbeth's character is much fuller and more explicit than that of Lady Macbeth's. The "fiend-like queen" appears on the stage only at intervals after the murder of Duncan; hence the history of her development as a dramatic character, the main feature of which is her deterioration as a strong-willed human being, is incompletely unfolded, with extensive gaps between the staged segments. Yet enough is shown that, surprisingly, we follow her course with considerably greater unanimity of critical opinion than has yet been achieved for Macbeth's character. If we cannot agree even on whether Macbeth has or has not a moral sense, we can be sure enough that Lady Macbeth's conscience is real and that it is even more potent than the "undaunted mettle" of her will, for it destroys that and ultimately destroys her as well. Bearing out the conspicuous pattern of paradox that runs throughout the play—"Fair is foul, and foul is fair," "So foul and fair a day I have not seen," "Lesser than Macbeth, and greater," "Not so happy, yet much happier," and so on—Lady Macbeth is at once stronger than her husband, and weaker; at once better, and worse. She is stronger in that when he falters, she provides the sustaining force; weaker in that her will ultimately disintegrates, whereas he, at the very end, can still throw his shield boldly before his body and cry, "Lay on, Macduff!" She is better than her husband in that she is capable of realizing the moral wrong of their deed whereas he can recognize only that it is risky, but she is also worse than he because, knowing that murder is wrong, she yet pushes him into committing it. Her early, "How easy is it, then!" easily persuades Macbeth, but it never can subdue her own inexorable conscience.

It is noteworthy, in this connection, that though most of the very greatest actors have played Macbeth, they have always mainly distinguished themselves rather as Hamlet than as Macbeth, whereas for actresses the pinnacle has usually been reached with Lady Macbeth, brief as the role is, but filled with high points. The play itself has an unbroken history of success on the stage from the seventeenth century to the present. Pepys records in his diary that he attended seven or eight performances in London between 1664 and 1668, three of them in a single year. *Macbeth* "plays" exceptionally well, not only because it contains such surefire theatrical wares as murders, witches, a ghost, an air-drawn dagger, and sundry other spectacular apparitions, but because it more than any other tragedy of Shakespeare's, even *Othello*, the nearest rival, is a true spellbinder. The central action is a single one, and it moves forward swiftly and relentlessly, building its force right up to the final confrontation of Macbeth and Macduff. Except for the brief episode of the Porter (the effect of which is brilliantly illuminated by DeQuincey in his "On the Knocking at the Gate in Macbeth"), the play provides virtually no moment for relaxation. In this respect it contrasts most markedly with *Hamlet*, which is leisurely and as filled with comic moments as most comedies, and with *King Lear*, which contains a secondary plot that provides great bustle and variety, with diversions of many sorts.

But perhaps what most contributes to the spellbinding effect is not the tight dramatic construction but the poetry of *Macbeth*. Not only the Witches, but Macbeth and his Lady also, during moments of greatest intensity, strike the hypnotic accents of incantation. The poetry of *Macbeth* is hardly lyrical, as in *Romeo and Juliet* and *Richard II*, nor is it resonantly musical, as in *Hamlet*. More often it is fierce and cruel, or dark and sinister in its sound. On occasion it hisses like a snake, as when Lady Macbeth advises her husband: "Look like the innocent flower,/ But be the serpent under 't." The example is characteristic: throughout the play, the language is remarkably suited to the occasion, the immediate subject, and the speaker.

But the richest poetry of the tragedy is spoken by Macbeth himself, who is quickly revealed as one of Shakespeare's pre-eminent poets. Surely no hero in any of the plays has a more fertile and vivid imagination, an imagination, of course, that is instrumental not only to his flow of sharp images and vivid words, but to his decisions and the action itself. Macbeth's poetic powers are enriched as his experience of life deepens in the course of his tragedy, as may be quickly recognized by comparing his facile but superficial and glittery description of the murdered Duncan in the death chamber (II, iii) with the famous "Tomorrow, and tomorrow, and tomorrow" speech at the death of his wife (V, v). But the boundless potentiality of his imagination, which is at once his blessing and his curse, is first and perhaps best revealed in the two major soliloquies that precede the murder of Duncan: "If it were done when 'tis done" (I, vii); and "Is this a dagger which I see before me" (II, i), wherein the terrifying excess of Macbeth's creative imagination is shown to be—paradoxically, again—the very seed of his undoing.

A NOTE ON THE COMPOSITION OF THE PLAY

According to the best available evidence, *Macbeth* was written in 1605–1606; it was first published in the Folio of 1623. Shakespeare's source was two episodes in Holinshed's *Chronicles*. The first episode tells the history of Macbeth; the second, from which were drawn details for the murder of Duncan, narrates the story of a King Duff by Donwald.

Coriolanus

DRAMATIS PERSONÆ

CAIUS MARCIUS   *afterwards* CAIUS MARCIUS
   CORIOLANUS
TITUS LARTIUS ⎫
COMINIUS   ⎬ *generals against the Volscians*
MENENIUS AGRIPPA   *friend to Coriolanus*
SICINIUS VELUTUS ⎫
JUNIUS BRUTUS   ⎬ *tribunes of the people*
YOUNG MARCIUS   *son of Coriolanus*
A ROMAN HERALD
TULLUS AUFIDIUS   *general of the Volscians*
LIEUTENANT   *to Aufidius*
CONSPIRATORS   *with Aufidius*

A CITIZEN   *of Antium*
TWO VOLSCIAN GUARDS
VOLUMNIA   *mother to Coriolanus*
VIRGILIA   *wife to Coriolanus*
VALERIA   *friend to Virgilia*
GENTLEWOMAN   *attending on Virgilia*
ROMAN *and* VOLSCIAN SENATORS, PATRICIANS,
   ÆDILES, LICTORS, SOLDIERS, CITIZENS,
   MESSENGERS, SERVANTS *to Aufidius, and other*
   ATTENDANTS
SCENE :   *Rome and the neighborhood; Corioli and*
   the neighborhood; Antium.

ACT I

SCENE i
Rome. A street.

[*Enter a company of mutinous* CITIZENS, *with
staves, clubs, and other weapons.*]
FIRST CITIZEN. Before we proceed any further, hear
   me speak.
ALL. Speak, speak.
FIRST CITIZEN. You are all resolved rather to die
5   than to famish?
ALL. Resolved, resolved.
FIRST CITIZEN. First, you know Caius Marcius is
   chief enemy to the people.
ALL. We know 't, we know 't.
10 FIRST CITIZEN. Let us kill him, and we'll have
   corn° at our own price. Is 't a verdict?
ALL. No more talking on 't. Let it be done. Away,
   away!

corn i.e., not our Indian corn, but wheat or other grain

SECOND CITIZEN. One word, good citizens.
FIRST CITIZEN. We are accounted poor citizens, the   15
   patricians, good. What authority surfeits on
   would relieve us. If they would yield us but the
   superfluity while it were wholesome, we might
   guess they relieved us humanely; but they
   think we are too dear.° The leanness that   20
   afflicts us, the object° of our misery, is as an
   inventory to particularize their abundance;°
   our sufferance is a gain to them. Let us revenge
   this with our pikes, ere we become rakes.° For
   the gods know I speak this in hunger for bread,   25
   not in thirst for revenge.
SECOND CITIZEN. Would you proceed especially
   against Caius Marcius?

dear expensive   *object* spectacle
inventory . . . abundance i.e., like a reverse image
  cataloguing the patricians' prosperity
pikes . . . rakes pitchforks, before we become as lean as
  rakes

ALL. Against him first. He's a very dog to the com-
30   monalty.
SECOND CITIZEN. Consider you what services he has
      done for his country?
FIRST CITIZEN. Very well, and could be content to
      give him good report for 't but that he pays
35   himself with being proud.
SECOND CITIZEN. Nay, but speak not maliciously.
FIRST CITIZEN. I say unto you, what he hath done
      famously, he did it to that end. Though soft-
      conscienced men can be content to say it was for
40   his country, he did it to please his mother and to
      be partly proud°—which he is, even to the
      altitude of his virtue.°
SECOND CITIZEN. What he cannot help in his
      nature, you account a vice in him. You must in
45   no way say he is covetous.
FIRST CITIZEN. If I must not, I need not be barren of
      accusations. He hath faults, with surplus, to tire
      in repetition. [Shouts within] What shouts are
      these? The other side o' the city is risen. Why
50   stay we prating here? To the Capitol!
ALL. Come, come.
FIRST CITIZEN. Soft! Who comes here?
              [Enter MENENIUS AGRIPPA.]
SECOND CITIZEN. Worthy Menenius Agrippa, one
      that hath always loved the people.
55 FIRST CITIZEN. He's one honest enough. Would all
      the rest were so!
MENENIUS. What work's, my countrymen, in
      hand? Where go you
      With bats and clubs? The matter? Speak, I
60   pray you.
FIRST CITIZEN. Our business is not unknown to the
      Senate. They have had inkling, this fortnight,
      what we intend to do, which now we'll show
      'em in deeds. They say poor suitors have strong
65   breaths. They shall know we have strong arms
      too.
MENENIUS. Why, masters, my good friends, mine
      honest neighbors,
      Will you undo yourselves?
FIRST CITIZEN. We cannot, sir, we are undone al-
      ready.
70 MENENIUS. I tell you, friends, most charitable care
      Have the patricians of you. For your wants,
      Your suffering in this dearth,° you may as well
      Strike at the heaven with your staves as lift them
      Against the Roman state, whose course will on
75   The way it takes, cracking ten thousand curbs
      Of more strong link asunder than can ever

Appear in your impediment. For the dearth,
      The gods, not the patricians, make it, and
      Your knees to them, not arms, must help. Alack,
      You are transported by calamity   80
      Thither where more attends you, and you
      slander
      The helms° o' the state, who care for you like
      fathers
      When you curse them as enemies.
FIRST CITIZEN. Care for us! True, indeed! They
      ne'er cared for us yet. Suffer us to famish, and   85
      their storehouses crammed with grain; make
      edicts for usury to support usurers; repeal daily
      any wholesome act established against the rich,
      and provide more piercing statutes daily to
      chain up and restrain the poor. If the wars eat us 90
      not up, they will, and there's all the love they
      bear us.
MENENIUS. Either you must
      Confess yourselves wondrous malicious,
      Or be accus'd of folly. I shall tell you   95
      A pretty tale. It may be you have heard it;
      But, since it serves my purpose, I will venture
      To stale 't° a little more.
FIRST CITIZEN. Well, I'll hear it, sir. Yet you must
      not think to fob off our disgrace° with a tale.   100
      But, an 't please you, deliver.
MENENIUS. There was a time when all the body's
      members
      Rebell'd against the belly, thus accus'd it:
      That only like a gulf it did remain
      I' the midst o' the body, idle and unactive,   105
      Still cupboarding the viand, never bearing
      Like labor with the rest, where th' other
      instruments
      Did see and hear, devise, instruct, walk, feel,
      And, mutually participate,° did minister
      Unto the appetite and affection° common   110
      Of the whole body. The belly answer'd—
FIRST CITIZEN. Well, sir, what answer made the
      belly?
MENENIUS. Sir, I shall tell you. With a kind of
      smile,
      Which ne'er came from the lungs, but even
      thus—
      For, look you, I may make the belly smile   115
      As well as speak—it tauntingly replied
      To the discontented members, the mutinous
      parts
      That envied his receipt;° even so most fitly

---

partly proud in part to be proud
altitude . . . virtue i.e., his pride is as high as his valor
dearth famine

helms helmsmen   stale 't make it stale
disgrace hardship
participate contributing   affection desires
receipt i.e., of foodstuff

As you malign our senators for that°
They are not such as you.
120 FIRST CITIZEN.   Your belly's answer? What!
The kingly-crowned head, the vigilant eye,
The counselor heart, the arm our soldier,
Our steed the leg, the tongue our trumpeter,
With other muniments and petty helps
In this our fabric, if that they—
125 MENENIUS.   What then?
'Fore me,° this fellow speaks! What then?
What then?
FIRST CITIZEN. Should by the cormorant belly be
restrain'd,
Who is the sink o' the body—
MENENIUS.   Well, what then?
FIRST CITIZEN. The former agents, if they did
complain,
What could the belly answer?
130 MENENIUS.   I will tell you.
If you'll bestow a small—of what you have
little—
Patience awhile, you'st hear the belly's answer.
FIRST CITIZEN. You're long about it.
MENENIUS.   Note me this, good friend.
Your most grave belly was deliberate,
135 Not rash like his accusers, and thus answer'd:
"True is it, my incorporate° friends," quoth he,
"That I receive the general food at first,
Which you do live upon; and fit it is,
Because I am the storehouse and the shop
140 Of the whole body. But, if you do remember,
I send it through the rivers of your blood,
Even to the court, the heart, to the seat o' the
brain;
And, through the cranks and offices° of man,
The strongest nerves and small inferior veins
145 From me receive that natural competency°
Whereby they live. And though that all at once,
You, my good friends"—this says the belly,
mark me—
FIRST CITIZEN. Aye, sir. Well, well.
MENENIUS.   "Though all at once cannot
See what I do deliver out to each,
150 Yet I can make my audit up that all
From me do back receive the flour of all
And leave me but the bran." What say you to 't?
FIRST CITIZEN. It was an answer. How apply you
this?
MENENIUS. The Senators of Rome are this good
belly,
155 And you the mutinous members. For examine

Their counsels and their cares, digest things
rightly
Touching the weal o' the common,° you shall
find
No public benefit which you receive
But it proceeds or comes from them to you
And no way from yourselves. What do you
think,   160
You, the great toe of this assembly?
FIRST CITIZEN. I the great toe! Why the great toe?
MENENIUS. For that, being one o' the lowest,
basest, poorest
Of this most wise rebellion, thou go'st foremost.
Thou rascal, that art worst in blood to run,   165
Lead'st first to win some vantage.
But make you ready your stiff bats and clubs.
Rome and her rats are at the point of battle;
The one side must have bale.°
             [Enter CAIUS MARCIUS.]
                                Hail, noble Marcius!
MARCIUS. Thanks. What's the matter, you dis-
sentious rogues,   170
That, rubbing the poor itch of your opinion,
Make yourselves scabs?
FIRST CITIZEN.   We have ever your good word.
MARCIUS. He that will give good words to thee will
flatter
Beneath abhorring. What would you have, you
curs,
That like nor peace nor war? The one affrights
you,   175
The other makes you proud. He that trusts to
you,
Where he should find you lions, finds you hares,
Where foxes, geese. You are no surer, no,
Than is the coal of fire upon the ice
Or hailstone in the sun. Your virtue is   180
To make him worthy whose offense subdues
him
And curse that justice did it.° Who deserves
greatness
Deserves your hate, and your affections are
A sick man's appetite who desires most that
Which would increase his evil. He that depends 185
Upon your favors swims with fins of lead
And hews down oaks with rushes. Hang ye!
Trust ye?
With every minute you do change a mind,
And call him noble that was now your hate,
Him vile that was your garland. What's the
matter,   190

---

for that because
'Fore me On my word!   *incorporate* united
cranks and offices passages and organs
competency allowance

weal o' the common common welfare   *bale* ruin
make him . . . did it glorify him whose offense brings
     penalty and curse the justice that imposed it

That in these several places of the city
You cry against the noble Senate, who,
Under the gods, keep you in awe, which else
Would feed on one another? What's their
  seeking?
MENENIUS. For corn at their own rates, whereof,
  they say,
195 The city is well stor'd.
MARCIUS.   Hang 'em! They say!
They'll sit by the fire and presume to know
What's done i' the Capitol, who's like to rise,
Who thrives, and who declines; side factions°
  and give out
200 Conjectural marriages, making parties strong
And feebling such as stand not in their liking
Below their cobbled° shoes. They say there's
  grain enough!
Would the nobility lay aside their ruth,°
And let me use my sword, I'd make a quarry°
205 With thousands of these quarter'd slaves, as high
As I could pick° my lance.
MENENIUS. Nay, these are almost thoroughly
  persuaded,
For though abundantly they lack discretion,
Yet are they passing° cowardly. But, I beseech
  you,
What says the other troop?
210 MARCIUS.   They are dissolv'd: hang 'em!
They said they were an-hungry; sigh'd forth
  proverbs,
That hunger broke stone walls, that dogs must
  eat,
That meat was made for mouths, that the gods
  sent not
Corn for the rich men only. With these shreds
They vented their complainings, which being
215   answer'd,
And a petition granted them, a strange one—
To break the heart of generosity
And make bold power look pale—they threw
  their caps
As they would hang them on the horns o' the
  moon,
Shouting their emulation.°
220 MENENIUS.   What is granted them?
MARCIUS. Five tribunes to defend their vulgar
  wisdoms,
Of their own choice. One's Junius Brutus,
Sicinius Velutus, and I know not—'Sdeath!°
The rabble should have first unroof'd the city

Ere so prevail'd with me. It will in time   225
Win upon power° and throw forth greater
  themes
For insurrection's arguing.
MENENIUS.   This is strange.
MARCIUS. Go get you home, you fragments!
    [Enter a MESSENGER, hastily.]
MESSENGER. Where's Caius Marcius?
MARCIUS.   Here. What's the matter?
MESSENGER. The news is, sir, the Volsces are in
  arms.   230
MARCIUS. I am glad on 't. Then we shall ha'
  means to vent
Our musty superfluity.° See, our best elders.
    [Enter COMINIUS, TITUS LARTIUS, and other
    SENATORS; JUNIUS BRUTUS and SICINIUS VELUTUS.]
FIRST SENATOR. Marcius, 'tis true that you have
  lately told us—
The Volsces are in arms.
MARCIUS.   They have a leader,
Tullus Aufidius, that will put you to 't.°   235
I sin in envying his nobility,
And were I anything but what I am,
I would wish me only he.
COMINIUS.   You have fought together?
MARCIUS. Were half to half the world by th' ears
  and he
Upon my party, I'd revolt to make   240
Only my wars with him. He is a lion
That I am proud to hunt.
FIRST SENATOR.   Then, worthy Marcius,
Attend upon Cominius to these wars.
COMINIUS. It is your former promise.
MARCIUS.   Sir, it is,
And I am constant. Titus Lartius, thou   245
Shalt see me once more strike at Tullus' face.
What, art thou stiff? Stand'st out?
TITUS.   No, Caius Marcius.
I'll lean upon one crutch and fight with t'other
Ere stay behind this business.
MENENIUS.   O, true-bred!
FIRST SENATOR. Your company to the Capitol,
  where I know   250
Our greatest friends attend us.
TITUS.   [To COMINIUS] Lead you on.
[To MARCIUS] Follow Cominius; we must follow
  you,
Right worthy you priority.°
COMINIUS.   Noble Marcius!

---

side factions take sides   cobbled repaired
ruth pity   quarry heap, as of wild game
pick hurl   passing surpassingly   emulation envy
'Sdeath by God's death

Win upon power rise above lawful authority
vent . . . superfluity i.e., solve our overpopulation
  problem
put you to 't test you to the utmost
Right . . . priority you well deserve to precede us

FIRST SENATOR. [*To the* CITIZENS] Hence to your
    homes. Be gone!
MARCIUS.   Nay, let them follow.
    The Volsces have much corn; take these rats
255   thither
    To gnaw their garners. Worshipful mutiners,
    Your valor puts well forth.° Pray, follow.
                [CITIZENS *steal away. Exeunt all*
                    but SICINIUS *and* BRUTUS.]
SICINIUS. Was ever man so proud as is this Marcius?
BRUTUS. He has no equal.
SICINIUS. When we were chosen tribunes for the
260   people—
BRUTUS. Mark'd you his lip and eyes?
SICINIUS.   Nay, but his taunts.
BRUTUS. Being mov'd, he will not spare to gird° the
    gods.
SICINIUS. Bemock the modest moon.
BRUTUS. The present wars devour him! He is
    grown
    Too proud to be so valiant.
265 SICINIUS.   Such a nature,
    Tickled with good success, disdains the shadow
    Which he treads on at noon. But I do wonder
    His insolence can brook to be commanded
    Under Cominius.
BRUTUS.   Fame, at the which he aims,
270   In whom already he's well grac'd, cannot
    Better be held, nor more attain'd, than by
    A place below the first. For what miscarries
    Shall be the general's fault, though he perform
    To th' utmost of a man, and giddy censure°
275   Will then cry out of Marcius, "O, if he
    Had borne the business!"
SICINIUS.   Besides, if things go well,
    Opinion, that so sticks on Marcius, shall
    Of his demerits° rob Cominius.
BRUTUS.   Come.
    Half all Cominius' honors are to Marcius,
    Though Marcius earn'd them not, and all his
280   faults
    To Marcius shall be honors, though indeed
    In aught he merit not.
SICINIUS.   Let's hence and hear
    How the dispatch is made,° and in what fashion,
    More than his singularity,° he goes
    Upon this present action.
285 BRUTUS.   Let's along.   [*Exeunt*]

---

puts well forth makes a good show
gird challenge, "take on"
giddy censure foolish public opinion
demerits just deserts
dispatch is made matter is dispatched
singularity i.e., usual strange way

SCENE ii
Corioli. The Senate House.

[*Enter* TULLUS AUFIDIUS, *with* SENATORS *of Corioli.*]
FIRST SENATOR. So, your opinion is, Aufidius,
    That they of Rome are enter'd in our counsels
    And know how we proceed.
AUFIDIUS.   Is it not yours?
    What ever have been thought on in this state
    That could be brought to bodily act ere Rome   5
    Had circumvention?° 'Tis not four days gone
    Since I heard thence. These are the words—I
    think
    I have the letter here—yes, here it is.

    [*Reads*] They have press'd° a power, but it is not
    known
    Whether for east or west. The dearth is great,   10
    The people mutinous, and it is rumor'd
    Cominius, Marcius your old enemy—
    Who is of Rome worse hated than of you—
    And Titus Lartius, a most valiant Roman,
    These three lead on this preparation   15
    Whither 'tis bent. Most likely 'tis for you.
    Consider of it.

FIRST SENATOR.   Our army's in the field.
    We never yet made doubt but Rome was ready
    To answer us.
AUFIDIUS.   Nor did you think it folly
    To keep your great pretenses° veil'd till when   20
    They needs must show themselves, which in the
    hatching,
    It seem'd, appear'd to Rome. By the discovery
    We shall be shorten'd in our aim, which was
    To take in many towns ere almost Rome
    Should know we were afoot.
SECOND SENATOR.   Noble Aufidius,   25
    Take your commission, hie you to your bands.
    Let us alone to guard Corioli.
    If they set down before 's, for the remove
    Bring up your army; but I think you'll find
    They've not prepar'd for us.
AUFIDIUS.   O, doubt not that.   30
    I speak from certainties. Nay, more,
    Some parcels of their power are forth already,
    And only hitherward. I leave your honors.
    If we and Caius Marcius chance to meet,
    'Tis sworn between us we shall ever strike   35
    Till one can do no more.
ALL.   The gods assist you!

---

circumvention i.e., preparation to circumvent made
    possible by forewarning
press'd a power levied an army   *pretenses* intentions

AUFIDIUS. And keep your honors safe!
FIRST SENATOR.   Farewell.
SECOND SENATOR.   Farewell.
ALL. Farewell.   [*Exeunt*]

SCENE iii
Rome. A room in MARCIUS' *house.*

[*Enter* VOLUMNIA *and* VIRGILIA. *They set them
down on two low stools and sew.*]

VOLUMNIA. I pray you, daughter, sing, or express
yourself in a more comfortable sort.° If my son
were my husband, I should freelier rejoice in
that absence wherein he won honor than in the
5   embracements of his bed where he would show
most love. When yet he was but tender-bodied
and the only son of my womb, when youth with
comeliness plucked all gaze his way, when for a
day of kings' entreaties a mother should not sell
10   him an hour from her beholding, I, considering
how honor would become such a person—that
it was no better than picturelike to hang by the
wall if renown made it not stir—was pleased to
let him seek danger where he was like to find
15   fame. To a cruel war I sent him, from whence he
returned, his brows bound with oak.° I tell thee,
daughter, I sprang not more in joy at first hearing he was a man-child than now in first seeing
he had proved himself a man.
20   VIRGILIA. But had he died in the business, madam,
how then?
VOLUMNIA. Then his good report should have been
my son; I therein would have found issue. Hear
me profess sincerely: had I a dozen sons, each in
25   my love alike, and none less dear than thine
and my good Marcius, I had rather had eleven
die nobly for their country than one voluptu-
ously surfeit out of action.
[*Enter a* GENTLEWOMAN.]
GENTLEWOMAN. Madam, the Lady Valeria is come
to visit you.
VIRGILIA. Beseech you, give me leave to retire
30   myself.
VOLUMNIA. Indeed, you shall not.
Methinks I hear hither your husband's drum,
See him pluck Aufidius down by the hair,
As children from a bear, the Volsces shunning
him.
35   Methinks I see him stamp thus, and call thus:
"Come on, you cowards! You were got° in fear,

Though you were born in Rome." His bloody
brow
With his mail'd hand then wiping, forth he
goes
Like to a harvestman that's task'd to mow
Or all, or° lose his hire.   40
VIRGILIA. His bloody brow! O Jupiter, no blood!
VOLUMNIA. Away, you fool! It more becomes a man
Than gilt his trophy.° The breasts of Hecuba,°
When she did suckle Hector, look'd not lovelier
Than Hector's forehead when it spit forth blood,   45
At Grecian sword contemning.° Tell Valeria
We are fit to bid her welcome.
[*Exit* GENTLEWOMAN.]
VIRGILIA. Heavens bless my lord from fell°
Aufidius!
VOLUMNIA. He'll beat Aufidius' head below his
knee
And tread upon his neck.   50
[*Enter* VALERIA, *with an* USHER *and*
GENTLEWOMAN.]
VALERIA. My ladies both, good day to you.
VOLUMNIA. Sweet madam.
VIRGILIA. I am glad to see your ladyship.
VALERIA. How do you both? You are manifest
housekeepers. What are you sewing here? A fine   55
spot,° in good faith. How does your little son?
VIRGILIA. I thank your ladyship, well, good madam.
VOLUMNIA. He had rather see the swords and hear a
drum than look upon his schoolmaster.
VALERIA. O' my word, the father's son. I'll swear,   60
'tis a very pretty boy. O' my troth, I looked
upon him o' Wednesday half an hour together;
has such a confirmed countenance. I saw him
run after a gilded butterfly, and when he
caught it, he let it go again, and after it again,   65
and over and over he comes, and up again,
catched it again. Or whether his fall enraged
him, or how 'twas, he did so set his teeth and
tear it. O, I warrant, how he mammocked° it!
VOLUMNIA. One on 's father's moods.   70
VALERIA. Indeed, la, 'tis a noble child.
VIRGILIA. A crack,° madam.
VALERIA. Come, lay aside your stitchery. I must
have you play the idle huswife° with me this
afternoon.   75
VIRGILIA. No, good madam, I will not out of doors.
VALERIA. Not out of doors!
VOLUMNIA. She shall, she shall.

Or . . . or either . . . or
gilt his trophy gilding becomes his monument
Hecuba queen of Troy and mother of Hector
contemning scorning   *fell* cruel
spot pattern   *mammocked* shredded
crack little rascal   *huswife* housewife

express . . . sort show greater cheerfulness
bound with oak i.e., the oaken garland for heroic deeds
got begotten

VIRGILIA. Indeed, no, by your patience. I'll not over
80   the threshold till my lord return from the wars.
VALERIA. Fie, you confine yourself most unreason-
    ably. Come, you must go visit the good lady that
    lies in.
VIRGILIA. I will wish her speedy strength and visit
85   her with my prayers, but I cannot go thither.
VOLUMNIA. Why, I pray you?
VIRGILIA. 'Tis not to save labor, nor that I want
    love.
VALERIA. You would be another Penelope.° Yet,
90   they say, all the yarn she spun in Ulysses'
    absence did but fill Ithaca full of moths. Come,
    I would your cambric were sensible as your
    finger, that you might leave pricking it for pity.
    Come, you shall go with us.
95   VIRGILIA. No, good madam, pardon me. Indeed, I
    will not forth.
VALERIA. In truth, la, go with me, and I'll tell you
    excellent news of your husband.
VIRGILIA. O, good madam, there can be none yet.
100 VALERIA. Verily, I do not jest with you; there came
    news from him last night.
VIRGILIA. Indeed, madam?
VALERIA. In earnest, it's true; I heard a senator
    speak it. Thus it is: the Volsces have an army
105 forth, against whom Cominius the general is
    gone with one part of our Roman power. Your
    lord and Titus Lartius are set down before their
    city Corioli. They nothing doubt prevailing,
    and to make it brief wars. This is true, on mine
110 honor; and so, I pray, go with us.
VIRGILIA. Give me excuse, good madam; I will obey
    you in everything hereafter.
VOLUMNIA. Let her alone, lady. As she is now, she
    will but disease our better mirth.
115 VALERIA. In troth, I think she would. Fare you well,
    then. Come, good sweet lady. Prithee, Virgilia,
    turn thy solemness out o' door, and go along
    with us.
VIRGILIA. No, at a word, madam; indeed, I must
120 not. I wish you much mirth.
VALERIA. Well then, farewell.   [Exeunt]

SCENE iv
Before Corioli.

[*Enter, with drum and colors,* MARCIUS, TITUS
    LARTIUS, CAPTAINS *and* SOLDIERS. *To them a*
    MESSENGER.]
MARCIUS. Yonder comes news. A wager they have
    met.
LARTIUS. My horse to yours, no.
MARCIUS.   'Tis done.
LARTIUS.   Agreed.
MARCIUS. Say, has our general met the enemy?
MESSENGER. They lie in view, but have not spoke
    as yet.
LARTIUS. So, the good horse is mine.
MARCIUS.   I'll buy him of you.   5
LARTIUS. No, I'll nor sell nor give him. Lend you
    him I will
For half a hundred years. Summon the town.
MARCIUS. How far off lie these armies?
MESSENGER.   Within this mile and half.
MARCIUS. Then shall we hear their 'larum and they
    ours.
Now, Mars, I prithee, make us quick in work,   10
That we with smoking swords may march
    from hence
To help our fielded friends! Come, blow thy
    blast.
    [*They sound a parley. Enter two* SENATORS *with*
        others, on the walls.]
Tullus Aufidius, is he within your walls?
FIRST SENATOR. No, nor a man that fears you less
    than he—
That's lesser than a little. Hark, our drums   15
    [*Drum afar off.*]
Are bringing forth our youth! We'll break our
    walls
Rather than they shall pound° us up. Our gates,
Which yet seem shut, we have but pinn'd with
    rushes;
They'll open of themselves. Hark you, far off!
    [*Alarum far off.*]
There is Aufidius; list what work he makes   20
Amongst your cloven army.
MARCIUS.   O, they are at it!
LARTIUS. Their noise be our instruction. Ladders'
    ho!
    [*Enter the army of the Volsces.*]
MARCIUS. They fear us not, but issue forth their
    city.
Now put your shields before your hearts and
    fight

Penelope   Ulysses' wife, whose weaving served to put off
    suitors during Ulysses' absence

pound   impound

With hearts more proof° than shields. Advance,
25   brave Titus.
They do disdain us much beyond our thoughts,
Which makes me sweat with wrath. Come on,
    my fellows.
He that retires, I'll take him for a Volsce,
And he shall feel mine edge.
    [*Alarum. The* ROMANS *are beat back to their*
        trenches. Re-enter MARCIUS, *cursing.*]
MARCIUS. All the contagion of the south° light on
30   you,
You shames of Rome! You herd of—Boils and
    plagues
Plaster you o'er, that you may be abhorr'd
Farther than seen, and one infect another
Against the wind a mile! You souls of geese
35   That bear the shapes of men, how have you run
From slaves that apes would beat! Pluto and
    hell!
All hurt behind! Backs red, and faces pale
With flight and agu'd° fear! Mend,° and charge
    home,
Or by the fires of heaven, I'll leave the foe
And make my wars on you. Look to 't. Come
40   on.
If you'll stand fast, we'll beat them to their
    wives,
As they us to our trenches. Follow 's!
    [*Another alarum. The Volsces fly, and* MARCIUS
        follows them to the gates.]
So, now the gates are ope. Now prove good
    seconds.
'Tis for the followers fortune widens them,
45   Not for the fliers. Mark me, and do the like.
                                    [*Enters the gates.*]
FIRST SOLDIER. Foolhardiness. Not I.
SECOND SOLDIER. Nor I.   [MARCIUS *is shut in.*]
FIRST SOLDIER. See, they have shut him in.
ALL.   To the pot,° I warrant him.
                                    [*Alarum continues.*]
            [*Re-enter* TITUS LARTIUS.]
LARTIUS. What is become of Marcius?
ALL.   Slain, sir, doubtless.
FIRST SOLDIER. Following the fliers at the very
50   heels,
With them he enters—who, upon the sudden,
Clapp'd to their gates. He is himself alone
To answer all the city.
LARTIUS.   O noble fellow!
Who sensibly outdares his senseless sword

And, when it bows, stands up! Thou art left,°
    Marcius.   55
A carbuncle entire, as big as thou art,
Were not so rich a jewel. Thou wast a soldier
Even to Cato's wish,° not fierce and terrible
Only in strokes, but, with thy grim looks and
The thunderlike percussion of thy sounds,   60
Thou mad'st thine enemies shake as if the world
Were feverous and did tremble.
    [*Re-enter* MARCIUS, *bleeding, assaulted by the*
        enemy.]
FIRST SOLDIER.   Look, sir.
LARTIUS.   O, 'tis Marcius!
Let's fetch him off, or make remain alike.
                    [*They fight, and all enter the city.*]

                    SCENE v
            Within Corioli. A street.

    [*Enter certain* ROMANS, *with spoils.*]
FIRST ROMAN. This will I carry to Rome.
SECOND ROMAN. And I this.
THIRD ROMAN. A murrain° on 't! I took this for
    silver.
                    [*Alarum continues still afar off.*]
    [*Enter* MARCIUS *and* TITUS LARTIUS *with a*
        trumpet.]
MARCIUS. See here these movers° that do prize
    their hours   5
At a crack'd drachma!° Cushions, leaden
    spoons,
Irons of a doit,° doublets that hangmen° would
Bury with those that wore them, these base
    slaves,
Ere yet the fight be done, pack up. Down with
    them!
And hark, what noise the general makes! To
    him!   10
There is the man of my soul's hate, Aufidius,
Piercing our Romans! Then, valiant Titus, take
Convenient numbers to make good the city,
Whilst I, with those that have the spirit, will
    haste
To help Cominius.

---

left lost
Cato's wish (Cato the Censor's ideal soldier made the
    enemy "afeared with the sound of his voice and
    grimness of his countenance")
murrain plague   *movers* i.e., of looted articles
crack'd drachma small Greek coin, worthless when
    cracked
Irons of a doit worthless wrought iron
hangmen who were awarded the victim's clothing

---

proof tested, sword-proof
south the pestilence-bearing south wind
agu'd trembling as with ague   *Mend* close ranks
To the pot i.e., "he's cooked"

15 LARTIUS.   Worthy sir, thou bleed'st.
    Thy exercise hath been too violent
    For a second course of fight.
   MARCIUS.   Sir, praise me not.
    My work hath yet not warm'd me. Fare you
      well.
    The blood I drop is rather physical°
20 Than dangerous to me. To Aufidius thus
    I will appear, and fight.
   LARTIUS.   Now the fair goddess Fortune
    Fall deep in love with thee, and her great
      charms
    Misguide thy opposers' swords! Bold gentle-
      man,
    Prosperity be thy page!
   MARCIUS.   Thy friend no less
25 Than those she placeth highest! So farewell.
   LARTIUS. Thou worthiest Marcius! [*Exit* MARCIUS.]
    Go sound thy trumpet in the marketplace.
    Call thither all the officers o' the town,
    Where they shall know our mind. Away!
                             [*Exeunt*]

SCENE vi
Near the camp of COMINIUS.

[*Enter* COMINIUS, *as it were in retire, with*
SOLDIERS.]
COMINIUS. Breathe you, my friends. Well fought.
      We are come off
    Like Romans, neither foolish in our stands
    Nor cowardly in retire. Believe me, sirs,
    We shall be charg'd again. Whiles we have
      struck,
5 By interims and conveying gusts° we have heard
    The charges of our friends. Ye Roman gods,
    Lead their successes as we wish our own,
    That both our powers, with smiling fronts en-
      countering,
    May give you thankful sacrifice!
               [*Enter a* MESSENGER.]
                           Thy news?
10 MESSENGER. The citizens of Corioli have issu'd
    And given to Lartius and to Marcius battle.
    I saw our party to their trenches driven,
    And then I came away.
   COMINIUS.   Though thou speak'st truth,
    Methinks thou speak'st not well. How long is 't
      since?
15 MESSENGER. Above an hour, my lord.
   COMINIUS. 'Tis not a mile. Briefly we heard their
      drums.

How couldst thou in a mile confound° an hour
    And bring thy news so late?
   MESSENGER.   Spies of the Volsces
    Held me in chase, that I was forc'd to wheel
    Three or four miles about; else had I, sir,   20
    Half an hour since brought my report.
               [*Enter* MARCIUS.]
   COMINIUS.   Who's yonder,
    That does appear as he were flay'd? O gods!
    He has the stamp° of Marcius, and I have
    Beforetime seen him thus.
   MARCIUS.   Come I too late?
   COMINIUS. The shepherd knows not thunder
      from a tabor°   25
    More than I know the sound of Marcius' tongue
    From every meaner man.
   MARCIUS.   Come I too late?
   COMINIUS. Aye, if you come not in the blood of
      others,
    But mantled in your own.
   MARCIUS.   O, let me clip° ye
    In arms as sound as when I woo'd, in heart   30
    As merry as when our nuptial day was done
    And tapers burn'd to bedward!
   COMINIUS.   Flower of warriors,
    How is 't with Titus Lartius?
   MARCIUS. As with a man busied about decrees,
    Condemning some to death and some to exile,   35
    Ransoming him or pitying, threatening th'
      other,
    Holding Corioli in the name of Rome,
    Even like a fawning greyhound in the leash,
    To let him slip at will.
   COMINIUS.   Where is that slave
    Which told me they had beat you to your
      trenches?   40
    Where is he? Call him hither.
   MARCIUS.   Let him alone;
    He did inform the truth. But for our gentlemen,
    The common file—a plague! Tribunes for them!
    The mouse ne'er shunn'd the cat as they did
      budge
    From rascals worse than they.
   COMINIUS.   But how prevail'd you?   45
   MARCIUS. Will the time serve to tell? I do not
      think.
    Where is the enemy? Are you lords o' the field?
    If not, why cease you till you are so?
   COMINIUS.   Marcius,
    We have at disadvantage fought, and did
    Retire to win our purpose.   50

---

physical purgative
By . . . gusts at intervals on the winds

confound waste
stamp form   *tabor* drum   *clip* embrace

Marcius. How lies their battle? Know you on
      which side
   They have plac'd their men of trust?
Cominius.   As I guess, Marcius,
   Their bands i' the vaward° are the Antiates,
   Of their best trust; o'er them Aufidius,
   Their very heart of hope.
55 Marcius.   I do beseech you,
   By all the battles wherein we have fought,
   By the blood we have shed together, by the
      vows
   We have made to endure friends, that you
      directly
   Set me against Aufidius and his Antiates,
60 And that you not delay the present, but,
   Filling the air with swords advanc'd and darts,
   We prove° this very hour.
Cominius.   Though I could wish
   You were conducted to a gentle bath
   And balms applied to you, yet dare I never
65 Deny your asking. Take your choice of those
   That best can aid your action.
Marcius.   Those are they
   That most are willing. If any such be here—
   As it were sin to doubt—that love this painting
   Wherein you see me smear'd, if any fear
70 Lesser his person than an ill report,
   If any think brave death outweighs bad life
   And that his country's dearer than himself,
   Let him alone, or so many so minded,
   Wave thus t' express his disposition,
75 And follow Marcius.
      [They all shout and wave their swords, take him
            up in their arms, and cast up their caps.]
   O, me alone, make you a sword of me?°
   If these shows be not outward,° which of you
   But is four Volsces? None of you but is
   Able to bear against the great Aufidius
80 A shield as hard as his. A certain number,
   Though thanks to all, must I select from all.
      The rest
   Shall bear the business in some other fight,
   As cause will be obey'd.° Please you to march,
   And four shall quickly draw out my command,°
   Which men are best inclin'd.
85 Cominius.   March on, my fellows.
   Make good this ostentation, and you shall
   Divide in all with us.   [Exeunt]

vaward vanguard   prove make trial
O me . . . me (unexplained and possibly corrupt line;
   however, soldiers have raised Marcius over their heads,
   like their swords)
shows . . . outward i.e., merely shows, not genuine
As . . . obey'd as occasion requires
draw . . . command select the volunteers to accompany me

SCENE vii
The gates of Corioli.

[Titus Lartius, having set a guard upon Corioli,
going with drum and trumpet toward Cominius
and Caius Marcius, enters with a Lieutenant,
      other Soldiers, and a Scout.]
Lartius. So, let the ports° be guarded. Keep your
      duties
   As I have set them down. If I do send, dispatch
   Those centuries° to our aid; the rest will serve
   For a short holding. If we lose the field,
   We cannot keep the town.
Lieutenant.   Fear not our care, sir.   5
Lartius. Hence, and shut your gates upon 's.
   Our guider, come; to the Roman camp conduct
      us.   [Exeunt]

SCENE viii
A field of battle between the Roman and the
Volscian camps.

[Alarum as in battle. Enter, from opposite sides,
      Marcius and Aufidius.]
Marcius. I'll fight with none but thee, for I do
      hate thee
   Worse than a promise-breaker.
Aufidius.   We hate alike.
   Not Afric owns a serpent I abhor
   More than thy fame and envy.° Fix thy foot.
Marcius. Let the first budger die the other's
      slave,   5
   And the gods doom him after!
Aufidius.   If I fly, Marcius,
   Holloa me like a hare.
Marcius.   Within these three hours, Tullus,
   Alone I fought in your Corioli walls
   And made what work I pleas'd. 'Tis not my
      blood
   Wherein thou seest me mask'd. For thy revenge   10
   Wrench up thy power to the highest.
Aufidius.   Wert thou the Hector
   That was the whip of your bragg'd progeny,°
   Thou shouldst not 'scape me here.
[They fight, and certain Volsces come in the aid of
Aufidius. Marcius fights till they be driven in
breathless.]

ports gates   centuries companies
envy i.e., that he has won by his deeds
Hector . . . progeny Trojans and their champion, Hector,
   were supposedly the Romans' ancestors

Officious and not valiant, you have sham'd me
15 In your condemned seconds.°   [*Exeunt*]

SCENE ix
The Roman camp.

[*Flourish. Alarum. A retreat is sounded. Enter, from
one side,* COMINIUS *with the* ROMANS; *from the
other side,* MARCIUS, *with his arm in a scarf.*]

COMINIUS. If I should tell thee o'er this thy day's
    work,
  Thou't not believe thy deeds. But I'll report it
  Where Senators shall mingle tears with smiles;
  Where great patricians shall attend, and shrug,
5 I' th' end admire; where ladies shall be frighted,
  And, gladly quak'd, hear more; where the dull
    tribunes,
  That, with the fusty° plebeians, hate thine
    honors,
  Shall say against their hearts, "We thank the
    gods
  Our Rome hath such a soldier."
10 Yet cam'st thou to a morsel of this feast,
  Having fully din'd before.
    [*Enter* TITUS LARTIUS, *with his power, from the
        pursuit.*]
LARTIUS.   O general,
  Here is the steed, we the caparison.°
  Hadst thou beheld—
MARCIUS.   Pray now, no more. My mother,
  Who has a charter to extol her blood,°
  When she does praise me grieves me. I have
15   done
  As you have done—that's what I can; induc'd
  As you have been—that's for my country.
  He that has but effected his good will°
  Hath overta'en mine act.
COMINIUS.   You shall not be
20 The grave of your deserving; Rome must know
  The value of her own. 'Twere a concealment
  Worse than a theft, no less than a traducement,°
  To hide your doings and to silence that
  Which, to the spire and top of praises vouch'd,
  Would seem but modest. Therefore, I beseech
25   you—
  In sign of what you are, not to reward
  What you have done—before our army hear me.

MARCIUS. I have some wounds upon me, and they
    smart
  To hear themselves remember'd.
COMINIUS.   Should they not,
  Well might they fester 'gainst ingratitude   30
  And tent° themselves with death. Of all the
    horses,
  Whereof we have ta'en good and good store, of
    all
  The treasure in this field achiev'd and city,
  We render you the tenth, to be ta'en forth
  Before the common distribution, at   35
  Your only choice.
MARCIUS.   I thank you, general,
  But cannot make my heart consent to take
  A bribe to pay my sword. I do refuse it,
  And stand upon my common part with those
  That have beheld the doing.   40
[*A long flourish. They all cry* "Marcius! Marcius!"
cast up their caps and lances. COMINIUS *and* LARTIUS
                                        stand bare.]
  May these same instruments, which you profane,
  Never sound more! When drums and trumpets
    shall
  I' the field prove flatterers, let courts and cities
    be
  Made all of false-fac'd° soothing!
  When steel grows soft as the parasite's silk,
  Let him be made a coverture for the wars!°   45
  No more, I say! For that I have not wash'd
  My nose that bled, or foil'd° some debile°
    wretch—
  Which without note here's many else have
    done—
  You shout me forth
  In acclamations hyperbolical,   50
  As if I lov'd my little should be dieted
  In praises sauc'd with lies.
COMINIUS.   Too modest are you,
  More cruel to your good report than grateful
  To us that give you truly. By your patience,
  If 'gainst yourself you be incens'd, we'll put you, 55
  Like one that means his proper° harm, in man-
    acles,
  Then reason safely with you. Therefore be it
    known,
  As to us, to all the world, that Caius Marcius
  Wears this war's garland.° In token of the which,

                                                    60

---

condemned seconds unwanted aid   *fusty* mouldy
caparison trappings
charter . . . blood special right to praise her own son
effected . . . will i.e., fought with conviction
traducement slander

tent cure
false-fac'd soothing i.e., fawning hypocrisy
Let him . . . wars (unsatisfactorily explained; Folio prints
  overture)
foil'd overthrown   *debile* feeble
proper own   *garland* chief honor

My noble steed, known to the camp, I give him,
With all his trim belonging. And from this time,
For what he did before Corioli, call him,
With all th' applause and clamor of the host,
65 CAIUS MARCIUS CORIOLANUS. Bear
Th' addition° nobly ever!
                    [*Flourish. Trumpets sound, and drums.*]
ALL. Caius Marcius Coriolanus!
CORIOLANUS. I will go wash,
And when my face is fair, you shall perceive
70 Whether I blush or no. Howbeit, I thank you.
I mean to stride your steed, and at all times
To undercrest° your good addition
To the fairness of my power.
COMINIUS.   So, to our tent,
Where, ere we do repose us, we will write
75 To Rome of our success. You, Titus Lartius,
Must to Corioli back. Send us to Rome
The best, with whom we may articulate°
For their own good and ours.
LARTIUS.   I shall, my lord.
CORIOLANUS. The gods begin to mock me. I, that
now
80 Refus'd most princely gifts, am bound to beg
Of my lord general.
COMINIUS.   Take 't; 'tis yours. What is 't?
CORIOLANUS. I sometime lay here in Corioli
At a poor man's house; he us'd me kindly.
He cried to me; I saw him prisoner.
85 But then Aufidius was within my view,
And wrath o'erwhelm'd my pity. I request you
To give my poor host freedom.
COMINIUS.   O, well begg'd!
Were he the butcher of my son, he should
Be free as is the wind. Deliver him, Titus.
LARTIUS. Marcius, his name?
90 CORIOLANUS.   By Jupiter, forgot.
I am weary; yea, my memory is tir'd.
Have we no wine here?
COMINIUS.   Go we to our tent.
The blood upon your visage dries; 'tis time
It should be look'd to. Come.   [*Exeunt*]

SCENE x
The camp of the Volsces.

[*A flourish. Cornets. Enter* TULLUS AUFIDIUS,
bloody, with two or three SOLDIERS.]
AUFIDIUS. The town is ta'en!
FIRST SOLDIER. 'Twill be deliver'd back on good
condition.
AUFIDIUS. Condition!
I would I were a Roman, for I cannot,
Being a Volsce, be that I am. Condition!   5
What good condition can a treaty find
I' the part that is at mercy?° Five times, Marcius,
I have fought with thee; so often hast thou beat
me,
And wouldst do so, I think, should we encounter
As often as we eat. By th' elements,   10
If e'er again I meet him beard to beard,
He's mine, or I am his. Mine emulation
Hath not that honor in 't it had, for where
I thought to crush him in an equal force,
True sword to sword, I'll potch° at him some
way.   15
Or wrath or° craft may get him.
FIRST SOLDIER.   He's the devil.
AUFIDIUS. Bolder, though not so subtle. My
valor's poison'd
With only suffering stain° by him, for him
Shall fly out of itself. Nor sleep nor° sanctuary,
Being naked, sick, nor fane° nor Capitol,   20
The prayers of priests nor times of sacrifice,
Embarquements all of fury,° shall lift up
Their rotten privilege and custom 'gainst
My hate to Marcius. Where I find him, were it
At home, upon my brother's guard, even there,   25
Against the hospitable canon,° would I
Wash my fierce hand in 's' heart. Go you to the
city;
Learn how 'tis held and what they are that must
Be hostages for Rome.
FIRST SOLDIER.   Will not you go?
AUFIDIUS. I am attended at the cypress grove. I
pray you—   30
'Tis south the city mills—bring me word thither
How the world goes, that to the pace of it
I may spur on my journey.
FIRST SOLDIER.   I shall, sir.   [*Exeunt*]

I' . . . mercy i.e., for the losers
potch thrust   *Or . . . or* Either . . . or
stain disgrace   *Nor . . . nor* neither . . . nor
fane temple
Embarquements . . . fury forces that restrain anger
hospitable canon law of hospitality

addition title
undercrest wear as a crest; i.e., "live up to"
articulate negotiate

ACT II

SCENE i
Rome. A public place.

[*Enter* MENENIUS, *with the two* TRIBUNES *of the people,* SICINIUS *and* BRUTUS.]

MENENIUS. The augurer tells me we shall have news tonight.

BRUTUS. Good or bad?

MENENIUS. Not according to the prayer of the
5　people, for they love not Marcius.

SICINIUS. Nature teaches beasts to know their friends.

MENENIUS. Pray you, who does the wolf love?

SICINIUS. The lamb.

10　MENENIUS. Aye, to devour him, as the hungry plebeians would the noble Marcius.

BRUTUS. He's a lamb indeed, that baas like a bear.

MENENIUS. He's a bear indeed, that lives like a lamb. You two are old men: tell me one thing
15　that I shall ask you.

BOTH. Well, sir.

MENENIUS. In what enormity° is Marcius poor in, that you two have not in abundance?

BRUTUS. He's poor in no one fault, but stored with
20　all.

SICINIUS. Especially in pride.

BRUTUS. And topping all others in boasting.

MENENIUS. This is strange now. Do you two know how you are censured° here in the city, I mean
25　of us o' the righthand file?° Do you?

BOTH. Why, how are we censured?

MENENIUS. Because you talk of pride now—will you not be angry?

BOTH. Well, well, sir, well.

30　MENENIUS. Why, 'tis no great matter, for a very little thief of occasion will rob you of a great deal of patience. Give your dispositions the reins, and be angry at your pleasures—at the least, if you take it as a pleasure to you in being so. You
35　blame Marcius for being proud?

BRUTUS. We do it not alone, sir.

MENENIUS. I know you can do very little alone, for your helps are many, or else your actions would grow wondrous single. Your abilities are too
40　infant-like for doing much alone. You talk of pride. O that you could turn your eyes toward

enormity fault　*censured* judged
file political group

the napes of your necks and make but an interior survey of your good selves! O that you could!

BOTH. What then, sir?　　　　　　　　　　　　45

MENENIUS. Why, then you should discover a brace of unmeriting, proud, violent, testy magistrates, alias fools, as any in Rome.

SICINIUS. Menenius, you are known well enough too.　　　　　　　　　　　　　　　　　　50

MENENIUS. I am known to be a humorous° patrician, and one that loves a cup of hot wine with not a drop of allaying Tiber° in 't; said to be something imperfect in favoring the first complaint,° hasty and tinderlike upon too　55
trivial motion;° one that converses more with the buttock of the night than with the forehead of the morning. What I think I utter, and spend my malice in my breath. Meeting two such wealsmen° as you are—I cannot call you Lycur-　60
guses°—if the drink you give me touch my palate adversely, I make a crooked face at it. I can't say your worships have delivered the matter well, when I find the ass in compound with the major part of your syllables.° And　65
though I must be content to bear with those that say you are reverend grave men, yet they lie deadly that tell you you have good faces. If you see this in the map of my microcosm,° follows it that I am known well enough too?　70
What harm can your bisson conspectuities° glean out of this character if I be known well enough too?

BRUTUS. Come, sir, come. We know you well enough.　　　　　　　　　　　　　　　　　　75

MENENIUS. You know neither me, yourselves, nor anything. You are ambitious for poor knaves' caps and legs. You wear out a good wholesome forenoon in hearing a cause between an orange-wife and a fosset-seller,° and then rejourn° the　80

humorous whimsical　　*allaying Tiber* diluting water
something . . . complaint somewhat quick to sympathize
motion cause　　*wealsmen* statesmen
Lycurguses great lawgivers
ass . . . syllables i.e., all that you say proves you a pair of
　asses
map . . . microcosm i.e., my face, which reveals all the
　inner qualities of my "little world"
bisson conspectuities bleary eyesights
orange . . . seller orange vendor and seller of barrel taps
rejourn adjourn

controversy of threepence to a second day of audience. When you are hearing a matter between party and party, if you chance to be pinched with the colic, you make faces like

85   mummers,° set up the bloody flag° against all patience, and, in roaring for a chamber-pot, dismiss the controversy bleeding,° the more entangled by your hearing. All the peace you make in their cause is calling both the parties

90   knaves. You are a pair of strange ones.

BRUTUS. Come, come, you are well understood to be a perfecter giber for the table than a necessary bencher in the Capitol.

MENENIUS. Our very priests must become mockers

95   if they shall encounter such ridiculous subjects as you are. When you speak best unto the purpose, it is not worth the wagging of your beards, and your beards deserve not so honorable a grave as to stuff a botcher's° cushion or to be

100   entombed in an ass's packsaddle. Yet you must be saying Marcius is proud, who, in a cheap estimation, is worth all your predecessors since Deucalion,° though peradventure some of the best of 'em were hereditary hangmen. God-den

105   to your worships. More of your conversation would infect my brain, being the herdsmen of the beastly plebeians. I will be bold to take my leave of you.

               [BRUTUS and SICINIUS go aside.]
           [Enter VOLUMNIA, VIRGILIA, and VALERIA.]

How now, my as fair as noble ladies—and the

110   moon, were she earthly, no nobler—whither do you follow your eyes so fast?

VOLUMNIA. Honorable Menenius, my boy Marcius approaches. For the love of Juno, let's go.

MENENIUS. Ha! Marcius coming home?

115 VOLUMNIA. Aye, worthy Menenius, and with most prosperous approbation.°

MENENIUS. Take my cap, Jupiter, and I thank thee. Hoo! Marcius coming home?

VIRGILIA and VALERIA. Nay, 'tis true.

120 VOLUMNIA. Look, here's a letter from him. The state hath another, his wife another, and I think there's one at home for you.

MENENIUS. I will make my very house reel tonight. A letter for me?

125 VIRGILIA. Yes, certain, there's a letter for you; I saw 't.

MENENIUS. A letter for me! It gives me an estate of seven years' health, in which time I will make a lip° at the physician. The most sovereign prescription in Galen° is but empiricutic,° and, to° 130 this preservation, of no better report than a horse-drench.° Is he not wounded? He was wont to come home wounded.

VIRGILIA. O, no, no, no.

VOLUMNIA. O, he is wounded; I thank the gods for't. 135

MENENIUS. So do I too, if it be not too much. Brings a' victory in his pocket? The wounds become him.

VOLUMNIA. On 's brows'. Menenius, he comes the third time home with the oaken garland. 140

MENENIUS. Has he disciplined Aufidius soundly?

VOLUMNIA. Titus Lartius writes they fought together, but Aufidius got off.

MENENIUS. And 'twas time for him too, I'll warrant him that. An he had stayed by him, I 145 would not have been so fidiused° for all the chests in Corioli and the gold that's in them. Is the Senate possessed° of this?

VOLUMNIA. Good ladies, let's go. Yes, yes, yes, the Senate has letters from the general wherein he 150 gives my son the whole name of the war. He hath in this action outdone his former deeds doubly.

VALERIA. In troth, there's wondrous things spoke of him. 155

MENENIUS. Wondrous! Aye, I warrant you, and not without his true purchasing.°

VIRGILIA. The gods grant them true!

VOLUMNIA. True! Pow, wow.

MENENIUS. True! I'll be sworn they are true. 160 Where is he wounded? [To the TRIBUNES] God save your good worships! Marcius is coming home. He has more cause to be proud. Where is he wounded?

VOLUMNIA. I' the shoulder and i' the left arm. There 165 will be large cicatrices to show the people when he shall stand for his place. He received in the repulse of Tarquin° seven hurts i' the body.

MENENIUS. One i' the neck and two i' the thigh; there's nine that I know. 170

VOLUMNIA. He had, before this last expedition, twenty-five wounds upon him.

MENENIUS. Now it's twenty-seven. Every gash was an enemy's grave. [A shout and flourish] Hark! The trumpets. 175

---

mummers pantomimists
set up . . . flag declare war
bleeding i.e., still raw and sore
botcher's clothes patcher
Deucalion the Greek Noah, legendary survivor of the great flood
prosperous approbation acclaimed success

make a lip scorn   *Galen* Greek physician
empiricutic quackish   *to* compared to
horse-drench dose of horse medicine
fidiused "Aufidiused"   *possessed* advised
true purchasing honest winning
Tarquin infamous Roman tyrant

VOLUMNIA. These are the ushers of Marcius.
Before him he carries noise, and behind him he
leaves tears.
Death, that dark spirit, in 's nervy° arm doth lie,
Which, being advanc'd, declines, and then men
180   die.
[*A sennet. Trumpets sound. Enter* COMINIUS *and*
TITUS LARTIUS; *between them,* CORIOLANUS,
crowned with an oaken garland; with CAPTAINS
and SOLDIERS, *and a* HERALD.]
HERALD. Know, Rome, that all alone Marcius did
fight
Within Corioli gates, where he hath won,
With fame, a name to Caius Marcius. These
In honor follows Coriolanus.
185 Welcome to Rome, renowned Coriolanus!
[*Flourish.*]
ALL. Welcome to Rome, renowned Coriolanus!
CORIOLANUS. No more of this; it does offend my
heart.
Pray now, no more.
COMINIUS.   Look, sir, your mother!
CORIOLANUS.   O,
You have, I know, petition'd all the gods
For my prosperity!   [*Kneels.*]
190 VOLUMNIA.   Nay, my good soldier, up,
My gentle Marcius, worthy Caius, and
By deed-achieving honor newly nam'd—
What is it?—Coriolanus must I call thee?—
But, O, thy wife!
CORIOLANUS.   My gracious silence, hail!
Wouldst thou have laugh'd had I come coffin'd
195   home,
That weep'st to see me triumph? Ah, my dear,
Such eyes the widows in Corioli wear,
And mothers that lack sons.
MENENIUS.   Now, the gods crown thee!
CORIOLANUS. And live you yet? [*To* VALERIA] O my
sweet lady, pardon.
VOLUMNIA. I know not where to turn. O, welcome
200   home.
And welcome, general. And ye're welcome all.
MENENIUS. A hundred thousand welcomes. I could
weep,
And I could laugh; I am light and heavy.
Welcome.
A curse begin at very root on 's heart
205 That is not glad to see thee! You are three
That Rome should dote on. Yet, by the faith of
men,
We have some old crab-trees° here at home that
will not

Be grafted to your relish.° Yet welcome, warriors.
We call a nettle but a nettle, and
The faults of fools but folly.
COMINIUS.   Ever right.   210
CORIOLANUS. Menenius, ever, ever.
HERALD. Give way there, and go on.
CORIOLANUS. [*To* VOLUMNIA *and* VIRGILIA] Your
hand, and yours.
Ere in our own house I do shade my head,
The good patricians must be visited,
From whom I have receiv'd not only greetings 215
But with them change° of honors.
VOLUMNIA.   I have liv'd
To see inherited my very wishes
And the buildings of my fancy. Only
There's one thing wanting, which I doubt not
but
Our Rome will cast upon thee.
CORIOLANUS.   Know, good mother, 220
I had rather be their servant in my way
Than sway° with them in theirs.
COMINIUS.   On, to the Capitol!
[*Flourish. Cornets. Exeunt in state, as before.*
BRUTUS *and* SICINIUS *come forward.*]
BRUTUS. All tongues speak of him, and the bleared
sights°
Are spectacled to see him. Your prattling nurse
Into a rapture lets her baby cry 225
While she chats° him. The kitchen malkin° pins
Her richest lockram° 'bout her reechy° neck,
Clambering the walls to eye him. Stalls, bulks,°
windows
Are smother'd up, leads° fill'd, and ridges
hors'd
With variable complexions,° all agreeing 230
In earnestness to see him. Seld-shown flamens°
Do press among the popular throngs, and puff
To win a vulgar station.° Our veil'd dames
Commit the war of white and damask in
Their nicely gawded cheeks to the wanton spoil 235
Of Phœbus' burning kisses.° Such a pother,°
As if that whatsoever god who leads him
Were slyly crept into his human powers
And gave him graceful posture.

---

grafted . . . relish i.e., rejoice at your success
change a variety   sway rule
bleared sights i.e., citizens with poor eyesight
chats talks of   malkin wench
lockram linen   reechy grimy   bulks shop fronts
leads leaden rooftops
hors'd . . . complexions straddled by all sorts of people
flamens priests
vulgar station any place in the crowd
veil'd . . . kisses elegant ladies subject their delicate
  white and pink complexions to the sun's hot rays
pother to-do

---

nervy sinewy
crab-trees crab-apples, i.e., the tribunes

SICINIUS.　　　　　　　　　　　On the sudden
　I warrant him consul.

240 BRUTUS.　　　　　　　　Then our office may,
　During his power, go sleep.

SICINIUS. He cannot temperately transport his
　　honors
　From where he should begin and end, but will
　Lose those he hath won.

BRUTUS.　　　　　　　　In that there's comfort.

SICINIUS.　　　　　　　　　　　Doubt not
245 The commoners, for whom we stand, but they
　Upon their ancient malice° will forget
　With the least cause these his new honors—
　　which
　That he will give them make I as little question
　As he is proud to do 't.°

BRUTUS.　　　　　　　　I heard him swear,
250 Were he to stand for consul, never would he
　Appear i' the marketplace, nor on him put
　The napless vesture° of humility,
　Nor showing, as the manner is, his wounds
　To the people, beg their stinking breaths.

SICINIUS.　　　　　　　　　　　'Tis right.
255 BRUTUS. It was his word. O, he would miss it rather
　Than carry it, but by the suit of the gentry to
　　him
　And the desire of the nobles.

SICINIUS.　　　　　　　　I wish no better
　Than have him hold that purpose and to put it
　In execution.

BRUTUS.　　　'Tis most like he will.

260 SICINIUS. It shall be to him then, as our good wills,°
　A sure destruction.

BRUTUS.　　　　　　So it must fall out
　To him or our authorities. For an end,°
　We must suggest the people in what hatred
　He still hath held them; that to 's power he
　　would
　Have made them mules, silenc'd their pleaders,
　　and
265 Dispropertied° their freedoms, holding them,
　In human action and capacity,
　Of no more soul nor fitness for the world
　Than camels in the war, who have their pro-
　　vand°
270 Only for bearing burthens, and sore blows
　For sinking under them.

Upon . . . malice　recalling their old hatred
which . . . do 't　that he will give them provocation
　(cause) to do it I have as little doubt as I have that he
　is proud
napless vesture　threadbare garment
as . . . wills　as our best interest requires
For an end　to ensure the result
Dispropertied　took away　　provand　provender

SICINIUS.　　　　　This, as you say, suggested
　At some time when his soaring insolence
　Shall touch the people—which time shall not
　　want,
　If he be put upon 't;° and that's as easy
　As to set dogs on sheep—will be his fire　　275
　To kindle their dry stubble; and their blaze
　Shall darken him forever.

　　　　　　[Enter a MESSENGER.]

BRUTUS.　　　　　　　　What's the matter?

MESSENGER. You are sent for to the Capitol. 'Tis
　　thought
　That Marcius shall be consul.
　I have seen the dumb men throng to see him and　280
　The blind to hear him speak. Matrons flung
　　gloves,
　Ladies and maids their scarfs and handkerchers
　Upon him as he pass'd. The nobles bended
　As to Jove's statue, and the commons made
　A shower and thunder with their caps and
　　shouts.　　　　　　　　　　　　　　285
　I never saw the like.

BRUTUS.　　　　　　Let's to the Capitol,
　And carry with us cars and eyes for the time,°
　But hearts for the event.°

SICINIUS.　　　　　　　Have with you.

　　　　　　　　　　　　　　　[Exeunt]

SCENE ii
The same. The Capitol.

[Enter two OFFICERS, to lay cushions.]

FIRST OFFICER. Come, come, they are almost here.
　How many stand for consulships?

SECOND OFFICER. Three, they say. But 'tis thought
　of everyone Coriolanus will carry it.

FIRST OFFICER. That's a brave fellow, but he's ven-　5
　geance° proud and loves not the common
　people.

SECOND OFFICER. Faith, there have been many
　great men that have flattered the people who
　ne'er loved them, and there be many that they　10
　have loved, they know not wherefore. So that, if
　they love they know not why, they hate upon no
　better a ground. Therefore, for Coriolanus
　neither to care whether they love or hate him
　manifests the true knowledge he has in their dis-　15
　position, and out of his noble carelessness lets
　them plainly see 't.

FIRST OFFICER. If he did not care whether he had
　their love or no, he waved indifferently° 'twixt

put upon 't　provoked　　time　i.e., opportune moment
event　outcome　　vengeance　i.e., intensely
waved indifferently　wavered disinterestedly

20 doing them neither good nor harm. But he seeks
their hate with greater devotion than they can
render it him, and leaves nothing undone that
may fully discover° him their opposite. Now, to
seem to affect° the malice and displeasure of the
25 people is as bad as that which he dislikes, to
flatter them for their love.

SECOND OFFICER. He hath deserved worthily of his
country, and his ascent is not by such easy degrees
as those who, having been supple and courteous
30 to the people, bonneted,° without any further
deed to have them° at all into their estimation
and report. But he hath so planted his honors in
their eyes and his actions in their hearts that for
their tongues to be silent and not confess so
35 much were a kind of ingrateful injury. To report
otherwise were a malice that, giving itself the
lie, would pluck reproof and rebuke from every
ear that heard it.

FIRST OFFICER. No more of him; he's a worthy man.
40 Make way, they are coming.

[A sennet. Enter, with LICTORS before them,
COMINIUS the Consul, MENENIUS, CORIOLANUS,
SENATORS, SICINIUS and BRUTUS. The SENATORS
take their places; the TRIBUNES take their places by
themselves. CORIOLANUS stands.]

MENENIUS. Having determin'd of° the Volsces and
To send for Titus Lartius, it remains
As the main point of this our after-meeting
To gratify his noble service that
Hath thus stood for his country. Therefore,
45   please you,
Most reverend and grave elders, to desire
The present consul, and last general
In our well-found successes, to report
A little of that worthy work perform'd
50 By Caius Marcius Coriolanus, whom
We met here both to thank and to remember
With honors like himself.

FIRST SENATOR.   Speak, good Cominius.
Leave nothing out for length, and make us think
Rather our state's defective for requital
Than we to stretch it out.° [To the TRIBUNES]
55   Masters o' the people,
We do request your kindest ears, and after,
Your loving motion toward the common body
To yield° what passes here.

SICINIUS.   We are convented

Upon a pleasing treaty and have hearts
Inclinable to honor and advance
The theme of our assembly.   60

BRUTUS.   Which the rather
We shall be bless'd to do if he remember
A kinder value of the people than
He hath hereto priz'd them at.

MENENIUS.   That's off, that's off.
I would you rather had been silent. Please you   65
To hear Cominius speak?

BRUTUS.   Most willingly.
But yet my caution was more pertinent
Than the rebuke you give it.

MENENIUS.   He loves your people,
But tie him not to be their bedfellow.
Worthy Cominius, speak. [CORIOLANUS offers to
go away] Nay, keep your place.   70

FIRST SENATOR. Sit, Coriolanus. Never shame to
hear
What you have nobly done.

CORIOLANUS.   Your honors' pardon.
I had rather have my wounds to heal again
Than hear say how I got them.

BRUTUS.   Sir, I hope
My words disbench'd you not.

CORIOLANUS.   No, sir. Yet oft,   75
When blows have made me stay, I fled from
words.
You sooth'd° not, therefore hurt not. But your
people,
I love them as they weigh.°

MENENIUS.   Pray now, sit down.

CORIOLANUS. I had rather have one scratch my
head i' the sun
When the alarum were struck° than idly sit   80
To hear my nothings monster'd.°   [Exit]

MENENIUS.   Masters of the people,
Your multiplying spawn how can he flatter—
That's° thousand to one good one—when you
now see
He had rather venture all his limbs for honor
Than one on 's ears to hear it? Proceed, Comi-
nius.   85

COMINIUS. I shall lack voice. The deeds of Corio-
lanus
Should not be utter'd feebly. It is held
That valor is the chiefest virtue and
Most dignifies the haver. If it be,
The man I speak of cannot in the world   90
Be singly counterpois'd.° At sixteen years,

discover show   affect cultivate
bonneted unbonneted, i.e., took their hats off
have them bring themselves
determin'd of decided issues concerning
state's . . . out i.e., that the state lacks means rather than
    that we lack the will to reward him fully
yield agree to

sooth'd flattered   weigh merit
have . . . struck i.e., sit idly by while the battle raged
monster'd exaggerated   That's who are
singly counterpois'd equalled by any one person

When Tarquin made a head for Rome, he fought
Beyond the mark of others. Our then dictator,
Whom with all praise I point at, saw him fight,
95 When with his Amazonian° chin he drove
The bristled lips before him. He bestrid
An o'er-press'd Roman, and i' the consul's view
Slew three opposers. Tarquin's self he met
And struck him on his knee.° In that day's feats,
100 When he might act the woman in the scene,
He proved best man i' the field, and for his meed
Was brow-bound with the oak. His pupil age
Man-enter'd° thus, he waxed like a sea,
And in the brunt of seventeen battles since
105 He lurch'd all swords° of the garland. For this
    last,
Before and in Corioli, let me say
I cannot speak him home.° He stopp'd the fliers,
And by his rare example made the coward
Turn terror into sport. As weeds before
110 A vessel under sail, so men obey'd
And fell below his stem. His sword, death's
    stamp,
Where it did mark, it took; from face to foot
He was a thing of blood, whose every motion
Was tim'd with dying cries. Alone he enter'd
115 The mortal gate of the city, which he painted
With shunless destiny;° aidless came off,
And with a sudden reinforcement struck
Corioli like a planet. Now all's his.
When by and by the din of war gan pierce
120 His ready sense, then straight his doubled spirit
Requicken'd what in flesh was fatigate,°
And to the battle came he, where he did
Run reeking o'er the lives of men as if
'Twere a perpetual spoil.° And till we call'd
125 Both field and city ours, he never stood
To ease his breast with panting.
MENENIUS.   Worthy man!
FIRST SENATOR. He cannot but with measure° fit the
    honors
Which we devise him.
COMINIUS.   Our spoils he kick'd at,
And look'd upon things precious as they were
130 The common muck of the world. He covets less
Than misery itself would give, rewards
His deeds with doing them, and is content
To spend the time to end it.°

MENENIUS.   He's right noble.
Let him be call'd for.
FIRST SENATOR.   Call Coriolanus.
OFFICER. He doth appear.   135
        [Re-enter CORIOLANUS.]
MENENIUS. The Senate, Coriolanus, are well
    pleas'd
To make thee consul.
CORIOLANUS.   I do owe them still
My life and services.
MENENIUS.   It then remains
That you do speak to the people.
CORIOLANUS.   I do beseech you,
Let me o'erleap that custom, for I cannot   140
Put on the gown, stand naked, and entreat them,
For my wounds' sake, to give their suffrage.
    Please you
That I may pass this doing.
SICINIUS.   Sir, the people
Must have their voices;° neither will they bate
One jot of ceremony.
MENENIUS.   Put them not to 't.   145
Pray you, go fit you to the custom, and
Take to you, as your predecessors have,
Your honor with your form.°
CORIOLANUS.   It is a part
That I shall blush in acting, and might well
Be taken from the people.
BRUTUS.   Mark you that?   150
CORIOLANUS. To brag unto them, thus I did, and
    thus;
Show them th' unaching scars which I should
    hide,
As if I had receiv'd them for the hire
Of their breath only!
MENENIUS.   Do not stand upon 't.
We recommend to you, tribunes of the people,   155
Our purpose to them, and to our noble consul
Wish we all joy and honor.
SENATORS. To Coriolanus come all joy and honor!
    [Flourish of cornets. Exeunt all but SICINIUS and
                                          BRUTUS.]
BRUTUS. You see how he intends to use the people.
SICINIUS. May they perceive 's intent! He will re-
    quire° them   160
As if he did contemn what he requested
Should be in them to give.
BRUTUS.   Come, we'll inform them
Of our proceedings here. On the marketplace
I know they do attend us.   [Exeunt]

Amazonian i.e., still beardless, like the female warrior's
on his knee to his knees
Man-enter'd entered into manhood
lurch'd all swords robbed all (other) warriors
speak him home praise him sufficiently
shunless destiny inescapable death   fatigate fatigued
spoil slaughter   with measure i.e., with full measure
to end it i.e., to get it over with

voices votes   form formality   require solicit

SCENE iii
The same. The Forum.

[*Enter seven or eight* CITIZENS.]

FIRST CITIZEN. Once if he do require our voices, we
ought not to deny him.

SECOND CITIZEN. We may, sir, if we will.

THIRD CITIZEN. We have power in ourselves to do
5   it, but it is a power that we have no power to do.
For if he show us his wounds and tell us his deeds,
we are to put our tongues into those wounds
and speak for them; so, if he tell us his noble
deeds, we must also tell him our noble accep-
10   tance of them. Ingratitude is monstrous, and for
the multitude to be ingrateful were to make a
monster of the multitude—of the which we
being members, should bring ourselves to be
monstrous members.

15 FIRST CITIZEN. And to make us no better thought
of, a little help will serve; for once we stood up
about the corn, he himself stuck not to call us the
many-headed multitude.

THIRD CITIZEN. We have been called so of many—
20   not that our heads are some brown, some black,
some auburn, some bald, but that our wits are so
diversely colored. And truly I think, if all our
wits were to issue out of one skull, they would
fly east, west, north, south, and their consent of
25   one direct way should be at once to all the points
o' the compass.

SECOND CITIZEN. Think you so? Which way do you
judge my wit would fly?

THIRD CITIZEN. Nay, your wit will not so soon out
30   as another man's will; 'tis strongly wedged up in
a block-head. But if it were at liberty, 'twould,
sure, southward.

SECOND CITIZEN. Why that way?

THIRD CITIZEN. To lose itself in a fog, where being
35   three parts melted away with rotten dews, the
fourth would return for conscience sake to help
to get thee a wife.

SECOND CITIZEN. You are never without your
tricks. You may, you may!°

40 THIRD CITIZEN. Are you all resolved to give your
voices? But that's no matter, the greater part
carries it. I say, if he would incline to the people,
there was never a worthier man.

[*Enter* CORIOLANUS *in a gown of humility, with*
MENENIUS.]

Here he comes, and in the gown of humility.
45   Mark his behavior. We are not to stay all together, but to come by him where he stands, by

ones, by twos, and by threes. He's to make his
requests by particulars, wherein every one of us
has a single honor in giving him our own voices
with our own tongues. Therefore follow me, and   50
I'll direct you how you shall go by him.

ALL. Content, content.   [*Exeunt* CITIZENS.]

MENENIUS. O sir, you are not right. Have you not
known
The worthiest men have done 't?

CORIOLANUS.   What must I say?—
"I pray, sir"—Plague upon 't! I cannot bring   55
My tongue to such a pace. "Look, sir, my
wounds!
I got them in my country's service, when
Some certain of your brethren roar'd and ran
From the noise of our own drums."

MENENIUS.   O me, the gods!
You must not speak of that. You must desire
them   60
To think upon you.

CORIOLANUS.   Think upon me! Hang 'em!
I would they would forget me, like the virtues
Which our divines lose by 'em.°

MENENIUS.   You'll mar all!
I'll leave you. Pray you, speak to 'em, I pray you,
In wholesome manner.   [*Exit*]

CORIOLANUS.   Bid them wash their faces   65
And keep their teeth clean. [*Re-enter two of the*
CITIZENS]   So, here comes a brace.

[*Re-enter a third* CITIZEN.]

You know the cause, sir, of my standing here.

THIRD CITIZEN. We do, sir. Tell us what hath
brought you to 't.

CORIOLANUS. Mine own desert.   70

SECOND CITIZEN. Your own desert!

CORIOLANUS. Aye, but not mine own desire.

THIRD CITIZEN. How! Not your own desire!

CORIOLANUS. No, sir, 'twas never my desire yet to
trouble the poor with begging.   75

THIRD CITIZEN. You must think, if we give you anything, we hope to gain by you.

CORIOLANUS. Well then, I pray, your price o' the
consulship?

FIRST CITIZEN. The price is to ask it kindly.   80

CORIOLANUS. Kindly! Sir, I pray, let me ha 't. I
have wounds to show you, which shall be yours
in private. Your good voice, sir. What say you?

SECOND CITIZEN. You shall ha 't, worthy sir.

CORIOLANUS. A match, sir. There's in all two   85
worthy voices begged. I have your alms. Adieu.

THIRD CITIZEN. But this is something odd.

SECOND CITIZEN. An 'twere to give again—but 'tis
no matter.   [*Exeunt the three* CITIZENS.]

---

you may   i.e., have your fun

lose by 'em   i.e., like casting pearls before swine

[*Re-enter two other* CITIZENS.]

90 CORIOLANUS. Pray you now, if it may stand with
the tune of your voices that I may be consul, I
have here the customary gown.

FOURTH CITIZEN. You have deserved nobly of your
country, and you have not deserved nobly.

95 CORIOLANUS. Your enigma?

FOURTH CITIZEN. You have been a scourge to her
enemies, you have been a rod to her friends; you
have not indeed loved the common people.

CORIOLANUS. You should account me the more vir-
100 tuous that I have not been common in my love. I
will, sir, flatter my sworn brother, the people, to
earn a dearer° estimation of them; 'tis a condition they account gentle. And since the wisdom
of their choice is rather to have my hat than my
105 heart, I will practice the insinuating nod, and be
off to them most counterfeitly; that is, sir, I will
counterfeit the bewitchment of some popular
man, and give it bountiful to the desirers. Therefore, beseech you, I may be consul.

110 FIFTH CITIZEN. We hope to find you our friend, and
therefore give you our voices heartily.

FOURTH CITIZEN. You have received many wounds
for your country.

CORIOLANUS. I will not seal° your knowledge with
115 showing them. I will make much of your voices,
and so trouble you no farther.

BOTH CITIZENS. The gods give you joy, sir, heartily!

[*Exeunt*]

CORIOLANUS. Most sweet voices!
Better it is to die, better to starve,
120 Than crave the hire which first we do deserve.
Why in this woolvish° toge should I stand here
To beg of Hob and Dick° that do appear
Their needless vouches? Custom calls me to 't.
What custom wills, in all things should we do 't,
125 The dust on antique time would lie unswept,
And mountainous error be too highly heap'd
For truth to o'erpeer. Rather than fool it so,
Let the high office and the honor go
To one that would do thus. I am half through.
130 The one part suffer'd, the other will I do.

[*Re-enter three* CITIZENS *more.*]

Here come moe voices.
Your voices! For your voices I have fought,
Watch'd° for your voices, for your voices bear
Of wounds two dozen odd. Battles thrice six
135 I have seen and heard of, for your voices have

Done many things, some less, some more. Your
voices!
Indeed, I would be consul.

SIXTH CITIZEN. He has done nobly, and cannot go
without any honest man's voice.

SEVENTH CITIZEN. Therefore let him be consul. The 140
gods give him joy, and make him good friend to
the people!

ALL. Amen, amen. God save thee, noble consul!

[*Exeunt*]

CORIOLANUS. Worthy voices!

[*Re-enter* MENENIUS, *with* BRUTUS *and* SICINIUS.]

MENENIUS. You have stood your limitation;° and
the tribunes   145
Endue you with the people's voice. Remains
That, in th' official marks° invested, you
Anon do meet the Senate.

CORIOLANUS.   Is this done?

SICINIUS. The custom of request you have dis-
charg'd.
The people do admit you, and are summon'd   150
To meet anon upon your approbation.°

CORIOLANUS. Where? At the Senate House?

SICINIUS.   There, Coriolanus.

CORIOLANUS. May I change these garments?

SICINIUS.   You may, sir.

CORIOLANUS. That I'll straight do, and, knowing
myself again,   155
Repair to the Senate House.

MENENIUS. I'll keep you company. Will you along?

BRUTUS. We stay here for the people.

SICINIUS.   Fare you well.

[*Exeunt* CORIOLANUS *and* MENENIUS.]

He has it now, and, by his looks, methinks
'Tis warm at 's heart.

BRUTUS.   With a proud heart he wore   160
His humble weeds. Will you dismiss the people?

[*Re-enter* CITIZENS.]

SICINIUS. How now, my masters! Have you chose
this man?

FIRST CITIZEN. He has our voices, sir.

BRUTUS. We pray the gods he may deserve your
loves.

SECOND CITIZEN. Amen, sir. To my poor unworthy
notice,   165
He mock'd us when he begg'd our voices.

THIRD CITIZEN.   Certainly
He flouted us downright.

FIRST CITIZEN. No, 'tis his kind of speech. He did not
mock us.

SECOND CITIZEN. Not one amongst us, save yourself, but says

---

dearer higher   *seal* confirm
woolvish i.e., deceptive, like a wolf in sheep's clothing
Hob and Dick i.e., just anyone who happens along
    (Shakespeare's Romans sometimes forget that they are
    not in England)
Watch'd stayed awake

limitation required time
official marks i.e., the robes of office
approbation confirmation

170 He us'd us scornfully. He should have show'd us
His marks of merit, wounds receiv'd for 's
    country.

SICINIUS. Why, so he did, I am sure.

CITIZENS. No, no. No man saw 'em.

THIRD CITIZEN. He said he had wounds which he
    could show in private,

175 And with his hat, thus waving it in scorn,
"I would be consul," says he. "Aged custom,
But by your voices, will not so permit me.
Your voices therefore." When we granted that,
Here was "I thank you for your voices. Thank
    you.
Your most sweet voices. Now you have left your
180   voices,
I have no further° with you." Was not this
    mockery?

SICINIUS. Why either were you ignorant to see 't,
Or, seeing it, of such childish friendliness
To yield your voices?

BRUTUS.   Could you not have told him,
185 As you were lesson'd: When he had no power,
But was a petty servant to the state,
He was your enemy, ever spake against
Your liberties and the charters° that you bear
I' the body of the weal? And now, arriving
190 A place of potency and sway o' the state,
If he should still malignantly remain
Fast foe to the plebeii, your voices might
Be curses to yourselves? You should have said
That as his worthy deeds did claim no less
195 Than what he stood for, so his gracious nature
Would think upon you for your voices, and
Translate his malice towards you into love,
Standing your friendly lord.

SICINIUS.   Thus to have said,
As you were foreadvis'd, had touch'd his spirit
200 And tried his inclination—from him pluck'd
Either his gracious promise, which you might,
As cause had call'd you up, have held him to;
Or else it would have gall'd his surly nature,
Which easily endures not article°
205 Tying him to aught. So, putting him to rage,
You should have ta'en th' advantage of his
    choler
And pass'd him unelected.

BRUTUS.   Did you perceive
He did solicit you in free contempt
When he did need your loves, and do you think
210 That his contempt shall not be bruising to you
When he hath power to crush? Why, had your
    bodies

No heart among you? Or had you tongues to cry
Against the rectorship° of judgment?

SICINIUS.   Have you
Ere now denied the asker—and now again,
Of him that did not ask but mock, bestow   215
Your su'd-for tongues?

THIRD CITIZEN. He's not confirm'd; we may deny
    him yet.

SECOND CITIZEN. And will deny him.
I'll have five hundred voices of that sound.

FIRST CITIZEN. I twice five hundred, and their
    friends to piece° 'em.   220

BRUTUS Get you hence instantly, and tell those
    friends
They have chose a consul that will from them
    take
Their liberties, make them of no more voice
Than dogs that are as often beat for barking
As therefore kept to do so.

SICINIUS.   Let them assemble,   225
And, on a safer° judgment, all revoke
Your ignorant election. Enforce° his pride
And his old hate unto you. Besides, forget not
With what contempt he wore the humble weed,
How in his suit he scorn'd you; but your loves, 230
Thinking upon his services, took from you
The apprehension of his present portance,°
Which most gibingly, ungravely, he did fashion
After th' inveterate hate he bears you.

BRUTUS.   Lay
A fault on us, your tribunes, that we labor'd,   235
No impediment between,° but that you must
Cast your election on him.

SICINIUS.   Say you chose him
More after our commandment than as guided
By your own true affections, and that your
    minds,
Preoccupied with what you rather must do   240
Than what you should, made you against the
    grain
To voice him consul. Lay the fault on us.

BRUTUS. Aye, spare us not. Say we read lectures to
    you,
How youngly he began to serve his country,
How long continu'd, and what stock he springs
    of—   245
The noble house o' the Marcians, from whence
    came
That Ancus Marcius, Numa's daughter's son,
Who after great Hostilius here was king;

---

no further no further use   *charters* rights
article conditions

rectorship rule   *piece* add to
safer more considered   *Enforce* stress
present portance immediate behavior
No impediment between setting all obstacles aside

Of the same house Publius and Quintus were,
250 That our best water brought by conduits hither;
And Censorinus, nobly named so,
Twice being by the people chosen censor,°
Was his great ancestor.
SICINIUS. One thus descended,
That hath beside well in his person wrought
255 To be set high in place, we did commend
To your remembrances; but you have found,
Scaling° his present bearing with his past,
That he's your fixed enemy, and revoke
Your sudden approbation.
BRUTUS. Say you ne'er had done 't—
260 Harp on that still—but by our putting on.
And presently, when you have drawn your num-
ber,

Repair to the Capitol.
CITIZENS. We will so. Almost all
Repent in their election. [Exeunt CITIZENS.]
BRUTUS. Let them go on,
This mutiny were better put in hazard°
Than stay, past doubt, for greater. 265
If, as his nature is, he fall in rage
With their refusal, both observe and answer
The vantage° of his anger.
SICINIUS. To the Capitol, come.
We will be there before the stream o' the
people;
And this shall seem, as partly 'tis, their own, 270
Which we have goaded onward. [Exeunt]

---

censor public recorder   Scaling balancing

put in hazard risked
answer the vantage seize the opportunity

ACT III

SCENE i
Rome. A street.

[Cornets. Enter CORIOLANUS, MENENIUS, all the
GENTRY, COMINIUS, TITUS LARTIUS, and other
SENATORS.]
CORIOLANUS. Tullus Aufidius then had made new
head?°
LARTIUS. He had, my lord, and that it was which
caus'd
Our swifter composition.°
CORIOLANUS. So then the Volsces stand but as at
first—
Ready, when time shall prompt them, to make
5 road°
Upon 's again.
COMINIUS. They are worn, lord consul, so,
That we shall hardly in our ages see
Their banners wave again.
CORIOLANUS. Saw you Aufidius?
LARTIUS. On safeguard he came to me and did
curse
10 Against the Volsces for they had so vilely
Yielded the town. He is retir'd to Antium.
CORIOLANUS. Spoke he of me?
LARTIUS. He did, my lord.
CORIOLANUS. How? What?

LARTIUS. How often he had met you sword to
sword,
That of all things upon the earth he hated
Your person most, that he would pawn his for-
tunes 15
To hopeless restitution, so he might
Be call'd your vanquisher.
CORIOLANUS. At Antium lives he?
LARTIUS. At Antium.
CORIOLANUS. I wish I had a cause to seek him there,
To oppose his hatred fully. Welcome home. 20
[Enter SICINIUS and BRUTUS.]
Behold. These are the tribunes of the people,
The tongues o' the common mouth. I do despise
them,
For they do prank them° in authority
Against all noble sufferance.°
SICINIUS. Pass no further.
CORIOLANUS. Ha! What is that? 25
BRUTUS. It will be dangerous to go on. No further.
CORIOLANUS. What makes this change?
MENENIUS. The matter?
COMINIUS. Hath he not pass'd the noble and the
common?
BRUTUS. Cominius, no.
CORIOLANUS. Have I had children's voices? 30

---

made new head raised a new army
composition agreement on terms   make road assault

prank them dress themselves
Against . . . sufferance beyond bearing

FIRST SENATOR. Tribunes, give way. He shall to the
  marketplace.
BRUTUS. The people are incens'd against him.
SICINIUS.   Stop,
  Or all will fall in broil.
CORIOLANUS.   Are these your herd?
  Must these have voices, that can yield them now
  And straight disclaim their tongues? What are
35 your offices?
  You being their mouths, why rule you not their
    teeth?
  Have you not set them on?
MENENIUS.   Be calm, be calm.
CORIOLANUS. It is a purpos'd° thing, and grows by
    plot
  To curb the will of the nobility.
40 Suffer 't, and live with such as cannot rule
  Nor ever will be rul'd.
BRUTUS.   Call 't not a plot.
  The people cry you mock'd them; and of late,
  When corn was given them gratis, you repin'd,
  Scandal'd the suppliants for the people, call'd
    them
45 Time-pleasers, flatterers, foes to nobleness.
CORIOLANUS. Why, this was known before.
BRUTUS.   Not to them all.
CORIOLANUS. Have you inform'd them sithence?
BRUTUS.   How! I inform them!
COMINIUS. You are like to do such business.
BRUTUS.   Not unlike,
  Each way, to better yours.°
CORIOLANUS. Why then should I be consul? By
50   yond clouds,
  Let me deserve so ill as you, and make me
  Your fellow tribune.
SICINIUS.   You show too much of that
  For which the people stir. If you will pass
  To where you are bound, you must inquire your
    way,
55 Which you are out of, with a gentler spirit,
  Or never be so noble as a consul,
  Nor yoke° with him for tribune.
MENENIUS.   Let's be calm.
COMINIUS. The people are abus'd,° set on. This
    paltering
  Becomes not Rome, nor has Coriolanus
60 Deserv'd this so dishonor'd rub, laid falsely
  I' the plain way of his merit.
CORIOLANUS.   Tell me of corn!
  This was my speech, and I will speak 't again—
MENENIUS. Not now, not now.
FIRST SENATOR.   Not in this heat, sir, now.

CORIOLANUS. Now, as I live, I will. My nobler
    friends,
  I crave their pardons.   65
  For the mutable, rank-scented many, let them
  Regard me as I do not flatter, and
  Therein behold themselves. I say again,
  In soothing them we nourish 'gainst our senate
  The cockle° of rebellion, insolence, sedition,   70
  Which we ourselves have plough'd for, sow'd,
    and scatter'd
  By mingling them with us, the honor'd number
  Who lack not virtue, no, nor power, but that
  Which they have given to beggars.
MENENIUS.   Well, no more.
FIRST SENATOR. No more words, we beseech you.
CORIOLANUS.   How! No more!   75
  As for my country I have shed my blood,
  Not fearing outward force, so shall my lungs
  Coin words till their decay against those measles°
  Which we disdain should tetter us,° yet sought
  The very way to catch them.
BRUTUS.   You speak o' the people   80
  As if you were a god to punish, not
  A man of their infirmity.
SICINIUS.   'Twere well
  We let the people know 't.
MENENIUS.   What, what? His choler?
CORIOLANUS. Choler!
  Were I as patient as the midnight sleep,
  By Jove, 'twould be my mind!   85
SICINIUS.   It is a mind
  That shall remain a poison where it is,
  Not poison any further.
CORIOLANUS.   Shall remain!
  Hear you this Triton° of the minnows? Mark you
  His absolute "shall"?
COMINIUS.   'Twas from the canon.°
CORIOLANUS.   "Shall"!   90
  O good but most unwise patricians! Why,
  You grave but reckless senators, have you thus
  Given Hydra° here to choose an officer,
  That with his peremptory "shall," being but
  The horn and noise o' the monster's, wants not
    spirit   95
  To say he'll turn your current in a ditch
  And make your channel his? If he have power,
  Then vail° your ignorance; if none, awake
  Your dangerous lenity. If you are learn'd,
  Be not as common fools; if you are not,   100

cockle weed (cocklebur)
measles i.e., loathsome spots
tetter us erupt on our skins
Triton Neptune's trumpeter
from the canon improper, illegal
Hydra many-headed beast   vail lower, subdue

purpos'd plotted   to better yours to outdo your efforts
yoke serve with   abus'd deceived

Let them have cushions by you. You are ple-
  beians,
If they be senators; and they are no less
When, both your voices blended, the great'st
  taste
Most palates theirs.° They choose their magis-
  trate—
105 And such a one as he, who puts his "shall,"
His popular "shall," against a graver bench
Than ever frown'd in Greece. By Jove himself,
It makes the consuls base! And my soul aches
To know, when two authorities are up,
110 Neither supreme, how soon confusion°
May enter 'twixt the gap of both and take
The one by th' other.°

COMINIUS.   Well, on to the marketplace.

CORIOLANUS. Whoever gave that counsel, to give
  forth
The corn o' the storehouse gratis, as 'twas us'd
Sometime in Greece—

115 MENENIUS.   Well, well, no more of that.

CORIOLANUS. Though there the people had more
  absolute power,
I say they nourish'd disobedience, fed
The ruin of the state.

BRUTUS.   Why, shall the people give
One that speaks thus their voice?

CORIOLANUS.   I'll give my reasons,
More worthier than their voices. They know the
120   corn
Was not our recompense, resting well assur'd
They ne'er did service for 't. Being press'd to the
  war,
Even when the naval of the state was touch'd,
They would not thread the gates.° This kind of
  service
125 Did not deserve corn gratis. Being i' the war,
Their mutinies and revolts, wherein they show'd
Most valor, spoke not for them.° Th' accusation
Which they have often made against the senate—
All cause unborn°—could never be the native°
130 Of our so frank donation. Well, what then?
How shall this bosom multiplied° digest
The senate's courtesy? Let deeds express
What's like to be their words: "We did request
  it;

We are the greater poll, and in true fear
They gave us our demands." Thus we debase   135
The nature of our seats and make the rabble
Call our cares fears, which will in time
Break ope the locks o' the senate and bring in
The crows to peck the eagles.

MENENIUS.   Come, enough.

BRUTUS. Enough, with over measure.

CORIOLANUS.   No, take more. 140
What may be sworn by, both divine and human,
Seal what I end withal! This double worship,°
Where one part does disdain with cause, the
  other
Insult without all reason; where gentry, title,
  wisdom
Cannot conclude but by the yea and no   145
Of general ignorance—it must omit°
Real necessities and give way the while
To unstable slightness.° Purpose° so barr'd, it
  follows
Nothing is done to purpose. Therefore, beseech
  you—
You that will be less fearful than discreet,   150
That love the fundamental part of state
More than you doubt° the change on 't, that pre-
  fer
A noble life before a long, and wish
To jump° a body with a dangerous physic
That's sure of death without it—at once pluck
  out   155
The multitudinous tongue. Let them not lick
The sweet which is their poison. Your dishonor
Mangles true judgment and bereaves the state
Of that integrity which should become 't,
Not having the power to do the good it would   160
For the ill which doth control 't.

BRUTUS.   Has said enough.

SICINIUS. Has spoken like a traitor, and shall answer
  As traitors do.

CORIOLANUS. Thou wretch, despite° o'erwhelm
  thee!
What should the people do with these bald tri-
  bunes,
On whom depending, their obedience fails   165
To the greater bench?° In a rebellion,
When what's not meet, but what must be, was
  law,
Then were they chosen. In a better hour,
Let what is meet be said it must be meet,
And throw their power i' the dust.   170

---

the great'st . . . theirs i.e., the prevailing voice is theirs, in
  which the most discriminating is reduced to the most
  common
confusion ruin
take . . . other use one to destroy the other
thread the gates i.e., pass through to fight
spoke . . . them i.e., did them no credit
cause unborn baseless   *native* birthplace; i.e., cause
bosom multiplied i.e., many-hearted, like many-headed

double worship divided rule   *omit* ignore
unstable slightness unpredictable whims
Purpose i.e., sober decision   *doubt* fear
jump risk   *despite* i.e., your own spite
greater bench i.e., the Senate

BRUTUS. Manifest treason!
SICINIUS.   This a consul? No.
BRUTUS. The ædiles,° ho!
                                        [*Enter an* ÆDILE.]
                                        Let him be apprehended.
SICINIUS. Go, call the people [*Exit* ÆDILE], in whose
      name myself
      Attach° thee as a traitorous innovator,°
175   A foe to the public weal. Obey, I charge thee,
      And follow to thine answer.°
CORIOLANUS.   Hence, old goat!
SENATORS, etc. We'll surety° him.
COMINIUS.   Ag'd sir, hands off.
CORIOLANUS. Hence, rotten thing, or I shall shake
      thy bones
      Out of thy garments.
SICINIUS.   Help, ye citizens!
                [*Enter a rabble of* CITIZENS, *with the* ÆDILES.]
180   MENENIUS. On both sides more respect.
SICINIUS. Here's he that would take from you all
      your power.
BRUTUS. Seize him, ædiles!
CITIZENS. Down with him! Down with him!
SENATORS, etc. Weapons, weapons, weapons!
                [*They all bustle about* CORIOLANUS.]
ALL. Tribunes!—Patricians!—Citizens!—What,
185   ho!—
      Sicinius!—Brutus!—Coriolanus!—Citizens!—
      Peace, peace, peace!—Stay! Hold! Peace!
MENENIUS. What is about to be? I am out of breath.
      Confusion's near. I cannot speak. You, tribunes
190   To the people! Coriolanus, patience!
      Speak, good Sicinius.
SICINIUS.   Hear me, people. Peace!
CITIZENS. Let's hear our tribune. Peace!—Speak,
      speak, speak.
SICINIUS. You are at point to lose your liberties.
      Marcius would have all from you—Marcius,
      Whom late you have nam'd for consul.
195   MENENIUS.   Fie, fie, fie!
      This is the way to kindle, not to quench.
FIRST SENATOR. T' unbuild the city, and to lay all
      flat.
SICINIUS. What is the city but the people?
CITIZENS.   True,
      The people are the city.
200   BRUTUS. By the consent of all, we were establish'd
      The people's magistrates.
CITIZENS.   You so remain.
MENENIUS. And so are like to do.

COMINIUS. That is the way to lay the city flat,
      To bring the roof to the foundation
      And bury all which yet distinctly ranges°   205
      In heaps and piles of ruin.
SICINIUS.   This deserves death.
BRUTUS. Or let us stand to our authority,
      Or let us lose it. We do here pronounce,
      Upon the part o' the people, in whose power
      We were elected theirs, Marcius is worthy   210
      Of present death.
SICINIUS.   Therefore lay hold of him.
      Bear him to the rock Tarpeian° and from thence
      Into destruction cast him.
BRUTUS.   Ædiles, seize him!
CITIZENS. Yield, Marcius, yield!
MENENIUS.   Hear me one word.
      Beseech you, tribunes, hear me but a word.   215
ÆDILES. Peace, peace!
MENENIUS. [*To* BRUTUS] Be that you seem, truly
      your country's friend,
      And temperately proceed to what you would
      Thus violently redress.
BRUTUS.   Sir, those cold ways
      That seem like prudent helps are very poisonous   220
      Where the disease is violent. Lay hands upon
      him
      And bear him to the rock.
CORIOLANUS.   No, I'll die here.
                                   [*Drawing his sword.*]
      There's some among you have beheld me fight-
      ing.
      Come, try upon yourselves what you have seen
      me.
MENENIUS. Down with that sword! Tribunes, with-
      draw awhile.   225
BRUTUS. Lay hands upon him.
MENENIUS.   Help Marcius, help,
      You that be noble. Help him, young and old!
CITIZENS. Down with him, down with him!
                [*In this mutiny, the* TRIBUNES, *the* ÆDILES, *and the*
                                   PEOPLE, *are beat in.*]
MENENIUS. Go, get you to your house; be gone,
      away!
      All will be naught else.
SECOND SENATOR.   Get you gone.
COMINIUS.   Stand fast; 230
      We have as many friends as enemies.
MENENIUS. Shall it be put to that?
FIRST SENATOR.   The gods forbid!
      I prithee, noble friend, home to thy house,
      Leave us to cure this cause.

ædiles police officers   *Attach* arrest
innovator agitator
answer i.e., place of answering the charge
surety stand good for

distinctly ranges stands in order
rock Tarpeian precipice from which traitors were thrown
      to death

MENENIUS.   For 'tis a sore upon us
235 You cannot tent° yourself. Be gone, beseech you.
COMINIUS. Come, sir, along with us.
CORIOLANUS. I would they were barbarians—as
 they are,
 Though in Rome litter'd—not Romans—as they
 are not,
 Though calved i' the porch o' the Capitol—
MENENIUS.   Be gone.
240 Put not your worthy rage into your tongue.
 One time will owe another.°
CORIOLANUS.   On fair ground
 I could beat forty of them.
MENENIUS.   I could myself
 Take up a brace o' the best of them; yea, the
 two tribunes.
COMINIUS. But now 'tis odds beyond arithmetic,
245 And manhood is call'd foolery when it stands
 Against a falling fabric. Will you hence
 Before the tag° return, whose rage doth rend
 Like interrupted waters and o'erbear
 What they are us'd to bear?
MENENIUS.   Pray you, be gone.
250 I'll try whether my old wit be in request
 With those that have but little. This must be
 patch'd
 With cloth of any color.°
COMINIUS.   Nay, come away.
 [*Exeunt* CORIOLANUS, COMINIUS, *and others.*]
FIRST PATRICIAN. This man has marr'd his fortune.
MENENIUS. His nature is too noble for the world.
255 He would not flatter Neptune for his trident
 Or Jove for 's power to thunder. His heart's his
 mouth.
 What his breast forges, that his tongue must
 vent,
 And, being angry, does forget that ever
 He heard the name of death.   [*A noise within.*]
 Here's goodly work!
SECOND PATRICIAN.   I would they were abed!
MENENIUS. I would they were in Tiber! What the
260 vengeance!
 Could he not speak 'em fair?
 [*Re-enter* BRUTUS *and* SICINIUS, *with the rabble.*]
SICINIUS.   Where is this viper
 That would depopulate the city and
 Be every man himself?
MENENIUS.   You worthy tribunes—
SICINIUS. He shall be thrown down the Tarpeian
 rock
265 With rigorous hands. He hath resisted law,

And therefore law shall scorn him further trial
Than the severity of the public power
Which he so sets at naught.
FIRST CITIZEN.   He shall well know
 The noble tribunes are the people's mouths,
 And we their hands.   270
CITIZENS. He shall, sure on 't.
MENENIUS.   Sir, sir—
SICINIUS. Peace!
MENENIUS. Do not cry havoc° where you should
 but hunt
 With modest warrant.
SICINIUS.   Sir, how comes 't that you
 Have holp to make this rescue?
MENENIUS.   Hear me speak.   275
 As I do know the consul's worthiness,
 So can I name his faults—
SICINIUS.   Consul! What consul?
MENENIUS. The consul Coriolanus.
BRUTUS.   He consul!
CITIZENS. No, no, no, no, no.
MENENIUS. If, by the tribunes' leave, and yours,
 good people,   280
 I may be heard, I would crave a word or two,
 The which shall turn you to no further harm
 Than so much loss of time.
SICINIUS.   Speak briefly then,
 For we are peremptory to dispatch
 This viperous traitor. To eject him hence   285
 Were but one danger, and to keep him here
 Our certain death. Therefore it is decreed
 He dies tonight.
MENENIUS.   Now the good gods forbid
 That our renowned Rome, whose gratitude
 Towards her deserved children is enroll'd   290
 In Jove's own book, like an unnatural dam
 Should now eat up her own!
SICINIUS. He's a disease that must be cut away.
MENENIUS. O, he's a limb that has but a disease:
 Mortal to cut it off; to cure it, easy.   295
 What has he done to Rome that's worthy death?
 Killing our enemies, the blood he hath lost—
 Which I dare vouch is more than that he hath
 By many an ounce—he dropp'd it for his coun-
 try;
 And what is left, to lose it by his country   300
 Were to us all that do 't and suffer it
 A brand° to th' end o' the world.
SICINIUS.   This is clean kam.°
BRUTUS. Merely awry. When he did love his
 country,
 It honor'd him.

tent cure *One . . . another* there will be another time
tag rabble
This . . . color we must fix it up in any way we can

cry havoc set slaughter afoot
brand mark of shame *clean kam* askew

MENENIUS.   The service of the foot
305   Being once gangrened, is not then respected
    For what before it was.
    BRUTUS.   We'll hear no more.
    Pursue him to his house and pluck him thence,
    Lest his infection, being of catching nature,
    Spread further.
    MENENIUS.   One word more, one word.
310   This tiger-footed rage, when it shall find
    The harm of unscann'd° swiftness, will, too late,
    Tie leaden pounds to 's heels. Proceed by process,
    Lest parties,° as he is belov'd, break out
    And sack great Rome with Romans.
    BRUTUS.   If it were so—
315   SICINIUS. What do ye talk?
    Have we not had a taste of his obedience?
    Our ædiles smote? Ourselves resisted? Come.
    MENENIUS. Consider this: he has been bred i' the wars
    Since he could draw a sword, and is ill school'd
320   In bolted° language; meal and bran together
    He throws without distinction. Give me leave,
    I'll go to him and undertake to bring him
    Where he shall answer, by a lawful form,
    In peace, to his utmost peril.
    FIRST SENATOR.   Noble tribunes,
325   It is the humane way. The other course
    Will prove too bloody, and the end of it
    Unknown to the beginning.
    SICINIUS.   Noble Menenius,
    Be you then as the people's officer.
    Masters, lay down your weapons.
    BRUTUS.   Go not home.
    SICINIUS. Meet on the marketplace. We'll attend
330   you there,
    Where, if you bring not Marcius, we'll proceed
    In our first way.
    MENENIUS.   I'll bring him to you.
    [To the SENATORS] Let me desire your company.
    He must come,
    Or what is worst will follow.
    FIRST SENATOR.   Pray you, let's to him.
                                        [Exeunt]

SCENE ii
A room in CORIOLANUS's house.

[Enter CORIOLANUS with PATRICIANS.]
CORIOLANUS. Let them pull all about mine ears,
    present me
    Death on the wheel or at wild horses' heels,
    Or pile ten hills on the Tarpeian rock,
    That the precipitation might stretch
    Below the beam of sight; yet will I still   5
    Be thus to them.
A PATRICIAN.   You do the nobler.
CORIOLANUS. I muse my mother
    Does not approve me further, who was wont
    To call them woolen vassals,° things created
    To buy and sell with groats,° to show bare heads   10
    In congregations, to yawn, be still, and wonder
    When one but of my ordinance° stood up
    To speak of peace or war.
                    [Enter VOLUMNIA.]
                              I talk of you.
    Why did you wish me milder? Would you have
    me
    False to my nature? Rather say I play   15
    The man I am.
VOLUMNIA.   O, sir, sir, sir,
    I would have had you put your power well on
    Before you had worn it out.
CORIOLANUS.   Let go.
VOLUMNIA. You might have been enough the man
    you are
    With striving less to be so. Lesser had been   20
    The thwartings of your dispositions if
    You had not show'd them how ye were dispos'd
    Ere they lack'd power to cross you.
CORIOLANUS.   Let them hang.
VOLUMNIA. Aye, and burn too.
        [Enter MENENIUS with the SENATORS.]
MENENIUS. Come, come, you have been too rough,
    something too rough.   25
    You must return and mend it.
FIRST SENATOR.   There's no remedy,
    Unless, by not so doing, our good city
    Cleave in the midst and perish.
VOLUMNIA.   Pray be counsel'd.
    I have a heart as little apt° as yours,
    But yet a brain that leads my use of anger   30
    To better vantage.
MENENIUS.   Well said, noble woman!
    Before he should thus stoop to the herd, but that

---

unscann'd unstudied   *parties* factions
bolted sifted; i.e., diplomatic

woolen vassals coarsely clothed slaves
groats four-penny coins   *ordinance* rank
apt i.e., given to yielding

The violent fit o' the time craves it as physic
For the whole state, I would put mine armor on,
Which I can scarcely bear.

35 CORIOLANUS.   What must I do?
MENENIUS. Return to the tribunes.
CORIOLANUS.   Well, what then? What then?
MENENIUS. Repent what you have spoke.
CORIOLANUS. For them! I cannot do it to the gods;
    Must I then do 't to them?
VOLUMNIA.   You are too absolute,
40 Though therein you can never be too noble
    But when extremities speak. I have heard you
        say
    Honor and policy,° like unsever'd friends,
    I' the war do grow together. Grant that, and tell
        me,
    In peace what each of them by the other lose,
    That they combine not there.
CORIOLANUS.   Tush, tush!
45 MENENIUS.   A good demand.
VOLUMNIA. If it be honor in your wars to seem
    The same you are not—which, for your best ends,
    You adopt your policy—how is it less or worse
    That it shall hold companionship in peace
50 With honor, as in war, since that to both
    It stands in like request?°
CORIOLANUS.   Why force you this?
VOLUMNIA. Because that now it lies you on° to
        speak
    To the people—not by your own instruction,
    Nor by the matter which your heart prompts
        you,
55 But with such words that are but roted° in
    Your tongue, though but bastards and syllables
    Of no allowance to your bosom's truth.
    Now this no more dishonors you at all
    Than to take in a town with gentle words
60 Which else would put you to your fortune and
    The hazard of much blood.
    I would dissemble with my nature where
    My fortunes and my friends at stake requir'd
    I should do so in honor. I am in this
65 Your wife, your son, these senators, the nobles—
    And you will rather show our general louts
    How you can frown than spend a fawn upon 'em
    For the inheritance of their loves and safeguard
    Of what that want might ruin.
MENENIUS.   Noble lady!
70 Come, go with us. Speak fair. You may salve so,
    Not° what is dangerous present, but the loss

Of what is past.
VOLUMNIA.   I prithee now, my son,
    Go to them with this bonnet in thy hand,
    And thus far having stretch'd it, here be° with
        them:
    Thy knee bussing the stones—for in such busi-
        ness   75
    Action is eloquence and the eyes of the ignorant
    More learned than the ears; waving° thy head—
    Which often thus, correcting thy stout heart,
    Now humble as the ripest mulberry
    That will not hold the handling. Or say to them 80
    Thou art their soldier, and being bred in broils
    Hast not the soft way which, thou dost confess,
    Were fit for thee to use, as they to claim,
    In asking their good loves; but thou wilt frame
    Thyself, forsooth, hereafter theirs, so far   85
    As thou hast power and person.
MENENIUS.   This but done
    Even as she speaks, why, their hearts were yours;
    For they have pardons, being ask'd, as free
    As words to little purpose.
VOLUMNIA.   Prithee now,
    Go, and be rul'd—although I know thou hadst
        rather   90
    Follow thine enemy in a fiery gulf
    Than flatter him in a bower.
            [Enter COMINIUS.]
                    Here is Cominius.
COMINIUS. I have been i' the marketplace, and sir,
    'tis fit
    You make strong party, or defend yourself
    By calmness or by absence. All's in anger.   95
MENENIUS. Only fair speech.
COMINIUS.   I think 'twill serve, if he
    Can thereto frame his spirit.
VOLUMNIA.   He must, and will.
    Prithee now, say you will, and go about it.
CORIOLANUS. Must I go show them my unbarbed
    sconce?° Must I,
    With my base tongue, give to my noble heart   100
    A lie that it must bear? Well, I will do 't.
    Yet, were there but this single plot to lose,
    This mould of Marcius, they to dust should
        grind it
    And throw 't against the wind. To the market-
        place!
    You have put me now to such a part which
        never   105
    I shall discharge to the life.°
COMINIUS.   Come, come, we'll prompt you.

---

policy political expediency
stands . . . request is equally needful
lies you on rests upon you   roted memorized
Not not only

here be be thus   waving bowing
unbarbed sconce bared head
discharge . . . life act convincingly

VOLUMNIA. I prithee now, sweet son, as thou hast
    said
    My praises made thee first a soldier, so,
    To have my praise for this, perform a part
    Thou hast not done before.

110 CORIOLANUS.   Well, I must do 't.
    Away, my disposition, and possess me
    Some harlot's spirit! My throat of war be turn'd,
    Which quired° with my drum, into a pipe
    Small as an eunuch, or the virgin voice
115   That babies lulls asleep! The smiles of knaves
    Tent° in my cheeks, and schoolboys' tears take
      up
    The glasses of my sight!° A beggar's tongue
    Make motion through my lips, and my arm'd
      knees,
    Who bow'd but in my stirrup, bend like his
120   That hath receiv'd an alms! I will not do 't,
    Lest I surcease° to honor mine own truth
    And by my body's action teach my mind
    A most inherent baseness.

    VOLUMNIA.   At thy choice then.
    To beg of thee, it is my more dishonor
125   Than thou of them. Come all to ruin. Let
    Thy mother rather feel thy pride than fear
    Thy dangerous stoutness,° for I mock at death
    With as big heart as thou. Do as thou list.
    Thy valiantness was mine, thou suck'dst it from
      me,
    But owe thy pride thyself.

130 CORIOLANUS.   Pray be content.
    Mother, I am going to the marketplace.
    Chide me no more. I'll mountebank their loves,°
    Cog° their hearts from them, and come home
      belov'd
    Of all the trades in Rome. Look, I am going.
135   Commend me to my wife. I'll return consul,
    Or never trust to what my tongue can do
    I' the way of flattery further.

    VOLUMNIA.   Do your will.
                              [Exit]
COMINIUS. Away! The tribunes do attend you. Arm
    yourself
    To answer mildly, for they are prepar'd
140   With accusations, as I hear, more strong
    Than are upon you yet.
CORIOLANUS. The word is "mildly." Pray you, let
    us go.
    Let them accuse me by invention, I

---

quired harmonized   *Tent* make abode
take up . . . sight overflow my eyeballs
surcease cease   *stoutness* stubbornness
mountebank their loves use a mountebank's tricks to win
    their affection
Cog cheat

    Will answer in mine honor.
MENENIUS.   Aye, but mildly.
CORIOLANUS. Well, mildly be it then. Mildly!   145
                              [Exeunt]

SCENE iii
The same. The Forum.

[*Enter* SICINIUS *and* BRUTUS.]
BRUTUS. In this point charge him home,° that he
    affects°
    Tyrannical power. If he evade us there,
    Enforce° him with his envy° to the people,
    And that the spoil got on° th' Antiates
    Was ne'er distributed.
            [*Enter an* ÆDILE.]
                  What, will he come?   5
ÆDILE. He's coming.
BRUTUS.   How accompanied?
ÆDILE. With old Menenius and those senators
    That always favor'd him.
SICINIUS.   Have you a catalogue
    Of all the voices that we have procur'd,
    Set down by the poll?°
ÆDILE.   I have; 'tis ready.   10
SICINIUS. Have you collected them by tribes?°
ÆDILE.   I have.
SICINIUS. Assemble presently the people hither,
    And when they hear me say "It shall be so
    I' the right and strength o' the commons," be it
      either
    For death, for fine, or banishment, then let them,   15
    If I say fine, cry "Fine," if death, cry "Death,"
    Insisting on the old prerogative
    And power i' the truth o' the cause.
ÆDILE.   I shall inform them.
BRUTUS. And when such time they have begun to
    cry,
    Let them not cease, but with a din confus'd   20
    Enforce the present° execution
    Of what we chance to sentence.
ÆDILE.   Very well.
SICINIUS. Make them be strong and ready for this
    hint
    When we shall hap to give 't them.
BRUTUS.   Go about it. [*Exit* ÆDILE.]
    Put him to choler straight. He hath been us'd   25
    Ever to conquer and to have his worth°
    Of contradiction. Being once chaf'd, he cannot

---

charge him home bait him   *affects* covets
Enforce confront   *envy* malice   *on* from
by the poll singly; i.e., to gain advantage
tribes electoral divisions; i.e., precincts
present immediate   *worth* weight

Be rein'd again to temperance; then he speaks
What's in his heart, and that is there which looks
With us to break his neck.

30 SICINIUS.   Well, here he comes.
[*Enter* CORIOLANUS, MENENIUS, *and* COMINIUS,
with SENATORS *and* PATRICIANS.]
MENENIUS. Calmly, I do beseech you.
CORIOLANUS. Aye, as an ostler, that for the poorest
    piece
    Will bear the knave by the volume.° The
        honor'd gods
    Keep Rome in safety and the chairs of justice
35 Supplied with worthy men! Plant love among's!
    Throng our large temples with the shows of
        peace,
    And not our streets with war!
FIRST SENATOR.   Amen, amen.
MENENIUS. A noble wish.
[*Re-enter* ÆDILE, *with* CITIZENS.]
SICINIUS. Draw near, ye people.
ÆDILE. List to your tribunes. Audience! Peace, I
40   say!
CORIOLANUS. First, hear me speak.
BOTH TRIBUNES.   Well, say. Peace, ho!
CORIOLANUS. Shall I be charg'd no further than this
    present?°
    Must all determine here?
SICINIUS.   I do demand
    If you submit you to the people's voices,
45 Allow° their officers, and are content
    To suffer lawful censure for such faults
    As shall be prov'd upon you.
CORIOLANUS.   I am content.
MENENIUS. Lo, citizens, he says he is content.
    The warlike service he has done, consider.
        Think
50 Upon the wounds his body bears, which show
    Like graves i' the holy churchyard.
CORIOLANUS.   Scratches with briers,
    Scars to move laughter only.
MENENIUS.   Consider further
    That when he speaks not like a citizen,
    You find him like a soldier. Do not take
55 His rougher accents for malicious sounds,
    But, as I say, such as become a soldier
    Rather than envy° you.
COMINIUS.   Well, well, no more.
CORIOLANUS. What is the matter
    That being pass'd for consul with full voice,
60 I am so dishonor'd that the very hour

You take if off again?
SICINIUS.   Answer to us.
CORIOLANUS. Say, then. 'Tis true, I ought so.
SICINIUS. We charge you that you have contriv'd
    to take
    From Rome all season'd office° and to wind
    Yourself into a power tyrannical,   65
    For which you are a traitor to the people.
CORIOLANUS. How! Traitor!
MENENIUS.   Nay, temperately; your promise.
CORIOLANUS. The fires i' the lowest hell fold in the
        people!
    Call me their traitor, thou injurious tribune!
    Within thine eyes sat twenty thousand deaths, 70
    In thy hands clutch'd as many millions, in
    Thy lying tongue both numbers, I would say
    "Thou liest" unto thee with a voice as free
    As I do pray the gods.
SICINIUS.   Mark you this, people?
CITIZENS. To the rock, to the rock with him!   75
SICINIUS. Peace!
    We need not put new matter to his charge.
    What you have seen him do and heard him
        speak,
    Beating your officers, cursing yourselves,
    Opposing laws with strokes, and here defying 80
    Those whose great power must try him, even
        this,
    So criminal and in such capital kind,
    Deserves th' extremest death.
BRUTUS.   But since he hath
    Serv'd well for Rome—
CORIOLANUS.   What do you prate of service?
BRUTUS. I talk of that, that know it.   85
CORIOLANUS. You?
MENENIUS. Is this the promise that you made your
        mother?
COMINIUS. Know, I pray you—
CORIOLANUS.   I'll know no further.
    Let them pronounce the steep Tarpeian death,
    Vagabond exile, flaying, pent to linger   90
    But with a grain a day, I would not buy
    Their mercy at the price of one fair word,
    Nor check my courage for what they can give,
    To have 't with saying "Good morrow."
SICINIUS.   For that° he has,
    As much as in him lies, from time to time   95
    Envied against° the people, seeking means
    To pluck away their power, as now at last
    Given° hostile strokes, and that not in the
        presence

---

bear . . . volume   submit to being called knave without
    limit
this present   on this occasion   *Allow*   acknowledge
envy   malice toward

season'd office   established authority
For that   because   *Envied against*   been hostile to
as . . . Given   and now has given

Of dreaded justice but on the ministers
100 That do distribute it, in the name o' the people
And in the power of us the tribunes, we
Even from this instant banish him our city
In peril of precipitation
From off the rock Tarpeian, never more
105 To enter our Rome gates. I' the people's name
I say it shall be so.
CITIZENS. It shall be so, it shall be so. Let him away.
He's banish'd, and it shall be so.
COMINIUS. Hear me, my masters, and my common
friends—
SICINIUS. He's sentenc'd; no more hearing.
110 COMINIUS.   Let me speak.
I have been consul, and can show for Rome
Her enemies' marks upon me. I do love
My country's good with a respect more tender,
More holy and profound, than mine own life,
115 My dear wife's estimate,° her womb's increase
And treasure of my loins; then if I would
Speak that—
SICINIUS.   We know your drift. Speak what?
BRUTUS. There's no more to be said but he is
banished
As enemy to the people and his country.
120 It shall be so.
CITIZENS. It shall be so, it shall be so.
CORIOLANUS. You common cry° of curs, whose
breath I hate
As reek o' the rotten fens, whose loves I prize

estimate value   cry pack

As the dead carcasses of unburied men
That do corrupt my air, I banish you,   125
And here remain° with your uncertainty!
Let every feeble rumor shake your hearts!
Your enemies, with nodding of their plumes,
Fan you into despair! Have the power still
To banish your defenders, till at length   130
Your ignorance, which finds not till it feels,
Making not reservation of yourselves,
Still° your own foes, deliver you as most
Abated° captives to some nation
That won you without blows! Despising,   135
For you, the city, thus I turn my back.
There is a world elsewhere.
        [Exeunt CORIOLANUS, COMINIUS,
            MENENIUS, SENATORS and PATRICIANS.]
ÆDILE. The people's enemy is gone, is gone!
CITIZENS. Our enemy is banish'd! He is gone! Hoo!
Hoo!
        [They all shout, and throw up their caps.]
SICINIUS. Go, see him out at gates, and follow him 140
As he hath follow'd you, with all despite.
Give him deserv'd vexation. Let a guard
Attend us through the city.
CITIZENS. Come, come, let's see him out at gates.
Come.
The gods preserve our noble tribunes! Come.   145
        [Exeunt]

remain may you remain   Still always
Abated wasted

ACT IV

SCENE i
Rome. Before a gate of the city.

[Enter CORIOLANUS, VOLUMNIA, VIRGILIA,
MENENIUS, COMINIUS, with the young nobility
of Rome.]
CORIOLANUS. Come, leave your tears; a brief
farewell. The beast
With many heads butts me away. Nay, mother,
Where is your ancient courage? You were us'd
To say extremity was the trier of spirits,
That common chances common men could
5   bear,
That when the sea was calm all boats alike
Show'd mastership in floating; fortune's blows,
When most struck home, being gentle wounded,
craves

A noble cunning.° You were us'd to load me
With precepts that would make invincible   10
The heart that conn'd° them.
VIRGILIA. O heavens! O heavens!
CORIOLANUS.   Nay, I prithee, woman—
VOLUMNIA. Now the red pestilence strike all trades
in Rome,
And occupations° perish!
CORIOLANUS.   What, what, what!
I shall be lov'd when I am lack'd. Nay, mother, 15
Resume that spirit when you were wont to say
If you had been the wife of Hercules,

fortune's . . . cunning i.e., to endure fortune's worst
    blows nobly requires real nobility
conn'd memorized
occupations i.e., trades and tradesmen

Six of his labors you'd have done, and sav'd
Your husband so much sweat. Cominius,
20　Droop not; adieu. Farewell, my wife, my
　　　mother.
I'll do well yet. Thou old and true Menenius,
Thy tears are salter than a younger man's,
And venomous to thine eyes. My sometime
　　　general,
I have seen thee stern, and thou hast oft beheld
25　Heart-hardening spectacles; tell these sad
　　　women
'Tis fond° to wail inevitable strokes
As 'tis to laugh at 'em. My mother, you wot
　　　well
My hazards still have been your solace, and
Believe 't not lightly—though I go alone,
30　Like to a lonely dragon that his fen
Makes fear'd and talk'd of more than seen—
　　　your son
Will or exceed the common or be caught
With cautelous baits and practice.°
VOLUMNIA.　　　　　　　　My first° son,
Whither wilt thou go? Take good Cominius
35　With thee awhile. Determine on some course
More than a wild exposure° to each chance
That starts i' the way before thee.
CORIOLANUS.　　　　　　　　O the gods!
COMINIUS. I'll follow thee a month, devise with thee
Where thou shalt rest, that thou mayst hear of
　　　us
40　And we of thee. So, if the time thrust forth
A cause for thy repeal,° we shall not send
O'er the vast world to seek a single man
And lose advantage, which doth ever cool
I' th' absence of the needer.
CORIOLANUS.　　　　　　　　Fare ye well.
Thou hast years upon thee, and thou art too
45　　　full
Of the wars' surfeits° to go rove with one
That's yet unbruis'd. Bring me but out at gate.
Come, my sweet wife, my dearest mother, and
My friends of noble touch,° when I am forth,
50　Bid me farewell and smile. I pray you, come.
While I remain above the ground, you shall
Hear from me still, and never of me aught
But what is like me formerly.
MENENIUS.　　　　　　　　That's worthily
As any ear can hear. Come, let's not weep.
55　If I could shake off but one seven years

---

fond　as foolish
cautelous . . . practice　treacherous devices and plotting
first　i.e., illustrious and only　　*exposure*　exposure
repeal　recall　　*surfeits*　deleterious effects
noble touch　i.e., proven noble, as gold tested by the
　　touchstone

From these old arms and legs, by the good gods
I'd with thee every foot.
CORIOLANUS.　　　　　　　Give me thy hand.
Come.　　　　　　　　　　　　　[*Exeunt*]

SCENE ii
The same. A street near the gate.

[*Enter the two* TRIBUNES, SICINIUS *and* BRUTUS,
with the ÆDILE.]
SICINIUS. Bid them all home; he's gone, and we'll
　no further.
The nobility are vex'd, whom we see have sided
In his behalf.
BRUTUS.　　　Now we have shown our power,
　Let us seem humbler after it is done
　Than when it was a-doing.
SICINIUS.　　　　　　　　Bid them home.　5
　Say their great enemy is gone, and they
　Stand in their ancient strength.
BRUTUS.　　　　　　　Dismiss them home.
　　　　　　　　　　　[*Exit* ÆDILE.]
　Here comes his mother.
　[*Enter* VOLUMNIA, VIRGILIA, *and* MENENIUS.]
SICINIUS.　　　　　　　Let's not meet her.
BRUTUS.　　　　　　　　　　Why?
SICINIUS. They say she's mad.
BRUTUS. They have ta'en note of us. Keep on your
　way.　　　　　　　　　　　　　　　　10
VOLUMNIA. O, ye're well met. The hoarded
　plague o' the gods
　Requite your love!
MENENIUS.　　　Peace, peace; be not so loud.
VOLUMNIA. If that I could for weeping, you should
　hear—
　Nay, and you shall hear some. [*To* BRUTUS] Will
　you be gone?
VIRGILIA. [*To* SICINIUS] You shall stay too. I would I
　had the power　　　　　　　　　　　15
　To say so to my husband.
SICINIUS.　　　　　　Are you mankind?°
VOLUMNIA. Aye, fool. Is that a shame? Note but this
　fool.
　Was not a man my father? Hadst thou foxship
　To banish him that struck more blows for Rome
　Than thou hast spoken words?
SICINIUS.　　　　　　O blessed heavens!　20
VOLUMNIA. Moe noble blows than ever thou wise
　words,
　And for Rome's good. I'll tell thee what; yet
　go—
　Nay, but thou shalt stay too. I would my son

---

mankind　i.e., of mankind, human

Were in Arabia,° and thy tribe before him,
His good sword in his hand.
SICINIUS.   What then?
25 VIRGILIA.   What then!
He'd make an end of thy posterity.
VOLUMNIA. Bastards and all.
Good man, the wounds that he does bear for
Rome!
MENENIUS. Come, come, peace.
30 SICINIUS. I would he had continued to his country
As he began, and not unknit himself
The noble knot he made.
BRUTUS.   I would he had.
VOLUMNIA. "I would he had!" 'Twas you incens'd
the rabble—
Cats, that can judge as fitly of his worth
35 As I can of those mysteries which heaven
Will not have earth to know.
BRUTUS.   Pray, let us go.
VOLUMNIA. Now, pray, sir, get you gone.
You have done a brave deed. Ere you go, hear
this:
As far as doth the Capitol exceed
40 The meanest house in Rome, so far my son—
This lady's husband here, this, do you see?—
Whom you have banish'd, does exceed you all.
BRUTUS. Well, well, we'll leave you.
SICINIUS.   Why stay we to be baited
With one that wants her wits?
VOLUMNIA.   Take my prayers with you.
                                    [Exeunt TRIBUNES.]
45 I would the gods had nothing else to do
But to confirm my curses! Could I meet 'em
But once a day, it would unclog my heart
Of what lies heavy to 't.
MENENIUS.   You have told them home,
And, by my troth, you have cause. You'll sup
with me?
50 VOLUMNIA. Anger's my meat; I sup upon myself,
And so shall starve with feeding. Come, let's go.
Leave this faint puling, and lament as I do,
In anger, Juno-like. Come, come, come.
                        [Exeunt VOLUMNIA and VIRGILIA.]
MENENIUS. Fie, fie, fie!   [Exit]

SCENE iii
A highway between Rome and Antium.

[Enter a ROMAN and a VOLSCE, meeting.]
A ROMAN. I know you well, sir, and you know me.
Your name, I think, is Adrian.
A VOLSCIAN. It is so, sir. Truly, I have forgot you.

Arabia i.e., the desert

A ROMAN. I am a Roman, and my services are, as
you are, against 'em. Know you me yet?   5
A VOLSCIAN. Nicanor, no?
A ROMAN. The same, sir.
A VOLSCIAN. You had more beard when I last saw
you, but your favor is well appeared by your
tongue.° What's the news in Rome? I have a   10
note from the Volscian state to find you out
there. You have well saved me a day's journey.
A ROMAN. There hath been in Rome strange insur-
rections—the people against the senators,
patricians, and nobles.   15
A VOLSCIAN. Hath been! Is it ended then? Our
state thinks not so. They are in a most warlike
preparation, and hope to come upon them in the
heat of their division.
A ROMAN. The main blaze of it is past, but a small 20
thing would make it flame again, for the nobles
receive so to heart the banishment of that
worthy Coriolanus, that they are in a ripe
aptness to take all power from the people and
to pluck from them their tribunes forever. This 25
lies glowing, I can tell you, and is almost mature
for the violent breaking out.
A VOLSCIAN. Coriolanus banished!
A ROMAN. Banished, sir.
A VOLSCIAN. You will be welcome with this   30
intelligence, Nicanor.
A ROMAN. The day serves well for them now. I
have heard it said the fittest time to corrupt a
man's wife is when she's fallen out with her
husband. Your noble Tullus Aufidius will   35
appear well in these wars, his great opposer,
Coriolanus, being now in no request of his
country.
A VOLSCIAN. He cannot choose. I am most fortunate, thus accidentally to encounter you. You   40
have ended my business, and I will merrily
accompany you home.
A ROMAN. I shall, between this and supper, tell you
most strange things from Rome, all tending to
the good of their adversaries. Have you an army 45
ready, say you?
A VOLSCIAN. A most royal one—the centurions
and their charges, distinctly billeted, already in
the entertainment,° and to be on foot at an
hour's warning.   50
A ROMAN. I am joyful to hear of their readiness
and am the man, I think, that shall set them in
present action. So, sir, heartily well met, and
most glad of your company.

favor . . . tongue face is made known by your speech
distinctly . . . entertainment individually enrolled,
enlisted in the service

55 A Volscian. You take my part from me, sir; I
   have the most cause to be glad of yours.
A Roman. Well, let us go together.   [Exeunt]

SCENE iv
Antium. Before Aufidius's house.

[Enter Coriolanus in mean apparel, disguised
and muffled.]

Coriolanus. A goodly city is this Antium. City,
   'Tis I that made thy widows. Many an heir
   Of these fair edifices 'fore my wars°
   Have I heard groan and drop. Then know me
      not,
   Lest that thy wives with spits and boys with
5   stones
   In puny battle slay me.
                     [Enter a Citizen.]
                           Save you, sir.
A Citizen. And you.
Coriolanus.   Direct me, if it be your will,
   Where great Aufidius lies. Is he in Antium?
A Citizen. He is, and feasts the nobles of the state
   At his house this night.
10 Coriolanus.   Which is his house, beseech you?
A Citizen. This, here, before you.
Coriolanus.   Thank you, sir. Farewell.
                              [Exit Citizen.]
   O world, thy slippery turns! Friends now fast
      sworn,
   Whose double bosoms seem to wear one heart,
   Whose hours, whose bed, whose meal and
      exercise
15 Are still together, who twin, as 'twere, in love
   Unseparable, shall within this hour,
   On a dissension of a doit,° break out
   To bitterest enmity. So, fellest° foes,
   Whose passions and whose plots have broke
      their sleep
20 To take the one the other, by some chance,
   Some trick not worth an egg, shall grow dear
      friends
   And interjoin their issues.° So with me.
   My birthplace hate I, and my love's upon
   This enemy town. I'll enter. If he slay me,
25 He does fair justice; if he give me way,
   I'll do his country service.   [Exit]

'fore my wars facing my assaults
dissension of a doit argument over nothing (half a cent)
fellest fiercest
interjoin . . . issues unite their descendants

SCENE v
The same. A hall in Aufidius's house.

[Music within. Enter a Servingman.]
First Servingman. Wine, wine, wine!—What
   service is here!
   I think our fellows are asleep.   [Exit]
             [Enter another Servingman.]
Second Servingman. Where's Cotus? My master
   calls for him.
   Cotus!   [Exit]
             [Enter Coriolanus.]
Coriolanus. A goodly house. The feast smells
   well. But I
   Appear not like a guest.   5
          [Re-enter the First Servingman.]
First Servingman. What would you have, friend?
   Whence are you?
   Here's no place for you. Pray go to the door.
                                     [Exit]
Coriolanus. I have deserv'd no better entertain-
   ment,
   In being Coriolanus.   10
          [Re-enter Second Servingman.]
Second Servingman. Whence are you, sir? Has the
   porter his eyes in his head, that he gives entrance
   to such companions?° Pray, get you out.
Coriolanus. Away!
Second Servingman. Away! Get you away.   15
Coriolanus. Now thou'rt troublesome.
Second Servingman. Are you so brave? I'll have
   you talked with anon.
[Enter a Third Servingman. The first meets him.]
Third Servingman. What fellow's this?
First Servingman. A strange one as ever I looked   20
   on. I cannot get him out o' the house. Prithee,
   call my master to him.   [Retires.]
Third Servingman. What have you to do here,
   fellow? Pray you, avoid the house.
Coriolanus. Let me but stand; I will not hurt your
   hearth.   25
Third Servingman. What are you?
Coriolanus. A gentleman.
Third Servingman. A marvelous poor one.
Coriolanus. True, so I am.
Third Servingman. Pray you, poor gentleman,   30
   take up some other station; here's no place for
   you. Pray you, avoid. Come.
Coriolanus. Follow your function,° go, and
   batten° on cold bits.
                     [Pushes him away from him.]

companions low fellows
follow . . . function get on with your job   batten fatten

35 THIRD SERVINGMAN. What, you will not? Prithee,
   tell my master what a strange guest he has here.
SECOND SERVINGMAN. And I shall.   [*Exit*]
THIRD SERVINGMAN. Where dwell'st thou?
CORIOLANUS. Under the canopy.°
40 THIRD SERVINGMAN. Under the canopy!
CORIOLANUS. Aye.
THIRD SERVINGMAN. Where's that?
CORIOLANUS. I' the city of kites and crows.
THIRD SERVINGMAN. I' the city of kites and crows!
45   What an ass it is! Then thou dwell'st with daws°
     too?
CORIOLANUS. No, I serve not thy master.
THIRD SERVINGMAN. How, sir! Do you meddle with
   my master?
CORIOLANUS. Aye. 'Tis an honester service than to
50   meddle with thy mistress. Thou pratest and
     pratest. Serve with thy trencher,° hence!
        [*Beats him away. Exit* THIRD SERVINGMAN.]
        [*Enter* AUFIDIUS *with the* SECOND SERVINGMAN.]
AUFIDIUS. Where is this fellow?
SECOND SERVINGMAN. Here, sir. I'd have beaten him
   like a dog, but for disturbing the lords within.
                                        [*Retires.*]
AUFIDIUS. Whence comest thou? What wouldst
55   thou? Thy name?
     Why speak'st not? Speak, man. What's thy
     name?
CORIOLANUS. [*Unmuffling*]   If, Tullus,
   Not yet thou knowest me, and, seeing me, dost
   not
   Think° me for the man I am, necessity
   Commands me name myself.
AUFIDIUS.   What is thy name?
CORIOLANUS. A name unmusical to the Volscians'
60   ears,
   And harsh in sound to thine.
AUFIDIUS.   Say, what's thy name?
   Thou hast a grim appearance, and thy face
   Bears a command in 't. Though thy tackle's
   torn,
   Thou show'st a noble vessel. What's thy name?
CORIOLANUS. Prepare thy brow to frown. Know'st
65   thou me yet?
AUFIDIUS. I know thee not. Thy name?
CORIOLANUS. My name is Caius Marcius, who hath
   done
   To thee particularly, and to all the Volsces,
   Great hurt and mischief; thereto witness may
70   My surname, Coriolanus. The painful service,
   The extreme dangers, and the drops of blood
   Shed for my thankless country are requited

But with that surname—a good memory°
And witness of the malice and displeasure
Which thou shouldst bear me. Only that name
   remains.   75
The cruelty and envy of the people,
Permitted by our dastard nobles, who
Have all forsook me, hath devour'd the rest
And suffer'd me by the voice of slaves to be
Hoop'd° out of Rome. Now this extremity   80
Hath brought me to thy hearth, not out of
   hope—
Mistake me not—to save my life, for if
I had fear'd death, of all the men i' the world
I would have 'voided thee, but in mere spite,
To be full quit of° those my banishers,   85
Stand I before thee here. Then if thou hast
A heart of wreak° in thee, that wilt revenge
Thine own particular wrongs and stop those
   maims
Of shame° seen through thy country, speed thee
   straight
And make my misery serve thy turn. So use it   90
That my revengeful services may prove
As benefits to thee, for I will fight
Against my canker'd° country with the spleen
Of all the underfiends. But if so be
Thou dar'st not this, and that to prove more
   fortunes   95
Th'art tir'd, then, in a word, I also am
Longer to live most weary, and present
My throat to thee and to thy ancient malice—
Which not to cut would show thee but a fool,
Since I have ever follow'd thee with hate,   100
Drawn tuns of blood out of thy country's breast,
And cannot live but to thy shame unless
It be to do thee service.
AUFIDIUS.   O Marcius, Marcius!
Each word thou hast spoke hath weeded from
   my heart
A root of ancient envy. If Jupiter   105
Should from yond cloud speak divine things,
And say "'Tis true," I'd not believe them more
Than thee, all noble Marcius. Let me twine
Mine arms about that body, where against
My grained ash° an hundred times hath broke,   110
And scarr'd the moon with splinters. Here I
   clip°
The anvil of my sword and do contest
As hotly and as nobly with thy love
As ever in ambitious strength I did

memory reminder   *Hoop'd* whooped
quit of revenged on   *heart of wreak* vengeful heart
maims Of shame shameful gashes
canker'd worm-eaten   *grained ash* wooden spear
clip embrace

canopy open sky   *daws* foolish birds (with pun)
trencher platter   *Think* recognize

638

115   Contend against thy valor. Know thou first,
      I lov'd the maid I married; never man
      Sigh'd truer breath. But that I see thee here,
      Thou noble thing, more dances my rapt heart
      Than when I first my wedded mistress saw
120   Bestride my threshold. Why, thou Mars! I tell
      thee
      We have a power on foot, and I had purpose
      Once more to hew thy target from thy brawn
      Or lose mine arm for 't. Thou hast beat me out
      Twelve several times, and I have nightly since
125   Dreamt of encounters 'twixt thyself and me.
      We have been down together in my sleep,
      Unbuckling helms, fisting each other's throat,
      And wak'd half dead with nothing. Worthy
        Marcius,
      Had we no quarrel else to Rome but that
130   Thou art thence banish'd, we would muster all
      From twelve to seventy, and pouring war
      Into the bowels of ungrateful Rome,
      Like a bold flood o'erbear. O, come, go in,
      And take our friendly Senators by the hands,
135   Who now are here taking their leaves of me,
      Who am prepar'd against your territories,
      Though not for Rome itself.
      CORIOLANUS.   You bless me, gods!
      AUFIDIUS. Therefore, most absolute° sir, if thou
        wilt have
      The leading of thine own revenges, take
140   The one half of my commission, and set down—
      As best thou art experienc'd, since thou know'st
      Thy country's strength and weakness—thine
        own ways,
      Whether to knock against the gates of Rome
      Or rudely visit them in parts remote,
145   To fright them ere destroy. But come in.
      Let me commend thee first to those that shall
      Say yea to thy desires. A thousand welcomes!
      And more a friend than e'er an enemy—
      Yet, Marcius, that was much. Your hand. Most
        welcome!   [Exeunt CORIOLANUS and AUFIDIUS.
                    The two SERVINGMEN come forward.]
150   FIRST SERVINGMAN. Here's a strange alteration!
      SECOND SERVINGMAN. By my hand, I had thought to
        have strucken him with a cudgel, and yet my
        mind gave me his clothes made a false report of
        him.
155   FIRST SERVINGMAN. What an arm he has! He turned
        me about with his finger and his thumb as one
        would set up a top.
      SECOND SERVINGMAN. Nay, I knew by his face that
        there was something in him. He had, sir, a kind
160   of face, methought—I cannot tell how to term it.

      absolute perfect

FIRST SERVINGMAN. He had so; looking as it were—
  Would I were hanged, but I thought there was
  more in him than I could think.
SECOND SERVINGMAN. So did I, I'll be sworn. He is
  simply the rarest man i' the world.   165
FIRST SERVINGMAN. I think he is. But a greater
  soldier then he, you wot one.
SECOND SERVINGMAN. Who? My master?
FIRST SERVINGMAN. Nay, it's no matter for that.
SECOND SERVINGMAN. Worth six on him.   170
FIRST SERVINGMAN. Nay, not so neither. But I take
  him to be the greater soldier.
SECOND SERVINGMAN. Faith, look you, one cannot
  tell how to say that. For the defense of a town,
  our general is excellent.   175
FIRST SERVINGMAN. Aye, and for an assault too.
            [Re-enter THIRD SERVINGMAN.]
THIRD SERVINGMAN. O slaves, I can tell you news.
  News, you rascals!
FIRST and SECOND SERVINGMAN. What, what, what?
  Let's partake.   180
THIRD SERVINGMAN. I would not be a Roman, of all
  nations. I had as lieve be a condemned man.
FIRST and SECOND SERVINGMAN. Wherefore? Where-
  fore?
THIRD SERVINGMAN. Why, here's he that was wont   185
  to thwack our general, Caius Marcius.
FIRST SERVINGMAN. Why do you say thwack our
  general?
THIRD SERVINGMAN. I do not say thwack our
  general; but he was always good enough for   190
  him.
SECOND SERVINGMAN. Come, we are fellows and
  friends. He was ever too hard for him; I have
  heard him say so himself.
FIRST SERVINGMAN. He was too hard for him   195
  directly,° to say the troth on 't. Before Corioli
  he scotched him and notched him like a carbonado.°
SECOND SERVINGMAN. An he had been cannibally
  given, he might have broiled and eaten him too.   200
FIRST SERVINGMAN. But more of thy news?
THIRD SERVINGMAN. Why, he is so made on here
  within as if he were son and heir to Mars. Set at
  upper end o' the table, no question asked him
  by any of the Senators, but they stand bald   205
  before him. Our general himself makes a
  mistress of him, sanctifies° himself with 's hand,
  and turns up the white o' the eye to his discourse.
  But the bottom of the news is, our general is cut
  i' the middle,° and but one half of what he was   210

directly i.e., head-on   *carbonado* steak
sanctifies i.e., as with a holy relic
cut . . . middle i.e., his command is divided

yesterday; for the other has half, by the entreaty and grant of the whole table. He'll go, he says, and sowl° the porter of Rome gates by the ears. He will mow all down before him and
215 leave his passage polled.°

SECOND SERVINGMAN. And he's as like to do 't as any man I can imagine.

THIRD SERVINGMAN. Do 't! He will do 't, for look you, sir, he has as many friends as enemies,
220 which friends, sir, as it were, durst not, look you, sir, show themselves, as we term it, his friends whilst he's in directitude.°

FIRST SERVINGMAN. Directitude! What's that?

THIRD SERVINGMAN. But when they shall see, sir,
225 his crest up again and the man in blood, they will out of their burrows like conies after rain and revel all with him.

FIRST SERVINGMAN. But when goes this forward?

THIRD SERVINGMAN. Tomorrow, today, presently.
230 You shall have the drum struck up this afternoon. 'Tis, as it were, a parcel° of their feast, and to be executed ere they wipe their lips.

SECOND SERVINGMAN. Why, then we shall have a stirring world again. This peace is nothing but
235 to rust iron, increase tailors, and breed balladmakers.

FIRST SERVINGMAN. Let me have war, say I; it exceeds peace as far as day does night. It's spritely, waking, audible, and full of vent.°
240 Peace is a very apoplexy, lethargy, mulled,° deaf, sleepy, insensible, a getter of more bastard children than war's a destroyer of men.

SECOND SERVINGMAN. 'Tis so. And as war, in some sort, may be said to be a ravisher, so it cannot be
245 denied but peace is a great maker of cuckolds.

FIRST SERVINGMAN. Aye, and it makes men hate one another.

THIRD SERVINGMAN. Reason—because they then less need one another. The wars for my money.
250 I hope to see Romans as cheap° as Volscians.— They are rising, they are rising.

FIRST and SECOND SERVINGMAN. In, in, in, in!

[Exeunt]

SCENE vi
Rome. A public place.

[*Enter the two* TRIBUNES, SICINIUS *and* BRUTUS.]

SICINIUS. We hear not of him, neither need we fear him.
His remedies are tame° i' the present peace
And quietness of the people, which before
Were in wild hurry. Here do we make his friends
Blush that the world goes well, who rather had,   5
Though they themselves did suffer by 't, behold
Dissentious numbers pest'ring° streets than see
Our tradesmen singing in their shops and going
About their functions friendly.

BRUTUS.   We stood to 't° in good time.

[*Enter* MENENIUS.]

                                   Is this Menenius?   10

SICINIUS. 'Tis he, 'tis he. O, he is grown most kind
Of late. Hail, sir!

MENENIUS.   Hail to you both!

SICINIUS. Your Coriolanus is not much miss'd,
But with his friends. The commonwealth doth stand,
And so would do were he more angry at it.   15

MENENIUS. All's well, and might have been much better if
He could have temporiz'd.°

SICINIUS.   Where is he, hear you?

MENENIUS. Nay, I hear nothing. His mother and his wife
Hear nothing from him.

[*Enter three of four* CITIZENS.]

CITIZENS. The gods preserve you both!

SICINIUS.   God-den, our neighbors.   20

BRUTUS. God-den to you all, god-den to you all.

FIRST CITIZEN. Ourselves, our wives, and children, on our knees,
Are bound to pray for you both.

SICINIUS.   Live, and thrive!

BRUTUS. Farewell, kind neighbors. We wish'd Coriolanus
Had lov'd you as we did.

CITIZENS.   Now the gods keep you!   25

BOTH TRIBUNES. Farewell, farewell.

[*Exeunt* CITIZENS.]

SICINIUS. This is a happier and more comely time
Than when these fellows ran about the streets
Crying confusion.

---

sowl pull out like a rabbit
polled i.e., like a shorn sheep
directitude blunder for *discredit*
in blood i.e., in lively action   *parcel* part
vent activity   *mulled* warm and insipid
cheap i.e., as commonly

remedies are tame chances of redress are negligible
pest'ring infesting   *stood to 't* stood firm
temporiz'd compromised

BRUTUS.   Caius Marcius was
30 A worthy officer i' the war, but insolent,
    O'ercome with pride, ambitious past all think-
      ing,
    Self-loving—
SICINIUS.   And affecting one sole throne
    Without assistance.°
MENENIUS.   I think not so.
SICINIUS. We should by this, to all our lamentation,
35 If he had gone forth consul, found it so.
BRUTUS. The gods have well prevented it, and
      Rome
    Sits safe and still without him.
              [Enter an ÆDILE.]
ÆDILE.   Worthy tribunes,
    There is a slave, whom we have put in prison,
    Reports the Volsces with two several° powers
40 Are enter'd in the Roman territories,
    And with the deepest malice of the war
    Destroy what lies before 'em.
MENENIUS.   'Tis Aufidius,
    Who, hearing of our Marcius' banishment,
    Thrusts forth his horns again into the world—
    Which were inshell'd° when Marcius stood for
45   Rome,
    And durst not once peep out.
SICINIUS.   Come, what talk you
    Of Marcius?
BRUTUS. Go see this rumorer whipp'd. It cannot be
    The Volsces dare break with us.
MENENIUS.   Cannot be!
50 We have record that very well it can,
    And three examples of the like have been
    Within my age. But reason with the fellow,
    Before you punish him, where he heard this,
    Lest you shall chance to whip your information
55 And beat the messenger who bids beware
    Of what is to be dreaded.
SICINIUS.   Tell not me.
    I know this cannot be.
BRUTUS.   Not possible.
              [Enter a MESSENGER.]
MESSENGER. The nobles in great earnestness are
      going
    All to the Senate House. Some news is come
    That turns their countenances.
60 SICINIUS.   'Tis this slave.
    Go whip him 'fore the people's eyes. His raising,°
    Nothing but his report.
MESSENGER.   Yes, worthy sir,
    The slave's report is seconded, and more,
    More fearful, is deliver'd.

SICINIUS.   What more fearful?
MESSENGER. It is spoke freely out of many mouths—   65
    How probable I do not know—that Marcius,
    Join'd with Aufidius, leads a power 'gainst
      Rome
    And vows revenge as spacious° as between
    The young'st and oldest thing.
SICINIUS.   This is most likely!
BRUTUS. Rais'd only that the weaker sort may
      wish   70
    Good Marcius home again.
SICINIUS.   The very trick on 't.
MENENIUS. This is unlikely.
    He and Aufidius can no more atone°
    Than violentest contrariety.
              [Enter a SECOND MESSENGER.]
SECOND MESSENGER. You are sent for to the Senate   75
    A fearful army, led by Caius Marcius
    Associated with Aufidius, rages
    Upon our territories and have already
    O'erborne their way, consum'd with fire, and
      took
    What lay before them.   80
              [Enter COMINIUS.]
COMINIUS. O, you have made good work!
MENENIUS.   What news? What news?
COMINIUS. You have holp to ravish your own
      daughters and
    To melt the city leads upon your pates,
    To see your wives dishonor'd to your noses—
MENENIUS. What's the news? What's the news?   85
COMINIUS. Your temples burn'd in their cement,
      and
    Your franchises,° whereon you stood, confin'd
    Into an auger's bore.°
MENENIUS.   Pray now, your news?—
    You have made fair work, I fear me.—Pray,
      your news?—
    If Marcius should be join'd with Volscians—
COMINIUS.   If!   90
    He is their god. He leads them like a thing
    Made by some other deity than nature,
    That shapes man better; and they follow him
    Against us brats with no less confidence
    Than boys pursuing summer butterflies   95
    Or butchers killing flies.
MENENIUS.   You have made good work,
    You and your apron-men. You that stood so
      much
    Upon the voice of occupation° and
    The breath of garlic-eaters!

And . . . assistance aspiring to be dictator
several separate   inshell'd retracted
His raising i.e., it is his doing

spacious all-inclusive   atone become one
franchises civil rights
confin'd . . . bore i.e., squeezed to nothing
voice of occupation tradesmen's votes

COMINIUS. He'll shake your Rome about your ears.

100 MENENIUS.   As Hercules
Did shake down mellow fruit.° You have made
  fair work!

BRUTUS. But is this true, sir?

COMINIUS.   Aye, and you'll look pale
Before you find it other. All the regions
Do smilingly revolt, and who resist

105 Are mock'd for valiant ignorance,
And perish constant° fools. Who is 't can blame
  him?
Your enemies and his find something in him.

MENENIUS. We are all undone unless
  The noble man have mercy.

COMINIUS.   Who shall ask it?

110 The tribunes cannot do 't for shame. The people
Deserve such pity of him as the wolf
Does of the shepherds. For his best friends, if
  they
Should say "Be good to Rome," they charg'd°
  him even
As those should do that had deserv'd his hate
And therein show'd like enemies.

115 MENENIUS.   'Tis true.
If he were putting to my house the brand
That should consume it, I have not the face
To say "Beseech you, cease." You have made
  fair hands,
You and your crafts! You have crafted fair!

COMINIUS.   You have brought

120 A trembling upon Rome such as was never
So incapable of help.

BOTH TRIBUNES.   Say not we brought it.

MENENIUS. How! Was it we? We lov'd him; but,
  like beasts
And cowardly nobles, gave way unto your
  clusters,
Who did hoot him out o' the city.

COMINIUS.   But I fear

125 They'll roar him in again. Tullus Aufidius,
The second name of men, obeys his points°
As if he were his officer. Desperation
Is all the policy, strength, and defense
That Rome can make against them.
            [Enter a troop of CITIZENS.]

MENENIUS.   Here come the clusters.

130 And is Aufidius with him? You are they
That made the air unwholesome when you
  cast
Your stinking greasy caps in hooting at

Coriolanus' exile. Now he's coming,
And not a hair upon a soldier's head
Which will not prove a whip. As many cox-
  combs   135
As you threw caps up will he tumble down,
And pay you for your voices. 'Tis no matter;
If he could burn us all into one coal,
We have deserv'd it.

CITIZENS. Faith, we hear fearful news.

FIRST CITIZEN.   For mine own part,   140
When I said banish him, I said 'twas pity.

SECOND CITIZEN. And so did I.

THIRD CITIZEN. And so did I, and, to say the truth,
  so did very many of us. That we did, we did for
  the best, and though we willingly consented to   145
  his banishment, yet it was against our will.

COMINIUS. Ye're goodly things, you voices!

MENENIUS.   You have made
Good work, you and your cry! Shall 's to the
  Capitol?

COMINIUS. O, aye, what else?
                    [Exeunt COMINIUS and MENENIUS.]

SICINIUS. Go, masters, get you home. Be not
  dismay'd.   150
These are a side that would be glad to have
This true which they so seem to fear. Go home,
And show no sign of fear.

FIRST CITIZEN. The gods be good to us! Come,
  masters, let's home. I ever said we were i' the   155
  wrong when we banished him.

SECOND CITIZEN. So did we all. But, come, let's
  home.   [Exeunt CITIZENS.]

BRUTUS. I do not like this news.

SICINIUS. Nor I.

BRUTUS. Let's to the Capitol. Would half my
  wealth   160
Would buy this for a lie!

SICINIUS.   Pray, let us go.
                                          [Exeunt]

SCENE vii
A camp, at a small distance from Rome.

[Enter AUFIDIUS with his LIEUTENANT.]

AUFIDIUS. Do they still fly to the Roman?

LIEUTENANT. I do not know what witchcraft's in
  him, but
Your soldiers use him as the grace 'fore meat,
Their talk at table, and their thanks at end,
And you are darken'd° in this action, sir,   5
Even by your own.

AUFIDIUS.   I cannot help it now,

As . . . fruit i.e., the eleventh labor, stealing apples of
  the Hesperides
constant loyal   charg'd would be asking
points orders

darken'd eclipsed

Unless, by using means, I lame the foot
Of our design. He bears himself more proudlier,
Even to my person, than I thought he would
10   When first I did embrace him. Yet his nature
In that's no changeling, and I must excuse
What cannot be amended.

LIEUTENANT.   Yet I wish, sir—
I mean for your particular°—you had not
Join'd in commission with him, but either
15   Had borne the action of yourself or else
To him had left it solely.

AUFIDIUS. I understand thee well, and be thou sure,
When he shall come to his account, he knows
    not
What I can urge against him. Although it seems,
20   And so he thinks, and is no less apparent
To the vulgar eye, that he bears all things fairly
And shows good husbandry for the Volscian
    state,
Fights dragon-like, and does achieve° as soon
As draw his sword, yet he hath left undone
25   That which shall break his neck or hazard mine
Whene'er we come to our account.

LIEUTENANT. Sir, I beseech you, think you he'll
    carry Rome?

AUFIDIUS. All places yield to him ere he sits down,°
And the nobility of Rome are his.
30   The senators and patricians love him too.
The tribunes are no soldiers, and their people
Will be as rash in the repeal as hasty
To expel him thence. I think he'll be to Rome
As is the osprey° to the fish, who takes it

By sovereignty of nature.° First he was   35
A noble servant to them, but he could not
Carry his honors even. Whether 'twas pride,
Which out of daily fortune° ever taints
The happy man; whether defect of judgment,
To fail in the disposing° of those chances   40
Which he was lord of; or whether nature,°
Not to be other than one thing, not moving
From the casque to the cushion,° but command-
    ing peace
Even with the same austerity and garb°
As he controll'd the war; but one of these—   45
As he hath spices of them all, not all,
For I dare so far free him—made him fear'd,
So hated, and so banish'd. But he has a merit
To choke it in the utt'rance.° So our virtues
Lie in th' interpretation of the time,   50
And power, unto itself most commendable,
Hath not a tomb so evident as a chair
T'extol what it hath done.°
One fire drives out one fire—one nail, one nail;
Rights by rights fouler, strengths by strengths
    do fail.   55
Come, let's away. When, Caius, Rome is thine,
Thou'rt poor'st of all; then shortly art thou
    mine.   [Exeunt]

sovereignty of nature   natural superiority
out . . . fortune   as result of unbroken successes
disposing   making the best use
nature   i.e., his nature
casque . . . cushion   helmet to senator's seat
austerity and garb   austere demeanor
But . . . utt'rance   he has merit enough to forbid mention
    of any fault
power . . . done   power, commendable in itself, has no
    surer way to destruction than public recognition

for your particular   for your own good
achieve   conquer   *sits down*   lays siege
osprey   fishawk

A C T   V

SCENE i
Rome. A public place.

[*Enter* MENENIUS, COMINIUS, SICINIUS *and* BRUTUS,
    the two TRIBUNES, *with others.*]

MENENIUS. No, I'll not go. You hear what he hath
    said
Which° was sometimes his general, who lov'd
    him
In a most dear particular.° He call'd me father:

But what o' that? Go, you that banish'd him;
A mile before his tent fall down, and knee   5
The way into his mercy. Nay, if he coy'd°
To hear Cominius speak, I'll keep at home.

COMINIUS. He would not seem to know me.

MENENIUS.   Do you hear?

COMINIUS. Yet one time he did call me by my
    name:
I urg'd our old acquaintance, and the drops   10
That we have bled together. Coriolanus

Which   who   *particular*   personal way

coy'd   was reluctant

He would not answer to, forbade all names.
He was a kind of nothing, titleless,
Till he had forg'd himself a name o' the fire
Of burning Rome.

15 MENENIUS. Why, so. You have made good work—
A pair of tribunes that have rack'd° for Rome
To make coals cheap! A noble memory!

COMINIUS. I minded° him how royal 'twas to pardon
When it was less expected. He replied

20 It was a bare petition° of a state
To one whom they had punish'd.

MENENIUS.   Very well.
Could he say less?

COMINIUS. I offer'd to awaken his regard
For 's private friends. His answer to me was

25 He could not stay to pick them in a pile
Of noisome musty chaff. He said 'twas folly,
For one poor grain or two, to leave unburnt
And still to nose th' offense.°

MENENIUS.   For one poor grain or two!
I am one of those; his mother, wife, his child,

30 And this brave fellow too, we are the grains.
You are the musty chaff, and you are smelt
Above the moon. We must be burnt for you.

SICINIUS. Nay, pray, be patient. If you refuse your aid
In this so never-needed help, yet do not

35 Upbraid 's with our distress. But sure, if you
Would be your country's pleader, your good tongue,
More than the instant army we can make,
Might stop our countryman.

MENENIUS.   No, I'll not meddle.

SICINIUS. Pray you, go to him.

MENENIUS.   What should I do?

40 BRUTUS. Only make trial what your love can do
For Rome, towards Marcius.

MENENIUS.   Well, and say that Marcius
Return me, as Cominius is return'd,
Unheard. What then?
But as a discontented friend, grief-shot
With his unkindness? Say 't be so?

45 SICINIUS.   Yet your goodwill
Must have that thanks from Rome after the measure
As you intended well.

MENENIUS.   I'll undertake 't.
I think he'll hear me. Yet to bite his lip
And hum at good Cominius much unhearts me.

He was not taken well;° he had not din'd. 50
The veins unfill'd, our blood is cold, and then
We pout upon the morning, are unapt
To give or to forgive. But when we have stuff'd
These pipes and these conveyances of our blood
With wine and feeding, we have suppler souls 55
Than in our priestlike fasts. Therefore I'll watch him
Till he be dieted to my request,
And then I'll set upon him.

BRUTUS. You know the very road into his kindness
And cannot lose your way.

MENENIUS.   Good faith, I'll prove° him, 60
Speed° how it will. I shall ere long have knowledge
Of my success.   [Exit]

COMINIUS.   He'll never hear him.

SICINIUS.   Not?

COMINIUS. I tell you, he does sit in gold,° his eye
Red as 'twould burn Rome, and his injury
The jailer to his pity. I kneel'd before him. 65
'Twas very faintly he said "Rise," dismiss'd me
Thus with his speechless hand. What he would do
He sent in writing after me; what he would not,
Bound with an oath to yield° to his conditions.
So that all hope is vain 70
Unless his noble mother and his wife,
Who, as I hear, mean to solicit him
For mercy to his country. Therefore let's hence
And with our fair entreaties haste them on.

                                        [Exeunt]

SCENE ii
Entrance to the Volscian camp before Rome.
Two SENTINELS *on guard.*

[*Enter to them,* MENENIUS.]

FIRST SENTINEL. Stay. Whence are you?

SECOND SENTINEL.   Stand, and go back.

MENENIUS. You guard like men; 'tis well. But, by your leave,
I am an officer of state, and come
To speak with Coriolanus.

FIRST SENTINEL.   From whence?

MENENIUS.   From Rome.

FIRST SENTINEL. You may not pass, you must return. Our general
Will no more hear from thence. 5

---

rack'd strained themselves
minded reminded   *bare petition* beggarly request
nose th' offense smell the offensive ones

taken well properly approached   *prove* try
Speed succeed   *sit in gold* on a throne of gold
to yield i.e., that we must yield

SECOND SENTINEL. You'll see your Rome embrac'd with fire before
   You'll speak with Coriolanus.
MENENIUS.   Good my friends,
   If you have heard your general talk of Rome,
10   And of his friends there, it is lots to blanks°
   My name hath touch'd your ears. It is Menenius.
FIRST SENTINEL. Be it so; go back. The virtue of your name
   Is not here passable.
MENENIUS.   I tell thee, fellow,
   Thy general is my lover. I have been
   The book° of his good acts, whence men have
15   read
   His fame unparallel'd haply amplified;
   For I have ever verified my friends,
   Of whom he's chief, with all the size° that verity
   Would without lapsing suffer. Nay, sometimes,
20   Like to a bowl upon a subtle° ground,
   I have tumbled past the throw, and in his praise
   Have almost stamp'd the leasing.° Therefore, fellow,
   I must have leave to pass.
FIRST SENTINEL. Faith, sir, if you had told as many
25   lies in his behalf as you have uttered words in
   your own, you should not pass here; no, though
   it were as virtuous to lie as to live chastely.
   Therefore go back.
MENENIUS. Prithee, fellow, remember my name is
30   Menenius, always factionary on the party of
   your general.
SECOND SENTINEL. Howsoever you have been his
   liar, as you say you have, I am one that, telling
   true under him, must say you cannot pass.
35   Therefore go back.
MENENIUS. Has he dined, canst thou tell? For I
   would not speak with him till after dinner.
FIRST SENTINEL. You are a Roman, are you?
MENENIUS. I am, as thy general is.
40   FIRST SENTINEL. Then you should hate Rome, as he
   does. Can you, when you have pushed out your
   gates the very defender of them, and, in a
   violent popular ignorance, given your enemy
   your shield, think to front° his revenges with the
45   easy groans of old women, the virginal palms of
   your daughters, or with the palsied intercession
   of such a decayed dotant as you seem to be?
   Can you think to blow out the intended fire
   your city is ready to flame in, with such weak
50   breath as this? No, you are deceived; therefore,
   back to Rome and prepare for your execution.

You are condemned; our general has sworn you
   out of reprieve and pardon.
MENENIUS. Sirrah, if thy captain knew I were here,
   he would use me with estimation.°   55
FIRST SENTINEL. Come, my captain knows you not.
MENENIUS. I mean, thy general.
FIRST SENTINEL. My general cares not for you.
   Back, I say, go, lest I let forth your half-pint of
   blood.—Back—that's the utmost of your having   60
   —back.
MENENIUS. Nay, but, fellow, fellow—
   [Enter CORIOLANUS and AUFIDIUS.]
CORIOLANUS. What's the matter?
MENENIUS. Now, you companion,° I'll say an errand
   for you. You shall know now that I am in estima-   65
   tion. You shall perceive that a Jack guardant°
   cannot office me from my son Coriolanus.
   Guess but by my entertainment with him, if
   thou standest not i' the state of hanging, or of
   some death more long in spectatorship and   70
   crueler in suffering. Behold now presently, and
   swoon for what's to come upon thee. The
   glorious gods sit in hourly synod° about thy
   particular prosperity, and love thee no worse
   than thy old father Menenius does! O my son,   75
   my son! Thou art preparing fire for us; look
   thee, here's water to quench it. I was hardly
   moved to come to thee, but being assured none
   but myself could move thee, I have been
   blown out of your gates with sighs, and conjure   80
   thee to pardon Rome and thy petitionary
   countrymen. The good gods assuage thy wrath,
   and turn the dregs of it upon this varlet here—
   this, who, like a block, hath denied my access to
   thee.   85
CORIOLANUS. Away!
MENENIUS. How! Away!
CORIOLANUS. Wife, mother, child I know not. My affairs
   Are servanted to others. Though I owe
   My revenge properly,° my remission lies   90
   In Volscian breasts. That we have been familiar,
   Ingrate forgetfulness shall poison rather
   Than pity note how much. Therefore be gone.
   Mine ears against your suits are stronger than
   Your gates against my force. Yet, for I lov'd thee,   95
   Take this along; I writ it for thy sake
   And would have sent it. [Gives him a letter]
   Another word, Menenius,
   I will not hear thee speak. This man, Aufidius,

---

lots to blanks i.e., winners to losers   *book* recorder
size i.e., exaggeration   *subtle* deceptive
stamp'd the leasing verified the false   *front* confront

estimation respect   *companion* rascal
Jack guardant knavish guard
synod council   *properly* for myself alone

Was my belov'd in Rome. Yet thou behold'st.
100 AUFIDIUS. You keep a constant temper.
            [*Exeunt* CORIOLANUS *and* AUFIDIUS.]
FIRST SENTINEL. Now, sir, is your name Menenius?
SECOND SENTINEL. 'Tis a spell, you see, of much
    power. You know the way home again.
FIRST SENTINEL. Do you hear how we are shent° for
105   keeping your greatness back?
SECOND SENTINEL. What cause do you think I have
    to swoon?
MENENIUS. I neither care for the world nor your
    general. For such things as you, I can scarce
110   think there's any, ye're so slight. He that hath a
    will to die by himself fears it not from another.
    Let your general do his worst. For you, be that
    you are, long, and your misery increase with
    your age! I say to you, as I was said to, Away!
                                    [*Exit*]
115 FIRST SENTINEL. A noble fellow, I warrant him.
SECOND SENTINEL. The worthy fellow is our
    general. He's the rock, the oak not to be wind-
    shaken.   [*Exeunt*]

SCENE iii
The tent of CORIOLANUS.

[*Enter* CORIOLANUS, AUFIDIUS, *and others*.]
CORIOLANUS. We will before the walls of Rome
    tomorrow
    Set down our host. My partner in this action,
    You must report to the Volscian lords how
        plainly°
    I have borne this business.
AUFIDIUS.   Only their ends
5   You have respected, stopp'd your ears against
    The general suit of Rome, never admitted
    A private whisper, no, not with such friends
    That thought them sure of you.
CORIOLANUS.   This last old man,
    Whom with a crack'd heart I have sent to Rome,
10 Lov'd me above the measure of a father,
    Nay, godded° me indeed. Their latest refuge°
    Was to send him, for whose old love I have,
    Though I show'd sourly to him, once more
        offer'd
    The first conditions, which they did refuse
15 And cannot now accept. To grace him only
    That thought he could do more, a very little
    I have yielded to. Fresh embassies and suits,
    Nor from the state nor° private friends, hereafter

Will I lend ear to. [*Shout within*] Ha! What
    shout is this?
Shall I be tempted to infringe my vow   20
In the same time 'tis made? I will not.
[*Enter, in mourning habits,* VIRGILIA, VOLUMNIA,
    leading young MARCIUS, VALERIA, *and*
        ATTENDANTS.]
My wife comes foremost, then the honor'd
    mould
Wherein this trunk was fram'd, and in her hand
The grandchild to her blood. But out, affection!
All bond and privilege of nature, break!   25
Let it be virtuous to be obstinate.
What is that curtsy worth? Or those doves' eyes,
Which can make gods forsworn? I melt, and am
    not
Of stronger earth than others. My mother bows,
As if Olympus to a molehill should   30
In supplication nod, and my young boy
Hath an aspect of intercession which
Great nature cries "Deny not." Let the Volsces
Plough Rome, and harrow Italy. I'll never
Be such a gosling to obey instinct, but stand   35
As if a man were author of himself
And knew no other kin.
VIRGILIA.   My lord and husband!
CORIOLANUS. These eyes are not the same I wore in
    Rome.
VIRGILIA. The sorrow that delivers° us thus chang'd
Makes you think so.
CORIOLANUS.   Like a dull actor now   40
    I have forgot my part, and I am out
    Even to a full disgrace.° Best of my flesh,
    Forgive my tyranny, but do not say,
    For that, "Forgive our Romans." O, a kiss
    Long as my exile, sweet as my revenge!   45
    Now, by the jealous queen° of heaven, that kiss
    I carried from thee, dear, and my true lip
    Hath virgin'd it e'er since. You gods! I prate,
    And the most noble mother of the world
    Leave unsaluted. Sink, my knee, i' th' earth; 50
                                    [*Kneels*]
    Of thy deep duty more impression show
    Than that of common sons.
VOLUMNIA.   O, stand up blest!
    Whilst, with no softer cushion than the flint,
    I kneel before thee, and unproperly
    Show duty, as mistaken all this while   55
    Between the child and parent.   [*Kneels*.]
CORIOLANUS.   What is this?
    Your knees to me? To your corrected° son?

shent chastised
plainly straightforwardly   godded made a god of
latest refuge last hope   Nor . . . nor neither . . . nor

delivers shows
I am . . . disgrace I have forgotten my lines completely
jealous queen Juno   corrected submissive

Then let the pebbles on the hungry° beach
Fillip° the stars; then let the mutinous winds
60 Strike the proud cedars 'gainst the fiery sun,
Murd'ring impossibility,° to make
What cannot be, slight work.
VOLUMNIA.   Thou art my warrior;
I holp to frame thee. Do you know this lady?
CORIOLANUS. The noble sister of Publicola,
65 The moon of Rome, chaste as the icicle
That's curdied° by the frost from purest snow
And hangs on Dian's° temple. Dear Valeria!
VOLUMNIA. This is a poor epitome° of yours,
Which by th' interpretation° of full time
May show like all yourself.
70 CORIOLANUS.   The god of soldiers,
With the consent of supreme Jove, inform
Thy thoughts with nobleness, that thou mayst
prove
To shame unvulnerable, and stick° i' the wars
Like a great sea-mark,° standing every flaw°
And saving those that eye thee!
75 VOLUMNIA.   Your knee, sirrah.
CORIOLANUS. That's my brave boy!
VOLUMNIA. Even he, your wife, this lady, and
myself
Are suitors to you.
CORIOLANUS.   I beseech you, peace;
Or, if you'd ask, remember this before:
80 The thing I have forsworn to grant may never
Be held by you denials.° Do not bid me
Dismiss my soldiers, or capitulate
Again with Rome's mechanics. Tell me not
Wherein I seem unnatural. Desire not
85 To allay my rages and revenges with
Your colder reasons.
VOLUMNIA.   O, no more, no more!
You have said you will not grant us anything,
For we have nothing else to ask but that
Which you deny already. Yet we will ask,
90 That, if you fail in our request, the blame
May hang upon your hardness. Therefore hear
us.
CORIOLANUS. Aufidius, and you Volsces, mark, for
we'll

Hear naught from Rome in private. Your
request?
VOLUMNIA. Should we be silent and not speak, our
raiment
And state of bodies would bewray° what life   95
We have led since thy exile. Think with thyself
How more unfortunate than all living women
Are we come hither, since that thy sight, which
should
Make our eyes flow with joy, hearts dance with
comforts,
Constrains them weep and shake with fear and
sorrow,   100
Making the mother, wife, and child to see
The son, the husband, and the father tearing
His country's bowels out. And to poor we
Thine enmity's most capital.° Thou barr'st us
Our prayers to the gods, which is a comfort   105
That all but we enjoy; for how can we,
Alas, how can we for our country pray,
Whereto we are bound, together with thy
victory,
Whereto we are bound? Alack, or we must lose
The country, our dear nurse, or else thy person, 110
Our comfort in the country. We must find
An evident calamity, though we had
Our wish which side should win; for either thou
Must, as a foreign recreant, be led
With manacles through our streets, or else   115
Triumphantly tread on thy country's ruin,
And bear the palm° for having bravely shed
Thy wife and children's blood. For myself, son,
I purpose not to wait on fortune till
These wars determine. If I cannot persuade thee 120
Rather to show a noble grace to both parts
Than seek the end of one, thou shalt no sooner
March to assault thy country than to tread—
Trust to 't, thou shalt not—on thy mother's
womb
That brought thee to this world.
VIRGILIA.   Aye, and mine   125
That brought you forth this boy to keep your
name
Living to time.
BOY.   A' shall not tread on me;
I'll run away till I am bigger, but then I'll
fight.
CORIOLANUS. Not of a woman's tenderness to be
Requires nor child nor woman's face to see.   130
I have sat too long.   [Rising.]
VOLUMNIA.   Nay, go not from us thus.
If it were so that our request did tend

---

hungry envious   *Fillip* strike at
Murd'ring impossibility i.e., proving nothing to be
   impossible
curdied congealed
Dian's Diana's, goddess of chastity and of the moon
poor epitome small model (Coriolanus's son)
interpretation elaboration, extension
stick stand firm   *sea-mark* navigator's fixed point
flaw gust
The thing . . . denials i.e., what I have already sworn not
   to grant, you must not regard as denial of your plea

bewray evince   *capital* deadly
palm emblem of triumph

To save the Romans, thereby to destroy
The Volsces whom you serve, you might condemn us
135 As poisonous of your honor. No, our suit
Is that you reconcile them. While the Volsces
May say "This mercy we have show'd," the Romans,
"This we receiv'd," and each in either side
Give the all-hail to thee, and cry "Be blest
For making up this peace!" Thou know'st,
140 great son,
The end of war's uncertain, but this certain:
That if thou conquer Rome, the benefit
Which thou shalt thereby reap is such a name
Whose repetition will be dogg'd with curses,
Whose chronicle thus writ, "The man was
145 noble,
But with his last attempt he wip'd it out,
Destroy'd his country, and his name remains
To th' ensuing age abhorr'd." Speak to me, son.
Thou hast affected the fine strains of honor,
150 To imitate the graces of the gods,
To tear with thunder the wide cheeks o' th' air,
And yet to change thy sulphur with a bolt
That should but rive an oak.° Why dost not
speak?
Think'st thou it honorable for a noble man
Still to remember wrongs? Daughter, speak
155 you;
He cares not for your weeping. Speak thou, boy;
Perhaps thy childishness will move him more
Than can our reasons. There's no man in the
world
More bound to 's mother, yet here he lets me
prate
Like one i' the stocks.° Thou hast never in thy
160 life
Show'd thy dear mother any courtesy,
When she, poor hen, fond of no second brood,
Has cluck'd thee to the wars and safely home,
Loaden with honor. Say my request's unjust,
165 And spurn me back. But if it be not so,
Thou art not honest,° and the gods will plague
thee
That thou restrain'st from me the duty which
To a mother's part belongs. He turns away.
Down, ladies! Let us shame him with our
knees.
170 To his surname Coriolanus 'longs more pride

Than pity to our prayers. Down, an end!
This is the last; so we will home to Rome
And die among our neighbors. Nay, behold 's!
This boy, that cannot tell what he would have,
But kneels and holds up hands for fellowship,°   175
Does reason° our petition with more strength
Than thou hast to deny 't. Come, let us go.
This fellow had a Volscian to his mother;
His wife is in Corioli, and his child
Like him by chance. Yet give us our dispatch.°   180
I am hush'd until our city be afire,
And then I'll speak a little.
CORIOLANUS. [After holding her by the hand, silent]
                               O mother, mother!
What have you done? Behold, the heavens do
ope,
The gods look down, and this unnatural scene
They laugh at. O my mother, mother! O!   185
You have won a happy victory to Rome,
But for your son, believe it, O, believe it,
Most dangerously you have with him prevail'd,
If not most mortal to him. But let it come.
Aufidius, though I cannot make true wars,   190
I'll frame convenient° peace. Now, good Aufidius,
Were you in my stead, would you have heard
A mother less? Or granted less, Aufidius?
AUFIDIUS. I was mov'd withal.
CORIOLANUS.   I dare be sworn you were.
And, sir, it is no little thing to make   195
Mine eyes to sweat compassion. But, good sir,
What peace you'll make, advise me. For my
part,
I'll not to Rome, I'll back with you; and pray
you,
Stand to me° in this cause. O mother! Wife!
AUFIDIUS. [Aside] I am glad thou hast set thy
mercy and thy honor   200
At difference in thee. Out of that I'll work
Myself a former fortune.°
                   [The LADIES make signs to CORIOLANUS.]
CORIOLANUS. [To VOLUMNIA, VIRGILIA, etc.] Aye, by
and by.
But we will drink together, and you shall bear
A better witness back than words, which we
On like conditions will have counterseal'd.   205
Come, enter with us. Ladies, you deserve
To have a temple built you. All the swords
In Italy and her confederate arms
Could not have made this peace.   [Exeunt]

And yet . . . oak (unsatisfactorily explained; possibly: to
  exchange your lightning for a thunderbolt that would
  only split an oak)
Like . . . stocks i.e., who has no claim to be heeded
honest honorable

fellowship i.e., like the rest of us   reason argue
dispatch dismissal
convenient suitable   Stand to me back me up
I'll . . . fortune I'll recover my former place

SCENE iv
Rome. A public place.

[*Enter* MENENIUS *and* SICINIUS.]

MENENIUS. See you yond coign o' the Captiol, yond
cornerstone?

SICINIUS. Why, what of that?

MENENIUS. If it be possible for you to displace it
with your little finger, there is some hope the
ladies of Rome, especially his mother, may
prevail with him. But I say there is no hope in 't.
Our throats are sentenced and stay upon°
execution.

SICINIUS. Is 't possible that so short a time can alter
the condition of a man?

MENENIUS. There is a differency between a grub
and a butterfly, yet your butterfly was a grub.
This Marcius is grown from man to dragon.
He has wings; he's more than a creeping thing.

SICINIUS. He loved his mother dearly.

MENENIUS. So did he me, and he no more remembers his mother now than an eight-year-
old horse. The tartness of his face sours ripe
grapes. When he walks, he moves like an
engine, and the ground shrinks before his
treading. He is able to pierce a corslet° with his
eye, talks like a knell, and his hum is a battery.°
He sits in his state° as a thing made for Alexander.° What he bids be done is finished with his
bidding. He wants° nothing of a god but eternity
and a heaven to throne in.

SICINIUS. Yes, mercy, if you report him truly.

MENENIUS. I paint him in the character.° Mark what
mercy his mother shall bring from him. There
is no more mercy in him than there is milk in a
male tiger; that shall our poor city find. And all
this is long of° you.

SICINIUS. The gods be good unto us!

MENENIUS. No, in such a case the gods will not be
good unto us. When we banished him, we
respected not them; and, he returning to break
our necks, they respect not us.

[*Enter a* MESSENGER.]

MESSENGER. Sir, if you'd save your life, fly to your
house.
The plebeians have got your fellow tribune
And hale him up and down, all swearing if
The Roman ladies bring not comfort home,

They'll give him death by inches.

[*Enter another* MESSENGER.]

SICINIUS.   What's the news?

SECOND MESSENGER. Good news, good news! The
ladies have prevail'd,
The Volscians are dislodg'd,° and Marcius gone.
A merrier day did never yet greet Rome,
No, not th' expulsion of the Tarquins.

SICINIUS.   Friend,
Art thou certain this is true? Is it most certain?

SECOND MESSENGER. As certain as I know the sun is
fire.
Where have you lurk'd, that you make doubt
of it?
Ne'er through an arch so hurried the blown°
tide
As the recomforted through the gates. Why,
hark you!

[*Trumpets; hautboys; drums beat; all together.*]

The trumpets, sackbuts,° psalteries,° and fifes,
Tabors and cymbals and the shouting Romans
Make the sun dance. Hark you!

[*A shout within.*]

MENENIUS.   This is good news.
I will go meet the ladies. This Volumnia
Is worth of consuls, senators, patricians
A city full; of tribunes such as you,
A sea and land full. You have pray'd well today.
This morning for ten thousand of your throats
I'd not have given a doit. Hark, how they joy!

[*Music still, with shouts.*]

SICINIUS. First, the gods bless you for your tidings;
next,
Accept my thankfulness.

SECOND MESSENGER.   Sir, we have all
Great cause to give great thanks.

SICINIUS.   They are near the city?

SECOND MESSENGER. Almost at point to enter.

SICINIUS.   We will meet them
And help the joy.   [*Exeunt*]

SCENE v.
The same. A street near the gates.

[*Enter two* SENATORS *with* VOLUMNIA, VIRGILIA,
VALERIA, *etc. passing over the stage, followed by*
PATRICIANS *and others.*]

FIRST SENATOR. Behold our patroness, the life of
Rome!
Call all your tribes together, praise the gods,

---

stay upon await   *corslet* breast armor
hum . . . battery his "hmm!" is a cannon volley
state chair of state
thing . . . Alexander statue of Alexander the Great
wants lacks   *in the character* i.e., as he is
long of because of

dislodg'd retired
blown swollen   *sackbuts* wind instruments
psalteries stringed instruments

And make triumphant fires. Strew flowers
before them.
Unshout the noise that banish'd Marcius;
5   Repeal him with the welcome of his mother.
Cry "Welcome, ladies, welcome!"

ALL.   Welcome, ladies,
Welcome!

[*A flourish with drums and trumpets. Exeunt.*]

SCENE vi.
Corioli. A public place.

[*Enter* TULLUS AUFIDIUS, *with* ATTENDANTS.]

AUFIDIUS. Go tell the lords o' the city I am here.
Deliver them this paper. Having read it,
Bid them repair to the marketplace, where I,
Even in theirs and in the commons' ears,
5   Will vouch the truth of it. Him I accuse
The city ports° by this hath enter'd and
Intends to appear before the people, hoping
To purge° himself with words. Dispatch.

[*Exeunt* ATTENDANTS.]

[*Enter three or four* CONSPIRATORS *of* AUFIDIUS'
faction.]

Most welcome!

FIRST CONSPIRATOR.   How is it with our general?

AUFIDIUS.   Even so
10   As with a man by his own alms empoison'd
And with his charity slain.

SECOND CONSPIRATOR.   Most noble sir,
If you do hold the same intent wherein
You wish'd us parties, we'll deliver you
Of your great danger.

AUFIDIUS.   Sir, I cannot tell.
15   We must proceed as we do find the people.

THIRD CONSPIRATOR. The people will remain
uncertain whilst
'Twixt you there's difference. But the fall of
either
Makes the survivor heir of all.

AUFIDIUS.   I know it,
And my pretext° to strike at him admits
20   A good construction.° I rais'd him, and I pawn'd
Mine honor for his truth, who being so
heighten'd,
He water'd his new plants with dews of flattery,
Seducing so my friends, and to this end
He bow'd his nature, never known before
25   But to be rough, unswayable, and free.

THIRD CONSPIRATOR. Sir, his stoutness

When he did stand for consul, which he lost
By lack of stooping—

AUFIDIUS.   That I would have spoke of.
Being banish'd for 't, he came unto my hearth,
Presented to my knife his throat. I took him,   30
Made him joint-servant° with me, gave him way
In all his own desires, nay, let him choose
Out of my files,° his projects to accomplish,
My best and freshest men, serv'd his design-
ments
In mine own person, holp to reap the fame   35
Which he did end° all his, and took some pride
To do myself this wrong—till at the last
I seem'd his follower, not partner, and
He wag'd me with his countenance° as if
I had been mercenary.

FIRST CONSPIRATOR.   So he did, my lord.   40
The army marvel'd at it, and in the last,
When he had carried Rome and that we look'd
For no less spoil than glory—

AUFIDIUS.   There was it
For which my sinews shall be stretch'd upon
him.°
At a few drops of women's rheum,° which are   45
As cheap as lies, he sold the blood and labor
Of our great action. Therefore shall he die,
And I'll renew me in his fall. But hark!

[*Drums and trumpets sound, with great shouts of
the people.*]

FIRST CONSPIRATOR. Your native town you enter'd
like a post°
And had no welcomes home. But he returns   50
Splitting the air with noise.

SECOND CONSPIRATOR.   And patient fools,
Whose children he hath slain, their base throats
tear
With giving him glory.

THIRD CONSPIRATOR.   Therefore, at your vantage,
Ere he express himself, or move the people
With what he would say, let him feel your
sword,
Which we will second. When he lies along,°   55
After your way his tale pronounc'd° shall bury
His reasons° with his body.

AUFIDIUS.   Say no more.
Here come the lords.

[*Enter the* LORDS *of the city.*]

ALL THE LORDS. You are most welcome home.

---

joint-servant partner   *files* ranks
end i.e., end by harvesting
wag'd . . . countenance paid me with condescension
my sinews . . . him my power will be used against him
rheum tears   *post* messenger   *along* stretched out
After . . . pronounc'd his doings told according to you
reasons extenuating arguments

---

ports gates   *purge* i.e., cleanse himself of guilt
pretext intent   *construction* justification

60 AUFIDIUS.   I have not deserv'd it.
   But, worthy lords, have you with heed perus'd
   What I have written to you?
   LORDS.   We have.
   FIRST LORD.   And grieve to hear 't.
   What faults he made before the last I think
   Might have found easy fines.° But there to end
65 Where he was to begin, and give away
   The benefit of our levies,° answering us
   With our own charge,° making a treaty where
   There was a yielding—this admits no excuse.
   AUFIDIUS. He approaches. You shall hear him.
      [Enter CORIOLANUS, marching with drum and
         colors, the commoners being with him.]
   CORIOLANUS. Hail, lords! I am return'd your
70   soldier,
   No more infected with my country's love
   Than when I parted hence, but still subsisting
   Under your great command. You are to know
   That prosperously I have attempted and
75 With bloody passage led your wars even to
   The gates of Rome. Our spoils we have brought
      home
   Do more than counterpoise° a full third part
   The charges of the action. We have made peace
   With no less honor to th' Antiates
   Than shame to the Romans, and we here
80   deliver,
   Subscribed by the consuls and patricians,
   Together with the seal o' the Senate, what
   We have compounded° on.
   AUFIDIUS.   Read it not, noble lords,
   But tell the traitor in the highest degree
85 He hath abus'd your powers.
   CORIOLANUS. Traitor! How now!
   AUFIDIUS.   Aye, traitor, Marcius!
   CORIOLANUS.   Marcius!
   AUFIDIUS. Aye, Marcius, Caius Marcius. Dost thou
      think
   I'll grace thee with that robbery, thy stol'n
      name
   Coriolanus in Corioli?
90 You lords and heads o' the state, perfidiously
   He has betray'd your business and given up
   For certain drops of salt, your city Rome—
   I say "your city"—to his wife and mother,
   Breaking his oath and resolution like
95 A twist° of rotten silk, never admitting
   Council o' the war, but at his nurse's tears

He whin'd and roar'd away your victory,
   That pages blush'd at him and men of heart
   Look'd wond'ring each at other.
CORIOLANUS.   Hear'st thou, Mars?
AUFIDIUS. Name not the god, thou boy of tears!
CORIOLANUS.   Ha! 100
AUFIDIUS. No more.
CORIOLANUS. Measureless liar, thou hast made my
      heart
   Too great for what contains it. "Boy!" O slave!
   Pardon me, lords, 'tis the first time that ever
   I was forc'd to scold. Your judgments, my grave
      lords,   105
   Must give this cur the lie, and his own notion°—
   Who wears my stripes impress'd upon him, that
   Must bear my beating to his grave—shall join
   To thrust the lie unto him.
FIRST LORD. Peace, both, and hear me speak.   110
CORIOLANUS. Cut me to pieces, Volsces. Men and
      lads,
   Stain all your edges on me. "Boy!" False
      hound!
   If you have writ your annals true, 'tis there°
   That like an eagle in a dovecote I
   Flutter'd your Volscians in Corioli.   115
   Alone I did it. "Boy!"
AUFIDIUS.   Why, noble lords,
   Will you be put in mind of his blind fortune,°
   Which was your shame, by this unholy braggart,
   'Fore your own eyes and ears?
ALL CONSPIRATORS. Let him die for 't.   120
ALL THE PEOPLE. Tear him to pieces!—Do it
   presently!—He killed my son!—My daughter!—
   He killed my cousin Marcus!—He killed my
   father!
SECOND LORD. Peace, ho! No outrage. Peace!   125
   The man is noble, and his fame folds in
   This orb o' th' earth. His last offenses to us
   Shall have judicious hearing. Stand, Aufidius,
   And trouble not the peace.
CORIOLANUS.   O that I had him,
   With six Aufidiuses or more, his tribe,   130
   To use my lawful sword!
AUFIDIUS.   Insolent villain!
ALL CONSPIRATORS. Kill, kill, kill, kill, kill him!
      [The CONSPIRATORS draw, and kill CORIOLANUS.
                    AUFIDIUS stands on his body.]
LORDS.   Hold, hold, hold, hold!
AUFIDIUS. My noble masters, hear me speak.
FIRST LORD.   O Tullus—
SECOND LORD. Thou hast done a deed whereat
      valor will weep.

---

fines penalties   levies i.e., levied troops
answering . . . charge repaying us with nothing but our
   expenses
counterpoise balance   compounded agreed
twist skein

notion awareness   there i.e., there recorded
blind fortune mere chance

THIRD LORD. Tread not upon him. Masters all, be
135   quiet.
    Put up your swords.
AUFIDIUS. My lords, when you shall know—as in
    this rage
    Provok'd by him, you cannot—the great
    danger
    Which this man's life did owe° you, you'll
    rejoice
140 That he is thus cut off. Please it your honors
    To call me to your Senate, I'll deliver°
    Myself your loyal servant or endure
    Your heaviest censure.
FIRST LORD.   Bear from hence his body.
    And mourn you for him. Let him be regarded

As the most noble corse° that ever herald   145
    Did follow to his urn.
SECOND LORD.   His own impatience
    Takes from Aufidius a great part of blame.
    Let's make the best of it.
AUFIDIUS.   My rage is gone,
    And I am struck with sorrow. Take him up.
    Help, three o' the chiefest soldiers; I'll be one.   150
    Beat thou the drum that it speak mournfully.
    Trail your steel pikes.° Though in this city he
    Hath widow'd and unchilded many a one,
    Which to this hour bewail the injury,
    Yet he shall have a noble memory.   155
    Assist.   [*Exeunt, bearing the body of* CORIOLANUS.
                    A dead march sounded.]

---

owe hold in store for   *deliver* prove   *corse* corpse   *Trail . . . pikes* i.e., in sign of mourning

AFTERWORD

The last of Shakespeare's tragedies, *Coriolanus* is also, for very special reasons peculiar to itself, one of the most challenging of them all. Never as widely read, subjected to as penetrating criticism, or staged as frequently as any one of the supreme tragedies, it indubitably falls short of these in important ways. Few readers or spectators become emotionally involved with the "lonely dragon," Coriolanus, as deeply as most involuntarily do with the fates of Hamlet, Othello, Lear, and Macbeth, all of whom have a way of insinuating themselves and their troubles into our very souls. "It is we," wrote Hazlitt, "who are Hamlet," and this insight is hardly less illuminating when applied to the other three profoundly and ingratiatingly human protagonists. To Coriolanus, at least in the experience of most readers, it would not apply at all. Who would be likely to assert, "It is we who are Coriolanus"?

The other heroes we come to know emotionally, from the inside out, as it were, through their own utterances that intertwine their passions with our own; but Coriolanus, if we ever come to know him well, we know from the outside in, and never quite to the center.

Yet on the evidence of nothing less than purely textual statistics it appears that Shakespeare never elsewhere worked so diligently, so pointedly, so systematically to delineate the character of a major tragic hero. The character of Coriolanus is the heart and substance, we may even say the main dramatic business, of more than half the total scenes of the play, and, at the end, indeed, it may seem to have been almost the whole play. "Plot" is here secondary not merely to the hero's character, but to the delineation of it. It is true, of course, that in the other tragedies also we often hear various persons speak, sometimes at considerable length, about Hamlet, or Othello, or Lear, or Macbeth, and unquestionably some part of our sense of what each of these is derives from what others say. But the fact does not contradict our basic argument here, which is that Shakespeare's emphasis on Coriolanus's character *as such*, and his method of divulging that character through repeated appraisals made by other participants, are startlingly different from his emphasis and method everywhere else. (A partial exception is *Timon of Athens*, which contains elaborate, repeated discussions and illustrations of Timon's character; but *Timon* emerges at last as unfinished and unsatisfactory, a dramatic disaster, whereas *Coriolanus* is a technical masterpiece.)

In the course of the tragedy, all the main characters take their turns at analyzing the nature of the hero, and most of them take not one but repeated turns at it; some, indeed, talk only of it. Again and again, in this way, Coriolanus's qualities are held up to our view, probed, sifted, balanced, assessed, praised, defended, lamented, condemned. His mother, Volumnia, never speaks but about her son. Menenius, his closest friend and substitute father, speaks at greater length and more often about him than does any other in the play. His partners in war, Cominius and Titus Lartius, comment steadily upon him. The two countervoices, the tribunes Sicinius and Brutus, who are great talkers, rarely utter any words but those that directly express their united verdict on Coriolanus. Aufidius, the Volscians' shrewd general, speaks almost exclusively on the subject of the hero, and at last (IV, vii, 28–55) delivers the most penetrating single analysis to be found anywhere in the text.

But, indeed, it is not only these, the principals, who give over whole and repeated speeches to diagnosing the hero's virtues and faults. The unnamed persons of the play also, the citizens, soldiers, servants, spies, messengers, whoever they are and whatever their business, wherever and whenever they meet, quickly find occasion to analyze

Coriolanus and to pronounce judgment. The play is only five lines underway when the First Citizen reminds his fellows (and informs us initially) that "Caius Marcius is chief enemy of the people," and all instantly agree (as if to dictate at once how the audience should see him) that "He's a very dog to the commonalty." True, they concede that he has rendered his country enormous services, but "he pays himself with being proud." And thus the diagnosis continues, line by line, scene by scene, act by act, throughout the tortuous route that leads inevitably at last, in flawless tragic order even by Shakespeare's best standards, to the catastrophe—the literal butchery of the *pièce de résistance*. All the while, Shakespeare has held the figure of Coriolanus under our scrutiny like some specimen spread-eagled upon a table while sharp lights probe its nature from every angle. No other Shakespearean character is ever subjected to anything like this unrelenting inspection.

Nor does the analysis of Coriolanus's character end with the extraordinary abundance of public discussion that is given to this function. Coriolanus himself, whenever he is shown in action, whenever he opens his mouth, is made to characterize himself—and, curiously, always appears to be acting and speaking primarily *for the purpose* of illustrating his own character, or demonstrating what has been said about him by others. Again excluding Timon of the imperfect *Timon of Athens*, he is the only Shakespearean hero whose actions and speeches appear consistently calculated to serve this purpose. (Certain of the speeches of Antony and Cleopatra are similarly designed.) Thus his very first words, spoken as he confronts the aroused rabble on the street, directly illustrate his character as we have just heard the Citizens describe it: "What's the matter, you dissentious rogues," he roars, "That, rubbing the poor itch of your opinion,/ Make yourself scabs?" But so, on the contrary side, does his action before Corioli illustrate what is said of him again and again by his staunch supporters; for on this occasion, at a crucial moment of battle, when the tide might turn either way, quite alone, abandoned to his death by cowardly followers, he fights his way within the city gates, is briefly shut inside—and shortly afterward fights his way out again, turning what the soldiers had scathingly labeled "foolhardiness" into decisive victory and great personal triumph.

Yet, though Shakespeare gives more meticulous attention to the character of Coriolanus than to that of other heroes, most of us never come to "feel" the man as we come virtually involuntarily to feel the characters of Hamlet, Othello, Lear, and Macbeth. Do we *like* him or not? Did Shakespeare *mean* that we should like him, or did he not? Is he a proud, insolent war-machine, a hater of the populace, as the tribunes insist? Or is he indeed, as Menenius flatly asserts, one whose nature "is too noble for the world"? We cannot easily decide—or, if we do decide, find difficulty in discovering anyone who agrees with us. Hamlet, we all know, remains and presumably will always remain the most famous Shakespearean puzzle and happiest hunting-ground for interpreters of dramatic character. Yet opinions on the character of Hamlet, though widely diverse and usually maintained with peculiar ferocity, are rarely, like those on the character of Coriolanus, diametrically opposed.

Coriolanus is Shakespeare's only exclusively *political* play, and at the very center of the conflict between political ideologies stands its hero's character. Perhaps this fact helps to explain why Shakespeare took such extraordinary measures to illuminate his primary object of study from so many angles. For Shakespeare is not here intent on "selling" his audience on a single point of view; it was rarely if ever his way, as a dramatist, to impose convictions upon us. Rather, he is intent upon exposing a perennial political issue to full light, leaving the problem of final judgment to reader or spectator; and reader and spectator, perhaps regrettably but inevitably, tend to judge Coriolanus by their own political biases.

Coriolanus is Shakespeare's only exclusively political play, but politics, of course, in one form and degree or another, enters most of the plays, even the romantic comedies, wherein wrongful dukes usurp their brothers' thrones and where factions spring up in support of this side and that. "Policy" is a favorite word of Shakespeare's everywhere. As for the history plays, they are sometimes designated "political plays," and politics and politicking are incessant in them. Similarly, the great tragedies are politically based: Claudius usurps his brother's throne; Macbeth usurps his rightful king's throne; opposing factions go to war over Lear's abdicated throne; the Venetian Senate's decision to give Othello command of Cyprus instead of lynching him is resolved by political expediency—the Turks are at their gates, as they suppose; *Antony and Cleopatra* depicts politics at the level of the highest professionals; *Julius Caesar* thrusts us into the midst of political turmoil at the outset and holds us there until the end. But none of these plays makes political ideology its very subject, as *Coriolanus* does. It is illuminating, if not perhaps wholly accurate, to see the play as one in which the particular hero (Coriolanus) and the particular time and place (ancient Rome) serve as incidental means (it might as easily have been another man, another time and place) used to debate what was foremost in Shakespeare's mind—a fundamental political question, specifically, whether the citizens of a society are capable of governing, and deserving of governing, themselves. Seen thus, *Coriolanus* is not primarily the personal story of its hero as *Hamlet* or *Othello* is the personal story of its hero; that is to say, Coriolanus is not himself what the story is essentially *about*. Perhaps it would be just to call the play "The Case of Coriolanus," wherein the central figure serves as focal point and primary illustration of the greater issue. The play is not unlike a trial, with Coriolanus's character supplying much of the body of evidence.

This perspective, then, casts readers and spectators in the roles of jurymen whose responsibility it is to decide the merits of the case. *Coriolanus* is the most challenging of tragedies because of the urgent demand it places upon us to determine the truth not according to our personal politics, but on the basis of all the evidence *as Shakespeare has presented it*. The best of critics, it must be acknowledged, have failed the test more often than not, and the history of *Coriolanus* includes much of the worst Shakespeare criticism on record. To cite only a famous example or two: Dr. Johnson, with aristocratic bias, quite predictably finds this "one of the most amusing of our author's performances," praises Volumnia's demeanor (if that is an apt word for it) as "a lofty lady's dignity," fondly caresses the "patrician and military haughtiness" of Coriolanus, but scathes the "plebeian malignity and tribunitian insolence in Brutus and Sicinius." At the other extreme, equally predictably, the great romantic and outspoken liberal, Hazlitt, often the most perceptive of Shakespeareans, writes off Coriolanus as a monster "of blows and big words" and insists that "The whole dramatic moral of *Coriolanus* is that those who have little shall have less and that those who have much shall take all that others have left." On the stage *Coriolanus* has suffered even worse abuses and distortions, for there the hero can readily be represented as best suits the particular political climate of time and country, or be shaped to fit the political bias of the director so that he appears as either a monster or an innocent—wolf or lamb. Perhaps therefore *Coriolanus* is the Shakespearean play about which we should be least content to let the stage make up our minds; we need to study the text.

Even so, probably few of us, whether editors or general readers, can sufficiently suppress our personal convictions to examine with perfect impartiality the elaborate and systematic balancing that Shakespeare devised, presumably quite deliberately, in the play. Did he load the scales just a little on one side or the other so that, if we had the formula, we could divine where he himself stood? In any event, *Coriolanus* (to paraphrase

Coleridge's famous dictum), more than most plays, requires "a willing suspension of personal bias" if we are to perceive what the text actually "says."

A NOTE ON THE COMPOSITION OF THE PLAY

Coriolanus was written in 1607–08; there is no record of an immediate performance. It was first published in the Folio of 1623. The source, as for the other "Roman plays," was North's translation of Plutarch's *Lives*.

The Winter's Tale

DRAMATIS PERSONÆ

LEONTES *King of Sicilia*
MAMILLIUS *young prince of Sicilia*
CAMILLO ⎫
ANTIGONUS ⎪
CLEOMENES ⎬ *Four lords of Sicilia*
DION ⎭
POLIXENES *King of Bohemia*
FLORIZEL *Prince of Bohemia*
ARCHIDAMUS *a lord of Bohemia*
OLD SHEPHERD *reputed father of Perdita*
CLOWN *his son*
AUTOLYCUS *a rogue*

A MARINER
A JAILER
HERMIONE *Queen to Leontes*
PERDITA *daughter to Leontes and Hermione*
PAULINA *wife to Antigonus*
EMILIA *a lady attending on Hermione*
MOPSA ⎫
DORCAS ⎬ *Shepherdesses*
Other LORDS *and* GENTLEMEN, LADIES, OFFICERS
and SERVANTS, SHEPHERDS *and* SHEPHERDESSES.
Time, as Chorus
SCENE: *Partly in Sicilia, and partly in Bohemia.*

ACT I

SCENE i
Antechamber in LEONTES' *palace.*

[*Enter* CAMILLO *and* ARCHIDAMUS.]

ARCHIDAMUS. If you shall chance, Camillo, to visit Bohemia on the like occasion whereon my services are now on foot,° you shall see, as I have said, great difference betwixt our Bohemia and your Sicilia.

5 CAMILLO. I think this coming summer the King of Sicilia means to pay Bohemia the visitation which he justly owes him.

ARCHIDAMUS. Wherein our entertainment shall shame us we will be justified in our loves,° for 10 indeed—

CAMILLO. Beseech you—

ARCHIDAMUS. Verily, I speak it in the freedom of my knowledge.° We cannot with such magnificence—in so rare—I know not what to say. 15 We will give you sleepy drinks, that° your senses, unintelligent of our insufficience, may, though they cannot praise us, as little accuse us.

CAMILLO. You pay a great deal too dear° for what's given freely. 20

ARCHIDAMUS. Believe me, I speak as my understanding instructs me and as mine honesty puts it to utterance.

CAMILLO. Sicilia cannot show himself overkind to Bohemia. They were trained together in their 25 childhoods, and there rooted betwixt them then

on . . . foot i.e., in attending your king as I am attending mine
Wherein . . . loves if we fall short of your lavishness, we shall make up for it in affection

Verily . . . knowledge truly, I know what I am talking about
that so that
You . . . dear i.e., you give too much praise

657

such an affection, which cannot choose but branch° now. Since their more mature dignities and royal necessities made separation of their
30 society,° their encounters, though not personal, have been royally attorneyed° with interchange of gifts, letters, loving embassies, that° they have seemed to be together, though absent, shook hands as over a vast, and embraced as it
35 were from the ends of opposed winds. The heavens continue their loves!

ARCHIDAMUS. I think there is not in the world either malice or matter to alter it. You have an unspeakable comfort of your young prince
40 Mamillius. It is a gentleman of the greatest promise that ever came into my note.

CAMILLO. I very well agree with you in the hopes of him. It is a gallant child, one that indeed physics the subject,° makes old hearts fresh.
45 They that went on crutches ere he was born desire yet their life to see him a man.

ARCHIDAMUS. Would they else be content to die?

CAMILLO. Yes, if there were no other excuse why they should desire to live.

50 ARCHIDAMUS. If the king had no son, they would desire to live on crutches till he had one.

[Exeunt]

SCENE ii
A room of state in the same.

[*Enter* LEONTES, HERMIONE, MAMILLIUS,
POLIXENES, CAMILLO, *and* ATTENDANTS.]

POLIXENES. Nine changes of the wat'ry star° hath been
 The shepherd's note° since we have left our throne
 Without a burthen.° Time as long again
 Would be fill'd up, my brother, with our thanks,
5 And yet we should for perpetuity
 Go hence in debt. And therefore, like a cipher,
 Yet standing in rich place,° I multiply
 With one "We thank you," many thousands moe°
 That go before it.

LEONTES.   Stay your thanks awhile,
 And pay them when you part.

POLIXENES.   Sir, that's tomorrow.   10
 I am question'd by my fears° of what may chance
 Or breed upon our absence, that may blow
 No sneaping winds at home, to make us say
 "This is put forth too truly."° Besides, I have stay'd
 To tire your royalty.

LEONTES.   We are tougher, brother,   15
 Than you can put us to't.

POLIXENES.   No longer stay.

LEONTES. One seven-night longer.

POLIXENES.   Very sooth,° tomorrow.

LEONTES. We'll part the time° between's, then, and in that
 I'll no gainsaying.

POLIXENES.   Press me not, beseech you, so.
 There is no tongue that moves, none, none i' the world,   20
 So soon as yours could win me. So it should now,
 Were there necessity in your request, although
 'Twere needful I denied it. My affairs
 Do even drag me homeward, which to hinder
 Were in your love a whip to me, my stay   25
 To you a charge and trouble. To save both,
 Farewell, our brother.

LEONTES.   Tongue-tied, our queen? Speak you.

HERMIONE. I had thought, sir, to have held my peace until
 You had drawn oaths from him not to stay. You, sir,
 Charge° him too coldly. Tell him you are sure   30
 All in Bohemia's well; this satisfaction
 The bygone day proclaim'd. Say this to him,
 He's beat from his best ward.°

LEONTES.   Well said, Hermione.

HERMIONE. To tell he longs to see his son were strong.
 But let him say so, then, and let him go;   35
 But let him swear so, and he shall not stay:
 We'll thwack him hence with distaffs.
 Yet of your royal presence I'll adventure°
 The borrow of a week. When at Bohemia
 You take my lord, I'll give him my commission°   40
 To let him there a month behind the gest

---

branch flourish   *society* i.e., comradeship
attorneyed represented   *that* so that
physics the subject is a tonic to all the king's subjects
wat'ry star moon
hath . . . note the shepherd has observed
burthen occupant
cipher . . . place i.e., a zero at the end of 1,000
 multiples the figure ten times
moe more

question'd . . . fears troubled
that . . . truly that (there) may occur no blighting
 mischances in Bohemia such as will prove my fears
 well grounded
sooth truth   *part the time* split the difference
Charge demand of   *ward* defense
adventure venture   *commission* permission

Prefix'd° for's parting. Yet, good deed,° Leontes,
I love thee not a jar° o' the clock behind
What lady she her lord. You'll stay?

POLIXENES.   No, madam.

HERMIONE. Nay, but you will?

45 POLIXENES.   I may not, verily.

HERMIONE. Verily!
You put me off with limber° vows; but I,
Though you would seek t' unsphere the stars
    with oaths,
Should yet say "Sir, no going." Verily,
50 You shall not go. A lady's "Verily" 's
As potent as a lord's. Will you go yet?
Force me to keep you as a prisoner,
Not like a guest; so you shall pay your fees°
When you depart, and save your thanks. How
    say you?
My prisoner? Or my guest? By your dread
55 "Verily,"
One of them you shall be.

POLIXENES.   Your guest, then, madam.
To be your prisoner should import offending,
Which is for me less easy to commit
Than you to punish.

HERMIONE.   Not your jailer, then,
60 But your kind hostess. Come, I'll question you
Of my lord's tricks and yours when you were
    boys.
You were pretty lordings then?

POLIXENES.   We were, fair queen,
Two lads that thought there was no more be-
    hind
But such a day tomorrow as today,
And to be boy eternal.

65 HERMIONE.   Was not my lord
The verier wag o' the two?

POLIXENES. We were as twinn'd lambs that did
    frisk i' the sun
And bleat the one at th' other. What we
    chang'd°
Was innocence for innocence; we knew not
70 The doctrine of ill-doing, nor dream'd
That any did. Had we pursu'd that life,
And our weak spirits ne'er been higher rear'd
With stronger blood,° we should have answer'd
    heaven
Boldly "not guilty," the imposition clear'd
Hereditary ours.°

75 HERMIONE.   By this we gather
You have tripp'd since.

POLIXENES.   O my most sacred lady!
Temptations have since then been born to's. For
In those unfledg'd days was my wife a girl;
Your precious self had then not cross'd the eyes
Of my young playfellow.

HERMIONE.   Grace to boot!°   80
Of this make no conclusion, lest you say
Your queen and I are devils. Yet go on;
Th' offenses we have made you do we'll answer,
If you first sinn'd with us, and that with us
You did continue fault, and that you slipp'd not 85
With any but with us.

LEONTES.   Is he won yet?

HERMIONE. He'll stay, my lord.

LEONTES.   At my request he would not.
Hermione, my dearest, thou never spok'st
To better purpose.

HERMIONE.   Never?

LEONTES.   Never but once.

HERMIONE. What! Have I twice said well? When
    was't before?   90
I prithee tell me; cram's with praise, and
    make's
As fat as tame things.° One good deed dying
    tongueless°
Slaughters a thousand waiting upon that.
Our praises are our wages. You may ride's
With one soft kiss a thousand furlongs ere   95
With spur we heat an acre.° But to the goal:
My last good deed was to entreat his stay.
What was my first? It has an elder sister,°
Or I mistake you. O, would her name were
    Grace!
But once before I spoke to the purpose. When? 100
Nay, let me have't; I long.

LEONTES.   Why, that was when
Three crabbed° months had sour'd themselves
    to death
Ere I could make thee open thy white hand
And clap° thyself my love. Then didst thou
    utter
"I am yours forever."

HERMIONE.   'Tis Grace indeed.   105
Why, lo you now, I have spoke to the purpose
    twice.
The one forever earn'd a royal husband,
The other for some while a friend.

LEONTES.   [Aside] Too hot, too hot!
To mingle friendship far is mingling bloods.
I have tremor cordis° on me. My heart dances, 110

---

gest Prefix'd prearranged time   good deed indeed
jar tick   limber limp
fees such as a prisoner paid his jailer when released
chang'd exchanged   blood passions
imposition . . . ours even original sin forgiven us

Grace to boot heaven help me
tame things i.e., fattened for slaughter
tongueless praiseless   heat an acre race a furlong
elder sister i.e., fellow   crabbed wretched
clap pledge   tremor cordis heart palpitations

But not for joy, not joy. This entertainment°
May a free° face put on, derive a liberty
From heartiness, from bounty,° fertile bosom,
And well become the agent; 't may, I grant.
115 But to be paddling palms and pinching fingers,
As now they are, and making practic'd smiles
As in a looking-glass, and then to sigh, as 'twere
The mort o' the deer°—O, that is entertainment
My bosom likes not, nor my brows!° Mamillius,
Art thou my boy?
    MAMILLIUS.   Aye, my good lord.
120 LEONTES.   I' fecks!°
Why, that's my bawcock.° What, hast smutch'd°
    thy nose?
They say it is a copy out of mine. Come, captain,
We must be neat—not neat,° but cleanly, cap-
    tain.
And yet the steer, the heifer, and the calf
125 Are all call'd neat.—Still virginalling°
Upon his palm!—How now, you wanton calf!
Art thou my calf?
    MAMILLIUS.   Yes, if you will, my lord.
LEONTES. Thou want'st a rough pash and the
    shoots° that I have
To be full like me; yet they say we are
130 Almost as like as eggs—women say so,
That will say anything. But were they false
As o'er-dy'd blacks,° as wind, as waters, false
As dice are to be wish'd by one that fixes
No bourn° 'twixt his and mine, yet were it true
135 To say this boy were like me. Come, sir page,
Look on me with your welkin° eye. Sweet vil-
    lain!
Most dear'st! My collop!° Can thy dam?°—
    May't be?—
Affection!° Thy intention stabs the center.°
Thou dost make possible things not so held,
Communicat'st with dreams.—How can this
140   be?—

entertainment cordiality   *free* innocent
bounty generosity   *fertile bosom* natural kindliness
mort . . . deer blast of the horn announcing death of the
  deer and end of the hunt
brows i.e., as if horns were sprouting, the sign of the
  cuckold
I' fecks in faith
bawcock fine fellow (French *beau coq*)
smutch'd smudged
not neat (neat is a general term for cattle; the word
  makes Leontes think of horns, sign of the cuckold)
virginalling playing
Thou . . . shoots you lack a rough head and horns
o'er-dy'd blacks materials rotted from too much dyeing
bourn boundary   *welkin* sky blue
collop slice (of me; "chip off the old block")
dam mother   *Affection* passion
stabs the center knows no limit

With what's unreal thou coactive art,
And fellow'st nothing.° Then 'tis very credent°
Thou mayst co-join with something; and thou
    dost,
And that beyond commission,° and I find it,
And that to the infection of my brains   145
And hardening of my brows.
POLIXENES.   What means Sicilia?
HERMIONE. He something° seems unsettled.
POLIXENES.   How, my lord!
What cheer? How is't with you, best brother?
HERMIONE.   You look
As if you held a brow of much distraction.
Are you mov'd, my lord?
LEONTES.   No, in good earnest.   150
How sometimes nature will betray its folly,
Its tenderness, and make itself a pastime
To harder bosoms! Looking on the lines
Of my boy's face, methought I did recoil
Twenty-three years and saw myself unbreech'd,° 155
In my green velvet coat, my dagger muzzled°
Lest it should bite its master and so prove,
As ornaments oft do, too dangerous.
How like, methought, I then was to this kernel,
This squash,° this gentleman. Mine honest
    friend,   160
Will you take eggs for money?°
MAMILLIUS. No, my lord, I'll fight.
LEONTES. You will! Why, happy man be's dole!°
    My brother,
Are you so fond of your young prince as we
Do seem to be of ours?
POLIXENES.   If at home, sir,   165
He's all my exercise, my mirth, my matter—
Now my sworn friend, and then mine enemy;
My parasite, my soldier, statesman, all.
He makes a July's day short as December,
And with his varying childness cures in me   170
Thoughts that would thick my blood.
LEONTES.   So stands this squire
Offic'd with me. We two will walk, my lord,
And leave you to your graver steps. Hermione,
How thou lov'st us, show in our brother's wel-
    come;
Let what is dear in Sicily be cheap.   175
Next to thyself and my young rover, he's

With . . . nothing you (passion) join with what is unreal
  and are companion to nothing
credent believable
beyond commission beyond what is permissible
something somewhat
unbreech'd not yet old enough for breeches
muzzled sheathed   *squash* unripe peapod
take . . . money i.e., be a "sucker"
happy . . . dole may happiness be your lot

Apparent° to my heart.
HERMIONE.   If you would seek us,
  We are yours i' the garden. Shall's attend you
    there?
LEONTES. To your own bents dispose you; you'll be
    found,
  Be you beneath the sky. [Aside] I am angling
180   now,
  Though you perceive me not how I give line.
  Go to, go to!
  How she holds up the neb,° the bill, to him!
  And arms her with the boldness of a wife
  To her allowing husband!
  [Exeunt POLIXENES, HERMIONE, and ATTENDANTS.]
185   Gone already!
  Inch-thick, knee-deep, o'er head and ears a
    fork'd° one!
  Go, play, boy, play. Thy mother plays, and I
  Play too, but so disgrac'd a part, whose issue°
  Will hiss me to my grave. Contempt and
    clamor
  Will be my knell. Go, play, boy, play. There
190   have been,
  Or I am much deceiv'd, cuckolds ere now,
  And many a man there is, even at this present,
  Now, while I speak this, holds his wife by the
    arm,
  That little thinks she has been sluic'd in's ab-
    sence
195 And his pond fish'd by his next neighbor, by
  Sir Smile, his neighbor. Nay, there's comfort in't
  Whiles° other men have gates and those gates
    open'd,
  As mine, against their will. Should all despair
  That have revolted wives, the tenth of mankind
  Would hang themselves. Physic for't there is
200   none;
  It is a bawdy planet, that will strike
  Where 'tis predominant,° and 'tis powerful,
    think it,
  From east, west, north and south. Be it con-
    cluded,
  No barricado° for a belly, know't.
205 It will let in and out the enemy
  With bag and baggage. Many thousand on's°
  Have the disease and feel't not. How now, boy!
MAMILLIUS. I am like you, they say.

LEONTES.   Why, that's some comfort.
  What, Camillo there?
CAMILLO. Aye, my good lord.   210
LEONTES. Go play, Mamillius; thou'rt an honest
    man.   [Exit MAMILLIUS.]
  Camillo, this great sir will yet stay longer.
CAMILLO. You had much ado to make his anchor
    hold.
  When you cast out, it still came home.
LEONTES.   Didst note it?
CAMILLO. He would not stay at your petitions—
    made   215
  His business more material.
LEONTES.   Didst perceive it?
  [Aside] They're here with me already, whisper-
    ing, rounding°
  "Sicilia is a so-forth." 'Tis far gone,
  When I shall gust° it last.—How came't, Camillo,
  That he did stay?
CAMILLO.   At the good queen's entreaty.   220
LEONTES. At the queen's be't; "good" should be
    pertinent,
  But, so it is, it is not. Was this taken°
  By any understanding pate but thine?
  For thy conceit is soaking,° will draw in
  More than the common blocks.° Not noted, is't,   225
  But of the finer natures? By some severals°
  Of head-piece extraordinary? Lower messes°
  Perchance are to this business purblind? Say.
CAMILLO. Business, my lord! I think most under-
    stand
  Bohemia stays here longer.
LEONTES.   Ha!
CAMILLO.   Stays here longer.   230
LEONTES. Aye, but why?
CAMILLO. To satisfy your highness, and the en-
    treaties
  Of our most gracious mistress.
LEONTES.   Satisfy!
  Th' entreaties of your mistress! Satisfy!
  Let that suffice. I have trusted thee, Camillo,   235
  With all the nearest things to my heart, as well°
  My chamber councils,° wherein, priest-like, thou
  Hast cleans'd my bosom; I from thee departed
  Thy penitent reform'd. But we have been
  Deceiv'd in thy integrity, deceiv'd   240
  In that which seems so.
CAMILLO.   Be it forbid, my lord!

apparent heir apparent   neb beak
fork'd horned   issue outcome
Whiles as long as
It is . . . predominant unfaithfulness in wives is like a
  bawdy planet that will blast all when it is
  ascendant (on planetary influence see King Lear, I, ii,
  Edmund's speech)
barricado defense   on's of us

rounding murmuring   gust taste (hear of)
taken noted
conceit is soaking apprehension is quick to absorb
blocks heads (blockheads)   severals individuals
Lower messes inferiors, who ate at the lower tables in the
  hall
as well as well as   chamber councils state affairs

LEONTES. To bide° upon't, thou art not honest; or,
    If thou inclin'st that way, thou art a coward,
    Which hoxes° honesty behind, restraining
    From course requir'd; or else thou must be
245   counted
    A servant grafted in my serious trust
    And therein negligent; or else a fool
    That seest a game play'd home,° the rich stake
        drawn,
    And tak'st it all for jest.
  CAMILLO.   My gracious lord,
250   I may be negligent, foolish, and fearful;
    In every one of these no man is free,
    But that his negligence, his folly, fear,
    Among the infinite doings of the world,
    Sometime puts forth.° In your affairs, my lord,
255   If ever I were wilful-negligent,
    It was my folly; if industriously
    I play'd the fool, it was my negligence,
    Not weighing well the end; if ever fearful
    To do a thing where I the issue doubted,
260   Whereof the execution did cry out
    Against the non-performance, 'twas a fear
    Which oft infects the wisest. These, my lord,
    Are such allow'd infirmities that honesty
    Is never free of. But, beseech your Grace,
265   Be plainer with me; let me know my trespass
    By its own visage.° If I then deny it,
    'Tis none of mine.
  LEONTES.   Ha' not you seen, Camillo—
    But that's past doubt, you have, or your eyeglass
    Is thicker than a cuckold's horn—or heard,
270   For to a vision so apparent rumor
    Cannot be mute—or thought, for cogitation
    Resides not in that man that does not think—
    My wife is slippery? If thou wilt confess—
    Or else be impudently negative,
    To have nor eyes nor ears nor thought—then
275   say
    My wife's a hobbyhorse,° deserves a name
    As rank as any flax-wench that puts to
    Before her troth-plight. Say't and justify't.
  CAMILLO. I would not be a stander-by to hear
280   My sovereign mistress clouded so, without
    My present° vengeance taken. Shrew° my heart,
    You never spoke what did become you less
    Than this, which to reiterate were sin
    As deep as that, though true.
  LEONTES.   Is whispering nothing?
285   Is leaning cheek to cheek? Is meeting noses?

Kissing with inside lip? Stopping the career
Of laughter with a sigh?—a note infallible
Of breaking honesty.° Horsing foot on foot?
Skulking in corners? Wishing clocks more swift?
Hours, minutes? Noon, midnight? And all eyes   290
Blind with the pin and web° but theirs, theirs
    only,
That would unseen be wicked? Is this nothing?
Why, then the world and all that's in't is no-
    thing;
The covering sky is nothing; Bohemia nothing;
My wife is nothing; nor nothing have these
    nothings,   295
If this be nothing.
  CAMILLO.   Good my lord, be cur'd
Of this diseas'd opinion, and betimes,
For 'tis most dangerous.
  LEONTES.   Say it be, 'tis true.
  CAMILLO. No, no, my lord.
  LEONTES.   It is. You lie, you lie!
I say thou liest, Camillo, and I hate thee,   300
Pronounce thee a gross lout, a mindless slave,
Or else a hovering° temporizer that
Canst with thine eyes at once see good and evil,
Inclining to them both. Were my wife's liver
Infected as her life, she would not live   305
The running of one glass.
  CAMILLO.   Who does infect her?
  LEONTES. Why, he that wears her like her medal,
    hanging
About his neck, Bohemia, who, if I
Had servants true about me, that bare eyes
To see alike mine honor as their profits,   310
Their own particular thrifts,° they would do that
Which should undo more doing. Aye, and thou,
His cupbearer—whom I from meaner form
Have bench'd° and rear'd to worship, who
    mayst see
Plainly as heaven sees earth and earth sees
    heaven,   315
How I am gall'd—mightst bespice a cup
To give mine enemy a lasting wink;
Which draught to me were cordial.°
  CAMILLO.   Sir, my lord,
I could do this, and that with no rash potion,
But with a lingering dram° that should not work   320
Maliciously° like poison. But I cannot
Believe this crack° to be in my dread mistress,
So sovereignly being honorable.

bide dwell
hoxes cripples   play'd home in grim earnest
puts forth i.e., sprouts, like plants
By . . . visage for what it is   hobbyhorse loose woman
present immediate   'Shrew beshrew, curse

breaking honesty crumbling virtue
pin and web cataracts
hovering vacillating   thrifts gains
bench'd given authority   cordial medicine
lingering dram poison that works slowly
Maliciously violently   crack flaw

I have lov'd thee—
LEONTES.   Make that thy question,° and go rot!
325 Dost think I am so muddy,° so unsettled,
T' appoint° myself in this vexation, sully
The purity and whiteness of my sheets,
Which to preserve is sleep, which being spotted
Is goads, thorns, nettles, tails of wasps,
330 Give scandal to the blood o' the prince my son,
Who I do think is mine and love as mine,
Without ripe moving° to 't? Would I do this?
Could man so blench?°
CAMILLO.   I must believe you, sir.
I do, and will fetch off Bohemia for 't,
Provided that, when he's remov'd, your high-
335   ness
Will take again your queen as yours at first,
Even for your son's sake, and thereby forsealing°
The injury of tongues in courts and kingdoms
Known and allied to yours.
LEONTES.   Thou dost advise me
340 Even so as I mine own course have set down.
I'll give no blemish to her honor, none.
CAMILLO. My lord,
Go then, and with a countenance as clear
As friendship wears at feasts, keep with Bohemia
345 And with your queen. I am his cupbearer:
If from me he have wholesome beverage,
Account me not your servant.
LEONTES.   This is all.
Do 't, and thou hast the one half of my heart;
Do 't not, thou split'st thine own.
CAMILLO.   I'll do 't, my lord.
LEONTES. I will seem friendly, as thou hast advis'd
350   me.   [Exit]
CAMILLO. O miserable lady! But, for me,
What case stand I in? I must be the poisoner
Of good Polixenes, and my ground to do 't
Is the obedience to a master, one
355 Who, in rebellion with himself, will have
All that are his so too. To do this deed,
Promotion follows. If° I could find example
Of thousands that had struck anointed kings
And flourish'd after, I'd not do 't; but since
Nor brass nor stone nor parchment bears not
360   one,
Let villainy itself forswear 't. I must
Forsake the court. To do 't or no is certain
To me a breakneck. Happy star reign now!
Here comes Bohemia.
          [Re-enter POLIXENES.]

POLIXENES.   This is strange; methinks
My favor here begins to warp. Not speak?   365
Good day, Camillo.
CAMILLO.   Hail, most royal sir!
POLIXENES. What is the news i' the court?
CAMILLO.   None rare, my lord.
POLIXENES. The king hath on him such a counte-
    nance
As he had lost some province, and a region
Lov'd as he loves himself. Even now I met him   370
With customary compliment, when he,
Wafting his eyes to the contrary and falling
A lip of much contempt, speeds from me and
So leaves me to consider what is breeding
That changes thus his manners.   375
CAMILLO. I dare not know, my lord.
POLIXENES. How! Dare not! Do not. Do you know,
    and dare not
Be intelligent° to me! 'Tis thereabouts—
For, to yourself, what you do know, you must,
And cannot say you dare not. Good Camillo,   380
Your chang'd complexions are to me a mirror
Which shows me mine chang'd too, for I must be
A party in this alteration, finding
Myself thus alter'd with 't.
CAMILLO.   There is a sickness
Which puts some of us in distemper. But   385
I cannot name the disease, and it is caught
Of you that yet are well.
POLIXENES.   How! Caught of me!
Make me not sighted like the basilisk.°
I have look'd on thousands who have sped° the
    better
By my regard, but kill'd none so. Camillo—   390
As you are certainly a gentleman, thereto
Clerk-like experienc'd,° which no less adorns
Our gentry than our parents' noble names,
In whose success° we are gentle°—I beseech you,
If you know aught which does behoove my
    knowledge   395
Thereof to be inform'd, imprison 't not
In ignorant concealment.
CAMILLO.   I may not answer.
POLIXENES. A sickness caught of me, and yet I well!
I must be answer'd. Dost thou hear, Camillo?
I conjure thee by all the parts of man   400
Which honor does acknowledge, whereof the
    least
Is not this suit of mine, that thou declare
What incidency° thou dost guess of harm

Make . . . question i.e., if you merely want to discuss that
  subject
muddy dull   *appoint* afflict
ripe moving strong cause   *blench* swerve
forsealing forestalling   *If* even if

intelligent informative
basilisk mythical serpent that killed with a look
sped prospered
Clerk-like experienc'd of scholarly experience
success succession   *gentle* noble   *incidency* incident

Is creeping toward me—how far off, how near,
405 Which way to be prevented, if to be;
If not, how best to bear it.
    CAMILLO.   Sir, I will tell you,
Since I am charg'd in honor and by him
That I think honorable. Therefore mark my
    counsel,
Which must be ev'n as swiftly follow'd as
410 I mean to utter it, or both yourself and me
Cry lost, and so good night!
    POLIXENES.   On, good Camillo.
CAMILLO. I am appointed him to murder you.
POLIXENES. By whom, Camillo?
CAMILLO.   By the king.
POLIXENES.   For what?
CAMILLO. He thinks—nay, with all confidence he
    swears,
415 As he had seen 't, or been an instrument
To vice° you to 't—that you have touch'd his
    queen
Forbiddenly.
    POLIXENES.   O, then my best blood turn
To an infected jelly, and my name
Be yok'd with his that did betray the Best!°
420 Turn then my freshest reputation to
A savor° that may strike the dullest nostril
Where I arrive, and my approach be shunn'd,
Nay, hated too, worse than the great'st infection
That e'er was heard or read!
    CAMILLO.   Swear this thought over
425 By each particular star in heaven and
By all their influences, you may as well
Forbid the sea for to obey the moon,
As or by oath remove or° counsel shake
The fabric of his folly, whose foundation
430 Is pil'd upon his faith and will continue
The standing of his body.
    POLIXENES.   How should this grow?
CAMILLO. I know not. But I am sure 'tis safer to

Avoid what's grown than question how 'tis born.
If therefore you dare trust my honesty,
That lies enclosed in this trunk° which you   435
Shall bear along impawn'd,° away tonight!
Your followers I will whisper to the business;
And will by twos and threes at several posterns°
Clear them o' the city. For myself, I'll put
My fortunes to your service, which are here   440
By this discovery lost. Be not uncertain,
For, by the honor of my parents, I
Have utter'd truth, which if you seek to prove,
I dare not stand by, nor shall you be safer
Than one condemned by the king's own mouth,
    thereon   445
His execution sworn.
    POLIXENES.   I do believe thee;
I saw his heart in's face. Give me thy hand.
Be pilot to me, and thy places° shall
Still neighbor mine. My ships are ready, and
My people did expect my hence departure   450
Two days ago. This jealousy
Is for a precious creature; as she's rare,
Must it be great; and, as his person's mighty,
Must it be violent; and as he does conceive
He is dishonor'd by a man which ever   455
Profess'd to him,° why, his revenges must
In that be made more bitter. Fear o'ershades me.
Good expedition° be my friend, and comfort°
The gracious queen, part of his theme but no-
    thing
Of his ill-ta'en suspicion!° Come, Camillo;   460
I will respect thee as a father if
Thou bear'st my life off hence. Let us avoid.
CAMILLO. It is in mine authority to command
The keys of all the posterns. Please your high-
    ness
To take the urgent hour. Come, sir, away.   465
                                        [Exeunt]

---

trunk i.e., his body   *impawn'd* as pledge of honesty
posterns gates   *places* dignities
Profess'd to him i.e., that he loved him
expedition speed
comfort may my successful departure give comfort to
part . . . suspicion i.e., who shares in the king's anger
    with me but is undeserving of his suspicions

vice force
his . . . Best Judas, who betrayed Christ
savor stench   *or . . . or* either . . . or

ACT II

SCENE i
A room in LEONTES' *palace.*

[*Enter* HERMIONE, MAMILLIUS, *and* LADIES.]
HERMIONE. Take the boy to you. He so troubles me,
    'Tis past enduring.
FIRST LADY.   Come, my gracious lord,
    Shall I be your playfellow?
MAMILLIUS.   No, I'll none of you.
FIRST LADY. Why, my sweet lord?
MAMILLIUS. You'll kiss me hard and speak to me as
5   if
    I were a baby still. I love you better.
SECOND LADY. And why so, my lord?
MAMILLIUS.   Not for because
    Your brows are blacker; yet black brows, they
        say,
    Become some women best, so that there be not
10   Too much hair there, but in a semicircle,
    Or a half-moon made with a pen.
SECOND LADY.   Who taught you this?
MAMILLIUS. I learn'd it out of women's faces. Pray
        now,
    What color are your eyebrows?
FIRST LADY.   Blue, my lord.
MAMILLIUS. Nay, that's a mock. I have seen a lady's
        nose
    That has been blue, but not her eyebrows.
15 FIRST LADY.   Hark ye,
    The queen your mother rounds apace. We shall
    Present our services to a fine new prince
    One of these days, and then you'd wanton° with
        us,
    If we would have you.
SECOND LADY.   She is spread of late
20   Into a goodly bulk. Good time encounter her!
HERMIONE. What wisdom stirs amongst you?
        Come, sir, now
    I am for you again. Pray you, sit by us
    And tell 's a tale.
MAMILLIUS.   Merry or sad shall 't be?
HERMIONE. As merry as you will.
25 MAMILLIUS. A sad tale's best for winter. I have one
    Of sprites and goblins.
HERMIONE.   Let's have that, good sir.
    Come on, sit down. Come on, and do your best

wanton play

To fright me with your sprites; you're powerful
    at it.
MAMILLIUS. There was a man—
HERMIONE.   Nay, come, sit down; then on.
MAMILLIUS. Dwelt by a churchyard. I will tell it
    softly;   30
    Yon crickets° shall not hear it.
HERMIONE.   Come on, then,
    And give 't me in mine ear.
    [*Enter* LEONTES, *with* ANTIGONUS, LORDS, *and*
            OTHERS.]
LEONTES. Was he met there? His train? Camillo
    with him?
FIRST LORD. Behind the tuft of pines I met them;
    never
    Saw I men scour° so on their way. I ey'd   35
    Them even to their ships.
LEONTES.   How blest am I
    In my just censure,° in my true opinion!
    Alack, for lesser knowledge! How accurs'd
    In being so blest! There may be in the cup
    A spider steep'd, and one may drink, depart,   40
    And yet partake no venom, for his knowledge
    Is not infected. But if one present
    Th' abhorr'd ingredient to his eye, make known
    How he hath drunk, he cracks his gorge, his
        sides,
    With violent hefts.° I have drunk, and seen the
        spider.   45
    Camillo was his help in this, his pander.°
    There is a plot against my life, my crown;
    All's true that is mistrusted.° That false villain
    Whom I employ'd was pre-employ'd by him.
    He has discover'd° my design, and I   50
    Remain a pinch'd thing,° yea, a very trick°
    For them to play at will. How came the posterns
    So easily open?
FIRST LORD.   By his great authority,
    Which often hath no less prevail'd than so
    On your command.
LEONTES.   I know 't too well.   55
    Give me the boy. I am glad you did not nurse
    him.

crickets i.e., the chattering ladies   *scour* scurry
censure judgment   *hefts* retchings
pander go-between   *mistrusted* suspected
discover'd revealed
pinch'd thing i.e., tormented like a puppet in cruel hands
trick toy

Though he does bear some signs of me, yet you
Have too much blood in him.
HERMIONE.   What is this? Sport?
LEONTES. Bear the boy hence; he shall not come
      about her.
60   Away with him! And let her sport herself
      With that she's big with; for 'tis Polixenes
      Has made thee swell thus.
HERMIONE.   But I'd say he had not,
      And I'll be sworn you would believe my saying,
      Howe'er you lean to the nayward.
LEONTES.   You, my lords,
65   Look on her, mark her well. Be but about
      To say "She is a goodly lady," and
      The justice of your hearts will thereto add
      "'Tis pity she's not honest,° honorable."
      Praise her but for this her without-door form,°
      Which on my faith deserves high speech, and
70   straight
      The shrug, the hum or ha, these petty brands
      That calumny doth use—O, I am out°—
      That mercy does, for calumny will sear
      Virtue itself. These shrugs, these hums and ha's,
      When you have said "she's goodly," come be-
75   tween
      Ere you can say "she's honest." But be 't known
      From him that has most cause to grieve it should
         be,
      She's an adult'ress.
HERMIONE.   Should a villain say so,
      The most replenish'd° villain in the world,
80   He were as much more villain. You, my lord,
      Do but mistake.
LEONTES.   You have mistook, my lady,
      Polixenes for Leontes. O thou thing!
      Which I'll not call a creature of thy place,°
      Lest barbarism,° making me the precedent,
85   Should a like language use to all degrees,°
      And mannerly distinguishment leave out
      Betwixt the prince and beggar. I have said
      She's an adult'ress; I have said with whom.
      More, she's a traitor, and Camillo is
90   A federary° with her, and one that knows
      What she should shame to know herself
      But with her most vile principal, that she's
      A bed-swerver, even as bad as those
      That vulgars give bold'st titles—aye, and privy
      To this their late escape.
95   HERMIONE.   No, by my life,

Privy to none of this. How will this grieve you
When you shall come to clearer knowledge, that
You thus have publish'd° me! Gentle my lord,
You scarce can right me throughly° then to say
You did mistake.
LEONTES.   No; if I mistake   100
In those foundations which I build upon,
The center° is not big enough to bear
A schoolboy's top. Away with her to prison!
He who shall speak for her is afar off guilty
But that he speaks.°
HERMIONE.   There's some ill planet reigns.   105
I must be patient till the heavens look
With an aspect favorable. Good my lords,
I am not prone to weeping, as our sex
Commonly are; the want° of which vain dew
Perchance shall dry your pities. But I have   110
The honorable grief lodg'd here which burns
Worse than tears drown. Beseech you all, my
   lords,
With thoughts so qualified as your charities
Shall best instruct you, measure° me; and so
The king's will be perform'd!
LEONTES.   Shall I be heard?   115
HERMIONE. Who is 't that goes with me? Beseech
   your highness
My women may be with me; for you see
My plight requires it. Do not weep, good fools;°
There is no cause. When you shall know your
   mistress
Has deserv'd prison, then abound in tears   120
As I come out. This action I now go on
Is for my better grace. Adieu, my lord.
I never wish'd to see you sorry; now
I trust I shall. My women, come; you have leave.
LEONTES. Go, do our bidding. Hence!   125
                  [Exit QUEEN, guarded; with LADIES.]
FIRST LORD. Beseech your highness, call the queen
   again.
ANTIGONUS. Be certain what you do, sir, lest your
   justice
Prove violence, in the which three great ones
   suffer,
Yourself, your queen, your son.
FIRST LORD.   For her, my lord,
I dare my life lay down and will do't, sir,   130
Please you t' accept it, that the queen is spotless
I' th' eyes of heaven and to you; I mean,
In this which you accuse her.

honest   chaste
without-door form   i.e., that she puts on publicly
I am out   I have the wrong word
replenish'd   complete   place   rank
barbarism   the common multitude
degrees   of social rank   federary   confederate

publish'd   proclaimed   throughly   thoroughly
center   earth
afar . . . speaks   shares her guilt merely by defending her
ill   evil   want   lack   measure   judge
fools   here a term of endearment

ANTIGONUS.   If it prove
  She's otherwise, I'll keep my stables where
135 I lodge my wife. I'll go in couples° with her,
  Than when I feel and see her no farther trust her.
  For every inch of woman in the world,
  Aye, every dram of woman's flesh is false
  If she be.
LEONTES. Hold your peaces.
FIRST LORD.   Good my lord—
140 ANTIGONUS. It is for you we speak, not for ourselves.
  You are abus'd, and by some putter-on
  That will be damn'd for 't. Would I knew the
    villain,
  I would land-damn° him. Be she honor-flaw'd,
  I have three daughters—the eldest is eleven,
145 The second and the third, nine and some five.
  If this prove true, they'll pay for 't. By mine
    honor,
  I'll geld 'em all; fourteen they shall not see,
  To bring false generations.° They are co-heirs,
  And I had rather glib° myself than they
  Should not produce fair issue.
150 LEONTES.   Cease; no more.
  You smell this business with a sense as cold
  As is a dead man's nose. But I do see 't and feel 't
  As you feel doing thus,° and see withal°
  The instruments° that feel.
ANTIGONUS.   If it be so,
155 We need no grave to bury honesty.
  There's not a grain of it the face to sweeten
  Of the whole dungy earth.
LEONTES.   What! Lack I credit?
FIRST LORD. I had rather you did lack than I, my
    lord,
  Upon this ground, and more it would content
    me
160 To have her honor true than your suspicion,
  Be blam'd for 't how you might.
LEONTES.   Why, what need we
  Commune with you of this, but rather follow
  Our forceful instigation?° Our prerogative
  Calls not your counsels, but our natural good-
    ness
165 Imparts this, which if you, or stupified
  Or seeming so in skill,° cannot or° will not
  Relish a truth like us, inform yourselves
  We need no more of your advice. The matter,

in couples linked together
land-damn him i.e., damn him utterly
false generations illegitimate offspring   *glib* geld
doing thus (Leontes evidently strikes himself or
  Antigonus)
withal therewith   *instruments* i.e., his hand or fingers
Our . . . instigation my royal inclination
skill cunning   *or . . . or* either . . . or

The loss, the gain, the ordering on 't° is all
  Properly ours.
ANTIGONUS.   And I wish, my liege,   170
  You had only in your silent judgment tried it,
  Without more overture.°
LEONTES.   How could that be?
  Either thou art most ignorant by age,
  Or thou wert born a fool. Camillo's flight,
  Added to their familiarity—   175
  Which was as gross as ever touch'd conjecture,
  That lack'd sight only, naught for approbation°
  But only seeing, all other circumstances
  Made up to the deed—doth push on this pro-
    ceeding.
  Yet, for a greater confirmation,   180
  For in an act of this importance 'twere
  Most piteous to be wild,° I have dispatch'd in
    post°
  To sacred Delphos,° to Apollo's temple,
  Cleomenes and Dion, whom you know
  Of stuff'd sufficiency.° Now from the oracle   185
  They will bring all, whose spiritual counsel had
  Shall stop or spur me. Have I done well?
FIRST LORD. Well done, my lord.
LEONTES. Though I am satisfied and need no more
  Than what I know, yet shall the oracle   190
  Give rest to the minds of others, such as he
  Whose ignorant credulity will not
  Come up to the truth. So have we thought it
    good
  From our free° person she should be confin'd,
  Lest that the treachery of the two fled hence   195
  Be left her to perform. Come, follow us.
  We are to speak in public, for this business
  Will raise° us all.
ANTIGONUS.   [*Aside*] To laughter, as I take it,
  If the good truth were known.   [*Exeunt*]

SCENE ii
A prison.

[*Enter* PAULINA, *a* GENTLEMAN, *and* ATTENDANTS.]
PAULINA. The keeper of the prison, call to him;
  Let him have knowledge who I am.
                    [*Exit* GENTLEMAN.]
                    Good lady,
  No court in Europe is too good for thee;
  What dost thou then in prison?

on 't of it
without . . . overture without making it public
approbation proof   *wild* rash   *post* haste
Delphos Delphi, site of the famed oracle
stuff'd sufficiency unimpeachable integrity
free openly accessible   *raise* rouse

[*Re-enter* GENTLEMAN, *with the* JAILER.]
                                        Now, good sir,
You know me, do you not?
5   JAILER.   For a worthy lady
And one who much I honor.
PAULINA.   Pray you, then,
Conduct me to the queen.
JAILER.   I may not, madam.
To the contrary I have express commandment.
PAULINA. Here's ado,
10   To lock up honesty and honor from
Th' access of gentle° visitors! Is 't lawful, pray
    you,
To see her women? Any of them? Emilia?
JAILER. So please you, madam,
To put apart these your attendants, I
Shall bring Emilia forth.
15   PAULINA.   I pray now, call her.
Withdraw yourselves.
            [*Exeunt* GENTLEMAN *and* ATTENDANTS.]
JAILER.   And, madam,
I must be present at your conference.
PAULINA. Well, be 't so, prithee.   [*Exit* JAILER.]
Here's such ado to make no stain a stain
As passes coloring.°
            [*Re-enter* JAILER, *with* EMILIA.]
20   Dear gentlewoman,
How fares our gracious lady?
EMILIA. As well as one so great and so forlorn
May hold together. On° her frights and griefs,
Which never tender lady hath borne greater,
25   She is something° before her time deliver'd.
PAULINA. A boy?
EMILIA.   A daughter; and a goodly babe,
Lusty and like to live. The queen receives
Much comfort in 't, says "My poor prisoner,
I am innocent as you."
PAULINA.   I dare be sworn.
These dangerous unsafe lunes° i' the king,
30   beshrew them!
He must be told on 't, and he shall. The office
Becomes a woman best; I'll take 't upon me.
If I prove honey-mouth'd, let my tongue blister,
And never to my red-look'd anger be
35   The trumpet any more. Pray you, Emilia,
Commend my best obedience to the queen.
If she dares trust me with her little babe,
I'll show 't the king and undertake to be
Her advocate to the loud'st. We do not know
40   How he may soften at the sight o' the child.

The silence often of pure innocence
Persuades when speaking fails.
EMILIA.   Most worthy madam,
Your honor and your goodness is so evident
That your free° undertaking cannot miss
A thriving issue. There is no lady living   45
So meet° for this great errand. Please your lady-
    ship
To visit the next room, I'll presently°
Acquaint the queen of your most noble offer,
Who but today hammer'd of° this design,
But durst not tempt a minister of honor°   50
Lest she should be denied.
PAULINA.   Tell her, Emilia,
I'll use that tongue I have. If wit° flow from 't
As boldness from my bosom, let 't not be
    doubted
I shall do good.
EMILIA.   Now be you blest for it!
I'll to the queen. Please you, come something
    nearer.   55
JAILER. Madam, if 't please the queen to send the
    babe,
I know not what I shall incur to pass it,°
Having no warrant.
PAULINA.   You need not fear it, sir.
This child was prisoner to the womb, and is
By law and process of great nature thence   60
Freed and enfranchis'd;° not a party to
The anger of the king nor guilty of,
If any be, the trespass of the queen.
JAILER. I do believe it.
PAULINA. Do not you fear. Upon mine honor, I   65
Will stand betwixt you and danger.   [*Exeunt*]

                    SCENE iii
            A room in LEONTES' *palace.*

        [*Enter* LEONTES, ANTIGONUS, LORDS, *and*
                    SERVANTS.]
LEONTES. Nor night nor day no rest. It is but
    weakness
To bear the matter thus, mere weakness. If
The cause were not in being—part o' the cause,
She th' adult'ress, for the harlot king
Is quite beyond mine arm, out of the blank°   5
And level of my brain, plot-proof. But she
I can hook to me. Say that she were gone,

---

gentle noble
passes coloring surpasses painting (glossing over)
On because of   something somewhat
lunes lunacies

free voluntary   meet fit
presently immediately   hammer'd of brooded over
tempt . . . honor attempt to win a highly placed envoy
wit wisdom   pass it i.e., out of the prison
enfranchis'd liberated   blank target, bullseye

Given to the fire, a moiety° of my rest
Might come to me again. Who's there?

FIRST SERVANT.   My lord?

LEONTES. How does the boy?

10 FIRST SERVANT.   He took good rest tonight;
'Tis hop'd his sickness is discharg'd.

LEONTES. To see his nobleness!
Conceiving the dishonor of his mother,
He straight declin'd, droop'd, took it deeply,
15 Fasten'd and fix'd the shame on 't° in himself,
Threw off his spirit, his appetite, his sleep,
And downright languish'd. Leave me solely.
  Go,
See how he fares. [Exit SERVANT] Fie, fie! No
  thought of him.
The very thought of my revenges that way
20 Recoil upon me—in himself too mighty,
And in his parties, his alliance. Let him be
Until a time may serve. For present vengeance,
Take it on her. Camillo and Polixenes
Laugh at me, make their pastime at my sorrow.
25 They should not laugh if I could reach them, nor
Shall she within my power.

            [Enter PAULINA, with a CHILD.]

FIRST LORD.   You must not enter.

PAULINA. Nay, rather, good my lords, be second to
  me.
Fear you his tyrannous passion more, alas,
Than the queen's life? A gracious innocent soul,
More free° than he is jealous.°

30 ANTIGONUS.   That's enough.

SECOND SERVANT. Madam, he hath not slept tonight, commanded
None should come at him.

PAULINA.   Not so hot, good sir!
I come to bring him sleep. 'Tis such as you,
That creep like shadows by him and do sigh
35 At each his needless heavings—such as you
Nourish the cause of his awaking. I
Do come with words as med'cinal as true,
Honest as either, to purge him of that humor°
That presses him from sleep.

LEONTES.   What noise there, ho?

PAULINA. No noise, my lord; but needful con-
40 ference
About some gossips° for your highness.

LEONTES.   How!
Away with that audacious lady! Antigonus,
I charg'd thee that she should not come about
  me.
I knew she would.

ANTIGONUS.   I told her so, my lord,
On your displeasure's peril and on mine,   45
She should not visit you.

LEONTES.   What, canst not rule her?

PAULINA. From all dishonesty he can. In this,
Unless he take the course that you have done—
Commit me for committing honor—trust it,
He shall not rule me.

ANTIGONUS.   La you now, you hear!   50
When she will take the rein, I let her run;
But she'll not stumble.

PAULINA.   Good my liege, I come—
And, I beseech you, hear me, who professes
Myself your loyal servant, your physician,
Your most obedient counselor, yet that dares   55
Less appear so in comforting° your evils
Than such as most seem yours—I say, I come
From your good queen.

LEONTES.   Good queen!

PAULINA.   Good queen, my lord,
Good queen. I say good queen,
And would by combat° make her good, so were I   60
A man, the worst° about you.

LEONTES.   Force her hence.

PAULINA. Let him that makes but trifles of his
  eyes
First hand me. On mine own accord I'll off,
But first I'll do my errand. The good queen,
For she is good, hath brought you forth a
  daughter.   65
Here 'tis; commends it to your blessing.

            [Laying down the CHILD.]

LEONTES.   Out!
A mankind° witch! Hence with her, out o' door.
A most intelligencing bawd!°

PAULINA.   Not so.
I am as ignorant in that as you
In so entitling me, and no less honest   70
Than you are mad—which is enough, I'll
  warrant,
As this world goes, to pass for honest.

LEONTES.   Traitors!
Will you not push her out? Give her the bastard.
Thou dotard! Thou art woman-tir'd,° unroosted
By thy Dame Partlet° here. Take up the bastard. 75
Take 't up, I say; give 't to thy crone.

comforting condoning
by combat in trial by combat, the chivalric way of
  proving truth
the worst the lowest in degree
mankind manlike, unfeminine
intelligencing bawd go-between, pander
woman-tir'd henpecked
Dame Partlet traditional name for the nagging hen (see
  "Reynard the Fox")

moiety part   on't of it   free innocent
jealous suspicious   humor disease
gossips godparents

PAULINA.　　　　　　　　　　　　　　Forever
　　Unvenerable be thy hands if thou
　　Tak'st up the princess by that forced baseness°
　　Which he has put upon 't!
LEONTES.　　　　　　　　　　　　He dreads his wife.
PAULINA. So I would you did; then 'twere past all
80　　doubt
　　You'd call your children yours.
LEONTES.　　　　　　　　　　　　A nest of traitors!
ANTIGONUS. I am none, by this good light.
PAULINA.　　　　　　　　　　　　Nor I, nor any
　　But one that's here, and that's himself. For he
　　The sacred honor of himself, his queen's,
85　　His hopeful son's, his babe's betrays to slander,
　　Whose sting is sharper than the sword's, and
　　　　will not—
　　For as the case now stands, it is a curse
　　He cannot be compell'd to 't—once remove
　　The root of his opinion, which is rotten
　　As ever oak or stone was sound.
90　LEONTES.　　　　　　　　　　　　A callat°
　　Of boundless tongue, who late hath beat her
　　　　husband
　　And now baits me! This brat is none of mine;
　　It is the issue of Polixenes.
　　Hence with it, and together with the dam
　　Commit them to the fire!
95　PAULINA.　　　　　　　　　　　　It is yours,
　　And, might we lay th' old proverb to your
　　　　charge,
　　"So like you, 'tis the worse." Behold, my lords,
　　Although the print be little, the whole matter
　　And copy of the father, eye, nose, lip,
　　The trick of 's frown, his forehead, nay, the
100　　valley,°
　　The pretty dimples of his chin and cheek, his
　　　　smiles,
　　The very mould and frame of hand, nail, finger.
　　And thou, good goddess Nature, which hast
　　　　made it
　　So like to him that got° it, if thou hast
　　The ordering of the mind too, 'mongst all
105　　colors
　　No yellow in 't,° lest she suspect, as he does,
　　Her children not her husband's!
LEONTES.　　　　　　　　　　　　A gross hag!
　　And, lozel,° thou art worthy to be hang'd,
　　That wilt not stay her tongue.
ANTIGONUS.　　　　　　　　Hang all the husbands

That cannot do that feat, you'll leave yourself　110
　　Hardly one subject.
LEONTES.　　　　　　　　Once more, take her hence.
PAULINA. A most unworthy and unnatural lord
　　Can do no more.
LEONTES.　　　　　　　　I'll ha' thee burnt.
PAULINA.　　　　　　　　　　　　I care not;
　　It is an heretic that makes the fire,
　　Not she which burns in 't. I'll not call you
　　　　tyrant,　　　　　　　　　　　　　　　　115
　　But this most cruel usage of your queen—
　　Not able to produce more accusation
　　Than your own weak-hing'd fancy—something
　　　　savors
　　Of tyranny and will ignoble make you,
　　Yea, scandalous to the world.
LEONTES.　　　　　　　　On your allegiance,　120
　　Out of the chamber with her! Were I a tyrant,
　　Where were her life? She durst not call me so
　　If she did know me one. Away with her!
PAULINA. I pray you, do not push me; I'll be gone.
　　Look to your babe, my lord; 'tis yours. Jove
　　　　send her　　　　　　　　　　　　　　　125
　　A better guiding spirit! What needs these
　　　　hands?°
　　You that are thus so tender o'er his follies
　　Will never do him good, not one of you.
　　So, so, farewell; we are gone.　　　　[Exit]
LEONTES. Thou, traitor, hast set on thy wife to this.　130
　　My child? Away with 't! Even thou, that hast
　　A heart so tender o'er it, take it hence
　　And see it instantly consum'd with fire;
　　Even thou and none but thou. Take it up
　　　　straight.
　　Within this hour bring me word 'tis done,　135
　　And by good testimony, or I'll seize thy life,
　　With what thou else call'st thine. If thou refuse
　　And wilt encounter with my wrath, say so;
　　The bastard brains with these my proper° hands
　　Shall I dash out. Go, take it to the fire,　140
　　For thou set'st on thy wife.
ANTIGONUS.　　　　　　　　I did not, sir.
　　These lords, my noble fellows, if they please,
　　Can clear me in 't.
LORDS.　　　　　　　　We can, my royal liege.
　　He is not guilty of her coming hither.
LEONTES. You're liars all.　　　　　　　　145
FIRST LORD. Beseech your highness, give us better
　　　　credit.
　　We have always truly serv'd you, and beseech
　　　　you
　　So to esteem of us; and on our knees we beg,

---

forced baseness proclaimed base birth
callat drab　　*valley* cleft　　*got* begot
No . . . in 't i.e., omit from the make-up of the child's
　mind the color of jealousy
lozel lout

What . . . hands i.e., of those who are forcing her out
proper own

As recompense of our dear services
Past and to come, that you do change this
  purpose,
150 Which being so horrible, so bloody, must
Lead on to some foul issue. We all kneel.

LEONTES. I am a feather for each wind that blows.
Shall I live on to see this bastard kneel
155 And call me father? Better burn it now
Than curse it then. But be it; let it live.
It shall not neither. You, sir, come you hither,
You that have been so tenderly officious
With Lady Margery your midwife there
160 To save this bastard's life—for 'tis a bastard,
So sure as this beard's grey—what will you
  adventure
To save this brat's life?

ANTIGONUS.   Anything, my lord,
That my ability may undergo
And nobleness impose. At least thus much:
165 I'll pawn the little blood which I have left
To save the innocent—anything possible.

LEONTES. It shall be possible. Swear by this sword
Thou wilt perform my bidding.

ANTIGONUS.   I will, my lord.

LEONTES. Mark and perform it. Seest thou? For the
  fail
170 Of any point in 't shall not only be
Death to thyself but to thy lewd-tongu'd wife,
Whom for this time we pardon. We enjoin thee,
As thou art liegeman° to us, that thou carry
This female bastard hence, and that thou bear it
175 To some remote and desert place, quite out
Of our dominions; and that there thou leave it,
Without more mercy, to it° own protection
And favor of the climate. As by strange fortune
It came to us, I do in justice charge thee,
180 On thy soul's peril and thy body's torture,

That thou commend it strangely° to some place
Where chance may nurse or end it. Take it up.

ANTIGONUS. I swear to do this, though a present°
  death
Had been more merciful. Come on, poor babe.
Some powerful spirit instruct the kites and
  ravens   185
To be thy nurses! Wolves and bears, they say,
Casting their savageness aside, have done
Like offices of pity. Sir, be prosperous
In more than this deed does require!° And
  blessing
Against this cruelty fight on thy side,   190
Poor thing, condemn'd to loss!
                              [Exit with the CHILD.]

LEONTES.   No, I'll not rear
Another's issue.
              [Enter a SERVANT.]

SERVANT.   Please your highness, posts
From those you sent to th' oracle are come
An hour since. Cleomenes and Dion,
Being well arriv'd from Delphos, are both
  landed,   195
Hasting to the court.

FIRST LORD.   So please you, sir, their speed
Hath been beyond account.

LEONTES.   Twenty three days
They have been absent. 'Tis good speed, fore-
  tells
The great Apollo suddenly will have
The truth of this appear. Prepare you, lords;   200
Summon a session, that we may arraign
Our most disloyal lady. For, as she hath
Been publicly accus'd, so shall she have
A just and open trial. While she lives,
My heart will be a burthen to me. Leave me,   205
And think upon my bidding.   [Exeunt]

liegeman true subject   it its

commend it strangely leave it as a stranger
present immediate   require merit

ACT III

SCENE i
A seaport in Sicilia.

[Enter CLEOMENES and DION.]

CLEOMENES. The climate's delicate, the air most
  sweet,
Fertile the isle, the temple much surpassing
The common praise it bears.

DION.   I shall report,
For most it caught me, the celestial habits°—
Methinks I so should term them—and the
  reverence   5
Of the grave wearers. O, the sacrifice!
How ceremonious, solemn, and unearthly
It was i' th' off'ring!

celestial habits heavenly garments

CLEOMENES.   But of all, the burst
   And the ear-deaf'ning voice o' th' oracle,
10 Kin to Jove's thunder, so surpris'd my sense
   That I was nothing.
DION.   If th' event° o' the journey
   Prove as successful to the queen—O be 't so!—
   As it hath been to us rare, pleasant, speedy,
   The time is worth the use on 't.
CLEOMENES.   Great Apollo
15 Turn all to the best! These proclamations,
   So forcing faults upon Hermione,
   I little like.
DION.   The violent carriage° of it
   Will clear or end the business. When the oracle,
   Thus by Apollo's great divine° seal'd up,
20 Shall the contents discover,° something rare
   Even then will rush to knowledge. Go. Fresh
      horses!
   And gracious be the issue!   [Exeunt]

                    SCENE ii
                 A court of Justice.

      [*Enter* LEONTES, LORDS, *and* OFFICERS.]
LEONTES. This sessions, to our great grief we
      pronounce,
   Even pushes 'gainst our heart: the party tried
   The daughter of a king, our wife, and one
   Of us too much belov'd. Let us be clear'd
5 Of being tyrannous, since we so openly
   Proceed in justice, which shall have due course,
   Even to the guilt or the purgation.°
   Produce the prisoner.
OFFICER. It is his highness' pleasure that the queen
10 Appear in person here in court. Silence!
   [*Enter* HERMIONE *guarded;* PAULINA *and* LADIES
                 attending.]
LEONTES. Read the indictment.
OFFICER.

   [*Reads*] Hermione, queen to the worthy
   Leontes, king of Sicilia, thou art here accused
   and arraigned of high treason, in committing
15 adultery with Polixenes, king of Bohemia, and
   conspiring with Camillo to take away the life of
   our sovereign lord the king, thy royal husband.
   The pretense° whereof being by circumstances
   partly laid open, thou, Hermione, contrary to
20 the faith and allegiance of a true subject, didst
   counsel and aid them, for their better safety, to
   fly away by night.

   event outcome   *carriage* management
   divine priest   *discover* disclose
   purgation acquittal   *pretense* intent

HERMIONE. Since what I am to say must be but
      that
   Which contradicts my accusation, and
   The testimony on my part no other   25
   But what comes from myself, it shall scarce
      boot° me
   To say "not guilty." Mine integrity,
   Being counted falsehood, shall, as I express it,
   Be so receiv'd. But thus: if powers divine
   Behold our human actions, as they do,   30
   I doubt not then but innocence shall make
   False accusation blush and tyranny
   Tremble at patience. You, my lord, best know,
   Who least will seem to do so, my past life
   Hath been as continent, as chaste, as true   35
   As I am now unhappy—which is more
   Than history can pattern,° though devis'd
   And play'd to take° spectators. For behold me
   A fellow of the royal bed, which owe°
   A moiety of the throne, a great king's daughter,   40
   The mother to a hopeful prince, here standing
   To prate and talk for life and honor 'fore°
   Who please to come and hear. For life, I prize it
   As I weigh grief, which I would spare. For honor,
   'Tis a derivative from me to mine,°   45
   And only that I stand for. I appeal
   To your own conscience, sir, before Polixenes
   Came to your court, how I was in your grace,
   How merited to be so; since he came,
   With what encounter so uncurrent° I   50
   Have strain'd,° t' appear thus.° If one jot beyond
   The bound of honor, or in act or° will
   That way inclining, harden'd be the hearts
   Of all that hear me, and my near'st of kin
   Cry fie upon my grave!
LEONTES.   I ne'er heard yet   55
   That any of these bolder vices wanted°
   Less impudence to gainsay° what they did
   Than to perform it first.
HERMIONE.   That's true enough,
   Though 'tis a saying, sir, not due to me.
LEONTES. You will not own it.
HERMIONE.   More than mistress of   60
   Which comes to me in name of fault, I must not
   At all acknowledge.° For Polixenes,
   With whom I am accus'd, I do confess

   boot avail   *pattern* parallel
   take move emotionally   *owe* own   *'fore* before
   derivative . . . mine a legacy from me to my children
   encounter so uncurrent meeting so unlawful
   strain'd transgressed   *appear thus* i.e., in court
   or . . . or either . . . or   *wanted* lacked
   gainsay deny
   More . . . acknowledge I must not acknowledge myself
      possessor of more faults than I do possess

I lov'd him as in honor he requir'd,°
65 With such a kind of love as might become
A lady like me, with a love even such,
So and no other, as yourself commanded—
Which not to have done I think had been in me
Both disobedience and ingratitude
70 To you and toward your friend, whose love had
    spoke,
Even since it could speak, from an infant, freely
That it was yours. Now, for conspiracy,
I know not how it tastes, though it be dish'd
For me to try how. All I know of it
75 Is that Camillo was an honest man;
And why he left your court, the gods them-
    selves,
Wotting° no more than I, are ignorant

LEONTES. You knew of his departure, as you know
What you have underta'en to do in 's absence.

80 HERMIONE. Sir,
You speak a language that I understand not.
My life stands in the level of your dreams,
Which I'll lay down.°

LEONTES.   Your actions are my dreams.
You had a bastard by Polixenes,
And I but dream'd it. As you were past all
85   shame—
Those of your fact° are so—so past all truth,
Which to deny concerns more than avails;° for
    as
Thy brat hath been cast out, like to itself,°
No father owning it—which is, indeed,
90 More criminal in thee than it—so thou
Shalt feel our justice, in whose easiest passage
Look for no less than death.

HERMIONE.   Sir, spare your threats.
The bug° which you would fright me with I seek.
To me can life be no commodity.°
95 The crown and comfort of my life, your favor,
I do give lost, for I do feel it gone
But know not how it went. My second joy
And first-fruits of my body, from his presence
I am barr'd like one infectious. My third com-
    fort,
100 Starr'd° most unluckily, is from my breast,
The innocent milk in it° most innocent mouth,
Hal'd° out to murder. Myself on every post

Proclaim'd a strumpet, with immodest° hatred
The childbed privilege° denied, which 'longs°
To women of all fashion; lastly, hurried   105
Here to this place, i' th' open air, before
I have got strength of limit.° Now, my liege,
Tell me what blessings I have here alive,
That I should fear to die? Therefore proceed.
But yet hear this, mistake me not: no life—   110
I prize it not a straw—but for mine honor,
Which I would free, if I shall be condemn'd
Upon surmises, all proofs sleeping else
But° what your jealousies awake, I tell you
'Tis rigor° and not law. Your honors all,   115
I do refer me to the oracle:
Apollo be my judge!

FIRST LORD.   This your request
Is altogether just. Therefore bring forth,
And in Apollo's name, his oracle.

                    [Exeunt certain OFFICERS.]

HERMIONE. The Emperor of Russia was my father. 120
O that he were alive and here beholding
His daughter's trial! That he did but see
The flatness° of my misery, yet with eyes
Of pity, not revenge!

[Re-enter OFFICERS, with CLEOMENES and DION.]

OFFICER. You here shall swear upon this sword of
    justice   125
That you, Cleomenes and Dion, have
Been both at Delphos and from thence have
    brought
This seal'd-up oracle, by the hand deliver'd
Of great Apollo's priest, and that since then
You have not dar'd to break the holy seal   130
Nor read the secrets in 't.

CLEOMENES and DION.   All this we swear.

LEONTES. Break up the seals and read.

OFFICER.

    [Reads] Hermione is chaste; Polixenes blame-
    less; Camillo a true subject; Leontes a jealous
    tyrant; his innocent babe truly begotten; and 135
    the king shall live without an heir if that which
    is lost be not found.

LORDS. Now blessed be the great Apollo!
HERMIONE.   Prais'd!
LEONTES. Hast thou read truth?
OFFICER.   Aye, my lord, even so
As it is here set down.   140
LEONTES. There is no truth at all i' th' oracle.

requir'd deserved   Wotting knowing
My . . . down my life stands within the shooting range
    (archery) of your lunacies, and I must therefore give it
    up
Those . . . fact those who commit your crime
concerns . . . avails requires more effort than it will
    serve your purpose   like to itself like an outcast
bug bugaboo   commodity asset   Starr'd fated
it its   Hal'd hauled

immodest immoderate
childbed privilege i.e., of "lying-in"   'longs belongs
strength of limit even limited strength
else But other than   rigor tyranny
flatness i.e., unrelieved and endless

The sessions shall proceed. This is mere falsehood.

[*Enter* SERVANT.]

SERVANT. My lord the king, the king!

LEONTES.   What is the business?

SERVANT. O sir, I shall be hated to report it!

145   The prince your son, with mere conceit° and fear
Of the queen's speed,° is gone.

LEONTES.   How! Gone!

SERVANT.   Is dead.

LEONTES. Apollo's angry, and the heavens themselves
Do strike at my injustice. [HERMIONE *faints*] How
now there!

PAULINA. This news is mortal to the queen. Look
down
And see what death is doing.

150   LEONTES.   Take her hence.
Her heart is but o'ercharg'd; she will recover.
I have too much believ'd mine own suspicion.
Beseech you, tenderly apply to her
Some remedies for life.

[*Exeunt* PAULINA *and* LADIES, *with* HERMIONE.]
Apollo, pardon

155   My great profaneness 'gainst thine oracle!
I'll reconcile me to Polixenes,
New woo my queen, recall the good Camillo,
Whom I proclaim a man of truth, of mercy;
For, being transported by my jealousies

160   To bloody thoughts and to revenge, I chose
Camillo for the minister to poison
My friend Polixenes, which had been done
But that the good mind of Camillo tardied
My swift command, though I with death and
with

165   Reward did threaten and encourage him,
Not doing it and being done.° He, most humane
And fill'd with honor, to my kingly guest
Unclasp'd my practice,° quit his fortunes here,
Which you knew great, and to the hazard

170   Of all incertainties himself commended,
No richer than his honor. How he glisters°
Thorough° my rust! And how his piety
Does my deeds make the blacker!

[*Re-enter* PAULINA.]

PAULINA.   Woe the while!
O, cut my lace, lest my heart, cracking it,
Break too!

175   FIRST LORD. What fit is this, good lady?

PAULINA. What studied torments, tyrant, hast for
me?
What wheels? Racks? Fires? What flaying?
Boiling?
In leads or oils? What old or newer torture
Must I receive, whose every word deserves
To taste of thy most worst? Thy tyranny   180
Together working with thy jealousies,
Fancies too weak for boys, too green and idle
For girls of nine, O, think what they have done
And then run mad indeed, stark mad! For all
Thy bygone fooleries were but spices of it.   185
That thou betray'dst Polixenes, 'twas nothing;
That did but show thee, of a fool, inconstant
And damnable ingrateful. Nor was 't much
Thou wouldst have poison'd good Camillo's
honor
To have him kill a king—poor trespasses,   190
More monstrous° standing by. Whereof I reckon
The casting forth to crows thy baby daughter
To be or none or° little, though a devil
Would have shed water out of fire° ere done 't.
Nor is 't directly laid to thee, the death   195
Of the young prince, whose honorable thoughts,
Thoughts high for one so tender, cleft the heart
That could conceive a gross and foolish sire
Blemish'd° his gracious dam. This is not, no,
Laid to thy answer. But the last—O lords,   200
When I have said,° cry "Woe!"—the queen, the
queen,
The sweet'st, dear'st creature's dead, and
vengeance for 't
Not dropp'd down yet.

FIRST LORD.   The higher powers forbid!

PAULINA. I say she's dead, I'll swear 't. If word nor
oath
Prevail not, go and see. If you can bring   205
Tincture or luster in her lip, her eye,
Heat outwardly or breath within, I'll serve you
As I would do the gods. But, O thou tyrant!
Do not repent these things, for they are heavier
Than all thy woes can stir. Therefore betake thee   210
To nothing but despair. A thousand knees
Ten thousand years together, naked, fasting
Upon a barren mountain, and still° winter
In storm perpetual, could not move the gods
To look that way thou wert.°

LEONTES.   Go on, go on;   215
Thou canst not speak too much; I have deserv'd
All tongues to talk their bitt'rest.

---

conceit imagination   *speed* fortune
Not . . . done i.e., death for not doing, reward for doing
Unclasp'd my practice revealed my plot
glisters glistens   *thorough* through

monstrous monstrous offenses   *or . . . or* either . . . or
shed . . . fire wept out of fiery eyes
Blemish'd defamed   *said* finished speaking
still always   *that . . . wert* in your direction

FIRST LORD.   Say no more.
   Howe'er the business goes, you have made fault
   I' the boldness of your speech.
   PAULINA.   I am sorry for 't.
   All faults I make, when I shall come to know
220   them,
   I do repent. Alas! I have show'd too much
   The rashness of a woman. He is touch'd
   To the noble heart. What's gone and what's
     past help
   Should be past grief. Do not receive affliction
225   At my petition; I beseech you, rather
   Let me be punish'd, that have minded° you
   Of what you should forget. Now, good my liege,
   Sir, royal sir, forgive a foolish woman.
   The love I bore your queen, lo, fool again!
230   I'll speak of her no more, nor of your children;
   I'll not remember° you of my own lord,
   Who is lost too. Take your patience to you,
   And I'll say nothing.
   LEONTES.   Thou didst speak but well
   When most the truth, which I receive much
     better
235   Than to be pitied of thee. Prithee, bring me
   To the dead bodies of my queen and son.
   One grave shall be for both; upon them shall
   The causes of their death appear, unto
   Our shame perpetual. Once a day I'll visit
240   The chapel where they lie, and tears shed there
   Shall be my recreation. So long as nature
   Will bear up with this exercise, so long
   I daily vow to use it. Come and lead me
   To these sorrows.   [Exeunt]

SCENE iii

Bohemia. A desert country near the sea.

[*Enter* ANTIGONUS *with a* CHILD, *and a* MARINER.]
ANTIGONUS. Thou art perfect,° then, our ship hath
   touch'd upon
   The deserts of Bohemia?
   MARINER.   Aye, my lord, and fear
   We have landed in ill time. The skies look
     grimly
   And threaten present° blusters. In my con-
     science,
   The heavens with that we have in hand are
5   angry
   And frown upon 's.
   ANTIGONUS. Their sacred wills be done! Go, get
     aboard;

---

minded reminded   *remember* remind
perfect positive   *present* immediate

Look to thy bark. I'll not be long before
I call upon thee.
MARINER. Make your best haste, and go not   10
   Too far i' the land. 'Tis like to be loud weather;
   Besides, this place is famous for the creatures
   Of prey that keep upon 't.
   ANTIGONUS.   Go thou away.
   I'll follow instantly.
MARINER.   I am glad at heart
   To be so rid o' the business.
ANTIGONUS.   Come, poor babe.   15
   I have heard, but not believ'd, the spirits o' the
     dead
   May walk again. If such thing be, thy mother
   Appear'd to me last night, for ne'er was dream
   So like a waking. To me comes a creature,
   Sometimes her head on one side, some another;   20
   I never saw a vessel of like sorrow
   So fill'd and so becoming.° In pure white robes,
   Like very sanctity, she did approach
   My cabin where I lay, thrice bow'd before me,
   And, gasping to begin some speech, her eyes   25
   Became two spouts. The fury spent, anon
   Did this break from her: "Good Antigonus,
   Since fate, against thy better disposition,
   Hath made thy person for the thrower-out
   Of my poor babe, according to thine oath,   30
   Places remote enough are in Bohemia.
   There weep and leave it crying; and, for the
     babe
   Is counted lost forever, Perdita,°
   I prithee, call 't. For this ungentle business
   Put on thee by my lord, thou ne'er shalt see   35
   Thy wife Paulina more." And so, with shrieks,
   She melted into air. Affrighted much,
   I did in time collect myself, and thought
   This was so, and no slumber. Dreams are toys,
   Yet for this once, yea, superstitiously,   40
   I will be squar'd° by this. I do believe
   Hermione hath suffer'd death, and that
   Apollo would—this being indeed the issue
   Of King Polixenes—it should here be laid,
   Either for life or death, upon the earth   45
   Of its right father. Blossom, speed thee well!
   There lie, and there thy character.° There
     these,
   Which may, if fortune please, both breed° thee,
     pretty,
   And still rest° thine. The storm begins. Poor
     wretch,

So . . . becoming so filled with sorrow and to whom
   sorrow was so becoming   *Perdita* "lost one"
squar'd directed
character identification   *breed* rear   *rest* remain

50 That for thy mother's fault art thus expos'd
To loss and what may follow! Weep I cannot,
But my heart bleeds, and most accurs'd am I
To be by oath enjoin'd to this. Farewell!
The day frowns more and more. Thou'rt like to have
55 A lullaby too rough: I never saw
The heavens so dim by day. A savage clamor!
Well may I get aboard! This is the chase.°
I am gone forever.   [*Exit, pursued by a bear.*]
                [*Enter a* SHEPHERD.]
SHEPHERD. I would there were no age between ten
60 and three-and-twenty, or that youth would
sleep out the rest. For there is nothing in the
between but getting wenches with child,
wronging the ancientry, stealing, fighting—
Hark you now! Would any but these boiled
65 brains of nineteen and two-and-twenty hunt
this weather? They have scared away two of my
best sheep, which I fear the wolf will sooner find
than the master. If anywhere I have them, 'tis by
the seaside, browsing of ivy. Good luck, an't° be
70 thy will! What have we here? Mercy on's, a
barne,° a very pretty barne! A boy or a child,° I
wonder? A pretty one, a very pretty one. Sure,
some scape.° Though I am not bookish, yet I can
read waiting-gentlewoman in the scape. This
75 has been some stairwork, some trunk-work,
some behind-door-work.° They were warmer
that got this than the poor thing is here. I'll take
it up for pity. Yet I'll tarry till my son come;
he hallooed but even now. Whoa, ho, hoa!
                [*Enter* CLOWN.]
80 CLOWN. Hilloa, loa!
SHEPHERD. What, art so near? If thou'lt see a
thing to talk on when thou art dead and rotten,
come hither. What ailest thou, man?
CLOWN. I have seen two such sights, by sea and by
85 land! But I am not to say it is a sea, for it is now
the sky. Betwixt the firmament and it you
cannot thrust a bodkin's° point.
SHEPHERD. Why, boy, how is it?
CLOWN. I would you did but see how it chafes,
90 how it rages, how it takes up the shore! But
that's not to the point. O, the most piteous cry
of the poor souls! Sometimes to see 'em, and
not to see 'em; now the ship boring the moon
with her mainmast, and anon swallowed with
95 yest° and froth, as you'd thrust a cork into a

hogshead. And then for the land-service,° to see
how the bear tore out his shoulder bone, how
he cried to me for help and said his name was
Antigonus, a nobleman. But to make an end of
the ship, to see how the sea flapdragoned° it. 100
But first, how the poor souls roared and the sea
mocked them, and how the poor gentleman
roared and the bear mocked him, both roaring
louder than the sea or weather.
SHEPHERD. Name of mercy, when was this, boy? 105
CLOWN. Now, now. I have not winked since I saw
these sights. The men are not yet cold under
water nor the bear half dined on the gentleman.
He's at it now.
SHEPHERD. Would I had been by, to have helped 110
the old man!
CLOWN. I would you had been by the ship side, to
have helped her. There your charity would have
lacked footing.°
SHEPHERD. Heavy matters! Heavy matters! But 115
look thee here, boy. Now bless thyself. Thou
met'st with things dying, I with things newborn.
Here's a sight for thee; look thee, a bearing-
cloth° for a squire's child! Look thee here, take
up, take up, boy, open't. So, let's see. It was told 120
me I should be rich by the fairies.° This is some
changeling.° Open't. What's within, boy?
CLOWN. You're a made old man. If the sins of your
youth are forgiven you, you're well to live.
Gold! All gold! 125
SHEPHERD. This is fairy gold, boy, and 'twill prove
so. Up with't, keep it close. Home, home, the
next way. We are lucky, boy, and to be so still
requires nothing but secrecy. Let my sheep go.
Come, good boy, the next way home. 130
CLOWN. Go you the next way with your findings.
I'll go see if the bear be gone from the gentleman and how much he hath eaten. They are
never curst° but when they are hungry. If there
be any of him left, I'll bury it. 135
SHEPHERD. That's a good deed. If thou mayest
discern by that which is left of him what he is,
fetch me to the sight of him.
CLOWN. Marry,° will I, and you shall help to put
him i' the ground. 140
SHEPHERD. 'Tis a lucky day, boy, and we'll do good
deeds on't.   [*Exeunt*]

---

the chase the hunted beast, pursued by "savage clamor"
an't if it   *barne* bairn, child   *child* baby girl
some scape escapade
stair-work . . . behind-door-work "hanky panky"
bodkin's pin's   *yest* foam

land-service action taking place on shore
flapdragoned gulped   *footing* basis for helping
bearing-cloth . . . child christening robe for a gentleman's child
rich . . . fairies made rich by fairies
changeling fairies were thought to steal mortal babies, leaving a "changeling"   *next* nearest
curst vicious   *Marry* by the Virgin Mary

ACT IV

SCENE i

[*Enter* TIME, *the Chorus.*]

TIME. I, that please some, try° all, both joy and
    terror
    Of good and bad that makes and unfolds error,
    Now take upon me, in the name of Time,
    To use my wings.° Impute it not a crime
5   To me or my swift passage that I slide
    O'er sixteen years and leave the growth untried°
    Of that wide gap, since it is in my power
    To o'erthrow law and in one self-born° hour
    To plant and o'erwhelm custom. Let me pass
10   The same I am, ere ancient'st order was
    Or what is now receiv'd.° I witness to
    The times that brought them in; so shall I do
    To the freshest things now reigning, and make
    stale
    The glist'ring of this present, as my tale
15   Now seems to it.° Your patience this allowing,
    I turn my glass° and give my scene such growing
    As° you had slept between. Leontes leaving,
    The effects of his fond° jealousies so grieving
    That he shuts up himself, imagine me,
20   Gentle spectators, that I now may be
    In fair Bohemia. And remember well,
    I mentioned a son o' the king's, which Florizel
    I now name to you, and with speed so pace
    To speak of Perdita, now grown in grace
25   Equal with wond'ring. What of her ensues
    I list not° prophesy, but let Time's news
    Be known when 'tis brought forth. A shepherd's
    daughter,
    And what to her adheres, which follows after,
    Is the argument° of Time. Of this allow
30   If ever you have spent time worse ere now;
    If never, yet that Time himself doth say
    He wishes earnestly you never may.   [*Exit.*]

SCENE ii
Bohemia. The palace of POLIXENES.

[*Enter* POLIXENES *and* CAMILLO.]

POLIXENES. I pray thee, good Camillo, be no more
    importunate. 'Tis a sickness denying thee any-
    thing; a death to grant this.

CAMILLO. It is fifteen° years since I saw my country.
    Though I have for the most part been aired   5
    abroad,° I desire to lay my bones there. Besides,
    the penitent king, my master, hath sent for me,
    to whose feeling sorrows I might be some allay,°
    or I o'erween° to think so, which is another spur
    to my departure.   10

POLIXENES. As thou lovest me, Camillo, wipe not
    out the rest of thy services by leaving me now.
    The need I have of thee, thine own goodness hath
    made; better not to have had thee than thus to
    want° thee. Thou, having made me business   15
    which none without thee can sufficiently
    manage, must either stay to execute them
    thyself or take away with thee the very services
    thou hast done—which if I have not enough
    considered, as too much I cannot, to be more   20
    thankful to thee shall be my study,° and my
    profit therein, the heaping friendships.° Of that
    fatal country, Sicilia, prithee speak no more,
    whose very naming punishes me with the
    remembrance of that penitent, as thou callest   25
    him, and reconciled king, my brother, whose
    loss of his most precious queen and children
    are even now to be afresh lamented. Say to me,
    when sawest thou the Prince Florizel, my son?
    Kings are no less unhappy, their issue not being   30
    gracious, than they are in losing them when they
    have approved° their virtues.

CAMILLO. Sir, it is three days since I saw the prince.
    What his happier affairs may be are to me
    unknown. But I have missingly noted he is of   35

---

try test
To . . . wings i.e., to overleap a wide expanse of time
growth untried the events unstaged
self-born self-same
Let me . . . receiv'd let me remain unchanged, as I have
    always been from the unrecorded past to the present
    moment
seems to it seems stale in comparison to the present
    moment (of the play)   *glass* hourglass   *As* as if
fond foolish   *list not* do not care to
argument plot, subject

fifteen (Camillo and the Chorus are in evident
    disagreement)
been . . . abroad breathed the air of a foreign country
allay comfort, alleviation
o'erween presume too much   *want* lack
study studious effort
heaping friendships i.e., the friendly acts of service
    rendered
approved proved

late much retired from court and is less fre-
quent° to his princely exercises than formerly he
hath appeared.

POLIXENES. I have considered so much, Camillo,
40 and with some care—so far that I have eyes
under my service which look upon his removed-
ness, from whom I have this intelligence, that he
is seldom from the house of a most homely°
shepherd, a man, they say, that from very
45 nothing, and beyond the imagination of his
neighbors, is grown into an unspeakable estate.

CAMILLO. I have heard, sir, of such a man, who hath
a daughter of most rare note. The report of her
is extended more than can be thought to begin
50 from such a cottage.

POLIXENES. That's likewise part of my intelligence.
But I fear the angle° that plucks our son thither.
Thou shalt accompany us to the place, where we
will, not appearing what we are, have some
55 question with the shepherd, from whose
simplicity I think it not uneasy to get the cause
of my son's resort thither. Prithee, be my
present partner in this business, and lay aside
the thoughts of Sicilia.

60 CAMILLO. I willingly obey your command.

POLIXENES. My best Camillo! We must disguise
ourselves.   [*Exeunt*]

SCENE iii
A road near the SHEPHERD's *cottage.*

[*Enter* AUTOLYCUS, *singing.*]

When daffodils begin to peer,
  With heigh! the doxy° over the dale,
Why, then comes in the sweet o' the year,
  For the red blood reigns in the winter's pale.

5 The white sheet bleaching on the hedge,
  With heigh! the sweet birds, O, how they sing!
Doth set my pugging° tooth on edge;
  For a quart of ale is a dish for a king.

The lark, that tirra-lyra chants,
10   With heigh! with heigh! the thrush and the jay,
Are summer songs for me and my aunts,°
  While we lie tumbling in the hay.

I have served Prince Florizel and in my time
wore three-pile.° But now I am out of service.

15 But shall I go mourn for that, my dear?
  The pale moon shines by night,
And when I wander here and there,
  I then do most go right.

If tinkers may have leave to live,
  And bear the sow-skin budget°   20
Then my account I well may give,
  And in the stocks avouch it.°

My traffic° is sheets; when the kite builds, look
to lesser linen.° My father named me Autolycus,
who being, as I am, littered under Mercury,°   25
was likewise a snapper-up of unconsidered
trifles. With die and drab I purchased this
caparison, and my revenue is the silly cheat.°
Gallows and knock are too powerful on the
highway; beating and hanging are terrors to   30
me.° For° the life to come, I sleep out the
thought of it. A prize! A prize!

[*Enter* CLOWN.]

CLOWN. Let me see. Every 'leven wether tods;°
every tod yields pound and odd shilling;
fifteen hundred shorn, what comes the wool to? 35

AUTOLYCUS. [*Aside*] If the springe° hold, the cock's°
mine.

CLOWN. I cannot do't without counters. Let me
see; what am I to buy for our sheep-shearing
feast? Three pound of sugar; five pound of   40
currants; rice—what will this sister of mine do
with rice? But my father hath made her mistress
of the feast, and she lays it on. She hath made me
four and twenty nosegays for the shearers,
three-man songmen° all, and very good ones,   45
but they are most of them means° and basses.
But one puritan amongst them, and he sings
psalms to hornpipes.° I must have saffron to
color the warden° pies; mace;° dates—none,
that's out of my note; nutmegs, seven; a race° 50

---

budget tool bag
in . . . it acknowledge my trade (thievery, not
  vagabondage) when imprisoned in the stocks
traffic trade
when . . . linen i.e., I will snatch your sheets from the
  clothesline even as the kite does
littered . . . Mercury born when the planet Mercury was
  ascendant (Mercury was, among other things, god of
  thieves, and his own son Autolycus was a sly thief)
With . . . cheat dice and loose women reduced me to this
  (ragged) outfit, and I live by petty thievery
Gallows . . . me hanging and beating, the penalties for
  highwaymen
For as for
'leven . . . tods eleven sheep yield a tod (28 lbs.) of wool
springe snare
cock woodcock, a stupid bird and Shakespeare's
  frequent symbol for stupidity
three-man songmen singers of three-part songs
means tenors
But . . . hornpipes (that even one "puritan" should be
  found in pagan Bohemia is at least as remarkable as the
  fact that he sings to hornpipes; a stroke of topical
  satire in defiance of the obvious anachronism)
warden pear   *mace* spice   *race* root

---

frequent regularly attentive   *homely* lowly
angle fishhook   *doxy* wench   *pugging* thieving
aunts i.e., lady friends   *three-pile* costly velvet

or two of ginger, but that I may beg; four
pound of prunes, and as many of raisins o' the
sun.°

AUTOLYCUS. O that ever I was born!

                              [*Groveling on the ground.*]

55 CLOWN. I' the name of me—

AUTOLYCUS. O, help me, help me! Pluck but off
these rags, and then death, death!

CLOWN. Alack, poor soul! Thou hast need of more
rags to lay on thee, rather than have these off.

60 AUTOLYCUS. O sir, the loathsomeness of them
offends me more than the stripes I have received,
which are mighty ones and millions.

CLOWN. Alas, poor man! A million of beating may
come to a great matter.

65 AUTOLYCUS. I am robbed, sir, and beaten, my
money and apparel ta'en from me, and these
detestable things put upon me.

CLOWN. What, by a horseman, or a footman?

AUTOLYCUS. A footman, sweet sir, a footman.

70 CLOWN. Indeed, he should be a footman by the
garments he has left with thee. If this be a horseman's coat, it hath seen very hot service. Lend
me thy hand, I'll help thee. Come, lend me thy
hand.   [*Helping him up.*]

75 AUTOLYCUS. O, good sir, tenderly, O!

CLOWN. Alas, poor soul!

AUTOLYCUS. O, good sir, softly, good sir! I fear, sir,
my shoulderblade is out.

CLOWN. How now! Canst stand?

80 AUTOLYCUS. Softly, dear sir [*Picks his pocket*]; good
sir, softly. You ha' done me a charitable office.

CLOWN. Dost lack any money? I have a little
money for thee.

AUTOLYCUS. No, good sweet sir; no, I beseech you,
85 sir. I have a kinsman not past three quarters of a
mile hence, unto whom I was going. I shall there
have money, or anything I want. Offer me no
money, I pray you; that kills my heart.

CLOWN. What manner of fellow was he that
90 robbed you?

AUTOLYCUS. A fellow, sir, that I have known to go
about with troll-my-dames.° I knew him once a
servant of the prince. I cannot tell, good sir, for
which of his virtues it was, but he was certainly
95 whipped out of the court.

CLOWN. His vices, you would say; there's no virtue
whipped out of the court. They cherish it to
make it stay there, and yet it will no more but
abide.°

AUTOLYCUS. Vices I would say, sir. I know this man   100
well. He hath been since an ape-bearer,° then a
process-server, a bailiff. Then he compassed a
motion of the Prodigal Son,° and married a
tinker's wife within a mile where my land and
living lies; and, having flown over many knavish   105
professions, he settled only in rogue. Some call
him Autolycus.

CLOWN. Out upon him! Prig,° for my life, prig. He
haunts wakes, fairs, and bear-baitings.

AUTOLYCUS. Very true, sir—he, sir, he. That's the   110
rogue that put me into this apparel.

CLOWN. Not a more cowardly rogue in all
Bohemia. If you had but looked big and spit at
him, he'd have run.

AUTOLYCUS. I must confess to you, sir, I am no   115
fighter. I am false of heart that way, and that he
knew, I warrant him.

CLOWN. How do you now?

AUTOLYCUS. Sweet sir, much better than I was; I
can stand and walk. I will even take my leave of   120
you, and pace softly towards my kinsman's.

CLOWN. Shall I bring thee on the way?

AUTOLYCUS. No, good-faced sir; no, sweet sir.

CLOWN. Then fare thee well. I must go buy spices
for our sheep-shearing.   125

AUTOLYCUS. Prosper you, sweet sir! [*Exit* CLOWN]
Your purse is not hot enough to purchase your
spice. I'll be with you at your sheep-shearing,
too. If I make not this cheat bring out another
and the shearers prove sheep, let me be unrolled   130
and my name put in the book of virtue!

                              Song
          Jog on, jog on, the foot-path way,
              And merrily hent° the stile-a;
          A merry heart goes all the day,
              Your sad tires in a mile-a.   [*Exit*]   135

                         SCENE iv
                    The SHEPHERD'S *cottage.*

                 [*Enter* FLORIZEL *and* PERDITA.]

FLORIZEL. These your unusual weeds° to each part
of you
Do give a life: no shepherdess, but Flora°
Peering in April's front.° This your sheep-
shearing

---

raisins . . . sun sun-dried
troll-my-dames a carnival-type game with balls and
  arches
no . . . abide stay only briefly

ape-bearer monkey-carrier (and exhibitor)
compassed . . . Son gained possession of a puppet show
  depicting the Prodigal Son's story
Prig thief   *hent* jump
weeds garments   *Flora* goddess of flowers
Peering . . . front i.e., when flowers shyly peer forth

Is as a meeting of the petty gods,
And you the queen on't.

5 PERDITA.   Sir, my gracious lord,
To chide at your extremes° it not becomes me.
O, pardon, that I name them! Your high self,
The gracious mark o' the land,° you have
    obscur'd
With a swain's wearing, and me, poor lowly
    maid,
Most goddess-like prank'd up.° But that our
10   feasts
In every mess have folly° and the feeders
Digest it with a custom,° I should blush
To see you so attir'd—swoon, I think,
To show myself a glass.°
FLORIZEL.   I bless the time
15 When my good falcon made her flight across
Thy father's ground.
PERDITA.   Now Jove afford you cause!°
To me the difference forges dread;° your
    greatness
Hath not been us'd to fear. Even now I tremble
To think your father, by some accident,
20 Should pass this way as you did. O, the Fates!
How would he look, to see his work, so noble,
Vilely bound up?° What would he say? Or how
Should I, in these my borrow'd flaunts,° behold
The sternness of his presence?
FLORIZEL.   Apprehend
25 Nothing but jollity. The gods themselves,
Humbling their deities to love, have taken
The shapes of beasts upon them. Jupiter
Became a bull, and bellow'd; the green Neptune
A ram, and bleated; and the fire-rob'd god,
30 Golden Apollo,° a poor humble swain,
As I seem now. Their transformations
Were never for a piece of beauty rarer,
Nor in a way so chaste, since my desires
Run not before mine honor, nor my lusts
Burn hotter than my faith.

PERDITA.   O, but, sir, 35
Your resolution cannot hold when 'tis
Oppos'd, as it must be, by the power of the king.
One of these two must be necessities,
Which then will speak, that you must change
    this purpose,
Or I my life.°
FLORIZEL.   Thou dearest Perdita, 40
With these forc'd thoughts, I prithee, darken
    not
The mirth o' the feast. Or I'll be thine, my fair,
Or not my father's. For I cannot be
Mine own, nor anything to any, if
I be not thine. To this I am most constant, 45
Though destiny say no. Be merry, gentle;
Strangle such thoughts as these with anything
That you behold the while. Your guests are
    coming.
Lift up your countenance as° it were the day
Of celebration of that nuptial which 50
We two have sworn shall come.
PERDITA.   O lady Fortune,
Stand you auspicious!
FLORIZEL.   See, your guests approach.
Address yourself to entertain them sprightly,
And let's be red with mirth.
    [Enter SHEPHERD, CLOWN, MOPSA, DORCAS,
        and others, with POLIXENES and CAMILLO
                disguised.]
SHEPHERD. Fie, daughter! When my old wife liv'd,
    upon 55
This day she was both pantler,° butler, cook,
Both dame and servant; welcom'd all, serv'd
    all;
Would sing her song and dance her turn; now
    here,
At upper end o' the table, now i' the middle;
On his shoulder, and his; her face o' fire 60
With labor, and the thing she took to quench it,
She would to each one sip. You are retir'd
As if you were a feasted one and not
The hostess of the meeting. Pray you, bid
These unknown friends to's welcome, for it is 65
A way to make us better friends, more known.
Come, quench your blushes and present your-
    self
That which you are, mistress o' the feast. Come
    on,
And bid us welcome to your sheep-shearing,
As° your good flock shall prosper.

---

extremes exaggerations
gracious . . . land the "glass of fashion and the mould of
    form"
prank'd up decked out
In . . . folly expect frivolity at every level
Digest . . . custom accept it as customary
To . . . glass i.e., my queenly garments reversely
    mirroring your homely ones
afford you cause i.e., for blessing the time
difference . . . dread the difference in our ranks frightens
    me
Vilely . . . up dressed in lowly shepherd's garb
flaunts fineries
Jupiter . . . Neptune . . . Apollo Jupiter as a bull carried
    off Europa; Neptune as a ram wooed Theophane;
    Apollo as a shepherd helped Admetus to win Alcestis

One . . . life one of these two must then prevail, either
    that you change your father's opposition or I give up
    my life
as as if   *pantler* manager of the pantry, supplier
As as you hope that

70 PERDITA.   [To POLIXENES] Sir, welcome.
It is my father's will I should take on me
The hostess-ship o' the day. [To CAMILLO] You're
     welcome, sir.
Give me those flowers there, Dorcas. Reverend
     sirs,
For you there's rosemary and rue; these keep
75 Seeming° and savor all the winter long.
Grace and remembrance be to you both,
And welcome to our shearing!
     POLIXENES.   Shepherdess,
A fair one are you. Well you fit our ages
With flowers of winter.
     PERDITA.   Sir, the year growing ancient,
80 Not yet on summer's death, nor on the birth
Of trembling winter, the fairest flowers o' the
     season
Are our carnations and streak'd gillyvors,°
Which some call nature's bastards. Of that kind
Our rustic garden's barren, and I care not
To get slips of them.
85 POLIXENES.   Wherefore, gentle maiden,
Do you neglect them?
     PERDITA.   For I have heard it said
There is an art which in their piedness shares
With great creating nature.°
     POLIXENES.   Say there be;
Yet nature is made better by no mean,°
90 But nature makes that mean. So over that art
Which you say adds to nature, is an art
That nature makes. You see, sweet maid, we
     marry
A gentler scion to the wildest stock,
And make conceive a bark of baser kind
95 By bud of nobler race.° This is an art
Which does mend° nature, change it rather, but
The art itself is nature.
     PERDITA.   So it is.
POLIXENES. Then make your garden rich in gilly-
     vors,
And do not call them bastards.
     PERDITA.   I'll not put
100 The dibble° in earth to set one slip of them,
No more than were I painted° I would wish
This youth should say 'twere well, and only
     therefore
Desire to breed by me. Here's flowers for you,
Hot lavender, mints, savory, marjoram,
105 The marigold that goes to bed wi' the sun

And with him rises weeping. These are flowers
Of middle summer, and I think they are given
To men of middle age. You're very welcome.
CAMILLO. I should leave grazing, were I of your
     flock,
And only live by gazing.
PERDITA.   Out, alas!   110
You'd be so lean that blasts of January
Would blow you through and through. Now,
     my fair'st friend,
I would I had some flowers o' the spring that
     might
Become your time of day, and yours, and yours,
That wear upon your virgin branches yet   115
Your maidenheads growing. O Proserpina,
For the flowers now that frighted thou let'st fall
From Dis's wagon!°—daffodils,
That come before the swallow dares, and take°
The winds of March with beauty; violets dim,   120
But sweeter than the lids of Juno's° eyes
Or Cytherea's° breath; pale primroses,
That die unmarried ere they can behold
Bright Phœbus in his strength, a malady
Most incident to maids; bold oxlips and   125
The crown imperial;° lilies of all kinds,
The flower-de-luce being one! O, these I lack
To make you garlands of, and my sweet friend,
To strew him o'er and o'er!
FLORIZEL.   What, like a corse?°
PERDITA. No, like a bank for love to lie and play on,   130
Not like a corse; or if, not to be buried,
But quick° and in mine arms. Come, take your
     flowers.
Methinks I play as I have seen them do
In Whitsun pastorals.° Sure this robe of mine
Does change my disposition.
FLORIZEL.   What you do   135
Still betters what is done. When you speak,
     sweet,
I'd have you do it ever. When you sing,
I'd have you buy and sell so, so give alms,
Pray so; and for the ordering your affairs,
To sing them too. When you do dance, I wish
     you   140
A wave o' the sea, that you might ever do
Nothing but that; move still, still so,

Seeming appearance   gillyvors gillyflowers, or pinks
art . . . nature i.e., artificial crossing   mean means
make . . . race thus make the baser kind produce a
     nobler strain
mend improve   dibble digger
painted i.e., artificially beautified

Proserpina . . . wagon Proserpina was gathering flowers
     when Pluto (Dis) carried her to the underworld
take charm   Juno queen of the gods
Cytherea Venus, goddess of love
crown imperial a kind of lily (Perdita wishes for spring
     flowers, rather than those of summer)
corse corpse   quick alive
Whitsun pastorals Whitsuntide festivals, seven weeks
     after Easter

And own no other function. Each your doing,
So singular in each particular,
145 Crowns what you are doing in the present deeds,°
That° all your acts are queens.
PERDITA.   O Doricles,
Your praises are too large. But that your youth
And the true blood which peeps fairly through't
Do plainly give you out an unstain'd shepherd,
150 With wisdom I might fear, my Doricles,
You woo'd me the false way.
FLORIZEL.   I think you have
As little skill° to fear as I have purpose
To put you to't. But come; our dance, I pray.
Your hand, my Perdita: so turtles° pair,
That never mean to part.
155 PERDITA.   I'll swear for 'em.
POLIXENES. This is the prettiest lowborn lass that
ever
Ran on the greensward. Nothing she does or
seems
But smacks of something greater than herself,
Too noble for this place.
CAMILLO.   He tells her something
That makes her blood look out. Good sooth, she
160 is
The queen of curds and cream.
CLOWN.   Come on, strike up!
DORCAS. Mopsa must be your mistress. Marry,
garlic,
To mend her kissing with!°
MOPSA.   Now, in good time!
CLOWN. Not a word, a word; we stand upon our
manners.
165 Come, strike up!
[*Music. Here a dance of* SHEPHERDS *and*
SHEPHERDESSES.]
POLIXENES. Pray, good shepherd, what fair swain is
this
Which dances with your daughter?
SHEPHERD. They call him Doricles, and boasts him-
self
To have a worthy feeding.° But I have it
170 Upon his own report, and I believe it.
He looks like sooth.° He says he loves my
daughter.
I think so too, for never gaz'd the moon
Upon the water as he'll stand and read
As 'twere my daughter's eyes. And, to be plain,
175 I think there is not half a kiss to choose
Who loves another° best.

POLIXENES.   She dances featly.°
SHEPHERD. So she does anything, though I report it
That should be silent. If young Doricles
Do light upon her, she shall bring him that
Which he not dreams of.   180
[*Enter* SERVANT.]
SERVANT. O master, if you did but hear the peddler
at the door, you would never dance again after
a tabor° and pipe; no, the bagpipe could not
move you. He sings several tunes faster than
you'll tell° money; he utters them as he had   185
eaten ballads and all men's ears grew to his
tunes.
CLOWN. He could never come better; he shall
come in. I love a ballad but even too well, if it be
doleful matter merrily set down, or a very   190
pleasant thing indeed and sung lamentably.
SERVANT. He hath songs for man or woman, of all
sizes; no milliner can so fit his customers with
gloves. He has the prettiest love songs for maids,
so without bawdry, which is strange; with such   195
delicate burthens of dildos and fadings, "jump
her and thump her,"° and where some stretch-
mouthed° rascal would, as it were, mean mischief and break a foul gap° into the matter, he
makes the maid to answer "Whoop, do me no   200
harm, good man," puts him off, slights him,
with "Whoop, do me no harm, good man."
POLIXENES. This is a brave° fellow.
CLOWN. Believe me, thou talkest of an admirable
conceited° fellow. Has he any unbraided° wares? 205
SERVANT. He hath ribbons of all the colors i' the
rainbow, points° more than all the lawyers in
Bohemia can learnedly handle, though they
come to him by the gross. Inkles,° caddises,°
cambrics, lawns°—why, he sings 'em over as   210
they were gods or goddesses. You would think a
smock were a she-angel, he so chants to the
sleeve-hand° and the work about the square°
on't.
CLOWN. Prithee bring him in, and let him approach 215
singing.
PERDITA. Forewarn him that he use no scurrilous
words in's tunes.   [*Exit* SERVANT.]
CLOWN. You have of° these peddlers that have
more in them than you'd think, sister.   220

---

featly gracefully   *tabor* drum   *tell* count
burthens . . . thump her familiar (and bawdy) refrains
stretch-mouthed big-mouthed
gap break in the song for interpolating some bawdy jest
brave fine   *conceited* ingenious
unbraided not shopworn
points lace points (with "legal" pun)   *Inkles* tapes
caddises tapes for garters   *lawns* fine linens
sleeve-hand cuff   *square* neck square   *of* some of

---

present deeds at present   *That* so that
skill reason   *turtles* turtledoves
To . . . with to improve her bad breath
feeding pasture land   *like sooth* honest
another the other

PERDITA. Aye, good brother, or go about° to think.
[*Enter* AUTOLYCUS, *singing*.]

Lawn as white as driven snow,
Cypress° black as e'er was crow,
Gloves as sweet as damask roses;
225 Masks for faces and for noses,
Bugle° bracelet, necklace amber,
Perfume for a lady's chamber,
Golden quoifs° and stomachers,°
For my lads to give their dears;
230 Pins and poking-sticks of steel,
What maids lack from head to heel.
Come buy of me, come, come buy, come buy;
Buy, lads, or else your lasses cry.
Come buy.

235 CLOWN. If I were not in love with Mopsa, thou
shouldst take no money of me; but being en-
thralled° as I am, it will also be the bondage of
certain ribbons and gloves.

MOPSA. I was promised them against° the feast, but
240 they come not too late now.

DORCAS. He hath promised you more than that, or
there be liars.

MOPSA. He hath paid you all he promised you.
May be he has paid you more, which will shame
245 you to give him again.°

CLOWN. Is there no manners left among maids?
Will they wear their plackets° where they
should bear their faces?° Is there not milking
time, when you are going to bed, or kiln hole,° to
250 whistle off these secrets, but you must be tittle-
tattling before all our guests? 'Tis well they are
whispering. Clamor° your tongues, and not a
word more.

MOPSA. I have done. Come, you promised me a
255 tawdry-lace° and a pair of sweet° gloves.

CLOWN. Have I not told thee how I was cozened°
by the way and lost all my money?

AUTOLYCUS. And indeed, sir, there are cozeners
abroad; therefore it behooves men to be wary.

260 CLOWN. Fear not thou, man, thou shalt lose
nothing here.

AUTOLYCUS. I hope so, sir, for I have about me many
parcels of charge.°

CLOWN. What hast here? Ballads?

MOPSA. Pray now, buy some. I love a ballad in 265
print, o' life,° for then we are sure they are true.

AUTOLYCUS. Here's one to a very doleful tune, how
a usurer's wife was brought to bed of twenty
money-bags at a burthen, and how she longed to
eat adders' heads and toads carbonadoed.° 270

MOPSA. Is it true, think you?

AUTOLYCUS. Very true, and but a month old.

DORCAS. Bless me from marrying a usurer!

AUTOLYCUS. Here's the midwife's name to't, one
Mistress Taleporter, and five or six honest wives 275
that were present. Why should I carry lies
abroad?

MOPSA. Pray you now, buy it.

CLOWN. Come on, lay it by, and let's first see moe°
ballads. We'll buy the other things anon. 280

AUTOLYCUS. Here's another ballad of a fish that
appeared upon the coast on Wednesday the
fourscore of April, forty thousand fathom above
water, and sung this ballad against the hard
hearts of maids. It was thought she was a woman, 285
and was turned into a cold fish for she would not
exchange flesh with one that loved her. The
ballad is very pitiful and as true.

DORCAS. Is it true too, think you?

AUTOLYCUS. Five justices' hands at it, and witnesses 290
more than my pack will hold.

CLOWN. Lay it by too. Another.

AUTOLYCUS. This is a merry ballad, but a very
pretty one.

MOPSA. Let's have some merry ones. 295

AUTOLYCUS. Why, this is a passing° merry one and
goes to the tune of "Two maids wooing a man."
There's scarce a maid westward but she sings it;
'tis in request, I can tell you.

MOPSA. We can both sing it. If thou'lt bear a part, 300
thou shalt hear; 'tis in three parts.

DORCAS. We had the tune on't a month ago.

AUTOLYCUS. I can bear my part; you must know 'tis
my occupation. Have at it with you.

Song

A. Get you hence, for I must go 305
Where it fits not you to know.
    D. Whither? M. O, whither? D. Whither?
M. It becomes thy oath full well,
Thou to me thy secrets tell.
    D. Me too, let me go thither. 310

M. Or thou goest to the grange or mill.
D. If to either, thou dost ill.
    A. Neither. D. What, neither? A. Neither.
D. Thou hast sworn my love to be;
M. Thou hast sworn it more to me. 315
    Then whither goest? Say, whither?

---

go about wish   Cypress crepe   Bugle beaded
quoifs headdresses   stomachers dress fronts
enthralled enslaved   against in time for
May be . . . again i.e., got you with child
plackets petticoats
wear . . . faces i.e., bare their secrets in public
kiln-hole chimney corner, convenient for gossips
Clamor silence   tawdry-lace neckerchief
sweet perfumed   cozened cheated
charge value

o' life on my life   carbonadoed broiled
moe more   passing surpassingly

CLOWN. We'll have this song out anon by ourselves. My father and the gentlemen are in sad°
talk, and we'll not trouble them. Come, bring
320 away thy pack after me. Wenches, I'll buy for
you both. Peddler, let's have the first choice.
Follow me, girls.
                          [*Exit with* DORCAS *and* MOPSA.]
AUTOLYCUS. And you shall pay well for 'em.
                          [*Follows singing.*]

      Will you buy any tape,
325   Or lace for your cape,
      My dainty duck, my dear-a?
      Any silk, any thread,
      Any toys for your head,
      Of the new'st, and finest, finest wear-a?
330   Come to the peddler;
      Money's a meddler,
      That doth utter°—all men's ware-a.
                                        [*Exit*]

         [*Re-enter* SERVANT.]
SERVANT. Master, there is three carters, three shepherds, three neatherds,° three swineherds that
335 have made themselves all men of hair. They call
themselves Saltiers,° and they have a dance
which the wenches say is a gallimaufry° of gambols, because they are not in't. But they themselves are o' the mind, if it be not too rough for
340 some that know little but bowling, it will please
plentifully.
SHEPHERD. Away! We'll none on't. Here has been
too much homely foolery already. I know, sir,
we weary you.
345 POLIXENES. You weary those that refresh us. Pray,
let's see these four threes of herdsmen.
SERVANT. One three of them, by their own report,
sir, hath danced before the king; and not the
worst of the three but jumps twelve foot and a
350 half by the squier.°
SHEPHERD. Leave your prating. Since these good
men are pleased, let them come in; but quickly
now.
SERVANT. Why, they stay at door, sir.   [*Exit*]
      [*Here a dance of twelve* SATYRS.]
POLIXENES. O, father, you'll know more of that
355 hereafter.
    [*To* CAMILLO] Is it not too far gone? 'Tis time to
part them.
He's simple and tells much. How now, fair shepherd!
Your heart is full of something that does take

Your mind from feasting. Sooth, when I was
    young
And handed° love as you do, I was wont   360
To load my she with knacks.° I would have ran-
    sack'd
The peddler's silken treasury and have pour'd it
To her acceptance; you have let him go
And nothing marted° with him. If your lass
Interpretation should abuse and call this   365
Your lack of love or bounty, you were straited°
For a reply, at least if you make a care
Of happy holding her.
FLORIZEL.   Old sir, I know
She prizes not such trifles as these are.
The gifts she looks from me are pack'd and
    lock'd   370
Up in my heart, which I have given already,
But not deliver'd. O, hear me breathe my life
Before this ancient sir, who, it should seem,
Hath sometime lov'd! I take thy hand, this hand,
As soft as dove's down and as white as it,   375
Or Ethiopian's tooth, or the fann'd snow that's
    bolted°
By the northern blasts twice o'er.
POLIXENES.   What follows this?
How prettily the young swain seems to wash
The hand was fair before! I have put you out.
But to your protestation; let me hear   380
What you profess.
FLORIZEL.   Do, and be witness to't.
POLIXENES. And this my neighbor too?
FLORIZEL.   And he, and more
Than he, and men, the earth, the heavens, and
    all:
That, were I crown'd the most imperial
    monarch,
Thereof most worthy, were I the fairest youth   385
That ever made eye swerve, had force and
    knowledge
More than was ever man's, I would not prize
    them
Without her love; for her, employ them all,
Commend them and condemn them to her ser-
    vice
Or to their own perdition.
POLIXENES.   Fairly offer'd.   390
CAMILLO. This shows a sound affection.
SHEPHERD.   But, my daughter,
Say you the like to him?
PERDITA.   I cannot speak
So well, nothing so well, no, nor mean better.

---

sad serious   *utter* sell
neat-herds cow herds   *Saltiers* satyrs
gallimaufry hodgepodge   *squier* square

handed dealt in   *knacks* knick-knacks
marted traded   *straited* "stuck"
bolted sifted, refined

By the pattern of mine own thoughts I cut out
The purity of his.

395 SHEPHERD.   Take hands, a bargain!
And, friends unknown, you shall bear witness
    to't:
I give my daughter to him, and will make
Her portion equal his.

FLORIZEL.   O, that must be
I' the virtue of your daughter. One being dead,
400 I shall have more than you can dream of yet—
Enough then for your wonder. But, come on,
Contract us 'fore these witnesses.

SHEPHERD.   Come, your hand;
And, daughter, yours.

POLIXENES.   Soft, swain, awhile, beseech you.
Have you a father?

FLORIZEL.   I have. But what of him?

POLIXENES. Knows he of this?

405 FLORIZEL.   He neither does nor shall.

POLIXENES. Methinks a father
Is at the nupital of his son a guest
That best becomes the table. Pray you once
    more,
Is not your father grown incapable
410 Of reasonable affairs? Is he not stupid
With age and alt'ring rheums?° Can he speak?
    Hear?
Know man from man? Dispute his own estate?
Lies he not bed-rid? And again does nothing
But what he did being childish?

FLORIZEL.   No, good sir.
415 He has his health and ampler strength indeed
Than most have of his age.

POLIXENES.   By my white beard,
You offer him, if this be so, a wrong
Something° unfilial. Reason° my son
Should choose himself a wife, but as good reason
420 The father, all whose joy is nothing else
But fair posterity, should hold some counsel
In such a business.

FLORIZEL.   I yield all this,
But for some other reasons, my grave sir,
Which 'tis not fit you know, I not acquaint
My father of this business.

425 POLIXENES.   Let him know't.

FLORIZEL. He shall not.

POLIXENES.   Prithee, let him.

FLORIZEL.   No, he must not.

SHEPHERD. Let him, my son. He shall not need to
    grieve
At knowing of thy choice.

FLORIZEL.   Come, come, he must not.
Mark our contract.

POLIXENES.   Mark your divorce, young sir,
                    [Discovering° himself.]
Whom son I dare not call; thou art too base   430
To be acknowledg'd, thou a scepter's heir,
That thus affects° a sheep-hook!° Thou old
    traitor,
I am sorry that by hanging thee I can
But shorten thy life one week. And thou, fresh
    piece
Of excellent witchcraft, who of force° must
    know   435
The royal fool thou cop'st° with—

SHEPHERD.   O, my heart!

POLIXENES. I'll have thy beauty scratch'd with
    briers and made
More homely than thy state.° For thee, fond°
    boy,
If I may ever know thou dost but sigh
That thou no more shalt see this knack,° as
    never   440
I mean thou shalt, we'll bar thee from succes-
    sion,
Not hold thee of our blood, no, not our kin,
Far than Deucalion off.° Mark thou my words.
Follow us to the court. Thou churl, for this time,
Though full of our displeasure, yet we free thee 445
From the dead° blow of it. And you, enchant-
    ment—
Worthy enough a herdsman; yea, him too
That makes himself, but for our honor therein,
Unworthy thee—if ever henceforth thou
These rural latches to his entrance open,   450
Or hoop his body more with thy embraces,
I will devise a death as cruel for thee
As thou art tender to't.   [Exit]

PERDITA.   Even here undone!
I was not much afeard, for once or twice
I was about to speak and tell him plainly   455
The selfsame sun that shines upon his court
Hides not his visage from our cottage, but
Looks on alike. Will't please you, sir, be gone?
I told you what would come of this. Beseech you,
Of your own state take care. This dream of
    mine—   460
Being now awake, I'll queen it no inch farther,
But milk my ewes and weep.

Discovering revealing   *affects* chooses
sheep-hook shepherd's crook   *of force* necessarily
cop'st are dealing with   *state* estate   *fond* foolish
knack plaything   *Far . . . off* as far back as
    Deucalion, the "Noah" of the classical flood; hence, of
    no kin at all
dead death

alt'ring rheums debilitating diseases
Something somewhat   *Reason* it is reasonable that

CAMILLO.   Why, how now, father!
　Speak ere thou diest.
SHEPHERD.   I cannot speak, nor think,
　Nor dare to know that which I know. O sir!
465　You have undone a man of fourscore three,
　That thought to fill his grave in quiet; yea,
　To die upon the bed my father died,
　To lie close by his honest bones. But now
　Some hangman must put on my shroud and lay
　　me
　Where no priest shovels in dust. O cursed
470　　wretch,
　That knew'st this was the prince, and wouldst
　　adventure
　To mingle faith with him! Undone! Undone!
　If I might die within this hour, I have liv'd
　To die when I desire.   [Exit]
FLORIZEL.   Why look you so upon me?
475　I am but sorry, not afeard; delay'd,
　But nothing alter'd. What I was, I am,
　More straining on for plucking back, not follow-
　　ing
　My leash unwillingly.
CAMILLO.   Gracious my lord,
　You know your father's temper. At this time
480　He will allow no speech, which I do guess
　You do not purpose to him, and as hardly
　Will he endure your sight as yet, I fear.
　Then, till the fury of his highness settle,
　Come not before him.
FLORIZEL.   I not purpose it.
　I think, Camillo?
485　CAMILLO.   Even he, my lord.
PERDITA. How often have I told you 'twould be
　　thus!
　How often said my dignity would last
　But till 'twere known!
FLORIZEL.   It cannot fail but by
　The violation of my faith, and then
490　Let nature crush the sides o' th' earth together
　And mar the seeds within! Lift up thy looks.
　From my succession wipe me, father; I
　Am heir to my affection.
CAMILLO.   Be advis'd.
FLORIZEL. I am, and by my fancy.° If my reason
495　Will thereto be obedient, I have reason;
　If not, my senses, better pleas'd with madness,
　Do bid it welcome.
CAMILLO.   This is desperate, sir.
FLORIZEL. So call it, but it does fulfil my vow;
　I needs must think it honesty. Camillo,
500　Not for Bohemia nor the pomp that may
　Be thereat glean'd, for all the sun sees or

The close earth wombs or the profound seas
　　hide
In unknown fathoms will I break my oath
To this my fair belov'd. Therefore I pray you,
As you have ever been my father's honor'd
　　friend,   505
When he shall miss me—as, in faith, I mean not
To see him anymore—cast your good counsels
Upon his passion. Let myself and fortune
Tug for the time to come. This you may know
And so deliver: I am put to sea   510
With her whom here I cannot hold on shore,
And most opportune to our need I have
A vessel rides fast by, but not prepar'd
For this design. What course I mean to hold
Shall nothing benefit your knowledge nor   515
Concern me the reporting.
CAMILLO.   O my lord!
　I would your spirit were easier for advice,
　Or stronger for your need.
FLORIZEL.   Hark, Perdita. [Drawing her aside.]
　I'll hear you by and by.
CAMILLO.   He's irremovable,
　Resolv'd for flight. Now were I happy if   520
　His going I could frame to serve my turn,
　Save him from danger, do him love and honor,
　Purchase the sight again of dear Sicilia
　And that unhappy king, my master, whom
　I so much thirst to see.
FLORIZEL.   Now, good Camillo,   525
　I am so fraught with curious° business that
　I leave out ceremony.
CAMILLO.   Sir, I think
　You have heard of my poor services i' the love
　That I have borne your father?
FLORIZEL.   Very nobly
　Have you deserv'd. It is my father's music   530
　To speak your deeds, not little of his care
　To have them recompens'd as thought on.
CAMILLO.   Well, my lord,
　If you may please to think I love the king,
　And through him what is nearest to him, which
　　is
　Your gracious self, embrace but my direction.   535
　If your more ponderous° and settled project
　May suffer alteration, on mine honor
　I'll point you where you shall have such re-
　　ceiving
　As shall become your highness; where you may
　Enjoy your mistress, from the whom, I see,   540
　There's no disjunction° to be made, but by—
　As heavens forefend!—your ruin. Marry her,

fancy love

curious exacting   ponderous considered
disjunction separation

And, with my best endeavors in your absence,
Your discontenting father strive to qualify°
And bring him up to liking.
545 FLORIZEL.   How, Camillo,
May this, almost a miracle, be done?—
That I may call thee something more than man
And after that trust to thee.
CAMILLO.   Have you thought on
A place whereto you'll go?
FLORIZEL.   Not any yet.
550 But as th' unthought-on accident is guilty
To what we wildly do, so we profess
Ourselves to be the slaves of chance, and flies
Of every wind that blows.
CAMILLO.   Then list to me.
This follows: if you will not change your pur-
pose,
555 But undergo this flight, make for Sicilia,
And there present yourself and your fair prin-
cess—
For so I see she must be—'fore Leontes.
She shall be habited° as it becomes
The partner of your bed. Methinks I see
560 Leontes opening his free arms and weeping
His welcomes forth; asks thee the son forgive-
ness
As 'twere i' the father's person; kisses the hands
Of your fresh princess; o'er and o'er divides him
'Twixt his unkindness and his kindness.° The one
565 He chides to hell and bids the other grow
Faster than thought or time.
FLORIZEL.   Worthy Camillo,
What color° for my visitation shall I
Hold up before him?
CAMILLO.   Sent by the king your father
To greet him and to give him comforts. Sir,
570 The manner of your bearing towards him, with
What you as from your father shall deliver,
Things known betwixt us three, I'll write you
down—
The which shall point you forth° at every sitting
What you must say, that° he shall not perceive
575 But that you have your father's bosom° there
And speak his very heart.
FLORIZEL.   I am bound to you.
There is some sap° in this.
CAMILLO.   A course more promising
Than a wild dedication of yourselves
To unpath'd waters, undream'd shores, most
certain

To miseries enough, no hope to help you   580
But as you shake off one to take another—
Nothing so certain as your anchors, who
Do their best office if they can but stay you
Where you'll be loath to be. Besides, you know
Prosperity's the very bond of love,   585
Whose fresh complexion and whose heart to-
gether
Affliction alters.
PERDITA.   One of these is true.
I think affliction may subdue the cheek,
But not take in the mind.
CAMILLO.   Yea, say you so?
There shall not at your father's house these
seven years°   590
Be born another such.
FLORIZEL.   My good Camillo,
She is as forward of° her breeding as
She is i' the rear o'° her birth.
CAMILLO.   I cannot say 'tis pity
She lacks instructions,° for she seems a mistress
To most that teach.
PERDITA.   Your pardon, sir; for this   595
I'll blush you thanks.
FLORIZEL.   My prettiest Perdita!
But O, the thorns we stand upon! Camillo,
Preserver of my father, now of me,
The med'cine of our house, how shall we do?
We are not furnish'd like Bohemia's son,   600
Nor shall appear° in Sicilia.
CAMILLO.   My lord,
Fear none of this. I think you know my fortunes
Do all lie there. It shall be so my care
To have you royally appointed° as if
The scene you play were mine. For instance, sir,   605
That you may know you shall not want, one
word.   [They talk aside.]
[Re-enter AUTOLYCUS.]
AUTOLYCUS. Ha, ha! What a fool Honesty is! And
Trust, his sworn brother, a very simple gentle-
man! I have sold all my trumpery—not a
counterfeit stone, not a ribbon, glass, pomander,°   610
brooch, table book, ballad, knife, tape, glove,
shoe tie, bracelet, horn ring to keep my pack
from fasting. They throng who should buy first,
as if my trinkets had been hallowed and brought
a benediction to the buyer. By which means I   615
saw whose purse was best in picture,° and what I

qualify mollify   _habited_ clothed
'Twixt . . . kindness i.e., his unkindness to Polixenes and
his kind welcome to you
color pretext   _point you forth_ direct you
that so that   _bosom_ secrets   _sap_ life, hope

these . . . years i.e., in a very long time
_as . . . of_ as far above   _i' . . . o'_ of low place in
instructions learning   _appear_ appear so
royally appointed equipped as becomes a prince
pomander perfume
best in picture most abundant in coins (with the royal
portrait)

saw, to my good use I remembered. My clown, who wants but something to be a reasonable man, grew so in love with the wenches' song that he would not stir his pettitoes° till he had both tune and words—which so drew the rest of the herd to me that all their other senses stuck in ears. You might have pinched a placket;° it was senseless. 'Twas nothing to geld a codpiece of a purse.° I could have filed keys off that hung in chains. No hearing, no feeling but my sir's° song and admiring the nothing of it. So that in this time of lethargy I picked and cut most of their festival purses, and had not the old man come in with a whoo-bub against his daughter and the king's son and scared my choughs° from the chaff, I had not left a purse alive in the whole army.

[CAMILLO, FLORIZEL, *and* PERDITA *come forward.*]

CAMILLO. Nay, but my letters, by this means being there

So soon as you arrive, shall clear that doubt.

FLORIZEL. And those that you'll procure from King Leontes—

CAMILLO. Shall satisfy your father.

PERDITA.   Happy be you! All that you speak shows fair.

CAMILLO.   Who have we here?

[*Seeing* AUTOLYCUS.]

We'll make an instrument of this; omit Nothing may give us aid.

AUTOLYCUS. If they have overheard me now, why, hanging.

CAMILLO. How now, good fellow! Why shakest thou so?

Fear not, man; here's no harm intended to thee.

AUTOLYCUS. I am a poor fellow, sir.

CAMILLO. Why, be so still; here's nobody will steal that from thee. Yet for the outside of thy poverty we must make an exchange; therefore discase° thee instantly—thou must think there's a necessity in't—and change garments with this gentleman. Though the pennyworth on his side be the worst, yet hold thee, there's some boot.

AUTOLYCUS. I am a poor fellow, sir. [*Aside*] I know ye well enough.

CAMILLO. Nay, prithee, dispatch. The gentleman is half flayed° already.

AUTOLYCUS. Are you in earnest, sir? [*Aside*] I smell the trick on't.

FLORIZEL. Dispatch, I prithee.

AUTOLYCUS. Indeed, I have had earnest,° but I cannot with conscience take it.

CAMILLO. Unbuckle, unbuckle.

[FLORIZEL *and* AUTOLYCUS *exchange garments.*]

Fortunate mistress—let my prophecy Come home to ye!—you must retire yourself Into some covert. Take your sweetheart's hat And pluck it o'er your brows, muffle your face, Dismantle° you, and, as you can, disliken° The truth of your own seeming, that you may— For I do fear eyes over°—to shipboard Get undescried.

PERDITA.   I see the play so lies That I must bear a part.

CAMILLO.   No remedy. Have you done there?

FLORIZEL.   Should I now meet my father, He would not call me son.

CAMILLO.   Nay, you shall have no hat.

[*Giving it to* PERDITA.]

Come, lady, come. Farewell, my friend.

AUTOLYCUS.   Adieu, sir.

FLORIZEL. O Perdita, what have we twain forgot! Pray you, a word.

CAMILLO. [*Aside*] What I do next shall be to tell the king Of this escape and whither they are bound, Wherein my hope is I shall so prevail To force him after, in whose company I shall review° Sicilia, for whose sight I have a woman's longing.

FLORIZEL.   Fortune speed us! Thus we set on, Camillo, to the seaside.

CAMILLO. The swifter speed the better.

[*Exeunt* FLORIZEL, PERDITA, *and* CAMILLO.]

AUTOLYCUS. I understand the business, I hear it. To have an open ear, a quick eye, and a nimble hand is necessary for a cutpurse; a good nose is requisite also, to smell out work for the other senses. I see this is the time that the unjust° man doth thrive. What an exchange had this been without boot!° What a boot is here with this exchange! Sure the gods do this year connive at° us, and we may do anything extempore. The prince himself is about a piece of iniquity, stealing away from his father with his clog° at his heels. If I thought it were a piece of honesty to acquaint the king withal, I would not do't. I hold it the more knavery to conceal it, and therein am I constant to my profession.

---

pettitoes feet   *pinched a placket* stolen a petticoat
geld . . . purse cut a purse from the front of men's breeches
my sir's i.e., the Clown's
choughs crows; but here, simpletons   *discase* undress
flayed skinned; but here, undressed

earnest part payment   *Dismantle* remove your cloak
disliken disguise   *eyes over* spying eyes
review revisit   *unjust* dishonest   *boot* extra gain
connive at side with   *clog* "ball and chain"

[*Re-enter* Clown *and* Shepherd.]

Aside, aside; here is more matter for a hot brain.
700 Every lane's end, every shop, church, session,
   hanging yields a careful man work.

Clown. See, see, what a man you are now! There
   is no other way but to tell the king she's a
   changeling and none of your flesh and blood.

705 Shepherd. Nay, but hear me.

Clown. Nay, but hear me.

Shepherd. Go to, then.

Clown. She being none of your flesh and blood,
   your flesh and blood has not offended the king,
710 and so your flesh and blood is not to be punished
   by him. Show those things you found about her,
   those secret things, all but what she has with
   her. This being done, let the law go whistle, I
   warrant you.

715 Shepherd. I will tell the king all, every word, yea,
   and his son's pranks too—who, I may say, is no
   honest man, neither to his father nor to me, to
   go about to make me the king's brother-in-law.

Clown. Indeed, brother-in-law was the farthest off
720 you could have been to him, and then your
   blood had been the dearer° by I know how
   much an ounce.

Autolycus. [*Aside*] Very wisely, puppies!

Shepherd. Well, let us to the king. There is that in
725 this fardel° will make him scratch his beard.

Autolycus. [*Aside*] I know not what impediment
   this complaint may be to the flight of my
   master.

Clown. Pray heartily he be at palace.

730 Autolycus. [*Aside*] Though I am not naturally
   honest, I am so sometimes by chance. Let me
   pocket up my peddler's excrement.° [*Takes off
   his false beard*] How now, rustic! Whither are you
   bound?

735 Shepherd. To the palace, an it like your worship.

Autolycus. Your affairs there, what, with whom,
   the condition of that fardel, the place of your
   dwelling, your names, your ages, of what
   having,° breeding, and anything that is fitting to
740 be known, discover.°

Clown. We are but plain fellows, sir.

Autolycus. A lie; you are rough and hairy. Let me
   have no lying. It becomes none but tradesmen,
   and they often give us soldiers the lie.° But we
745 pay them for it with stamped coin, not stabbing
   steel; therefore they do not give us the lie.°

Clown. Your worship had like to have given us
   one if you had not taken yourself with the manner.°

750 Shepherd. Are you a courtier, an't like you, sir?

Autolycus. Whether it like me or no, I am a
   courtier. Seest thou not the air of the court in
   these enfoldings?° Hath not my gait in it the
   measure° of the court? Receives not thy nose
755 court-odor from me? Reflect I not on thy baseness court-contempt? Thinkest thou, for that I
   insinuate,° or toaze° from thee thy business, I am
   therefore no courtier? I am courtier cap-a-pe,°
   and one that will either push on or pluck back
760 thy business there; whereupon I command thee
   to open thy affair.

Shepherd. My business, sir, is to the king.

Autolycus. What advocate hast thou to him?

Shepherd. I know not, an't like you.

765 Clown. Advocate's the court word for a pheasant.°
   Say you have none.

Shepherd. None, sir; I have no pheasant, cock nor
   hen.

Autolycus. How bless'd are we that are not simple
   men!
   Yet nature might have made me as these are;
770 Therefore I will not disdain.

Clown. This cannot be but a great courtier.

Shepherd. His garments are rich, but he wears
   them not handsomely.

Clown. He seems to be the more noble in being
775 fantastical.° A great man, I'll warrant; I know by
   the picking on's teeth.°

Autolycus. The fardel there? What's i' the fardel?
   Wherefore that box?

Shepherd. Sir, there lies such secrets in this fardel
780 and box which none must know but the king,
   and which he shall know within this hour if I
   may come to the speech of him.

Autolycus. Age, thou hast lost thy labor.

Shepherd. Why, sir?

785 Autolycus. The king is not at the palace; he is
   gone aboard a new ship to purge melancholy
   and air himself. For, if thou beest capable of

---

dearer more precious   *fardel* bundle
excrement growth; here, hair   *having* property
discover reveal   *give . . . lie* call us liars
But . . . lie i.e., whereas soldiers ordinarily respond by
   stabbing the one who "gave them the lie," they
   respond to being cheated by tradesmen by paying up

Your . . . manner you might have told us a lie if you had
   not caught yourself in time (Autolycus reversed himself
   after saying that tradesmen "give" soldiers the lie)
enfoldings fancy garments   *measure* movement
insinuate pry into   *toaze* extract
cap-a-pe head to foot
Advocate's . . . pheasant i.e., at court, *advocate* is
   synonymous with *bribe*
fantastical eccentric
picking . . . teeth the way he picks his teeth (elegant
   gentlemen, especially Continental travelers, sported
   toothpicks, often worn in the cap)

things serious, thou must know the king is full of grief.

790 SHEPHERD. So 'tis said, sir—about his son, that should have married a shepherd's daughter.

AUTOLYCUS. If that shepherd be not in handfast,° let him fly. The curses he shall have, the tortures he shall feel, will break the back of man, the
795 heart of monster.

CLOWN. Think you so, sir?

AUTOLYCUS. Not he alone shall suffer what wit can make heavy and vengeance bitter, but those that are germane° to him, though removed fifty
800 times, shall all come under the hangman, which though it be great pity, yet is is necessary. An old sheep-whistling rogue, a ram-tender, to offer to have his daughter come into grace! Some say he shall be stoned; but that death is too soft for
805 him, say I. Draw our throne into a sheepcote! All deaths are too few, the sharpest too easy.

CLOWN. Has the old man e'er a son, sir, do you hear, an't like you, sir?

AUTOLYCUS. He has a son, who shall be flayed alive,
810 then 'nointed° over with honey, set on the head of a wasp's nest, then stand till he be three quarters and a dram dead, then recovered again with aqua-vitæ° or some other hot infusion, then, raw as he is, and in the hottest day prognostica-
815 tion proclaims, shall he be set against a brick wall, the sun looking with a southward eye upon him, where he is to behold him with flies blown to death. But what talk we of these traitorly rascals, whose miseries are to be smiled at, their
820 offenses being so capital? Tell me, for you seem to be honest plain men, what you have to the king. Being something gently considered, I'll bring you where he is aboard, tender your persons to his presence, whisper him in your be-
825 halfs, and if it be in man besides the king to effect your suits, here is man shall do it.

CLOWN. He seems to be of great authority. Close with° him, give him gold, and though authority be a stubborn bear, yet he is oft led by the nose
830 with gold. Show the inside of your purse to the outside of his hand, and no more ado. Remember "stoned," and "flayed alive."

SHEPHERD. An't please you, sir, to undertake the business for us, here is that gold I have. I'll make it as much more and leave this young man in 835 pawn till I bring it you.

AUTOLYCUS. After I have done what I promised?

SHEPHERD. Aye, sir.

AUTOLYCUS. Well, give me the moiety.° Are you a party in this business? 840

CLOWN. In some sort, sir. But though my case° be a pitiful one, I hope I shall not be flayed out of it.

AUTOLYCUS. O, that's the case of the shepherd's son. Hang him, he'll be made an example.

CLOWN. Comfort, good comfort! We must to the 845 king and show our strange sights. He must know 'tis none of your daughter nor my sister; we are gone else. Sir, I will give you as much as this old man does when the business is performed, and remain, as he says, your pawn till it be brought 850 you.

AUTOLYCUS. I will trust you. Walk before toward the seaside; go on the right hand. I will but look upon the hedge and follow you.

CLOWN. We are blest in this man, as I may say, 855 even blest.

SHEPHERD. Let's before as he bids us. He was provided to do us good.

[*Exeunt* SHEPHERD *and* CLOWN.]

AUTOLYCUS. If I had a mind to be honest, I see Fortune would not suffer me. She drops booties in 860 my mouth. I am courted now with a double occasion, gold and a means to do the prince my master good—which who knows how that may turn back to my advancement? I will bring these two moles, these blind ones, aboard him. 865 If he think it fit to shore them again and that the complaint they have to the king concerns him nothing, let him call me rogue for being so far officious, for I am proof against that title and what shame else belongs to't. To him will I 870 present them. There may be matter in it.

[*Exit*]

---

handfast custody   germane related
'nointed anointed   aqua-vitæ spirits   moiety portion
Close with come to terms with   case legal situation; but also, skin

A C T   V

SCENE i
A room in LEONTES' *palace.*

[*Enter* LEONTES, CLEOMENES, DION, PAULINA, *and*
SERVANTS.]

CLEOMENES. Sir, you have done enough, and have
    perform'd
A saintlike sorrow. No fault could you make
Which you have not redeem'd, indeed, paid
    down
More penitence than done trespass. At the last,
5 Do as the heavens have done, forget your evil;
With them forgive yourself.
LEONTES.   Whilst I remember
Her and her virtues, I cannot forget
My blemishes° in them, and so still think of
The wrong I did myself, which was so much
10 That heirless it hath made my kingdom and
Destroy'd the sweet'st companion that e'er man
Bred his hopes out of.
PAULINA.   True, too true, my lord.
If, one by one, you wedded all the world,
Or from the all that are took something good
15 To make a perfect woman, she you kill'd
Would be unparallel'd.
LEONTES.   I think so. Kill'd!
She I kill'd! I did so. But thou strik'st me
Sorely to say I did; it is as bitter
Upon thy tongue as in my thought. Now, good
    now,
Say so but seldom.
20 CLEOMENES.   Not at all, good lady.
You might have spoken a thousand things that
    would
Have done the time more benefit and grac'd
Your kindness better.
PAULINA.   You are one of those
Would have him wed again.
DION.   If you would not so,
25 You pity not the state nor the remembrance
Of his most sovereign name, consider little
What dangers, by his highness' fail of issue,
May drop upon his kingdom and devour
Incertain lookers on. What were more holy
30 Than to rejoice the former queen is well?
What holier than, for royalty's repair,
For present comfort and for future good,

To bless the bed of majesty again
With a sweet fellow to't?
PAULINA.   There is none worthy,
Respecting° her that's gone. Besides, the gods   35
Will have fulfill'd their secret purposes;
For has not the divine Apollo said,
Is't not the tenor of his oracle,
That King Leontes shall not have an heir
Till his lost child be found? Which that it shall 40
Is all as monstrous° to our human reason
As my Antigonus to break his grave
And come again to me, who, on my life,
Did perish with the infant. 'Tis your counsel
My lord should to the heavens be contrary,   45
Oppose against their wills. [*To* LEONTES] Care
    not for issue;
The crown will find an heir. Great Alexander
Left his to the worthiest; so, his successor
Was like to be the best.
LEONTES.   Good Paulina,
Who hast the memory of Hermione,   50
I know, in honor, O, that ever I
Had squar'd me to thy counsel!—Then, even
    now,
I might have look'd upon my queen's full eyes,
Have taken treasure from her lips—
PAULINA.   And left them
More rich for what they yielded.
LEONTES.   Thou speak'st truth. 55
No more such wives; therefore, no wife. One
    worse,
And better us'd, would make her sainted spirit
Again possess her corpse, and on this stage
Where we offended, now appear soul-vex'd,
And begin, "Why to me?"
PAULINA.   Had she such power, 60
She had just cause.
LEONTES.   She had, and would incense me
To murder her I married.
PAULINA.   I should so.
Were I the ghost that walk'd, I'd bid you mark
Her eye and tell me for what dull part in't
You chose her; then I'd shriek, that even your
    ears   65
Should rift° to hear me, and the words that
    follow'd

---

blemishes in wrongs to

Respecting compared with   *monstrous* unthinkable
rift split

Should be "Remember mine."

LEONTES.   Stars, stars,
And all eyes else dead coals! Fear thou no wife;
I'll have no wife, Paulina.

PAULINA.   Will you swear
70 Never to marry but by my free leave?

LEONTES. Never, Paulina, so be blest my spirit!

PAULINA. Then, good my lords, bear witness to his
    oath.

CLEOMENES. You tempt him overmuch.

PAULINA.   Unless another
    As like Hermione as is her picture
    Affront° his eye.

CLEOMENES.   Good madam—

75 PAULINA.   I have done.
    Yet if my lord will marry—if you will, sir,
    No remedy, but you will—give me the office
    To choose you a queen. She shall not be so young
    As was your former, but she shall be such
    As, walk'd your first queen's ghost, it should
80   take joy
    To see her in your arms.

LEONTES.   My true Paulina,
    We shall not marry till thou bid'st us.

PAULINA.   That
    Shall be when your first queen's again in breath.
    Never till then.

                [Enter a GENTLEMAN.]

GENTLEMAN. One that gives out himself Prince
85   Florizel,
    Son of Polixenes, with his princess, she
    The fairest I have yet beheld, desires access
    To your high presence.

LEONTES.   What with him? He comes not
    Like to his father's greatness. His approach,
90 So out of circumstance° and sudden, tells us
    'Tis not a visitation fram'd,° but forc'd
    By need and accident. What train?°

GENTLEMAN.   But few,
    And those but mean.

LEONTES.   His princess, say you, with him?

GENTLEMAN. Aye, the most peerless piece of earth, I
    think,
    That e'er the sun shone bright on.

95 PAULINA.   O Hermione,
    As every present time doth boast itself
    Above a better gone, so must thy grave
    Give way to what's seen now! Sir, you yourself
    Have said and writ so, but your writing now
100 Is colder than that theme. "She had not been,
    Nor was not to be equall'd"—thus your verse

Flow'd with her beauty once. 'Tis shrewdly
    ebb'd,
To say you have seen a better.

GENTLEMAN.   Pardon, madam.
    The one I have almost forgot—your pardon—
    The other, when she has obtain'd your eye,   105
    Will have your tongue too. This is a creature,
    Would she begin a sect, might quench the zeal
    Of all professors else,° make proselytes
    Of who she but bid follow.

PAULINA.   How! Not women?

GENTLEMAN. Women will love her, that she is a
    woman   110
    More worth than any man; men, that she is
    The rarest of all women.

LEONTES.   Go, Cleomenes;
    Yourself, assisted with your honor'd friends,
    Bring them to our embracement.

                [Exeunt CLEOMENES and others.]
                                  Still, 'tis strange
    He thus should steal upon us.

PAULINA.   Had our prince,   115
    Jewel of children, seen this hour, he had pair'd
    Well with this lord. There was not full a month
    Between their births.

LEONTES. Prithee, no more; cease; thou know'st
    He dies to me again when talk'd of. Sure,   120
    When I shall see this gentleman, thy speeches
    Will bring me to consider that which may
    Unfurnish me of reason. They are come.

[Re-enter CLEOMENES and others, with FLORIZEL
                and PERDITA.]
    Your mother was most true to wedlock, prince,
    For she did print your royal father off,   125
    Conceiving you. Were I but twenty-one,
    Your father's image is so hit in you,
    His very air, that I should call you brother
    As I did him, and speak of something wildly
    By us perform'd before. Most dearly welcome!   130
    And your fair princess—goddess!—O, alas!
    I lost a couple that 'twixt heaven and earth
    Might thus have stood begetting wonder, as
    You, gracious couple, do. And then I lost,
    All° mine own folly, the society,   135
    Amity too, of your brave father, whom,
    Though bearing misery, I desire my life
    Once more to look on him.

FLORIZEL.   By his command
    Have I here touch'd Sicilia, and from him
    Give you all greetings that a king, a friend,   140
    Can send his brother. And, but° infirmity,

Affront confront
out of circumstance lacking ceremony
fram'd planned   *train* attendants

professors else followers of other faiths
All all through
but but that

Which waits upon worn times,° hath something°
    seiz'd
His wish'd ability, he had himself
The lands and waters 'twixt your throne and his
145 Measur'd to look upon you, whom he loves,
He bade me say so, more than all the scepters
And those that bear them living.
    LEONTES.   O my brother,
Good gentleman! The wrongs I have done thee
    stir
Afresh within me, and these thy offices,°
150 So rarely kind, are as interpreters°
Of my behind-hand slackness! Welcome hither
As is the spring to the earth. And hath he too
Expos'd this paragon to the fearful usage,
At least ungentle, of the dreadful Neptune,
155 To greet a man not worth her pains, much less
Th' adventure° of her person?
    FLORIZEL.   Good my lord,
She came from Libya.
    LEONTES.   Where the warlike Smalus,
That noble honor'd lord, is fear'd and lov'd?
    FLORIZEL. Most royal sir, from thence; from him,
    whose daughter
His tears proclaim'd his, parting with her.
160   Thence,
A prosperous southwind friendly, we have
    cross'd
To execute the charge my father gave me
For visiting your highness. My best train
I have from your Sicilian shores dismiss'd,
165 Who for Bohemia bend, to signify
Not only my success in Libya, sir,
But my arrival, and my wife's, in safety
Here where we are.
    LEONTES.   The blessed gods
Purge all infection from our air whilst you
170 Do climate° here! You have a holy father,
A graceful gentleman, against whose person,
So sacred as it is, I have done sin
For which the heavens, taking angry note,
Have left me issueless, and your father's blest,
175 As he from heaven merits it, with you
Worthy his goodness. What might I have been,
Might I a son and daughter now have look'd on,
Such goodly things as you!
            [Enter a LORD.]
    LORD.   Most noble sir,
That which I shall report will bear no credit,
180 Were not the proof so nigh. Please you, great sir,

Bohemia greets you from himself by me,
Desires you to attach° his son, who has—
His dignity and duty both cast off—
Fled from his father, from his hopes, and with
A shepherd's daughter.
    LEONTES.   Where's Bohemia? Speak. 185
    LORD. Here in your city; I now came from him.
I speak amazedly, and it becomes
My marvel and my message. To your court
Whiles he was hastening, in the chase, it seems,
Of this fair couple, meets he on the way   190
The father of this seeming lady and
Her brother, having both their country quitted
With this young prince.
    FLORIZEL.   Camillo has betray'd me,
Whose honor and whose honesty till now
Endur'd all weathers.
    LORD.   Lay't so to his charge.   195
He's with the king your father.
    LEONTES.   Who? Camillo?
    LORD. Camillo, sir. I spake with him, who now
Has these poor men in question. Never saw I
Wretches so quake. They kneel, they kiss the
    earth,
Forswear themselves as often as they speak.   200
Bohemia stops his ears, and threatens them
With divers deaths° in death.
    PERDITA.   O my poor father!
The heaven sets spies upon us, will not have
Our contract celebrated.
    LEONTES.   You are married?
    FLORIZEL. We are not, sir, nor are we like to be;   205
The stars, I see, will kiss the valleys first.
The odds for high and low's alike.
    LEONTES.   My lord,
Is this the daughter of a king?
    FLORIZEL.   She is,
When once she is my wife.
    LEONTES. That "once," I see by your good father's
    speed,   210
Will come on very slowly. I am sorry,
Most sorry, you have broken from his liking
Where you were tied in duty, and as sorry
Your choice is not as rich in worth as beauty,
That you might well enjoy her.
    FLORIZEL.   Dear, look up.   215
Though Fortune, visible° an enemy,
Should chase us with my father, power no jot
Hath she to change our loves. Beseech you, sir,
Remember since° you ow'd no more to time
Than I do now. With thought of such affections,   220

worn times   old age
something   somewhat   *offices*   courtesies
interpreters . . . slackness   reminders of my negligence
adventure   risk   *climate*   reside

attach   arrest
divers deaths   various forms of death
visible   manifestly   *since*   when

Step forth mine advocate; at your request
My father will grant precious things as trifles.
LEONTES. Would he do so, I'd beg your precious
    mistress,
Which he counts but a trifle.
PAULINA.   Sir, my liege,
225   Your eye hath too much youth in't. Not a month
'Fore your queen died, she was more worth such
    gazes
Than what you look on now.
LEONTES.   I thought of her
Even in these looks I made. [To FLORIZEL] But
    your petition
Is yet unanswer'd. I will to your father.
230   Your honor not o'erthrown by your desires,
I am friend to them and you, upon which errand
I now go toward him; therefore follow me
And mark what way I make. Come, good my
    lord.   [Exeunt]

SCENE ii
Before LEONTES' palace.

[Enter AUTOLYCUS and a GENTLEMAN.]
AUTOLYCUS. Beseech you, sir, were you present at
    this relation?
FIRST GENTLEMAN. I was by at the opening of the
    fardel, heard the old shepherd deliver the man-
5   ner how he found it. Whereupon, after a little
    amazedness, we were all commanded out of the
    chamber. Only this methought I heard the shep-
    herd say—he found the child.
AUTOLYCUS. I would most gladly know the issue of
10   it.
FIRST GENTLEMAN. I make a broken delivery of the
    business, but the changes I perceived in the king
    and Camillo were very notes of admiration.°
    They seemed almost, with staring on one
15   another, to tear the cases of their eyes. There
    was speech in their dumbness, language in their
    very gesture; they looked as they had heard of a
    world ransomed, or one destroyed. A notable
    passion of wonder appeared in them, but the
20   wisest beholder that knew no more but seeing°
    could not say if the importance° were joy or sor-
    row; but in the extremity of the one, it must
    needs be.
                  [Enter another GENTLEMAN.]
Here comes a gentleman that haply° knows
25   more. The news, Rogero?

SECOND GENTLEMAN. Nothing but bonfires. The
    oracle is fulfilled; the king's daughter is found.
    Such a deal of wonder is broken out within this
    hour that ballad-makers cannot be able to ex-
    press it.   30
                [Enter a third GENTLEMAN.]
Here comes the Lady Paulina's steward. He can
    deliver you more. How goes it now, sir? This
    news which is called true is so like an old tale
    that the verity of it is in strong suspicion. Has the
    king found his heir?   35
THIRD GENTLEMAN. Most true, if ever truth were
    pregnant° by circumstance. That which you hear
    you'll swear you see, there is such unity in the
    proofs. The mantle of Queen Hermione's, her
    jewel about the neck of it, the letters of Anti- 40
    gonus found with it, which they know to be his
    character,° the majesty of the creature in resem-
    blance of the mother, the affection° of nobleness
    which nature shows above her breeding, and
    many other evidences proclaim her with all cer- 45
    tainty to be the king's daughter. Did you see the
    meeting of the two kings?
SECOND GENTLEMAN. No.
THIRD GENTLEMAN. Then have you lost a sight
    which was to be seen, cannot be spoken of. 50
    There might you have beheld one joy crown
    another, so and in such manner that it seemed
    sorrow wept to take leave of them, for their joy
    waded in tears. There was casting up of eyes,
    holding up of hands, with countenance of such 55
    distraction that they were to be known by gar-
    ment, not by favor.° Our king, being ready to
    leap out of himself for joy of his found daughter,
    as if that joy were now become a loss, cries "O,
    thy mother, thy mother!" then asks Bohemia 60
    forgiveness, then embraces his son-in-law, then
    again worries he his daughter with clipping her,°
    now he thanks the old shepherd, which stands
    by like a weather-bitten conduit° of many kings'
    reigns. I never heard of such another encounter, 65
    which lames report to follow it and undoes
    description to do it.
SECOND GENTLEMAN. What, pray you, became of
    Antigonus, that carried hence the child?
THIRD GENTLEMAN. Like an old tale still, which will 70
    have matter to rehearse, though credit° be
    asleep and not an ear open. He was torn to
    pieces with a bear. This avouches the shepherd's
    son, who has not only his innocence, which

---

admiration wonder
knew . . . seeing knew only what he saw
importance effect   *haply* perhaps

pregnant manifest   *character* handwriting
affection attitude   *favor* features
clipping hugging   *conduit* fountain
credit belief

75   seems much, to justify him, but a handkerchief
      and rings of his that Paulina knows.

FIRST GENTLEMAN. What became of his bark and his
      followers?

THIRD GENTLEMAN. Wrecked the same instant of
80   their master's death and in the view of the shep-
      herd, so that all the instruments which aided to
      expose the child were even then lost when it was
      found. But O, the noble combat that 'twixt joy
      and sorrow was fought in Paulina! She had one
85   eye declined for the loss of her husband, another
      elevated that the oracle was fulfilled. She lifted
      the princess from the earth, and so locks her in
      embracing as if she would pin her to her heart
      that she might no more be in danger of losing.

90 FIRST GENTLEMAN. The dignity of this act was worth
      the audience of kings and princes, for by such
      was it acted.

THIRD GENTLEMAN. One of the prettiest touches of
      all, and that which angled for mine eyes—
95   caught the water though not the fish—was
      when, at the relation of the queen's death, with
      the manner how she came to't bravely confessed
      and lamented by the king, how attentiveness
      wounded his daughter till, from one sign of
100   dolor to another, she did, with an "Alas," I
      would fain say, bleed tears, for I am sure my
      heart wept blood. Who was most marble there
      changed color; some swooned, all sorrowed. If
      all the world could have seen't, the woe had
105   been universal.

FIRST GENTLEMAN. Are they returned to the court?

THIRD GENTLEMAN. No. The princess hearing of her
      mother's statue, which is in the keeping of
      Paulina—a piece many years in doing and now
110   newly performed by that rare Italian master,
      Julio Romano,° who, had he himself eternity
      and could put breath into his work, would be-
      guile Nature of her custom,° so perfectly he is
      her ape—he so near to Hermione hath done Her-
115   mione that they say one would speak to her and
      stand in hope of answer.—Thither with all
      greediness of affection° are they gone, and there
      they intend to sup.

SECOND GENTLEMAN. I thought she had some great
120   matter there in hand, for she hath privately
      twice or thrice a day, ever since the death of Her-
      mione, visited that removed house. Shall we
      thither and with our company piece° the re-
      joicing?

125 FIRST GENTLEMAN. Who would be thence that has
      the benefit of access? Every wink of an eye, some

new grace will be born. Our absence makes us
unthrifty to our knowledge.° Let's along.
                        [Exeunt GENTLEMEN.]

AUTOLYCUS. Now, had I not the dash of my former
      life in me, would preferment° drop on my head.   130
      I brought the old man and his son aboard the
      Prince, told him I heard them talk of a fardel and
      I know not what. But he at that time, overfond
      of the shepherd's daughter, so he then took her
      to be, who began to be much seasick, and him-   135
      self little better, extremity of weather con-
      tinuing, this mystery remained undiscovered.°
      But 'tis all one to me, for had I been the finder
      out of this secret, it would not have relished
      among° my other discredits.   140
                  [Enter SHEPHERD and CLOWN.]
      Here come those I have done good to against my
      will, and already appearing in the blossoms of
      their fortune.

SHEPHERD. Come, boy; I am past moe children, but
      thy sons and daughters will be all gentlemen   145
      born.

CLOWN. You are well met, sir. You denied to fight
      with me this other day because I was no gentle-
      man born. See you these clothes? Say you see
      them not, and think me still no gentleman born. 150
      You were best say these robes are not gentlemen
      born. Give me the lie, do, and try whether I am
      not now a gentleman born.

AUTOLYCUS. I know you are now, sir, a gentleman
      born.   155

CLOWN. Aye, and have been so anytime these four
      hours.

SHEPHERD. And so have I, boy.

CLOWN. So you have. But I was a gentleman born
      before my father, for the king's son took me by 160
      the hand and called me brother, and then the
      two kings called my father brother, and then the
      prince my brother and the princess my sister
      called my father father, and so we wept, and
      there was the first gentlemanlike tears that ever 165
      we shed.

SHEPHERD. We may live, son, to shed many more.

CLOWN. Aye, or else 'twere hard luck, being in so
      preposterous estate as we are.

AUTOLYCUS. I humbly beseech you, sir, to pardon   170
      me all the faults I have committed to your wor-
      ship and to give me your good report to the
      prince my master.

SHEPHERD. Prithee, son, do, for we must be gentle,
      now we are gentlemen.   175

---

unthrifty . . . knowledge wasteful of opportunity to
      expand our knowledge
preferment advancement   *undiscovered* unrevealed
relished among suited with

Julio Romano Italian painter, 1492–1546
custom trade   *affection* emotion   *piece* add to

CLOWN. Thou wilt amend thy life?

AUTOLYCUS. Aye, an it like your good worship.

CLOWN. Give me thy hand. I will swear to the
prince thou art as honest a true fellow as any is in
180 Bohemia.

SHEPHERD. You may say it, but not swear it.

CLOWN. Not swear it, now I am a gentleman? Let
boors° and franklins° say it, I'll swear it.

SHEPHERD. How if it be false, son?

185 CLOWN. If it be ne'er so false, a true gentleman may
swear it in the behalf of his friend. And I'll
swear to the prince thou art a tall° fellow of thy
hands and that thou wilt not be drunk; but I
know thou art no tall fellow of thy hands and
190 that thou wilt be drunk. But I'll swear it, and I
would thou wouldst be a tall fellow of thy hands.

AUTOLYCUS. I will prove so, sir, to my power.

CLOWN. Aye, by any means prove a tall fellow. If I
do not wonder how thou darest venture to be
195 drunk, not being a tall fellow, trust me not.
Hark! The kings and the princes, our kindred,
are going to see the queen's picture.° Come, follow us. We'll be thy good masters.   [*Exeunt*]

SCENE iii
A chapel in PAULINA'S *house.*

[*Enter* LEONTES, POLIXENES, FLORIZEL, PERDITA,
CAMILLO, PAULINA, LORDS, *and* ATTENDANTS.]

LEONTES. O grave and good Paulina, the great
comfort
That I have had of thee!

PAULINA.   What, sovereign sir,
I did not well, I meant well. All my services
You have paid home. But that you have vouch-
saf'd,°
With your crown'd brother and these your con-
tracted
5   Heirs of your kingdoms, my poor house to visit,
It is a surplus of your grace which never
My life may last to answer.

LEONTES.   O Paulina,
We honor you with trouble, but we came
10   To see the statue of our queen. Your gallery
Have we pass'd through, not without much con-
tent
In many singularities,° but we saw not
That which my daughter came to look upon,
The statue of her mother.

PAULINA.   As she liv'd peerless,
So her dead likeness, I do well believe,   15
Excels whatever yet you look'd upon
Or hand of man hath done; therefore I keep it
Lonely, apart. But here it is. Prepare
To see the life as lively mock'd° as ever
Still sleep mock'd death. Behold, and say 'tis
well.   20
[PAULINA *draws a curtain, and discovers* HERMIONE
standing like a statue.]
I like your silence; it the more shows off
Your wonder. But yet speak; first, you, my liege.
Comes it not something near?

LEONTES.   Her natural posture!
Chide me, dear stone, that I may say indeed
Thou art Hermione; or rather, thou art she   25
In thy not chiding, for she was as tender
As infancy and grace. But yet, Paulina,
Hermione was not so much wrinkled, nothing
So aged as this seems.

POLIXENES.   O, not by much.

PAULINA. So much the more our carver's excel-
lence,   30
Which lets go by some sixteen years and makes
her
As° she liv'd now.

LEONTES.   As now she might have done,
So much to my good comfort as it is
Now piercing to my soul. O, thus she stood,
Even with such life of majesty, warm life,   35
As now it coldly stands, when first I woo'd her!
I am asham'd. Does not the stone rebuke me
For being more stone than it? O royal piece,
There's magic in thy majesty, which has
My evils conjur'd to remembrance, and   40
From thy admiring° daughter took the spirits,
Standing like stone with thee.

PERDITA.   And give me leave—
And do not say 'tis superstition—that
I kneel and then implore her blessing. Lady,
Dear queen, that ended when I but began,   45
Give me that hand of yours to kiss.

PAULINA.   O, patience!
The statue is but newly fix'd,° the color's
Not dry.

CAMILLO. My lord, your sorrow was too sore laid
on,
Which sixteen winters cannot blow away,   50
So many summers dry. Scarce any joy
Did ever so long live, no sorrow
But kill'd itself much sooner.

---

boors peasants   *franklins* farmers
tall . . . hands brave man of action
picture i.e., statue
vouchsaf'd granted   *singularities* rarities

mock'd imitated   *As* as if
admiring wondering   *fix'd* painted

POLIXENES.   Dear my brother,
  Let him that was the cause of this have power
55 To take off so much grief from you as he
  Will piece up° in himself.
PAULINA.   Indeed, my lord,
  If I had thought the sight of my poor image
  Would thus have wrought° you—for the stone is
    mine—
  I'd not have show'd it.
LEONTES.   Do not draw the curtain.
PAULINA. No longer shall you gaze on't, lest your
60   fancy
  May think anon it moves.
LEONTES.   Let be, let be.
  Would I were dead, but that, methinks, al-
    ready—
  What was he that did make it? See, my lord,
  Would you not deem it breath'd? And that those
    veins
  Did verily bear blood?
65 POLIXENES.   Masterly done.
  The very life seems warm upon her lip.
LEONTES. The fixure° of her eye has motion in't,
  As° we are mock'd with art.
PAULINA.   I'll draw the curtain.
  My lord's almost so far transported that
  He'll think anon it lives.
70 LEONTES.   O sweet Paulina,
  Make me to think so twenty years together!
  No settled senses of the world can match
  The pleasure of that madness. Let't alone.
PAULINA. I am sorry, sir, I have thus far stirr'd you.
    But
  I could afflict you farther.
75 LEONTES.   Do, Paulina,
  For this affliction has a taste as sweet
  As any cordial comfort. Still, methinks,
  There is an air comes from her. What fine chisel
  Could ever yet cut breath? Let no man mock me,
  For I will kiss her.
80 PAULINA.   Good my lord, forbear.
  The ruddiness upon her lip is wet;
  You'll mar it if you kiss it, stain your own
  With oily painting. Shall I draw the curtain?
LEONTES. No, not these twenty years.
PERDITA.   So long could I
  Stand by, a looker on.
85 PAULINA.   Either forbear,
  Quit presently° the chapel, or resolve you
  For more amazement. If you can behold it,
  I'll make the statue move indeed, descend,

piece up make up   wrought moved
fixure fixed gaze   As as if
presently immediately

And take you by the hand. But then you'll
  think,
  Which I protest against, I am assisted   90
  By wicked powers.
LEONTES.   What you can make her do,
  I am content to look on; what to speak,
  I am content to hear; for 'tis as easy
  To make her speak as move.
PAULINA.   It is requir'd
  You do awake your faith. Then all stand still. 95
  Or those that think it is unlawful business
  I am about, let them depart.
LEONTES.   Proceed.
  No foot shall stir.
PAULINA.   Music, awake her; strike!
                                    [Music.]
  'Tis time; descend; be stone no more; approach;
  Strike all that look upon with marvel. Come,   100
  I'll fill your grave up. Stir, nay, come away,
  Bequeath to death your numbness, for from
    him
  Dear life redeems you. You perceive she stirs.
                        [HERMIONE comes down.]
  Start not; her actions shall be holy as
  You hear my spell is lawful. Do not shun her   105
  Until you see her die again, for then
  You kill her double. Nay, present your hand.
  When she was young you woo'd her; now in age
  Is she become the suitor?
LEONTES.   O, she's warm!
  If this be magic, let it be an art   110
  Lawful as eating.
POLIXENES.   She embraces him.
CAMILLO. She hangs about his neck.
  If she pertain to life let her speak too.
POLIXENES. Aye, and make't manifest where she
    has liv'd,
  Or how stolen from the dead.
PAULINA.   That she is living, 115
  Were it but told you, should be hooted at
  Like an old tale. But it appears she lives,
  Though yet she speak not. Mark a little while.
  Please you to interpose, fair madam. Kneel
  And pray your mother's blessing. Turn, good
    lady,   120
  Our Perdita is found.
HERMIONE.   You gods, look down,
  And from your sacred vials pour your graces
  Upon my daughter's head! Tell me, mine own,
  Where hast thou been preserv'd? Where liv'd?
    How found
  Thy father's court? For thou shalt hear that I, 125
  Knowing by Paulina that the oracle
  Gave hope thou wast in being, have preserv'd
  Myself to see the issue.

PAULINA.   There's time enough for that,
Lest they desire upon this push° to trouble
130 Your joys with like relation. Go together,
You precious winners all; your exultation
Partake to every one. I, an old turtle,°
Will wing me to some wither'd bough and there
My mate, that's never to be found again,
Lament till I am lost.
135 LEONTES.   O, peace, Paulina!
Thou shouldst a husband take by my consent,
As I by thine a wife: this is a match,
And made between's by vows. Thou hast found
mine,
But how is to be question'd, for I saw her,
140 As I thought, dead, and have in vain said many
A prayer upon her grave. I'll not seek far—
For him, I partly know his mind—to find thee

An honorable husband. Come, Camillo,
And take her by the hand whose worth and
honesty
Is richly noted and here justified   145
By us, a pair of kings. Let's from this place.
What! Look upon my brother. Both your par-
dons
That e'er I put between your holy looks
My ill suspicion. This your son-in-law,
And son unto the king, whom heavens directing 150
Is troth-plight to your daughter. Good Paulina,
Lead us from hence, where we may leisurely
Each one demand and answer to his part
Perform'd in this wide gap of time since first
We were dissever'd. Hastily lead away.   155

                                [*Exeunt*]

upon this push   on top of this excitement
turtle   turtledove

AFTERWORD

With the English chronicle plays, romantic comedies, "dark comedies," and tragedies behind him, Shakespeare turned finally to a species of drama that owes elements to all the preceding genres but that is unmistakably unique, profoundly different from anything that he had written before, and, though clearly adapted to the dramatic fashion currently being exploited by his younger contemporaries, markedly distinguishable from their productions also.

Pericles, in 1608, inaugurated Shakespeare's final period; it was followed in yearly succession by *Cymbeline, The Winter's Tale,* and *The Tempest.* The four plays are appropriately classified as comedies, in that all end happily; but they are frequently identified somewhat more specifically as "dramatic romances," or, along with the earlier group of "dark" comedies, as "tragi-comedies." Like the plays of this earlier group (*All's Well That Ends Well, Measure for Measure,* and *Troilus and Cressida*) all are potentially tragic, narrowly skirt disaster, and predominantly appeal to emotions not usually associated with comedy, though comic moments also abound in them.

Like the earlier romantic comedies, the dramatic romances deal in the perennially attractive commodities of youth, love, and beauty. Though not, as in the romantic comedies, the be-all and end-all of the drama, a love story is an integral part of each, and there are lovers as young and splendid in these latest works as any among those who populate Shakespeare's early plays, when the dramatist himself was young. The lovers of *The Tempest*, Ferdinand and Miranda, are, like Romeo and Juliet, spellbound at first meeting: "At the first sight," says Prospero, "They have chang'd eyes." Ferdinand and Miranda are the most famous couple among the lovers of the dramatic romances, and deserve to be; but they are no more resplendent than the Prince and Princess of *The Winter's Tale*, Florizel and Perdita, who share moments when they shine like stars.

But in the dramatic romances, and not in the romantic comedies, the older generation figures as prominently as the younger. True, in *As You Like It*, both Rosalind and Celia have fathers, the rival dukes whose affairs affect the careers of their children. Yet essentially the stories of the romantic comedies are the stories of the young, wherein parents, if they are allowed to show at all, appear only incidentally. On the other hand, in the dramatic romances the parents' affairs are important too; they share at least equal billing, and sometimes they even predominate. *Pericles* is essentially the story of Pericles, the father; and the story of the daughter, Marina, is but one of the trials by which he is beset. *Cymbeline* again swings the scale to children, for Imogen, the daughter, is central, and the unhappy relations of her father and stepmother are only causal. But *The Winter's Tale* is essentially the story of Leontes and Hermione—parents—to whose bitter experience the romance of Florizel and Perdita is at best corollary. As for *The Tempest*, it is centrally Prospero, the father, by whose high art, ultimately, the joyous union of the young lovers is effected.

Thus the prevailing theme of the dramatic romances is not young love only, but parents and children. It is also separation and reconciliation: in *Pericles*, the father is separated from both his wife and his daughter, but regains them at the end. In *Cymbeline* father, daughter, son-in-law—all are estranged until the fifth act, when they are happily rejoined. In *The Winter's Tale* father and mother are separated, both are separated from their daughter, the Prince and his father are estranged, and all are miraculously reconciled at last. In *The Tempest* Prospero is cast out of his dukedom, the usurper is separated from his son, but ultimately the union achieved is richer than that which had been lost. In all the romances, what was once lost by the older generation is revived, restored, and enriched by the younger. Life, in short, by some all-preserving force, is renewed and carries on. "Now bless thyself," says the old Shepherd of *The Winter's Tale* to his son, "Thou met'st with things dying, I with things newborn." The old generation and the new, separation and reconciliation, rebirth, regeneration: these are the prevailing concerns of the four dramatic romances.

None of the romances better exemplifies the characteristic qualities of all than does *The Winter's Tale*. Yet it is a play that has often been criticized for inaccuracies, anachronisms, lack of motivation, improbability. Ben Jonson, though he loved Shakespeare "this side Idolatry, as much as any," lampooned the attribution of a seacoast to Bohemia, "wher ther is no Sea neer by some 100 miles." Dr. Johnson found the play entertaining "with all its absurdities." In between these two, Pope, editing the play, doubted that it could be Shakespeare's because it was so filled with mistakes. But Hazlitt, a century later, settled that issue: "These slips or blemishes do not prove it not to be Shakespeare's; for he was as likely to fall into them as any body." And of course he was, and never more appropriately, or at least excusably, than in *The Winter's Tale*, wherein errors at the level of mundane fact are even less relevant to the work as a work of art than is the famous error of John Keats in his sonnet, when he has "stout Cortez," not Balboa, gazing down upon the Pacific. The seacoast of Bohemia is not Shakespeare's only factual mishap in *The Winter's Tale*: Perdita, a child of sixteen years spent in Bohemia, speaks of playing "as I have seen them do/ In Whitsun pastorals"—British festivals of later date. And sharp Autolycus—the only character on whose comic supremacy classical, romantic, and modern critics agree—speaks as casually of "puritans" as if they were as well known to medieval Bohemians as to seventeenth-century Englishmen.

More pertinently, critics have sometimes attacked Leontes' sudden fit of jealousy as unmotivated and unfounded, hence unconvincing and improbable. And of course none of us can deny that Leontes' jealous lunacy erupts without provocation: Hermione, standing in full view of husband and court, openly entreats Polixenes to remain in Sicilia yet another month, even as Leontes had instructed her. Her sole fault, and Leontes' sole evidence of "infidelity," is that her plea succeeds where his had failed. Not only the groundlessness but also the suddenness of Leontes' fit is startling: within five minutes of playing time onstage, the jovial king is transformed to an utter madman. Obsession seizes him without warning either to himself, his fellow actors on the stage, or spectators in the audience. Even old King Lear's raving fury when Cordelia crosses him flares less abruptly and more predictably. Possibly those critics are justified who have questioned the dramatic verisimilitude of this representation of jealousy.

But lest we prove ourselves as guilty as Leontes of making a too sudden and irrational judgment we should pause for a moment to consider what manner of dramatic piece we are confronted with in *The Winter's Tale*. It is not, after all, a chronicle play, a grave and proper tragedy, or even a romantic comedy; it is something else, a genre of different character, rightly demanding to be considered on its own terms. And these terms are unlike any that Shakespeare had previously set, at least until *Pericles*, the first of these strange plays we call dramatic romances. For them all, *strange* is a key word.

Early in Act II, young Prince Mamillius converses with his mother:

> HERMIONE. Come, sir, now
>   I am for you again. Pray you, sit by us
>   And tell's a tale.
> MAMILLIUS. Merry or sad shall't be?
> HERMIONE. As merry as you will.
> MAMILLIUS. A sad tale's best for winter. I have one
>   Of sprites and goblins.

But Mamillius gets no farther in his tale than the beginning: "There was a man . . . dwelt by a churchyard." Here Leontes enters, raving with groundless jealousy, charges his queen with adultery, and cries, "Away with her to prison." With no warning, king, queen, prince, royal visitor, and the Sicilian court are caught up in a nightmarish action: the "winter's tale" has begun, perhaps just such a tale as Mamillius was about to tell.

Leontes is not a man in "real life," or even a character in a play the function of which is to make make everything as plausible as it is in real life. He is a figure in an "old tale," where, if he acted like a commonplace man, he would be grotesquely out of accord with events in this particular dramatic world in which nothing is commonplace. For *The Winter's Tale* is truly a wild play, Shakespeare's wildest, and Shakespeare's plays are all, if the truth must be told, among the wildest in the world, never populated with commonplace people engaged in commonplace activities in a stable milieu. If there were a better term for them than *wild*, it must be the modern *far out*. (Even his lone realistic domestic comedy, *The Merry Wives of Windsor*, set in a community of established middle-class English society, where, if ever, we might expect stodgy citizens and well-ordered events, erupts soon in a wonderful kind of madness: the suspicious husband, Ford, becomes nearly as incoherent as Leontes; the wives are fantastically inventive and bear twinkles in their eyes; the romance of the hero, Fenton, and the heroine, "sweet Anne Page," touches wild extremes and concludes with a bizarre elopement; and the whole frenzy ends with a swirl of satyrs, fairies, ouphes, and elves dancing about Sir John Falstaff, wearing a buck's head, in the dead of night at "Herne's Oak" in Windsor Forest. If *The Merry Wives* represents Shakespeare's most commonplace exhibition, what, indeed, is *The Winter's Tale*, his wildest? In between the extremes are the romantic comedies, with their Illyrias, their fabulous Belmonts equipped with gold, silver, and lead caskets, their Forests of Arden, their Oberons and Titanias; the tragedies, with their air-drawn daggers, ghosts, witches, magic potions, blackamoors, and Cleopatras. To say that *The Winter's Tale* exhibits the Shakespearean imagination in its most unbridled surge is therefore to say much.)

At the end of Act III, Antigonus, ordered to abandon a newborn baby girl in "some remote and desert place," lays down the Princess Perdita, "the lost one," and thereafter makes what is assuredly the most extraordinary exit in Shakespeare: "Exit, pursued by a bear." Then follows the Clown's account of the wild scene at the seashore, where simultaneously the mariners who had brought Antigonus to Bohemia, and Antigonus himself, meet their several dooms:

> . . . now the ship boring the moon with her main-mast, and anon swallowed with yest and froth, as you'd thrust a cork into a hogshead. And then for the land-service, to see how the bear tore out his shoulder-bone; how he cried to me for help and said his name was Antigonus, gentleman. But to make an end of the ship, to see how the sea flap-dragoned it; but, first, how the poor souls roared, and the sea mocked them; and how the poor gentleman roared and the bear mocked him, both roaring louder than the sea or weather.

Meanwhile, the old Shepherd has found "a barne; a very pretty barne," and has taken it up "for pity." Thus a small spark of the old life survives to link the generations.

Of such stuff is the whole drama made, and Leontes' sudden fit of madness, which ends as abruptly as it began, is of a kind with all the rest. In Act V, some sixteen years after Perdita is placed on the seashore of Bohemia, as the truths of what has occurred begin to come to light, the participants themselves come to recognize that they have lived an "old tale." Says the Second Gentleman, "This news which is called true is so like an old tale that the verity of it is in strong suspicion." The Second Gentleman's wonder grows with each new turn of news: "What, pray you, became of Antigonus, that carried hence the child?" "Like an old tale still," replies the Third Gentleman, "which will have matter to rehearse though credit be asleep and not an ear open." And, finally, when the very last one of the strange and wonderful secrets has been divulged, Paulina, who has worked marvels of her own during those sixteen years, sums up the universal astonishment that greets the proof of Hermione's survival:

> That she is living,
> Were it but told you, should be hooted at
> Like an old tale.

If the wild rage of Leontes and the bizarre death of Antigonus are extremes in their kind, so are the qualities that distinguish the two heroines, Hermione and Perdita. All Shakespeare's heroines—from the gentle Julia and the exquisite Silvia ("Who is Silvia, What is she?") of *The Two Gentlemen of Verona*, down through Hermia and Helena of *A Midsummer Night's Dream* ("Two lovely berries molded on one stem") to Bassanio's Portia, Orlando's Rosalind, Orsino's Viola, and yet on to the matchless princesses of the first two romances, Marina of *Pericles* and Imogen of *Cymbeline*—are brilliant and beautiful women, no less splendid within than without. Not one of them falls short of the ultimate adjective, *peerless*. Yet by some rare magic that perhaps even he could never quite master before, Shakespeare manages to elevate both Hermione and Perdita, mother and daughter, to a single pinnacle that tops all others. "When you do dance," says Florizel to Perdita,

> I wish you
> A wave o' the sea, that you might ever do
> Nothing but that; move still, still so,
> And own no other function.

These are a lover's words, of course, and might deserve to be discounted; but here speaks a gentleman of Leontes' court who has just glimpsed Perdita for the first time:

> Women will love her that she is a woman
> More worth than any man; men, that she is
> The rarest of all women.

But even this is only a testimonial at second hand; the best evidence of Perdita's quality is that provided by herself, in all her language and actions. Heredity and environment have shaped in her a flawless blend of princess and unsophisticated shepherdess, simultaneously gorgeous and good as Nature herself. Perdita is at her transcendent best in the famous sheep-shearing festival of Act IV—itself, for comedy, pathos, and spectacle, one of the richest scenes in all Shakespeare.

Hermione, on the other hand, is no shepherdess, but is purely royal. As with Perdita, praise spoken of her, extravagant as it is—and Shakespeare never wrote praise more extravagant—touches only the surface. We best know her by her own utterances, as when, for example, she confronts Leontes' insane charges of infidelity with a degree of dignity and forbearance that might be the very emblem of queenliness and that, were he not totally mad, should instantly overwhelm and silence him utterly. In the middle of the present century, an American critic observed that the trouble with *The Winter's Tale* is "that Hermione talks too much." But this was a critic who somehow totally missed the spirit of the play and of the genre.

For Perdita and Hermione are creatures of romance, as is the instantly mad Leontes; the female titan, Paulina, who "tells off" the mad king as if he were a naughty boy tearing butterflies; the fairy-tale prince, Florizel, beside whom Prince Charming had as well remained a frog; Camillo, the loyal retainer whose loyalty is exceeded only by his resourcefulness; Autolycus, a rogue to end all rogues; and Polixenes, whose surge of irrational fury that shatters the idyllic glory of the sheep-shearing parallels the sudden storm with which Leontes precipitated this "winter's tale."

Finally, as "right" for an "old tale" as are the characters and the strange and wonderful events of the plot is the poetic language of the play. We do not hear its characteristic tones immediately; the opening scene is tortured with linguistic gymnastics as hosts and guests vie in exchanging compliments in courtly terms. The dominant notes start when the first notion of Hermione's infidelity taints Leontes' wits. The king's obsession expresses itself in fits and starts, incoherent phrases, violent images that sting, shock, or disgust:

> Is whispering?
> Is leaning cheek to cheek? Is meeting noses?
> Kissing with inside lip? . . . Horsing foot on foot?
> Skulking in corners? Wishing clocks more swift?
> Hours, minutes? Noon, midnight? And all eyes
> Blind with the pin and web but theirs, theirs only,
> That would unseen be wicked?

Leontes' utterances erupt in sudden, ugly figures; thus, when he urges Camillo to murder Polixenes: "Do 't and thou hast the one half of my heart;/ Do 't not, thou split'st thine own." And to the attendants who are reluctant to credit his false suspicion: "You smell this business with a sense as cold/ As is a dead man's nose." Out of his madness, as he describes the feelings of a husband who has had proof of his wife's guilt, comes one of the most vivid images in Shakespeare:

> There may be in the cup
> A spider steep'd, and one may drink, depart,
> And yet partake no venom, for his knowledge
> Is not infected. But if one present
> Th' abhorr'd ingredient to his eye, make known
> How he hath drunk, he cracks his gorge, his sides
> With violent hefts. I have drunk, and seen the spider.

Leontes' extremes of expression are matched by those of Florizel and others in their extravagant praise of Perdita, by the absolute oaths of Camillo and Polixenes, by the ungoverned and ungovernable tongue of Paulina. Excepting the momentary lull during the sheep-shearing idyll, nothing is mild or moderate in this wild tale.

Thus all the principal elements of the drama—character, incident, language—harmonize within their frame. What Shakespeare early establishes is the illusionary world of an "old tale," and once we recognize the fact and accept the terms of this world, we find ourselves committed to accept what goes on there. *The Winter's Tale* proffers a strange new reality wherein the incredible grows credible as we surrender to its spell. On the stage, well performed, it provides an experience that is immediately fascinating and permanently haunting. Hazlitt rightly recognized the work as "one of the best-acting of our author's plays."

A NOTE ON THE COMPOSITION OF THE PLAY

One of Shakespeare's last plays, *The Winter's Tale* was written in 1610–1611 and performed in 1611. It was first published in the Folio of 1623. Shakespeare's source was Robert Greene's romance, *Pandosto or the Triumph of Time* (1588), reprinted in 1607 as *Dorasmus and Fawnia.*

Sonnets

1

From fairest creatures we desire increase,
That thereby beauty's rose° might never die,
But as the riper should by time decease,
His tender heir might bear his memory.
5 But thou, contracted° to thine own bright eyes,
Feed'st thy light's flame with self-substantial° fuel,
Making a famine where abundance lies,
Thyself thy foe, to thy sweet self too cruel.
Thou that art now the world's fresh ornament
10 And only herald to the gaudy spring,
Within thine own bud buriest thy content°
And, tender churl, mak'st waste in niggarding.
    Pity the world, or else this glutton be,
    To eat the world's due, by the grave and thee.°

rose i.e., perfection   contracted betrothed
self-substantial of your own substance
content that which is contained—offspring, the copy of
   yourself
To eat . . . thee i.e., by dying without offspring rob the
   future of its due

2

When forty winters shall besiege thy brow
And dig deep trenches in thy beauty's field,
Thy youth's proud livery,° so gaz'd on now,
Will be a tatter'd weed,° of small worth held.
5 Then being ask'd where all thy beauty lies,
Where all the treasure of thy lusty days,
To say within thine own deep-sunken eyes
Were an all-eating shame and thriftless praise.
How much more praise deserv'd thy beauty's use°
10 If thou couldst answer, "This fair child of mine
Shall sum my count° and make my old excuse,"°
Proving his beauty by succession thine!
    This were to be new-made when thou art old,
    And see thy blood warm when thou feel'st it
    cold.

youth's . . . livery i.e., the garment of youthfulness
tatter'd weed rag   use investment, profit
count account   old excuse excuse for my old age

3

Look in thy glass and tell the face thou viewest
Now is the time that face should form another,
Whose fresh repair° if now thou not renewest,
Thou dost beguile the world, unbless° some
   mother.
For where is she so fair whose unear'd° womb   5
Disdains the tillage of thy husbandry?
Or who is he so fond° will be the tomb
Of his self-love, to stop posterity?
Thou art thy mother's glass,° and she in thee
Calls back the lovely April of her prime.   10
So thou through windows of thine age shalt see,
Despite of wrinkles, this thy golden time.
    But if thou live remember'd not to be,°
    Die single, and thine image dies with thee.

fresh repair freshness   unbless leave unblessed
unear'd untilled   fond foolish
glass reflection
remember'd . . . be not to be remembered

4

Unthrifty loveliness, why dost thou spend
Upon thyself thy beauty's legacy?°
Nature's bequest gives nothing, but doth lend,
And being frank, she lends to those are free.°
Then, beauteous niggard, why dost thou abuse   5
The bounteous largess given thee to give?
Profitless usurer, why dost thou use
So great a sum of sums, yet canst not live?
For having traffic with thyself alone,
Thou of thyself thy sweet self dost deceive.   10
Then how, when nature calls thee to be gone,
What acceptable audit canst thou leave?
    Thy unus'd beauty must be tomb'd with thee,
    Which, used, lives th' executor to be.

beauty's legacy the beauty that you inherited
frank . . . free generous . . . generous

5

Those hours that with gentle work did frame
The lovely gaze where every eye doth dwell
Will play the tyrants to the very same
And that unfair° which fairly doth excel.
5 For never-resting time leads summer on
To hideous winter and confounds° him there,
Sap check'd with frost and lusty leaves quite gone,
Beauty o'ersnow'd and bareness everywhere.
Then, were not summer's distillation° left,
10 A liquid prisoner pent in walls of glass,
Beauty's effect with beauty were bereft,°
Nor it, nor no remembrance what it was.°
    But flowers distill'd, though they with winter
      meet,
    Leese° but their show; their substance still lives
      sweet.

unfair make no longer fair   *confounds* destroys
summer's distillation perfume derived from summer's
    flowers
Beauty's . . . bereft the product of beauty (perfume) as well
    as beauty itself would be lost
Nor . . . was neither it nor remembrance of it would
    remain
Leese lose

6

Then let not winter's ragged hand deface
In thee thy summer ere thou be distill'd.
Make sweet some vial; treasure thou some place
With beauty's treasure ere it be self-kill'd.
5 That use is not forbidden usury
Which happies those that pay the willing loan;
That's for thyself to breed another thee,
Or ten times happier, be it ten for one;
Ten times thyself were happier than thou art
10 If ten of thine ten times refigur'd° thee.
Then what could death do if thou shouldst depart,
Leaving thee living in posterity?
    Be not self-will'd, for thou art much too fair
    To be death's conquest and make worms thine
      heir.

refigur'd reincarnated

7

Lo, in the orient when the gracious light°
Lifts up his burning head, each under-eye°
Doth homage to his new-appearing sight,
Serving with looks his sacred majesty;
And having climb'd the steep-up heavenly hill,   5
Resembling strong youth in his middle age,
Yet mortal looks adore his beauty still,
Attending on his golden pilgrimage.
But when from highmost pitch, with weary car,°
Like feeble age, he reeleth from the day,   10
The eyes, 'fore duteous, now converted are
From his low tract,° and look another way.
    So thou, thyself out-going° in thy noon,
    Unlook'd on diest unless thou get a son.

gracious light the sun   *under-eye* mortal eye
car i.e., the chariot of the sun
tract track, course   *out-going* declining

8

Music to hear,° why hear'st thou music sadly?
Sweets with sweets war not, joy delights in joy.
Why lov'st thou that which thou receiv'st not
    gladly,
Or else receiv'st with pleasure thine annoy?
If the true concord of well tuned sounds,   5
By unions married, do offend thine ear,
They do but sweetly chide thee who confounds°
In singleness the parts that thou shouldst bear.
Mark how one string, sweet husband to another,
Strikes each in each by mutual ordering,°   10
Resembling sire and child and happy mother,
Who, all in one, one pleasing note do sing,
    Whose speechless song, being many, seeming
      one,
    Sings this to thee: "Thou single wilt prove
      none."

Music to hear you whose sound is music
confounds destroys
mutual ordering i.e., harmony

9

Is it for fear to wet a widow's eye
That thou consum'st thyself in single life?
Ah, if thou issueless shalt hap to die,
The world will wail thee like a makeless° wife.
The world will be thy widow and still weep   5
That thou no form of thee hast left behind
When every private widow well may keep
By children's eyes her husband's shape in mind.
Look, what an unthrift in the world doth spend
Shifts but his° place, for still the world enjoys it;   10
But beauty's waste hath in the world an end,

And kept unus'd, the user so destroys it.
  No love toward others in that bosom sits
  That on himself such murd'rous shame com-
    mits.

makeless mateless   *his* its

10

For shame! Deny that thou bear'st love to any,
Who for thyself art so unprovident.
Grant, if thou wilt, thou art belov'd of many,
But that thou none lov'st is most evident;
5 For thou art so possess'd with murd'rous hate
That 'gainst thyself thou stick'st not° to conspire,
Seeking that beauteous roof° to ruinate
Which to repair should be thy chief desire.
O, change thy thought, that I may change my
    mind!
10 Shall hate be fairer lodg'd than gentle love?
Be, as thy presence is, gracious and kind,
Or to thyself at least kind-hearted prove.
    Make thee another self, for love of me,
    That beauty still may live in thine or thee.

stick'st not do not object   *roof* i.e., your body

11

As fast as thou shalt wane, so fast thou grow'st
In one of thine from that which thou depart'st,
And that fresh blood which youngly thou be-
    stow'st
Thou mayst call thine when thou from youth
    convert'st.°
5 Herein lives wisdom, beauty, and increase;
Without this, folly, age, and cold decay.
If all were minded so, the times should cease
And threescore year would make the world away.
Let those whom Nature hath not made for store,
10 Harsh, featureless, and rude, barrenly perish.
Look, whom she best endow'd she gave the more,
Which bounteous gift thou shouldst in bounty
    cherish.
    She carv'd thee for her seal,° and meant thereby
    Thou shouldst print more, not let that copy die.

convert'st change   *seal* stamp

12

When I do count the clock that tells the time
And see the brave° day sunk in hideous night;
When I behold the violet past prime
And sable° curls all silver'd o'er with white;
When lofty trees I see barren of leaves,   5
Which erst from heat did canopy the herd,
And summer's green all girded up in sheaves,
Borne on the bier with white and bristly beard,
Then of thy beauty do I question make°
That thou among the wastes of time must go,   10
Since sweets and beauties do themselves forsake
And die as fast as they see others grow.
    And nothing 'gainst Time's scythe can make
        defense
    Save breed,° to brave° him when he takes thee
        hence.

brave fine   *sable* black
question make make a subject of though
breed offspring   *brave* defy

13

O that you were yourself! But, love, you are
No longer yours than you yourself here live.
Against° this coming end you should prepare,
And your sweet semblance to some other give.
So should that beauty which you hold in lease   5
Find no determination;° then you were
Yourself again, after yourself's decease,
When your sweet issue your sweet form should
    bear.
Who lets so fair a house fall to decay,
Which husbandry° in honor might uphold   10
Against the stormy gusts of winter's day
And barren rage of death's eternal cold?
    O, none but unthrifts. Dear my love, you know
    You had a father; let your son say so.

Against in anticipation of
Find no determination not come to an end
husbandry thrift; but also, marriage

14

Not from the stars do I my judgment pluck,
And yet methinks I have astronomy,°
But not to tell of good or evil luck,
Of plagues, of dearths, or seasons' quality;

5 Nor can I fortune to brief minutes tell,
  Pointing° to each his° thunder, rain, and wind,
  Or say with princes if it shall go well,
  By oft predict° that I in heaven find.
  But from thine eyes my knowledge I derive,
10 And, constant stars, in them I read such art°
  As° truth and beauty shall together thrive,
  If from thyself to store thou wouldst convert.°
    Or else of thee this I prognosticate:
    Thy end is truth's and beauty's doom and date.

have astronomy know astrology
Pointing appointing   *his* its
oft predict numerous portents   *art* knowledge
As as that
If . . . convert i.e., if you would pass yourself along by
  means of progeny

15

When I consider everything that grows
Holds in° perfection but a little moment,
That this huge stage presenteth naught but shows
Whereon the stars in secret influence comment;°
5 When I perceive that men as plants increase,
Cheered and check'd even by the self-same sky,
Vaunt in their youthful sap, at height decrease,
And wear their brave° state out of memory;
Then the conceit° of this inconstant stay
10 Sets you most rich in youth before my sight,
Where wasteful Time debateth with Decay
To change your day of youth to sullied night.
    And all in war with Time for love of you,
    As he takes from you I engraft you new.°

Holds in maintains its
in . . . comment silently influence   *brave* fine
conceit idea
engraft you new renew your youth (through verse)

16

But wherefore do not you a mightier way
Make war upon this bloody tyrant Time
And fortify yourself in your decay
With means more blessed than my barren rhyme?
5 Now stand you on the top of happy hours,
And many maiden gardens, yet unset,
With virtuous wish would bear your living
    flowers
Much liker than your painted counterfeit.°
So should the lines of life° that life repair

Which this time's pencil,° or my pupil pen,   10
Neither in inward worth nor outward fair
Can make you live yourself in eyes of men.
    To give away yourself keeps yourself still,
    And you must live drawn by your own sweet
     skill.

painted counterfeit i.e., as drawn by painter or poet
lines of life i.e., descendants
this . . . pencil i.e., of the contemporary artist

17

Who will believe my verse in time to come
If it were fill'd with your most high deserts?
Though yet, heaven knows, it is but as a tomb
Which hides your life and shows not half your
    parts.
If I could write the beauty of your eyes   5
And in fresh numbers° number all your graces,
The age to come would say "This poet lies;
Such heavenly touches ne'er touch'd earthly
    faces."
So should my papers, yellow'd with their age,
Be scorn'd like old men of less truth than tongue,   10
And your true rights be term'd a poet's rage
And stretched meter° of an antique song.
    But were some child of yours alive that time,
    You should live twice, in it and in my rhyme.

numbers meters   *stretched meter* exaggeration

18

Shall I compare thee to a summer's day?
Thou art more lovely and more temperate.
Rough winds do shake the darling buds of May,
And summer's lease hath all too short a date.
Sometime too hot the eye of heaven shines,   5
And often is his gold complexion dimm'd;
And every fair from fair sometime declines,
By chance or nature's changing course untrimm'd.°
But thy eternal summer shall not fade,
Nor lose possession of that fair thou owest;°   10
Nor shall Death brag thou wander'st in his shade
When in eternal lines to time thou grow'st.
    So long as men can breathe or eyes can see,
    So long lives this, and this gives life to thee.

untrimm'd i.e., bereft of its beauties
owest possess, own

19

Devouring Time, blunt thou the lion's paws
And make the earth devour her own sweet brood;
Pluck the keen teeth from the fierce tiger's jaws,
And burn the long-liv'd phœnix° in her blood;
5 Make glad and sorry seasons as thou fleet'st,
And do whate'er thou wilt, swift-footed Time,
To the wide world and all her fading sweets.
But I forbid thee one most heinous crime:
O, carve not with thy hours my love's fair brow,
10 Nor draw no lines there with thine antique pen;
Him in thy course untainted do allow
For beauty's pattern to succeeding men.
     Yet do thy worst, old Time. Despite thy wrong,
     My love shall in my verse ever live young.

long-liv'd phoenix mythical bird that lives for five hundred
     years, is consumed by flames, and rises again from its
     own ashes

20

A woman's face with Nature's own hand painted
Hast thou, the master-mistress of my passion;
A woman's gentle heart, but not acquainted
With shifting change, as is false women's fashion;
5 An eye more bright than theirs, less false in
     rolling,°
Gilding the object whereupon it gazeth;
A man in hue, all hues in his controlling,°
Which steals men's eyes and women's souls
     amazeth.
And for a woman wert thou first created,
10 Till Nature, as she wrought thee, fell a-doting,
And by addition me of thee defeated
By adding one thing to my purpose nothing.
     But since she prick'd thee out° for women's
          pleasure,
     Mine be thy love, and thy love's use their
          treasure.

rolling roving
A man . . . controlling of manly complexion excelling
     all others
prick'd . . . out selected you (with obvious secondary
     meaning)

21

So is it not with me as with that Muse°
Stirr'd by a painted beauty to his verse,
Who heaven itself for ornament doth use

And every fair with his fair doth rehearse,°
Making a couplement of proud compare°   5
With sun and moon, with earth and sea's rich
     gems,
With April's first-born flowers and all things rare
That heaven's air in this huge rondure° hems.
O, let me, true in love, but truly write,
And then believe me, my love is as fair   10
As any mother's child, though not so bright
As those gold candles fix'd in heaven's air.
     Let them say more that like of hearsay well;
     I will not praise that° purpose not to sell.

Muse poet   *rehearse* compare
Making . . . compare joining together in exaggerated
     comparison
rondure orb (the earth)   *that* who

22

My glass shall not persuade me I am old
So long as youth and thou are of one date,
But when in thee time's furrows I behold,
Then look I death my days should expiate.°
For all that beauty that doth cover thee   5
Is but the seemly raiment of my heart,
Which in thy breast doth live, as thine in me.
How can I then be elder than thou art?
O, therefore, love, be of thyself so wary
As I, not for myself, but for thee will,   10
Bearing thy heart, which I will keep so chary°
As tender nurse her babe from faring ill.
     Presume not on thy heart when mine is slain;
     Thou gav'st me thine not to give back again.

Then . . . expiate then I look forward to death's ending
     my days
chary carefully

23

As an unperfect actor on the stage
Who with his fear is put besides his part,°
Or some fierce thing replete with too much rage
Whose strength's abundance weakens his own
     heart,
So I, for fear of trust, forget to say   5
The perfect ceremony of love's rite,°
And in mine own love's strength seem to decay,
O'ercharg'd with burthen of mine own love's
     might.
O let my books be then the eloquence
And dumb presagers° of my speaking breast,   10
Who plead for love and look for recompense

More than that tongue that more hath more
  express'd.
  O learn to read what silent love hath writ;
  To hear with eyes belongs to love's fine wit.

Who . . . part whose stage fright causes him to forget his
  lines
forget . . . rite fearing to trust myself, neglect to express
  my love
presagers interpreters

24

Mine eye hath play'd the painter and hath stell'd°
Thy beauty's form in table of my heart;
My body is the frame wherein 'tis held,
And perspective it is best painter's art.°
5 For through the painter° must you see his skill
To find where your true image pictur'd lies,
Which in my bosom's shop is hanging still
That hath his windows glazed with thine eyes.
Now see what good turns eyes for eyes have done:
10 Mine eyes have drawn thy shape, and thine for me
Are windows to my breast, wherethrough the sun
Delights to peep, to gaze therein on thee.
    Yet eyes this cunning want° to grace their art;
    They draw but what they see, know not the
    heart.

stell'd emplaced
perspective . . . art perspective (lent by the frame) is the
  best feature of the painter's art
through the painter (here with literal meaning)
want lack

25

Let those who are in favor with their stars
Of public honor and proud titles boast,
Whilst I, whom fortune of such triumph bars,
Unlook'd for joy in that° I honor most.
5 Great princes' favorites their fair leaves spread
But as the marigold° at the sun's eye,
And in themselves their pride lies buried,
For at a frown they in their glory die.
The painful warrior famoused for fight,
10 After a thousand victories once foil'd,
Is from the book of honor razed quite,
And all the rest forgot for which he toil'd.
    Then happy I, that love and am belov'd
    Where I may not remove nor be remov'd.

Unlook'd . . . that unexpectedly enjoy that which
marigold which opens only while in sunlight

26

Lord of my love, to whom in vassalage
Thy merit hath my duty strongly knit,
To thee I send this written ambassage°
To witness duty, not to show my wit;
Duty so great, which wit so poor as mine   5
May make seem bare in wanting° words to show
  it,
But that I hope some good conceit of thine
In thy soul's thought, all naked, will bestow° it;
Till whatsoever star that guides my moving°
Points° on me graciously with fair aspect°   10
And puts apparel on my tatter'd loving
To show me worthy of thy sweet respect.
    Then may I dare to boast how I do love thee;
    Till then not show my head where thou mayst
    prove° me.

ambassage envoy   *wanting* lacking
bestow house, accommodate
guides my moving directs my destiny   *Points* shines
aspect influence   *prove* test

27

Weary with toil, I haste me to my bed,
The dear repose for limbs with travel tir'd;
But then begins a journey in my head
To work my mind when body's work's expir'd.
For then my thoughts, from far where I abide,   5
Intend a zealous pilgrimage to thee
And keep my drooping eyelids open wide,
Looking on darkness which the blind do see,
Save that my soul's imaginary° sight
Presents thy shadow° to my sightless view,   10
Which like a jewel hung in ghastly night
Makes black night beauteous and her old face
  new.
    Lo thus by day my limbs, by night my mind
    For thee and for myself no quiet find.

imaginary imaginative   *shadow* image

28

How can I then return in happy plight
That am debarr'd the benefit of rest
When day's oppression is not eas'd by night,
But day by night and night by day oppress'd?
And each, though enemies to either's reign,   5
Do in consent shake hands to torture me,

The one by toil, the other to complain
How far I toil, still farther off from thee.
I tell the day, to please him° thou art bright,
And dost him grace when clouds do blot the
10   heaven.
So flatter I the swart-complexion'd night:
When sparkling stars twire° not, thou gild'st the
          even.
    But day doth daily draw my sorrows longer,
    And night doth nightly make grief's strength
    seem stronger.

to . . . him   that it is to please him   *twire*   twinkle

29

When, in disgrace with fortune and men's eyes,
I all alone beweep my outcast state
And trouble deaf heaven with my bootless° cries
And look upon myself and curse my fate,
5   Wishing me like to one more rich in hope,
Featur'd like him, like him with friends possess'd
Desiring this man's art and that man's scope,
With what I most enjoy contented least,
Yet in these thoughts myself almost despising—
10 Haply° I think on thee, and then my state,
Like to the lark at break of day arising
From sullen earth, sings hymns at heaven's gate;
    For thy sweet love remember'd such wealth
    brings
    That then I scorn to change my state with
    kings.

bootless   useless   *Haply*   perhaps

30

When to the sessions° of sweet silent thought
I summon up remembrance of things past,
I sigh the lack of many a thing I sought,
And with old woes new wail my dear time's
          waste.
5   Then can I drown an eye unus'd to flow
For precious friends hid in death's dateless night,
And weep afresh love's long since cancell'd woe,
And moan th' expense of many a vanish'd sight.
Then can I grieve at grievances foregone,
10 And heavily from woe to woe tell o'er
The sad account of fore-bemoaned moan,
Which I new pay as if not paid before.
    But if the while I think on thee, dear friend,
    All losses are restor'd and sorrows end.

sessions   court sessions

31

Thy bosom is endeared with all hearts
Which I by lacking have supposed dead;
And there reigns love and all love's loving parts
And all those friends which I thought buried.
How many a holy and obsequious° tear   5
Hath dear religious° love stol'n from mine eye
As interest of the dead, which now appear
But things remov'd that hidden in thee lie!
Thou art the grave where buried love doth live,
Hung with the trophies of my lovers gone,   10
Who all their parts of me to thee did give;
That due of many now is thine alone.
    Their images I lov'd I view in thee,
    And thou, all they, hast all the all of me.

obsequious   mourning   *religious*   devoted

32

If thou survive my well-contented day
When that churl Death my bones with dust shall
          cover
And shalt by fortune once more re-survey
These poor rude lines of thy deceased lover,
Compare them with the bett'ring of the time,   5
And though they be outstripp'd by every pen,
Reserve them for my love, not for their rhyme,
Exceeded by the height of happier men.°
O then vouchsafe° me but this loving thought:
"Had my friend's Muse grown with this growing
          age,   10
A dearer birth than this his love had brought,
To march in ranks of better equipage.°
    But since he died and poets better prove,
    Theirs for their style I'll read, his for his love."

height . . . men   achievement of poets more gifted
vouchsafe   grant   *equipage*   furnishings

33

Full many a glorious morning have I seen
Flatter the mountain-tops with sovereign eye,
Kissing with golden face the meadows green,
Gilding pale streams with heavenly alchemy,
Anon permit the basest clouds to ride   5
With ugly rack° on his celestial face
And from the forlorn world his visage hide,
Stealing unseen to west with this disgrace.
Even so my sun one early morn did shine

10   With all-triumphant splendor on my brow;
     But, out, alack! He was but one hour mine;
     The region° cloud hath mask'd him from me now.
        Yet him for this my love no whit disdaineth;
        Suns of the world may stain° when heaven's sun
           staineth.

rack cloud mass   *region* i.e., of the upper air
stain be obscured, suffer disgrace

34

     Why didst thou promise such a beauteous day
     And make me travel forth without my cloak
     To let base clouds o'ertake me in my way,
     Hiding their bravery° in their rotten smoke?°
5   'Tis not enough that through the cloud thou break
     To dry the rain on my storm-beaten face,
     For no man well of such a salve can speak
     That heals the wound and cures not the disgrace,
     Nor can thy shame give physic to my grief;
10   Though thou repent, yet I have still the loss.
     Th' offender's sorrow lends but weak relief
     To him that bears the strong offense's cross.
        Ah, but those tears are pearl which thy love
           sheds,
        And they are rich and ransom all ill deeds.

bravery finery   *smoke* mist

35

     No more be griev'd at that which thou hast done:
     Roses have thorns, and silver fountains mud;
     Clouds and eclipses stain both moon and sun,
     And loathsome canker° lives in sweetest bud.
5   All men make faults, and even I in this,
     Authorizing thy trespass with compare,°
     Myself corrupting, salving thy amiss,
     Excusing thy sins more than thy sins are;
     For to thy sensual fault I bring in sense°—
10   Thy adverse party° is thy advocate—
     And 'gainst myself a lawful plea commence;
     Such civil war is in my love and hate
        That I an accessory needs must be
        To that sweet thief which sourly robs from me.

canker cankerworm
Authorizing . . . compare justifying your fault by using
   (the preceding) comparisons
sense reason, argument
adverse party i.e., I, the injured one

36

     Let me confess that we two must be twain,
     Although our undivided loves are one;
     So shall those blots that do with me remain,
     Without thy help, by me be borne alone.
5   In our two loves there is but one respect,°
     Though in our lives a separable spite,°
     Which though it alter not love's sole effect,°
     Yet doth it steal sweet hours from love's delight.
     I may not evermore acknowledge thee,
10   Lest my bewailed guilt should do thee shame,
     Nor thou with public kindness honor me,
     Unless thou take that honor from thy name.
        But do not so; I love thee in such sort,
        As thou being mine, mine is thy good report.

respect entity
separable spite separating malignity
sole effect unique character

37

     As a decrepit father takes delight
     To see his active child do deeds of youth,
     So I, made lame by fortune's dearest° spite,
     Take all my comfort of thy worth and truth.
5   For whether beauty, birth, or wealth, or wit,
     Or any of these all, or all, or more,
     Entitled in thy parts do crowned sit,°
     I make my love engrafted to° this store;
     So then I am not lame, poor, nor despis'd,
10   Whilst that this shadow doth such substance give
     That I in thy abundance am suffic'd
     And by a part of all thy glory live.
        Look, what is best, that best I wish in thee:
        This wish I have; then ten times happy me!

dearest most malicious
Entitled in . . . sit sits like a king among your qualities
engrafted to in addition to

38

     How can my Muse want subject to invent,°
     While thou dost breathe, that pour'st into my
        verse
     Thine own sweet argument,° too excellent
     For every vulgar paper to rehearse?
5   O give thyself the thanks if aught in me

Worthy perusal stand against thy sight;
For who's so dumb that cannot write to thee,
When thou thyself dost give invention° light?
Be thou the tenth Muse, ten times more in worth
10 Than those old nine which rhymers invocate;
And he that calls on thee, let him bring forth
Eternal numbers to outlive long date.
    If my slight Muse do please these curious days,
    The pain be mine, but thine shall be the praise.

want . . . invent lack poetic subject matter
argument substance   *invention* poetic invention

To bear love's wrong than hate's known injury.
    Lascivious grace, in whom all ill well shows,°
    Kill me with spites; yet we must not be foes.

loves mistresses
for . . . receiv'st because of love for me you take my
    mistress
for . . . usest because you use my mistress
By . . . refusest by sampling the fruits of the wedlock that
    you refuse
all my poverty i.e., my small having
Lascivious . . . shows you in whom even lasciviousness is
    becoming

39

O how thy worth with manners° may I sing
When thou art all the better part of me?
What can mine own praise to mine own self
        bring?
And what is 't but mine own when I praise thee?
5 Even for this° let us divided live,
And our dear love lose name of single one,
That by this separation I may give
That due to thee which thou deserv'st alone.
O absence, what a torment wouldst thou prove,
10 Were it not thy sour leisure gave sweet leave
To entertain the time with thoughts of love,
Which time and thoughts so sweetly doth deceive,°
    And that thou teachest how to make one twain
    By praising him here who doth hence remain!°

with manners graciously   *for this* therefore
Which . . . deceive love, which so sweetly beguiles time
    and thoughts
And that . . . remain i.e., absence teaches me to make one
    person of two by imagining (while praising him) the
    absent one to be present

40

Take all my loves,° my love, yea, take them all;
What hast thou then more than thou hadst before?
No love, my love, that thou mayst true love call;
All mine was thine before thou hadst this more.
Then, if for my love thou my love receiv'st,°
5 I cannot blame thee for my love thou usest;°
But yet be blam'd if thou thyself deceiv'st°
By wilful taste of what thyself refusest.°
I do forgive thy robbery, gentle thief,
Although thou steal thee all my poverty;°
10 And yet, love knows, it is a greater grief

41

Those pretty wrongs that liberty° commits
When I am sometime absent from thy heart,
Thy beauty and thy years full well befits,
For still° temptation follows where thou art.
Gentle° thou art, and therefore to be won;   5
Beauteous thou art, therefore to be assail'd.
And when a woman woos, what woman's son
Will sourly leave her till she have prevail'd?
Aye me! But yet thou mightst my seat° forbear,
And chide thy beauty and thy straying youth,   10
Who lead thee in their riot° even there
Where thou art forc'd to break a twofold truth,
    Hers, by thy beauty tempting her to thee,
    Thine, by thy beauty being false to me.

liberty lasciviousness   *still* always   *Gentle* noble
seat place   *riot* revel

42

That thou hast her, it is not all my grief,
And yet it may be said I lov'd her dearly;
That she hath thee is of my wailing chief,
A loss in love that touches me more nearly.
Loving offenders, thus I will excuse ye: 5
Thou dost love her because thou know'st I love
        her;
And for my sake even so doth she abuse me,
Suff'ring my friend for my sake to approve° her.
If I lose thee, my loss is my love's gain,
And losing her, my friend hath found that loss;   10
Both find each other, and I lose both twain,
And both for my sake lay on me this cross.
    But here's the joy: my friend and I are one;
    Sweet flattery! Then she loves but me alone.

approve make trial of

43

When most I wink,° then do mine eyes best see,
For all the day they view things unrespected;°
But when I sleep, in dreams they look on thee,
And, darkly bright, are bright in dark directed.°
5   Then thou, whose shadow° shadows doth make
      bright,
How would thy shadow's form form happy show
To the clear day with thy much clearer light,
When to unseeing eyes thy shade shines so!
How would, I say, mine eyes be blessed made
10 By looking on thee in the living day,
When in dead night thy fair imperfect° shade
Through heavy sleep on sightless eyes doth stay!
    All days are nights to see till I see thee,
    And nights bright days when dreams do show
       thee me.

wink i.e., sleep   *unrespected* unnoticed
And . . . directed and, bright in the darkness, are directed
  in the darkness by (your) brightness
shadow image   *imperfect* i.e., because only a shadow

44

If the dull substance of my flesh were thought,
Injurious distance should not stop my way;
For then, despite of space, I would be brought,
From limits far remote, where thou dost stay.
5 No matter then although my foot did stand
Upon the farthest earth remov'd from thee;
For nimble thought can jump both sea and land
As soon as think the place where he would be.
But, ah, thought kills me that I am not thought,
10 To leap large lengths of miles when thou art gone,
But that, so much of earth and water wrought,°
I must attend time's leisure with my moan,
    Receiving naught by elements° so slow
    But heavy tears, badges of either's woe.

wrought composed   *elements* i.e., earth and water

45

The other two,° slight air and purging fire,
Are both with thee, wherever I abide;
The first my thought, the other my desire,
These present-absent with swift motion slide.
5 For when these quicker elements are gone
In tender embassy of love to thee,

My life, being made of four, with two alone
Sinks down to death, oppress'd with melancholy
Until life's composition° be recur'd
By those swift messengers return'd from thee,   10
Who even but now come back again, assur'd
Of thy fair health, recounting it to me.
    This told, I joy; but then no longer glad,
    I send them back again, and straight grow sad.

two i.e., elements
composition i.e., of the four elements
recur'd restored

46

Mine eye and heart are at a mortal war
How to divide the conquest of thy sight;
Mine eye my heart thy picture's sight would bar,
My heart mine eye the freedom of that right.
My heart doth plead that thou in him dost lie,   5
A closet never pierc'd with crystal eyes;
But the defendant doth that plea deny,
And says in him thy fair appearance lies.
To 'cide this title is impaneled
A quest° of thoughts, all tenants to the heart;   10
And by their verdict is determined
The clear eye's moiety and the dear heart's part,
    As thus: mine eye's due is thine outward part,
    And my heart's right thine inward love of
      heart.

quest inquest, jury

47

Betwixt mine eye and heart a league is took,°
And each doth good turns now unto the other:
When that mine eye is famish'd for a look
Or heart in love with sighs himself doth smother,
With my love's picture then my eye doth feast   5
And to the painted banquet bids my heart;
Another time mine eye is my heart's guest
And in his thoughts of love doth share a part.
So, either by thy picture or my love,
Thyself away art present still with me,   10
For thou not farther than my thoughts canst
    move,
And I am still with them and they with thee;
    Or, if they sleep, thy picture in my sight
    Awakes my heart to heart's and eye's delight.

league is took compact is made

48

How careful was I, when I took my way,
Each trifle under truest bars to thrust,
That to my use it might unused stay
From hands of falsehood, in sure wards of trust!°
5 But thou, to whom my jewels trifles are,
Most worthy comfort, now my greatest grief,
Thou, best of dearest and mine only care,
Art left the prey of every vulgar° thief.
Thee have I not lock'd up in any chest,
10 Save where thou art not, though I feel thou art,
Within the gentle closure of my breast,
From whence at pleasure thou mayst come and
    part;
    And even thence thou wilt be stol'n, I fear,
    For truth proves thievish for a prize so dear.

in . . . trust i.e., under lock and key
vulgar common

49

Against° that time, if ever that time come,
When I shall see thee frown on my defects,
When as thy love hath cast his utmost sum,°
Call'd to that audit by advis'd respects;°
5 Against that time when thou shalt strangely pass,
And scarcely greet me with that sun, thine eye,
When love, converted from the thing it was,
Shall reasons find of settled gravity;
Against that time do I ensconce me here
10 Within the knowledge of mine own desert,
And this my hand against myself uprear
To guard the lawful reasons on thy part.
    To leave poor me thou hast the strength of
    laws,
    Since why to love I can allege no cause.

Against in preparation for
cast . . . sum balanced its books
advis'd respects sober considerations

50

How heavy° do I journey on the way,
When what I seek, my weary travel's end,
Doth teach that ease and that repose to say,
"Thus far the miles are measur'd from thy
    friend!"
5 The beast that bears me, tired with my woe,

Plods dully on, to bear that weight in me,
As if by some instinct the wretch did know
His rider lov'd not speed, being made from° thee.
The bloody spur cannot provoke him on
That sometimes anger thrusts into his hide,   10
Which heavily he answers with a groan
More sharp to me than spurring to his side;
    For that same groan doth put this in my mind:
    My grief lies onward, and my joy behind.

heavy sadly   *from* away from

51

Thus can my love excuse the slow offense
Of my dull bearer when from thee I speed.
From where thou art why should I haste me
    thence?
Till I return, of posting° is no need.
O, what excuse will my poor beast then find,   5
When swift extremity° can seem but slow?
Then should I spur, though mounted on the wind;
In winged speed no motion shall I know.
Then can no horse with my desire keep pace;
Therefore desire, of perfect'st love being made,   10
Shall neigh—no dull flesh—in his fiery race;°
But love, for love, thus shall excuse my jade:
    Since from thee going he went wilful-slow,
    Towards thee I'll run and give him leave to go.°

posting hurrying
swift extremity extreme swiftness
Shall . . . race i.e., my desire shall neigh like a swift steed
  in its passionate race
go walk

52

So am I as the rich, whose blessed key
Can bring him to his sweet up-locked treasure,
The which he will not every hour survey,
For blunting the fine point of seldom pleasure.
Therefore are feasts so solemn and so rare,   5
Since, seldom coming, in the long year set,
Like stones of worth they thinly placed are,
Or captain° jewels in the carcanet.°
So is the time that keeps you as my chest,
Or as the wardrobe which the robe doth hide,   10
To make some special instant special blest
By new unfolding his imprison'd pride.
    Blessed are you, whose worthiness gives scope,
    Being had, to triumph, being lack'd, to hope.

captain chief   *carcanet* necklace

53

What is your substance, whereof are you made,
That millions of strange shadows° on you tend?
Since every one hath, every one, one shade,
And you, but one, can every shadow lend.°
5   Describe Adonis,° and the counterfeit°
Is poorly imitated after you;
On Helen's° cheek all art of beauty set,
And you in Grecian tires° are painted new;
Speak of the spring and foison° of the year,
10 The one doth shadow of your beauty show,
The other as your bounty° doth appear,
And you in every blessed shape we know.
    In all external grace you have some part,
    But you like none, none you, for constant heart.

shadows (used with various meanings in the course of the
    poem: ordinary shadow, image, reflection, picture)
lend present
Adonis youth beloved of Venus (see Shakespeare's
    "Venus and Adonis")
counterfeit description   *Helen* of Troy
tires attire   *foison* harvest time
bounty bountiful gift

54

O, how much more doth beauty beauteous seem
By that sweet ornament which truth doth give!
The rose looks fair, but fairer we it deem
For that sweet odor which doth in it live.
5   The canker-blooms° have full as deep a dye
As the perfumed tincture of the roses,
Hang on such thorns, and play as wantonly
When summer's breath their masked buds
    discloses.
But, for their virtue only is their show,
10 They live unwoo'd and unrespected° fade,
Die to themselves. Sweet roses do not so.
Of their sweet deaths are sweetest odors made.
    And so of you, beauteous and lovely youth,
    When that shall vade,° my verse distills your
    truth.

canker-blooms odorless wild roses
unrespected unvalued   *vade* fade

✓

55

Not marble nor the gilded monuments
Of princes shall outlive this powerful rhyme,
But you shall shine more bright in these contents
Than unswept stone besmear'd with sluttish time.

When wasteful war shall statues overturn,   5
And broils root out the work of masonry,
Nor Mars his° sword nor war's quick fire shall burn
The living record of your memory.
'Gainst death and all-oblivious° enmity
Shall you pace forth; your praise shall still find
    room   10
Even in the eyes of all posterity
That wear this world out to the ending doom.
    So, till the judgment that° yourself arise,
    You live in this, and dwell in lovers' eyes.

Nor Mars his neither Mars'
all-oblivious all-obliterating   *that* when

56

Sweet love, renew thy force. Be it not said
Thy edge should blunter be than appetite,
Which but today by feeding is allay'd,
Tomorrow sharpen'd in his° former might.
So, love, be thou; although today thou fill   5
Thy hungry eyes even till they wink° with fullness,
Tomorrow see again, and do not kill
The spirit of love with a perpetual dullness.
Let this sad interim like the ocean be
Which parts the shore, where two contracted
    new°   10
Come daily to the banks, that, when they see
Return of love, more blest may be the view.
    Or call it winter, which, being full of care,
    Makes summer's welcome thrice more wish'd,
    more rare.

his its   *wink* close
contracted new newly betrothed

57

Being your slave, what should I do but tend°
Upon the hours and times of your desire?
I have no precious time at all to spend,
Nor services to do, till you require.
Nor dare I chide the world-without-end hour   5
Whilst I, my sovereign, watch the clock for you,
Nor think the bitterness of absence sour
When you have bid your servant once adieu.
Nor dare I question with my jealous thought
Where you may be, or your affairs suppose,   10
But, like a sad slave, stay and think of naught
Save where you are how happy you make those.
    So true a fool is love that in your will,
    Though you do anything, he thinks no ill.

tend attend, wait

716

58

That god forbid that made me first your slave,
I should in thought control your times of pleasure,
Or at your hand th' account of hours to crave,
Being your vassal, bound to stay your leisure!
O, let me suffer, being at your beck,
Th' imprison'd absence of your liberty,°
And patience, tame to suff'rance,° bide each check°
Without accusing you of injury.
Be where you list,° your charter° is so strong
That you yourself may privilege your time
To what you will; to you it doth belong
Yourself to pardon of self-doing crime.
　　I am to wait, though waiting so be hell,
　　Not blame your pleasure, be it ill or well.

Th' imprison'd . . . liberty i.e., my imprisonment (in
　waiting) that results from your license to do as you wish
tame to suff'rance inured to suffering
check rebuke　　*list* like　　*charter* privilege

59

If there be nothing new, but that which is
Hath been before, how are our brains beguil'd,
Which, laboring for invention,° bear amiss
The second burthen of a former child!°
O, that record could with a backward look,
Even of five hundred courses of the sun,
Show me your image in some antique book,
Since mind at first in character° was done,
That I might see what the old world could say
To this composed wonder° of your frame—
Whether we are mended,° or whether better they,
Or whether revolution be the same.°
　　O, sure I am, the wits of former days
　　To subjects worse have given admiring praise.

invention poetic invention
former child i.e., what has been said before
character letters, writing
composed wonder wonderful composition
mended improved
revolution . . . same i.e., the cycle merely repeats itself

60

Like as the waves make towards the pebbled
　　　shore,
So do our minutes hasten to their end;
Each changing place with that which goes before,
In sequent toil all forwards do contend.
Nativity, once in the main of light,°

Crawls to maturity, wherewith being crown'd,
Crooked eclipses° 'gainst his glory fight,
And Time that gave doth now his gift confound.°
Time doth transfix° the flourish set on youth
And delves the parallels in beauty's brow,　　　10
Feeds on the rarities of nature's truth,
And nothing stands but for his scythe to mow.
　　And yet to times in hope° my verse shall stand,
　　Praising thy worth, despite his cruel hand.

Nativity . . . light the newborn child once brought into the
　light of day
Crooked eclipses destructive influences
confound destroy　　*transfix* pierce through
times in hope future ages

61

Is it thy will thy image should keep open
My heavy eyelids to the weary night?
Dost thou desire my slumbers should be broken
While shadows like to thee do mock my sight?
Is it thy spirit that thou send'st from thee　　　5
So far from home into my deeds to pry,
To find out shames and idle hours in me,
The scope and tenor of thy jealousy?°
O, no! Thy love, though much, is not so great:
It is my love that keeps mine eye awake,　　　10
Mine own true love that doth my rest defeat
To play the watchman ever for thy sake.
　　For thee watch I whilst thou dost wake else-
　　　where,
　　From me far off, with others all too near.

scope . . . jealousy range and direction of your suspicion

62

Sin of self-love possesseth all mine eye
And all my soul and all my every part;
And for this sin there is no remedy,
It is so grounded inward in my heart.
Methinks no face so gracious is as mine,　　　5
No shape so true, no truth of such account,
And for myself mine own worth do define,°
As I all other in all worths surmount.
But when my glass shows me myself indeed,
Beated° and chopp'd° with tann'd antiquity,　　　10
Mine own self-love quite contrary I read;
Self so self-loving were iniquity.
　　'Tis thee, myself, that for myself° I praise,
　　Painting my age with beauty of thy days.

And . . . define i.e., self-love defines my worth for me
Beated battered　　*chopp'd* chapped
myself thee, my other self

63

Against° my love shall be as I am now,
With Time's injurious hand crush'd and o'erworn;
When hours have drain'd his blood and fill'd his
    brow
With lines and wrinkles; when his youthful morn
5 Hath travel'd on to age's steepy night,
And all those beauties whereof now he's king
Are vanishing or vanish'd out of sight,
Stealing away the treasure of his spring:
For such a time do I now fortify
10 Against confounding° age's cruel knife,
That he shall never cut from memory
My sweet love's beauty, though my lover's life.
    His beauty shall in these black lines be seen,
    And they shall live, and he in them still green.°

Against in anticipation of the time when
confounding destroying   *green* youthful

64

When I have seen by Time's fell hand defac'd
The rich-proud cost of outworn buried age;
When sometime° lofty towers I see down-raz'd,
And brass eternal slave to mortal rage;
5 When I have seen the hungry ocean gain
Advantage on the kingdom of the shore,
And the firm soil win of the watery main,
Increasing store with loss and loss with store:
When I have seen such interchange of state,
10 Or state itself confounded to decay,
Ruin hath taught me thus to ruminate,
That Time will come and take my love away.
    This thought is as a death, which cannot choose
    But weep to have that which it fears to lose.

sometime formerly

65

Since brass, nor stone, nor earth, nor boundless sea
But sad mortality o'er-sways their power,
How with this rage shall beauty hold a plea,
Whose action° is no stronger than a flower?
5 O how shall summer's honey breath hold out
Against the wrackful° siege of battering days,
When rocks impregnable are not so stout
Nor gates of steel so strong, but Time decays?

O fearful meditation! Where, alack,
Shall Time's best jewel from Time's chest lie hid? 10
Or what strong hand can hold his swift foot back?
Or who his spoil of beauty can forbid?
    O, none, unless this miracle have might,
    That in black ink my love may still shine
    bright.

action case (legal image)   *wrackful* wreckful

66

Tir'd with all these, for restful death I cry,
As, to behold desert a beggar born,
And needy nothing trimm'd in jollity,
And purest faith unhappily forsworn,°
And gilded honor shamefully misplac'd,   5
And maiden virtue rudely strumpeted,
And right perfection wrongfully disgrac'd,
And strength by limping sway° disabled,
And art made tongue-tied by authority,
And folly, doctor-like,° controlling skill,   10
And simple truth miscall'd simplicity,
And captive good attending captain ill.
    Tir'd with all these, from these would I be gone,
    Save that, to die, I leave my love alone.

forsworn betrayed   *sway* authority
doctor-like i.e., affecting learned authority

67

Ah, wherefore with infection° should he live
And with his presence grace impiety,
That sin by him advantage should achieve
And lace° itself with his society?
Why should false painting imitate his cheek,   5
And steal dead seeing° of his living hue?
Why should poor beauty indirectly seek
Roses of shadow,° since his rose is true?
Why should he live, now Nature bankrupt is,
Beggar'd of blood to blush through lively veins? 10
For she hath no exchequer now but his,°
And, proud of many, lives upon his gains.
    O, him she stores, to show what wealth she had
    In days long since, before these last so bad.

infection corruption   *lace* ornament
steal . . . seeing steal the appearance of life
indirectly . . . shadow deceptively use imitation coloring—
    i.e., cosmetics
she . . . his i.e., Nature has only his beauty left in her
    treasury

68

Thus is his cheek the map of days outworn,
When beauty liv'd and died as flowers do now,
Before these bastard signs° of fair were born,
Or durst inhabit on a living brow;
Before the golden tresses of the dead,   5
The right of sepulchres, were shorn away
To live a second life on second head,
Ere beauty's dead fleece made another gay.
In him those holy antique hours are seen,
Without all ornament, itself and true,   10
Making no summer of another's green,
Robbing no old to dress his beauty new.
    And him as for a map doth Nature store
    To show false Art what beauty was of yore.

bastard signs i.e., cosmetics

69

Those parts of thee that the world's eye doth view
Want° nothing that the thought of hearts can
    mend;°
All tongues, the voice of souls, give thee that due,
Uttering bare truth, even so as foes commend.°
Thy outward thus with outward praise is crown'd,   5
But those same tongues that give thee so thine own
In other accents do this praise confound
By seeing farther than the eye hath shown.
They look into the beauty of thy mind,
And that, in guess, they measure by thy deeds.   10
Then, churls, their thoughts, although their eyes
    were kind,
To thy fair flower add the rank smell of weeds.
    But why thy odor matcheth not thy show,
    The soil° is this, that thou dost common° grow.

Want lack   *mend* improve
commend would agree   *soil* ground, cause
common i.e., accessible to all

70

That thou art blam'd shall not be thy defect,
For slander's mark was ever yet the fair;
The ornament of beauty is suspect,
A crow that flies in heaven's sweetest air.
So thou be good, slander doth but approve°   5
Thy worth the greater, being woo'd of time;

For canker vice the sweetest buds° doth love,
And thou present'st a pure unstained prime.
Thou hast pass'd by the ambush of young days,
Either not assail'd, or victor being charg'd.   10
Yet this thy praise cannot be so thy praise
To tie up° envy evermore enlarg'd.°
    If some suspect of ill mask'd not thy show,
    Then thou alone kingdoms of hearts shouldst
        owe.

approve prove
canker . . . buds the cankerworm attacks buds, "the worm
    i' the bud"
so . . . tie up so much your praise as to restrain
enlarg'd at liberty

71

No longer mourn for me when I am dead
Than you shall hear the surly sullen bell
Give warning to the world that I am fled
From this vile world, with vilest worms to dwell.
Nay, if you read this line, remember not   5
The hand that writ it, for I love you so
That I in your sweet thoughts would be forgot
If thinking on me then should make you woe.
O, if, I say, you look upon this verse
When I perhaps compounded am with clay,   10
Do not so much as my poor name rehearse,
But let your love even with my life decay,
    Lest the wise world should look into your moan
    And mock you with me after I am gone.

72

O, lest the world should task you to recite
What merit liv'd in me, that you should love
After my death, dear love, forget me quite,
For you in me can nothing worthy prove
Unless you would devise some virtuous lie   5
To do more for me than mine own desert
And hang more praise upon deceased I
Than niggard truth would willingly impart.
O, lest your true love may seem false in this,
That you for love speak well of me untrue,°   10
My name be buried where my body is
And live no more to shame nor me nor you.
    For I am sham'd by that which I bring forth,
    And so should you, to love things nothing worth.

untrue untruly

73 ✓ TIME AGE

That time of year thou mayst in me behold
When yellow leaves, or none, or few, do hang
Upon those boughs which shake against the cold,
Bare ruin'd choirs where late the sweet birds sang.
5 In me thou see'st the twilight of such day
As after sunset fadeth in the west,
Which by and by black night doth take away,
Death's second self, that seals up all in rest.
In me thou see'st the glowing of such fire
10 That on the ashes of his youth doth lie
As the death-bed whereon it must expire,
Consum'd with that which it was nourish'd by.
      This thou perceiv'st, which makes thy love
         more strong,
      To love that well which thou must leave ere
         long.

74

But be contented. When that fell° arrest
Without all bail shall carry me away,
My life hath in this line° some interest,
Which for memorial still with thee shall stay.
5 When thou reviewest this, thou dost review
The very part was consecrate to thee.
The earth can have but earth, which is his due;
My spirit is thine, the better part of me.
So then thou hast but lost the dregs of life,
10 The prey of worms, my body being dead,
The coward conquest of a wretch's knife,
Too base of thee to be remembered.
      The worth of that is that which it contains,°
         And that is this,° and this with thee remains.

fell cruel   *line* of verse
The worth . . . contains the value of the body lies in the soul
   that it contains
that is this i.e., my soul is in my verse

75

So are you to my thoughts as food to life,
Or as sweet-season'd showers are to the ground.
And for the peace of you I hold such strife
As 'twixt a miser and his wealth is found,
5 Now proud as an enjoyer, and anon
Doubting° the filching age will steal his treasure;
Now counting best to be with you alone,

Then better'd that the world may see my
   pleasure;
Sometime all full with feasting on your sight,
And by and by clean starved for a look,   10
Possessing or pursuing no delight
Save what is had or must from you be took.
      Thus do I pine and surfeit day by day,
         Or gluttoning on all, or° all away.

Doubting suspecting   *Or . . . or* either . . . or

76

Why is my verse so barren of new pride,°
So far from variation or quick change?
Why with the time do I not glance aside
To new-found methods and to compounds
   strange?
Why write I still all one, ever the same,   5
And keep invention in a noted weed,°
That every word doth almost tell my name,
Showing their birth and where they did proceed?
O, know, sweet love, I always write of you,
And you and love are still my argument.°   10
So all my best is dressing old words new,
Spending again what is already spent.
      For as the sun is daily new and old,
         So is my love still telling what is told.

new pride showy novelty   *noted weed* familiar dress
argument subject matter

77

Thy glass will show thee how thy beauties wear,
Thy dial° how thy precious minutes waste;
The vacant leaves° thy mind's imprint will bear,
And of this book this learning mayst thou taste.
The wrinkles which thy glass will truly show   5
Of mouthed° graves will give thee memory;
Thou by thy dial's shady stealth° mayst know
Time's thievish progress to eternity.
Look, what thy memory cannot contain
Commit to these waste blanks, and thou shalt find   10
Those children nurs'd, deliver'd from thy brain,
To take a new acquaintance of thy mind.
      These offices,° so oft as thou wilt look,
         Shall profit thee and much enrich thy book.

dial sundial   *vacant leaves* empty pages
mouthed gaping
shady stealth stealthily moving shadow
These offices i.e., looking in the glass and at the sundial,
   and writing in these blank pages

720

78

So oft have I invok'd thee for my Muse
And found such fair assistance in my verse
As° every alien pen hath got my use
And under thee° their poesy disperse.
5 Thine eyes, that taught the dumb on high to sing
And heavy ignorance aloft to fly,
Have added feathers to the learned's wing
And given grace a double majesty.
Yet be most proud of that which I compile,
10 Whose influence is thine and born of thee.
In others' works thou dost but mend the style,
And arts with thy sweet graces graced be.
    But thou art all my art, and dost advance
    As high as learning my rude ignorance.

As that   *under thee* under your patronage

79

Whilst I alone did call upon thy aid,
My verse alone had all thy gentle grace;
But now my gracious numbers are decay'd,
And my sick Muse doth give another place.°
5 I grant, sweet love, thy lovely argument°
Deserves the travail of a worthier pen;
Yet what of thee thy poet doth invent
He robs thee of, and pays it thee again.
He lends thee virtue, and he stole that word
10 From thy behavior; beauty doth he give,
And found it in thy cheek. He can afford
No praise to thee but what in thee doth live.
    Then thank him not for that which he doth say,
    Since what he owes thee thou thyself dost pay.

give . . . place yield to another
thy . . . argument the theme of your beauty

80

O, how I faint when I of you do write,
Knowing a better spirit° doth use your name,
And in the praise thereof spends all his might
To make me tongue-tied, speaking of your fame!
5 But since your worth, wide as the ocean is,
The humble as° the proudest sail doth bear,
My saucy bark,° inferior far to his,
On your broad main° doth wilfully appear.
Your shallowest help will hold me up afloat,
Whilst he upon your soundless deep doth ride; 10
Or, being wreck'd, I am a worthless boat,
He of tall building and of goodly pride.
    Then if he thrive and I be cast away,
    The worst was this: my love was my decay.

better spirit greater genius   *as* as well as
bark small boat   *main* ocean

81

Or I shall live your epitaph to make,
Or° you survive when I in earth am rotten;
From hence your memory death cannot take,
Although in me each part will be forgotten.
Your name from hence immortal life shall have, 5
Though I, once gone, to all the world must die.
The earth can yield me but a common grave,
When you entombed in men's eyes shall lie.
Your monument shall be my gentle verse,
Which eyes not yet created shall o'er-read, 10
And tongues to be your being shall rehearse
When all the breathers of this world are dead.
    You still shall live—such virtue hath my pen—
    Where breath most breathes, even in the
        mouths of men.

Or . . . or either . . . or

82

I grant thou wert not married to my Muse,
And therefore mayst without attaint° o'erlook°
The dedicated° words which writers use
Of their fair subject, blessing every book.
Thou art as fair in knowledge as in hue, 5
Finding thy worth a limit past my praise,°
And therefore art enforc'd to seek anew
Some fresher stamp of the time-bettering days.°
And do so, love; yet when they have devis'd
What strained° touches rhetoric can lend, 10
Thou truly fair wert truly sympathiz'd°
In true plain words by thy true-telling friend.
    And their gross painting might be better us'd
    Where cheeks need blood; in thee it is abus'd.

attaint disgrace   *o'erlook* read over
dedicated dedicatory
a limit . . . praise beyond my ability to praise
time-bettering days i.e., days of improved verse
strained exaggerated   *sympathiz'd* represented

83

I never saw that you did painting need,
And therefore to your fair no painting set;
I found, or thought I found, you did exceed
The barren tender° of a poet's debt.
5 And therefore have I slept in your report,°
That you yourself, being extant, well might show
How far a modern° quill doth come too short,
Speaking of worth, what worth in you doth grow.
This silence for my sin you did impute,
10 Which shall be most my glory, being dumb;
For I impair not beauty being mute,
When others would give life and bring a tomb.
    There lives more life in one of your fair eyes
    Than both your poets can in praise devise.

tender offer of repayment
slept . . . report refrained from praising you
modern slight

84

Who is it that says most? Which can say more
Than this rich praise, that you alone are you?—
In whose confine immured is the store
Which should example where your equal grew.°
5 Lean penury within that pen doth dwell
That to his subject lends not some small glory;
But he that writes of you, if he can tell
That you are you, so dignifies his story.
Let him but copy what in you is writ,
10 Not making worse what nature made so clear,
And such a counterpart shall fame° his wit,
Making his style admired everywhere.
    You to your beauteous blessings add a curse,
    Being fond on° praise, which makes your praises
      worse.

In . . . grew within you is contained all that must set the
  pattern for any being that is to be your equal
fame make famous   *on* of

85

My tongue-tied Muse in manners holds her still,°
While comments of your praise, richly compil'd,
Reserve° their character with golden quill,
And precious phrase by all the Muses fil'd.°
5 I think good thoughts, whilst other° write good
      words,
And, like unletter'd clerk, still cry "Amen"
To every hymn that able spirit° affords
In polish'd form of well refined pen.
Hearing you prais'd, I say, "'Tis so, 'tis true,"

And to the most° of praise add something more;   10
But that is in my thought, whose love to you,
Though words come hindmost, holds his rank
      before.
    Then others for the breath of words respect,
    Me for my dumb thoughts, speaking in effect.°

in . . . still modestly remains silent
Reserve preserve   *fil'd* polished   *other* others
able spirit i.e., the rival poet   *most* utmost
in effect i.e., by their silence

86

Was it the proud full sail of his great verse,
Bound for the prize of all too precious you,
That did my ripe thoughts in my brain inhearse,°
Making their tomb the womb wherein they grew?
Was it his spirit, by spirits taught to write   5
Above a mortal pitch, that struck me dead?
No, neither he, nor his compeers by night
Giving him aid, my verse astonished.°
He, nor that affable familiar ghost°
Which nightly gulls him with intelligence,°   10
As victors, of my silence cannot boast;
I was not sick of any fear from thence.
    But when your countenance° fill'd up his line,
    Then lack'd I matter; that enfeebled mine.

inhearse entomb   *astonished* struck dumb
ghost attending spirit
gulls . . . intelligence deceives him with (false) information
countenance face, features; but also, approval

87

Farewell! Thou art too dear for my possessing,
And like enough thou know'st thy estimate.°
The charter° of thy worth gives thee releasing;
My bonds in thee are all determinate.°
For how do I hold thee but by thy granting?   5
And for that riches where is my deserving?
The cause of this fair gift in me is wanting,
And so my patent back again is swerving.°
Thyself thou gav'st, thy own worth then not
      knowing,
Or me, to whom thou gav'st it, else mistaking;   10
So thy great gift, upon misprision growing,°
Comes home again, on better judgment making.
    Thus have I had thee as a dream doth flatter:
    In sleep a king, but waking no such matter.

estimate value   *charter* privilege
determinate ended
patent . . . swerving the privilege granted me is returning
  to you
upon . . . growing based upon error

88

When thou shalt be dispos'd to set me light°
And place my merit in the eye of scorn,
Upon thy side against myself I'll fight
And prove thee virtuous though thou art forsworn.
5   With mine own weakness being best acquainted,
Upon thy part I can set down a story
Of faults conceal'd, wherein I am attainted,°
That° thou in losing me shalt win much glory.
And I by this will be a gainer too;
10   For bending all my loving thoughts on thee,
The injuries that to myself I do,
Doing thee vantage, double-vantage me.
    Such is my love, to thee I so belong
    That for thy right myself will bear all wrong.

set me light   regard me with little favor
attainted   dishonored   *That*   so that

89

Say that thou didst forsake me for some fault,
And I will comment upon that offense.
Speak of my lameness, and I straight will halt,°
Against thy reasons making no defense.
5   Thou canst not, love, disgrace me half so ill,
To set a form upon desired change,°
As I'll myself disgrace; knowing thy will,
I will acquaintance strangle and look strange,°
Be absent from thy walks, and in my tongue
10   Thy sweet beloved name no more shall dwell,
Lest I, too much profane, should do it wrong
And haply° of our old acquaintance tell.
    For thee, against myself I'll vow debate,
    For I must ne'er love him whom thou dost hate.

halt   limp
To set . . . change   by identifying the change that you desire
strange   i.e., as if I never knew you   *haply*   perhaps

90

Then hate me when thou wilt; if ever, now;
Now while the world is bent my deeds to cross,
Join with the spite of fortune, make my bow,
And do not drop in for an after-loss.
Ah, do not, when my heart hath 'scap'd this
5   sorrow,

Come in the rearward of a conquer'd woe;
Give not a windy night a rainy morrow,
To linger out a purpos'd overthrow.
If thou wilt leave me, do not leave me last,
When other petty griefs have done their spite,   10
But in the onset come: so shall I taste
At first the very worst of fortune's might;
    And other strains of woe, which now seem woe,
    Compar'd with loss of thee will not seem so.

91

Some glory in their birth, some in their skill,
Some in their wealth, some in their body's force,
Some in their garments, though new-fangled ill,°
Some in their hawks and hounds, some in their
     horse;
And every humor° hath his adjunct° pleasure   5
Wherein it finds a joy above the rest.
But these particulars are not my measure;°
All these I better in one general best.
Thy love is better than high birth to me,
Richer than wealth, prouder than garments' cost,   10
Of more delight than hawks or horses be;
And having thee, of all men's pride I boast:
    Wretched in this alone, that thou mayst take
    All this away and me most wretched make.

new-fangled ill   ugly in the latest fashion
humor   disposition   *adjunct*   attendant, particular
are . . . measure   i.e., fall short of my extreme of pleasure

92

But do thy worst to steal thyself away,
For term of life thou art assured mine,
And life no longer than thy love will stay,
For it depends upon that love of thine.
Then need I not to fear the worst of wrongs,   5
When in the least of them my life hath end.
I see a better state to me belongs
Than that which on thy humor doth depend.
Thou canst not vex me with inconstant mind,
Since that my life on thy revolt° doth lie.   10
O what a happy title° do I find,
Happy to have thy love, happy to die!
    But what's so blessed-fair that fears no blot?
    Thou mayst be false, and yet I know it not.

revolt   desertion   *happy title*   claim to happiness

93

So shall I live, supposing thou art true,
Like a deceived husband; so love's face
May still seem love to me, though alter'd new,
Thy looks with me, thy heart in other place.
5 For there can live no hatred in thine eye;
Therefore in that I cannot know thy change.
In many's looks the false heart's history
Is writ in moods and frowns and wrinkles strange,
But heaven in thy creation did decree
10 That in thy face sweet love should ever dwell;
Whate'er thy thoughts or thy heart's workings be,
Thy looks should nothing thence but sweetness
    tell.
    How like Eve's apple° doth thy beauty grow
    If thy sweet virtue answer not° thy show!

Eve's apple i.e., attractive but ruinous
answer not does not match

94

They that have power to hurt and will do none,
That do not do the things they most do show,°
Who, moving others, are themselves as stone,
Unmoved, cold, and to temptation slow,
5 They rightly do inherit heaven's graces
And husband° nature's riches from expense;°
They are the lords and owners of their faces,
Others but stewards of their excellence.
The summer's flower is to the summer sweet,
10 Though to itself it only live and die,
But if that flower with base infection meet,
The basest weed outbraves his dignity.
    For sweetest things turn sourest by their deeds;
    Lilies that fester smell far worse than weeds.

show appear to do   *husband* preserve
expense waste

95

How sweet and lovely dost thou make the shame
Which, like a canker in the fragrant rose,
Doth spot the beauty of thy budding name!
O, in what sweets dost thou thy sins enclose!
5 That tongue that tells the story of thy days,
Making lascivious comments on thy sport,

Cannot dispraise but in a kind of praise;
Naming thy name blesses an ill report.
O, what a mansion have those vices got
Which for their habitation chose out thee,   10
Where beauty's veil doth cover every blot
And all things turn to fair that eyes can see!
    Take heed, dear heart, of this large privilege;°
    The hardest knife ill us'd doth lose his edge.

privilege license

96

Some say thy fault is youth, some wantonness;
Some say thy grace is youth and gentle sport.
Both grace and faults are lov'd of more and less:°
Thou mak'st faults graces that to thee resort.
As on the finger of a throned queen   5
The basest jewel will be well esteem'd,
So are these errors that in thee are seen
To truths translated° and for true things deem'd.
How many lambs might the stern wolf betray
If like a lamb he could his looks translate!   10
How many gazers mightst thou lead away
If thou wouldst use the strength of all thy state!
    But do not so; I love thee in such sort
    As thou being mine, mine is thy good report.°

more and less of high and low rank
translated transformed
But . . . report (the couplet also ends Sonnet 36)

97

How like a winter hath my absence been
From thee, the pleasure of the fleeting year!
What freezings have I felt, what dark days seen!
What old December's bareness everywhere!
And yet this time remov'd was summer's time,   5
The teeming autumn, big with rich increase,
Bearing the wanton burthen of the prime
Like widow'd wombs after their lords' decease.
Yet this abundant issue seem'd to me
But hope of orphans and unfather'd fruit.   10
For summer and his pleasures wait on thee,
And, thou away, the very birds are mute,
    Or, if they sing, 'tis with so dull a cheer
    That leaves look pale, dreading the winter's
    near.

98

From you have I been absent in the spring,
When proud-pied° April, dress'd in all his trim,
Hath put a spirit of youth in everything,
That heavy Saturn° laugh'd and leap'd with him.
5   Yet nor the lays° of birds nor the sweet smell
Of different flowers in odor and in hue
Could make me any summer's story tell
Or from their proud lap pluck them where they grew.
Nor did I wonder at the lily's white,
10   Nor praise the deep vermilion in the rose;
They were but sweet, but figures of delight
Drawn after you, you pattern of all those.
     Yet seem'd it winter still, and, you away,
     As with your shadow I with these did play.

proud-pied i.e., proud of its varied colors
heavy Saturn (the gloomy planet whose influence was thought to cause melancholy)
lays songs

99

The forward° violet thus did I chide:
Sweet thief, whence didst thou steal thy sweet that smells,
If not from my love's breath? The purple pride
Which on thy soft cheek for complexion dwells,
5   In my love's veins thou hast too grossly dy'd.
The lily I condemned for thy hand,°
And buds of marjoram had stol'n thy hair;
The roses fearfully on thorns did stand,
One blushing shame, another white despair;
10   A third, nor red nor white, had stol'n of both,
And to his robbery had annex'd thy breath;
But for his theft, in pride of all his growth,
A vengeful canker eat him up to death.
     More flowers I noted, yet I none could see
     But sweet or color it had stol'n from thee.

forward early
for thy hand i.e., for stealing its whiteness

100

Where art thou, Muse, that thou forget'st so long
To speak of that which gives thee all thy might?
Spend'st thou thy fury° on some worthless song,
Dark'ning thy power to lend base subjects light?
5   Return, forgetful Muse, and straight redeem
In gentle numbers time so idly spent;
Sing to the ear that doth thy lays esteem
And gives thy pen both skill and argument.
Rise, resty° Muse: my love's sweet face survey
If Time have any wrinkle graven there;   10
If any, be a satire to decay,°
And make Time's spoils despised everywhere.
     Give my love fame faster than Time wastes life;
     So thou prevent'st his scythe and crooked knife.

fury poetic frenzy   *resty* lazy
be . . . decay satirize Time's ravages

101

O truant Muse, what shall be thy amends
For thy neglect of truth in beauty dy'd?
Both truth and beauty on my love depends;
So dost thou too, and therein dignified.°
Make answer, Muse: wilt thou not haply say   5
"Truth needs no color, with his color fix'd;
Beauty no pencil, beauty's truth to lay;°
But best is best if never intermix'd"?
Because he needs no praise, wilt thou be dumb?
Excuse not silence so, for 't lies in thee   10
To make him much outlive a gilded tomb
And to be prais'd of ages yet to be.
     Then do thy office, Muse; I teach thee how
     To make him seem long hence as he shows now.

dignified you are dignified   *lay* paint

102

My love is strengthen'd, though more weak in seeming;
I love not less, though less the show appear.
That love is merchandis'd whose rich esteeming
The owner's tongue doth publish everywhere.
Our love was new, and then but in the spring,   5
When I was wont to greet it with my lays,
As Philomel° in summer's front° doth sing,
And stops her pipe in growth of riper days.
Not that the summer is less pleasant now
Than when her mournful hymns did hush the night,   10
But that wild music burthens every bough,
And sweets grown common lose their dear delight.
     Therefore, like her, I sometime hold my tongue
     Because I would not dull you with my song.

Philomel the nightingale
summer's front early summer

103

Alack, what poverty my Muse brings forth,
That having such a scope to show her pride,
The argument,° all bare, is of more worth
Than when it hath my added praise beside!
5 O blame me not if I no more can write!
Look in your glass, and there appears a face
That overgoes° my blunt invention quite,
Dulling my lines and doing me disgrace.
Were it not sinful then, striving to mend,°
10 To mar the subject that before was well?
For to no other pass° my verses tend
Than of your graces and your gifts to tell,
    And more, much more, than in my verse can
      sit,
    Your own glass shows you when you look in it.

argument subject   *overgoes* outdoes
mend improve   *pass* end

104

To me, fair friend, you never can be old,
For as you were when first your eye I ey'd,
Such seems your beauty still. Three winters cold
Have from the forests shook three summers' pride,
5 Three beauteous springs to yellow autumn turn'd
In process of the seasons have I seen,
Three April perfumes in three hot Junes burn'd,
Since first I saw you fresh which yet are green.
Ah yet doth beauty like a dial-hand
10 Steal from his figure° and no pace perceiv'd.
So your sweet hue, which methinks still doth
    stand,
Hath motion, and mine eye may be deceiv'd;
    For fear of which, hear this, thou age unbred:
    Ere you were born was beauty's summer dead.

Steal . . . figure move on past the numeral on the dial

105

Let not my love be call'd idolatry,
Nor my beloved as an idol show,
Since all alike my songs and praises be
To one, of one, still such, and ever so.
5 Kind is my love today, tomorrow kind,
Still constant in a wondrous excellence;
Therefore my verse, to constancy confin'd,
One thing expressing, leaves out difference.°
"Fair, kind, and true" is all my argument,
10 "Fair, kind, and true," varying to other words;
And in this change is my invention spent,

Three themes in one, which wondrous scope
    affords.
    "Fair, kind, and true" have often liv'd alone,
    Which three till now never kept seat in one.

difference variety

106

When in the chronicle of wasted° time
I see descriptions of the fairest wights°
And beauty making beautiful old rhyme
In praise of ladies dead and lovely knights,
5 Then in the blazon° of sweet beauty's best
Of hand, of foot, of lip, of eye, of brow,
I see their antique pen would have express'd
Even such a beauty as you master now.
So all their praises are but prophecies
10 Of this our time, all you prefiguring,
And, for they look'd but with divining° eyes,
They had not skill enough your worth to sing.
    For° we which now behold these present days
    Have eyes to wonder, but lack tongues to praise.

wasted past   *wights* men
blazon display, as on a coat of arms
divining prophetic   *For* i.e., whereas

107

Not mine own fears nor the prophetic soul
Of the wide world dreaming on things to come
Can yet the lease° of my true love control,
Suppos'd as forfeit to a confin'd doom.°
5 The mortal moon° hath her eclipse endur'd,°
And the sad augurs mock their own presage;°
Incertainties now crown themselves assur'd,
And peace proclaims olives° of endless age.
Now with the drops of this most balmy time
10 My love looks fresh, and Death to me subscribes,°
Since, spite of him, I'll live in this poor rhyme
While he insults° o'er dull and speechless tribes.
    And thou in this shaft find thy monument
    When tyrants' crests and tombs of brass are
      spent.

lease duration
Suppos'd . . . doom supposedly nearing the end of its
    allotted time
mortal moon (possible allusion to Queen Elizabeth, who
    survived various crises, including serious illness, in the
    1590's)
endur'd survived
And . . . presage those who had predicted doom now mock
    their own prediction
olives symbols of peace   *subscribes* yields
insults tyrannizes

108

What's in the brain that ink may character°
Which hath not figur'd to thee my true spirit?
What's new to speak, what new to register,
That may express my love or thy dear merit?
5   Nothing, sweet boy; but yet, like prayers divine,
I must each day say o'er the very same,
Counting no old thing old, thou mine, I thine,
Even as when first I hallow'd thy fair name.
So that eternal love in love's fresh case°
10   Weighs not the dust and injury of age
Nor gives to necessary wrinkles place,
But makes antiquity for aye his page,°
    Finding the first conceit° of love there bred
    Where time and outward form would show it
      dead.°

character write
love's . . . case i.e., case that preserves love always fresh
makes . . . page makes age his servant forever
conceit inspiration, idea
Where . . . dead i.e., in an aged face which would seem
  unlikely to inspire love

109

O, never say that I was false of heart,
Though absence seem'd my flame to qualify.°
As easy might I from myself depart
As from my soul, which in thy breast doth lie.
5   That is my home of love. If I have rang'd,
Like him that travels I return again,
Just to the time,° not with the time exchang'd,°
So that myself bring water for my stain.°
Never believe, though in my nature reign'd
10   All frailties that besiege all kinds of blood,
That it could so preposterously be stain'd
To leave for nothing all thy sum of good.
    For nothing this wide universe I call,
    Save thou, my rose; in it thou art my all.

my . . . qualify to suggest that my ardor had cooled
Just . . . time punctually   *exchang'd* changed
bring . . . stain justify my absence

110

Alas, 'tis true I have gone here and there
And made myself a motley° to the view,
Gor'd mine own thoughts, sold cheap what is
    most dear,
Made old offenses of affections new.
5   Most true it is that I have look'd on truth
Askance and strangely. But by all above,

These blenches° gave my heart another youth,
And worse essays° prov'd thee my best of love.
Now all is done, have what shall have no end.
Mine appetite I never more will grind   10
On newer proof to try an older friend,
A god in love, to whom I am confin'd.
    Then give me welcome, next my heaven the
      best,
    Even to thy pure and most most loving breast.

motley jester   *blenches* side-glances
worse essays less happy trials

111

O, for my sake do you with Fortune chide,
The guilty goddess of my harmful deeds
That did not better for my life provide
Than public means, which public manners breeds.
Thence comes it that my name receives a brand,°   5
And almost thence my nature is subdu'd
To what it works in, like the dyer's hand.
Pity me then and wish I were renew'd,
Whilst like a willing patient I will drink
Potions of eisel° 'gainst my strong infection;   10
No bitterness that I will bitter think,
Nor double penance, to correct correction.°
    Pity me then, dear friend, and I assure ye
    Even that your pity is enough to cure me.

brand stigma
eisel vinegar (used as a plague remedy)
correct correction make correction doubly sure

112

Your love and pity doth th' impression fill°
Which vulgar scandal stamp'd upon my brow;
For what care I who calls me well or ill,
So you o'er-green my bad, my good allow?
You are my all the world, and I must strive   5
To know my shames and praises from your
      tongue;
None else to me, nor I to none alive,
That my steel'd sense or changes right or wrong.°
In so profound abysm I throw all care
Of others' voices that my adder's sense°   10
To critic and to flatt'rer stopped are.
Mark how with my neglect I do dispense:
    You are so strongly in my purpose bred
    That all the world besides methinks are dead.

fill cover over
or . . . wrong affects my mind one way or the other
adder's sense adders were thought to be deaf (see
  Psalm 58:4)

113

Since I left you mine eye is in my mind,
And that which governs me to go about
Doth part° his function and is partly blind,
Seems seeing, but effectually is out;
5   For it no form delivers to the heart
Of bird, of flower, or shape which it doth latch.°
Of his quick° objects hath the mind no part,
Nor his own vision holds what it doth catch;
For if it see the rud'st or gentlest sight,
10 The most sweet favor° or deformed'st creature,
The mountain or the sea, the day or night,
The crow or dove, it shapes them to your feature.
   Incapable of more, replete with you,
   My most true mind thus maketh mine° untrue.

part part from, neglect   *latch* seize upon
his quick its fleeting   *favor* face
mine i.e., my eye

114

Or whether doth° my mind, being crown'd with
      you,
Drink up the monarch's plague, this flattery?
Or whether shall I say mine eye saith true,
And that your love taught it this alchemy
5   To make of monsters and things indigest°
Such cherubins as your sweet self resemble,
Creating every bad a perfect best
As fast as objects to his beams assemble?
O 'tis the first; 'tis flattery in my seeing,
10 And my great mind most kingly drinks it up.
Mine eye well knows what with his gust° is 'gree-
      ing,
And to his palate doth prepare the cup.
   If it be poison'd, 'tis the lesser sin
   That mine eye loves it and doth first begin.°

Or . . . doth or is it that   *indigest* shapeless
gust taste   *first begin* i.e., tastes first

115

Those lines that I before have writ do lie,
Even those that said I could not love you dearer.
Yet then my judgment knew no reason why
My most full flame should afterwards burn
      clearer.
5   But reckoning Time, whose million'd accidents°
Creep in 'twixt vows and change decrees of kings,
Tan sacred beauty, blunt the sharp'st intents,
Divert strong minds to the course of altering
      things—

Alas, why, fearing of Time's tyranny,
Might I not then say "Now I love you best,"   10
When I was certain o'er incertainty,
Crowning the present, doubting of the rest?
   Love is a babe; then might I not say so,°
   To give full growth to that which still doth
      grow?

reckoning . . . accidents remembering Time, whose
   countless events
so i.e., "I love you best"

116

Let me not to the marriage of true minds
Admit impediments. Love is not love
Which alters when it alteration finds
Or bends with the remover° to remove.
O, no! It is an ever-fixed mark   5
That looks on tempests and is never shaken;
It is the star to every wand'ring bark,
Whose worth's° unknown, although his height be
      taken.
Love's not Time's fool,° though rosy lips and
      cheeks
Within his bending sickle's compass come;   10
Love alters not with his brief hours and weeks,
But bears it out even to the edge of doom.
   If this be error and upon me prov'd,
   I never writ, nor no man ever lov'd.

remover inconstant one
worth i.e., value to navigators   *fool* plaything

117

Accuse me thus: that I have scanted all
Wherein I should your great deserts repay,
Forgot upon your dearest love to call,
Whereto all bonds do tie me day by day;
That I have frequent been with unknown minds,°   5
And given to time your own dear-purchas'd right;°
That I have hoisted sail to all the winds
Which should transport me farthest from your
      sight.
Book° both my wilfulness and errors down,
And on just proof surmise accumulate.°   10
Bring me within the level of your frown,
But shoot not at me in your waken'd hate,
   Since my appeal says I did strive to prove
   The constancy and virtue of your love.

frequent . . . minds frequented the society of unselected
   persons
given . . . right wasted time that was rightly yours
Book record
on . . . accumulate add what is surmised to what is fact

118

Like as, to make our appetites more keen,
With eager° compounds we our palate urge—
As, to prevent° our maladies unseen,
We sicken° to shun sickness when we purge—
5 Even so, being full of your ne'er-cloying sweetness,
To bitter sauces did I frame my feeding,
And sick of welfare° found a kind of meetness
To be diseas'd ere that there was true needing.
Thus policy in love, t' anticipate
10 The ills that were not, grew to faults assur'd,°
And brought to medicine° a healthful state
Which, rank of° goodness, would by ill be cur'd.
    But thence I learn, and find the lesson true,
    Drugs poison him that so fell sick of you.

eager sharp   *prevent* forestall
sicken i.e., take sickening medicine
sick of welfare surfeited with being healthy
faults assur'd real ills
brought to medicine i.e., brought to a need for
rank of surfeited with

119

What potions have I drunk of Siren° tears
Distill'd from limbecks° foul as hell within,
Applying fears to hopes and hopes to fears,
Still losing when I saw myself to win!
5 What wretched errors hath my heart committed,
Whilst it hath thought itself so blessed never!
How have mine eyes out of their spheres been
    fitted°
In the distraction of this madding fever!
O benefit of ill! Now I find true
10 That better is by evil still made better,
And ruin'd love, when it is built anew,
Grows fairer than at first, more strong, far greater.
    So I return rebuk'd to my content,
    And gain by ill thrice more than I have spent.

Siren tempting (the Sirens lured seafarers to destruction)
limbecks alembics, distilling vessels
fitted i.e., by fits, convulsions

120

That you were once unkind befriends me now,
And for that sorrow which I then did feel
Needs must I under my transgression bow,
Unless my nerves were brass or hammer'd steel.
5 For if you were by my unkindness shaken
As I by yours, you've pass'd a hell of time;
And I, a tyrant, have no leisure taken
To weigh how once I suffer'd in your crime.

O that our night of woe might have remember'd°
My deepest sense how hard true sorrow hits,   10
And soon to you, as you to me, then tender'd°
The humble salve which wounded bosoms fits!
    But that your trespass now becomes a fee;
    Mine ransoms yours, and yours must ransom
    me.

remember'd reminded   *then tender'd* had then offered

121

'Tis better to be vile than vile esteem'd,
When not to be receives reproach of being,
And the just pleasure lost which is so deem'd°
Not by our feeling but by others' seeing.
For why should others' false adulterate eyes   5
Give salutation to° my sportive blood?
Or on my frailties why are frailer spies°
Which in their wills count bad what I think good?
No, I am that I am, and they that level
At my abuses reckon up their own.   10
I may be straight, though they themselves be
    bevel;°
By their rank thoughts my deeds must not be
    shown;
    Unless this general evil they maintain,
    All men are bad and in their badness reign.

so deem'd i.e., deemed vile
Give . . . to i.e., welcome as of their own kind
frailer spies i.e., spies with greater frailties
bevel slanted, i.e., crooked

122

Thy gift, thy tables,° are within my brain
Full character'd° with lasting memory,
Which shall above that idle rank° remain
Beyond all date, even to eternity.
Or, at the least, so long as brain and heart   5
Have faculty by nature to subsist,
Till each to raz'd oblivion° yield his part
Of thee, thy record never can be miss'd.
That poor retention° could not so much hold,
Nor need I tallies thy dear love to score;   10
Therefore to give them from me was I bold,
To trust those tables° that receive thee more.
    To keep an adjunct° to remember thee
    Were to import° forgetfulness in me.

tables notebook   *character'd* inscribed
idle rank series of vacant leaves
raz'd oblivion i.e., nothingness
retention i.e., the notebook
those tables i.e., my mind and heart
adjunct aiding device   *import* imply

123

No, Time, thou shalt not boast that I do change.
Thy pyramids° built up with newer might
To me are nothing novel, nothing strange;
They are but dressings° of a former sight.
5 Our dates° are brief, and therefore we admire°
What thou dost foist upon us that is old,
And rather make them born to our desire
Than think that we before have heard them told.°
Thy registers° and thee I both defy,
10 Not wond'ring at the present nor the past,
For thy records and what we see doth lie,
Made more or less° by thy continual haste.
    This I do vow, and this shall ever be:
    I will be true, despite thy scythe and thee.

pyramids (probably here standing for large structures in
    general)
dressings i.e., redressings   *dates* lifetimes
admire wonder at
And . . . told i.e., tend to regard new things as our own
    inventions rather than recognize them as repetitions of
    the past
registers records
Made . . . less increasing and decreasing

124

If my dear love° were but the child of state,°
It might for Fortune's bastard be unfather'd,
As subject to Time's love or to Time's hate,
Weeds among weeds, or flowers with flowers
    gather'd.
5 No, it was builded far from accident;
It suffers not in smiling pomp, nor falls
Under the blow of thralled discontent,°
Whereto th' inviting time our fashion calls.°
It fears not policy,° that heretic,
10 Which works on leases of short-number'd hours,
But all alone stands hugely politic,
That° it nor grows with heat nor° drowns with
    showers.
    To this I witness call the fools° of time,
    Which die for goodness° who have liv'd for
        crime.

love i.e., the emotion, not the beloved
child of state creature of circumstance, accident
thralled discontent i.e., the discontent of being held in
    thrall, enslaved
Whereto . . . calls i.e., which is fashionable nowadays
    (as in the tradition of the lover disdained)
policy craft   *That* so that
nor . . . nor neither . . . nor   *fools* playthings
for goodness i.e., piously

125

Were 't aught to me I bore the canopy,°
With my extern the outward honoring,°
Or laid great bases for eternity,°
Which prove more short than waste or ruining?
5 Have I not seen dwellers on form and favor°
Lose all, and more, by paying too much rent,°
For compound sweet forgoing simple savor,
Pitiful thrivers, in their gazing spent?
No, let me be obsequious° in thy heart,
10 And take thou my oblation,° poor but free,
Which is not mix'd with seconds,° knows no art°
But mutual render,° only me for thee.
    Hence, thou suborn'd informer!° A true soul
    When most impeach'd stands least in thy
        control.

bore the canopy i.e., above the head of some eminent
    personage; hence, made outward show of respect
With . . . honoring honoring the outward with outward
    show
laid . . . eternity raised aspirations for eternal fame
dwellers . . . favor i.e., those enamored of outward show
paying . . . rent i.e., buying favor at too great expense
obsequious devoted   *oblation* offering
seconds baser elements   *art* artifice
render surrender, exchange
suborn'd informer false witness, i.e., suspicion, jealousy

126

O thou, my lovely boy, who in thy power
Dost hold Time's fickle glass,° his sickle, hour;
Who hast by waning grown,° and therein show'st
Thy lovers withering as thy sweet self grow'st;
5 If Nature, sovereign mistress over wrack,°
As thou goest onwards, still will pluck thee back,
She keeps thee to this purpose, that her skill
May Time disgrace and wretched minutes kill.
Yet fear her, O thou minion° of her pleasure!
10 She may detain, but not still° keep, her treasure:
    Her audit, though delay'd, answer'd must be,
    And her quietus° is to render° thee.

glass mirror
waning grown grown more lovely in growing older
wrack ruin   *minion* darling   *still* always
quietus final closing of the account
render surrender

127

In the old age black was not counted fair,°
Or if it were, it bore not beauty's name;
But now is black beauty's successive° heir,
And beauty° slander'd with a bastard shame:
5 For since each hand hath put° on nature's power,
Fairing the foul with art's false borrow'd face,°
Sweet beauty hath no name, no holy bower,
But is profan'd, if not lives in disgrace.
Therefore my mistress' brows are raven black,
10 Her eyes so suited, and they mourners seem
At such who, not born fair, no beauty lack,°
Sland'ring creation with a false esteem.°
    Yet so they mourn, becoming of° their woe,
    That every tongue says beauty should look so.

black . . . fair brunette, dark-complexioned . . . beautiful,
    light-complexioned
successive legitimate   *beauty* i.e., "fair" beauty
put taken, assumed
Fairing . . . face beautifying the ugly with cosmetics
no . . . lack i.e., thanks to cosmetics
esteem reputation   *becoming of* gracing

128

How oft when thou, my music, music play'st
Upon that blessed wood° whose motion sounds
With thy sweet fingers, when thou gently sway'st
The wiry concord° that mine ear confounds,°
5 Do I envy those jacks° that nimble leap
To kiss the tender inward of thy hand,
Whilst my poor lips, which should that harvest
    reap,
At the wood's boldness by thee blushing stand!
To be so tickled, they would change their state
10 And situation with those dancing chips,
O'er whom thy fingers walk with gentle gait,
Making dead wood more blest than living lips.
    Since saucy jacks so happy are in this,
    Give them thy fingers, me thy lips to kiss.

wood keys of the virginal
wiry concord i.e., harmony of the wires
confounds overwhelms   *jacks* keys

129

Th' expense° of spirit in a waste of shame
Is lust in action; and till action,° lust
Is perjur'd, murd'rous, bloody, full of blame,
Savage, extreme, rude, cruel, not to trust;
5 Enjoy'd no sooner but despised straight;

Past reason hunted, and no sooner had,
Past reason hated, as a swallow'd bait
On purpose laid to make the taker mad;
Mad in pursuit, and in possession so;
Had, having, and in quest to have, extreme;   10
A bliss in proof,° and prov'd, a very woe;
Before, a joy propos'd; behind, a dream.
    All this the world well knows; yet none knows
        well
    To shun the heaven that leads men to this hell.

expense expenditure
till action until it is expressed in action
in proof in the experiencing

130

My mistress' eyes are nothing like the sun;
Coral is far more red than her lips' red.
If snow be white, why then her breasts are dun;
If hairs be wires, black wires grow on her head.
I have seen roses damask'd, red and white,   5
But no such roses see I in her cheeks;
And in some perfumes is there more delight
Than in the breath that from my mistress reeks.
I love to hear her speak, yet well I know
That music hath a far more pleasing sound.   10
I grant I never saw a goddess go;°
My mistress, when she walks, treads on the
        ground.
    And yet, by heaven, I think my love as rare
    As any she belied with false compare.°

go walk
belied . . . compare dishonestly represented with
    exaggerated comparisons

131

Thou art as tyrannous, so as thou art,°
As those whose beauties proudly make them cruel;
For well thou know'st to my dear doting heart
Thou art the fairest and most precious jewel.
Yet, in good faith, some say that thee behold,   5
Thy face hath not the power to make love groan;
To say they err I dare not be so bold,
Although I swear it to myself alone.
And to be sure that is not false I swear,
A thousand groans, but thinking on thy face,   10
One on another's neck,° do witness bear
Thy black is fairest in my judgment's place.
    In nothing art thou black save in thy deeds,
    And thence this slander, as I think, proceeds.

so . . . art being as you are   *on . . . neck* successively

132

Thine eyes I love, and they, as pitying me,
Knowing thy heart torments me with disdain,
Have put on black, and loving mourners be,
Looking with pretty ruth upon my pain.
5   And truly not the morning sun of heaven
Better becomes the grey cheeks of the east,
Nor that full star that ushers in the even
Doth half that glory to the sober west
As those two mourning° eyes become thy face.
10   O, let it then as well beseem° thy heart
To mourn for me, since mourning doth thee
        grace,
And suit thy pity like° in every part.
    Then will I swear beauty herself is black,
    And all they foul that thy complexion lack.

mourning (with obvious pun)
beseem suit   *like* alike

133

Beshrew° that heart that makes my heart to groan
For that deep wound it gives my friend and me!
Is 't not enough to torture me alone,
But slave to slavery my sweet'st friend must be?
5   Me from myself thy cruel eye hath taken,
And my next self° thou harder hast engross'd.°
Of him, myself, and thee, I am forsaken,
A torment thrice threefold thus to be cross'd.
Prison my heart in thy steel bosom's ward,°
But then my friend's heart let my poor heart
10   bail;°
Whoe'er keeps me, let my heart be his guard;
Thou canst not then use rigor° in my jail.
    And yet thou wilt; for I, being pent in thee,
    Perforce am thine, and all that is in me.

Beshrew mischief on   *next self* i.e., my friend
engross'd made captive   *ward* cell
bail i.e., bail out   *rigor* cruel treatment

134

So, now I have confess'd that he is thine
And I myself am mortgag'd to thy will,
Myself I'll forfeit, so that other mine
Thou wilt restore to be my comfort still.
5   But thou wilt not, nor he will not° be free,
For thou art covetous and he is kind;
He learn'd but surety-like° to write° for me,

Under that bond that him as fast doth bind.
The statute° of thy beauty thou wilt take,
Thou usurer, that put'st forth all to use,   10
And sue a friend came° debtor for my sake;
So him I lose through my unkind abuse.
    Him have I lost; thou hast both him and me:
    He pays the whole, and yet am I not free.

will not does not wish to   *surety-like* as guarantor
write i.e., underwrite   *statute* security
came who became

135

Whoever hath her wish, thou hast thy "Will,"°
And "Will" to boot, and "Will" in overplus;
More than enough am I that vex thee still,
To thy sweet will making addition thus.
Wilt thou, whose will is large and spacious,   5
Not once vouchsafe° to hide my will in thine?
Shall will in others seem right gracious,
And in my will no fair acceptance shine?
The sea, all water, yet receives rain still,
And in abundance addeth to his store.   10
So thou, being rich in "Will," add to thy "Will"
One will of mine, to make thy large "Will" more.
    Let no unkind "No" fair beseechers kill;
    Think all but one,° and me in that one "Will."

"Will" (with puns throughout the poem, meaning the
    poet's name, possibly the friend's name, also desire,
    volition)
vouchsafe grant
Think . . . one think all wills are only one

136

If thy soul check° thee that I come so near,
Swear to thy blind soul that I was thy "Will,"
And will, thy soul knows, is admitted there;
Thus far for love, my love-suit, sweet, fulfil.
"Will" will fulfil the treasure of thy love,   5
Aye, fill it full with wills, and my will one.
In things of great receipt° with ease we prove
Among a number one is reckon'd none:
Then in the number let me pass untold,°
Though in thy store's account I one must be.   10
For nothing hold me, so it please thee hold
That nothing me, a something sweet to thee.
    Make but my name thy love, and love that still,
    And then thou lov'st me, for my name is
        "Will."

check rebuke   *receipt* capacity
untold uncounted

137

Thou blind fool, Love, what dost thou to mine
　　eyes,
That they behold, and see not what they see?
They know what beauty is, see where it lies,
Yet what the best is take the worst to be.
5　If eyes, corrupt by over-partial looks,
Be anchor'd in the bay where all men ride,°
Why of eyes' falsehood hast thou forged hooks
Whereto the judgment of my heart is tied?
Why should my heart think that a several plot°
10　Which my heart knows the wide world's common
　　place?
Or mine eyes seeing this, say this is not,
To put fair truth upon so foul a face?
　　In things right true my heart and eyes have err'd,
　　And to this false plague are they now trans-
　　ferr'd.

all men ride　i.e., all ships pass
several plot　private place

138

When my love swears that she is made of truth,
I do believe her, though I know she lies,
That she might think me some untutor'd youth,
Unlearned in the world's false subtleties.
5　Thus vainly thinking that she thinks me young,
Although she knows my days are past the best,
Simply I credit her false-speaking tongue.
On both sides thus is simple truth suppress'd.
But wherefore says she not she is unjust?°
10　And wherefore say not I that I am old?
O, love's best habit° is in seeming° trust,
And age in love loves not to have years told.
　　Therefore I lie with her and she with me,
　　And in our faults by lies we flatter'd be.

unjust　untrue　　*habit*　manner, fashion
seeming　simulating

139

O, call not me to justify the wrong
That thy unkindness lays upon my heart;
Wound me not with thine eye, but with thy
　　tongue;
Use power with power,° and slay me not by art.°
5　Tell me thou lov'st elsewhere; but in my sight,
Dear heart, forbear to glance thine eye aside.
What need'st thou wound with cunning, when thy
　　might

Is more than my o'er-press'd defense can bide?
Let me excuse thee: ah, my love well knows
Her pretty looks have been mine enemies,　　10
And therefore from my face she turns my foes,°
That they elsewhere might dart their injuries.
　　Yet do not so; but since I am near slain,
　　Kill me outright with looks, and rid my pain.

with power　outrightly　　*art*　i.e., subtle means
my foes　i.e., her eyes

140

Be wise as thou art cruel; do not press
My tongue-tied patience with too much disdain,
Lest sorrow lend me words, and words express
The manner of my pity-wanting° pain.
If I might teach thee wit, better it were,　　5
Though not to love,° yet, love, to tell me so,
As testy sick men, when their deaths be near,
No news but health from their physicians know.°
For, if I should despair, I should grow mad,
And in my madness might speak ill of thee.　　10
Now this ill-wresting° world is grown so bad,
Mad slanderers by mad ears believed be.
　　That I may not be so, nor thou belied,
　　Bear thine eyes straight, though thy proud heart
　　go wide.

pity-wanting　unpitied
Though . . . to love　though you do not love me
know　i.e., are told
ill-wresting　i.e., given to malicious misrepresentation

141

In faith, I do not love thee with mine eyes,
For they in thee a thousand errors note;
But 'tis my heart that loves what they despise,
Who, in despite of view, is pleas'd to dote;
Nor are mine ears with thy tongue's tune de-
　　lighted;　　5
Nor tender feeling, to base touches prone,
Nor taste, nor smell, desire to be invited
To any sensual feast with thee alone.
But my five wits° nor my five senses can
Dissuade one foolish heart from serving thee,　　10
Who leaves unsway'd° the likeness of a man,
Thy proud heart's slave and vassal wretch to be.
　　Only my plague thus far I count my gain,
　　That she that makes me sin awards me pain.

five wits　common sense, imagination, fancy, judgment,
　memory
unsway'd　uncontrolled, off balance

142

Love is my sin, and thy dear° virtue hate,
Hate of my sin, grounded on sinful loving.
O, but with mine compare thou thine own state,
And thou shalt find it merits not reproving;
5   Or, if it do, not from those lips of thine,
That have profan'd their scarlet ornaments°
And seal'd false bonds of love as oft as mine,
Robb'd others' beds' revenues of their rents.
Be it lawful I love thee, as thou lov'st those
10 Whom thine eyes woo as mine importune thee:
Root pity in thy heart, that, when it grows,
Thy pity may deserve to pitied be.
     If thou dost seek to have what thou dost hide,°
     By self-example mayst thou be denied!

dear special
scarlet ornaments i.e., their own glory
hide deny; i.e., pity

143

Lo, as a careful housewife runs to catch
One of her feather'd creatures broke away,
Sets down her babe, and makes all swift dispatch
In pursuit of the thing she would have stay,
5   Whilst her neglected child holds her in chase,°
Cries to catch her whose busy care is bent
To follow that which flies before her face,
Not prizing° her poor infant's discontent,
So runn'st thou after that which flies from thee,
10 Whilst I thy babe chase thee afar behind.
But if thou catch thy hope, turn back to me
And play the mother's part, kiss me, be kind.
     So will I pray that thou mayst have thy "Will"°
     If thou turn back and my loud crying still.

holds . . . chase runs after her   *prizing* heeding
"Will" i.e., the poet, the friend, or both

144

Two loves I have of comfort and despair,
Which like two spirits do suggest° me still.
The better angel is a man right fair,
The worser spirit a woman color'd ill.
5   To win me soon to hell, my female evil
Tempteth my better angel from my side,
And would corrupt my saint to be a devil,

Wooing his purity with her foul pride.
And whether that my angel be turn'd fiend
Suspect I may, yet not directly tell;   10
But being both from° me, both to each° friend,
I guess one angel in another's hell.
     Yet this shall I ne'er know, but live in doubt,
     Till my bad angel fire my good one out.

suggest prompt, attract   *from* away from
each each other

145

Those lips that Love's own hand did make
Breath'd forth the sound that said "I hate"
To me that languish'd for her sake.
But when she saw my woeful state,
Straight in her heart did mercy come,   5
Chiding that tongue that ever sweet
Was us'd in giving gentle doom,
And taught it thus anew to greet.
"I hate" she alter'd with an end
That follow'd it as gentle day   10
Doth follow night, who, like a fiend,
From heaven to hell is flown away.
     "I hate" from hate away she threw,
     And sav'd my life, saying "not you."

146

Poor soul, the center of my sinful earth,°
Thrall to° these rebel powers that thee array,
Why dost thou pine within and suffer dearth,
Painting thy outward walls so costly gay?
Why so large cost, having so short a lease,   5
Dost thou upon thy fading mansion spend?
Shall worms, inheritors of this excess,
Eat up thy charge?° Is this thy body's end?
Then, soul, live thou upon thy servant's loss,
And let that pine to aggravate° thy store;   10
Buy terms divine° in selling hours of dross;
Within be fed, without be rich no more.
     So shalt thou feed on Death, that feeds on men,
     And Death once dead, there's no more dying
     then.

earth i.e., body
Thrall to (a conjectured reading for the Quarto reading,
    which repeats "sinful earth" from preceding line)
charge expense; but also, the body, recipient of the
    expense
aggravate increase   *terms divine* i.e., eternal life

147

My love is as a fever, longing still°
For that which longer nurseth the disease,
Feeding on that which doth preserve the ill,
Th' uncertain sickly appetite to please.
5   My reason, the physician to my love,
Angry that his prescriptions are not kept,
Hath left me, and I desperate now approve°
Desire is death, which physic did except.°
Past cure I am, now reason is past care,
10 And frantic-mad with evermore unrest.
My thoughts and my discourse as madmen's are,
At random from the truth vainly express'd;
      For I have sworn thee fair and thought thee
         bright
      Who art as black as hell, as dark as night.

still always   *approve* prove that   *except* refuse

148

O me, what eyes hath Love put in my head,
Which have no correspondence with true sight!
Or, if they have, where is my judgment fled,
That censures° falsely what they see aright?
5   If that be fair whereon my false eyes dote,
What means the world to say it is not so?
If it be not, then love doth well denote
Love's eye is not so true as all men's. No,
How can it? O, how can Love's eye be true,
10 That is so vex'd with watching° and with tears?
No marvel then, though I mistake my view;
The sun itself sees not till heaven clears.
      O cunning Love! With tears thou keep'st me
         blind,
      Lest eyes well-seeing thy foul faults should find.

censures judges   *watching* staying awake

149

Canst thou, O cruel! say I love thee not,
When I against myself with thee partake?°
Do I not think on thee when I forgot
Am of myself, all tyrant,° for thy sake?
5   Who hateth thee that I do call my friend?
On whom frown'st thou that I do fawn upon?
Nay, if thou lour'st on me, do I not spend

Revenge upon myself with present° moan?
What merit do I in myself respect,
That is so proud thy service to despise,   10
When all my best doth worship thy defect,
Commanded by the motion of thine eyes?
      But, love, hate on, for now I know thy mind:
      Those that can see, thou lov'st; and I am blind.

partake take part
all tyrant i.e., you who are all tyrant
present immediate

150

O, from what power hast thou this powerful might
With insufficiency my heart to sway?°
To make me give the lie to my true sight,
And swear that brightness doth not grace the day?
Whence hast thou this becoming of things ill,°   5
That in the very refuse of thy deeds
There is such strength and warrantize° of skill
That, in my mind, thy worst all best exceeds?
Who taught thee how to make me love thee more,
The more I hear and see just cause of hate?   10
O, though I love what others do abhor,
With others thou shouldst not abhor my state.
      If thy unworthiness rais'd love in me,
      More worthy I to be belov'd of thee.

With . . . sway to rule my heart despite your defects
becoming . . . ill power to make ill things look well
warrantize warrant

151

Love is too young to know what conscience is;
Yet who knows not conscience is born of love?
Then, gentle cheater, urge° not my amiss,°
Lest guilty of my faults thy sweet self prove.
For, thou betraying me, I do betray   5
My nobler part to my gross body's treason;
My soul doth tell my body that he may
Triumph in love; flesh stays° no farther reason,
But rising at thy name doth point out thee
As his triumphant prize. Proud of this pride,   10
He is contented thy poor drudge to be,
To stand in thy affairs, fall by thy side.
      No want of conscience hold it that I call
      Her "love" for whose dear love I rise and fall.

urge make a point of   *amiss* transgression
stays waits for

152

In loving thee thou know'st I am forsworn,°
But thou art twice forsworn, to me love swearing,
In act thy bed-vow broke, and new faith torn,
In vowing new hate after new love bearing.
5 But why of two oaths' breach do I accuse thee,
When I break twenty? I am perjur'd most,
For all my vows are oaths but to misuse° thee,
And all my honest faith in thee is lost.
For I have sworn deep oaths of thy deep kindness,
10 Oaths of thy love, thy truth, thy constancy;
And, to enlighten° thee, gave eyes to blindness,°
Or made them swear against the thing they see,
    For I have sworn thee fair. More perjur'd I,
    To swear against the truth so foul a lie!

forsworn i.e., because married to another
misuse misrepresent
enlighten i.e., make you light who are dark
gave . . . blindness forbade my eyes to see

153

Cupid laid by his brand° and fell asleep.
A maid of Dian's° this advantage° found,
And his love-kindling fire did quickly steep
In a cold valley-fountain of that ground;
5 Which borrow'd from this holy fire of Love
A dateless lively heat, still° to endure,
And grew a seething bath,° which yet men prove

Against strange maladies a sovereign cure.
But at my mistress' eye Love's brand new-fir'd,
The boy for trial° needs would touch my breast; 10
I, sick withal,° the help of bath desir'd,
And thither hied, a sad distemper'd guest,
    But found no cure. The bath for my help lies
    Where Cupid got new fire, my mistress' eyes.

brand torch   *Dian* Diana, goddess of chastity
advantage opportunity   *still* forever
bath (probably Bath, famed spa)
for trial i.e., as a test
sick withal lovesick from it

154

The little Love-god lying once asleep
Laid by his side his heart-inflaming brand,
Whilst many nymphs that vow'd chaste life to
    keep
Came tripping by. But in her maiden hand
The fairest votary° took up that fire   5
Which many legions of true hearts had warm'd,
And so the general° of hot desire
Was sleeping by a virgin hand disarm'd.
This brand she quenched in a cool well by,
Which from Love's fire took heat perpetual,   10
Growing a bath and healthful remedy
For men diseas'd. But I, my mistress' thrall,
    Came there for cure, and this by that I prove:
    Love's fire heats water, water cools not love.

votary chaste one   *general* i.e., Cupid

AFTERWORD

In his *Palladis Tamia, Wit's Treasury* (1598) Francis Meres made the first recorded comment that we have on Shakespeare's sonnets: "...the sweet, witty soul of Ovid lives in mellifluous and honey-tongued Shakespeare, witness his *Venus and Adonis*, his *Lucrece*, his sugred Sonnets among his private friends." In the following year two of the sonnets (138, 144) were printed in *The Passionate Pilgrim*; but the full collection of one hundred fifty-four was not printed until 1609, by one Thomas Thorpe, with a dedication that raises the first, but not the last, mystery about the sonnets:

TO.THE.ONLIE.BEGETTER.OF.

THESE.INSUING.SONNETS.

MR.W.H.ALL.HAPPINESSE.

AND.THAT.ETERNITIE.

PROMISED.

BY

OUR.EVER-LIVING.POET.

WISHETH.

THE.WELL-WISHING

ADVENTURER.IN.

SETTING.

FORTH.

T.T.

Who was "Mr. W. H."? And why is he called the "onlie begetter" of these sonnets? Was he the unknown young man with a "woman's face" whom, in the first seventeen poems, the poet urges to marry and have children, and whom, with a few exceptions, the poet addresses directly in the first one hundred twenty-six? Was he William Herbert, Earl of Pembroke, as has often been argued? Or the Earl of Southampton, Henry Wriothesley (with initials curiously reversed), as has been argued no less strenuously? Or was he merely one William Hall, a printer, who conceivably was the "begetter" in some quite mundane sense involving a business transaction by which he procured the poems for publication?

Other, and deeper, mysteries grow as the reader pursues his course through the sonnets and their half-told story, or rather stories, wherein relationships are rather hinted than divulged, left in the dark rather than dragged into the light. Did the poet mean to vex and tantalize future ages—about which he evidently thought consciously, for he repeatedly insists that these very verses will preserve his friend's beauty to the world "So long as men can breathe or eyes can see"—by means of shadowy allusions and elaborately figurative poetic invention? Or were details of all these intrigues so well known among the "private friends" mentioned by Meres that, for them, details would have been superfluous, and ruinous to the sonnets? Who was the rival poet who, for a time, drove a wedge between our poet and his handsome friend? What were, in terms of plain biographical fact, the relationships of the poet, his friend and recipient of extravagant praise in the first one hundred twenty-six sonnets, and the Cleopatra of the sonnets, the "dark lady" who, though "foul" and "black as hell," seemingly enslaves both, imprisons them in her "hell," and separates the poet's eyes from his judgment? Was this lady indeed one of the ladies-in-waiting of Queen Elizabeth, as has been argued? Did she *see* the twenty-odd devastating sonnets in which the poet charges her with every sort of evil, besides physical ugliness? And what, if any, is the connection of the mystifying final two sonnets, wherein it seems to be recorded that the poet went to Bath, where "strange maladies" are cured, to the preceding twenty and more that seemingly record a period of degradation and sin in the poet's life?

Such questions partly account for the fact that, as one modern editor states, "the sonnets are the most discussed and disputed of all collections of poetry in the English language." But there is a question that lies deeper than any of these, and that is whether the sonnets are, as a whole, truth or fiction. "With this key Shakespeare unlocked his heart," wrote Wordsworth of the sonnet form, but Browning retorted, "If so, the less Shakespeare he." Are the sonnets indeed autobiographical? Do they give us, in fact, our only direct contact with the poet's personal experiences, our only profound insights into his mental, moral, spiritual life, which is otherwise barricaded from us by the hundreds of dramatic portraits and unnumbered historical or fictional events that are depicted in the plays? Or are the sonnets themselves a "fantasy of the mind," lyric in form but essentially dramatic in conception—creations of the poet's imagination as purely as is *A Midsummer Night's Dream* or *Love's Labor's Lost*? Are they all "invention"—the handsome friend, the rival poet, the "dark lady," even the "poet" himself, who is imagined as experiencing all this vast range of ecstasy and despair, love and hate, jealousy and trust, admiration and revulsion?

Both views continue to be tempting. We would like to believe that the sonnets "speak true," and give us a look into the heart of Shakespeare—and, curiously more than that, give us occasional glimpses of his mundane, daily life that is otherwise hidden. And indeed as we examine the details of many of the sonnets we are likely to say to ourselves suddenly, "This one *has* to be real. He would never have thought to say it just this way if he had not actually experienced it." Sonnet 50, for example: must he not *really* have ridden between London and Stratford? Is not this, at least, a direct recording of experience? And yet, who can say? Might not the imagination that "invented" the speeches of Hamlet, Macbeth, Lear, Othello, Antony, Bottom, Jaques, Falstaff, and all the rest, *ad infinitum*—have just as easily "bodied forth" the image of a fictitious, troubled poet journeying "heavy" on his way, not between a real London and a real Stratford, but only between an imaginary grief that lies onward and an imaginary joy that lies behind?

Are the sonnets greater if they are autobiographical, or are they greater if they are "dramatic"? Perhaps the question itself is nonsense, for they are in any event what they are. The search for any item that may open a window upon the life of Shakespeare has continued for a long while and will inevitably continue much longer. But it is doubtless damaging to our personal experience of the sonnets as poems, as works of art, if we read them like detectives searching for clues. It is one thing (and not bad) to scrutinize every scrap of a line in endeavoring to ascertain whether the "rival poet" was Drayton, Chapman, Spenser, Daniel, or some other; it is quite another (and certainly better) to drink up the power of the best of the sonnets as individual works of art, independently of questions that tend to intrude upon and may entirely block the aesthetic experience that they have to give.

In this latter regard the sonnets are not uniformly potent. It is noteworthy that selective anthologists regularly choose their representatives from a list of twenty or fewer, on the force and beauty of which there seems to be something like a critical consensus; thus any editor's choice of a few sonnets, with allowance for some variations, is likely to be made among "When I do count the clock" (12), "When I consider everything that grows" (15), "Shall I compare thee" (18), "When in disgrace" (29), "When to the sessions" (30), "Not marble nor the gilded monuments" (55), "Like as the waves" (60), "When I have seen by Time's fell hand defac'd" (64), "Since brass, nor stone" (65), "That time of year" (73), "How like a winter" (97), "When in the chronicle" (106), "Not mine own fears" (107), "Th' expense of spirit" (129), "My mistress' eyes" (130, which burlesques two hundred years of sonnet imagery), and "Poor soul" (146). The greater number of these are distinguished by generalized, hence readily understandable, human emotions; by that special harmony of sound often heard in the plays, especially those of the highly lyrical years of the mid-1590's, and aptly identified by George Bernard Shaw as "the Shakespearean music"; by a steady and glittering flow of imagery, sometimes fully as extravagant as the impassioned utterances of *Romeo and Juliet*, but generally "right" and true to the sense and the mood that they are meant to communicate; and, finally, by a high degree of self-containment, for each sonnet poses its essential idea, works intently at its ramifications, then abruptly reaches its resolution, leaving behind what seems indeed a genuine experience shaped to form a miniature work of art that is finished and complete and that attests to the validity of Rossetti's striking definition: "A sonnet is a moment's monument."

Of course no reader should be, and no receptive reader will be, intimidated by any critic's list of "best twenty" from which anthologists so often choose their sparse representation. Probably among these twenty are some that, by and large, recommend themselves to more readers than do others, at least in part because they treat universal experiences in readily understood terms. But it is a special distinction of the sonnets that they sometimes come home to men's business and bosoms in unpredictable and quite individual ways: in the mood of a given moment, a single line or phrase from the least-quoted one among the hundred fifty-four sonnets may cut through to the quick and leave the reader gasping who has been impervious to the assault of all the "greatest" sonnets. It is useless here to hazard any suggestions: among the hundred fifty-four sonnets is not a single one that lacks the potential, given the right circumstances, to strike home; when, why, how—who can anticipate? Perhaps it is the source of this unpredictable power that is the real mystery of the sonnets.

When Shakespeare took up the sonnet form, it had already lived about sixty years in England after being introduced into the country by Wyatt and Surrey early in the century. In Italy, the country of its origin, it had been practiced by Dante and Petrarch; and it had a history in France. In England, before Shakespeare, its most noteworthy practitioners were Spenser (*Amoretti*) and Sidney (*Astrophel and Stella*). Originating as a love lyric, it developed in England as a popular device for the expression (and exploitation) of several major themes—lovers' complaints to their disdainful mistresses, the tyranny of time, the praise of beauty, contempt of the world and the worldly (*contemptu mundi*). Before Shakespeare took up the form, it had become encrusted with conventions: others, too, had urged a young man to marry, had lauded a noble patron, insisted that the poet's verse could bestow immortality, flagellated themselves in the service of faithless mistresses. Residues of all that had preceded him in the form are readily discernible in most of Shakespeare's sonnets—and perhaps it is not unjust to assert that in the very least impressive of them, the conventions dominate the utterance and blunt whatever fresh and vibrant experience the sonnet may have been meant to communicate. Where the encrustation is heaviest, the sonnets read very much like riddles, the idea emerges tortuously through labyrinthian figures and topical allusions—and the reader makes his way painfully, consulting a great many footnotes that may yet leave the main idea obscure or even buried.

But in the great ones—and there are at very least fifty of these, something like a third of the total—the poet unfolds his idea like a flower, surely, naturally, and beautifully. For these, gratefully, an editor requires few footnotes, or none. The great ones not only are superb examples of Shakespeare's lyric voice, but are also superb examples of sparkling-clear exposition, which makes its point economically and lets it stand. Even without consideration of what they do or do not reveal of the poet's personal life and thought, taken wholly on their own merit, all these stand easily beside the finest two or three sonnets each of Spenser, Milton, Wordsworth, and Keats. They are hardly a mean accomplishment for Shakespeare's left hand while his right hand was busy with *Romeo and Juliet*, *A Midsummer Night's Dream*, *Richard II*, and as many more plays on either side of these.

SOME SUGGESTED REFERENCES

SHAKESPEARE'S AGE

BINDOFF, S. T. *Tudor England*. Baltimore: Penguin Books, Inc., 1950. (The Pelican History of England, $5.)

BYRNE, M. ST. CLARE. *Elizabethan Life in Town and Country*, rev. ed. New York: Barnes & Noble, Inc., 1961.

CRAIG, HARDIN. *The Enchanted Glass: the Elizabethan Mind in Literature*. New York: Oxford University Press, 1936.

FORD, BORIS (ed.). *The Age of Shakespeare*. Baltimore: Penguin Books, Inc., 1955. (The Pelican Guide to English Literature, $2.)

HALLIDAY, F. E. *Shakespeare in his Age*. Duckworth, 1956.

TILLYARD, E. M. W. *The Elizabethan World Picture*. New York: The Macmillan Company, 1944.

WILSON, JOHN DOVER (ed.). *Life in Shakespeare's England*, 2nd ed. New York: The Macmillan Company, 1913.

SHAKESPEARE'S LIFE

ADAMS, J. Q. *A Life of William Shakespeare*. Boston: Houghton Mifflin Company, 1923.

CHUTE, MARCHETTE. *Shakespeare of London*. New York: E. P. Dutton & Co., 1949.

HALLIDAY, F. E. *The Life of Shakespeare*. Baltimore: Penguin Books, Inc., 1963.

SPENCER, HAZELTON. *The Art and Life of William Shakespeare*. New York: Harcourt Brace Jovanovich, Inc., 1940.

WILSON, JOHN DOVER. *The Essential Shakespeare*. New York: Cambridge University Press, 1932.

SHAKESPEARE'S THEATER

CHAMBERS, E. K. *The Elizabethan Stage*, 4 vols. New York: Oxford University Press, 1923, 1945.

HODGES, C. WALTER. *The Globe Restored*. New York: Coward-McCann, 1954.

NAGLER, A. M. *Shakespeare's Stage*. New Haven: Yale University Press, 1958.

SHAKESPEARE'S PLAYS

BRADLEY, A. C. *Shakespearean Tragedy*. New York: The Macmillan Company, 1904. (Meridian paperback, 1957.)

CHARLTON, H. B. *Shakespearean Comedy*. New York: The Macmillan Company, 1938.

CHARLTON, H. B. *Shakespearean Tragedy*. New York: Cambridge University Press, 1949.

CLEMEN, WOLFGANG H. *The Development of Shakespeare's Imagery*. Cambridge, Mass.: Harvard University Press, 1951.

EVANS, BERTRAND. *Shakespeare's Comedies*. Oxford: Clarendon Press, 1960. (Oxford paperback, 1967.)

FARNHAM, WILLARD. *Shakespeare's Tragic Frontier*. Berkeley: University of California Press, 1950.

GRANVILLE-BARKER, HARLEY. *Prefaces to Shakespeare*, 2 vols. Princeton, N.J.: Princeton University Press, 1946–1947.

HALLIDAY, F. E. *The Poetry of Shakespeare's Plays*. Duckworth, 1954.

KNIGHTS, L. C. *Some Shakespearean Themes*. London: Chatto & Windus, 1959.

LAWRENCE, WILLIAM W. *Shakespeare's Problem Comedies*. New York: The Macmillan Company, 1931.

MUIR, KENNETH. *Shakespeare's Sources*. London: Methuen, 1957.

PARROTT, THOMAS MARC. *Shakespearean Comedy*. New York: Oxford University Press, 1949.

RICHMOND, HUGH. *Shakespeare's Political Plays*. New York: Random House, Inc., 1967.

SPENCER, THEODORE. *Shakespeare and the Nature of Man*. New York: The Macmillan Company, 1942.

SPURGEON, CAROLINE F. E. *Shakespeare's Imagery and What It Tells Us*. New York: The Macmillan Company, 1935.

TILLYARD, E. M. W. *Shakespeare's History Plays*. New York: The Macmillan Company, 1946.

TILLYARD, E. M. W. *Shakespeare's Last Plays*. London: Chatto & Windus, 1938.

VAN DOREN, MARK. *Shakespeare*. New York: Holt, Rinehart & Winston, Inc., 1939.

SHAKESPEARE'S SONNETS

BOOTH, STEPHEN. *An Essay on Shakespeare's Sonnets.* New Haven: Yale University Press, 1969.

HUBLER, EDWARD. *The Sense of Shakespeare's Sonnets.* Princeton, N.J.: Princeton University Press, 1952.

LANDRY, HILTON. *Interpretations in Shakespeare's Sonnets.* Berkeley: University of California Press, 1963.

INDEX OF FIRST LINES OF
THE SONNETS